...the earth serves me to walk upon,
the sun to light me... Montaigne

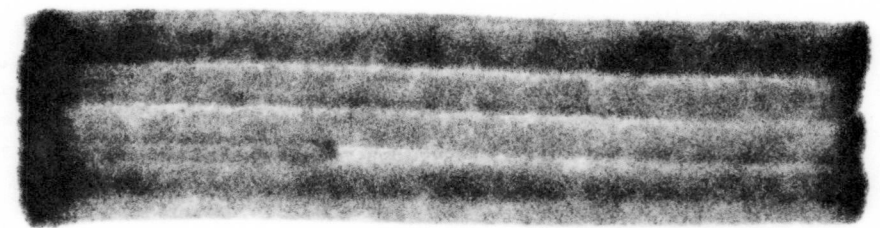

Hammond Incorporated

HAMMOND®

STANDARD
WORLD ATLAS

Latest and most Authentic
Geographical and Statistical Information

HAMMOND INCORPORATED
MAPLEWOOD, NEW JERSEY

New York   Chicago   Boston   Cleveland   San Francisco

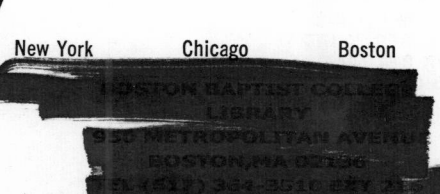

Hammond Publications Advisory Board

Africa — South of the Sahara: IRENE S. VAN DONGEN
Assistant Professor, Department of Geography and Earth Science,
California State College (Pennsylvania)

Anglo-America: DANIEL JACOBSON
Director, Social Science Teaching Institute,
Michigan State University

Australia, New Zealand and the Pacific Area: TOM L. MC KNIGHT
Professor, Department of Geography,
University of California, Los Angeles

Biblical Archaeology: HARRY THOMAS FRANK
Professor, Department of Religion,
Oberlin College

Cartography: GERARD L. ALEXANDER
Chief, Map Division,
The New York Public Library

East Asia: CHRISTOPHER L. SALTER
Assistant Professor, Department of Geography
University of Oregon

Flags: WHITNEY SMITH
Executive Director,
The Flag Research Center

Latin and Middle America: JOHN P. AUGELLI
Dean, International Programs,
University of Kansas

Northern and Central Europe: VINCENT H. MALMSTROM
Professor, Department of Geography and Geology,
Middlebury College

Population and Demography: KINGSLEY DAVIS
Director, International Population and Urban Research,
Institute of International Studies,
University of California, Berkeley

South and Southeast Asia: P. P. KARAN
Chairman, Department of Geography,
University of Kentucky

Soviet Union and Eastern Europe: THEODORE SHABAD
Editor and Translator,
Soviet Geography: Review and Translation

Western and Southern Europe: NORMAN J. W. THROWER
Professor, Department of Geography,
University of California, Los Angeles

Contents

Gazetteer-Index of the World

This alphabetical list of grand divisions, countries, states, colonial possessions, etc., gives area, population, capital or chief town, and index references and page numbers on which they are shown on the largest scale. The index reference shows the square on the respective map in which the name of the entry may be located.

Country	Area (Sq. Miles)	Population	Capital or Chief Town	Index Ref.	Plate No.
Afars and Issas, Terr.	8,498	125,050	Djibouti	H 5	111
*Afghanistan	250,000	17,078,263	Kabul	A 2	68
Africa	11,682,000	345,000,000			102
Alabama, U.S.A.	51,609	3,444,165	Montgomery	J 4	188
Alaska, U.S.A.	586,412	302,173	Juneau	C 5	188
*Albania	11,100	2,126,000	Tiranë	E 5	45
Alberta, Canada	255,285	1,627,874	Edmonton		182
*Algeria	919,595	13,547,000	Algiers	D 3	106
American Samoa	76	27,159	Pago Pago	J 7	87
Andorra	175	19,000	Andorra la Vella	G 1	33
Angola	481,351	5,430,000	Luanda	C 6	115
Antarctica	5,500,000				5
Antigua & Dependencies	171	63,000	St. Johns	E11	161
*Argentina	1,072,070	23,983,000	Buenos Aires		143
Arizona, U.S.A.	113,909	1,772,482	Phoenix	D 4	188
Arkansas, U.S.A.	53,104	1,923,295	Little Rock	H 3	188
Ascension	34	1,486	Georgetown	A 5	102
Asia	17,032,000	2,043,997,000			54
*Australia	2,967,741	12,630,000	Canberra		88
*Austria	32,374	7,419,341	Vienna		41
Bahama Islands	4,404	168,838	Nassau	C 1	156
*Bahrain	231	207,000	Manama	F 4	59
Bangladesh	55,126	70,000,000	Dacca	G 4	68
*Barbados	166	253,620	Bridgetown	B 8	161
*Belgium	11,779	9,660,154	Brussels		27
Bermuda	21	52,000	Hamilton	H 3	156
*Bhutan	18,000	1,034,774	Thimphu	G 3	68
*Bolivia	424,163	4,804,000	La Paz, Sucre		136
*Botswana	219,815	629,000	Gaborone	C 4	118
*Brazil	3,284,426	90,840,000	Brasília		132
British Columbia, Canada	366,255	2,184,621	Victoria		184
British Honduras	8,867	122,000	Belmopan	C 2	154
British Indian Ocean Terr.	30	2,000	Victoria (Seychelles)	L10	54
Brunei	2,226	130,000	Bandar Seri Begawan	E 4	85
*Bulgaria	42,829	8,501,000	Sofia	F 4	45
*Burma	261,789	27,000,000	Rangoon	B 2	72
*Burundi	10,747	3,475,000	Bujumbura	E 4	115
California, U.S.A.	158,693	19,953,134	Sacramento	B 3	188
*Cambodia	69,898	6,701,000	Phnom Penh	E 4	72
*Cameroon	183,568	5,836,000	Yaoundé	B 2	115
*Canada	3,851,809	21,568,311	Ottawa		162
Canal Zone	647	44,198	Balboa Heights	G 6	154
Cape Verde Islands	1,557	250,000	Praia	B 8	106
Cayman Islands	100	10,652	Georgetown	B 3	156
*Central African Republic	240,534	1,518,000	Bangui	C 2	115
Central America	196,928	16,090,000			154
*Ceylon (Sri Lanka)	25,332	12,300,000	Colombo	E 7	68
*Chad	495,753	3,510,000	Fort-Lamy	C 4	111
Channel Islands	75	117,000	St. Helier	E 7	13
*Chile	292,257	8,834,820	Santiago		138
*China (People's Rep.)	3,691,506	740,000,000	Peking		77
China (Taiwan)	13,948	14,577,000	Taipei	K 7	77
*Colombia	439,513	21,117,000	Bogotá		126
Colorado, U.S.A.	104,247	2,207,259	Denver	E 3	188
Comoro Is.	838	270,000	Moroni	G 2	118
*Congo, Rep. of	132,046	915,000	Brazzaville	B 4	115
Connecticut, U.S.A.	5,009	3,032,217	Hartford	M 2	188
Cook Islands	93	20,000	Avarua	K 7	87
*Costa Rica	19,575	1,800,000	San José	E 5	154
*Cuba	44,206	8,553,395	Havana		158
*Cyprus	3,473	649,000	Nicosia	E 5	63
*Czechoslovakia	49,370	14,497,000	Prague		41
*Dahomey	44,290	2,640,000	Porto-Novo	E 7	106
Delaware, U.S.A.	2,057	548,104	Dover	L 3	188
*Denmark	16,625	4,912,865	Copenhagen		21
District of Columbia, U.S.A.	67	756,510	Washington	L 3	188
Dominica	290	70,302	Roseau	E 7	161
*Dominican Republic	18,704	4,011,589	Santo Domingo		158
*Ecuador	109,483	6,144,000	Quito		128
*Egypt	386,100	33,329,000	Cairo	E 2	111
*El Salvador	8,260	3,418,455	San Salvador	C 4	154
England, U.K.	50,327	46,102,300	London		13
*Equatorial Guinea	10,832	286,000	Santa Isabel	A 3	115
*Ethiopia	471,776	24,764,000	Addis Ababa	G 5	111
Europe	4,063,000	652,000,000			7
Faerøe Islands, Den.	540	38,000	Tórshavn	B 2	21
Falkland Islands	4,618	2,000	Stanley	E 8	120
*Fiji	7,015	519,000	Suva	H 8	87
*Finland	130,128	4,706,000	Helsinki		18
Florida, U.S.A.	58,560	6,789,443	Tallahassee	K 5	188
*France	212,841	50,770,000	Paris		28
French Guiana	35,135	48,000	Cayenne	E 3	131
French Polynesia	1,544	109,000	Papeete	L 8	87
*Gabon	103,346	500,000	Libreville	B 4	115
*Gambia	4,003	357,000	Bathurst	A 6	106
Georgia, U.S.A.	58,876	4,589,575	Atlanta	K 4	188
Germany, East (German Democratic Republic)	41,814	17,117.000	Berlin		22
Germany, West (Federal Republic)	95,959	61,194,600	Bonn		22
*Ghana	91,843	8,545,561	Accra	D 7	106
Gibraltar	2	27,000	Gibraltar	D 4	33
Gilbert and Ellice Is.	369	55,185	Bairiki	J 6	87
*Great Britain and Northern Ireland (United Kingdom)	94,214	55,534,000	London		10
*Greece	50,548	8,838,000	Athens	F 6	45
Greenland	840,000	47,000	Godthåb	B12	4
Grenada	133	105,000	St. George's	D 9	161
Guadeloupe and Dependencies	687	324,000	Basse-Terre	A 5	161
Guam	209	84,996	Agaña	F 4	87
*Guatemala	42,042	5,200,000	Guatemala	B 3	154
*Guinea	94,925	3,890,000	Conakry	B 6	106
*Guyana	83,000	763,000	Georgetown	B 3	131
*Haiti	10,694	4,867,190	Port-au-Prince		158
Hawaii, U.S.A.	6,450	769,913	Honolulu	E 5	188
*Holland (Netherlands)	13,958	13,077,000	Amsterdam, The Hague		27
*Honduras	43,277	2,495,000	Tegucigalpa	D 3	154
Hong Kong	398	4,089,000	Victoria	H 7	77
*Hungary	35,915	10,315,597	Budapest		41
*Iceland	39,768	204,578	Reykjavík	B 1	21
Idaho, U.S.A.	83,557	713,008	Boise	D 2	188
Illinois, U.S.A.	56,400	11,113,976	Springfield	J 3	188
*India	1,261,483	546,955,945	New Delhi		68
Indiana, U.S.A.	36,291	5,193,669	Indianapolis	J 3	188
*Indonesia	735,264	119,572,000	Djakarta		85
Iowa, U.S.A.	56,290	2,825,041	Des Moines	H 2	188
*Iran	636,293	28,448,000	Tehran		66
*Iraq	167,924	9,431,000	Baghdad		66
*Ireland	26,600	2,944,000	Dublin		17
Ireland, Northern, U.K.	5,459	1,512,500	Belfast		17
Isle of Man, U.K.	227	50,000	Douglas	C 3	13
*Israel	7,993	2,911,000	Jerusalem		65
*Italy	116,303	54,504,000	Rome		34
*Ivory Coast	124,503	4,800,000	Abidjan	C 7	106
*Jamaica	4,411	1,972,000	Kingston		158
*Japan	143,622	104,665,171	Tokyo		81
*Jordan	37,297	2,300,000	Amman		65
Kansas, U.S.A.	82,264	2,249,071	Topeka	G 3	188
Kentucky, U.S.A.	40,395	3,219,311	Frankfort	J 3	188
*Kenya	224,960	10,880,200	Nairobi	G 3	115
Korea, North	46,540	13,300,000	P'yŏngyang		81
Korea, South	38,452	31,683,000	Seoul		81
*Kuwait	6,177	733,196	Al Kuwait	E 4	59
*Laos	91,459	2,900,000	Vientiane	D 3	72
*Lebanon	4,015	2,800,000	Beirut	F 6	63
*Lesotho	11,716	930,000	Maseru	D 5	118
*Liberia	43,000	1,200,000	Monrovia	C 7	106
*Libya	679,359	1,900,000	Tripoli		111
Liechtenstein	61	21,000	Vaduz	J 2	39
Louisiana, U.S.A.	48,523	3,643,180	Baton Rouge	H 4	188
*Luxembourg	999	339,000	Luxembourg	J 9	27

*Members of the United Nations

Gazetteer-Index of the World

Country	Area (Sq. Miles)	Population	Capital or Chief Town	Index Ref.	Plate No.
Macao	6.2	292,000	Macao	H 7	77
Maine, U.S.A.	33,215	993,663	Augusta	N 1	188
*Malagasy Republic	226,657	7,011,563	Tananarive	H 3	118
*Malawi	45,483	4,530,000	Zomba	F 6	115
Malaya, Malaysia	50,670	9,000,000	Kuala Lumpur	D 6	72
*Malaysia	128,308	10,583,000	Kuala Lumpur		72,85
*Maldives	115	110,770	Male	L 9	54
*Mali	463,948	4,929,000	Bamako	C 6	106
*Malta	122	321,000	Valletta	E 7	34
Manitoba, Canada	251,000	988,247	Winnipeg		179
Martinique	425	332,000	Fort-de-France	D 5	161
Maryland, U.S.A.	10,577	3,922,399	Annapolis	L 3	188
Massachusetts, U.S.A.	8,257	5,689,170	Boston	M 2	188
*Mauritania	397,954	1,140,000	Nouakchott	B 5	106
*Mauritius & Dependencies	787	823,000	Port Louis	G 5	118
*Mexico	761,601	48,313,438	Mexico City		150
Michigan, U.S.A.	58,216	8,875,083	Lansing	J 1	188
Midway Islands	2	2,220		J 3	87
Minnesota, U.S.A.	84,068	3,805,069	St. Paul	H 1	188
Mississippi, U.S.A.	47,716	2,216,912	Jackson	J 4	188
Missouri, U.S.A.	69,686	4,677,399	Jefferson City	H 3	188
Monaco	368 acres	23,035	Monaco	G 6	28
*Mongolia	604,247	1,300,000	Ulan Bator		77
Montana, U.S.A.	147,138	694,409	Helena	D 1	188
Montserrat	38	12,300	Plymouth	F 3	156
*Morocco	172,413	15,577,000	Rabat	C 2	106
Mozambique	302,328	7,376,000	Lourenço Marques	E 4	118
Nauru	8.2	7,000	Uaboe dist.	G 6	87
Nebraska, U.S.A.	77,227	1,483,791	Lincoln	F 2	188
*Nepal	54,362	10,845,000	Kathmandu	E 3	68
*Netherlands	13,958	13,077,000	Amsterdam, The Hague		27
Netherlands Antilles	390	220,000	Willemstad	E 4	156
Nevada, U.S.A.	110,540	488,738	Carson City	C 3	188
New Brunswick, Canada	28,354	634,557	Fredericton		170
New Caledonia & Dependencies	8,548	100,579	Nouméa	G 8	87
Newfoundland, Canada	156,185	522,104	St. John's		166
New Guinea, Terr. of (Aust. Trust.)	92,160	1,722,572	Port Moresby		85,87
New Hampshire, U.S.A.	9,304	737,681	Concord	M 2	188
New Hebrides	5,700	80,000	Vila	G 7	87
New Jersey, U.S.A.	7,836	7,168,164	Trenton	M 3	188
New Mexico, U.S.A.	121,666	1,016,000	Santa Fe	E 4	188
New York, U.S.A.	49,576	18,241,266	Albany	L 2	188
*New Zealand	103,736	2,815,000	Wellington		100
*Nicaragua	45,698	1,984,000	Managua	D 4	154
*Niger	489,189	4,016,000	Niamey	F 5	106
*Nigeria	356,669	66,174,000	Lagos	F 6	106
Niue	100	5,323	Alofi	K 7	87
North America	9,363,000	314,000,000			146
North Carolina, U.S.A.	52,586	5,082,059	Raleigh	K 3	188
North Dakota, U.S.A.	70,665	617,761	Bismarck	F 1	188
Northern Ireland, U.K.	5,459	1,512,500	Belfast		17
Northwest Territories, Canada	1,304,903	34,807	Yellowknife		187
*Norway	125,181	3,893,000	Oslo		18
Nova Scotia, Canada	21,425	788,960	Halifax		168
Ohio, U.S.A.	41,222	10,652,017	Columbus	K 2	188
Oklahoma, U.S.A.	69,919	2,559,253	Oklahoma City	G 3	188
*Oman	82,000	565,000	Muscat	G 5	59
Ontario, Canada	412,582	7,703,106	Toronto		175,177
Oregon, U.S.A.	96,981	2,091,385	Salem	B 2	188
Pacific Islands, U.S. Trust Terr. of the	687	94,900	Garapan	F 5	87
*Pakistan	310,403	60,000,000	Islamabad		68
*Panama	29,209	1,425,343	Panamá	G 6	154
Papua, Australia	86,100	648,000	Port Moresby		85,87
*Paraguay	157,047	2,314,000	Asunción		144
Pennsylvania, U.S.A.	45,333	11,793,909	Harrisburg	L 2	188
*Persia (Iran)	636,293	28,448,000	Tehran		66
*Peru	496,222	13,586,300	Lima		128
*Philippines	115,707	39,079,000	Quezon City		82
Pitcairn Islands	18	74	Adamstown	O 8	87
*Poland	120,664	32,889,000	Warsaw		47
*Portugal	35,510	9,560,000	Lisbon		33
Portuguese Guinea	13,948	530,000	Bissau	A 6	106
Portuguese Timor	5,762	590,000	Dili	H 7	85
Prince Edward Island, Canada	2,184	111,641	Charlottetown	E 2	168
Puerto Rico	3,435	2,712,033	San Juan		161
*Qatar	8,500	100,000	Doha	F 4	59
Québec, Canada	594,860	6,027,764	Québec		172,174
Réunion	969	436,000	St-Denis	F 5	118
Rhode Island, U.S.A.	1,214	949,723	Providence	M 2	188
Rhodesia	150,332	5,310,000	Salisbury	D 3	118

Country	Area (Sq. Miles)	Population	Capital or Chief Town	Index Ref.	Plate No.
*Rumania	91,699	20,394,000	Bucharest	F 3	45
*Rwanda	10,169	3,500,000	Kigali	E 4	115
Sabah, Malaysia	29,388	633,000	Kota Kinabalu	F 4	85
St. Christopher-Nevis-Anguilla	138	56,000	Basseterre		156,161
St. Helena & Dependencies	47	4,707	Jamestown	B 6	102
St. Lucia	238	110,000	Castries	G 6	161
St-Pierre and Miquelon	93.5	5,235	St-Pierre	C 4	166
St. Vincent	150	89,129	Kingstown	A 8	161
San Marino	23.4	19,000	San Marino	D 3	34
São Tomé e Príncipe	372	66,000	São Tomé	F 8	106
Sarawak, Malaysia	48,250	950,000	Kuching	E 5	85
Saskatchewan, Canada	251,700	926,242	Regina		181
*Saudi Arabia	920,000	7,200,000	Riyadh, Mecca	D 4	59
Scotland, U.K.	30,411	5,194,000	Edinburgh		15
*Senegal	75,750	3,780,000	Dakar	A 5	106
Seychelles	109	51,396	Victoria	H 5	118
*Siam (Thailand)	198,456	35,448,000	Bangkok	D 3	72
*Sierra Leone	27,925	2,512,000	Freetown	B 7	106
*Singapore	226	2,034,000	Singapore	F 6	72
Solomon Islands Prot.	10,983	161,525	Honiara	F 6	87
*Somalia	246,200	2,730,000	Mogadishu	H 3	115
*South Africa	471,663	21,282,000	Cape Town, Pretoria	C 5	118
South America	6,875,000	186,000,000			120
South Carolina, U.S.A.	31,055	2,590,516	Columbia	K 4	188
South Dakota, U.S.A.	77,047	666,257	Pierre	F 2	188
South-West Africa	317,838	615,000	Windhoek	B 3	118
*Spain	194,896	33,290,000	Madrid		33
Spanish Sahara, Spain	102,702	63,000	El Aaiún	B 4	106
*Sri Lanka	25,332	12,300,000	Colombo	E 7	68
*Sudan	967,495	15,312,000	Khartoum	E 4	111
Surinam	55,144	389,000	Paramaribo	C 3	131
*Swaziland	6,704	411,879	Mbabane	E 5	118
*Sweden	173,665	7,978,000	Stockholm		18
Switzerland	15,941	6,230,000	Bern		39
*Syria	71,498	5,866,000	Damascus	G 5	63
*Tanzania	362,819	12,896,000	Dar es Salaam	F 5	115
Tennessee, U.S.A.	42,244	3,924,164	Nashville	J 3	188
Texas, U.S.A.	267,339	11,196,730	Austin	G 4	188
*Thailand	198,456	35,448,000	Bangkok	D 3	72
*Togo	21,853	2,004,711	Lomé	E 7	106
Tokelau Islands	3.9	2,000	Fakaofo	J 6	87
Tonga	270	83,000	Nuku'alofa	J 8	87
*Trinidad and Tobago	1,980	1,040,000	Port of Spain	A10	161
Tristan da Cunha	40	269	Edinburgh	G10	2
*Tunisia	63,378	5,027,000	Tunis	F 2	106
*Turkey	301,381	34,375,000	Ankara		63
Turks and Caicos Is.	166	6,000	Cockburn Town	D 2	156
*Uganda	92,674	9,764,000	Kampala	F 3	115
*Ukrainian S.S.R., U.S.S.R.	232,046	47,126,517	Kiev	D 5	52
*Union of Soviet Socialist Republics	8,649,498	241,748,000	Moscow		48,52
*United Arab Emirates	32,278	179,126	Abu Dhabi	F 5	59
*United Kingdom	94,214	55,534,000	London		10
*United States of America, land	3,554,609	203,235,298	Washington, D.C.		188
land and water	3,615,123				
*Upper Volta	105,841	5,330,000	Ouagadougou	D 6	106
*Uruguay	72,172	2,900,000	Montevideo		145
Utah, U.S.A.	84,916	1,059,273	Salt Lake City	D 3	188
Vatican City	109 acres	1,000		B 6	34
*Venezuela	352,143	10,398,907	Caracas		124
Vermont, U.S.A.	9,609	444,732	Montpelier	M 2	188
Vietnam, North	61,293	21,340,000	Hanoi	E 3	72
Vietnam, South	66,263	16,543,434	Saigon	F 4	72
Virginia, U.S.A.	40,817	4,648,494	Richmond	L 3	188
Virgin Islands, British	59	10,484	Road Town	H 1	156
Virgin Islands, U.S.A.	133	62,468	Charlotte Amalie		161
Wake Island, U.S.A.	2.5	1,647		G 4	87
Wales, U.K.	8,017	2,754,540	Cardiff		13
Washington, U.S.A.	68,192	3,409,169	Olympia	B 1	188
Western Samoa	1,133	139,810	Apia	J 7	87
West Virginia, U.S.A.	24,181	1,744,237	Charleston	K 3	188
*White Russian S.S.R. (Byelorussian S.S.R.), U.S.S.R.	80,154	9,002,338	Minsk	C 4	52
Wisconsin, U.S.A.	56,154	4,417,933	Madison	H 2	188
World	57,491,000	3,782,000,000			1,2
Wyoming, U.S.A.	97,914	332,416	Cheyenne	E 2	188
*Yemen Arab Republic	75,000	5,000,000	San'a	D 7	59
*Yemen, Peoples Dem. Rep. of	111,075	1,220,000	Aden	E 7	59
*Yugoslavia	98,766	20,586,000	Belgrade	C 3	45
Yukon Territory, Canada	207,076	18,388	Whitehorse	E 3	187
*Zaire	905,563	21,637,876	Kinshasa	D 4	115
*Zambia	290,586	4,056,995	Lusaka	E 7	115

Introduction to the Maps and Indexes

The following notes have been added to aid the reader in making the best use of this atlas. Though he may be familiar with maps and map indexes, the publisher believes that a quick review of the material below will add to his enjoyment of this reference work.

Arrangement — The Plan of the Atlas. The atlas has been designed with maximum convenience for the user as its objective. All geographically related information pertaining to a country or region appears on adjacent pages, eliminating the task of searching throughout the entire volume for data on a given area. Thus, the reader will find, conveniently assembled, political, topographic, economic and special maps of a political area or region, accompanied by detailed map indexes, statistical data, and illustrations of the national flags of the area.

The sequence of country units in this American-designed atlas is international in arrangement. Units on the world as a whole are followed by a section on the polar regions which, in turn, is followed by pages devoted to Europe and its countries. Every continent map is accompanied by special population distribution, climatic and vegetation maps of that continent. Following the maps of the European continent and its countries, the geographic sequence plan proceeds as follows: Asia, the Pacific and Australia, Africa, South America, and ends with North America.

Political Maps — The Primary Reference Tool. The most detailed maps in each country unit are the *political maps.* It is our feeling that the reader is likely to refer to these maps more often than to any other in the book when confronted by such questions as — Where? How big? What is it near? Answering these common queries is the function of the political maps. Each political map stresses *political* phenomena — countries, internal political divisions, boundaries, cities and towns. The major political unit or units, shown on the map, are banded in distinctive colors for easy identification and delineation. First-order political subdivisions (states, provinces, counties on the state maps) are shown, scale permitting.

The reader is advised to make use of the *legend* appearing under the title on each political map. Map *symbols,* the special "language" of maps, are explained in the legend. Each variety of dot, circle, star or interrupted line has a special meaning which should be clearly understood by the user so that he may interpret the map data correctly.

Each country has been portrayed at a *scale* commensurate with its political, areal, economic or tourist importance. In certain cases, a whole map unit may be devoted to a single nation if that nation is considered to be of prime interest to most atlas users. In other cases, several nations will be shown on a single map if, as separate entities, they are of lesser relative importance. Areas of dense settlement and important significance within a country have been enlarged and portrayed in inset maps inserted on the margins of the main map. The reader is advised to refer to the linear or "bar" scale appearing on each map or map inset in order to ascertain the basic scale of the map or to determine the distance between points.

The *projection* system used for each map is noted near the title of the map. Map projections are the special graphic systems used by cartographers to render the curved three-dimensional surface of the globe on a flat surface. Optimum map projections determined by the attributes of the area have been used by the publishers for each map in the atlas.

A word here as to the choice of place names on the maps. Throughout the atlas names appear, with a few exceptions, in their local official spellings. However, conventional Anglicized spellings are used for major geographical divisions and for towns and topographic features for which English forms exist; i.e., "Spain" instead of "España" or "Munich" instead of "München." Names of this type are normally followed by the local official spelling in

parentheses. As an aid to the user the indexes are cross-referenced for all current and most former spellings of such names.

It is the belief of the publishers that the boundaries shown in a general reference atlas should reflect current geographic and political realities. This policy has been followed consistently in the atlas. The presentation of *de facto* boundaries in cases of territorial dispute between various nations does not imply the political endorsement of such boundaries by the publisher, but simply the honest representation of boundaries as they exist at the time of the printing of the atlas maps.

Indexes — Pinpointing a Location. Each political map is accompanied by a comprehensive index of the place names appearing on the map. If you are unfamiliar with the location of a particular geographical place and wish to find its position within the confines of the subject area of the map, consult the map index as your first step. The name of the feature sought will be found in its proper alphabetical sequence with a key reference letter-number combination corresponding to its location on the map. After noting the key reference letter-number combination for the place name, turn to the map. The place name will be found within the square formed by the two lines of latitude and the two lines of longitude which enclose the co-ordinates — i.e., the marginal letters and numbers. The diagram below illustrates the system of indexing.

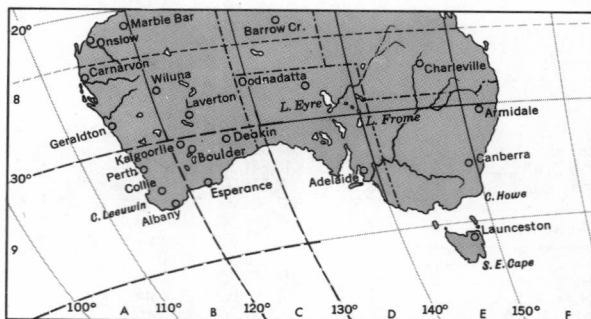

In the case of maps consisting entirely of insets, the place name is found near the intersection point of the imaginary lines connecting the co-ordinates at right angles. See below.

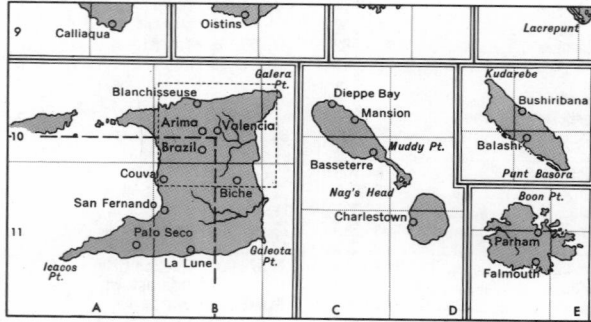

Where space on the map has not permitted giving the complete form of the place name, the complete form is shown in the index. Where a place is known by more than one name or by various spellings of the same name, the different forms have been included in the index. Physical features are listed under their proper names and not according to their generic terms; that is to say, Rio Negro will be found under Negro and not under Rio Negro. On the other hand, Rio Grande will be found under Rio Grande. Accompanying most index entries for cities and towns, and for other political units, are *population figures* for the particular entries. The large number of population figures in the atlas makes this work one of the most comprehensive statistical sources available to the public today. The population figures have been taken from the latest official censuses and estimates of the various nations.

Population and area figures for countries and major political units are listed in bold type *fact lists* on the margins of the indexes. In addition, the capital, largest city, highest point, monetary unit, principal languages and the prevailing religions of the country concerned are also listed. The Gazetteer-Index of the World on the preceding pages provides a quick reference index for countries and other important areas. Though population and area figures for each major unit area also found in the map section, the Gazetteer-Index provides a conveniently arranged statistical comparison contained in two pages.

Relief Maps. Accompanying each political map is a relief map of the area. The purpose of the relief map is to illustrate the surface configuration (TOPOGRAPHY) of the region. A shading technique in color simulates the relative ruggedness of the terrain — plains, plateaus, valleys, hills and mountains. Graded colors, ranging from greens for lowlands, yellows for intermediate elevations to browns in the highlands, indicate the height above sea level of each part of the land. A vertical scale at the margin of the map shows the approximate height in meters and feet represented by each color.

Economic Maps — Agriculture, Industry and Resources. One of the most interesting features that will be found in each country unit is the economic map. From this map one can determine the basic activities of a nation as expressed through its economy. A perusal of the map yields a full under-

standing of the area's economic geography and natural resources.

The agricultural economy is manifested in two ways: color bands and commodity names. The color bands express broad categories of *dominant land use,* such as, cereal belts, forest lands, livestock range lands, nonagricultural wastes. The red commodity names, on the other hand, pinpoint the areas of production of *specific* crops; i.e., wheat, cotton, sugar beets, etc.

Major mineral occurrences are denoted by standard letter symbols appearing in blue. The relative size of the letter symbols signifies the relative importance of the deposit.

The manufacturing sector of the economy is presented by means of diagonal line patterns expressing the various *industrial areas* of consequence within a country. The products of each major industrial area are listed in boxes at the margin of the map.

The fishing industry is represented by names of commercial fish species appearing offshore in blue letters. Major waterpower sites are designated by blue symbols.

The publishers have tried to make this work the most comprehensive and useful atlas available, and it is hoped that it will prove a valuable reference work. Any constructive suggestions from the reader will be welcomed.

Sources and Acknowledgments

A multitude of sources goes into the making of a large-scale reference work such as this. To list them all would take many pages and would consume space better devoted to the maps and reference materials themselves. However, certain general sources were very useful in preparing this work and are listed below.

STATISTICAL OFFICE OF THE UNITED NATIONS.
Demographic Yearbook. New York. Issued annually.

STATISTICAL OFFICE OF THE UNITED NATIONS.
Statistical Yearbook. New York. Issued annually.

THE GEOGRAPHER, U.S. DEPARTMENT OF STATE.
International Boundary Study papers. Washington. Various dates.

THE GEOGRAPHER, U.S. DEPARTMENT OF STATE.
Geographic Notes. Washington. Various dates.

UNITED STATES BOARD ON GEOGRAPHIC NAMES.
Official Standard Names Gazetteers. Washington. Various dates.

CANADIAN PERMANENT COMMITTEE ON GEOGRAPHICAL NAMES.
Gazetteer of Canada series. Ottawa. Various dates.

UNITED STATES DEPARTMENT OF THE INTERIOR. BUREAU OF MINES.
Minerals Yearbook. 4 vols. Washington. Various dates.

UNITED STATES DEPARTMENT OF COMMERCE. JOINT PUBLICATIONS RESEARCH SERVICE.
JPRS reports dealing with foreign geography. Washington. Various dates.

CARTACTUAL.
Cartactual — Topical Map Service. Budapest.. Issued bimonthly

AMERICAN GEOGRAPHICAL SOCIETY.
Focus. New York. Issued ten times a year.

A sample list of sources used for <u>specific</u> countries follows:

Algeria
COMMISSARIAT NATIONAL AU RECENSEMENT DE LA POPULATION.
Résultats Préliminaires du Recensement Général de la Population Effectué en 1966. Oran.

Barbados
BARBADOS STATISTICAL SERVICE.
1970 Census. St. Michael.

Chile
INSTITUTO NACIONAL DE ESTADÍSTICAS.
XIV Censo Nacional de Población y III de Vivienda. 1970. Santiago.

Dominican Republic
OFICINA NACIONAL DE ESTADÍSTICA.
Censo Nacional de Población y Habitación. 9 y 10 Enero de 1970. Santo Domingo.

France
INSTITUT NATIONAL DE LA STATISTIQUE ET DES ÉTUDES ÉCONOMIQUES.
Recensement de 1968. Population de la France. Paris.

Ghana
CENSUS OFFICE.
1970 Population Census of Ghana. Accra.

Iran
IRANIAN STATISTICAL CENTER.
National Census of Population and Housing, 1966. Tehran.

Ireland
THE CENTRAL STATISTICS OFFICE.
Census of Population of Ireland 1966. Dublin.

Kenya
MINISTRY OF ECONOMIC PLANNING AND DEVELOPMENT. STATISTICS DIVISION.
Provisional Results of the 1969 Population Census. Nairobi.

Kuwait
MINISTRY OF GUIDANCE & INFORMATION.
Population Census 1970. Kuwait.

Mexico
DIRECCIÓN GENERAL DE ESTADÍSTICA.
IX Censo General de Población 1970. México, D. F.

New Caledonia
INSTITUT NATIONAL DE LA STATISTIQUE ET DES ÉTUDES ÉCONOMIQUES (France).
Recensement de 1969. Paris.

Panama
DIRECCIÓN DE ESTADÍSTICA Y CENSO.
Censos Nacionales de 1970. Panamá.

Rhodesia
CENTRAL STATISTICAL OFFICE.
1969 Population Censuses. Salisbury.

Tanzania
CENTRAL STATISTICAL BUREAU.
1967 Population Census. Dar es Salaam.

Togo
DIRECTION DE LA STATISTIQUE.
Résultats Provisoires du Recensement Général de la Population 1970. Lomé.

U.S.S.R.
CENTRAL STATISTICAL ADMINISTRATION.
Preliminary Results of the All-Union Census of Population 1970. Moscow.

United States
BUREAU OF THE CENSUS.
1970 Census of Population. Washington.

CORPS OF ENGINEERS.
Reservoir status lists and maps. Various districts.

Zaire
MINISTÈRE DE L'INTÉRIEUR ET DES AFFAIRES COUTUMIÈRES.
Recensement Général de la Population 1970. Kinshasa.

Zambia
CENTRAL STATISTICAL OFFICE.
Population and Housing Census — 1969. Lusaka.

GLOSSARY OF ABBREVIATIONS

A

A. A. F. — Army Air Field
Acad. — Academy
A. C. T. — Australian Capital Territory
adm. — administration; administrative
adm. city-co. — administrative city-county
A. F. B. — Air Force Base
Afgh., Afghan. — Afghanistan
Afr. — Africa
A. & I. — Terr. of the Afars and Issas
Ala. — Alabama
Alb. — Albania
Alg. — Algeria
Alta. — Alberta
Amer. — American
Amer. Samoa — American Samoa
And. — Andorra
Ant. — Antarctica
Ar. — Arabia
arch. — archipelago
Arg. — Argentina
Ariz. — Arizona
Ark. — Arkansas
A. S. S. R. — Autonomous Soviet
　　　　Socialist Republic
Austr., Austral. — Australian, Australia
aut. — autonomous
Aut. Obl. — Autonomous Oblast
aut. prov. — autonomous province

B

B. — bay
Bah. Is. — Bahama Islands
Barb. — Barbados
Battlef. — Battlefield
Bch. — Beach
Belg. — Belgium
Berm. — Bermuda
Bol. — Bolivia
Bots. — Botswana
Br. — Branch
Br. — British
Braz. — Brazil
Br. Col. — British Columbia
Br. Ind. Oc. Terr. — British Indian
　　　　Ocean Territory
Bulg. — Bulgaria

C

C. — cape
Calif. — California
can. — canal
cap. — capital
Cent. Afr. Rep. — Central African
　　　　Republic
Cent. Amer. — Central America
C. G. Sta. — Coast Guard Station
C. H. — Court House
chan. — channel
Chan. Is. — Channel Islands
Chem. Ctr. — Chemical Center
co. — county
C. of G. H. — Cape of Good Hope
Col. — Colombia
Colo. — Colorado
comm. — commissary
Conn. — Connecticut
cont. — continent
cord. — cordillera (mountain range)
C. Rica — Costa Rica
C. S. — County Seat
C. Verde Is. — Cape Verde Islands
Cy. — City
C. Z. — Canal Zone
Czech. — Czechoslovakia

D

D. C. — District of Columbia
Del. — Delaware
Dem. — Democratic
Den. — Denmark
depr. — depression
dept. — department
des. — desert
dist., dist's — district, districts
div. — division
Dom. Rep. — Dominican Republic
dry riv. — dry river

E

E. — East
Ec., Ecua. — Ecuador
E. Ger. — East Germany
elec. div. — electoral division

El Salv. — El Salvador
Eng. — England
Eq. Guin. — Equatorial Guinea
escarp. — escarpment
est. — estuary
Eth. — Ethiopia

F

Falk. Is. — Falkland Islands
Fin. — Finland
Fk., Fks. — Fork, Forks
Fla. — Florida
for. — forest
Fr. — France, French
Fr. Gui. — French Guiana
Fr. Poly. — French Polynesia
Ft. — Fort

G

G. — gulf
Ga. — Georgia
Game Res. — Game Reserve
Ger. — Germany
geys. — geyser
Gibr. — Gibraltar
Gilb. & Ell. Is. — Gilbert and Ellice
　　　　Islands
glac. — glacier
gov. — governorate
Gr. — Group
Greenl. — Greenland
Gt. Brit. — Great Britain
Guad. — Guadeloupe
Guat. — Guatemala
Guy. — Guyana

H

har., harb., hbr. — harbor
hd. — head
highl. — highland, highlands
Hist. — Historic, Historical
Hond. — Honduras
Hts. — Heights
Hung. — Hungary

I

i., isl., — island, isle
Ice., Icel. — Iceland
Ida. — Idaho
Ill. — Illinois
Ind. — Indiana
ind. city — independent city
Indon. — Indonesia
Ind. Res. — Indian Reservation
int. div. — internal division
inten. — intendency
interm. str. — intermittent stream
Int'l — International
Ire. — Ireland
is., isls. — islands
Isr. — Israel
isth. — isthmus

J

Jam. — Jamaica
Jct. — Junction

K

Kans. — Kansas
Ky. — Kentucky

L

L. — Lake, Loch, Lough
La. — Louisiana
Lab. — Laboratory
lag. — lagoon
Ld. — Land
Leb. — Lebanon
Les. — Lesotho
Liecht. — Liechtenstein
Lux. — Luxembourg

M

Malag. Rep. — Malagasy Republic
Man. — Manitoba
Mart. — Martinique
Mass. — Massachusetts
Maur. — Mauritania
Md. — Maryland
met. area — metropolitan area
Mex. — Mexico
Mich. — Michigan
Minn. — Minnesota
Miss. — Mississippi

Mo. — Missouri
Mon. — Monument
Mong. — Mongolia
Mont. — Montana
Mor. — Morocco
Moz., Mozamb. — Mozambique
mt. — mount
mtn. — mountain

N

N., No. — North, Northern
N. Amer. — North America
N. A. S. — Naval Air Station
Nat'l — National
Nat'l Cem. — National Cemetery
Nat'l Mem. Park — National Memorial
　　　　Park
Nat'l Mil. Park — National Military
　　　　Park
Nat'l Pkwy. — National Parkway
Nav. Base — Naval Base
Nav. Sta. — Naval Station
N. B., N. Br. — New Brunswick
N. C. — North Carolina
N. Dak. — North Dakota
Nebr. — Nebraska
Neth. — Netherlands
Neth. Ant. — Netherlands Antilles
Nev. — Nevada
New Cal. — New Caledonia
Newf. — Newfoundland
New Hebr. — New Hebrides
N. H. — New Hampshire
Nic. — Nicaragua
N. Ire. — Northern Ireland
N. J. — New Jersey
N. Mex. — New Mexico
Nor. — Norway, Norwegian
No. Terr. — Northern Territory
　　　　(Australia)
N. S. — Nova Scotia
N. S. W. — New South Wales
N. W. T. — Northwest Territories
　　　　(Canada)
N. Y. — New York
N. Z. — New Zealand

O

Obl. — Oblast
O. F. S. — Orange Free State
Okla. — Oklahoma
Okr. — Okrug
Ont. — Ontario
Ord. Depot — Ordnance Depot
Oreg. — Oregon

P

Pa. — Pennsylvania
Pac. — Pacific
Pac. Is. — Pacific Islands,
　　　　Territory of the
Pak. — Pakistan
Pan. — Panama
Par. — Paraguay
par. — parish
passg. — passage
P.D.R. Yemen — Peoples Democratic
　　　　Republic of Yemen
P. E. I. — Prince Edward Island
pen. — peninsula
Phil., Phil. Is. — Philippines
Pk. — Park
pk. — peak
plat. — plateau
Port. — Portugal, Portuguese
P. Rico — Puerto Rico
pref. — prefecture
prom. — promontory
prov. — province, provincial
prov. dist. — provincial district
pt. — point

Q

Que. — Québec
Queens. — Queensland

R

R. — River
ra. — range
Rec., Recr. — Recreation, Recreational
reg. — region
Rep. — Republic
Rep. of Congo — Republic of Congo
res. — reservoir
Res. — Reservation, Reserve

Rhod. — Rhodesia
R. I. — Rhode Island
riv. — river
Rum. — Rumania

S

S. — South
Sa. — Sierra, Serra
S. Afr., S. Africa — South Africa
salt dep. — salt deposit
salt des. — salt desert
S. Amer. — South America
São T. & Pr. — São Tomé
　　　　and Príncipe
Sask. — Saskatchewan
Saudi Ar. — Saudi Arabia
S. Aust., S. Austral. — South Australia
S. C. — South Carolina
Scot. — Scotland
Sd. — Sound
S. Dak. — South Dakota
Sen. — Senegal
sen. dist. — senatorial district
Seych. — Seychelles
S. F. S. R. — Soviet Federated Socialist
　　　　Republic
Sing. — Singapore
S. Leone — Sierra Leone
S. Marino — San Marino
Sol. Is. Prot. — Solomon Islands
　　　　Protectorate, British
Sp. — Spanish
Spr., Sprs. — Spring, Springs
S. S. R. — Soviet Socialist Republic
St., Ste. — Saint, Sainte
Sta. — Station
St. Chr.-N.-A. — Saint Christopher-
　　　　Nevis-Anguilla
St. P. & M. — Saint Pierre and
　　　　Miquelon
str., strs. — strait, straits
Sur. — Surinam
S. W. Afr. — South-West Africa
Swaz. — Swaziland
Switz. — Switzerland

T

Tanz. — Tanzania
Tas. — Tasmania
Tenn. — Tennessee
terr., terrs. — territory, territories
Terr. N. G. — New Guinea, Territory of
Tex. — Texas
Thai. — Thailand
Trin. & Tob. — Trinidad and Tobago
Tun. — Tunisia
twp. — township

U

U. A. E. — Union of (United)
　　　　Arab Emirates
U. K. — United Kingdom
Upp. Volta — Upper Volta
urb. area — urban area
Urug. — Uruguay
U. S. — United States
U. S. S. R. — Union of Soviet Socialist
　　　　Republics

V

Va. — Virginia
Vall. — Valley
Ven., Venez. — Venezuela
V. I. (Br.) — Virgin Islands (British)
V. I. (U. S.) — Virgin Islands (U. S.)
Vic. — Victoria
Vill. — Village
vol. — volcano
Vt. — Vermont

W

W. — West, Western
Wash. — Washington
W. Aust., W. Austral. — Western
　　　　Australia
W. Ger. — West Germany
Wis. — Wisconsin
W. Samoa — Western Samoa
W. Va. — West Virginia
Wyo. — Wyoming

Y

Yugo. — Yugoslavia
Yukon — Yukon Territory

Environment & life

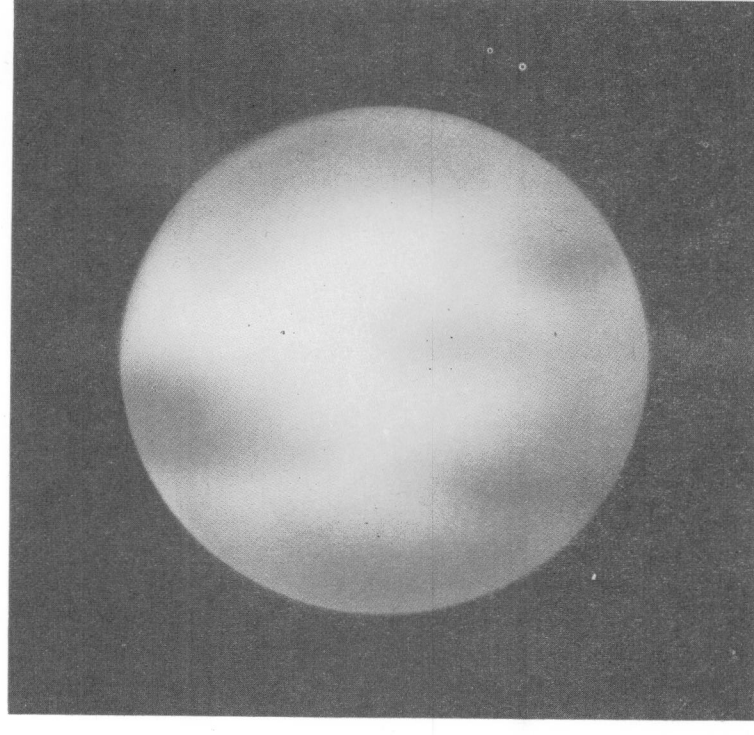

The Sun: *Energy Source of the Solar System*
*For longer than the memory of man, a
glowing furnace of nuclear activity has held our solar
system within its gravitational orbit and,
deep within its interior, fused the nuclei of
hydrogen and helium, dispensing them as heat, light and the
other forms of radiation which nurture the very elements of
life on earth. The sun—with radiant energy so fierce that
it was deified by ancient man—still dominates the
lives of laymen and the minds of
scientists who seek to comprehend its nature
and utilize its mighty force.*

The Earth:
ITS PERSPECTIVE IN SPACE

Tilted and spinning on its invisible axis, revolving with measured pace in orbit around the sun, moving with the sun and the other members of its solar system as it works its way through space toward the constellation Hercules, the earth in "perpetual motion" defines day and night and the seasons of the year with all their variations.

Like a giant gyroscope, the base of its axis rooted in the atmosphere, it tips its rounded surface to catch the direct rays of sun which begin to warm the Northern Hemisphere in March, as the earth angles its southern surface away from the source of heat and light. The 365¼-day procession of the seasons begins once more.

With more rapid motion the earth rotates from west to east, turning first one face and then the other toward the sun, measuring out the hours of day and night — man's labor and man's rest.

Neither flat nor completely round, our almost spherical planet is itself a gravitational force attracting all things toward itself and is subject to the effects of its rotations. Where the speed is greatest at the center of its mass it bulges out at the Equator and flattens somewhat in the slower moving polar areas.

Wrapped in a protective blanket of atmosphere which shields it from destruction by bombardment of high energy atomic particles released by the sun's giant magnetic storms, the earth in an otherwise hostile universe provides the only known environment capable of nurturing intelligent life or, as far as we know, any life at all.

But man has never been content with safety in his quest for understanding and now seeks beyond the atmosphere and beyond the stars to know — perhaps to conquer — all of his environment and find perhaps another, stranger universe.

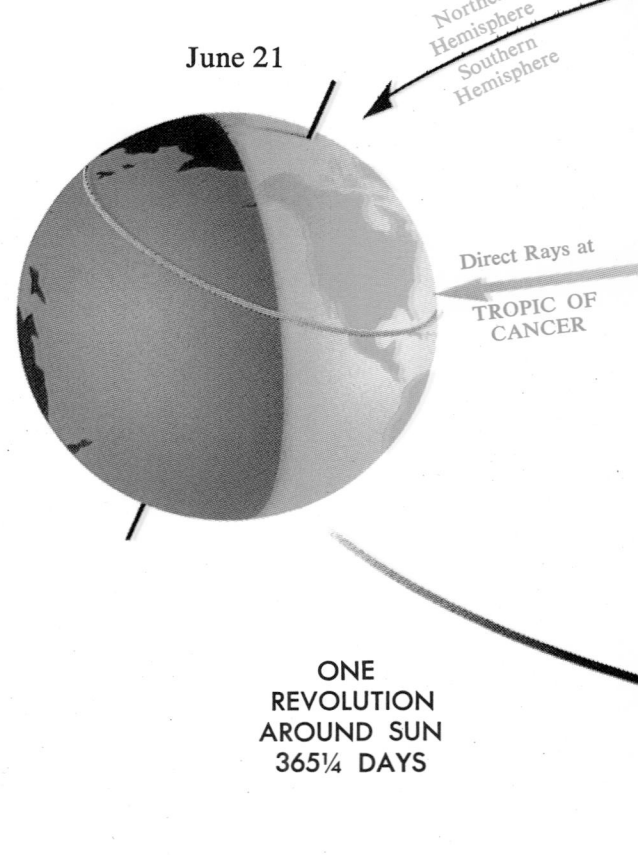

June 21

Northern Hemisphere
Southern Hemisphere

Direct Rays at
TROPIC OF CANCER

ONE
REVOLUTION
AROUND SUN
365¼ DAYS

SATELLITE VIEWS OF THE EARTH

From Sunrise to Sunset

7:30 A.M.

10:30 A.M.

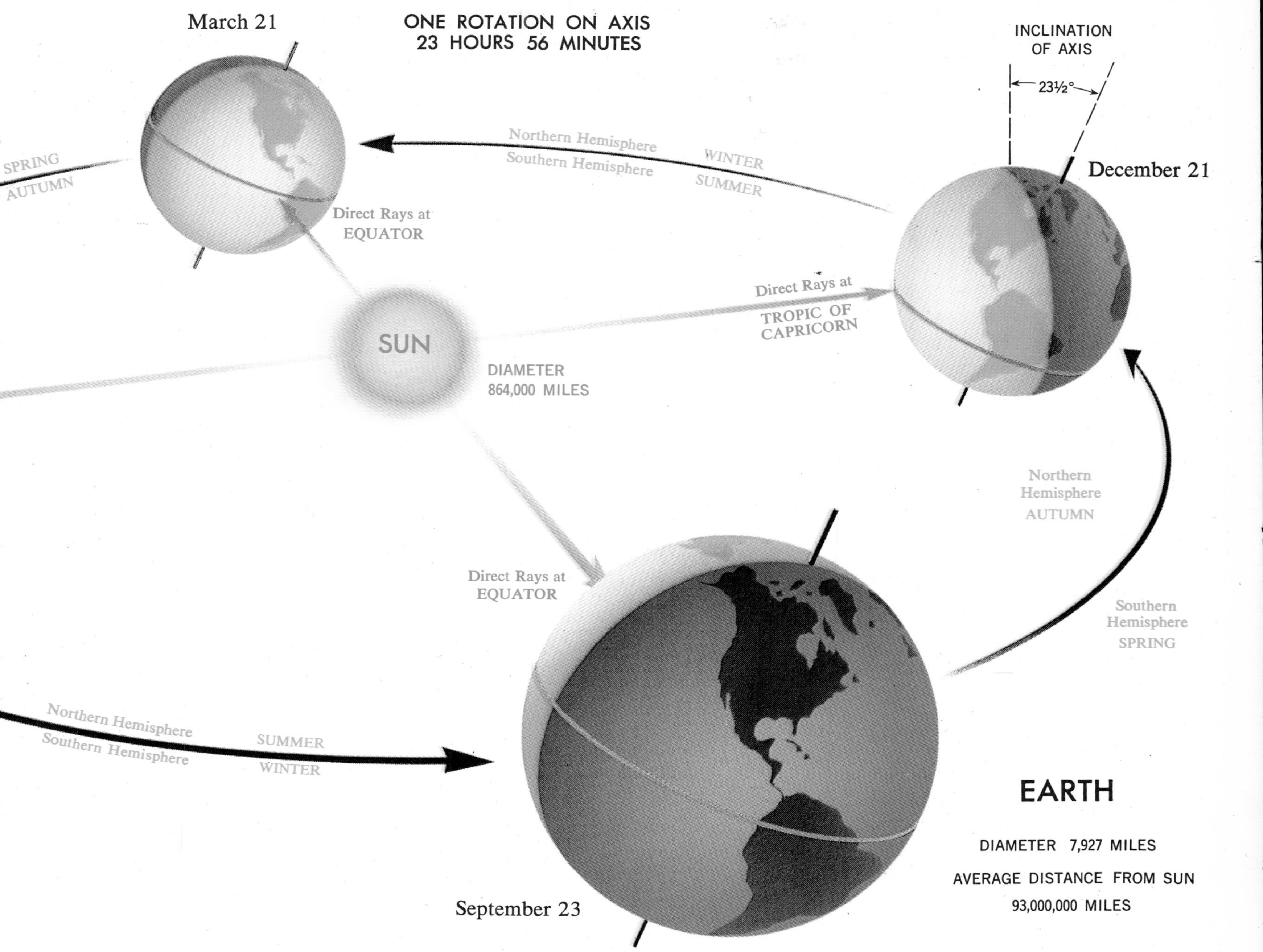

March 21

**ONE ROTATION ON AXIS
23 HOURS 56 MINUTES**

INCLINATION
OF AXIS

23½°

Northern Hemisphere WINTER
Southern Hemisphere SUMMER

SPRING
AUTUMN

December 21

Direct Rays at
EQUATOR

Direct Rays at
TROPIC OF
CAPRICORN

SUN

DIAMETER
864,000 MILES

Direct Rays at
EQUATOR

Northern
Hemisphere
AUTUMN

Southern
Hemisphere
SPRING

Northern Hemisphere SUMMER
Southern Hemisphere WINTER

EARTH

DIAMETER 7,927 MILES

AVERAGE DISTANCE FROM SUN
93,000,000 MILES

September 23

NASA

NOON

3:30 P.M.

7:30 P.M.

Structure of the Earth

The photographs (opposite) reveal views of the world seen only since the advent of satellites and space vehicles. Pictures such as these greatly increase man's understanding of the earth's structure and the visible forces which act upon it.

If man were big enough he could peel the earth somewhat like a complicated grape, finding at its heart what some scientists believe is the remains of its most primitive beginnings — a solid core of iron and nickel. Wrapped around this solid mass is a second, molten outer core which, set in motion by the earth's rotations, may be the source of its magnetic field. The solid rock mantle, extending to about 1,800 miles from the surface of the earth, is the next layer which in turn is covered by the crust and separated from it by a distinct boundary known as the Mohorovicic discontinuity. The crust, which is as deep as 40 miles under the continents, is only about 5 miles thick beneath the oceans.

To simplify the complex layerings of solids, liquids and gases which make up the structure of the earth, geologists have divided them into three zones: the lithosphere, containing all solids from the land surface to the earth's center; the hydrosphere, all surface water areas; and the atmosphere, the layered gaseous envelope extending about 600 miles above the earth's surface. From each of these three spheres the biologist has selected those parts which contain organic matter, plant as well as animal, and has grouped them together into a comprehensive zone known as the Biosphere. Here, in this world of life, man survives in relationship, however indirectly, with every other living organism.

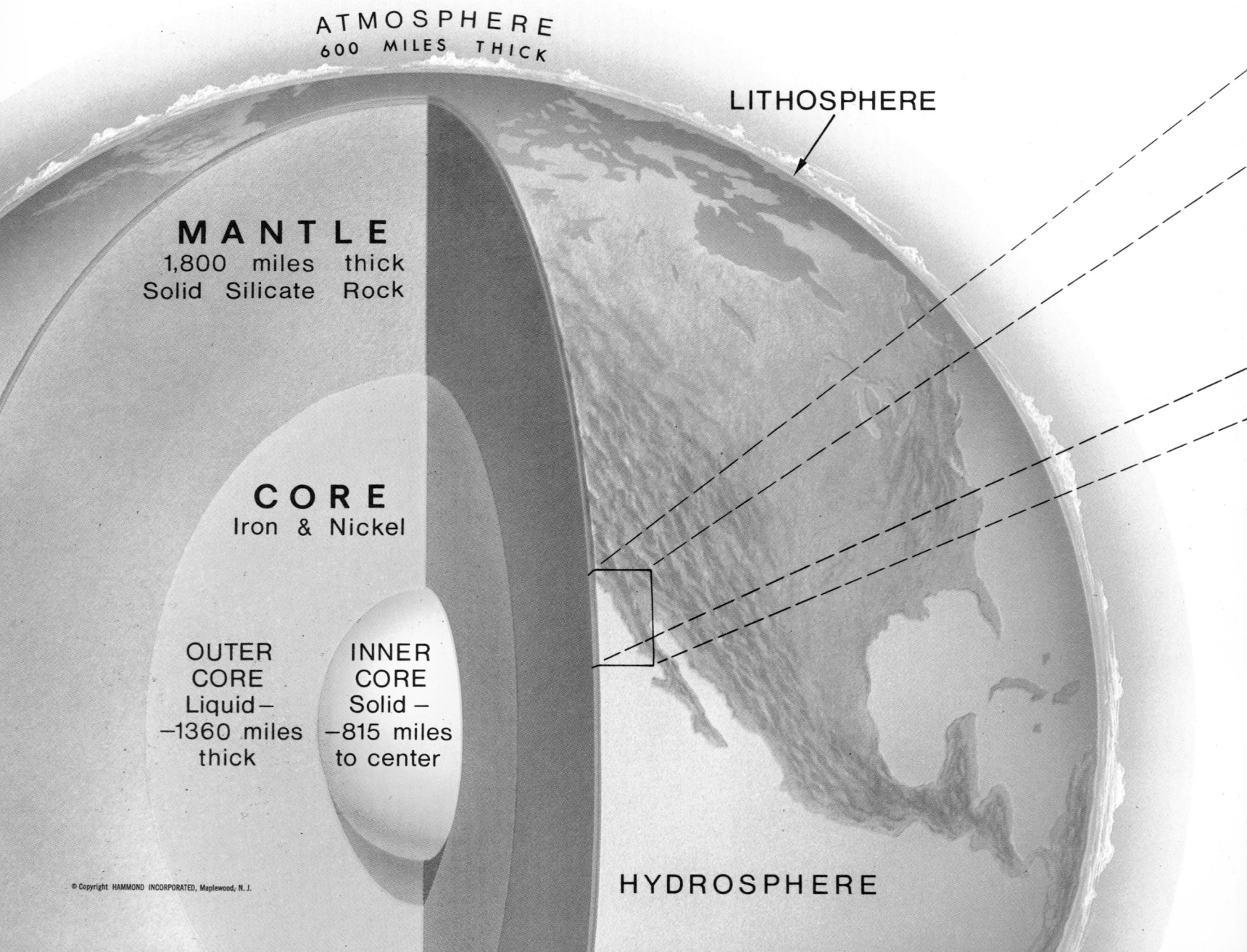

ATMOSPHERE
600 MILES THICK

LITHOSPHERE

MANTLE
1,800 miles thick
Solid Silicate Rock

CORE
Iron & Nickel

OUTER CORE
Liquid —
—1360 miles thick

INNER CORE
Solid —
—815 miles to center

© Copyright HAMMOND INCORPORATED, Maplewood, N. J.

HYDROSPHERE

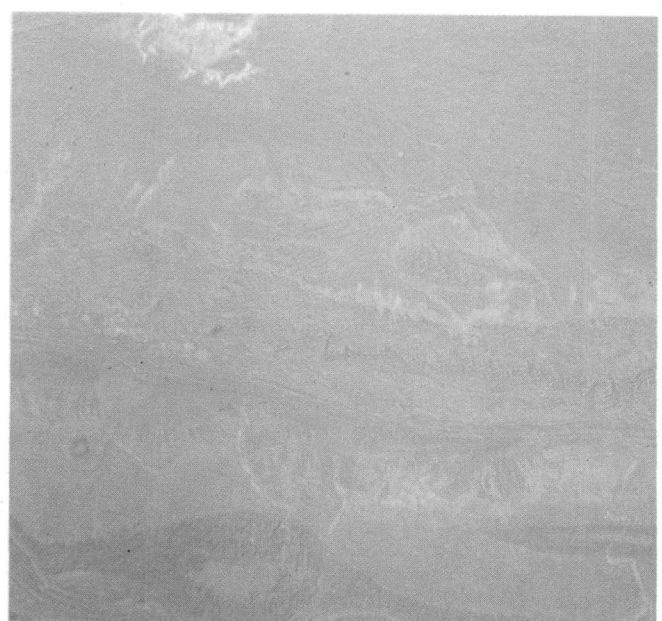

Complex geologic structures, Northern Territory, Australia   NASA

Ocean-bottom topography of the Great Bahama Bank   NASA

CRUST
Average — 25 miles thick

SIAL (Granitic)

SIMA (Basaltic)

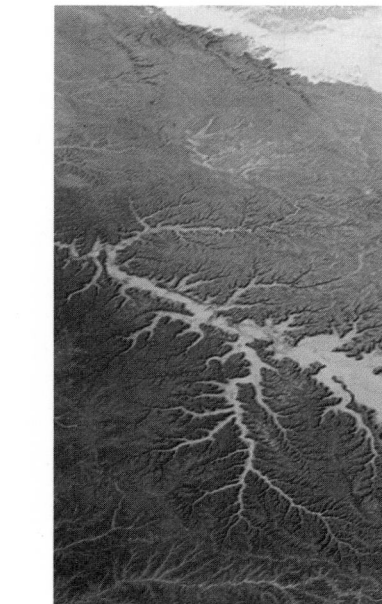

Classic dendritic drainage patterns, Saudi Arabia   NASA

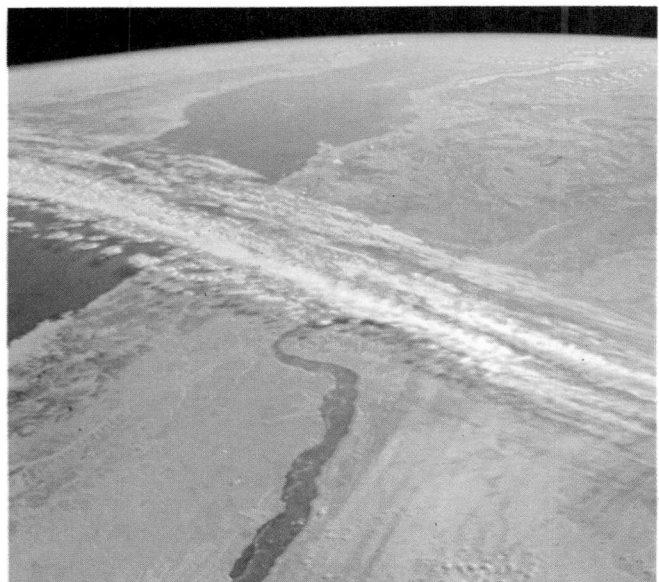

Jet stream over the Red Sea and Nile Valley   NASA

Cloud formations affecting the Indian Subcontinent   NASA

Development of Continents and Oceans

If we can envision the continents of the world as seated firmly on massive rafts of rock and moving across the surface of the earth at a rate of about 6 feet every 60 years we have a basic notion of what is meant by continental drift and the manner in which land and sea masses have been formed.

The original concept of continental drift was proposed in the 1920s, but only during the past three years or so have geologists and geophysicists accepted as fact the seemingly preposterous notion that the surface of the earth is constantly in motion.

The making of the continents began more than 200 million years ago during the Permian period with the splitting of a gigantic landmass known as Pangaea. Two con-

tinents, Laurasia to the north and Gondwana to the south, were formed by the initial division. Over a period of many millions of years these landmasses subdivided into smaller parts approximately the shapes of Africa, Eurasia, North and South America, Australia, and Antarctica as we know them today.

Although, if he could go back in time, a 20th century cartographer would recognize these landmasses by their profiles, their positions relative to each other would probably seem like a puzzle maker's bad joke. New York would rest on the Equator; Japan would be in the Arctic; and Australia and India would touch the Antarctic.

Earth's traditional timetable — rock — has provided much of the scientific basis for the theory of continental

(continued)

CRUSTAL STRUCTURE AND MOVEMENT

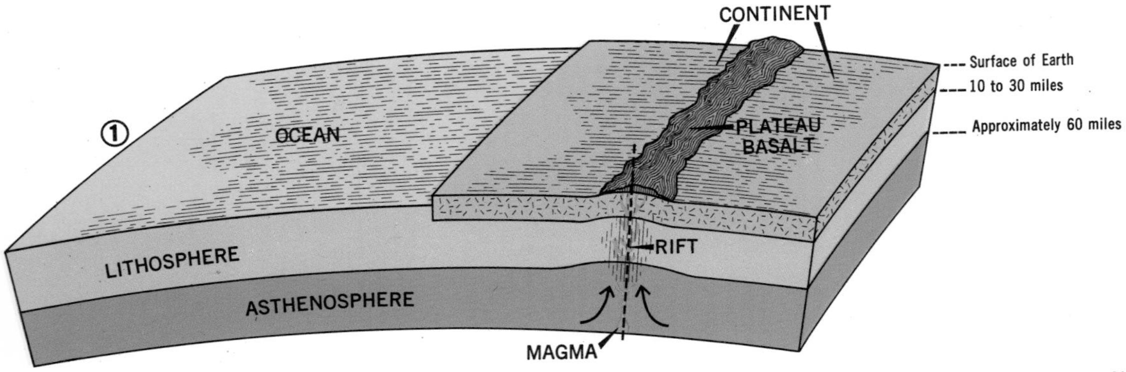

The concept of movement within the earth's crust assumes that the earth's outer layer has a firm lithosphere divided up into individual pieces called plates. These plates "float" above a weaker interior layer, the **asthenosphere**, and over vast periods of time noticeably change position, shape, size and direction depending upon forces exerted from within the earth.

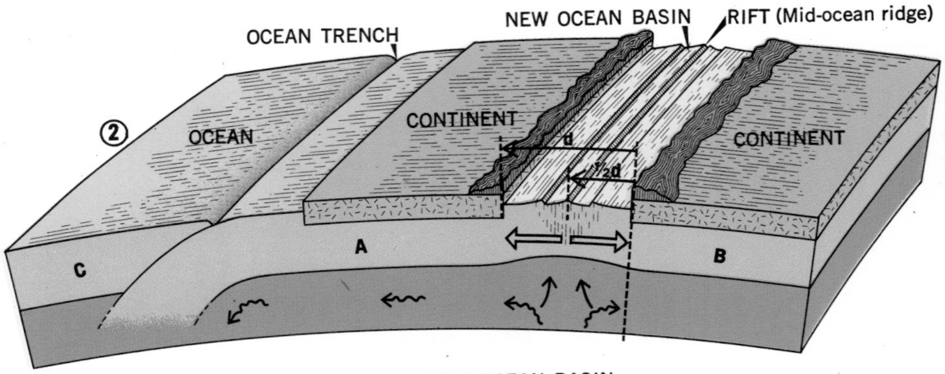

① A rift or split in a lithosphere plate has caused a break in the overlying continental landmass. The pressure exerted by the outpouring of magma onto the earth's surface results in a spreading apart of the lithosphere plates.

② Continued pressure from the rift area forces plates A and B to separate and "raft" with them their accompanying continental areas. As the continents move away from each other, an ever-widening new ocean basin (d) is formed.

③ A neighboring plate, C, separated from plate A by a trench, is confronted by the rafted continental mass. The continent could be absorbed directly down into the trench or, as this diagram shows, collide with the edge of the trench, causing its downward slope angle to be reversed in direction.

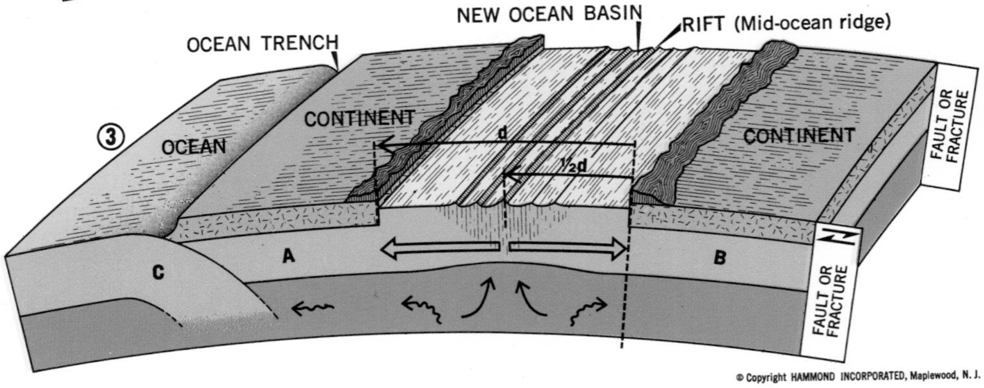

PERMIAN
225 Million Years Ago

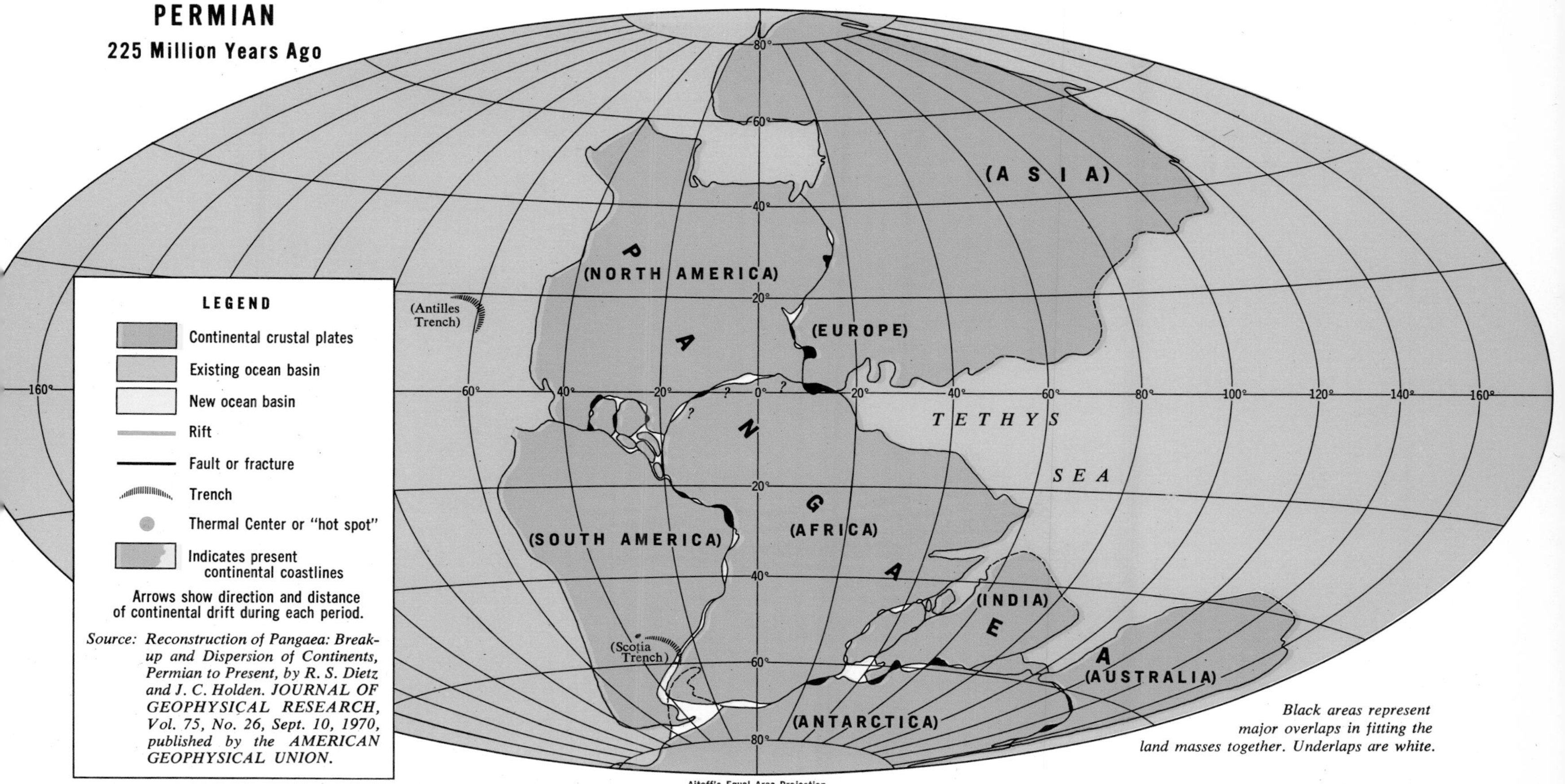

(A S I A)

P (NORTH AMERICA)

(EUROPE)

A

N

G

(SOUTH AMERICA)

(AFRICA)

E

A

T E T H Y S

S E A

(INDIA)

A

(AUSTRALIA)

(ANTARCTICA)

(Antilles Trench)

(Scotia Trench)

LEGEND

	Continental crustal plates
	Existing ocean basin
	New ocean basin
	Rift
	Fault or fracture
	Trench
●	Thermal Center or "hot spot"
	Indicates present continental coastlines

Arrows show direction and distance of continental drift during each period.

Source: Reconstruction of Pangaea: Break-up and Dispersion of Continents, Permian to Present, by R. S. Dietz and J. C. Holden. JOURNAL OF GEOPHYSICAL RESEARCH, Vol. 75, No. 26, Sept. 10, 1970, published by the AMERICAN GEOPHYSICAL UNION.

Black areas represent major overlaps in fitting the land masses together. Underlaps are white.

Aitoff's Equal Area Projection

A single earth landmass, Pangaea, is reconstructed by fitting together present-day continents at their offshore slope depths of about 2,000 meters. This line is believed to approximate the location of the original continental breaks.

TRIASSIC
180 Million Years Ago

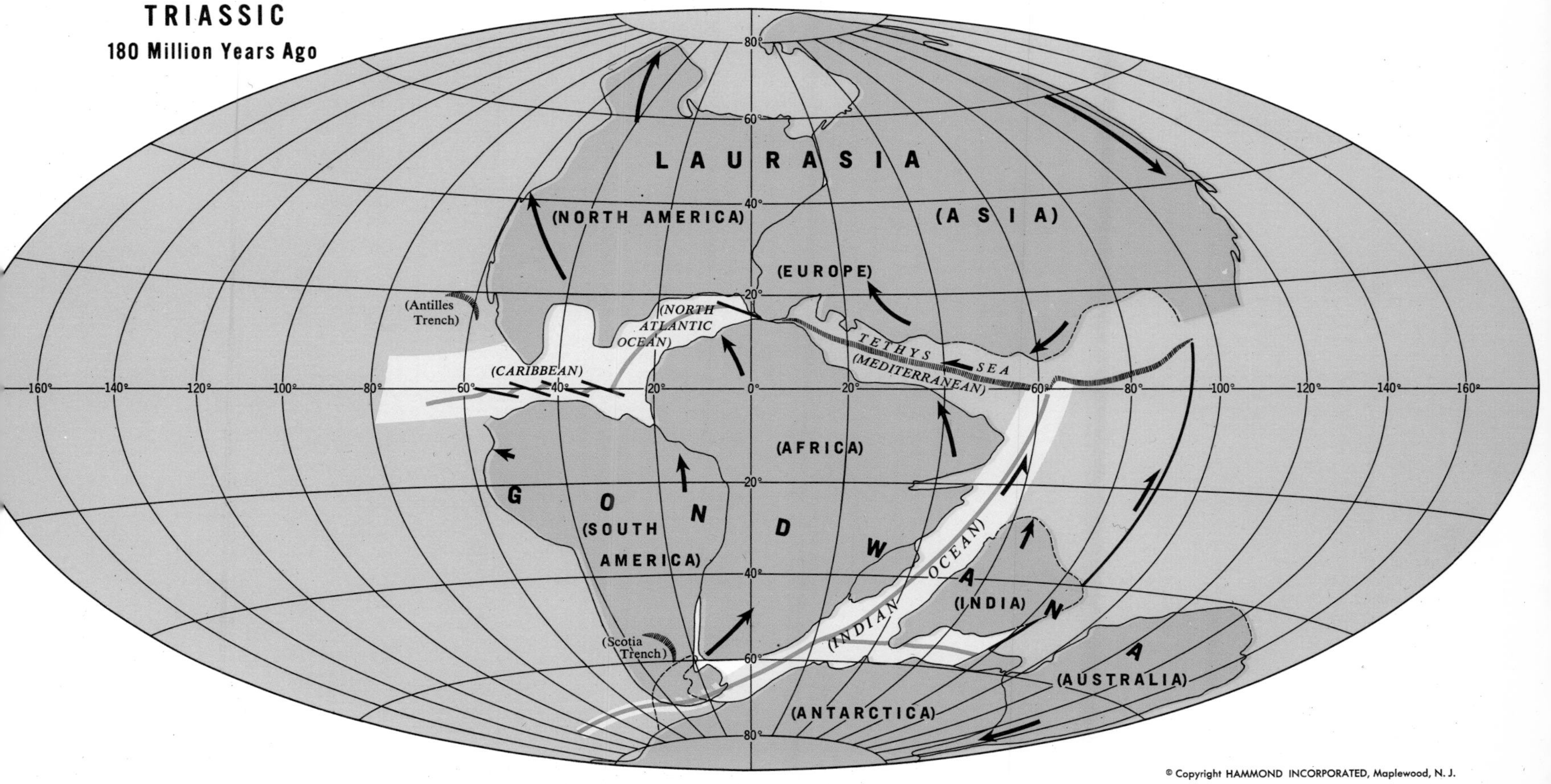

L A U R A S I A

(NORTH AMERICA)

(A S I A)

(EUROPE)

(Antilles Trench)

(NORTH ATLANTIC OCEAN)

(CARIBBEAN)

T E T H Y S   S E A
(MEDITERRANEAN)

G

O

N

D

W

A

N

A

(SOUTH AMERICA)

(AFRICA)

(INDIA)

(INDIAN OCEAN)

(AUSTRALIA)

(ANTARCTICA)

(Scotia Trench)

© Copyright HAMMOND INCORPORATED, Maplewood, N. J.

During the Triassic Period the northern group of continents, Laurasia, moves away from the southern landmass, Gondwana. Splitting off from Gondwana are areas which will eventually become India, Australia and Antarctica.

JURASSIC
135 Million Years Ago

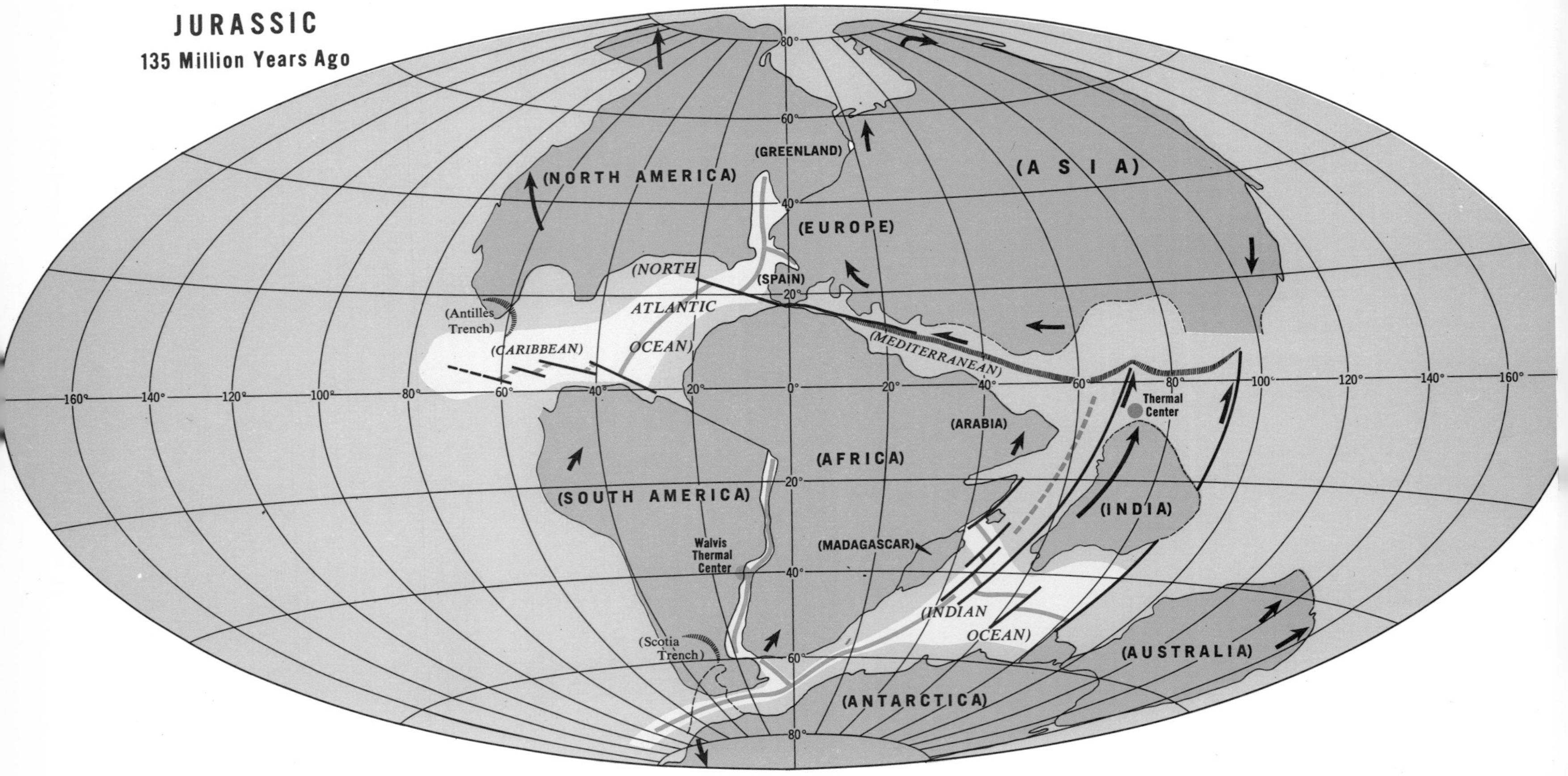

Further drifting opens up the North Atlantic Ocean and creates a wide break between South America and Africa.
The India landmass continues its rapid movement toward Asia.

CRETACEOUS
70 Million Years Ago

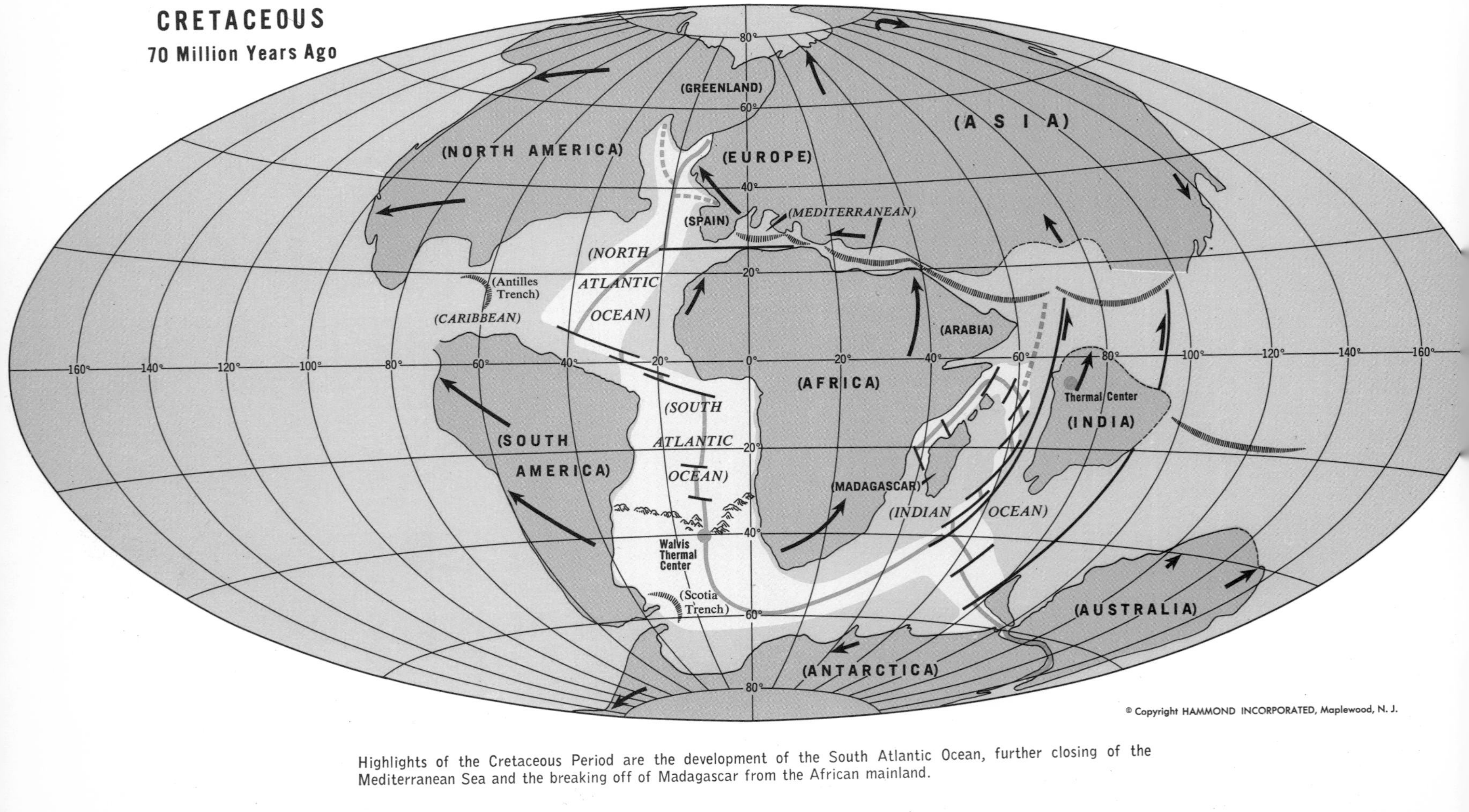

© Copyright HAMMOND INCORPORATED, Maplewood, N. J.

Highlights of the Cretaceous Period are the development of the South Atlantic Ocean, further closing of the
Mediterranean Sea and the breaking off of Madagascar from the African mainland.

(continued)

movement and the formation of land and sea masses. When it was in a molten state, rock captured and preserved the minerals and the primitive life of millions of years ago. In a similar fashion, it has retained the magnetic orientation present in the various geologic periods during which it became solid and stratified.

Through a study of ancient rocks, scientists are able to discover the locations of the magnetic poles at stages of the earth's development. By comparing the magnetic orientation of rock found on different continents but solidified during the same geologic periods, they have determined that magnetic pole locations vary from continent to continent. If continents had retained their original positions without shifting in their relationships, the direction of their magnetic poles would be the same.

But how do continents move? The concept of tremendous masses of land floating across the face of the earth staggers the imagination. One explanation of the continental drift mechanism can be made in terms of plate tectonics and seafloor spreading.

The lithosphere, or outer surface of the earth, is composed of rock about 60 miles thick. Beneath the lithosphere lies the relatively weak upper layer of the earth's mantle called the asthenosphere. For reasons which are not com-

pletely clear, forces generated in the asthenosphere during the Permian period caused the earth's outer surface to break into 10 major and a number of minor sections called plates. It is on these plates that the continents rest.

The rifts between the plates filled with molten material from the mantle, pushing the plates to either side and farther and farther apart as the material continued to seep through. Since material from the mantle is heavier than lithospheric rock, it leveled off below sea level forming ocean floors as water from the Pacific, or "mother" ocean, flowed in. Study of the floors of the Atlantic and Indian oceans reveal a ridge or rift running almost directly north to south at their centers indicating that they developed in this fashion.

During the past 65 million years (the Cenozoic era)—a relatively short period of geological time—nearly half of the ocean floors were created and the continents continued to move in a generally westward direction into their present positions.

Sea bottoms continue to be shoved away from the sides of rifts and continents continue in their monolithic movements. In 50 million years, if our cartographer could return, he would have to begin again to plot his pictures of the changing world.

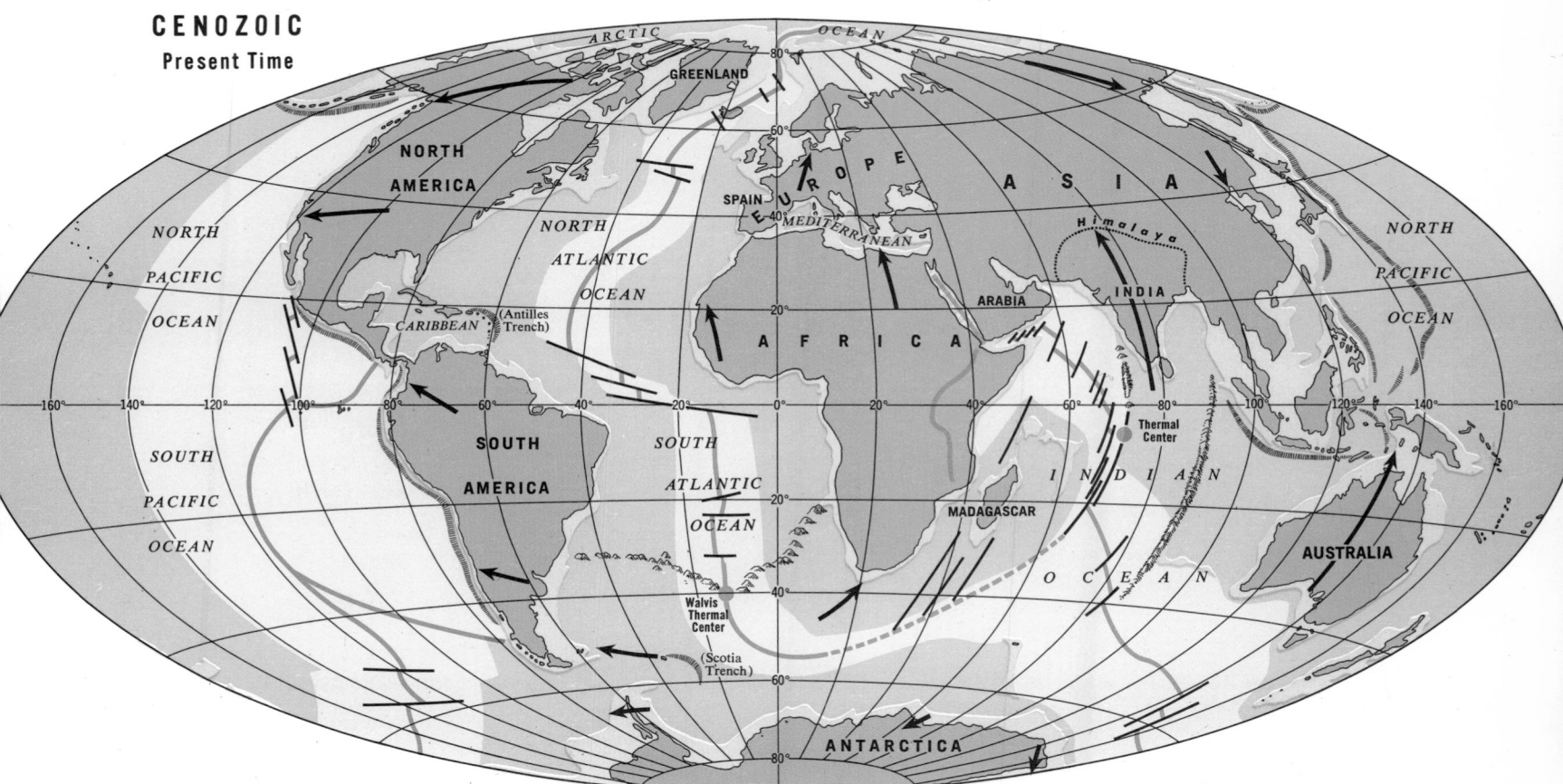

The work of the past 70 million years has shaped the world as it appears today. India has collided with Asia, and Laurasia has been split apart in the North Atlantic. Movements on and within the earth's crust continue to alter the face of our planet.

The Ice Ages

Far from being an isolated instance, the movement of glaciers over the face of the earth has been a natural phenomenon for many thousands of years. Stimulated by changes in climate and resulting changes in sea level — perhaps induced by shifts in the earth's axis — glaciers have followed a rather unpredictable course of advance and retreat continuing into the 20th century.

At some point in unrecorded history during the greatest ice age, or the Pleistocene epoch, as much as 27 percent of the earth's surface was covered by glacial ice to a depth of up to 10,000 feet. The icy masses moved across the earth as far south as New York City and the Missouri River in North America, burying much of Europe and blanketing vast areas in northern Asia.

Many of the great ice sheets retreated as the climate became warmer, leaving deposits of soil and rock picked up as they traveled southward in the Northern Hemisphere. The landscape changed as the glaciers left behind their typical U-shaped valleys, amphitheater-like hollows and jagged mountain ridges, altering to a large extent the former ecological zones which changed again and again as the ice reformed and melted.

Although not enough is known about glaciers to predict accurately their future behavior, we do know that they react to climatic changes. Glaciers were advancing in Alpine regions during the 19th century until a global warm up in the beginning of this century caused their retreat. Recently the trend has been toward cooler and moister climate and, on a limited scale, glaciers are beginning to advance once more.

An imaginary scene during the Pleistocene Epoch shows an advancing continental glacier virtually covering all terrain in its path. (Courtesy of The American Museum of Natural History)

During an interglacial period of the Pleistocene, the retreating glaciers left a scoured landscape laden with ice-transported deposits. (Courtesy of The American Museum of Natural History)

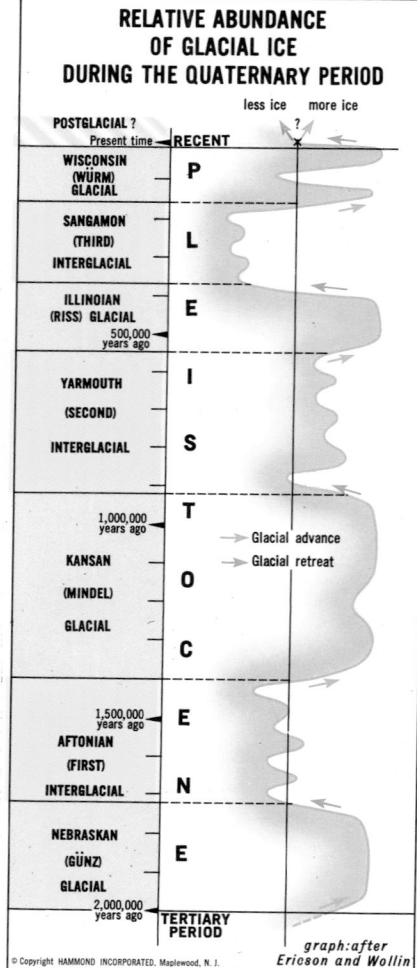

RELATIVE ABUNDANCE OF GLACIAL ICE DURING THE QUATERNARY PERIOD

less ice   more ice

POSTGLACIAL ?
Present time — RECENT   ?

WISCONSIN (WÜRM) GLACIAL   P

SANGAMON (THIRD) INTERGLACIAL   L

ILLINOIAN (RISS) GLACIAL   E
500,000 years ago

YARMOUTH (SECOND) INTERGLACIAL   I S

1,000,000 years ago   T

→ Glacial advance
→ Glacial retreat

KANSAN (MINDEL) GLACIAL   O

C

1,500,000 years ago   E

AFTONIAN (FIRST) INTERGLACIAL   N

NEBRASKAN (GÜNZ) GLACIAL   E

2,000,000 years ago   TERTIARY PERIOD

© Copyright HAMMOND INCORPORATED, Maplewood, N. J.

graph:after Ericson and Wollin

Four major glacial periods highlight the last 2,000,000 years of history. Future glaciation will depend upon those factors which control the earth's climate.

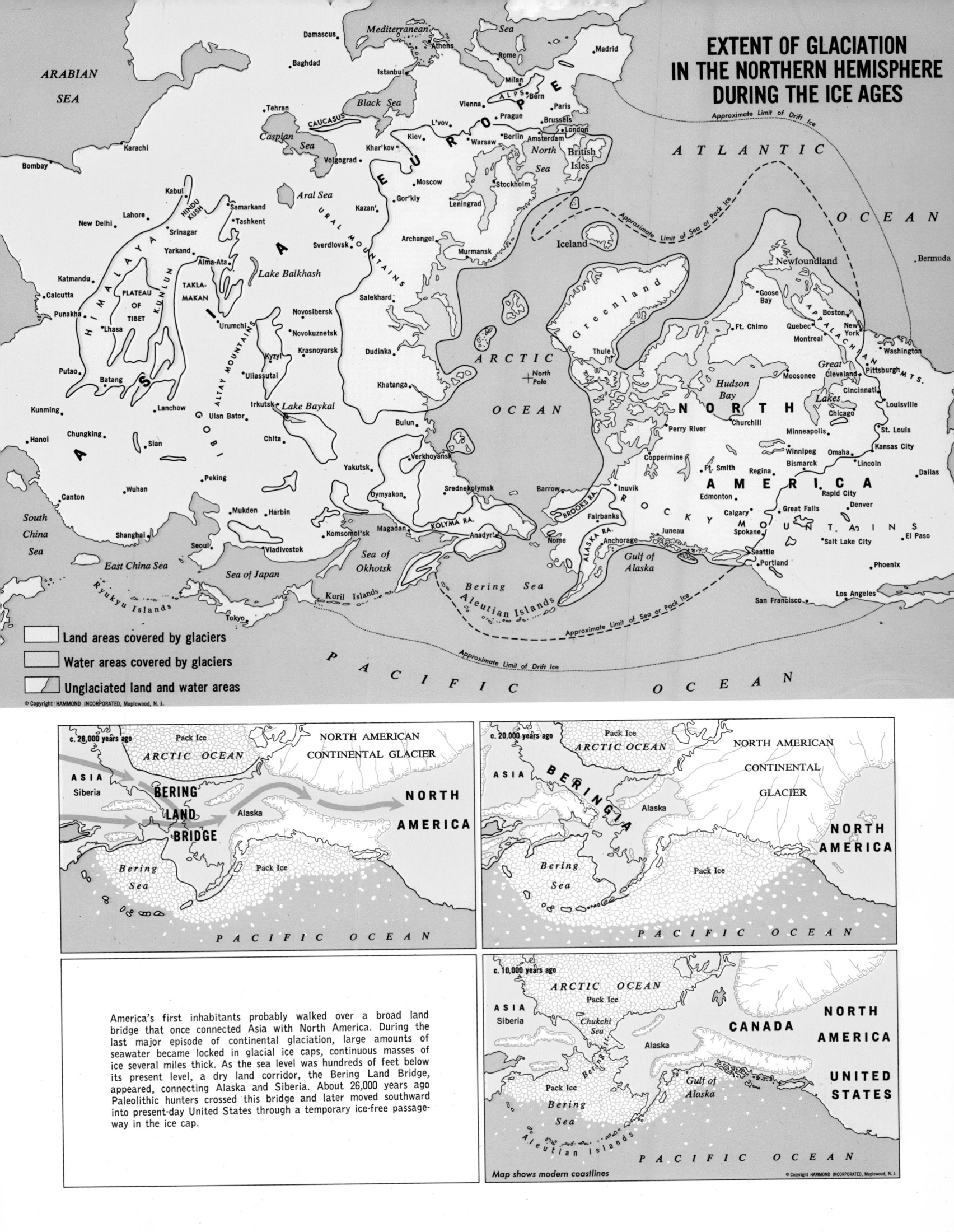

EXTENT OF GLACIATION IN THE NORTHERN HEMISPHERE DURING THE ICE AGES

Land areas covered by glaciers

Water areas covered by glaciers

Unglaciated land and water areas

© Copyright HAMMOND INCORPORATED, Maplewood, N. J.

c. 26,000 years ago — ARCTIC OCEAN — Pack Ice — NORTH AMERICAN CONTINENTAL GLACIER — ASIA Siberia — BERING LAND BRIDGE — Alaska — NORTH AMERICA — Bering Sea — Pack Ice — PACIFIC OCEAN

c. 20,000 years ago — ARCTIC OCEAN — Pack Ice — NORTH AMERICAN CONTINENTAL GLACIER — ASIA — BERINGIA — Alaska — NORTH AMERICA — Bering Sea — Pack Ice — PACIFIC OCEAN

America's first inhabitants probably walked over a broad land bridge that once connected Asia with North America. During the last major episode of continental glaciation, large amounts of seawater became locked in glacial ice caps, continuous masses of ice several miles thick. As the sea level was hundreds of feet below its present level, a dry land corridor, the Bering Land Bridge, appeared, connecting Alaska and Siberia. About 26,000 years ago Paleolithic hunters crossed this bridge and later moved southward into present-day United States through a temporary ice-free passageway in the ice cap.

c. 10,000 years ago — ARCTIC OCEAN — Pack Ice — ASIA Siberia — Chukchi Sea — NORTH AMERICA CANADA — Alaska — Pack Ice — Bering Sea — Gulf of Alaska — UNITED STATES — Aleutian Islands — PACIFIC OCEAN — Map shows modern coastlines — © Copyright HAMMOND INCORPORATED, Maplewood, N. J.

Changing the Face of the Earth

The face of the earth, like man himself, is continually changing — the victim of stress and counterstress, thrust and counterthrust from within and from without. The opposing forces of uplift, and weathering and erosion are constantly at work sculpturing the face of the land. The forces to which a given landscape is subject can be read on the surface at various stages in much the same way that a man's character can be traced in his face.

The infant's skin is relatively smooth and unbroken; as he grows toward manhood, the structure of his facial bones becomes more apparent as the jawline and cheekbones assume their clear-cut definition. So too an "infant landscape"— the consequence of the raising of land for whatever reason — is smooth. Gradually small streams and rivers develop and their narrow valleys begin to deepen and widen as water makes its way toward the sea.

With maturity, laugh lines or the markings of innumerable frowns begin to furrow a man's skin. As he grows older and muscles weaken, much of the underlying structure disappears as the skin is smoothed down by the continual tugs of gravity. When valleys have reached their base limit their straightforward routes are ended and they begin to dissect the landscape with lateral cuts. Broad valleys result and eventually widen until old age, when the entire landscape has been flattened to an almost uninterrupted valley called a floodplain. If this flattening process, the result of weathering and erosion, were to go unchecked for several thousands of years, the earth's surface would be uninterestingly flat and covered by shallow water. But the nature of the earth is to rebuild itself.

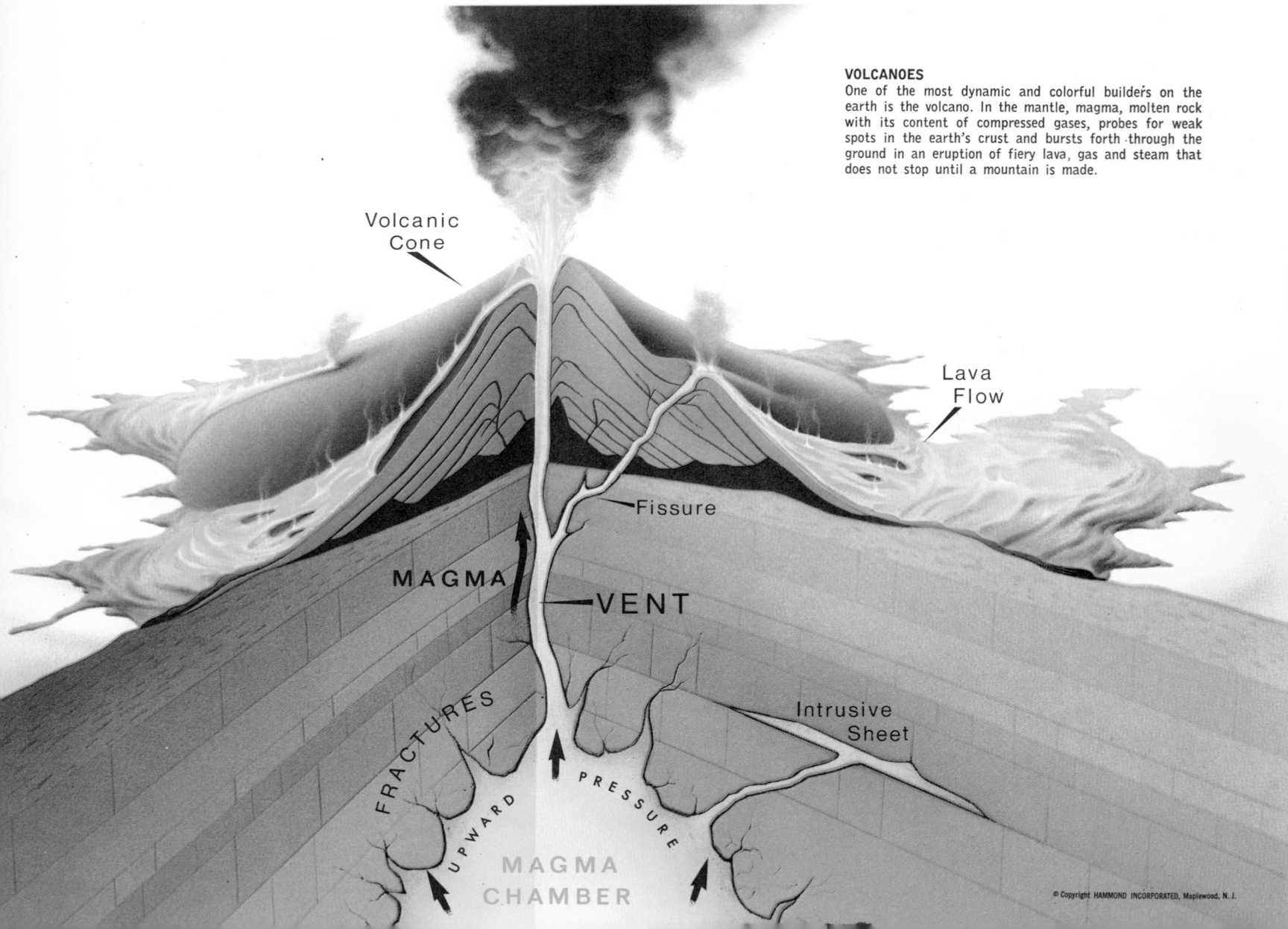

VOLCANOES
One of the most dynamic and colorful builders on the earth is the volcano. In the mantle, magma, molten rock with its content of compressed gases, probes for weak spots in the earth's crust and bursts forth through the ground in an eruption of fiery lava, gas and steam that does not stop until a mountain is made.

Volcanic Cone

Lava Flow

Fissure

MAGMA

VENT

FRACTURES

Intrusive Sheet

UPWARD PRESSURE

MAGMA CHAMBER

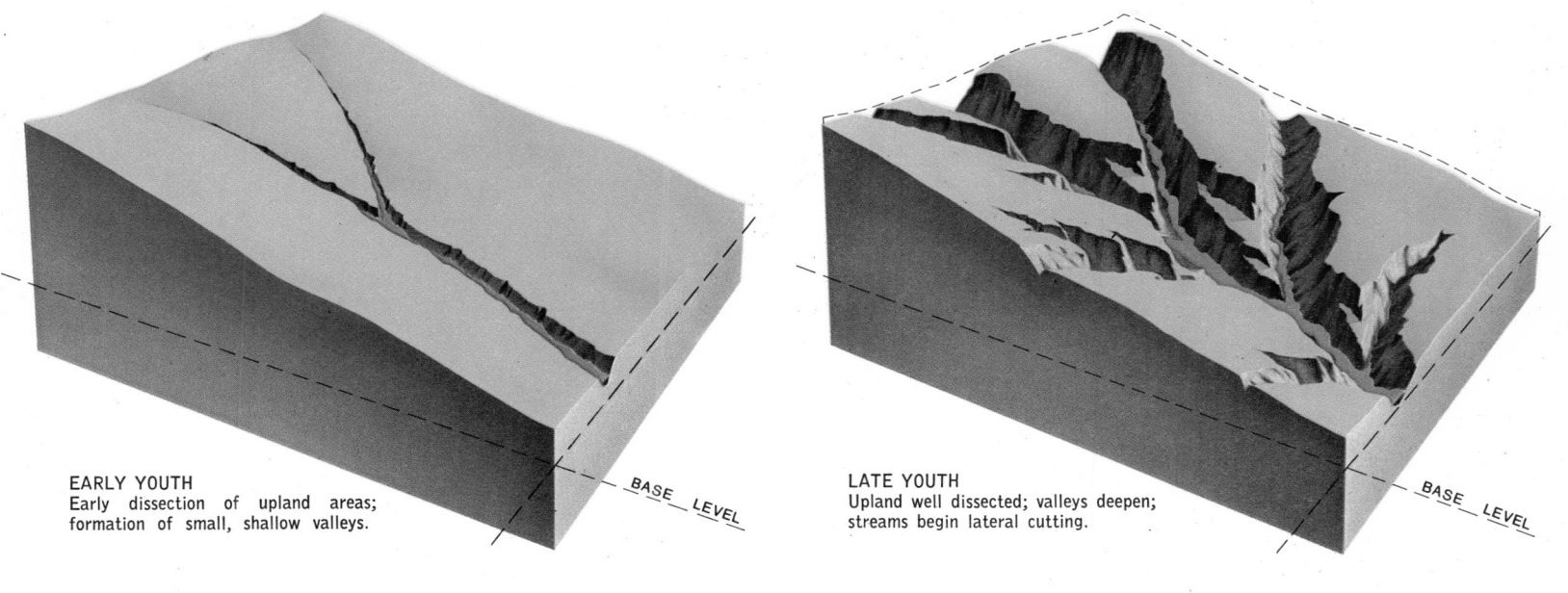

EARLY YOUTH
Early dissection of upland areas; formation of small, shallow valleys.

BASE LEVEL

LATE YOUTH
Upland well dissected; valleys deepen; streams begin lateral cutting.

BASE LEVEL

RUNNING WATER
Beginning as rainfall, running water is a prolific sculptor of the face of the land. Laden with picked-up abrasive materials, it flows downhill to the sea, carving and widening valleys until ultimately it reduces all the terrain in its path to near base level.

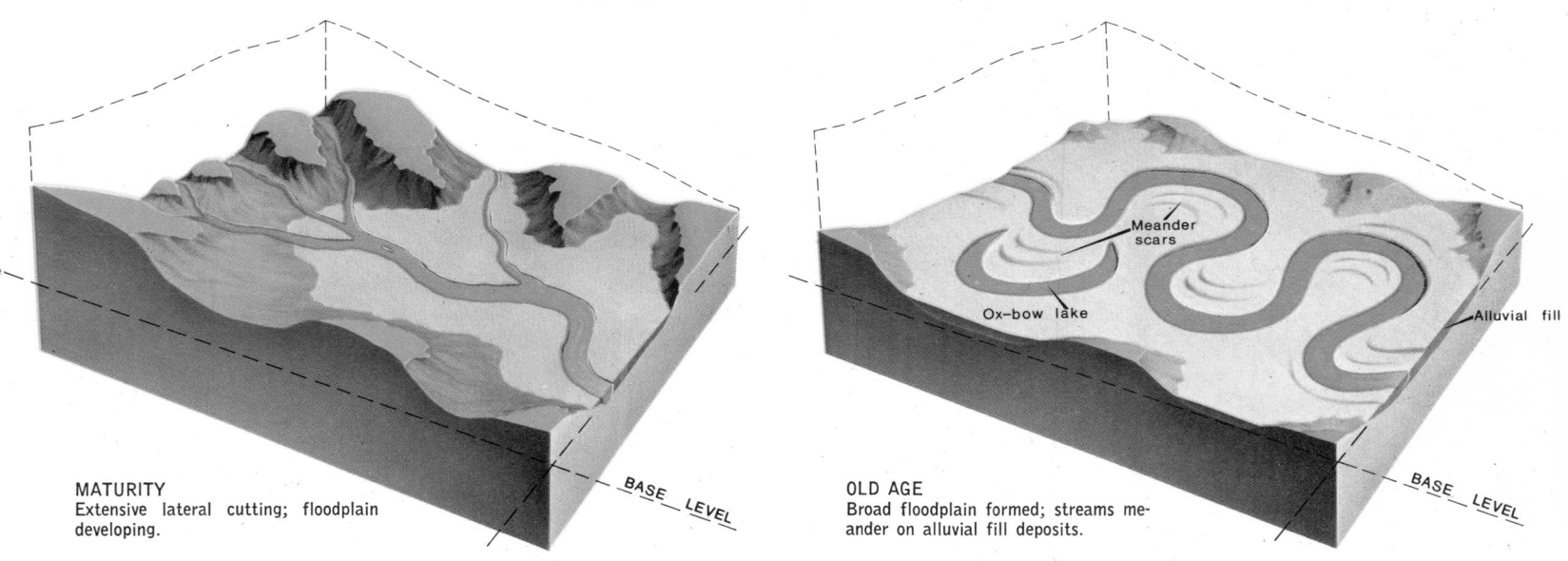

MATURITY
Extensive lateral cutting; floodplain developing.

BASE LEVEL

OLD AGE
Broad floodplain formed; streams meander on alluvial fill deposits.

Meander scars

Ox-bow lake

Alluvial fill

BASE LEVEL

Uplift, or the building process, can be as violent as erosion is passive. Uplift is the result of unbearable forces or stresses within the depths of the earth which demand to be loosed on the surface. We do not know for certain whether the energy results from cooling of the earth's core, from movement within the mantle, or from the pressures of accumulating silt deposits on the ocean floors. We do know that when the tremendous energy of a volcano or an earthquake is released, the growing pains of earth can become a disaster to mankind.

The volcano "blows its stack" when it can no longer contain the pressure of steam and other gases within the sealed chamber of its interior. As these materials seek to expand, they exert unbearable forces on the rocks overlying the chamber. Fissures are created. As the pressure continues, one of the fissures breaks through to the surface and an eruption occurs, spewing gases and molten rock — material from the magma chamber — through the main vent and through subsidiary fissures. With each subsequent eruption the volcanic cone — or the sides of the "mountain"— increase in height and depth until the volcano ceases its external activity and becomes dormant.

Sometimes volcanic mountains, such as the enigmatic Fonuafoou in the Kingdom of Tonga, rise rapidly from the depths of the sea, belch forth their complement of lava, gases and ash, and then mysteriously disappear. More often the volcanic mountain rises slowly, growing larger as it feeds on its own eruptions. Eventually the mountain quiets and supports new life until it wears away through the process of weathering and erosion.

For scientists the volcanic builders of the earth are interesting because they extend our knowledge of the workings of the earth's interior. In some instances life caught in death has been preserved for the archaeologist and anthropologist in historic cities like Pompeii, whose swift destruction was preserved by an airless blanket of lava and ash. Nothing survived the satanic blast when the top blew off the volcanic island of Krakatoa in 1882. However, the very lack of a single living organism gave us an opportunity to observe the island's recolonization and study the beginnings of life in a "primeval" territory.

Fortunately not all mountains or mountain ranges are

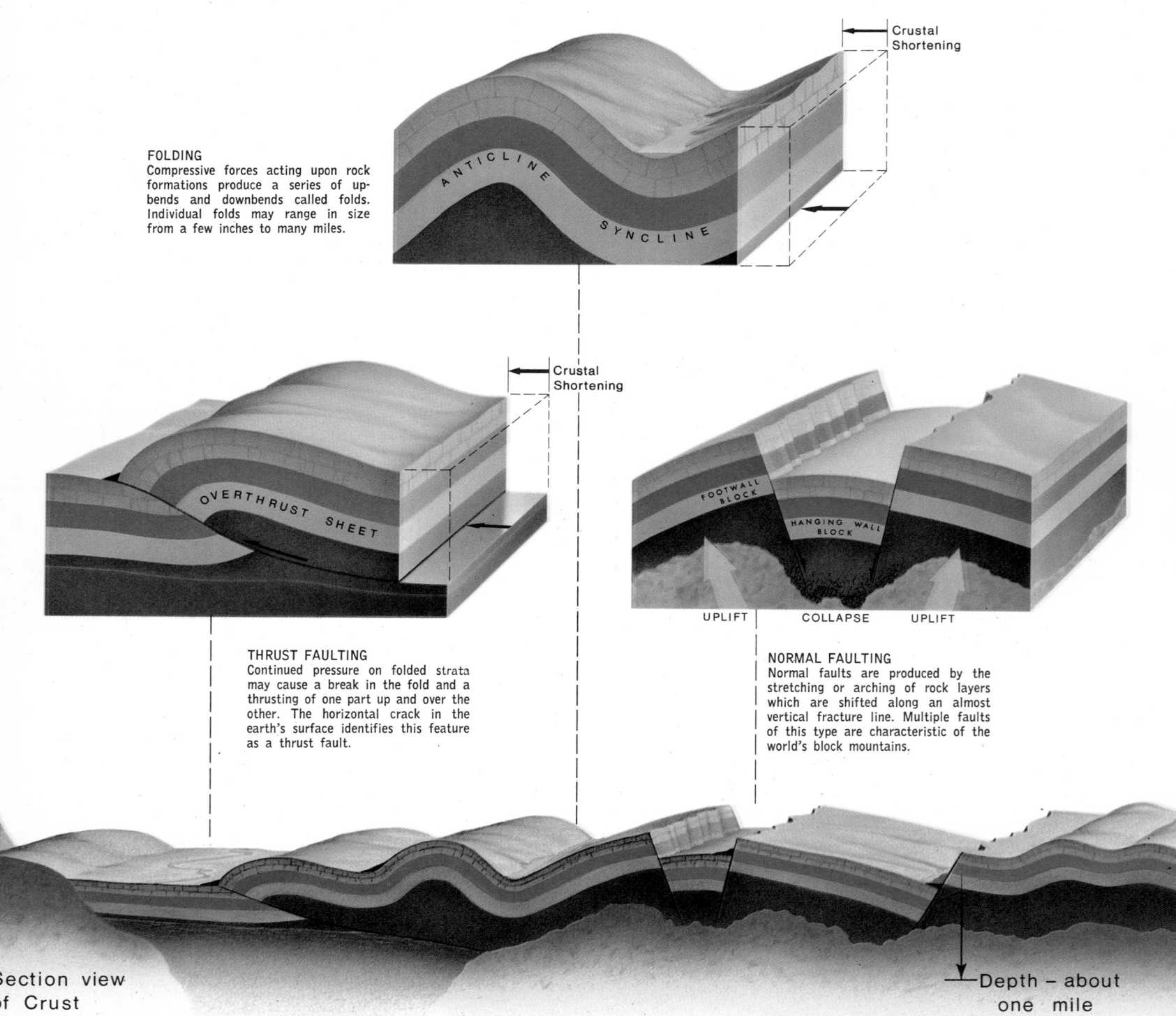

CRUSTAL DEFORMATION
Stress within the earth manifests itself in a variety of ways on the earth's crust. Most typical of these are the warped and cracked features seen on the earth's surface.

Crustal Shortening

FOLDING
Compressive forces acting upon rock formations produce a series of up-bends and downbends called folds. Individual folds may range in size from a few inches to many miles.

ANTICLINE

SYNCLINE

Crustal Shortening

OVERTHRUST SHEET

THRUST FAULTING
Continued pressure on folded strata may cause a break in the fold and a thrusting of one part up and over the other. The horizontal crack in the earth's surface identifies this feature as a thrust fault.

FOOTWALL BLOCK

HANGING WALL BLOCK

UPLIFT   COLLAPSE   UPLIFT

NORMAL FAULTING
Normal faults are produced by the stretching or arching of rock layers which are shifted along an almost vertical fracture line. Multiple faults of this type are characteristic of the world's block mountains.

Section view of Crust

Depth – about one mile

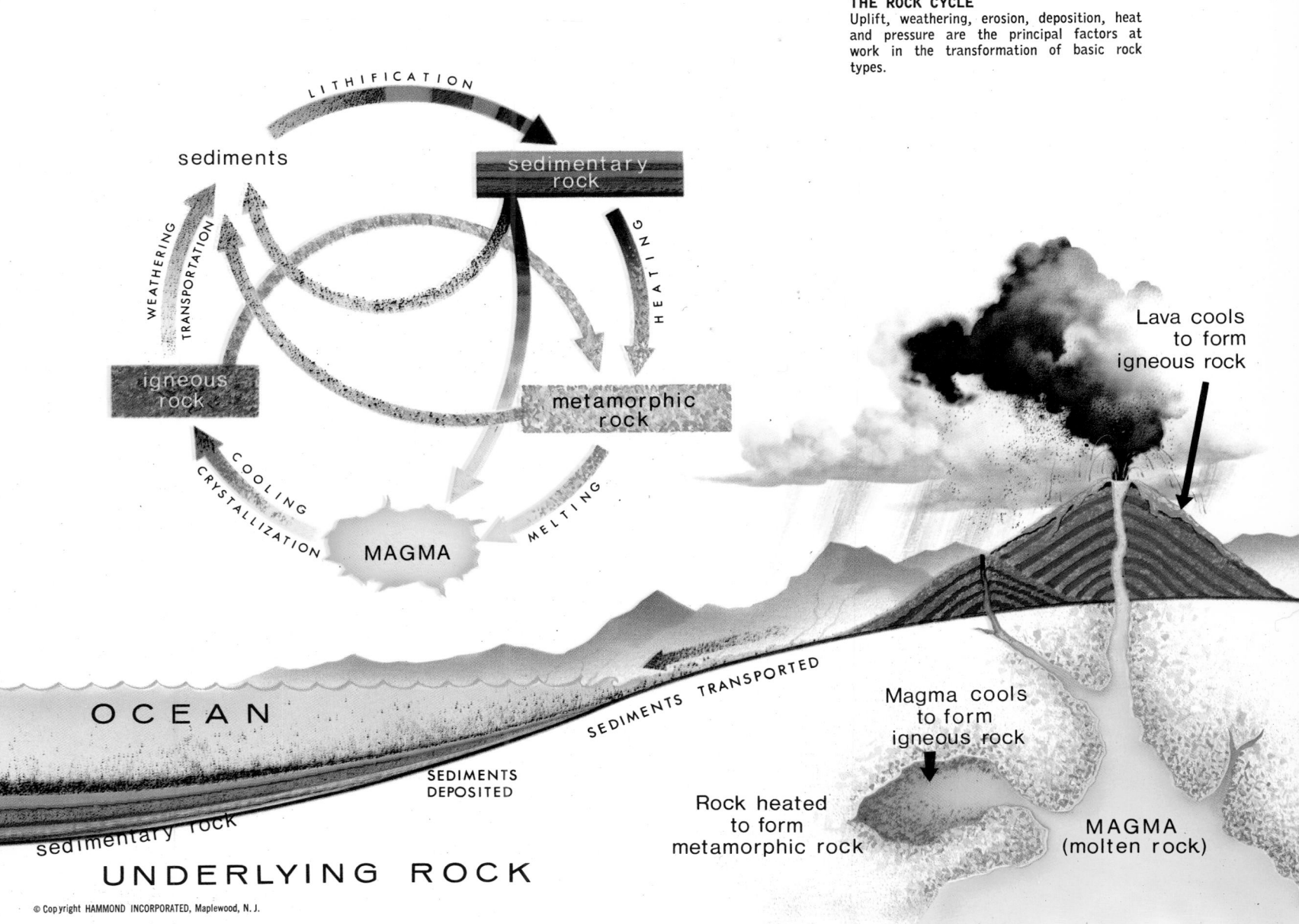

THE ROCK CYCLE
Uplift, weathering, erosion, deposition, heat and pressure are the principal factors at work in the transformation of basic rock types.

© Copyright HAMMOND INCORPORATED, Maplewood, N.J.

built with so much haste and violence. Often flat lands, reacting to compressive forces, grow into mountains or mountain ranges almost imperceptibly over a period of millions of years. The tides of the mantle, the layer of still-molten rock under the earth's surface, continue to flow under tremendous pressure. Sometimes this pressure creates folds or faults in the crustal rock. As pressure increases wave-like formations called folds are produced. If the underlying stress becomes too great the rock fractures or breaks creating a fault.

In recorded history as many as 100,000 people have lost their lives in a single incident as the rock on one or both sides of a fault shifted, creating an earthquake. Fracture or fault zones occur throughout the world, but

the Pacific area, where most volcanoes are located, also contains the greatest concentration of major fracture zones, many connected with structures on the North American continent. Movement along the San Andreas Fault, extending more than 600 miles in California, destroyed San Francisco in 1906 and was responsible for the damage in Los Angeles during early 1971.

Clearly, men who say there is nothing new on the face of the earth have never watched it open up beneath their feet or lived long enough to see a mountain grow and wash away again. They cannot understand that time will turn the barren rock beneath their feet to soil as, often gently, sometimes violently, the face of the earth is continually altered.

GEOLOGIC TIME

TIME DIVISION			YEARS AGO	MAJOR GEOLOGIC DEVELOPMENTS
CENOZOIC ERA	QUATERNARY PERIOD	RECENT	10,000	GREAT LAKES
		PLEISTOCENE	1-2 million	NORWEGIAN FJORDS ICE AGES BLACK SEA
	TERTIARY PERIOD	PLIOCENE	11 million	CASPIAN SEA
		MIOCENE	25 million	HIMALAYAS
		OLIGOCENE	40 million	ALPS
		EOCENE	60 million	
		PALEOCENE	70 million	
MESOZOIC ERA		CRETACEOUS PERIOD	135 million	ANDES MOUNTAINS ROCKY MOUNTAINS CHALK DEPOSITS
		JURASSIC PERIOD	180 million	COAST RANGES SIERRA NEVADA JURA MOUNTAINS NEW JERSEY PALISADES
		TRIASSIC PERIOD	225 million	CAUCASUS URAL MOUNTAINS APPALACHIAN MOUNTAINS
PALEOZOIC ERA		PERMIAN PERIOD	270 million	POTASH DEPOSITS
		PENNSYLVANIAN PERIOD	300 million	COAL DEPOSITS
		MISSISSIPPIAN PERIOD	350 million	ACADIAN MOUNTAINS
		DEVONIAN PERIOD	400 million	
		SILURIAN PERIOD	440 million	NIAGARA FALLS CAPROCK TACONIC MOUNTAINS
		ORDOVICIAN PERIOD	500 million	LIMESTONE DEPOSITS VERMONT MOUNTAINS
		CAMBRIAN PERIOD	600 million	ARIZONA MOUNTAINS
		PRE-CAMBRIAN		METALLIC ORE DEPOSITS LAURENTIAN MOUNTAINS ADIRONDACK MOUNTAINS

© Copyright HAMMOND INCORPORATED, Maplewood, N. J.

Like a giant Rosetta stone the secrets of the earth's creation lie spread in strata beneath our feet, revealing their hieroglyphic message to a few of the initiated.

For billions of years layers of rock — the sedimentary deposits of ages — have piled up on the earth's surface, entrapping the characteristics of time. Time when a lifeless nature prepared for the first microscopic living organisms; time when these organisms were destroyed or became extinct; time when, through endless subtle mutations, they evolved into new forms of life.

The Paleozoic, ancient era; Mesozoic, middle era; and Cenozoic, recent era, are the designations used for the broad periods of time during which life evolved. Locked within strata of rock, vestiges of life are found in the fossilized remains of creatures over a billion years old. In succeeding layers geologists and anthropologists find other clues to the mystery of time and life: the appearance of the lowest forms of animal life; the evolution of fish, amphibians, reptiles, birds and mammals. Late in the schedule of creation traces of a strange and wonderful animal appear, for it was only one million years ago that man left his first imprint on the geologic record.

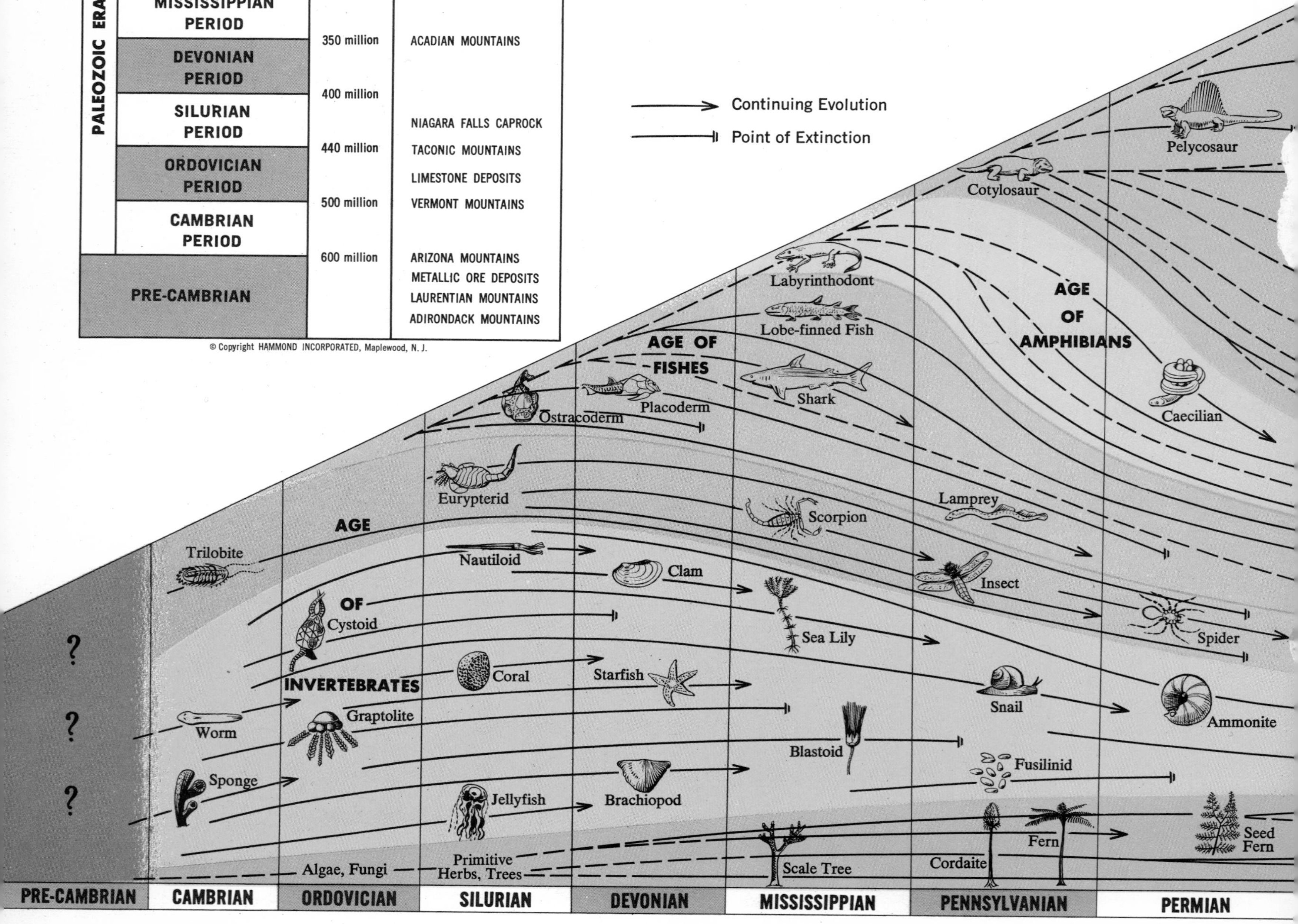

→ Continuing Evolution
⊣ Point of Extinction

Pelycosaur
Cotylosaur
Labyrinthodont
Lobe-finned Fish
AGE OF FISHES
Shark
AGE OF AMPHIBIANS
Caecilian
Ostracoderm
Placoderm
Eurypterid
Scorpion
Lamprey
Insect
Spider
AGE
Trilobite
Nautiloid
Clam
OF
Cystoid
Sea Lily
Starfish
Coral
Snail
Ammonite
INVERTEBRATES
Graptolite
Blastoid
Worm
Fusilinid
Sponge
Jellyfish
Brachiopod
Fern
Seed Fern
Algae, Fungi
Primitive Herbs, Trees
Scale Tree
Cordaite

| PRE-CAMBRIAN | CAMBRIAN | ORDOVICIAN | SILURIAN | DEVONIAN | MISSISSIPPIAN | PENNSYLVANIAN | PERMIAN |

The Geologic Record

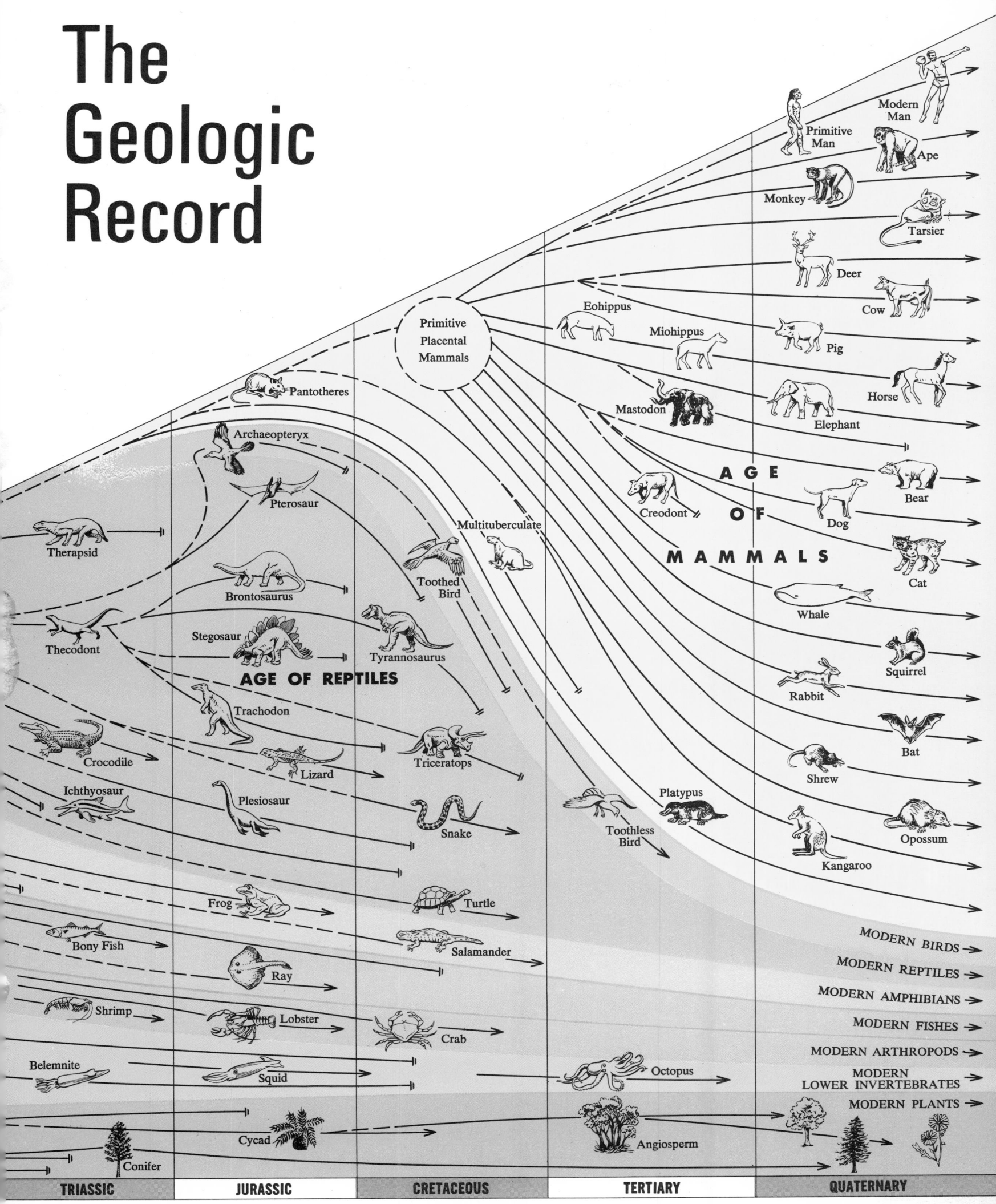

| TRIASSIC | JURASSIC | CRETACEOUS | TERTIARY | QUATERNARY |

The Biosphere: Realm of Living Things

Polar and mountainous regions of perpetual **ice and snow** cover one-tenth of the earth's land areas. Windswept, always below freezing, it can support life only peripherally, if at all.

A place of mosses, lichens and stunted flowering plants and trees, the **tundra** is an area so marginal that only specially adapted life-forms, such as reindeer, can live there.

As favorable climates produce and sustain an abundance of vegetation, the **mid-latitude forest** regions of the world continue to serve as home for a majority of the world's population.

Ranging from the luxuriant vegetation of the rainforest to scrub-like woodlands in drier areas, the **tropical forest** is noted for containing a wide variety of insects, birds and small animals.

The **savanna** or tropical grassland is a land of tall grass interspersed with trees. A place of winter droughts and summer rainfall, it is the true jungle home of big-game animals.

On the **mid-latitude grasslands** are found many of the sheep and cattle ranches of the earth, and, where the land has been successfully cultivated, the great grain fields.

Except in scattered oases and irrigated lands, the **deserts** of the world are inhabited only by livestock-herding nomads and wildlife capable of surviving in moisture-deficient areas.

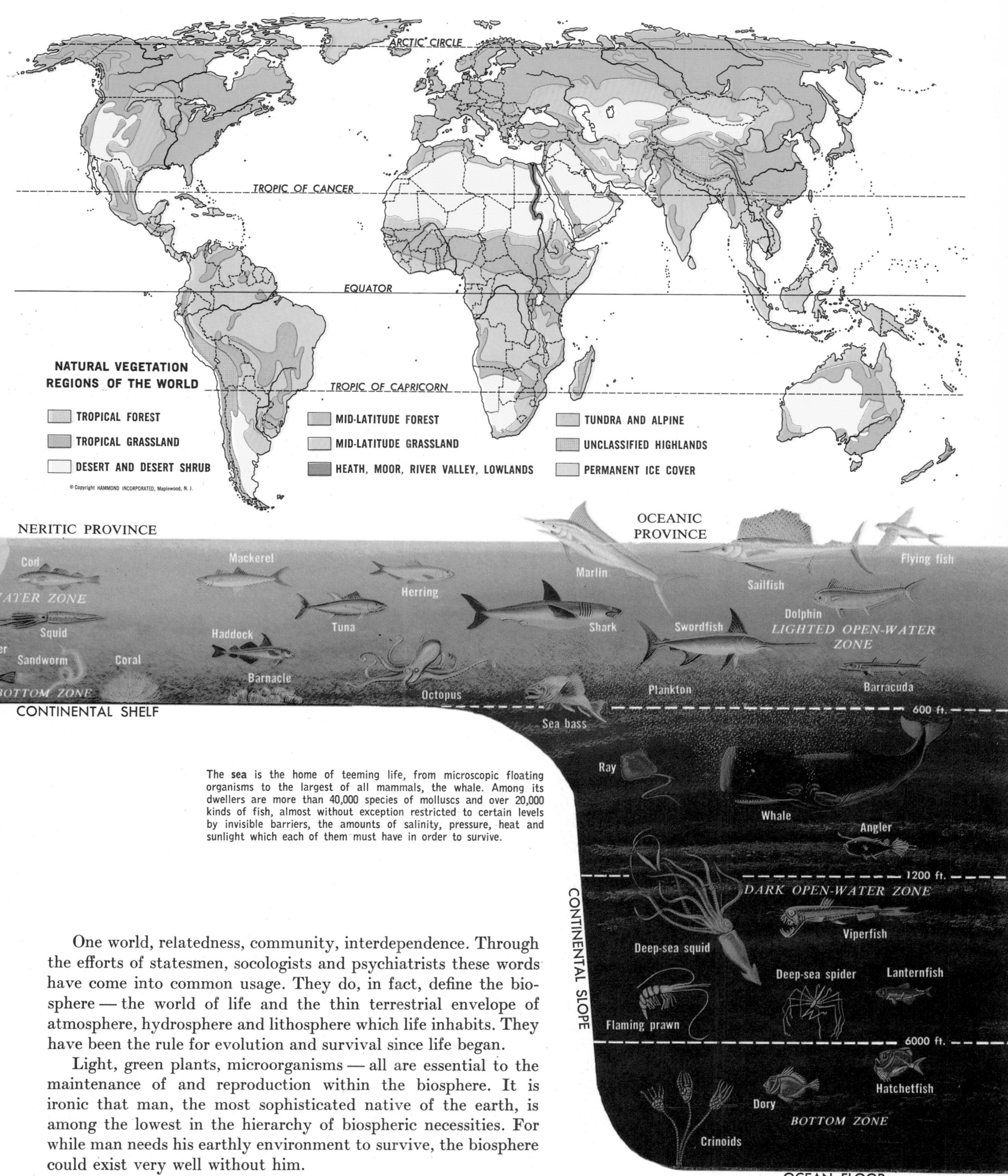

NATURAL VEGETATION REGIONS OF THE WORLD

ARCTIC CIRCLE

TROPIC OF CANCER

EQUATOR

TROPIC OF CAPRICORN

- TROPICAL FOREST
- TROPICAL GRASSLAND
- DESERT AND DESERT SHRUB
- MID-LATITUDE FOREST
- MID-LATITUDE GRASSLAND
- HEATH, MOOR, RIVER VALLEY, LOWLANDS
- TUNDRA AND ALPINE
- UNCLASSIFIED HIGHLANDS
- PERMANENT ICE COVER

© Copyright HAMMOND INCORPORATED, Maplewood, N. J.

NERITIC PROVINCE

OCEANIC PROVINCE

WATER ZONE

LIGHTED OPEN-WATER ZONE

Cod, Mackerel, Marlin, Flying fish, Herring, Sailfish, Squid, Tuna, Shark, Swordfish, Dolphin, Haddock, Sandworm, Coral, Barnacle, Octopus, Plankton, Barracuda

BOTTOM ZONE

CONTINENTAL SHELF

Sea bass

600 ft.

Ray

Whale

Angler

1200 ft.

DARK OPEN-WATER ZONE

Deep-sea squid

Viperfish

Deep-sea spider

Lanternfish

Flaming prawn

6000 ft.

Dory

Hatchetfish

BOTTOM ZONE

Crinoids

OCEAN FLOOR

CONTINENTAL SLOPE

The **sea** is the home of teeming life, from microscopic floating organisms to the largest of all mammals, the whale. Among its dwellers are more than 40,000 species of molluscs and over 20,000 kinds of fish, almost without exception restricted to certain levels by invisible barriers, the amounts of salinity, pressure, heat and sunlight which each of them must have in order to survive.

One world, relatedness, community, interdependence. Through the efforts of statesmen, socologists and psychiatrists these words have come into common usage. They do, in fact, define the biosphere — the world of life and the thin terrestrial envelope of atmosphere, hydrosphere and lithosphere which life inhabits. They have been the rule for evolution and survival since life began.

Light, green plants, microorganisms — all are essential to the maintenance of and reproduction within the biosphere. It is ironic that man, the most sophisticated native of the earth, is among the lowest in the hierarchy of biospheric necessities. For while man needs his earthly environment to survive, the biosphere could exist very well without him.

© Copyright HAMMOND INCORPORATED, Maplewood, N. J.

Environmental Controls

Primitive man worshiped the sun, danced for rain, and trembled when the angry gods unleashed the force of hurricane or hid the face of the sun in clouds. Modern man curses the drought, hides from the wind and snow and builds walls against the onslaught of flood.

Little has changed in the impact of climate and environment on the life of man. There are no vegetarians in the desert or in the ice-bound regions of the far north. Houses exposing vast expanses of glass to the burning fingers of the sun are not found in the Sahara, at the Equator or near the Poles. Man does not die of malaria in regions too dry or too cold to support the larvae of mosquitoes; swollen goiterous necks are never seen in areas where local water is naturally supplied with iodine.

Men who live near lakes or seas build boats while those near mountains climb or ski. The plainsman nurtures cattle or grain; the farmer in the valley cultivates tomatoes or legumes. In work, in play, in sickness and varying degrees of health — even in the formation of national traditions — the world of man is subject to the force of nature.

By a variety of adaptations man wrestles with the problems of his environment. He can air-condition or heat his home, refrigerate his food, quench parts of the thirsty deserts with irrigated water, drain the swamps and navigate the seas. He has developed intricate technologies to forecast earthquakes, blizzards, floods and hurricanes.

But the ancient sun still governs the movements of the earth within its orbit, determining heat and cold, the progress of the winds and ocean currents, the levels of the seas — the glacier's trail. Man continues to bow before the "god of day."

The interactions of sun, rain and wind are so closely related that they function as a single entity which is, perhaps, the most dominant force in creating man's environment.

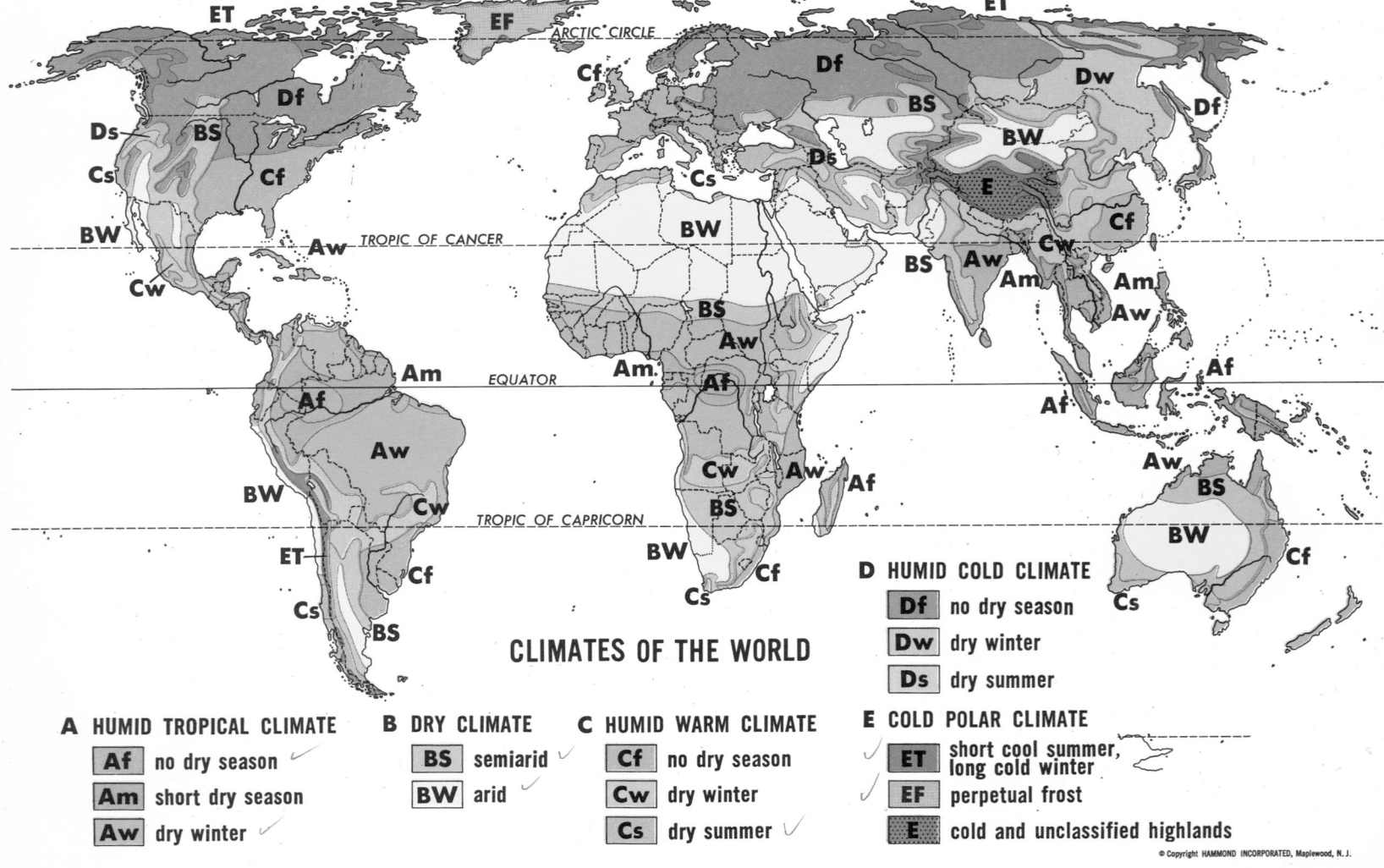

CLIMATES OF THE WORLD

A HUMID TROPICAL CLIMATE
- **Af** no dry season
- **Am** short dry season
- **Aw** dry winter

B DRY CLIMATE
- **BS** semiarid
- **BW** arid

C HUMID WARM CLIMATE
- **Cf** no dry season
- **Cw** dry winter
- **Cs** dry summer

D HUMID COLD CLIMATE
- **Df** no dry season
- **Dw** dry winter
- **Ds** dry summer

E COLD POLAR CLIMATE
- **ET** short cool summer, long cold winter
- **EF** perpetual frost
- **E** cold and unclassified highlands

© Copyright HAMMOND INCORPORATED, Maplewood, N. J.

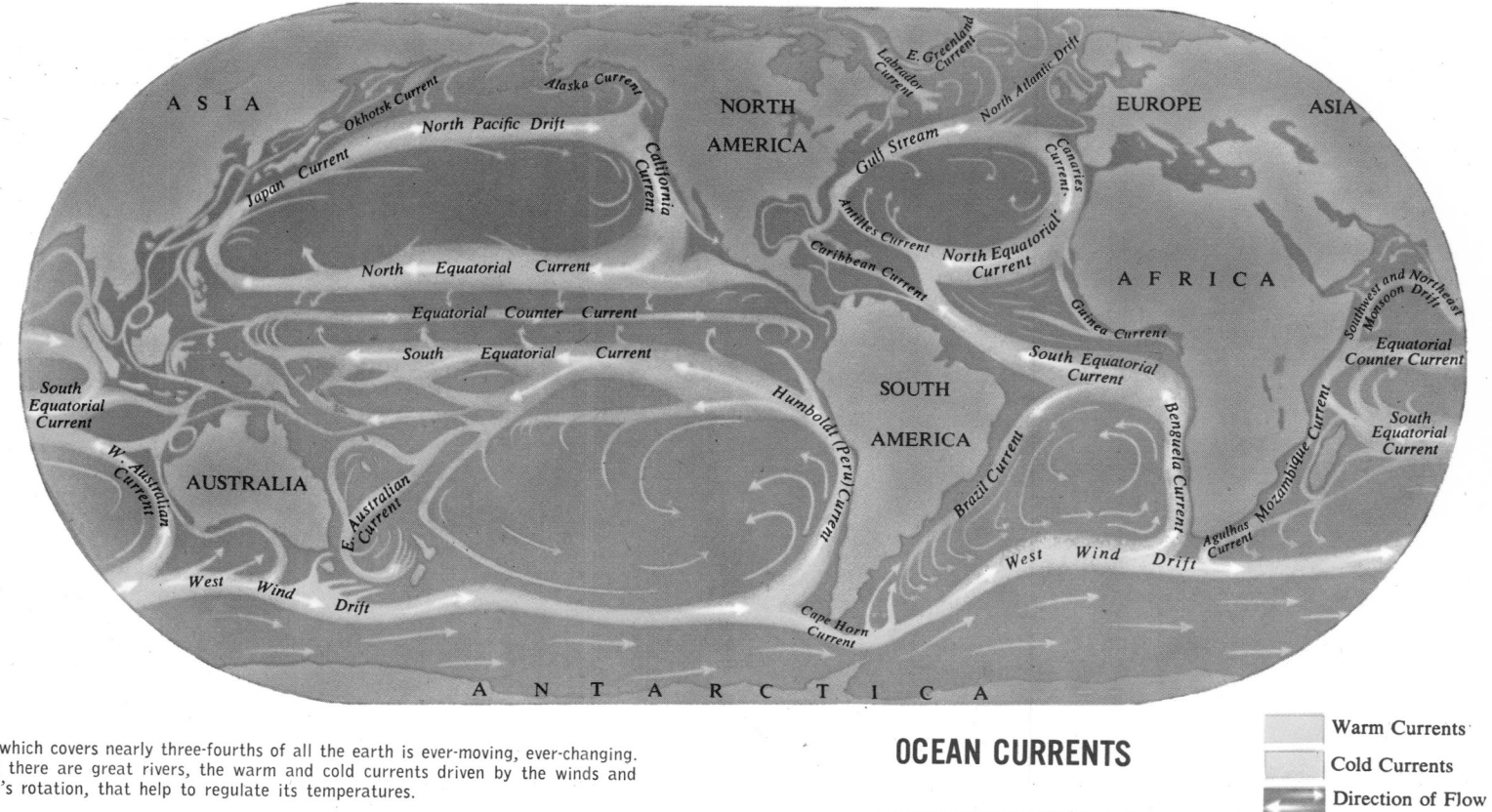

The sea, which covers nearly three-fourths of all the earth is ever-moving, ever-changing. Within it there are great rivers, the warm and cold currents driven by the winds and the earth's rotation, that help to regulate its temperatures.

OCEAN CURRENTS

Warm Currents
Cold Currents
Direction of Flow

© Copyright HAMMOND INCORPORATED, Maplewood, N. J.

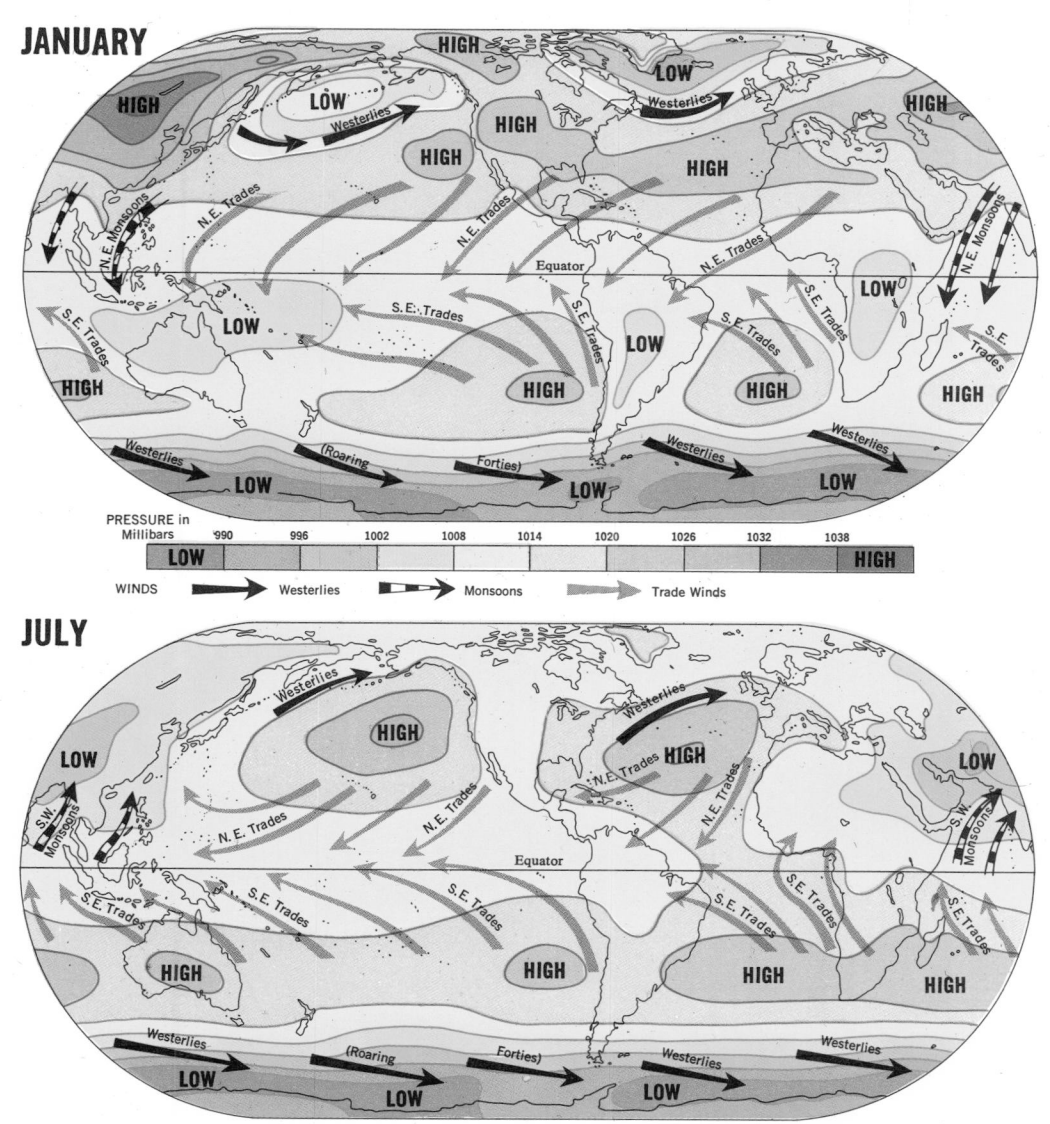

JANUARY

PRESSURE in Millibars 990 996 1002 1008 1014 1020 1026 1032 1038

LOW   HIGH

WINDS   → Westerlies   ⇒ Monsoons   ⇒ Trade Winds

JULY

AIR PRESSURE AND WINDS

Just as the atmosphere tends to equalize heat distribution, it tends to maintain equal pressure over the earth. Whenever this equilibrium, or balance, is disturbed, air flows from areas of higher pressure to areas of lower pressure. In the Northern Hemisphere winds flow clockwise around a high pressure area (high) and counterclockwise around the center of a low pressure area (low). These movements are reversed in the Southern Hemisphere.

© Copyright HAMMOND INCORPORATED, Maplewood, N. J.

Life Support Cycles

With an intuition clearly beyond their scientific knowledge, the ancients of India developed a theory of reincarnation which, in some philosophic ways, parallels what science has learned of the workings of the biosphere. In the remarkable thrift of nature nothing is lost — in tremendous complex cycles atoms from the first life on earth still move through the biosphere.

The miracle of energy is constantly performed in the cycles of the "life-giving" elements. Carbon, hydrogen, oxygen, nitrogen, sulfur and phosphorus act together to produce all living matter. While many other elements such as calcium, iodine and iron are also found in living things, they are not absolute essentials in all cases. Carbon, hydrogen and oxygen are vital for photosynthesis and are the components of the basic food substances — carbohydrates and fats. Carbon, in its common gaseous form, carbon dioxide, is absorbed by green plants and triggers

the production of carbohydrate compounds by reacting with molecules of water.

Some "energy" is stored within the plant in the form of new tissue; other "energy," in the form of oxygen is released into the air to be used by other organisms. The seemingly inexhaustible supply of carbon dioxide available for use is replenished in the atmosphere through the respiration of all living things, and in the soil as bacteria and fungi break down plant and animal cells,

Nitrogen, sulfur and phosphorus are essential to animals and plants for the production and maintenance of protein. Nitrogen, with carbon, hydrogen and oxygen, is used for the growth and repair of tissue. Sulfur acts as a "stiffening" agent in all protein. To perform their functions proteins must be folded and shaped in a particular way, and their structure is maintained by bonds between sulfur atoms. While phosphorus is not a constituent of protein,

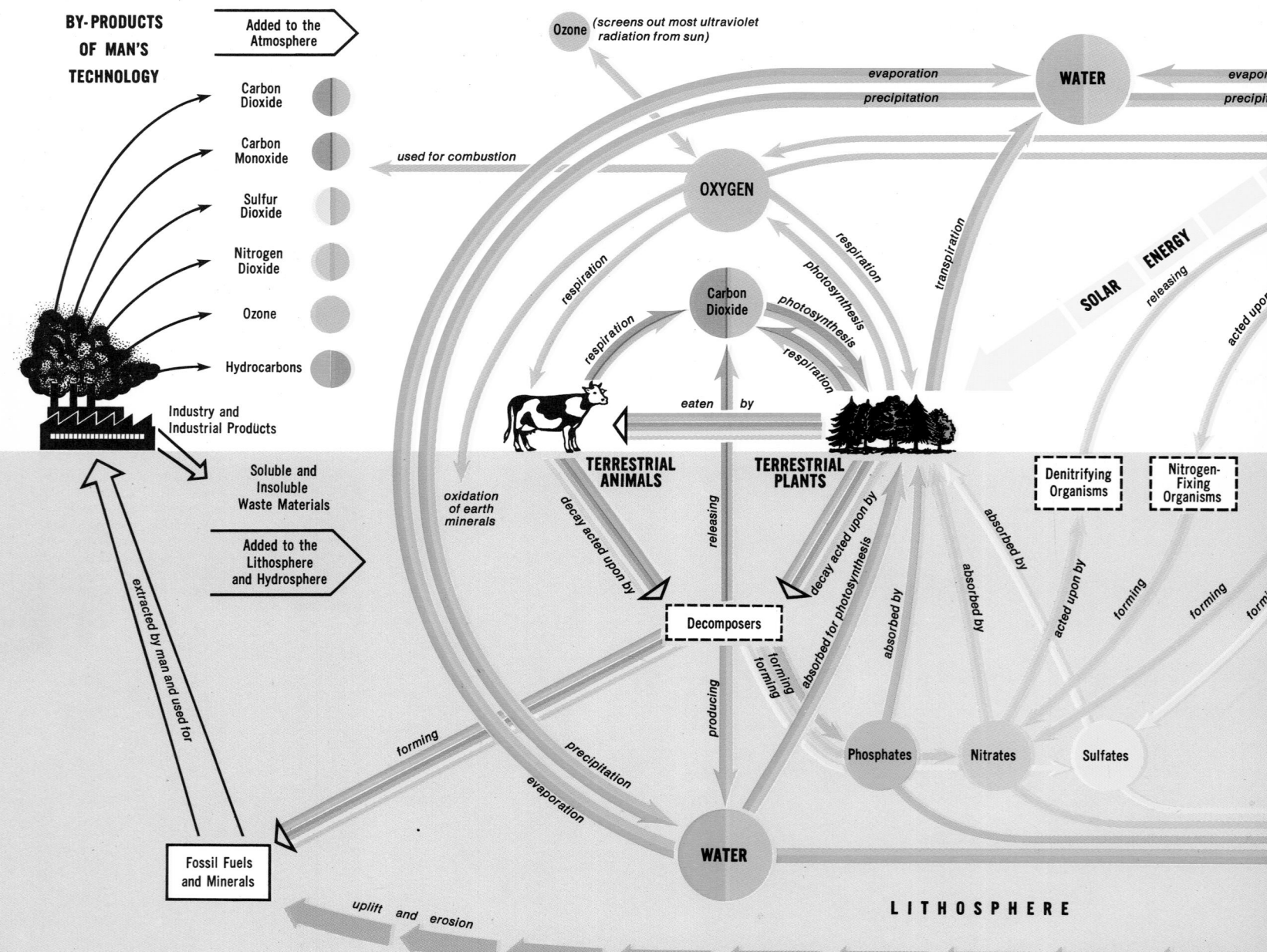

no protein can be made without it. Special phosphate compounds are the "fuel" for all biochemical work within the cell.

Although about four-fifths of the atmosphere is nitrogen, higher forms of life cannot make use of it in its "free" state and must absorb it at one or more points in its biospheric cycle. The decomposers — bacteria and fungi — act on waste matter, breaking down complex compounds into simpler usable forms including nitrogen. Some nitrogen-fixing bacteria are able to utilize atmospheric nitrogen in their own metabolism, while others convert it to those nitrogen-enriched substances necessary for all plant growth.

In nature, no part is greater than the whole and almost every element is dependent on another for some essential part of its cycle. Water, which is incorporated into every organism, is essential in the formation of free oxygen which in turn sustains the life of that organism. Water is also the principal "carrier" in the cycling of all elements. When it evaporates, water returns certain elements to the atmosphere; when it seeps through the soil on its return to the sea, water distributes nutrients to plant roots.

Carbon monoxide, sulfur and nitrogen oxides, hydrocarbons — by-products of man's industry — are being injected into the biosphere in ever-increasing amounts. There, as the "new compounds," they must in some way co-exist with the life-support cycles established throughout millions of years of evolution. Their compatability with these cycles and the organisms they nurture will determine the future of life on our planet.

Already man has learned one thing. Although the question of reincarnation or any form of life after death remains unanswered for many, science has proved that there is no natural end to the raw materials of nature or to the "new compounds" man has made from them.

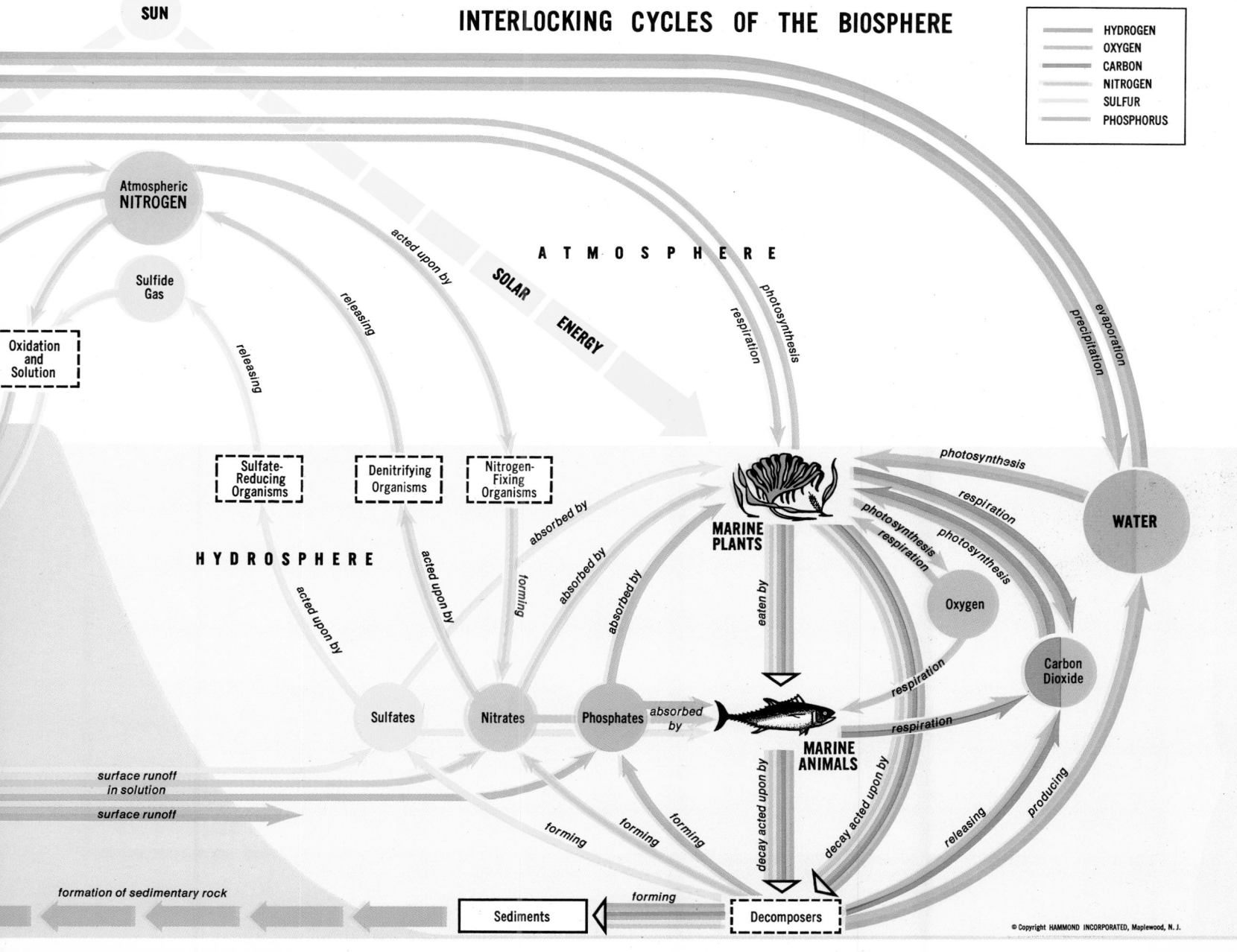

INTERLOCKING CYCLES OF THE BIOSPHERE

PHOTOSYNTHESIS: Converting the sun's energy

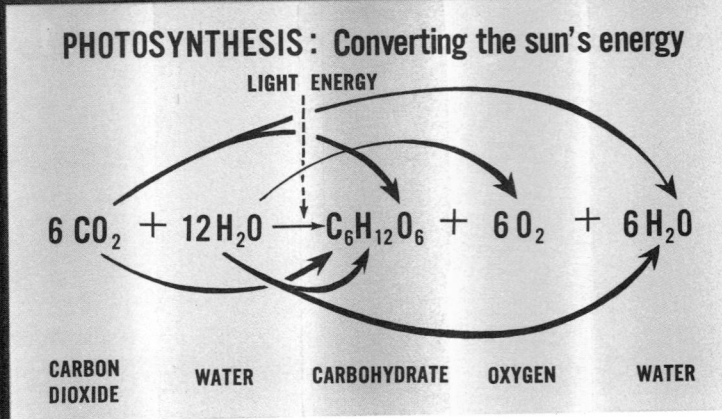

LIGHT ENERGY

$$6 CO_2 + 12H_2O \rightarrow C_6H_{12}O_6 + 6O_2 + 6H_2O$$

| CARBON DIOXIDE | WATER | CARBOHYDRATE | OXYGEN | WATER |

Using light energy, green plants build up organic foods such as carbohydrates — stored chemical energy to be used by the entire community — from the simple inorganic substances of carbon dioxide and water. The important by-product of this reaction is the release of oxygen, an element vital to the respiration of all living things.

THE LEAF: An organ of photosynthesis
CROSS SECTION

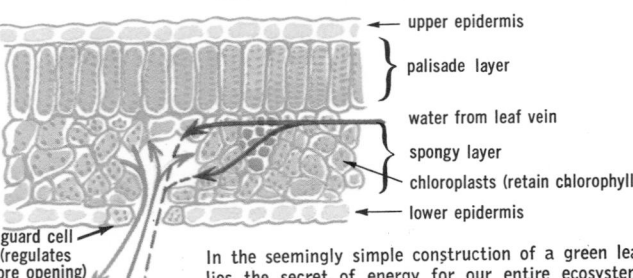

- upper epidermis
- palisade layer
- water from leaf vein
- spongy layer
- chloroplasts (retain chlorophyll)
- lower epidermis
- guard cell (regulates pore opening)
- oxygen
- carbon dioxide
- water vapor

In the seemingly simple construction of a green leaf lies the secret of energy for our entire ecosystem. Within the microscopic chloroplasts of plant cells, which contain the vital green pigment known as chlorophyll, carbon dioxide and water are absorbed, decomposed and converted into carbohydrate and oxygen molecules. Special "guard cells" control the surface pore openings to regulate the intake and output of materials.

PRODUCER - CONSUMER FOOD WEB

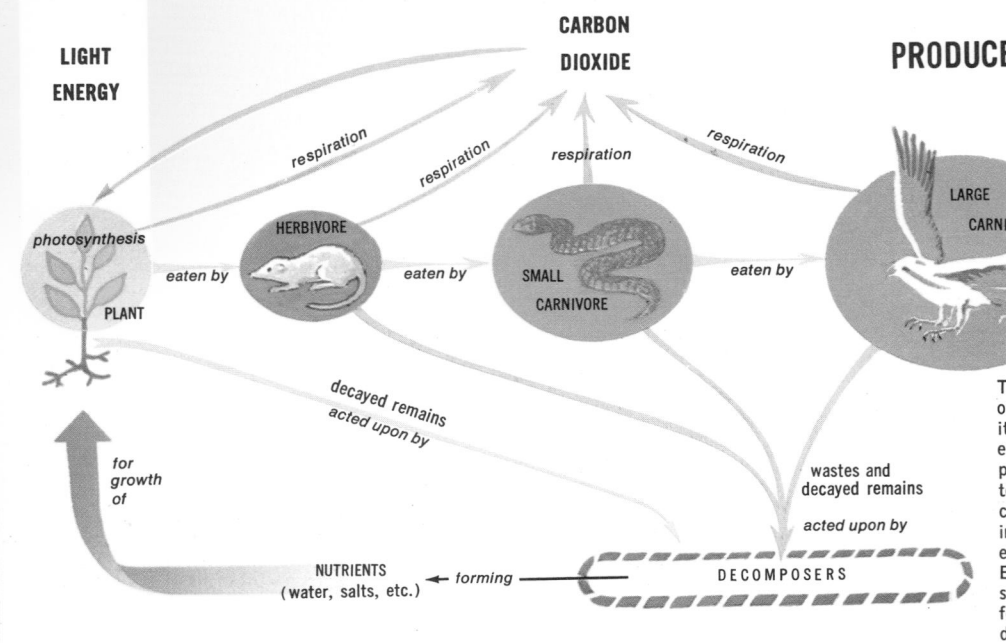

LIGHT ENERGY

CARBON DIOXIDE

respiration

photosynthesis

PLANT — eaten by — HERBIVORE — eaten by — SMALL CARNIVORE — eaten by — LARGE CARNIVORE

decayed remains acted upon by

for growth of

wastes and decayed remains

acted upon by

NUTRIENTS (water, salts, etc.) ← forming — DECOMPOSERS

Some of the complex relationships of life in an ecological system can be described by tracing the passage of energy through a simplified community in what is called a food chain or web.

The primary food source is the producer, that organism which uses light energy to manufacture its own food from inorganic substances (nutrients). This producer or plant is consumed by a plant-eating animal which in turn may fall prey to a flesh-eating animal or carnivore. A larger carnivore may extend the food chain further. During this process part of the consumed organism's energy is passed on to the consuming animal. Energy not passed on is released to the atmosphere during respiration or to the soil in the form of waste materials. Eventually, death and decay of all organisms lead to a recycling of nutrient compounds to be used by the producers.

CHAIN OF LIFE IN THE SEA

Although community members are constructed to adapt to their watery habitat, the chain of life in the sea is quite similar to the chain of life on land.

The most important members of the oceanic community are those that contain chlorophyll or a chlorophyll-like substance and thus are able to make organic matter from inorganic ingredients. Algae and phytoplankton are the ocean's principal producers. In the open seas the initial consumers are tiny crustacea only a few centimeters long, while in coastal waters these consumers include the more familiar starfish, sea urchins, molluscs and some worms.

Just as on land, where the smaller or weaker animal is consumed by the larger and stronger, members of the oceanic community feed upon each other. Nutrients are returned to the atmosphere through respiration and to the hydrosphere through a breakdown of complex organisms by the work of decomposing organisms.

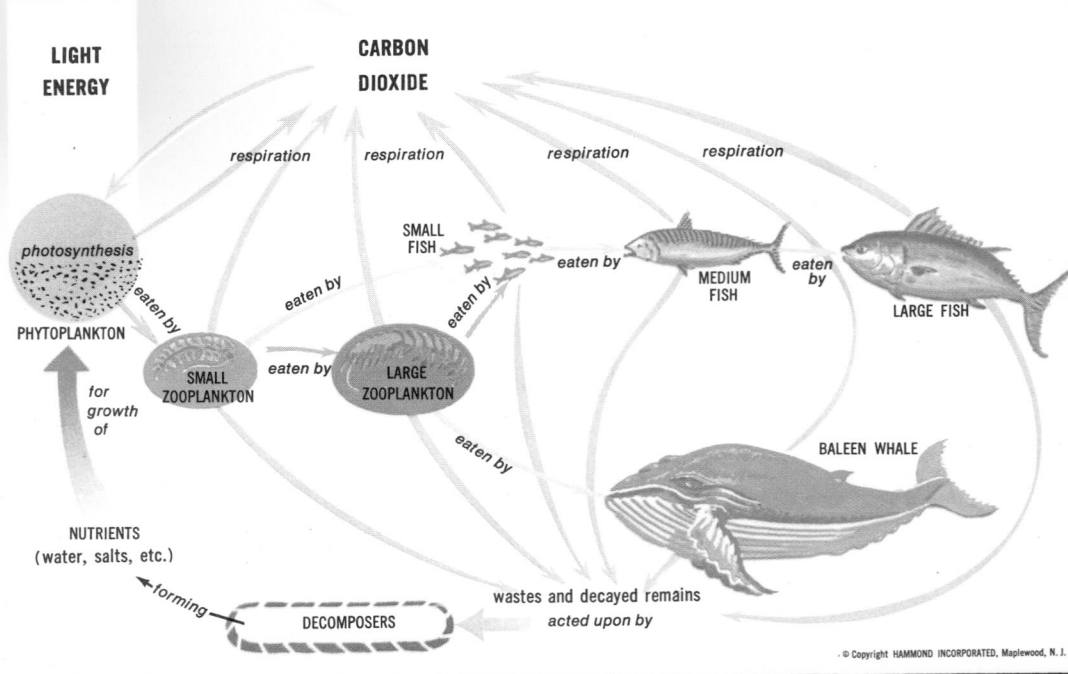

LIGHT ENERGY

CARBON DIOXIDE

respiration

photosynthesis

PHYTOPLANKTON — eaten by — SMALL ZOOPLANKTON — eaten by — LARGE ZOOPLANKTON

SMALL FISH — eaten by — MEDIUM FISH — eaten by — LARGE FISH

eaten by — BALEEN WHALE

for growth of

NUTRIENTS (water, salts, etc.)

forming — DECOMPOSERS

wastes and decayed remains acted upon by

Ecology:
INTERRELATION OF LIVING THINGS AND THEIR SURROUNDINGS

Freedom and independence do not exist in the universe except in the creative reaches of man's intellect which distinguishes him from the other living organisms with which he shares a portion of the biosphere.

Dependent on the sun for its creation, the earth is dependent on it still for solar energy to sustain and move all living things. The amount and types of earthly life are determined by the amounts and patterns of flow of this energy which is fixed by green plants and converted into the organic compounds to maintain the plants themselves and every other organism.

In a seemingly tangled web of forces — in competition, cooperation, neutrality — in a constantly changing and more or less suitable climate, and in the processes of evolution continually in flux throughout the thin layers of atmosphere, earth and sea, strands of mutual dependence have been woven. Each form of life, from the simple one-celled organism to the complexity of man, is subject to the same laws of nature, depending one upon the other for energy and food — creating it as they destroy it and are destroyed themselves.

The word "ecology" comes from two Greek words meaning "the study of the home," and in modern times has signified the study of all living things in relation to their environments — or homes — and to each other. Western man, particularly, has romanticised his notion of a home and often chose to think of it as a solitary fortress snug against intrusion by other men and the forces of nature. But the making and maintaining of a home for man as for other forms of life is a subtle combination and balance of light, heat, moisture and food any one of which may be disturbed or destroyed by natural calamity or inadvertent act.

Through a closer study of ecology and ecological systems man is learning, hopefully not too late, that even the "lilies of the field," which neither sow nor reap, are as essential to him as are the insects clinging to their leaves, the rodents burrowing at their feet, and the soil and air that they enrich.

A TYPICAL FOOD CHAIN

1. Through the process of photosynthesis a green plant or primary producer begins the food chain.

2. A cricket, feeding upon the plant, becomes a primary consumer.

3. A secondary consumer is the frog who devours the cricket.

4. It is the fate of the frog to turn into a meal for the snake, the third or tertiary consumer.

5. The food chain ends with a snake-eating hawk, the fourth consumer, who has no predator other than man.

Photos: Ernst G. Hofmann

Man's Impact Upon Nature

Since he could think man has been at war with death. He has fought his battles against destruction with science and technology as his weapons, virtually eliminating his own annihilation by predatory animals and from diseases such as leprosy, tuberculosis and diphtheria. He has walked into many valleys of death to fight malaria and yellow fever, and he has resolved that each year more of his own kind will live to finish out their threescore years and ten.

However, the victory over nature, which had balanced population with food supply and space, is bitter, for the population has "exploded" leaving man with the seemingly insolvable problem of providing more food and space for himself or reducing his numbers by starvation or by war.

Man outsmarted himself in many ways as he worked toward creating a more perfect world for himself without understanding that natural laws go beyond human manipulation. He has destroyed forests and meadows, polluted the water and air, eliminated organisms that tried to share his bread. However, he has yet to learn to recreate the wood and brush or the interdependent communities of bacteria, insects and animals that he learned — too late — enrich the air, the soil and the water and without which he cannot function.

Modern man knows how to manufacture "miraculous" materials to work for his pleasure or his seemingly insatiable needs, but the sophistications of technology have yet to control effectively the by-products. These new materials, still subject to the order of nature's cycles, penetrate the biosphere and eventually come to roost in his own vulnerable body.

New battles are being fought throughout the world and new standards bearing the slogans of ecology float in the "unsafe" air. It is somehow ironic to find that many people now believe that man has been fighting the wrong fight in his gigantic struggle with nature. That, after all, nature never was his enemy.

Man cannot turn back to his beginnings when he lived with, and not against, the natural world. But a compromise between technology and nature must take place for our "plundered planet" cries out for the day of reckoning.

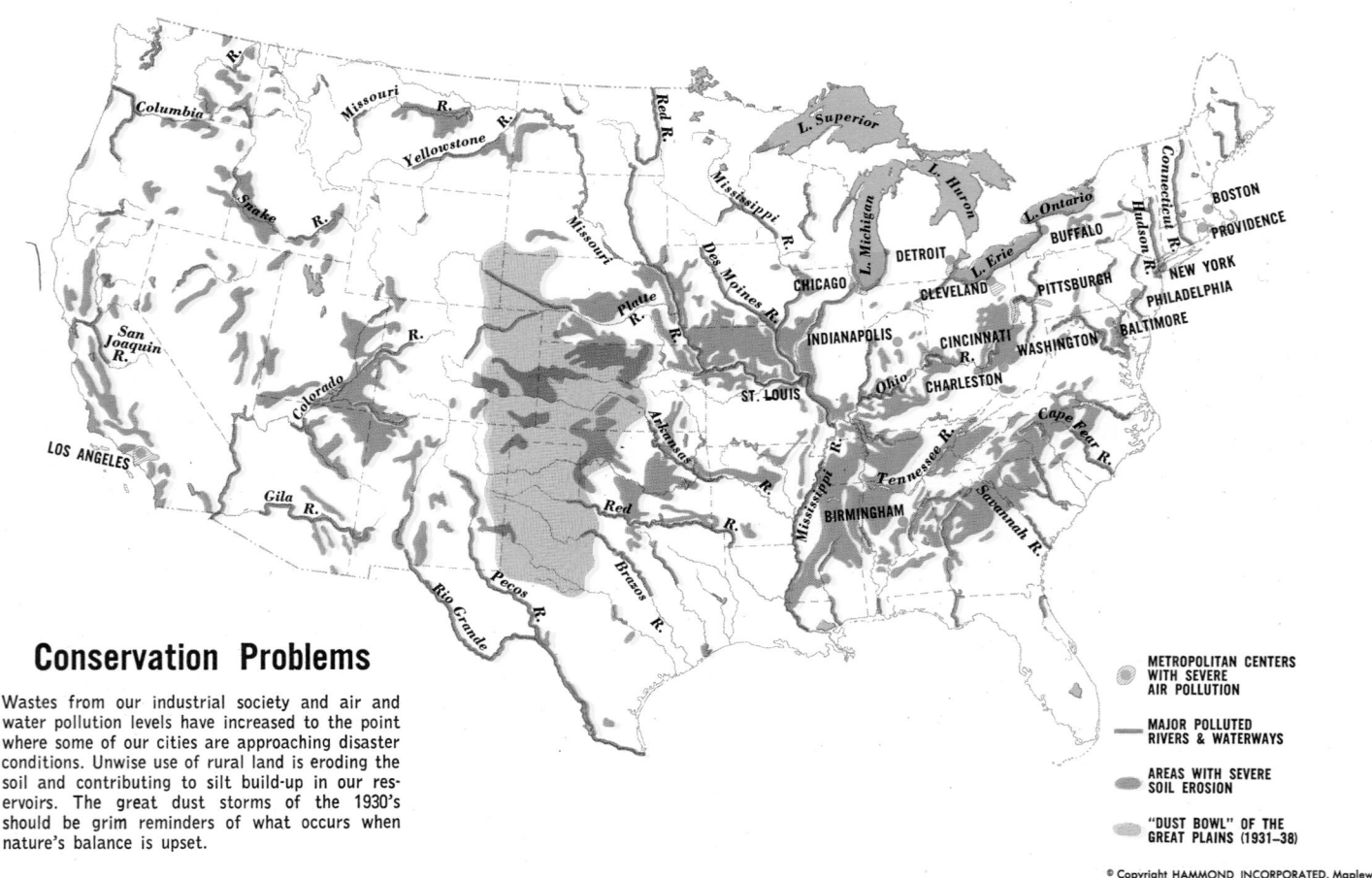

Conservation Problems

Wastes from our industrial society and air and water pollution levels have increased to the point where some of our cities are approaching disaster conditions. Unwise use of rural land is eroding the soil and contributing to silt build-up in our reservoirs. The great dust storms of the 1930's should be grim reminders of what occurs when nature's balance is upset.

METROPOLITAN CENTERS
WITH SEVERE
AIR POLLUTION

MAJOR POLLUTED
RIVERS & WATERWAYS

AREAS WITH SEVERE
SOIL EROSION

"DUST BOWL" OF THE
GREAT PLAINS (1931–38)

A sloping barnyard provides a convenient runoff for chemical and organic fertilizers, causing overenrichment (eutrophication) of the pond.

Trash burning billows clouds of air pollution over the nation's capital.

A forest stripped of trees reduces the supply of oxygen-producing greenery and inhibits good soil development and maintenance.

Poor drainage procedures near a housing development produce unstable soil, resulting in earth slides.

Unauthorized dumping affects the beauty of the countryside and later will pollute the nearby river.

Photos: U.S. Department of Agriculture

This stream is rapidly becoming polluted because of the direct discharge of soap and detergent suds into it.

POLLUTION CIRCLE
TYPES OF POLLUTION AND THEIR EFFECT ON THE TOTAL ENVIRONMENT

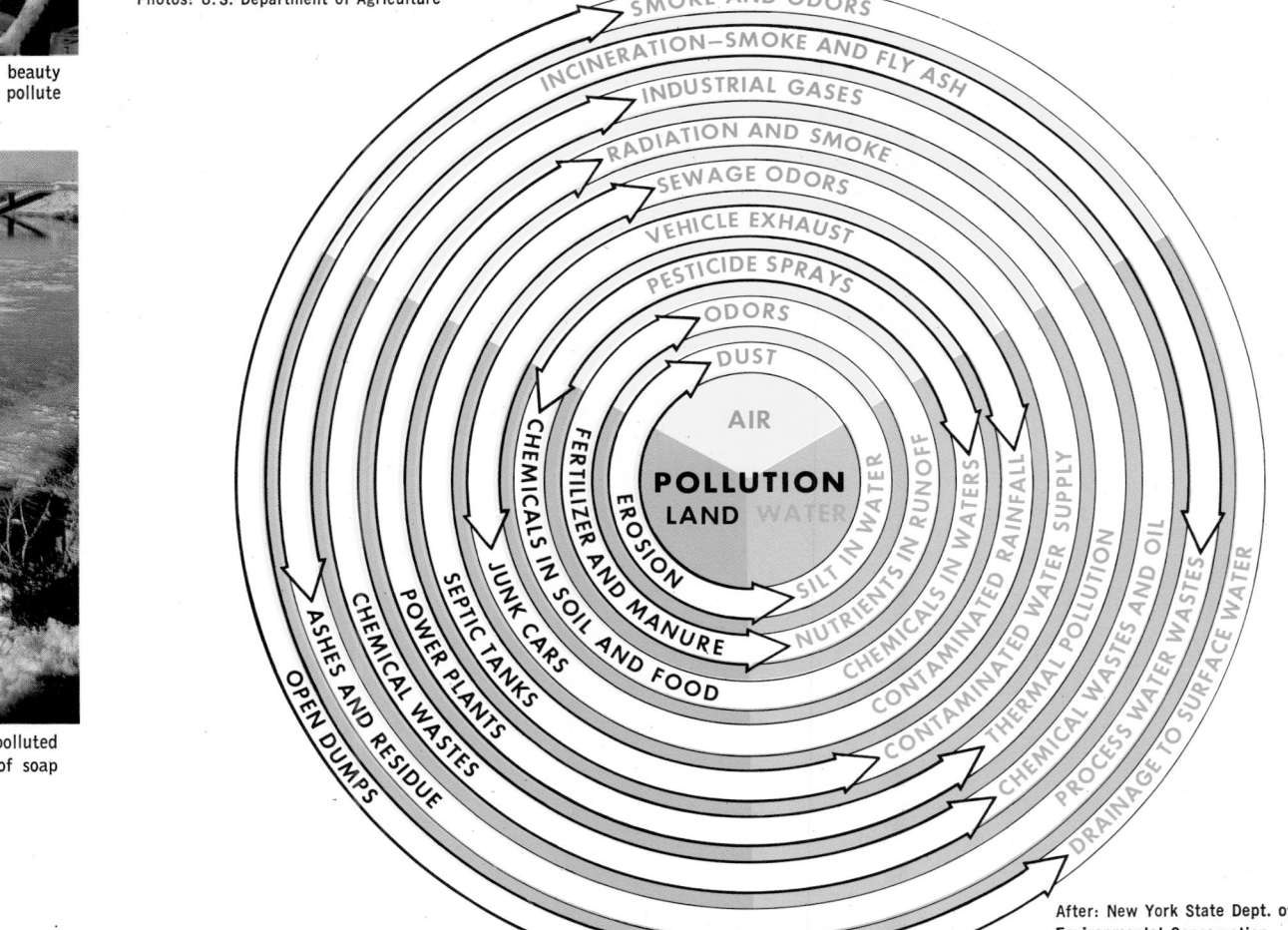

After: New York State Dept. of Environmental Conservation

The Moon:
MAN'S FIRST SPACE ODYSSEY

From the physicist to the clothes designer, from the astronomer to the welder, working in close cooperation or in isolated laboratories on almost every continent of the world, men have been involved in a mighty labor to secure their first steps into outer space.

Tantalizing and always beyond reach, the sun, the moon, the stars and the planets had been examined only by instruments, unmanned spacecraft and the earthbound imagination. For no man could live in the hazardous environment of space. The heat of friction, the deadly cold of the outer skies and the destructive girdles of radiation surrounding the earth maintained an atmosphere where no earthly organism could survive. But with the enigmatic world of space always before his eyes and prodding his imagination, man had determined to recreate and maintain his earthly environment for life beyond his normal realm.

The mysterious and "inconstant" moon, for centuries the territory of lovers and poets, became the target of technology. On July 20, 1969, two men, bundled beyond recognition in their protective lunar skins, wandered over the airless, waterless wastes of the moon's surface. They picked up rocks as they might have done as children while people the world over waited and prayed, thinking of different poems to be written in the vocabulary of the new age of enlightenment.

Bits of lunar soil, samples of rock and dust returned to earth with the lunar voyagers. As they were studied and analyzed new questions waited to be answered.

Man returned again to the lunar steppes, proving beyond doubt that he can carry his environment beyond terrestrial boundaries — proving perhaps that he will carry out his dream to live among the stars.

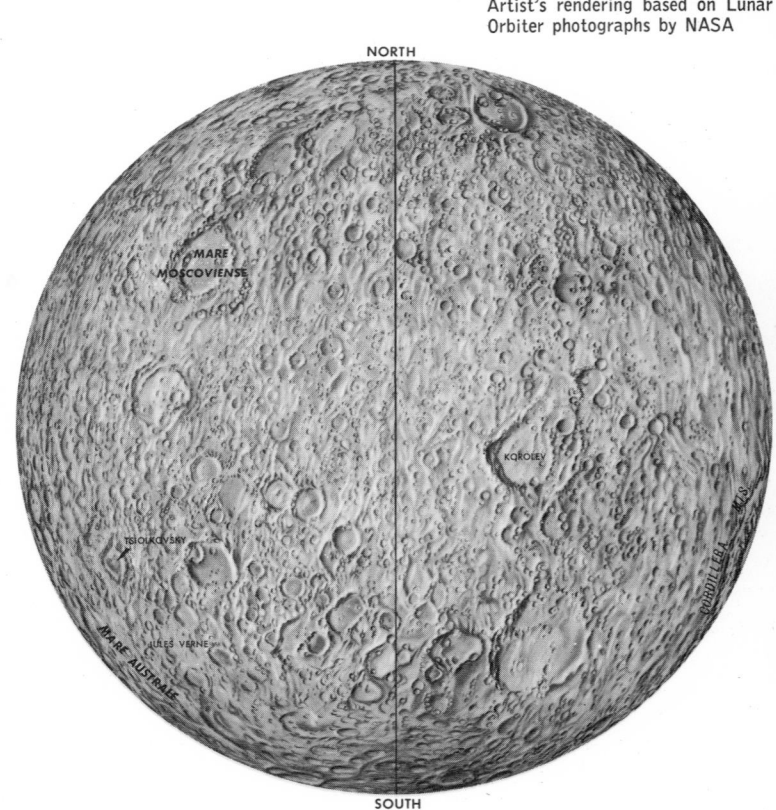

FAR SIDE MOON HEMISPHERE
Artist's rendering based on Lunar Orbiter photographs by NASA

A spacecraft's view of the moon shows portions of both the near and far sides. While appearing almost "full" to a visiting astronaut, the moon would only be entering its first-quarter phase to an observer on earth.

NASA

An oblique view depicts the forbidding rugged terrain encountered on the moon. A crescent earth is seen just above the horizon.

NASA

The crater Langrenus is pictured from an altitude of about 170 miles. Note the conspicuous terrace features visible on the inner crater wall.

NASA

A closeup of lunar surface material is seen. Chemical analysis of samples shows a resemblance to terrestrial igneous rocks, although percentages of specific elements may vary considerably.

NEAR SIDE MOON HEMISPHERE
Base photo mosaic supplied by Aeronautical Chart and Information Service, U.S. Air Force

NORTH

SOUTH

Widening Horizons

Luminous sirens of space — the ancient Loreleis of night — still beckon modern man with mysteries unsolved since the beginning of human thought. Steadfastly, first through observation, later with the aid of sophisticated mathematics and technology, astronomers have pursued the elusive inhabitants of space to the 20th century only to find that the more they learn the less they seem to know. It was not long ago that man believed that if he was not yet master of all he saw, at least he saw all there was to master. Now he knows that the earthly solar system, extending about three and a half billion miles in space, is but a tiny part of a universe only dimly perceived during the last few years.

Some 5,000 stars can be seen with the naked eye on a clear night. The perceptive lens of the Palomar telescope discloses billions of other heavenly bodies at distances be-yond all but the wildest imaginings of most earthlings. And beyond them? Again some millions more stretching out in space yet undisclosed to human measurement.

The terms of time and space with which the earth scientist is familiar have no meaning as the horizons of the expanding universe retreat. With what perspective can he view the distant galaxies as they rush away from his at speeds proportionate to their distance from earth's solar system? How far will they travel and where? How can he judge their place in time when their light already has traveled millions of years to reach his eyes?

Today's cosmologist has learned to deal with speculations and assumptions as he gropes through the twilight of uncharted worlds, returning again and again to the unsolved puzzle of infinity.

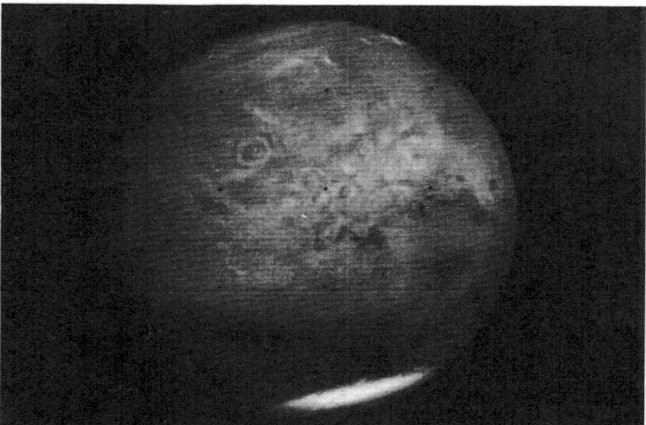

CLOSEUP VIEWS OF MARS
Except for its familiar white south polar cap, Mars has surface features strikingly similar to lunar topography.

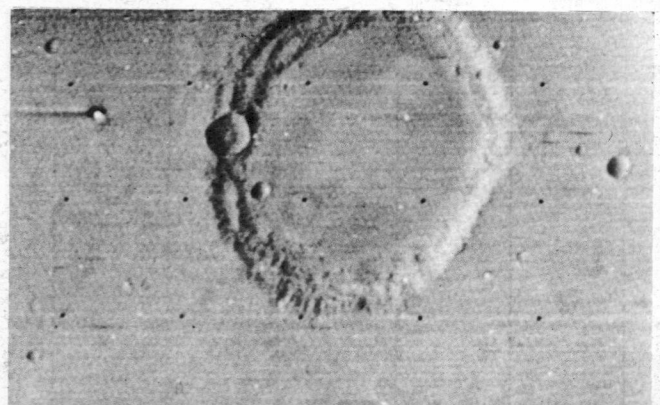

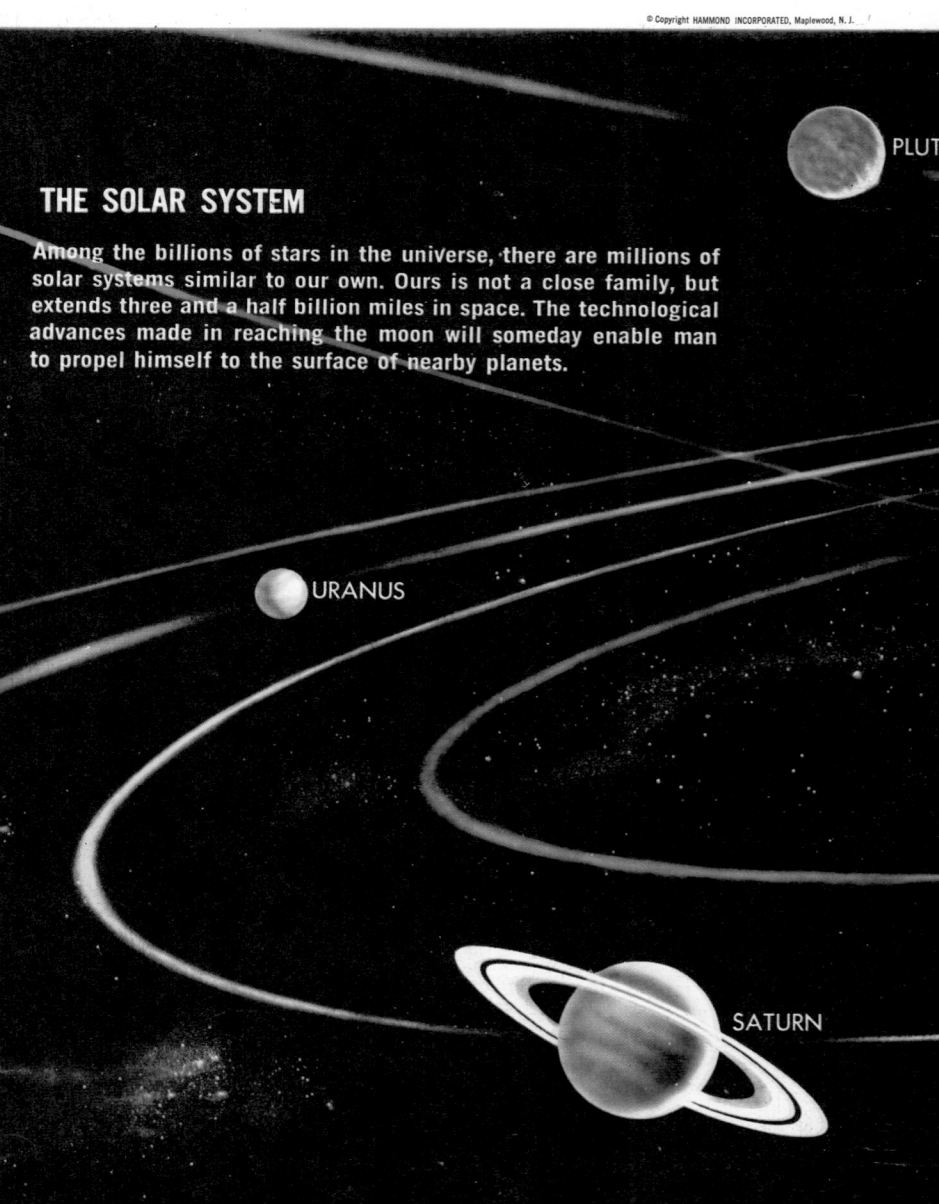

© Copyright HAMMOND INCORPORATED, Maplewood, N. J.

PLUTO

THE SOLAR SYSTEM

Among the billions of stars in the universe, there are millions of solar systems similar to our own. Ours is not a close family, but extends three and a half billion miles in space. The technological advances made in reaching the moon will someday enable man to propel himself to the surface of nearby planets.

URANUS

SATURN

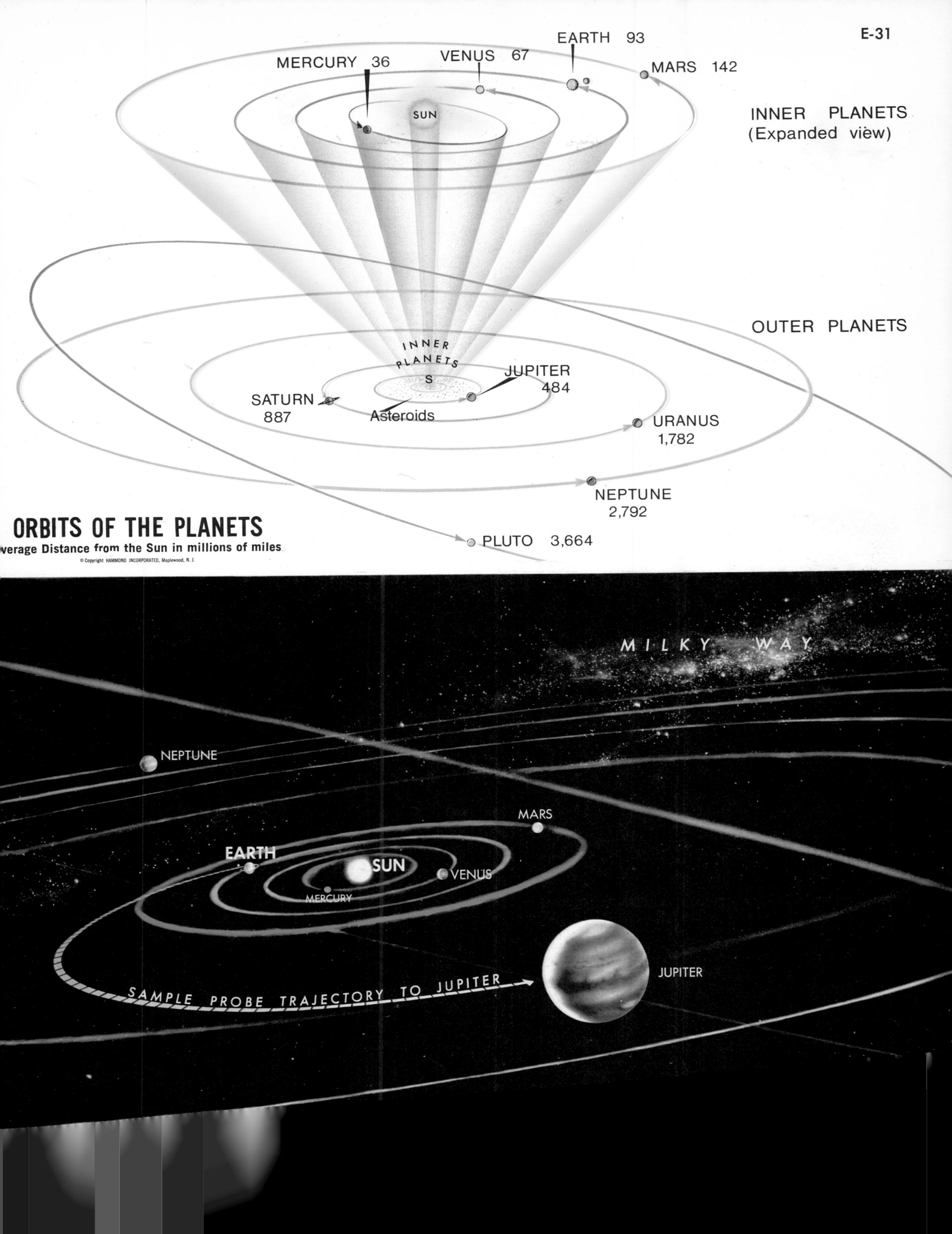

INNER PLANETS
(Expanded view)

MERCURY 36
VENUS 67
EARTH 93
MARS 142

SUN

OUTER PLANETS

INNER
PLANETS
S

JUPITER
484

SATURN
887

Asteroids

URANUS
1,782

NEPTUNE
2,792

PLUTO 3,664

ORBITS OF THE PLANETS
verage Distance from the Sun in millions of miles

MILKY WAY

NEPTUNE

MARS

EARTH

SUN

MERCURY

VENUS

SAMPLE PROBE TRAJECTORY TO JUPITER →

JUPITER

In soaring cities, in golden plains of wheat, in the meanderings of highways, in the warmth of firesides — in homes, factories, forests, farms and seasides — we see the tracings of man's intellect and imagination. Unlike other creatures man's energies are not directed merely toward survival but to the challenge of creating his own environment.

For too many years man has played games with his environment without knowing nature's ground rules and it has become apparent, even to children, that the tools that mold the stuffs of nature to man's liking are double-edged.

It is unlikely that man will turn his wits and his technology toward a return to a simple and primitive way of life. It is also unlikely that man can stand still and survive.

Now man must begin to grapple with causes that have more than one effect. It is time for man to meditate on his heritage and to act, remembering that "knowledge is a fountain of life to him who possesses it."

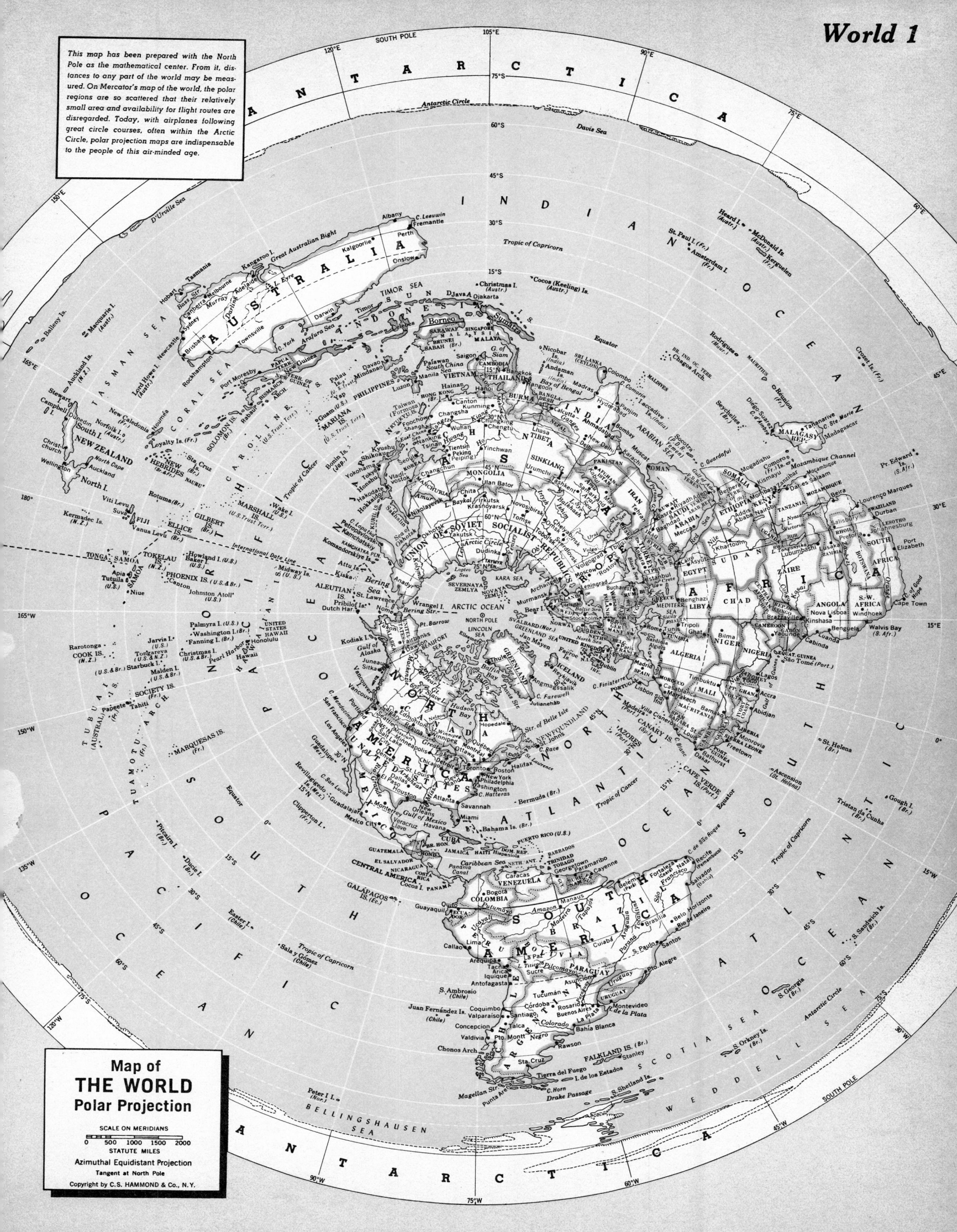

World 1

This map has been prepared with the North Pole as the mathematical center. From it, distances to any part of the world may be measured. On Mercator's map of the world, the polar regions are so scattered that their relatively small area and availability for flight routes are disregarded. Today, with airplanes following great circle courses, often within the Arctic Circle, polar projection maps are indispensable to the people of this air-minded age.

Map of THE WORLD Polar Projection

SCALE ON MERIDIANS

0   500   1000   1500   2000

STATUTE MILES

Azimuthal Equidistant Projection
Tangent at North Pole
Copyright by C.S. Hammond & Co., N.Y.

THE WORLD

BRIESEMEISTER ELLIPTICAL EQUAL-AREA PROJECTION

Capitals of Countries .... ⊗
International Boundaries .... ─ ─ ─

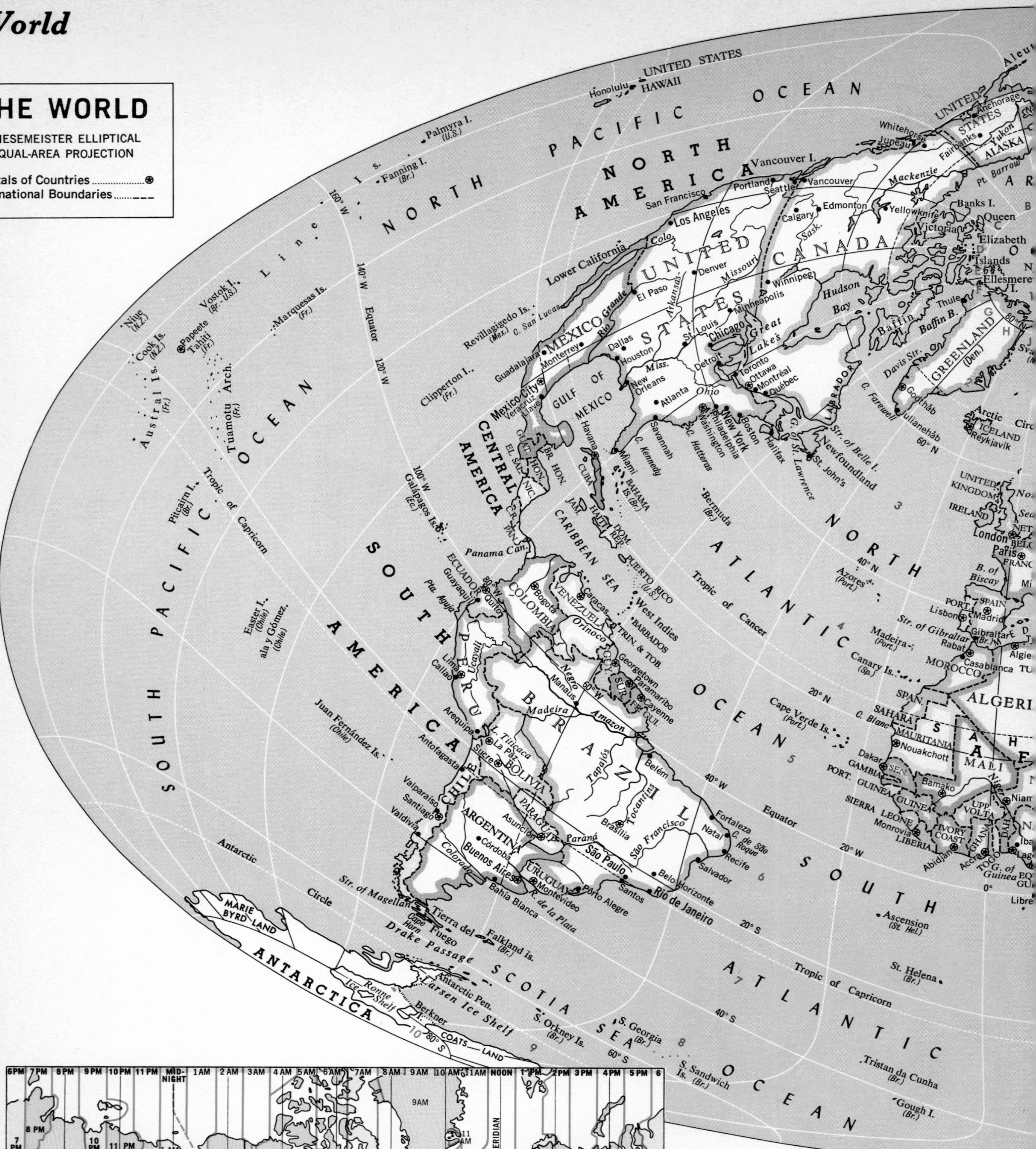

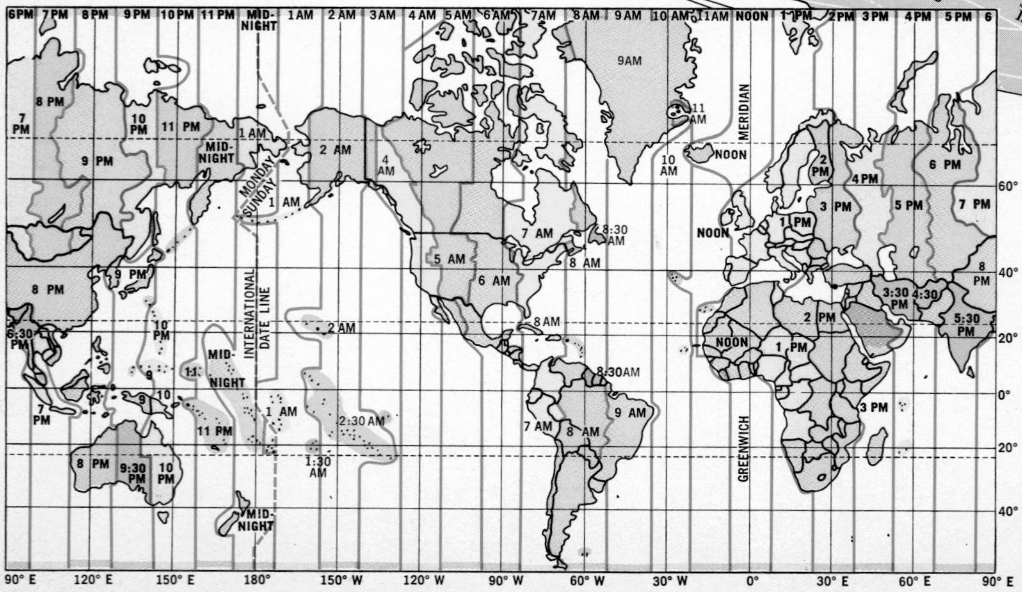

TIME ZONES

STANDARD	Areas using half hour deviations.
TIME	Areas not using zone system.
ZONES	

NOTE: Standard time zones in the U.S.S.R. are always advanced one hour.

Time zone strip labels (top): 6PM 7PM 8PM 9PM 10PM 11PM MIDNIGHT 1AM 2AM 3AM 4AM 5AM 6AM 7AM 8AM 9AM 10AM 11AM NOON 1PM 2PM 3PM 4PM 5PM 6

Longitude labels (bottom): 90° E 120° E 150° E 180° 150° W 120° W 90° W 60° W 30° W 0° 30° E 60° E 90° E

Latitude labels: 60° N, 40° N, 20° N, 0°, 20° S, 40° S

INTERNATIONAL DATE LINE — GREENWICH MERIDIAN

MONDAY / SUNDAY

Map labels (selected):

NORTH PACIFIC OCEAN — NORTH AMERICA — SOUTH PACIFIC OCEAN — SOUTH AMERICA — NORTH ATLANTIC OCEAN — SOUTH ATLANTIC OCEAN — ANTARCTICA — CARIBBEAN SEA — GULF OF MEXICO — SCOTIA SEA — Drake Passage

UNITED STATES — CANADA — MEXICO — CENTRAL AMERICA — GREENLAND (Den.) — ICELAND — UNITED KINGDOM — IRELAND — FRANCE — SPAIN — PORTUGAL — MOROCCO — ALGERIA — SAHARA — MAURITANIA — MALI — SENEGAL — GAMBIA — PORT. GUINEA — GUINEA — SIERRA LEONE — LIBERIA — IVORY COAST — GHANA — TOGO — GUINEA

COLOMBIA — VENEZUELA — ECUADOR — PERU — BRAZIL — BOLIVIA — CHILE — ARGENTINA — PARAGUAY — URUGUAY — SURINAM — FR. GUI. — GUYANA — MARIE BYRD LAND — COATS LAND

Honolulu, HAWAII — Palmyra I. (U.S.) — Fanning I. (Br.) — Line Is. — Niue (N.Z.) — Cook Is. (N.Z.) — Austral Is. (Fr.) — Papeete, Tahiti (Fr.) — Vostok I. (Br.-U.S.) — Marquesas Is. (Fr.) — Tuamotu Arch. (Fr.) — Pitcairn I. (Br.) — Easter I. (Chile) — Sala y Gómez (Chile) — Juan Fernández Is. (Chile) — Galápagos Is. (Ec.) — Clipperton I. (Fr.) — Revillagigedo Is. (Mex.)

Anchorage — Whitehorse — Juneau — Fairbanks — ALASKA — Pt. Barrow — Yukon — Mackenzie — Banks I. — Victoria I. — Queen Elizabeth Islands — Ellesmere I. — Baffin I. — Baffin B. — Thule — Davis Str. — Godthåb — Julianehåb — Arctic Circle — Reykjavik

Vancouver I. — Vancouver — Portland — Seattle — San Francisco — Los Angeles — Lower California — Calgary — Edmonton — Yellowknife — Winnipeg — Minneapolis — Denver — El Paso — Dallas — Houston — Colorado — Missouri — Arkansas — Rio Grande — St. Louis — Chicago — Detroit — Great Lakes — Hudson Bay — Toronto — Ottawa — Montréal — Québec — Labrador — Newfoundland — St. John's — Halifax — St. Lawrence — Str. of Belle I. — New York — Boston — Philadelphia — Washington — Atlanta — Savannah — Miami — New Orleans — C. Kennedy — C. Hatteras — Ohio

Guadalajara — Monterrey — Mexico City — Veracruz — Havana — CUBA — JAMAICA — BAHAMA IS. — HAITI — DOM. REP. — PUERTO RICO (U.S.) — West Indies — BARBADOS — TRIN. & TOB. — Panama Can. — BR. HON. — GUAT. — EL SALV. — HON. — NIC. — C.R. — Bermuda — Azores (Port.) — Madeira (Port.) — Canary Is. (Sp.) — Cape Verde Is. (Port.) — C. Blanco — Tropic of Cancer — Tropic of Capricorn — Equator — 40° N — 20° N — 20° S — 40° S

Bogotá — Caracas — Quito — Guayaquil — Pta. Aguja — Lima — Callao — Arequipa — Antofagasta — Valparaíso — Santiago — Valdivia — Córdoba — Buenos Aires — Asunción — Sucre — La Paz — L. Titicaca — Ucayali — Negro — Madeira — Amazon — Manaus — Tapajós — Tocantins — São Francisco — Brasília — São Paulo — Santos — Porto Alegre — Belém — Fortaleza — Natal — Recife — Salvador — Belo Horizonte — Rio de Janeiro — Montevideo — R. de la Plata — Bahía Blanca — Colorado — Tierra del Fuego — Cape Horn — Falkland Is. (Br.) — Str. of Magellan — S. Georgia (Br.) — S. Orkney Is. (Br.) — S. Sandwich Is. (Br.) — Tristan da Cunha (Br.) — Gough I. (Br.) — Ascension (St. Hel.) — St. Helena (Br.)

Antarctic Circle — Antarctic Pen. — Ronne Ice Shelf — Larsen Ice Shelf — Berkner I.

London — Paris — Lisbon — Madrid — Gibraltar (Br.) — Rabat — Casablanca — B. of Biscay — Str. of Gibraltar — Dakar — Nouakchott — Bamako — Monrovia — Abidjan — Accra — Lagos — Libreville

WORLD
LAND AREA 57,491,000 sq. mi.
WATER AREA 139,459,000 sq. mi.
TOTAL SURFACE AREA 196,950,000 sq. mi.
POPULATION 3,782,000,000

ANTARCTICA

AZIMUTHAL EQUIDISTANT PROJECTION

© Copyright HAMMOND INCORPORATED, Maplewood, N.J.

4 Arctic Ocean

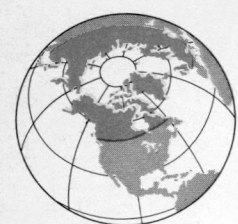

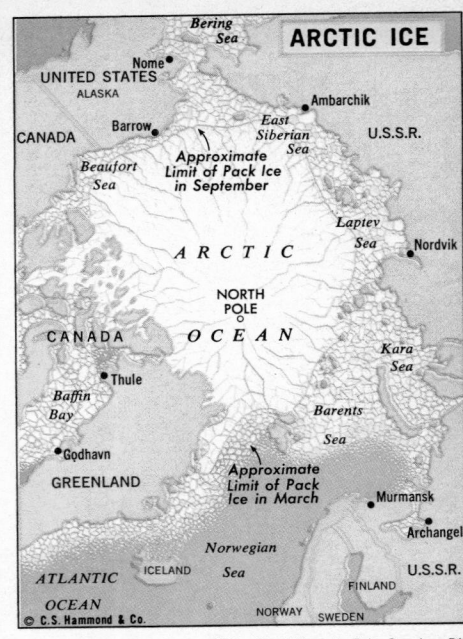

ARCTIC ICE

ARCTIC OCEAN

AZIMUTHAL EQUIDISTANT PROJECTION

SCALE OF MILES
0 100 200 400 600

SCALE OF KILOMETRES
0 200 400 600 800 1000

Copyright by C.S. Hammond & Co., N.Y.

EXPLORERS' ROUTES

Peary 1909
Byrd 1926
Amundsen, Ellsworth & Nobile 1926
Anderson in U.S.S. Nautilus 1958

By ship — By sledge
By airplane — By dirigible
By nuclear submarine

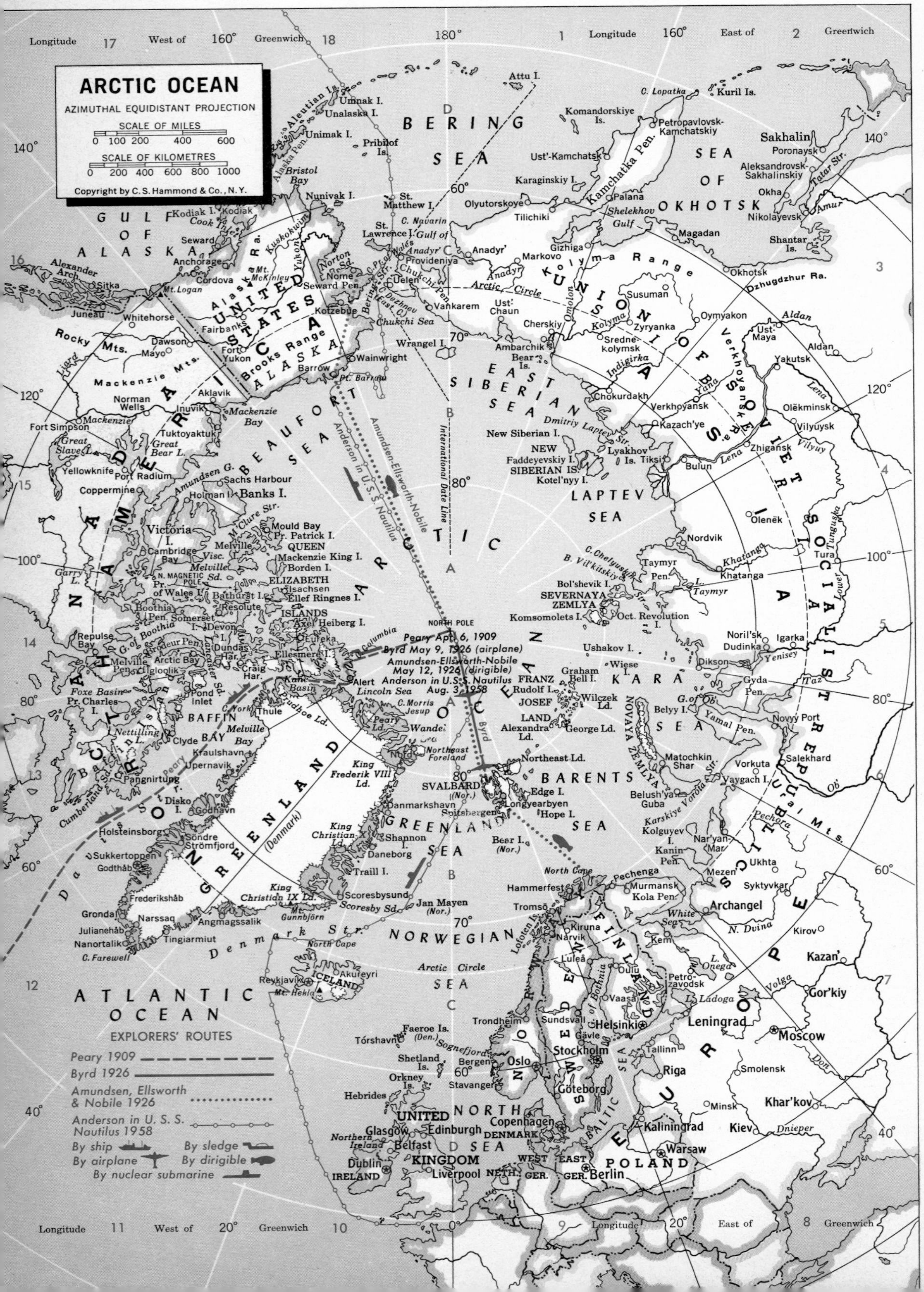

Antarctica 5

ANTARCTICA
AZIMUTHAL EQUIDISTANT PROJECTION

SCALE OF MILES
0 200 400 600 800

SCALE OF KILOMETRES
0 200 400 600 800 1000

© C. S. HAMMOND & Co., N.Y.

ATLANTIC OCEAN

INDIAN OCEAN

PACIFIC OCEAN

SCOTIA SEA

WEDDELL SEA

Ross Sea

Amundsen Sea

Bellingshausen Sea

SOUTH AMERICA

NEW ZEALAND

AUSTRALIA

Tasmania

Melbourne

Hobart

Dunedin

Adare (cape)	B 9	Luitpold Coast (region)	B17
Adelaide (isl.)	C15	Lützow-Holm (bay)	C 3
Adélie Coast (region)	C 7	Mackenzie (bay)	C 4
Alexander (isl.)	B15	Mac-Robertson Land (region)	C 4
American Highland	B 4	Marguerite (bay)	C15
Amery Ice Shelf	C 4	Marie Byrd Land (region)	B12
Amundsen (sea)	B13	Markham (mt.)	A 8
Antarctic (pen.)	C15	Mawson	C 4
Balleny (isls.)	C 9	McMurdo (sound)	B 9
Banzare Coast (region)	C 7	Mertz (glacier)	C 8
Barr Smith (mt.)	A 8	Mirnyy	C 5
Batterbee (cape)	C 3	New Schwabenland	B 1
Beardmore (glacier)	A 8	Ninnis (glacier)	C 8
Bellingshausen (sea)	C14	Norvegia (cape)	B18
Berkner (isl.)	B16	Oates Coast (region)	B 8
Biscoe (isls.)	C16	Palmer (arch.)	C15
Bouvet (isl.)	D 1	Palmer Land (region)	B15
Bransfield (strait)	C16	Palmer Station	C15
Budd Coast (region)	C 6	Peter I (isl.)	C14
Byrd Station	A12	Prince Olav Coast (region)	C 3
Caird Coast (region)	B17	Princess Astrid Coast	B 1
Charcot (isl.)	C15	Princess Martha Coast	B18
Clarie Coast (region)	C 7	Princess Ragnhild Coast	B 2
Coats Land (region)	B18	Prydz (bay)	C 4
Colbeck (cape)	B10	Queen Mary Coast	C 5
Coronation (isl.)	C16	Queen Maud Land	
Daly (cape)	C 4	Riiser-Larsen (pen.)	C 2
Darnley (cape)	C 4	Ronne Entrance (bay)	B15
Dart (cape)	B12	Roosevelt (isl.)	A10
Davis (sea)	C 5	Ross (isl.)	B 9
Davis (sta.)	C 4	Ross (sea)	B10
Drake (passage)	C15	Ross Ice Shelf	A10
Dumont d'Urville (sta.)	C 7	Sabine (mt.)	B 9
Edith Ronne Ice Shelf	B16	Sabrina Coast (region)	C 6
Edward VII (pen.)	B11	Sanae (sta.)	B18
Eights Coast (region)	B14	Scotia (sea)	D16
Elephant (isl.)	C16	Scott (isl.)	C10
Ellsworth Land (reg.)	A14	Shackleton Ice Shelf	C 5
Enderby Land (region)	B14	Sidley (mt.)	B12
English Coast (reg.)	B15	Siple (mt.)	B12
Executive Committee (range)	B12	South Georgia (isl.)	D17
Farr (bay)	C 5	South Magnetic Polar Area	C 8
Filchner Ice Shelf	B16	South Orkney (isls.)	C16
Ford (ranges)	B11	South Polar (plateau)	A 1
Gaussberg (mt.)	C 5	South Pole	A 4
George V Coast (region)	C 8	South Sandwich (isls.)	D17
Getz Ice Shelf	B12	South Shetland (isls.)	C15
Goodenough (cape)	C 7	Sulzberger (bay)	B11
Graham Land (region)	C15	Thurston (isl.)	C14
Grytviken	D17	Transantarctic (mts.)	A11
Hilton Inlet (bay)	B16	Victoria Land (region)	B 8
Hobbs Coast (region)	B12	Vincennes (bay)	C 6
Hollick-Kenyon (plateau)	B13	Vinson Massif (mt.)	B14
Hope (bay)	C15	Walgreen Coast (region)	B13
Joinville (isl.)	C16	Weddell (sea)	C17
Kainan (bay)	B10	West Ice Shelf	C 5
Keltie (cape)	C 7	Wilhelm II Coast (region)	C 5
Kemp Coast (region)	C 3	Wilkes Land (region)	C 7
King George (isl.)	C16		
Kirkpatrick (mt.)	A 8		
Knox Coast (region)	A 6		
Larsen Ice Shelf	C16		
Lazarev (sta.)	C 1		
Levick (mt.)	B 8		
Lister (mt.)	B 8		
Little America	B10		

EXPLORERS' ROUTES
Palmer 1820
Amundsen 1910-12
Scott 1910-13
Byrd 1928-30
Fuchs 1957-58
By ship   By sledge   By airplane
By snow tractor

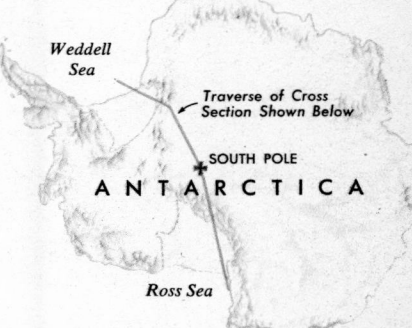

Weddell Sea
Traverse of Cross Section Shown Below
SOUTH POLE
ANTARCTICA
Ross Sea

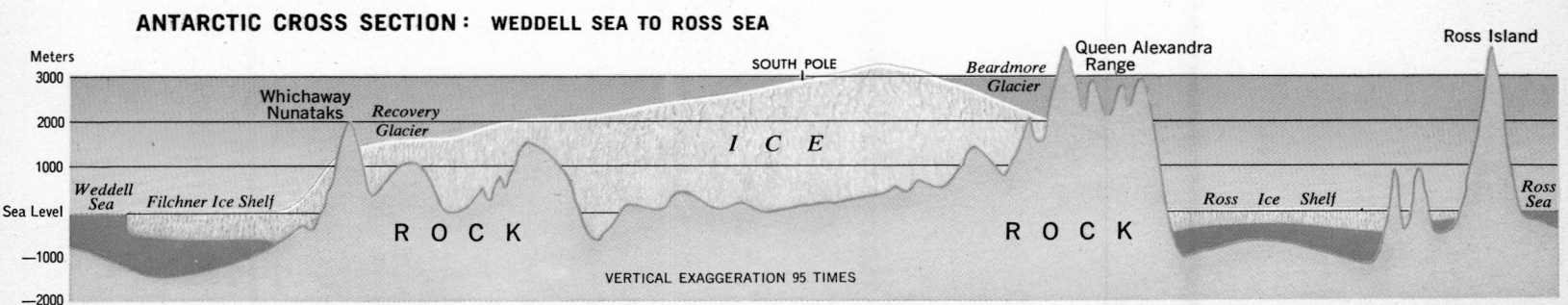

ANTARCTIC CROSS SECTION: WEDDELL SEA TO ROSS SEA

VERTICAL EXAGGERATION 95 TIMES

Information Based on American Geographical Society's "Antarctic Map Folio Series"

The government of the United States has
not recognized the incorporation of Estonia,
Latvia and Lithuania into the Soviet Union,
nor does it recognize as final the de facto
western limit of Polish administration in
Germany (the Oder-Neisse line).

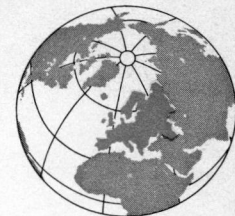

AREA 4,063,000 sq. mi.
POPULATION 652,000,000
LARGEST CITY London
HIGHEST POINT El'brus 18,481 ft.
LOWEST POINT Caspian Sea -92 ft.

POPULATION DISTRIBUTION

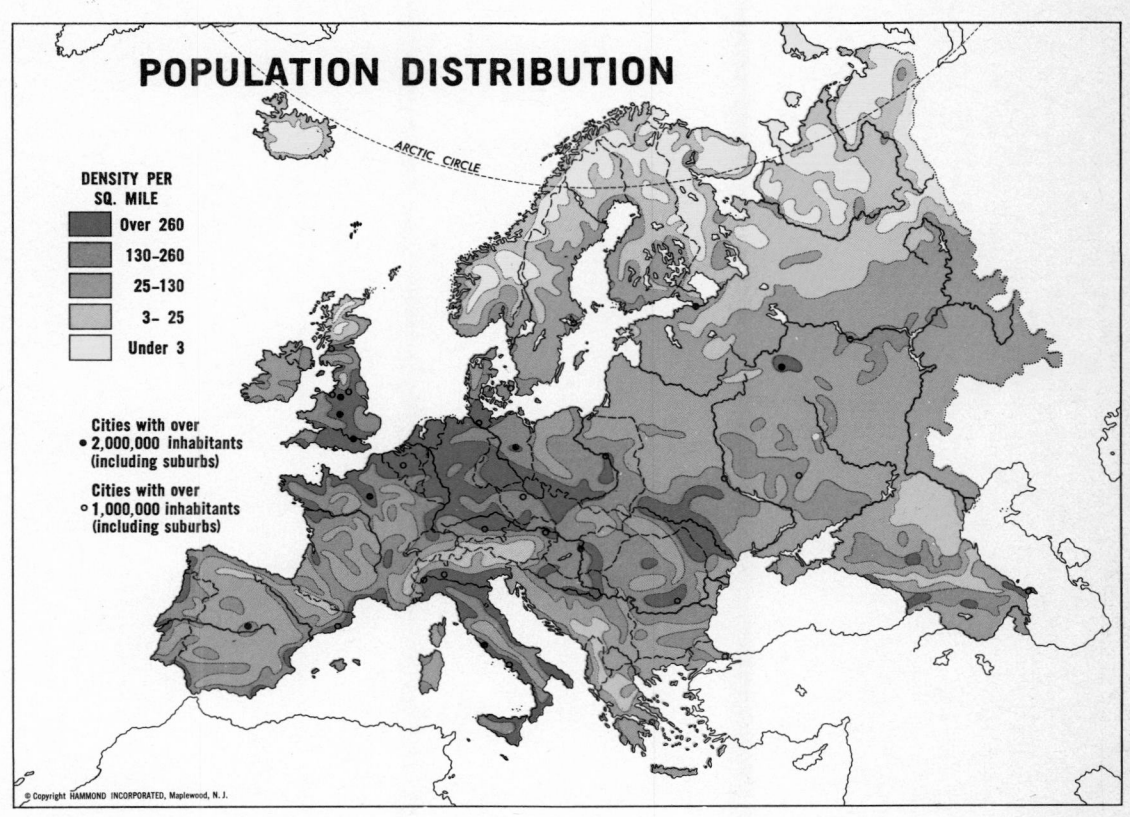

DENSITY PER SQ. MILE
- Over 260
- 130–260
- 25–130
- 3– 25
- Under 3

● Cities with over 2,000,000 inhabitants (including suburbs)

○ Cities with over 1,000,000 inhabitants (including suburbs)

© Copyright HAMMOND INCORPORATED, Maplewood, N.J.

VEGETATION

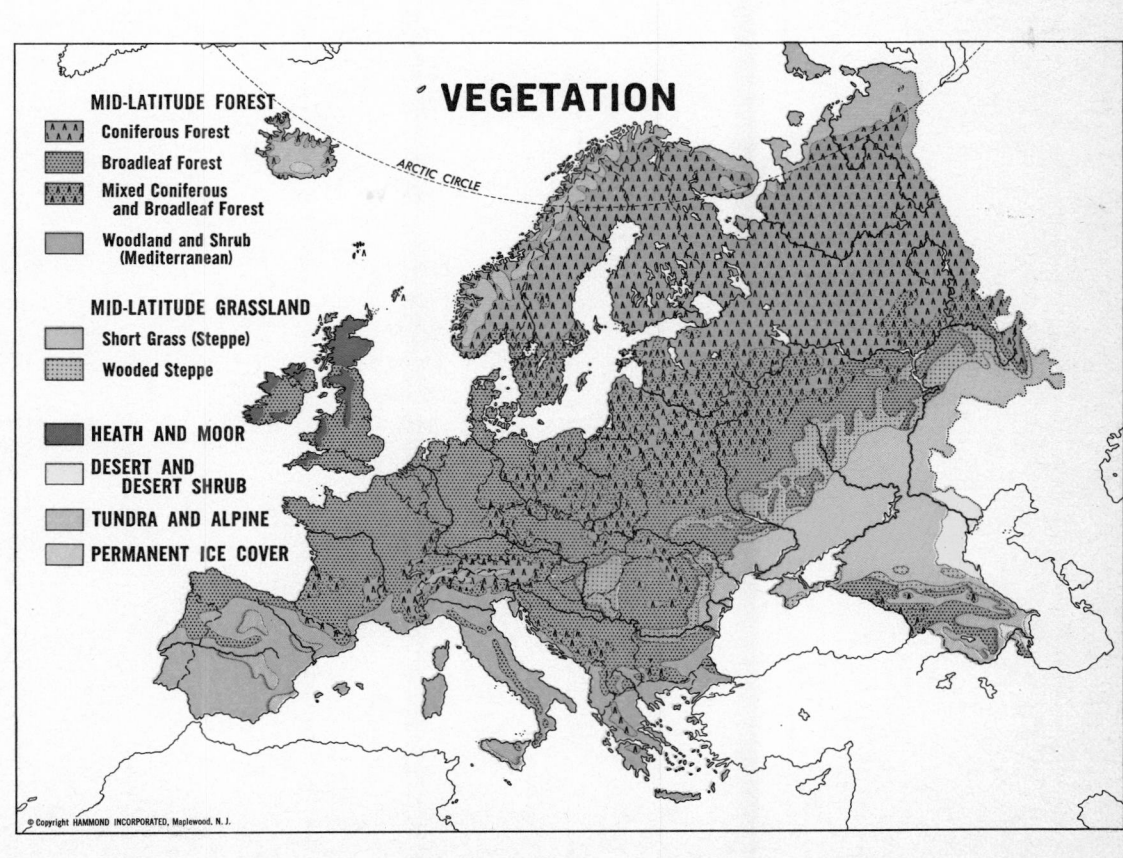

MID-LATITUDE FOREST
- Coniferous Forest
- Broadleaf Forest
- Mixed Coniferous and Broadleaf Forest
- Woodland and Shrub (Mediterranean)

MID-LATITUDE GRASSLAND
- Short Grass (Steppe)
- Wooded Steppe

HEATH AND MOOR

DESERT AND DESERT SHRUB

TUNDRA AND ALPINE

PERMANENT ICE COVER

© Copyright HAMMOND INCORPORATED, Maplewood, N.J.

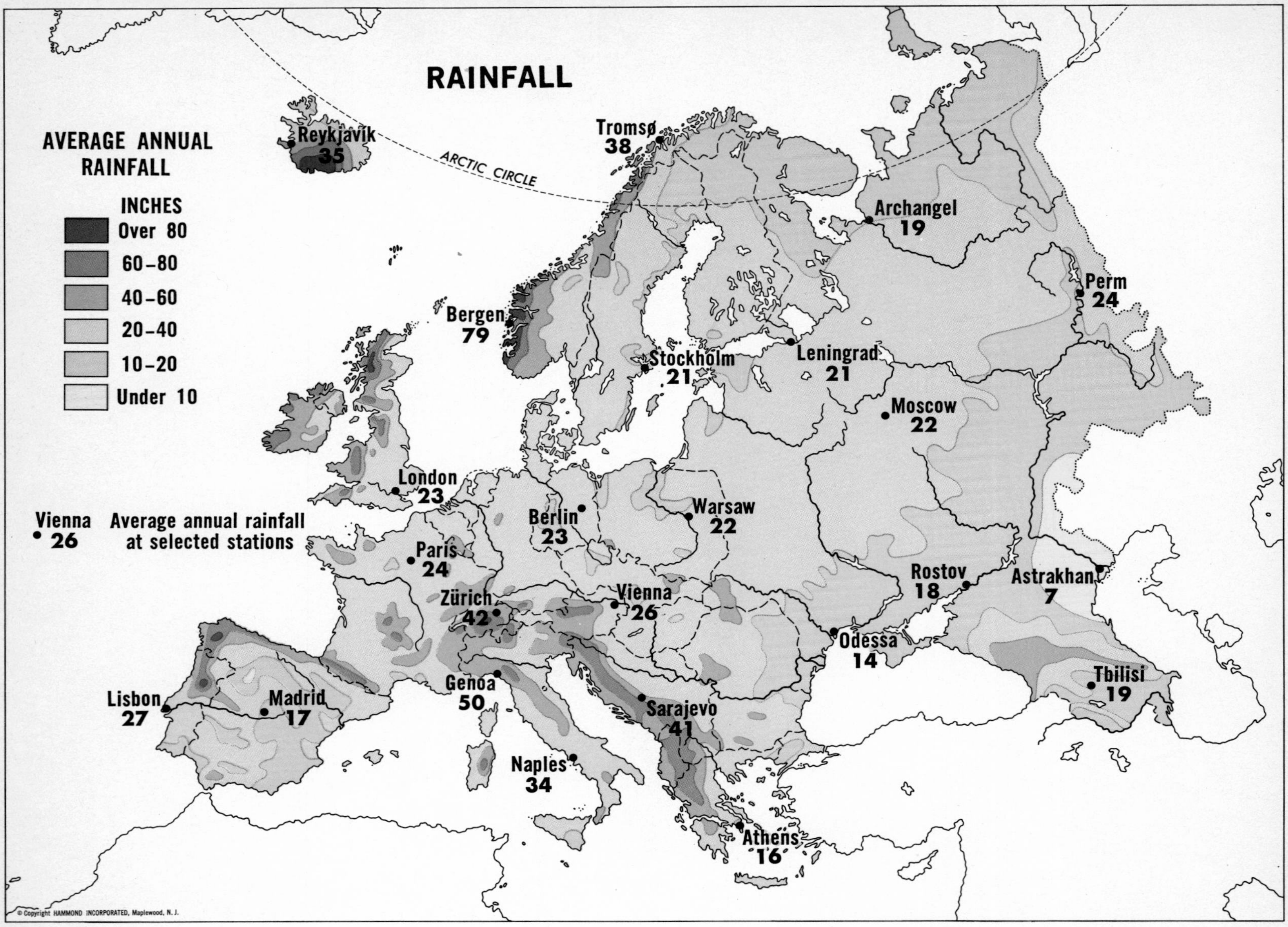

RAINFALL

AVERAGE ANNUAL
RAINFALL

INCHES
Over 80
60–80
40–60
20–40
10–20
Under 10

Reykjavík
35

Tromsø
38

ARCTIC CIRCLE

Archangel
19

Perm
24

Bergen
79

Stockholm
21

Leningrad
21

Moscow
22

London
23

Vienna
• 26   Average annual rainfall
at selected stations

Berlin
23

Warsaw
22

Paris
24

Zürich
42

Vienna
26

Rostov
18

Astrakhan
7

Odessa
14

Tbilisi
19

Lisbon
27

Madrid
17

Genoa
50

Sarajevo
41

Naples
34

Athens
16

© Copyright HAMMOND INCORPORATED, Maplewood, N.J.

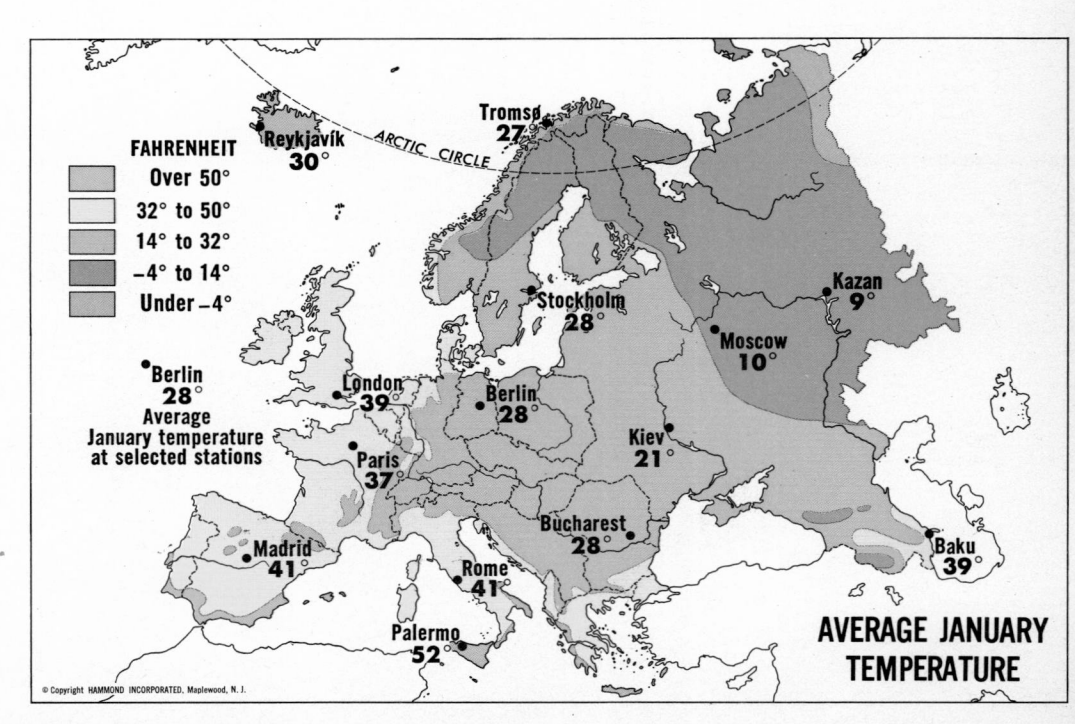

FAHRENHEIT
Over 50°
32° to 50°
14° to 32°
−4° to 14°
Under −4°

Tromsø
27

ARCTIC CIRCLE

Reykjavík
30

Kazan
9°

Stockholm
28

Moscow
10°

Berlin
28°
Average
January temperature
at selected stations

London
39°

Berlin
28°

Kiev
21°

Paris
37°

Madrid
41°

Bucharest
28°

Baku
39°

Rome
41°

Palermo
52°

© Copyright HAMMOND INCORPORATED, Maplewood, N.J.

AVERAGE JANUARY
TEMPERATURE

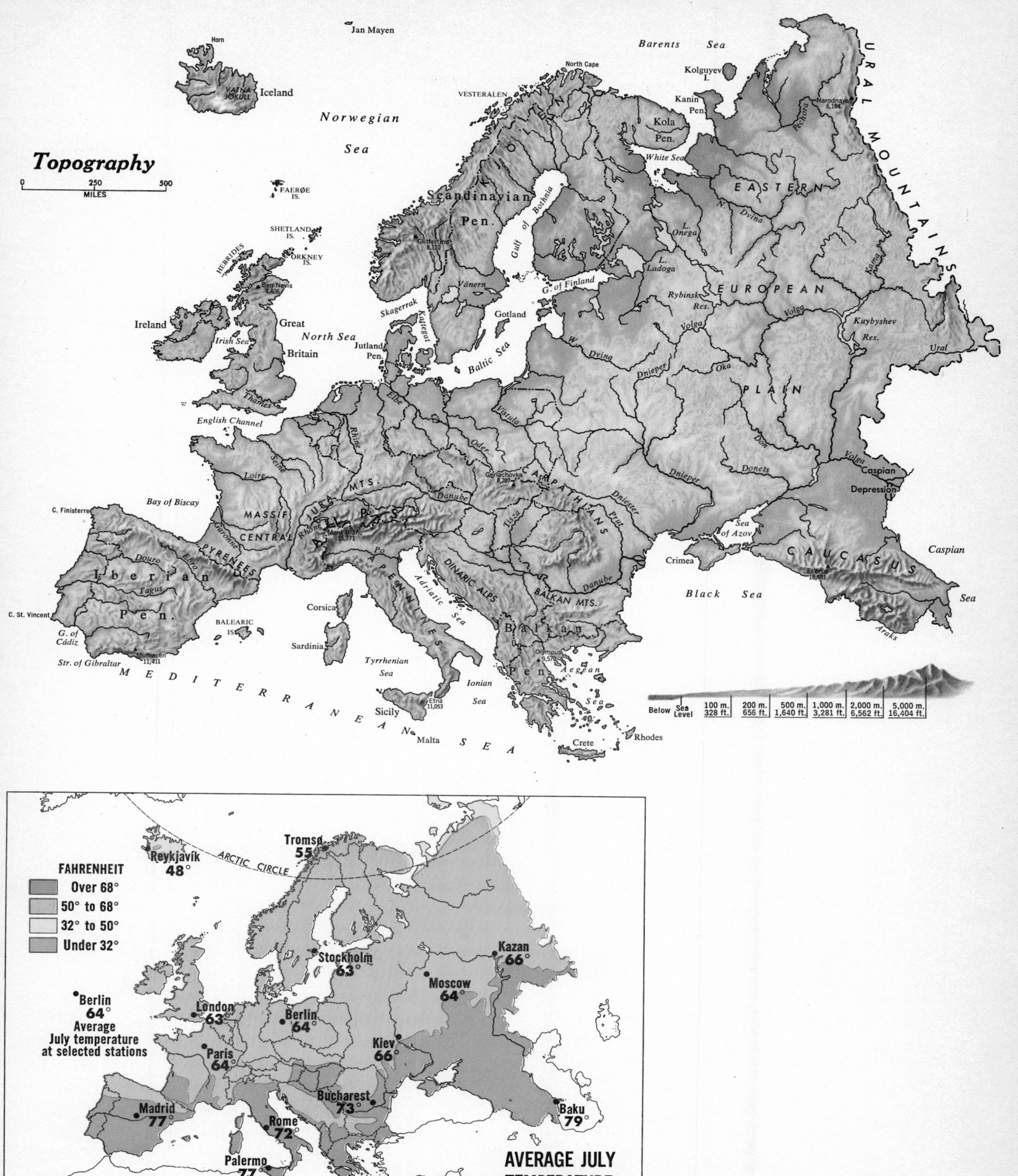

Topography

Horn

Jan Mayen

Barents Sea

Iceland
VATNA JÖKULL

Norwegian

Sea

North Cape

VESTERÅLEN

Kolguyev I.

Kola Pen.

Kanin Pen.

White Sea

EASTERN

0   250   500
MILES

FAERØE IS.

Scandinavian Pen.

Gulf of Bothnia

L. Onega

N. Dvina

EUROPEAN

SHETLAND IS.

Glittertind 8,110

ORKNEY IS.

HEBRIDES

Ben Nevis 4,406

Vänern

L. Ladoga

Rybinsk Res.

Kama

Narodnaya 6,184

URAL MOUNTAINS

Ireland

Great

G. of Finland

Gotland

Volga

Volga

Kuybyshev Res.

Irish Sea

North Sea

Britain

Jutland Pen.

Baltic Sea

W. Dvina

Dnieper

Oka

PLAIN

Ural

Thames

Elbe

Oder

Vistula

Don

English Channel

Rhine

Donets

Volga

Caspian

C. Finisterre

Bay of Biscay

Loire

Seine

JURA MTS.

ALPS

Danube

Tisza

CARPATHIANS

Dniester

Prut

Depression

MASSIF CENTRAL

Garonne

Rhône

Mont Blanc 15,771

Po

Gerlachovka 8,707

Danube

Sea of Azov

Caspian

PYRENEES

Crimea

CAUCASUS

Iberian

Douro

Ebro

DINARIC ALPS

Adriatic

BALKAN MTS.

Black Sea

El Brus 18,481

Sea

Tagus

APENNINES

Sea

Balkan

Araks

Pen.

C. St. Vincent

Pen.

Corsica

BALEARIC IS.

Sardinia

Tyrrhenian Sea

Ionian Sea

Olympus 9,570

Aegean Sea

G. of Cádiz

Mulhacén 11,411

Str. of Gibraltar

M E D I T E R R A N E A N   S E A

Sicily

Etna 11,053

Malta

Crete

Rhodes

Below Sea Level | 100 m. 328 ft. | 200 m. 656 ft. | 500 m. 1,640 ft. | 1,000 m. 3,281 ft. | 2,000 m. 6,562 ft. | 5,000 m. 16,404 ft.

FAHRENHEIT
Over 68°
50° to 68°
32° to 50°
Under 32°

Tromsö 55°

Reykjavík 48°

ARCTIC CIRCLE

Kazan 66°

Stockholm 63°

Moscow 64°

Berlin 64°
Average July temperature at selected stations

London 63°

Berlin 64°

Kiev 66°

Paris 64°

Bucharest 73°

Baku 79°

Madrid 77°

Rome 72°

Palermo 77°

AVERAGE JULY TEMPERATURE

© Copyright HAMMOND INCORPORATED, Maplewood, N.J.

UNITED KINGDOM and IRELAND

BONNE PROJECTION

SCALE OF MILES

SCALE OF KILOMETRES

Capitals of Countries .... ☆
International Boundaries ....
Other Boundaries ....
Canals ....

SHETLAND ISLANDS

SHETLAND ISLANDS
Same scale as main map.

GREATER LONDON

UNITED KINGDOM

AREA 94,214 sq. mi.
POPULATION 55,534,000
CAPITAL London
LARGEST CITY London
HIGHEST POINT Ben Nevis 4,406 ft.
MONETARY UNIT pound sterling
MAJOR LANGUAGES English, Gaelic, Welsh
MAJOR RELIGIONS Protestantism, Roman Catholicism

IRELAND

AREA 26,600 sq. mi.
POPULATION 2,944,000
CAPITAL Dublin
LARGEST CITY Dublin
HIGHEST POINT Carrantuohill 3,414 ft.
MONETARY UNIT Irish pound
MAJOR LANGUAGES English, Gaelic
MAJOR RELIGION Roman Catholicism

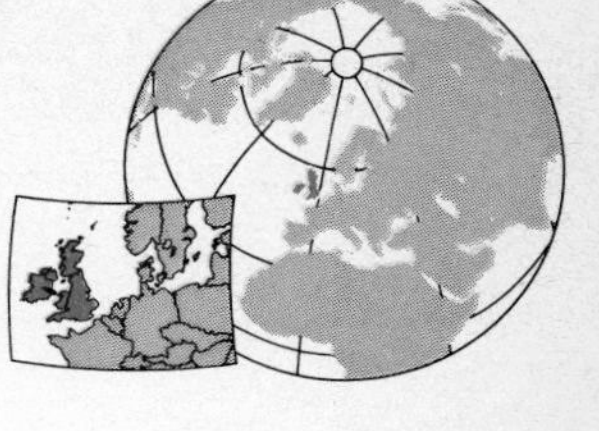

UNITED KINGDOM

IRELAND

GREATER LONDON

CITIES and TOWNS

Banstead, 44,790	B 6
Barking, 167,960	C 5
Barnet, 314,530	B 5
Bexley, 215,610	C 5
Brent, 281,530	B 5
Brentwood, 58,250	C 5
Bromley, 303,550	B 5
Bushey, 25,290	B 5
Camden, 228,080	B 5
Caterham and Warlingham, 37,760	B 6
Chertsey, 45,250	B 6
Cheshunt, 43,890	B 5
Chigwell, 56,030	C 5
Croydon, 327,130	B 6
Dartford, 46,280	C 5
Ealing, 297,910	B 5
Egham, 30,800	B 5
Enfield, 265,600	B 5
Epping, 11,380	C 5
Epsom and Ewell, 72,190	B 6
Esher, 63,190	B 6
Gravesend, 55,310	C 5
Greenwich, 228,030	C 5
Hackney, 238,530	B 5
Hammersmith, 192,810	B 5
Haringey, 242,300	B 5
Harrow, 207,700	B 5
Havering, 252,860	C 5
Hillingdon, 237,050	B 5
Hounslow, 205,060	B 5
Islington, 235,990	B 5
Kensington and Chelsea, 208,480	B 5
Kingston-upon-Thames, 143,670	B 6
Lambeth, 325,070	B 5
Leatherhead, 39,200	B 6
Lewisham, 282,080	B 5
London (cap.), 7,703,410	B 5
London, ‡12,956,440	B 5
Merton, 183,570	B 5
Newham, 252,090	B 5
Northfleet, 25,450	C 5
Potters Bar, 25,240	B 5
Redbridge, 244,800	C 5
Richmond-upon-Thames, 176,600	B 5
Rickmansworth, 30,360	A 5
Sevenoaks, 18,150	C 6
Southwark, 290,530	B 5
Staines, 56,610	B 5
Sunbury-on-Thames, 40,120	B 6
Sutton, 166,430	B 6
Thurrock, 124,830	C 5
Waltham Forest, 235,880	B 5
Waltham Holy Cross, 13,670	B 5
Walton and Weybridge, 52,530	B 6
Wandsworth, 319,190	B 5
Watford, 76,700	B 5
Westminster, 240,360	B 5
Wimbledon, 57,312	B 5
Woking, 78,180	B 6

OTHER FEATURES

Colne (river)	A 5
Thames (river)	C 5

BIRMINGHAM AREA

CITIES and TOWNS

Aldridge-Brownhills, 87,530	G 3
Bewdley, 6,400	F 3
Birmingham, 1,086,400	G 3
Birmingham, *2,440,540	G 3
Brewood, 5,751	F 2
Bromsgrove, 39,440	G 3
Burntwood, †12,085	G 2
Burton-on-Trent, 50,850	G 2
Cannock, 54,540	G 2
Castle Bromwich, 9,205	G 3
Dudley, 181,380	G 3
Halesowen, 51,930	G 3
Kenilworth, 21,000	G 3
Kidderminster, 46,740	G 3
Lichfield, 22,930	G 2
Redditch, 37,910	G 3
Rugeley, 19,320	G 2
Shenstone, 5,174	G 3
Solihull, 110,350	G 3
Stafford, 54,200	G 2
Stourbridge, 52,290	G 3
Stourport-on-Severn, 16,090	G 3
Sutton Coldfield, 82,220	G 3
Swadlincote, 20,130	G 2
Tamworth, 37,360	G 3
Walsall, 184,260	G 3
Warley, 167,810	G 3
West Bromwich, 171,850	G 3
Wolverhampton, 264,520	G 3

OTHER FEATURES

Anker (river)	G 3
Penk (river)	G 2
Severn (river)	F 3
Tame (river)	G 3
Trent (river)	G 2

LIVERPOOL-MANCHESTER AREA

CITIES and TOWNS

Accrington, 36,340	G 1
Altrincham, 41,000	G 2
Ashton-under-Lyne, 48,180	G 2
Bacup, 16,270	G 1
Bakewell, 4,170	G 2
Bebington, 57,060	F 2
Birkenhead, 141,950	F 2
Blackburn, 100,010	G 1
Blackpool, 146,700	F 1
Bollington, 6,150	G 2
Bolton, 152,500	G 2
Bootle, 79,950	F 2
Bradford, 293,210	H 1
Brierfield, 7,290	G 1
Burnley, 76,610	G 1
Burtonwood, †2,766	G 2
Bury, 67,070	G 2
Buxton, 20,100	G 2
Cheadle and Gatley, 57,290	G 2
Chester, 60,880	F 2
Chorley, 30,990	G 2
Clitheroe, 12,910	G 1
Colne, 18,890	G 1
Colne Valley, 21,000	G 2
Congleton, 19,610	G 2
Crewe, 51,960	G 2
Crosby, 58,580	F 2
Darwen, 28,500	G 1
Dewsbury, 51,560	H 2
Eccles, 39,830	G 2
Ellesmere Port, 56,750	F 2
Formby, 21,730	F 2
Fulwood, 19,880	G 1
Glossop, 21,830	G 2
Halifax, 93,570	G 1
Hebden Royd, 8,800	G 1
Hoylake, 32,190	F 2
Huddersfield, 130,600	G 2
Hyde, 38,710	G 2
Keighley, 55,400	H 1
Kirkby, 65,260	F 2
Kirkham, 6,380	F 1
Knutsford, 11,900	G 2
Leigh, 46,200	G 2
Leyland, 23,100	F 1
Litherland, 24,540	F 2
Liverpool, 677,450	F 2
Liverpool, *1,341,660	F 2
Longridge, 6,170	G 1
Lymm, 9,380	G 2
Lytham Saint Anne's, 37,000	F 1
Macclesfield, 41,870	G 2
Manchester, 593,770	G 2
Manchester, *2,433,370	G 2
Marple, 24,100	G 2
Middleton, 57,510	G 2
Middlewich, 8,000	G 2
Nantwich, 11,200	G 2
Nelson, 31,230	G 1
Neston, 16,940	F 2
New Mills, 8,880	G 2
Northwich, 18,940	G 2
Oldham, 108,280	G 2
Ormskirk, 25,900	F 2
Parbold, †976	G 2
Poulton le Fylde, 16,150	F 1
Preston, 102,100	F 1
Rawtenstall, 21,640	G 2
Rochdale, 86,600	G 2
Runcorn, 31,560	G 2
Saddleworth, 19,620	G 2
Saint Helens, 102,770	F 2
Salford, 137,750	G 2
Sandbach, 12,160	G 2
Skelmersdale and Holland, 23,640	F 2
Southport, 79,430	F 2
Sowerby Bridge, 16,610	G 2
Stalybridge, 21,620	G 2
Stockport, 140,030	G 2
Thornton Cleveleys, 26,250	F 1
Todmorden, 15,430	G 2
Wallasey, 101,360	F 2
Warrington, 70,870	F 2
Whaley Bridge, 5,390	G 2
Widnes, 55,120	F 2
Wigan, 79,780	G 2
Wilmslow, 28,790	G 2
Winsford, 22,040	G 2
Wirral, 26,000	F 2

OTHER FEATURES

Dee (river)	F 2
Irish (sea)	F 2
Mersey (river)	F 2
Ribble (river)	G 1

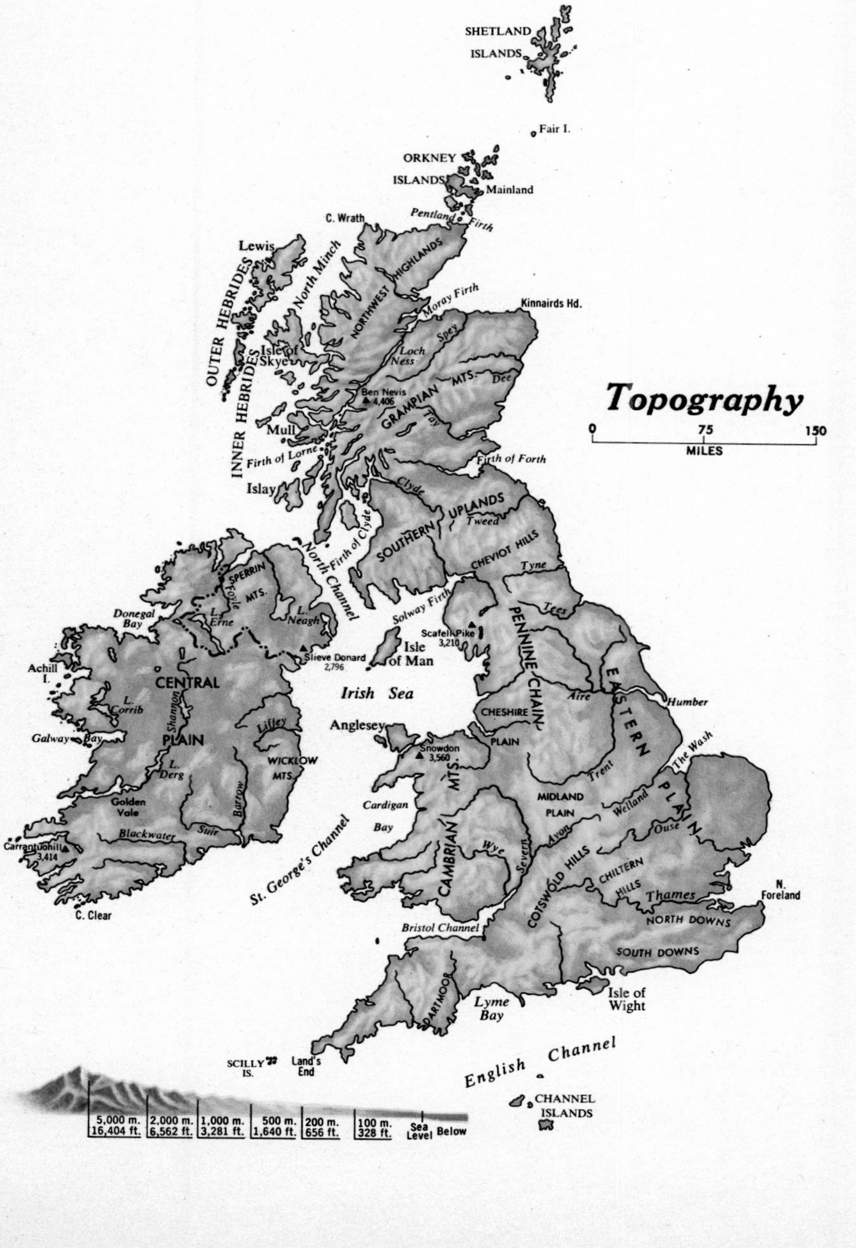
Topography
0
75
150
MILES
SHETLAND ISLANDS
Fair I.
ORKNEY ISLANDS
Mainland
C. Wrath
Pentland Firth
Lewis
North Minch
OUTER HEBRIDES
NORTHWEST HIGHLANDS
Moray Firth
Kinnairds Hd.
Isle of Skye
Loch Ness
Spey
Ben Nevis 4,406
GRAMPIAN MTS.
Dee
Tay
INNER HEBRIDES
Mull
Firth of Lorne
Firth of Forth
Islay
Clyde
Firth of Clyde
SOUTHERN UPLANDS
Tweed
CHEVIOT HILLS
Tyne
North Channel
SPERRIN MTS.
L. Neagh
L. Erne
Donegal Bay
Solway Firth
Scafell Pike 3,210
Tees
PENNINE CHAIN
Slieve Donard 2,796
Isle of Man
Achill I.
CENTRAL PLAIN
L. Corrib
Shannon
Irish Sea
EASTERN PLAIN
Humber
Aire
CHESHIRE PLAIN
Galway Bay
Liffey
Anglesey
Snowdon 3,560
WICKLOW MTS.
L. Derg
Barrow
Trent
The Wash
Golden Vale
CAMBRIAN MTS.
MIDLAND PLAIN
Welland
Ouse
Cardigan Bay
Wye
Severn
Avon
Blackwater
Suir
Carrantuohill 3,414
St. George's Channel
COTSWOLD HILLS
CHILTERN HILLS
Thames
N. Foreland
C. Clear
NORTH DOWNS
Bristol Channel
SOUTH DOWNS
DARTMOOR
Lyme Bay
Isle of Wight
SCILLY IS.
Land's End
English Channel
CHANNEL ISLANDS
5,000 m. 16,404 ft.
2,000 m. 6,562 ft.
1,000 m. 3,281 ft.
500 m. 1,640 ft.
200 m. 656 ft.
100 m. 328 ft.
Sea Level
Below

ENGLAND
(map on page 13)

COUNTIES

Bedfordshire, 443,960	G 5
Berkshire, 623,540	F 6
Buckinghamshire, 578,210	G 6
Cambridgeshire and Isle of Ely, 302,560	H 5
Cheshire, 1,512,820	E 4
Cornwall, 362,180	C 7
Cumberland, 295,530	D 3
Derbyshire, 891,570	F 4
Devon, 881,590	D 7
Dorset, 348,840	E 7
Durham, 1,433,990	F 3
Essex, 1,314,680	H 6
Gloucestershire, 1,078,050	E 6
Hampshire (Hants), 1,551,900	F 6
Herefordshire, 142,060	E 5
Hertfordshire, 903,390	G 6
Huntingdon and Peterborough, 196,670	G 5
Isle of Wight, 102,100	F 7
Kent, 1,388,820	H 6
Lancashire, 5,182,380	E 4
Leicestershire, 740,170	F 5
Lincolnshire-Holland, 105,170	G 5
Lincolnshire-Kesteven, 233,040	G 5
Lincolnshire-Lindsey, 464,350	G 4
London (greater), 7,703,410	G 6
Norfolk, 609,930	H 5
Northamptonshire, 453,920	G 5
Northumberland, 823,030	E 2
Nottinghamshire, 969,730	F 4
Oxfordshire, 374,610	F 6
Rutland, 29,860	G 5
Shropshire (Salop), 332,330	E 5
Somerset, 664,690	E 6
Southampton (Hampshire), 1,551,900	F 6
Staffordshire, 1,846,970	E 5
Suffolk, East, 384,210	J 5
Suffolk, West, 163,760	G 7
Surrey, 1,002,140	G 6
Sussex, East, 736,050	H 7
Sussex, West, 469,900	G 7
Warwickshire, 2,139,640	F 5
Westmorland, 71,710	E 3
Wight, Isle of, 102,100	F 7
Wiltshire, 496,930	F 6
Worcestershire, 683,820	E 5
Yorkshire-East Riding, 545,430	G 4
Yorkshire-North Riding, 721,870	F 3
Yorkshire-West Riding, 3,800,750	F 4

CITIES and TOWNS

Abingdon, 17,820	F 6
Accrington, 36,340	E 4
Aldershot, 38,120	G 6
Alfreton, 22,440	F 4
Andover, 24,780	F 6
Arnold, 31,780	G 4
Ashford, 35,360	H 6
Ashington, 25,830	F 2
Aylesbury, 36,730	G 6
Banbury, 27,900	F 5
Barnet, 314,530	G 6
Barnsley, 74,880	F 4
Barnstaple, 16,850	C 6
Barrow-in-Furness, 63,460	D 3
Basildon, 122,760	H 6
Basingstoke, 43,570	F 6
Bath, 84,760	E 6
Batley, 40,276	F 4
Bedford, 68,650	G 5
Bedlington Station (Bedlingtonshire), 30,040	F 2
Bedworth, 40,700	F 5
Beeston and Stapleford, 63,600	F 5
Belper, 16,360	F 4
Benfleet, 46,270	H 6
Berwick-upon-Tweed, 11,530	F 2
Beverley, 17,320	G 4
Bexhill, 33,470	H 7
Bideford, 11,240	C 6
Birkenhead, 141,950	D 4
Birmingham, 1,086,400	F 5
Birmingham, *2,440,540	F 5
Bishop Auckland, 34,480	F 3
Bishop's Stortford, 21,270	H 6
Blackburn, 100,010	E 4
Blackpool, 146,700	D 4
Blaydon, 32,000	F 3
Bletchley, 28,300	G 5
Blyth, 35,130	F 2
Bognor Regis, 31,710	G 7
Bolsover, 11,770	F 4
Bolton, 152,500	E 4
Bootle, 79,950	D 4
Boston, 25,260	H 5
Bournemouth, 149,820	F 7
Bracknell, 20,378	G 6
Bradford, 293,210	F 4
Braintree and Bocking, 23,380	H 6
Brandon and Byshottles, 18,490	F 3
Brentwood, 58,250	H 6
Bridgwater, 26,800	D 6
Bridlington, 26,430	G 3
Brighouse, 33,130	F 4
Brighton, 163,600	G 7
Bristol, 427,230	E 6
Broadstairs and St. Peter's, 20,900	J 6
Bromsgrove, 39,440	E 5
Burgess Hill, 17,980	G 7
Burnham-on-Sea, 11,530	D 6
Burnley, 76,610	E 4
Burton-upon-Trent, 50,850	F 5
Bury, 67,070	E 4
Bury Saint Edmunds, 25,140	H 5
Buxton, 20,100	F 4
Camborne-Redruth, 38,380	B 7
Cambridge, 100,200	H 5
Cannock, 54,540	E 5
Canterbury, 33,140	J 6
Carlisle, 71,090	D 3
Carlton, 42,640	G 5
Castleford, 39,160	F 4

(continued on following page)

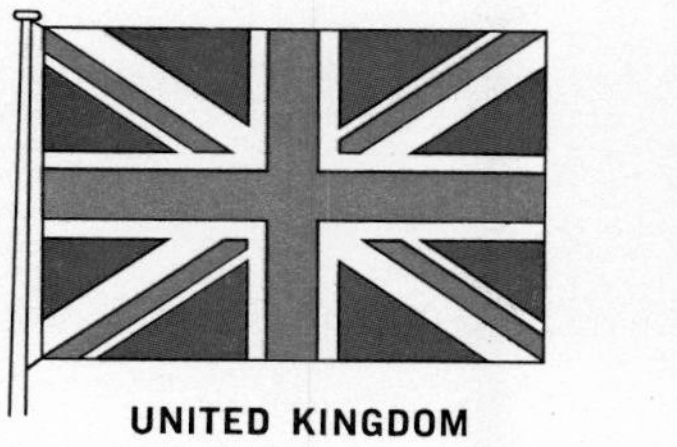

UNITED KINGDOM

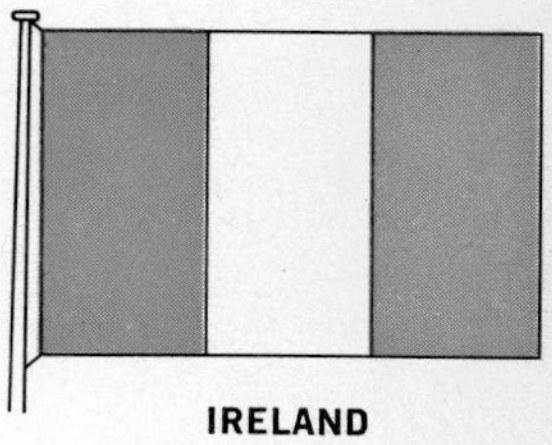

IRELAND

ENGLAND

AREA 50,327 sq. mi.
POPULATION 46,102,300
CAPITAL London
LARGEST CITY London
HIGHEST POINT Scafell Pike 3,210 ft.

WALES

AREA 8,017 sq. mi.
POPULATION 2,724,540
LARGEST CITY Cardiff
HIGHEST POINT Snowdon 3,560 ft.

SCOTLAND

AREA 30,411 sq. mi.
POPULATION 5,194,700
CAPITAL Edinburgh
LARGEST CITY Glasgow
HIGHEST POINT Ben Nevis 4,406 ft.

NORTHERN IRELAND

AREA 5,459 sq. mi.
POPULATION 1,512,500
CAPITAL Belfast
LARGEST CITY Belfast
HIGHEST POINT Slieve Donard 2,796 ft.

(continued)

ENGLAND (continued)

Caterham and Warlingham, 37,760 ... G 6
Chatham, 55,460 ... H 6
Cheadle and Gatley, 57,290 ... F 5
Chelmsford, 56,900 ... H 6
Cheltenham, 76,000 ... F 6
Chesham, 20,750 ... G 6
Cheshunt, 43,890 ... G 6
Chester, 60,880 ... E 4
Chesterfield, 70,420 ... F 4
Chester-le-Street, 20,800 ... F 3
Chichester, 20,740 ... G 7
Chippenham, 18,970 ... F 6
Chorley, 30,990 ... E 4
Christchurch, 31,780 ... F 7
Cirencester, 13,080 ... F 6
Clacton, 35,730 ... J 6
Cleethorpes, 35,370 ... H 4
Clevedon, 13,980 ... E 6
Clitheroe, 12,910 ... E 4
Coalville, 28,470 ... F 5
Colchester, 75,210 ... H 6
Colne, 18,890 ... E 4
Congleton, 19,610 ... E 4
Consett, 37,010 ... F 3
Corby, 49,210 ... G 5
Coventry, 335,650 ... F 5
Cowes, 18,000 ... F 7
Crawley, 64,520 ... G 6
Crewe, 51,960 ... E 4
Crook and Willington, 23,050 ... F 3
Croydon, 327,130 ... G 6
Cuckfield, 24,640 ... G 6
Dalton-in-Furness, 11,000 ... D 3
Darlington, 84,700 ... F 3
Dawley, 24,240 ... E 5
Deal, 27,130 ... J 6
Derby, 221,240 ... F 5
Dewsbury, 51,560 ... F 4
Doncaster, 84,050 ... G 4
Dorchester, 13,660 ... E 7
Dorking, 22,850 ... G 6
Dover, 35,640 ... J 6
Dunstable, 29,780 ... G 6
Durham, 25,780 ... F 3
Ealing, 297,910 ... G 6
East Grinstead, 8,390 ... G 6
East Retford, 18,860 ... G 4
Eastbourne, 69,290 ... H 7
Eastleigh, 45,100 ... F 7
Ellesmere Port, 56,750 ... E 4
Ely, 10,020 ... H 5
Epping, 11,380 ... H 6
Evesham, 13,170 ... F 5
Exeter, 92,880 ... D 7
Exmouth, 23,630 ... D 7
Falmouth, 17,350 ... C 7
Fareham, 79,740 ... F 7
Farnborough, 42,060 ... G 6
Farnham, 30,150 ... G 6
Faversham, 14,610 ... J 6
Felixstowe, 19,310 ... J 6
Fleet, 21,900 ... G 6
Fleetwood, 28,970 ... D 4
Folkestone, 45,270 ... J 6
Frinton and Walton, 12,060 ... J 6
Frome, 12,600 ... E 6
Gainsborough, 17,680 ... G 4
Gateshead, 100,060 ... F 3
Gillingham, 90,840 ... H 6
Glossop, 21,830 ... F 4
Gloucester, 90,530 ... E 6
Godalming, 18,230 ... G 6
Goole, 18,430 ... G 4
Gosport, 76,160 ... F 7
Grantham, 26,630 ... G 5
Gravesend, 55,310 ... H 6
Great Yarmouth, 50,760 ... J 5
Greenwich, 228,030 ... H 6
Grimsby, 96,500 ... H 4
Guildford, 55,890 ... G 6
Guisborough, 13,000 ... G 3
Halifax, 93,570 ... F 4
Haltemprice, 51,790 ... G 4
Harlow, 76,240 ... H 6
Harrogate, 62,680 ... F 4
Hartlepool, 98,710 ... F 3
Harwich, 14,870 ... J 6
Haslemere, 13,560 ... G 6
Haslingden, 14,280 ... E 4
Hastings, 69,020 ... H 7
Heanor, 24,470 ... F 5
Hemel Hempstead, 66,200 ... G 6
Hereford, 47,170 ... E 5
Herne Bay, 24,510 ... J 6
Hertford, 19,180 ... G 6
Hetton, 17,250 ... F 3
Heysham (Morecambe and Heysham), 40,880 ... D 3
High Wycombe, 57,360 ... G 6
Hinckley, 45,070 ... F 5
Hitchin, 27,410 ... G 6
Horsham, 26,360 ... G 6
Hove, 71,190 ... G 7
Hoylake, 32,190 ... D 4
Hucknall, 26,440 ... F 4
Huddersfield, 130,600 ... F 4
Hull (Kingston-upon-Hull), 292,600 ... G 4
Huntingdon and Godmanchester, 15,650 ... G 5
Hythe, 11,700 ... H 6
Ilkeston, 35,400 ... F 5
Ilkley, 19,820 ... F 4
Ipswich, 122,050 ... J 5
Jarrow, 29,370 ... F 3
Keighley, 55,400 ... F 4
Kendal, 20,160 ... E 3
Kenilworth, 21,000 ... F 5
Kettering, 40,040 ... G 5
Keynsham, 18,670 ... E 6
Kidderminster, 46,740 ... E 5
King's Lynn, 30,650 ... H 5
Kingston-upon-Hull (Hull), 292,600 ... G 4
Kingston-upon-Thames, 143,670 ... G 6
Kingswood, 29,340 ... E 6
Kirkby-in-Ashfield, 22,610 ... F 4
Knottingley, 17,010 ... F 4
Knutsford, 11,900 ... E 4
Lancaster, 48,170 ... E 3
Leamington (Royal Leamington Spa), 45,090 ... F 5
Leatherhead, 39,200 ... G 6
Leeds, 503,720 ... F 4
Leeds, *1,727,300 ... F 4
Leek, 19,180 ... E 4
Leicester, 278,470 ... G 5
Leigh, 46,200 ... E 4
Leighton-Linslade, 19,370 ... G 6
Letchworth, 29,870 ... G 6
Lewes, 14,030 ... H 7
Leyland, 23,100 ... E 4
Lichfield, 22,930 ... F 5
Lincoln, 75,570 ... G 4
Littlehampton, 18,200 ... G 7
Liverpool, 677,450 ... D 4
Liverpool, *1,341,660 ... D 4
London (cap.), 7,703,410 ... G 6
London, ‡12,956,440 ... G 6
Long Eaton, 33,170 ... F 5
Loughborough, 40,190 ... F 5
Louth, 11,480 ... H 4
Lowestoft, 50,730 ... J 5
Luton, 156,690 ... G 6
Lymington, 33,510 ... F 7
Lytham Saint Anne's, 37,000 ... D 4
Macclesfield, 41,870 ... F 4
Maidenhead, 46,050 ... G 6
Maidstone, 67,400 ... H 6
Maldon, 12,920 ... H 6
Malvern, 29,810 ... E 5
Manchester, 593,770 ... E 4
Manchester, *2,433,370 ... E 4
Mangotsfield, 23,530 ... E 6
Mansfield, 56,210 ... F 4
March, 14,080 ... H 5
Margate, 49,080 ... J 6
Maryport, 12,000 ... D 3
Matlock, 20,240 ... F 4
Melton Mowbray, 18,440 ... G 5
Morecambe and Heysham, 40,880 ... E 3
Morley, 44,120 ... F 4
Morpeth, 14,620 ... F 2
Nantwich, 11,200 ... E 4
Nelson, 31,230 ... E 4
New Windsor, 31,270 ... G 6
Newark, 24,580 ... G 4
Newbury, 22,170 ... F 6
Newcastle (Newcastle-under-Lyme), 76,570 ... E 5
Newcastle upon Tyne, 240,340 ... F 2
Newcastle upon Tyne, *839,910 ... F 2
Newham, 252,090 ... H 6
Newmarket, 12,190 ... H 5
Newport, 21,440 ... F 7
Newquay, 12,420 ... B 7
Newton Abbot, 18,660 ... D 7
Northampton, 123,800 ... G 5
Northfleet, 25,450 ... H 6
Northwich, 18,940 ... E 4
Norton-Radstock, 14,540 ... E 6
Norwich, 118,800 ... J 5
Nottingham, 303,090 ... F 5
Nuneaton, 64,650 ... F 5
Oakengates, 15,770 ... E 5
Old Fletton, 13,330 ... G 5
Oldham, 108,280 ... E 4
Ormskirk, 25,900 ... E 4
Otley, 13,090 ... F 4
Oxfored, 109,720 ... F 6
Penrith, 11,170 ... E 3
Penzance, 18,790 ... B 7
Peterborough, 66,800 ... G 5
Plymouth, 248,470 ... D 7
Pontefract, 30,820 ... F 4
Poole, 101,930 ... E 7
Portland, 12,780 ... E 7
Portslade-by-Sea, 18,420 ... G 7
Portsmouth, 214,800 ... G 7
Preston, 102,100 ... E 4
Prudhoe, 10,930 ... F 3
Queensborough-in-Sheppey, 28,790 ... G 5
Ramsgate, 39,140 ... J 6
Rawmarsh, 19,740 ... F 4
Reading, 127,530 ... F 6
Redditch, 37,910 ... F 5
Reigate, 57,830 ... G 6
Ripley, 17,910 ... F 4
Ripon, 11,840 ... F 3
Rochdale, 86,600 ... E 4
Rochester, 55,810 ... H 6
Rotherham, 86,450 ... F 4
Rugby, 57,700 ... F 5
Rugeley, 19,320 ... E 5
Runcorn, 31,560 ... E 4
Rushden, 18,130 ... G 5
Ryde, 22,290 ... F 7
Saint Albans, 52,680 ... G 6
Saint Austell with Fowey, 29,900 ... C 7
Saint Helens, 102,770 ... E 4
Salisbury, 36,440 ... F 6
Saltburn and Marske-by-the-Sea, 17,820 ... G 3
Sandbach, 12,160 ... E 4
Sandown-Shanklin, 14,030 ... F 7
Scarborough, 42,500 ... G 3
Scunthorpe, 69,720 ... G 4
Seaford, 15,600 ... H 7
Seaham, 24,800 ... F 3
Selby, 11,340 ... F 4
Sevenoaks, 18,150 ... H 6
Sheffield, 528,860 ... F 4
Shildon, 13,660 ... F 3
Shipley, 29,010 ... F 4
Shoreham-by-Sea, 18,050 ... G 7
Shrewsbury, 54,190 ... E 5
Sidmouth, 12,180 ... D 7
Sittingbourne and Milton, 30,820 ... H 6
Skegness, 12,680 ... H 4
Skelton and Brotton, 14,270 ... G 3
Skipton, 12,940 ... E 3
Slough, 92,750 ... G 6
South Shields, 106,150 ... F 3
Southampton, 210,000 ... F 7
Southend-on-Sea, 164,700 ... H 6
Southport, 79,430 ... D 4
Southwick, 11,360 ... G 7
Spalding, 16,300 ... G 5
Spennymoor, 18,400 ... F 3
Stafford, 54,200 ... F 5
Stalybridge, 21,620 ... F 4
Stamford, 14,000 ... G 5
Stockport, 140,030 ... E 4
Stoke-on-Trent, 272,260 ... E 4
Stourbridge, 52,290 ... E 5
Stourport-on-Severn, 16,090 ... E 5
Stratford-upon-Avon, 19,110 ... F 5
Stretford, 58,820 ... E 4
Stroud, 18,970 ... E 6
Sunderland, 218,970 ... F 3
Sutton-in-Ashfield, 40,570 ... F 4
Swindon, 98,290 ... F 6
Tamworth, 37,360 ... F 5
Taunton, 37,420 ... D 6
Teesside, 393,810 ... F 3
Teignmouth, 12,260 ... D 7
Thurrock, 124,830 ... H 6
Tiverton, 14,810 ... D 7
Tonbridge, 28,970 ... H 6
Torbay, 100,820 ... D 7
Trowbridge, 17,940 ... E 6
Truro, 14,590 ... C 7
Tunbridge Wells (Royal Tunbridge Wells), 44,930 ... H 6
Tynemouth, 72,390 ... F 2
Ulverston, 10,850 ... D 3
Wakefield, 59,630 ... F 4
Wallasey, 101,360 ... D 4
Wallsend, 47,120 ... F 2
Walsall, 184,260 ... F 5
Ware, 14,240 ... H 6
Warminster, 12,710 ... E 6
Warrington, 70,870 ... E 4
Warwick, 18,720 ... F 5
Watford, 76,700 ... G 6
Wellingborough, 35,680 ... G 5
Wellington, 16,890 ... E 5
Welwyn (Welwyn Garden City), 41,230 ... G 6
West Bromwich, 171,850 ... F 5
Weston-super-Mare, 47,960 ... E 6
Weymouth and Melcombe Regis, 42,120 ... E 7
Whitby, 12,130 ... G 3
Whitehaven, 26,760 ... D 3
Whitley Bay, 38,040 ... F 2
Whitstable, 23,780 ... J 6
Widnes, 55,120 ... E 4
Wigan, 79,780 ... E 4
Wigston, 28,130 ... G 5
Wilmslow, 28,790 ... E 4
Winchester, 31,070 ... F 6
Windsor (New Windsor), 31,270 ... G 6
Winsford, 22,050 ... E 4
Wisbech, 17,510 ... G 5
Witham, 13,080 ... H 6
Woking, 78,180 ... G 6
Wokingham, 19,580 ... F 6
Wolverhampton, 264,520 ... E 5
Wolverton, 13,600 ... G 5
Wombwell, 18,970 ... F 4
Worcester, 71,540 ... E 5
Workington, 29,710 ... D 3
Worksop, 35,660 ... F 4
Worthing, 83,100 ... G 7
Yeovil, 25,740 ... E 7
York, 107,940 ... F 4

OTHER FEATURES

Aire (river) ... F 4
Avon (river) ... F 5
Avon (river) ... F 6
Axe Edge (mt.) ... F 4
Beachy (head) ... H 7
Bigbury (bay) ... C 7
Blackwater (river) ... J 6
Bridlington (bay) ... G 3
Bristol (channel) ... C 6
Brown Willy (mt.) ... C 7
Carter Fell (mt.) ... E 2
Cheviot (hills) ... E 2
Cornish Heights (hills) ... B 7
Cotswold (hills) ... E 6
Cross Fell (mt.) ... E 3
Cumbrian (mts.) ... D 3
Dartmoor (forest) ... C 7
Dee (river) ... D 4
Derwent (river) ... G 4
Don (river) ... F 4
Dorset Heights (hills) ... E 7
Dover (strait) ... J 6
Dukeries, The (dist.) ... F 4
Dungeness (prom.) ... J 7
East Anglian Heights (hills) ... H 5
Eddystone (rocks) ... C 7
Eden (river) ... E 3
English (channel) ... D 8
Esk (river) ... D 2
Exmoor (forest) ... D 6
Flamborough (head) ... H 3
Formby (head) ... D 4
Foulness (isl.), 316 ... J 6
Hartland (point) ... C 6
High Willhays (mt.) ... C 7
Holy (Lindisfarne) (isl.), 190 ... F 2
Humber (river) ... H 4
Isle of Purbeck (pen.) ... F 7
Land's End (prom.) ... B 7
Liddel Water (river) ... F 2
Lincoln Wolds (hills) ... G 4
Lindisfarne (Holy) (isl.), 190 ... F 2
Little Ouse (river) ... H 5
Lizard (head) ... B 8
Lundy (isl.), 32 ... C 6
Lune (river) ... E 3
Lyme (bay) ... E 7
Manacles, The (rocks) ... C 7
Mendip (hills) ... E 6
Mersea (isl.), 3,840 ... J 6
Morte (point) ... C 6
Mounts (bay) ... B 8
Naze, The (prom.) ... J 6
Nene (river) ... H 5
New Forest (dist.) ... F 7
Nidd (river) ... F 3
North Foreland (prom.) ... J 6
North Tyne (river) ... E 2
Orfordness (prom.) ... J 5
Ouse (river) ... F 3
Ouse (river) ... H 5
Parrett (river) ... E 6
Peak, The (mt.) ... F 4
Peel Fell (mt.) ... E 2
Pennine (range) ... E 3
Portland (pen.) ... E 7
Prawle (point) ... D 7
Ribble (river) ... D 4
Saint Austell (bay) ... C 7
Saint Bees (head) ... D 3
Saint Mary's (isl.), 1,736 ... A 8
Scafell Pike (mt.) ... D 3
Scilly (isls.), 1,980 ... A 8
Selsey Bill (point) ... G 7
Severn (river) ... E 6
Sheppey (isl.), 28,790 ... H 6
Skiddaw (mt.) ... D 3
Solent (channel) ... F 7
Solway (firth) ... D 3
South Downs (hills) ... G 7
South Tyne (river) ... E 3
Spithead (channel) ... F 7
Spurn (head) ... H 4
Swale (river) ... F 3
Tamar (river) ... C 7
Tees (river) ... F 3
Thames (river) ... H 6
Till (river) ... F 2
Trent (river) ... G 4
Tresco (isl.), 283 ... A 7
Trevose (head) ... B 7
Tweed (river) ... E 2
Tyne (river) ... F 3
Ure (river) ... F 3
Walney (isl.), 9,811 ... D 3
Wash, The (bay) ... H 4
Waveney (river) ... J 5
Wear (river) ... F 3
Wharfe (river) ... F 4
Widemouth (bay) ... C 7
Wight (isl.), 102,100 ... F 7
Witham (river) ... G 4
Wye (river) ... D 5
Yare (river) ... J 5

WALES

COUNTIES

Anglesey, 58,210 ... C 4
Breconshire, 54,940 ... D 6
Caernarvonshire, 120,620 ... C 5
Cardiganshire, 53,500 ... C 5
Carmarthenshire, 163,600 ... C 6
Denbighshire, 182,050 ... D 4
Flintshire, 169,210 ... D 4
Glamorganshire, 1,258,450 ... D 6
Merionethshire, 37,700 ... D 5
Monmouthshire, 463,990 ... E 6
Montgomeryshire, 42,870 ... D 5
Pembrokeshire, 101,150 ... C 6
Radnorshire, 18,250 ... D 5

CITIES and TOWNS

Aberaeron, 1,220 ... C 5
Aberdare, 38,210 ... D 6
Abergavenny, 9,600 ... E 6
Abergele, 11,520 ... D 4
Abertillery, 22,610 ... E 6
Aberystwyth, 10,420 ... C 5
Amlwch, 3,890 ... C 4
Ammanford, 5,940 ... C 6
Bala, 1,600 ... D 5
Bangor, 14,930 ... C 4
Barmouth, 2,210 ... C 5
Barry, 42,500 ... D 6
Beaumaris, 2,060 ... C 4
Bethesda, 4,210 ... C 4
Betwys-y-Coed, 800 ... C 4
Brecknock, 6,380 ... D 6
Bridgend, 15,260 ... D 6
Brynmawr, 6,530 ... D 6
Builth Wells, 1,560 ... D 5
Burry Port, 5,900 ... C 6
Caerleon, 6,030 ... E 6
Caernarvon, 9,130 ... C 4
Caerphilly, 39,890 ... D 6
Cardiff, 285,860 ... E 6
Cardigan, 3,830 ... C 5
Carmarthen, 12,820 ... C 6
Chepstow, 7,840 ... E 6
Colwyn Bay, 25,060 ... D 4
Conway, 11,910 ... D 4
Cowbridge, 1,430 ... D 6
Criccieth, 1,580 ... C 5
Cwmamman, 4,050 ... D 6
Denbigh, 8,600 ... D 4
Dolgellau, 2,670 ... D 5
Ebbw Vale, 26,470 ... D 6
Ffestiniog, 6,350 ... D 5
Fishguard and Goodwick, 4,940 ... B 6
Flint, 14,650 ... D 4
Haverfordwest, 10,490 ... C 6
Hay, 1,340 ... D 5
Holyhead, 10,970 ... C 4
Holywell, 8,750 ... D 4
Kidwelly, 2,950 ... C 6
Knighton, 2,120 ... D 5
Lampeter, 2,120 ... C 5
Llandeilo, 1,880 ... C 6
Llandovery, 2,090 ... D 6
Llandrindod Wells, 3,240 ... D 5
Llandudno, 16,610 ... D 4
Llanelli, 27,570 ... C 6
Llanfairfechan, 3,230 ... C 4
Llanfyllin, 1,110 ... D 5
Llangefni, 3,580 ... C 4
Llangollen, 3,030 ... D 5
Llanidloes, 2,320 ... D 5
Llanrwst, 2,590 ... D 4
Llwchwr, 26,030 ... D 6
Machynlleth, 1,760 ... D 5
Menai Bridge, 2,390 ... C 4
Merthyr Tydfil, 56,360 ... D 6
Milford Haven, 13,670 ... B 6
Mold, 8,040 ... D 4
Monmouth, 6,280 ... E 6
Montgomery, 1,000 ... D 5
Mountain Ash, 28,130 ... D 6
Narberth, 1,040 ... C 6
Neath, 29,690 ... D 6
New Quay, 870 ... C 5
Newcastle Emlyn, 670 ... C 6
Newport, 112,000 ... E 6
Newtown, 5,590 ... D 5
Neyland, 2,410 ... C 6
Pembroke, 14,200 ... B 6
Penarth, 23,120 ... D 6
Penmaenmawr, 3,970 ... C 4
Pontypool, 36,600 ... E 6
Pontypridd, 35,010 ... D 6
Port Talbot, 50,970 ... D 6
Porthcawl, 13,410 ... D 6
Portmadoc, 3,840 ... C 5
Prestatyn, 13,670 ... D 4
Presteigne, 1,300 ... D 5
Pwllheli, 3,790 ... C 5
Rhondda, 94,300 ... D 6
Rhyl, 21,510 ... D 4
Risca, 16,030 ... D 6
Ruthin, 4,180 ... D 4
Swansea, 171,320 ... C 6
Tenby, 4,580 ... C 6
Tywyn, 4,440 ... C 5
Welshpool, 6,820 ... D 5
Wrexham, 37,620 ... E 4

OTHER FEATURES

Bardsey (isl.), 17 ... C 5
Berwyn (mts.) ... D 5
Braich-y-Pwll (prom.) ... C 5
Bristol (channel) ... E 5
Cader Idris (mts.) ... D 5
Caldy (isl.), 61 ... C 6
Cambrian (mts.) ... D 5
Cardigan (bay) ... C 5
Carmel (head) ... C 4
Clwyd (river) ... D 4
Dee (river) ... D 4
Gower (pen.), 16,100 ... C 6
Great Ormes (head) ... C 4
Holyhead (Holy) (isl.), 12,550 ... C 4
Lleyn (pen.), 19,840 ... C 5
Menai (strait) ... C 4
Pencilan (head) ... C 5
Plynlimon (mt.) ... D 5
Ramsey (isl.) ... B 6
Saint Brides (bay) ... B 6
Saint David's (head) ... B 6
Saint George's (channel) ... B 5
Saint Gowans (head) ... B 6
Severn (river) ... D 5
Skerries (isls.) ... C 4
Skomer (isl.) ... B 6
Snowdon (mt.) ... D 4
Snowdonia Nat'l Park ... D 5
Swansea (bay) ... C 6
Teifi (river) ... C 5
Towy (river) ... D 6
Tremadoc (bay) ... C 5
Usk (river) ... D 6
Wye (river) ... D 5

ISLE OF MAN

Total Population 50,000

CITIES and TOWNS

Douglas (cap.), 19,517 ... C 3
Michael, 353 ... C 3
Onchan, 3,609 ... C 3
Peel, 2,739 ... C 3
Ramsey, 3,880 ... C 3

OTHER FEATURES

Ayre (point) ... C 3
Calf of Man (isl.) ... B 3
Langness (prom.) ... C 3
Snaefell (mt.) ... C 3
Spanish (head) ... C 4

CHANNEL ISLANDS

Total Population 117,000

CITIES and TOWNS

Saint Anne, Alderney, †1,472 ... E 8
Saint Helier (cap.), Jersey, 19,661 ... E 8
Saint Peter Port (cap.), Guernsey, 15,804 ... E 8
Saint Sampson's, Guernsey, †5,916 ... E 8

OTHER FEATURES

Alderney (isl.), 1,472 ... E 8
Guernsey (isl.), 48,000 ... E 8
Herm (isl.), 90 ... E 8
Jersey (isl.), 68,000 ... E 8
Sark (isl.), 550 ... E 8

*City and suburbs.
†Population of parish.
‡Population of conurbation.

SCOTLAND

(map on page 15)

COUNTIES

Aberdeen, 317,803 ... L 5
Angus, 277,279 ... K 6
Argyll, 58,360 ... F 7
Ayr, 354,005 ... H 9
Banff, 43,753 ... K 5
Berwick, 20,499 ... L 8
Bute, 12,465 ... F 8
Caithness, 28,202 ... J 3
Clackmannan, 44,084 ... J 7
Dumfries, 87,276 ... J 9
Dunbarton, 277,635 ... G 7
East Lothian, 55,070 ... L 8
Fife, 325,139 ... K 7
Forfar (Angus), 277,279 ... K 6
Inverness, 84,786 ... G 5
Kincardine, 25,694 ... M 6
Kinross, 6,347 ... K 7
Kirkcudbright, 27,899 ... H 9
Lanark, 1,541,455 ... J 8
Midlothian, 595,590 ... K 8
Moray, 52,241 ... K 5
Nairn, 7,991 ... J 5
Orkney, 17,264 ... K 1
Peebles, 13,339 ... K 8
Perth, 124,199 ... H 7
Renfrew, 359,090 ... G 8
Ross and Cromarty, 56,641 ... F 4
Roxburgh, 42,619 ... L 9
Selkirk, 20,273 ... K 9
Stirling, 203,977 ... H 7
Sutherland, 12,995 ... G 3
West Lothian, 106,030 ... J 8
Wigtown, 27,611 ... G10
Zetland, 17,089 ... M 3

CITIES and TOWNS

Abbotsford, 15 ... L 8
Aberchirder, 838 ... L 4
Aberdeen, 181,089 ... N 5
Aberfeldy, 1,542 ... J 6
Aberfoyle, 853 ... H 7
Aberlour, 801 ... K 5
Abernethy, 772 ... K 7
Aboyne, 1,012 ... L 5
Acharacle, 93 ... E 6
Achiltibuie, 49 ... F 3
Achmore, 158 ... C 3
Achnasheen, 50 ... F 4
Airdrie, 36,188 ... D 2
Alexandria, 8,229 ... B 2
Alford, 758 ... L 5
Alloa, 14,205 ... E 1
Alness, 1,177 ... H 4
Alva, 4,100 ... J 7
Alyth, 1,705 ... K 6
Annan, 6,019 ... K10
Applecross, 25 ... E 5
Arbroath, 21,632 ... L 6
Ardcharnich, 16 ... F 4
Ardgour, 21 ... F 6
Ardrishaig, 1,047 ... F 8
Ardrossan, 9,946 ... G 8
Arinagour, 54 ... C 6
Arisaig, 174 ... E 6
Armadale, 6,384 ... E 2
Arrochar, 100 ... G 7
Auchinleck, 5,694 ... H 9
Auchterarder, 2,343 ... J 7
Auchtermuchty, 1,331 ... K 7
Auldearn, 359 ... J 4
Aultbea, 99 ... E 4
Aviemore, 635 ... J 5
Avoch, 899 ... H 4
Ayr, 47,635 ... G 9
Ayton, 425 ... M 8
Badachro, 35 ... E 4
Badcall, 17 ... F 3
Ballachulish, 381 ... F 6
Ballantrae, 420 ... F 9
Ballater, 1,076 ... K 5
Balmaha, 40 ... C 1
Balmoral Castle, 66 ... K 5
Balquhidder, 38 ... H 7
Baltasound, 240 ... M 2
Banavie, 197 ... F 6
Banchory, 2,066 ... M 5
Banff, 3,492 ... L 4
Bannockburn, 3,887 ... D 1
Barr, 224 ... G 9
Barrhead, 17,560 ... C 2
Barvas, 378 ... D 3
Bathgate, 14,763 ... J 8
Bearsden, 23,143 ... C 2
Beauly, 1,386 ... G 5
Beith, 4,993 ... B 2
Bellshill, 16,527 ... D 2
Berriedale, 30 ... K 3
Bettyhill, 99 ... H 3
Biggar, 1,668 ... J 8
Bishopbriggs, 19,779 ... D 2
Blair-Atholl, 509 ... J 6
Blairgowrie and Rattray, 5,071 ... J 6
Blantyre, 16,288 ... D 2
Boddam, 854 ... N 5
Bonar Bridge, 437 ... H 4
Bo'ness, 13,493 ... J 7
Bonhill, 4,024 ... B 2
Bonnybridge, 5,742 ... D 2
Bonnyrigg and Lasswade, 7,017 ... K 8
Bowmore, 840 ... D 8
Bracadale, 246 ... D 5
Braemar, 468 ... K 5
Brechin, 6,775 ... L 6
Bridge of Allan, 4,285 ... D 1
Broadford, 293 ... E 5
Brodick, 647 ... F 8
Brora, 1,256 ... J 3
Buckhaven and Methil, 18,815 ... L 7
Buckie, 7,697 ... L 4
Bunessan, 107 ... D 7
Burghead, 1,368 ... J 4
Burntisland, 5,451 ... K 7
Burravoe, 136 ... N 2
Cairnryan, 167 ... G10
Callander, 1,777 ... H 7
Cambuslang, 18,868 ... D 2
Campbeltown, 6,285 ... E 9
Cannich, 197 ... G 5
Canonbie, 194 ... K 9
Carbost, 118 ... C 5
Cargill, 21 ... K 7
Carloway, 232 ... C 3
Carluke, 8,110 ... E 2
Carnoustie, 5,663 ... L 6
Carnwath, 1,072 ... J 8
Carsphairn, 61 ... H 9
Carstairs Jct., 1,353 ... J 8
Castlebay, 122 ... B 6
Castle Douglas, 3,264 ... H10
Cawdor, 136 ... J 5
Ceres, 609 ... L 7
Chirnside, 821 ... M 8
Clackmannan, 2,476 ... J 7
Closeburn, 218 ... J 9
Clydebank, 49,997 ... C 2
Coatbridge, 52,804 ... D 2
Cockburnspath, 261 ... M 8
Cockenzie and Port Seton, 3,565 ... L 8
Coldingham, 392 ... M 8
Coldstream, 1,267 ... M 8
Colmonell, 231 ... G 9
Corpach, 376 ... F 6
Coupar Angus, 1,978 ... K 6
Cove and Kilcreggan, 1,292 ... B 1
Cowdenbeath, 10,480 ... K 7
Coylton, 233 ... H 9
Craignure, 43 ... E 7
Crail, 968 ... L 7
Crawford, 417 ... J 9
Creetown, 829 ... H10
Crieff, 5,569 ... J 7
Crinan, 34 ... E 7
Cromarty, 587 ... J 4
Cruden Bay, 489 ... N 5
Cullen, 1,253 ... L 4
Cults, 2,448 ... M 5
Cumbernauld, 26,678 ... D 2
Cumnock and Holmhead, 5,920 ... H 9
Cupar, 6,559 ... K 7
Dalbeattie, 3,229 ... J10
Dalkeith, 9,368 ... K 8
Dalmally, 155 ... G 7
Dalmellington, 2,130 ... H 9
Dalry, Ayr, 5,623 ... B 2
Dalry, Kirkcudbright, 448 ... H 9
Dalwhinnie, 132 ... H 6
Darvel, 3,165 ... H 8
Daviot, 38 ... H 5
Denny and Dunipace, 8,587 ... D 1
Dervaig, 82 ... D 6
Dingwall, 3,912 ... H 4
Dores, 143 ... H 5
Dornie, 102 ... F 5
Dornoch, 930 ... H 4
Douglas, 2,075 ... J 8
Doune, 758 ... H 7
Drummore, 390 ... G10
Dufftown, 1,536 ... K 5
Dumbarton, 25,510 ... B 2
Dumfries, 28,149 ... J 9
Dunbar, 2,931 ... M 8
Dunbeath, 159 ... K 3
Dunblane, 3,884 ... D 1
Dundee, 181,950 ... K 7
Dundonald, 1,293 ... H 8
Dunfermline, 50,305 ... J 7
Dunkeld, 279 ... J 6
Dunnet, 72 ... K 2
Dunoon, 9,431 ... A 2
Duns, 1,885 ... M 8
Dunscore, 169 ... J 9
Dunvegan, 157 ... D 5
Durness, 97 ... G 2
Dyce, 1,530 ... M 5
Earlston, 1,367 ... L 8
East Kilbride, 62,243 ... C 2
East Linton, 912 ... L 7
Ecclefechan, 834 ... K 9
Edderton, 52 ... H 4
Eddleston, 181 ... K 8
Edinbain, 149 ... D 5
Edinburgh (cap.), 465,421 ... K 8
Edzell, 644 ... L 6
Elderslie, 4,616 ... C 2
Elgin, 16,416 ... K 4
Elie and Earlsferry, 802 ... L 7
Ellon, 1,877 ... M 5
Elvanfoot, 85 ... J 9
Eriboll, 24 ... G 3
Errol, 744 ... K 7
Ettrick, 38 ... K 9
Evanton, 484 ... H 4
Ewes, 20 ... K 9
Eyemouth, 2,257 ... M 8
Falkirk, 38,625 ... E 1
Fearn, 210 ... J 4
Fetteresso, 20 ... M 6
Findhorn, 629 ... K 4
Findochty, 1,207 ... K 4
Findon, 77 ... M 5
Fochabers, 1,054 ... K 4
Ford, 50 ... F 7
Fordoun, 126 ... M 6
Forfar, 9,870 ... L 6
Forres, 4,711 ... K 4
Fort Augustus, 372 ... G 5
Fort William, 4,006 ... F 6
Fortingall, 33 ... H 6
Fortrose, 1,027 ... H 4
Fraserburgh, 10,898 ... N 4
Gairloch, 104 ... E 4
Galashiels, 12,073 ... L 8
Galston, 4,058 ... H 8
Gardenstown, 906 ... M 4
Garelochhead, 1,042 ... A 1
Gatehouse-of-Fleet, 797 ... H10
Girvan, 6,868 ... G 9
Glamis, 205 ... L 6
Glasgow, 927,948 ... D 2
Glasgow, *1,746,313 ... D 2
Glenbarr, 56 ... E 8
Glenelg, 290 ... E 5
Glenisla, 25 ... K 6
Glenluce, 706 ... G10
Glenrothes, 26,700 ... K 7
Golspie, 1,167 ... H 4
Gourock, 10,618 ... B 2
Grangemouth, 22,701 ... J 8
Grantown-on-Spey, 1,600 ... J 5
Greenlaw, 544 ... M 8
Greenock, 70,267 ... A 2
Gretna Green, 86 ... K 9
Haddington, 4,070 ... L 8
Halkirk, 608 ... K 3
Hamilton, 46,397 ... D 2
Harris (Tarbert), 416 ... C 4
Hawick, 16,685 ... L 9
Helensburgh, 13,594 ... B 1
Helmsdale, 768 ... K 3
Hillswick, 64 ... M 2
Hobkirk, 25 ... L 9
Hopeman, 1,146 ... K 4
Howmore, 38 ... A 5
Huntly, 3,878 ... L 5
Hurlford, 4,152 ... H 8
Hutton, 78 ... K 9
Innerleithen, 2,275 ... K 8
Insch, 917 ... L 5
Insh, 26 ... J 5
Inveraray, 468 ... F 7
Inverbervie, 885 ... M 6
Invergordon, 2,074 ... M 4
Inverie, 36 ... E 5
Inverkeilor, 224 ... M 6
Inverkeithing, 5,367 ... K 7
Inverness, 32,058 ... H 5
Inverurie, 5,351 ... M 5
Irvine, 21,382 ... G 8
Jamestown, 1,193 ... C 1
Jedburgh, 3,714 ... M 9
John O'Groats, 184 ... K 2
Johnshaven, 625 ... M 6
Johnstone, 22,633 ... B 2
Keiss, 364 ... K 2
Keith, 4,091 ... L 4
Kelso, 4,411 ... M 8
Kentallen, 91 ... F 6
Kilbarchan, 2,330 ... B 2
Kilbirnie, 8,158 ... B 2
Kildonan, 22 ... J 3
Kildrummy, 273 ... L 5
Kilfinan, 30 ... F 8
Killin, 583 ... H 7
Kilmacolm, 2,902 ... B 2
Kilmarnock, 47,631 ... G 8
Kilmelford, 69 ... F 7
Kilmore, 78 ... F 7
Kilmory, 81 ... F 9
Kilmuir, 87 ... D 5
Kilrenny and Anstruther, 2,814 ... L 7
Kilsyth, 9,659 ... D 2
Kincardine, 26 ... H 4
Kincardine O'Neil, 166 ... L 5
Kingussie, 1,013 ... H 5
Kinloch Rannoch, 236 ... H 6
Kinlochbervie, 117 ... G 3
Kinlochleven, 1,515 ... G 6
Kinross, 2,361 ... K 7
Kintore, 783 ... M 5
Kirkcaldy, 52,097 ... K 7
Kirkcolm, 318 ... F10
Kirkcowan, 401 ... G10
Kirkcudbright, 2,730 ... H10
Kirkintilloch, 24,601 ... C 2
Kirkoswald, 296 ... G 9
Kirkpatrick Fleming, 231 ... K 9
Kirkwall, 4,688 ... K 2
Kirriemuir, 4,107 ... L 6
Kyle of Lochalsh, 606 ... E 5
Laggan, 43 ... H 5
Lairg, 538 ... H 3
Lamlash, 528 ... F 8
Lanark, 8,407 ... J 8
Langholm, 2,393 ... K 9
Larbert, 4,167 ... D 1
Largs, 8,908 ... B 2
Larkhall, 13,931 ... D 2
Latheron, 51 ... K 3
Lauder, 564 ... L 8
Laurencekirk, 1,365 ... M 6
Leith, 51,378 ... K 8
Lennoxtown, 3,155 ... C 2
Lerwick, 5,919 ... N 3
Leslie, 3,229 ... K 7
Lesmahagow, 3,558 ... H 8
Leuchars, 1,332 ... L 7
Leven, 8,987 ... L 7
Leverburgh, 175 ... C 4
Linlithgow, 5,191 ... K 8
Livingston, 8,100 ... C 1
Lochaline, 200 ... E 6
Lochboisdale, 316 ... B 5
Lochcarron, 210 ... E 5
Lochgelly, 8,021 ... K 7
Lochgilphead, 1,253 ... F 7
Lochinver, 240 ... F 3
Lochmaben, 1,265 ... J 9
Lochmaddy, 303 ... B 4
Lochranza, 95 ... F 8
Lochwinnoch, 2,066 ... B 2
Lockerbie, 2,878 ... K 9
Logierait, 104 ... J 6
Lossiemouth and Branderburgh, 6,419 ... K 4
Lothbeg, 9 ... J 3
Luss, 140 ... B 1
Lybster, 534 ... K 3
Macduff, 3,502 ... M 4
Mallaig, 849 ... E 5
Markinch, 2,349 ... K 7
Marykirk, 126 ... M 6
Mauchline, 3,538 ... H 8
Maybole, 4,548 ... G 9
Meigle, 347 ... K 6
Melrose, 2,242 ... L 8
Melvaig, 36 ... E 4
Melvich, 130 ... H 2
Methlick, 299 ... M 5
Methven, 796 ... J 7
Mid Yell, 166 ... N 2
Millport, 1,159 ... A 2
Milngavie, 9,955 ... C 2
Moffat, 1,866 ... K 9
Moniaive, 409 ... J 9
Monifieth, 5,170 ... L 7
Montrose, 10,269 ... M 6
Motherwell and Wishaw, 75,022 ... D 2
Muirkirk, 3,409 ... H 9
Musselburgh, 17,244 ... L 8
Muthill, 726 ... J 7
Nairn, 4,986 ... J 4
Neilston, 3,795 ... C 2
New Abbey, 352 ... J10
Newarthill, 6,840 ... D 2
Newburgh, Aberdeen, 458 ... N 2
Newburgh, Fife, 2,107 ... K 7
New Cumnock, 5,508 ... H 9
New Deer, 619 ... M 5
New Galloway, 339 ... H 9
Newmilns and Greenholm, 3,506 ... H 8
Newport-on-Tay, 3,427 ... L 7
Newton-Stewart, 1,810 ... G10
Nigg, 33 ... J 4

(continued)

ENGLAND and WALES

CONIC PROJECTION

SCALE OF MILES

0 10 20   40   60   80

SCALE OF KILOMETRES

0 10 20   40   60   80

Capitals of Countries _____ ☆
Other Capitals _____ ◉
Administrative Centers _____ △
County Boundaries _____
Canals _____

Copyright by C.S. HAMMOND & CO., N.Y.

(continued)

SCOTLAND (continued)

North Berwick, 4,534 .... L 7
Oban, 6,743 .... F 7
Old Meldrum, 1,126 .... M 5
Oykel Bridge, 45 .... G 4
Paisley, 95,182 .... C 2
Peebles, 5,598 .... K 8
Penicuik, 81,293 .... K 8
Perth, 41,654 .... J 7
Peterhead, 13,332 .... N 4
Pierowall, 108 .... K 1
Pitlochry, 2,482 .... J 6
Pittenweem, 1,445 .... L 7
Plockton, 254 .... E 5
Poolewe, 81 .... E 4
Port Appin, 96 .... F 6
Portaskaig, 30 .... D 8
Port Ellen, 721 .... D 8
Port Glasgow, 21,985 .... B 2
Portknockie, 1,122 .... L 4
Portlethen, 75 .... M 5
Portmahomack, 207 .... J 4
Portobello, 27,141 .... K 8
Port of Ness, 93 .... D 3
Portpatrick, 681 .... F10
Portree, 1,356 .... D 5
Portsoy, 1,698 .... L 4
Port William, 528 .... G10
Prestonpans, 6,816 .... L 8
Prestwick, 13,741 .... G 9
Queensferry, 4,256 .... K 8
Quendale, 11 .... M 3
Rackwick, 12 .... K 2
Reay, 187 .... J 2
Renfrew, 19,114 .... C 2
Renton, 3,898 .... B 2
Rhynie, 363 .... L 5
Rosehearty, 1,144 .... M 4
Rosneath, 222 .... A 1
Rothes, 1,099 .... K 4
Rothesay, 6,329 .... F 8
Rothiemay, 24 .... L 4
Rutherglen, 25,213 .... C 2
Ruthwell, 96 .... K 9
Saddell, 44 .... E 8
Saint Andrews, 10,890 .... L 7
Saint Boswells, 1,007 .... L 8
Saint Combs, 713 .... N 4
Saint Cyrus, 347 .... M 6
Saint Margaret's Hope, 205 .... L 2
Saint Mary's, 151 .... L 2
Salen, 171 .... E 7
Saltcoats, 14,170 .... G 8
Sandness, 27 .... M 3
Sandwick, 43 .... N 3
Sanquhar, 2,066 .... J 9
Scalasaig, 45 .... D 7
Scalloway, 878 .... M 3
Scarinish, 103 .... C 7
Scone, 3,047 .... K 7
Scourie, 71 .... F 3
Scrabster, 129 .... J 2
Selkirk, 5,527 .... L 8
Shieldaig, 68 .... E 5
Shotts, 10,304 .... E 2
Skipness, 69 .... F 8
Spean Bridge, 229 .... G 6
Stevenston, 11,281 .... G 8
Stewarton, 4,156 .... H 8
Stirling, 28,786 .... D 1
Stonehaven, 4,573 .... M 6
Stonehouse, 3,686 .... M 8
Stoneykirk, 196 .... G10
Stornoway, 5,352 .... C 3
Stow, 453 .... L 8
Strachur, 36 .... F 7
Stranraer, 9,401 .... G10
Strathaven, 4,321 .... H 8
Strichen, 967 .... M 4
Stromness, 1,556 .... K 2
Strontian, 39 .... E 6
Tain, 1,719 .... H 4
Tarbert, Argyll, 1,236 .... F 8
Tarbert, Inverness, 416 .... C 4
Tarland, 396 .... L 5
Tayport, 2,916 .... L 7
Thornhill, 1,482 .... J 9
Thurso, 9,167 .... K 2
Tillicoultry, 4,125 .... J 7
Tobermory, 616 .... D 6
Tomintoul, 278 .... K 5
Tongue, 108 .... H 3
Torridon, 13 .... F 5
Tranent, 6,988 .... L 8
Traquair, 55 .... K 8
Troon, 10,906 .... G 8
Turriff, 2,784 .... M 4
Tweedsmuir, 30 .... J 9
Uig, Inverness, 107 .... D 4
Uig, Ross and Cromarty, 166 .... B 3
Ullapool, 676 .... F 4
Voe, 147 .... M 3
Walls, 132 .... M 3
Watten, 251 .... K 2
West Calder, 1,535 .... K 8
West Kilbride, 3,042 .... G 8
West Linton, 667 .... K 8
Whitburn, 9,596 .... E 2
Whithorn, 998 .... H10
Wick, 7,346 .... K 3
Wigtown, 1,149 .... H10
Yarrow, 30 .... K 8
Yetholm, 426 .... M 8

OTHER FEATURES

Abbey (head) J10
A'Chralaig (mt.) .... F 5
Affric (lake) .... G 5
Ailsa Craig (isl.), 10 .... F 9
Aird (pt.) .... D 4
Almond (riv.) .... J 7
Alness (riv.) .... H 4
Alsh (inlet) .... E 5
Annan (riv.) .... K 9
Appin (dist.), 429 .... F 6
Ardgour (dist.), 299 .... F 6
Ardivachar (pt.) .... A 5
Ardle (riv.) .... K 6
Ardnamurchan (dist.), 772 .... D 6
Ardnamurchan (pt.) .... D 6
Argyll (dist.), 4,435 .... F 7
Arisaig (dist.), 682 .... E 6
Arkaig (lake) .... F 6
Arran (isl.), 3,700 .... F 8
Askival (mt.) .... D 6
Assynt (dist.), 831 .... F 3
Assynt (lake) .... G 3
Athol (dist.), 1,458 .... H 6
Auskerry (isl.), 3 .... M 1
Avon (riv.) .... K 5
Awe (lake) .... F 7
Ayr (riv.) .... H 9
Badenoch (dist.), 6,473 .... H 6
Baleshare (isl.), 59 .... A 4
Barra (head) .... A 6
Barra (isl.), 1,369 .... A 5
Barra (isls.), 1,469 .... B 6
Barra (passg.) .... B 6
Battock (mt.) .... L 6
Beauly (firth) .... H 5
Beinn Bheigeir (mt.) .... D 8
Bell Rock (isl.), 3 .... M 7
Ben Alder (mt.) .... G 6
Ben Avon (mt.) .... K 5
Benbecula (isl.), 1,358 .... A 5
Benbecula (sound) .... A 5
Ben Dearg (mt.) .... G 4
Benderloch (dist.) .... F 7
Beneveian (lake) .... G 5
Ben Griam More (mt.) .... H 3
Ben Hee (mt.) .... G 3
Ben Hope (mt.) .... G 3
Ben Klibreck (mt.) .... H 3
Ben Lawers (mt.) .... H 6
Ben Macdhui (mt.) .... J 5
Ben Mhor (mt.) .... B 5
Ben More (mt.), Argyll .... E 7
Ben More (mt.), Perth .... G 7
Ben More Assynt (mt.) .... G 3
Ben Nevis (mt.) .... F 6
Ben Vorlich (mt.) .... H 7
Ben Wyvis (mt.) .... G 4
Bernera (isl.), 317 .... C 3
Berneray (isl.), 3 .... A 6
Berneray (isl.), 201 .... B 4
Black Isle (dist.), 5,673 .... H 4
Blackwater (res.) .... G 6
Boisdale (inlet) .... B 5
Boreray (isl.), 5 .... B 4
Bracadale (inlet) .... C 5
Braemar (dist.), 5,091 .... K 5
Bran (falls) .... J 6
Breadalbane (dist.), 3,877 .... H 7
Bressay (isl.), 269 .... N 3
Brims Ness (prom.) .... J 2
Broad (bay) .... D 3
Broad Law (mt.) .... K 9
Broom (inlet) .... F 4
Brora (riv.) .... H 3
Brough (head) .... K 1
Brough Ness (prom.) .... L 2
Buchan (dist.), 53,172 .... M 4
Buchan Ness (prom.) .... N 5
Buddon Ness (prom.) .... L 7
Burrow (head) H10
Bute (isl.), 9,793 .... F 8
Bute (sound) .... F 8
Butt of Lewis (prom.) .... D 3
Cairn Gorm (mt.) .... J 5
Cairngorm (mts.) .... J 5
Cairn Mor (mt.) .... K 5
Cairnsmore (mt.) .... H 9
Cairn Toul (mt.) .... J 5
Caledonian (canal) .... G 5
Canna (isl.), 24 .... C 5
Canna (sound) .... C 6
Caolisport (inlet) .... E 8
Carn Eige (mt.) .... F 5
Carrick (dist.), 21,867 .... G 9
Carron (inlet) .... E 5
Carron (river) .... G 4
Cellar (head) .... D 3
Cheviot (hills) .... L 9
Clar Nan (lake) .... J 3
Clisham (mt.) .... C 4
Clyde (falls) .... J 8
Clyde (firth) .... F 9
Clyde (river) .... G 8
Cnoc Moy (mt.) .... E 9
Coire (lake) .... H 3
Coll (isl.), 147 .... C 6
Colonsay (isl.), 164 .... C 7
Conon (river) .... H 4
Copinsay (isl.), 3 .... L 2
Corryvreckan (gulf) .... E 7
Corsewall (pt.) .... F 9
Cowal (dist.), 16,247 .... F 7
Creag Meagaidh (mt.) .... G 6
Cree (river) .... G 9
Creran (inlet) .... F 7
Cromarty (firth) .... H 4
Cuillin (hills) .... D 5
Cumbraes (isls.), 1,646 .... A 2
Dee (riv.) .... H 9
Dee (riv.) .... M 5
Dennis (head) .... M 1
Deveron (riv.) .... L 5
Dhuheartach (isl.), 3 .... C 7
Don (riv.) .... L 5
Doon (lake) .... G 9
Dornoch (firth) .... J 4
Duich (inlet) .... F 5
Duirinish (dist.), 1,268 .... C 5
Dulnain (riv.) .... J 5
Duncansby (head) .... L 2
Dunnet (head) .... J 2
Dunvegan (head) .... C 4
Durness, Kyle of (inlet) .... G 2
Earn (lake) .... H 7
Earn (riv.) .... J 7
East Loch Tarbert (inlet) .... C 4
Eck (lake) .... F 7
Eday (isl.), 198 .... L 1
Eddrachillis (bay) .... F 3
Eden (riv.) .... L 7
Egilsay (isl.), 54 .... L 1
Eigg (isl.), 74 .... D 6
Eil (inlet) .... F 6
Eishort (inlet) .... D 5
Enard (bay) .... F 3
Eport (inlet) .... B 4
Eriboll (inlet) .... G 2
Ericht (lake) .... H 6
Eriskay (isl.), 231 .... B 5
Erisort (inlet) .... D 3
Esk (riv.) .... L 9
Etive (inlet) .... F 7
Ettrick Pen (mt.) .... K 9
Eye (pen.) .... D 3
Eynhallow (sound) .... K 1
Eynort (inlet) .... B 5
Fair (isl.), 64 .... L 3
Fannich (lake) .... F 4
Farrar (riv.) .... G 5
Fetlar (isl.), 127 .... N 2
Fife Ness (prom.) .... L 7
Findhorn (riv.) .... J 5
Fionn (lake) .... F 4
Flannan (isls.), 3 .... A 3
Fleet (inlet) .... J 4
Foinaven (mt.) .... G 3
Formartine (dist.), 15,010 .... M 5
Forth (firth) .... L 7
Forth (riv.) .... H 7
Forth and Clyde (canal) .... H 8
Foula (isl.), 54 .... L 3
Foyers (falls) .... H 5
Fyne (inlet) .... F 8
Gair (inlet) .... E 4
Gairloch (dist.), 1,788 .... E 4
Gallan (head) .... B 3
Galloway (dist.), 57,994 .... H10
Galloway, Mull of (prom.) G10
Garioch (dist.), 7,950 .... L 5
Garry (lake) .... G 5
Garry (riv.) .... J 6
Gigha (isl.), 163 .... E 8
Gigha (sound) .... E 8
Girdle Ness (prom.) .... N 5
Glas Maol (mt.) .... K 6
Glass (lake) .... G 4
Glass (riv.) .... G 5
Glenelg (dist.), 1,549 .... E 5
Goat Fell (mt.) .... F 8
Grampian (mts.) .... G 6
Greenstone (pt.) .... E 4
Grimsay (isl.), 239 .... B 5
Gruinard (bay) .... E 4
Gruinard (dist.) .... F 4
Gruinart (inlet) .... D 8
Gulvain (mt.) .... F 6
Gunna (sound) .... C 6
Halladale (riv.) .... J 3
Harris (dist.), 2,493 .... C 4
Harris (sound) .... B 4
Hebrides (isls.), 43,676 .... A 5
Hebrides, Inner (isls.), 13,964 .... D 5
Hebrides, Outer (isls.), 29,712 .... A 5
Hebrides (sea) .... C 5
Helmsdale (riv.) .... J 3
Herma Ness (prom.) .... M 2
Holm (sound) .... L 2
Holy (isl.), 7 .... F 9
Holy Loch (inlet) .... A 2
Hope (lake) .... G 3
Hourn (inlet) .... F 5
Hoy (isl.), 511 .... K 2
Hynish (bay) .... C 7
Hyskier (isl.), 3 .... C 6
Inchard (inlet) .... F 3
Inchcape (Bell) Rock (isl.), 3 .... M 7
Inchkeith (isl.), 3 .... K 7
Indaal (inlet) .... D 8
Inner (sound) .... E 5
Inner Hebrides (isls.), 13,964 .... D 5
Inver (inlet) .... F 3
Iona (isl.), 130 .... D 7
Isla (riv.) .... K 6
Islay (isl.), 3,860 .... D 8
Jura (isl.), 249 .... E 7
Katrine (lake) .... G 7
Keal, Na (inlet) .... D 7
Kebock (head) .... D 3
Kilbrennan (sound) .... F 9
Kinnairds (head) .... N 4
Kintyre (dist.), 9,914 .... E 9
Kintyre, Mull of (prom.) .... E 9
Knapdale (dist.), 2,711 .... E 8
Knoydart (dist.), 1,234 .... E 5
Kyle (dist.) .... H 9
Laggan (bay) .... D 8
Lammermuir (hills) .... L 8
Langavat (lake) .... C 3
Laxford (inlet) .... F 3
Lennox (hills) .... C 1
Leven (inlet) .... F 6
Leven (lake) .... K 7
Lewis (dist.), 21,614 .... C 3
Lewis, Butt of (prom.) .... D 3
Liddel Water (riv.) .... L 9
Linnhe (inlet) .... F 6
Lismore (isl.), 155 .... F 7
Little Minch (sound) .... C 4
Lochaber (dist.), 7,591 .... F 6
Lochalsh (dist.), 1,651 .... E 5
Lochnager (mt.) .... K 6
Lochy (lake) .... G 6
Lomond (lake) .... G 7
Long (inlet) .... B 1
Lorne (dist.), 12,656 .... F 7
Lorne (firth) .... E 7
Lothians (dist.) .... K 8
Loyal (lake) .... H 3
Lubnaig (lake) .... H 7
Luce (bay) G10
Lyon (riv.) .... H 6
Maddy (inlet) .... B 4
Mainland (isl.), 13,282 .... N 3
Mainland (isl.), 13,495 .... K 1
Mam Soul (mt.) .... F 5
Mar (dist.), 16,918 .... E 4
Maree (lake) .... F 4
May (isl.), 7 .... M 7
Merrick (mt.) .... H 9
Mhor (lake) .... H 5
Minginish (dist.), 578 .... D 5
Moidart (dist.), 247 .... E 6
Monach (isls.) .... A 4
Monach (sound) .... A 4
Monadhliath (mts.) .... H 5
Monar (lake) .... F 5
Morar (dist.), 1,106 .... E 6
Morar (lake) .... E 6
Moray (firth) .... J 4
More (lake) .... G 3
Moriston (riv.) .... G 5
Morven (dist.), 422 .... E 6
Morven (mt.) .... J 3
Muck (isl.), 29 .... D 6
Muirnag (hill) .... D 3
Mull (head) .... L 1
Mull (head) .... L 2
Mull (isl.), 2,149 .... E 7
Mull (sound) .... E 7
Nairn (riv.) .... J 5
Na Keal (inlet) .... D 7
Nan Clar (lake) .... J 3
Naver (lake) .... H 3
Naver (riv.) .... H 3
Neist (pt.) .... C 5
Ness (lake) .... H 5
Ness (riv.) .... H 5
Nevis (inlet) .... E 5
Nith (riv.) .... J 9
North (chan.) .... E 9
North (sound) .... L 1
North Esk (riv.) .... L 6
North Minch (sound) .... E 3
North Ronaldsay (firth) .... M 1
North Ronaldsay (isl.), 161 .... M 1
North Uist (isl.), 1,620 .... A 4
Noss (head) .... L 3
Noup (head) .... K 1
Oa, Mull of (prom.) .... D 8
Ochil (hills) .... J 7
Oich (riv.) .... G 5
Orchy (riv.) .... G 7
Orkney (isls.), 17,264 .... J 1
Oronsay (isl.), 2 .... D 7
Oronsay (passg.) .... D 7
Orrin (riv.) .... G 5
Outer Hebrides (isls.), 29,712 .... A 5
Oykell (riv.) .... G 4
Pabbay (isl.), 2 .... B 4
Papa Stour (isl.), 55 .... L 3
Papa Westray (isl.), 139 .... L 1
Paps of Jura (peaks) .... E 8
Park (dist.), 797 .... C 3
Peel Fell (mt.) .... L 9
Pentland (firth) .... K 2
Pladda (isl.), 6 .... F 9
Queensberry (mt.) .... J 9
Quoich (lake) .... F 5
Raasay (isl.), 211 .... D 5
Raasay (sound) .... D 5
Rannoch (dist.), 832 .... H 6
Rannoch (lake) .... H 6
Rattray (head) .... N 4
Renish (pt.) .... C 4
Resort (inlet) .... B 3
Rhinns (pt.) .... C 8
Rhu Coigach (cape) .... E 3
Roag (inlet) .... C 3
Rona (isl.), 49 .... D 4
Ross of Mull (pen.), 471 .... D 7
Rousay (isl.), 237 .... K 1
Rudha Hunish (cape) .... D 4
Rudh Re (cape) .... E 4
Rum (isl.), 40 .... D 6
Rum (sound) .... D 6
Ryan (inlet) .... F 9
Saint Abb's (head) .... M 8
Saint Andrews (bay) .... L 7
Saint Kilda (isl.), 65 .... B 8
Saint Magnus (bay) .... M 3
Saint Mary's Loch (lake) .... K 9
Sanda (isl.), 7 .... E 9
Sanday (isl.), Inverness .... D 5
Sanday (isl.), Orkney, 670 .... M 1
Sanday (sound) .... L 1
Scalpay (isl.), 470 .... C 4
Scalpay (isl.), 2 .... E 5
Scapa Flow (chan.) .... K 2
Scarba (isl.), 5 .... E 7
Scarp (isl.), 46 .... B 3
Scavaig (inlet) .... D 5
Scradain (inlet) .... D 7
Scurdie Ness (prom.) .... M 6
Seaforth (inlet) .... C 4
Sgurr a Choir Ghlais (mt.) .... G 5
Sgurr Mhor (mt.) .... F 4
Sgurr Na Ciche (mt.) .... F 5
Sgurr Na Lapaich (mt.) .... F 5
Shapinsay (isl.), 416 .... L 1
Shee Water (riv.) .... J 6
Shell (inlet) .... D 4
Shetland (isls.), 17,089 .... M 3
Shiel (lake) .... E 6
Shin (falls) .... H 4
Shin (lake) .... G 3
Shona (isl.), 11 .... E 6
Sidlaw (hills) .... K 6
Sinclair's (bay) .... K 2
Skeir Graitich (isl.) .... D 4
Skerryvore (isl.), 3 .... B 7
Skye (isl.), 7,478 .... D 5
Sleat (dist.), 524 .... E 5
Sleat (pt.) .... D 5
Sleat (sound) .... E 5
Small (isls.), 143 .... C 6
Snizort (inlet) .... D 4
Soay (isl.), 11 .... D 5
Solway (firth) J10
South Esk (riv.) .... K 6
South Ronaldsay (isl.), 980 .... L 2
South Uist (isl.), 2,376 .... A 5
Spean (riv.) .... G 6
Spey (riv.) .... K 4
Staffin (bay) .... D 4
Start (pt.) .... M 1
Stinchar (riv.) .... G 9
Stoer (pt.) .... F 3
Stornoway (harb.) .... D 3
Storr, The (mt.) .... D 4
Strathbogie (dist.), 9,152 .... L 5
Strathmore (dist.) .... J 7
Strathy (pt.) .... H 2
Stroma (isl.), 12 .... K 2
Stronsay (firth) .... L 1
Stronsay (isl.), 497 .... M 1
Sumburgh (head) .... M 3
Sunart (inlet) .... E 6
Swona (isl.), 3 .... K 2
Taransay (isl.), 5 .... B 4
Tarbat Ness (prom.) .... J 4
Tarbert (inlet) .... D 8
Tay (firth) .... L 7
Tay (lake) .... H 7
Tay (riv.) .... K 7
Teith (riv.) .... H 7
Teviot (riv.) .... L 9
Thurso (riv.) .... J 3
Tilt (riv.) .... J 6
Tiree (isl.), 993 .... C 6
Tirry (riv.) .... H 3
Tiumpan (head) .... D 3
Toe (head) .... B 4
Tolsta (head) .... D 3
Ton Mhor (pt.) .... C 8
Tongue, Kyle of (inlet) .... G 2
Tor Ness (prom.) .... K 2
Torridon (inlet) .... E 4
Treig (lake) .... G 6
Trossachs, The (valley) .... H 7
Trotternish (dist.), 389 .... D 4
Troup (head) .... M 4
Tuath (inlet) .... D 7
Tummel (falls) .... J 6
Tummel (river) .... J 6
Turnberry (pt.) .... G 9
Tweed (riv.) .... M 8
Tyne (riv.) .... M 7
Ugie (riv.) .... N 4
Ulva (isl.), 28 .... D 7
Unst (isl.), 1,148 .... N 2
Vaternish (dist.), 198 .... C 4
Vaternish (pt.) .... C 4
Vatersay (isl.), 95 .... A 6
Voil (lake) .... G 7
Watten (lake) .... K 3
West Burra (isl.), 561 .... M 3
West Loch Tarbert (inlet) .... B 4
Westray (firth) .... K 1
Westray (isl.), 872 .... K 1
Whalsay (isl.), 764 .... N 3
Whiten (head) .... G 2
Wide (firth) .... L 1
Wigtown (bay) H10
Wrath (cape) .... F 2
Yarrow Water (riv.) .... L 8
Yell (isl.), 1,155 .... M 2
Yell (sound) .... M 2
Ythan (riv.) .... M 5

*City and suburbs.

Agriculture, Industry and Resources

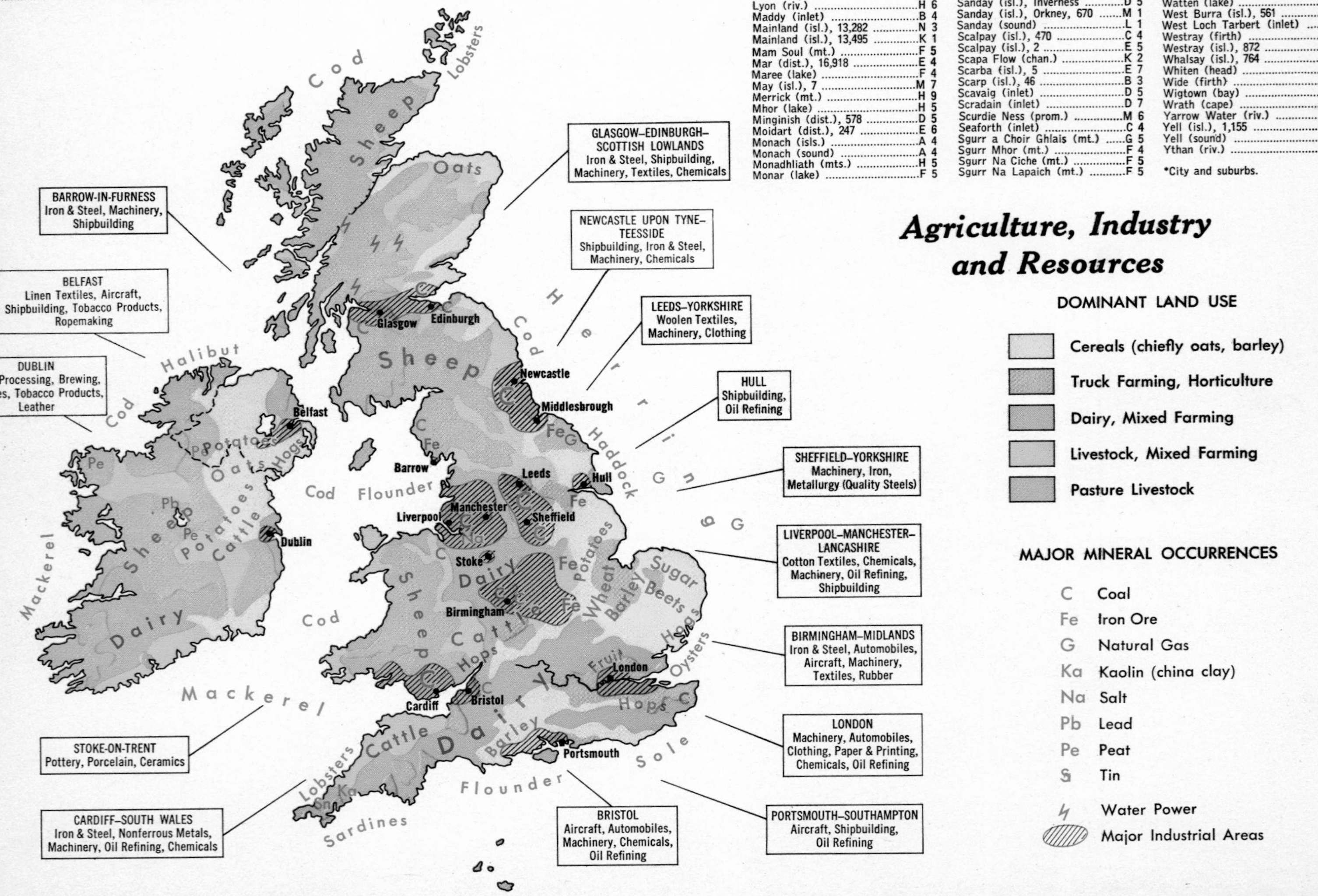

DOMINANT LAND USE
Cereals (chiefly oats, barley)
Truck Farming, Horticulture
Dairy, Mixed Farming
Livestock, Mixed Farming
Pasture Livestock
MAJOR MINERAL OCCURRENCES
C Coal
Fe Iron Ore
G Natural Gas
Ka Kaolin (china clay)
Na Salt
Pb Lead
Pe Peat
Sn Tin
Water Power
Major Industrial Areas
GLASGOW–EDINBURGH–SCOTTISH LOWLANDS
Iron & Steel, Shipbuilding, Machinery, Textiles, Chemicals
BARROW-IN-FURNESS
Iron & Steel, Machinery, Shipbuilding
NEWCASTLE UPON TYNE–TEESSIDE
Shipbuilding, Iron & Steel, Machinery, Chemicals
BELFAST
Linen Textiles, Aircraft, Shipbuilding, Tobacco Products, Ropemaking
LEEDS–YORKSHIRE
Woolen Textiles, Machinery, Clothing
DUBLIN
Food Processing, Brewing, Textiles, Tobacco Products, Leather
HULL
Shipbuilding, Oil Refining
SHEFFIELD–YORKSHIRE
Machinery, Iron, Metallurgy (Quality Steels)
LIVERPOOL–MANCHESTER–LANCASHIRE
Cotton Textiles, Chemicals, Machinery, Oil Refining, Shipbuilding
BIRMINGHAM–MIDLANDS
Iron & Steel, Automobiles, Aircraft, Machinery, Textiles, Rubber
STOKE-ON-TRENT
Pottery, Porcelain, Ceramics
LONDON
Machinery, Automobiles, Clothing, Paper & Printing, Chemicals, Oil Refining
CARDIFF–SOUTH WALES
Iron & Steel, Nonferrous Metals, Machinery, Oil Refining, Chemicals
BRISTOL
Aircraft, Automobiles, Machinery, Chemicals, Oil Refining
PORTSMOUTH–SOUTHAMPTON
Aircraft, Shipbuilding, Oil Refining
Cod
Lobsters
Oats
Sheep
Glasgow
Edinburgh
Herring
Halibut
Newcastle
Middlesbrough
Belfast
Potatoes
Oats
Hogs
Barrow
Leeds
Hull
Haddock
Flounder
Manchester
Liverpool
Sheffield
Dublin
Cattle
Mackerel
Stoke
Dairy
Birmingham
Wheat
Barley
Sugar Beets
Fruit
Hops
London
Oysters
Cardiff
Bristol
Portsmouth
Sole
Sardines

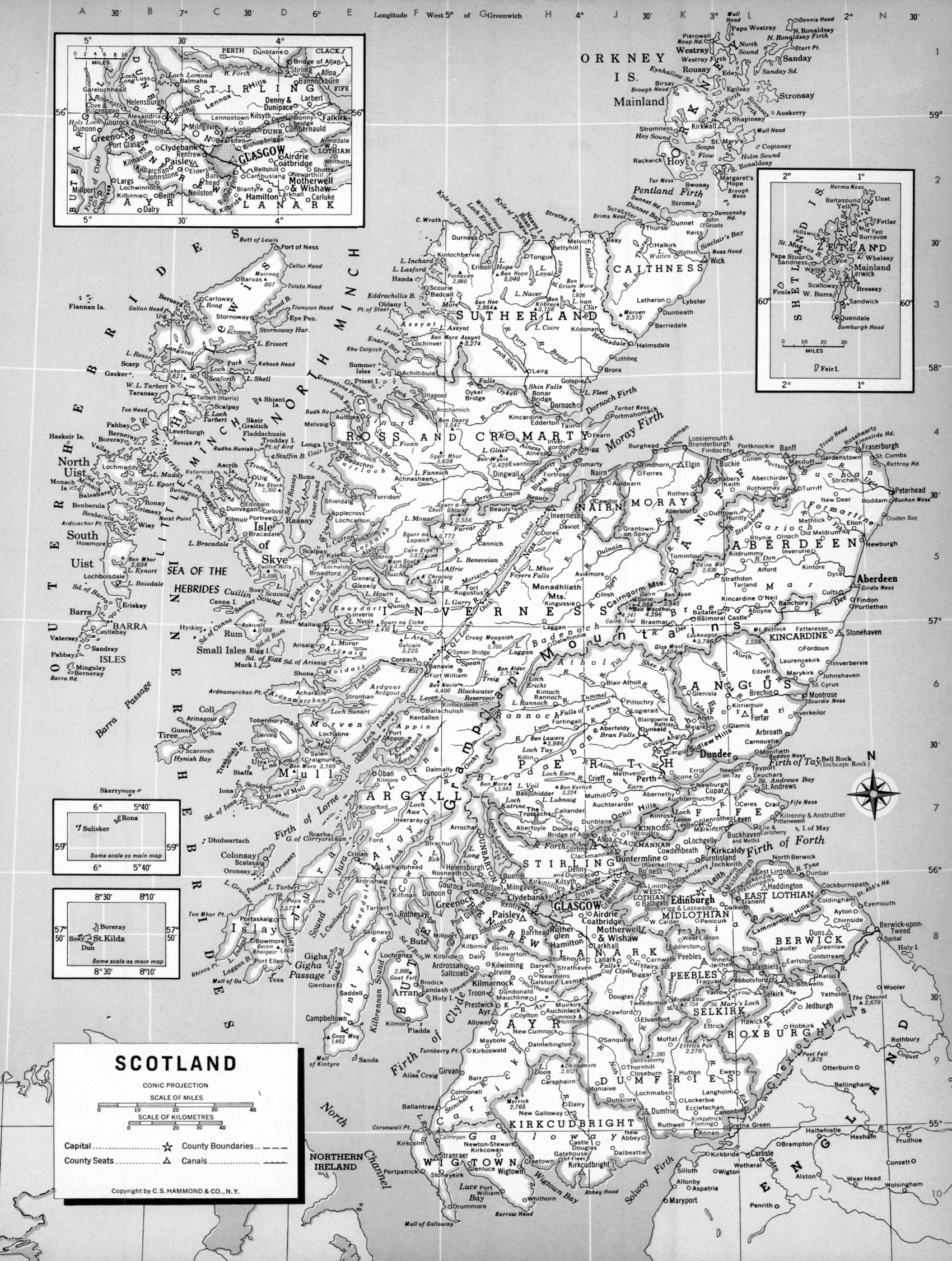

SCOTLAND

CONIC PROJECTION

SCALE OF MILES

SCALE OF KILOMETRES

| Capital | ★ | County Boundaries | - - - - |
| County Seats | △ | Canals | |

Copyright by C.S. HAMMOND & CO., N.Y.

16 United Kingdom and Ireland
(continued)

IRELAND

COUNTIES

Carlow, 33,342 H 6
Cavan, 56,594 G 4
Clare, 73,702 D 6
Cork, 330,443 D 7
Galway, 149,887 D 5
Donegal, 113,842 F 2
Dublin, 718,332 J 5
Kerry, 116,458 B 7
Kildare, 64,402 H 5
Kilkenny, 61,668 G 6
Laoighis, 45,069 G 6
Leitrim, 33,470 E 3
Leix (Laoighis), 45,069 G 6
Limerick, 133,339 D 7
Longford, 30,643 F 4
Louth, 67,378 J 4
Mayo, 123,330 C 4
Meath, 65,122 H 4
Monaghan, 47,088 H 3
Offaly, 51,533 F 5
Roscommon, 59,217 E 4
Sligo, 53,561 D 3
Tipperary, 123,822 F 6
Waterford, 71,439 F 7
Westmeath, 52,861 G 5
Wexford, 83,308 H 7
Wicklow, 58,473 J 5

CITIES and TOWNS

Abbeydorney, 164 B 7
Abbeyfeale, 1,272 C 7
Abbeylara, 113 F 4
Abbeyleix, 1,085 G 6
Achill Sound, 277 B 4
Aclare, 117 D 3
Adare, 590 D 6
Aghadoe, †371 C 7
Aghagower, †558 C 4
Ahascragh, 234 E 5
Annagassan, 194 J 4
Annascaul, 212 B 7
An Uaimh, 3,998 H 4
Ardagh, Limerick, 122 C 7
Ardagh, Longford, 102 F 4
Ardara, 547 E 2
Ardee, 2,710 H 4
Ardfinnan, 428 F 7
Ardmore, 290 F 8
Arklow, 5,390 J 6
Arthurstown, 136 H 7
Arva, 512 F 4
Ashford, 309 J 5
Askeaton, 706 D 6
Athboy, 680 H 4
Athea, 299 C 7
Athenry, 1,266 D 5
Athleague, 132 E 4
Athlone, 9,624 F 5
Athy, 3,842 H 6
Aughrim, 528 J 6
Avoca, 248 J 6
Bagenalstown (Muinebeag), 2,071 H 6
Baile Atha Cliath (Dublin) (cap.), 537,448 K 5
Bailieborough, 1,136 G 4
Balbriggan, 2,943 J 4
Balla, 324 C 4
Ballaghaderreen, 1,308 E 4
Ballina, 6,027 C 3
Ballinagh, 389 G 4
Ballinakill, 315 G 6
Ballinamore, 793 F 3
Ballinasloe, 5,711 E 5
Ballincollig, 960 D 8
Ballindine, 222 C 4
Ballingarry, Limerick, 360 D 7
Ballingarry, Tipperary, 209 F 6
Ballinlough, 252 D 4
Ballinrobe, 1,165 C 4
Ballintober, †938 E 4
Ballintra, 250 E 2
Ballisodare, 529 E 3
Ballybay, 716 G 3
Ballybofey, 1,030 F 2
Ballybunion, 1,163 B 7
Ballycanew, 168 J 6
Ballycastle, 191 C 3
Ballyconnell, 592 F 3
Ballycotton, 412 F 8
Ballydehob, 303 C 8
Ballydesmond, 178 C 7
Ballyduff, 379 B 7
Ballygar, 315 E 4
Ballyhaunis, 1,174 D 4
Ballyheigue, 417 B 7
Ballyjamesduff, 581 G 4
Ballylanders, 280 E 7
Ballylongford, 594 B 6
Ballymahon, 830 F 4
Ballymakeery-Ballyvourney, 321 C 8
Ballymore, 179 F 5
Ballymore Eustace, 348 J 5
Ballymote, 965 D 3
Ballynacargy, 288 G 4
Ballyporeen, 270 E 7
Ballyragget, 478 G 6
Ballyroan, 122 G 6
Ballyshannon, 2,322 E 3
Ballytore, 269 H 5
Ballyvaughn, 152 C 5
Balrothery, 102 J 4
Baltimore, 188 C 9
Baltinglass, 116 H 6
Banagher, 1,050 F 5
Bandon, 2,308 D 8
Bannow, †820 H 7
Bantry, 2,234 C 8
Barna, 143 C 5
Belmullet, 724 B 3
Belturbet, 1,093 G 3
Birr, 3,221 F 5
Blackwater, 216 J 7
Blarney, 995 D 8
Blessington, 491 J 5
Borris, 413 H 6
Borrisokane, 750 E 6
Boyle, 1,739 E 4
Bray (Brí Chualann), 11,688 K 5
Bruff, 545 D 7
Bunclody-Carrickduff, 891 H 6
Buncrana, 2,960 G 1
Bundoran, 1,326 E 3
Bunmahon, 265 G 7
Burtonport, 224 E 2
Buttevant, 981 D 7
Cahir, 1,662 F 7
Cahirciveen, 1,659 A 8
Callan, 1,346 G 7
Cappamore, 501 E 6
Cappawhite, 318 E 6
Cappoquin, 806 F 7
Carbury, †926 H 5
Carlingford, 471 J 3
Carlow, 7,708 H 6
Carndonagh, 1,016 G 1
Carnew, 551 H 6
Carrick, 153 D 2
Carrickmacross, 1,940 H 4
Carrick-on-Shannon, 1,497 F 4
Carrick-on-Suir, 4,672 F 7
Carrigaholt, 160 B 6
Carrigallen, 202 F 4
Carrigart, 196 F 1
Carrowkeel, 118 G 1
Cashel, 2,679 F 7
Castlebar, 5,482 C 4
Castlebellingham, 656 J 4
Castleblayney, 2,127 H 3
Castlebridge, 181 J 7
Castlecomer-Donaguile, 1,129 G 6
Castledermot, 551 H 6
Castlefin, 565 F 2
Castlegregory, 235 A 7
Castleisland, 1,718 B 7
Castlemaine, 171 B 7
Castlepollard, 778 G 4
Castlerea, 1,568 D 4
Castletown, 264 F 6
Castletownbere, 721 B 8
Castletownroche, 381 D 7
Castletownshend, 177 C 9
Cavan, 3,208 G 3
Ceanannus Mór, 2,193 G 4
Celbridge, 1,305 H 5
Charlestown-Bellahy, 727 D 4
Charleville (Rathluirc), 1,956 D 7
Clara, 2,477 F 5
Claregalway, 627 D 5
Claremorris, 1,519 C 4
Clashmore, 175 F 8
Clifden, 1,025 B 5
Cloghan, 399 G 6
Clogh-Chatsworth, 303 F 5
Clogheen, 576 F 7
Clogherhead, 585 J 4
Clonakilty, 2,417 D 8
Clonaslee, 275 F 5
Clondalkin, 3,434 J 5
Clones, 2,107 G 3
Clonmacnoise, †411 F 5
Clonmany, 238 G 1
Clonmel, 10,640 F 7
Clonroche, 193 H 7
Cloon, 106 F 4
Cloughjordan, 479 E 6
Cloyne, 612 E 8
Coachford, 275 D 8
Cóbh, 5,266 E 8
Coill Dubh, 645 H 5
Collooney, 553 E 3
Cong, 178 C 4
Convoy, 616 F 2
Coolaney, 124 D 3
Coole, 344 G 4
Coolgreany, 124 J 6
Cootehill, 1,296 G 3
Cork, 77,980 E 8
Corofin, 362 C 6
Courtmacsherry, 205 D 8
Courtown Harbour-Riverchapel, 396 J 6
Crookhaven, 62 B 9
Croom, 720 D 6
Crosshaven, 858 E 8
Crossmolina, 777 C 3
Culdaff, 108 G 1
Cullen, 113 C 7
Daingean, 679 G 5
Delvin, 165 G 4
Dingle, 1,460 A 7
Doaghbeg, †795 F 1
Donabate, 318 J 5
Donegal, 1,458 F 2
Doneraile, 725 D 7
Dooagh, 387 A 4
Douglas, †3,113 D 8
Drishane, †1,511 C 7
Drogheda, 17,085 J 4
Droichead Nua, 3,668 H 5
Dromahair, 229 E 3
Dromore West, 99 D 3
Drumcar, †1,205 J 4
Drumcliffe, 772 E 3
Drumconrath, 195 H 4
Drumkeerin, 136 E 3
Drumlish, 343 F 4
Drumshanbo, 565 E 3
Dublin (cap.), 537,448 K 5
Dublin, *595,288 K 5
Duleek, 379 J 4
Dunboyne, 521 H 5
Duncannon, 226 H 7
Dundalk, 19,790 H 3
Dunfanaghy, 324 F 1
Dungarvan, 5,188 F 7
Dungloe, 793 E 2
Dunkineely, 261 E 2
Dún Laoghaire, 47,792 K 5
Dunlavin, 416 H 5
Dunleer, 529 J 4
Dunmanway, 1,411 C 8
Dunmore, 500 D 4
Dunmore East, 547 G 7
Dunshaughlin, 231 H 5
Durrow, Laoighis, 439 G 6
Durrow, Westmeath, 435 F 5
Easky, 317 D 3
Edenderry, 2,691 G 5
Elphin, 494 E 4
Emyvale, 255 G 3
Ennis, 5,699 D 6
Enniscorthy, 5,754 J 7
Enniskerry, 652 J 5
Ennistymon, 1,145 C 6
Eyrecourt, 355 E 5
Fahan, 322 G 1
Feakle, 129 D 6
Fenit, 308 B 7
Ferbane, 896 F 5
Fermoy, 3,241 E 7
Ferns, 557 J 6
Fethard, Tipperary, 962 F 7
Fethard, Wexford, 218 H 7
Fiddown, 152 G 7
Foxford, 876 C 4
Foynes, 686 C 6
Frankford (Kilcormac), 1,018 F 5
Frenchpark, 155 E 4
Freshford, 656 G 6
Galbally, 266 E 7
Galway, 22,028 C 5
Geashill, 170 G 5
Glandore, 151 C 8
Glencolumbkille, 95 D 2
Glenculleen, 161 J 5
Glengarriff, 392 C 8
Glenties, 828 E 2
Glenville, 146 E 7
Glin, 763 C 6
Golden, 153 F 7
Gorey, 2,671 J 6
Gort, 1,044 D 5
Gowran, 365 G 6
Granard, 1,040 F 4
Greencastle, 233 H 1
Greenore, 142 J 4
Greystones-Delgany, 3,551 K 5
Hacketstown, 509 H 6
Holycross, 921 F 6
Hospital, 572 E 7
Inchigeela, 157 C 8
Inniscrone, 533 C 3
Johnstown, 326 G 6
Kanturk, 1,985 D 7
Keel, 459 A 4
Kells, 128 G 7
Kells (Ceanannus Mór), 2,193 G 4
Kenmare, 1,046 B 8
Kilbeggan, 799 G 5
Kilbehenny, 86 E 7
Kilcar, 229 D 2
Kilcock, 739 H 5
Kilconnell, 113 E 5
Kilcoole, 549 K 5
Kilcormac, 1,018 F 5
Kilcullen, 637 H 5
Kildare, 2,551 H 5
Kildysart, 295 C 6
Kilfenora, 135 C 6
Kilfinane, 565 D 7
Kilgarvan, 183 B 8
Kilkee, 1,392 B 6
Kilkelly, 257 D 4
Kilkenny, 10,159 G 6
Killala, 337 C 3
Killaloe, 835 D 6
Killarney, 6,825 C 7
Killavullen, 167 D 7
Killenaule, 531 F 6
Killeshandra, 397 F 3
Killimor, 195 E 5
Killorglin, 1,100 B 7
Killucan-Rathwire, 314 G 4
Killybegs, 1,065 E 2
Kilmacrennan, 251 F 1
Kilmacthomas, 446 G 7
Kilmallock, 1,159 D 7
Kilmeaden, 77 G 7
Kilmihill, 264 C 6
Kilnaleck, 279 G 4
Kilronan, 231 B 5
Kilrush, 2,861 C 6
Kilsheelan, 172 F 7
Kiltimagh, 980 C 4
Kilworth, 334 E 7
Kingscourt, 793 H 4
Kingstown (Dún Laoghaire), 47,792 K 5
Kinlough, 203 E 3
Kinnegad, 251 G 5
Kinnitty, 275 F 5
Kinsale, 1,587 D 8
Kinvara, 338 D 5
Knightstown, 337 A 8
Knock, 218 D 4
Knocklong, 289 D 7
Knocktopher, 127 G 7
Labasheeda, 142 C 6
Laghey, 184 E 2
Lahinch, 389 C 6
Lanesborough-Ballyleague, 720 E 4
Laracor, 386 H 4
Laytown-Bettystown, 766 J 4
Leenane, 123 B 4
Leighlinbridge, 457 H 6
Leitrim, 111 F 3
Leixlip, 915 H 5
Letterkenny, 4,329 F 2
Lifford, 864 F 2
Limerick, 50,786 D 6
Liscarroll, 228 D 7
Lisdoonvarna, 625 C 5
Lismore, 810 F 7
Listowel, 7,859 C 7
Littleton, 274 F 6
Longford, 3,558 F 4
Lorrha, 84 E 5
Loughrea, 2,784 E 5
Louisburgh, 346 B 4
Louth, 207 J 4
Lucan-Doddsborough, 1,657 J 5
Luimneach (Limerick), 50,786 D 6
Lusk, 495 J 4
Macroom, 2,169 C 8
Malahide, 2,534 J 5
Malin, 164 G 1
Mallow, 5,545 D 7
Manorhamilton, 920 E 3
Manulla, †774 C 4
Maryborough (Portlaoighise), 3,133 G 5
Maynooth, 1,753 H 5
Meathas Truim, 624 G 4
Midleton, 2,772 E 8
Milford, 611 F 1
Millstreet, 1,283 D 7
Miltown Malbay, 700 C 6
Mitchelstown, 2,655 E 7
Moate, 1,261 F 5
Mohill, 905 F 4
Monaghan, 4,013 G 3
Monasterevan, 1,273 H 5
Moneygall, 284 F 6
Monivea, 222 D 5
Mooncoin, 507 G 7
Mount Bellew, 306 D 5
Mountcharles, 400 E 2
Mountmellick, 2,436 G 5
Mountrath, 1,051 F 5
Moville, 1,097 G 1
Moycullen, 127 C 5
Moynalty, 128 H 4
Muff, 219 G 1
Muinebeag, 2,071 H 6
Mullagh, 213 H 4
Mullaghmore, 137 D 3
Mullinahone, 322 F 7
Mullinavat, 339 G 7
Mullingar, 5,834 G 4
Naas, 4,023 H 5
Navan (An Uaimh), 3,998 H 4
Nenagh, 4,317 E 6
Newbliss, 192 G 3
Newbridge (Droichead Nua), 3,668 H 5
Newcastle, 2,527 D 7
New Inn, 164 F 7
Newmarket, 791 C 7
Newmarket-on-Fergus, 807 D 6
New Pallas, 171 E 6
Newport, Mayo, 459 C 4
Newport, Tipperary, 581 E 6
New Ross, 4,494 H 7
Newtownforbes, 318 F 4
Newtownmountkennedy-Killadreenan, 935 J 5
Newtownsandes, 304 C 6
O'Briensbridge-Montpelier, 232 D 6
Oola, 314 E 6
Oranmore, 346 D 5
Oughterard, 618 C 5
Passage East, 494 G 7
Passage West, 2,561 E 8
Patrickswell, 305 D 6
Pettigo, 313 F 2
Portarlington, 2,846 G 5
Portlaoighise, 3,133 G 5
Portlaw, 1,113 G 7
Portmarnock, 669 J 5
Portumna, 836 E 5
Queenstown (Cóbh), 5,266 E 8
Quilty, 190 C 6
Rahan, †635 F 5
Ramelton, 759 F 1
Raphoe, 818 F 2
Rathangan, 569 G 5
Rathcormac, 267 E 7
Rathdowney, 896 F 6
Rathdrum, 1,128 J 6
Rathkeale, 1,459 D 7
Rathluirc, 1,956 D 7
Rathmore, 417 C 7
Rathmullen, 491 F 1
Rathnew-Merrymeeting, 861 J 6
Rathowen, 119 F 4
Rathvilly, 293 H 6
Ratoath, 289 J 5
Riverstown, 203 E 3
Rockcorry, 190 H 3
Rosapenna, †905 F 1
Roscommon, 1,600 E 4
Roscrea, 3,372 F 6
Rosscarbery, 380 C 8
Rosslare, 529 J 7
Roundstone, 250 A 5
Rush, 2,118 J 4
Saggart, 426 F 2
Saint Johnstown, 458 F 2
Sallybrook-Riverstown, 563 E 8
Scariff-Tuamgraney, 600 E 6
Schull, 419 B 8
Scotstown, 199 H 3
Shannon Airport, 234 D 6
Shercock, 254 G 4
Shillelagh, 202 J 6
Shinrone, 402 F 5
Shrule, 250 C 4
Silvermines, 222 E 6
Sixmilebridge, 448 D 6
Skerries, 2,721 J 4
Skibbereen, 2,028 C 8
Slane, 421 H 4
Sligo, 13,145 E 3
Smithborough, 94 G 3
Sneem, 282 B 8
Spiddal, 134 C 5
Stradbally, Laoighis, 792 G 5
Stradbally, Waterford, 213 F 7
Stranorlar, 848 F 2
Strokestown, 707 E 4
Swanlinbar, 306 F 3
Swinford, 1,115 C 4
Swords, 1,816 J 5
Taghmon, 347 H 7
Tallow, 819 F 7
Tarbert, 455 C 6
Teltown, †684 H 4
Templemore, 1,779 F 6
Templetouhy, 156 F 6
Termonfeckin, 300 J 4
Thomastown, 1,209 G 7
Thurles, 6,421 F 6
Timoleague, 291 D 8
Tinahely, 417 H 6
Tipperary, 4,684 E 7
Toomevara, 231 E 6
Tralee, 10,723 B 7
Tramore, 2,882 G 7
Trim, 1,371 H 4
Tuam, 3,500 D 4
Tubbercurry, 878 D 3
Tulla, 389 D 6
Tullamore, 6,243 G 5
Tullaroan, 118 G 6
Tullow, 1,725 H 6
Tyrellspass, 259 G 5
Urlingford, 562 F 6
Virginia, 515 G 4
Waterford, 28,216 G 7
Waterville-Spunkane, 702 A 8
Westport, 2,882 C 4
Wexford, 11,328 H 7
Whitegate, 397 E 8
Wicklow, 3,125 K 6
Woodford, 264 E 5
Youghal, 5,043 F 8

OTHER FEATURES

Achill (isl.), 4,220 A 4
Aherlow (riv.) E 7
Allen (lake) E 3
Allen, Bog of (marsh) H 5
Allow (riv.) D 7
Annalee (riv.) G 3
Anner (riv.) F 7
Aran (isl.), 948 D 2
Aran (isls.), 1,651 B 5
Arrow (lake) E 3
Awbeg (riv.) D 7
Ballinskelligs (bay) A 8
Ballyhoura (hills) E 7
Ballynakill (harb.) A 4
Ballysadare (bay) D 3
Ballyteige (bay) H 7
Bandon (riv.) D 8
Bann (riv.) J 6
Bantry (bay) B 8
Barrow (riv.) H 7
Baurtregaum (mt.) A 7
Bear (isl.), 382 B 8
Beltra (lake) C 4
Ben Dash (hill) C 6
Benwee (head) B 3
Bertraghboy (bay) A 5
Black (head) C 5
Blacksod (bay) A 3
Blackstairs (mt.) H 6
Blackwater (riv.) D 7
Blackwater (riv.) H 4
Blasket (isls.) A 7
Bloody Foreland (prom.) E 1
Blue Stack (mts.) E 2
Boderg (lake) E 4
Boggeragh (mts.) D 7
Bolus (head) A 8
Bonet (riv.) E 3
Boyne (riv.) J 4
Brandon (bay) A 7
Brandon (mt.) A 7
Brannock (isls.) A 5
Bray (head) A 8
Bride (riv.) E 7
Broad Haven (harb.) B 3
Brosna (riv.) F 5
Bull, The (isl.) A 8
Caha (mts.) B 8
Cahore (pt.) J 6
Cark (mt.) F 2
Carlingford (inlet) J 3
Carnsore (pt.) J 7
Carra (lake) C 4
Carrantuohill (mt.) B 7
Carrigan (head) D 2
Carrowmore (lake) B 3
Clare (riv.) D 5
Clare with Inishturk (isls.), 313 A 4
Clear (cape) B 9
Clear (isl.) C 9
Clew (bay) B 4
Comeragh (mts.) F 7
Conn (lake) C 3
Connacht (prov.), 419,465 C 4
Connemara (dist.), 23,841 B 5
Corrib (lake) C 5
Courtmacsherry (bay) D 8
Croagh Patrick (mt.) C 4
Crossfarnoge (pt.) J 7
Cuilcagh (mt.) F 3
Cullin (lake) C 4
Curragh, The H 5
Cutra (lake) D 5
Dee (riv.) H 4
Deel (riv.) C 3
Deel (riv.) D 7
Deel (riv.) F 2
Derg (lake) E 6
Derg (lake) F 2
Derravaragh (lake) G 4
Derryveagh (mts.) E 2
Devilsbit (mt.) F 6
Dingle (bay) A 7
Donegal (bay) D 3
Donegal (pt.) B 6
Doulus (head) A 8
Downpatrick (head) C 3
Drum (hills) F 7
Dublin (bay) J 5
Dunaff (head) F 1
Dunany (pt.) J 4
Dundalk (bay) J 4
Dunkellin (riv.) D 5
Dunmanus (bay) B 8
Dursey (isl.) A 8
Eask (lake) E 2
Ennell (lake) G 5
Erkina (riv.) G 6
Erne (riv.) E 3
Erris (head) A 3
Errigal (mt.) E 1
Fanad (head) F 1
Fastnet Rock (isl.) B 9
Feale (riv.) C 7
Feeagh (lake) B 4
Fergus (riv.) D 6
Finn (riv.) F 2
Finn (riv.) G 3
Flesk (riv.) C 7
Foul (sound) B 5
Foyle (inlet) G 1
Foyle (riv.) G 2
Galley (head) D 9
Galtee (mts.) E 7
Galtymore (mt.) E 7
Galway (bay) C 5
Gara (lake) D 4
Garadice (lake) F 3
Gartan (lake) F 2
Garvan (isls.) G 1
Gill (lake) E 3
Glen (lake) F 1
Glyde (riv.) H 4
Gola (isl.) E 1
Golden Vale (plain) E 7
Gorumna (isl.), †1,730 B 5
Gowna (lake) G 4
Grand (canal) G 5
Great Blasket (isl.) A 7
Greenore (pt.) J 7
Gregory's (sound) B 5
Gweebarra (bay) D 2
Gweebarra (riv.) E 2
Hags (head) B 6
Helvick (head) G 7
High (isl.) A 4
Hook (head) H 7
Horn (head) E 1
Iar Connaught (dist.), 4,051 C 5
Inishbofin (isl.), 248 A 4
Inishbofin (isl.) E 1
Inisheer (isl.), 358 B 5
Inishmaan (isl.), 357 C 5
Inishmore (isl.), 936 B 5
Inishmurray (isl.) D 3
Inishowen (head) H 1
Inishowen (pen.) G 1
Inishshark (isl.) A 4
Inishtrahull (isl.) G 1
Inishturk with Clare (isls.), 313 A 4
Inny (riv.) A 8
Inny (riv.) F 4
Inver (bay) E 2
Ireland's Eye (isl.) K 5
Irish (sea) K 4
Joyce's Country (dist.), 2,425 B 4
Keeper (hill) E 6
Kenmare (riv.) A 8
Kerry (head) A 7
Key (lake) E 3
Kilkieran (bay) B 5
Killary (harb.) A 4
Kinsale, Old Head of (head) E 8
Kippure (mt.) J 5
Knockadoon (head) F 8
Knockanefune (mt.) C 7
Knockboy (mt.) B 8
Knockmealdown (mts.) F 7
Lady's Island Lake (inlet) J 7
Lambay (isl.) K 5
Lamb's (head) A 8
Laune (riv.) B 7
Leane (lake) B 7
Leane (lake) G 4
Lee (riv.) D 8
Leinster (mt.) H 6
Leinster (prov.), 1,332,149 G 5
Lettermullen (isl.) B 5
Liffey (riv.) H 5
Liscannor (bay) B 6
Little Brosna (riv.) E 5
Long Island (bay) B 9
Loop (head) A 6
Loughros More (bay) D 2
Lugnaquillia (mt.) J 5
Lung (riv.) D 4
Macgillicuddy's Reeks (mts.) B 7
Macnean (lake) F 3
Maigue (riv.) D 6
Maine (riv.) C 7
Malin (head) F 1
Mangerton (mt.) C 8
Mask (lake) C 4
Maumakeogh (mt.) C 3
Maumturk (mts.) B 5
Melvin (lake) E 3
Mine (head) F 8
Mizen (head) B 9
Mizen (head) K 6
Moher (cliffs) B 6
Monavullagh (mts.) F 7
Moy (riv.) C 3
Muckish (mt.) E 1
Muckno (lake) H 3
Mulkear (riv.) E 6
Mullaghareirk (mts.) C 7
Mulroy (bay) F 1
Munster (prov.), 849,203 D 7
Mutton (isl.) B 6
Mweelrea (mt.) B 4
Mweenish (isl.) B 5
Nagles (mts.) E 7
Nephin (mt.) C 3
Nephin Beg (mt.) B 3
Nore (riv.) G 7
North (sound) B 5
North Inishkea (isl.) A 3
Omey (isl.) A 5
Oughter (lake) G 3
Ovoca (riv.) J 6
Owell (lake) G 4
Owenmore (riv.) B 3
Owenmore (riv.) D 3
Owey (isl.) D 1
Ox (Slieve Gamph) (mts.) D 3
Paps, The (mt.) C 7
Partry (mts.) C 4
Pollaphuca (res.) J 5
Puffin (isl.) A 8
Punchestown H 5
Ramor (lake) G 4
Rathlin O'Birne (isl.) C 2
Ree (lake) F 5
Rinn (lake) F 4
Roaringwater (bay) B 9
Rosses (bay) D 1
Rosskeeragh (pt.) D 3
Rosslare (bay) J 7
Royal (canal) G 4
Saint Finan's (bay) A 8
Saint George's (chan.) K 7
Saint John's (pt.) D 2
Saltee (isls.) H 7
Scarriff (isl.) A 8
Seven (heads) D 8
Seven Hogs, The (isls.) A 7
Shannon (riv.) E 6
Shannon, Mouth of the (est.) B 6
Sheeffry (hills) B 4
Sheep Haven (harb.) F 1
Sheeps (head) B 8
Shehy (mts.) C 8
Sherkin (isl.) C 9
Silvermine (mts.) E 6
Slaney (riv.) H 7
Slieve Anierin (mt.) F 3
Slieve Aughty (mts.) D 5
Slieve Bernagh (mt.) D 6
Slieve Bloom (mts.) F 5
Slieve Callan (mt.) C 6
Slievecar (mt.) B 3
Slieve Elva (mt.) C 5
Slievefelim (mts.) E 6
Slieve Gamph (mts.) D 3
Slieve League (mt.) D 2
Slieve Mishkish (mts.) B 8
Slievenaman (mt.) F 7
Slyne (head) A 5
Smerwick (harb.) A 7
South (sound) C 5
Stacks (mts.) B 7
Suck (riv.) E 5
Sugarloaf (mt.) B 8
Suir (riv.) G 7
Swilly (inlet) F 1
Tara (hill) H 4
Tawin (isl.) C 5
Toe (head) C 9
Tory (isl.) E 1
Tralee (bay) B 7
Tramore (bay) G 7
Trawbreaga (bay) F 1
Truskmore (mt.) E 3
Twelve Pins (mt.) B 4
Ulster (prov.), 217,524 G 2
Valentia (Valencia) (isl.), 926 A 8
Veagh (lake) F 1
Wexford (bay) J 7
Wicklow (mts.) J 6
Wicklow (head) K 6
Youghal (bay) F 8

NORTHERN IRELAND

COUNTIES

Antrim, 333,800 J 2
Armagh, 128,200 H 3
Belfast (city), 385,900 K 2
Down, 300,800 J 3
Fermanagh, 49,900 F 3
Londonderry, 177,300 H 2
Tyrone, 136,600 G 2

CITIES and TOWNS

Aghadowey, †679 H 1
Ahoghill, 885 J 2
Annalong, 553 K 3
Antrim, 33,980 J 2
Ardglass, 737 K 3
Armagh, 11,920 H 3
Armoy, 383 J 1
Augher, 222 G 3
Aughnacloy, 805 H 3
Ballycastle, 2,960 J 1
Ballyclare, 4,690 J 2
Ballygally, 276 K 2
Ballygawley, 427 G 3
Ballykelly, 367 G 1
Ballymena, 16,730 J 2
Ballymoney, 3,700 J 1
Ballynahinch, 2,042 J 3
Ballynure, 291 K 2
Ballywalter, 789 K 2
Banbridge, 6,620 J 3
Bangor, 30,030 K 2
Belfast (cap.), 385,900 J 2
Belfast, *528,700 J 2
Bellaghy, 663 H 2
Belleek, 162 E 3
Beragh, 349 G 2
Bessbrook, 3,199 J 3
Brookeborough, 294 G 3
Broughshane, 716 J 2
Bushmills, 936 J 1
Caledon, 350 H 3
Carnlough, 586 J 2
Carrickfergus, 13,130 K 2
Carrowdore, 297 K 2
Castledawson, 906 H 2
Castlederg, 1,367 F 2
Castlewellan, 1,241 K 3
Claudy, 286 G 2
Clogher, 197 G 3
Coalisland, 1,351 H 2
Coleraine, 14,090 H 1
Comber, 3,987 K 2
Cookstown, 6,190 H 2
Craigavon, 11,140 J 3
Crossgar, 842 K 3
Crossmaglen, 932 H 3
Crumlin, 394 J 2
Cullybackey, 758 J 2
Cushendall, 618 J 1
Derrygonnelly, 296 F 3
Dervock, 558 J 1
Doagh, 486 J 2
Donaghdee, 3,730 K 2
Downpatrick, 5,290 K 3
Draperstown, 592 H 2
Dromara, 280 J 3
Dromore, Down, 1,980 J 3
Dromore, Tyrone, 503 G 3
Drumquin, 307 F 2
Dunbarton, 905 J 3
Dundrum, 641 K 3
Dungannon, 7.590 H 3
Dungiven, 1,102 H 2
Dunnamanagh, 352 G 2
Ederny, 227 F 2
Enniskillen, 7,020 F 3
Feeny, 206 H 2
Fintona, 990 G 3
Fivemiletown, 77 G 3
Garvagh, 550 H 2
Gilford, 780 J 3
Glenarm, 673 J 2
Glenavy, 1,306 J 2
Glynn, 389 K 2
Gortin, 261 G 2
Greyabbey, 611 K 2
Hillsborough, 806 J 3
Hilltown, 309 J 3
Holywood, 7,930 K 2
Irvinestown, 934 F 3
Jonesborough, 274 J 3
Keady, 1,960 H 3
Kells, 495 J 2
Kesh, †689 F 3
Kilkeel, 2,570 K 3
Killeter, †442 F 2
Killough, 504 K 3
Killyleagh, 1,876 K 3
Kilrea, 952 H 2
Kircubbin, 843 K 3
Lack, †571 F 2
Larne, 17,840 K 2
Limavady, 5,230 H 1
Lisburn, 24,870 J 2
Lisnaskea, 977 G 3
Londonderry, 55,000 G 2
Loughbrickland, 300 J 3
Loughgall, †1,086 H 3
Maghera, 1,607 H 2
Magherafelt, 2,459 H 2
Maguire's Bridge, 339 G 3
Markethill, 813 H 3
Middletown, 161 H 3
Millisle, 386 K 2
Moira, 501 J 3
Moneymore, 807 H 2
Moy, 751 H 3
Moygashel, 1,146 H 3
Newcastle, 4,450 J 3
Newry, 11,960 J 3
Newtownabbey, 53,450 K 2
Newtownards, 14,180 K 2
Newtownbutler, 358 G 3
Newtownhamilton, 589 H 3
Newtownstewart, 1,125 G 2
Omagh, 10,710 G 2
Pettigoe, 76 F 2
Pomeroy, 349 H 2
Portaferry, 1,406 K 3
Portavogie, 1,071 K 3
Portglenone, 613 H 2
Portrush, 4,420 H 1
Portstewart, 4,660 H 1
Randalstown, 1,579 J 2
Rasharkin, 799 J 2
Rathfriland, 1,558 J 3
Rostrevor, 1,265 J 3
Saintfield, 702 K 3
Sion Mills, 1,616 G 2
Sixmilecross, 245 H 2
Stewartstown, 621 H 2
Strabane, 9,040 G 2
Strangford, 413 K 3
Tandragee, 1,570 H 3
Templepatrick, †775 J 2
Tempo, 269 G 3
Trillick, 220 G 3
Tynan, †805 H 3
Warrenpoint, 3,750 J 3
Whitehead, 2,760 K 2

OTHER FEATURES

Arney (riv.) F 3
Bann (riv.) H 2
Beg (lake) J 2
Belfast (inlet) K 2
Binevenagh (mt.) H 1
Blackwater (riv.) H 3
Bush (riv.) H 1
Copeland (isl.) K 2
Derg (riv.) F 2
Erne (lake) F 3
Fair (head) J 1
Foyle (inlet) G 1
Foyle (riv.) G 2
Garron (pt.) K 1
Giant's Causeway H 1
Knocklayd (mt.) J 1
Lagan (riv.) K 2
Larne (inlet) K 2
Macnean (lake) F 3
Magee, Island (pen.) K 2
Magilligan (pt.) H 1
Maidens, The (isls.) K 2
Main (riv.) J 2
Mourne (mts.) J 3
Mourne (riv.) G 2
Neagh (lake) J 2
North (chan.) K 1
Owenkillew (riv.) G 2
Rathlin (isl.), 159 J 1
Red (bay) K 1
Roe (riv.) H 1
Saint John's (pt.) K 3
Slemish (mt.) J 2
Slieve Beagh (mt.) G 3
Slieve Donard (mt.) K 3
Slieve Gullion (mt.) J 3
Sperrin (mts). G 2
Strangford (inlet) K 3
Torr (head) K 1
Trostan (mt.) J 1
Ulster (prov.), 1,512,500 G 2
Upper Lough Erne (lake) F 3

*City and suburbs.
†Population of district.

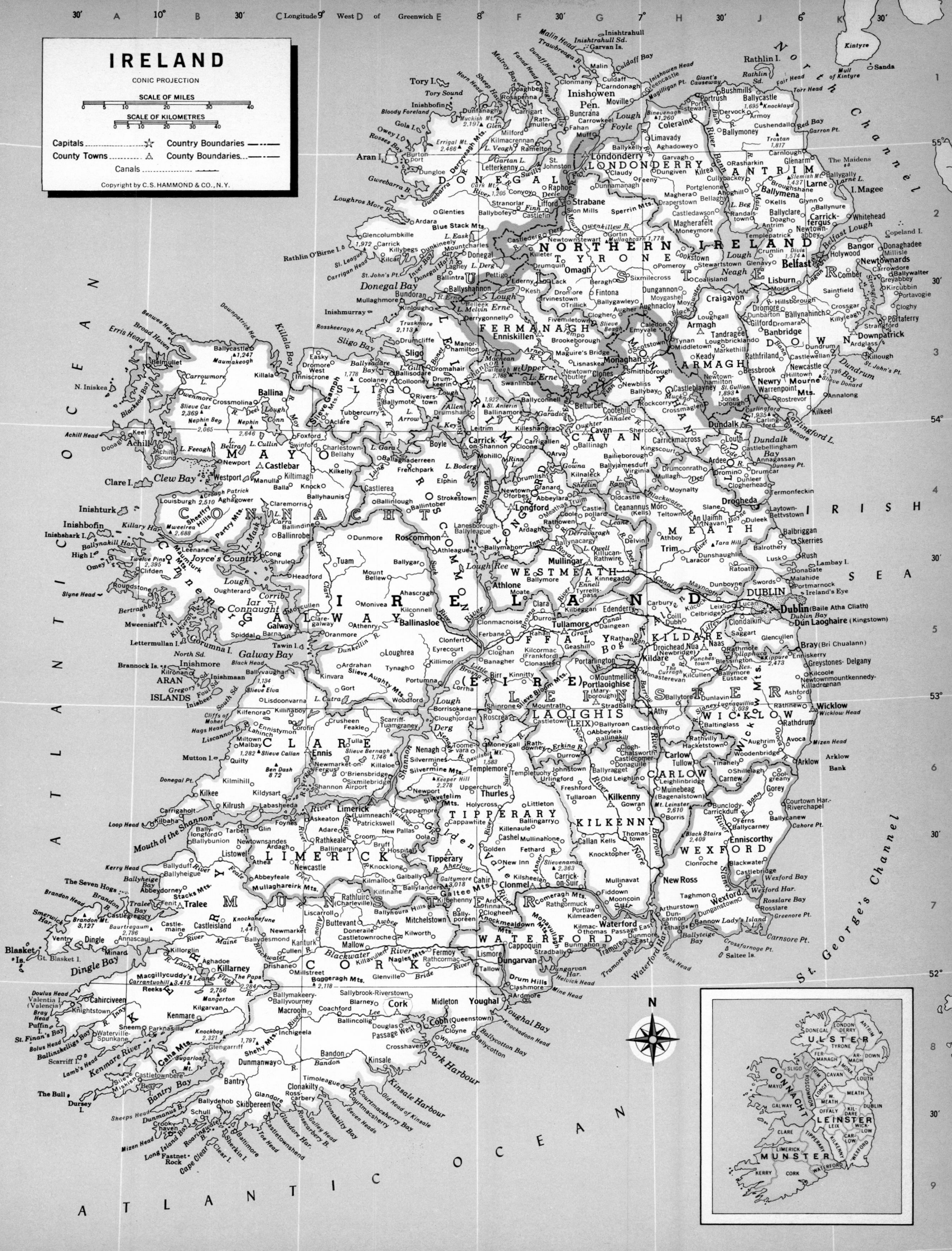

IRELAND

CONIC PROJECTION

SCALE OF MILES

SCALE OF KILOMETRES

Capitals .... ☆   Country Boundaries ___
County Towns .... △   County Boundaries ___
Canals ....

Copyright by C.S. HAMMOND & CO., N.Y.

NORWAY, SWEDEN, FINLAND and DENMARK

CONIC PROJECTION

SCALE OF MILES

SCALE OF KILOMETRES

Capitals of Countries .... ★
Administrative Centers .... △
International Boundaries .... ▬ ▬ ▬
Internal Boundaries .... ▬ · ▬ · ▬
Canals ....

© C. S. HAMMOND & Co., N.Y.

SUBDIVISIONS
indicated by Numbers
Fylker in NORWAY
1 Akershus   G6
2 Vestfold   G7
3 Østfold   G7
4 Oslo   G7
5 Bergen   D6
Oslo is the administrative
center for Akershus and
Oslo Fylker; Bergen for
Hordaland and Bergen
Fylker.
Län in SWEDEN
6 Göteborg och
Bohus   G7
7 Västmanland   K7
8 Södermanland   K7
9 Östergötland   J7
10 Malmöhus   H9
11 Kristianstad   J8

SVALBARD

Longitude East of Greenwich

NORWAY

AREA 125,181 sq. mi.
POPULATION 3,893,000
CAPITAL Oslo
LARGEST CITY Oslo
HIGHEST POINT Glittertind 8,110 ft.
MONETARY UNIT krone (crown)
MAJOR LANGUAGE Norwegian
MAJOR RELIGION Protestantism

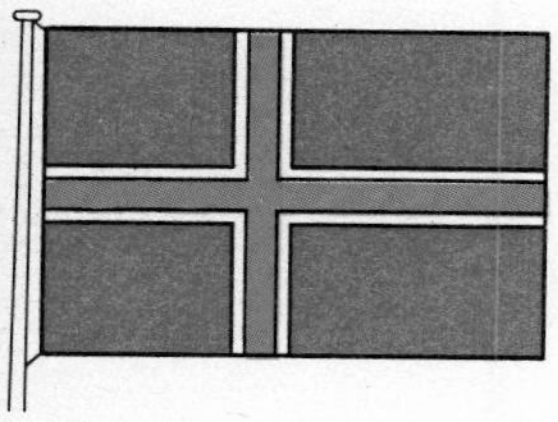

SWEDEN

AREA 173,665 sq. mi.
POPULATION 7,978,000
CAPITAL Stockholm
LARGEST CITY Stockholm
HIGHEST POINT Kebnekaise 6,946 ft.
MONETARY UNIT krona (crown)
MAJOR LANGUAGE Swedish
MAJOR RELIGION Protestantism

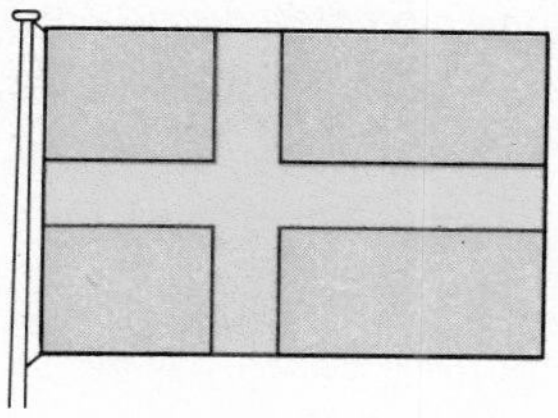

FINLAND

AREA 130,128 sq. mi.
POPULATION 4,706,000
CAPITAL Helsinki
LARGEST CITY Helsinki
HIGHEST POINT Mt. Haltia 4,343 ft.
MONETARY UNIT Markka (Mark)
MAJOR LANGUAGES Finnish, Swedish
MAJOR RELIGION Protestantism

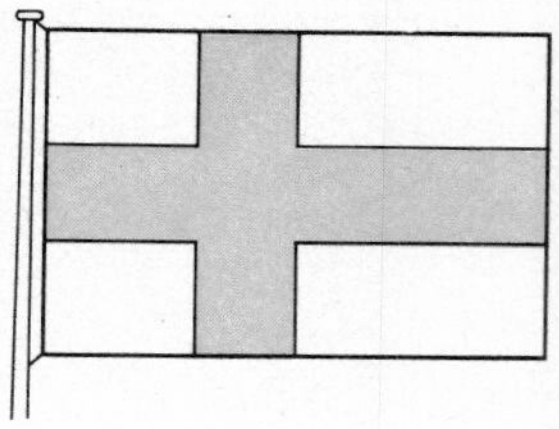

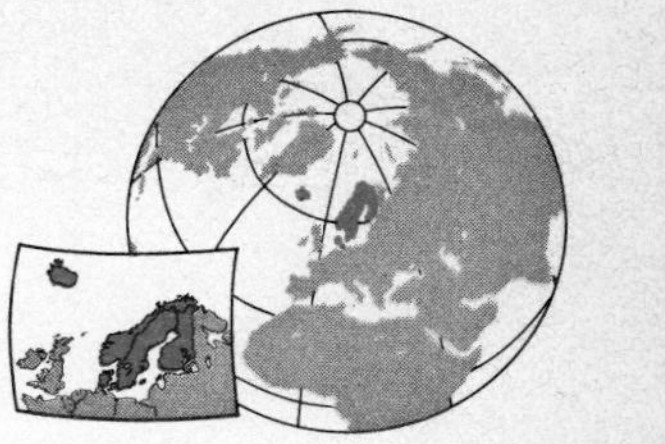

FINLAND

PROVINCES

Ahvenanmaa, 21,584 .... L 6
Häme, 623,756 .... O 6
Keski-Suomi, 248,599 .... O 5
Kuopio, 265,434 .... P 5
Kymi, 348,989 .... Q 6
Lappi, 220,755 .... P 3
Mikkeli, 225,685 .... P 6
Oulu, 422,828 .... P 4
Pohjois-Karjala, 193,199 .... Q 5
Turku-Pori, 680,713 .... N 6
Uusimaa, 999,053 .... O 6
Vaasa, 447,785 .... N 5

CITIES and TOWNS

Äänekoski, 10,977 .... O 5
Åbo (Turku), 155,000 .... N 6
Alavus (Alavo), †11,139 .... N 5
Björneborg (Pori), 71,972 .... M 6
Borgå (Porvoo), 15,738 .... O 6
Brahestad (Raahe), 7,637 .... O 4
Ekenäs (Tammisaari), 6,401 .... N 6
Espoo (Esbo), 88,086 .... O 6
Forssa, 15,260 .... N 6
Fredrikshamn (Hamina), 10,872 .... P 6
Gamlakarleby (Kokkola), 20,715 .... N 5
Haapajärvi, 8,943 .... O 5
Haapamäki, 2,200 .... O 5
Hämeenlinna (Tavastehus), 37,333 .... O 6
Hamina, 10,872 .... P 6
Hangö (Hanko), 9,668 .... N 7
Harjavalta, 8,191 .... N 6
Heinola, 13,696 .... P 6
Helsinki (Helsingfors) (cap.), 531,286 .... O 6
Helsinki, *700,000 .... O 6
Himanka, †3,260 .... N 5
Hyrynsalmi, †5,629 .... Q 4
Hyvinkää (Hyvinge), 33,062 .... O 6
Iisalmi, 7,551 .... P 5
Ilomantsi, †12,050 .... R 5
Imatra, 35,054 .... Q 6
Ivalo .... P 2
Jakobstad (Pietarsaari), 19,114 .... N 5
Joensuu, 35,385 .... R 5
Juuka, †9,925 .... Q 5
Jyväskylä, 56,824 .... O 5
Kajaani, 19,131 .... P 4
Kalajoki, †7,314 .... N 4
Karis (Karjaa), 7,940 .... N 6
Karkkila, 8,504 .... N 6
Kaskö (Kaskinen), 1,436 .... M 5
Kauttua .... M 6
Kemi, 30,199 .... O 4
Kemijärvi, 6,546 .... P 3
Kerava (Kervo), 13,322 .... O 6
Kittilä, †8,347 .... O 3
Kokemäki, †10,922 .... N 6
Kokkola (Gamlakarleby), 20,715 .... N 5
Kotka, 33,953 .... P 6
Kouvola, 25,275 .... P 6
Kristiinankaupunki (Kristinestad), 2,726 .... N 5
Kuhmo, †14,847 .... Q 4
Kuopio, 63,800 .... Q 5
Kurikka, 11,373 .... M 5
Kuusamo, †20,324 .... Q 4
Lahti, 87,237 .... O 6
Lappeenranta, 50,543 .... P 6
Lieksa, 4,703 .... R 5
Loimaa, 6,366 .... N 6
Lovisa (Loviisa), 6,695 .... P 6
Maarianhamina (Mariehamn), 8,512 .... M 7
Mänttä, 7,277 .... O 6
Mariehamn (Maarianhamina), 8,512 .... M 7
Mikkeli (Sankt Michel), 24,962 .... P 6
Muonio, †3,226 .... O 3
Naantali (Nådendal), 6,784 .... M 6
Nivala, †10,784 .... O 5
Nokia, 19,200 .... N 6
Nurmes, 2,329 .... Q 5
Nykarleby (Uusikaarlepyy), 1,289 .... N 5
Nyslott (Savonlinna), 17,618 .... Q 6
Nystad (Uusikaupunki), 6,845 .... M 6
Oulainen, 7,898 .... O 4
Oulu (Uleåborg), 85,094 .... O 4
Outokumpu, 10,862 .... Q 5
Parikkala, †7,052 .... Q 6
Parkano, †8,587 .... N 6
Pello, †7,139 .... O 3
Pieksämäki, 12,821 .... P 5
Pietarsaari (Jakobstad), 19,114 .... N 5
Pori (Björneborg), 71,972 .... M 6
Porvoo (Borgå), 15,738 .... O 6
Posio, †7,454 .... Q 3
Pudasjärvi, †15,622 .... P 4
Raahe (Brahestad), 7,637 .... O 4
Rauma (Raumo), 25,218 .... M 6
Riihimäki, 22,442 .... O 6
Rovaniemi, 28,680 .... O 3
Saarijärvi, †11,586 .... O 5
Salo, 16,715 .... N 6
Sankt Michel (Mikkeli), 24,962 .... P 6
Savonlinna, 17,618 .... Q 6
Savukoski, †2,392 .... Q 3
Seinäjoki, 19,836 .... N 5
Sodankylä, †11,745 .... P 3
Sotkamo, †14,127 .... Q 4
Suolahti, 5,563 .... O 5
Suomussalmi, †15,507 .... Q 4
Suonenjoki, 10,012 .... P 5
Tammerfors (Tampere), 156,100 .... N 6
Tammisaari (Ekenäs), 6,401 .... N 6
Tampere (Tammerfors), 156,000 .... N 6
Tapiola .... O 6
Tavastehus (Hämeenlinna), 37,333 .... O 6
Teuva, †8,280 .... N 5
Toijala, 7,505 .... N 6
Tornio (Torneå), 7,325 .... O 4
Turku (Åbo), 155,000 .... N 6
Uleåborg (Oulu), 85,094 .... O 4
Ulvila (Ulvsby), †7,800 .... N 6
Utsjoki, †1,436 .... P 2
Uusikaarlepyy (Nykarleby), 1,289 .... N 5
Uusikaupunki (Nystad), 6,845 .... M 6
Vaala, †6,675 .... P 4
Vaasa (Vasa), 49,109 .... M 5
Valkeakoski, 15,949 .... N 6
Vammala, 5,605 .... N 6
Varkaus, 24,619 .... Q 5
Vasa (Vaasa), 48,262 .... M 5

OTHER FEATURES

Ahvenanmaa (Åland) (isls.), 21,584 .... L 6
Finland (gulf) .... P 7
Haltia (mt.) .... M 2
Hangöudd (prom.) .... N 7
Hauki (lake) .... Q 5
Ii (river) .... O 4
Inari (lake) .... P 2
Juo (lake) .... Q 5
Kala (river) .... O 4
Kalla (lake) .... P 5
Keitele (lake) .... O 5
Kemi (lake) .... Q 3
Kemi (river) .... O 3
Kianta (lake) .... Q 4
Kilpis (lake) .... M 2
Kitinen (river) .... P 3
Kivi (lake) .... O 5
Koitere (lake) .... R 5
Kuusamo (lake) .... Q 4
Längelmä (lake) .... O 6
Lapland (reg.) .... O 2
Lapuan (river) .... N 5
Lesti (lake) .... O 5
Lokka (res.) .... P 3
Muo (lake) .... R 4
Muonio (river) .... M 2
Nasi (lake) .... O 6
Onkivesi (lake) .... P 5
Orihvesi (lake) .... Q 5
Oulu (river) .... O 4
Ounas (river) .... O 3
Päijänne (lake) .... O 6
Pasvik (river) .... Q 2
Pielinen (lake) .... Q 5
Puru (lake) .... Q 6
Puula (lake) .... P 5
Pyhä (lake) .... M 6
Pyhä (lake) .... O 5
Saimaa (lake) .... Q 6
Siika (river) .... O 4
Simo (lake) .... P 3
Simo (river) .... O 4
Tana (Teno) (river) .... P 2
Tornio (river) .... O 3
Vallgrund (isl.), 2,063 .... M 5
Ylikitka (lake) .... Q 3

NORWAY

COUNTIES

Akershus, 282,928 .... D 4
Aust-Agder, 78,184 .... E 7
Bergen, 117,465 .... D 6
Buskerud, 191,789 .... F 6
Finnmark, 75,553 .... O 2
Hedmark, 177,300 .... G 6
Hordaland, 243,545 .... E 6
Møre og Romsdal, 219,384 .... E 5
Nord-Trøndelag, 117,376 .... H 4
Nordland, 244,165 .... J 3
Oppland, 168,819 .... F 6
Oslo (city), 485,200 .... D 3
Østfold, 212,450 .... D 4
Rogaland, 256,501 .... E 7
Sogn og Fjordane, 100,711 .... E 6
Sør-Trøndelag, 224,654 .... G 5
Telemark, 155,834 .... F 7
Troms, 132,407 .... L 2
Vest-Agder, 117,226 .... E 7
Vestfold, 167,778 .... D 4

CITIES and TOWNS

Åfjord, †4,105 .... G 5
Ål, †4,377 .... F 6
Ålesund, 18,558 .... D 5
Åndalsnes, 2,202 .... F 5
Arendal, 11,579 .... F 7
Askim, †9,673 .... E 4
Bamble, †8,338 .... F 7
Barentsburg .... C 2
Bergen, 117,465 .... D 6
Bergen, *270,000 .... D 6
Bodø, 14,048 .... J 3
Borre, 6,636 .... D 4
Drammen, 47,261 .... C 4
Drammen, *48,700 .... C 4
Drøbak, 2,683 .... D 4
Eigersund, 9,730 .... D 7
Elverum, †13,604 .... G 6
Farsund, 7,697 .... E 7
Flekkefjord, 8,616 .... E 7
Flora, 7,836 .... D 6
Fredrikstad, 30,006 .... D 4
Gjøvik, 24,256 .... G 6
Grimstad, 2,610 .... F 7
Gulen, †3,212 .... D 6
Halden, 10,006 .... G 7
Hamar, 14,712 .... G 6
Hammerfest, 6,806 .... N 1
Harstad, 18,892 .... K 2
Haugesund, 27,569 .... D 7
Holmestrand, 6,857 .... C 4
Honningsvåg, 2,813 .... O 1
Horten, 13,387 .... D 4
Kirkenes, 4,433 .... Q 2
Kongsberg, 17,578 .... F 7
Kongsvinger, 13,080 .... H 6
Kragerø, †10,067 .... F 7
Kristiansand, 52,542 .... F 8
Kristiansand, *54,900 .... F 8
Kristiansund, 18,466 .... E 5
Kvinnherad, †9,848 .... E 6
Larvik, 10,728 .... C 4
Lenvik, †10,209 .... L 2
Lesja, †2,755 .... F 5
Lillehammer, 19,808 .... F 6
Lillesand, †4,975 .... F 7
Lillestrøm, 10,547 .... E 3
Løkken, †5,054 .... F 5
Longyearbyen .... D 2
Lysaker, 5,393 .... D 3
Mandal, 10,622 .... E 7
Mo, 8,348 .... J 3
Molde, 17,862 .... E 5
Moss, 23,198 .... D 4
Mysen, 2,500 .... G 7
Namsos, 10,998 .... G 4
Narvik, 13,543 .... K 2
Nesttun, 3,827 .... D 6
Notodden, 13,680 .... F 7
Odda, †10,444 .... E 6
Orkanger, 2,874 .... F 5
Oslo (cap.), 483,196 .... D 3
Oslo, *635,700 .... D 3
Porsgrunn, 28,167 .... G 7
Ringerike, 28,577 .... C 3
Risør, 6,110 .... F 7
Rjukan, 6,308 .... F 7
Røros, †5,259 .... G 5
Sandefjord, 6,085 .... C 4
Sandnes, 28,534 .... D 7
Sandvika, 3,751 .... C 3
Sarpsborg, 13,185 .... D 4
Ski, †12,337 .... D 4
Skien, 47,302 .... F 7
Skjåk, †2,692 .... F 6
Stavanger, 79,700 .... D 7
Stavanger, *80,800 .... D 7
Stavern, 2,148 .... D 4
Steinkjer, 19,874 .... G 4
Stor-Elvdal, †4,151 .... G 6
Sulitjelma, 2,129 .... K 3
Sunndalsøra, 2,376 .... F 5
Svolvaer, 3,812 .... J 2
Tana, †3,286 .... Q 1
Telemark .... C 4
Tønsberg, 11,566 .... D 4
Tromsø, 34,600 .... L 2
Trondheim, 118,703 .... F 5
Trondheim, *123,600 .... F 5
Ullensvang, †4,940 .... E 6
Vadsø, 5,320 .... Q 1
Vardø, 4,185 .... R 1
Volda, 2,647 .... E 5
Voss, †13,473 .... E 6

OTHER FEATURES

Alst (fjord) .... G 3
Alsten (isl.), 4,348 .... H 4
Alta (river) .... N 2
Alte (lake) .... L 2
Ands (fjord) .... K 2
Bardu (river) .... L 2
Barentsöya (isl.) .... D 2
Bellsund (bay) .... C 2
Bjørna (fjord) .... D 6
Bjørnøya (isl.) .... D 3
Bokn (fjord) .... D 7
Bremanger (isl.), 2,028 .... D 6
Dønna (isl.), 1,978 .... H 3
Dovrefjeld (mts.) .... F 5
Edgeøya (isl.) .... E 2
Femund (lake) .... G 5
Folda (fjord) .... G 4
Folda (fjord) .... J 3
Frohavet (bay) .... F 5
Frøya (isl.), 4,034 .... F 5
Glittertind (mt.) .... F 6
Glomma (river) .... G 6
Hadsel (fjord) .... J 2
Hardanger (fjord) .... D 7
Hardanger (mts.) .... E 6
Hinlopen (strait) .... C 1
Hinnøy (isl.), 27,599 .... K 2
Hitra (isl.), 3,134 .... F 5
Hopen (isl.) .... E 2
Hornsund (bay) .... C 2
Hortens (fjord) .... G 4
Is (fjord) .... B 2
Jostedals (glacier) .... E 6
Karmøy (isl.), 19,234 .... D 7
Kob (fjord) .... O 1
Kong Karls Land (isls.) .... E 1
Kvaløy (isl.), 6,869 .... O 1
Lagen (river) .... G 6
Lakse (fjord) .... P 1
Langøy (isl.), 16,500 .... J 2
Lapland (reg.) .... K 2
Lindesnes (cape) .... E 8
Lista (pen.), 7,702 .... E 7
Lofoten (isls.), 28,980 .... H 2
Lopphavet (bay) .... M 1
Magerøy (isl.), 5,545 .... P 1
Mohn (cape) .... E 1
Moskenesøy (isl.), 2,318 .... H 3
Namsen (river) .... H 4
Nord (fjord) .... E 6
Nordaustlandet (isl.) .... D 1
Nordkyn (cape) .... Q 1
North (cape) .... P 1
Norwegian (sea) .... F 3
Ofot (fjord) .... K 2
Otter (river) .... E 7
Pasvik (river) .... Q 2
Platen (cape) .... D 1
Porsanger (fjord) .... O 1
Rana (river) .... J 3
Ran (fjord) .... H 3
Rauma (river) .... F 5
Reisa (river) .... M 2
Ringvassøy (isl.), 1,472 .... L 2
Romsdals (fjord) .... E 5
Salt (fjord) .... J 3
Seiland (isl.), 769 .... N 1
Senja (isl.), 10,541 .... K 2
Skagerrak (strait) .... E 8
Smøla (isl.), 2,840 .... E 5
Snåsa (lake) .... H 4
Sogne (fjord) .... D 6
Sørkapp (cape) .... C 2
Sørøy (isl.), 2,350 .... N 1
South Kvaløy (isl.), 3,444 .... K 2
Spitsbergen (isl.) .... C 2
Steinneset (cape) .... E 2
Stor (fjord) .... D 2
Sunn (fjord) .... D 6
Tana (river) .... P 1
Tjuv (fjord) .... D 2
Tunn (lake) .... H 4
Tyri (fjord) .... C 3
Vågå (lake) .... F 6
Vannøy (isl.), 1,112 .... L 1
Varanger (fjord) .... Q 1
Vega (isl.) .... G 4
Vest (fjord) .... H 3

(continued on following page)

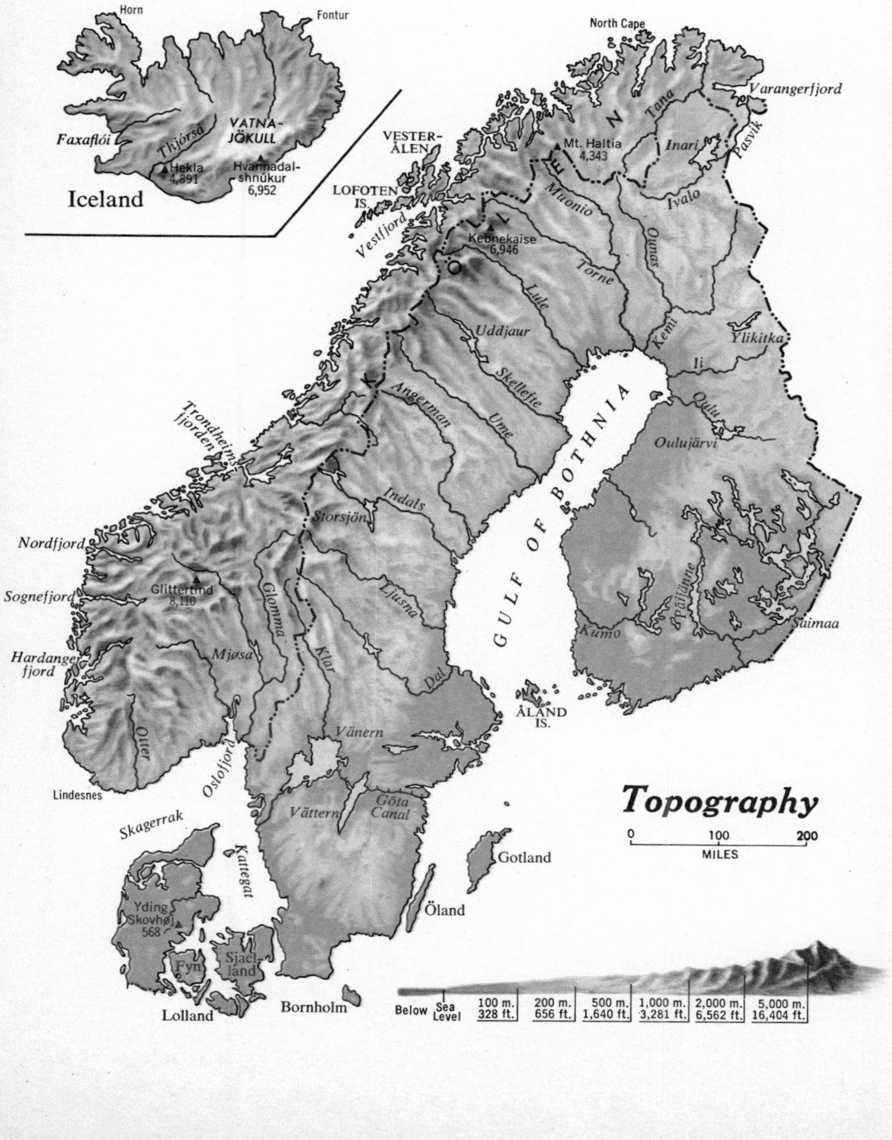
Horn
Fontur
Faxaflói
Thjórsá
VATNA-
JÖKULL
Hekla
4,891
Hvannadal-
shnúkur
6,952
Iceland
North Cape
Varangerfjord
VESTER-
ÅLEN
LOFOTEN
IS.
Vestfjord
Mt. Haltia
4,343
Inari
Tana
Pasvik
Ivalo
Muonio
Ounas
Kebnekaise
6,946
Torne
Lule
Kemi
Ylikitka
Uddjaur
Ii
Skellefte
Ume
Oulu
Oulujärvi
Ångerman
GULF OF BOTHNIA
Trondheimsfjorden
Indals
Storsjön
Nordfjord
Glittertind
8,110
Sognefjord
Glomma
Ljusna
Päijänne
Saimaa
Kiemo
Hardanger
fjord
Mjøsa
Klar
Dal
ÅLAND
IS.
Vänern
Otter
Lindesnes
Oslofjord
Vättern
Göta
Canal
Topography
0
100
200
MILES
Skagerrak
Kattegat
Gotland
Öland
Yding
Skovhøj
568
Fyn
Sjælland
Lolland
Bornholm
Below
Sea
Level
100 m.
328 ft.
200 m.
656 ft.
500 m.
1,640 ft.
1,000 m.
3,281 ft.
2,000 m.
6,562 ft.
5,000 m.
16,404 ft.

Norway, Sweden, Finland, Denmark and Iceland
(continued)

NORWAY (continued)

Vesterålen (isls.), 34,385 ....J 2
Vestvågøy (isl.), 11,749 ....H 3
Vikna (isl.), 3,411 ....G 4

SWEDEN

COUNTIES

Älvsborg, 391,851 ....H 7
Blekinge, 150,901 ....J 8
Gävleborg, 294,916 ....K 6
Göteborg och Bohus, 685,449 ....G 7
Gotland, 50,438 ....L 8
Halland, 185,810 ....H 8
Jämtland, 121,552 ....J 5
Jönköping, 292,303 ....H 8
Kalmar, 234,175 ....K 8
Kopparberg, 270,971 ....J 6
Kristianstad, 258,295 ....J 8
Kronoberg, 164,309 ....J 8
Malmöhus, 683,752 ....H 9
Norrbotten, 261,410 ....L 3
örebro, 259,794 ....J 7
östergötland, 369,374 ....J 7
Skaraborg, 248,970 ....H 7
Södermanland, 239,451 ....K 7
Stockholm, 1,406,580 ....L 7
Uppsala, 191,821 ....K 6
Värmland, 273,139 ....H 7
Västerbotten, 235,307 ....K 4
Västernorrland, 277,715 ....K 5
Västmanland, 255,142 ....K 7

CITIES and TOWNS

Åhus, 4,758 ....J 9
Alingsås, 19,810 ....H 7
Älmhult, 6,023 ....H 8
Alvesta, 8,957 ....J 8
Älvsbyn, 4,343 ....M 4
Åmål, 9,397 ....H 7
Anderstorp, 3,960 ....H 8
Ånge, 4,000 ....J 5
Ängelholm, 13,985 ....H 8
Arboga, 12,266 ....J 7
Årjäng, 2,893 ....H 7
Arvidsjaur, 7,767 ....L 4
Arvika, 15,901 ....H 7
Åseda, 3,629 ....J 8
Åsele, 4,727 ....K 4
Åtvidaberg, 9,010 ....K 7
Avesta, 29,232 ....J 6
Båstad, 2,202 ....H 8
Bengtsfors, 3,411 ....H 7
Boden, 24,912 ....M 4
Bollnäs, 17,123 ....K 6
Borås, 70,238 ....H 8
Borlänge, 29,097 ....J 6
Bräcke, 2,658 ....J 5
Brunflo, 2,700 ....J 5
Bureå, 4,583 ....M 4
Burträsk, 6,747 ....M 4
Charlottenberg, 3,112 ....H 6
Danderyd, 15,657 ....H 1
Djursholm, 7,681 ....H 1
Dorotea, 3,964 ....K 4
Edsbyn, 7,132 ....J 6
Eksjö, 9,897 ....J 8
Emmaboda, 3,697 ....J 8
Enköping, 17,684 ....G 1
Eskilstuna, 65,580 ....K 7
Eslöv, 14,737 ....H 9
Fagersta, 16,609 ....J 6
Falkenberg, 12,920 ....H 8
Falköping, 16,032 ....H 7
Falun, 33,840 ....J 6
Filipstad, 7,559 ....H 7
Finspång, 17,616 ....J 7
Flen, 9,112 ....K 7
Forshaga, 4,655 ....H 7
Frösö, 9,520 ....J 5
Frövi, 3,082 ....J 7
Gällivare, 9,718 ....M 3
Gamleby, 3,949 ....K 8
Gävle, 60,868 ....K 6
Gnesta, 3,275 ....G 2
Göteborg, 444,131 ....G 8
Göteborg, *647,122 ....G 8
Gränna, 3,195 ....J 8
Hagfors, 8,964 ....H 6
Hällefors, 12,011 ....J 7
Hallsberg, 12,121 ....J 7
Hallstahammar, 14,099 ....K 7
Halmstad, 46,655 ....H 8
Hälsingborg, 80,801 ....H 8
Haparanda, 9,429 ....N 4
Härnösand, 16,637 ....L 5
Hässleholm, 16,031 ....H 8
Hedemora, 17,744 ....K 6
Hjo, 4,783 ....J 7
Höganäs, 13,846 ....H 8
Holmsund, 5,778 ....M 5
Hudiksvall, 16,057 ....K 6
Hultsfred, 4,979 ....K 8
Huskvarna, 18,198 ....J 8
Järna, 4,591 ....G 2
Järpen, 2,962 ....H 5
Järvsö, 4,850 ....K 6
Jokkmokk, 4,869 ....L 3
Jönköping, 53,774 ....H 8
Jörn, 4,275 ....M 4
Kalmar, 37,938 ....K 8
Karlshamn, 12,351 ....J 8
Karlskoga, 38,284 ....J 7
Karlskrona, 37,358 ....K 8
Karlstad, 54,321 ....H 7
Katrineholm, 21,660 ....K 7
Kinna, 6,386 ....H 8
Kiruna, 29,210 ....L 3
Kisa, 4,353 ....J 8
Köping, 20,807 ....J 7
Kopparberg, 7,985 ....J 7
Kramfors, 11,729 ....K 5
Kristianstad, 27,527 ....J 9
Kristinehamn, 21,925 ....H 7
Kumla, 15,039 ....J 7
Kungälv, 11,213 ....G 8
Kungsbacka, 7,205 ....G 8
Laholm, 3,853 ....H 8
Landskrona, 32,079 ....H 9
Långsele, 4,640 ....K 5
Långshyttan, 3,124 ....K 6
Laxå, 9,498 ....J 7
Leksand, 8,608 ....J 6
Lidingö, 35,400 ....H 1
Lidköping, 19,700 ....H 7
Lindesberg, 6,863 ....J 7
Linköping, 77,881 ....K 7
Ljungby, 11,930 ....J 8
Ljusdal, 10,630 ....J 6
Ljusne, 4,808 ....K 6
Ludvika, 21,989 ....J 6
Luleå, 36,428 ....N 4
Lund, 50,494 ....H 9
Lycksele, 6,333 ....L 4
Lysekil, 8,000 ....G 7
Malmberget, 12,384 ....M 3
Malmköping, 3,450 ....F 1
Malmö, 256,064 ....H 9
Malmö, *428,338 ....H 9
Markaryd, 5,980 ....H 8
Mariefred, 2,502 ....G 1
Mariestad, 15,700 ....H 7
Mellerud, 4,317 ....H 7
Mjölby, 12,790 ....J 7
Mölndal, 31,072 ....H 8
Mönsterås, 6,687 ....K 8
Mora, 13,307 ....J 6
Motala, 27,907 ....J 7
Nacka, 25,798 ....H 1
Nässjö, 20,000 ....J 8
Nora, 9,215 ....J 7
Norberg, 6,160 ....K 6
Norrköping, 94,296 ....K 7
Norrsundet, 4,575 ....K 6
Norrtälje, 11,803 ....L 7
Norsjö, 5,171 ....L 4
Nybro, 10,956 ....J 8
Nyköping, 31,195 ....K 7
Nynäshamn, 10,676 ....L 7
Ockelbo, 5,819 ....K 6
Olofström, 16,218 ....J 8
örbyhus, 2,266 ....K 6
örebro, 86,977 ....J 7
öregrund, 2,026 ....L 6
örnsköldsvik, 16,539 ....L 5
Oskarshamn, 24,873 ....K 8
östersund, 26,600 ....J 5
östhammar, 8,858 ....L 6
övertorneå, 3,589 ....N 3
överum, 2,533 ....K 7
Oxelösund, 14,835 ....K 7
Pajala, 3,871 ....N 3
Piteå, 8,476 ....M 4
Ramnäs, 4,092 ....J 7
Ramsele, 4,547 ....K 5
Rättvik, 7,551 ....J 6
Rimbo, 3,426 ....L 7
Ronneby, 10,125 ....J 8
Ryd, 4,100 ....J 8
Säffle, 12,599 ....H 7
Sala, 11,800 ....K 7
Saltsjöbaden, 6,507 ....J 1
Sandviken, 25,476 ....K 6
Säter, 4,629 ....J 6
Sävsjö, 5,547 ....J 8
Sigtuna, 3,970 ....H 1
Simrishamn, 7,966 ....J 9
Skänninge, 4,482 ....J 7
Skara, 10,376 ....H 7
Skellefteå, 61,880 ....M 4
Skövde, 27,976 ....H 7
Smedjebacken, 10,504 ....J 6
Söderhamn, 13,778 ....K 6
Söderköping, 5,954 ....K 7
Södertälje, 52,601 ....G 1
Sollefteå, 9,715 ....K 5
Sollentuna, 35,038 ....H 1
Solna, 57,707 ....H 1
Sölvesborg, 6,782 ....J 9
Sorsele, 3,550 ....K 4
Stockholm (cap.), 756,697 ....G 1
Stockholm, *1,288,769 ....G 1
Storvik, 2,432 ....K 6
Strängnäs, 9,506 ....F 1
Strömstad, 9,817 ....G 7
Strömsund, 6,058 ....K 5
Sundbyberg, 28,773 ....G 1
Sundsvall, 62,222 ....K 5
Sunne, 11,018 ....H 7
Sveg, 4,975 ....J 5
Svenljunga, 2,925 ....H 8
Täby, 33,694 ....H 1
Tidaholm, 7,250 ....J 7
Tierp, 4,303 ....K 6
Tillberga, 270 ....K 7
Timrå, 12,800 ....K 5
Tomelilla, 6,349 ....J 9
Torsby, 6,796 ....H 6
Torshälla, 7,939 ....K 7
Tranås, 18,845 ....J 7
Trelleborg, 35,249 ....H 9
Trollhättan, 40,945 ....H 7
Uddevalla, 36,510 ....G 7
Ulricehamn, 8,504 ....H 8
Umeå, 51,955 ....M 5
Uppsala, 97,315 ....L 7
Vadstena, 6,893 ....J 7
Vaggeryd, 4,840 ....J 8
Valdemarsvik, 3,590 ....K 7
Vänersborg, 19,975 ....H 7
Vännäs, 4,045 ....L 5
Vansbro, 2,941 ....H 6
Vara, 11,056 ....H 7
Varberg, 18,451 ....G 8
Värnamo, 15,939 ....J 8
Västerås, 110,539 ....J 7
Västerhaninge, 9,814 ....H 1
Västervik, 23,014 ....K 8
Vaxholm, 4,322 ....J 1
Vaxjö, 32,760 ....J 8
Vetlanda, 10,780 ....J 8
Vilhelmina, 9,426 ....K 4
Vimmerby, 7,257 ....J 8
Virserum, 4,650 ....J 8
Visby, 18,338 ....L 8
Vislanda, 2,594 ....H 8
Wallhamn ....G 7
Ystad, 14,002 ....H 9

OTHER FEATURES

Angerman (river) ....K 5
Asnen (lake) ....J 8
Bothnia (gulf) ....M 5
Byske (river) ....L 4
Fårö (isl.), 790 ....L 8
Göta (river) ....H 7
Gotland (isl.), 50,438 ....L 8
Hornslandet (pen.) ....K 6
Kalix (river) ....N 3
Kalmarsund (sound) ....K 8
Kattegat (strait) ....G 8
Kebnekaise (mt.) ....L 3
Lainio (river) ....N 3
Lapland (dist.) ....K 2
Lule (river) ....M 3
Muonio (river) ....M 2
öland (isl.), 20,416 ....K 8
Ornö (isl.), 224 ....J 1
österdal (river) ....H 6
Pite (river) ....M 4
Skellefte (river) ....L 4
Stora Lulevatten (lake) ....L 3
Storuman (lake) ....K 4
Sulitjelma (mt.) ....K 3
Torne (river) ....M 3
Torneträsk (lake) ....L 2
Uddjaur (lake) ....L 4
Ume (river) ....L 4
Vänern (lake) ....H 7
Vättern (lake) ....J 7
Vesterdal (river) ....H 6
Vindel (river) ....L 4
Vojmsjön (lakes) ....J 4

*City and suburbs.
†Population of parish or commune.

DENMARK

INTERNAL DIVISIONS

Århus (county), 525,167 ....D 5
Bornholm (county), 47,405 ....F 9
Copenhagen (commune), 634,500 ....F 6
Færøe Islands, 38,000 ....B 2
Frederiksberg (commune), 102,751 ....F 6
Frederiksborg (county), 252,557 ....F 5
Fyn (county), 430,958 ....D 7
København (Copenhagen) (commune), 634,500 ....F 6
København (county), 609,469 .....F 6
Nordjylland (county), 455,062 ....D 4
Ribe (county), 196,894 ....B 6
Ringkøbing (county), 240,014 ....B 5
Roskilde (county), 147,434 ....E 6
Sønderjylland (county), 237,270 ....C 7
Storstrøm (county), 251,815 ......E 7
Vejle (county), 304,358 ....C 6
Vestsjælland (county), 256,997 ....E 6
Viborg (county), 220,214 ....B 4

CITIES and TOWNS

Åbenrå, 15,156 ....C 7
Åbybro, 6,309 ....C 3
Ærøskøbing, 1,228 ....D 8
Agerbæk, 804, ...B 6
Åkirkeby, 1,549 ....F 9
Ålborg, 82,346 ....D 4
Ålborg, *153,307 ....D 4
Ålestrup, 5,228 ....C 4
Allingåbro, 1,352 ....D 5
Allinge-Sandvig, 2,023 ....F 8
Ansager, 1,123 ....B 6
Arden, 1,353 ....C 4
Århus, 109,498 ....D 5
Århus, *232,173 ....D 5
Års, 5,075 ....C 4
Årup, †5,033 ....D 7
Aså, 1,348 ....D 3
Askov, 725 ....C 7
Asnæs, 2,493 ....E 6
Assens, Århus, 1,266 ....D 4
Assens, Fyn, †10,777 ....D 7
Augustenborg, 3,537 ....D 8
Auning, 1,367 ....D 5
Avlum, 3,694 ....B 5
Bælum, 1,922 ....D 4
Bagenkop, 774 ....D 8
Ballerup, †50,128 ....F 6
Bandholm, 1,248 ....E 8
Bested, 1,886 ....B 4
Birkerød, †20,835 ....F 6
Bjerringbro, 6,469 ....C 5
Bogense, †6,450 ....D 6
Bolderslev, 729 ....C 8
Børkop, †9,053 ....C 6
Borup, 2,344 ....E 7
Brabrand, 12,514 ....C 5
Brædstrup, 3,925 ....C 6
Bramminge, 5,937 ....B 7
Brande, 6,814 ....B 6
Bredebro, †3,747 ....B 7
Broager, †5,387 ....C 8
Brønderslev, 10,274 ....C 3
Brøns, 867 ....B 7
Brørup, 4,066 ....C 7
Brovst, †8,086 ....C 3
Christiansfeld, 958 ....C 7
Copenhagen (cap.), 634,500 ....F 6
Copenhagen, *1,346,720 ....F 6
Dronninglund, 9,179 ....D 3
Dybvad, 793 ....D 3
Ebeltoft, 3,168 ....D 5
Egernsund, 1,360 ....C 8
Egtved, 2,857 ....C 6
Ejby, 3,265 ....D 7
Esbjerg, 62,483 ....B 7
Fåborg, 5,630 ....D 7
Fakse, 7,268 ....F 7
Fakse Ladeplads, 1,639 ....F 7
Farsø, 4,126 ....C 4
Farum, †9,583 ....F 6
Fjerritslev, 2,686 ....C 3
Fredensborg, 3,977 ....F 6
Fredericia, 34,464 ....C 6
Frederiksberg, 102,751 ....F 6
Frederikshavn, 24,640 ....D 3
Frederikssund, 7,835 ....E 6
Frederiksværk, 4,385 ....E 6
Fuglebjerg, 5,082 ....E 7
Gedser, 1,195 ....F 8
Gedsted, 1,924 ....C 4
Gelsted, 2,461 ....C 7
Gentofte, †78,641 ....F 6
Gilleleje, 4,300 ....F 5
Give, 8,573 ....C 6
Gjerlev, 1,209 ....D 4
Glamsbjerg, †5,677 ....D 7
Glostrup, †28,169 ....F 6
Glumsø, 819 ....E 7
Glyngøre, 1,047 ....C 4
Gørding, 2,422 ....B 7
Gørlev, 2,437 ....E 6
Græsted, 2,899 ....F 5
Gram, 3,935 ....C 7
Gråsten, †6,336 ....C 8
Grenå, 13,277 ....D 5
Grindsted, 9,345 ....B 6
Gylling, 990 ....D 6
Haderslev, 20,291 ....C 7
Hadsten, 6,919 ....C 5
Hadsund, 6,862 ....D 4
Hals, 3,016 ....D 3
Hammel, 7,456 ....C 5
Hammerum, 2,415 ....C 5
Hanstholm, 3,358 ....B 3
Harboør, 2,224 ....A 4
Hårby, †4,671 ....D 7
Hårlev, 980 ....F 7
Hasle, 1,542 ....F 8
Haslev, 10,173 ....E 7
Havdrup, 5,163 ....F 6
Hedensted, 4,791 ....C 6
Hellebæk, 2,240 ....F 5
Helsinge, 4,707 ....F 6
Helsingør, 30,211 ....F 6
Herning, 32,512 ....B 5
Hillerød, 23,500 ....F 6
Hinnerup, †5,614 ....D 5
Hirtshals, 8,598 ....C 2
Hjallerup, 1,385 ....C 3
Hjerm, 1,421 ....B 5
Hjørring, 15,699 ....C 3
Hobro, 8,845 ....C 4
Højer, 1,407 ....B 8
Højslev, 2,863 ....C 4
Holbæk, 17,892 ....E 6
Holeby, 4,359 ....E 8
Holstebro, 24,009 ....B 5
Holsted, 2,773 ....B 6
Høng, †7,355 ....E 7
Hornslet, 3,371 ....D 5
Horsens, 35,621 ....C 6
Hørsholm, 18,060 ....F 6
Hørve, 2,829 ....E 6
Hov, 607 ....D 6
Humlum, 2,357 ....B 4
Hundested, †6,301 ....E 6
Hurup, 2,560 ....B 4
Hvidbjerg, 2,361 ....B 4
Hvide Sande, 1,775 ....A 6
Hviding, 750 ....B 7
Ikast, 11,110 ....C 5
Jelling, 4,780 ....C 6
Jerslev, 2,672 ....D 3
Juelsminde, 7,245 ....D 6
Jyderup, 3,246 ....E 6
Kalundborg, 11,762 ....D 6
Karby, 2,302 ....B 4
Karise, 1,733 ....F 7
Karup, 1,891 ....C 5
Kastrup ....F 6
Kerteminde, †10,296 ....D 7
Kibæk, 1,179 ....B 5
Kjellerup, 3,506 ....C 5
Klaksvík, Færøe Is., 3,894 ....B 2
København (Copenhagen), (cap.), 634,500 ....F 6
Køge, 17,360 ....F 7
Kolding, 39,609 ....C 7
Kolind, 2,590 ....D 5
Kørsør, 15,550 ....E 7
Kværndrup, 1,963 ....D 7
Langå, 2,801 ....C 5
Lem, 1,060 ....B 5
Lemvig, 6,766 ....B 4
Løgstør, 3,666 ....C 4
Løgumkloster, 2,089 ....B 7
Lohals, 634 ....D 7
Løjt Kirkeby, 2,724 ....C 7
Løkken, 1,388 ....C 3
Løsning, 2,418 ....C 6
Lundby, 2,392 ....E 7
Lunderskov, †4,402 ....C 7
Lyngby, †61,245 ....F 6
Malling, 4,332 ....D 5
Mariager, 3,733 ....D 4
Maribo, 5,235 ....E 8
Marstal, 4,095 ....D 8
Middelfart, 9,015 ....C 7
Møgeltønder, 1,181 ....B 8
Næstved, 24,831 ....E 7
Nakskov, 15,994 ....E 8
Neksø, 3,499 ....F 9
Nibe, 2,786 ....C 4
Nordborg, 3,016 ....C 7
Nordby, 2,353 ....B 7
Nørre Åby, †5,195 ....C 7
Nørre Alslev, 1,939 ....E 8
Nørre Broby, 858 ....D 7
Nørre Nebel, 867 ....B 6
Nørre Snede, 3,019 ....C 6
Nørresundby, 23,848 ....D 3
Nørre Vorupør, 632 ....B 4
Nyborg, 11,698 ....D 7
Nykøbing, Storstrøm, 17,364 ....E 8
Nykøbing, Vestsjælland, 4,905 ....E 6
Nykøbing, Viborg, 8,710 ....B 4
Nysted, 1,211 ....E 8
Odder, 8,144 ....D 6
Odense, 102,698 ....D 7
Odense, *163,593 ....D 7
Ølgod, 7,091 ....B 6
Ørsted, 1,925 ....D 5
Øster Vrå, 931 ....D 3
Otterup, †10,462 ....D 7
Ovtrup, 549 ....B 6
Pandrup, 1,383 ....C 3
Pedersborg, 1,560 ....E 7

Agriculture, Industry and Resources

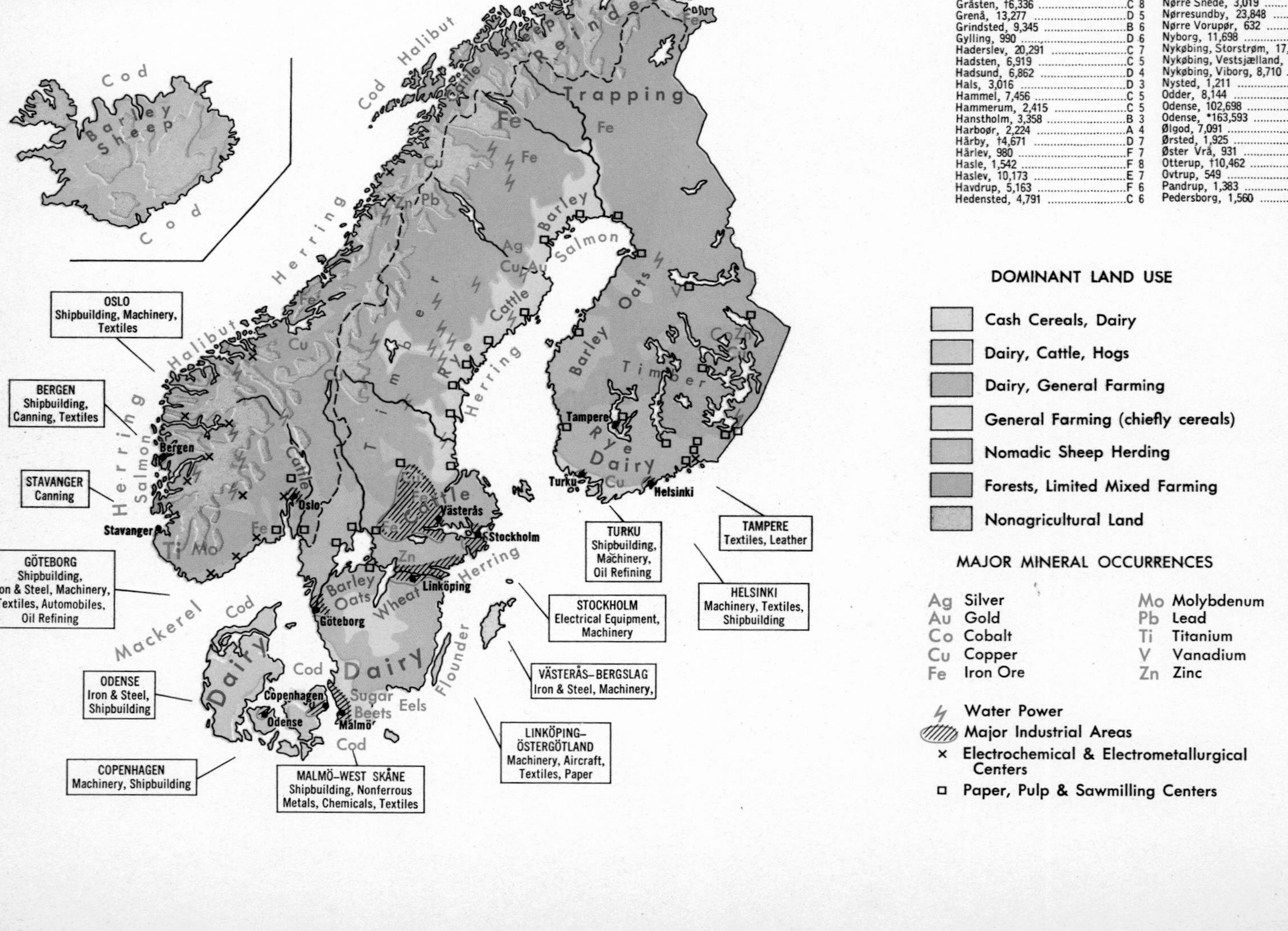

Shrimp
Haddock
Cod
Halibut
Reindeer
Trapping
Barley
Sheep
Herring
Salmon
Cattle
Oats
Rye
Dairy
Timber
Wheat
Mackerel
Flounder
Sugar Beets
Eels
OSLO
Shipbuilding, Machinery, Textiles
BERGEN
Shipbuilding, Canning, Textiles
STAVANGER
Canning
GÖTEBORG
Shipbuilding, Iron & Steel, Machinery, Textiles, Automobiles, Oil Refining
ODENSE
Iron & Steel, Shipbuilding
COPENHAGEN
Machinery, Shipbuilding
MALMÖ–WEST SKÅNE
Shipbuilding, Nonferrous Metals, Chemicals, Textiles
LINKÖPING–ÖSTERGÖTLAND
Machinery, Aircraft, Textiles, Paper
VÄSTERÅS–BERGSLAG
Iron & Steel, Machinery,
STOCKHOLM
Electrical Equipment, Machinery
TURKU
Shipbuilding, Machinery, Oil Refining
HELSINKI
Machinery, Textiles, Shipbuilding
TAMPERE
Textiles, Leather
Bergen
Stavanger
Oslo
Göteborg
Copenhagen
Odense
Malmö
Linköping
Västerås
Stockholm
Turku
Tampere
Helsinki
DOMINANT LAND USE
Cash Cereals, Dairy
Dairy, Cattle, Hogs
Dairy, General Farming
General Farming (chiefly cereals)
Nomadic Sheep Herding
Forests, Limited Mixed Farming
Nonagricultural Land
MAJOR MINERAL OCCURRENCES
Ag Silver
Au Gold
Co Cobalt
Cu Copper
Fe Iron Ore
Mo Molybdenum
Pb Lead
Ti Titanium
V Vanadium
Zn Zinc
Water Power
Major Industrial Areas
× Electrochemical & Electrometallurgical Centers
▫ Paper, Pulp & Sawmilling Centers

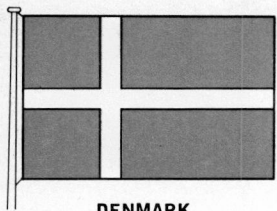

DENMARK

ICELAND

DENMARK

- **AREA** 16,614 sq. mi.
- **POPULATION** 4,912,865
- **CAPITAL** Copenhagen
- **LARGEST CITY** Copenhagen
- **HIGHEST POINT** Yding Skovhøj 568 ft.
- **MONETARY UNIT** krone (crown)
- **MAJOR LANGUAGE** Danish
- **MAJOR RELIGION** Protestantism

ICELAND

- **AREA** 39,768 sq. mi.
- **POPULATION** 204,578
- **CAPITAL** Reykjavík
- **LARGEST CITY** Reykjavík
- **HIGHEST POINT** Hvannadalshnúkur 6,952 ft.
- **MONETARY UNIT** króna (crown)
- **MAJOR LANGUAGE** Icelandic
- **MAJOR RELIGION** Protestantism

Præstø, 4,926	E 7
Ramme, 1,560	B 4
Randers, 41,253	C 4
Ranum, 2,320	C 3
Ribe, 8,224	B 7
Ringe, 6,907	D 7
Ringkøbing, 6,536	B 5
Ringsted, 12,499	E 7
Rødby, 4,751	E 8
Rødding, 2,826	B 7
Rødekro, 17,874	C 7
Rødkærsbro, 992	C 4
Rødvig Ladeplads, 1,068	F 7
Rømø, 817	A 7
Rønde, 4,487	D 4
Rønne, 12,440	F 9
Rørby, 1,081	E 6
Roskilde, 39,984	E 6
Roslev, 1,260	B 4
Rudkøbing, 17,069	D 8
Ruds Vedby, 954	E 6
Ry, 5,945	C 5
Ryomgård, 947	D 3
Sæby, 4,378	D 2
Sakskøbing, 2,523	E 8
Silkeborg, 26,129	C 4
Sindal, 18,695	D 3
Skælskør, 8,776	E 7
Skærbæk, 3,016	B 7
Skagen, 11,699	D 2
Skals, 1,968	C 4
Skanderborg, 11,227	D 5
Skårup, 2,215	D 7
Skibby, 14,585	E 6
Skive, 17,980	B 4
Skjern, 6,058	B 6
Skodborg, 1,728	C 7
Skørping, 2,347	C 4
Slagelse, 22,973	E 6
Slangerup, 2,701	E 6
Snedsted, 2,571	B 3
Søllested, 857	E 8
Sønderborg, 23,069	C 8
Sønderho, 352	A 7
Sønder Nissum, 1,236	A 5
Sønder Omme, 2,449	B 6
Sønderså, 19,479	D 7
Sorø, 5,591	E 7
Stege, 3,872	F 8
Stenlille, 1,617	E 6
Stenstrup, 1,993	D 7
Stoholm, 1,178	C 4
Store Heddinge, 2,245	F 7
Støvring, 1,980	C 4
Strandby, 1,752	D 3
Struer, 9,263	B 5
Stubbekøbing, 2,061	F 8
Sulsted, 5,006	C 3
Svaneke, 1,164	F 9
Svendborg, 23,149	D 7
Svenstrup, 3,530	C 4
Svinninge, 15,681	E 6
Tarm, 2,702	B 6
Tårnby, 145,868	F 6
Tåstrup, †29,154	F 6
Them, 2,419	C 5
Thisted, 8,730	B 4
Thyborøn, 2,404	A 4
Thyregod, 2,441	C 6
Tim, 1,175	B 5
Tingley, 2,825	C 7
Tistrup, 653	B 6
Toftlund, 3,311	B 7
Tølløse, 18,036	E 6
Tommerup, 16,076	D 7
Tønder, 7,489	B 8
Tørring, 2,453	C 6
Tórshavn (cap.), Færøe Is., 9,738	A 3
Tranebjerg, 701	D 5
Troense, 631	D 7
Trustrup, 801	D 5
Tversted, 1,973	D 2
Uldum, 1,182	C 6
Ulfborg, 2,053	B 5
Vamdrup, 4,760	C 7
Varde, 11,456	B 6
Vejen, 7,470	C 7
Vejle, 31,763	C 6
Vemb, 1,937	B 5
Vester Skerninge, 503	D 7
Vestervig, 2,513	B 4
Viborg, 25,468	C 4
Viby, 1,038	F 7
Videbæk, †10,368	B 5
Vig, 2,678	E 6
Vildbjerg, 2,698	B 5
Vinderup, 17,857	B 5
Vodskov, 2,327	D 3
Vojens, 6,975	C 7
Vorbasse, 1,952	B 6
Vordingborg, 11,640	E 7
Vrå, 4,371	C 3

OTHER FEATURES

Ærø (isl.), 9,295	D 8
Ålborg (bay)	D 4
Als (isl.), 50,518	C 7
Amager (isl.), 177,818	F 6
Anholt (isl.), 196	E 4
Årø (isl.), 259	C 7
Båga (isl.), 113	C 7
Blåvands Huk (point)	A 7
Bornholm (isl.), 47,405	F 9
Dovns Klint (prom.)	D 8
Endelave (isl.), 257	D 6
Eysturoy (isl.), Færøe Is., 7,714	B 3
Fakse (bay)	F 7
Falster (isl.), 49,405	E 8
Fanø (isl.), 2,705	B 7
Fehmarn (strait)	E 9
Fejø (isl.), 933	E 8

Femø (isl.), 381	E 8
Frisian, North (isls.), 3,653	B 7
Fyn (isl.), 397,234	D 7
Fyns Hoved (prom.)	D 6
Gedser Odde (point)	E 9
Gelså (river)	C 7
Gilbjerg Hoved (prom.)	F 5
Gjerrild Klint (prom.)	D 5
Gudenå (river)	D 4
Horsens (fjord)	D 6
Isefjord (fjord)	E 6
Jammerbugt (bay)	C 3
Jutland (Jylland) (pen.), 2,088,642	C 5
Jyske Ås (hills)	D 3
Kattegat (strait)	E 4
Knøsen (mt.)	D 3
Knudshoved (prom.)	D 7
Køge (bay)	F 7
Læsø (isl.), 2,722	E 3
Langeland (isl.), 17,132	D 8
Langelands Bælt (channel)	D 8
Lille Bælt (channel)	C 7
Lilleå (river)	C 4
Limfjorden (fjord)	A, D 4
Løgstør Bredning (fjord)	C 4
Lolland (isl.), 74,819	E 8
Mariager (fjord)	D 4
Mollebjerg (mt.)	C 6
Møn (isl.), 12,436	F 8
Møns Klint (prom.)	F 8
Mors (isl.), 25,026	B 4
Nissum (fjord)	A 5
North Frisian (isls.), 3,653	B 7
Odense (fjord)	D 7
Omme (river)	B 6
Omø (isl.), 241	E 7
Øresund (sound)	F 6
Ringkøbing (fjord)	B 6
Rømø (isl.), 817	B 7
Røsnæs (prom.)	E 6
Samsø (isl.), 5,192	D 6
Samsø Bælt (channel)	D 6
Sandoy (isl.), Færøe Is., 1,684	B 3
Sejerø (isl.), 561	E 6
Sjælland (isl.), 2,116,294	E 6
Sjællands Odde (point)	E 5
Skagens Odde (The Skaw) (point)	D 2
Skagerrak (strait)	C 2
Skive (river)	C 4
Stevns Klint (prom.)	F 7
Storå (river)	B 5
Store Bælt (channel)	D 6
Streymoy (isl.), Færøe Is., 14,078	A 2
Sudhuroy (isl.), Færøe Is., 5,734	B 3
Susá (river)	E 7
Tannis (bay)	D 2
Tranebjerg (mt.)	C 6
Varde (river)	B 6
Vejle (fjord)	C 6
Vigsø (bay)	B 3
Vorgod (river)	B 5
Yding Skovhøj (mt.)	C 6

ICELAND

CITIES and TOWNS

Akranes, 4,253	B 1
Akureyri, 10,755	C 1
Hafnarfjördhur, 9,696	B 1
Húsavík, 1,993	C 1
Isafjördhur, 2,880	B 1
Keflavík, 5,663	B 1
Neskaupstadhur (Nes), 1,552	D 1
Olafsfjördhur, 1,086	C 1
Reykjavík (capital), 81,693	B 1
Reykjavík, *98,521	B 1
Saudhárkrókur, 1,600	C 1
Seydhisfjördhur, 884	D 1
Siglufjördhur, 2,161	C 1
Vestmannaeyjar, 5,186	B 2

OTHER FEATURES

Bjargtangur (point)	A 1
Breidhafjördhur (fjord)	B 1
Faxaflói (bay)	B 1
Fontur (prom.)	D 1
Gerpir (cape)	D 1
Grimsey (isl.), 79	C 1
Hekla (volcano)	C 2
Hofsjökull (glacier)	C 1
Horn (cape)	B 1
Hornafjördhur (fjord)	D 1
Húnaflói (bay)	B 1
Hvannadalshnúkur (mt.)	C 1
Hvítá (river)	B 1
Isafjördhur (fjord)	B 1
Jökulsá (river)	C 1
Lagarfljót (stream)	D 1
Langjökull (glacier)	C 1
Mýrdalsjökull (glacier)	C 2
Önduðharnes (mt.)	A 1
Reykjanestá (cape)	A 2
Rifstangi (cape)	C 1
Skagata (cape)	C 1
Skjálfandafljót (river)	C 1
Surtsey (isl.)	B 2
Thjórsá (river)	C 2
Vatnajökull (glacier)	C 1
Vopnafjördhur (fjord)	D 1

*City and suburbs.

†Population of rural municipality.

DENMARK and ICELAND

CONIC PROJECTION

SCALE OF MILES
0 10 20 30 40 50

SCALE OF KILOMETERS

Capitals of Countries _____ ☆
Capitals of Counties (amter) _____ ⚓
International Boundaries _____
Internal Boundaries _____

Denmark is divided into fourteen counties plus Copenhagen and Frederiksberg communes.

© Copyright HAMMOND INCORPORATED, Maplewood, N.J.

FAERØE ISLANDS

Streymoy
Klaksvík
Eysturoy
Tórshavn
Sandoy
Sudhuroy
MILES

BORNHOLM

Same scale as main map
Allinge-Sandvig
Hasle
Svaneke
Bornholm
Rønne
Akirkeby
Neksø

GERMANY

CONIC PROJECTION
SCALE OF MILES

SCALE OF KILOMETERS

Capitals of Countries .... ☆
State and District Capitals .... ⊙
International Boundaries .... —··—··—
State and District Boundaries .... —·—·—·
Canals ....

East Germany is divided into districts bearing the same name as their respective capitals.

BERLIN

Copyright by C.S. HAMMOND & Co., Maplewood, N.J.

WEST GERMANY

AREA 95,959 sq. mi.
POPULATION 61,194,600
CAPITAL Bonn
LARGEST CITY Berlin (West)
HIGHEST POINT Zugspitze 9,718 ft.
MONETARY UNIT West German Deutsch mark
MAJOR LANGUAGE German
MAJOR RELIGIONS Protestantism, Roman Catholicism

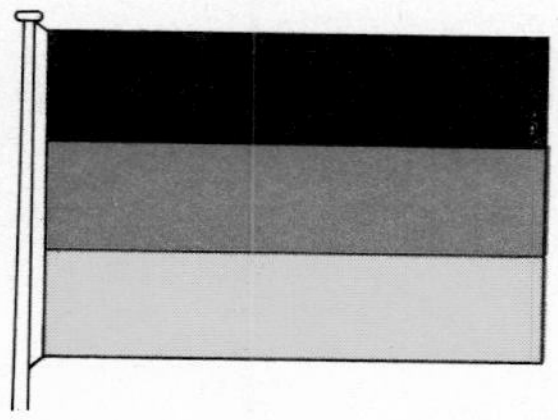

EAST GERMANY

AREA 41,814 sq. mi.
POPULATION 17,117,000
CAPITAL Berlin (East)
LARGEST CITY Berlin (East)
HIGHEST POINT Fichtelberg 3,983 ft.
MONETARY UNIT East German Deutsch mark
MAJOR LANGUAGE German
MAJOR RELIGIONS Protestantism, Roman Catholicism

EAST GERMANY

DISTRICTS

Berlin (East), 1,084,000 ....F 4
Cottbus, 839,133 ....F 3
Dresden, 1,887,739 ....E 3
Erfurt, 1,249,540 ....D 3
Frankfurt, 660,666 ....F 2
Gera, 735,175 ....D 3
Halle, 1,932,733 ....E 3
Karl-Marx-Stadt, 2,082,927 ....E 3
Leipzig, 1,510,773 ....E 3
Magdeburg, 1,323,644 ....D 2
Neubrandenburg, 633,209 ....E 2
Potsdam, 1,127,498 ....E 2
Rostock, 842,743 ....D 1
Schwerin, 594,786 ....D 2
Suhl, 549,398 ....D 3

CITIES and TOWNS

Aken, 12,126 ....D 3
Altenburg, 47,462 ....E 3
Angermünde, 12,200 ....E 2
Anklam, 19,436 ....E 2
Annaberg-Buchholz, 28,663 ....E 3
Apolda, 29,735 ....D 3
Arnstadt, 27,674 ....D 3
Aschersleben, 36,777 ....D 3
Aue, 31,723 ....E 3
Auerbach, 19,673 ....E 3
Bad Doberan, 13,197 ....D 1
Bad Dürrenberg, 16,500 ....D 3
Bad Freienwalde, 11,845 ....F 2
Bad Langensalza, 16,952 ....D 3
Bad Salzungen, 12,722 ....C 3
Barth, 12,688 ....E 1
Bautzen, 44,041 ....F 3
Bergen, 10,979 ....E 1
Berlin (East) (capital), 1,084,000 ....F 4
Bernau, 14,078 ....E 2
Bernburg, 45,885 ....D 3
Bischofswerda, 11,345 ....F 3
Bitterfeld, 30,916 ....E 3
Blankenburg, 19,595 ....D 3
Boizenburg, 11,370 ....D 2
Borna, 20,669 ....E 3
Brandenburg, 90,753 ....E 2
Burg, 29,906 ....D 2
Calbe, 16,464 ....D 3
Chemnitz (Karl-Marx-Stadt), 295,443 ....D 3
Coswig, 18,600 ....E 3
Cottbus, 75,541 ....F 3
Crimmitschau, 30,752 ....E 3
Delitzsch, 23,480 ....E 3
Demmin, 16,755 ....E 2
Dessau, 95,682 ....E 3
Döbeln, 28,430 ....E 3
Dresden, 499,848 ....E 3
Ebersbach, 11,293 ....F 3
Eberswalde, 33,680 ....E 2
Eilenburg, 21,366 ....E 3
Eisenach, 50,234 ....D 3
Eisenberg, 13,858 ....D 3
Eisenhüttenstadt, 38,138 ....F 2
Eisleben, 32,402 ....D 3
Erfurt, 193,745 ....D 3
Falkensee, 29,884 ....E 3
Falkenstein, 15,269 ....E 3
Finsterwalde, 22,441 ....E 3
Forst, 29,823 ....F 3
Frankfurt-an-der-Oder, 58,866 ....F 2
Freiberg, 49,122 ....E 3
Freital, 42,675 ....E 3
Fürstenwalde, 30,527 ....F 2
Gardelegen, 13,218 ....D 2
Genthin, 15,619 ....E 2
Gera, 109,989 ....E 3
Glauchau, 33,103 ....E 3
Görlitz, 88,632 ....F 3
Gotha, 57,692 ....D 3
Greifswald, 47,402 ....E 1
Greiz, 39,313 ....E 3
Grevesmühlen, 10,914 ....D 2
Grimma, 16,509 ....E 3
Grimmen, 12,943 ....E 1
Grossenhain, 19,848 ....E 3
Grossräschen, 12,737 ....E 3
Guben (Wilhelm-Pieck-Stadt), 26,586 ....F 3
Güstrow, 38,185 ....E 2
Hagenow, 10,434 ....D 2
Halberstadt, 46,071 ....D 3
Haldensleben, 20,547 ....D 2
Halle, 263,928 ....D 3
Heidenau, 20,161 ....E 3
Heiligenstadt, 12,627 ....D 3
Hennigsdorf, 21,398 ....E 3
Hettstedt, 19,218 ....D 3
Hoyerswerda, 43,922 ....F 3
Ilmenau, 19,852 ....D 3
Jena, 85,032 ....D 3
Johanngeorgenstadt, 10,801 ....E 3
Jüterbog, 14,416 ....E 3
Kamenz, 16,236 ....F 3
Karl-Marx-Stadt, 295,443 ....E 3
Kleinmachnow, 13,919 ....E 4
Klingenthal, 14,748 ....E 3
Köpenick, 52,294 ....F 4
Köthen, 38,154 ....E 3
Kottbus (Cottbus), 75,541 ....F 3
Lauchhammer, 28,680 ....E 3
Leipzig, 590,291 ....E 3
Lichtenberg, 62,841 ....F 4
Limbach-Oberfrohna, 26,053 ....E 3
Löbau, 17,068 ....F 3
Lübben, 12,742 ....E 3
Lübbenau, 16,976 ....F 3
Luckenwalde, 29,282 ....E 2
Ludwigslust, 11,512 ....D 2
Magdeburg, 268,269 ....D 2
Markkleeberg, 21,854 ....E 3
Meerane, 24,262 ....E 3
Meiningen, 25,025 ....D 3
Meissen, 47,166 ....E 3
Merseburg, 55,562 ....D 3
Meuselwitz, 10,582 ....E 3
Mittweida, 20,440 ....E 3
Mücheln, 10,842 ....D 3
Mühlhausen, 46,155 ....D 3
Nauen, 12,017 ....E 2
Naumburg, 37,990 ....D 3
Neubrandenburg, 38,740 ....E 2
Neuenhagen, 13,116 ....F 4
Neugersdorf, 11,889 ....F 3
Neuruppin, 22,424 ....E 2
Neustadt, 10,085 ....D 3
Neustrelitz, 27,624 ....E 2
Nordhausen, 42,279 ....D 3
Oelsnitz, 15,954 ....E 3
Oelsnitz im Erzgebirge, 18,377 ....E 3
Olbernhau, 14.240 ....E 3
Oranienburg, 20,401 ....E 2
Oschatz, 15,582 ....E 3
Oschersleben, 18,078 ....D 2
Pankow, 68,785 ....F 3
Parchim, 19,226 ....D 2
Pasewalk, 14,086 ....F 2
Perleberg, 13,707 ....D 2
Pirna, 42,562 ....E 3
Plauen, 81,739 ....E 3
Pössneck, 19,468 ....D 3
Potsdam, 110,671 ....E 2
Prenzlau, 20,276 ....F 2
Quedlinburg, 30,840 ....D 3
Radeberg, 17,410 ....E 3
Radebeul, 41,437 ....E 3
Rathenow, 28,979 ....E 2
Reichenbach, 29,372 ....E 3
Ribnitz-Damgarten, 15,301 ....E 1
Riesa, 43,322 ....E 3
Rosslau, 16,256 ....E 3
Rosswein, 10,649 ....E 3
Rostock, 190,275 ....E 1
Rüdersdorf, 11,837 ....E 2
Rudolstadt, 30,433 ....D 3
Saalfeld, 32,145 ....D 3
Salzwedel, 19,534 ....D 2
Sangerhausen, 29,373 ....D 3
Sassnitz, 13,253 ....E 1
Schkeuditz, 17,131 ....E 3
Schmalkalden, 14,569 ....D 3
Schmölln, 13,992 ....E 3
Schneeberg, 21,225 ....E 3
Schönebeck, 44,551 ....D 2
Schöneiche, 10,101 ....E 2
Schwedt, 23,359 ....F 2
Schwerin, 92,356 ....D 2
Sebnitz, 14,655 ....F 3
Senftenberg, 24,532 ....F 3
Sömmerda, 16,061 ....D 3
Sondershausen, 22,456 ....D 3
Sonneberg, 29,804 ....D 3
Spremberg, 23,367 ....F 3
Stassfurt, 25,622 ....D 3
Stendal, 36,193 ....D 2
Stralsund, 68,925 ....E 1
Strausberg, 17,985 ....F 2
Suhl, 28,698 ....D 3
Tangermünde, 12,992 ....D 2
Teltow, 13,735 ....E 4
Templin, 11,203 ....E 2
Teterow, 11,039 ....E 2
Thale, 17,273 ....D 3
Torgau, 20,941 ....E 3
Torgelow, 13,584 ....F 2
Treptow, 22,302 ....F 4
Ueckermünde, 11,614 ....F 2
Zwickau, 127,688 ....E 3
Waltershausen, 14,250 ....D 3
Waren, 20,008 ....E 2
Weida, 11,950 ....D 3
Weimar, 64,300 ....D 3
Weissenfels, 47,704 ....D 3
Weissensee, 50,691 ....F 3
Weisswasser, 16,016 ....F 3
Werdau, 23,783 ....E 3
Wernigerode, 32,579 ....D 3
Wilhelm-Pieck-Stadt, 26,586 ....F 3
Wismar, 55,235 ....D 2
Wittenberg, 46,816 ....E 3
Wittenberge, 32,621 ....D 2
Wittstock, 10,358 ....E 2
Wolgast, 14,955 ....E 1
Wurzen, 24,349 ....E 3
Zehdenick, 12,306 ....E 2
Zeitz, 46,393 ....E 3
Zella-Mehlis, 17,121 ....D 3
Zerbst, 19,527 ....E 3
Zeulenroda, 18,534 ....D 3
Zittau, 43,259 ....F 3
Zwickau, 127,688 ....E 3

OTHER FEATURES

Altmark (reg.), 288,928 ....D 2
Arkona (cape) ....E 1
Baltic (sea) ....F 1
Black Elster (riv.) ....E 3
Brandenburg (region), 3,726,413 ....E 2
Brocken (mt.) ....D 3
Darsser Ort (point) ....E 1
Elbe (riv.) ....D 2
Elster (riv.) ....E 3
Erzgebirge (mts.) ....E 3
Fichtelberg (mt.) ....E 3
Havel (riv.) ....E 2
Kummerowersee (lake) ....E 2
Lusatia (reg.) ....F 3
Malchinersee (lake) ....E 2
Mecklenburg (reg.), 1,226,685....E 2
Mecklenburg (bay) ....D 1
Mulde (riv.) ....E 3
Müritzee (lake) ....E 2
Neisse (riv.) ....F 3
Oder (riv.) ....F 2
Penne (riv.) ....E 2
Plauersee (lake) ....E 2
Pomerania (region), 711,075 ....E 2
Pomeranian (bay) ....F 1
Rhön (mts.) ....D 3
Rügen (isl.), 92,348 ....E 1
Saale (riv.) ....D 3
Saxony (region), 5,318,661 ....E 3
Schaalsee (lake) ....D 2
Schwerinersee (lake) ....D 2
Spree (riv.) ....F 3
Spreewald (forest) ....F 3
Stettin (bay) ....F 2
Stubbenkammer (point) ....E 1
Thüringer Wald (forest) ....D 3
Thuringia (Thüringen) (reg.), 2,017,924 ....D 3
Tollensee (lake) ....E 2
Ücker (riv.) ....E 2
Unstrut (riv.) ....D 3
Usedom (isl.) ....F 1
Warnow (riv.) ....D 2
Werra (riv.) ....D 3
White Elster (riv.) ....E 3

WEST GERMANY

STATES

Baden-Württemberg, 8,909,700 ....C 4
Bavaria, 10,568,900 ....D 4
Berlin (West) (free city), 2,134,256 ....E 4
Bremen, 755,977 ....C 2
Hamburg, 1,817,122 ....D 2
Hesse, 5,422,600 ....C 3
Lower Saxony, 7,100,400 ....C 2
North Rhine-Westphalia, 17,129,800 ....B 3
Rhineland-Palatinate, 3,671,300 ....B 4
Saarland, 1,127,400 ....B 4
Schleswig-Holstein, 2,557,200 ....C 1

CITIES and TOWNS

Aachen, 177,642 ....B 3
Aalen, 35,102 ....D 4
Ahlen, 50,411 ....B 3
Ahrensburg, 25,829 ....D 2
Alfeld, 13,726 ....C 2
Alsdorf, 31,726 ....B 3
Altena, 31,164 ....B 3
Altona ....C 2
Alzey, 12,749 ....C 4
Amberg, 42,141 ....E 4
Andernach, 22,367 ....B 3
Ansbach, 30,083 ....D 4
Arnsberg, 22,577 ....C 3
Aschaffenburg, 56,236 ....C 4
Augsburg, 214,376 ....D 4
Aurich, 12,299 ....B 2
Backnang, 28,086 ....C 4
Bad Dürkheim, 15,792 ....C 4
Baden-Baden, 38,852 ....C 4
Bad Harzburg, 11,356 ....D 3
Bad Hersfeld, 23,494 ....C 3
Bad Homburg vor der Höhe, 41,236 ....C 3
Bad Honnef am Rhein, 20,649 ....B 3
Bad Kissingen, 12,672 ....D 3

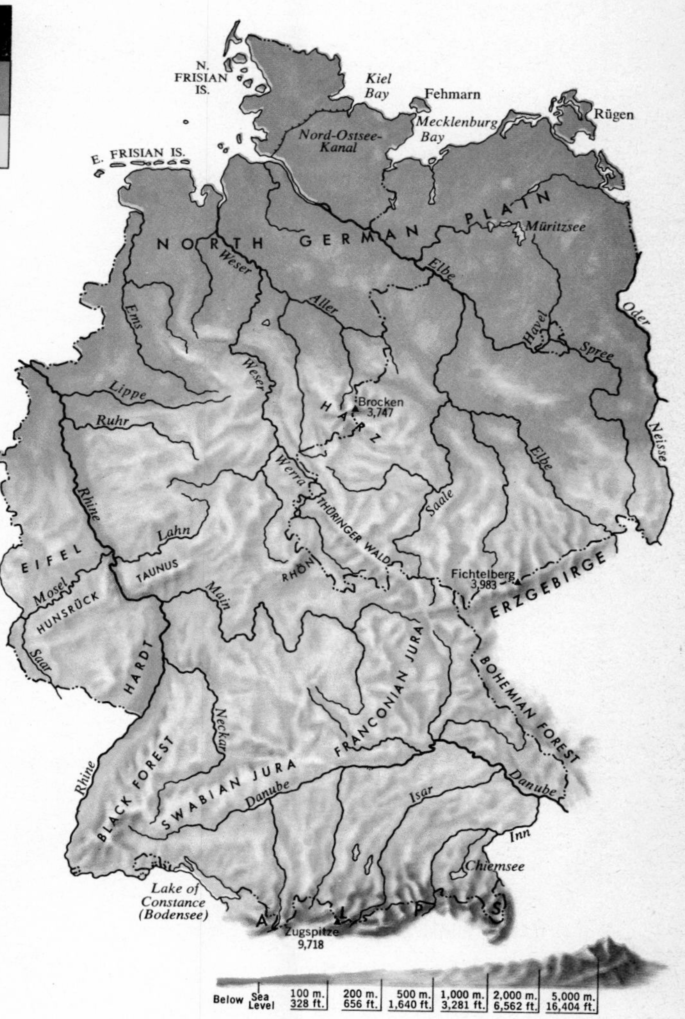

Bad Kreuznach, 42,707 ....B 4
Bad Mergentheim, 12,552 ....D 4
Bad Nauheim, 15,222 ....C 3
Bad Oeynhausen, 14,127 ....C 2
Bad Oldesloe, 18,915 ....D 2
Bad Pyrmont, 16,527 ....C 2
Bad Reichenhall, 14,894 ....E 5
Bad Salzuflen, 49,030 ....C 2
Bad Schwartau, 16,909 ....D 2
Bad Segeberg, 12,494 ....D 2
Bad Tölz, 12,468 ....D 5
Bad Vilbel, 18,315 ....C 3
Bad Wildungen, 12,189 ....C 3
Balingen, 13,693 ....C 4
Bamberg, 68,713 ....D 4
Bayreuth, 63,387 ....D 4
Bendorf, 14,361 ....B 3
Bensheim, 27,495 ....C 4
Berchtesgaden, 4,074 ....E 5
Bergisch Gladbach, 50,095 ....B 3
Berlin (West), 2,134,256 ....E 4
Betzdorf, 10,388 ....B 3
Biberach an der Riss, 25,597 ....C 4
Bielefeld, 169,347 ....C 2
Bietigheim, 22,488 ....C 4
Bingen, 24,452 ....B 4
Böblingen, 36,644 ....C 4
Bocholt, 48,134 ....B 3
Bochum, 346,886 ....B 3
Bonn (cap.), 299,376 ....B 3
Borghorst, 17,072 ....B 2
Borken, 30,614 ....B 3
Bottrop, 108,161 ....B 3
Brackwede, 40,254 ....C 3
Brake, 19,388 ....C 2
Bramsche, 10,733 ....B 2
Braunschweig (Brunswick), 225,168 ....D 2
Bremen, 607,184 ....C 2
Bremerhaven, 148,793 ....C 2
Brilon, 15,301 ....C 3
Bruchsal, 27,103 ....C 4
Brühl, 41,782 ....B 3
Brunswick, 225,168 ....D 2
Bückeburg, 13,396 ....C 2
Burghausen, 16,630 ....E 4
Burgsteinfurt, 12,554 ....B 2
Buxtehude, 23,140 ....C 2
Celle, 56,335 ....D 2
Charlottenburg ....F 4
Clausthal-Zellerfeld, 15,744 ....D 3
Cloppenburg, 18,162 ....B 2
Coburg, 41,369 ....D 3
Coesfeld, 26,565 ....B 3
Cologne, 866,308 ....B 3
Crailsheim, 16,687 ....D 4
Cuxhaven, 45,218 ....C 2
Dachau, 33,093 ....D 4
Darmstadt, 141,075 ....C 4
Deggendorf, 18,601 ....E 4
Delmenhorst, 63,685 ....C 2
Detmold, 64,473 ....C 3
Diepholz, 11,639 ....C 2
Dillenburg, 10,236 ....C 3
Dillingen an der Donau, 11,606 ....D 4
Dingolfing, 10,747 ....E 4
Donaueschingen, 11,643 ....C 5
Donauwörth, 11,266 ....D 4
Dorsten, 39,393 ....B 3
Dortmund, 648,883 ....B 3
Duderstadt, 10,421 ....D 3
Dudweiler, 30,078 ....B 4
Duisburg, 457,891 ....B 3
Dülmen, 21,094 ....B 3
Düren, 54,867 ....B 3
Düsseldorf, 680,806 ....B 3
Eberbach, 14,369 ....C 4
Ebingen, 22,004 ....C 4
Eckernförde, 21,971 ....D 1
Ehingen, 12,957 ....C 4
Eichstätt, 10,040 ....D 4
Einbeck, 18,618 ....C 3
Eiserfeld, 22,490 ....B 1
Ellwangen, 13,128 ....D 4
Elmshorn, 41,353 ....C 2
Emden, 48,313 ....B 2
Emmendingen, 15,986 ....B 4
Emmerich, 24,512 ....B 3
Erkelenz, 12,275 ....B 3
Erlangen, 85,727 ....D 4
Eschwege, 22,219 ....D 3
Eschweiler, 39,622 ....B 3
Espelkamp, 12,309 ....C 2
Essen, 704,769 ....B 3
Esslingen am Neckar, 86,497 ....C 4
Ettlingen, 21,342 ....C 4
Euskirchen, 41,965 ....B 3
Eutin, 18,177 ....D 1
Fellbach, 29,343 ....C 4
Flensburg, 96,778 ....C 1
Forchheim, 21,582 ....D 4
Frankenthal, 40,505 ....C 4
Frankfurt am Main, 660,410 ....C 3
Frechen, 30,786 ....B 3
Freiburg im Breisgau, 165,960 ....B 5
Freising, 30,264 ....D 4
Freudenstadt, 14,356 ....C 4
Friedberg, 17,401 ....C 3
Friedrichshafen, 42,483 ....C 5
Fulda, 44,262 ....C 3
Fürstenfeldbruck, 22,495 ....D 4
Fürth, 94,310 ....D 4
Füssen, 10,891 ....D 5
Gaggenau, 14,773 ....C 4
Garmisch-Partenkirchen, 27,313 ....D 5
Geesthacht, 23,594 ....D 2
Geislingen an der Steige, 27,209 ....C 4
Geldern, 22,602 ....B 3
Gelsenkirchen, 348,620 ....B 3
Giessen, 74,731 ....C 3
Gifhorn, 23,001 ....D 2
Glückstadt, 16,199 ....C 2
Goch, 27,721 ....B 3
Göggingen, 15,840 ....D 4
Göppingen, 46,899 ....C 4
Goslar, 41,653 ....D 3
Göttingen, 115,227 ....D 3
Grevenbroich, 28,197 ....B 3
Griesheim, 16,392 ....C 4
Gronau, 26,596 ....B 2
Gummersbach, 45,026 ....B 3
Günzburg, 13,449 ....D 4
Gütersloh, 76,343 ....C 3
Haar, 12,388 ....D 4
Hagen, 203,048 ....B 3
Haltern, 15,264 ....B 3
Hamburg, 1,817,122 ....D 2
Hameln, 47,114 ....C 2
Hamm, 84,302 ....B 3
Hanau, 55,674 ....C 3
Hannover, 517,783 ....C 2
Harburg-Wilhelmsburg ....C 2
Hassloch, 17,852 ....C 4
Haunstetten, 22,205 ....D 4
Heide, 23,419 ....C 1
Heidelberg, 121,929 ....C 4
Heidenheim an der Brenz, 50,170 ....D 4
Heilbronn, 99,440 ....C 4
Helmstedt, 27,161 ....D 2
Hennef, 26,589 ....B 3
Herborn, 10,395 ....C 3
Herford, 67,267 ....C 2
Herne, 100,798 ....B 3
Hildesheim, 95,926 ....D 2
Hockenheim, 15,615 ....C 4
Hof, 54,805 ....D 3
Holzminden, 22,273 ....C 3
Homburg, 32,258 ....B 4
Höxter, 32,823 ....C 3
Hürth, 52,011 ....B 3
Husum, 25,037 ....C 1
Hüttental, 40,287 ....C 3
Ibbenbüren, 17,780 ....B 2
Idar-Oberstein, 32,590 ....B 4
Immenstadt, 10,775 ....D 5
Ingolstadt, 71,954 ....D 4
Iserlohn, 57,792 ....B 3
Itzehoe, 35,678 ....C 2
Jülich, 20,152 ....B 3
Kaiserslautern, 99,859 ....B 4
Karlsruhe, 257,144 ....C 4
Kassel, 213,494 ....C 3
Kaufbeuren, 39,940 ....D 5
Kehl, 15,958 ....B 4
Kelheim, 11,701 ....D 4
Kempten, 44,617 ....D 5
Kevelaer, 20,257 ....B 3
Kiel, 276,600 ....C 1
Kirchheim unter Teck, 28,878 ....C 4
Kitzingen, 18,308 ....D 4
Kleve, 44,150 ....B 3
Koblenz, 106,189 ....B 3
Köln (Cologne), 866,308 ....B 3
Konstanz, 61,617 ....C 5
Korbach, 17,324 ....C 3
Kornwestheim, 28,574 ....C 4
Krefeld, 228,726 ....B 3
Kulmbach, 22,768 ....D 3
Lage, 30,949 ....C 3
Lahr, 25,028 ....B 4
Lampertheim, 24.053 ....C 4
Landau in der Pfalz, 32,318 ....C 4
Landsberg am Lech, 14,378 ....D 4
Landshut, 51.393 ....E 4
Langen, 30,230 ....C 4
Langenhagen, 37.077 ....C 2
Lauenburg, 11,445 ....D 2
Lauf an der Pegnitz, 15,771 ....D 4
Leer, 29,919 ....B 2
Lehrte, 21,792 ....D 2
Lemgo, 38,526 ....C 2
Lengerich, 21,451 ....B 2
Leverkusen, 111,588 ....B 3
Lichtenfels, 11,218 ....D 3
Limburg an der Lahn, 14,889 ....C 3
Lindau, 26,260 ....C 5
Lingen, 25,810 ....B 2
Lippstadt, 42,299 ....C 3
Lohr am Main, 11,291 ....C 4
Lörrach, 32,939 ....B 5
Lübbecke, 11,433 ....C 2
Lübeck, 242,191 ....D 2
Lüdenscheid, 80,096 ....B 3
Ludwigsburg, 79,538 ....C 4
Ludwigshafen am Rhein, 174,698 ....C 4
Lüneburg, 59,944 ....D 2
Lünen, 72,195 ....B 3

(continued on following page)

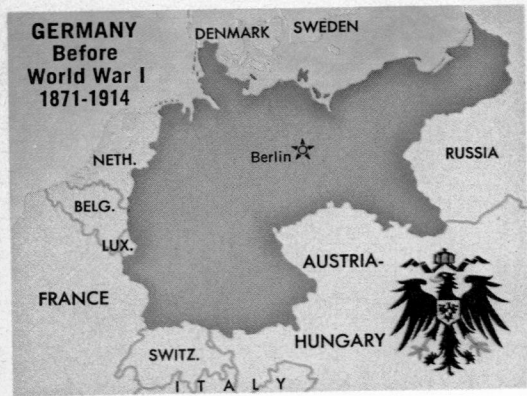

GERMANY Before World War I 1871-1914

GERMANY Between Wars 1919-1937

Occupied GERMANY 1945-1949

WEST GERMANY (continued)

Mainz, 176,720 ....C 4
Mannheim, 330,920 ....C 4
Marburg an der Lahn, 51,382 ....C 3
Marktredwitz, 15,605 ....E 3
Marl, 75,779 ....B 3
Mayen, 18,485 ....B 3
Memmingen, 35,454 ....D 5
Meppen, 17,892 ....B 2
Merzig, 12,443 ....B 4
Meschede, 16,222 ....C 3
Metzingen, 14,093 ....C 4
Minden, 51,527 ....C 2
Mittenwald, 10,026 ....D 5
Mölln, 15,307 ....D 2
Mönchengladbach, 152,172 ....B 3
Moosburg an der Isar, 11,730 ....D 4
Mosbach, 13,871 ....C 4
Mühldorf am Inn, 10,998 ....E 4
Mülheim an der Ruhr, 191,080 ....B 3
Münden, 19,111 ....C 3
Munich (München), 1,326,331 ....D 4
Münster, 204,571 ....B 3
Neckarsulm, 18,523 ....C 4
Neheim-Hüsten, 36,864 ....C 3
Neuburg an der Donau, 18,530 ....D 4
Neu-Isenburg, 36,014 ....C 3
Neumarkt in der Oberpfalz, 18,930 ....D 4
Neumünster, 84,636 ....C 1
Neunkirchen, 44,326 ....B 4
Neuss, 117,599 ....B 3
Neustadt an der Weinstrasse, 51,058 ....C 4
Neustadt bei Coburg, 12,496 ....D 3
Neustadt in Holstein, 16,222 ....D 1
Neu-Ulm, 27,710 ....D 4
Neuwied, 31,359 ....B 3

Nienburg, 22,467 ....C 2
Norden, 16,355 ....B 2
Nordenham, 27,368 ....C 2
Nordhorn, 42,895 ....B 2
Nördlingen, 14,238 ....D 4
Northeim, 19,150 ....C 3
Nuremberg (Nürnberg), 477,108 ....D 4
Nürtingen, 21,284 ....C 4
Oberammergau, 4,641 ....D 5
Oberhausen, 249,045 ....B 3
Oberlahnstein, 20,131 ....B 3
Oberursel, 24,933 ....C 3
Ochtrup, 15,823 ....B 2
Offenbach am Main, 118,754 ....C 3
Offenburg, 32,628 ....B 4
Oldenburg, 131,434 ....C 2
Opladen, 43,531 ....B 3
Osterholz-Scharmbeck, 15,211 ....C 2
Osterode am Harz, 16,757 ....D 3
Paderborn, 68,735 ....C 3
Papenburg, 16,714 ....B 2
Passau, 31,574 ....E 4
Peine, 30,882 ....D 2
Penzberg, 10,784 ....D 5
Pforzheim, 90,780 ....C 4
Pfullingen, 15,967 ....C 4
Pinneberg, 36,439 ....C 2
Pirmasens, 56,172 ....B 4
Plettenberg, 30,233 ....C 3
Plön, 11,142 ....D 1
Porz am Rhein, 78,076 ....B 3
Preetz, 14,653 ....C 1
Radolfzell, 15,512 ....C 5
Rastatt, 29,102 ....B 4
Rastede, 16,851 ....C 2
Ratingen, 43,420 ....B 3
Ratzeburg, 12,335 ....D 2
Ravensburg, 31,819 ....C 5
Recklinghausen, 125,535 ....B 3
Regensburg, 128,083 ....E 4
Rehau, 10,565 ....D 3

Remscheid, 137,374 ....B 3
Rendsburg, 35,453 ....C 1
Reutlingen, 77,853 ....C 4
Rheine, 51,167 ....B 2
Rheinfelden, 16,547 ....B 5
Rheinhausen, 71,698 ....B 3
Rheydt, 100,633 ....B 3
Rosenheim, 36,376 ....D 5
Rotenburg, 16,664 ....C 2
Roth bei Nürnberg, 11,550 ....D 4
Rothenburg ob der Tauber, 12,002 ....D 4
Rottenburg am Neckar, 13,495 ....C 4
Rottweil, 19,881 ....C 4
Rüsselsheim, 57,308 ....C 4
Saarbrücken, 130,765 ....B 4
Saarlouis (Saarlautern), 36,251 ....B 4
Säckingen, 12,614 ....C 5
Salzgitter, 118,020 ....D 2
Sankt Ingbert, 28,774 ....B 4
Sankt Wendel, 10,138 ....B 4
Schleswig, 33,317 ....C 1
Schönebeck ....E 4
Schöningen, 14,551 ....D 2
Schramberg, 19,050 ....C 4
Schwabach, 25,774 ....D 4
Schwäbisch Gmünd, 44,628 ....C 4
Schwäbisch Hall, 23,765 ....C 4
Schwandorf in Bayern, 15,995 ....E 4
Schweinfurt, 59,293 ....D 3
Schwelm, 34,199 ....B 3
Schwenningen am Neckar, 35,487 ....C 4
Schwetzingen, 16,613 ....C 4
Seesen, 13,027 ....D 3
Selb, 18,498 ....E 3
Sennestadt, 20,518 ....C 3
Siegburg, 34,586 ....B 3
Siegen, 57,996 ....C 3
Sindelfingen, 41,029 ....C 4
Singen, 39,719 ....C 5

Soest, 40,580 ....C 3
Solingen, 175,895 ....B 3
Soltau, 14,981 ....C 2
Sonthofen, 16,504 ....D 5
Spandau ....E 3
Speyer, 42,323 ....C 4
Springe, 12,698 ....C 2
Stade, 31,637 ....C 2
Stadthagen, 16,876 ....C 2
Starnberg, 10,622 ....D 4
Stolberg, 39,589 ....B 3
Straubing, 36,943 ....E 4
Stuttgart, 628,412 ....C 4
Sulzbach-Rosenberg, 18,691 ....D 4
Tailfingen, 16,787 ....C 4
Tempelhof ....F 4
Traunstein, 14,117 ....E 5
Trier, 103,412 ....B 4
Tübingen, 56,008 ....C 4
Tuttlingen, 26,587 ....C 5
Überlingen, 12,837 ....C 5
Uelzen, 23,775 ....D 2
Uetersen, 16,734 ....C 2
Ulm, 92,486 ....C 4
Varel, 12,759 ....C 2
Vechta, 16,326 ....C 2
Verden, 16,741 ....C 2
Viersen, 83,988 ....B 3
Villingen im Schwarzwald, 37,652 ....C 4
Völklingen, 39,763 ....B 4
Waldshut, 16,011 ....C 5
Walsrode, 13,904 ....C 2
Wangen im Allgäu, 14,159 ....C 5
Wanne-Eickel, 99,923 ....B 3
Warendorf, 18,969 ....B 3
Wedel, 31,134 ....C 2
Weiden in der Oberpfalz, 43,097 ....D 4
Weilheim in Oberbayern, 14,433 ....D 5
Weingarten, 18,420 ....C 4
Weinheim, 29,544 ....C 4
Weissenburg in Bayern, 13,718 ....D 4

Wertheim, 12,035 ....C 4
Wesel, 44,710 ....B 3
Westerstede, 16,387 ....C 3
Wetzlar, 37,230 ....C 3
Wiesbaden, 260,614 ....C 4
Wilhelmshaven, 103,150 ....B 2
Witten, 97,807 ....B 3
Wolfenbüttel, 41,225 ....D 2
Wolfsburg, 89,442 ....D 2
Worms, 78,004 ....C 4
Wunstorf, 17,589 ....C 2
Wuppertal, 414,722 ....B 3
Würzburg, 120,317 ....C 4
Zirndorf, 15,363 ....D 4
Zweibrücken, 32,883 ....B 4
Zwischenahn, 19,906 ....C 2

OTHER FEATURES

Aller (riv.) ....C 2
Allgäu (reg.) ....D 5
Alz (riv.) ....E 4
Ammersee (lake) ....D 4
Amrum (isl.), 2,155 ....B 1
Baltrum (isl.), 924 ....B 2
Bavarian (forest) ....E 4
Bavarian Alps (mts.) ....D 5
Black (forest) ....B 4
Bodensee (Constance) (lake) ....C 5
Bohemian (forest) ....E 4
Borkum (isl.), 5,348 ....B 2
Breisgau (reg.), 675,500 ....B 5
Chiemsee (lake) ....E 5
Constance (lake) ....C 5
Danube (Donau) (riv.) ....C 4
Dümmer (lake) ....C 2
East Friesland (region), 599,700 ....B 2
East Frisian (isls.), 20,962 ....B 2
Eder (res.) ....C 3
Eider (riv.) ....C 1

Eifel (mts.) ....B 3
Elbe (riv.) ....C 2
Ems (riv.) ....B 2
Fehmarn (isl.), 12,586 ....D 1
Feldberg (mt.) ....B 5
Fichtelgebirge (mts.) ....D 3
Föhr (isl.), 8,585 ....C 1
Franconian Jura (mts.) ....D 4
Frankenwald (forest) ....D 3
Fulda (riv.) ....C 3
Grosser Arber (mt.) ....E 4
Halligen, The (isls.), 5,112 ....C 1
Hardt (mts.) ....B 4
Harz (mts.) ....D 3
Hegau (reg.) ....C 5
Helgoland (isl.), 3,184 ....B 1
Hunsrück (mts.) ....B 4
Iller (riv.) ....D 4
Inn (riv.) ....E 4
Isar (riv.) ....D 4
Jade (bay) ....C 2
Juist (isl.), 2,147 ....B 2
Kaiserstuhl (mt.) ....B 4
Kiel (canal) ....C 1
Königssee (lake) ....E 5
Lahn (riv.) ....C 3
Langeoog (isl.), 2,611 ....B 2
Lech (riv.) ....D 4
Leine (riv.) ....C 2
Lippe (riv.) ....C 3
Lüneburger Heide (dist.) ....C 2
Main (riv.) ....C 3
Mecklenburg (bay) ....D 1
Mosel (riv.) ....B 3
Neckar (riv.) ....C 4
Nord-Ostsee (Kiel) (canal) ....C 1
Norderney (isl.), 8,983 ....B 2

Nordstrand (isl.), 3,079 ....C 1
North (sea) ....A 1
North Friesland (reg.), 163,800 ....C 1
North Frisian (islands), 36,259 ....B 1
Oberpfälzer Wald (forest) ....E 4
Odenwald (forest) ....C 4
Pellworm (isl.), 2,033 ....C 1
Regen (riv.) ....E 4
Regnitz (riv.) ....D 4
Rhine (Rhein) (riv.) ....B 3
Rhön (mts.) ....C 3
Ruhr (riv.) ....B 3
Saar (riv.) ....B 4
Salzach (riv.) ....E 5
Sauer (riv.) ....B 4
Sauerland (reg.) ....B 3
Schwarzwald (Black) (forest) ....C 4
Spessart (range) ....C 4
Spiekeroog (isl.), 823 ....B 2
Starnbergersee (lake) ....D 5
Steigerwald (forest) ....D 4
Steinhuder (lake) ....C 2
Swabian Jura (mts.) ....C 4
Sylt (isl.), 20,407 ....C 1
Tauber (riv.) ....C 4
Taunus (range) ....C 3
Tegernsee (lake) ....D 5
Teutoburger Wald (forest) ....C 2
Vechte (riv.) ....B 2
Vogelsberg (mt.) ....C 3
Walchensee (lake) ....D 5
Wangerooge (isl.), 2,126 ....B 2
Wasserkuppe (mt.) ....C 3
Watzmann (mt.) ....E 5
Werra (riv.) ....D 3
Weser (riv.) ....C 2
Westerwald (forest) ....B 3
Wurmsee (Starnbergersee) (lake) ....D 5
Zugspitze (mt.) ....D 5

Agriculture, Industry and Resources

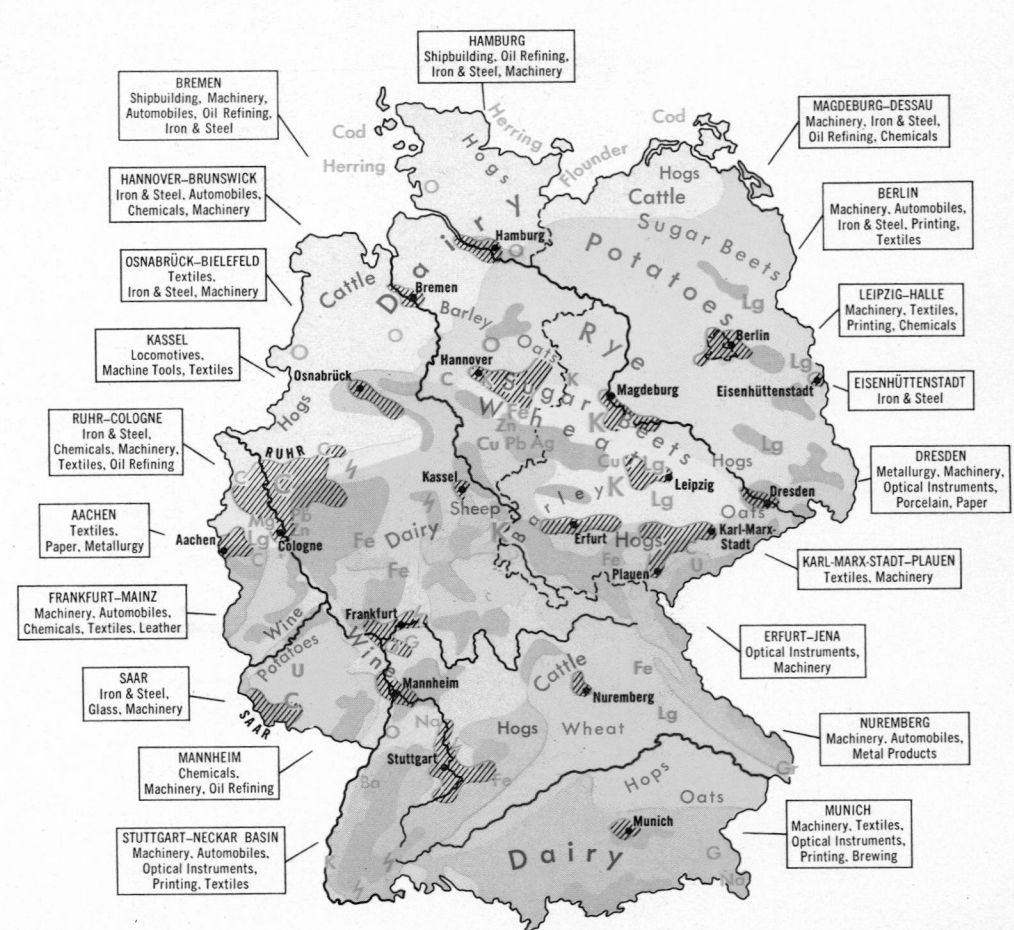

DOMINANT LAND USE

- Wheat, Sugar Beets
- Cereals (chiefly rye, oats, barley)
- Potatoes, Rye
- Dairy, Livestock
- Mixed Cereals, Dairy
- Truck Farming
- Grapes, Fruit
- Forests

MAJOR MINERAL OCCURRENCES

Ag Silver
Ba Barite
C Coal
Cu Copper
Fe Iron Ore
G Natural Gas
Gr Graphite
K Potash
Lg Lignite
Mg Magnesium
Na Salt
O Petroleum
Pb Lead
U Uranium
Zn Zinc

⚡ Water Power
▨ Major Industrial Areas

HAMBURG
Shipbuilding, Oil Refining, Iron & Steel, Machinery

BREMEN
Shipbuilding, Machinery, Automobiles, Oil Refining, Iron & Steel

MAGDEBURG-DESSAU
Machinery, Iron & Steel, Oil Refining, Chemicals

HANNOVER-BRUNSWICK
Iron & Steel, Automobiles, Chemicals, Machinery

BERLIN
Machinery, Automobiles, Iron & Steel, Printing, Textiles

OSNABRÜCK-BIELEFELD
Textiles, Iron & Steel, Machinery

LEIPZIG-HALLE
Machinery, Textiles, Printing, Chemicals

KASSEL
Locomotives, Machine Tools, Textiles

EISENHÜTTENSTADT
Iron & Steel

RUHR-COLOGNE
Iron & Steel, Chemicals, Machinery, Textiles, Oil Refining

DRESDEN
Metallurgy, Machinery, Optical Instruments, Porcelain, Paper

AACHEN
Textiles, Paper, Metallurgy

KARL-MARX-STADT-PLAUEN
Textiles, Machinery

FRANKFURT-MAINZ
Machinery, Automobiles, Chemicals, Textiles, Leather

ERFURT-JENA
Optical Instruments, Machinery

SAAR
Iron & Steel, Glass, Machinery

NUREMBERG
Machinery, Automobiles, Metal Products

MANNHEIM
Chemicals, Machinery, Oil Refining

MUNICH
Machinery, Textiles, Optical Instruments, Printing, Brewing

STUTTGART-NECKAR BASIN
Machinery, Automobiles, Optical Instruments, Printing, Textiles

NETHERLANDS
AREA 13,958 sq. mi.
POPULATION 13,077,000
CAPITALS The Hague, Amsterdam
LARGEST CITY Amsterdam
HIGHEST POINT Vaalserberg, 1,056 ft.
MONETARY UNIT guilder
MAJOR LANGUAGE Dutch
MAJOR RELIGIONS Protestantism, Roman Catholicism

BELGIUM
AREA 11,779 sq. mi.
POPULATION 9,660,154
CAPITAL Brussels
LARGEST CITY Brussels (greater)
HIGHEST POINT Botrange 2,277 ft.
MONETARY UNIT Belgian franc
MAJOR LANGUAGES French (Walloon), Flemish
MAJOR RELIGION Roman Catholicism

LUXEMBOURG
AREA 999 sq. mi.
POPULATION 339,000
CAPITAL Luxembourg
LARGEST CITY Luxembourg
HIGHEST POINT Ardennes Plateau, 1,825 ft.
MONETARY UNIT Luxembourg franc
MAJOR LANGUAGES Luxembourgeois (German dialect), French, German
MAJOR RELIGION Roman Catholicism

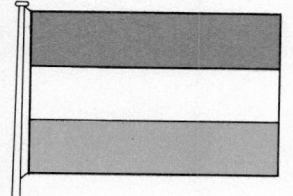
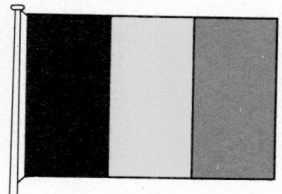

BELGIUM

PROVINCES

Antwerp, 1,529,826 ....F 6
Brabant, 2,166,372 ....F 7
East Flanders, 1,310,638 ....D 7
Hainault, 1,331,810 ....D 7
Liège, 1,016,131 ....H 7
Limburg, 650,338 ....G 6
Luxembourg, 219,369 ....G 9
Namur, 383,618 ....F 8
West Flanders, 1,052,052 ....B 7

CITIES and TOWNS†

Aalst, 45,900 ....D 7
Aalter, 8,569 ....C 6
Aarlen (Arlon), 14,191 ....H 9
Aarschot, 12,329 ....F 7
Aat (Ath), 11,094 ....D 7
Adinkerke, 2,713 ....A 6
Alken, 8,054 ....G 7
Alost (Aalst), 45,900 ....D 7
Amay, 7,561 ....G 7
Andenne, 8,068 ....G 7
Anderlecht, 103,832 ....B 9
Anderlues, 12,930 ....D 8
Antoing, 3,435 ....C 7
Antwerp (Antwerpen), 234,099 ..E 6

Antwerp, *673,259 ....E 6
Ardooie, 7,163 ....C 7
Arendonk, 9,516 ....G 6
Arlon, 14,191 ....H 9
As, 4,087 ....G 6
Asse, 12,631 ....E 7
Assebroek, 15,195 ....C 6
Assesse, 1,138 ....G 8
Ath, 11,094 ....D 7
Athus, 7,185 ....H 9
Audenarde (Oudenaarde),
  21,980 ....D 7
Auderghem, 32,782 ....B 9
Autelbas, 1,606 ....H 9
Auvelais, 8,412 ....F 8
Aywaille, 3,813 ....H 8
Baerle-Duc, 2,171 ....F 6
Balen, 14,719 ....G 6
Barvaux, 1,727 ....H 8
Basècles, 4,245 ....D 7
Bastogne (Bastenaken),
  6,476 ....H 9
Beaumont, 1,762 ....E 8
Beauraing, 2,703 ....F 8
Berchem, 49,880 ....E 6
Berchem-Sainte-Agathe,
  17,689 ....B 9
Bergen (Mons), 27,042 ....E 8
Bertrix, 4,481 ....G 9
Beveren, 15,350 ....E 6

Bilzen, 7,000 ....G 7
Binche, 10,340 ....E 8
Blankenberge, 10,400 ....C 6
Bocholt, 5,582 ....H 6
Boom, 17,280 ....E 6
Borgerhout, 50,226 ....E 6
Borgloon, 3,543 ....G 7
Borgworm (Waremme),
  7,623 ....G 7
Bouillon, 3,089 ....G 9
Bourg-Leopold (Leopoldsburg),
  9,621 ....G 6
Boussu, 11,626 ....D 8
Bovigny, 1,015 ....H 8
Braine-l'Alleud, 16,028 ....F 7
Braine-le-Comte, 11,343 ....D 7
Bredene, 9,381 ....B 6
Bree, 10,462 ....H 6
Bruges (Brugge), 52,249 ....C 6
Bruges, *112,611 ....C 6
Brussels (Bruxelles) (cap.),
  *1,073,111 ....C 9
Charleroi, 24,895 ....E 8
Charleroi, *218,089 ....E 8
Châtelet, 15,314 ....F 8
Châtelineau, 20,293 ....F 8
Chièvres, 3,154 ....D 7
Chimay, 3,309 ....E 8
Ciney, 7,431 ....G 8
Comblain-au-Pont, 3,538 ......G 8

Comines, 8,219 ....B 7
Couillet, 15,055 ....E 8
Courcelles, 17,157 ....E 8
Courtrai, 45,310 ....C 7
Couvin, 4,192 ....F 8
Cul-des-Sarts, 993 ....E 9
Deinze, 6,214 ....D 7
Denderleeuw, 9,699 ....E 7
Dendermonde, 9,663 ....E 6
De Panne, 6,792 ....A 6
Dessel, 7,170 ....G 6
Deurne, 75,819 ....F 6
Diegem, 4,760 ....C 9
Diest, 9,587 ....F 7
Diksmuide, 6,557 ....B 6
Dilbeek, 13,620 ....B 9
Dinant, 9,700 ....G 8
Dison, 8,809 ....H 7
Dixmude (Diksmuide),
  6,557 ....B 6
Doel, 1,395 ....E 6
Doornik (Tournai), 33,309 .....C 7
Dour, 10,407 ....D 8
Drogenbos, 4,648 ....B 9
Drongen, 8,312 ....D 6
Dudzele, 2,112 ....C 6
Duffel, 13,560 ....F 6
Ecaussinnes d'Enghien,
  6,557 ....E 7
Edingen (Enghien), 4,279 .....D 7

Eeklo, 19,007 ....D 6
Eernegem, 5,865 ....B 6
Eigenbrakel (Braine-l'Alleud),
  16,028 ....E 7
Ekeren, 24,535 ....E 6
Ellezelles, 3,676 ....D 7
Enghien, 4,279 ....D 7
Ensival, 5,515 ....H 7
Erquelinnes, 4,812 ....E 8
Esneux, 5,923 ....H 7
Essen, 10,515 ....F 6
Etalle, 1,179 ....H 9
Etterbeek, 52,299 ....C 9
Eupen, 14,856 ....J 7
Evere, 24,289 ....C 9
Evergem, 12,329 ....D 6
Flémalle-Haute, 7,800 ....G 7
Fleurus, 8,475 ....F 8
Florennes, 4,070 ....F 8
Florenville, 2,526 ....G 9
Forest, 55,799 ....B 9
Fosses-la-Ville, 3,887 ....F 8
Frameries, 11,624 ....D 8
Frasnes-lez-Buissenal, 2,672 ..D 7
Furnes (Veurne), 7,475 ....B 6
Ganshoren, 19,154 ....B 9
Gaurain-Ramecroix, 3,599 ....D 7
Gedinne, 1,021 ....F 9
Geel, 28,484 ....F 6
Geldenaken (Jodoigne), 4,194 ..F 7

Gembloux, 11,030 ....F 7
Gemmenich, 2,608 ....H 7
Genk, 55,596 ....H 7
Gent (Ghent), 153,301 ....D 6
Gentbrugge, 22,986 ....D 7
Geraardsbergen, 9,201 ....D 7
Ghent, 153,301 ....D 6
Ghent, *229,687 ....D 6
Gilly, 24,155 ....E 8
Gosselies, 10,970 ....E 8
Grammont (Geraardsbergen),
  9,201 ....D 7
Haacht, 4,372 ....F 7
Hal (Halle), 20,071 ....E 7
Halen, 5,321 ....G 7
Halle, 20,071 ....E 7
Hamme, 17,083 ....E 6
Hamont, 6,626 ....H 6
Hannut (Hannuit), 3,069 ......G 7
Harelbeke, 17,981 ....C 7
Hasselt, 38,773 ....G 7
Havelange, 1,495 ....G 8
Heer, 578 ....F 8
Heist, 9,289 ....C 6
Heist-op-den-Berg,
  13,206 ....F 6
Herbeumont, 590 ....G 9
Herentals, 18,377 ....F 6
Herstal, 29,602 ....H 7
Herve, 4,357 ....H 7
Hoboken, 31,815 ....E 6
Hoei (Huy), 13,398 ....G 7
Hoeselt, 5,570 ....H 7
Hoogstraten, 4,376 ....F 6
Hornu, 10,905 ....D 8
Houffalize, 1,297 ....H 8
Huy, 13,398 ....G 7
Ieper, 18,461 ....B 7
Ingelmunster, 9,973 ....C 7
Ixelles, 92,532 ....C 9
Izegem, 22,729 ....C 7
Jambes, 14,924 ....G 7
Jemappes, 12,906 ....D 8
Jemeppe, 12,232 ....G 7
Jette, 37,354 ....B 9
Jodoigne, 4,194 ....F 7
Jumet, 28,811 ....E 8
Kain, 4,900 ....C 7
Kalmthout, 12,122 ....F 6
Kapellen, 12,297 ....F 6
Kessel-Lo, 21,351 ....F 7
Knokke, 14,268 ....C 6
Koekelare, 6,423 ....B 6
Koekelberg, 17,348 ....B 9
Koersel, 10,756 ....G 6
Kontich, 13,193 ....E 6
Kortemark, 5,839 ....C 6
Kortrijk (Courtrai),
  45,310 ....C 7
Kraainem, 10,560 ....C 9
La Louvière, 23,447 ....E 8
La Louvière, *113,795 ....E 8
La Roche-en-Ardenne,
  1,894 ....H 8
Lanaken, 8,216 ....H 7
Landen, 5,247 ....G 7
Langemark, 4,787 ....B 7
Lede, 10,229 ....D 7
Ledeberg, 11,056 ....D 7
Lens, 1,790 ....D 7
Leopoldsburg, 9,621 ....G 6
Lessines (Lessen), 9,047 .....D 7
Leuven (Louvain), 32,125 .....F 7
Leuze, 7,128 ....D 7
Libramont, 2,774 ....G 9
Lichtervelde, 7,372 ....C 7
Liedekerke, 10,273 ....E 7
Liège, 150,127 ....H 7
Liège, *446,990 ....H 7
Lier (Lierre), 28,557 ....F 6
Lierneux, 2,847 ....H 8
Limburg (Limburg),
  3,973 ....J 7
Linkebeek, 4,096 ....C10
Lokeren, 26,654 ....E 6
Lommel, 20,567 ....G 6
Looz (Borgloon), 3,543 ....G 7
Louvain, 32,125 ....F 7
Luik (Liège), 150,127 ....H 7
Maaseik, 8,383 ....H 6
Machelen, 7,331 ....C 9
Maldegem, 14,182 ....D 6
Malines (Mechelen),
  65,728 ....F 6
Malmédy, 6,482 ....J 8
Marche-en-Famenne, 4,423 ..G 8
Marchin, 4,361 ....G 7
Marcinelle, 25,992 ....E 8
Mariembourg, 1,776 ....F 8
Martelange, 1,594 ....H 9
Mechelen, 65,728 ....F 6
Meerhout, 8,359 ....F 6
Meerle, 2,809 ....F 6
Melsbroek, 2,034 ....D 9
Menen (Menin), 22,458 ......C 7
Merchtem, 8,772 ....E 7
Merelbeke, 13,755 ....D 7

Merksem, 39,011 ....E 6
Merksplas, 4,950 ....F 6
Messancy, 3,064 ....H 9
Mettet, 3,366 ....F 8
Meulebeke, 10,619 ....C 7
Moeskroen (Mouscron),
  37,624 ....C 7
Mol, 27,320 ....G 6
Molenbeek-Saint-Jean,
  67,271 ....B 9
Mons, 27,042 ....E 8
Montegnée, 11,882 ....G 7
Montignies-sur-Sambre,
  24,048 ....F 8
Mortsel, 27,999 ....E 6
Mouscron, 37,624 ....C 7
Namur (Namen), 32,621 ......F 8
Neerlinter, 1,431 ....F 7
Neerpelt, 8,273 ....G 6
Neufchâteau, 2,739 ....G 9
Nieuwpoort (Nieuport),
  7,165 ....B 6
Ninove, 12,087 ....D 7
Niveles (Nijvel), 15,384 ......E 7
Oostende (Ostend), 57,749 ...B 6
Oostkamp, 8,560 ....C 6
Ophoven, 2,487 ....H 6
Opwijk, 9,622 ....E 7
Ostend, 57,749 ....B 6
Oud-Turnhout, 8,219 ....F 6
Oudenaarde, 21,980 ....D 7
Ougrée, 21,152 ....H 7
Overijse, 14,119 ....F 7
Overpelt, 10,002 ....G 6
Peer, 5,882 ....G 6
Péruwelz, 7,814 ....D 8
Perwez (Perwijs), 2,858 ......F 7
Philippeville, 1,822 ....E 8
Poperinge, 12,619 ....B 7
Poppel, 2,246 ....G 6
Putte, 6,856 ....F 6
Quaregnon, 18,289 ....D 8
Quiévrain, 5,685 ....D 8
Raeren, 3,490 ....J 7
Rance, 1,443 ....E 8
Rebecq-Rognon, 3,831 ....E 7
Renaix (Ronse), 25,371 ....D 7
Retie, 6,339 ....G 6
Riezes, 307 ....E 9
Rochefort, 4,242 ....G 8
Roeselare, 40,077 ....C 7
Roeulx, 2,605 ....E 8
Ronse, 25,371 ....D 7
Roulers (Roeselare), 40,077 ..C 7
Ruisbroek, 5,685 ....B 9
's Gravenbrakel (Braine-le-Comte),
  11,343 ....D 7
Saint-Georges, 6,085 ....G 7
Saint-Gérard, 1,626 ....F 8
Saint-Gilles, 57,238 ....B 9
Saint-Hubert, 3,104 ....G 8
Saint-Josse-ten-Noode,
  24,335 ....C 9
Saint-Léger, 1,600 ....H 9
Saint-Vith (Sankt-Vith),
  2,935 ....J 8
Schaerbeek, 120,650 ....C 9
Schoten, 28,543 ....F 6
Seraing, 40,937 ....G 7
Sint-Amandsberg, 24,778 ....D 6
Sint-Andries, 15,062 ....C 6
Sint-Lenaarts, 4,464 ....F 6
Sint-Niklaas, 48,851 ....E 6
Sint-Pieters-Leeuw, 15,978 ..B 9
Sint-Truiden (Saint-Trond),
  21,131 ....G 7
Sivry, 1,384 ....E 8
Soignies, 11,320 ....D 7
Spa, 9,683 ....H 8
Staden, 5,581 ....B 7
Stavelot, 4,661 ....H 8
Steenokkerzeel, 3,877 ....C 9
Stene, 9,304 ....B 6
Stokkem, 3,380 ....H 6
Strombeek-Bever, 10,027 ....C 9
Tamines, 8,139 ....F 8
Tamise (Temse), 14,559 ......E 6
Templeuve, 3,737 ....C 7
Temse, 14,559 ....E 6
Termonde (Dendermonde),
  9,663 ....E 6
Tessenderlo, 10,665 ....G 6
Theux, 5,491 ....H 8
Thuin, 5,877 ....E 8
Tielt, Brabant, 3,813 ....F 7
Tielt, West Flanders,
  13,887 ....C 7
Tienen (Tirlemont), 22,660 ...F 7
Tongeren (Tongres), 16,880 ..G 7
Torhout, 14,301 ....C 6
Tournai, 33,309 ....C 7
Tronchiennes (Drongen),
  8,312 ....D 6
Tubize (Tubeke),
  10,269 ....E 7
Turnhout, 37,828 ....F 6
Uccle (Ukkel), 76,579 ....B 9
Verviers, 35,730 ....H 7

(continued on following page)

Agriculture, Industry and Resources

DOMINANT LAND USE

- Dairy, Truck Farming
- Cash Crops, Livestock
- Mixed Cereals, Dairy
- Specialized Horticulture
- Grapes, Wine
- Forests
- Sand Dunes

MAJOR MINERAL OCCURRENCES

C   Coal   Na Salt
Fe Iron Ore   O   Petroleum
G   Natural Gas

///// Major Industrial Areas

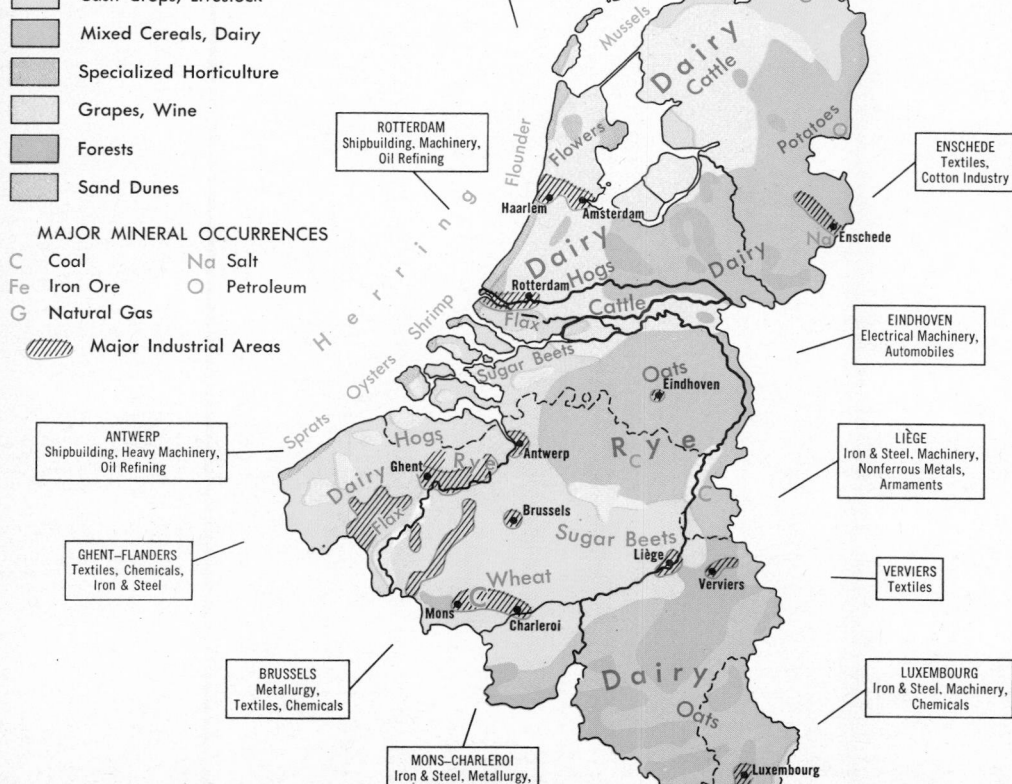

AMSTERDAM–HAARLEM
Shipbuilding, Machinery, Iron & Steel

ROTTERDAM
Shipbuilding, Machinery, Oil Refining

ENSCHEDE
Textiles, Cotton Industry

EINDHOVEN
Electrical Machinery, Automobiles

ANTWERP
Shipbuilding, Heavy Machinery, Oil Refining

LIÈGE
Iron & Steel, Machinery, Nonferrous Metals, Armaments

GHENT–FLANDERS
Textiles, Chemicals, Iron & Steel

VERVIERS
Textiles

BRUSSELS
Metallurgy, Textiles, Chemicals

MONS–CHARLEROI
Iron & Steel, Metallurgy, Machinery, Chemicals

LUXEMBOURG
Iron & Steel, Machinery, Chemicals

BELGIUM (continued)

Veurne, 7,475 ....B 6
Vielsalm, 3,702 ....J 8
Villers-devant-Orval, 777 ....G 9
Vilvoorde (Vilvorde), 34,040 ..H 9
Virton, 3,956 ....H 9
Visé, 6,595 ....J 8
Vorst (Forest), 55,799 ......D 9
Waarschoot, 7,852 ......D 6
Waasten (Warneton), 3,215 ..B 7
Waha, 2,664 ....G 8
Waimes, 2,787 ....J 8
Walcourt, 2,077 ....F 8
Wandre, 6,833 ....J 7
Waregem, 16,928 ....C 7
Waremme, 7,623 ....G 7
Warneton, 3,215 ....B 7
Wasmes, 13,933 ....D 7
Waterloo, 14,615 ....F 7
Watermael-Boitsfort, 24,730 ..C 9
Watervliet, 1,812 ....D 6
Wavre (Waver), 11,007 ......F 7
Weismes (Waimes), 2,787 ....J 8
Wemmel, 11,404 ....B 9
Wenduine, 1,756 ....C 6
Wervik, 12,728 ....B 7
Westende, 2,746 ....B 6
Westerlo, 7,630 ....F 7
Wetteren, 20,775 ....D 7
Wezembeek-Oppem, 10,536 ..D 9
Wezet (Visé), 6,595 ....H 7
Willebroek, 15,650 ....E 7
Wilrijk, 42,109 ....F 6
Wingene, 7,178 ....C 6
Woluwe-Saint-Lambert, 44,102 ..C 9
Woluwe-Saint-Pierre, 37,314 ..C 9
Wolvertem, 5,326 ....E 7
Ypres (Ieper), 18,461 ......B 7
Yvoir, 2,837 ....F 8
Zaventem, 9,941 ....C 9
Zeebrugge ....C 6
Zele, 18,386 ....E 7
Zellik, 5,165 ....B 9
Zelzate, 11,751 ....D 6
Zinnik (Soignies), 11,320 ....D 7
Zonhoven, 12,910 ....G 7
Zottegem, 6,905 ....D 7

OTHER FEATURES

Albert (canal) ....F 6
Ardennes (plateau) ....J 8
Botrange (mt.) ....J 8
Dender (river) ....D 7
Dyle (river) ....F 7
Hohe Venn (plateau) ....H 8
Lesse (river) ....F 8
Mark (river) ....F 6
Meuse (river) ....H 7
Nethe (river) ....F 6
Ourthe (river) ....H 8
Rupel (river) ....F 7
Scheldt (Schelde) (river) ..C 7
Schnee Eifel (plateau) ......J 9
Semois (river) ....G 9
Senne (river) ....E 7
Vesdre (river) ....H 7
Weissenstein (mt.) ....J 8
Yser (river) ....B 7
Zitterwald (plateau) ....J 8

LUXEMBOURG

CITIES and TOWNS

Clervaux, 933 ....J 8

Diekirch, 4,899 ....J 9
Differdange, 9,808 ....H 9
Dudelange, 14,849 ....J10
Echternach, 3,472 ....J 9
Esch-sur-Alzette, 27,921 ....J 9
Esch-sur-Sauer, 265 ....J 9
Ettelbrück, 5,557 ....J 9
Grevenmacher, 2,850 ....J 9
Luxembourg (cap.), 77,458 ..J 9
Mersch, 1,682 ....J 9
Pétange, 6,251 ....H 9
Redange, 990 ....H 9
Remich, 1,958 ....J 9
Troisvierges, 928 ....J 9
Vianden, 1,381 ....J 9
Wasserbillig, 2,047 ....J 9
Wiltz, 1,538 ....H 9

OTHER FEATURES

Alzette (river) ....J 9
Clerf (river) ....H 9
Eisling (mts.) ....H 9
Mosel (river) ....J 9
Our (river) ....J 9
Sauer (river) ....J 9

NETHERLANDS

PROVINCES

Drenthe, 366,590 ....K 3
Friesland, 521,751 ....H 2
Gelderland, 1,505,760 ......H 4
Groningen, 517,305 ....K 2
Limburg, 998,570 ....H 6
North Brabant,
   1,787,783 ....F 5
North Holland,
   2,244,456 ....F 3
Overijssel, 920,882 ....J 4
South Holland,
   2,968,670 ....E 4
Utrecht, 801,285 ....G 4
Zeeland, 305,754 ....D 6

CITIES and TOWNS

Aalsmeer, †18,166 ....F 4
Aalst, 4,423 ....G 6
Aalten, †16,295 ....K 5
Aardenburg, †3,853 ....C 6
Akkrum, 2,296 ....H 2
Alkmaar, †52,091 ....F 3
Almelo, †58,941 ....K 4
Amersfoort, †78,189 ....G 4
Amstelveen, †69,167 ....B 5
Amsterdam (cap.),
   831,463 ....B 4
Amsterdam, *918,676 ....B 4
Andijk, †4,602 ....G 3
Anjum, 939 ....J 2
Apeldoorn, 123,628 ....H 4
Apeldoorn, *214,974 ....H 4
Appelscha, 1,622 ....J 3
Appingedam, †10,987 ......K 2
Arnhem, 132,531 ....H 4
Arnhem, *232,860 ....H 4
Asten, †38,956 ....K 3
Asten, †11,209 ....H 6
Axel, †8,904 ....D 6
Baarle-Nassau,
   †4,948 ....F 6
Baarn, 124,106 ....G 4
Badhoevedorp, 8,699 ....H 4
Balkbrug, 2,468 ....J 3

Barneveld, †30,046 ....H 4
Bath, 128 ....E 5
Beilen, †12,289 ....K 3
Bergeijk (Hof), †7,816 ......G 6
Bergen, †13,060 ....F 3
Bergen op Zoom,
   139,051 ....E 5
Bergum, †4,252 ....H 2
Berkel, 15,936 ....F 5
Berkhout, †3,941 ....F 3
Beverwijk, †41,357 ....F 4
Blerick, 14,593 ....J 6
Bloemendaal, †19,253 ......E 4
Blokzijl, †1,375 ....H 3
Bodegraven, †14,083 ......F 4
Bolsward, †9,247 ....H 2
Borculo, †8,510 ....J 4
Borger, †10,972 ....K 3
Borne, †15,423 ....K 4
Boskoop, †11,600 ....F 4
Boxmeer, †10,850 ....H 5
Boxtel, †19,000 ....G 5
Breda, †21,009 ....F 5
Breda, *233,704 ....F 5
Breezand, 1,962 ....F 3
Breskens, †3,857 ....C 6
Brielle, †8,314 ....E 4
Broek, †2,260 ....C 4
Brouwershaven, †3,256 ....D 5
Brummen, †18,077 ....J 4
Buiksloot, 23,738 ....B 4
Bussum, †41,787 ....G 4
Callantsoog, †11,698 ......F 3
Coevorden, †12,488 ....K 3
Colijnsplaat, 1,477 ....D 5
Culemborg, †11,083 ......G 5
Cuyk, †12,144 ....H 5
Dalen, †4,823 ....K 3
De Bilt, †29,153 ....G 4
Dedemsvaart, †6,384 ......J 3
De Koog, 701 ....E 2
Delft, 83,698 ....E 4
Delfzijl, †21,990 ....K 2
Den Burg, 3,579 ....F 2
Den Helder, †60,612 ......F 3
Denekamp, †10,919 ....L 4
Deurne, †23,949 ....H 6
Deventer, †65,319 ....J 4
De Wijk, †4,120 ....J 3
Diemen, †9,558 ....C 5
Dieren, 8,612 ....J 4
Diever, †3,180 ....J 3
Dinxperlo, †6,248 ....K 5
Dirksland, †6,092 ....E 5
Doesburg, †9,451 ....J 4
Doetinchem, †31,097 ......J 4
Dokkum, †9,886 ....H 2
Domburg, †3,154 ....C 5
Dongen, †16,231 ....F 5
Doorn, †10,084 ....G 4
Doornspijk, †10,463 ......H 4
Dordrecht, †88,699 ....F 5
Dordrecht, *99,284 ....F 5
Drachten, 16,529 ....J 2
Driebergen, †15,828 ......G 4
Druten, †9,761 ....H 5
Duivendrecht, 2,656 ......C 5
Durgerdam, 640 ....C 4
Echt, †16,795 ....H 6
Edam, †18,184 ....G 3
Ede, †71,952 ....H 4
Eefde, 2,396 ....J 4
Egmond aan Zee,
   †5,554 ....E 3
Eindhoven, 188,631 ......G 5
Eindhoven, *301,049 ......G 5
Elburg, †5,135 ....H 4
Elst, †15,182 ....H 5

LAND from the SEA

NORTH SEA — WADDENZEE — WEST FRISIAN ISLANDS — Leeuwarden — Enclosing Dam 1932 — IJSSELMEER (ZUIDER ZEE) — North East Polder 1942 — Wieringermeer Polder 1930 — Markerwaard (planned) — East Flevoland 1957 — South Flevoland 1969 — Amsterdam — Haarlemmer Lake 1852

1600, 1400, 1280, 1242, 1200, 1427, 1847, 1824, 1599, 1610, 1456, 1844, 1927, 1564, 1631, 1608, 1635, 1612, 1683, 1626, 1622, 1628, 1872

Reclaimed Land and Dates of Completion
Future Polders
= 10 Square Miles

For centuries the Dutch have been renowned for the drainage of marshes and the construction of polders, i.e., arable land reclaimed from the sea. Future projects will convert much of the present IJsselmeer to agricultural land.

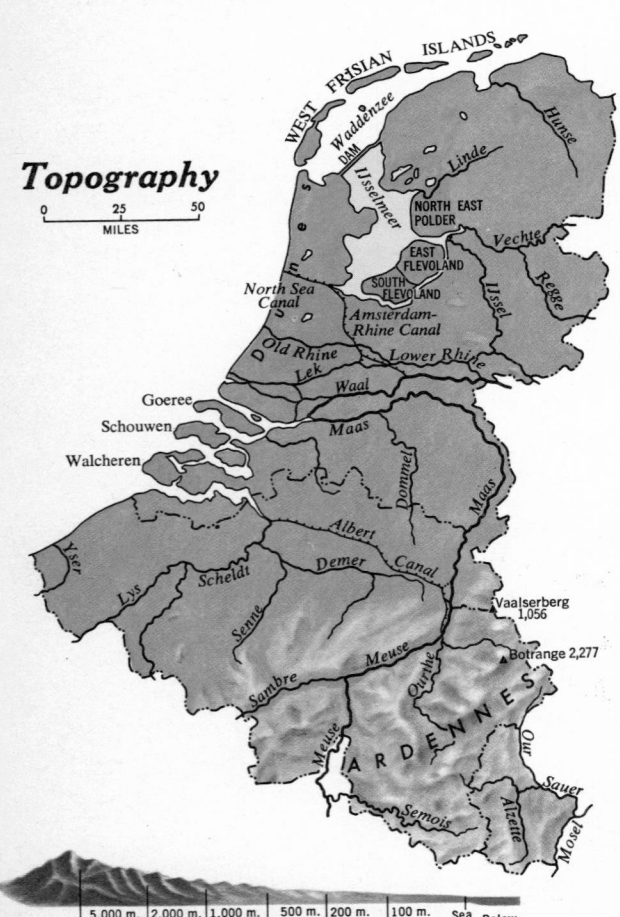

Topography

0 25 50 MILES

WEST FRISIAN ISLANDS — Waddenzee — IJsselmeer — DAM — Linde — Humse — Vecht — NORTH EAST POLDER — EAST FLEVOLAND — SOUTH FLEVOLAND — Regge — IJssel — Amsterdam-Rhine Canal — North Sea Canal — Old Rhine — Lek — Lower Rhine — Waal — Goeree — Schouwen — Walcheren — Maas — Dommel — Maas — Albert Canal — Demer — Scheldt — Senne — Yser — Lys — Sambre — Meuse — Ourthe — Dommel — Meuse — Vaalserberg 1,056 — Botrange 2,277 — ARDENNES — Semois — Alzette — Our — Sauer — Mosel

5,000 m. 16,404 ft. | 2,000 m. 6,562 ft. | 1,000 m. 3,281 ft. | 500 m. 1,640 ft. | 200 m. 656 ft. | 100 m. 328 ft. | Sea Level | Below

NETHERLANDS, BELGIUM and LUXEMBOURG

CONIC PROJECTION

SCALE OF MILES

0 5 10   20   30   40

SCALE OF KILOMETRES

0 5 10   20   30   40   50

Capitals of Countries . . . . ☆
Provincial Capitals . . . . △
International Boundaries . . . . . . —·—·—
Provincial Boundaries . . . . —··—··—
Canals . . . .

Copyright by C. S. Hammond & Co., N.Y.

AMSTERDAM

BRUSSELS

FRANCE

CONIC PROJECTION

SCALE OF MILES

SCALE OF KILOMETRES

Capitals of Countries..............★
Capitals of Departments..........△
International Boundaries..........—·—·—
Department Boundaries............—··—··—
Canals................................——————

© C.S. HAMMOND & Co., N.Y.

PARIS and ENVIRONS

CORSICA

Same Scale as Main Map

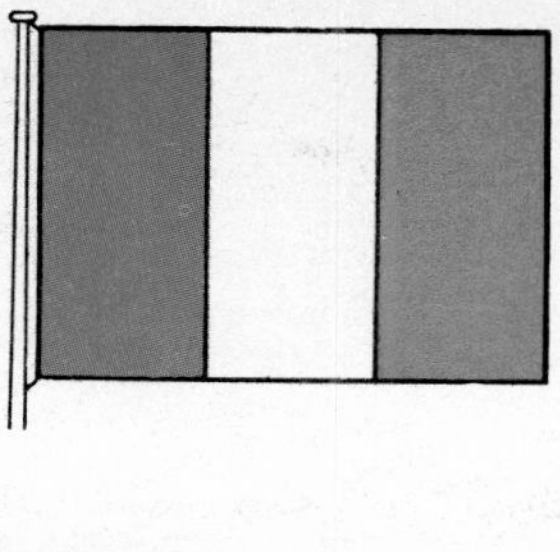

AREA 212,841 sq. mi.
POPULATION 50,770,000
CAPITAL Paris
LARGEST CITY Paris
HIGHEST POINT Mont Blanc 15,771 ft.
MONETARY UNIT franc
MAJOR LANGUAGE French
MAJOR RELIGION Roman Catholicism

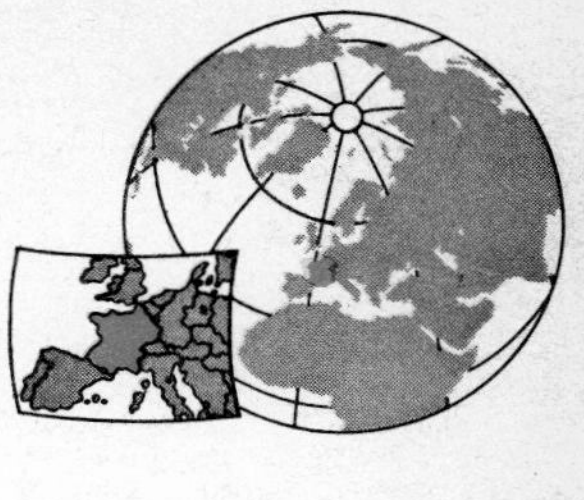

Topography

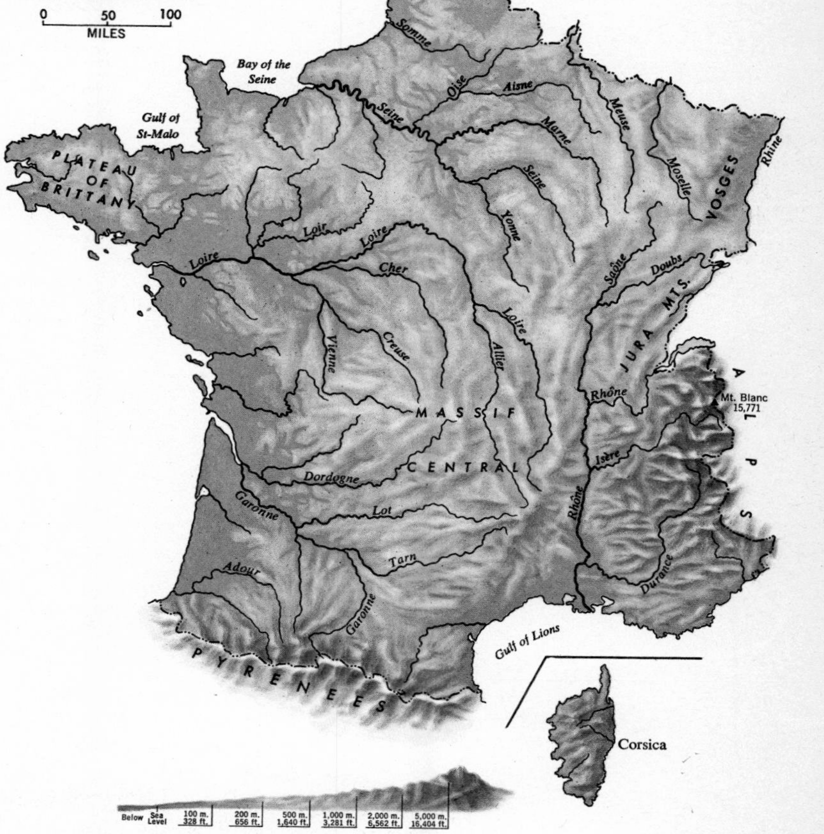

DEPARTMENTS

Ain, 339,262 .... F 4
Aisne, 526,346 .... E 3
Allier, 386,533 .... E 4
Alpes-de-Haute-Provence, 104,813 .... G 5
Alpes-Maritimes, 722,070 .... G 6
Ardèche, 256,927 .... F 5
Ardennes, 309,380 .... F 3
Ariège, 138,478 .... D 6
Aube, 270,325 .... E 3
Aude, 278,323 .... E 6
Aveyron, 281,568 .... E 5
Bas-Rhin, 827,367 .... G 3
Belfort (terr.), 118,450 .... G 4
Bouches-du-Rhône, 1,470,271 .... F 6
Calvados, 519,695 .... C 3
Cantal, 169,330 .... E 5
Charente, 331,016 .... D 5
Charente-Maritime, 483,622 .... C 5
Cher, 304,601 .... E 4
Corrèze, 237,858 .... D 5
Corsica (Corse), 269,831 .... B 6
Côte-d'Or, 421,192 .... F 4
Côtes-du-Nord, 506,102 .... B 3
Creuse, 156,876 .... D 4
Deux-Sèvres, 326,462 .... C 4
Dordogne, 374,073 .... D 5
Doubs, 426,363 .... G 4
Drôme, 342,891 .... F 5
Essonne, 674,157 .... E 3
Eure, 383,385 .... D 3
Eure-et-Loir, 302,207 .... D 3
Finistère, 768,929 .... A 3
Gard, 478,544 .... F 6
Gers, 181,577 .... D 6
Gironde, 1,009,390 .... C 5
Haut-Rhin, 585,018 .... G 4
Haute-Garonne, 690,712 .... D 6
Haute-Loire, 208,337 .... E 5
Haute-Marne, 214,336 .... F 3
Haute-Saône, 214,176 .... G 4
Haute-Savoie, 378,550 .... G 5
Haute-Vienne, 341,589 .... D 5
Hautes-Alpes, 91,790 .... G 5
Hautes-Pyrénées, 225.730 .... D 6
Hauts-de-Seine, 1,461,619 .... A 2
Hérault, 591,397 .... E 6
Ille-et-Vilaine, 652,722 .... C 3
Indre, 247,178 .... D 4
Indre-et-Loire, 437,870 .... D 4
Isère, 768,450 .... F 5
Jura, 233,547 .... F 4
Landes, 277,381 .... C 5
Loir-et-Cher, 267,896 .... D 4
Loire, 722,383 .... F 5
Loire-Atlantique, 861,452 .... C 4
Loiret, 430,629 .... E 4
Lot, 151,198 .... D 5
Lot-et-Garonne, 290,592 .... D 5
Lozère, 77,258 .... E 5
Maine-et-Loire, 584,709 .... C 4
Manche, 451,939 .... C 3
Marne, 485,388 .... F 3
Mayenne, 252,762 .... C 3
Meurthe-et-Moselle, 705,413 .... G 3
Meuse, 209,513 .... F 3
Morbihan, 540,474 .... B 4
Moselle, 971,314 .... G 3
Nièvre, 247,702 .... E 4
Nord, 2,417,899 .... E 2
Oise, 540,988 .... E 3
Orne, 288,524 .... C 3
Paris, 2,590,771 .... B 2
Pas-de-Calais, 1,397,159 .... E 2
Puy-de-Dôme, 547,743 .... E 5
Pyrénées-Atlantiques, 508,734 .... C 6
Pyrénées-Orientales, 281,976 .... E 6
Rhône, 1,325,611 .... F 5
Saône-et-Loire, 550,362 .... F 4
Sarthe, 461,839 .... D 3
Savoie, 288,921 .... G 5
Seine-et-Marne, 604,340 .... E 3
Seine-Maritime, 1,113,977 .... D 3
Seine-Saint-Denis, 1,251,792 .... B 1
Somme, 512,113 .... E 3
Tarn, 332,011 .... E 6
Tarn-et-Garonne, 183,572 .... D 5
Val-de-Marne, 1,121,340 .... B 2
Val-d'Oise, 693,269 .... E 3
Var, 555,926 .... G 6
Vaucluse, 353,966 .... F 6
Vendée, 421,250 .... C 4
Vienne, 340,256 .... D 4
Vosges, 388,201 .... G 3
Yonne, 283,376 .... E 4
Yvelines, 853,386 .... D 3

CITIES and TOWNS

Abbeville, 23,770 .... D 2
Agde, 8,812 .... E 6
Agen, 34,592 .... D 5
Aix-en-Provence, 74,948 .... F 6
Aix-les-Bains, 20,594 .... G 5
Ajaccio, 38,776 .... B 7
Albert, 10,937 .... E 2
Albertville, 15,422 .... G 5
Albi, 38,867 .... E 6
Alençon, 30,368 .... D 3
Aléria, 1,000 .... B 6
Alès, 31,948 .... E 5
Ambérieu-en-Bugey, 8,570 .... F 5
Amboise, 8,408 .... D 4
Amiens, 116,107 .... D 3
Angers, 127,415 .... C 4
Angoulême, 46,584 .... D 5
Annecy, 53,361 .... G 5
Annonay, 19,591 .... F 5
Antibes, 47,393 .... G 6
Antony, 56,556 .... B 2
Apt, 8,502 .... F 6
Arcachon, 14,852 .... C 5
Argentan, 14,418 .... D 3
Argenteuil, 87,106 .... A 1
Arles, 33,575 .... F 6
Armentières, 24,460 .... E 2
Arras, 48,494 .... E 2
Asnières, 79,942 .... A 1
Aubagne, 17,055 .... F 6
Aubenas, 10,480 .... F 5
Aubervilliers, 73,559 .... B 1
Aubusson, 5,641 .... E 4
Auch, 18,072 .... D 6
Audincourt, 13,487 .... G 4
Aulnay-sous-Bois, 61,384 .... B 1
Auray, 8,180 .... B 4
Aurignac, 783 .... D 6
Aurillac, 26,776 .... E 5
Autun, 17,194 .... F 4
Auxerre, 33,700 .... E 4
Avallon, 6,615 .... E 4
Avesnes-sur-Helpe, 6,253 .... F 2
Avignon, 78,871 .... F 6
Avion, 22,390 .... E 2
Avranches, 9,751 .... C 3
Bagnères-de-Bigorre, 9,139 .... D 6
Bagnères-de-Luchon, 4,079 .... D 6
Bagnolet, 33,607 .... B 2
Bagnols-sur-Cèze, 15,336 .... F 5
Bar-le-Duc, 18,874 .... F 3
Bar-sur-Seine, 2,642 .... F 3
Barfleur, 825 .... C 3
Bastia, 48,800 .... B 6
Bayeux, 11,190 .... C 3
Bayonne, 39.761 .... C 6
Beaucaire, 8,820 .... F 6
Beaune, 16,441 .... F 4
Beauvais, 46,284 .... E 3
Bédarieux, 6,929 .... E 6
Belfort, 53,001 .... G 4
Belley, 5,958 .... F 5
Berck, 13,658 .... D 2
Bergerac, 24,184 .... D 5
Bernay, 9,298 .... D 3
Besançon, 107,939 .... G 4
Bessèges, 5,421 .... F 5
Béthune, 26,144 .... E 2
Béziers, 74,517 .... E 6
Biarritz, 26,628 .... C 6
Blois, 39,279 .... D 4
Bobigny, 39,321 .... B 1
Bolbec, 12,517 .... D 3
Bondy, 51,555 .... B 1
Bordeaux, 263,808 .... C 5
Bordeaux, †648,000 .... C 5
Boulogne-Billancourt, 108,846 .... A 2
Boulogne-sur-Mer, 49,064 .... D 2
Bourg-en-Bresse, 35,064 .... F 4
Bourges, 67,137 .... E 4
Bressuire, 8,010 .... C 4
Brest, 150,696 .... A 3
Briançon, 7,551 .... G 5
Briare, 4,725 .... E 4
Brignoles, 8,010 .... G 6
Brive-la-Gaillarde, 45,314 .... D 5
Bruay-en-Artois, 38,608 .... E 2
Caen, 106,790 .... C 3
Cahors, 17,775 .... D 5
Calais, 70,153 .... D 2
Caluire-et-Cuire, 37,541 .... F 5
Calvi, 2,523 .... B 6
Cambrai, 37,290 .... E 2
Cannes, 66,590 .... G 6
Carcassonne, 40,580 .... D 6
Carentan, 5,207 .... C 3
Carmaux, 13,423 .... E 5
Carpentras, 18,092 .... F 5
Castelnaudary, 8,550 .... E 6
Castelsarrasin, 7,912 .... D 6
Castres, 35,975 .... E 6
Cavaillon, 14,815 .... F 6
Cayeux-sur-Mer, 2,489 .... D 2
Chalon-sur-Saône, 47,004 .... F 4
Châlons-sur-Marne, 48,558 .... F 3
Chambéry, 49,858 .... F 5
Chambord, 200 .... D 4
Chamonix-Mont Blanc, 5,907 .... G 5
Champigny-sur-Marne, 70,353 .... C 2
Chantilly, 10,156 .... E 3
Charenton-le-Pont, 22,220 .... B 2
Charleville-Mézières, 55,230 .... F 3
Chartres, 34,128 .... D 3
Château-du-Loir, 5,239 .... D 4
Château-Gontier, 7,881 .... C 4
Château-Renault, 5,082 .... D 4
Château-Thierry, 10,858 .... E 3
Châteaubriant, 11,196 .... C 4
Châteaudun, 13,715 .... D 3
Châteauneuf-sur-Loire, 4,603 .... E 4
Châteauroux, 48,867 .... D 4
Châtellerault, 33,491 .... D 4
Châtillon, 24,468 .... B 2
Châtillon-sur-Seine, 6,128 .... F 4
Chatou, 22,495 .... A 1
Chaumont, 25,602 .... F 3
Chauny, 13,714 .... E 3
Chelles, 22,111 .... C 1
Cherbourg, 37,933 .... C 3
Chinon, 5,435 .... D 4
Choisy-le-Roi, 41,080 .... B 2
Cholet, 40,224 .... C 4
Clamart, 54,866 .... A 2
Clermont, 7,119 .... E 3
Clermont-Ferrand, 145,856 .... E 5
Clichy, 52,398 .... B 1
Cluny, 3,552 .... F 4
Cluses, 12,391 .... G 4
Cognac, 21,137 .... C 5
Colmar, 58,623 .... G 3
Colombes, 80,224 .... A 1
Commentry, 8,129 .... E 4
Commercy, 7,043 .... F 3
Compiègne, 28,881 .... E 3
Concarneau, 16,458 .... A 4
Cosne-sur-Loire, 8,931 .... E 4
Coudekerque-Branche, 22,972 .... E 2
Coulommiers, 11.182 .... E 3
Courbevoie, 57,998 .... A 1
Coutances, 8,599 .... C 3
Coutras, 4,251 .... C 5
Creil, 31,792 .... E 3
Crépy-en-Valois, 8,506 .... E 3
Créteil, 48,757 .... B 2
Cusset, 12,286 .... E 4
Dax, 18,185 .... C 6
Deauville, 5,103 .... C 3
Decazeville, 9,581 .... E 5
Denain, 27,840 .... E 2
Dieppe, 29,829 .... D 3
Digne, 11,973 .... G 5
Digoin, 9,585 .... F 4
Dijon, 143,120 .... F 4
Dinan, 12,999 .... B 3
Dinard, 9,042 .... B 3
Dôle, 25,620 .... F 4
Domrémy-la-Pucelle, 184 .... F 3
Douai, 47,347 .... E 2
Douarnenez, 18,442 .... A 3
Draguignan, 16,139 .... G 6
Drancy, 69,226 .... B 1
Dreux, 28,156 .... D 3
Dunkirk (Dunkerque), 26,038 .... E 2
Elbeuf, 19,110 .... D 3
Embrun, 3,986 .... G 5
Épernay, 26,094 .... E 3
Épinal, 36,219 .... G 3
Épinay-sur-Seine, 41,538 .... B 1
Étampes, 15,542 .... E 3
Étaples, 9,092 .... D 2
Eu, 7,866 .... D 3
Évreux, 41,004 .... D 3
Évry, 7,047 .... E 3
Falaise, 6,977 .... C 3
Fécamp, 21,098 .... D 3
Figeac, 8,462 .... D 5
Firminy, 24,545 .... F 5
Flers, 16,677 .... C 3
Foix, 9,061 .... D 6
Fontainebleau, 17,565 .... E 3
Fontenay-le-Comte, 10,884 .... C 4
Fontenay-sous-Bois, 38,737 .... C 2
Forbach, 23,062 .... G 3
Fougères, 25,745 .... C 3
Fourmies, 14,895 .... F 2
Fréjus, 22,567 .... G 6
Gagny, 35,745 .... C 1
Gap, 22,027 .... G 5
Gardanne, 12,601 .... F 6
Gennevilliers, 45,925 .... B 1
Gentilly, 18,638 .... B 2
Gex, 3,078 .... G 4
Gien, 11,655 .... E 4
Gisors, 7,024 .... D 3
Givet, 7,697 .... F 2
Givors, 17,545 .... F 5
Granville, 12,315 .... C 3
Grasse, 24,398 .... G 6
Graulhet, 10,318 .... E 6
Gray, 7,782 .... F 4
Grenoble, 161,230 .... F 5
Guebwiller, 10,684 .... G 4
Guéret, 12,441 .... D 4
Guingamp, 9,091 .... B 3
Guise, 6,732 .... E 3
Haguenau, 22,335 .... G 3
Ham, 5,565 .... E 3
Harfleur, 15,503 .... D 3
Hautmont, 17,818 .... F 2
Hayange, 10,218 .... F 3
Hazebrouck, 16,768 .... E 2
Hendaye, 7,536 .... C 6
Hénin-Liétard, 25,067 .... E 2
Hennebont, 7,605 .... B 4
Héricourt, 7,376 .... G 4
Hirson, 11,764 .... F 3
Honfleur, 9,017 .... D 3
Hyères, 27,600 .... G 6
Issoire, 11,745 .... E 5
Issoudun, 14,559 .... D 4
Issy-les-Moulineaux, 50,260 .... A 2
Istres, 8,713 .... F 6
Ivry-sur-Seine, 60,342 .... B 2
Joigny, 9,609 .... E 3
La Baule-Escoublac, 11,962 .... B 4
La Ciotat, 19,485 .... F 6
La Courneuve, 42,812 .... B 1
La Flèche, 9,536 .... C 4
La Grand-Combe, 8,608 .... E 5
La Roche-sur-Yon, 32,279 .... C 4
La Rochelle, 72,075 .... C 4
La Seyne-sur-Mer, 42,958 .... F 6
La Tour-du-Pin, 5,649 .... F 5
L'Aigle, 7,478 .... D 3
Landerneau, 12,356 .... B 3
Langeac, 4,584 .... E 5
Langres, 8,945 .... F 4
Lannion, 10,066 .... B 3
Laon, 25,623 .... E 3
Laval, 45,051 .... C 3
Lavelanet, 8,512 .... E 6
Le Blanc-Mesnil, 48,212 .... B 1
Le Bourget, 9,625 .... B 1
Le Cateau, 8,922 .... E 2
Le Chesnay, 13,586 .... A 2
Le Creusot, 33,581 .... F 4
Le Croisic, 4,092 .... B 4
Le Havre, 198,021 .... C 3
Le Mans, 140,520 .... C 3
Le Puy, 24,816 .... F 5
Le Teil, 7,872 .... F 5
Le Touquet-Paris-Plage, 4,403 .... D 2
Le Tréport, 6,194 .... D 2
Lens, 41,800 .... E 2
Les Andelys, 6,292 .... D 3
Les Sables-d'Olonne, 17,856 .... B 4
Levallois-Perret, 58,890 .... B 1
Lézignan-Corbières, 7,101 .... E 6
Libourne, 19,981 .... C 5
Liévin, 35,733 .... E 2
Lille, 189,697 .... E 2
Lille, †1,042,000 .... E 2
Limoges, 127,605 .... D 5
Limoux, 9,150 .... E 6
Lisieux, 23,337 .... D 3
Livry-Gargan, 32,015 .... C 1
Lodève, 6,899 .... E 6
Longwy, 21,052 .... F 3
Lons-le-Saunier, 18,649 .... F 4
Lorient, 66,023 .... B 4
Loudun, 6,118 .... D 4
Lourdes, 17,627 .... C 6
Louviers, 15,159 .... D 3
Lunel, 10,178 .... E 6
Lunéville, 22,961 .... G 3
Luxeuil-les-Bains, 9,203 .... G 4
Lyon, 524,500 .... F 5
Lyon, †1,305,000 .... F 5
Mâcon, 33,266 .... F 4
Maisons-Alfort, 53,118 .... B 2
Maisons-Laffitte, 24,041 .... A 1
Malakoff, 36,198 .... B 2
Manosque, 13,352 .... G 6
Mantes-la-Jolie, 25,842 .... D 3
Marmande, 12,145 .... C 5
Marseille, 880,527 .... F 6
Marseille, †1,015,000 .... F 6
Martigues, 17,771 .... F 6
Maubeuge, 31,992 .... F 2
Mayenne, 10,010 .... C 3
Mazamet, 14,650 .... E 6
Meaux, 29,966 .... E 3
Melun, 33,345 .... E 3
Mende, 9,424 .... E 5
Menton, 23,401 .... G 6
Metz, 105,533 .... G 3
Meudon, 30,735 .... A 2
Millau, 21,420 .... E 5
Moissac, 7,694 .... D 5
Mont-de-Marsan, 22,771 .... C 6
Mont-Dore, 2,045 .... E 5
Mont-Saint-Michel, 72 .... C 3
Montargis, 18,087 .... E 3
Montauban, 33,945 .... D 5
Montbéliard, 23,402 .... G 4
Montbrison, 8,733 .... E 5
Montceau-les-Mines, 18,621 .... F 4
Montdidier, 5,785 .... E 3
Montélimar, 23,831 .... F 5
Montfort, 2,563 .... C 3
Montigny-les-Metz, 24,417 .... G 3
Montluçon, 57,638 .... E 4
Montpellier, 152,105 .... E 6
Montreuil, 95,420 .... B 2
Montrouge, 44,788 .... B 2
Morlaix, 16,750 .... B 3
Moulins, 25,778 .... E 4
Moûtiers, 4,066 .... G 5
Moyeuvre-Grande, 14,559 .... G 3
Mulhouse, 115,632 .... G 4
Muret, 10,515 .... D 6
Nancy, 121,910 .... G 3
Nanterre, 90,124 .... A 1
Nantes, 253,105 .... C 4
Narbonne, 35,236 .... E 6
Nemours, 8,081 .... E 3
Neufchâteau, 7,656 .... F 3
Neufchâtel-en-Bray, 5,734 .... D 3
Neuilly-sur-Seine, 70,787 .... B 1
Nevers, 42,092 .... E 4
Nice, 301,400 .... G 6
Nîmes, 115,561 .... F 6
Niort, 46,749 .... C 4
Nogent-le-Rotrou, 11,040 .... D 3
Nogent-sur-Seine, 4,271 .... E 3
Noisy-le-Sec, 34,058 .... B 1
Noyon, 11,567 .... E 3
Nyons, 4,311 .... F 5
Oloron-Sainte-Marie, 12,597 .... C 6
Orange, 17,582 .... F 5
Orléans, 94,382 .... D 3
Orly, 30,151 .... B 2
Orthez, 8,778 .... C 6
Oullins, 26,520 .... F 5
Oyonnax, 19,571 .... F 4
Pamiers, 13,183 .... D 6
Pantin, 47,580 .... B 1
Paray-le-Monial, 10,324 .... F 4
Paris (cap.), 2,580,010 .... B 2
Paris, *7,953,065 .... B 2
Paris, †9,283,000 .... B 2
Parthenay, 11,177 .... C 4
Pau, 71,865 .... C 6
Périgueux, 36,991 .... D 5
Perpignan, 100,086 .... E 6
Pessac, 35,343 .... C 5
Ploërmel, 3,720 .... B 4
Poitiers, 68,082 .... D 4
Pont-à-Mousson, 13,283 .... G 3
Pont-l'Abbé, 6,227 .... A 4
Pont-l'Évêque, 2,823 .... D 3
Pontarlier, 16,250 .... G 4
Pontivy, 9,674 .... B 3
Pontoise, 16,633 .... E 3
Port-de-Bouc, 13,447 .... F 6
Port-Louis, 3,921 .... B 4

(continued on following page)

HISTORIC PROVINCES

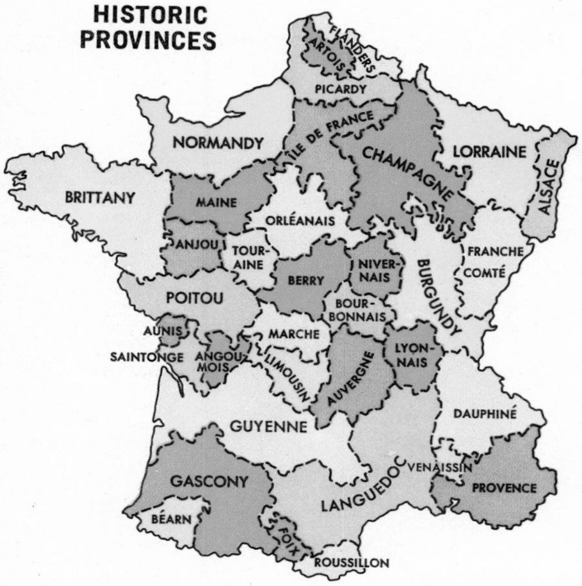

A resident of the city of Caen thinks of himself as a Norman rather than as a citizen of the modern department of Calvados. In spite of the passing of nearly two centuries, the historic provinces which existed before 1790 command the local patriotism of most Frenchmen.

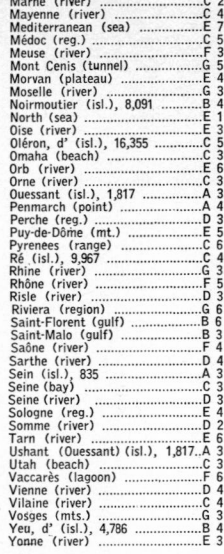

WINE REGIONS

CALVADOS
(distilled from cider)

Caen
Reims
CHAMPAGNE
ALSACE
Colmar
Chablis
Angers · Anjou · Touraine · Tours
LOIRE VALLEY
POUILLY SANCERRE
BURGUNDY
Côte-d'Or
Beaune
JURA
QUINCY REUILLY
Mâcon
COGNAC
Mâconnais
Cognac
Beaujolais
Saône
BORDEAUX
Médoc
Graves · Sauternes
Bordeaux
Bergerac
CÔTES DE DURAS
Valence
CÔTES DU RHÔNE
ARMAGNAC
Auch
GAILLAC
Avignon
PROVENCE
Pau
JURANÇON
Béziers
LANGUEDOC
Toulon
LIMOUX
ROUSSILLON

Climate, soil and variety of grape planted determine the quality of wine. Long, hot and fairly dry summers with cool, humid nights constitute an ideal climate. The nature of the soil is such a determining influence that identical grapes planted in Bordeaux, Burgundy and Champagne, will yield wines of widely different types.

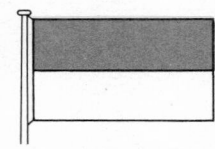

MONACO
AREA   368 acres
POPULATION   23,035

Agriculture, Industry and Resources

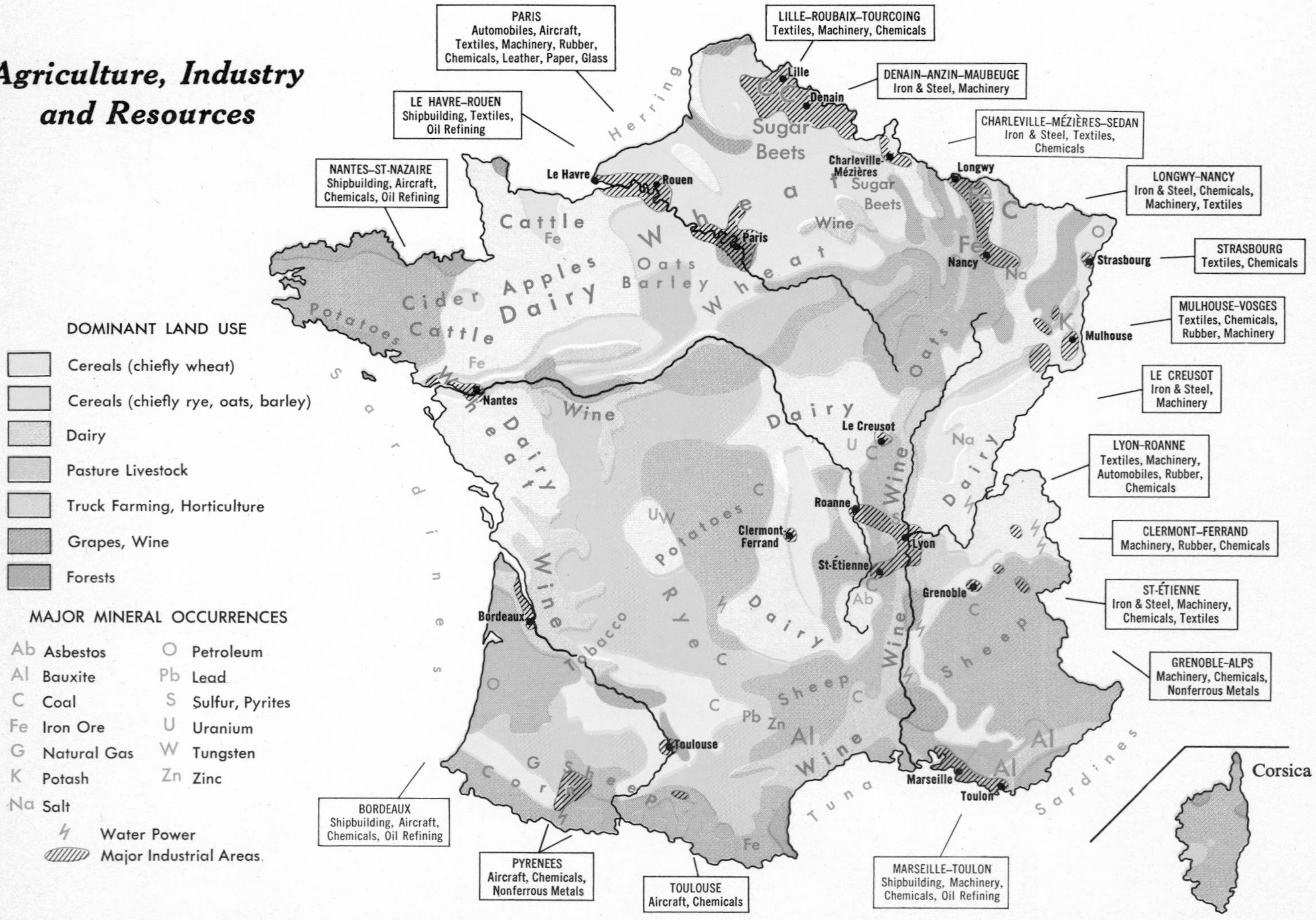

DOMINANT LAND USE

- Cereals (chiefly wheat)
- Cereals (chiefly rye, oats, barley)
- Dairy
- Pasture Livestock
- Truck Farming, Horticulture
- Grapes, Wine
- Forests

MAJOR MINERAL OCCURRENCES

Ab	Asbestos	O	Petroleum
Al	Bauxite	Pb	Lead
C	Coal	S	Sulfur, Pyrites
Fe	Iron Ore	U	Uranium
G	Natural Gas	W	Tungsten
K	Potash	Zn	Zinc
Na	Salt		

⚡ Water Power
▨ Major Industrial Areas

PARIS
Automobiles, Aircraft, Textiles, Machinery, Rubber, Chemicals, Leather, Paper, Glass

LILLE–ROUBAIX–TOURCOING
Textiles, Machinery, Chemicals

LE HAVRE–ROUEN
Shipbuilding, Textiles, Oil Refining

DENAIN–ANZIN–MAUBEUGE
Iron & Steel, Machinery

CHARLEVILLE–MÉZIÈRES–SEDAN
Iron & Steel, Textiles, Chemicals

NANTES–ST-NAZAIRE
Shipbuilding, Aircraft, Chemicals, Oil Refining

LONGWY–NANCY
Iron & Steel, Chemicals, Machinery, Textiles

STRASBOURG
Textiles, Chemicals

MULHOUSE–VOSGES
Textiles, Chemicals, Rubber, Machinery

LE CREUSOT
Iron & Steel, Machinery

LYON–ROANNE
Textiles, Machinery, Automobiles, Rubber, Chemicals

CLERMONT–FERRAND
Machinery, Rubber, Chemicals

ST-ÉTIENNE
Iron & Steel, Machinery, Chemicals, Textiles

GRENOBLE–ALPS
Machinery, Chemicals, Nonferrous Metals

BORDEAUX
Shipbuilding, Aircraft, Chemicals, Oil Refining

PYRENEES
Aircraft, Chemicals, Nonferrous Metals

TOULOUSE
Aircraft, Chemicals

MARSEILLE–TOULON
Shipbuilding, Machinery, Chemicals, Oil Refining

Herring
Lille
Denain
Charleville-Mézières
Longwy
Nancy
Strasbourg
Mulhouse
Sugar Beets
Le Havre
Rouen
Paris
Wine
Cattle
Cider Apples
Dairy
Potatoes
Cattle
Oats
Barley
Wheat
Oats
Nantes
Wine
Dairy
Le Creusot
Roanne
Clermont Ferrand
St-Étienne
Lyon
Grenoble
Bordeaux
Potatoes
Rye
Dairy
Wine
Tobacco
Sheep
Sheep
Toulouse
Wine
Marseille
Toulon
Tuna
Sardines
Corsica

ANDORRA

CITIES and TOWNS

Andorra la Vella (cap.), 2,250....G 1

GIBRALTAR

PHYSICAL FEATURES

Europa (point) ....D 4

PORTUGAL

PROVINCES

Algarve, 315,300 ....B 4
Alto Alentejo, 410,200 ....C 3
Baixo Alentejo, 275,000 ....B 3
Beira Alta, 761,500 ....C 2
Beira Baixa, 321,100 ....C 3
Beira Litoral, 1,448,800 ....B 2
Douro Litoral, 1,352,600 ....B 2
Estremadura, 1,998,600 ....B 3
Madeira, 268,700 ....A 2
Minho, 944,800 ....B 2
Ribatejo, 479,400 ....B 3
Trás-os-Montes e Alto Douro, 586,500 ....C 2

CITIES and TOWNS

Águeda, 8,345 ....B 2
Alcácer do Sal, 14,733 ....B 3
Alcântara, 30,625 ....A 1
Alcobaça, 5,166 ....B 3
Aldeia Nova, 7,678 ....C 4
Algés, 14,517 ....A 1
Alhos Vedros, 19,606 ....B 3
Aljezur, 5,333 ....B 4
Aljustrel, 9,913 ....B 4
Almada, 30,688 ....A 1
Almeirim, 8,902 ....B 3
Alpiarça, 7,856 ....B 3
Amadora, 36,331 ....A 1
Amareleja, 4,816 ....C 3
Aveiro, 16,011 ....B 2
Baixa da Banheira, 12,525..........B 3
Barcelos, 5,420 ....B 2
Batalha, 7,053 ....B 3
Beja, 15,702 ....C 3
Belas, 7,509 ....A 1
Belém, 20,416 ....A 1
Benfica, 23,161 ....A 1
Braga, 40,977 ....B 2
Bragança, 8,075 ....C 2
Caldas da Rainha, 10,635 ....B 3
Calheta, 5,404 ....A 2
Campo Maior, 8,807 ....C 3
Cantanhede, 6,630 ....B 2
Caparica, 10,363 ....A 1
Carnaxide, 28,301 ....A 1
Cartaxo, 6,665 ....B 3
Cascais, 10,861 ....B 3
Castelo Branco, 14,838 ....C 3
Castro Marim, 5,347 ....C 4
Chaves, 13,156 ....C 2
Coimbra, 46,313 ....B 2
Cova da Piedade, 15,720 ....A 1
Covilhã, 23,091 ....C 2
Elvas, 11,742 ....C 3
Espinho, 13,503 ....B 2
Estoril, 11,193 ....B 3
Estremoz, 10,122 ....C 3
Évora, 24,144 ....C 3
Fafe, 7,126 ....B 2
Faro, 18,909 ....B 4
Fátima, 5,852 ....B 3
Ferreira do Alentejo, 8,108..........B 3
Figueira da Foz, 10,855 ....B 2
Funchal, 43,301 ....A 2
Gondomar, 11,182 ....B 2
Guarda, 9,094 ....C 2
Guimarães, 23,229 ....B 2
Ilhavo, 12,646 ....B 2
Lagos, 10,008 ....B 4
Lamego, 10,236 ....C 2
Lavos, 5,744 ....B 2
Leiria, 7,477 ....B 3
Lisbon (Lisboa) (cap.), 828,000..A 1
Loulé, 16,152 ....B 4
Louriçal, 5,608 ....B 3
Lourinhã, 8,677 ....B 3
Lousã, 8,191 ....B 2
Machico, 11,608 ....A 2
Marinha Grande, 15,699 ....B 3
Matosinhos, 37,694 ....B 2
Mértola, 5,682 ....C 4
Miranda do Corvo, 5,103 ....B 2
Montargil, 6,357 ....B 3
Montemor-o-Novo, 13,115 ....B 3
Montijo, 17,751 ....B 3
Moscavide, 22,065 ....A 1
Mourão, 12,126 ....C 3
Muge, 5,546 ....B 3
Nazaré, 9,189 ....B 3
Nisa, 5,262 ....C 3
Óbidos, 4,599 ....B 3
Odivelas, 27,423 ....A 1
Oeiras, 6,857 ....B 3
Olhão, 16,017 ....C 4
Olivais, 11,896 ....A 1
Oporto, 324,400 ....B 2
Ovar, 14,128 ....B 2
Peniche, 11,357 ....B 3
Pombal, 9,973 ....B 3
Ponta do Sol, 7,426 ....A 2
Ponte de Sor, 13,010 ....B 3
Portalegre, 11,017 ....C 3
Portimão, 12,129 ....B 4
Porto (Oporto), 324,400 ....B 2
Povoa de Varzim, 17,696 ....B 2
Proença-a-Nova, 6,060 ....B 3
Queluz, 14,703 ....A 1
Ribeira Brava, 8,726 ....A 2
Sacavém, 10,624 ....A 1
Santa Cruz, 9,858 ....A 2
Santarém, 16,449 ....B 3
Santiago do Cacém, 6,939 ....B 3
São Brás de Alportel, 9,058..........C 4
São João da Madeira, 11,921 ....B 2
São Teotónio, 8,183 ....B 4
Serpa, 10,967 ....C 4
Sertã, 6,909 ....B 3
Sesimbra, 16,837 ....B 3
Setúbal, 44,435 ....B 3
Sines, 8,866 ....B 4
Sintra, 19,930 ....B 3
Soure, 9,655 ....B 2
Tavira, 12,046 ....C 4
Tomar, 12,974 ....B 3
Tôrres Novas, 11,974 ....B 3
Tôrres Vedras, 13,091 ....B 3
Vagos, 8,281 ....B 2
Vendas Novas, 9,675 ....B 3
Viana do Castelo, 14,371 ....B 2
Vila do Conde, 12,771 ....B 2
Vila Franca de Xira, 13,404..........B 3
Vila Nova de Gaia, 45,739..........B 2
Vila Real, 10,263 ....C 2
Vila Real de Sto. António, 11,096 ....C 4
Viseu, 16,961 ....C 2

OTHER FEATURES

Carvoeiro (cape) ....B 3
Desertas (isls.) ....A 2
Douro (river) ....C 2
Estrela, Serra da (mts.) ....C 2
Foia (mt.) ....B 4
Guadiana (river) ....C 4
Lima (river) ....B 2
Madeira (isl.), 265,432 ....A 2
Minho (river) ....B 2
Mira (river) ....B 4
Monchique (mts.) ....B 4
Mondego (cape) ....B 3
Mondego (river) ....C 2
Monsanto (hill) ....A 1
Ossa (mts.) ....C 3
Palha, Mar da (bay) ....A 1
Roca (cape) ....B 3
Sado (river) ....B 3
Saint Vincent (cape) ....B 4
Santa María (cape) ....C 4
Setúbal (bay) ....B 3
Tagus (river) ....B 3
Tâmega (river) ....C 2
Tejo (Tagus) (river) ....B 3
Xarrama (river) ....B 3

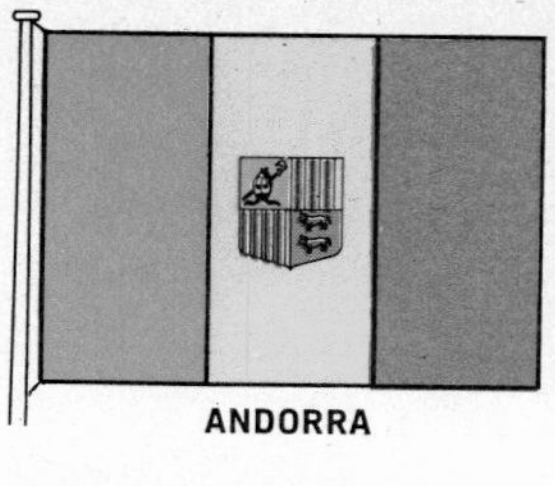

ANDORRA

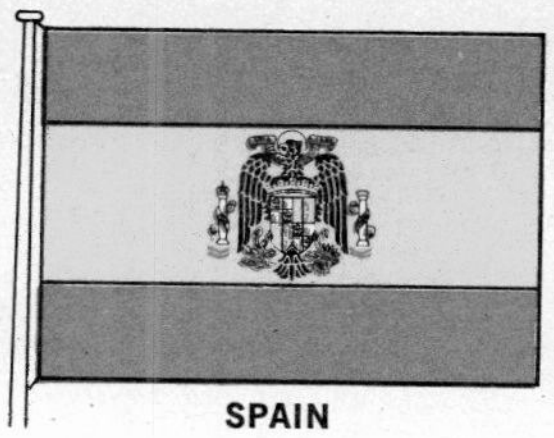

SPAIN

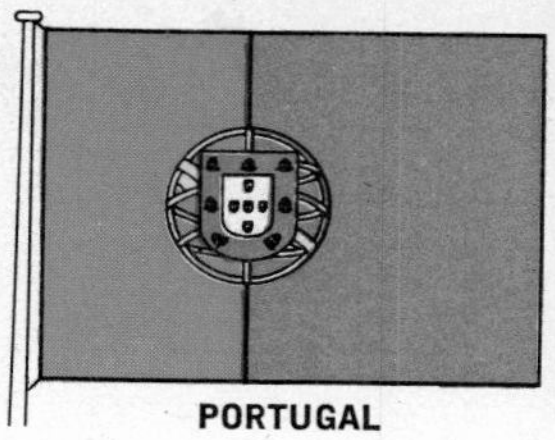

PORTUGAL

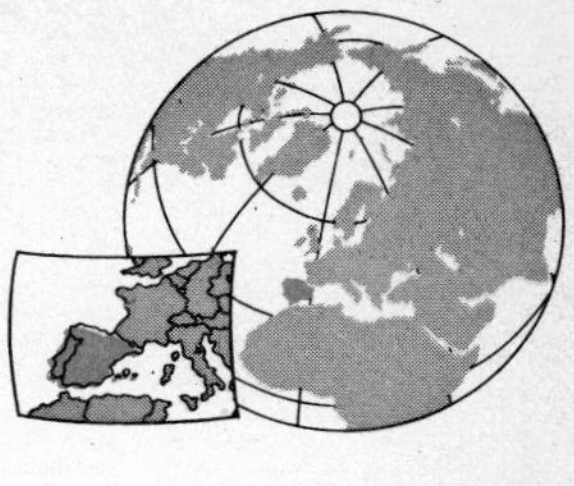

SPAIN

AREA 194,896 sq. mi.
POPULATION 33,290,000
CAPITAL Madrid
LARGEST CITY Madrid
HIGHEST POINT Pico de Teide 12,172 ft. (Canary Is.); Mulhacén 11,411 ft. (mainland)
MONETARY UNIT peseta
MAJOR LANGUAGES Spanish, Catalan, Basque
MAJOR RELIGION Roman Catholicism

ANDORRA

AREA 175 sq. mi.
POPULATION 19,000
CAPITAL Andorra la Vella
MONETARY UNIT French franc, Spanish peseta
MAJOR LANGUAGE Catalan
MAJOR RELIGION Roman Catholicism

PORTUGAL

AREA 35,510 sq. mi.
POPULATION 9,560,000
CAPITAL Lisbon
LARGEST CITY Lisbon
HIGHEST POINT Malhão da Estrêla 6,532 ft.
MONETARY UNIT escudo
MAJOR LANGUAGE Portuguese
MAJOR RELIGION Roman Catholicism

GIBRALTAR

AREA 2 sq. mi.
POPULATION 27,000
CAPITAL Gibraltar
MONETARY UNIT pound sterling
MAJOR LANGUAGES English, Spanish
MAJOR RELIGION Roman Catholicism

SPAIN

PROVINCES

Álava, 148,899 ....E 1
Albacete, 358,290 ....E 3
Alicante, 746,917 ....F 3
Almería, 360,798 ....E 4
Ávila, 231,916 ....D 2
Badajoz, 839,363 ....C 3
Baleares (Balearic Is.), 451,343..H 3
Barcelona, 3,213,212 ....G 2
Burgos, 372,138 ....E 1
Cáceres, 540,060 ....C 3
Cádiz, 874,837 ....D 4
Castellón, 344,350 ....G 2
Ciudad Real, 589,262 ....D 3
Córdoba, 802,633 ....D 3
Cuenca, 305,432 ....E 2
Gerona, 361,250 ....H 1
Granada, 760,210 ....E 4
Guadalajara, 174,572 ....E 2
Guipúzcoa, 532,095 ....E 1
Huelva, 413,459 ....C 4
Huesca, 231,376 ....F 1
Jaén, 720,559 ....E 4
La Coruña, 1,004,149 ....B 1
Las Palmas, 492,466 ....C 4
León, 600,935 ....C 1
Lérida, 336,818 ....G 2
Logroño, 228,922 ....E 1
Lugo, 464,922 ....C 1
Madrid, 2,973,619 ....E 2
Málaga, 783,436 ....D 4
Murcia, 817,545 ....F 4
Navarra, 409,239 ....F 1
Orense, 442,420 ....C 1
Oviedo, 1,034,244 ....C 1
Palencia, 230,426 ....D 1
Pontevedra, 681,295 ....B 1
Salamanca, 401,276 ....C 2
Santa Cruz de Tenerife, 525,095 ....B 5
Santander, 443,113 ....D 1
Saragossa, 670,357 ....F 2
Segovia, 192,229 ....D 2
Seville, 1,295,094 ....D 4
Soria, 140,517 ....E 2
Tarragona, 363,830 ....G 2
Teruel, 205,565 ....F 2
Toledo, 516,870 ....D 3
Valencia, 1,462,005 ....F 3
Valladolid, 368,685 ....D 2
Vizcaya, 852,768 ....E 1
Zamora, 293,489 ....D 2

CITIES and TOWNS

Adra, 10,211 ....E 4
Aguilar, 13,760 ....D 4
Aguilas, 11,970 ....F 4
Alagón, 5,270 ....F 2
Alayor, 4,988 ....J 3
Albacete, 61,635 ....F 3
Albox, 4,036 ....E 4
Alburqerque, 9,540 ....C 3
Alcalá de Chivert, 4,049 ....G 2
Alcalá de Guadaira. 27,378 ....D 4
Alcalá de Henares, 20,572 ....G 4
Alcalá de los Gazules, 7,015 ....D 4
Alcalá la Real, 8,351 ....E 4
Alcanar, 6,332 ....G 2
Alcañiz, 9,489 ....F 2
Alcántara, 3,564 ....C 3
Alcantarilla, 15,748 ....F 4
Alcaudete, 9,280 ....E 4
Alcázar de San Juan, 23,788..........E 3
Alcira, 22,417 ....F 3
Alcoy, 48,712 ....F 3
Alfaro, 8,570 ....F 1
Algeciras, 51,096 ....D 4
Algemesí, 16,683 ....F 3
Alhama de Granada, 6,989 ....E 4
Alhama de Murcia, 7,175 ....F 4
Alicante, 103,289 ....F 3
Almadén, 13,206 ....D 3
Almagro, 9,232 ....E 3
Almansa, 15,391 ....F 3
Almendralejo, 20,867 ....C 3
Almería, 76,643 ....E 4
Almodóvar del Campo, 8,115..........D 3
Almonte, 9,444 ....C 4
Almuñécar, 5,644 ....E 4
Álora, 6,459 ....D 4
Amposta, 11,026 ....G 2
Andújar, 23,897 ....D 3
Antequera, 28,400 ....D 4
Aracena, 5,605 ....C 4
Aranda de Duero, 12,623 ....E 2
Aranjuez, 25,988 ....E 2
Archena, 5,802 ....F 3
Archidona. 7.262 ....D 4
Arcos de la Frontera, 13,536 ......D 4
Arenas de San Pedro, 5,585........D 2
Arenys de Mar, 6,665 ....H 2
Argamasilla de Alba, 6,411 ....E 3
Arganda, 5,253 ....G 4
Arnedo, 7,958 ....E 1
Aroche, 5,319 ....C 4
Arrecife, 12,748 ....C 4
Arroyo de la Luz, 9,781 ....C 3
Arta, 5,173 ....H 3
Arucas, 10,917 ....B 5
Aspe, 9,742 ....F 3
Astorga, 10,101 ....C 1
Ávila de los Caballeros, 26,738 ....D 2
Avilés, 19,992 ....C 1
Ayamonte, 9,608 ....C 4
Ayora, 5,635 ....F 3
Azpeitia, 8,219 ....E 1
Azuaga, 15,477 ....D 3
Badajoz, 23,715 ....C 3
Badalona, 90,655 ....H 2
Baena, 17,612 ....D 4
Baeza, 13,329 ....E 4
Bailén, 11,144 ....E 3
Balaguer, 8,342 ....G 2
Bañolas, 7,531 ....H 1
Barajas, 9,058 ....F 4
Barbastro, 9,730 ....F 1
Barcarrota, 7,443 ....C 3
Barcelona, 1,555,564 ....H 2
Barruelo de Santullán, 3,761......D 1
Baza, 13,323 ....E 4
Beas de Segura, 8,194 ....E 3
Béjar, 14,225 ....D 2
Bélmez, 6,907 ....D 3
Benavente, 11,061 ....D 1
Benicarló, 10,627 ....G 2
Berga, 8,923 ....G 1
Berja, 7,989 ....E 4
Bermeo, 12,398 ....E 1
Betanzos, 6,999 ....B 1
Bilbao, 293,939 ....E 1
Blanes, 9,256 ....H 2
Borja, 4,335 ....F 2
Borjas Blancas, 5,086 ....G 2
Brozas, 5,634 ....C 3
Bujalance, 10,465 ....D 4
Bullas, 7,326 ....F 4
Burgos, 79,810 ....E 1
Burriana, 15,670 ....G 3
Cabeza del Buey, 10,734 ....D 3
Cabra, 15,688 ....D 4
Cáceres, 42,903 ....C 3
Cádiz, 117,871 ....C 4
Calahorra, 14,400 ....E 1
Calasparra, 7,543 ....F 3
Calatayud, 15,777 ....F 2
Calella, 7,947 ....H 2
Callosa de Ensarria, 4,617 ....G 3
Calzada de Calatrava, 7,536..........E 3
Campanario, 8,910 ....D 3
Campillos, 8,791 ....D 4
Campo de Criptana, 13,616..........E 3
Candeleda, 6,507 ....D 2
Cangas, 4,059 ....B 1
Caniles, 5,026 ....E 4
Caravaca, 10,016 ....E 3
Carcagente, 15,791 ....F 3
Carmona, 26,368 ....D 4
Cartagena, 42,424 ....F 4
Casar de Cáceres, 4,560 ....C 3
Caspe, 8,251 ....G 2
Castellón de la Plana, 52,868......G 3
Castro del Río, 11,200 ....D 4
Castro-Urdiales, 7,128 ....E 1
Castuera, 9,905 ....D 3
Caudete, 7,481 ....F 3
Cazalla de la Sierra, 9,414..........D 4
Cazorla, 7,932 ....E 4
Cebreros, 3,898 ....D 2
Ceclavín, 4,778 ....C 3
Cehegín, 10,467 ....F 3
Cervera, 5,215 ....G 2
Cervera del Río Alhama, 3,648....E 1
Ceuta, 88,000 ....D 5
Chiclana de la Frontera, 19,155..C 4
Chinchón, 4,432 ....G 5
Chiva, 3,978 ....F 3
Ciempozuelos, 9,042 ....F 5
Cieza, 20,620 ....F 3
Ciudadela, 10,872 ....H 2
Ciudad Real, 35,015 ....D 3
Cocentaina, 7,405 ....F 3
Coín, 11,441 ....D 4
Colmenar de Oreja, 5,119 ....G 5
Colmenar Viejo, 8,133 ....F 4
Constantina, 12,015 ....D 4
Consuegra, 10,572 ....E 3
Córdoba, 167,808 ....D 4
Corella, 5,591 ....F 1
Coria del Río, 13,781 ....C 4
Corral de Almaguer, 8,621 ....E 3
Crevillente, 12,025 ....F 3
Cuéllar, 5,703 ....D 2
Cuenca, 26,663 ....E 2
Cúllar de Baza, 3,769 ....E 4
Cullera, 13,040 ....F 3
Daimiel, 19,485 ....E 3
Denia, 8,281 ....G 3
Don Benito, 22,642 ....C 3
Dos Hermanas, 21,517 ....D 4
Durango, 11,882 ....E 1
Écija, 29,262 ....D 4
Eibar, 31,371 ....E 1
Ejea de los Caballeros, 9,000..........F 1
El Arahal, 15,107 ....D 4
El Bonillo, 5,215 ....E 3
Elche, 50,989 ....F 3
Elda, 24,182 ....F 3
El Ferrol del Caudillo, 62,010..........B 1
El Puerto de Santa María, 31,848 ....C 4
Énguera, 4,606 ....F 3
Espejo, 8,006 ....D 4
Estella, 8,142 ....E 1
Estepa, 8,628 ....D 4
Estepona, 11,309 ....D 4
Felanitx, 7,860 ....H 3
Fermoselle, 3,885 ....C 2
Figueras, 16,460 ....H 1
Fraga, 8,264 ....G 2

Agriculture, Industry and Resources

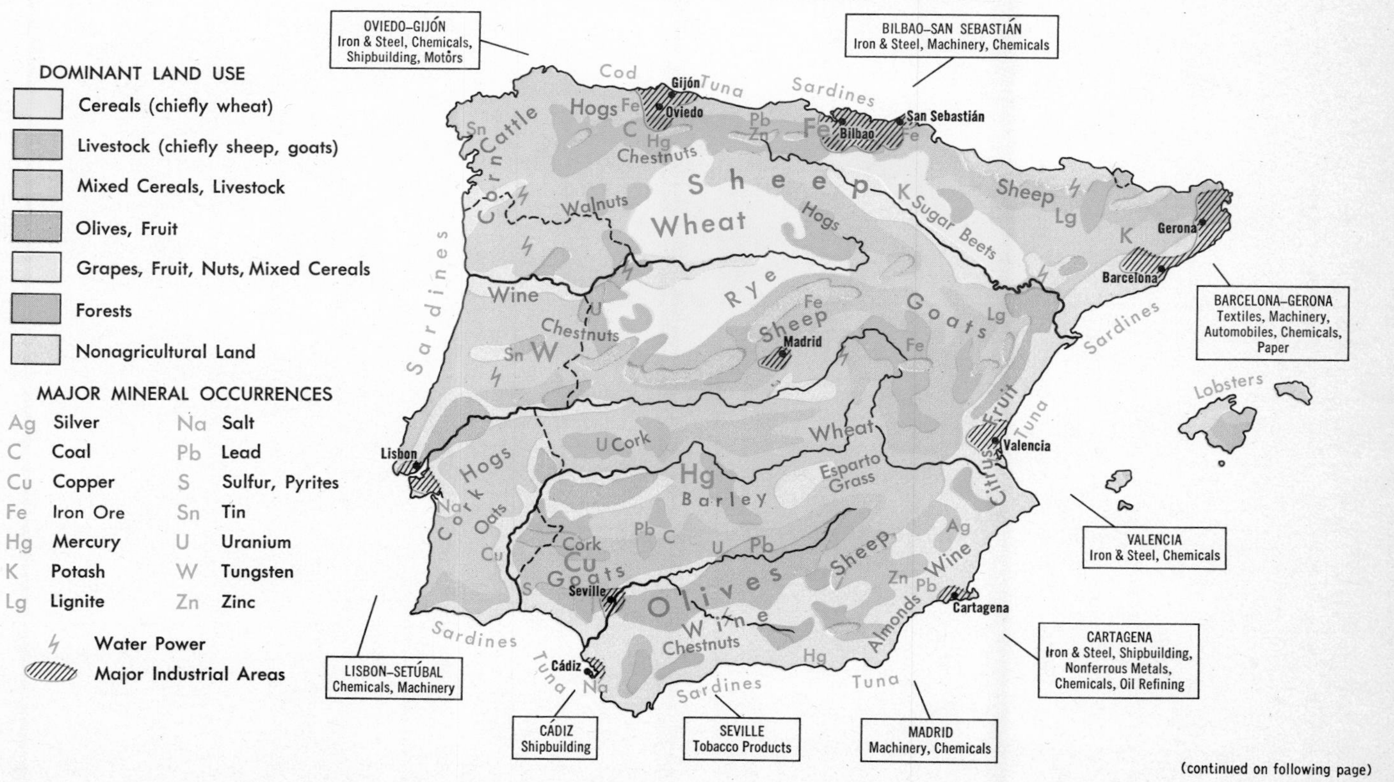
DOMINANT LAND USE
Cereals (chiefly wheat)
Livestock (chiefly sheep, goats)
Mixed Cereals, Livestock
Olives, Fruit
Grapes, Fruit, Nuts, Mixed Cereals
Forests
Nonagricultural Land
MAJOR MINERAL OCCURRENCES
Ag Silver
C Coal
Cu Copper
Fe Iron Ore
Hg Mercury
K Potash
Lg Lignite
Na Salt
Pb Lead
S Sulfur, Pyrites
Sn Tin
U Uranium
W Tungsten
Zn Zinc
Water Power
Major Industrial Areas
OVIEDO–GIJÓN
Iron & Steel, Chemicals, Shipbuilding, Motors
BILBAO–SAN SEBASTIÁN
Iron & Steel, Machinery, Chemicals
BARCELONA–GERONA
Textiles, Machinery, Automobiles, Chemicals, Paper
VALENCIA
Iron & Steel, Chemicals
CARTAGENA
Iron & Steel, Shipbuilding, Nonferrous Metals, Chemicals, Oil Refining
LISBON–SETÚBAL
Chemicals, Machinery
CÁDIZ
Shipbuilding
SEVILLE
Tobacco Products
MADRID
Machinery, Chemicals
Gijón
Oviedo
Bilbao
San Sebastián
Gerona
Barcelona
Madrid
Valencia
Lisbon
Seville
Cádiz
Cartagena
Cod
Tuna
Sardines
Lobsters
Cattle
Corn
Hogs
Chestnuts
Walnuts
Wheat
Sheep
Sugar Beets
Wine
Rye
Goats
Fruit
Citrus Fruit
Cork
Oats
Barley
Esparto Grass
Olives
Almonds

(continued on following page)

SPAIN (continued)

Fregenal de la Sierra, 9,506......C 3
Fuengirola, 5,622 ....D 4
Fuensalida, 4,697 ....D 3
Fuente de Cantos, 8,484 ....C 3
Fuente-Obejuna, 5,353 ....C 3
Fuentes de Andalucía, 8,357.......D 4
Gálvez, 3,828 ....D 3
Gándara, 400 ....C 1
Gandía, 15,940 ....F 3
Garrovillas, 5,665 ....C 3
Gerona, 28,134 ....H 2
Getafe, 21,066 ....D 4
Gijón, 92,020 ....D 1
Granada, 150,186 ....E 4
Granollers, 18,810 ....H 2
Guadalajara, 20,135 ....E 2
Guadalcanal, 5,483 ....D 3
Guadix, 15,897 ....E 4
Guareña, 8,438 ....C 3
Guernica y Luno, 4,855 ....E 1
Haro, 8,375 ....E 1
Hellín, 17,071 ....F 3
Herencia, 8,606 ....E 3
Herrera del Duque, 5,404 ....D 3
Hinojosa del Duque, 14,074.......D 3
Hortaleza, 8,552 ....G 4
Hospitalet, 122,813 ....H 2
Huelma, 6,382 ....E 4
Huelva, 56,548 ....C 4
Huércal-Overa, 4,406 ....F 4
Huesca, 5,097 ....F 1
Huéscar, 24,338 ....E 4
Huéscar, 5,097 ....E 4
Ibiza, 11,259 ....G 3
Igualada, 19,866 ....G 2
Illora, 5,586 ....E 4
Inca, 13,816 ....H 3
Iniesta, 4,292 ....F 3
Irún, 20,212 ....E 1
Isla Cristina, 9,616 ....C 4
Jaca, 9,821 ....F 1
Jaén, 59,699 ....E 4
Jaraiz, 8,130 ....D 2

Jativa, 19,195 ....F 3
Jávea, 4,929 ....G 3
Jerez de la Frontera, 96,209.....C 4
Jerez de los Caballeros, 12,349..C 3
Jijona, 5,147 ....F 3
Jódar, 14,289 ....E 4
Jumilla, 15,703 ....F 3
La Bañeza, 7,869 ....C 1
La Bisbal, 5,194 ....H 1
La Carolina, 10,915 ....E 3
La Coruña, 161,260 ....B 1
La Gineta, 3,237 ....E 3
La Línea, 58,169 ....D 4
La Orotava, 8,019 ....B 4
La Palma del Condado, 8,526......C 4
La Puebla, 9,931 ....H 3
La Puebla de Montalbán, 7,286....D 3
La Rambla, 8,057 ....D 4
La Roda, 11,739 ....E 3
La Solana, 14,948 ....E 3
Las Palmas, 166,236 ....B 4
Las Pedroñeras, 6,418 ....E 3
La Unión, 19,705 ....F 4
Lavaderos, 9,708 ....B 1
Lebrija, 13,663 ....C 4
Ledesma, 2,527 ....C 2
Leganés, 8,064 ....F 4
Lena, Pola de, 3,966 ....D 1
León, 73,483 ....D 1
Lérida, 50,047 ....G 2
Linares, 50,527 ....E 3
Liria, 9,723 ....F 3
Llerena, 7,854 ....C 3
Lluchmayor, 9,827 ....H 3
Logrosán, 58,545 ....E 1
Logroña, 6,595 ....D 3
Loja, 11,441 ....D 4
Lora del Río, 15,086 ....D 4
Lorca, 19,854 ....F 4
Los Navalmorales, 4,686 ....D 3
Los Navalucillos, 4,823 ....D 3
Los Santos de Maimona, 8,910.....C 3

Los Yébenes, 6,596 ....E 3
Luarca, 4,070 ....C 1
Lucena, 19,975 ....D 4
Lugo, 45,497 ....C 1
Madrid (cap.), 2,850,631 ....F 4
Madridejos, 9,795 ....E 3
Madroñera, 5,256 ....D 3
Mahón, 14,836 ....J 3
Málaga, 259,245 ....D 4
Malagón, 9,246 ....E 3
Malpartida de Cáceres, 5,751.....C 2
Malpartida de Plasencia, 6,757...C 2
Manacor, 17,544 ....H 3
Mancha Real, 7,587 ....E 4
Manlleu, 8,489 ....H 1
Manresa, 46,105 ....G 2
Manzanares, 16,639 ....E 3
Marbella, 7,302 ....D 4
Marchena, 15,879 ....D 4
Marín, 8,838 ....B 1
Martos, 16,442 ....E 4
Mataró, 29,937 ....H 2
Mazarrón, 3,379 ....F 4
Medina del Campo, 13,640 ....D 2
Medina de Ríoseco, 4,897 ....D 2
Medina-Sidonia, 6,869 ....D 4
Menasalbas, 4,407 ....D 3
Mérida, 28,791 ....C 3
Miajadas, 8,632 ....D 3
Mieres, 19,308 ....D 1
Miranda de Ebro, 22,836 ....E 1
Moguer, 6,776 ....C 4
Monasterio, 7,559 ....C 4
Monforte, 13,737 ....C 1
Monóvar, 7,972 ....F 3
Montánchez, 4,190 ....D 3
Montefrío, 4,917 ....D 4
Montehermoso, 6,006 ....C 2
Montellano, 8,694 ....D 4
Montijo, 12,519 ....C 3
Montilla, 19,830 ....D 4
Montoro, 11,243 ....D 3
Mora, 10,613 ....E 3

Moratalla, 5,675 ....E 3
Morón de la Frontera, 29,096.....D 4
Mota del Cuervo, 5,403 ....E 3
Motril, 18,624 ....E 4
Mula, 9,912 ....F 3
Munera, 5,931 ....E 3
Murcia, 83,190 ....F 4
Nava del Rey, 3,815 ....D 2
Navalcarnero, 4,681 ....F 4
Navalmoral de la Mata, 8,978.....D 2
Navalucillos, Los, 4,823 ....D 3
Nerja, 5,767 ....E 4
Nerva, 11,974 ....C 3
Novelda, 11,003 ....F 3
Nules, 7,626 ....F 3
Ocaña, 6,592 ....E 3
Oliva, 13,342 ....F 3
Oliva de la Frontera, 11,141.....C 3
Olivenza, 8,304 ....C 3
Olot, 13,099 ....H 1
Olvera, 9,088 ....D 4
Onda, 10,666 ....F 3
Onteniente, 18,787 ....F 3
Orellana la Vieja, 6,925 ....D 3
Orense, 40,517 ....C 1
Orihuela, 15,873 ....F 3
Osuna, 17,671 ....D 4
Oviedo, 91,550 ....D 1
Padul, 6,868 ....E 4
Palafrugell, 7,476 ....H 2
Palamós, 5,481 ....H 2
Palencia, 48,144 ....D 2
Palma, 136,431 ....H 3
Palma del Río, 14,053 ....D 4
Pamplona, 59,227 ....F 1
Paredes de Nava, 4,065 ....D 1
Pego, 8,291 ....F 3
Peñafiel, 5,333 ....E 2
Peñaranda de Bracamonte, 5,943 ..D 2
Peñarroya-Pueblonuevo, 17,449....D 3
Piedrabuena, 5,453 ....D 3
Pinos-Puente, 8,311 ....E 4
Plasencia, 21,297 ....C 2
Pollensa, 7,370 ....H 3

Ponferrada, 17,042 ....C 1
Pontevedra, 19,739 ....B 1
Porcuna, 9,671 ....D 4
Portugalete, 20,514 ....E 1
Posadas, 8,440 ....D 3
Pozoblanco, 14,728 ....D 3
Priego de Córdoba, 13,469 ....D 4
Puebla de Don Fadrique, 3,771....E 4
Puebla de Montalbán, La, 7,286...D 3
Puente-Genil, 24,836 ....D 4
Puertollano, 48,528 ....D 3
Puerto Real, 12,717 ....C 4
Quesada, 6,503 ....E 4
Quintana de la Serena, 7,160.....D 3
Quintanar de la Orden, 9,483.....E 3
Reinosa, 10,044 ....D 1
Requena, 8,278 ....F 3
Reus, 32,037 ....G 2
Ripoll, 7,821 ....H 1
Ronda, 17,703 ....D 4
Rota, 14,236 ....C 4
Rute, 8,945 ....D 4
Sabadell, 98,049 ....H 2
Sagunto, 15,210 ....F 3
Salamanca, 90,388 ....D 2

Sallent, 7,462 ....H 2
Sama, 7,149 ....D 1
San Carlos de la Rápita, 6,844...G 2
San Clemente, 6,411 ....E 3
San Felíu de Guixols, 9,077......H 2
San Fernando, 51,406 ....C 4
San Lorenzo de El Escorial,7,455 E 2
Sanlúcar de Barrameda, 32,580....C 4
Sanlúcar la Mayor, 6,094 ....C 4
San Sebastián, 98,603 ....E 1
Santa Cruz de la Palma, 9,928....B 4
Santa Cruz de la Mudela, 8,724...E 3
Santa Cruz de la Zarza, 5,588....E 3
Santa Cruz de Tenerife, 82,620...B 4
Santa Eugenia, 5,336 ....B 1
Santafé, 8,212 ....E 4
Santander, 98,784 ....D 1
Santiago, 37,916 ....B 1
Santoña, 7,535 ....E 1
Seglorbe, 7,136 ....F 3
Segovia, 33,360 ....D 2
Seville (Sevilla), 423,762.......D 4

Sitges, 6,796 ....G 2
Socuéllamos, 14,742 ....E 3
Sóller, 6,011 ....H 3
Sonseca, 5,994 ....E 3
Soria, 18,872 ....E 2
Sueca, 19,005 ....F 3
Tabernes de Valldigna, 12,890....G 3
Tafalla, 7,320 ....E 1
Talavera de la Reina, 28,107.....D 2
Tarancón, 7,678 ....E 2
Tarazona de Aragón, 11,004.......F 2
Tarazona de la Mancha, 6,850.....E 3
Tarifa, 9,147 ....D 4
Tarragona, 35,689 ....G 2
Tarrasa, 89,128 ....H 2
Tárrega, 7,317 ....G 2
Tauste, 6,544 ....F 2
Telde, 6,711 ....B 5
Teruel, 18,304 ....F 2
Toledo, 39,367 ....D 3
Tolosa, 10,980 ....E 1
Tomelloso, 27,715 ....E 3
Toro, 9,123 ....D 2
Torredonjimeno, 12,848 ....D 4

Topography

0 50 100
MILES

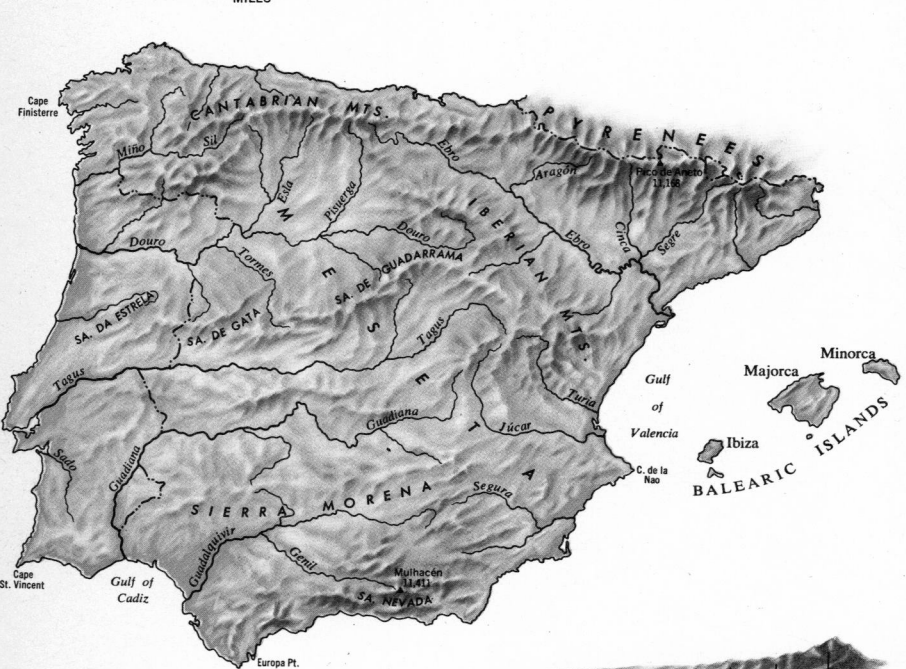

Below Sea Level | 100 m. 328 ft. | 200 m. 656 ft. | 500 m. 1,640 ft. | 1,000 m. 3,281 ft. | 2,000 m. 6,562 ft. | 5,000 m. 16,404 ft.

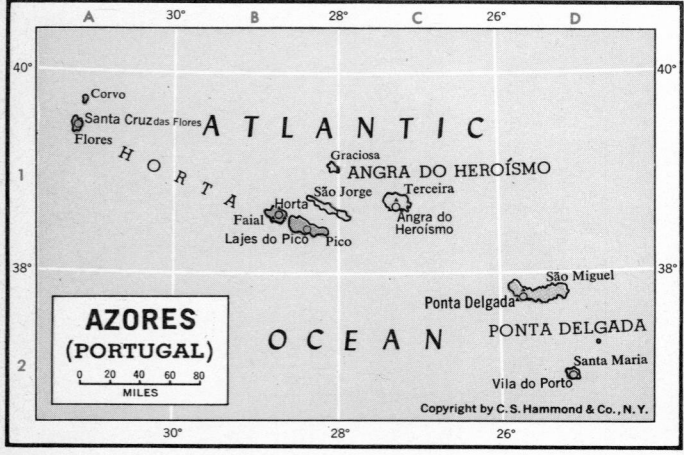

AZORES
(PORTUGAL)

0 20 40 60 80
MILES

AZORES

DISTRICTS

Angra do Heroísmo, 103,800......C 1
Horta, 44,900 ....A 1
Ponta Delgada, 185,600 ....D 2

CITIES and TOWNS

Angra do Heroísmo, 13,502 ......C 1
Horta, 7,109 ....B 1
Lajes do Pico, 2,508 ....B 1
Ponta Delgada, 22,316 ....D 2
Santa Cruz das Flores, 1,898....A 1
Vila do Porto, 5,373 ....D 2

OTHER FEATURES

Corvo (isl.), 681 ....A 1
Faial (isl.), 20,281 ....B 1
Flores (isl.), 6,583 ....A 1
Graciosa (isl.), 8,669 ....C 1
Pico (isl.), 21,831 ....C 1
Santa Maria (isl.), 13,233......D 2
São Jorge (isl.), 15,895 ....B 1
São Miguel (isl.), 168,691......D 2
Terceira (isl.), 71,610.........C 1

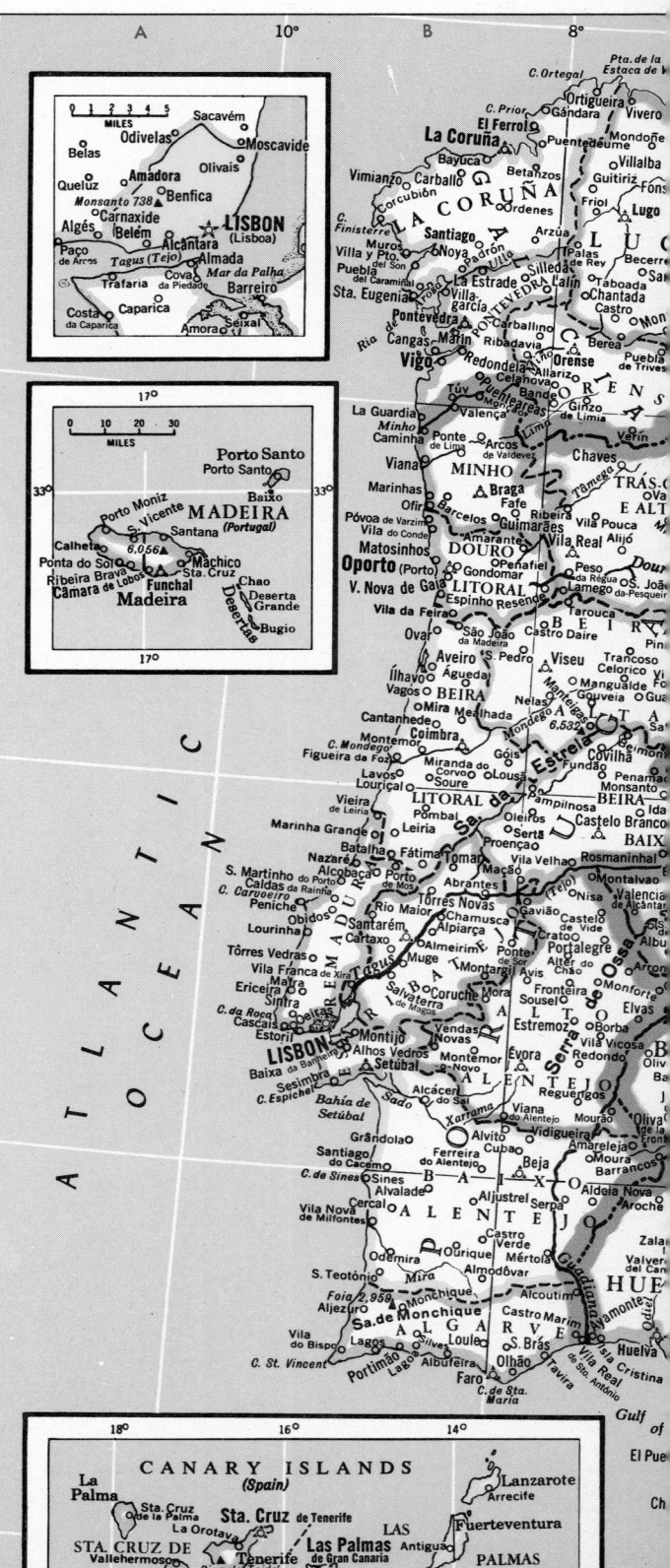

Torrejoncillo, 5,499 .... C 3
Torrelavega, 13,612 .... D 1
Torremolinos, 7,980 .... D 4
Torrente, 23,432 .... F 3
Torrevieja, 8,961 .... F 4
Torrox, 5,211 .... E 4
Tortosa, 18,674 .... G 2
Totana, 10,156 .... F 4
Trigueros, 6,151 .... C 4
Trujillo, 13,326 .... D 3
Tudela, 16,422 .... F 1
Úbeda, 26,930 .... E 3
Ubrique, 8,915 .... D 4
Urda, 5,479 .... E 3
Utiel, 9,720 .... F 3
Utrera, 25,935 .... D 4
Valdepeñas, 24,462 .... E 3
Valdevereja, 3,607 .... D 2
Valencia, 466,571 .... F 3
Valencia de Alcántara, 13,159 .... C 3
Valladolid, 133,486 .... D 2
Vall de Uxó, 18,577 .... F 3
Vallehermoso, 887 .... A 5
Valls, 10,890 .... G 2
Valverde del Camino, 10,843 .... C 4

Vejer de la Frontera, 11,853 .... C 4
Vélez-Málaga, 14,348 .... D 4
Vélez Rubio, 4,113 .... E 4
Vich, 18,184 .... H 2
Vigo, 69,429 .... B 1
Villacañas, 10,113 .... E 3
Villacarrillo, 10,970 .... E 3
Villafranca de los Barros, 14,591 .... C 3
Villafranca del Panadés, 11,306 .... G 2
Villagarcía, 4,391 .... B 1
Villahermosa, 5,496 .... E 3
Villajoyosa, 7,508 .... F 3
Villanueva de Córdoba, 15,719 .... D 3
Villanueva del Arzobispo, 9,307 .... E 3
Villanueva de la Serena, 17,647 .... D 3
Villanueva de los Infantes, 9,909 .... E 3
Villanueva y Geltrú, 25,669 .... G 2
Villar del Arzobispo, 3,876 .... F 3
Villarreal de los Infantes, 20,025 .... G 3
Villarrobledo, 19,585 .... E 3
Villarrubia de los Ojos, 9,043 .... E 3
Villena, 18,333 .... F 3
Vinaroz, 10,968 .... G 2

Yecla, 17,955 .... F 3
Zafra, 9,950 .... C 3
Zalamea de la Serena, 8,543 .... D 3
Zamora, 41,319 .... D 2
Zaragoza (Saragossa), 295,080 .... F 2
Zarza la Mayor, 3,728 .... C 3
Zorita, 5,718 .... D 3

OTHER FEATURES

Alagón (river) .... C 2
Alborán (isl.) .... E 5
Alcudia (bay) .... H 3
Almanzor (mt.) .... D 2
Almanzora (river) .... F 4
Andalusia (reg.), 6,011,026 .... D 4
Aneto (mt.) .... G 1
Aragón (river) .... F 1
Aragón (reg.), 1,107,298 .... F 2
Asturias (reg.), 1,034,244 .... D 1
Autza (mt.) .... F 1
Balearic (isls.), 451,343 .... H 3
Bañuelo (mt.) .... D 4
Barbate (river) .... D 4
Biscay (bay) .... E 1

Cádiz (gulf) .... C 4
Canary (isls.), 1,017,361 .... B 4
Cantabrian (mts.) .... D 1
Castile, New (reg.), 4,559,755 .... E 3
Castile, Old (reg.), 2,207,946 .... D 2
Catalonia (reg.), 4,275,110 .... G 2
Cinca (river) .... G 2
Columbretes (isls.) .... G 3
Costa Brava (reg.) .... H 2
Costa del Sol (reg.) .... D 4
Creus (cape) .... H 1
Cuenca (mts.) .... F 3
Demanda (mts.) .... E 1
Douro (Duero) (river) .... C 2
Duratón (river) .... E 2
Ebro (river) .... G 2
Eresma (river) .... D 2
Esla (river) .... D 1
Estremadura (region), 1,379,423 .... C 3
Finisterre (cape) .... B 1
Formentor (cape) .... H 2
Fuerteventura (isl.), 18,138 .... C 4
Galicia (reg.), 2,592,786 .... B 1
Gata (cape) .... E 4
Gata (mts.) .... C 3

Genil (river) .... D 4
Gibraltar (strait) .... D 5
Gomera (isl.), 27,790 .... A 5
Gran Canaria (isl.), 400,837 .... B 5
Gredos (mts.) .... D 3
Guadalimar (river) .... E 3
Guadalquivir (river) .... C 4
Guadarrama (mts.) .... E 2
Guadiana (river) .... D 3
Gúdar, Sierra da (mts.) .... F 2
Henares (river) .... E 2
Hierro (isl.), 7,957 .... A 5
Huelva (river) .... C 4
Ibiza (Iviza) (isl.), 34,495 .... G 3
Jalón (river) .... F 2
Jarama (river) .... E 2
Júcar (river) .... F 3
Lanzarote (isl.), 34,805 .... C 4
León (reg.), 1,295,700 .... D 1
Lima (river) .... B 1
Llobregat (river) .... H 2
Majorca (isl.), 363,199 .... H 3
Mallorca (Majorca) (isl.), 363,199 .... H 3

Mancha, La (dist.) .... E 3
Manzanares (river) .... F 4
Marismas, Las (marsh) .... C 4
Menor, Mar (lagoon) .... F 4
Menorca (Minorca) (isl.), 42,954 .... J 2
Miño (river) .... B 1
Minorca (isl.), 42,954 .... J 2
Moncayo (mt.) .... F 2
Montserrat (mt.) .... G 2
Morena, Sierra (range) .... D 3
Mulhacén (mt.) .... E 4
Murcia (reg.), 1,175,835 .... F 4
Nao (cape) .... G 3
Navia (river) .... C 1
Nevada, Sierra (range) .... E 4
Orbigo (river) .... D 1
Ortegal (cape) .... B 1
Palma (isl.), 67,141 .... A 4
Peñalara (mt.) .... E 2
Penibética (mts.) .... E 4
Peñarroya (mt.) .... F 2
Perales (river) .... F 4
Perdido (mt.) .... G 1
Puigmal (mt.) .... H 1

Pyrenees (mts.) .... G 1
Rosas (gulf) .... H 1
Rouge (mt.) .... G 1
San Jorge (gulf) .... G 2
San Pedro (cape) .... C 3
Sebollera (mt.) .... E 2
Segre (river) .... G 1
Segura (river) .... F 3
Sil (river) .... C 1
Tagus (Tajo) (river) .... C 3
Teide (peak) .... B 5
Tenerife (isl.), 387,767 .... B 5
Ter (river) .... H 1
Tinto (river) .... C 4
Toledo (mts.) .... D 3
Torote (river) .... F 2
Trafalgar (cape) .... C 4
Turia (river) .... F 3
Ulla (river) .... B 1
Urgel (plain) .... G 2
Valencia (reg.) .... F 3
Valencia (gulf) .... G 3
Valencia (lagoon) .... F 3
Valencia (reg.), 2,553,272 .... F 3
Vascongadas (reg.), 1,533,762 .... E 1

*City and suburbs.

SPAIN and PORTUGAL

CONIC PROJECTION

SCALE OF MILES

SCALE OF KILOMETRES

Capitals of Countries _____☆
Provincial Capitals _____△
International Boundaries _____
Provincial Boundaries _____

© Copyright by C.S. HAMMOND & Co., Maplewood, N.J.

ITALY
CONIC PROJECTION

SCALE OF MILES
0 20 40 60 80 100

SCALE OF KILOMETERS
0 20 40 60 80 100

Capitals of Countries _____ ☆
Regional Capitals _____ ⌖
Provincial Capitals _____ △
International Boundaries _·_··_··_
Regional Boundaries _·_·_·_·_

ITALY is divided for administrative purposes into 20 regions, shown on the map in separate colors.

The regions are subdivided into provinces bearing the same names as their respective capitals, except:

PROVINCE	CAPITAL
MASSA-CARRARA	Massa
PESARO-URBINO	Pesaro

Copyright by C.S. HAMMOND & Co., N.Y.

VATICAN CITY

SCALE
0 300 600 ft.

ROME and ENVIRONS

MILES
0 5 10 15

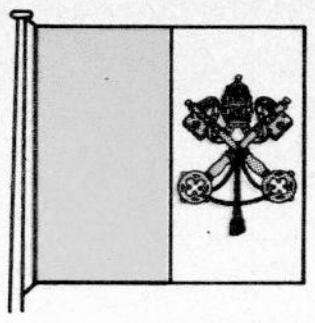

VATICAN CITY
AREA 109 acres
POPULATION 1,000

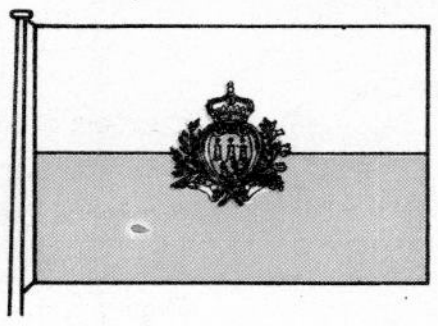

SAN MARINO
AREA 23.4 sq. mi.
POPULATION 19,000

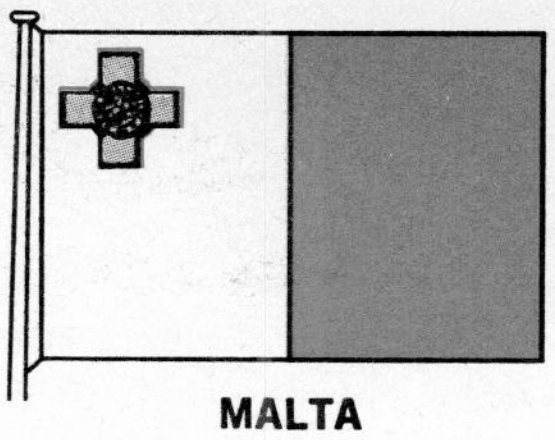

MALTA

AREA 122 sq. mi.
POPULATION 321,000
CAPITAL Valletta
LARGEST CITY Sliema
HIGHEST POINT 787 ft.
MONETARY UNIT Maltese pound
MAJOR LANGUAGES Maltese, English
MAJOR RELIGION Roman Catholicism

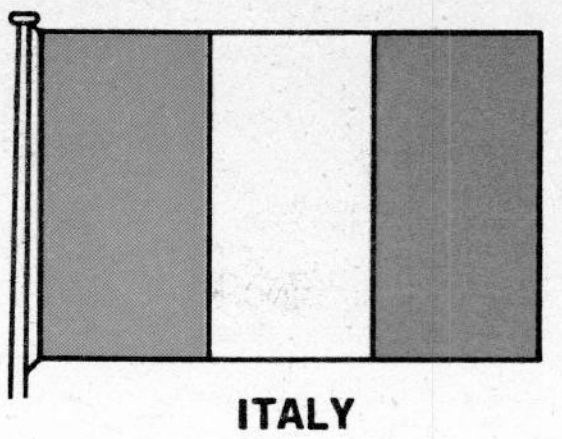

ITALY

AREA 116,303 sq. mi.
POPULATION 54,504,000
CAPITAL Rome
LARGEST CITY Rome
HIGHEST POINT Dufourspitze (Mte. Rosa) 15,203 ft.
MONETARY UNIT lira
MAJOR LANGUAGE Italian
MAJOR RELIGION Roman Catholicism

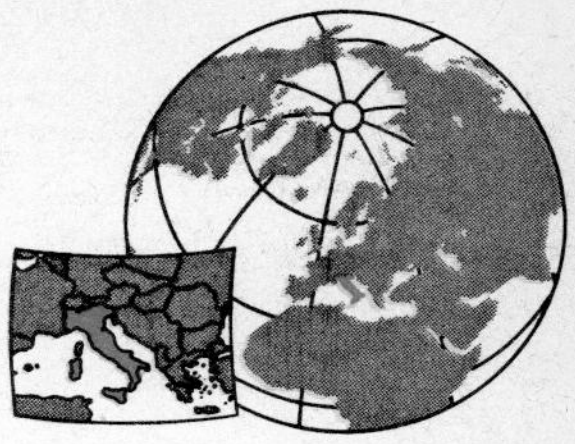

ITALY

REGIONS

Abruzzi, 1,206,266 .... D 3
Aosta, 100,959 .... A 2
Apulia, 3,421,217 .... F 4
Basilicata, 644,297 .... F 4
Calabria, 2,045,047 .... F 5
Campania, 4,760,759 .... E 4
Emilia-Romagna, 3,666,680 .... C 2
Friuli-Venezia Giulia, 1,204,298 ... D 1
Latium, 3,958,957 .... D 4
Liguria, 1,735,349 .... B 2
Lombardy, 7,406,152 .... B 2
Marche, 1,347,489 .... D 3
Molise, 358,052 .... E 4
Piedmont, 3,914,250 .... A 2
Puglia (Apulia), 3,421,217 .... F 4
Sardinia, 1,419,362 .... B 4
Sicily, 4,721,001 .... E 6
Trentino-Alto Adige, 785,967 .... C 1
Tuscany, 3,286,160 .... C 3
Umbria, 794,745 .... D 3
Venetia, 3,846,562 .... C 2

PROVINCES

Agrigento, 472,945 .... D 6
Alessandria, 478,613 .... B 2
Ancona, 405,709 .... D 3
Aosta, 100,959 .... A 2
Arezzo, 308,964 .... C 3
Ascoli Piceno, 335,627 .... D 3
Asti, 214,604 .... B 2
Avellino, 464,904 .... E 4
Bari, 1,263,245 .... F 4
Belluno, 234,921 .... D 1
Benevento, 313,020 .... E 4
Bergamo, 744,670 .... B 2
Bologna, 841,474 .... C 2
Bolzano, 373,863 .... C 1
Brescia, 882,949 .... C 2
Brindisi, 345,635 .... G 4
Cagliari, 754,965 .... B 5
Caltanissetta, 302,513 .... D 6
Campobasso, 358,052 .... E 4
Caserta, 649,327 .... E 4
Catania, 893,542 .... E 6
Catanzaro, 741,509 .... F 5
Chieti, 373,632 .... E 3
Como, 622,132 .... B 2
Cosenza, 694,398 .... F 5
Cremona, 351,160 .... B 2
Cuneo, 536,356 .... A 2
Enna, 229,126 .... E 6
Ferrara, 403,218 .... C 2
Florence, 1,012,703 .... C 3
Foggia, 665,286 .... E 4
Forlì, 521,128 .... D 2
Frosinone, 438,254 .... D 4
Genoa, 1,031,091 .... B 2
Gorizia, 137,745 .... D 2
Grosseto, 220.305 .... C 3
Imperia, 202,160 .... B 3
L'Aquila, 328,989 .... D 3
La Spezia, 239,256 .... B 2
Latina, 319,056 .... D 4
Lecce, 678,338 .... G 4
Leghorn, 310,210 .... C 3
Lucca, 365,540 .... C 3
Macerata, 291,412 .... D 3
Mantua, 387,255 .... C 2
Massa-Carrara, 202,981 .... C 2
Matera, 200,131 .... F 4
Messina, 685,260 .... E 5
Milan, 3,156,815 .... B 2
Modena, 511,355 .... C 2
Naples, 2,421,243 .... E 4
Novara, 460,190 .... B 2
Nuoro, 283,206 .... B 4
Padua, 694,017 .... C 2
Palermo, 1,111,397 .... D 5
Parma, 389,199 .... C 2
Pavia, 518,193 .... B 2
Perugia, 570,149 .... D 3
Pesaro e Urbino, 314,741 .... D 3
Pescara, 242,958 .... E 3
Piacenza, 291,059 .... B 2
Pisa, 362,396 .... C 3
Pistoia, 232,999 .... C 2
Pordenone, 241,724 .... D 2
Potenza, 444,166 .... E 4
Ragusa, 252,769 .... E 6
Ravenna, 329,559 .... D 2
Reggio di Calabria, 609,140 .... E 5
Reggio nell'Emilia, 379,688 .... C 2
Rieti, 162,405 .... D 3
Rome, 2,775,380 .... F 6
Rovigo, 277,811 .... C 2
Salerno, 912,265 .... E 4
Sassari, 381,191 .... B 4
Savona, 262,842 .... B 2
Siena, 270,062 .... C 3
Sondrio, 161,450 .... B 1
Syracuse, 345,777 .... E 6
Taranto, 468,713 .... F 4
Teramo, 260,687 .... D 3
Terni, 224,596 .... D 3
Trapani, 427,672 .... D 5
Trento, 412,104 .... C 1
Treviso, 607,616 .... D 2
Trieste, 298,645 .... E 2
Turin, 1,824,254 .... A 2
Udine, 526,184 .... D 1
Varese, 581,528 .... B 2
Venice, 749,173 .... D 2
Vercelli, 400,233 .... B 2
Verona, 667,517 .... C 2
Vicenza, 615,507 .... C 2
Viterbo, 263,862 .... C 3

CITIES and TOWNS

Acireale, 26,744 .... E 6
Acqui Terme, 14,070 .... B 2
Acri, 7,660 .... F 5
Adrano, 31,411 .... E 6
Adria, 11,456 .... D 2
Agira, 13,157 .... E 6
Agrigento, 46,947 .... D 6
Agropoli, 7,200 .... E 4
Alassio, 10,492 .... A 2
Alatri, 5,311 .... D 4
Alba, 16,396 .... B 2
Albano Laziale, 13,007 .... F 7
Albenga, 9,429 .... B 3
Albino, 6,875 .... B 2
Alcamo, 42,974 .... D 6
Alessandria, 65,908 .... B 2
Alghero, 22,139 .... B 4
Altamura, 41,528 .... F 4
Amalfi, 5,183 .... E 4
Amantea, 5,910 .... E 5
Ancona, 77,748 .... D 3
Andria, 69,499 .... F 4
Anzio, 12,102 .... D 4
Aosta, 28,637 .... A 2
Aprilia, 8,784 .... D 4
Aragona, 12,119 .... D 6
Arezzo, 43,868 .... C 3
Ariano Irpino, 11,302 .... E 4
Ascoli Piceno, 33,825 .... D 3
Assisi, 5,302 .... D 3
Asti, 44,455 .... B 2
Augusta, 25,774 .... E 6
Avellino, 31,744 .... E 4
Aversa, 40,245 .... E 4
Avezzano, 24,120 .... D 3
Avigliano, 5,119 .... E 4
Avola, 27,197 .... E 6
Bagheria, 31,435 .... D 5
Barcellona Pozzo di Gotto, 32,147 .... D 5
Bari, 293,963 .... F 4
Barletta, 67,419 .... F 4
Bassano del Grappa, 24,077 .... C 2
Belluno, 15,400 .... D 1
Benevento, 41,467 .... E 4
Bergamo, 110,666 .... B 2
Biancavilla, 19,858 .... E 6
Biella, 42,994 .... B 2
Bisceglie, 40,520 .... F 4
Bitonto, 34,160 .... F 4
Bitti, 5,623 .... B 4
Bologna, 443,178 .... C 2
Bolzano, 84,685 .... C 1
Bondeno, 6,413 .... C 2
Bonorva, 6,192 .... B 4
Bordighera, 9,045 .... A 3
Borgomanero, 11,843 .... B 2
Borgo San Lorenzo, 6,135 .... C 2
Bosa, 7,890 .... B 4
Bra, 14,472 .... A 2
Bracciano, 6,460 .... C 3
Brescia, 140,518 .... C 2
Bressanone, 10,095 .... C 1
Brindisi, 63,480 .... G 4
Bronte, 19,418 .... E 6
Busto Arsizio, 58,483 .... B 2
Cagliari, 172,925 .... B 5
Caltagirone, 37,634 .... E 6
Caltanissetta, 51,699 .... D 6
Camaiore, 7,130 .... C 3
Campobasso, 27,568 .... E 4
Campo Tures, 1,162 .... C 1
Canicatti, 29,613 .... E 6
Canosa di Puglia, 32,908 .... E 4
Cantù, 17,298 .... B 2
Capua, 13,334 .... E 4
Caravaggio, 9,938 .... B 2
Carbonia, 26,227 .... B 5
Carini, 15,486 .... D 5
Carloforte, 7,153 .... B 5
Carmagnola, 6,583 .... A 2
Carpi, 27,647 .... C 2
Carrara, 37,386 .... C 2
Casale Monferrato, 31,226 .... B 2
Casalmaggiore, 5,995 .... C 2
Cascina-Navacchio, 23,739 .... C 3
Caserta, 36,337 .... E 4
Cassano allo Ionio, 9,250 .... F 5
Cassino, 11,369 .... E 4
Castelfranco Veneto, 9,978 .... D 2
Castel Gandolfo, 2,861 .... F 7
Castellammare del Golfo, 16,581 .... D 5
Castellammare di Stabia, 49,064 .... E 4
Castel San Pietro Terme, 4,824 .. C 2
Castelvetrano, 30,009 .... D 6
Castrovillari, 13,063 .... F 5
Catania, 358,700 .... E 6
Catanzaro, 44,198 .... F 5
Cava de'Tirreni, 19,883 .... E 4
Cavarzere, 6,109 .... D 2
Cecina, 13,749 .... C 3
Cefalù, 10,360 .... E 5
Ceglie Messapico, 17,891 .... F 4
Celano, 9,743 .... D 3
Cerignola, 43,345 .... E 4
Cernobbio, 6,857 .... B 2
Cesena, 31,153 .... D 2
Cesenatico, 7,684 .... D 2
Chiari, 9,552 .... C 2
Chiavari, 22,835 .... B 2
Chieri, 15,358 .... A 2
Chieti, 31,374 .... E 3
Chioggia, 25,058 .... D 2
Chivasso, 11,806 .... A 2
Ciampino, 10,012 .... F 7
Cittadella, 5,698 .... C 2
Città di Castello, 15,564 .... D 3
Cittanova, 11,567 .... F 5
Cividale del Friuli, 7,698 .... D 1
Civitavecchia, 34,996 .... C 3
Clusone, 5,729 .... C 2
Codriopo, 5,064 .... D 2
Colle di Val d'Elsa, 7,329 .... C 3
Comacchio, 9,743 .... D 2
Comiso, 24,016 .... E 6
Como, 64,301 .... B 2
Conegliano, 16,910 .... D 2
Conversano, 15,543 .... F 4
Corato, 38,774 .... F 4
Cori, 6,930 .... F 7
Corigliano Calabro, 13,526 .... F 5
Corleone, 14,185 .... D 6
Correggio, 8,146 .... C 2
Cortina d'Ampezzo, 4,291 .... D 1
Cosenza, 70,201 .... F 5
Courmayeur, 1,013 .... A 2
Crema, 20,679 .... B 2
Cremona, 64,775 .... B 2
Crotone, 36,516 .... F 5
Cuneo, 32,978 .... A 2
Desenzano del Garda, 8,017 .... C 2
Domodossola, 15,097 .... B 1
Dorgali, 6,976 .... B 4
Eboli, 19,550 .... E 4
Empoli, 22,484 .... C 3
Enna, 26,206 .... E 6
Este, 11,007 .... C 2
Fabriano, 15,127 .... D 3
Faenza, 40,425 .... D 2
Fano, 24,591 .... D 3
Fasano, 17,990 .... F 4
Favara, 27,523 .... D 6
Feltre, 9,446 .... C 1
Fermo, 14,453 .... D 3
Ferrandina, 8,381 .... F 4
Ferrara, 90,419 .... C 2
Fidenza, 13,567 .... B 2
Finale Emilia, 6,711 .... C 2
Finale Ligure, 9,789 .... B 2
Firenze (Florence), 413,455 .... C 3
Fiumicino, 9,489 .... F 7
Florence, 413,455 .... C 3
Floridia, 16,104 .... E 6
Foggia, 108,682 .... E 4
Foligno, 23,094 .... D 3
Fondi, 14,991 .... D 4
Forlì, 65,376 .... D 2
Formia, 15,048 .... D 4
Fossano, 12,563 .... A 2
Francavilla Fontana, 27,629 .... F 4
Frascati, 12,602 .... F 6
Frosinone, 20,998 .... D 4
Gaeta, 20,436 .... D 4
Galatina, 19,654 .... G 4
Galatone, 13,487 .... F 4
Gallarate, 34,870 .... B 2
Gallipoli, 15,958 .... F 4
Gela, 54,526 .... E 6
Gemona, 7,698 .... D 1
Genoa (Genova), 747,794 .... B 2
Genzano di Roma, 11,666 .... F 7
Giarre, 11,859 .... E 6
Gioia del Colle, 23,734 .... F 4
Giovinazzo, 14,189 .... F 4
Giulianova, 11,220 .... E 3
Gorizia, 35,307 .... D 2
Gravina in Puglia, 30,615 .... F 4
Grosseto, 36,558 .... C 3
Grottaferrata, 5,356 .... F 7
Grottaglie, 22,218 .... F 4
Guastalla, 7,511 .... C 2
Gubbio, 9,730 .... D 3
Iesi, 26,018 .... D 3
Iglesias, 20,518 .... B 5
Imola, 32,148 .... C 2
Imperia, 30,522 .... B 3
Isernia, 9,689 .... E 4
Ivrea, 19,344 .... B 2
La Maddalena, 10,414 .... B 4
Lanciano, 15,182 .... E 3
Lanusei, 5,208 .... B 5
L'Aquila, 29,462 .... D 3
La Spezia, 111,768 .... B 2
Latina, 26,171 .... D 4
Lavello, 12,857 .... E 4
Lecce, 68,385 .... G 4
Lecco, 47,468 .... B 2
Leghorn, 152,517 .... C 3
Legnago, 10,126 .... C 2
Lendinara, 6,475 .... C 2
Lentini, 31,788 .... E 6
Leonforte, 17,690 .... E 6
Licata, 38,222 .... D 6
Lido di Ostia, 25,662 .... F 7
Lido di Venezia, 16,581 .... D 2
Lipari, 3,852 .... E 5
Livorno (Leghorn), 152,517 .... C 3
Lodi, 34,281 .... B 2
Lonigo, 5,774 .... C 2
Lucca, 45,398 .... C 3
Lucera, 24,399 .... E 4
Lugo, 16,550 .... D 2
Macerata, 27,054 .... D 3
Macomer, 7,782 .... B 4
Maglie, 12,205 .... G 4
Manduria, 23,971 .... F 4
Manfredonia, 34,583 .... F 4
Mantua, 55,806 .... C 2
Marino, 9,798 .... F 7
Marsala, 34,294 .... D 6
Martina Franca, 27,588 .... F 4
Massa, 46,992 .... C 2
Massafra, 18.884 .... F 4
Massa Marittima, 6,804 .... C 3
Matera, 36,727 .... F 4
Mazara del Vallo, 35,356 .... D 6
Mazzarino, 17,195 .... E 6
Melfi, 15,122 .... E 4
Menfi, 12,335 .... D 6
Merano, 29,196 .... C 1
Mesagne, 25,042 .... G 4
Messina, 202,095 .... E 5
Mestre, 138,822 .... D 2
Milan, 1,573,009 .... B 2
Milazzo, 14,034 .... E 5
Mirandola, 9,272 .... C 2
Mira Taglio, 8,380 .... D 2
Mistretta, 9,979 .... E 6
Modena, 107,814 .... C 2
Modica, 28,998 .... E 6
Mola di Bari, 22,397 .... F 4
Molfetta, 61,226 .... F 4
Moncalieri, 14,339 .... A 2
Mondovì Breo, 9,893 .... A 2
Monfalcone, 26,708 .... D 2
Monopoli, 25,161 .... F 4
Monreale, 18,881 .... D 5
Monselice, 7,766 .... C 2
Montebelluna, 6,088 .... D 2
Montefiascone, 6,428 .... D 3
Monterotondo, 9,616 .... F 6
Monte Sant'Angelo, 20,512 .... F 4
Montevarchi, 12,413 .... C 3
Monza, 79,715 .... B 2
Mortara, 12,243 .... B 2
Naples, 1,119,392 .... E 4
Nardò, 23,006 .... F 4
Narni, 5,551 .... D 3
Naro, 14,295 .... D 6
Nettuno, 16,187 .... D 4
Nicastro, 21,240 .... F 5
Nicosia, 16,624 .... E 6
Niscemi, 24,468 .... E 6
Nizza Monferrato, 6,229 .... B 2
Nocera Inferiore, 38,690 .... E 4
Noto, 21,586 .... E 6
Novara, 79,188 .... B 2
Novi Ligure, 23,349 .... B 2
Nuoro, 22,559 .... B 4
Olbia, 13,795 .... B 4
Oliena, 6,974 .... B 4
Orbetello, 6,800 .... C 3
Oristano, 16,305 .... B 5
Ortona, 11,315 .... E 3
Orvieto, 9,617 .... D 3
Osimo, 9,406 .... D 3
Ostuni, 25,190 .... F 4
Otranto, 3,510 .... G 4
Ozieri, 10,194 .... B 4
Pachino, 20,645 .... E 6
Padua, 169,298 .... C 2
Palazzolo Acreide, 10,802 .... E 6
Palermo, 531,306 .... D 5
Palestrina, 7,897 .... F 7
Palma di Montechiaro, 20,425 .... D 6
Palmi, 14,576 .... E 5
Pantelleria, 3,100 .... C 6
Paola, 9,701 .... E 5
Parma, 118,602 .... C 2
Partanna, 12,931 .... D 6
Partinico, 25,924 .... D 6
Paterno, 39,912 .... E 6
Patti, 6,748 .... E 5
Pavia, 69,581 .... B 2
Penne, 5,709 .... D 3
Pergine Valsugana, 4,877 .... C 1
Perugia, 52,534 .... D 3
Pesaro, 47,185 .... D 3
Pescara, 81,697 .... E 3
Pescia, 8,737 .... C 3
Piacenza, 78,985 .... B 2
Piazza Armerina, 23,915 .... E 6
Pietrasanta, 6,785 .... B 3
Pinerolo, 25,262 .... A 2
Piombino, 30,843 .... C 3
Piove di Sacco, 6,230 .... C 2
Pisa, 76,846 .... C 3
Pisticci, 11,469 .... F 4
Pistoia, 41,058 .... C 2
Poggibonsi, 12,932 .... C 3
Pont-Canavese, 4,071 .... A 2
Pontecorvo, 5,845 .... D 4
Pontremoli, 4,839 .... C 2
Popoli, 6,749 .... E 3
Pordenone, 29,461 .... D 2
Porto Civitanova, 18,288 .... D 3
Porto Empedocle, 16,110 .... D 6
Portoferraio, 6,318 .... C 3
Portofino, 735 .... B 2
Portogruaro, 8,913 .... D 2
Portomaggiore, 5,532 .... C 2
Porto Recanati, 4,986 .... D 3
Porto Torres, 10,108 .... B 4
Potenza, 34,216 .... F 4
Pozzallo, 11,862 .... E 6
Pozzuoli, 44,038 .... D 4
Prato, 75,402 .... C 3
Prima Porta, 9,978 .... F 6
Priverno, 9,154 .... D 4
Putignano, 15,976 .... F 4
Quartu Sant'Elena, 22,271 .... B 5
Ragusa, 50,718 .... E 6
Rapallo, 16,628 .... B 2
Ravenna, 56,815 .... D 2
Recanati, 7,242 .... D 3
Reggio di Calabria, 93,964 .... E 5
Reggio nell'Emilia, 83,073 .... C 2
Rho, 27,586 .... B 2
Riesi, 17,899 .... E 6
Rieti, 21,278 .... D 3
Rimini, 72,720 .... D 2
Rionero in Vulture, 13,567 .... E 4
Riva, 7,626 .... C 2
Rome (cap.), 2,043,055 .... F 6
Rome, *2,656,104 .... F 6
Ronciglione, 5,772 .... C 3
Rossano, 13,323 .... F 5
Rovereto, 20,505 .... C 2
Rovigo, 22,804 .... C 2
Ruvo di Puglia, 23,216 .... F 4
Sala Consilina, 6,742 .... E 4
Salemi, 12,237 .... D 6
Salerno, 103,778 .... E 4
Salsomaggiore Terme, 10,376 .... B 2
Saluzzo, 11,991 .... A 2
Sambiase, 11,551 .... F 5
San Bartolomeo in Galdo, 8,745 .. E 4
San Benedetto del Tronto, 28,053 .... E 3
San Cataldo, 21,778 .... D 6
San Giovanni in Fiore, 16,528 .... F 5
San Giovanni in Persiceto, 8,692 .... C 2
San Marco in Lamis, 17,933 .... E 4
Sannicandro Garganico, 17,238 .... E 4
San Remo, 40,068 .... A 3
Sansepolcro, 10,063 .... D 3
San Severino Marche, 5,582 .... D 3
San Severo, 47,897 .... E 4
Santa Maria Capua Vetere, 29,925 .... E 4
Santeramo in Colle, 19,587 .... F 4
San Vito al Tagliamento, 5,278 D 2

(continued on following page)

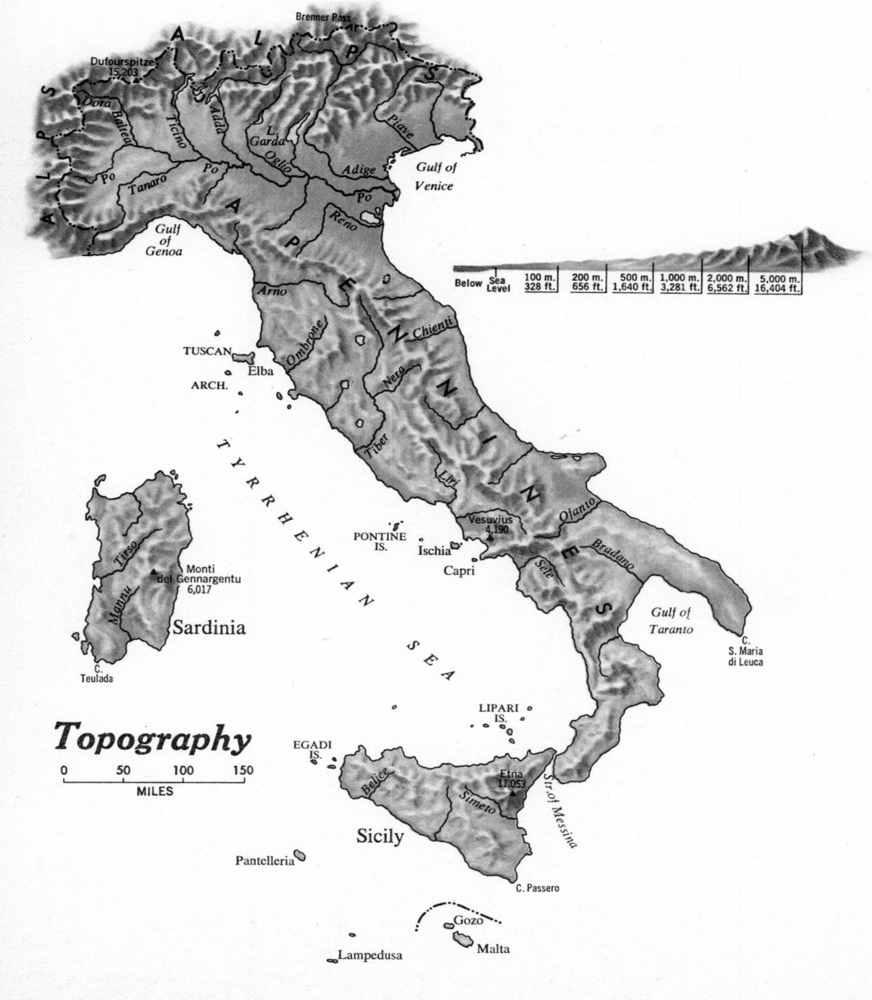
Brenner Pass
Dufourspitze 15,203
ALPS
Dora Baltea
Ticino
Adda
L. Garda
Oglio
Piave
Adige
Gulf of Venice
Po
Tanaro
Reno
Gulf of Genoa
APENNINES
Arno
Ombrone
Chienti
Nera
Tiber
Liri
TUSCAN ARCH.
Elba
TYRRHENIAN SEA
Vesuvius 4,190
PONTINE IS.
Ischia
Capri
Ofanto
Sele
Bradano
Gulf of Taranto
C. S. Maria di Leuca
Tirso
Monti del Gennargentu 6,017
Mannu
Sardinia
C. Teulada
LIPARI IS.
EGADI IS.
Belice
Simeto
Etna 11,053
Str. of Messina
Sicily
Pantelleria
C. Passero
Gozo
Malta
Lampedusa
Below Sea Level
100 m. 328 ft.
200 m. 656 ft.
500 m. 1,640 ft.
1,000 m. 3,281 ft.
2,000 m. 6,562 ft.
5,000 m. 16,404 ft.
Topography
0 50 100 150
MILES

(continued)

OTHER FEATURES

MALTA

CITIES and TOWNS

OTHER FEATURES

SAN MARINO

CITIES and TOWNS

VATICAN CITY

*City and suburbs.

Agriculture, Industry and Resources

VERONA
Textiles, Machinery
MILAN–BRESCIA–ASTI
Textiles, Automobiles, Iron & Steel, Machinery, Chemicals
TRIESTE
Iron & Steel, Shipbuilding, Machinery, Oil Refining
TURIN–BIELLA
Automobiles, Textiles, Machinery, Iron & Steel
VENICE
Shipbuilding, Nonferrous Metals, Textiles
GENOA–LIGURIA
Shipbuilding, Iron & Steel, Oil Refining
BOLOGNA–PARMA
Machinery, Chemicals, Automobiles.
LEGHORN–FLORENCE
Textiles, Shipbuilding, Machinery, Chemicals
TERNI
Iron & Steel, Machinery, Textiles
PIOMBINO
Iron & Steel
BARI
Chemicals, Oil Refining
ROME
Chemicals, Machinery, Printing, Paper, Tobacco Products
NAPLES
Iron & Steel, Machinery, Chemicals, Shipbuilding
TARANTO
Iron & Steel
Milan
Brescia
Turin
Asti
Verona
Venice
Trieste
Genoa
Bologna
Florence
Leghorn
Piombino
Terni
Rome
Naples
Bari
Taranto
Cattle
Wheat
Rice
Corn
Dairy
Sugar Beets
Olives
Chestnuts
Wine
Potatoes
Sheep
Hemp
Almonds
Tobacco
Goats
Sardines
Tuna
Citrus Fruit

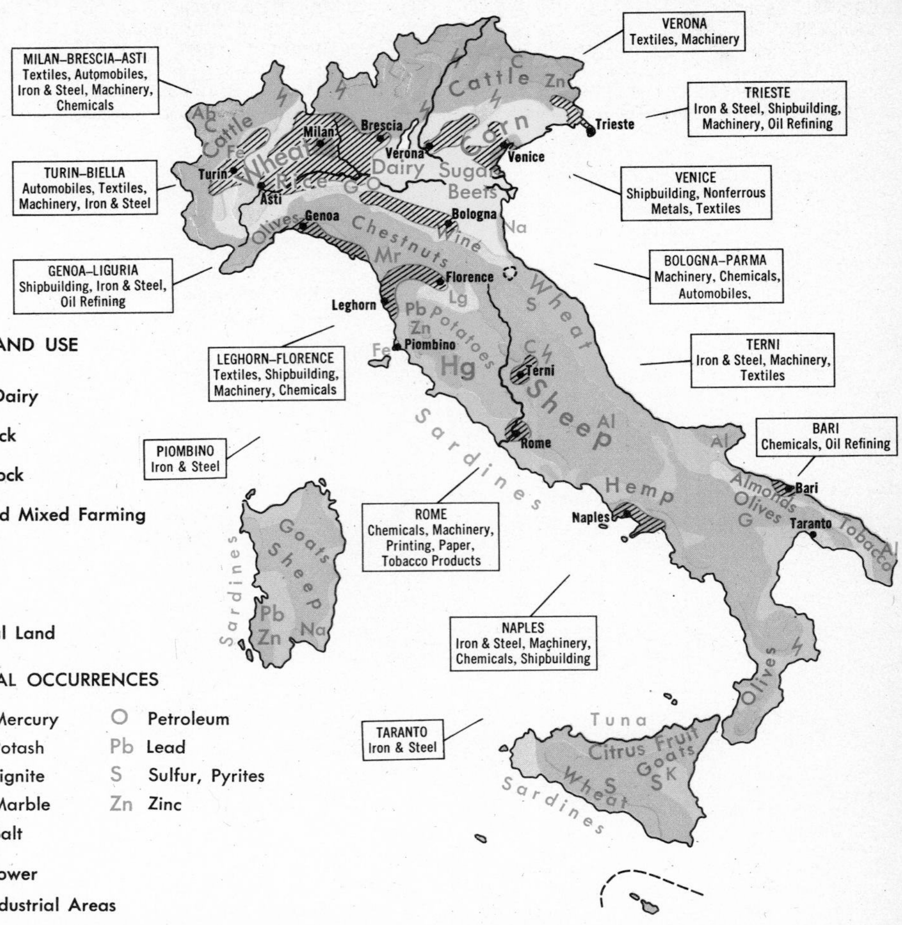

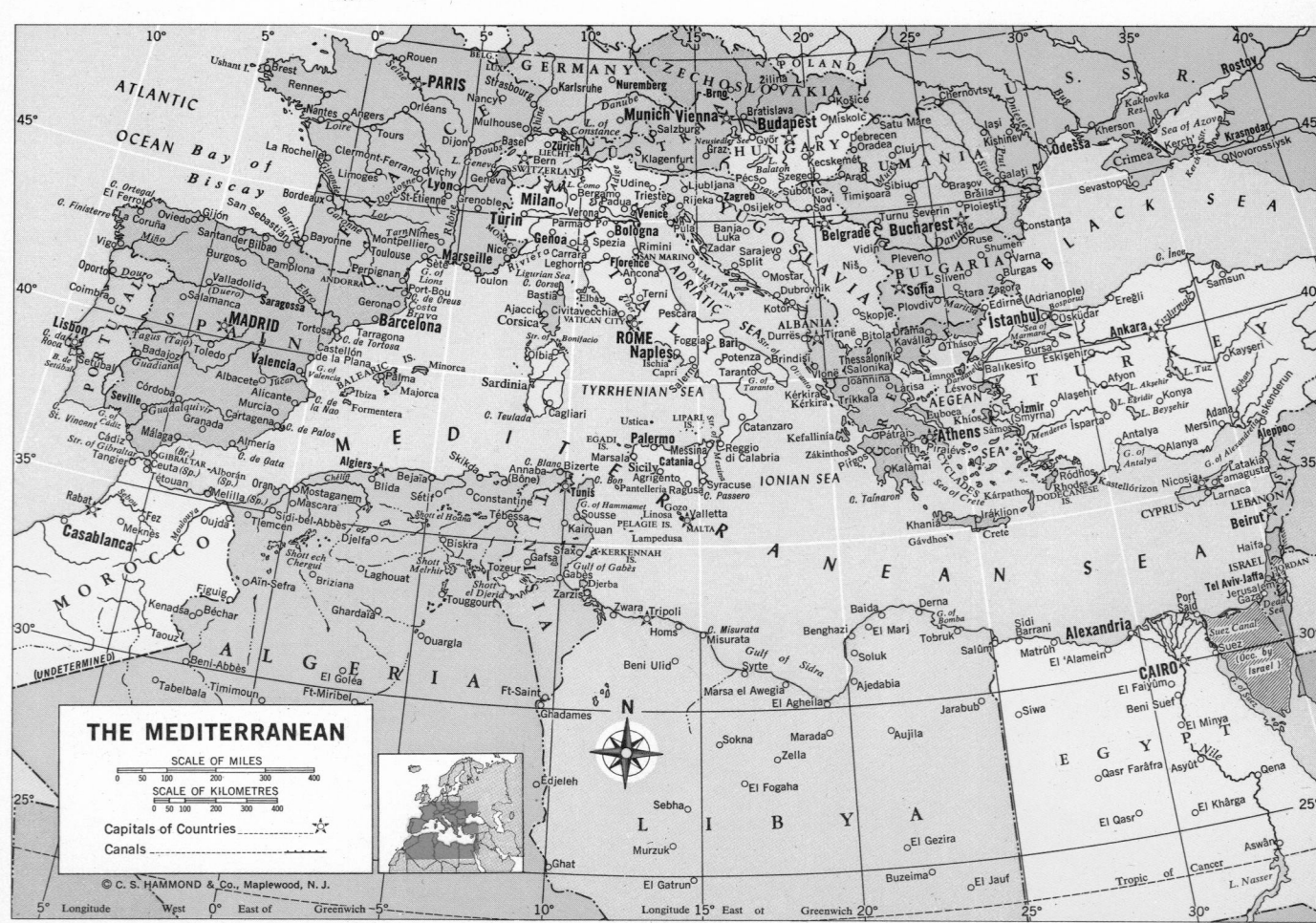

DOMINANT LAND USE

- Wheat, Rice, Dairy
- Pasture Livestock
- Cereals, Livestock
- Fruit, Truck and Mixed Farming
- Grapes, Wine
- Forests
- Nonagricultural Land

MAJOR MINERAL OCCURRENCES

Ab	Asbestos	Hg	Mercury	O	Petroleum
Al	Bauxite	K	Potash	Pb	Lead
C	Coal	Lg	Lignite	S	Sulfur, Pyrites
Fe	Iron Ore	Mr	Marble	Zn	Zinc
G	Natural Gas	Na	Salt		

Water Power

Major Industrial Areas

THE MEDITERRANEAN
SCALE OF MILES
0 50 100 200 300 400
SCALE OF KILOMETRES
0 50 100 200 300 400
Capitals of Countries
Canals
© C. S. HAMMOND & Co., Maplewood, N. J.
ATLANTIC OCEAN
Bay of Biscay
MEDITERRANEAN SEA
TYRRHENIAN SEA
IONIAN SEA
ADRIATIC SEA
AEGEAN SEA
BLACK SEA
MOROCCO
ALGERIA
LIBYA
EGYPT
TURKEY
YUGOSLAVIA
BULGARIA
RUMANIA
HUNGARY
GERMANY
PARIS
MADRID
ROME
Algiers
Tunis
Tripoli
Athens
Istanbul
Ankara
Sofia
Belgrade
Bucharest
Budapest
Vienna
Alexandria
CAIRO
Longitude West 0° East of Greenwich

SWITZERLAND

AREA 15,941 sq. mi.
POPULATION 6,230,000
CAPITAL Bern
LARGEST CITY Zürich
HIGHEST POINT Dufourspitze (Mte. Rosa) 15,203 ft.
MONETARY UNIT Swiss franc
MAJOR LANGUAGES German, French, Italian, Romansch
MAJOR RELIGIONS Protestantism, Roman Catholicism

LIECHTENSTEIN

AREA 61 sq. mi.
POPULATION 21,000
CAPITAL Vaduz
LARGEST CITY Vaduz
HIGHEST POINT Naafkopf 8,445 ft.
MONETARY UNIT Swiss franc
MAJOR LANGUAGE German
MAJOR RELIGION Roman Catholicism

SWITZERLAND

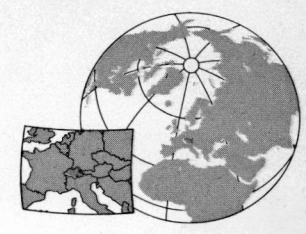

LIECHTENSTEIN

LANGUAGES

- German
- French
- Italian
- Romansch

Switzerland is a multilingual nation with four official languages. 70% of the people speak German, 19% French, 10% Italian and 1% Romansch.

SWITZERLAND

CANTONS

Aargau, 397,000	F 2
Appenzell, Ausser-Rhoden, (canton), 50,000	H 2
Appenzell, Inner-Rhoden, (canton), 13,500	H 2
Baselland (canton) 177,900	E 2
Baselstadt (canton) 237,300	E 1
Bern, 958,000	D 2
Fribourg, 163,000	D 3
Geneva, 304,400	B 4
Glarus, 42,000	H 3
Graubünden (Grisons), 155,000	J 3
Luzern (Lucerne), 274,000	F 2
Neuchâtel, 161,000	C 3
Nidwalden, 25,000	F 3
Obwalden, 25,000	F 3
Sankt Gallen, 363,000	H 2
Schaffhausen, 72,000	G 1
Schwyz, 84,800	G 2
Solothurn (Soleure), 220,000	E 2
Thurgau, 183,000	H 1
Ticino, 220,000	G 5
Uri, 33,000	G 3
Valais, 191,000	E 4
Vaud, 486,000	C 3
Zug, 61,000	G 2
Zürich, 1,048,000	G 2

CITIES and TOWNS

Aadorf, 2,258	G 2
Aarau, 17,400	F 2
Aarau, *47,800	F 2
Aarberg, 2,355	D 2
Aarburg, 5,302	F 2
Adelboden, 2,881	E 3
Aeschi bei Spiez, 1,319	E 3
Aigle, 4,381	C 4
Airolo, 2,023	G 4
Alle, 1,471	D 2
Allschwil, 15,500	D 1
Alpnach, 3,211	F 3
Altdorf, 7,477	G 3
Altstätten, 8,751	J 2
Amriswil, 6,752	H 1
Andermatt, 1,523	G 3
Appenzell, 5,082	H 2
Arbedo-Castione, 1,467	G 4
Arbon, 13,100	H 1
Ardon, 1,432	D 4
Arlesheim, 5,219	E 2
Arosa, 2,600	J 3
Arth, 6,321	G 3
Ascona, 3,053	G 4
Attalens, 1,023	C 4
Aubonne, 1,766	B 4
Avenches, 1,776	C 3
Baar, 9,114	G 2
Baden, 14,900	F 2
Baden, *54,500	F 2
Bad Ragaz, 2,699	H 2
Balerna, 3,040	G 5
Balsthal, 5,735	E 2
Bäretswil, 2,577	G 2
Basel, 213,200	E 1
Basel, *364,800	E 1
Bassecourt, 2,284	D 2
Bätterkinden, 1,916	E 2
Bauma, 3,214	G 2
Beatenberg, 1,303	E 3
Beckenried, 2,042	G 3
Beinwil am See, 2,346	F 2
Bellinzona, 14,900	H 4
Bellinzona, *25,700	H 4
Belp, 4,922	D 3
Bergün-Bravuogn, 551	J 3
Bern (cap.), 166,800	D 3
Bern, *258,000	D 3
Beromünster, 1,443	F 2
Bex, 4,667	D 4
Biasca, 3,349	H 4
Biberist, 7,188	D 2
Biel (Bienne), 67,800	D 2
Biel, *87,000	D 2
Bière, 1,166	B 3
Binningen, 13,800	D 1
Bischofszell, 3,811	H 1
Blumenstein, 1,121	E 3
Bodio, 1,276	G 4
Bolligen, 19,400	D 3
Boltigen, 1,691	D 3
Boncourt, 1,493	C 2
Bönigen, 1,883	E 3
Boswil, 1,663	F 2
Boudry, 3,086	C 3
Bourg-Saint-Pierre, 524	D 5
Breil-Brigels, 1,272	H 3
Breitenbach, 1,851	E 2
Bremgarten, 4,555	F 2
Brienz, 2,864	F 3
Brig, 4,647	E 4
Brissago, 1,845	G 4
Brittnau, 3,070	F 2
Brugg, 6,683	F 2
Brusio, 1,445	K 4
Bubendorf, 1,690	E 2
Bubikon, 2,612	G 2
Buchs, 6,345	H 2
Bülach, 8,188	G 2
Bulle, 5,983	D 3
Buochs, 2,733	G 3
Büren an der Aare, 2,432	D 2
Burgdorf, 15,600	E 2
Bürglen, 3,175	G 3
Bürglen, 1,899	H 1
Bussigny-près-Lausanne, 2,381	B 3
Bütschwil, 3,414	H 2
Carouge, 15,600	B 4
Castagnola, 3,775	G 4
Cazis, 1,553	H 3
Cernier, 1,545	C 2
Chalais, 1,597	E 4
Cham, 6,483	F 2
Chamoson, 2,088	D 4
Charmey, 1,144	D 3
Châteaux-d'Oex, 3,378	D 4
Châtel-Saint-Denis, 2,666	C 3
Chavornay, 1,414	C 3
Chexbres, 1,449	C 3
Chiasso, 7,377	G 5
Chur, 29,100	J 3
Churwalden, 877	J 3
Coire (Chur), 29,100	J 3
Conthey, 3,563	D 4
Coppet, 774	B 4
Corcelles-près-Payerne, 1,253	C 3
Corgémont, 1,414	D 2
Cossonay, 1,284	C 3
Courgenay, 1,666	D 2
Courroux, 1,667	D 2
Court, 1,493	D 2
Courtelary, 1,330	D 2
Courtételle, 1,618	D 2
Couvet, 3,450	C 3
Cully, 1,375	C 4
Därstetten, 900	D 3
Davos (Dorf and Platz), 9,588	J 3
Degersheim, 3,221	H 2
Delémont, 9,542	E 2
Derendingen, 4,463	E 2
Diemtigen, 1,934	D 3
Diessenhofen, 2,222	G 1
Dietikon, 20,600	F 2
Disentis-Mustèr, 2,376	G 3
Dombresson, 1,040	C 2
Dornach, 4,260	E 2
Dübendorf, 17,100	G 2
Düdingen, 4,248	D 3
Dürnten, 4,271	G 2
Dürrenroth, 1,221	E 2
Ebnat-Kappel, 4,979	H 2
Echallens, 1,428	C 3
Egg, 3,018	G 2
Eggiwil, 2,591	E 3
Eglisau, 1,911	G 2
Egnach, 3,483	H 1
Einsiedeln, 8,792	G 2
Elgg, 2,643	G 2
Emmen, 21,400	F 2
Engelberg, 2,646	G 3
Engi, 1,064	H 3
Ennenda, 3,076	H 3
Entlebuch, 3,318	F 3
Erlenbach im Simmental, 1,471	E 3
Ermatingen, 1,857	H 1
Erstfeld, 4,126	G 3
Eschenbach, 2,866	G 2
Escholzmatt, 3,257	E 3
Estavayer-le-Lac, 2,583	C 3
Evolène, 1,786	D 4
Faido, 1,441	G 4

(continued on following page)

Agriculture, Industry and Resources

DOMINANT LAND USE

- Cereals, Dairy
- Pasture Livestock
- General Farming, Livestock
- Fruit, Truck, Mixed Farming
- Forests
- Nonagricultural Land

⚡ Water Power
▨ Major Industrial Areas

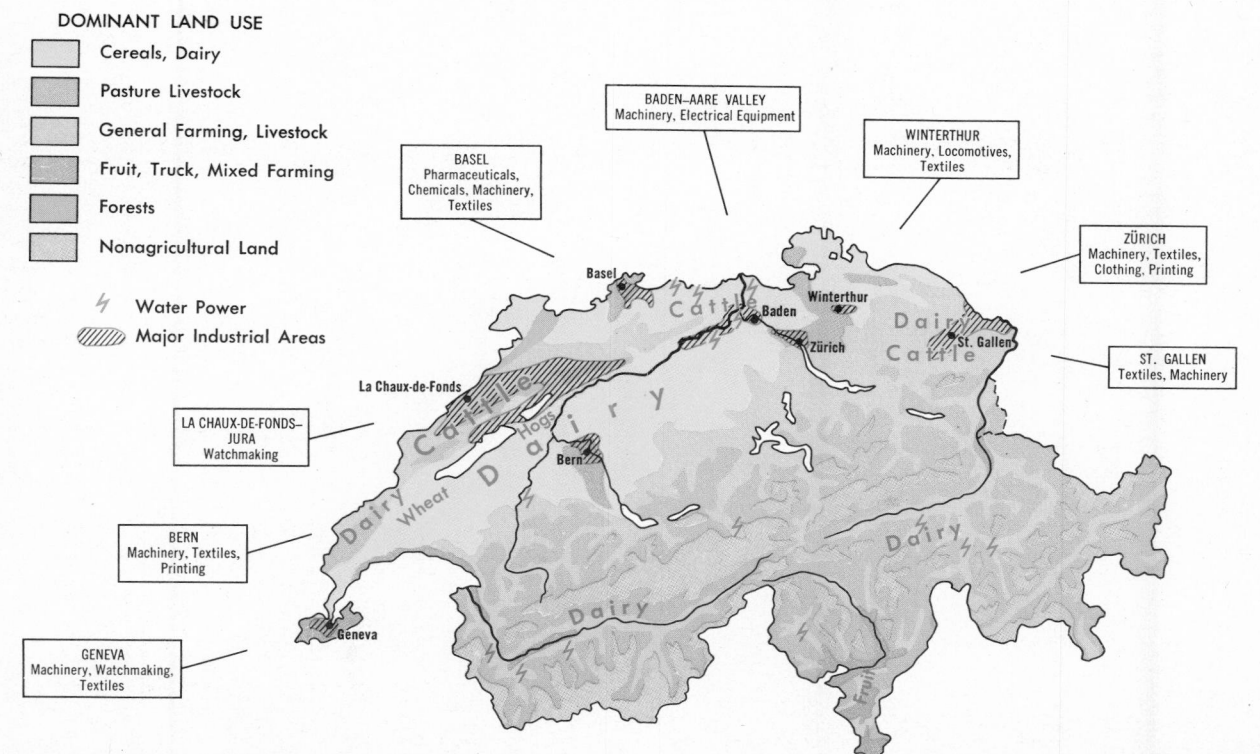

BADEN–AARE VALLEY
Machinery, Electrical Equipment

WINTERTHUR
Machinery, Locomotives, Textiles

BASEL
Pharmaceuticals, Chemicals, Machinery, Textiles

ZÜRICH
Machinery, Textiles, Clothing, Printing

ST. GALLEN
Textiles, Machinery

LA CHAUX-DE-FONDS–JURA
Watchmaking

BERN
Machinery, Textiles, Printing

GENEVA
Machinery, Watchmaking, Textiles

(continued)

Topography

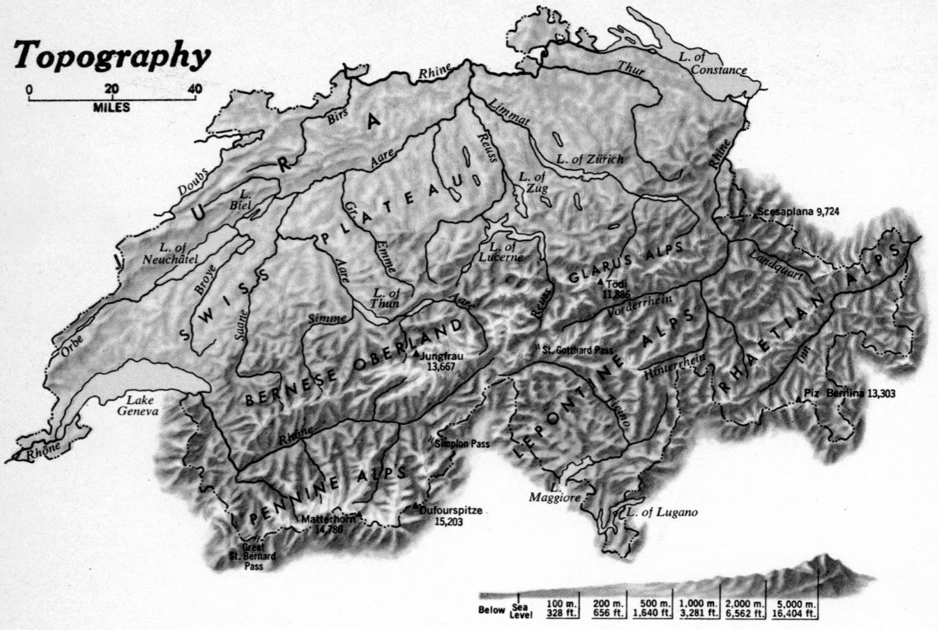

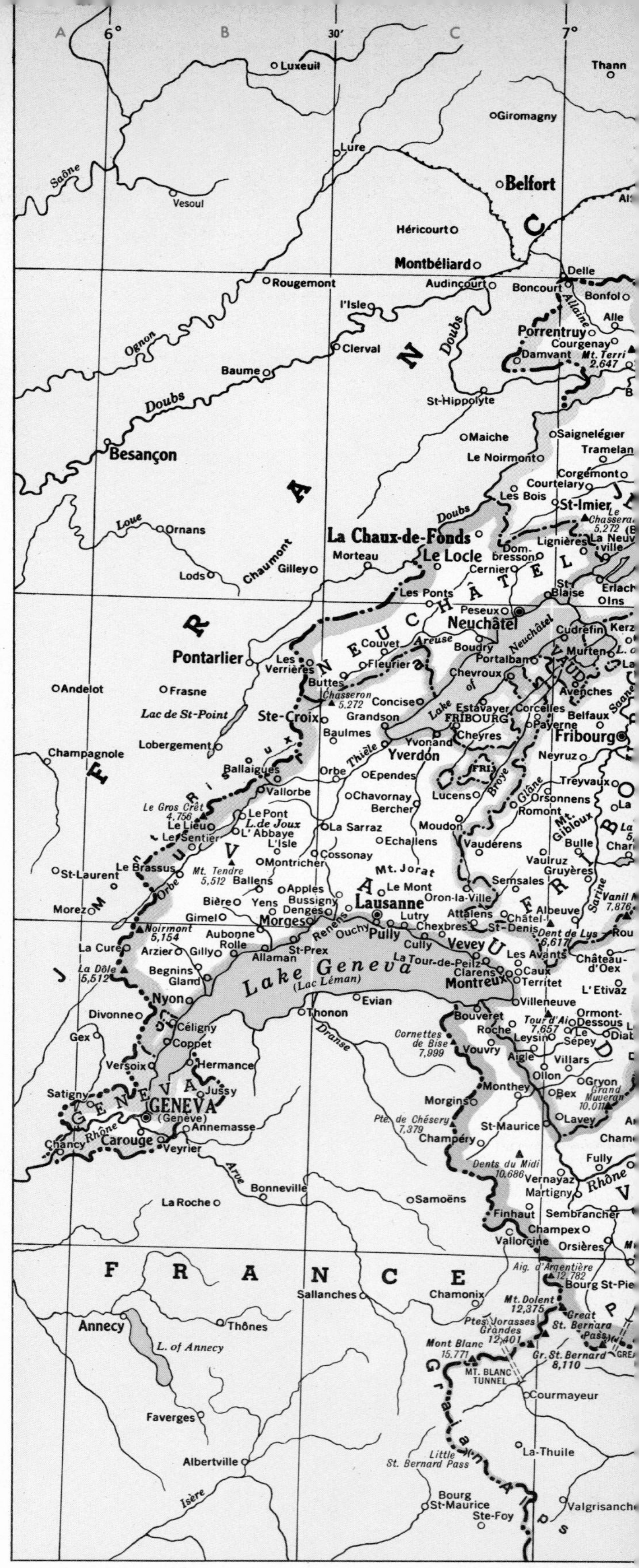

SWITZERLAND (continued)

Flawil, 7,256 .... H 2
Fleurier, 3,814 .... C 3
Flims, 1,444 .... H 3
Flüelen, 1,717 .... G 3
Flums, 4,462 .... H 2
Frauenfeld, 16,800 .... G 1
Fribourg, 38,500 .... D 3
Fribourg, *47,300 .... D 3
Frick, 2,123 .... E 1
Frutigen, 5,565 .... E 3
Fully, 3,419 .... D 4
Gais, 2,488 .... H 2
Gelterkinden, 3,870 .... E 2
Geneva (Genève), 169,500 .... B 4
Geneva, *307,500 .... B 4
Gersau, 1,754 .... G 2
Gimel, 1,091 .... B 3
Giornico, 1,063 .... G 4
Giswil, 2,656 .... F 3
Giubiasco, 4,281 .... H 4
Gland, 1,545 .... B 4
Glarus, 5,852 .... H 2
Glattfelden, 2,426 .... F 1
Gordola, 1,794 .... G 4
Göschenen, 1,284 .... G 3
Gossau, 9,731 .... H 2
Grabs, 4,218 .... H 2
Grandson, 2,091 .... C 3
Gränichen, 4,411 .... F 2
Grenchen, 19,800 .... D 2
Grenchen, *23,400 .... D 2
Grindelwald, 3,244 .... E 3
Grossandelfingen, 1,102 .... G 1
Grosswangen, 2,373 .... F 2
Gruyères, 1,349 .... D 3
Gsteig, 937 .... D 4
Guggisberg, 2,021 .... D 3
Gurtnellen, 1,048 .... G 3
Hallau, 1,966 .... F 1
Heiden, 3,158 .... H 2
Heimberg, 2,125 .... E 3
Hemberg, 1,011 .... H 2
Henau (Uzwil), 7,828 .... H 2
Hérémence, 1,868 .... D 4
Herisau, 15,500 .... H 2
Hermance, 512 .... B 4
Herzogenbuchsee, 4,641 .... E 2
Hinwil, 4,811 .... G 2
Hochdorf, 4,452 .... F 2
Horgen, 15,300 .... G 2
Hospental, 289 .... F 3
Huttwil, 4,664 .... E 2
Igis, 3,902 .... J 3
Ilanz, 1,843 .... H 3
Illnau, 6,160 .... G 2
Ingenbohl, 5,046 .... G 2
Innertkirchen, 1,230 .... F 3
Ins, 2,486 .... D 2
Interlaken, 4,738 .... E 3
Jegenstorf, 1,397 .... D 2
Jenaz, 1,143 .... J 3
Jona, 5,686 .... G 2
Jungfraujoch .... E 3
Kaltbrunn, 2,527 .... H 2
Kandersteg, 937 .... E 4
Kerns, 3,553 .... F 3
Kerzers, 2,228 .... D 3
Kilchberg, 6,784 .... F 2
Kirchberg, 3,304 .... E 2
Kirchberg, 5,554 .... G 2
Kleinlützel, 1,269 .... D 2
Klingnau, 2,192 .... F 1
Klosters, 3,181 .... J 3
Kloten, 8,446 .... G 2
Koblenz, 1,114 .... F 1
Kölliken, 3,007 .... F 2
Köniz, 30,600 .... D 3
Kreuzlingen, 14,900 .... H 1
Kriens, 17,200 .... F 2
Küsnacht, 12,800 .... G 2
Küssnacht, 12,400 .... F 2
Küttigen, 3,457 .... F 2
L'Abbaye, 1,124 .... B 3
La Chaux-de-Fonds, 42,800 .... C 2
Lachen, 3,913 .... G 2
La Neuveville, 3,216 .... D 2
Langenthal, 12,400 .... E 2
Langnau, 9,201 .... E 3
Langnau am Albis, 2,850 .... G 2
La Roche, 1,043 .... D 3
La Sarraz, 1,026 .... C 3
La Tour-de-Peilz, 6,820 .... C 4
Läufelfingen, 1,176 .... E 2
Laufen, 3,955 .... D 2
Laufenburg, 1,850 .... F 1
Laupen, 1,607 .... D 3
Lauperswil, 2,652 .... E 3
Lausanne, 138,300 .... C 3
Lausanne, *214,900 .... C 3
Lauterbrunnen, 3,216 .... E 3
Le Brassus (Le Chenit), 5,242 .... B 3
Le Châble, 4,237 .... D 4
Le Lieu, 970 .... B 3
Le Locle, 15,100 .... C 2
Le Mont, 1,719 .... C 3
Lengnau, 3,524 .... D 2
Lenk, 1,900 .... D 4
Le Noirmont, 1,559 .... C 2
Lens, 1,743 .... D 4
Lenzburg, 6,378 .... F 2
Les Bois, 1,098 .... C 2
Les Ponts-de-Martel, 1,429 .... C 2
Les Verrières, 1,084 .... B 3
Leuk, 2,546 .... E 4
Leukerbad, 619 .... E 4
Leysin, 2,241 .... C 4
Liestal, 11,300 .... E 2
Linthal, 2,645 .... H 3
Littau, 8,715 .... F 2
Locarno, 12,200 .... G 4
Locarno, *21,000 .... G 4
Lucens, 1,620 .... C 3
Lucerne, 73,000 .... F 2
Lucerne, *148,500 .... F 2
Lugano, 21,100 .... G 4
Lugano, *50,000 .... G 4
Lungern, 1,794 .... F 3
Luthern, 1,801 .... E 2
Lutry, 3,481 .... C 3
Lützelflüh, 3,960 .... E 3
Luzein, 1,013 .... J 3
Luzern (Lucerne), 73,000 .... F 2
Lyss, 5,616 .... D 2
Maienfeld, 1,488 .... J 2
Malans, 1,358 .... J 3
Malters, 4,579 .... F 2
Malvaglia, 1,120 .... H 4
Männedorf, 6,182 .... G 2
Marbach, 1,347 .... E 3
Martigny, 7,593 .... C 4
Meilen, 8,203 .... G 2
Meiringen, 3,749 .... F 3
Melchnau, 1,511 .... E 2
Melide, 1,046 .... G 5
Mellingen, 1,941 .... F 2
Mels, 5,254 .... H 2
Mendrisio, 5,100 .... G 5
Menzingen, 3,340 .... G 2
Menznau, 2,275 .... E 2
Mesocco, 1,324 .... H 4
Minusio, 3,663 .... G 4
Möhlin, 4,681 .... E 1
Mollis, 2,303 .... H 2
Montana-Vermala, 1,543 .... E 4
Monthey, 6,834 .... C 4
Montreux-Le Châtelard, 20,100 .... C 4
Morges, 8,420 .... B 3
Moudon, 2,806 .... C 3
Moutier, 7,472 .... D 2
Müllheim, 1,475 .... G 1
Mümliswil-Ramiswil, 2,714 .... E 2
Münchenbuchsee, 3,652 .... E 2
Münsingen, 6,051 .... E 3
Muotathal, 2,592 .... G 3
Muri, 3,957 .... F 2
Muri bei Bern, 7,855 .... E 3
Murten, 3,330 .... D 3
Müstair, 717 .... K 3
Muttenz, 14,000 .... E 1
Näfels, 3,617 .... H 2
Naters, 3,797 .... E 4
Nebikon, 1,206 .... F 2
Nesslau, 2,002 .... H 2
Netstal, 2,925 .... H 2
Neuchâtel, 36,300 .... C 3
Neuchâtel, *52,600 .... C 3
Neuenegg, 2,921 .... D 3
Neuhausen am Rheinfall, 11,800 .... G 1
Neunkirch, 1,208 .... F 1
Niederbipp, 3,141 .... E 2
Niederurnen, 3,347 .... G 2
Niederweningen, 1,027 .... F 1
Nunningen, 1,372 .... E 2
Nyon, 7,643 .... B 4
Oberägeri, 2,656 .... G 2
Oberburg, 3,030 .... E 2
Oberdiessbach, 1,927 .... E 3
Oberdorf, 1,132 .... E 2
Oberriet, 5,498 .... J 2
Obersaxen, 710 .... H 3
Oberuzwil, 4,394 .... H 2
Oensingen, 2,907 .... E 2
Ollon, 4,126 .... D 4
Olten, 21,900 .... E 2
Olten, *47,100 .... E 2
Orbe, 3,824 .... C 3
Ormont-Dessous, 996 .... D 4
Orsières, 2,281 .... D 4
Payerne, 6,024 .... C 3
Peseux, 4,933 .... C 3
Pfäffikon, 5,735 .... G 2
Pfaffnau, 2,575 .... E 2
Pieterlen, 2,978 .... D 2
Pontresina, 1,067 .... J 3
Porrentruy, 7,095 .... C 2
Poschiavo, 3,743 .... J 4
Pratteln, 9,492 .... E 1
Pully, 15,900 .... C 4
Quinto, 1,365 .... G 3
Rafz, 1,925 .... G 1
Ramsen, 1,181 .... G 1
Rapperswil, 7,585 .... G 2
Raron, 1,077 .... E 4
Rechthalten, 1,015 .... D 3
Regensdorf, 4,997 .... F 2
Reichenbach, 2,829 .... E 3
Reiden, 2,795 .... F 2
Reigoldswil, 1,192 .... E 2
Reinach, 5,174 .... F 2
Renens, 15,200 .... C 3
Rheinau, 2,363 .... G 1
Rheineck, 3,047 .... J 2
Rheinfelden, 5,197 .... E 1
Richterswil, 5,842 .... G 2
Riehen, 20,100 .... E 1
Riggisberg, 1,949 .... E 3
Riva San Vitale, 1,358 .... G 5
Rivera, 950 .... G 4
Roggwil, 3,420 .... E 2
Rohrbach, 1,534 .... E 2
Rolle, 2,942 .... B 4
Romanshorn, 7,755 .... H 1
Romont, 2,982 .... C 3
Rorschach, 13,400 .... H 2
Rorschach, *24,500 .... H 2
Rosenlaui .... F 3
Rothrist, 5,048 .... E 2
Rougemont, 860 .... D 4
Roveredo, 1,878 .... H 4
Rüeggisberg, 2,035 .... E 3
Rüschegg, 1,628 .... D 3
Ruswil, 4,657 .... F 2
Rüthi, 1,521 .... J 2
Rüti, Glarus, 738 .... H 3
Rüti, Zürich, 8,282 .... G 2
Saanen, 5,649 .... D 4
Saas-Fee, 739 .... E 4
Sachseln, 2,721 .... F 3
Saignelégier, 1,636 .... D 2
Saint-Blaise, 2,412 .... D 2
Sainte-Croix, 6,925 .... B 3
Saint-Imier, 6,704 .... D 2
Saint-Martin, 1,155 .... E 4
Saint-Maurice, 3,196 .... C 4
Saint Moritz, 3,751 .... J 3
Saint Niklaus, 2,071 .... E 4
Saint-Prex, 1,897 .... B 4
Saint-Stephan, 1,227 .... D 3
Saint-Ursanne, 1,304 .... D 2
Samedan, 2,106 .... J 3
Sankt Gallen, 78,900 .... H 2
Sargans, 2,571 .... H 2
Sarnen, 6,554 .... F 3
Satigny, 1,594 .... A 4
Savièse, 3,203 .... D 4
Savognin, 632 .... J 3
Saxon, 2,305 .... D 4
Schaffhausen, 37,400 .... G 1
Schaffhausen, *56,900 .... G 1
Schangnau, 1,031 .... E 3
Schänis, 2,328 .... H 2
Schiers, 2,363 .... J 3
Schinznach-Dorf, 1,081 .... F 2
Schlarigna-Celerina, 868 .... J 3
Schleitheim, 1,494 .... G 1
Schlieren, 11,600 .... F 2
Schönenwerd, 4,561 .... E 2
Schüpfheim, 3,771 .... F 3
Schwanden, 3,020 .... H 2
Schwyz, 12,200 .... G 2
Scuol-Schuls, 1,429 .... K 3
Sedrun, 1,855 .... G 3
Seewis, 969 .... J 3
Sembrancher, 710 .... D 4
Sempach, 1,345 .... F 2
Semsales, 762 .... C 3
Seon, 3,006 .... F 2
Sevelen, 2,370 .... H 2
Sierre, 8,690 .... D 4
Siggenthal, 7,376 .... F 1
Signau, 2,555 .... E 3
Sigriswil, 3,739 .... E 3
Silenen, 2,261 .... G 3
Sils im Domleschg, 737 .... H 3
Silvaplana, 346 .... J 4
Sins, 2,195 .... F 2
Sion, 18,900 .... D 4
Sirnach, 3,075 .... G 2
Sissach, 4,574 .... E 2
Solothurn (Soleure), 18,900 .... E 2
Solothurn, *36,400 .... E 2
Sonvico, 1,005 .... G 4
Spiez, 8,168 .... E 3
Stäfa, 6,947 .... G 2
Stalden, 1,007 .... E 4
Stammheim, 1,460 .... G 1
Stans, 4,337 .... F 3
Steckborn, 3,514 .... G 1
Steffisburg, 12,100 .... E 3
Stein, 1,060 .... E 1
Stein am Rhein, 2,588 .... G 1
Sulgen, 1,252 .... H 1
Sulz, 1,022 .... F 1
Sumiswald, 5,525 .... E 2
Sursee, 5,324 .... F 2
Tafers, 1,621 .... D 3
Täuffelen, 1,500 .... D 2
Tavannes, 3,939 .... D 2
Thalwil, 13,200 .... G 2
Thayngen, 3,013 .... G 1
Therwil, 1,946 .... E 1
Thun, 33,700 .... E 3
Thun, *56,700 .... E 3
Thusis, 1,998 .... H 3
Trachselwald, 1,269 .... E 2
Tramelan, 5,567 .... D 2
Trogen, 2,101 .... H 2
Trub, 1,981 .... E 3
Trun, 1,583 .... G 3
Turbenthal, 2,685 .... G 2
Turgi, 1,860 .... F 1
Ueberstorf, 1,536 .... D 3
Uetendorf, 2,810 .... E 3
Unterägeri, 3,832 .... G 2
Unterkulm, 2,149 .... F 2
Unterseen, 3,783 .... E 3
Untervaz, 1,142 .... H 3
Urnäsch, 2,330 .... H 2
Uster, 20,800 .... G 2
Utzenstorf, 2,821 .... E 2
Uznach, 3,173 .... H 2
Uzwil, 7,828 .... H 2
Vallorbe, 3,990 .... B 3
Vals, 968 .... H 3
Vaz-Obervaz, 1,568 .... J 3
Vechigen, 3,153 .... E 3
Vernayaz, 1,188 .... D 4
Versoix, 3,426 .... B 4
Vevey, 18,000 .... C 4
Vevey, *29,600 .... C 4
Veyrier, 2,705 .... B 4
Villeneuve, 2,366 .... C 4
Visp, 3,658 .... E 4
Vouvry, 1,368 .... C 4
Wädenswil, 14,300 .... G 2
Wahlern, 4,723 .... D 3
Wald, 7,778 .... G 2
Waldenburg, 1,284 .... E 2
Waldkirch, 2,487 .... H 2
Wallenstadt, 3,296 .... H 2
Walzenhausen, 2,345 .... J 2
Wangen an der Aare, 1,936 .... E 2
Wängi, 1,681 .... H 1
Wartau, 3,284 .... H 2
Wattwil, 7,480 .... H 2
Weesen, 1,280 .... H 2
Weggis, 2,243 .... F 2
Weinfelden, 6,954 .... H 1
Wettingen, 19,700 .... F 2
Wetzikon, 12,600 .... G 2
Wil, 12,900 .... H 2
Wilchingen, 1,061 .... F 1
Wilderswil, 1,701 .... E 3
Wildhaus, 1,179 .... H 2
Willisau, 2,508 .... F 2
Wimmis, 1,756 .... E 3
Windisch, 5,377 .... F 1
Winterthur, 92,500 .... G 1
Winterthur, *104,600 .... G 1
Wohlen, 8,636 .... F 2
Wohlen bei Bern, 2,985 .... D 3
Wolfenschiessen, 1,647 .... F 3
Wolhusen, 3,446 .... F 2
Wollerau, 2,415 .... G 2
Worb, 5,885 .... E 3
Wynigen, 2,221 .... E 2
Yverdon, 19,200 .... C 3
Yvonand, 1,290 .... C 3
Zäziwil, 1,265 .... E 3
Zell, Luzern, 1,582 .... E 2
Zell, Zürich, 3,347 .... G 2
Zermatt, 2,731 .... E 4
Zizers, 1,290 .... J 3
Zofingen, 1,290 .... F 2
Zollikofen, 6,237 .... E 3
Zollikon, 12,100 .... G 2
Zug, 22,300 .... G 2
Zuoz, 1,001 .... J 3
Zürich, 432,400 .... F 2
Zürich, *671,500 .... F 2
Zurzach, 2,694 .... F 1
Zweisimmen, 2,676 .... D 3

OTHER FEATURES

Aa (river) .... F 3
Aare (river) .... E 3
Ägerisee (lake) .... G 2
Albristhorn (mt.) .... D 4
Aletschhorn (mt.) .... F 4
Allaine (river) .... D 2
Areuse (river) .... C 3
Ault (peak) .... H 3
Baldeggersee (lake) .... F 2
Balmhorn (mt.) .... E 4
Bärenhorn (mt.) .... H 3
Basodino (mt.) .... G 4
Bernese Oberland (region) .... E 3
Bernina, Piz (mt.) .... J 4
Bernina (pass) .... K 4
Bernina (river) .... J 4
Beverin (mt.) .... H 3
Biel (lake) .... D 2
Birs (river) .... D 2
Blindenhorn (mt.) .... F 4
Blümlisalp (mt.) .... E 3
Bodensee (Constance) (lake) .... H 1
Borgne (river) .... D 4
Breithorn (mt.) .... E 5
Breithorn (mt.) .... E 4
Brienz (lake) .... F 3
Brienzer Rothorn (mt.) .... F 3
Broye (river) .... C 3
Brulé (mt.) .... D 4
Buchegg (mts.) .... D 2
Bürkelkopf (mt.) .... K 3
Bütschelegg (mt.) .... D 3
Calancasca (river) .... H 4
Campo Tencia (peak) .... G 4
Ceneri (mt.) .... G 4
Cheville (pass) .... D 4
Churfirsten (mt.) .... H 2
Claridenstock (mt.) .... G 3
Collon (mt.) .... D 5
Constance (lake) .... H 1
Dammastock (mt.) .... F 3
Davos (valley) .... J 3
Dent Blanche (mt.) .... E 4
Dent de Lys (mt.) .... D 4
Dent de Ruth (mt.) .... D 3
Dent d'Hérens (mt.) .... E 5
Dents du Midi (mt.) .... C 4
Diablerets (mt.) .... D 4
Doldenhorn (mt.) .... E 4
Dolent (mt.) .... C 5
Dom (mt.) .... E 4
Doubs (river) .... C 2
Drance (river) .... D 4
Dufourspitze (mt.) .... E 5
Emmental (valley) .... E 3
Engadine (valley) .... J-K 3-4
Err (mt.) .... J 3
Finsteraarhorn (mt.) .... F 3
Finstermünz (pass) .... K 3
Fletschhorn (mt.) .... F 4
Flüela (pass) .... J 3
Fluhberg (mt.) .... G 2
Fort (mt.) .... D 4
Furka (pass) .... F 3
Generoso (mt.) .... H 5
Geneva (lake) .... C 4
Giacomo (pass) .... G 4
Gibloux (mt.) .... D 3
Glâne (river) .... C 3
Glärnisch (mt.) .... H 2

SWITZERLAND and LIECHTENSTEIN

CONIC PROJECTION

SCALE OF MILES

0   5   10   20   30

SCALE OF KILOMETRES

0   5   10   20   30   40   50

Capitals of Countries .... ☆
Capitals of Cantons .... ◉
International Boundaries .... ▬ ▪ ▬ ▪
Canals .... ⌇⌇⌇⌇⌇⌇

Copyright by C.S. HAMMOND & Co., N.Y.

AUSTRIA

PROVINCES

Burgenland, 271,001 ....D 3
Carinthia, 495,226 ....C 3
Lower Austria, 1,374,012 ....C 2
Salzburg, 347,292 ....B 3
Styria, 1,137,865 ....C 3
Tirol, 462,899 ....A 3
Upper Austria 1,131,623 ....B 2
Vienna (city), 1,631,423 ....D 2
Vorarlberg, 226,323 ....A 3

CITIES and TOWNS

Admont, 3,057 ....C 3
Aigen, 1,941 ....B 2
Alt Aussee, 2,026 ....B 3
Altheim, 4,271 ....B 2
Althofen, 3,221 ....C 3
Amstetten, 12,086 ....C 2
Andau, 3,011 ....D 3
Arnoldstein, 6,229 ....B 3
Aspang, 2,359 ....D 3
Attnang-Puchheim, 7,525 ....B 2
Bad Aussee, 5,144 ....B 3
Bad Goisern, 6,028 ....B 3
Bad Hofgastein, 4,700 ....B 3
Bad Ischl, 12,703 ....B 3
Bad Sankt Leonhard, 1,939 ....C 3
Baden, 22,484 ....D 2
Badgastein, 5,742 ....B 3
Berndorf, 8,992 ....C 2
Bischofshofen, 8,287 ....B 3
Bludenz, 11,127 ....A 3
Bramberg, 2,620 ....B 3
Braunau, 14,449 ....B 2
Bregenz, 21,428 ....A 3
Bruck an der Leitha, 6,791 ....D 2
Bruck an der Mur, 16,087 ....C 3
Deutsch Feistritz, 3,427 ....C 3
Deutsch Landsberg, 5,227 ....C 3
Deutsch Wagram, 4,207 ....D 2
Deutschkreutz, 3,901 ....D 3
Dornbirn, 28,075 ....A 3
Ebenfurth, 2,342 ....D 2
Ebensee, 9,602 ....B 3
Eferding, 3,151 ....B 2
Eggenburg, 3,338 ....C 2
Eisenerz, 12,435 ....C 3

Horn, 4,705 ....C 2
Hüttenberg, 2,257 ....C 3
Imst, 5,057 ....A 3
Innsbruck, 113,468 ....A 3
Jenbach, 5,479 ....A 3
Judenburg, 9,869 ....C 3
Kapfenberg, 23,859 ....C 3
Kappl, 1,970 ....A 3
Kaprun, 2,164 ....B 3
Kindberg, 5,766 ....C 3
Kirchdorf an der Krems, 2,964 ..C 3
Kitzbühel, 7,744 ....B 3
Klagenfurt, 69,218 ....C 3
Klosterneuburg, 22,787 ....D 2
Knittelfeld, 14,259 ....C 3
Köflach, 12,367 ....C 3
Königswiesen, 2,707 ....C 2
Korneuburg, 8,276 ....D 2
Kössen, 2,361 ....B 3
Kötschach-Mauthen, 2,763 ....B 3
Krems, 21,046 ....C 2
Kufstein, 11,215 ....B 3
Kundl, 2,508 ....A 3
Laa an der Thaya, 4,925 ....D 2
Laakirchen, 6,722 ....B 3
Lambach, 3,019 ....B 2
Landeck, 6,514 ....A 3
Landskron, 9,058 ....A 3
Längenfeld, 2,314 ....A 3
Langenlois, 4,655 ....C 2
Langenwang, 3,734 ....C 3
Laxenburg ....
Leibnitz, 6,356 ....C 3
Lenzing, 5,372 ....B 2
Leoben, 36,257 ....C 3
Leonfelden, 2,546 ....C 2
Lienz, 11,132 ....B 3
Liezen, 5,444 ....C 3
Lilienfeld, 3,307 ....C 2
Linz, 205,762 ....C 2
Lustenau, 12,582 ....A 3
Mannersdorf, 3,909 ....D 2
Marchegg, 2,159 ....D 2
Mariazell, 2,181 ....C 3
Matrei, 3,430 ....B 3
Mattersburg, 4,270 ....D 3
Mattighofen, 3,919 ....B 2
Mauerkirchen, 2,175 ....B 2
Mautern, 2,365 ....C 2
Mauthausen, 3,836 ....C 2
Mauthen-Kötschach, 2,763 ....B 3
Mayrhofen, 2,523 ....A 3

Schärding, 5,710 ....B 2
Scheibbs, 3,231 ....C 2
Schladming, 3,249 ....B 3
Schrems, 3,080 ....C 2
Schruns, 3,304 ....A 3
Schwarzach, 3,186 ....B 3
Schwaz, 9,455 ....A 3
Schwertberg, 3,369 ....C 2
Sierning, 7,527 ....C 2
Sillian, 1,948 ....B 3
Solbad Hall, 10,750 ....A 3
Spital, 2,421 ....C 3
Spittal, 10,045 ....B 3
Steinach, 2,155 ....A 3
Steyr, 38,306 ....C 2
Stockerau, 11,853 ....D 2
Strassburg, 2,972 ....C 3
Tamsweg, 4,431 ....B 3
Telfs, 5,438 ....A 3
Ternitz, 9,032 ....D 3
Traiskirchen, 7,026 ....D 2
Traun, 16,026 ....C 2
Trieben, 4,023 ....C 3
Trofaiach, 6,909 ....C 3
Tulln, 6,306 ....D 2
Velden, 2,039 ....C 3
Vienna (capital), 1,642,072 ....D 2
Villach, 32,971 ....B 3
Vöcklabruck, 9,353 ....B 2
Voitsberg, 9,353 ....C 3
Völkermarkt, 3,678 ....C 3
Vorarlberg, 2,896 ....C 3
Waidhofen an der Thaya,
3,748 ....C 2
Waidhofen an der Ybbs,
5,586 ....C 2
Weitensfeld, 2,998 ....C 3
Weiz, 8,146 ....C 3
Wels, 41,060 ....C 2
Weyer, 2,367 ....C 2
Wiener Neustadt, 33,845 ....D 3
Wildon, 2,020 ....C 3
Wilhelmsburg, 6,196 ....C 2
Wolfsberg, 9,470 ....C 3
Wörgl, 6,828 ....A 3
Ybbs, 5,324 ....C 2
Zams, 2,782 ....A 3
Zell am See, 6,455 ....B 3
Zeltweg, 7,340 ....C 3
Zirl, 3,165 ....A 3
Zistersdorf, 3,011 ....D 2
Zwettl, 3,836 ....C 2

OTHER FEATURES

Allgäu Alps (mts.) ....A 3
Atter (lake) ....B 3
Bavarian Alps (mts.) ....A 3
Bodensee (Constance) (lake) ....A 3
Brenner (pass) ....A 3
Carnic Alps (mts.) ....B 3
Coglians (Hohe Warte) (peak)..B 3
Constance (lake) ....A 3
Danube (river) ....C 2
Donau (Danube) (river) ....D 2
Drau (river) ....C 3
Enns (river) ....C 3
Fertő tó (Neusiedler) (lake) ....D 3
Greiner (forest) ....
Grossglockner (mt.) ....B 3
Gross Höllkogel (mt.) ....B 3
Gross Peilstein (mt.) ....B 2
Hochgolling (mt.) ....B 3
Hohe Tauern (range) ....B 3
Hohe Warte (peak) ....B 3
Inn (river) ....A 3
Kamp (river) ....C 2
Karawanken (mts.) ....C 3
Laufnitz (river) ....D 2
March (river) ....D 2
Mühlviertel (region),
196,037 ....C 2
Mur (river) ....C 3
Mürz (river) ....C 3
Niedere Tauern (range) ....B 3
Olsa (river) ....
Ötztal Alps (mts.) ....A 3
Parseierspitze (mt.) ....A 3
Raab (river) ....C 3
Rhine (river) ....A 3
Salzach (river) ....B 3
Salzkammergut (region) ....B 3
Semmering (pass) ....C 3
Thaya (river) ....C 2
Traun (river) ....B 2
Traun (lake) ....B 3
Wildspitze (mt.) ....A 3
Zugspitze (mt.) ....A 3

CZECHOSLOVAKIA

REPUBLICS

Czech Soc. Rep., 9,778,000 ....B 1
Slovak Soc. Rep., 4,421,000 ....E 2

REGIONS

Jihočeský, 659,000 ....C 2
Jihomoravský, 1,941,000 ....D 2
Prague (city), 1,025,000 ....C 1
Severočeský, 1,122,000 ....C 1
Severomoravský, 1,695,000 ....D 1
Středočeský, 1,271,000 ....C 2
Středoslovenský, 1,379,000 ....D 2
Východočeský, 1,213,000 ....C 1
Východoslovenský, 1,199,000 ....F 2
Západočeský, 852,000 ....B 2
Západoslovenský, 1,843,000 ....D 2

CITIES and TOWNS

Aš, 10,000 ....B 1
Austerlitz (Slavkov), 4,869 ....D 2
Bánovce, 3,563 ....E 2
Banská Bystrica, 29,000 ....E 2
Banská Štiavnica, 10,381 ....E 2
Bardejov, 11,000 ....F 2
Bechyně, 2,398 ....C 2
Benešov, 10,000 ....C 2
Beroun, 17,000 ....C 2
Bílina, 12,000 ....B 1
Blansko, 11,000 ....D 2
Blatná, 3,596 ....C 2
Blovice, 2,629 ....B 2
Bojkovice, 2,902 ....D 2
Bor, 2,257 ....B 2
Boskovice, 6,396 ....D 2

Brandýs nad Labem-Stará
Boleslav, 13,161 ....C 1
Bratislava, 278,835 ....D 2
Břeclav, 13,000 ....D 2
Březnice, 2,634 ....C 2
Brezno, 11,000 ....E 2
Brno, 333,831 ....D 2
Broumov, 6,370 ....D 1
Brtnice, 2,176 ....C 2
Bruntál, 9,000 ....D 2
Bučovice, 3,381 ....D 2
Budišov, 2,573 ....D 2
Bystřice nad Pernštejnem,
2,653 ....D 2
Bystřice pod Hostýnem, 4,973 ....D 2
Bytča, 4,528 ....D 2
Čadca, 13,000 ....D 2
Čáslov, 4,536 ....C 2
Fil'akovo, 5,950 ....E 2
Františkovy Lázně, 5,212 ....B 1
Frýdek-Místek, 32,000 ....D 1
Frýdlant nad Ostravicí, 4,178 ....D 1
Frýdlant v Čechách, 5,460 ....C 1
Fulnek, 2,765 ....D 1
Galanta, 8,000 ....D 2
Gelnica, 3,240 ....E 2
Golčův Jeníkov, 1,920 ....C 2
Gottwaldov, 63,000 ....D 2
Handlová, 16,000 ....D 2
Havířov, 72,000 ....D 1
Havlíčkův Brod, 16,000 ....C 2
Hlinsko, 5,189 ....C 2
Hlohovec, 14,000 ....D 2
Hlučín, 11,000 ....D 1
Hodonín, 19,000 ....D 2

Cukmantl, 2,362 ....D 1
Dačice, 2,810 ....C 2
Děčín, 42,000 ....B 1
Detva, 7,786 ....E 2
Dobřany, 4,905 ....B 2
Dobříš, 4,390 ....C 2
Dobrá Voda, 4,093 ....D 1
Dobšiná, 3,957 ....E 2
Doksy, 3,061 ....C 1
Dolný Kubín, 5,000 ....D 2
Domažlice, 8,000 ....B 2
Dubnica nad Váhom, 11,250 ....D 2
Duchcov, 8,229 ....B 1
Dunajská Streda, 9,000 ....D 2
Dvory, 5,475 ....C 2
Dvůr Králové nad Labem, 16,000 ....C 1
Falknov (Sokolov), 20,000 ....B 1

(continued)

Austria CITIES and TOWNS (continued)

Eisenstadt, 7,167 ....D 3
Enns, 8,919 ....C 2
Feldbach, 3,687 ....C 3
Feldkirch, 17,343 ....A 3
Feldkirchen in Kärnten, 3,181 ..B 3
Ferlach, 5,672 ....C 3
Fieberbrunn, 3,010 ....B 3
Fohnsdorf, 11,571 ....C 3
Frankenmarkt, 2,565 ....B 2
Frauenkirchen, 2,812 ....D 3
Friesach, 3,388 ....C 3
Freistadt, 5,375 ....C 2
Frohnleiten, 4,969 ....C 3
Fulpmes, 2,282 ....A 3
Fürstenfeld, 6,415 ....C 3
Gaming, 4,218 ....C 2
Gänserndorf, 3,378 ....D 2
Gleisdorf, 4,385 ....C 3
Gloggnitz, 7,228 ....C 3
Gmünd, Carinthia, 2,195 ....B 3
Gmünd, Lower Austria, 6,522 ..C 2
Gmunden, 12,518 ....B 2
Golling an der Salzach,
2,845 ....B 3
Götzis, 7,034 ....A 3
Gratwein, 2,515 ....C 3
Graz, 253,000 ....C 3
Grein, 2,518 ....C 2
Grieskirchen, 4,137 ....B 2
Gross Siegharts, 2,599 ....C 2
Grünburg, 3,609 ....C 2
Güssing, 2,715 ....D 3
Haag, 4,671 ....C 2
Hainburg, 6,437 ....D 2
Hainfeld, 3,883 ....C 2
Hallein, 13,329 ....B 3
Hallstatt, 1,373 ....B 3
Hartberg, 5,529 ....C 3
Haslach an der Mühl, 2,565 ....C 2
Heidenreichstein, 3,653 ....C 2
Heiligenblut, 1,195 ....B 3
Hermagor, 2,778 ....B 3
Herzogenburg, 5,166 ....C 2
Hieflau, 2,003 ....C 3
Hohenau an der March, 3,907 ..D 2
Hohenberg, 2,093 ....C 2
Hohenems, 9,188 ....A 3
Hollabrunn, 5,832 ....C 2
Hopfgarten in Nordtirol, 4,163 ..B 3

Melk, 3,534 ....C 2
Mistelbach an der Zaya, 5,434..D 2
Mittersill, 3,502 ....B 3
Mödling, 17,274 ....D 2
Mondsee, 2,050 ....B 3
Murau, 2,755 ....C 3
Mürzzuschlag, 11,586 ....C 3
Nassereith, 1,744 ....A 3
Neuberg an der Mürz, 2,411 ..C 3
Neumarkt, Styria, 1,880 ....C 3
Neumarkt am Wallersee, 2,877..B 3
Neunkirchen, 10,027 ....C 3
Neusiedl am See, 3,826 ....D 3
Neustift im Stubaital, 2,195 ....A 3
Ober Grafendorf, 3,825 ....C 2
Oberndorf bei Salzburg, 3,084..B 3
Obervellach, 2,371 ....B 3
Oberwart, 4,740 ....C 3
Paternion, 5,581 ....B 3
Perg, 4,116 ....C 2
Peuerbach, 2,105 ....B 2
Pinkafeld, 3,826 ....C 3
Pöchlarn, 2,921 ....C 2
Pörtschach, 2,449 ....C 3
Poysdorf, 2,738 ....D 2
Pregarten, 2,818 ....C 2
Radenthein, 5,651 ....B 3
Radstadt, 3,311 ....B 3
Rankweil, 6,451 ....A 3
Rechnitz, 3,374 ....C 3
Reichenau an der Rax, 4,441 ..C 3
Retz, 2,941 ....C 2
Reutte, 4,285 ....A 3
Ried im Innkreis, 9,471 ....B 2
Rottenmann, 4,139 ....C 3
Saalfelden, 8,901 ....B 3
Salzburg, 120,204 ....B 3
Sankt Aegyd am Neuwalde,
3,206 ....C 2
Sankt Anton am Arlberg, 1,741..A 3
Sankt Johann, 4,713 ....B 3
Sankt Michael, 3,433 ....C 3
Sankt Michael im Lungau,
2,422 ....B 3
Sankt Paul, 1,808 ....C 3
Sankt Pölten, 40,112 ....C 2
Sankt Valentin, 7,750 ....C 2
Sankt Veit an der Glan, 10,950 ..C 3
Sankt Wolfgang, 2,234 ....B 3

AUSTRIA
AREA 32,374 sq. mi.
POPULATION 7,419,341
CAPITAL Vienna
LARGEST CITY Vienna
HIGHEST POINT Grossglockner 12,457 ft.
MONETARY UNIT schilling
MAJOR LANGUAGE German
MAJOR RELIGION Roman Catholicism

CZECHOSLOVAKIA
AREA 49,370 sq. mi.
POPULATION 14,497,000
CAPITAL Prague
LARGEST CITY Prague
HIGHEST POINT Gerlachovka 8,707 ft.
MONETARY UNIT koruna (crown)
MAJOR LANGUAGES Czech, Slovak
MAJOR RELIGIONS Roman Catholicism, Protestantism

HUNGARY
AREA 35,915 sq. mi.
POPULATION 10,315,597
CAPITAL Budapest
LARGEST CITY Budapest
HIGHEST POINT Kékes 3,330 ft.
MONETARY UNIT forint
MAJOR LANGUAGE Hungarian
MAJOR RELIGIONS Roman Catholicism, Protestantism

AUSTRIA

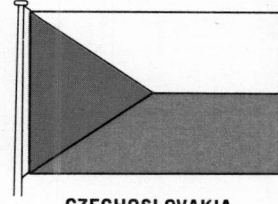

CZECHOSLOVAKIA

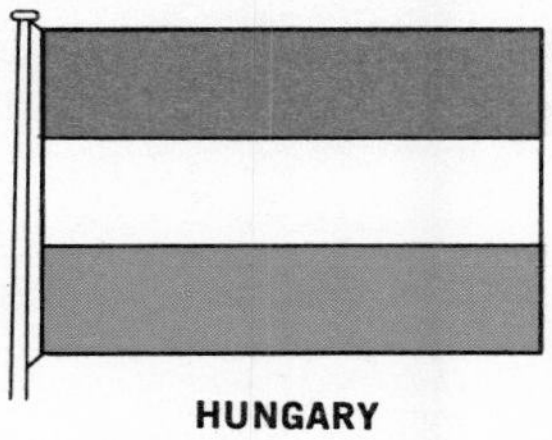

HUNGARY

AUSTRIA, CZECHOSLOVAKIA and HUNGARY

CONIC PROJECTION

SCALE OF MILES
0 10 20   40   60   80

SCALE OF KILOMETRES
0 10 20   40   60   80

Capitals of Countries ....☆   International Boundaries _____
Republic Capital ....◎   Internal Boundaries _____
Administrative Centers ...△   Canals ....

Czechoslovakia is divided internally into two republics, Czech (capital-Prague) and Slovak (capital-Bratislava), ten regions (Kraj) and the independent cities of Prague and Bratislava.

© C. S. HAMMOND & Co., N.Y.

CZECHOSLOVAKIA (continued)

Holešov, 6,599	D 2	
Holíč, 5,881	D 2	
Holice, 5,695	D 1	
Horazďovice, 3,098	C 2	
Hořice, 7,133	C 1	
Horní Benešov, 3,181	D 2	
Horní Libina, 4,583	D 2	
Hořovice, 4,697	C 2	
Horšovský Týn, 3,475	B 2	
Hostinné, 4,412	C 1	
Hradec Králové, 62,000	C 1	
Hranice, 12,000	D 2	
Hronov, 11,000	D 1	
Hrušovany, 3,128	C 2	
Humenné, 14,000	G 2	
Humpolec, 5,083	C 2	
Hurbanovo, 3,578	E 3	
Hustopeče, 2,698	D 2	
Ilava, 2,043	E 2	
Ivančice, 4,742	D 2	
Jablonec nad Nisou, 33,000	C 1	
Jablunkov, 4,467	E 2	
Jáchymov, 6,806	B 1	
Jaroměř, 12,000	C 1	
Jelšava, 2,456	F 2	
Jemnice, 3,383	C 2	
Jeseník, 5,873	D 1	
Jesenské, 1,567	F 2	
Jevíčko, 2,881	D 2	
Jičín, 13,000	C 1	
Jihlava, 37,000	C 2	
Jilemnice, 3,362	C 1	
Jindřichův Hradec, 12,000	C 2	
Jirkov, 21,000	B 1	
Kadaň, 5,062	B 1	
Kamenice, 2,692	C 2	
Kaplice, 1,931	C 2	
Karlovy Vary, 45,000	B 1	
Karviná, 70,000	E 2	
Kašperské Hory, 2,814	B 2	
Kdyně, 2,609	B 2	
Kežmarok, 7,372	F 2	
Kladno, 55,000	B 1	
Klatovy, 16,000	B 2	
Kojetín, 5,292	D 2	
Kokava, 5,398	E 2	
Kolárovo, 11,000	D 3	
Kolín, 25,000	C 1	
Mělník, 15,000	C 1	
Michalovce, 18,000	G 2	
Mikulov, 5,220	D 2	
Milevsko, 3,754	C 2	
Mimoň, 5,349	C 1	
Mladá Boleslav, 27,000	C 1	
Mladá Vožice, 1,732	C 2	
Mnichovo Hradiště, 4,647	C 1	
Modra, 6,239	D 2	
Modrý Kameň, 1,836	E 2	
Mohelnice, 4,949	D 2	
Moldava, 2,241	F 2	
Moravská Třebová, 5,844	D 2	
Moravské Budějovice, 4,348	C 2	
Moravský Krumlov, 2,897	C 2	
Most, 56,000	B 1	
Mučeníkov, 5,207	D 2	
Myjava, 9,935	D 2	
Náchod, 18,000	D 1	
Neded, 4,553	D 3	
Nejdek, 5,748	B 1	
Nepomuk, 1,860	B 2	
Nesvady, 5,070	E 3	
Nitra, 32,000	E 2	
Nová Baňa, 5,113	E 2	
Nová Bystřice, 2,418	C 2	
Nové Město na Moravě, 3,250	D 2	
Nové Město nad Váhom, 14,000	D 2	
Nové Strašecí, 3,288	B 1	
Nové Zamky, 24,000	D 3	
Nové Bohumín, 12,000	E 2	
Nový Bor, 5,994	C 1	
Nový Bydžov, 6,120	C 1	
Nový Hrozenkov, 5,302	E 2	
Nový Jičín, 17,000	E 2	
Nymburk, 13,000	C 1	
Nýřany, 4,420	B 2	
Nýrsko, 4,124	B 2	
Odry, 5,340	D 2	
Olomouc, 77,000	D 2	
Opava, 46,000	D 2	
Oslavany, 3,606	C 2	
Ostrava, 271,905	E 2	
Ostrov, 19,000	B 1	
Otrokovice-Kvítkovice, 11,000	D 2	
Pacov, 2,775	C 2	
Pardubice, 65,000	C 1	
Rýmařov, 4,328	D 2	
Sabinov, 3,909	F 2	
Šafaříkovo, 3,180	F 2	
Šahy, 4,019	E 2	
Šaľa, 4,397	D 2	
Sečovce, 3,354	F 2	
Sedlčany, 2,083	C 2	
Semily, 6,549	C 1	
Senec, 6,184	D 2	
Senica, 8,000	D 2	
Sereď, 6,208	D 2	
Skalica, 5,440	D 2	
Skuteč, 3,348	C 2	
Slaný, 12,000	C 1	
Slavkov, 4,869	D 2	
Snina, 5,002	G 2	
Soběslav, 4,643	C 2	
Sobotka, 2,147	C 1	
Sokolov, 20,000	B 1	
Spišská Belá, 3,072	F 2	
Spišská Nová Ves, 20,000	F 2	
Stará Ľubovňa, 1,989	F 2	
Staré Město, 6,350	D 2	
Sternberk, 12,000	D 2	
Stod, 2,502	B 2	
Strakonice, 16,000	B 2	
Strážnice, 5,147	D 2	
Stříbro, 4,659	B 2	
Stropkov, 2,506	F 2	
Štúrovo, 4,082	E 3	
Šumperk, 22,000	D 1	
Šurany, 5,381	E 2	
Sušice, 6,973	B 2	
Svárov, 3,381	C 1	
Svitavy, 14,000	D 2	
Tábor, 21,000	C 2	
Tachov, 8,000	B 2	
Tardošked, 6,689	C 2	
Telč, 4,381	C 2	
Teplá u Toužimě, 2,500	B 2	
Teplice, 52,000	B 1	
Terchová, 4,400	E 2	
Tišnov, 4,885	C 2	
Tisovec, 3,988	E 2	
Topoľčany, 12,000	D 2	
Třebíč, 21,000	C 2	
Trebišov, 10,000	F 2	
Třeboň, 4,663	C 2	
Trenčín, 26,000	E 2	
Třešť, 4,900	C 2	
Zbiroh, 1,718	B 2	
Zborov, 1,551	F 2	
Žďár nad Sázavou, 12,000	C 2	
Železovce, 3,748	E 2	
Žiar nad Hronom, 11,000	E 2	
Zidlochovice, 2,696	C 2	
Žilina, 38,000	E 2	
Zlaté Moravce, 4,003	E 2	
Zlín (Gottwaldov), 63,000	D 2	
Žlutice, 2,114	B 1	
Znojmo, 25,000	C 2	
Zvolen, 23,000	E 2	

OTHER FEATURES

Berounka (river)	C 2	
Beskids, East (mts.)	F 2	
Beskids, West (mts.)	E 2	
Bohemia (region), 6,142,000	C 2	
Bohemian (forest)	B 2	
Bohemian-Moravian Heights	C 2	
Dudváh (river)	D 2	
Dunajec (river)	F 2	
Dyje (river)	C 2	
Erzgebirge (mts.)	B 1	
Gerlachovka (mt.)	F 2	
Hornád (river)	F 2	
Hron (river)	E 2	
Ipel' (river)	E 2	
Jablunka (pass)	E 2	
Jeseníky (mts.)	D 1	
Jihlava (river)	C 2	
Kamýcká (res.)	C 2	
Krušné Hory (Erzgebirge) (mts.)	B 1	
Labe (river)	C 2	
Laborec (river)	F 2	
Lipno (res.)	C 2	
Lužnice (river)	C 2	
Moldau (Vltava) (river)	C 2	
Morava (river)	D 2	
Moravia (region), 3,636,000	D 2	
Nitra (river)	D 2	
Oder (Odra) (river)	D 2	
Ohře (river)	B 1	
Orava (res.)	E 2	
Orava (river)	E 2	
Orlice (river)	C 1	
Orlická (res.)	C 2	
Otava (river)	B 2	

Agriculture, Industry and Resources

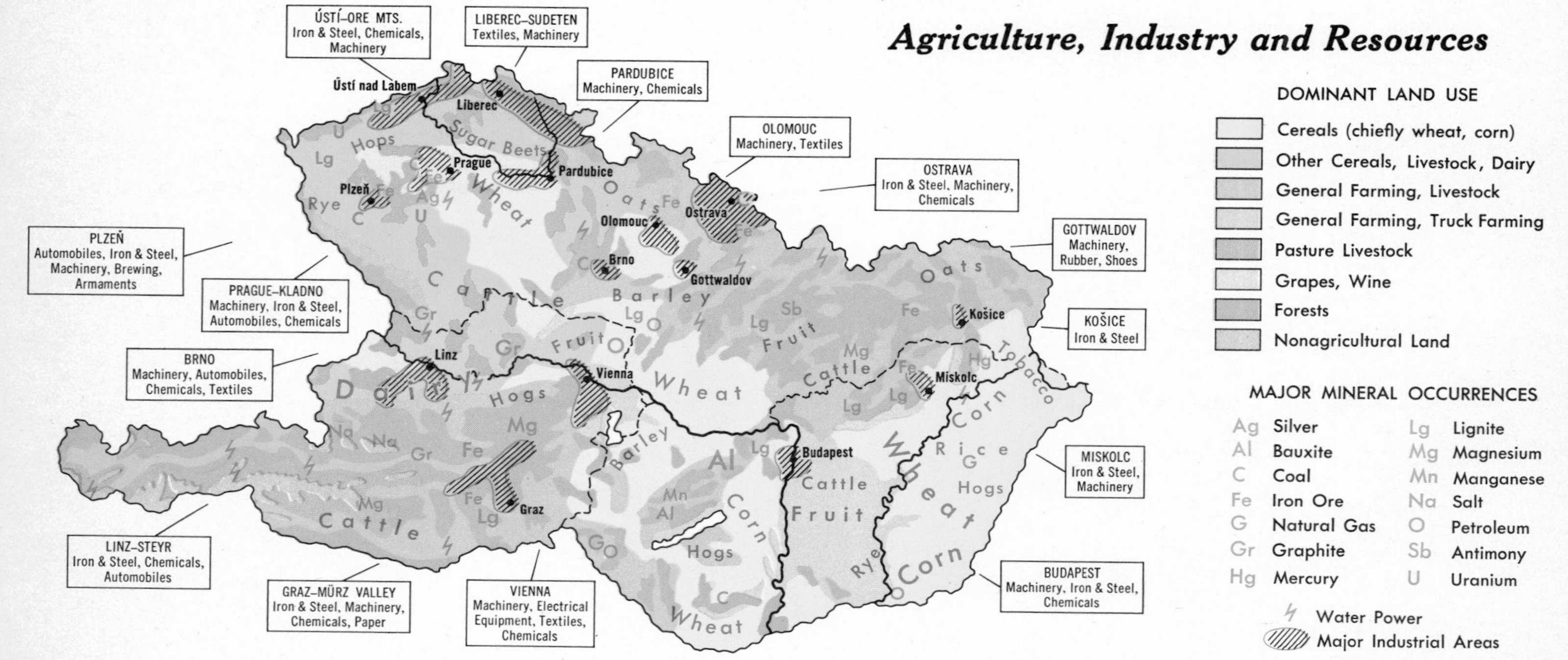

ÚSTÍ-ORE MTS.
Iron & Steel, Chemicals, Machinery

LIBEREC–SUDETEN
Textiles, Machinery

PARDUBICE
Machinery, Chemicals

OLOMOUC
Machinery, Textiles

OSTRAVA
Iron & Steel, Machinery, Chemicals

GOTTWALDOV
Machinery, Rubber, Shoes

KOŠICE
Iron & Steel

MISKOLC
Iron & Steel, Machinery

BUDAPEST
Machinery, Iron & Steel, Chemicals

PLZEŇ
Automobiles, Iron & Steel, Machinery, Brewing, Armaments

PRAGUE–KLADNO
Machinery, Iron & Steel, Automobiles, Chemicals

BRNO
Machinery, Automobiles, Chemicals, Textiles

LINZ–STEYR
Iron & Steel, Chemicals, Automobiles

GRAZ–MÜRZ VALLEY
Iron & Steel, Machinery, Chemicals, Paper

VIENNA
Machinery, Electrical Equipment, Textiles, Chemicals

DOMINANT LAND USE

- Cereals (chiefly wheat, corn)
- Other Cereals, Livestock, Dairy
- General Farming, Livestock
- General Farming, Truck Farming
- Pasture Livestock
- Grapes, Wine
- Forests
- Nonagricultural Land

MAJOR MINERAL OCCURRENCES

Ag	Silver	Lg	Lignite
Al	Bauxite	Mg	Magnesium
C	Coal	Mn	Manganese
Fe	Iron Ore	Na	Salt
G	Natural Gas	O	Petroleum
Gr	Graphite	Sb	Antimony
Hg	Mercury	U	Uranium

⚡ Water Power
▨ Major Industrial Areas

Komárno, 26,000	D 3	
Košice, 115,332	F 2	
Kostelec nad Černými, Lesy, 3,616	C 2	
Kostelec nad Orlicí, 5,539	D 1	
Králíky, 3,895	D 1	
Kralovice, 2,268	B 2	
Kráľovský Chlmec, 3,410	G 2	
Kralupy nad Vltavou, 14,000	C 1	
Kraslice, 6,294	B 1	
Krásna Lípa, 5,041	C 1	
Kremnica, 4,979	E 2	
Krnov, 22,000	D 1	
Kroměříž, 22,000	D 2	
Krompachy, 3,340	F 2	
Krupina, 5,418	E 2	
Krupka, 10,000	B 1	
Kutná Hora, 17,000	C 2	
Kúty, 3,348	D 2	
Kyjov, 5,620	D 2	
Kynšperk, 5,398	B 1	
Kysucké Nové Mesto, 2,318	E 2	
Lanškroun, 6,558	D 2	
Ledeč, 2,625	C 2	
Levice, 15,000	E 2	
Levoča, 7,584	F 2	
Libáň, 2,261	C 1	
Liberec, 71,000	C 1	
Libochovice, 2,879	B 1	
Lidice, 478	C 1	
Lipník, 6,887	D 2	
Liptovský Mikuláš, 14,000	E 2	
Lišov, 2,691	C 2	
Litoměřice, 8,000	C 1	
Litomyšl, 6,384	D 1	
Litovel, 4,962	C 1	
Litvínov, 22,000	B 1	
Lomnice, 2,228	C 2	
Louny, 13,000	C 1	
Lovosice, 4,962	C 1	
L'ubica, 3,335	F 2	
Lučenec, 18,000	E 2	
Lysá, 6,500	C 1	
Malacky, 11,000	D 2	
Mariánské Lázně, 13,000	B 1	
Martin, 29,000	E 2	
Partizánske, 3,171	E 2	
Pelhřimov, 8,000	C 2	
Pezinok, 12,000	D 2	
Piešťany, 21,000	D 2	
Písek, 22,000	C 2	
Planá, 5,216	B 2	
Plánice, 1,718	B 2	
Plasy, 1,472	B 2	
Plzeň, 143,945	B 2	
Počátky, 2,141	C 2	
Podbořany, 3,893	B 1	
Poděbrady, 13,000	C 1	
Pohořelice, 3,068	C 2	
Polička, 5,600	D 2	
Polná, 4,005	C 2	
Poprad, 18,000	F 2	
Poruba, 21,179	D 2	
Povážská Bystrica, 13,000	E 2	
Prachatice, 6,000	C 2	
Prague (Praha) (capital), 1,031,870	C 1	
Přelouč, 4,228	C 2	
Přerov, 35,000	D 2	
Prešov, 39,000	F 2	
Přeštice, 4,616	B 2	
Příbor, 5,491	E 2	
Příbram, 29,000	C 2	
Přibyslav, 2,950	C 2	
Prievidza, 24,000	E 2	
Prostějov, 35,000	D 2	
Protivín, 3,217	C 2	
Púchov, 4,316	E 2	
Radnice, 2,342	B 2	
Rajec, 2,753	E 2	
Rakovník, 13,000	B 1	
Říčany, 6,376	C 2	
Rimavská Sobota, 13,000	F 2	
Rokycany, 13,000	B 2	
Roknytnice nad Jizerou, 3,893	C 1	
Rosice, 4,900	C 2	
Roudnice nad Labem, 11,000	C 1	
Rožňava, 11,000	F 2	
Rožnov, 3,989	E 2	
Rumburk, 6,759	C 1	
Ružomberok, 20,000	E 2	
Rychnov nad Kněžnou, 6,000	D 1	
Trhové Sviny, 2,953	C 2	
Třinec, 27,000	E 2	
Trnava, 35,000	D 2	
Trstená, 2,468	E 2	
Trutnov, 24,000	D 1	
Turnov, 12,000	C 1	
Turzovka, 9,823	E 2	
Týn, 4,135	C 2	
Uherské Hradiště, 15,000	D 2	
Uherský Brod, 6,457	D 2	
Uhlířské Janovice, 1,979	C 2	
Uničov, 3,325	D 2	
Úpice, 5,498	C 1	
Ústí nad Labem, 72,000	C 1	
Ústí nad Orlicí, 11,000	D 1	
Valašské Klobouky, 2,525	D 2	
Valašské Meziříčí, 15,000	D 2	
Varnsdorf, 14,000	C 1	
Vasrec, 2,747	E 2	
Vejprty, 5,476	B 1	
Velká Bíteš, 1,714	C 2	
Velká Bystřice, 4,459	D 2	
Veľké Kapušany, 2,371	G 2	
Velké Meziříčí, 6,217	C 2	
Veselí nad Lužnicí, 4,382	C 2	
Veselí nad Moravou, 4,636	D 2	
Vítkov, 2,685	D 2	
Vizovice, 3,583	D 2	
Vlašim, 5,066	C 2	
Vodňany, 5,374	C 2	
Volary, 5,034	B 2	
Volyně, 3,019	B 2	
Votice, 2,191	C 2	
Vráble, 3,498	E 2	
Vracov, 4,171	D 2	
Vranov, 3,964	F 2	
Vrchlabí, 11,000	C 1	
Vrútky, 5,927	E 2	
Vsetín, 20,000	E 2	
Vysoké Mýto, 7,983	D 2	
Vysoké Tatry, 14,445	F 2	
Žabřeh, 5,847	D 2	
Žamberk, 4,278	D 1	
Žatec, 16,000	B 1	

HUNGARY

COUNTIES

Bács-Kiskun, 560,000	E 3	
Baranya, 280,000	E 4	
Békés, 440,000	F 3	
Borsod-Abaúj-Zemplén, 600,000	F 2	
Budapest (city), 1,990,000	E 3	
Csongrád, 320,000	E 3	
Fejér, 390,000	E 3	
Győr-Sopron, 400,000	D 3	
Hajdú-Bihar, 360,000	F 3	
Heves, 340,000	E 3	
Komárom, 300,000	D 3	
Nógrád, 240,000	E 3	
Pest, 870,000	E 3	
Somogy, 360,000	D 3	
Szabolcs-Szatmár, 540,000	G 3	
Szolnok, 440,000	F 3	
Tolna, 260,000	E 3	
Vas, 280,000	D 3	
Veszprém, 420,000	D 3	
Zala, 260,000	D 3	

CITIES and TOWNS

Aba, 4,369	E 3	
Abádszalók, 7,257	F 3	
Abaújszántó, 4,586	F 3	
Abony, 16,048	E 3	
Ács, 8,507	D 3	
Adony, 4,211	E 3	
Ajka, 21,000	D 3	
Albertirsa, 11,490	E 3	
Aszód, 5,361	E 3	
Bácsalmás, 9,514	E 3	
Baja, 34,000	E 3	
Balassagyarmat, 13,000	E 3	
Balatonfüred, 7,561	D 3	
Balkány, 8,224	G 3	
Balmazújváros, 18,645	F 3	
Barcs, 7,245	D 3	
Bátaszék, 7,378	E 3	
Battonya, 11,019	F 3	
Békés, 21,296	F 3	
Békéscsaba, 53,000	F 3	
Berettyóújfalu, 11,577	F 3	
Berzence, 3,651	D 3	
Bicske, 9,106	E 3	
Biharkeresztes, 4,844	F 3	
Biharnagybajom, 4,762	F 3	
Bőhönye, 3,809	D 3	
Bonyhád, 9,354	E 3	
Budafok, 39,870	E 3	
Budaörs, 12,682	E 3	
Budapest (capital), 1,990,000	S 3	
Cegléd, 37,000	E 3	
Celldömölk, 9,762	D 3	
Cigánd, 5,220	G 2	
Csákvár, 5,135	E 3	
Csanádpalota, 5,264	F 3	
Csenger, 4,835	G 3	
Csepel, 86,287	E 3	
Csepreg, 4,348	D 3	
Csongrád, 20,000	E 3	
Csorna, 9,192	D 3	
Csorvás, 7,622	F 3	
Csurgó, 5,400	D 3	
Debrecen, 160,000	F 3	
Derecske, 9,980	F 3	
Deváványa, 12,137	F 3	
Devecser, 5,741	D 3	
Dombóvár, 15,605	D 3	
Dombrád, 6,868	F 3	
Dömsöd, 6,532	E 3	
Dorog, 9,994	E 3	
Dunaföldvár, 11,039	E 3	
Dunaharaszti, 13,655	E 3	
Dunakeszi, 15,636	E 3	
Dunaújváros, 45,000	E 3	
Dunavecse, 4,908	E 3	
Edelény, 6,851	F 3	
Eger, 45,000	F 3	
Egyek, 8,678	F 3	
Elek, 6,325	F 3	
Emőd, 5,233	F 3	
Endrőd, 9,263	F 3	
Enying, 6,406	E 3	
Ercsi, 7,850	E 3	
Érd, 25,900	E 3	
Erdőtelek, 4,634	F 3	
Esztergom, 26,000	E 3	
Fegyvernek, 7,835	F 3	
Fehérgyarmat, 6,024	G 3	
Földeák, 4,275	F 3	
Füzesabony, 7,125	F 3	
Füzesgyarmat, 7,807	F 3	
Gödöllő, 22,000	E 3	
Gönc, 3,093	F 2	
Gyoma, 10,921	F 3	
Gyöngyös, 32,000	E 3	
Gyónk, 2,684	E 3	
Győr, 81,000	D 3	
Gyula, 25,000	F 3	
Hajdúböszörmény, 30,000	F 3	
Hajdúdorog, 10,559	F 3	
Hajdúhadház, 13,030	F 3	
Hajdúnánás, 17,000	F 3	
Hajdúsámson, 7,284	F 3	
Hajdúszoboszló, 22,000	F 3	
Hajós, 5,584	E 3	
Hatvan, 21,000	E 3	
Heves, 11,349	F 3	
Hódmezővásárhely, 53,000	F 3	
Hogyesz, 3,501	E 3	
Izsák, 8,609	E 3	
Jánoshalma, 12,897	E 3	
Jánosháza, 3,468	D 3	
Jászapáti, 10,495	F 3	
Jászárokszállás, 10,745	F 3	
Jászberény, 30,000	F 3	
Jászfényszaru, 5,052	E 3	
Jászkarajenő, 4,955	E 3	
Jászkisér, 7,280	F 3	
Jászladány, 8,841	F 3	
Kalocsa, 15,000	E 3	
Kapuvár, 52,000	D 3	
Karád, 3,438	D 3	
Karcag, 24,000	F 3	
Kazincbarcika, 29,000	F 2	
Kecel, 10,193	E 3	
Kecskemét, 76,000	E 3	
Kemecse, 4,681	G 3	
Keszthely, 17,000	D 3	
Kisbér, 4,567	D 3	
Kiskőrös, 12,954	E 3	
Kiskunfélegyháza, 33,000	E 3	
Kiskunhalas, 28,000	E 3	
Kiskunmajsa, 12,311	E 3	
Kispest, 66,547	E 3	
Kistelek, 8,925	E 3	
Kisújszállás, 13,000	F 3	
Kisvárda, 13,050	G 3	
Komádi, 9,850	F 3	
Komárom, 11,000	E 3	
Komló, 28,000	E 3	
Kondoros, 7,462	F 3	
Körmend, 7,548	D 3	
Körösladány, 7,302	F 3	
Kőszeg, 10,000	D 3	
Kunágota, 5,547	F 3	
Kunhegyes, 10,792	F 3	
Kunmadaras, 8,463	F 3	
Kunszentmárton, 13,383	F 3	
Kunszentmiklós, 8,198	E 3	
Lajosmizse, 12,617	E 3	
Lébény, 3,568	D 3	
Lengyeltóti, 3,392	D 3	
Letenye, 4,507	D 3	
Lökösháza, 2,511	F 3	
Lőrinci, 11,142	E 3	
Madaras, 5,177	E 3	
Makó, 29,000	F 3	
Mándok, 4,828	G 2	
Marcali, 7,877	D 3	
Mátészalka, 11,496	G 3	
Mélykút, 8,168	E 3	
Mezőberény, 12,830	F 3	
Mezőcsát, 6,583	F 3	
Mezőfalva, 4,951	E 3	
Mezőhegyes, 9,137	F 3	
Sándorfalva, 5,815	F 3	
Sárbogárd, 6,853	E 3	
Sarkad, 12,169	F 3	
Sárospatak, 12,799	F 2	
Sárvár, 11,247	D 3	
Sátoraljaújhely, 17,000	F 2	
Siklós, 5,897	E 4	
Siófok, 10,322	E 3	
Solt, 7,199	E 3	
Soltvadkert, 8,244	E 3	
Sopron, 45,000	D 3	
Sümeg, 5,925	D 3	
Szabadszállás, 8,799	E 3	
Szarvas, 19,000	F 3	
Szécsény, 4,410	E 2	
Szeged, 120,000	E 3	
Szeghalom, 10,093	F 3	
Szegvár, 6,970	F 3	
Székesfehérvár, 71,000	E 3	
Szekszárd, 23,000	E 3	
Szendrő, 3,773	F 2	
Szentendre, 12,000	E 3	
Szentes, 32,000	F 3	
Szentgotthárd, 5,421	D 3	
Szerencs, 7,789	F 2	
Szigetvár, 10,000	D 3	
Szikszó, 6,110	F 2	
Szolnok, 61,000	F 3	
Szombathely, 62,000	D 3	
Tab, 4,265	D 3	
Tamási, 7,689	E 3	
Tápiószele, 5,632	E 3	
Tapolca, 10,000	D 3	
Tarpa, 3,906	G 2	
Tata, 19,000	E 3	
Tatabánya, 64,000	E 3	
Tét, 4,861	D 3	
Tiszacsege, 7,002	F 3	
Tiszaföldvár, 12,377	F 3	
Tiszafüred, 11,214	F 3	
Tiszakécske, 12,834	E 3	
Tiszalök, 6,125	F 3	
Tiszavasvári, 12,201	F 3	
Tokaj, 5,031	F 2	
Tolna, 8,741	E 3	
Törökszentmiklós, 24,000	F 3	
Tótkomlós, 9,368	F 3	
Tura, 8,169	E 3	
Túrkeve, 11,000	F 3	
Újfehértó, 14,386	F 3	
Mezőkövesd, 18,160	F 3	
Mezőszilas, 3,434	E 3	
Mezőtúr, 22,000	F 3	
Mindszent, 9,179	F 3	
Miskolc, 180,000	F 2	
Mohács, 18,000	E 4	
Monor, 15,360	E 3	
Mór, 11,622	E 3	
Mosonmagyaróvár, 25,000	D 3	
Nádudvar, 10,006	F 3	
Nagyatád, 8,791	D 3	
Nagybajom, 4,972	D 3	
Nagyecsed, 8,348	G 3	
Nagyhalász, 6,650	F 3	
Nagykálló, 11,329	F 3	
Nagykanizsa, 38,000	D 3	
Nagykőrös, 26,000	E 3	
Nagyléta, 6,902	F 3	
Nagymágocs, 7,439	F 3	
Nyírábrány, 4,517	G 3	
Nyirádony, 7,325	G 3	
Nyírbátor, 10,167	G 3	
Nyíregyháza, 65,000	F 3	
Nyírmada, 4,826	G 3	
Örkény, 5,001	E 3	
Oroháza, 33,000	F 3	
Oroszlány, 20,000	E 3	
Ózd, 40,000	F 2	
Paks, 11,919	E 3	
Pannonhalma, 3,529	D 3	
Pápa, 27,000	D 3	
Pásztó, 8,091	E 3	
Pécs, 140,000	E 3	
Pécsvárad, 3,199	E 3	
Pétervására, 2,727	F 3	
Pilis, 8,458	E 3	
Pilisvörösvár, 6,967	E 3	
Polgár, 9,353	F 3	
Püspökladány, 15,488	F 3	
Putnok, 6,440	F 2	
Ráckeve, 7,456	E 3	
Rakamaz, 5,383	F 3	
Rákospalota, 63,344	E 3	
Sajószentpéter, 12,846	F 2	
Salgótarján, 37,000	E 2	
Újpest, 79,961	E 3	
Vác, 29,000	E 3	
Várpalota, 27,000	E 3	
Vasvár, 4,293	D 3	
Vecsés, 16,411	E 3	
Veszprém, 33,000	D 3	
Vésztő, 10,463	F 3	
Villány, 2,769	E 4	
Zahony, 2,117	G 3	
Zalaegerszeg, 33,000	D 3	
Zalaszentgrót, 4,470	D 3	
Zirc, 5,427	D 3	

OTHER FEATURES

Bakony (mts.)	D 3	
Balaton (lake)	D 3	
Berettyó (river)	F 3	
Börsöny (mts.)	E 3	
Bükk (mts.)	F 3	
Cserehát (mts.)	F 2	
Csepelsziget (isl.)	E 3	
Danube (river)	E 3	
Dráva (river)	D 3	
Duna (Danube) (river)	E 3	
Fertő tó (Neusiedler) (lake)	D 3	
Great Alföld (plain)	F 3	
Hernád (river)	F 2	
Ipoly (river)	E 3	
Kapos (river)	E 3	
Kőrishegy (mt.)	D 3	
Körös (river)	F 3	
Little Alföld (plain)	D 3	
Maros (river)	F 3	
Mátra (mts.)	E 3	
Mecsek (mts.)	E 3	
Neusiedler (lake)	D 3	
Rába (river)	D 3	
Sajó (river)	F 2	
Sebes Körös (river)	F 3	
Sió (canal)	E 3	
Szentendreisziget (isl.)	E 3	
Tarna (river)	E 3	
Tisza (river)	F 3	
Zala (river)	D 3	

YUGOSLAVIA

AREA 98,766 sq. mi.
POPULATION 20,586,000
CAPITAL Belgrade
LARGEST CITY Belgrade
HIGHEST POINT Triglav 9,393 ft.
MONETARY UNIT Yugoslav dinar
MAJOR LANGUAGES Serbo-Croatian, Slovenian, Macedonian, Albanian
MAJOR RELIGIONS Eastern Orthodoxy, Roman Catholicism, Islam

ALBANIA

AREA 11,100 sq. mi.
POPULATION 2,126,000
CAPITAL Tiranë
LARGEST CITY Tiranë
HIGHEST POINT Korab 9,026 ft.
MONETARY UNIT lek
MAJOR LANGUAGE Albanian
MAJOR RELIGIONS Islam, Eastern Orthodoxy, Roman Catholicism

RUMANIA

AREA 91,699 sq. mi.
POPULATION 20,394,000
CAPITAL Bucharest
LARGEST CITY Bucharest
HIGHEST POINT Moldoveanul 8,343 ft.
MONETARY UNIT leu
MAJOR LANGUAGES Rumanian, Hungarian
MAJOR RELIGION Eastern Orthodoxy

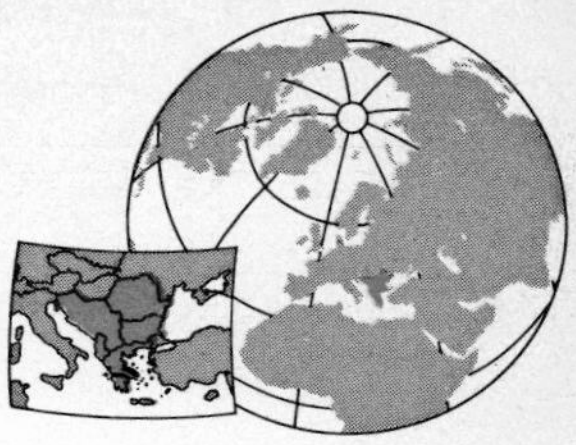

BULGARIA

AREA 42,829 sq. mi.
POPULATION 8,501,000
CAPITAL Sofia
LARGEST CITY Sofia
HIGHEST POINT Musala 9,597 ft.
MONETARY UNIT lev
MAJOR LANGUAGE Bulgarian
MAJOR RELIGION Eastern Orthodoxy

GREECE

AREA 50,548 sq. mi.
POPULATION 8,838,000
CAPITAL Athens
LARGEST CITY Athens
HIGHEST POINT Olympus 9,570 ft.
MONETARY UNIT drachma
MAJOR LANGUAGE Greek
MAJOR RELIGION Eastern (Greek) Orthodoxy

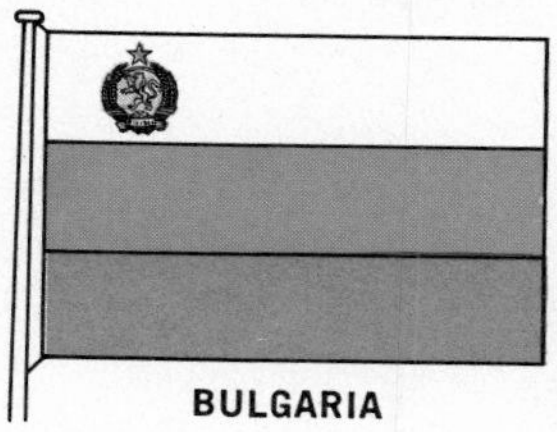

BULGARIA

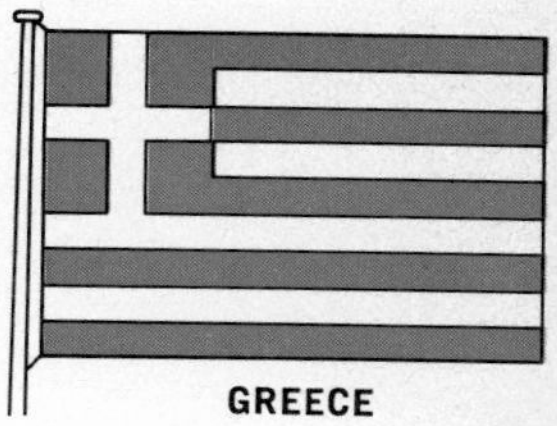

GREECE

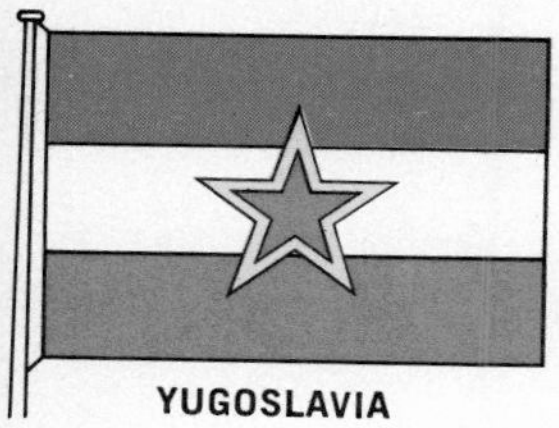

YUGOSLAVIA

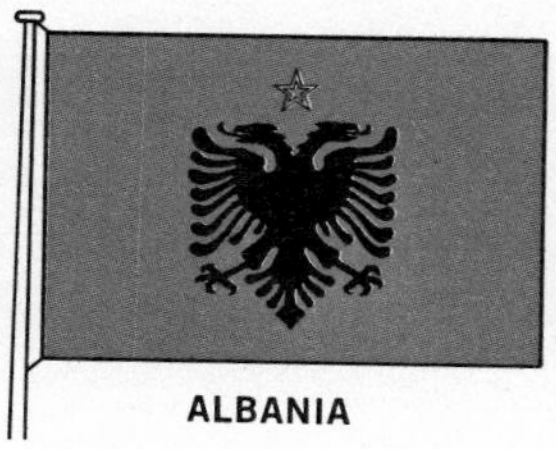

ALBANIA

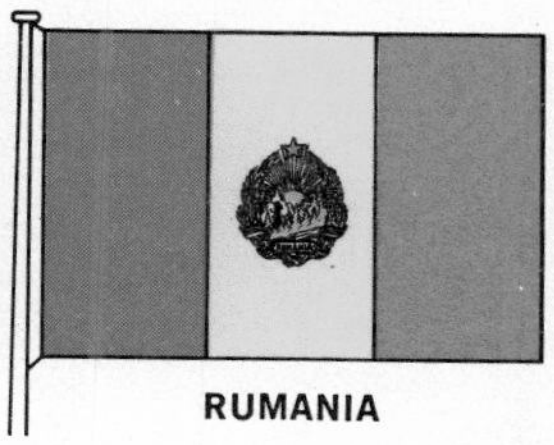

RUMANIA

Agriculture, Industry and Resources

DOMINANT LAND USE

- Cereals (chiefly wheat, corn)
- Mixed Farming, Horticulture
- Pasture Livestock
- Tobacco, Cotton
- Grapes, Wine
- Forests
- Nonagricultural Land

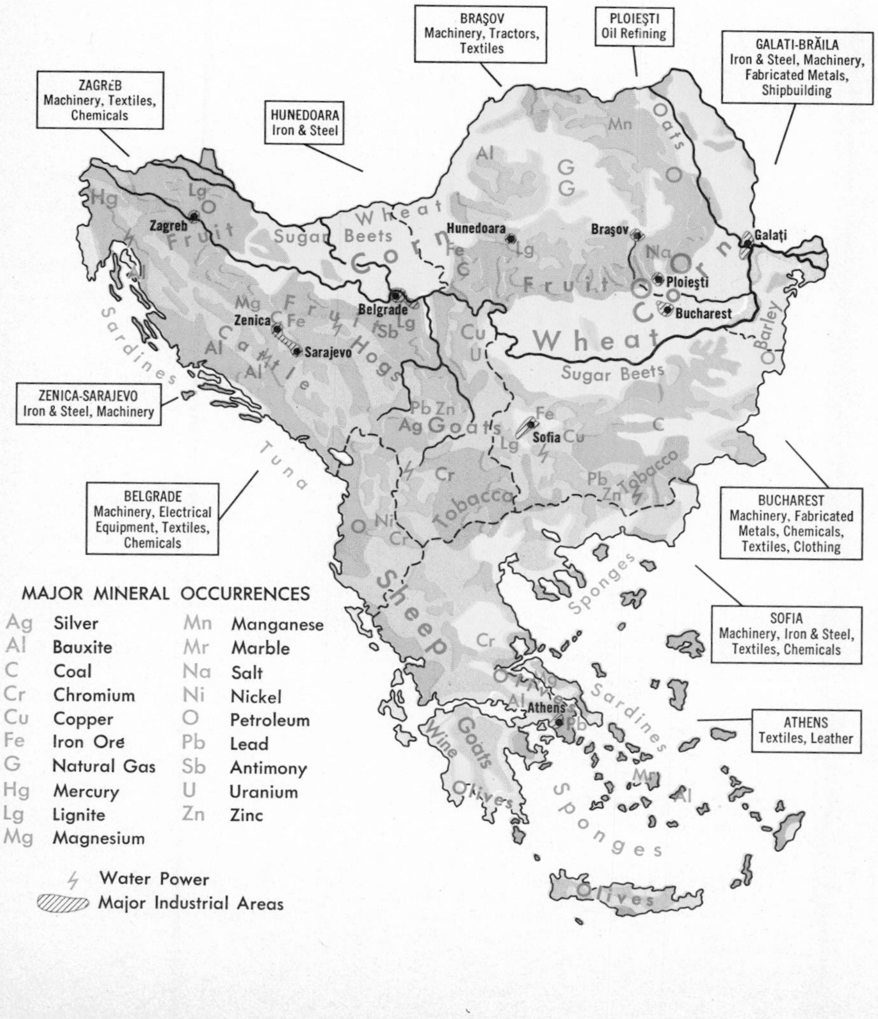
BRAŞOV
Machinery, Tractors, Textiles
PLOIEŞTI
Oil Refining
GALATI-BRĂILA
Iron & Steel, Machinery, Fabricated Metals, Shipbuilding
ZAGREB
Machinery, Textiles, Chemicals
HUNEDOARA
Iron & Steel
ZENICA-SARAJEVO
Iron & Steel, Machinery
BELGRADE
Machinery, Electrical Equipment, Textiles, Chemicals
BUCHAREST
Machinery, Fabricated Metals, Chemicals, Textiles, Clothing
SOFIA
Machinery, Iron & Steel, Textiles, Chemicals
ATHENS
Textiles, Leather
Zagreb
Hunedoara
Braşov
Galaţi
Ploieşti
Bucharest
Belgrade
Zenica
Sarajevo
Sofia
Athens
Wheat
Corn
Fruit
Sugar Beets
Beets
Hogs
Cattle
Goats
Sheep
Tobacco
Barley
Oats
Olives
Wine
Sardines
Tuna
Sponges

MAJOR MINERAL OCCURRENCES

Ag	Silver	Mn	Manganese
Al	Bauxite	Mr	Marble
C	Coal	Na	Salt
Cr	Chromium	Ni	Nickel
Cu	Copper	O	Petroleum
Fe	Iron Ore	Pb	Lead
G	Natural Gas	Sb	Antimony
Hg	Mercury	U	Uranium
Lg	Lignite	Zn	Zinc
Mg	Magnesium		

Water Power
Major Industrial Areas

ALBANIA

CITIES and TOWNS

Berat, 22,000	D 5
Bajram Cur, 1,795	D 4
Burrel, 3,150	D 5
Çorovodë, 1,790	E 5
Delvinë, 5,700	D 6
Durrës, 47,900	D 5
Elbasan, 35,300	E 5
Ersekë, 2,150	E 5
Fier, 17,900	D 5
Gjirokastër, 15,000	D 5
Kavajë, 17,700	D 5
Korcë, 43,700	E 5
Kruë, 6,700	D 5
Kucovë (Stalin), 12,300	D 5
Kukës, 3,900	E 4
Leskovik, 1,625	E 5
Lezh, 3,000	D 5
Lushnje, 16,000	D 5
Peqin, 3,800	D 5
Përmet, 4,000	E 5
Peshkopi, 5,500	E 5
Pogradec, 8,900	E 5
Pukë, 1,700	E 4
Sarandë, 7,700	E 6
Shijak, 5,100	D 5
Shkodër, 47,000	D 5
Stalin, 12,300	D 5
Tepelenë, 2,500	D 5
Tiranë (Tirana) (cap.), 170,000	E 5
Vlorë, 46,900	D 5

OTHER FEATURES

Adriatic (sea)	B 4
Drin (riv.)	E 4
Korab (mt.)	E 5
Ohrid (lake)	E 5
Otranto (str.)	D 5
Prespa (lake)	E 5
Sazan (isl.)	D 5
Scutari (lake)	D 4
Tomor (mt.)	E 5
Vijosë (riv.)	D 5

BULGARIA

CITIES and TOWNS

Alfatar, 3,650	H 4
Akhtopol, 1,058	H 4
Alfatar, 4,042	H 4
Ardino, 2,558	G 5
Asenovgrad, 37,411	G 5
Aytos, 17,769	H 4
Balchik, 8,714	H 4
Bansko, 7,851	F 5
Belogradchik, 5,174	F 4
Berkovitsa, 11,553	F 4
Blagoyevgrad, 32,744	F 5
Botevgrad, 12,051	F 4
Bregovo, 4,725	F 3
Breznik, 4,093	F 4
Burgas, 122,212	H 4
Byala, 9,347	G 4
Byala Slatina, 14,942	F 4
Chirpan, 17,857	G 4
Devin, 4,475	G 5
Dimitrovgrad, 41,787	G 4
Dobrich (Tolbukhin), 55,111	H 4
Dryanovo, 8,187	G 4
Elena, 4,071	G 4
Elin Pelin, 8,074	F 4
Elkhovo, 11,315	H 4
Gabrovo, 57,758	G 4
General Toshevo, 8,251	H 4
Godech, 4,074	F 4
Gorna Dzhumaya (Blagoyevgrad), 32,744	F 5
Gorna Oryakhovitsa, 26,290	G 4
Gotse Delchev, 14,457	F 5
Grudovo, 9,177	F 4
Ikhtiman, 10,325	F 4
Isperikh, 8,445	H 4
Ivaylovgrad, 2,907	H 5
Karapelit, 2,033	H 4
Karlovo (Levskigrad), 20,287	G 4
Karnobat (Polyanovgrad), 18,727	H 4
Kavarna, 8,291	J 4
Kazanlŭk, 44,418	G 4
Kharmanlii, 15,478	H 5
Khaskovo, 57,682	G 5
Kolarovgrad (Shumen), 59.362	H 4
Kotel, 7,209	H 4
Krumovgrad, 2,230	G 5
Kubrat, 7,531	H 4
Kula, 6,474	F 4
Kŭrdzhali, 33,319	G 5
Kyustendil, 38,199	F 4
Levskigrad, 20,287	G 4
Lom, 28,189	F 4
Lovech, 30,843	G 4
Lukovit, 9,716	G 4
Mallco Tŭrnovo, 3,744	H 4
Maritsa, 8,532	H 4
Mıchurin, 2,783	H 4
Mikhaylovgrad, 27,240	F 4
Momchilgrad, 6,084	G 5
Nesebŭr, 2,333	H 4
Nikopol, 5,763	G 4
Nova Zagora, 19,257	H 4
Novi Pazar, 12,476	H 4
Omurtag, 8,148	H 4
Oryakhovo, 7,498	F 4
Panagyurishte, 18,298	F 4
Pazardzhik, 55,410	G 4
Pernik, 75,844	F 4
Peshtera, 14,606	G 4
Petrich, 20,653	F 5
Pirdop, 8,252	G 4
Pleven, 79,234	G 4
Plovdiv, 234,547	G 4
Polyanovgrad, 18,727	H 4
Pomorie, 9,567	H 4
Popina, 2,699	H 3
Popovo, 15,609	H 4
Provadiya, 13,837	H 4
Radomir, 8,458	F 4
Razgrad, 26,297	H 4
Razlog, 10,425	F 5
Rositsa, 1,505	H 4
Ruse, 142,894	H 4
Samokov, 21,585	F 4
Sandanski, 14,590	F 5
Sevlievo, 20,396	G 4
Shabla, 3,788	J 4
Shumen, 59,362	H 4
Silistra, 32,996	H 3
Simeonovgrad (Maritsa), 8,532	H 4
Sliven, 68,331	H 4
Smolyan, 17,479	G 5
Smyadovo, 5,349	H 4
Sofia (cap.), 840,113	F 4
Sofia, *923,400	F 4
Sozopol, 3,257	H 4
Stanke Dimitrov, 35,813	F 4
Stara Zagora, 100,565	G 4
Sveti Vrach (Sandanski), 14,590	F 5
Svilengrad, 12,438	G 5
Svishtov, 21,522	G 4
Teteven, 9,807	G 4
Tolbukhin, 55,111	H 4
Topolovgrad, 6,633	H 4
Troyan, 18,982	G 4
Trŭn, 2,922	F 4
Tŭrgovishte, 25,528	H 4
Tutrakan, 9,909	H 4
Varna, 200,827	J 4
Veliko Tŭrnovo, 37,269	G 4
Vidin, 36,820	F 4
Vratsa, 39,052	F 4
Yambol, 58,405	H 4
Zlatograd, 6,508	G 5

OTHER FEATURES

Balkan (mts.)	G 4
Black (sea)	J 4
Danube (Dunav) (riv.)	H 4
Emine (cape)	J 4
Iskŭr (riv.)	G 4
Kaliakra (cape)	J 4
Lom (riv.)	H 4
Maritsa (riv.)	G 4
Mesta (riv.)	F 5
Musala (mt.)	F 4
Osŭm (riv.)	G 4
Rhodope (mts.)	G 5
Ruen (mt.)	F 4
Struma (riv.)	F 5
Timok (riv.)	F 3
Tundzha (riv.)	G 4
Vit (riv.)	G 4

GREECE

REGIONS

Aegean Islands, 477,476	G 6
Áyion Óros (aut. dist.), 2,687	G 5
Central Greece and Euboea, 2,823,658	F 6
Crete, 483,258	G 8
Epirus, 352,604	E 6
Greater Athens, 1,852,709	F 7
Ionian Islands, 212,573	D 6
Macedonia, 1,890,654	F 5
Pelopónnisos, 1,096,390	F 7
Thessalía, 695,385	F 6
Thrace, 356,555	G 5

CITIES and TOWNS

Agrínion, 24,763	E 6
Aíyina, 4,989	F 7
Aíyion, 17,762	F 6
Alexandroúpolis, 18,712	H 5
Alivérion, 3,523	G 6
Almirós, 6,010	F 6
Amaliás, 15,468	E 7
Amfilokhía, 5,408	E 6
Ámfissa, 6,076	F 6
Ándissa, 2,530	H 6
Andravídha, 3,155	E 6
Ándros, 2,032	G 7
Áno Viánnos, 1,820	G 8
Anóyia, 2,461	G 8
Ardhéa, 3,222	F 5
Argalastí, 1,864	F 6
Árgos, 16,712	F 7
Argostólion, 7,322	E 6
Arkhángelos, 2,918	J 7
Arnaía, 2,612	F 5
Árta, 16,899	E 6
Astipálaia, 1,205	H 7
Atalándi, 4,552	F 6
Athens (cap.), 627,564	F 7
Athens, *2,347,000	F 7
Áyios Matthaíos, 1,892	D 6
Áyios Nikólaos, 3,709	G 8
Candia (Iráklion), 63,458	G 8
Canea (Khaniá), 38,467	G 8
Chalcis (Khalkís), 24,745	F 6
Corinth, 15,892	F 7
Delvinákion, 1,076	E 6
Dhidhimótikhon, 7,287	H 5
Dhíkaia, 1,181	H 5
Dhimitsána, 1,300	F 7
Dhomokós, 2,017	F 6
Dráma, 32,195	F 5
Édhessa, 15,534	F 5
Elassón, 6,501	F 6
Elevtheroúpolis, 5,448	G 5
Ermoúpolis, 14,402	G 7
Fársala, 6,356	F 6
Filiátes, 3,065	E 6
Filiatrá, 6,753	E 7
Flórina, 11,933	E 5
Gargaliánoi, 6,637	E 7
Grevená, 6,892	E 5
Ídhra, 2,546	F 7
Ierápetra, 6,488	G 8
Igoumenítsa, 3,235	E 6
Ioánnina, 34,997	E 6
Iráklion, 63,458	G 8
Istiaía, 3,882	F 6
Itháki, 2,632	E 6
Kalámai, 38,211	F 7
Kalampáka, 4,640	E 6
Kalávrita, 2,039	F 6
Kálimnos, 10,211	H 7
Kardhítsa, 23,708	E 6
Kariá, 1,739	E 6
Kariaí, 429	G 5
Káristos, 3,335	G 6
Karpenísion, 3,523	E 6
Kastéllion, 2,071	F 8
Kastéllion, 1,351	G 8
Kastoría, 10,162	E 5
Kateríni, 28,046	F 5
Kaválla, 44,517	G 5
Kéa, 1,788	G 7
Kérkira, 26,991	D 6
Khalkís, 24,745	F 6
Khaniá, 38,467	G 8
Khíos, 24,053	G 6
Kiáton, 6,069	F 6
Kilkís, 10,963	F 5
Kími, 3,252	F 6
Kiparissía, 4,602	E 7
Kíthira, 469	F 7
Komotiní, 28,355	G 5
Kónitsa, 3,485	E 5
Koropí, 7,862	G 7
Kos, 8,138	H 7

(continued on following page)

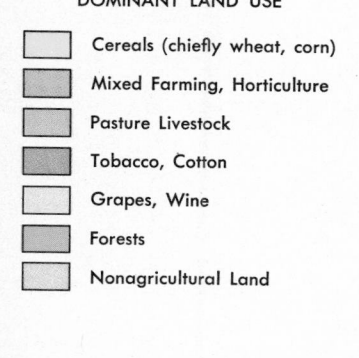

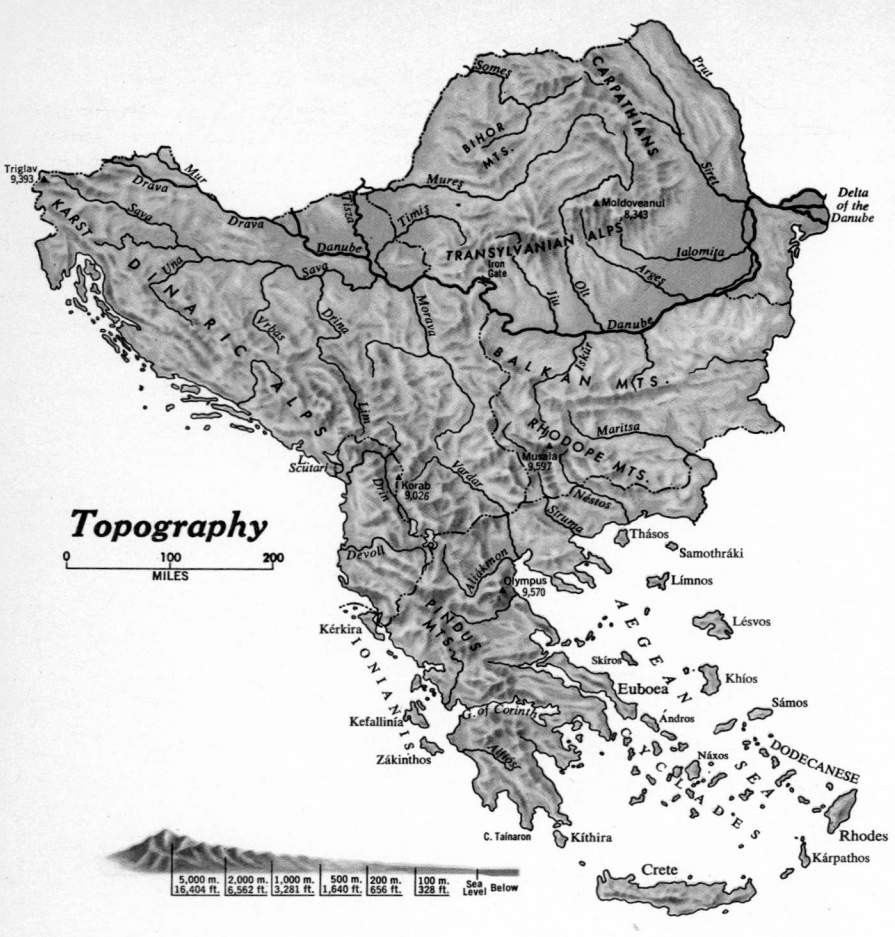

Topography

Triglav 9,393

Delta of the Danube

0   100   200
MILES

5,000 m. | 2,000 m. | 1,000 m. | 500 m. | 200 m. | 100 m. | Sea Level | Below
16,404 ft. | 6,562 ft. | 3,281 ft. | 1,640 ft. | 656 ft. | 328 ft.

Thásos
Samothráki
Límnos
Lésvos
Skíros
Khíos
Euboea
Sámos
Ándros
Náxos
DODECANESE
Rhodes
Kárpathos
Kíthira
Crete

Kérkira
Kefallinía
Zákinthos

Giurgiu, *55,471	G 3
Hațeg, 3,853	F 3
Hîrșova, 4,761	J 3
Hunedoara, 68,303	F 3
Hunedoara, *100,953	J 2
Huși, 20,703	J 2
Iași, 173,569	H 2
Iași, *196,167	H 2
Isaccea, 5,203	J 3
Jimbolia, 11,281	E 3
Lipova, 10,064	E 2
Lugoj, 35,388	F 3
Lupeni, 29,377	F 3
Mangalia, 4,792	J 3
Medgidia, 27,989	J 3
Mediaș, 46,396	G 2
Miercurea Ciuc, 11,996	G 2
Mizil, 11,887	H 3
Moinești, 12,934	H 2
Moldova Nouă, 3,582	E 3
Moreni, 11,687	G 3
Năsăud, 5,725	G 2
Ocna Mureș, 10,701	G 2
Odobești, 4,977	H 3
Odorhei, 14,162	G 2
Oltenița, 14,111	H 3
Oradea, 132,266	E 2
Oradea, *136,375	E 2
Orăștie, 10,488	F 3
Orașul Gheorghe Gheorghiu-Dej, 35,689	H 2
Oravița, 8,175	E 3
Orșova, 6,527	F 3
Panciu, 7,679	H 3
Pașcani, 15,008	H 2
Petrila, 24,804	F 3
Petroșeni, 35,237	F 3
Petroșeni, *130,111	F 3
Piatra Neamț, 45,925	H 2
Piatra Neamț, *58,397	G 2
Pitești, 60,094	G 3
Pitești, *78,784	G 3
Ploiești, 156,382	H 3
Ploiești, *191,663	H 3
Pucioasa, 9,259	G 3
Rădăuti, 15,949	H 2
Reghin, 23,317	G 2
Reșița, 58,683	E 3
Reșița, *121,458	H 3
Rîmnicu Sărat, 22,325	H 3
Rîmnicu Vîlcea, 23,880	F 3
Roman, 38,990	H 2
Roman, *49,496	H 2
Roșiori de Vede, 21,707	G 3
Săcele, 22,822	G 3
Salonta, 16,276	E 2
Satu Mare, 68,257	F 2
Sebeș, 11,626	F 2
Sfîntu Gheorge, 20,759	G 3
Sibiu, 117,020	G 3
Sighetul-Marmației, 29,768	F 2
Sighișoara, 25,100	G 2
Șimleu Silvaniei, 8,560	F 2
Sinaia, 9,006	G 3
Sînnicolau Mare, 9,566	E 2
Siret, 5,664	G 1
Slănic, 6,842	H 3
Slatina, 13,381	G 3
Slobozia, 9,632	H 3
Solca, 2,904	H 2
Strehaia, 8,545	F 3
Suceava, 37,715	G 2
Suceava, *76,327	H 2
Sulina, 3,622	J 3
Techirghiol, 2,705	J 3
Tecuci, 28,458	H 3
Timișoara, 184,797	E 3
Timișoara, *194,159	F 3
Tîrgoviște, 29,754	G 3
Tîrgoviște, *48,005	G 3
Tîrgu Jiu, *33,019	F 3
Tîrgu Mureș, 86,458	G 2
Tîrgu Mureș, *104,922	G 2
Tîrgu Neamț, 10,373	H 2
Tîrgu Ocna, 11,227	H 2
Tîrgu Secuiesc, 7,500	H 2
Tîrnăveni, 20,354	F 2
Toplița, 8,944	G 2
Tulcea, 35,552	J 3
Turda, 42,318	G 2
Turda, *69,768	G 2
Turnu Măgurele, 26,409	G 3
Turnu Severin, 45,394	F 3
Turnu Severin, *52,497	F 3
Urlați, 8,658	H 3
Urziceni, 6,061	H 3
Vasile Roaită, 3,286	J 3
Vaslui, 14,850	H 2
Vatra Dornei, 10,822	G 2
Vișeu de Sus, 13,956	F 2
Zalău, 13,378	F 2
Zărnești, 6,673	G 3
Zimnicea, 12,445	G 4

OTHER FEATURES

Argeș (riv.)	G 3
Buzău (riv.)	H 3
Carpathian (mts.)	G 2
Crișul Alb (riv.)	F 2
Crișul Repede (riv.)	F 2
Danube (river)	H 4
Ialomița (marshes)	J 3
Jiu (riv.)	F 3
Moldoveanul (mt.)	G 3
Mureș (riv.)	G 2
Negoiul (mt.)	G 3
Olt (riv.)	G 3
Pietrosul (mt.)	H 2
Prut (riv.)	J 2
Siret (riv.)	H 2
Someș (riv.)	F 2
Timiș (riv.)	E 3
Transylvanian Alps (mts.)	G 3

YUGOSLAVIA

INTERNAL DIVISIONS

Bosnia and Hercegovina (rep.), 3,594,000	C 3
Croatia (rep.), 4,281,000	C 3
Kosovo-Mitohiyan (aut. prov.), 1,089,000	E 4
Macedonia (rep.), 1,506,000	E 5
Montenegro (rep.), 471,894	D 4
Serbia (rep.), 7,637,800	E 3
Slovenia (rep.), 1,624,900	B 2
Voyvodina (aut. prov.), ,1,880,000	D 3

CITIES and TOWNS

Aleksinac, 8,828	E 4
Apatin, 17,000	D 3
Bačka Topola, 14,000	D 3
Bakar,	B 3
Banja Luka, 55,000	C 3
Bar, 2,184	D 4
Bečej, 22,000	E 3
Bela Crkva, 11,000	E 3
Belgrade (Beograd) (cap.),	E 3
Belgrade, *1,050,000	E 3
Bihać, 17,000	B 3
Bijeljina, 19,000	D 3
Bijelo Polje, 5,856	D 4
Bileća, 2,491	D 4
Biograd, 2,418	B 4
Bitola (Bitolj), 52,000	E 5
Bjelovar, 16,000	C 3
Bled, 4,156	A 2
Bor, 19,000	E 3
Bosanska Dubica, 6,259	C 3
Bosanska Gradiška, 6,363	C 3
Bosanska Kostajnica, 2,034	B 3
Bosanska Krupa, 6,191	C 3
Bosanski Brod, 7,350	D 3
Bosanski Novi, 7,023	C 3
Bosanski Petrovac, 3,473	C 3
Bosanski Šamac, 3,654	D 3
Brčko, 20,000	D 3
Brežice, 2,641	B 3
Brod, 30,000	D 3
Bugojno, 5,453	C 3
Buje, 1,955	A 3
Čačak, 30,000	D 4
Čapljina, 3,275	C 4
Caribrod (Dimitrovgrad), 3,665	F 4
Celje, 28,000	B 2
Cetinje, 9,359	D 4
Ćuprija, 12,000	E 4
Debar, 6,323	E 5
Derventa, 9,843	D 3
Dimitrovgrad, 3,665	F 4
Djakovica, 22,000	E 4
Djakovo, 13,000	D 3
Donji Vakuf, 3,764	C 3
Drvar, 3,646	C 3
Dubrovnik, 24,000	C 4
Fiume (Rijeka), 108,000	B 3
Foča, 6,000	D 4
Fojnica, 1,549	C 4
Gacko, 1,368	D 4
Gevgelija, 7,332	F 5
Gnjilane, 14,000	E 4
Gornji Vafuf, 1,860	C 4
Gospić, 6,767	B 3
Gostivar, 14,000	E 5
Gračac, 2,183	B 3
Gračanica, 7,656	D 3
Gradačac, 5,878	D 3
Grubišno Polje, 2,655	C 3
Gusinje, 2,756	D 4
Hercegnovi, 3,797	C 4
Ivangrad, 6,969	E 4
Jajce, 6,853	C 3
Jesenice, 16,000	A 2
Kamnik, 5,262	B 2
Kanjiža, 10,000	D 3
Kardeljevo, 3,267	C 4
Karlovac, 35,000	B 3
Kavadarci, 13,000	E 5
Kičevo, 11,000	E 5
Kikinda, 32,000	D 3
Kladanj, 2,825	D 3
Ključ, 2,320	C 3
Knin, 5,116	C 3
Knjaževac, 7,448	F 3
Kočevje, 5,819	B 3
Konjic, 5,927	D 4
Koper, 12,000	A 3
Koprivnica, 12,000	C 3
Korčula, 2,458	C 4
Kosovska Mitrovica, 29,000	E 4
Kostajnica, 2,080	C 3
Kotor, 4,764	D 4
Kragujevac, 56,000	E 4
Kraljevo (Rankovičevo), 26,000	E 4
Kranj, 23,000	B 2
Križevci, 6,642	C 3
Krk, 1,280	B 3
Krško, 3,518	B 3
Kruševac, 33,000	E 4
Kumanovo, 33,000	E 4
Leskovac, 37,000	E 4
Livno, 5,181	C 4
Ljubljana, 183,000	B 3
Ljubuški, 2,168	C 4
Loznica, 12,000	D 3
Maglaj, 4,556	D 3
Makarska, 3,634	C 4
Maribor, 89,000	B 2
Medvedac, 12,000	C 4
Modriča, 5,053	D 3
Mostar, 53,000	C 4
Našice, 4,187	D 3
Negotin, 8,635	F 3
Nevesinje, 2,349	D 4
Nikšić, 25,000	D 4
Niš, 92,000	E 4
Nova Gradiška, 9,229	C 3
Novi, 2,075	B 3
Novi Pazar, 23,000	E 4
Novi Sad, 119,000	D 3
Novo Mesto, 6,885	B 3
Novska, 3,844	C 3
Ogulin, 3,522	B 3
Ohrid, 18,000	E 5
Omiš, 2,970	C 4
Opatija, 7,974	A 3
Osijek, 78,000	D 3

Pag, 2,431	B 3
Pančevo, 49,000	E 3
Paraćin, 17,000	E 4
Peć, 30,000	E 4
Petrinja, 7,366	C 3
Piran, 5,474	A 3
Pirot, 20,000	F 4
Plav, 2,535	D 4
Pljevlja, 12,000	D 4
Podgorica (Titograd), 37,000	D 4
Pola (Pula), 40,000	A 3
Poreč, 3,006	A 3
Postojna, 4,857	B 3
Požarevac, 23,000	E 3
Požega, 14,000	C 3
Preševo, 5,680	E 4
Priboj, 5,490	D 4
Prijedor, 21,000	C 3
Prijepolje, 4,566	D 4
Prilep, 40,000	E 5
Priština, 43,000	E 4
Prizren, 29,000	E 4
Prokuplje, 15,000	E 4
Prozor, 1,052	C 4
Ptuj, 7,392	B 2
Pula, 40,000	A 3
Rab, 1,548	B 3
Rača, 1,351	E 3
Radeče, 1,500	B 3
Radovič, 6,246	F 5
Ragusa (Dubrovnik), 24,000	C 4
Rankovičevo, 26,000	E 4
Raška, 2,278	E 4
Rijeka, 108,000	B 3
Rogatica, 3,040	D 4
Rovinj, 7,155	A 3
Ruma, 21,000	D 3
Šabac, 30,000	D 3
Sanski Most, 5,096	C 3
Sarajevo, 223,000	D 3
Senj, 3,903	B 3
Senta, 22,000	D 3
Šibenik, 27,000	C 4
Sinj, 4,134	C 4
Sisak, 29,000	C 3
Škofja Loka, 3,429	A 2
Skopje, 230,000	E 4
Skradin, 1,118	C 4
Smederevo, 29,000	E 3
Sombor, 31,000	D 3
Split, 106,000	C 4
Srebrenica, 1,859	D 3
Sremska Mitrovica, 22,000	D 3
Sremski Karlovci, 6,390	D 3
Stari Majdan, 1,445	C 3
Štip, 22,000	E 5
Stolac, 2,970	D 4
Struga, 6,857	E 5
Strumica, 17,000	F 5
Subotica, 76,000	D 3
Surdulica, 5,007	F 4
Svetozarevo, 22,000	E 4
Svilajnac, 5,895	E 3
Tešanj, 3,148	D 3
Tetovo, 27,000	E 5
Titograd, 37,000	D 4
Titovo Užice, 26,000	D 4
Titov Veles, 29,000	E 5
Travnik, 12,000	C 3
Trbovlje, 16,000	B 3
Trebinje, 4,073	D 4
Trogir, 5,003	C 4
Tržič, 4,881	B 2
Tuzla, 56,000	D 3
Ulcinj, 5,705	D 5
Valjevo, 27,000	D 3
Varaždin, 28,000	B 2
Vareš, 7,647	D 3
Veliki Bečkerek (Zrenjanin), 56,000	E 3
Vinkovci, 24,000	D 3
Virovitica, 10,000	C 3
Višegrad, 3,309	D 4
Vranje, 18,000	F 4
Vrbas, 19,000	D 3
Vršac, 32,000	E 3
Vukovar, 25,000	D 3
Zabari, 1,984	E 3
Zadar, 28,000	B 3
Zagreb, 503,000	C 3
Zaječar, 18,000	F 3
Zara (Zadar), 28,000	B 3
Zenica, 50,000	D 3
Žepče, 2,709	D 3
Zrenjanin, 56,000	E 3
Zvornik, 5,444	D 3

OTHER FEATURES

Adriatic (sea)	B 4
Bobotov Kuk (mt.)	D 4
Bosna (riv.)	C 3
Brač (isl.), 14,227	C 4
Čazma (riv.)	C 3
Cres (isl.), 4,949	B 3
Danube (riv.)	E 3
Dinaric Alps (mts.)	C 3
Drava (riv.)	B 2
Drina (riv.)	D 3
Dugi Otok (isl.), 4,873	B 3
Hvar (isl.), 12,147	C 4
Ibar (riv.)	E 4
Kamenjak (mt.)	A 3
Korab (mt.)	E 5
Korčula (isl.), 10,245	C 4
Kornat (isl.)	B 4
Krk (isl.), 14,548	B 3
Kvarner (gulf)	B 3
Lastovo (Lagosta) (isl.), 1,449	C 4
Lim (riv.)	D 4
Lošinj (isl.), 5,068	B 3
Mljet (isl.), 1,963	C 4
Morava (riv.)	E 4
Mur (riv.)	B 2
Neretva (riv.)	C 4
Ohrid (lake)	E 5
Pag (isl.), 8,017	B 3
Pelagruž (Pelagosa) (isl.)	C 4
Prespa (lake)	E 5
Rab (isl.), 8,400	B 3
Ruen (mt.)	F 4
Sava (riv.)	C 3
Scutari (lake)	D 4
Solta (isl.), 2,735	C 4
Tara (riv.)	D 4
Timok (riv.)	F 3
Tisza (riv.)	D 3
Triglav (mt.)	A 2
Una (riv.)	C 3
Vardar (riv.)	E 5
Vis (isl.), 7,004	C 4
Vrbas (riv.)	C 3
Žirje (isl.), 506	B 4

*City and suburbs.

GREECE (continued)

Kozáni, 21,537	F 5
Kraniídhion, 3,942	F 7
Lamía, 21,509	F 6
Langadhás, 6,739	F 5
Lárisa, 55,391	F 6
Lávrion, 6,553	G 7
Leonídhion, 3,297	F 7
Levádheia, 12,609	F 6
Levkás, 6,552	E 6
Limenária, 1,999	G 5
Limín Vathéos, 5,469	H 7
Límni, 2,394	F 6
Litókhoron, 5,032	F 5
Lixoúrion, 3,977	E 6
Loutrá Aidhipsoú, 1,859	F 6
Marathón, 2,167	G 6
Megalópolis, 2,235	F 7
Mégara, 15,450	F 7
Meligalá, 1,960	F 7
Mesolóngion, 11,266	E 6
Messíni, 8,249	F 7
Métsovon, 2,976	E 6
Mikinai, 361	F 7
Mílos, 944	G 7
Mírina, 3,460	G 6
Missolonghi (Mesolóngion), 11,266	E 6
Míthimna, 1,828	G 6
Mitilíni, 25,758	H 6
Moláoi, 2,526	F 7
Monólithos, 496	H 8
Moúdhros, 1,236	G 6
Náousa, 15,492	F 5
Návpaktos, 7,080	F 6
Návplion, 8,918	F 7
Náxos, 2,458	G 7
Néa Filippiás, 3,001	E 6
Neápolis, 2,464	G 7
Neméa, 4,720	F 7
Néon Karlóvasi, 5,308	H 7
Nigríta, 9,979	F 5
Olimbía, 771	E 7
Orestiás, 10,281	H 5
Paramithiá, 2,827	E 6
Pátrai, 95,364	E 6
Péta, 2,522	E 6
Pigádhia, 1,281	H 8
Pílos, 2,434	E 7
Piraiévs (Piraeus), 183,877	F 7
Pírgos, 20,558	E 7
Piryí, 1,914	G 6
Píthion, 1,535	H 5
Plomárion, 5,172	H 6
Políkastron, 3,821	F 5
Políkhnitos, 5,131	G 6
Polýiros, 3,541	F 5
Póros, 4,392	F 7
Préveza, 11,172	E 6
Psakhná, 4,433	F 6
Ptolemaís, 12,747	E 5
Réthimnon, 14,999	G 8
Ródhos (Rhodes), 27,393	J 7
Salamís, 11,161	F 7
Salonika (Thessaloníki), 448,000	F 5
Sámi, 1,065	E 6
Sápai, 2,589	G 5
Sérrai, 40,063	F 5
Sérvia, 4,132	F 5
Siátista, 4,727	E 5
Sidhirókastron, 8,177	F 5
Sími, 2,982	H 7

Sitía, 5,327	H 8
Skíros, 2,411	G 6
Skópelos, 2,955	F 6
Soúflion, 6,693	H 5
Sparta, 10,412	F 7
Spétsai, 3,314	F 7
Stilís, 4,673	F 6
Thebes (Thívai), 15,779	F 6
Thessaloníki, 448,000	F 5
Thásos, 1,875	G 5
Thíra, 1,481	G 7
Thívai, 15,779	F 6
Timbákion, 2,816	G 8
Tínos, 2,882	G 6
Tírnavos, 10,805	F 6
Tríkkala, 27,876	E 6
Trípolis, 18,500	F 7
Vartholomión, 3,244	E 7
Vathí, 3,161	H 7
Velvendós, 4,158	F 5
Vérroia, 25,765	F 5
Vólos, 49,221	F 6
Vólos, *67,424	F 6
Vónitsa, 2,996	E 6
Vrondádhes, 4,685	G 6
Xánthi, 26,377	G 5
Yiannitsá, 19,693	F 5
Yíthion, 4,992	F 7
Zákinthos, 9,506	E 7
Zante (Zákinthos), 9,506	E 7

OTHER FEATURES

Aegean (sea)	G 6
Akrítas (cape)	F 7
Aktí (pen.)	G 5
Amorgós (isl.), 2,396	G 7
Anáfi (isl.), 471	G 7
Andikíthira (isl.), 178	F 8
Ándros (isl.), 12,928	G 6
Arda (riv.)	G 5
Argolís (gulf)	F 7
Astipálaia (isl.), 1,539	H 7
Athos (isl.)	G 5
Ayios Evstrátios (isl.), 1,061	G 6
Ayios Yeóryios (cape)	F 6
Cephalonia (Kefallinía) (isl.), 39,793	E 6
Chios (Khíos) (isl.), 60,061	G 6
Corfu (Kérkira) (isl.), 99,092	D 6
Corinth (gulf)	F 6
Crete (isl.), 483,075	G 8
Crete (sea)	G 7
Cyclades (isls.), 99,959	G 7
Dhrépanon (cape)	G 6
Dodecanese (isls.), 123,021	H 8
Euboea (isl.), 163,215	G 6
Évros (riv.)	H 5
Gávdhos (isl.), 198	G 8
Ikaría (isl.), 9,577	H 7
Ionian (sea)	D 7
Íos (isl.), 1,343	G 7
Itháki (Ithaca) (isl.), 5,210	E 6
Kálimnos (isl.), 10,211	H 7
Kafirévs (cape)	G 6
Kárpathos (isl.), 6,689	H 8
Kásos (isl.), 1,422	H 8

Kassándra (pen.)	F 6
Kéa (isl.), 2,361	G 7
Kefallinía (isl.), 39,793	E 6
Kérkira (isl.), 99,092	D 6
Khálki (isl.), 501	H 7
Khani, (gulf)	G 8
Khíos (isl.), 60,061	G 6
Kiparissía (gulf)	E 7
Kíthira (isl.), 5,340	F 7
Kíthnos (isl.), 2,064	G 7
Kos (isl.), 18,187	H 7
Kriós (cape)	F 8
Lakonía (gulf)	F 7
Léros (isl.), 6,611	H 7
Lésvos (isl.), 117,371	G 6
Levítha (isl.), 7	H 7
Levkás (isl.), 2,697	E 6
Límnos (isl.), 21,808	G 6
Maléa (cape)	F 7
Matapan (Taínaron) (cape)	F 7
Merabéllou (gulf)	H 8
Mesará (gulf)	G 8
Messíni (gulf)	F 7
Míkonos (isl.), 3,633	G 7
Mílos (isl.), 4,910	G 7
Mirtóón (sea)	F 7
Náxos (isl.), 16,703	G 7
Néstos (riv.)	G 5
Nísiros (isl.), 1,788	H 7
Northern Sporades (isls.), 9,810	F 6
Olympus (mt.)	F 5
Óssa (mt.)	F 6
Parnassus (mt.)	F 6
Páros (isl.), 7,830	G 7
Pátmos (isl.), 2,564	H 7
Paxoí (isl.), 2,678	D 6
Pindus (mts.)	E 6
Piniós (riv.)	F 6
Prespa (lake)	E 5
Psará (isl.), 576	G 6
Rhodes (isl.), 63,951	H 7
Rhodope (mts.)	G 5
Salonika (Thermaic) (gulf)	F 6
Sámos (isl.), 41,124	H 7
Samothráki (isl.), 3,830	G 5
Saría (isl.), 18	H 8
Saronit (gulf)	F 7
Sérifos (isl.), 1,878	G 7
Sídheros (cape)	H 8
Sífnos (isl.), 2,258	G 7
Sími (isl.), 3,123	H 7
Síros (isl.), 19,570	G 7
Sithoniá (pen.)	F 6
Skíros (isl.), 2,882	G 6
Spátha (cape)	G 8
Strímon (gulf)	F 5
Strofádhes (isl.), 10	E 7
Taínaron (cape)	F 7
Thásos (isl.), 15,916	G 5
Thermaic (gulf)	F 5
Thíra (isl.), 7,751	G 7
Tílos (isl.), 789	H 7
Tínos (isl.), 9,273	G 7
Toronaic (gulf)	F 6
Vardar (riv.)	F 5

Voïviís (lake)	F 6
Vólvi (lake)	F 5
Voúxa (cape)	F 8
Zákinthos (Zante) (isl.), 35,499	E 7

RUMANIA

CITIES and TOWNS

Aiud, 11,886	F 2
Alba Iulia, 22,225	F 2
Alexandria, 21,907	G 3
Anina, 11,837	E 3
Arad, 132,757	E 2
Arad, *137,444	E 2
Babadag, 5,549	J 3
Bacău, 73,481	H 2
Bacău, *87,465	H 2
Baia Mare, 62,769	F 2
Baia Mare, *108,709	F 2
Băilești, 15,932	F 3
Balș, 6,956	G 3
Beiuș, 6,467	F 2
Bîrlad, 41,061	H 2
Bîrlad, *52,497	H 2
Bistrița, 25,534	G 2
Blaj, 8,731	G 2
Botoșani, 35,185	H 2
Botoșani, *50,204	H 2
Brad, 9,963	F 2
Brăila, 147,495	H 3
Brașov, 175,264	G 3
Brașov, *264,537	G 3
Bucharest (București) (cap.), 1,431,993	G 3
Bucharest, *1,518,725	G 3
Buhuș, 12,382	H 2
Buzău, 56,380	H 3
Buzău, *82,454	H 3
Buziaș, 5,140	E 3
Călafat, 8,069	F 3
Călărași, 35,698	H 3
Caracal, 22,715	G 3
Caransebeș, 15,195	F 3
Carei, 16,780	F 2
Cernavodă, 8,802	J 3
Cîmpia Turzii, 11,514	F 2
Cîmpina, 22,862	G 3
Cîmpulung, 24,891	G 3
Cîmpulung Moldovenesc, 13,627	G 2
Cisnădie, 12,246	G 3
Cluj, 193,375	F 2
Cluj, *223,519	F 2
Comănești, 12,392	H 2
Constanța, 165,245	J 3
Constanța, *202,024	J 3
Corabia, 11,502	G 3
Craiova, 166,249	F 3
Craiova, *174,669	F 3
Curtea de Argeș, 10,764	G 3
Dej, 26,968	F 2
Deva, 26,952	F 2
Deva, *45,836	F 2
Dorohoi, 14,771	H 2
Drăgășani, 9,963	G 3
Făgăraș, 8,640	G 3
Fălticeni, 13,305	H 2
Fetești, 21,425	H 3
Focșani, 35,075	H 3
Găești, 7,179	G 3
Galați, 160,097	J 2
Gheorgheni, 11,969	G 2
Gherla, 7,617	G 2
Giurgiu, 39,225	G 3

THE BALKAN STATES

CONIC PROJECTION

SCALE OF MILES

0 25 50 75 100 125 150 175

SCALE OF KILOMETRES

0 25 50 75 100 125 150 175

Capitals of Countries _____ ⭐
Administrative Centers _____ △
International Boundaries _____
Major Internal Boundaries _____
Minor Internal Boundaries _____
Canals _____

BULGARIA and GREECE are divided into counties and
departments, respectively. Because of the scale no
attempt has been made to delimit and name these subdivisions; their administrative centers have, however,
been designated.
    The larger divisions named in Greece are well-known
geographical regions, without administrative function.
    RUMANIA consists of thirty-nine counties and
three cities of regional status, Bucharest, Constanța
and Petroșeni. Scale does not permit delimiting
these counties.
    ALBANIA is divided into twenty-seven districts. Scale
does not permit the delimitation of these divisions.
    YUGOSLAVIA is a federation of six republics. The
Serbian republic includes an autonomous province
(Voyvodina), and an autonomous region (Kosovo-
Mitohiyan).

© C. S. HAMMOND & Co., N. Y.

Topography

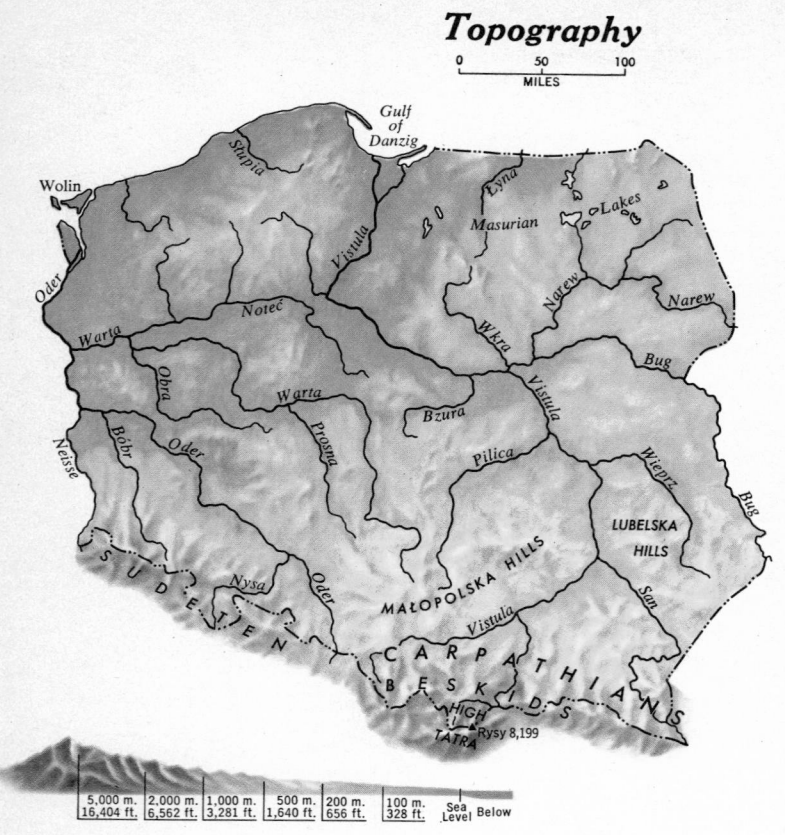

0   50   100
MILES

| 5,000 m. | 2,000 m. | 1,000 m. | 500 m. | 200 m. | 100 m. | Sea | Below |
| 16,404 ft. | 6,562 ft. | 3,281 ft. | 1,640 ft. | 656 ft. | 328 ft. | Level | |

PROVINCES		
Białystok, 1,177,000		F 2
Bydgoszcz, 1,871,000		D 2
Cracow (Kraków),		
2,159,000		D 4
Cracow (Kraków) (city),		
540,200		D 4
Gdańsk, 1,393,000		C 1
Katowice, 3,585,000		D 3
Kielce, 1,910,000		E 3
Koszalin, 774,000		C 2
Łódź, 1,675,000		D 3
Łódź (city),		
750,400		D 3
Lublin, 1,920,000		F 3
Olsztyn, 973,000		E 2
Opole, 1,027,000		C 3
Poznań, 2,159,000		C 2
Poznań (city),		
446,700		C 2
Rzeszów, 1,720,000		E 4
Szczecin, 872,000		B 2
Warsaw, 2,483,000		E 2
Warsaw (city),		
1,282,600		E 2
Wrocław, 1,994,000		C 3

Wrocław (city),		
487,000		C 3
Zielona Góra, 866,000		B 2
CITIES and TOWNS		
Aleksandrów Łódzki,		
13,800		D 3
Allenstein (Olsztyn),		
80,700		E 2
Augustów, 18,400		F 2
Auschwitz (Oświęcim),		
36,900		D 3
Będzin, 41,800		C 4
Belgard (Białogard),		
20,100		
Beuthen (Bytom),		
191,000		B 4
Biała Podlaska,		
23,500		F 2
Białogard, 20,100		C 2
Białystok, 149,000		F 2
Bielawa, 31,500		C 3
Bielsk Podlaski,		
13,000		F 2
Bielsko-Biała, 86,300		D 4

Bochnia, 13,600		E 4
Bogatynia, 12,800		B 3
Bolesławiec, 28,400		B 3
Breslau (Wrocław),		
487,000		C 3
Brieg (Brzeg), 28,600		C 3
Brodnica, 16,300		D 2
Bromberg (Bydgoszcz),		
264,400		D 2
Brzeg, 28,600		C 3
Bydgoszcz,		
264,400		D 2
Bytom, 191,000		B 4
Chełm, 35,300		F 3
Chełmno, 17,800		D 2
Chełmza, 14,800		D 2
Chodziez, 13,100		C 2
Chojnice, 23,100		C 2
Chojnów, 10,900		B 3
Chorzów, 153,100		B 4
Chrzanów, 24,800		D 3
Ciechanów, 21,500		E 2
Cieplice Śląskie-Zdrój,		
15,700		B 3
Cieszyn, 24,700		D 4
Cracow (Kraków),		
540,200		E 3

POLAND 1938

0   50   100
MILES

Agriculture, Industry and Resources

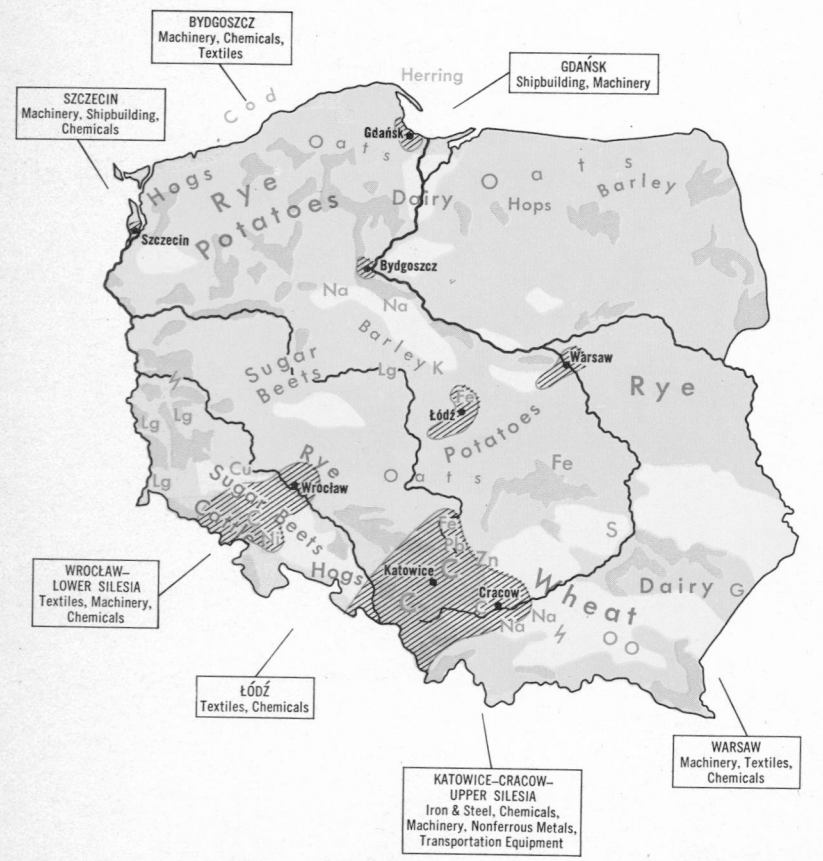

BYDGOSZCZ
Machinery, Chemicals, Textiles

GDAŃSK
Shipbuilding, Machinery

SZCZECIN
Machinery, Shipbuilding, Chemicals

WROCŁAW—LOWER SILESIA
Textiles, Machinery, Chemicals

ŁÓDŹ
Textiles, Chemicals

KATOWICE—CRACOW—UPPER SILESIA
Iron & Steel, Chemicals, Machinery, Nonferrous Metals, Transportation Equipment

WARSAW
Machinery, Textiles, Chemicals

POLAND 1945

0   50   100
MILES

DOMINANT LAND USE

- Cereals (chiefly wheat)
- Rye, Oats, Barley, Potatoes
- General Farming, Livestock
- Forests

MAJOR MINERAL OCCURRENCES

C	Coal	Na	Salt
Cu	Copper	Ni	Nickel
Fe	Iron Ore	O	Petroleum
G	Natural Gas	Pb	Lead
K	Potash	S	Sulfur
Lg	Lignite	Zn	Zinc

⚡ Water Power

⫽ Major Industrial Areas

AREA 120,664 sq. mi.
POPULATION 32,889,000
CAPITAL Warsaw
LARGEST CITY Warsaw
HIGHEST POINT Rysy 8,199 ft.
MONETARY UNIT zloty
MAJOR LANGUAGE Polish
MAJOR RELIGION Roman Catholicism

Place	Pop.	Key
Czechowice-Dziedzice, 24,600		D 4
...zeladź, 31,400		B 4
...zęstochowa, 179,400		D 3
Dąbrowa Górnicza, 60,100		D 4
Danzig (Gdańsk), 333,500		D 1
Dębica, 12,700		E 3
Deblin, 11,700		E 3
Dirschau (Tczew), 38,000		D 1
Dzierżoniów, 31,900		C 3
Debno, 10,200		B 2
86,700		D 1
Frankenstein (Ząbkowice Śląskie), 13,000		C 3
Gdańsk, 333,500		D 1
Gdynia, 171,900		D 1
Giżycko, 16,600		E 1
Glatz (Kłodzko), 25,600		C 3
Gliwice (Gleiwitz), 164,900		A 4
Głowno, 12,700		D 3
Głuchołazy, 14,000		C 3
Gniezno (Gnesen), 48,000		C 2
Gorlice, 14,000		E 4
Görlitz (Zgorzelec), 26,400		B 3
Gorzów Wielkopolski, 69,700		B 2
Gostyń, 12,200		C 3
Gostynin, 10,900		D 2
Graudenz (Grudziądz), 73,700		D 2
Grodziec, 10,500		B 3
Grodzisk Mazowiecki, 19,200		E 2
Grodzisk Wielkopolski, 8,300		C 2
Grudziądz, 73,700		D 2
Grünberg (Zielona Góra), 66,200		B 3
Gryfice, 12,500		C 2
Hajnówka, 14,400		F 2
Haynau (Chojnów), 10,900		B 3
Hindenburg (Zabrze), 197,600		A 4
Hirschberg (Jelenia Góra), 54,900		B 3
Hohensalza (Inowrocław), 52,000		C 2
Hrubieszów, 13,400		F 3
Inowrocław, 52,000		C 2
Jarosław, 27,300		F 3
Jaworów, 15,300		D 3
Jaworzno, 63,000		D 4
Jędrzejów, 13,700		E 3
Jelenia Góra, 54,900		B 3
Kalisz, 77,500		D 3
Kamienna Góra, 21,100		C 3
Katowice, 291,600		B 4
Kędzierzyn, 27,900		D 3
Kętrzyn, 17,400		E 1
Kielce, 113,200		E 3
Kłobuck, 11,500		D 3
Kłodzko, 25,600		C 3
Kluczbork, 16,300		D 3
Knurów, 23,500		A 4
Koło, 12,100		D 2
Kołobrzeg, 23,000		B 1
Königshütte (Chorzów), 153,100		B 4
Konin, 29,300		D 2
Końskie, 11,700		E 3
Konstantynów, 12,500		D 3
Kościan, 12,500		C 2
Kościerzyna, 13,500		C 1
Koszalin, 56,800		C 1
Kraków (Cracow), 540,200		E 3
Kraśnik, 13,700		E 3
Krasnystaw, 11,800		F 3
Krosno, 24,600		E 4
Krotoszyn, 20,900		C 3
Krynica, 9,300		E 4
Kutno, 28,100		D 2
Kwidzyń, 22,800		D 2
Łańcut, 11,300		F 3
Landeshut (Kamienna Góra), 21,100		C 3
Landsberg (Gorzów Wielkopolski), 69,700		B 2
Langenbielau (Bielawa), 31,500		C 3
Lauban (Lubań), 16,800		B 3
Lębork (Lauenburg), 24,100		C 1
Łęczyca, 13,700		D 2
Lędziny, 13,600		B 4
Legionowo, 20,100		E 2
Legnica, 73,400		C 3
Leszno, 32,500		C 3
Lidzbark Warmiński, 12,200		E 1
Liegnitz (Legnica), 73,400		C 3
Lipno, 11,200		D 2
Łódź, 750,400		D 3
Łomża, 23,700		F 2
Łowicz, 18,800		D 2
Lubań, 16,800		B 3
Lublin, 211,900		F 3
Lubliniec, 18,500		D 3
Łuków, 16,100		E 2
Łuków, 13,400		F 2
Lyck (Ełk), 13,400		F 2
Malbork, 29,500		D 2
Marienburg (Malbork), 29,500		D 2
Marienwerder (Kwidzyń), 22,800		D 2
Międzyrzec Podlaski, 12,900		F 3
Międzyrzecz, 12,200		B 2
Mielec, 26,000		E 3
Mików, 20,000		B 4
Mińsk Mazowiecki, 21,700		E 2
Mława, 17,900		E 2
Mrągowo, 12,600		E 2
Mysłowice (Myslowitz), 44,200		B 4
Nakło nad Notecią, 16,000		C 2
Neisse (Nysa), 29,000		C 3
Neusalz (Nowa Sól), 30,700		B 3
Neustadt (Prudnik), 19,200		C 3
Neustettin (Szczecinek), 27,000		C 2
Nowa Ruda, 18,900		C 3
Nowa Sól, 30,700		B 3
Nowy Dwór, 14,900		E 2
Nowy Sącz, 38,600		E 4
Nowy Targ, 20,600		E 4
Nysa, 29,000		C 3
Oels (Oleśnica), 24,700		C 3
Oława (Ohlau), 15,300		C 3
Oleśnica, 24,700		C 3
Olkusz, 14,500		D 3
Opoczno, 11,600		E 3
Opole (Oppeln), 78,800		C 3
Osterode (Ostróda)		D 2
Ostrołęka, 18,600		E 2
Ostrów Mazowiecka, 14,300		E 2
Ostrów Wielkopolski, 47,100		C 3
Ostrowiec Świętokrzyski, 45,600		E 3
Oświęcim, 37,300		D 3
Otwock, 38,200		E 2
Ozorków, 17,400		D 2
Pabianice, 60,100		D 3
Piekary Śląskie, 36,000		B 4
Piła, 40,700		C 2
Pionki, 13,600		E 3
Piotrków Trybunalski, 58,200		D 3
Pleszew, 12,200		C 3
Płock, 60,300		D 2
Płońsk, 10,900		E 2
Poznań (Posen), 446,700		C 2
Pruszków, 19,200		E 2
Prudnik, 19,200		C 3
Przemyśl, 51,000		F 4
Pszczyna, 17,400		B 4
Puławy, 26,100		E 3
Pułtusk, 11,900		E 2
Pyskowice, 22,900		A 4
Racibórz, 37,800		C 3
Radom, 148,400		E 3
Radomsko, 29,600		D 3
Ratibor (Racibórz), 37,800		C 3
Rawicz, 13,600		C 3
Ruda Śląska, 142,800		B 4
Rumia, 21,500		D 1
Rybnik, 39,500		D 3
Rzeszów, 72,200		F 3
Sandomierz, 15,600		E 3
Sanok, 19,300		F 4
Schneidemühl (Piła), 40,700		C 2
Schweidnitz (Świdnica), 46,700		C 3
Siedlce, 36,500		F 2
Siemianowice Śląskie, 67,000		B 4
Sieradz, 16,300		D 3
Sierpc, 12,200		D 2
Skarżysko-Kamienna, 38,200		E 3
Skierniewice, 24,900		D 2
Słupsk, 61,800		C 1
Sochaczew, 18,300		E 2
Sopot, 44,900		D 1
Sorau (Żary), 28,400		B 3
Sosnowiec, 143,300		B 4
Śrem, 12,900		C 2
Środa Wielkopolska, 13,900		C 2
Stalowa Wola, 27,300		E 3
Starachowice, 40,600		E 3
Stargard Szczeciński, 40,600		B 2
Starogard Gdański, 30,600		D 1
Stettin (Szczecin), 322,000		B 2
Stolp (Słupsk), 61,800		C 1
Strzegom, 14,000		C 3
Strzelce Opolskie, 14,000		D 3
Suwałki, 22,900		F 1
Świdnica, 46,700		C 3
Świdnik, 19,300		E 3
Świdwin, 11,500		B 2
Świebodzin, 14,000		B 2
Świecie, 15,700		D 2
Świętochłowice		B 4
Świnoujście (Swinemünde), 24,100		B 2
Szamotuły, 12,700		C 2
Szczecin, 322,000		B 2
Szczecinek, 27,000		C 2
Szczytno, 15,600		E 2
Tarnów, 81,000		E 3
Tarnowskie Góry, 32,600		B 4
Tczew, 38,000		D 1
Teschen (Cieszyn), 24,700		D 4
Thorn (Toruń), 117,800		D 2
Tomaszów Mazowiecki, 53,200		E 3
Toruń (Thorn), 117,800		D 2
Turek, 17,500		D 2
Tychy, 35,200		B 4
Wąbrzeźno, 12,100		D 2
Wągrowiec, 14,400		C 2
Wałbrzych, 126,600		C 3
Wałcz, 18,000		C 2
Waldenburg (Wałbrzych), 126,600		C 3
Warsaw (capital), 1,282,600		E 2
Warszawa (Warsaw) (cap.), 1,282,600		E 2
Wejherowo, 30,600		D 1
Wieliczka, 12,800		E 3
Wieluń, 12,500		D 3
Włocławek, 70,200		D 2
Wołomin, 22,800		E 2
Wrocław, 487,000		C 3
Września, 16,100		C 2
Ząbkowice Śląskie, 13,000		C 3
Zabrze, 197,600		A 4
Zagań, 21,100		B 3
Zakopane, 26,100		D 4
Zambrów, 13,200		F 2
Zamość, 31,500		F 3
Żary, 28,400		B 3
Zawiercie, 37,700		D 3
Zduńska Wola, 28,000		D 3
Zgierz, 40,900		D 3
Zgorzelec, 26,400		B 3
Zielona Góra, 66,200		B 3
Złotoryja, 13,700		B 3
Złocieniec, 10,100		C 2
Zoppot (Sopot), 44,900		D 1
Żyrardów, 31,500		D 2
Żywiec, 21,700		D 4

OTHER FEATURES

Alle (Łyna) (river)	E 1
Baltic (sea)	B 1
Beskids (mts.)	E 4
Brda (river)	C 2
Bug (river)	F 2
Bzura (river)	D 2
Danzig (Gdańsk) (gulf)	D 1
Drawa (river)	C 2
Drwęca (river)	D 2
Dukla (pass)	E 4
Dunajec (river)	E 4
Gdańsk (Danzig) (gulf)	D 1
Gwda (river)	C 2
Hel (pen.)	D 1
High Tatra (mts.)	D 4
Kłodnica (river)	A 4
Łyna (river)	E 1
Mamry (Mauer) (lake)	E 1
Mauer (Mamry) (lake)	E 1
Neisse (Nysa Łużycka) (river)	B 3
Nitze (Noteć) (river)	C 2
Noteć (Nitze) (river)	C 2
Nysa Kłodzka (river)	C 3
Nysa Łużycka (Neisse) (river)	B 3
Oder (Odra) (river)	D 1
Odra (Oder) (river)	D 1
Orava (res.)	D 4
Pilica (river)	E 3
Pomeranian (bay)	B 1
Prosna (river)	C 3
Rysy (mt.)	E 4
San (river)	F 3
Śniardwy (Spirding) (lake)	E 2
Sołokija (river)	F 3
Spirding (Śniardwy) (lake)	E 2
Sudeten (range)	C 3
Uznam (Usedom) (isl.)	B 1
Vistula (Wisła) (river)	C 2
Warta (Warthe) (river)	C 2
Wieprz (river)	F 3
Wisła (Vistula) (river)	D 2
Wkra (river)	B 2
Wolin (Wollin) (isl.), 38,400	B 2

POLAND
CONIC PROJECTION
SCALE OF MILES
0 20 40 60 80 100
SCALE OF KILOMETRES
0 20 40 60 80 100 120 140 160
International Boundaries
Internal Boundaries
Capitals of Countries ☆
Administrative Centers ◉
Canals
© C. S. HAMMOND & Co., N. Y.

GLOSSARY

PRESENT POLISH	FORMER GERMAN	KEY
Brzeg	Brieg	C-3
Bytom	Beuthen	B-4
Elbląg	Elbing	D-1
Gdańsk	Danzig	D-1
Gliwice	Gleiwitz	A-4
Głogów	Glogau	C-3
Gorzów Wlkp.	Landsberg	B-2
Gubin	Guben	B-3
Jelenia Góra	Hirschberg	B-3
Kołobrzeg	Kolberg	B-1
Kostrzyn	Küstrin	B-2
Koszalin	Köslin	C-1
Legnica	Liegnitz	C-3
Malbork	Marienburg	D-2
Nysa	Neisse	C-3
Olsztyn	Allenstein	E-2
Opole	Oppeln	C-3
Piła	Schneidemühl	C-2
Racibórz	Ratibor	C-3
Słupsk	Stolp	C-1
Świdnica	Schweidnitz	C-3
Świnoujście	Swinemünde	B-2
Szczecin	Stettin	B-2
Wałbrzych	Waldenburg	C-3
Wrocław	Breslau	C-3
Zabrze	Hindenburg	D-3
Zielona Góra	Grünberg	B-3

Post-war territorial changes shown on this map do not necessarily represent the final status of such boundaries. Only after the signing of the Peace Treaties can changes be considered official and definite.

UNION REPUBLICS

Armenian S.S.R., 2,491,900 ....E 6
Azerbaidzhan S.S.R., 5,117,100 ....E 5
Estonian S.S.R., 1,356,100 ....C 4
Georgian S.S.R., 4,686,000 ....D 5
Kazakh S.S.R., 12,849,000 ....F 5
Kirgiz S.S.R., 2,932,800 ....H 5
Latvian S.S.R., 2,364,100 ....C 4
Lithuanian S.S.R., 3,128,000 ....C 4
Moldavian S.S.R., 3,568,900 ....C 5
Russian S.F.S.R., 130,079,210 ....D 4
Tadzhik S.S.R., 2,900,000 ....G 6
Turkmen S.S.R., 2,158,880 ....F 6
Ukrainian S.S.R., 47,126,517 ....C 5
Uzbek S.S.R., 11,960,000 ....G 5
White Russian S.S.R., 9,002,338 ....C 4

INTERNAL DIVISIONS

Abkhaz A.S.S.R., 487,000 ....E 5
Adygey Aut. Oblast, 385,000 ....D 5
Adzhar A.S.S.R., 310,000 ....E 5
Aginsk-Buryat Nat'l Okrug, 66,000 ....M 4
Bashkir A.S.S.R., 3,818,000 ....F 4
Buryat A.S.S.R., 812,000 ....M 4
Chechen-Ingush A.S.S.R., 1,065,000 ....E 5

Chukchi Nat'l Okrug, 101,000 ....R 3
Chuvash A.S.S.R., 1,224,000 ....E 4
Dagestan A.S.S.R., 1,429,000 ....E 5
Evenki Nat'l Okrug, 13,000 ....K 3
Gorno-Altay Aut. Oblast, 168,000 ....J 4
Gorno-Badakhshan Aut. Oblast, 98,000 ....H 6
Jewish Aut. Oblast, 172,000 ....O 5
Kabardin-Balkar A.S.S.R., 588,000 ....E 5
Kalmuck A.S.S.R., 268,000 ....E 5
Karachay-Cherkess Aut. Oblast, 345,000 ....E 5
Karakalpak A.S.S.R., 702,000 ....G 5
Karelian A.S.S.R., 713,000 ....D 3
Khakass Aut. Oblast, 446,000 ....J 4
Khanty-Mansi Nat'l Okrug, 271,000 ....F 3
Komi A.S.S.R., 965,000 ....F 3
Komi-Permyak Nat'l Okrug, 212,000 ....F 4
Koryak Nat'l Okrug, 31,000 ....R 3
Mari A.S.S.R., 685,000 ....F 4
Mordvinian A.S.S.R., 1,029,000 ....E 4

Nagorno-Karabakh Aut. Oblast, 150,000 ....E 5
Nakhichevan' A.S.S.R., 202,000 ....E 5
Nenets Nat'l Okrug, 39,000 ....F 3
North Ossetian A.S.S.R., 552,000 ....E 5
South Ossetian Aut. Oblast, 99,000 ....E 5
Tatar A.S.S.R., 3,131,000 ....F 4
Taymyr Nat'l Okrug, 38,000 ....K 2
Tuvinian A.S.S.R., 231,000 ....K 4
Udmurt A.S.S.R., 1,418,000 ....F 4
Ust'-Ordynsk-Buryat Nat'l Okrug, 146,000 ....M 4
Yakut A.S.S.R., 664,000 ....N 3
Yamal-Nenets Nat'l Okrug, 80,000 ....H 3

CITIES and TOWNS

Abakan, 90,000 ....J 4
Achinsk, 97,000 ....K 4
Adimi ....P 5
Aginskoye, 9,000 ....M 4
Akmolinsk (Tselinograd), 180,000 ....H 4
Aktyubinsk, 150,000 ....F 4
Aldan, 19,000 ....N 4
Aleksandrovsk-Sakhalinskiy, 22,000 ....P 5
Aleysk, 32,000 ....J 4
Alga, 17,000 ....F 5
Allakh-Yun' ....O 3
Alma-Ata, 730,000 ....H 5

Ambarchik ....R 3
Amderma ....F 3
Amursk, 15,000 ....O 4
Anadyr', 8,000 ....T 3
Andizhan, 188,000 ....H 5
Angarsk, 203,000 ....L 4
Anzhero-Sudzhensk, 106,000 ....J 4
Aral'sk, 26,000 ....G 5
Archangel, 343,000 ....E 3
Arkalyk, 15,000 ....G 4
Armavir, 145,000 ....E 5
Artem, 61,000 ....O 5
Artemovskiy ....M 4
Arzamas, 67,000 ....E 4
Ashkhabad, 253,000 ....F 6
Ashkhabad, *256,000 ....F 6
Asino, 30,000 ....J 4
Astrakhan', 410,000 ....E 5
Atbasar, 41,000 ....G 4
Atka ....Q 3
Ayaguz, 40,000 ....H 5
Ayan ....O 4
Aykhal ....M 3
Bagdarin ....M 4
Baku, 852,000 ....F 5
Baku, *1,266,000 ....F 5
Balashov, 83,000 ....E 4
Balkhash, 76,000 ....H 5
Balturino, 10,000 ....K 4
Barabinsk, 40,000 ....H 4
Baranovichi, 101,000 ....C 4
Barnaul, 439,000 ....J 4
Batumi, 101,000 ....E 5
Baykit ....K 3
Baykonur ....G 5

Bayram-Ali, 33,000 ....G 6
Belgorod, 151,000 ....D 4
Belogorsk, 57,000 ....N 4
Belomorsk, 18,000 ....D 3
Beloretsk, 67,000 ....F 4
Belovo, 108,000 ....J 4
Berdichev, 71,000 ....C 5
Berdsk, 53,000 ....J 4
Berezniki, 146,000 ....F 4
Berezovo, 6,000 ....G 3
Beringovskiy ....T 3
Bilibino, 13,000 ....R 3
Birobidzhan, 56,000 ....O 5
Biysk, 186,000 ....J 4
Blagoveshchensk, 128,000 ....N 4
Bobruysk, 138,000 ....C 4
Bodaybo, 19,000 ....M 4
Borisoglebsk, 64,000 ....E 4
Borzya, 28,000 ....M 4
Boshchakul' ....H 4
Bratsk, 155,000 ....L 4
Brest, 122,000 ....C 4
Bryansk, 318,000 ....D 4
Bugul'ma, 72,000 ....F 4
Bukhara, 112,000 ....G 5
Bulun ....N 2
Buzuluk, 67,000 ....F 4
Chapayevo ....H 4
Chapayevsk, 86,000 ....E 4
Chardzhou, 96,000 ....G 6
Chardzhara, 216,000 ....H 4
Chelkar, 25,000 ....F 5
Chelyabinsk, 875,000 ....G 4

Cheremkhovo, 99,000 ....L 4
Cherepovets, 188,000 ....D 4
Cherkessk, 67,000 ....E 5
Chernigov, 159,000 ....C 4
Chernovtsy, 187,000 ....C 5
Chernyshevsk, 10,000 ....M 4
Chernyshevskiy, 10,000 ....M 3
Cherskiy ....Q 3
Chimbay, 20,000 ....G 5
Chimkent, 247,000 ....G 5
Chirchik, 107,000 ....H 5
Chita, 241,000 ....M 4
Chokurdakh ....P 2
Chul'man ....N 4
Chumikan ....O 4
Dalnegorsk, 33,500 ....O 5
Dalnerechensk, 30,000 ....O 5
Daugavpils, 100,400 ....C 4
Dikson ....J 2
Dimitrovgrad, 81,000 ....F 4
Dnepropetrovsk, 862,000 ....D 5
Dolinsk, 18,000 ....P 5
Donetsk, 879,000 ....D 5
Drogobych, 56,000 ....C 5
Druzhina ....P 3
Dudinka, 22,000 ....J 3
Dushanbe, 376,000 ....G 6
Dzerzhinsk, 221,000 ....E 4
Dzhalal-Abad, 44,000 ....H 5
Dzhalinda ....N 4
Dzhambul, 187,000 ....H 5
Dzhetygara, 39,000 ....G 4
Dzhezkazgan, 62,000 ....G 5

Ekimchan ....O 4
El'dikan ....O 3
Elista, 50,000 ....E 5
Engel's, 130,000 ....E 4
Erivan, 767,000 ....E 5
Evensk ....Q 3
Fergana, 111,000 ....H 5
Fort-Shevchenko, 12,000 ....F 5
Frolovo, 30,000 ....E 4
Frunze, 430,600 ....H 5
Gasan-Kuli ....F 6
Gizhiga ....Q 3
Gol'chikha ....J 2
Gomel', 272,000 ....D 4
Gor'kiy, 1,170,000 ....E 4
Gorno-Altaysk, 34,000 ....J 4
Grodno, 132,000 ....C 4
Groznyy, 341,000 ....E 5
Gubakha, 40,000 ....F 4
Gulistan, 31,000 ....H 5
Gur'yev, 114,000 ....F 5
Gusinoozersk, 10,000 ....M 4
Gydy ....H 2
Igarka, 22,000 ....J 3
Ilanskiy, 24,000 ....K 4
Iliysk, 17,000 ....H 5
Indiga ....F 3
Inta, 50,000 ....F 3
Iolotan', 10,000 ....G 6
Irkutsk, 451,000 ....L 4
Ishim, 56,000 ....G 4
Ishimbay, 54,000 ....F 4
Isil'-Kul', 26,000 ....H 4
Ivano-Frankovsk, 105,000 ....C 5

UNION OF SOVIET SOCIALIST REPUBLICS

CONIC PROJECTION

SCALE OF MILES
0 100 200 300 400 500 600

SCALE OF KILOMETERS
0 100 200 300 400 500 600

Capitals   Boundaries
★ National
☆ Union Republic
◉ A.S.S.R.
◎ Autonomous Oblast
⊙ National Okrug

ADMINISTRATIVE DIVISIONS NOT NAMED ON MAP

Division	Ref.	Division	Ref.
1. Abkhaz A.S.S.R.	E5	13. Khakass Aut. Oblast	J4
2. Adygey Aut. Oblast	D5	14. Komi-Permyak Nat'l Okrug	F4
3. Adzhar A.S.S.R.	E5	15. Mari A.S.S.R.	F4
4. Aginsk-Buryat Nat'l Okrug	M4	16. Mordivian A.S.S.R.	E4
5. Chechen-Ingush A.S.S.R.	E5	17. Nagorno-Karabakh Aut. Oblast	E5
6. Chuvash A.S.S.R.	E4	18. Nakhichevan' A.S.S.R.	E5
7. Gorno-Altay Aut. Oblast	J4	19. North Ossetian A.S.S.R.	E5
8. Gorno-Badakhshan Aut. Oblast	H6	20. South Ossetian Aut. Oblast	E5
9. Jewish Aut. Oblast	O5	21. Tatar A.S.S.R.	F4
10. Kabardin-Balkar A.S.S.R.	E5	22. Tuvinian A.S.S.R.	K4
11. Karachay-Cherkess Aut. Oblast	E5	23. Udmurt A.S.S.R.	F4
12. Karakalpak A.S.S.R.	G5	24. Ust'-Ordynsk-Buryat Nat'l Okrug	L4

AREA 8,649,498 sq. mi.
POPULATION 241,748,000
CAPITAL Moscow
LARGEST CITY Moscow
HIGHEST POINT Communism Peak 24,590 ft.
MONETARY UNIT ruble
MAJOR LANGUAGES Russian, Ukrainian, White Russian,
Uzbek, Azerbaidzhani, Tatar, Georgian, Lithuanian,
Armenian, Yiddish, Latvian, Mordvinian, Kirghiz,
Tadzhik, Estonian, Kazakh, Moldavian, German,
Chuvash, Turkmenian, Bashkir
MAJOR RELIGIONS Eastern (Russian) Orthodoxy, Islam,
Judaism, Protestantism (Baltic States)

UNION REPUBLICS

	AREA (sq. mi.)	POPULATION	CAPITAL and LARGEST CITY
RUSSIAN S.F.S.R.	6,592,819	130,079,210	Moscow 6,942,000
KAZAKH S.S.R.	1,048,301	12,849,000	Alma-Ata 730,000
UKRAINIAN S.S.R.	232,046	47,126,517	Kiev 1,632,000
TURKMEN S.S.R.	188,456	2,158,880	Ashkhabad 253,000
UZBEK S.S.R.	173,591	11,960,000	Tashkent 1,385,000
WHITE RUSSIAN S.S.R.	80,154	9,002,338	Minsk 907,000
KIRGIZ S.S.R.	76,641	2,932,800	Frunze 430,600
TADZHIK S.S.R.	55,251	2,900,000	Dushanbe 376,000
AZERBAIDZHAN S.S.R.	33,436	5,117,100	Baku 852,000
GEORGIAN S.S.R.	26,911	4,686,000	Tbilisi 889,000
LITHUANIAN S.S.R.	25,174	3,128,000	Vilna 371,700
LATVIAN S.S.R.	24,595	2,364,100	Riga 731,800
ESTONIAN S.S.R.	17,413	1,356,100	Tallinn 362,706
MOLDAVIAN S.S.R.	13,012	3,568,900	Kishinev 356,900
ARMENIAN S.S.R.	11,500	2,491,900	Erivan 767,000

Ivanovo, 420,000 ....E 4
Izhevsk, 422,000 ....F 4
Izmail, 70,000 ....C 5
Kachug ....L 4
Kalachinsk, 24,000 ....H 4
Kalakan ....M 4
Kalinin, 345,000 ....D 4
Kaliningrad, 297,000 ....B 4
Kalmykovo ....F 5
Kaluga, 211,000 ....D 4
Kamenskoye ....R 3
Kamensk-Ural'skiy,
169,000 ....G 4
Kamyshin, 97,000 ....E 4
Kamyshlov, 34,000 ....G 4
Kansk, 95,000 ....K 4
Karabekaul ....G 6
Karaganda, 523,000 ....H 5
Karasuk, 26,000 ....H 4

Karazhal, 18,000 ....H 5
Karkaralinsk, 9,000 ....H 5
Karshi, 71,000 ....G 6
Kaunas, 306,200 ....C 4
Kazach'ye ....O 2
Kazalinsk, 22,000 ....G 5
Kazan', 869,000 ....F 4
Kazandzhik ....F 6
Kem, 55,000 ....D 3
Kemerovo, 385,000 ....J 4
Kentau, 55,000 ....G 5
Kerki, 23,000 ....G 6
Kezhma ....K 4
Khabarovsk, 436,000 ....O 5
Khandyga ....O 3
Khanty-Mansiysk,
25,000 ....H 3
Khar'kov, 1,223,000 ....D 4
Kharovsk, 10,000 ....D 3

Khatanga ....L 2
Kherson, 261,000 ....D 5
Khilok, 17,000 ....M 4
Khiva, 25,000 ....F 5
Khodzheyli, 36,000 ....F 5
Kholmsk, 42,000 ....P 5
Khorog, 12,300 ....H 6
Kiev, 1,632,000 ....D 4
Kirensk, 10,000 ....L 4
Kirov, 333,000 ....E 4
Kirovabad, 189,800 ....E 5
Kirovograd, 189,000 ....D 5
Kiselevsk, 127,000 ....J 4
Kishinev, 356,900 ....C 5
Kizel, 49,000 ....F 4
Kizyl-Arvat, 24,000 ....F 6
Klaipeda, 139,900 ....B 4
Kokand, 133,000 ....H 5
Kokchetav, 81,000 ....H 4
Kolomna, 135,900 ....D 4
Kolpashevo, 27,000 ....J 4
Komsomol'sk, 218,000 ....O 4
Kondopoga, 25,000 ....D 3
Kopeysk, 156,000 ....G 4
Korf ....R 3
Korsakov, 35,000 ....P 5
Koslan ....E 3
Kostroma, 223,000 ....E 4
Kotlas, 56,000 ....E 3

Kovel', 35,000 ....C 4
Kovrov, 123,000 ....E 4
Kozhevnikovo ....L 2
Krasino ....F 2
Krasnodar, 464,000 ....E 5
Krasnokamsk, 55,000 ....F 4
Krasnotur'insk, 59,000 ....G 3
Krasnoural'sk, 42,000 ....G 4
Krasnovishersk, 16,000 ....F 3
Krasnovodsk, 49,000 ....E 5
Krasnoyarsk, 648,000 ....K 4
Kremenchug, 148,000 ....D 5
Krivoy Rog, 573,000 ....D 5
Kudymkar, 20,000 ....F 4
Kul'sary, 14,000 ....F 5
Kungur, 74,000 ....F 4
Kupino, 24,000 ....H 4
Kurgan, 244,000 ....G 4
Kurgan-Tyube, 34,600 ....G 6
Kuril'sk, 2,000 ....P 5
Kursk, 284,000 ....D 4
Kushka ....G 6
Kustanay, 124,000 ....G 4
Kutaisi, 161,000 ....E 5
Kuybyshev, 1,045,000 ....F 4
Kyakhta ....L 4
Kyusyur ....N 2
Kyzyl, 52,000 ....K 4
Kzyl-Orda, 122,000 ....G 5

Labytnangi ....G 3
Leninabad, 103,200 ....G 5
Leninakan, 165,000 ....E 5
Leningrad, 3,513,000 ....D 4
Leningrad,
*3,950,000 ....D 4
Leninogorsk, 72,000 ....J 5
Leninsk-Kuznetskiy,
128,000 ....J 4
Leninskoye ....O 5
Lenkoran', 35,500 ....E 5
Lensk, 21,000 ....M 3
Lesozavodsk, 37,000 ....O 5
Liepāja, 92,800 ....B 4
Lipetsk, 289,000 ....E 4
Luga, 30,000 ....D 4
Lutsk, 94,000 ....C 4
Luza, 10,000 ....E 3
L'vov, 553,000 ....C 4
Lys'va, 73,000 ....F 4
Magadan, 92,000 ....P 4
Magdagachi, 10,000 ....N 4
Magnitogorsk,
364,000 ....G 4
Makhachkala,
186,000 ....E 5
Makinsk, 28,000 ....H 4
Maklakovo, 20,000 ....K 4
Mama ....M 4

Markovo ....S 3
Mary, 62,000 ....G 6
Maykop, 110,000 ....D 5
Mednogorsk, 41,000 ....F 4
Medvezh'yegorsk,
18,000 ....D 3
Megion ....H 3
Mezen' ....E 3
Miass, 131,000 ....G 4
Michurinsk, 94,000 ....E 4
Millerovo, 38,000 ....E 5
Minusinsk, 47,000 ....K 4
Mirnyy, 24,000 ....M 3
Mogilev, 202,000 ....D 4
Mogocha, 16,000 ....N 4
Molodechno, 50,000 ....C 4
Monchegorsk,
49,000 ....C 3
Moscow (capital),
6,942,000 ....D 4
Moscow, *7,061,000 ....D 4
Motygino, 10,000 ....K 4
Mozyr', 49,000 ....C 4
Murgab ....H 6
Murmansk, 309,000 ....D 4
Muvnak, 12,000 ....F 5
Nadym ....H 3

Nagornyy ....N 4
Nakhichevan',
33,200 ....E 6
Nakhodka, 104,000 ....O 5
Nal'chik, 146,000 ....E 5
Namangan, 175,000 ....H 5
Naminga, 5,000 ....M 4
Napas ....J 4
Nar'yan-Mar, 15,000 ....F 3
Naryn, 21,000 ....H 5
Navoi, 61,000 ....G 6
Nebit-Dag, 56,000 ....F 6
Nel'kan ....O 4
Nepa ....L 4
Nerchinsk, 10,000 ....M 4
Nikolayev, 331,000 ....D 5
Nikolayevsk, 34,000 ....P 4
Nikol'skoye ....R 4
Nimnyrskiy ....N 4
Nizhne-Angarsk ....M 4
Nizhneudinsk, 39,000 ....K 4
Nizhniy Tagil, 378,000 ....G 4
Nordvik ....M 2
Noril'sk, 135,000 ....J 3
Novaya Kazanka ....F 5
Novgorod, 128,000 ....D 4
Novokuznetsk, 499,000 ....J 4
Novomoskovsk,
134,000 ....E 4

Topography

(continued on following page)

© C. S. HAMMOND & CO., Maplewood, N.J.

Agriculture, Industry and Resources

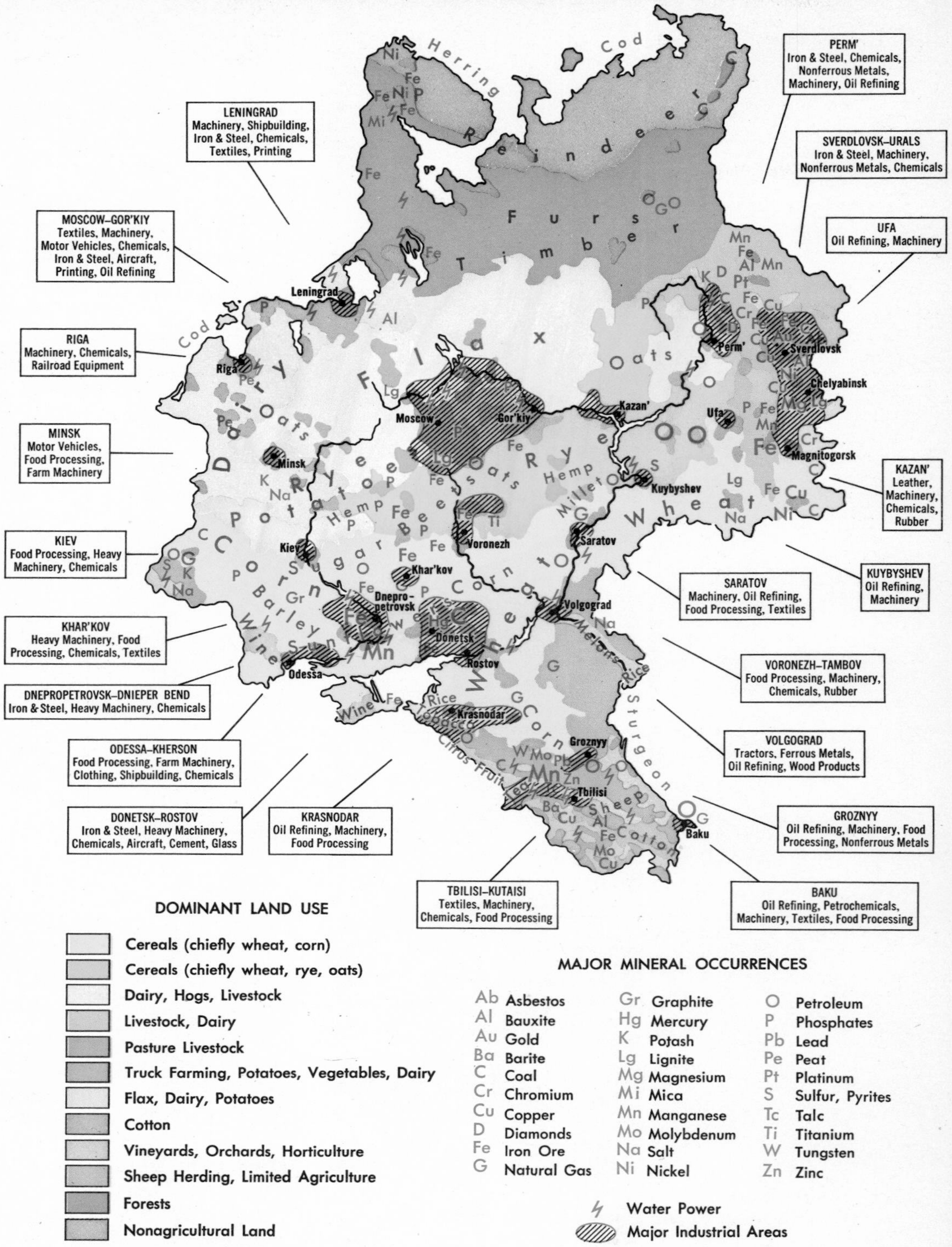

Industrial Area Descriptions (map labels)

PERM' — Iron & Steel, Chemicals, Nonferrous Metals, Machinery, Oil Refining

SVERDLOVSK–URALS — Iron & Steel, Machinery, Nonferrous Metals, Chemicals

UFA — Oil Refining, Machinery

LENINGRAD — Machinery, Shipbuilding, Iron & Steel, Chemicals, Textiles, Printing

MOSCOW–GOR'KIY — Textiles, Machinery, Motor Vehicles, Chemicals, Iron & Steel, Aircraft, Printing, Oil Refining

RIGA — Machinery, Chemicals, Railroad Equipment

MINSK — Motor Vehicles, Food Processing, Farm Machinery

KIEV — Food Processing, Heavy Machinery, Chemicals

KHAR'KOV — Heavy Machinery, Food Processing, Chemicals, Textiles

DNEPROPETROVSK–DNIEPER BEND — Iron & Steel, Heavy Machinery, Chemicals

ODESSA–KHERSON — Food Processing, Farm Machinery, Clothing, Shipbuilding, Chemicals

DONETSK–ROSTOV — Iron & Steel, Heavy Machinery, Chemicals, Aircraft, Cement, Glass

KRASNODAR — Oil Refining, Machinery, Food Processing

KAZAN' — Leather, Machinery, Chemicals, Rubber

KUYBYSHEV — Oil Refining, Machinery

SARATOV — Machinery, Oil Refining, Food Processing, Textiles

VORONEZH–TAMBOV — Food Processing, Machinery, Chemicals, Rubber

VOLGOGRAD — Tractors, Ferrous Metals, Oil Refining, Wood Products

GROZNYY — Oil Refining, Machinery, Food Processing, Nonferrous Metals

TBILISI–KUTAISI — Textiles, Machinery, Chemicals, Food Processing

BAKU — Oil Refining, Petrochemicals, Machinery, Textiles, Food Processing

DOMINANT LAND USE

- Cereals (chiefly wheat, corn)
- Cereals (chiefly wheat, rye, oats)
- Dairy, Hogs, Livestock
- Livestock, Dairy
- Pasture Livestock
- Truck Farming, Potatoes, Vegetables, Dairy
- Flax, Dairy, Potatoes
- Cotton
- Vineyards, Orchards, Horticulture
- Sheep Herding, Limited Agriculture
- Forests
- Nonagricultural Land

MAJOR MINERAL OCCURRENCES

Ab	Asbestos	Gr	Graphite	O	Petroleum
Al	Bauxite	Hg	Mercury	P	Phosphates
Au	Gold	K	Potash	Pb	Lead
Ba	Barite	Lg	Lignite	Pe	Peat
C	Coal	Mg	Magnesium	Pt	Platinum
Cr	Chromium	Mi	Mica	S	Sulfur, Pyrites
Cu	Copper	Mn	Manganese	Tc	Talc
D	Diamonds	Mo	Molybdenum	Ti	Titanium
Fe	Iron Ore	Na	Salt	W	Tungsten
G	Natural Gas	Ni	Nickel	Zn	Zinc

Water Power

Major Industrial Areas

Agriculture, Industry and Resources

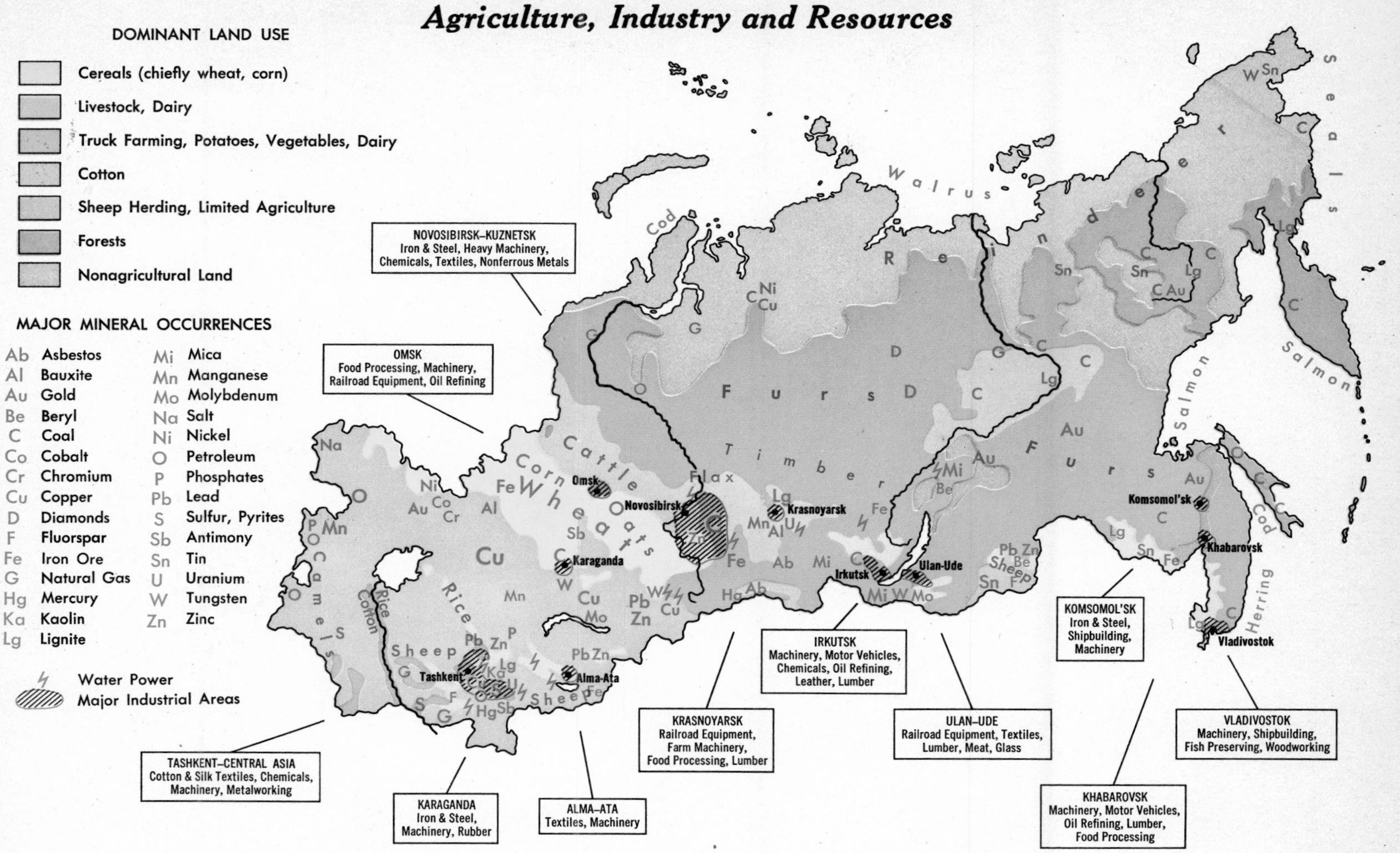
DOMINANT LAND USE
Cereals (chiefly wheat, corn)
Livestock, Dairy
Truck Farming, Potatoes, Vegetables, Dairy
Cotton
Sheep Herding, Limited Agriculture
Forests
Nonagricultural Land
MAJOR MINERAL OCCURRENCES
Ab Asbestos
Al Bauxite
Au Gold
Be Beryl
C Coal
Co Cobalt
Cr Chromium
Cu Copper
D Diamonds
F Fluorspar
Fe Iron Ore
G Natural Gas
Hg Mercury
Ka Kaolin
Lg Lignite
Mi Mica
Mn Manganese
Mo Molybdenum
Na Salt
Ni Nickel
O Petroleum
P Phosphates
Pb Lead
S Sulfur, Pyrites
Sb Antimony
Sn Tin
U Uranium
W Tungsten
Zn Zinc
Water Power
Major Industrial Areas
NOVOSIBIRSK–KUZNETSK
Iron & Steel, Heavy Machinery, Chemicals, Textiles, Nonferrous Metals
OMSK
Food Processing, Machinery, Railroad Equipment, Oil Refining
TASHKENT–CENTRAL ASIA
Cotton & Silk Textiles, Chemicals, Machinery, Metalworking
KARAGANDA
Iron & Steel, Machinery, Rubber
ALMA–ATA
Textiles, Machinery
KRASNOYARSK
Railroad Equipment, Farm Machinery, Food Processing, Lumber
IRKUTSK
Machinery, Motor Vehicles, Chemicals, Oil Refining, Leather, Lumber
ULAN–UDE
Railroad Equipment, Textiles, Lumber, Meat, Glass
KOMSOMOL'SK
Iron & Steel, Shipbuilding, Machinery
KHABAROVSK
Machinery, Motor Vehicles, Oil Refining, Lumber, Food Processing
VLADIVOSTOK
Machinery, Shipbuilding, Fish Preserving, Woodworking
Walrus
Reindeer
Seals
Cod
Salmon
Herring
Furs
Timber
Flax
Cattle
Corn
Wheat
Oats
Rice
Cotton
Sheep
Camels
Omsk
Novosibirsk
Krasnoyarsk
Karaganda
Tashkent
Alma-Ata
Irkutsk
Ulan-Ude
Komsomol'sk
Khabarovsk
Vladivostok

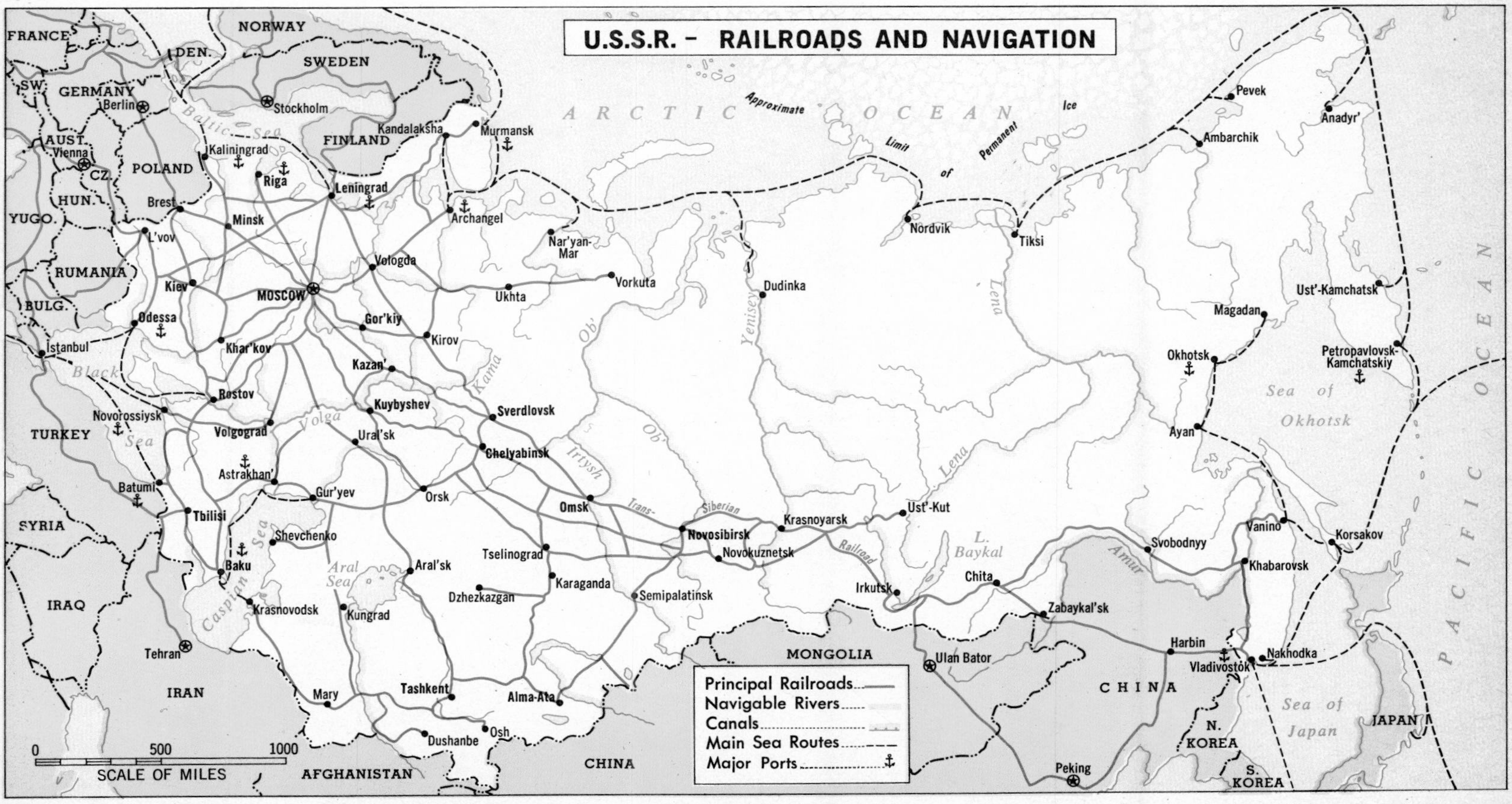
U.S.S.R. - RAILROADS AND NAVIGATION
Principal Railroads
Navigable Rivers
Canals
Main Sea Routes
Major Ports
0 500 1000
SCALE OF MILES
ARCTIC OCEAN
Approximate Limit of Permanent Ice
PACIFIC OCEAN
Sea of Okhotsk
Sea of Japan
Baltic Sea
Black Sea
Caspian Sea
Aral Sea
L. Baykal
Trans-Siberian Railroad
FRANCE
NORWAY
SWEDEN
DEN.
SW.
GERMANY
FINLAND
POLAND
AUST.
CZ.
HUN.
YUGO.
RUMANIA
BULG.
TURKEY
SYRIA
IRAQ
IRAN
AFGHANISTAN
CHINA
MONGOLIA
N. KOREA
S. KOREA
JAPAN
Berlin
Stockholm
Vienna
Kaliningrad
Riga
Leningrad
Kandalaksha
Murmansk
Archangel
Brest
Minsk
L'vov
Kiev
MOSCOW
Vologda
Odessa
Istanbul
Khar'kov
Gor'kiy
Kirov
Rostov
Kazan'
Novorossiysk
Volgograd
Kuybyshev
Sverdlovsk
Ural'sk
Chelyabinsk
Astrakhan'
Batumi
Tbilisi
Gur'yev
Orsk
Omsk
Baku
Shevchenko
Krasnovodsk
Kungrad
Aral'sk
Tselinograd
Karaganda
Dzhezkazgan
Semipalatinsk
Novosibirsk
Novokuznetsk
Krasnoyarsk
Ust'-Kut
Irkutsk
Chita
Zabaykal'sk
Ulan Bator
Harbin
Vladivostok
Nakhodka
Khabarovsk
Svobodnyy
Vanino
Korsakov
Ayan
Okhotsk
Magadan
Petropavlovsk-Kamchatskiy
Ust'-Kamchatsk
Anadyr'
Pevek
Ambarchik
Tiksi
Nordvik
Dudinka
Nar'yan-Mar
Vorkuta
Ukhta
Tehran
Mary
Tashkent
Alma-Ata
Dushanbe
Osh
Peking
Volga
Kama
Ob'
Irtysh
Yenisey
Lena
Amur

(continued on following page)

UNION OF SOVIET SOCIALIST REPUBLICS
European Part
CONIC PROJECTION

SCALE OF MILES
0 50 100 200 300

SCALE OF KILOMETRES
0 50 100 200 300

National Capitals .... ★
Capitals of Union Republics ....
Administrative Centers ....
International boundaries ....
Union Republic boundaries ....
A.S.S.R., Oblast, Kray boundaries ......
Autonomous Oblast boundaries ....
National Okrug boundaries ....
Canals ....

The government of the United States has not recognized the
incorporation of Estonia, Latvia and Lithuania into the Soviet
Union, nor does it recognize as final the de facto western limit
of Polish administration in Germany (the Oder-Neisse line).

Copyright by C.S. HAMMOND & CO., N.Y.

Administrative Divisions bear same
names as their respective Capitals
or Centers, except:

Abkhaz A.S.S.R.	Sukhumi	F6
Adygey Aut. Oblast	Maykop	F6
Adzhar A.S.S.R.	Batumi	F6
Bashkir A.S.S.R.	Ufa	J4
Chechen-Ingush A.S.S.R.	Groznyy	G6
Chuvash A.S.S.R.	Cheboksary	G3
Crimean Oblast	Simferopol'	D6
Dagestan A.S.S.R.	Makhachkala	G6
Kabardin-Balkar A.S.S.R.	Nal'chik	F6
Kalmuck A.S.S.R.	Elista	F5
Karachay-Cherkess Aut. Obl.	Cherkessk	F6
Karelian A.S.S.R.	Petrozavodsk	D2
Komi A.S.S.R.	Syktyvkar	H2
Komi-Permyak Nat'l Okrug	Kudymkar	H3
Mari A.S.S.R.	Yoshkar-Ola	G4
Mordvinian A.S.S.R.	Saransk	G4
Nagorno-Karabakh Aut. Obl.	Stepanakert	G7
Nenets Nat'l Okrug	Nar'yan-Mar	H1
North Ossetian A.S.S.R.	Ordzhonikidze	F6
South Ossetian Aut. Obl.	Tskhinvali	F6
Tatar A.S.S.R.	Kazan'	G3
Trans-Carpathian Oblast	Uzhgorod	B5
Udmurt A.S.S.R.	Izhevsk	H3
Volyn Oblast	Lutsk	C4

U.S.S.R. - EUROPEAN

UNION REPUBLICS

Armenian S.S.R., 2,491,900 .... F 6
Azerbaidzhan S.S.R., 5,117,100 .. G 6
Estonian S.S.R., 1,356,100 .... C 3
Georgian S.S.R., 4,686,000 .... F 6
Latvian S.S.R., 2,364,100 .... B 3
Lithuanian S.S.R., 3,128,000 ..... B 3
Moldavian S.S.R., 3,568,900 ...... C 5
Russian S.F.S.R., 130,079,210 .... F 3
Ukrainian S.S.R., 47,126,517 ..... D 5
White Russian S.S.R., 9,002,338.. C 4

INTERNAL DIVISIONS

Abkhaz A.S.S.R., 487,000 .... F 6
Adygey Aut. Oblast, 385,000 ...... F 6
Adzhar A.S.S.R., 310,000 .... F 6
Bashkir A.S.S.R., 3,818,000 ... ... J 4
Chechen-Ingush A.S.S.R., 1,065,000 ... G 6
Chuvash A.S.S.R., 1,224,000 ...... G 3
Crimean Oblast, 1,813,000 .... D 6
Dagestan A.S.S.R., 1,429,000 .... G 6
Kabardin-Balkar A.S.S.R., 588,000 ... F 6
Kalmuck A.S.S.R., 268,000 .... F 5
Karachay-Cherkess Aut. Oblast, 345,000 ... F 6
Karelian A.S.S.R., 713,000 .... D 2
Komi A.S.S.R., 965,000 .... H 2
Komi-Permyak Nat'l Okrug, 212,000 ... H 3
Mari A.S.S.R., 685,000 .... G 3
Mordvinian A.S.S.R., 1,029,000 .. G 4
Nagorno-Karabakh Aut. Oblast, 150,000 ... G 7
Nakhichevan' A.S.S.R., 202,000.. F 7
Nenets Nat'l Okrug, 39,000 .... H 1
North Ossetian A.S.S.R., 552,000 F 6
South Ossetian Aut. Oblast, 99,000 ... F 6
Tatar A.S.S.R., 3,131,000 .... G 3
Trans-Carpathian Oblast, 1,057,000 ... B 5
Udmurt A.S.S.R., 1,418,000 ...... H 3
Volyn Oblast, 974,000 .... C 4

CITIES and TOWNS

Abdulino, 27,000 ... H 4
Agdam, 21,300 ... G 6
Agryz, 21,000 ... H 3
Akhaltsikhe, 20,000 ... F 6
Akhtubinsk, 33,000 ... G 5
Akhtyrka, 42,000 ... E 4
Alagir, 18,000 ... F 6
Alatyr', 47,000 ... G 4
Aleksandriya, 69,000 ... D 5
Alekseyevka, 24,000 ... E 4
Aleksin, 61,000 ... E 4
Ali-Bayramly, 33,900 ... G 7
Al'met'yevsk, 87,000 ... H 3
Alushta, 21,000 ... D 6
Anapa, 25,000 ... E 6
Apatity, 40,000 ... D 1
Apsheronsk, 36,000 ... F 6
Archangel (Arkhangel'sk), 343,000 ... F 2
Armavir, 145,000 ... F 5
Arzamas, 67,000 ... F 3
Astrakhan', 410,000 ... G 5
Atkarsk, 30,000 ... G 4
Azov, 59,000 ... E 5
Bakhchisaray, 12,000 ... D 6
Bakhmach, 14,000 ... D 4
Baku, 852,000 ... H 6
Baku, *1,266,000 ... H 6
Balakhna, 36,000 ... F 3
Balaklava, 5,000 ... D 6
Balakovo, 103,000 ... G 4
Balashoy, 83,000 ... F 4
Baltiysk, 18,000 ... A 4
Baranovichi, 101,000 ... C 4
Barysh, 21,000 ... G 4
Bataysk, 85,000 ... E 5
Batumi, 101,000 ... F 6
Belaya Tserkov', 109,000 ... C 5
Belebey, 35,000 ... H 4
Belev, 18,000 ... E 4
Belgorod, 151,000 ... E 4
Belgorod-Dnestrovskiy, 30,000 ... D 5
Belomorsk, 18,000 ... D 2
Beloretsk, 67,000 ... J 4
Bel'tsy, 101,800 ... C 5
Bendery, 72,300 ... C 5
Berdichev, 71,000 ... C 5
Berdyansk, 100,000 ... E 5
Beregovo, 30,000 ... B 5
Berezniki, 146,000 ... J 3
Beslan, 28,000 ... F 6
Bezhetsk, 31,000 ... E 3
Birsk, 36,000 ... J 3
Blagoveshchensk, 15,000 ... J 4
Bobruysk, 138,000 ... C 4
Bologoye, 32,000 ... D 3
Bor, 55,000 ... F 3
Borislav, 36,000 ... B 5
Borisoglebsk, 64,000 ... F 4
Borisov, 84,000 ... C 4
Borovichi, 55,000 ... D 3
Borzhomi, 17,000 ... F 6
Brest, 122,000 ... B 4
Bryansk, 318,000 ... D 4
Bugul'ma, 72,000 ... H 4
Buguruslan, 49,000 ... H 4
Buy, 25,000 ... F 3
Buynaksk, 41,000 ... G 6
Buzuluk, 67,000 ... H 4
Bykhov, 16,000 ... C 4
Cēsis, 17,700 ... C 3
Chadyr-Lunga, 20,200 ... C 5
Chapayevsk, 86,000 ... G 4
Chaykovskiy, 48,000 ... H 3
Cheboksary, 216,000 ... G 3
Cherepovets, 188,000 ... E 3
Cherkassy, 158,000 ... D 5
Cherkessk, 67,000 ... F 6
Chernigov, 159,000 ... D 4
Chernovtsy, 187,000 ... C 5
Chervonograd, 41,000 ... B 4
Chiatura, 30,000 ... F 6
Chistopol', 60,000 ... H 3
Chkalov (Orenburg), 344,000 ... J 4
Chortkov, 21,000 ... B 5
Chusovoy, 58,000 ... J 3
Danilov, 17,000 ... E 3
Daugavpils, 100,400 ... C 3
Davlekanovo, 22,000 ... H 4
Derbent, 57,000 ... G 6
Dimitrovgrad, 81,000 ... G 4
Dneprodzerzhinsk, 227,000 ... D 5
Dnepropetrovsk, 862,000 ... D 5
Dobrush, 17,000 ... D 4
Donetsk, 879,000 ... E 5
Drogobych, 56,000 ... B 5
Dubna, 43,700 ... E 3
Dubna, 8,000 ... E 4
Dvinsk (Daugavpils), 100,400 ... C 3
Dzerzhinsk, 221,000 ... F 3
Dzhankoy, 42,000 ... D 5
Elektrostal', 123,100 ... E 3
Elista, 50,000 ... F 5
Engel's, 130,000 ... G 4
Erivan, 767,000 ... F 6
Ertil', 20,000 ... F 4
Fastov, 42,000 ... C 4
Feodosiya, 65,000 ... D 5
Frolovo, 30,000 ... F 5
Furmanov, 44,000 ... F 3
Gagarin, 15,000 ... D 3
Gagra, 23,000 ... E 6
Galich, 20,000 ... F 3
Gandzha (Kirovabad), 189,800 ... G 6
Gatchina, 63,000 ... D 3
Gay, 35,000 ... J 4
Gaysin, 23,000 ... C 5
Gelendzhik, 24,000 ... E 6
Genichesk, 19,000 ... E 5
Georgiu-Dezh, 48,000 ... E 4
Glazov, 68,000 ... H 3
Glukhov, 30,000 ... D 4
Gomel', 272,000 ... D 4
Gori, 45,000 ... F 6
Gorki, 24,000 ... D 4
Gor'kiy, 1,170,000 ... F 3
Gorlovka, 335,000 ... E 5
Gornyatskiy, 30,000 ... K 1
Gorodets, 34,000 ... F 3
Gremyachinsk, 34,000 ... J 3
Grodno, 132,000 ... B 4
Groznyy, 341,000 ... G 6
Gryazi, 40,000 ... F 4
Gubakha, 40,000 ... J 3
Gubkin, 54,000 ... E 4
Gudauta, 14,000 ... F 6
Gukovo, 65,000 ... F 5
Gus'-Khrustal'nyy, 65,000 ... F 3
Ichnya, 14,000 ... D 4
Inta, 50,000 ... K 1
Inza, 20,000 ... G 4
Ishimbay, 54,000 ... J 4
Ivano-Frankovsk, 105,000 ... B 5
Ivanovo, 420,000 ... E 3
Izhevsk, 422,000 ... H 3
Izmail, 70,000 ... C 5
Izyum, 52,000 ... E 5
Jelgava, 55,300 ... B 3
Kadiyevka, 137,000 ... E 5
Kagul, 26,000 ... C 5
Kakhovka, 25,000 ... D 5
Kalach, 23,000 ... F 5
Kalinin, 345,000 ... E 3
Kaliningrad, 297,000 ... B 4
Kaliningrad, 105,900 ... E 3
Kalinkovichi, 22,000 ... C 4
Kaluga, 211,000 ... E 4
Kamenets-Podol'skiy, 57,000 ... C 5
Kamenka, 30,000 ... F 4
Kamensk-Shakhtinskiy, 68,000 ... F 5
Kamyshin, 97,000 ... F 4
Kanash, 45,000 ... G 3
Kandalaksha, 42,000 ... D 1
Kapsukas, 28,700 ... B 4
Kashin, 19,000 ... E 3
Kasimov, 37,000 ... F 4
Kaspiysk, 39,000 ... G 6
Kaunas, 306,200 ... B 4
Kazan', 869,000 ... G 3
Kazatin, 28,000 ... C 5
Kem', 21,000 ... D 2
Kerch', 128,000 ... E 5
Khachmas, 22,300 ... G 6
Khar'kov, 1,223,000 ... E 5
Khasavyurt, 54,000 ... G 6
Kherson, 261,000 ... D 5
Khmel'nitskiy, 113,000 ... C 5
Khorol, 13,000 ... D 5
Khvalynsk, 19,000 ... G 4
Kiev, 1,632,000 ... D 4
Kiliya, 26,000 ... C 5
Kimovsk, 44,000 ... E 4
Kimry, 53,000 ... E 3
Kinel', 38,000 ... H 4
Kineshma, 96,000 ... F 3
Kirov, 30,000 ... D 4
Kirov, 333,000 ... G 3
Kirovabad, 189,800 ... G 6
Kirovakan, 107,000 ... G 6
Kirovo-Chepetsk, 51,000 ... H 3
Kirovograd, 189,000 ... D 5
Kirovsk, 48,000 ... D 1
Kirsanov, 24,000 ... F 4
Kishinev, 356,900 ... C 5
Kislovodsk, 90,000 ... F 6
Kizel, 49,000 ... J 3
Kizlyar, 30,000 ... G 6
Klaipėda, 139,900 ... B 3
Klimovichi, 13,000 ... D 4
Klintsy, 58,000 ... D 4
Kobrin, 25,000 ... B 4
Kobuleti, 18,000 ... F 6
Kohtla-Järve, 68,318 ... C 3
Kolomna, 135,900 ... E 4
Kolpino, 70,000 ... D 3
Kommunarsk, 123,000 ... E 5
Komrat, 21,400 ... C 5
Kondopoga, 25,000 ... D 2
Königsberg (Kaliningrad), 297,000 ... B 4
Konotop, 68,000 ... D 4
Konstantinovka, 105,000 ... E 5
Korosten', 56,000 ... C 4
Kostroma, 223,000 ... F 3
Kotel'nich, 30,000 ... G 3
Kotel'nikovo, 21,000 ... F 5
Kotlas, 56,000 ... G 2
Kotovo, 20,000 ... G 4
Kotovsk, 38,000 ... C 5
Kotovsk, 32,000 ... F 4
Kovel', 35,000 ... C 4
Kovrov, 123,000 ... F 3
Kramatorsk, 150,000 ... E 5
Krasnoarmeysk, 21,000 ... G 4
Krasnodar, 464,000 ... E 6
Krasnograd, 18,000 ... E 5
Krasnokamsk, 55,000 ... H 3
Krasnovishersk, 16,000 ... J 2
Krasnyy Kut, 17,000 ... G 4
Krasnyy Luch, 103,000 ... E 5
Kremenchug, 148,000 ... D 5
Krichev, 26,000 ... D 4
Krivoy Rog, 573,000 ... D 5
Krolevets, 18,000 ... D 4
Kropotkin, 68,000 ... F 5
Krymsk, 44,000 ... E 6
Kuba, 18,900 ... G 6
Kudymkar, 20,000 ... H 3
Kulebaki, 48,000 ... F 3
Kumertau, 42,000 ... J 4
Kungur, 74,000 ... J 3
Kupyansk, 28,000 ... E 5
Kursk, 284,000 ... E 4
Kutaisi, 161,000 ... F 6

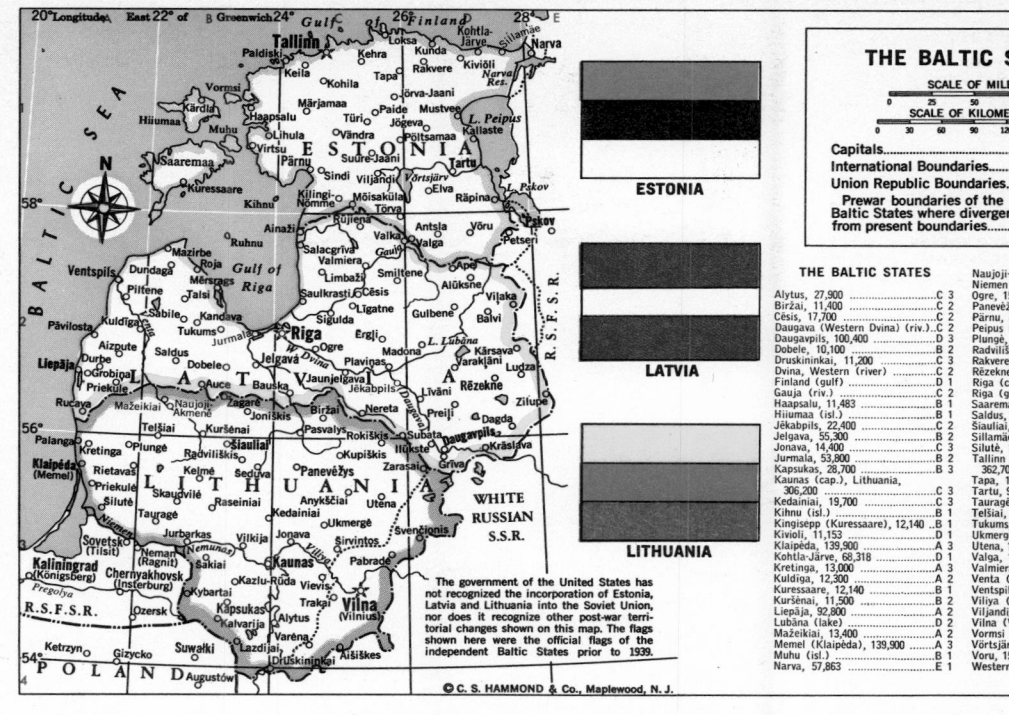

The government of the United States has not recognized the incorporation of Estonia, Latvia and Lithuania into the Soviet Union, nor does it recognize other post-war territorial changes shown on this map. The flags shown here were the official flags of the independent Baltic States prior to 1939.

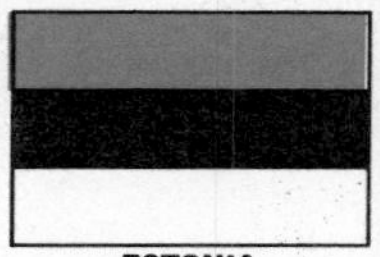

ESTONIA

LATVIA

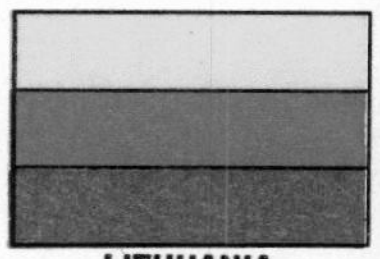

LITHUANIA

THE BALTIC STATES

SCALE OF MILES: 0 25 50 75 100
SCALE OF KILOMETRES: 0 30 60 90 120 150 180

Capitals ☆
International Boundaries
Union Republic Boundaries
Prewar boundaries of the Baltic States where divergent from present boundaries

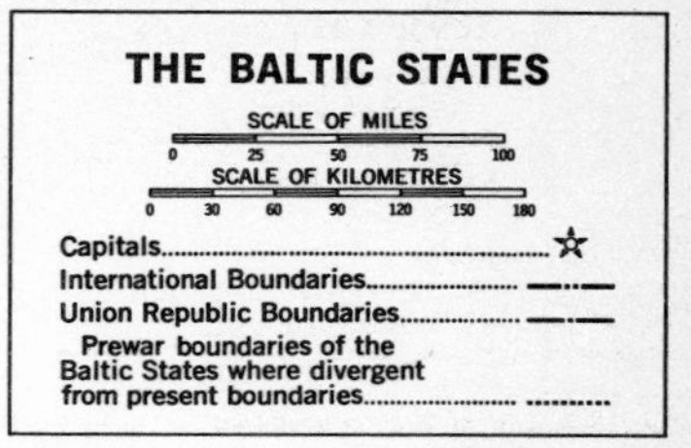

THE BALTIC STATES

Alytus, 27,900 ... C 3
Biržai, 11,400 ... C 2
Cēsis, 17,700 ... C 2
Daugava (Western Dvina) (riv.).. C 2
Daugavpils, 100,400 ... D 3
Dobele, 10,100 ... B 2
Druskininkai, 11,200 ... C 3
Dvina, Western (river) ... C 2
Finland (gulf) ... D 1
Gauja (riv.) ... C 2
Haapsalu, 11,483 ... B 1
Hiiumaa (isl.) ... B 1
Jēkabpils, 22,400 ... C 2
Jelgava, 55,300 ... B 2
Jonava, 14,400 ... C 3
Jurmala, 53,800 ... B 2
Kapsukas, 28,700 ... B 3
Kaunas (cap.), Lithuania, 306,200 ... C 3
Kedainiai, 19,700 ... C 3
Kihnu (isl.) ... B 1
Kingisepp (Kuressaare), 12,140 .. B 1
Kivioli, 11,153 ... D 1
Klaipėda, 139,900 ... A 3
Kohtla-Järve, 68,318 ... D 1
Kretinga, 13,000 ... A 3
Kuldīga, 12,300 ... A 2
Kuressaare, 12,140 ... B 1
Kuršėnai, 11,500 ... B 2
Liepāja, 92,800 ... A 2
Lubāna (lake) ... D 2
Mažeikiai, 13,400 ... A 2
Memel (Klaipėda), 139,900 ... A 3
Muhu (isl.) ... B 1
Narva, 57,863 ... E 1
Naujoji-Akmene, 10,200 ... B 2
Niemen (Nemunas) (riv.) ... A 3
Ogre, 15,700 ... C 2
Panevėžys, 73,500 ... C 3
Pärnu, 46,316 ... C 1
Peipus (lake) ... D 1
Plungė, 13,600 ... B 3
Radviliškis, 16,900 ... B 3
Rakvere, 17,891 ... D 1
Rēzekne, 30,800 ... D 2
Riga (cap.), Latvia, 731,800 ... C 2
Riga (gulf) ... B 2
Saaremaa (isl.) ... B 1
Saldus, 10,000 ... B 2
Šiauliai, 92,800 ... B 3
Sillamäe, 13,505 ... D 1
Silutė, 12,400 ... A 3
Tallinn (cap.), Estonia, 362,706 ... C 1
Tapa, 10,037 ... C 1
Tartu, 90,459 ... D 1
Tauragė, 19,500 ... B 3
Telšiai, 20,200 ... B 2
Tukums, 14,800 ... B 2
Ukmergė, 21,600 ... C 3
Utena, 13,300 ... C 3
Valga, 16,795 ... D 2
Valmiera, 20,300 ... C 2
Venta (riv.) ... B 2
Ventspils, 40,500 ... A 2
Viliya (riv.) ... C 3
Viljandi, 20,814 ... C 1
Vilna (Vilnius), 371,700 ... C 3
Vormsi (isl.) ... B 1
Võrtsjärv (lake) ... D 1
Voru, 15,398 ... D 2
Western Dvina (riv.) ... C 2

Kuvandyk, 24,000 ... J 4
Kuybyshev, 1,045,000 ... H 4
Kuznetsk, 84,000 ... G 4
Labinsk, 50,000 ... F 6
Lebedin, 29,000 ... D 4
Leninakan, 165,000 ... F 6
Leningrad, 3,513,000 ... C 3
Leningrad, *3,950,000 ... C 3
Leninogorsk, 45,000 ... H 4
Lenkoran', 35,500 ... G 7
L'gov, 28,000 ... E 4
Lida, 48,000 ... C 4
Liepāja, 92,800 ... B 3
Lipetsk, 289,000 ... E 4
Lisichansk, 118,000 ... E 5
Livny, 37,000 ... E 4
Lodeynoye Pole, 20,000 ... D 2
Lozovaya, 34,000 ... E 5
Lubny, 39,000 ... D 4
Luga, 30,000 ... C 3
Lutsk, 94,000 ... B 4
L'vov (Lwów), 553,000 ... B 5
Lys'va, 73,000 ... J 3
Lyubertsy, 139,400 ... E 3
Lyubotin, 38,000 ... E 4
Lyudinovo, 33,000 ... D 4
Makeyevka, 392,000 ... E 5
Makhachkala, 186,000 ... G 6
Makharadze, 24,000 ... F 6
Manturovo, 21,000 ... F 3
Marganets, 47,000 ... E 5
Mariupol' (Zhdanov), 417,000 ... E 5
Marks, 18,000 ... G 4
Maykop, 110,000 ... F 6
Mednogorsk, 41,000 ... J 4
Medvezh'yegorsk, 18,000 ... D 2
Melenki, 19,000 ... F 3
Meleuz, 28,000 ... J 4
Melitopol', 137,000 ... D 5
Memel (Klaipėda), 139,900 ... B 3
Merefa, 32,000 ... E 5
Michurinsk, 94,000 ... F 4
Mikhaylovka, 50,000 ... F 4
Millerovo, 38,000 ... F 5
Mineralnye Vody, 55,000 ... F 6
Mingechaur, 43,100 ... G 6
Minsk, 907,000 ... C 4
Minsk, *917,000 ... C 4
Mirgorod, 28,000 ... D 5
Mogilev, 202,000 ... C 4
Mogilev-Podol'skiy, 27,000 ... C 5
Molodechno, 50,000 ... C 4
Molotov (Perm'), 850,000 ... J 3
Monchegorsk, 49,000 ... D 1
Morshansk, 45,000 ... F 4
Moscow (Moskva) (cap.), 6,942,000 ... E 3
Moscow, *7,061,000 ... E 3
Mozhaysk, 20,300 ... E 3
Mozhga, 34,000 ... H 3
Mozyr', 49,000 ... C 4
Mtsensk, 24,000 ... E 4
Mukachevo, 57,000 ... B 5
Murmansk, 309,000 ... D 1
Murom, 99,000 ... F 3
Mytishchi, 118,700 ... E 3
Naberezhnye Chelny, 38,000 ... H 3
Nakhichevan', 33,200 ... F 7
Nal'chik, 146,000 ... F 6
Narva, 57,863 ... C 3
Nar'yan-Mar, 15,000 ... H 1
Neftekamsk, 35,000 ... J 3
Nelidovo, 30,000 ... D 3
Nerekhta, 28,000 ... F 3
Nevinnomyssk, 85,000 ... F 6
Nezhin, 56,000 ... D 4
Nikel', 17,000 ... C 1
Nikolayev, 331,000 ... D 5
Nikopol', 125,000 ... D 5
Nizhnekamsk, 49,000 ... H 3
Nizhniy Lomov, 19,000 ... F 4
Nosovka, 23,000 ... D 4
Novaya Kakhovka, 40,000 ... D 5
Novgorod, 128,000 ... D 3
Novoanninskiy, 21,000 ... F 4
Novocherkassk, 162,000 ... F 5
Novograd-Volynskiy, 36,000 ... C 4
Novogrudok, 20,000 ... C 4
Novokuybyshevsk, 104,000 ... G 4
Novomoskovsk, 134,000 ... E 4
Novopolotsk, 40,000 ... C 3
Novorossiysk, 133,000 ... E 6
Novoshakhtinsk, 102,000 ... E 5
Novotroitsk, 83,000 ... J 4
Novoukrainka, 22,000 ... D 5
Novovolynsk, 40,000 ... B 4
Novozybkov, 33,000 ... D 4
Nyandoma, 24,000 ... F 2
Obninsk, 49,000 ... E 3
Ochamchire, 20,000 ... F 6
Odessa, 892,000 ... D 5
Oktyabr'sk, 36,000 ... G 4
Oktyabr'skiy, 77,000 ... H 4
Olenegorsk, 21,000 ... D 1
Omutninsk, 29,000 ... H 3
Onega, 27,000 ... E 2
Ordzhonikidze, 236,000 ... F 6
Orel, 232,000 ... E 4
Orenburg, 344,000 ... J 4
Orgeyev, 25,800 ... C 5
Orsha, 101,000 ... C 4
Orsk, 225,000 ... J 4
Osipenko (Berdyansk), 100,000 ... E 5
Osipovichi, 19,000 ... C 4
Ostashkov, 22,000 ... D 3
Ostrogozhsk, 35,000 ... E 4
Ostrov, 19,000 ... C 3
Otradnyy, 46,000 ... H 4
Panevėžys, 73,500 ... B 3
Pärnu, 46,316 ... C 3
Pavlovo, 63,000 ... F 3
Pechora, 41,000 ... J 1
Penza, 374,000 ... F 4
Perm', 850,000 ... J 3
Pervomaysk, 59,000 ... D 5
Pervomayskiy, 18,000 ... F 2
Petrovsk, 32,000 ... G 4
Petrozavodsk, 184,000 ... D 2
Pinsk, 62,000 ... C 4
Piryatin, 18,000 ... D 4
Pochep, 16,000 ... D 4
Podol'sk, 168,700 ... E 3
Polonnoye, 23,000 ... C 4
Polotsk, 64,000 ... C 3
Poltava, 220,000 ... D 5
Postavy, 13,000 ... C 3
Poti, 48,000 ... F 6
Povorino, 22,000 ... F 4
Prikumsk, 36,000 ... F 6
Priluki, 57,000 ... D 4
Primorsko-Akhtarsk, 30,000 ... E 5
Priyutovo, 20,000 ... H 4
Promyshlennyy, 22,000 ... K 1
Pskov, 127,000 ... C 3
Pugachev, 38,000 ... G 4
Pushkin, 79,000 ... C 3
Pyatigorsk, 93,000 ... F 6
Pyatikhatki, 20,000 ... D 5
Radomyshl', 12,000 ... C 4
Rakhov, 11,000 ... B 5
Rakvere, 17,891 ... C 3
Rasskazovo, 40,000 ... F 4
Rechitsa, 48,000 ... C 4
Revel (Tallinn), 362,706 ... B 3
Rēzekne, 30,800 ... C 3
Riga, 731,800 ... B 3
Rogachev, 12,000 ... D 4
Romny, 48,000 ... D 4
Roslavl', 48,000 ... D 4
Rossosh', 36,000 ... E 4
Rostov, 32,000 ... E 3
Rostov, 789,000 ... F 5
Rovno, 116,000 ... C 4
Rtishchevo, 40,000 ... F 4
Rubezhnoye, 58,000 ... E 5
Rustavi, 98,000 ... G 6
Ruzayevka, 38,000 ... F 4
Ryazan', 350,000 ... E 4
Rybinsk, 218,000 ... E 3
Rybnitsa, 32,400 ... C 5
Rzhev, 61,000 ... D 3
Safonovo, 44,000 ... D 3
Saki, 23,000 ... D 5
Salavat, 114,000 ... H 4
Sal'sk, 50,000 ... F 5
Sal'yany, 24,200 ... G 7
Samara (Kuybyshev), 1,045,000.. H 4
Saransk, 191,000 ... G 4
Sarapul, 97,000 ... H 3
Saratov, 757,000 ... G 4
Sarny, 10,000 ... C 4
Sasovo, 28,000 ... F 4
Segezha, 30,000 ... D 2
Semenov, 25,000 ... F 3
Serdobel (Sortavala), 23,000 ... D 2
Serdobsk, 33,000 ... F 4
Serpukhov, 124,300 ... E 4
Sevastopol', 229,000 ... D 6
Severodonetsk, 90,000 ... E 5
Severodvinsk, 145,000 ... E 2
Severomorsk, 45,000 ... D 1
Shakhty, 205,000 ... F 5
Shakhun'ya, 22,000 ... G 3
Shar'ya, 25,000 ... G 3
Shchekino, 61,000 ... E 4
Shcherbakov (Rybinsk), 218,000.. E 3
Sheki, 43,200 ... G 6
Shemakha, 17,900 ... G 6
Shepetovka, 39,000 ... C 4
Shostka, 64,000 ... D 4
Shumerlya, 33,000 ... G 3
Shuya, 69,000 ... F 3
Šiauliai, 92,800 ... B 3
Sibay, 42,000 ... J 4
Simferopol', 249,000 ... D 6
Skopin, 23,000 ... F 4
Slantsy, 40,000 ... C 3
Slavuta, 24,000 ... C 4
Slavyansk, 124,000 ... E 5
Slavyansk-na-Kubani, 52,000 ... E 5
Slobodskoy, 37,000 ... H 3
Slonim, 30,000 ... B 4
Slutsk, 36,000 ... C 4
Smela, 55,000 ... D 5
Smolensk, 211,000 ... D 4
Sochi, 224,000 ... E 6
Sokol, 49,000 ... F 3
Solikamsk, 89,000 ... J 3
Sol'-Iletsk, 25,000 ... J 4
Sorochinsk, 25,000 ... H 4
Soroki, 21,700 ... C 5
Sortavala, 23,000 ... D 2
Sosnogorsk, 25,000 ... H 2
Sovetsk, 38,000 ... B 4
Sovetsk, 19,000 ... G 3
Stalingrad (Volgograd), 818,000 ... F 5
Staraya Russa, 34,000 ... D 3
Staryy Oskol, 52,000 ... E 4
Stavropol', 198,000 ... F 5
Stepanakert, 30,300 ... G 7
Stepnoy (Elista), 50,000 ... G 5
Sterlitamak, 185,000 ... J 4
Stupino, 59,300 ... E 4
Sukhumi, 102,000 ... F 6
Sumgait, 124,400 ... G 6
Sumy, 159,000 ... E 4
Svetlogorsk, 40,000 ... C 4
Svetlograd, 30,000 ... F 5
Syktyvkar, 125,000 ... H 2
Syzran', 173,000 ... G 4
Taganrog, 254,000 ... E 5
Tallinn, 362,706 ... B 3
Tambov, 230,000 ... F 4
Tartu, 90,459 ... C 3
Tauragė, 19,500 ... B 3
Tbilisi, 889,000 ... F 6
Telavi, 23,000 ... G 6
Telšiai, 20,200 ... B 3
Temryuk, 28,000 ... E 5
Ternopol', 85,000 ... C 5
Teykovo, 34,000 ... E 3
Tiflis (Tbilisi), 889,000 ... F 6
Tighina (Bendery), 72,300 ... C 5
Tikhoretsk, 60,000 ... F 5
Tikhvin, 29,000 ... D 3
Timashevsk, 35,000 ... E 5
Tiraspol', 105,700 ... D 5
Togliatti, 251,000 ... G 4
Tokmak, 39,000 ... E 5
Torzhok, 47,000 ... D 3
Tskhinvali, 30,000 ... F 6
Tuapse, 51,000 ... E 6
Tula, 462,000 ... E 4
Tul'chin, 14,000 ... C 5
Tuymazy, 35,000 ... H 4
Tyrnyauz, 19,000 ... F 6
Uchaly, 18,000 ... J 4
Ufa, 771,000 ... J 4
Uglich, 36,000 ... E 3
Ukhta, 63,000 ... H 2
Ukmergė, 21,600 ... C 3
Ul'yanovsk, 351,000 ... G 4
Uman', 63,000 ... D 5
Uryupinsk, 37,000 ... F 4
Usman', 19,000 ... E 4
Uzhgorod, 65,000 ... B 5
Uzlovaya, 62,000 ... E 4
Valga, 16,795 ... C 3
Valmiera, 20,300 ... C 3
Valuyki, 29,000 ... E 4
Vasil'kov, 27,000 ... D 4
Velikiye Luki, 85,000 ... D 3
Velikiy Ustyug, 35,000 ... F 2
Vel'sk, 20,000 ... F 2
Ventspils, 40,500 ... B 3
Vichuga, 53,000 ... F 3
Viipuri (Vyborg), 65,000 ... C 2
Vilna (Vilnius), 371,700 ... C 4
Vinnitsa, 212,000 ... C 5
Vitebsk, 231,000 ... C 3
Vladimir, 234,000 ... F 3
Volgodonsk, 25,000 ... F 5
Volgograd, 818,000 ... F 5
Volkhov, 46,000 ... D 3
Volkovysk, 22,000 ... B 4
Vologda, 178,000 ... F 3
Vol'sk, 69,000 ... G 4
Volzhsk, 44,000 ... G 3
Volzhskiy, 142,000 ... G 5
Vorkuta, 90,000 ... K 1
Voronezh, 660,000 ... E 4
Voroshilovgrad, 383,000 ... F 5
Voskresensk, 66,900 ... E 3
Votkinsk, 74,000 ... H 3
Voznesensk, 36,000 ... D 5
Vyatskiye Polyany, 33,000 ... H 3
Vyaz'ma, 42,000 ... D 3
Vyborg, 65,000 ... C 2
Vyksa, 46,000 ... F 3
Vyshniy Volochek, 74,000 ... D 3
Yalta, 62,000 ... D 6
Yanaul, 18,000 ... J 3
Yaroslavl', 517,000 ... E 3
Yartsevo, 37,000 ... D 3
Yefremov, 47,000 ... E 4
Yelabuga, 36,000 ... H 3
Yelets, 101,000 ... E 4
Yenakiyevo, 92,000 ... E 5
Yershov, 20,000 ... G 4
Yessentuki, 65,000 ... F 6
Yevpatoria, 79,000 ... D 5
Yeysk, 64,000 ... E 5
Yoshkar-Ola, 166,000 ... G 3
Yur'yevets, 23,000 ... F 3
Zagorsk, 92,400 ... E 3
Zaporozh'ye, 658,000 ... E 5
Zelenodol'sk, 77,000 ... G 3
Zhdanov, 417,000 ... E 5
Zherdevka, 20,000 ... F 4
Zhigulevsk, 52,000 ... G 4
Zhitomir, 161,000 ... C 4
Zhlobin, 25,000 ... D 4
Zhmerinka, 34,000 ... C 5
Zhodino, 17,000 ... C 4
Znamenka, 30,000 ... D 5
Zolotonosha, 27,000 ... D 5
Zugdidi, 39,000 ... F 6
Zvenigorodka, 21,000 ... D 5

OTHER FEATURES

Apsheron (pen.) ... H 6
Araks (river) ... G 7
Azov (sea) ... E 5
Baltic (sea) ... B 3
Barents (sea) ... E 1
Belaya (river) ... H 3
Beloye (lake) ... E 2
Berezina (river) ... C 4
Black (sea) ... D 6
Bug (river) ... B 4
Bug (river) ... D 5
Caspian (sea) ... G 6
Caucasus (mts.) ... F 6
Central Ural (mts.) ... J 2
Chir (river) ... F 5
Crimea (pen.), 1,813,000 ... D 5
Dagö (Hiiumaa) (isl.) ... B 3
Denezhkin Kamen' (mt.) ... K 2
Desna (river) ... D 4
Dnieper (river) ... D 5
Dniester (river) ... C 5
Don (river) ... F 5
Donets (river) ... E 5
Dvina (bay) ... E 2
Dvina, Northern (river) ... F 2
Dvina, Western (river) ... C 3
Dykh-Tau (mt.) ... F 6
El'brus (mt.) ... F 6
Finland (gulf) ... C 3
Goryn' (river) ... C 4
Hiiumaa (isl.) ... B 3
Ilek (river) ... J 4
Il'men (lake) ... D 3
Izhma (river) ... H 2
Kakhovka (res.) ... D 5
Kama (river) ... H 3
Kandalaksha (gulf) ... D 1
Kanin (pen.) ... G 1
Kapydzhik (mt.) ... G 7
Kara (sea) ... K 1
Kazbek (mt.) ... F 6
Khoper (river) ... F 4
Kil'din (isl.) ... D 1
Kinel' (river) ... H 4
Kola (pen.) ... E 1
Kolguyev (isl.) ... G 1
Kolva (river) ... J 1
Kuban' (river) ... E 5
Kubeno (lake) ... E 3
Kura (river) ... G 6
Kuyto (lake) ... D 2
Ladoga (lake) ... D 2
Lapland (reg.) ... C 1
Lovat' (river) ... D 3
Mansel'ka (mts.) ... C 1
Manych-Gudilo (lake) ... F 5
Matveyev (isl.) ... J 1
Medveditsa (river) ... F 4
Mezen' (river) ... G 1
Mezhdusharskiy (isl.) ... G 1
Moksha (river) ... F 4
Moskva (river) ... E 3
Msta (river) ... D 3
Niemen (river) ... B 4
North Ural (mts.) ... K 1
Northern Dvina (river) ... F 2
Novaya Zemlya (isls.) ... H 1
Oka (river) ... F 4
Onega (bay) ... E 2
Onega (lake) ... E 2
Ösel (Saaremaa) (isl.) ... B 3
Pay-Yer (mt.) ... K 1
Pechora (river) ... H 1
Pechora (sea) ... H 1
Peipus (lake) ... C 3
Pinega (river) ... G 2
Ponoy (river) ... E 1
Pripet (marsh) ... C 4
Pripyat' (river) ... C 4
Prut (river) ... C 5
Psel (river) ... D 4
Riga (gulf) ... B 3
Russkiy Zavorot (cape) ... H 1
Rybachiy (pen.) ... D 1
Saaremaa (isl.) ... B 3
Samara (river) ... H 4
Seg (lake) ... D 2
Sevan (lake) ... G 6
Seym (river) ... D 4
Solovetskiye (isls.) ... E 1
South Ural (mts.) ... J 4
Suda (river) ... E 3
Sukhona (river) ... F 2
Sura (river) ... G 4
Svir' (river) ... D 2
Sysola (river) ... H 2
Tel'pos-Iz (mt.) ... K 2
Timan Ridge (mts.) ... H 1
Top (lake) ... D 1
Tuloma (river) ... D 1
Ufa (river) ... J 3
Undzha (river) ... F 3
Ural (mts.) ... J 2
Ural (river) ... J 4
Usa (river) ... K 1
Vaga (river) ... F 2
Valday (hills) ... D 3
Vaygach (isl.) ... K 1
Velikaya (river) ... C 3
Vetluga (river) ... G 3
Vodl (lake) ... E 2
Volga (river) ... G 5
Volga-Don (canal) ... F 5
Volkhov (river) ... D 3
Vorona (river) ... F 4
Vorskla (river) ... E 4
Vozhe (lake) ... F 2
Vyatka (river) ... H 3
Vychegda (river) ... G 2
Vyg (lake) ... E 2
Vym' (river) ... H 2
Western Dvina (river) ... C 3
White (sea) ... E 1
Yamantau (mt.) ... J 4
Yug (river) ... G 2
Yugorskiy (pen.) ... K 1

*City and suburbs.

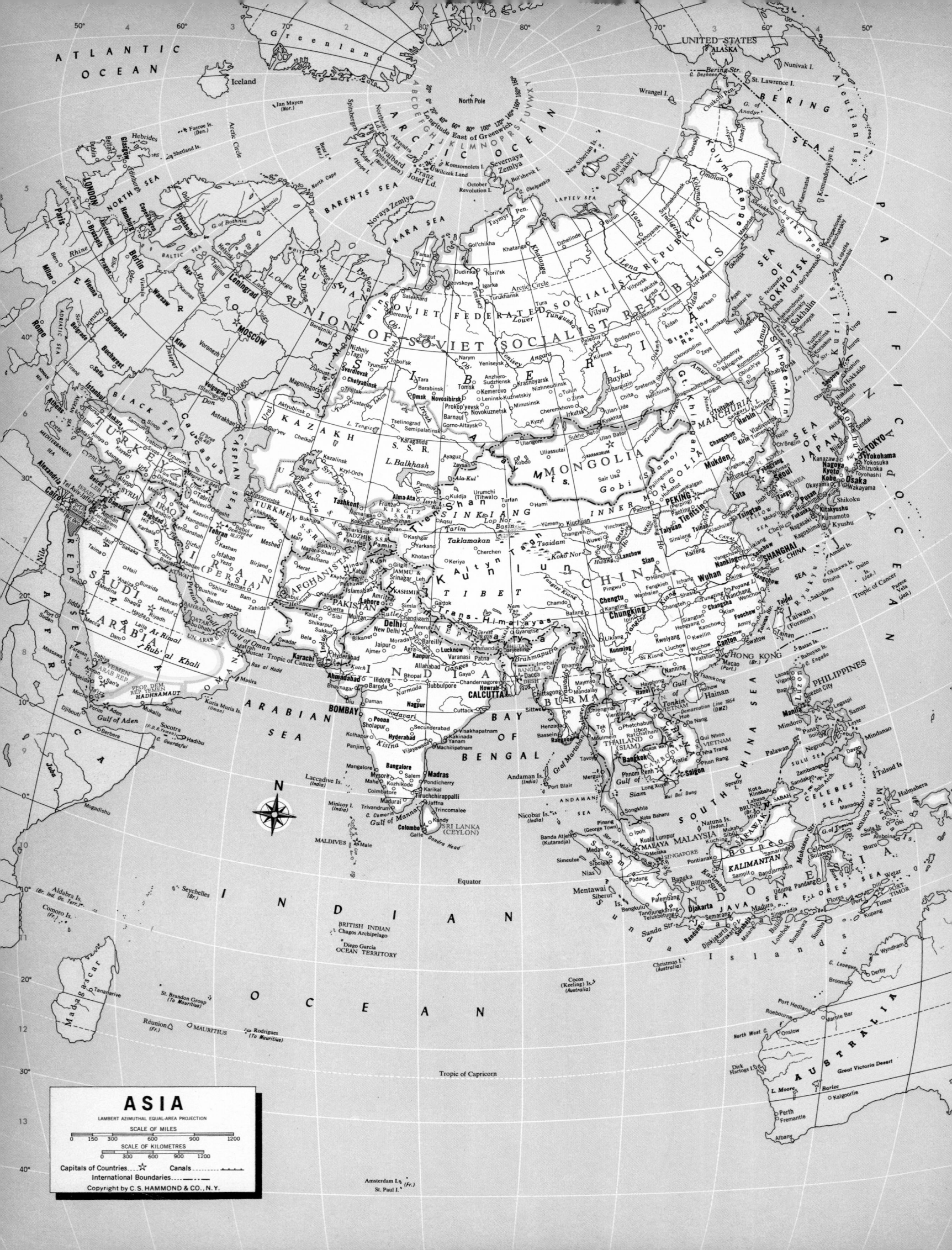

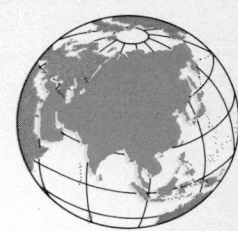

POPULATION DISTRIBUTION

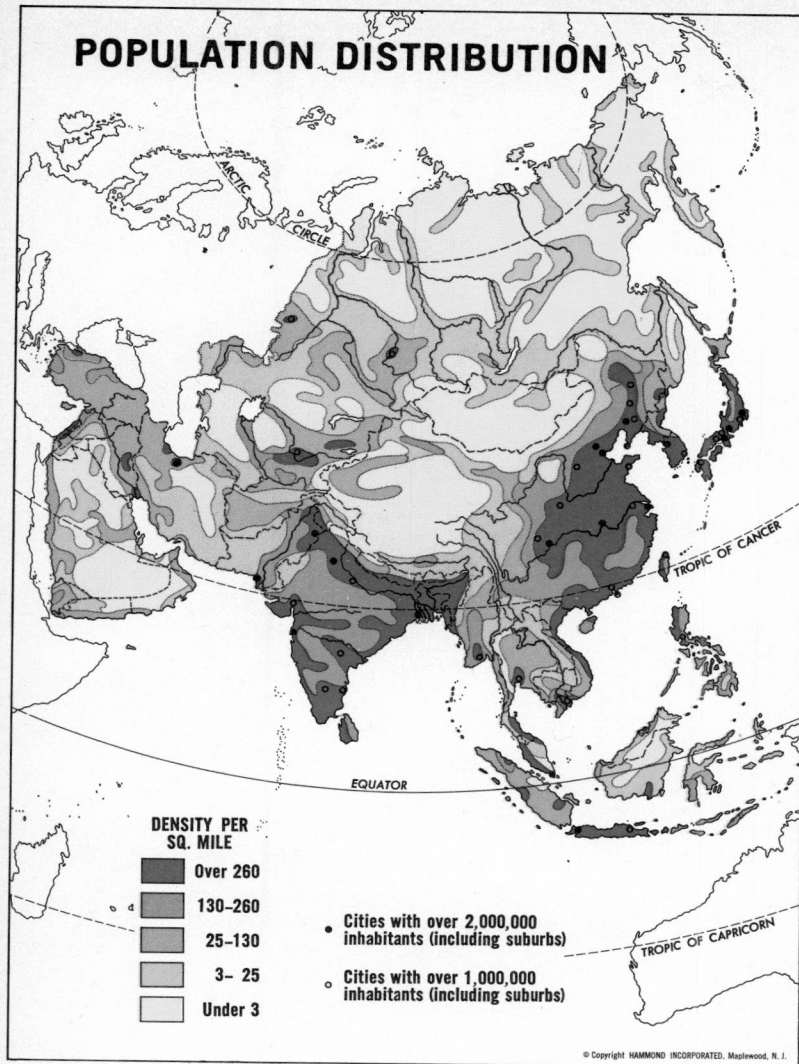

AREA 17,032,000 sq. mi.
POPULATION 2,043,997,000
LARGEST CITY Tokyo
HIGHEST POINT Mt. Everest 29,028 ft.
LOWEST POINT Dead Sea -1,290 ft.

DENSITY PER SQ. MILE

- Over 260
- 130–260
- 25–130
- 3–25
- Under 3

• Cities with over 2,000,000 inhabitants (including suburbs)

○ Cities with over 1,000,000 inhabitants (including suburbs)

© Copyright HAMMOND INCORPORATED, Maplewood, N. J.

VEGETATION

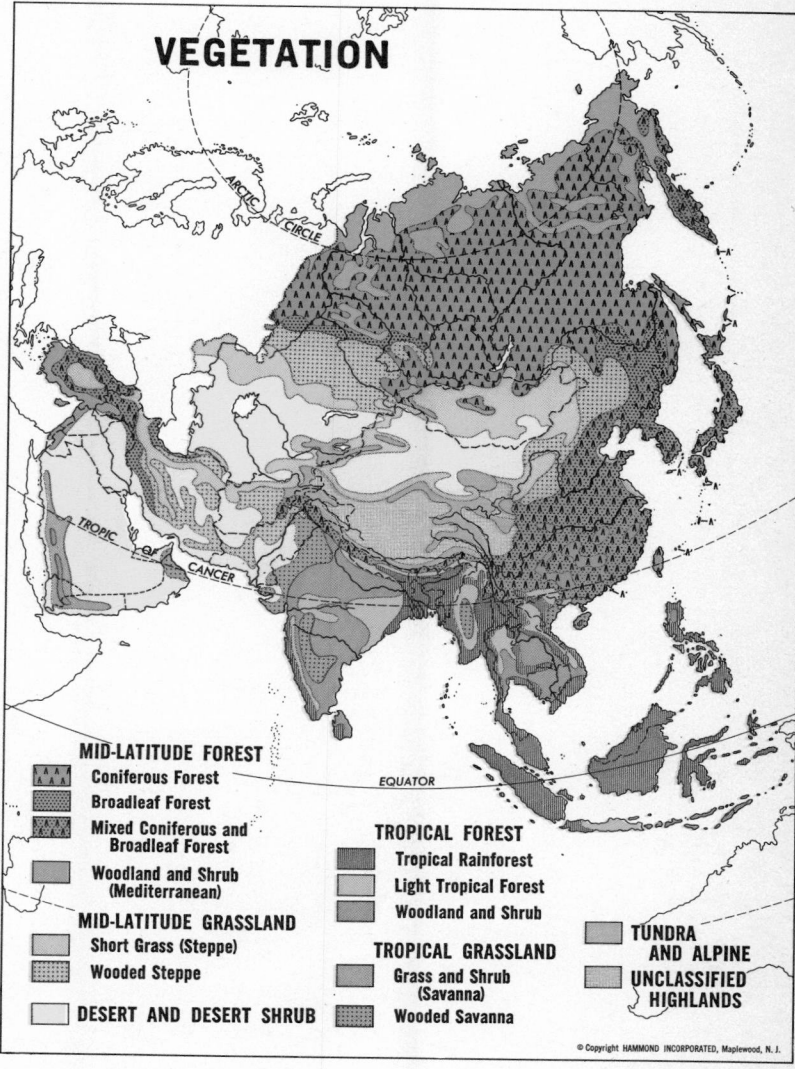

MID-LATITUDE FOREST
- Coniferous Forest
- Broadleaf Forest
- Mixed Coniferous and Broadleaf Forest
- Woodland and Shrub (Mediterranean)

MID-LATITUDE GRASSLAND
- Short Grass (Steppe)
- Wooded Steppe

DESERT AND DESERT SHRUB

TROPICAL FOREST
- Tropical Rainforest
- Light Tropical Forest
- Woodland and Shrub

TROPICAL GRASSLAND
- Grass and Shrub (Savanna)
- Wooded Savanna

- TUNDRA AND ALPINE
- UNCLASSIFIED HIGHLANDS

© Copyright HAMMOND INCORPORATED, Maplewood, N. J.

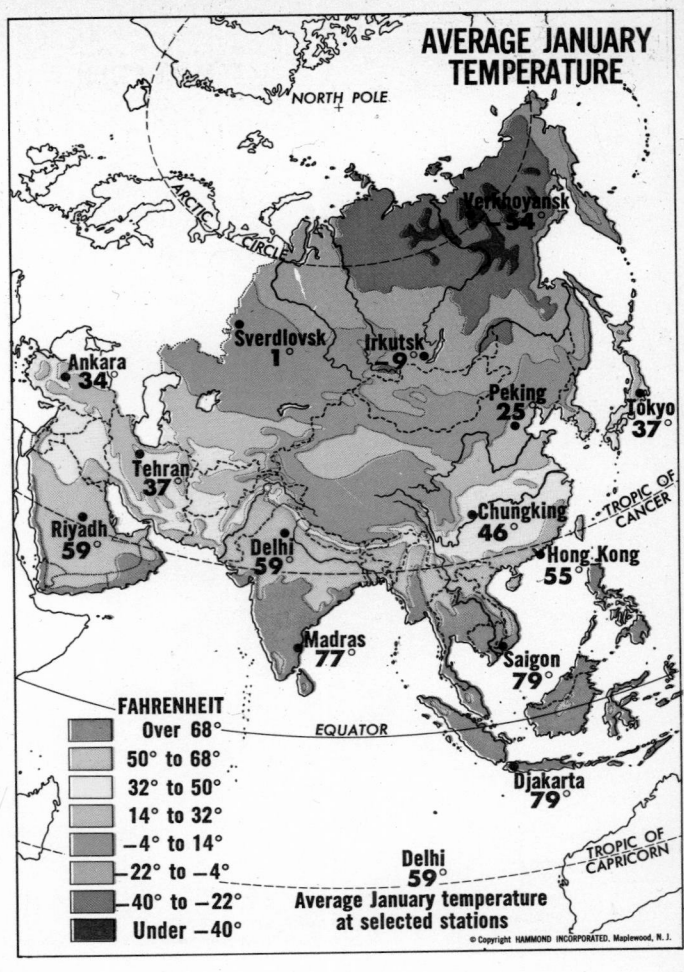

AVERAGE JANUARY TEMPERATURE

NORTH POLE

Verkhoyansk
-54°

Sverdlovsk
1°

Irkutsk
-9°

Ankara
34°

Peking
25°

Tokyo
37°

Tehran
37°

Chungking
46°

Riyadh
59°

Delhi
59°

Hong Kong
55°

Madras
77°

Saigon
79°

Djakarta
79°

EQUATOR

FAHRENHEIT
- Over 68°
- 50° to 68°
- 32° to 50°
- 14° to 32°
- -4° to 14°
- -22° to -4°
- -40° to -22°
- Under -40°

Delhi
59°
Average January temperature
at selected stations

© Copyright HAMMOND INCORPORATED, Maplewood, N.J.

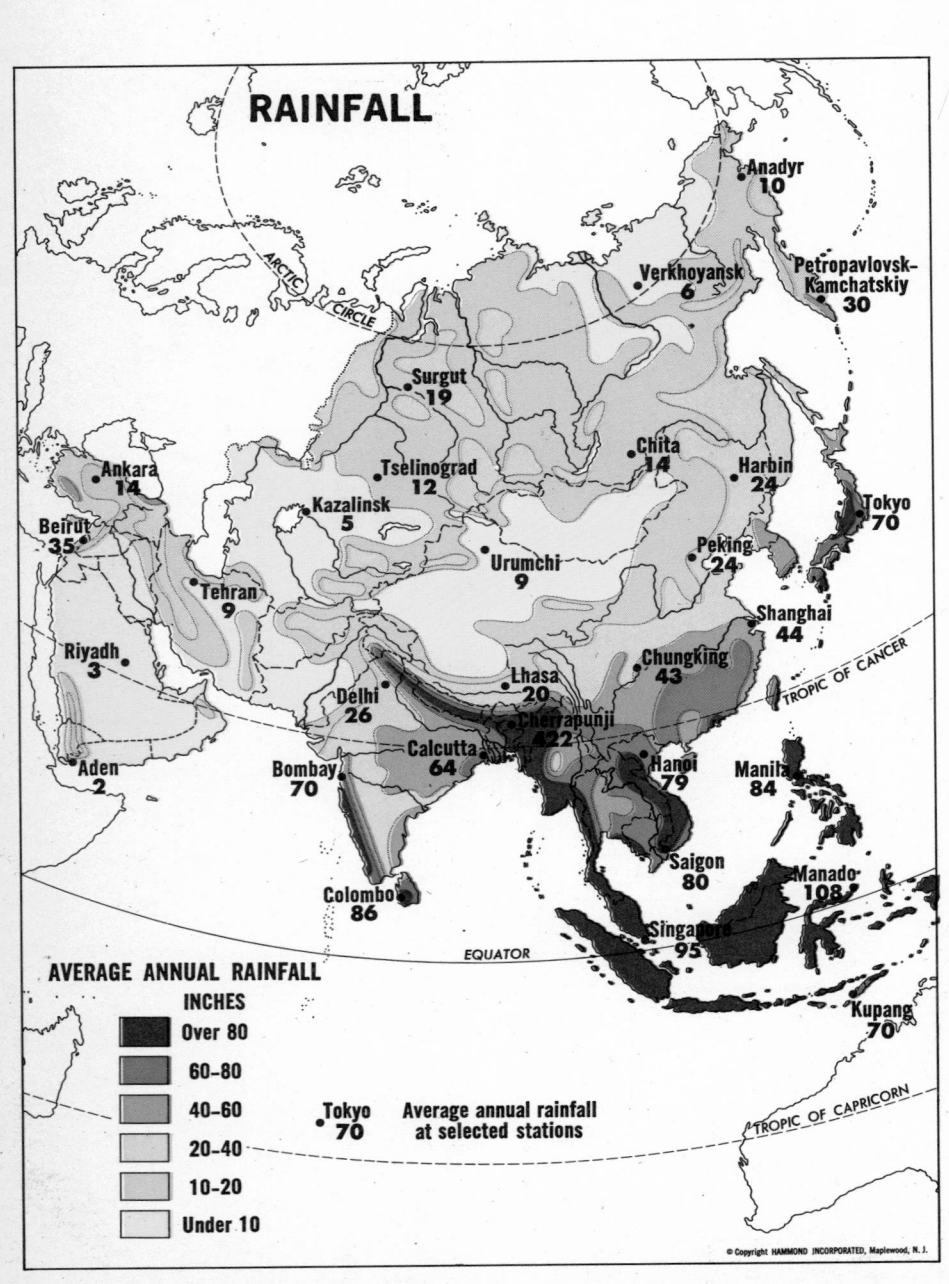

RAINFALL

Anadyr
10

Verkhoyansk
6

Petropavlovsk-
Kamchatskiy
30

Surgut
19

Chita
14

Harbin
24

Tokyo
70

Tselinograd
12

Ankara
14

Kazalinsk
5

Urumchi
9

Peking
24

Beirut
35

Tehran
9

Shanghai
44

Riyadh
3

Lhasa
20

Chungking
43

Delhi
26

Cherrapunji
422

Aden
2

Bombay
70

Calcutta
64

Hanoi
79

Manila
84

TROPIC OF CANCER

Saigon
80

Colombo
86

Manado
108

Singapore
95

EQUATOR

Kupang
70

TROPIC OF CAPRICORN

AVERAGE ANNUAL RAINFALL
INCHES
- Over 80
- 60–80
- 40–60
- 20–40
- 10–20
- Under 10

Tokyo
70
Average annual rainfall
at selected stations

© Copyright HAMMOND INCORPORATED, Maplewood, N.J.

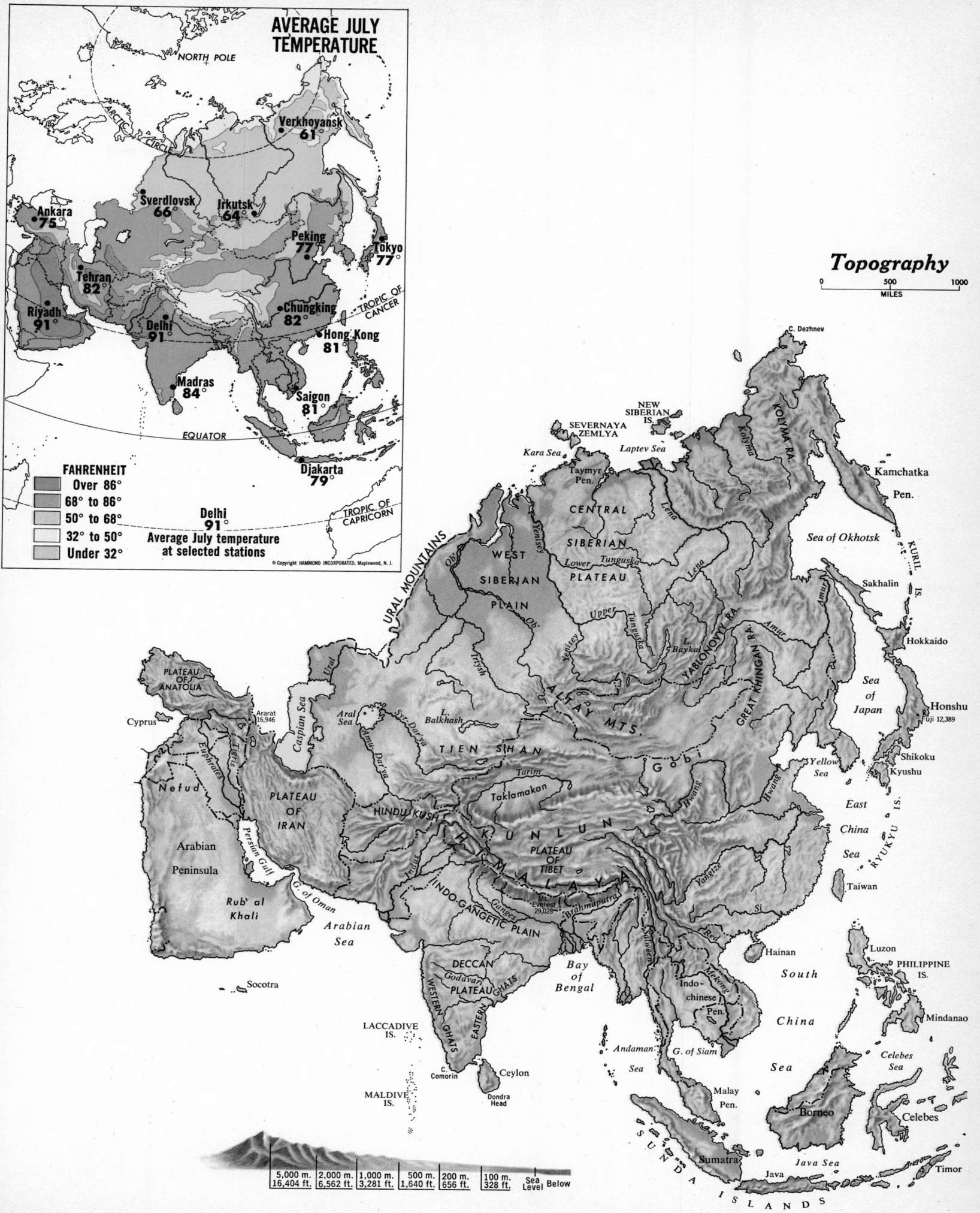

AVERAGE JULY TEMPERATURE

NORTH POLE

Verkhoyansk
61°

Sverdlovsk
66°
Irkutsk
64°

Ankara
75°

Peking
77°
Tokyo
77°

Tehran
82°

Chungking
82°

Riyadh
91°

Delhi
91°

Hong Kong
81°

Madras
84°

Saigon
81°

TROPIC OF CANCER

EQUATOR

Djakarta
79°

TROPIC OF CAPRICORN

FAHRENHEIT
- Over 86°
- 68° to 86°
- 50° to 68°
- 32° to 50°
- Under 32°

Delhi
91°
Average July temperature
at selected stations

© Copyright HAMMOND INCORPORATED, Maplewood, N. J.

Topography

0   500   1000
MILES

C. Dezhnev

NEW SIBERIAN IS.

SEVERNAYA ZEMLYA

Kara Sea

Laptev Sea

Taymyr Pen.

KOLYMA RA.

Kamchatka Pen.

CENTRAL SIBERIAN PLATEAU

Kolyma

Lena

Sea of Okhotsk

URAL MOUNTAINS

Ob

Yenisey

Lower Tunguska

Lena

KURIL IS.

WEST SIBERIAN PLAIN

Upper Tunguska

Sakhalin

Hokkaido

Trtysh

Ob

Yenisey

L. Baykal

YABLONOVYY RA.

Amur

Sea of Japan

PLATEAU OF ANATOLIA

Ararat 16,946

Ural

ALTAY MTS.

GREAT KHINGAN RA.

Amur

Honshu
Fuji 12,389

Cyprus

Caspian Sea

Aral Sea

Syr-Darya

L. Balkhash

TIEN SHAN

Gobi

Hwang

Yellow Sea

Shikoku
Kyushu

Euphrates
Tigris

Amu-Darya

Tarim

Taklamakan

KUNLUN

Hwang

East China Sea

RYUKYU IS.

Nefud

PLATEAU OF IRAN

HINDU KUSH

PLATEAU OF TIBET

Yangtze

Si

Arabian Peninsula

Persian Gulf

Indus

HIMALAYA

Mt. Everest 29,028

Brahmaputra

Hainan

South China Sea

Taiwan

Rub' al Khali

G. of Oman

INDO-GANGETIC PLAIN

Ganges

Salween

Red

Indo-chinese Pen.

Luzon

PHILIPPINE IS.

Arabian Sea

DECCAN PLATEAU

Godavari

WESTERN GHATS

EASTERN GHATS

Bay of Bengal

Mekong

Mindanao

Socotra

LACCADIVE IS.

C. Comorin

Ceylon

Andaman Sea

G. of Siam

Malay Pen.

Borneo

Celebes Sea

Celebes

MALDIVE IS.

Dondra Head

SUNDA ISLANDS

Sumatra

Java

Java Sea

Timor

5,000 m.   2,000 m.   1,000 m.   500 m.   200 m.   100 m.   Sea
16,404 ft. 6,562 ft. 3,281 ft. 1,640 ft. 656 ft. 328 ft. Level   Below

58 Near and Middle East

SAUDI ARABIA KUWAIT YEMEN ARAB REPUBLIC BAHRAIN QATAR OMAN PEOPLES DEM. REP. OF YEMEN

AFGHANISTAN

CITIES and TOWNS

Andkhui, 30,000 ....J 2
Baghlan, 92,000 ....J 2
Bala Murghab, 10,000 ...J 2
Balkh, 15,000 ....J 2
Bamian, 25,000 ....J 3
Chahar Burjak, 500 ....H 3

Charikar, 83,700 ....J 2
Daulatabad, 15,000 ...J 2
Daulat Yar, 2,000 ....J 3
Doshi, 5,000 ....K 2
Faizabad, 57,000 ....K 2
Farah, 26,400 ....H 3
Gardez, 33,000 ....J 3
Ghazni, 39,900 ....J 3
Ghurian, 10,000 ....H 3
Girishk, 10,000 ....H 3

Haibak, 35,200 ....J 2
Herat, 71,563 ....H 3
Jalalabad, 48,919 ....K 3
Jurm, 10,000 ....K 2
Juwain, 2,000 ....H 3
Kabul (capital),
   472,313 ....J 3
Kabul, *600,000 ...J 3
Kala Bist, 26,100 ....H 3
Kalat-i-Ghilzai, 40,500 ...J 3

Kandahar, 127,036 ....J 3
Kandahar, *142,000 ...J 3
Khanabad, 30,000 ....J 2
Kushk, 10,000 ....H 3
Landi Muhammad Amin Khan,
   1,000 ....H 3
Maimana, 48,750 ....J 2
Matun, 15,000 ....J 3
Mazar-i-Sharif, 43,197 ...J 2
Mukur, 10,000 ....J 3

Obeh, 5,000 ....H 3
Panjao, 3,000 ....J 3
Qala Panja, 1,000 ....K 2
Qaleh-i-Kang, 15,600 ...H 3
Rudbar, 1,000 ....H 3
Rustak, 10,000 ....J 2
Sabzawar, 5,000 ....H 3
Sar-i-Pul, 5,000 ....J 2
Shahjui, 5,000 ....J 3
Shibarghan, 50,440 ....H 2

Shindand (Sabzawar),
   5,000 ....H 3
Taiwara, 5,000 ....J 3
Tashkurghan, 30,000 ...J 2
Zebak, 3,000 ....K 2

OTHER FEATURES

Chagai (hills) ....H 4
Farah Rud (river) ....H 3

Gaud-i-Zirreh (marsh) ...H 4
Hari Rud (river) ....H 2
Hindu Kush (mts.) ....J 2
Jam (mt.) ....J 3
Kabul (river) ....K 3
Kunar (river) ....K 2
Kunduz (river) ....J 2
Lora (river) ....J 3
Margo, Dasht-i (desert) ...H 3

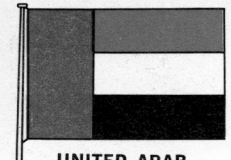

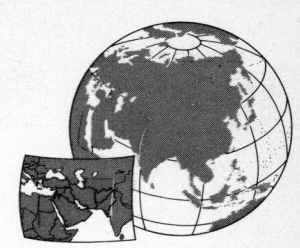

UNITED ARAB EMIRATES

Murghab (river) .... H 2
Namaksar (salt lake) .... H 3
Paropamisus (range) .... H 3
Pyandzh (river) .... K 2
Registan (desert) .... H 3

BAHRAIN

CITIES and TOWNS

Manama (capital),
79,098 .... F 4
Muharraq, 34,430 .... F 4

IRAN

CITIES and TOWNS

Abadan, 272,962 .... E 3
Abadeh, 16,000 .... F 3

Abarquh, 8,000 .... F 3
Ahwaz, 206,375 .... E 3
Amul, 40,076 .... F 2
Anarak, 2,038 .... F 3
Arak, 71,925 .... E 3
Ardebil, 83,596 .... E 2
Ardistan, 6,645 .... F 3
Asterabad (Gurgan),
51,181 .... F 2
Babol, 49,973 .... F 2

Bafq, 5,000 .... G 3
Baft, 6,000 .... G 4
Bahramabad, 21,000 .... G 3
Bam, 22,000 .... G 4
Bandar 'Abbas, 34,627 ...... G 4
Bandar Shah, 13,000 .... F 2
Bandar Shahpur, 6,000 ..... E 3
Barfrush (Babol),
49,973 .... F 2
Birjand, 25,854 .... G 3

Borazjun, 20,000 .... F 4
Bujnurd, 31,248 .... G 2
Burujird, 71,476 .... E 3
Bushire, 26,032 .... F 4
Chalus, 15,000 .... F 2
Damghan, 13,000 .... F 2
Darab, 13,000 .... G 4
Dizful, 84,499 .... E 3
Duzdab (Zahidan),
40,000 .... H 4

(continued on following page)

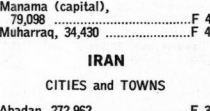

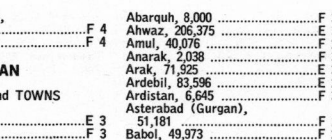

SAUDI ARABIA
AREA 920,000 sq. mi.
POPULATION 7,200,000
CAPITALS Riyadh, Mecca
MONETARY UNIT riyal
MAJOR LANGUAGE Arabic
MAJOR RELIGION Islam

KUWAIT
AREA 8,000 sq. mi.
POPULATION 733,196
CAPITAL Al Kuwait
MONETARY UNIT Kuwaiti dinar
MAJOR LANGUAGE Arabic
MAJOR RELIGION Islam

YEMEN ARAB REPUBLIC
AREA 75,000 sq. mi.
POPULATION 5,000,000
CAPITAL San'a
MONETARY UNIT bakcha
MAJOR LANGUAGE Arabic
MAJOR RELIGION Islam

PEOPLES DEMOCRATIC REPUBLIC OF YEMEN
AREA 111,075 sq. mi.
POPULATION 1,220,000
CAPITAL Aden
MONETARY UNIT East African shilling
MAJOR LANGUAGE Arabic
MAJOR RELIGION Islam

BAHRAIN
AREA 231 sq. mi.
POPULATION 207,000
CAPITAL Manama
MONETARY UNIT Bahrain dinar
MAJOR LANGUAGE Arabic
MAJOR RELIGION Islam

QATAR
AREA 8,500 sq. mi.
POPULATION 100,000
CAPITAL Doha
MONETARY UNIT Qatar-Dubai riyal
MAJOR LANGUAGE Arabic
MAJOR RELIGION Islam

UNITED ARAB EMIRATES
AREA 31,628 sq. mi.
POPULATION 155,881
CAPITAL Abu Dhabi
MONETARY UNIT rupee, Bahrain dinar, Qatar-Dubai riyal
MAJOR LANGUAGE Arabic
MAJOR RELIGION Islam

OMAN
AREA 82,000 sq. mi.
POPULATION 565,000
CAPITAL Muscat
MONETARY UNIT rial saidi
MAJOR LANGUAGE Arabic
MAJOR RELIGION Islam

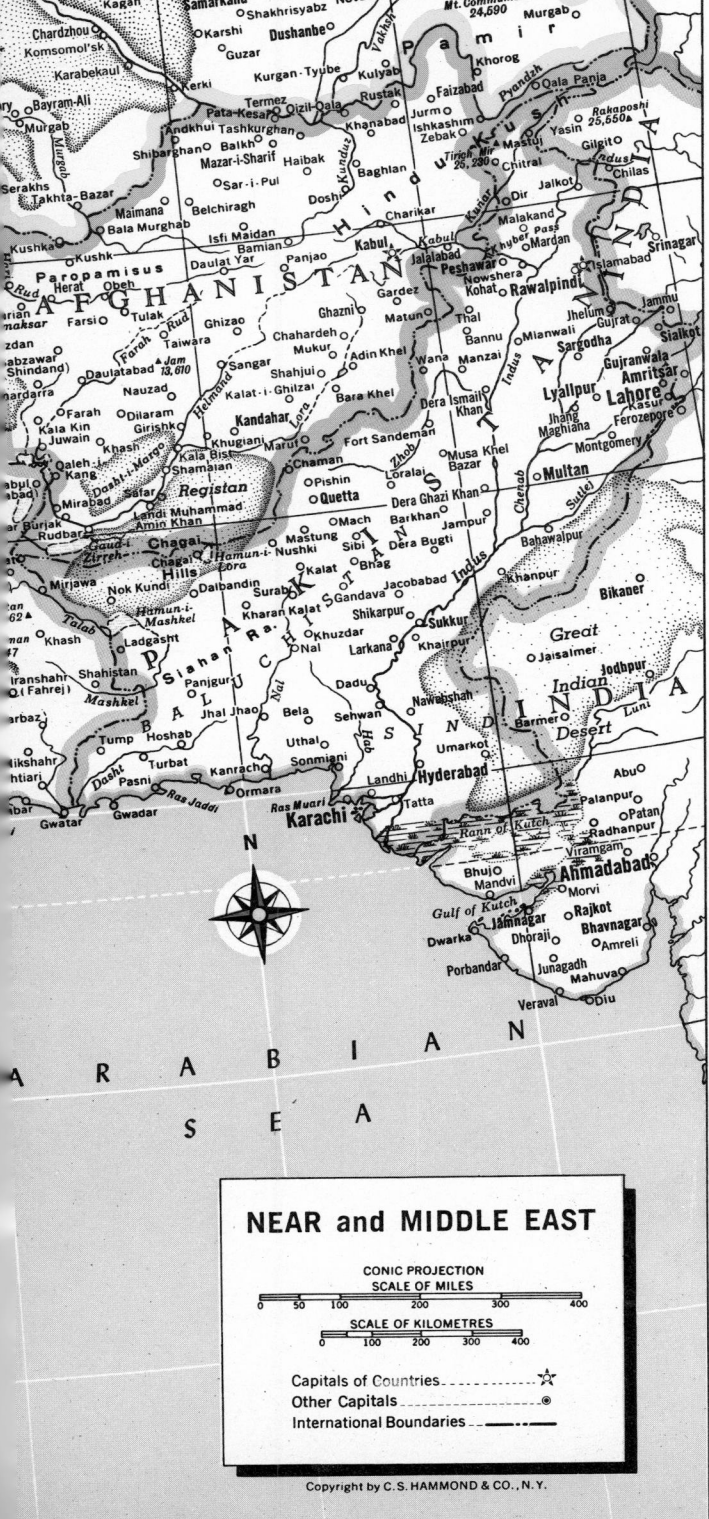

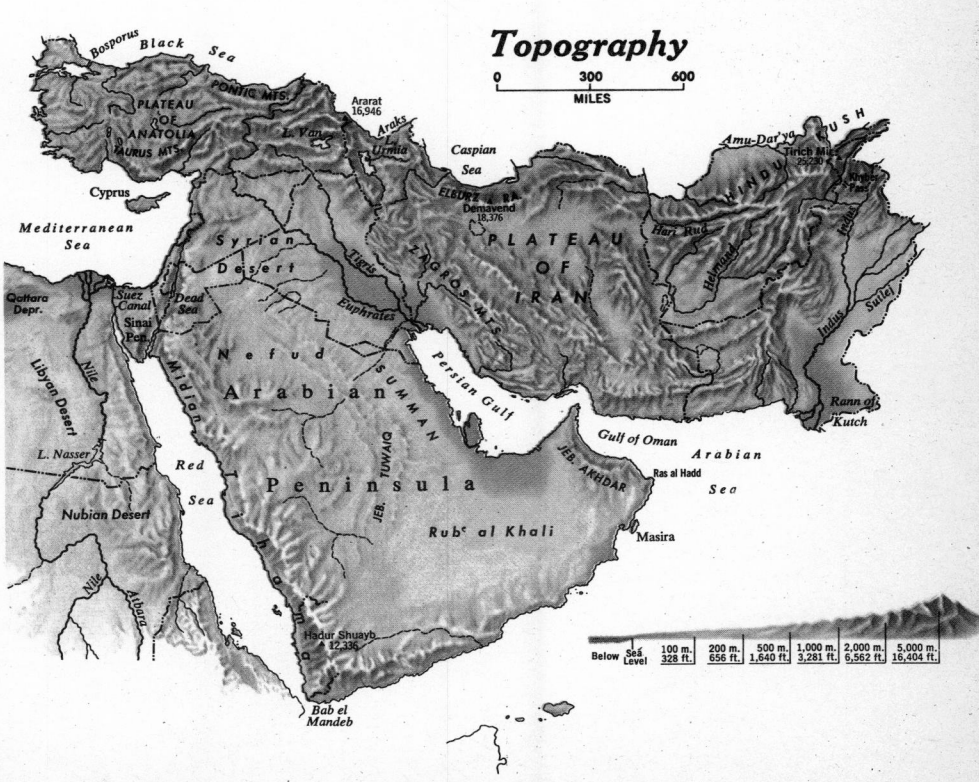

Topography

0   300   600
MILES

NEAR and MIDDLE EAST

CONIC PROJECTION
SCALE OF MILES
0   50   100   200   300   400

SCALE OF KILOMETRES
0   100   200   300   400

Capitals of Countries ---------- ☆
Other Capitals ---------------- ◉
International Boundaries --------

Below Sea Level | Sea Level | 100 m. 328 ft. | 200 m. 656 ft. | 500 m. 1,640 ft. | 1,000 m. 3,281 ft. | 2,000 m. 6,562 ft. | 5,000 m. 16,404 ft.

IRAN (continued)

Enzeli (Pahlevi), 41,785 E 2
Estahbanat, 18,187 F 4
Fahrej (Iranshahr), 5,000 H 4
Fasa, 19,000 F 4
Firdaus, 11,000 G 3
Gach Saran F 3
Garmsar, 4,723 F 2
Gulpaigan, 20,515 F 3
Gunabad, 8,000 G 3
Gurgan, 51,181 F 2
Hamadan, 124,167 E 3
Iranshahr, 5,000 H 4
Isfahan, 424,045 F 3
Jahrum, 38,236 F 4
Juimand (Gunabad), 8,000 G 3
Kangavar, 9,414 E 3
Kashan, 58,468 F 3
Kashmar, 17,000 G 2
Kazerun, 39,758 F 4
Kazvin, 88,106 E 2
Kerman, 85,404 G 3
Kermanshah, 187,930 E 3
Khaf, 5,000 H 3
Khoi, 47,648 E 2
Khorramshahr, 88,536 E 3
Khur, 2,912 G 3
Khurramabad, 59,578 E 3
Lar, 22,000 F 4
Mahabad, 28,610 E 2
Maragheh, 54,106 E 2
Marand, 24,000 E 2
Meshed, 409,616 H 2
Mianeh, 28,447 E 2
Mirjawa, 11,000 H 4
Na'in, 5,925 F 3
Naishapur (Nishapur), 33,482 G 2
Nasratabad (Zabul), 20,000 H 3
Natanz, 4,370 F 3
Nehavend, 24,000 E 3
Nejafabad, 43,384 F 3
Nishapur, 33,482 G 2
Pahlevi, 41,785 E 2
Qain, 6,000 G 3
Quchan, 29,133 G 2
Qum, 134,292 F 3
Ravar, 7,000 G 3
Resht, 143,557 E 2
Reza'iyeh, 110,749 D 2
Sabzawar, 42,415 G 2
Sabzawaran, 7,000 G 4
Samnan, 31,058 F 2
Sanandaj, 54,578 E 2
Saqqiz, 17,000 E 2
Sari, 44,547 F 2
Saveh, 17,565 F 2
Shahr-i-Tajan (Sari), 44,547 F 2
Shahriza, 34,220 F 3
Shahrud, 30,767 G 2
Shahsawar, 12,000 F 2
Shiraz, 269,865 F 4
Shirvan, 11,000 G 2
Shushtar, 24,000 E 3
Sirjan, 12,160 G 4
Sultanabad (Arak), 71,925 E 3
Sultanabad (Kashmar), 17,000 G 2
Susangird, 21,000 E 3
Tabas (Tabas-Masina), 10,000 H 3
Tabriz, 403,413 E 2
Tehran (capital), 2,719,730 F 2
Tun (Firdaus), 11,000 G 3
Turbat-i-Haidari, 30,106 G 2
Turbat-i-Shaikh Jam, 13,000 H 2
Turshiz (Kashmar), 17,000 G 2
Turun G 2
Urmia (Reza'iyeh), 110,749 D 2
Yezd, 93,241 F 3
Zabul, 20,000 H 3
Zahidan, 39,732 H 4
Zarand, 5,000 G 3
Zenjan, 58,714 E 2

OTHER FEATURES

Araks (river) E 2
Atrek (river) G 2
Bazman, Kuh-i-(mt.) H 4
Demavend (mt.) F 2
Diz, Ab-i- (river) E 3
Elburz (mts.) F 2
Galvkhaneh (lake) F 3
Gurgan (river) F 2
Haliri (river) G 4
Jaz Murian, Hamun-i- (marsh) G 4
Karun (river) E 3
Kavir, Dasht-i- (salt desert) G 3
Kavir-i-Namak (salt desert) G 3
Lut, Dasht-i- (desert) G 3
Maidani, Ras (cape) G 4
Mand Rud (river) F 4
Mashkel (river) H 4
Mehran (river) F 4
Namak, Darya-i- (salt lake) F 3
Namaksar (salt lake) H 3
Namakzar (marsh) G 3
Nezwar (mt.) F 2
Oman (gulf) G 5
Persian (gulf) F 4
Qais (isl.) F 4
Qishm (isl.) G 4
Qizil Uzun (river) E 2
Safidar, Kuh-i- (mt.) F 4
Shaikh Shu'aib (isl.) F 4
Shir (mt.) F 3
Taftan (mt.) H 4
Talab (river) H 4
Tashk (lake) F 4
Urmia (lake) E 2
Zagros (mts.) E 3

IRAQ

CITIES and TOWNS

Al 'Aziziya, 7,450 E 3
Al Falluja, 38,072 D 3
Al Musaiyib, 15,955 E 3
Al Qurna, 5,638 E 3
'Amadiya, 2,578 D 2
'Amara, 64,847 E 3
An Najaf, 128,096 D 3
An Nasiriya, 60,405 E 3
'Ana, 6,884 D 3
Ar Rahhaliya D 3
Arbela (Erbil), 90,320 D 2
As Salman, 1,789 E 3
Baghdad (capital), 502,503 E 3
Baghdad, *1,745,328 E 3
Ba'quba, 34,575 D 3
Basra, 313,327 E 3
Erbil, 90,320 D 2
Habbaniya, 14,405 D 3
Haditha, 6,870 D 3
Hai, 16,988 E 3
Hilla, 84,717 D 3
Hit, 9,131 D 3
Karbala', 83,301 D 3
Khanaqin, 23,522 D 3
Kirkuk, 167,413 D 2
Kut, 42,116 E 3
Maidan, 354 E 3
Mosul, 315,157 D 2
Qal'a Sharqat, 2,434 D 2
Ramadi, 28,723 D 3
Rutba, 5,091 D 3
Samarra, 24,746 D 3
Samawa, 33,473 D 3
Shithatha, 2,326 D 3
Sulaimaniya, 86,822 E 2
Tikrit, 9,921 D 3

OTHER FEATURES

Al Batin, Wadi (river) E 4
'Aneiza, Jebel (mt.) C 3
'Ar'ar, Wadi (dry river) D 3
El Hamad (desert) D 3
Euphrates (river) E 3
Hauran, Wadi (dry river) D 3
Mesopotamia (reg.) D 3
Tigris (river) E 3

KUWAIT

CITIES and TOWNS

Al Kuwait (capital), 80,008 E 4
Al Kuwait, *217,364 E 4
Mina al-Ahmadi E 4

OTHER FEATURES

Bubiyan (isl.) E 4
Persian (gulf) E 4

OMAN

CITIES and TOWNS

Adam G 5
Buraimi G 5
Dhank G 5
Ibra G 5
'Ibri G 5
Juwara G 6
Kamil G 5
Khaluf G 5
Khasab G 4
Manah G 5
Matrah, 15,000 G 5
Mina al Fahal G 5
Murbat G 6
Muscat (capital), 7,500 G 5
Nizwa G 5
Quryat G 5
Risut F 6
Salala, 4,000 F 6
Sarur G 5
Shinas G 5
Sohar G 5
Sur G 5
Suwaiq G 5

OTHER FEATURES

Akhdar, Jebel (range) G 5
Arabian (sea) H 5
Batina (reg.) G 5
Dhofar (reg.), 120,000 F 6
Hadd, Ras al (cape) G 5
Hallaniya (isl.), 78 G 6
Jibsh, Ras (cape) G 5
Kuria Muria (isls.), 78 G 6
Madraka, Ras (cape) G 6
Masira (gulf) G 6
Masira (isl.) G 5
Musandam, Ras (cape) G 4
Nus, Ras (cape) G 6
Oman (gulf) G 5
Oman (reg.) G 5
Ruus al Jibal (dist.) G 4
Sauqira (bay) G 6
Sauqira, Ras (cape) G 6
Sham, Jebel (mt.) G 5
Sharbatat, Ras (cape) G 6

QATAR

CITIES and TOWNS

Doha (capital), 45,000 F 4
Dukhan, 2,500 F 4
Umm Sa'id, 3,500 F 5

OTHER FEATURES

Persian (gulf) F 4
Rakan, Ras (cape) F 4

SAUDI ARABIA

PROVINCES

'Asir, 900,000 D 6
Eastern, 2,250,000 E 4
Hejaz, 1,250,000 C 4
Nejd, 1,500,000 D 4

CITIES and TOWNS

Abha D 6
Abqaiq E 4
Abu 'Arish D 6
Abu Hadriya E 4
'Ain al Mubarrak C 5
Al 'Ain C 5
Al 'Ala C 4
Al 'Auda E 4
Al Lith C 5
Al Muadhdham C 4
Al Qahm D 6
'Anaiza D 4
Artawiya D 4
Badr C 5
Buraida D 4
Buraimi G 5
Dam D 5
Dammam, 3,000 F 4
Dar al Hamra C 4
Dhaba C 4
Dhahran, 12,500 E 4
Dharma D 5
Dilam E 5
Doqa D 6
Duwadami D 5
Er Ras D 4
Faid D 4
Haddar D 5
Hadiya C 4
Hafar al Batin E 4
Hail, 20,000 D 4
Halli D 6
Hamar E 5
Hanakiya D 5
Haql C 4
Haradh E 5
Haraja D 6
Hariq E 5
Hauta E 5
Hofuf, 83,000 E 4
Jabrin E 5
Jauf, 5,000 C 4
Jidda, 194,000 C 5
Jubail E 4
Jubba D 4
Junaina D 5
Kaf C 3
Khaibar D 4
Khamis Mushait D 6
Khurma D 5
Khurs E 5
Laila E 5
Majma'a D 4
Maqna C 4
Mastaba C 5
Mastura C 5
Mecca (capital), 185,000 C 5
Medain Salih C 4
Medina, 72,000 C 5
Mendak D 5
Mina Sa'ud E 4
Mubarraz E 4
Mudhnib D 4
Muwailih C 4
Najran D 6
Nisab D 4
Oqair E 4
Qadhima C 5
Qafar D 4
Qasr al Haiyanya D 4
Qatif E 4
Qizan D 6
Qunfidha D 6
Qusaiba D 4
Rabigh C 5
Ras Tanura F 4
Riyadh (capital), 225,000 E 5
Rumaihiya E 4
Sabya D 6
Saihat E 4
Sakaka D 4
Salwa E 5
Shaqra D 4
Shuqaiq D 6
Sufeina D 5
Sulaiyil E 5
Taif, 54,000 D 5
Taima C 4
Tamra D 5
Tebuk C 4
Truba D 5
Turaba D 5
Umm Lajj C 4
Wejh C 4
Yamama E 5
Yenbo C 5
Zilfi E 4

OTHER FEATURES

Abu-mad (cape) C 5
'Ar'ar, Wadi (dry river) D 3
Al Ahqaf (Bahr es Safi) (desert) E 6
'Aneiza, Jebel (mt.) C 3
'Aqaba (gulf) C 4
Arafat, Jebel (mt.) C 5
Ar'ar, Wadi (dry river) D 3
Arma (plateau) E 4
Aswad, Ras al (cape) C 5
Bahr es Safi (desert) E 6
Barida, Ras (cape) C 5
Bisha, Wadi (dry river) D 5
Dahana (desert) E 4
Dawasir, Wadi (dry river) E 5
Dawasir, Hadb (range) D 5
Farasan (isls.) D 6
Hasa (reg.) E 4
Hatiba, Ras (cape) C 5
Jafura (desert) F 5
Mashabi (isl.) C 4
Midian (district) C 4
Misha'ab, Ras (cape) E 4
Nefud (desert) D 4
Nefud Dahi (desert) D 5
Persian (gulf) F 4
Ranya, Wadi (dry river) D 5
Red (Nefud) (desert) D 4
Red (sea) C 5
Rima, Wadi (river) D 4
Rimal, Ar (desert) F 5
Rub' al Khali (desert) F 5
Safaniya, Ras (cape) E 4
Salma, Jebel (mts.) D 4
Shaibara (isl.) C 4
Shammar, Jebel (plateau) D 4
Sirhan, Wadi (dry river) C 3
Subh, Jebel (mt.) C 5
Summan (plateau) E 4
Tihama (reg.) C 5
Tiran (isl.) B 4
Tiran (str.) B 4
Tuwaiq, Jebel (range) E 5

UNITED ARAB EMIRATES

CITIES and TOWNS

Abu Dhabi (capital), 22,000 F 5
Abu Dhabi, *35,000 F 5
'Ajman, 3,725 G 4
'Arada F 5
Buraimi G 5
Dubai, 13,092 F 4
Dubai, *57,400 F 4
Fujairah, 761 G 4
Jebel Dhanna F 5
Ras al Khaimah, 5,244 F 4
Sharjah, 19,198 F 4
Sharjah, *20,621 F 4
Umm al Qaiwain, 2,928 F 4

OTHER FEATURES

Das (isl.) F 4
Persian (gulf) F 4
Yas (isl.) F 5
Zirko (isl.) F 5

YEMEN ARAB REP.

CITIES and TOWNS

'Amran D 6
Bait al Faqih D 7
Dhamar D 7
Harib E 6
Hodeida, 40,000 D 7
Huth D 6
Ibb D 7
Luhaiya (Loheia) D 6
Maida, 2,500 D 6
Manakha D 6
Marib D 6
Mocha D 7
Sa'ada D 6
Safir E 6
San'a (capital), 100,000 D 6
Sheikh Sa'id D 7
Ta'izz, 80,000 D 7
Yarim, 5,000 D 7
Zabid, 8,000 D 7

OTHER FEATURES

Hanish (isls.) D 7
Manar, Jebel (mt.) D 7
Red (sea) C 5
Sabir, Jebel (mt.) D 7
Tihama (reg.) C 5
Zuqar (isl.) D 7

YEMEN, PEOPLES DEM. REPUBLIC OF

CITIES and TOWNS

Aden (capital), 150,000 E 7
Aden, *225,000 E 7
Ahwar E 7
Al Qatn E 6
Balhaf E 7
Bir 'Ali E 7
Damqut F 6
'Einat E 6
Ghaida F 6
Hadibu F 7
Hajarain E 6
Haura E 6
Hureidha E 6
'Irqa E 7
Lahej E 7
Leijun E 6
Lodar E 7
Madinat ash Sha'b, 29,897 E 7
Maqatin E 7
Meifa E 7
Mukalla, 30,000 E 7
Nisab E 7
Nuqub E 6
Qishn F 6
Riyan E 7
Saihut, 10,000 F 6
Seiyun E 6
Shabwa E 6
Shibam, 6,000 E 6
Shihr E 7
Shuqra E 7
Taburkum E 6
Tarim E 6
Yeshbum E 6
Zinjibar E 7

OTHER FEATURES

Fartak, Ras (cape) F 6
Hadhramaut (dist.), 350,000 E 7
Hadhramaut, Wadi (dry river) F 7
Kamaran (island), 2,200 D 6
Mandeb, Bab el (strait) D 7
Perim (isl.), 381 D 7
Socotra (island), 14,000 F 7

*City and suburbs.

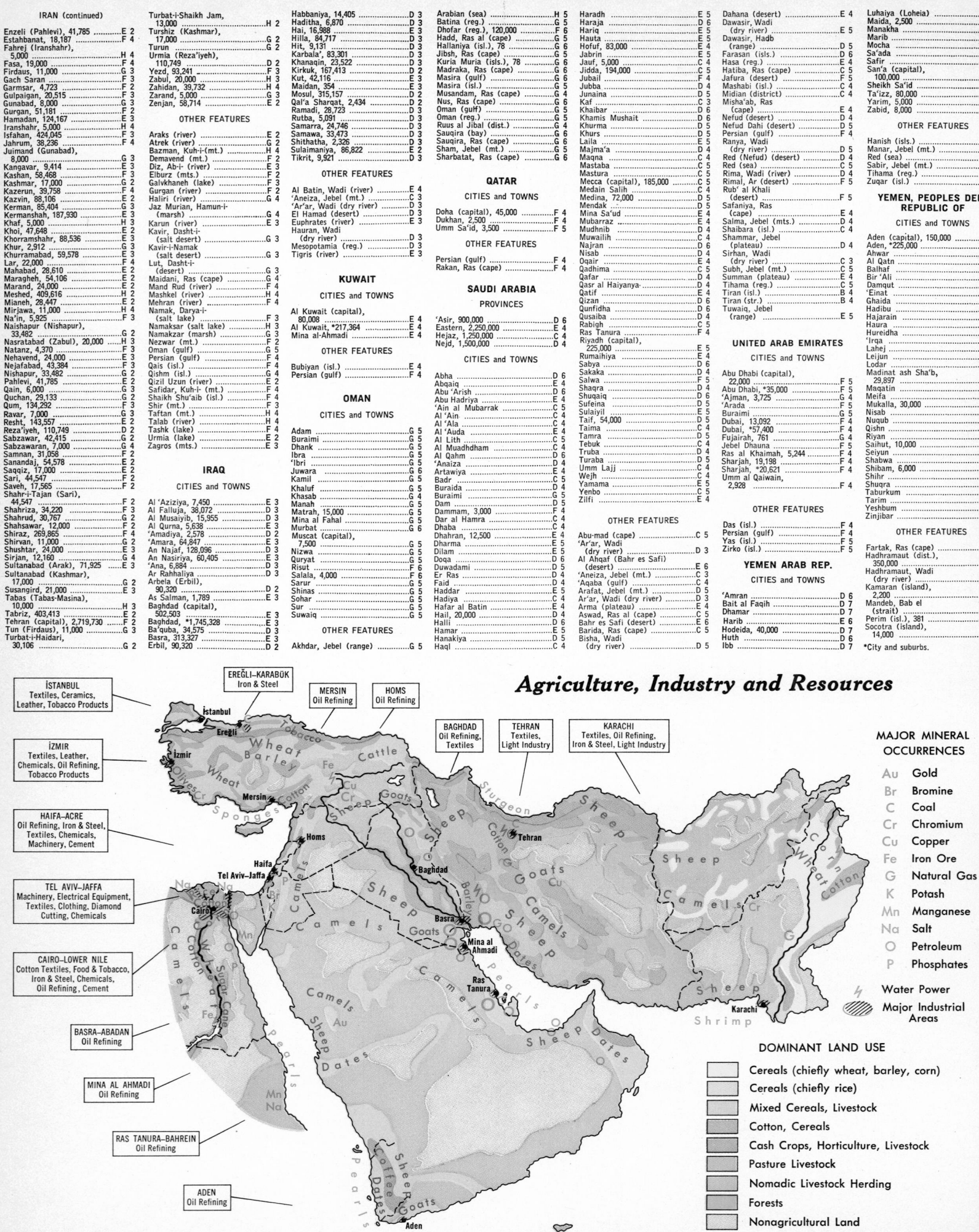

Agriculture, Industry and Resources

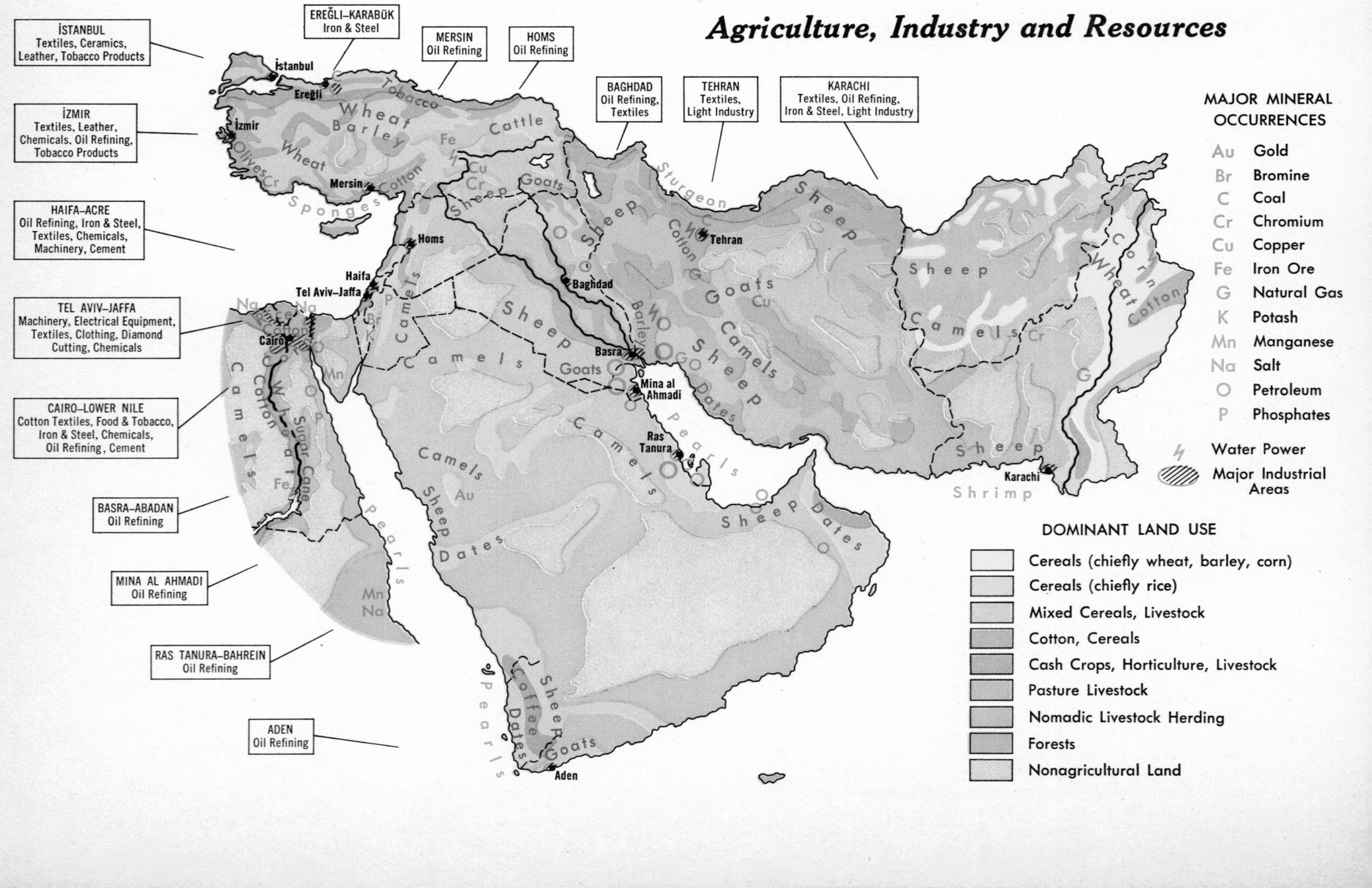

İSTANBUL
Textiles, Ceramics, Leather, Tobacco Products
EREĞLI–KARABÜK
Iron & Steel
MERSIN
Oil Refining
HOMS
Oil Refining
BAGHDAD
Oil Refining, Textiles
TEHRAN
Textiles, Light Industry
KARACHI
Textiles, Oil Refining, Iron & Steel, Light Industry
İZMIR
Textiles, Leather, Chemicals, Oil Refining, Tobacco Products
HAIFA–ACRE
Oil Refining, Iron & Steel, Textiles, Chemicals, Machinery, Cement
TEL AVIV–JAFFA
Machinery, Electrical Equipment, Textiles, Clothing, Chemicals
CAIRO–LOWER NILE
Cotton Textiles, Food & Tobacco, Iron & Steel, Chemicals, Oil Refining, Cement
BASRA–ABADAN
Oil Refining
MINA AL AHMADI
Oil Refining
RAS TANURA–BAHREIN
Oil Refining
ADEN
Oil Refining
İstanbul
Ereğli
İzmir
Mersin
Homs
Haifa
Tel Aviv–Jaffa
Cairo
Baghdad
Tehran
Basra
Mina al Ahmadi
Ras Tanura
Karachi
Aden
Wheat
Barley
Tobacco
Cattle
Olives
Sponges
Cotton
Sheep
Goats
Camels
Sturgeon
Dates
Pearls
Sugar Cane
Corn
Rice
Coffee
Shrimp
MAJOR MINERAL OCCURRENCES
Au Gold
Br Bromine
C Coal
Cr Chromium
Cu Copper
Fe Iron Ore
G Natural Gas
K Potash
Mn Manganese
Na Salt
O Petroleum
P Phosphates
Water Power
Major Industrial Areas
DOMINANT LAND USE
Cereals (chiefly wheat, barley, corn)
Cereals (chiefly rice)
Mixed Cereals, Livestock
Cotton, Cereals
Cash Crops, Horticulture, Livestock
Pasture Livestock
Nomadic Livestock Herding
Forests
Nonagricultural Land

TURKEY

SYRIA

LEBANON

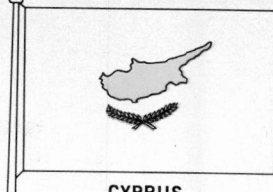
CYPRUS

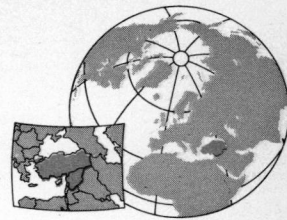

TURKEY
AREA 301,381 sq. mi.
POPULATION 34,375,000
CAPITAL Ankara
LARGEST CITY İstanbul (greater)
HIGHEST POINT Ararat 16,914 ft.
MONETARY UNIT Turkish pound (lira)
MAJOR LANGUAGE Turkish
MAJOR RELIGION Islam

SYRIA
AREA 71,498 sq. mi.
POPULATION 5,866,000
CAPITAL Damascus
LARGEST CITY Damascus
HIGHEST POINT Hermon 9,232 ft.
MONETARY UNIT Syrian pound
MAJOR LANGUAGES Arabic, Kurdish, Armenian
MAJOR RELIGIONS Islam, Christianity

LEBANON
AREA 4,015 sq. mi.
POPULATION 2,800,000
CAPITAL Beirut
LARGEST CITY Beirut
HIGHEST POINT Qurnet es Sauda 10,131 ft.
MONETARY UNIT Lebanese pound
MAJOR LANGUAGE Arabic
MAJOR RELIGIONS Christianity, Islam

CYPRUS
AREA 3,473 sq. mi.
POPULATION 649,000
CAPITAL Nicosia
LARGEST CITY Nicosia
HIGHEST POINT Troodos 6,406 ft.
MONETARY UNIT Cypriot pound
MAJOR LANGUAGES Greek, Turkish
MAJOR RELIGIONS Eastern (Greek) Orthodoxy, Islam

CYPRUS
CITIES and TOWNS

Famagusta, 38,000 .....F 5
Famagusta, *41,000 .....F 5
Kyrenia, 3,500 .....E 5
Kyrenia, *4,500 .....E 5
Larnaca, 20,000 .....E 5
Larnaca, *21,000 .....E 5
Lefka, 3,673 .....E 5
Lefkara, 2,075 .....E 5
Limassol, 46,500 .....E 5
Limassol, *50,000 .....E 5
Morphou, 6,642 .....E 5
Nicosia (capital), 47,000 .....E 5
Nicosia, *112,000 .....E 5
Paphos, 10,000 .....E 5
Paphos, *11,500 .....E 5
Yialousa, 2,541 .....F 5

OTHER FEATURES

Andreas (cape) .....F 5
Arnauti (cape) .....E 5
Famagusta (bay) .....F 5
Gata (cape) .....E 5
Greco (cape) .....F 5
Klides (isls.) .....F 5
Kormakiti (cape) .....E 5
Larnaca (bay) .....E 5
Morphou (bay) .....E 5
Sovereign Base Area, 3,602 .....E 5
Troodos (mt.) .....E 5

LEBANON
CITIES and TOWNS

'Aleih, 18,630 .....F 6
Amyun, 7,926 .....G 5
Ba'albek, 15,560 .....G 5
Batrun, 5,976 .....F 5
Beirut (capital), 700,000 .....F 6
Beirut, *840,000 .....F 6
En Naqura, 967 .....F 6
Hermil, 2,652 .....G 5

Merj 'Uyun, 9,318 .....F 6
Rasheiya, 6,731 .....F 6
Rayak, 1,480 .....G 6
Saida (Saida), 32,200 .....F 6
Sidon (Saida), 32,200 .....F 6
Sur, 16,483 .....F 6
Tarabulus (Tripoli), 127,611 .....F 5
Tyre (Sur), 16,483 .....F 6
Zahle, 53,121 .....F 6
Zegharta, 18,210 .....G 5

OTHER FEATURES

Hermon (mt.) .....F 6
Lebanon (range) .....F 6
Litani (Leontes) (river) .....F 6
Sauda, Qurnet es (mt.) .....G 5

SYRIA
GOVERNORATES

Aleppo, 1,131,854 .....G 4
Damascus, 1,060,484 .....G 6
Damascus (municipality), 630,063 .....G 6
Deir ez Zor, 286,010 .....H 5
Der'a, 221,275 .....G 6
El Quneitra, 6,396 .....F 6
Es Suweida, 151,500 .....G 6
Hama, 390,084 .....G 5
Haseke, 309,279 .....J 4
Homs, 504,098 .....G 5
Idlib, 374,751 .....G 5
Latakia, 625,473 .....G 5
Rashid, 124,876 .....H 5

CITIES and TOWNS

Abu Kemal, 6,907 .....J 5
Aleppo, 566,770 .....G 4
A'zaz, 13,923 .....G 4
Baniyas, 8,537 .....F 5
Damascus (cap.), 789,840 .....G 6
Deir ez Zor, 60,335 .....H 5
Der'a, 20,465 .....G 6

Dimishq (Damascus) (capital), 789,840 .....G 6
Duma, 30,050 .....G 6
El Bab, 27,366 .....G 4
El Haseke, 23,074 .....J 4
El Ladhiqiya (Latakia), 72,378 .....F 5
El Quneitra, 206 .....F 6
El Rashid, 11,998 .....H 5
En Nebk, 16,334 .....G 6
Es Suweida, 17,592 .....G 6
Haleb (Aleppo), 566,770 .....G 4
Hama, 196,224 .....G 5
Harim, 6,837 .....G 4
Homs, 231,877 .....G 5
Idlib, 37,501 .....F 5
Jeble, 15,715 .....F 5
Jerablus, 8,610 .....G 4
Jisr esh Shughur, 13,131 .....G 5
Latakia, 72,378 .....F 5
Masyaf, 7,058 .....G 5
Membij, 13,796 .....G 4
Meyadin, 12,515 .....J 5
Palmyra (Tadmor), 10,670 .....H 5
Qamishliye, 31,448 .....J 4
Quteife, 4,993 .....G 6
Raqqa (El Rashid), 11,998 .....H 5
Safita, 9,650 .....G 5
Selemiya, 25,728 .....G 5
Tadmor, 10,670 .....H 5
Tartus, 19,137 .....F 5
Zebdani, 10,010 .....G 6

OTHER FEATURES

'Abdul 'Aziz, Jebel (mts.) .....J 4
Abu Rujmein, Jebel (mts.) .....H 5
'Asi (river) .....G 5
Druz, Jebel ed (mts.) .....G 6
Euphrates (El Furat) (river) .....J 5
Furat, El (river) .....H 4
Hermon (mt.) .....F 6
Khabur (river) .....J 5
Orontes ('Asi) (river) .....G 5
Ruad (island) .....F 5
Sharqi, Jebel esh (range) .....G 5
Tigris (river) .....K 4

TURKEY
PROVINCES

Adana, 902,712 .....F 4
Adıyaman, 267,288 .....H 4
Afyon-Karahisar, 502,248 .....D 3
Ağrı, 246,961 .....K 3
Amasya, 285,729 .....F 2
Ankara, 1,644,302 .....E 3
Antalya, 486,910 .....D 4
Artvin, 210,065 .....J 2
Aydın, 524,918 .....B 4
Balıkesir, 708,342 .....B 3
Bilecik, 139,041 .....D 2
Bingöl, 150,521 .....J 3
Bitlis, 154,069 .....J 3
Bolu, 383,939 .....D 2
Burdur, 194,950 .....D 4
Bursa, 755,504 .....C 2
Çanakkale, 350,317 .....B 2
Çankırı, 250,706 .....E 2
Çorum, 485,567 .....F 2
Denizli, 463,369 .....C 4
Diyarbakır, 475,916 .....H 4
Edirne, 303,234 .....B 2
Elâzığ, 322,727 .....H 3
Erzincan, 258,586 .....H 3
Erzurum, 628,001 .....J 3
Eskişehir, 415,101 .....D 3
Gaziantep, 511,026 .....G 4
Giresun, 428,615 .....H 2
Gümüşhane, 262,731 .....H 2
Hakkâri, 83,937 .....K 4
Hatay, 506,154 .....G 4
İçel, 511,273 .....F 4
Isparta, 266,240 .....D 4
İstanbul, 2,293,823 .....C 2
İzmir, 1,234,667 .....B 3
Kars, 606,313 .....K 2
Kastamonu, 441,638 .....E 2
Kayseri, 536,206 .....F 3
Kırklareli, 258,386 .....B 2
Kırşehir, 196,836 .....F 3
Kocaeli, 335,518 .....D 2
Konya, 1,122,622 .....E 4
Kütahya, 398,081 .....C 3

Malatya, 452,624 .....H 3
Manisa, 748,545 .....B 3
Maraş, 438,423 .....G 4
Mardin, 397,880 .....J 4
Muğla, 334,973 .....C 4
Muş, 198,716 .....J 3
Nevşehir, 203,316 .....F 3
Niğde, 362,044 .....F 3
Ordu, 543,863 .....G 2
Rize, 281,099 .....J 2
Sakarya, 404,078 .....D 2
Samsun, 755,946 .....F 2
Siirt, 264,832 .....J 4
Sinop, 266,069 .....F 2
Sivas, 705,186 .....G 3
Tekirdağ, 287,381 .....B 2
Tokat, 495,352 .....G 2
Trabzon, 595,782 .....H 2
Tunceli, 154,175 .....H 3
Urfa, 450,798 .....H 4
Uşak, 190,536 .....C 3
Van, 266,840 .....K 3
Yozgat, 437,883 .....F 3
Zonguldak, 650,191 .....D 2

CITIES and TOWNS

Abana, 2,455 .....F 1
Acıgol, 3,265 .....F 3
Acıpayam, 4,118 .....C 4
Adalia (Antalya), 71,833 .....D 4
Adana, 289,919 .....F 4
Adapazarı, 86,124 .....D 2
Adilcevaz, 6,148 .....J 3
Adıyaman, 22,153 .....H 4
Afşin, 8,069 .....G 3
Afyon, 44,026 .....D 3
Ağlasun, 3,730 .....D 4
Ağrı, 3,425 .....K 3
Ağrı (Karaköse), 24,168 .....K 3
Ahlat, 5,879 .....J 3
Akçaabat, 7,600 .....H 2
Akçadağ, 5,995 .....H 3
Akçakale, 4,526 .....H 4
Akçakoca, 7,179 .....D 2
Akdağmadeni, 4,321 .....F 3
Akhisar, 46,167 .....B 3
Aksaray, 24,414 .....F 3

Akşehir, 25,269 .....D 3
Akseki, 2,505 .....D 4
Akviran, 3,786 .....D 2
Akyazı, 9,090 .....D 2
Alaca, 8,288 .....F 2
Alaçam, 7,833 .....F 2
Alanya, 12,436 .....D 4
Alaşehir, 16,012 .....C 3
Alexandretta (İskenderun), 69,382 .....G 4
Aliağa, 3,087 .....B 3
Alibeyköyü, 15,199 .....D 6
Almus, 4,110 .....G 2
Alpu, 2,709 .....D 3
Altındağ, 89,838 .....E 2
Altınova, 6,368 .....B 3
Altıntaş, 2,361 .....C 3
Amasya, 34,168 .....F 2
Anadoluhisari, 13,959 .....D 6
Anamur, 11,246 .....E 4
Andırın, 3,695 .....G 3
Ankara (capital), 905,660 .....E 3
Antâkya, 57,855 .....G 4
Antalya, 71,833 .....D 4
Araç, 2,820 .....E 2
Aralık, 2,879 .....L 3
Arapkir, 7,056 .....H 3
Ardahan, 9,117 .....K 2
Ardeşen, 5,488 .....J 2
Arnavutköy, 22,468 .....D 6
Arsin, 4,028 .....H 2
Artova, 2,863 .....G 2
Artvin, 9,847 .....J 2
Aşkale, 6,943 .....J 3
Aslanköy, 3,656 .....F 4
Avanos, 5,675 .....F 3
Ayancık, 5,320 .....F 2
Ayas, 3,873 .....E 2
Aybastı, 7,450 .....G 2
Aydın, 43,483 .....B 3
Ayvacık, 2,277 .....B 3
Ayvalık, 16,283 .....B 3
Babadağ, 5,511 .....C 4
Babaeski, 13,879 .....B 2
Bafra, 26,239 .....F 2
Bahçe, 2,264 .....G 4
Bakırköy, 65,285 .....D 6

Baklan, 2,680 .....C 4
Balâ, 3,646 .....E 3
Balıkesir, 69,341 .....B 3
Banaz, 3,495 .....C 3
Bandırma, 33,116 .....C 2
Barak, 3,117 .....G 4
Bartın, 14,259 .....E 2
Başkale, 4,007 .....K 3
Başmakçı, 5,093 .....D 4
Batman, 24,990 .....J 4
Bayburt, 15,184 .....H 2
Bayındır, 11,273 .....B 3
Bayramiç, 4,607 .....B 3
Bergama, 24,121 .....B 3
Beşiktaş, 58,814 .....D 6
Besni, 11,625 .....G 4
Beykoz, 37,730 .....D 5
Beylerbeyi, 21,741 .....D 6
Beyoğlu, 39,984 .....D 6
Beypazarı, 9,860 .....D 2
Beyşehir, 7,456 .....D 4
Biga, 12,063 .....B 2
Bigadiç, 4,820 .....C 3
Bilecik, 9,722 .....C 3
Bingöl (Çapakçur), 11,727 .....J 3
Birecik, 15,317 .....H 4
Bismil, 4,444 .....H 4
Bitlis, 18,725 .....J 3
Bodrum, 5,136 .....B 4
Boğazlıyan, 7,925 .....F 3
Bolu, 21,700 .....D 2
Bolvadin, 20,139 .....D 3
Bor, 14,309 .....F 4
Borçka, 3,763 .....J 2
Bornova, 30,445 .....B 3
Boyabat, 9,418 .....F 2
Bozdoğan, 6,739 .....C 4
Bozkır, 3,112 .....E 4
Bozkurt, 2,954 .....F 2
Bozova, 3,425 .....H 4
Bozüyük, 10,842 .....D 3
Bucak, 10,094 .....D 4
Bulancak, 9,343 .....H 2
Bulanık, 6,186 .....K 3
Buldan, 9,813 .....C 3
Bünyan, 8,467 .....F 3
Burdur, 29,268 .....D 4
Burhaniye, 12,597 .....B 3

(continued on following page)

Agriculture, Industry and Resources

DOMINANT LAND USE

- Cereals (chiefly wheat, barley), Livestock
- Cash Crops, Horticulture, Livestock
- Pasture Livestock
- Nomadic Livestock Herding
- Forests
- Nonagricultural Land

MAJOR MINERAL OCCURRENCES

- Ab Asbestos
- C Coal
- Cr Chromium
- Cu Copper
- Fe Iron Ore
- Hg Mercury
- Na Salt
- O Petroleum
- Pb Lead
- Sb Antimony
- Zn Zinc

⚡ Water Power
▨ Major Industrial Areas

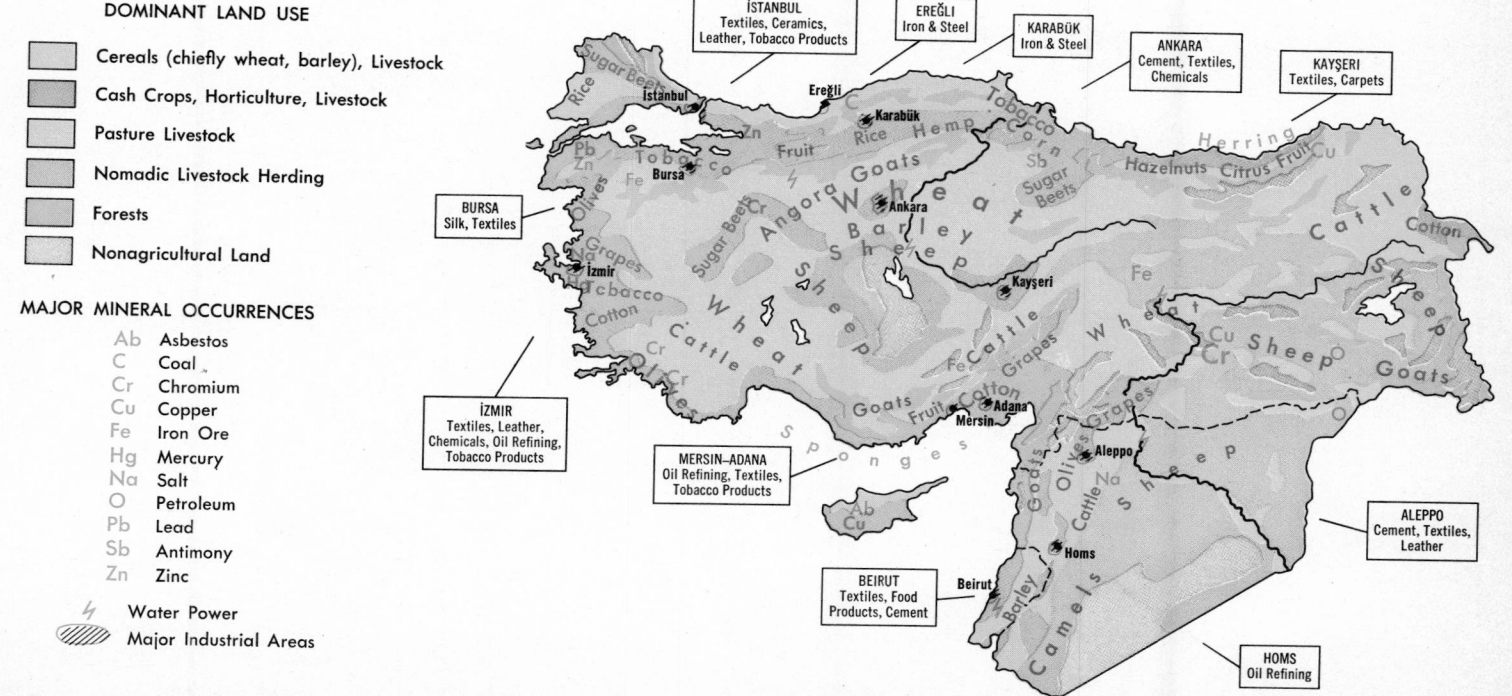

62 Turkey, Syria, Lebanon and Cyprus
(continued)

TURKEY (continued)

Bursa, 211,644	C 2	Çermik, 5,420	H 3
Büyükada, 5,261	D 6	Çeşme, 4,068	A 3
Büyükdere	D 5	Çetinkaya, 2,525	H 3
Çal, 2,925	C 3	Çevizli, 2,580	D 4
Çalköy, 2,232	C 2	Ceyhan, 41,124	F 4
Çan, 5,486	B 2	Ceylanpınar, 12,508	H 4
Çanakkale, 22,789	B 6	Cide, 2,130	E 2
Çandır, 21,450	F 3	Cifteler, 5,901	D 3
Çankaya, 161,804	E 2	Cihanbeyli, 6,739	E 3
Çankırı, 21,450	E 2	Çıldır, 2,040	K 2
Çapakçur, 11,727	J 3	Çimin, 1,405	H 3
Çardak, 2,410	C 6	Çine, 8,271	B 4
Çarşamba, 18,003	F 2	Çivril, 5,780	C 3
Çatalca, 5,811	C 2	Cizre, 8,662	J 4
Çay, 9,761	D 3	Çölemerik, 6,129	K 4
Çayeli, 11,496	J 2	Çorlu, 27,187	B 2
Çayıralan, 4,357	F 3	Çorum, 41,574	F 2
Cebeci, 204,592	E 2	Çubuk, 8,857	E 2
Çekerek, 3,286	F 2	Çukur, 4,045	F 3
Çelikhan, 3,305	H 4	Cumra, 10,299	E 4
Çemişkezek, 2,235	H 3	Darende, 7,643	G 3
Çerkeş, 2,865	E 2	Demirci, 10,050	C 3
Çerkezköy, 5,355	C 2	Demirkent, 3,855	C 4
		Demirköy, 3,309	C 2
		Denizli, 64,331	C 4
		Derik, 6,684	J 4

Derinkuyu, 4,056	F 3
Develi, 13,411	F 3
Devrek, 5,058	D 2
Dicle, 3,577	J 3
Dikili, 5,805	B 3
Dinar, 11,298	C 3
Dirmil, 2,736	C 4
Diváği, 9,160	H 3
Diyadin, 2,934	K 3
Diyarbakır, 102,653	H 4
Doğanbey, 3,058	D 3
Doğanhisar, 5,966	D 3
Doğanşehir, 4,944	G 3
Döger, 2,913	D 3
Doğubayazıt, 8,523	K 3
Dörtyol, 11,595	F 4
Dumlu, 3,416	J 2
Dursunbey, 6,533	C 3
Düzce, 22,274	D 2
Eceabat, 2,842	B 2
Edirne, 46,091	B 2
Edremit, 25,003	B 3
Eğirdir, 8,912	D 4
Elazığ, 78,605	H 3
Elbistan, 13,492	G 3
Eldivan, 3,344	E 2

Eleşkirt, 6,019	K 3
Elmalı, 8,482	C 4
Emet, 4,815	C 3
Emirdağ, 10,914	D 3
Emirgazi, 3,509	E 3
Enez, 1,808	B 2
Erbaa, 11,300	F 2
Erciş, 14,072	K 3
Erdek, 7,813	B 2
Erdemli, 10,304	F 4
Ereğli, 38,362	F 4
Ereğli, 18,978	D 2
Erenköy, 35,980	D 6
Ergani, 10,528	H 3
Erkilet, 3,223	F 3
Ermenak, 8,017	E 4
Eruh, 3,298	K 4
Erzin, 10,257	G 4
Erzincan, 45,197	H 3
Erzurum, 105,317	J 3
Eskimalatya, 4,244	H 3
Eskişehir, 173,882	D 3
Esme, 5,035	C 3
Espiye, 5,318	H 2
Eynesil, 5,210	H 2
Eyüp, 58,244	D 6

Ezbider, 3,185	H 3
Ezine, 7,819	B 3
Fakıl, 3,377	D 6
Fatih, 71,965	D 6
Fatsa, 9,738	G 2
Feke, 3,030	F 4
Fethiye, 8,386	C 4
Fevzipaşa, 3,917	G 4
Fındıklı, 3,928	J 2
Finike, 4,352	C 4
Foça, 2,953	B 3
Gallipoli, 12,945	B 2
Gaziantep, 160,152	G 4
Gaziapaşa, 3,524	E 4
Gebze, 9,269	D 2
Gediz, 7,486	C 3
Gelibolu (Gallipoli), 12,945	B 2
Gemerek, 4,660	G 3
Gemlik, 15,716	C 2
Genç, 3,114	J 3
Genezin, 4,691	F 3
Gerçüş, 2,593	J 4
Gerede, 6,677	E 2
Germencik, 7,344	B 4
Gerze, 5,387	F 2
Gevaş, 4,019	K 3

Geyve, 5,001	D 2
Giresun, 25,331	H 2
Göksun, 4,511	G 3
Gölbaşı, 5,044	G 3
Gölcük, 21,544	D 2
Göle, 3,826	K 2
Gölhisar, 5,562	C 4
Gölköy, 5,852	G 2
Gölmarmara, 8,301	C 3
Gölpazarı, 3,960	D 2
Gönen, 11,666	C 2
Gördes, 5,665	C 3
Görele, 5,687	H 2
Göynük, 2,084	D 2
Güdül, 4,385	E 2
Gülnar, 4,983	E 4
Gülşehir, 3,549	F 3
Gümüş, 2,949	F 2
Gümüşhacıköy, 10,199	F 2
Gümüşhane, 8,092	H 2
Güney, 7,416	C 3
Gürün, 6,374	G 3
Hacıbektaş, 3,739	F 3
Hacılar, 10,149	F 3
Hadım, 7,176	E 4
Hafik, 2,634	G 3

Hakkâri (Çölemerik), 6,129	K 4
Halfeti, 2,622	G 4
Hani, 4,802	H 3
Harput, 2,205	H 3
Haruniye, 5,198	G 4
Hatay (Antákya), 57,855	G 4
Havran, 7,205	B 3
Havza, 10,338	F 2
Haymana, 5,396	E 2
Hayrabolu, 8,444	B 2
Hazro, 3,483	J 3
Hekimhan, 4,288	H 3
Helete, 3,636	G 3
Hendek, 10,788	D 2
Hilvan, 3,390	H 4
Hınıs, 5,263	J 3
Hisarönü, 3,730	E 2
Hopa, 5,703	J 2
Horasan, 5,236	J 3
Hozat, 2,680	H 3
İçel (Mersin), 86,692	F 4
İçme, 2,680	H 3
İdil, 2,109	J 4
Iğdır, 15,701	K 3
Ilgaz, 2,924	E 2
Ilgın, 10,196	D 3

Ilıca, 7,612 ....J 3
İmranlı, 3,176 ....H 3
İmroz, 2,721 ....B 2
İncesu, 5,775 ....F 3
İnebolu, 5,935 ....E 2
İnegöl, 27,777 ....C 2
İnönü, 4,246 ....D 3
İpsala, 6,544 ....B 2
İpsile, 2,246 ....G 2
İskenderun, 69,382 ....G 4
İskilip, 12,400 ....F 2
İslâhiye, 13,775 ....G 4
Isparta, 42,901 ....D 4
İspir, 2,294 ....J 2
İstanbul, 1,742,978 ....D 6
İstanbul, *2,043,447 ....D 6
İzmir, 263,521 ....B 3
İzmir, *411,626 ....B 3
İzmit, 89,547 ....C 2
İznik, 8,213 ....C 2
Kadıköy, 81,945 ....D 6
Kadınhanı, 8,398 ....E 3
Kadirli, 15,926 ....F 4
Kağıthane, 56,157 ....D 6
Kağızman, 9,417 ....K 2
Kâhta, 6,885 ....H 4
Kalan, 5,825 ....H 3
Kale, 3,166 ....C 4
Kalecik, 4,022 ....E 2
Kaman, 10,067 ....E 3
Kandıra, 5,992 ....D 2
Kangal, 4,412 ....G 3
Karabük, 46,169 ....E 2
Karacabey, 18,368 ....C 2
Karahallı, 4,987 ....C 3
Karakoçan, 2,965 ....J 3
Karaköse, 24,168 ....K 3
Karaman, 26,051 ....E 4
Karamanlı, 4,694 ....C 4
Karapınar, 12,989 ....E 4
Karasu, 7,060 ....D 2
Karataş, 3,686 ....F 4
Karayaka, 3,631 ....G 2
Kargı, 3,954 ....F 2
Kars, 41,376 ....K 2
Karşıyaka, 82,574 ....B 3
Kartal, 20,139 ....D 6
Kastamonu, 23,485 ....F 2
Kavak, 2,135 ....C 5
Kavak, 2,473 ....F 2
Kayseri, 126,653 ....F 3
Kazanlı, 3,360 ....F 4

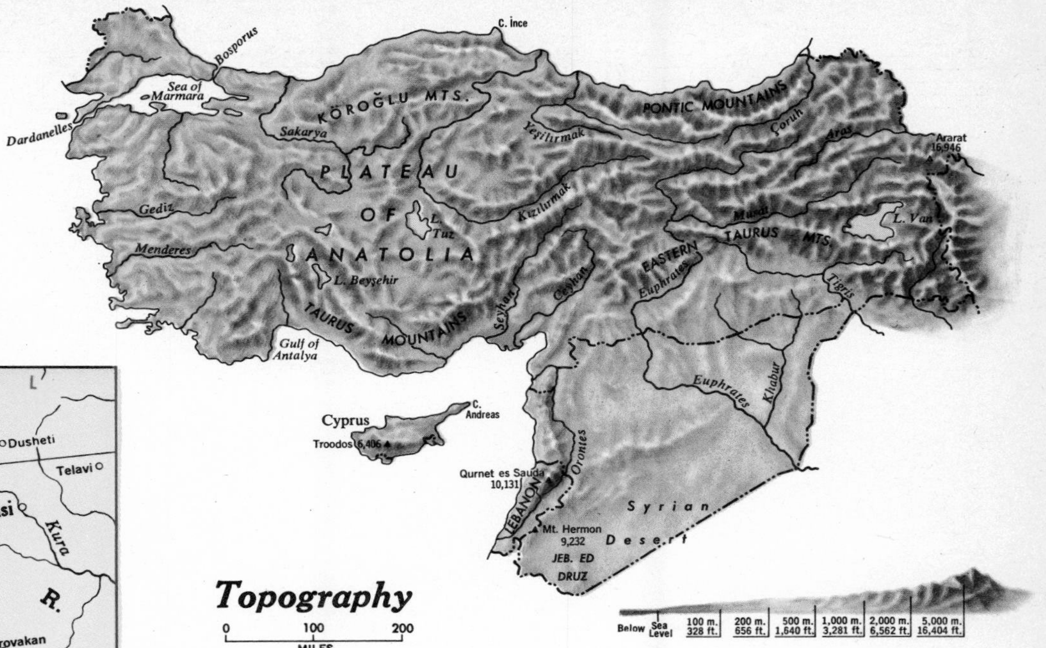

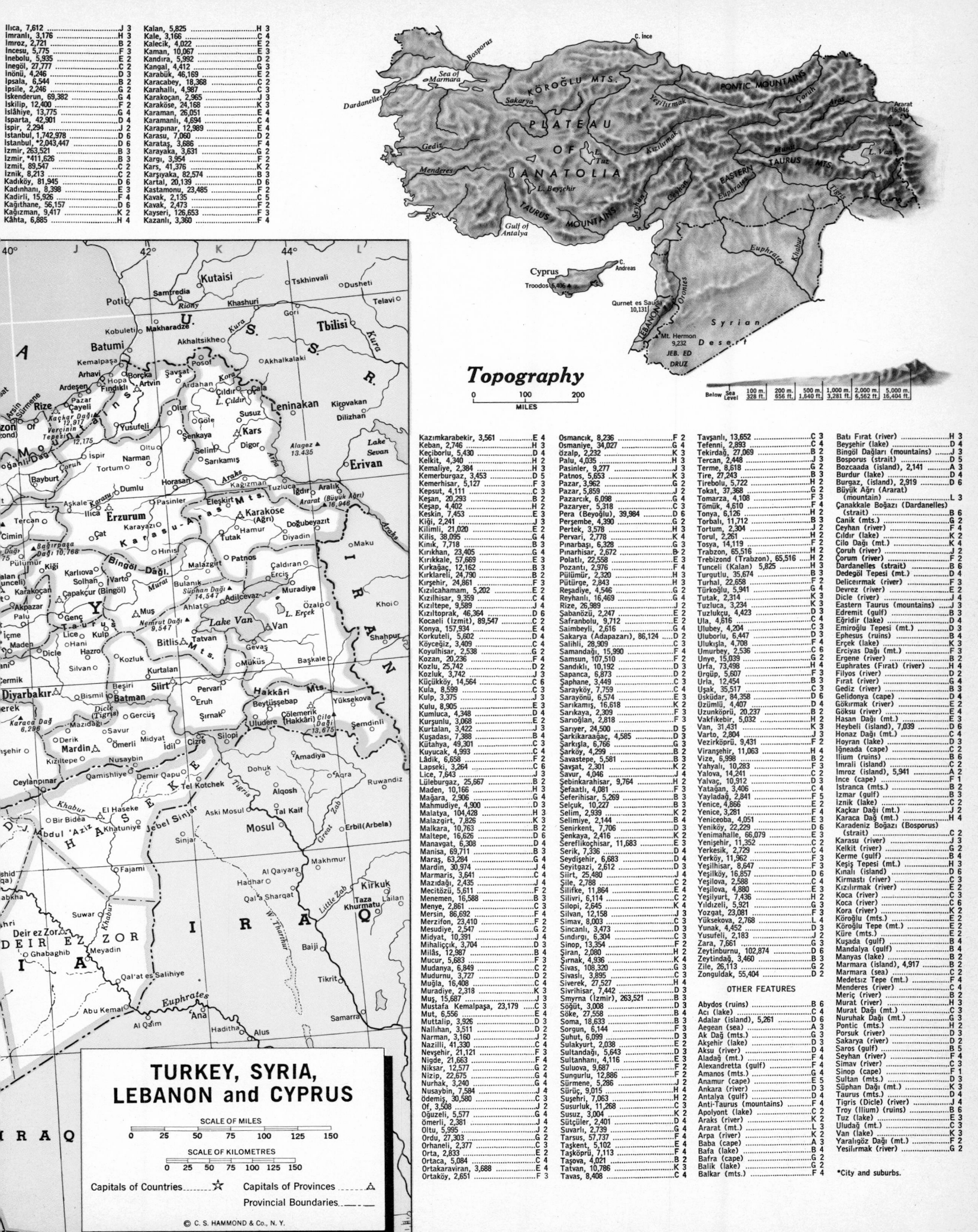

Topography

0 100 200 MILES

Kazımkarabekir, 3,561 ....E 4
Keban, 2,746 ....H 3
Keçiborlu, 5,430 ....D 4
Kelkit, 4,340 ....H 2
Kemaliye, 2,384 ....H 3
Kemerburgaz, 3,453 ....D 5
Kemerhisar, 5,127 ....F 3
Kepsut, 4,111 ....C 3
Keşan, 20,293 ....B 2
Keşap, 4,402 ....H 2
Keskin, 7,453 ....E 3
Kiğı, 2,241 ....J 3
Kilimli, 21,020 ....E 2
Kilis, 38,095 ....G 4
Kınık, 7,718 ....B 3
Kırıkhan, 23,405 ....G 4
Kırıkkale, 57,669 ....E 3
Kırkağaç, 12,162 ....B 3
Kırklareli, 24,790 ....B 2
Kırşehir, 24,861 ....F 3
Kızılcahamam, 5,202 ....E 2
Kızılhisar, 9,359 ....C 4
Kızıltepe, 9,589 ....J 4
Kızıltoprak, 46,364 ....D 6
Kocaeli (İzmit), 89,547 ....C 2
Konya, 157,934 ....E 4
Korkuteli, 5,602 ....D 4
Köyceğiz, 3,409 ....C 4
Koyulhisar, 2,538 ....G 2
Kozan, 20,236 ....F 4
Kozlu, 25,742 ....D 2
Kozluk, 3,742 ....J 3
Küçükköy, 14,564 ....C 6
Kula, 8,599 ....C 3
Kulp, 3,375 ....J 3
Kulu, 8,905 ....E 3
Kumluca, 4,348 ....D 4
Kurşunlu, 3,068 ....E 2
Kurtalan, 3,422 ....J 3
Kuşadası, 7,388 ....B 4
Kütahya, 49,301 ....C 3
Kuyucak, 4,993 ....C 4
Lâdik, 6,658 ....F 2
Lapseki, 3,264 ....C 6
Lice, 7,643 ....J 3
Lüleburgaz, 25,667 ....B 2
Maden, 10,166 ....H 3
Mağara, 2,906 ....G 4
Mahmudiye, 4,900 ....D 3
Malatya, 104,428 ....H 3
Malazgirt, 7,826 ....K 3
Malkara, 10,763 ....B 2
Maltepe, 16,626 ....D 6
Manavgat, 6,308 ....D 4
Manisa, 69,711 ....B 3
Maraş, 63,284 ....G 4
Mardin, 30,974 ....J 4
Marmaris, 3,641 ....C 4
Mazıdağı, 2,435 ....J 4
Mecitözü, 5,611 ....F 2
Menemen, 16,588 ....B 3
Menye, 2,861 ....C 3
Mersin, 86,692 ....F 4
Merzifon, 23,410 ....F 2
Mesudiye, 2,547 ....G 2
Midyat, 10,391 ....J 4
Mihaliççık, 3,704 ....D 3
Milâs, 12,987 ....B 4
Mucur, 5,683 ....F 3
Mudanya, 6,849 ....C 2
Mudurnu, 3,727 ....D 2
Muğla, 16,408 ....C 4
Muradiye, 2,318 ....K 3
Muş, 15,687 ....J 3
Mustafa Kemalpaşa, 23,179 ....C 3
Mut, 6,556 ....E 4
Muttalip, 3,926 ....D 3
Nallıhan, 3,511 ....D 2
Narman, 3,160 ....J 2
Nazilli, 41,330 ....C 4
Nevşehir, 21,121 ....F 3
Nigde, 21,663 ....F 4
Niksar, 12,577 ....G 2
Nizip, 22,675 ....G 4
Nurhak, 3,240 ....G 4
Nusaybin, 7,584 ....J 4
Ödemiş, 30,580 ....C 3
Of, 3,508 ....J 2
Oğuzeli, 5,577 ....G 4
Ömerli, 2,381 ....J 4
Oltu, 5,995 ....J 2
Ordu, 27,303 ....G 2
Orhaneli, 2,377 ....C 3
Orta, 2,833 ....E 2
Ortaca, 5,084 ....C 4
Ortakaraviran, 3,688 ....E 4
Ortaköy, 2,651 ....F 3

Osmancık, 8,236 ....F 2
Osmaniye, 34,027 ....G 4
Özalp, 2,232 ....K 3
Palu, 4,035 ....H 3
Pasinler, 9,277 ....J 3
Patnos, 5,653 ....K 3
Pazar, 3,962 ....G 2
Pazar, 5,859 ....J 2
Pazarcık, 6,098 ....G 4
Pazaryer, 5,318 ....C 3
Pera (Beyoğlu), 39,984 ....D 6
Perşembe, 4,390 ....G 2
Pertek, 3,578 ....H 3
Pervari, 2,778 ....K 4
Pınarbaşı, 6,328 ....G 3
Pınarhisar, 2,672 ....B 2
Polatlı, 22,558 ....E 3
Pozantı, 2,976 ....F 4
Pülümür, 2,320 ....H 3
Pütürge, 2,843 ....H 3
Reşadiye, 4,546 ....G 2
Reyhanlı, 16,469 ....G 4
Rize, 26,989 ....J 2
Şabanözü, 2,247 ....E 2
Safranbolu, 9,712 ....E 2
Saimbeyli, 2,616 ....G 4
Sakarya (Adapazarı), 86,124 ....D 2
Salihli, 28,909 ....C 3
Samandağı, 15,990 ....F 4
Samsun, 107,510 ....F 2
Sandıklı, 10,192 ....D 3
Sapanca, 6,873 ....D 2
Şaphane, 3,449 ....C 3
Sarayköy, 7,759 ....C 4
Sarayönü, 6,574 ....E 3
Sarıkamış, 16,618 ....K 2
Sarıkaya, 2,309 ....F 3
Sarıoğlan, 2,818 ....F 3
Sarıyer, 24,500 ....D 5
Şarkikaraağaç, 4,585 ....D 3
Şarkışla, 6,766 ....G 3
Şarköy, 4,299 ....B 2
Savastepe, 5,581 ....B 3
Şavşat, 2,301 ....K 2
Savur, 4,046 ....J 4
Şebinkarahisar, 9,764 ....H 2
Şefaatlı, 4,081 ....F 3
Seferihisar, 5,269 ....B 3
Selçuk, 10,227 ....B 3
Selim, 2,939 ....K 2
Selimiye, 2,144 ....B 4
Senirkent, 7,706 ....D 3
Şenkaya, 2,416 ....K 2
Şereflikoçhisar, 11,683 ....E 3
Serik, 7,336 ....D 4
Seydişehir, 6,683 ....D 4
Seyitgazi, 2,612 ....D 3
Siirt, 25,480 ....J 4
Şile, 2,788 ....C 2
Silifke, 11,864 ....E 4
Silivri, 6,114 ....C 2
Silopi, 2,645 ....K 4
Silvan, 12,158 ....J 3
Simav, 8,003 ....C 3
Sincanlı, 3,473 ....D 3
Sındırgı, 6,304 ....C 3
Sinop, 13,354 ....F 2
Şiran, 2,080 ....H 2
Şırnak, 4,936 ....K 4
Sivas, 108,320 ....G 3
Sivaslı, 3,895 ....C 3
Siverek, 27,527 ....H 4
Sivrihisar, 7,442 ....D 3
Smyrna (İzmir), 263,521 ....B 3
Söğüt, 3,008 ....D 3
Söke, 27,558 ....B 4
Soma, 18,633 ....B 3
Sorgun, 6,144 ....F 3
Şuhut, 6,099 ....D 3
Sulakyurt, 2,038 ....E 2
Sultandağı, 5,643 ....D 3
Sultanhanı, 4,116 ....E 3
Suluova, 9,687 ....F 2
Sungurlu, 12,886 ....F 2
Sürmene, 5,286 ....J 2
Sürüç, 9,015 ....H 4
Suşehri, 7,063 ....H 2
Susurluk, 11,268 ....C 3
Susuz, 3,004 ....K 2
Sütçüler, 2,401 ....D 4
Suvarlı, 2,739 ....G 4
Tarsus, 57,737 ....F 4
Taşkent, 5,102 ....E 4
Taşköprü, 7,113 ....F 4
Taşova, 4,021 ....B 2
Tatvan, 10,786 ....K 3
Tavas, 8,408 ....C 4

Tavşanlı, 13,652 ....C 3
Tefenni, 2,893 ....C 4
Tekirdağ, 27,069 ....B 2
Tercan, 2,448 ....J 3
Terme, 8,618 ....G 2
Tire, 27,243 ....B 3
Tirebolu, 5,722 ....H 2
Tokat, 37,368 ....G 2
Tomarza, 4,108 ....F 3
Tömük, 4,610 ....F 4
Tonya, 6,126 ....H 2
Torbalı, 11,712 ....B 3
Tortum, 2,304 ....J 2
Torul, 2,261 ....H 2
Tosya, 14,119 ....F 2
Trabzon, 65,516 ....H 2
Trebizond (Trabzon), 65,516 ....H 2
Tunceli (Kalan) 5,825 ....H 3
Turgutlu, 35,674 ....B 3
Turhal, 22,658 ....F 2
Türkoğlu, 5,941 ....G 4
Tutak, 2,314 ....K 3
Tuzluca, 3,234 ....K 3
Tuzlukçu, 4,423 ....D 3
Ula, 4,616 ....C 4
Ulubey, 4,204 ....C 3
Uluborlu, 6,447 ....D 3
Ulukışla, 4,708 ....F 4
Umurbey, 2,536 ....C 6
Unye, 15,039 ....G 2
Urfa, 73,498 ....H 4
Ürgüp, 5,607 ....F 3
Urla, 12,454 ....B 3
Uşak, 35,517 ....C 3
Üsküdar, 84,358 ....D 6
Üzümlü, 4,407 ....D 4
Uzunköprü, 20,237 ....B 2
Vakfıkebir, 5,032 ....H 2
Van, 31,431 ....K 3
Varto, 2,804 ....J 3
Vezirköprü. 9,431 ....F 2
Viranşehir, 11,063 ....H 4
Vize, 6,998 ....B 2
Yahyalı, 10,283 ....F 3
Yalova, 14,241 ....C 2
Yalvaç, 10,912 ....D 3
Yatağan, 3,406 ....C 4
Yayladağ, 2,841 ....F 5
Yenice, 4,866 ....E 2
Yenice, 3,281 ....F 4
Yeniceoba, 4,051 ....E 3
Yeniköy, 22,229 ....D 6
Yenimahalle, 66,079 ....E 3
Yenişehir, 11,352 ....C 2
Yerkesik, 2,729 ....C 4
Yerköy, 11,962 ....F 3
Yeşilhisar, 8,647 ....F 3
Yeşilköy, 16,857 ....D 6
Yeşilova, 2,588 ....C 4
Yeşilova, 4,880 ....E 3
Yeşilyurt, 7,436 ....H 2
Yıldızeli, 5,921 ....G 3
Yozgat, 23,081 ....F 3
Yüksekova, 2,768 ....L 4
Yunak, 4,452 ....D 3
Yusufeli, 2,183 ....J 2
Zara, 7,661 ....G 3
Zeytinburnu, 102,874 ....D 6
Zeytindağ, 3,460 ....B 3
Zile, 26,113 ....G 2
Zonguldak, 55,404 ....D 2

OTHER FEATURES

Abydos (ruins) ....B 6
Acı (lake) ....C 4
Adalar (island), 5,261 ....D 6
Aegean (sea) ....A 3
Ak Dağ (mts.) ....G 3
Akşehir (lake) ....D 3
Aksu (river) ....D 4
Aladağ (mt.) ....F 4
Alexandretta (gulf) ....F 4
Amanos (mts.) ....G 4
Anamur (cape) ....E 5
Ankara (river) ....D 3
Antalya (gulf) ....D 4
Anti-Taurus (mountains) ....F 4
Apolyont (lake) ....C 2
Araks (river) ....K 2
Ararat (mt.) ....L 3
Arpa (river) ....K 2
Baba (cape) ....A 3
Bafa (lake) ....B 4
Bafra (cape) ....G 2
Balik (lake) ....G 2
Balkar (mts.) ....F 4
Batı Fırat (river) ....H 3
Beyşehir (lake) ....D 4
Bingöl Dağları (mountains) ....J 3
Bosporus (strait) ....D 5
Bozcaada (island), 2,141 ....A 3
Burdur (lake) ....D 4
Burgaz, (island), 2,919 ....D 6
Büyük Ağrı (Ararat) (mountain) ....L 3
Çanakkale Boğazı (Dardanelles) (strait) ....B 6
Canik (mts.) ....G 2
Ceyhan (river) ....F 4
Cıldır (lake) ....K 2
Cilo Dağı (mt.) ....K 4
Çoruh (river) ....J 2
Çorum (river) ....F 2
Dardanelles (strait) ....B 6
Dedegöl Tepesi (mt.) ....D 4
Deliceırmak (river) ....F 3
Devrez (river) ....E 2
Dicle (river) ....J 4
Eastern Taurus (mountains) ....J 3
Edremit (gulf) ....B 3
Eğridir (lake) ....D 4
Emiroğlu Tepesi (mt.) ....D 3
Ephesus (ruins) ....B 4
Erçek (lake) ....K 3
Erciyas Dağı (mt.) ....F 3
Ergene (river) ....B 2
Euphrates (Fırat) (river) ....H 4
Filyos (river) ....D 2
Fırat (river) ....G 4
Gediz (river) ....B 3
Gelidonya (cape) ....D 4
Gökırmak (river) ....E 2
Göksu (river) ....E 4
Hasan Dağı (mt.) ....E 3
Heybeli (island), 7,039 ....D 6
Honaz Dağı (mt.) ....C 4
Hoyran (lake) ....D 3
İğneada (cape) ....C 2
Ilium (ruins) ....B 6
İmrali (island) ....C 2
İmroz (island), 5,941 ....A 2
İnce (cape) ....F 1
Istranca (mts.) ....B 2
İzmar (gulf) ....B 3
İznik (lake) ....C 2
Kaçkar Dağı (mt.) ....J 2
Karaca Dağ (mt.) ....H 4
Karadeniz Boğazı (Bosporus) (strait) ....C 2
Karasu (river) ....J 3
Kelkit (river) ....G 2
Kerme (gulf) ....B 4
Keşiş Tepesi (mt.) ....H 3
Kınalı (island) ....D 6
Kirmastı (river) ....C 3
Kızılırmak (river) ....E 2
Koca (river) ....C 3
Koca (river) ....C 6
Kora (river) ....K 2
Köroğlu (mts.) ....E 2
Köroğlu Tepe (mt.) ....E 2
Küre (mts.) ....E 2
Kuşada (gulf) ....B 4
Mandalya (gulf) ....B 4
Manyas (lake) ....B 2
Marmara (island), 4,917 ....B 2
Marmara (sea) ....C 2
Medetsız Tepe (mt.) ....F 4
Menderes (river) ....C 4
Meriç (river) ....B 2
Murat (river) ....H 3
Murat Dağı (mt.) ....C 3
Nuruhak Dağı (mt.) ....G 3
Pontic (mts.) ....H 2
Porsuk (river) ....D 3
Sakarya (river) ....D 2
Saros (gulf) ....B 5
Seyhan (river) ....F 4
Simav (river) ....C 3
Sinop (cape) ....F 1
Sultan (mts.) ....D 3
Süphan Dağı (mt.) ....K 3
Taurus (mts.) ....D 4
Tigris (Dicle) (river) ....J 4
Troy (Ilium) (ruins) ....B 6
Tuz (lake) ....E 3
Uludağ (mt.) ....C 3
Van (lake) ....K 3
Yaralıgöz Dağı (mt.) ....F 2
Yesilırmak (river) ....G 2

*City and suburbs.

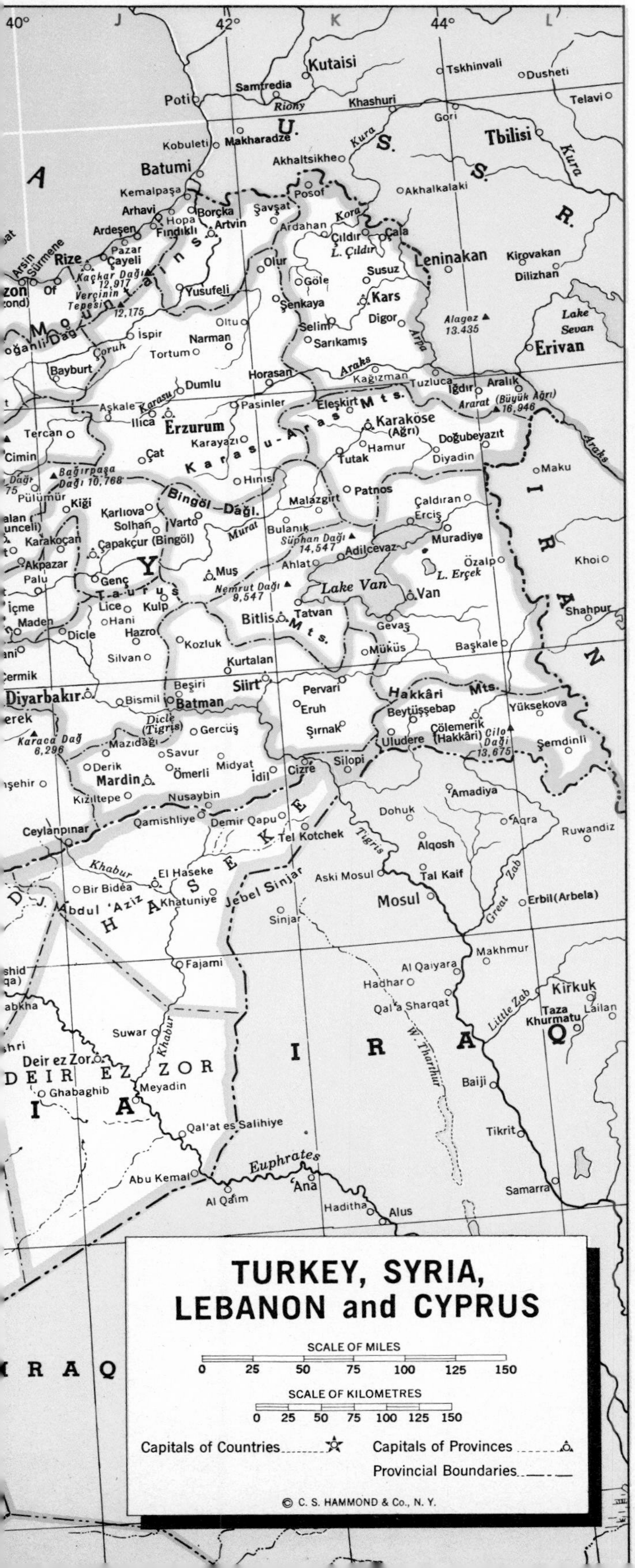

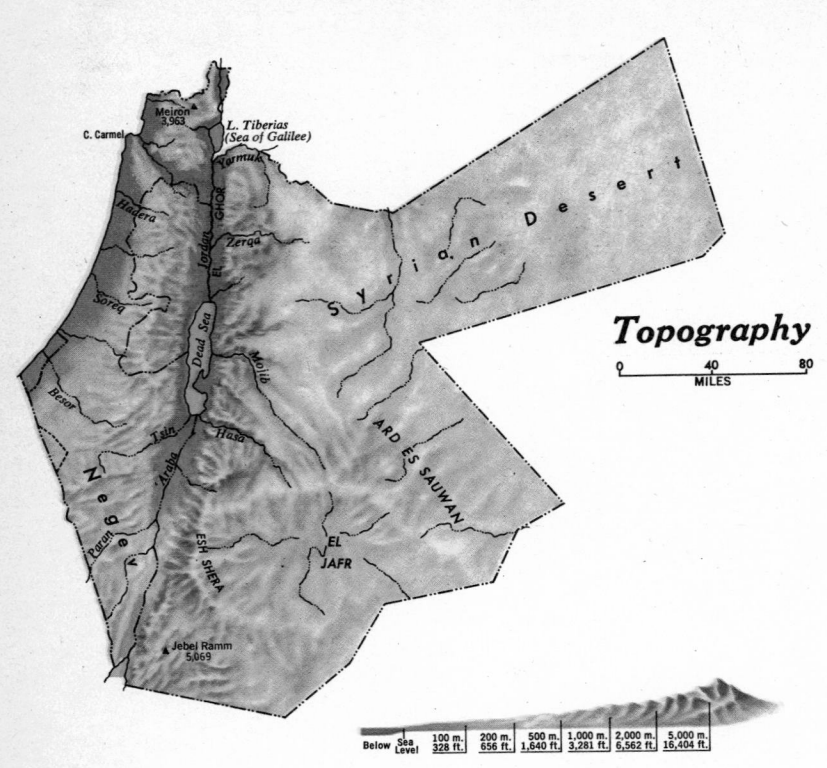

Topography

0   40   80
MILES

| Below Sea Level | 100 m. 328 ft. | 200 m. 656 ft. | 500 m. 1,640 ft. | 1,000 m. 3,281 ft. | 2,000 m. 6,562 ft. | 5,000 m. 16,404 ft. |

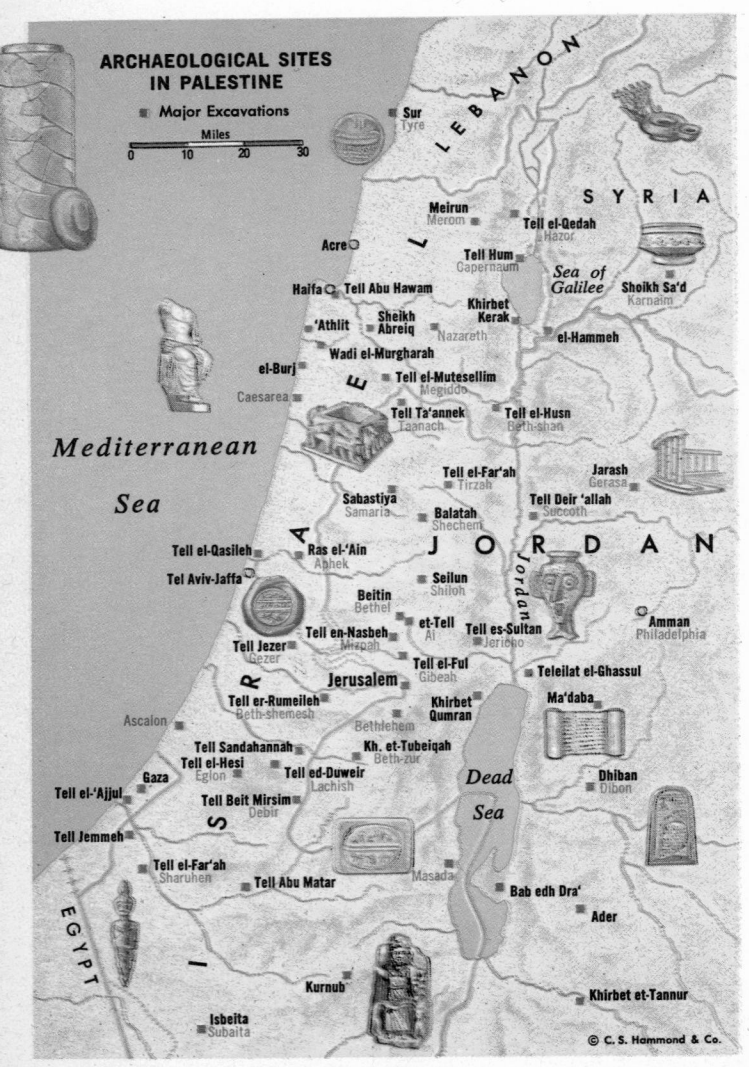

ARCHAEOLOGICAL SITES IN PALESTINE

■ Major Excavations

Miles
0   10   20   30

Mediterranean Sea

© C. S. Hammond & Co.

Agriculture, Industry and Resources

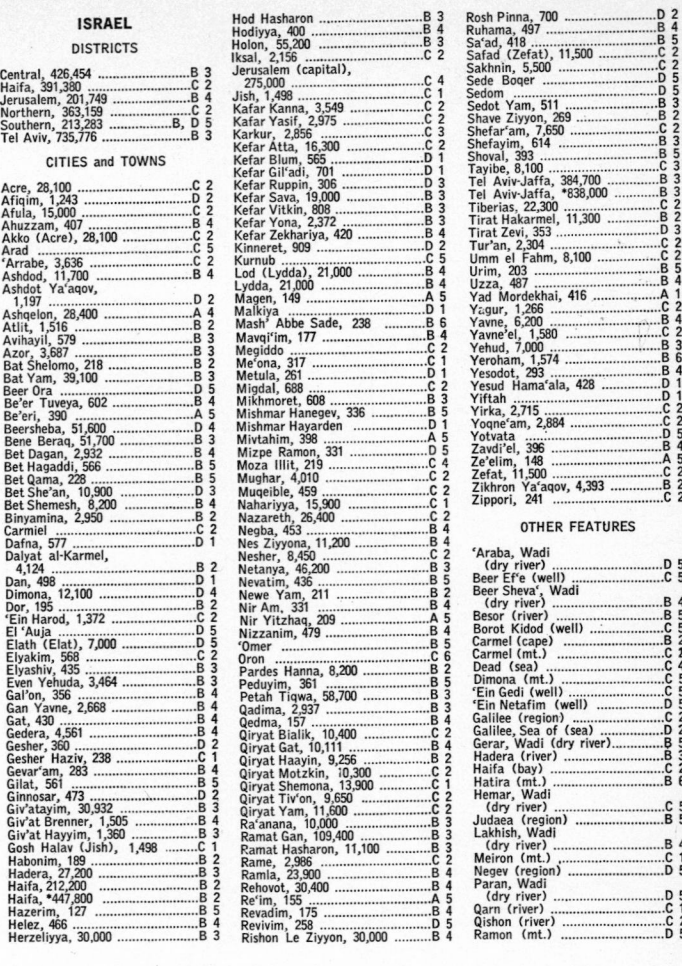

ACRE
Iron & Steel, Chemicals, Textiles

HAIFA
Oil Refining, Textiles, Cement, Machinery

NETANYA
Diamond Cutting

TEL AVIV–JAFFA
Machinery, Electrical Equipment, Textiles, Clothing, Diamond Cutting, Chemicals

JERUSALEM
Ceramics, Textiles, Leather

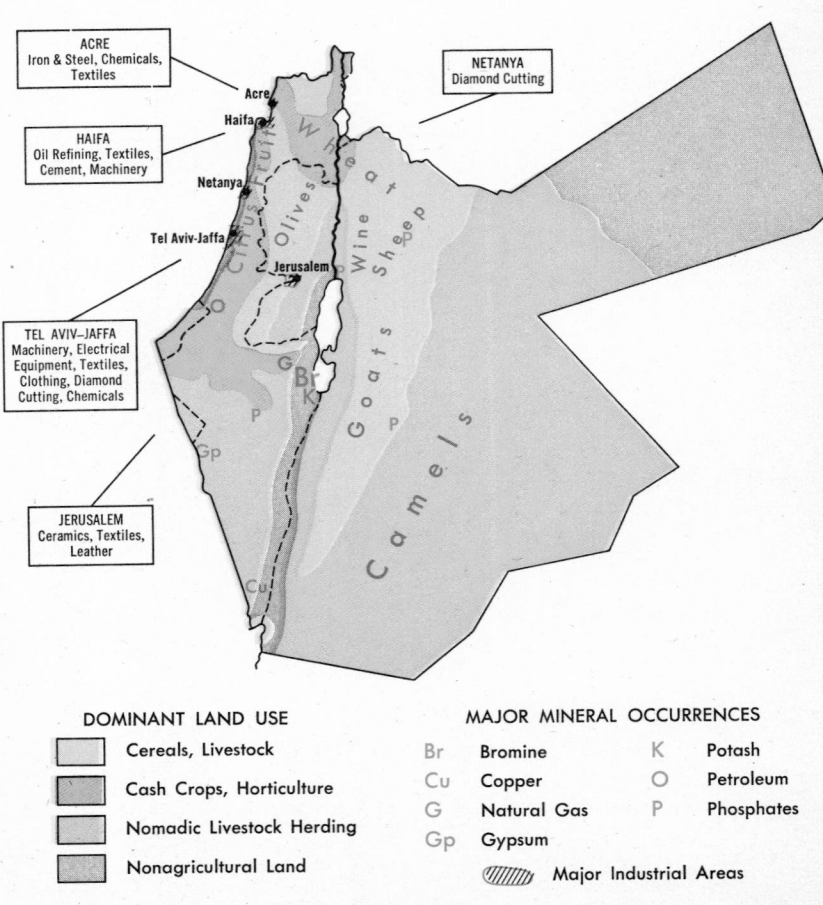

DOMINANT LAND USE

- Cereals, Livestock
- Cash Crops, Horticulture
- Nomadic Livestock Herding
- Nonagricultural Land

MAJOR MINERAL OCCURRENCES

Br   Bromine
Cu   Copper
G   Natural Gas
Gp   Gypsum

K   Potash
O   Petroleum
P   Phosphates

⧅ Major Industrial Areas

ISRAEL

JORDAN

ISRAEL
AREA 7,993 sq. mi.
POPULATION 2,911,000
CAPITAL Jerusalem
LARGEST CITY Tel Aviv-Jaffa
HIGHEST POINT Meiron 3,963 ft.
MONETARY UNIT Israeli pound
MAJOR LANGUAGES Hebrew, Arabic
MAJOR RELIGIONS Judaism, Islam, Christianity

JORDAN
AREA 37,297 sq. mi.
POPULATION 2,300,000
CAPITAL Amman
LARGEST CITY Amman
HIGHEST POINT Jeb. Ramm 5,069 ft.
MONETARY UNIT Jordanian dinar
MAJOR LANGUAGE Arabic
MAJOR RELIGION Islam

ISRAEL and JORDAN

CYLINDRICAL PROJECTION

SCALE OF MILES
0   5   10 15 20 25 30

SCALE OF KILOMETRES
0   5 10 15 20 25 30

Capitals of Countries .... ☆
District Capitals .... ◉
International Boundaries _____
District Boundaries _ _ _ _ _ _
Demilitarized Zone Boundaries _ . _ . _
Neutral Zone Boundaries _ _ _ _ _

Copyright by C. S. Hammond & Co., N.Y.

Rubin, Wadi
  (dry river) ....B 4
Shiqma (river) ....B 4
Tabor (mt.) ....D 2
Tiberias (Galilee) (sea) ....D 2
Tseelim, Wadi
  (dry river) ....C 5
Tsin, Wadi
  (dry river) ....D 5
Yarmuk (river) ....D 3
Yarqon (river) ....B 3

JORDAN

DISTRICTS

'Ajlun, 334,000 ....D 3
Amman, 526,000 ....D 4
El Balqa, 95,000 ....D 4
El Karak, 81,000 ....E 5
Hebron, 145,000 ....C 4
Jerusalem, 418,000 ....C 4
Ma'an, 58,000 ....D 5
Nablus, 414,000 ....C 3

CITIES and TOWNS

'Ajja, 1,322 ....C 3
'Ajlun, 5,390 ....D 3
Amman (capital),
  330,220 ....D 4
'Anabta, 4,018 ....C 3
Anin, 914 ....C 2
'Anjara, 3,163 ....D 3
'Anza, 807 ....C 3
'Aqaba, 8,908 ....D 6
Aqraba, 2,501 ....C 3
Ariha (Jericho), 5,312 ....C 4
'Arraba, 4,231 ....C 3
'Arura, 849 ....C 4
'Attil, 3,808 ....C 3
Bal'ama, 769 ....E 3
Baqura, 3,042 ....D 2
Beit Fajjar, 2,474 ....C 4
Beit Hanina, 3,067 ....C 4
Beit Jala, 6,041 ....C 4
Beit Lahm (Bethlehem),
  14,439 ....C 4
Beit Nuba, 1,350 ....B 4
Beit Sahur, 5,380 ....C 4
Bethlehem, 14,439 ....C 4
Biddu, 1,259 ....C 4
Bir Zeit, 2,311 ....C 4
Birqin, 2,036 ....C 3
Burqa, 2,477 ....C 3
Damiya, 483 ....D 3
Deir Abu Sa'id, 1,927 ....D 3
Deir Ballut, 1,058 ....C 4
Deir Sharaf, 973 ....C 3
Dhahiriya, 4,875 ....B 5
Dhira, 214 ....D 5
Duma, 524 ....C 3
Dura, 4,954 ....C 4
El 'Al, 492 ....D 4
El Bira, 9,674 ....C 4
El Husn, 3,728 ....D 3
El Karak, 7,422 ....E 4
El Khalil (Hebron),
  38,309 ....C 4
El Kitta, 987 ....D 3
El Madwar, 10,791 ....E 3
El Mafraq, 9,499 ....E 3
El Majdal, 259 ....C 3
El Quweira, 268 ....E 5
El Yaduda, 251 ....D 4
Er Ramtha, 10,791 ....D 2
Er Rihya, 559 ....D 3
Er Rumman, 293 ....D 3
Er Ruseifa, 6,200 ....E 4
Es Sahab, 2,580 ....E 4
Es Salt, 16,176 ....D 3
Es Sukhna, 649 ....E 3
Esh Shaubak ....E 5
Et Tafila, 4,506 ....E 5
Et Taiyiba, 2,606 ....C 3
Ez Zababida, 1,474 ....C 3
Ez Zarqa', 121,303 ....E 3
Falama, 162 ....C 3
Halhul, 6,041 ....C 4
Harima, 635 ....D 2
Haris, 641 ....C 3
Hawara, 2,342 ....C 3
Hebron, 38,309 ....C 4
Hisban, 718 ....D 4
'Ibbin, 1,364 ....D 3
Idna, 3,713 ....B 4
Irbid, 44,685 ....D 2
Jaba', 2,817 ....C 3
Jabir, 135 ....E 2
Jalama, 784 ....C 3
Jalbun, 914 ....D 3
Jalud, 221 ....D 3
Jarash, 3,796 ....D 3
Jenin, 8,346 ....C 3
Jericho, 5,312 ....C 4
Jerusalem (old city),
  60,488 ....C 4
Jifna, 655 ....C 4

Kharas, 1,364 ....C 4
Kitim, 1,026 ....D 3
Kuraiyima ....D 3
Ma'ad, 125 ....D 2
Ma'an, 6,643 ....E 5
Ma'daba, 11,224 ....D 4
Ma'in, 1,271 ....D 4
Manja, 353 ....C 5
Mazra', 1,194 ....C 5
Nablus, 41,709 ....C 3
Nabulus (Nablus). 41,709 ....C 3
Nahhalin, 1,109 ....C 4
Na'ur, 2,382 ....D 4
Ni'lin, 1,227 ....C 4
Nitil, 348 ....D 4
Qabalan, 1,970 ....C 3
Qabatiya, 6,005 ....C 3
Qaffin, 2,480 ....C 3
Qalqiliya, 8,926 ....C 3
Qibya, 926 ....C 4
Qumeim, 955 ....D 2
Rafidiya, 1,123 ....C 3
Ramallah, 12,134 ....C 4
Rammun, 1,198 ....C 4
Rantis, 897 ....C 4
Ra's en Naqb, 225 ....E 5
Safi, 3,468 ....C 5
Safut, 421 ....D 3
Salfit, 3,201 ....C 3
Samar, 716 ....D 2
Samu, 3,784 ....C 5
Sarih, 3,390 ....D 2
Shu'fat, 2,732 ....C 4
Shunat Nimrin, 109 ....D 4
Shuweika, 2,332 ....C 3
Silat Dhahr, 3,566 ....C 3
Sinjil, 1,823 ....C 3
Siris, 1,285 ....C 3
Subeihi, 514 ....D 3
Suf, 3,259 ....D 3
Suweilih, 3,457 ....D 4
Suweima, 315 ....D 4
Tammun, 2,952 ....C 3
Tarqumiya, 2,412 ....C 4
Tubas, 5,262 ....C 3
Tulkarm, 10,255 ....C 3
Tur, 4,289 ....C 4
Um Jauza, 582 ....D 3
Wadi es Sir, 4,455 ....D 4
Wadi Musa, 654 ....E 5
Waqqas, 2,321 ....D 2
Ya'bad, 4,857 ....C 3
Yabrud, 277 ....C 4
Yamun, 4,173 ....C 3
Yatta, 7,281 ....C 4
Zububa, 633 ....C 3
Zuweiza, 126 ....D 4

OTHER FEATURES

'Ajlun (range) ....D 3
Anabta (mt.) ....C 3
'Aqaba (gulf) ....D 6
'Araba, Wadi
  (dry river) ....D 5
Dead (sea) ....C 4
Ebal (mt.) ....C 3
El Ghor (reg.) ....C 3
El Lisan (pen.) ....C 5
Hasa, Wadi
  (dry river) ....E 5
Hebron (mt.) ....C 4
Jordan (river) ....D 3
Judaea (region) ....C 4
Khirbet Qumran
  (site) ....D 4
Kufrinja (mt.) ....D 3
Kufrinja, Wadi
  (dry river) ....D 3
Mashash, Wadi
  (dry river) ....C 4
Nebo (mt.) ....D 4
Petra (ruins) ....D 5
Samaria (region) ....C 3
Shallala, Wadi ....D 2
Shu'eib, Wadi
  (dry river) ....D 4
Tell Asur (mt.) ....C 4
Tur (mt.) ....C 4
Yabis, Wadi
  (dry river) ....D 3
Yamun (mt.) ....D 3
Zarqa' (river) ....D 3

GAZA STRIP

Total Population, 480,000

CITIES and TOWNS

'Abasan, 1,481 ....A 5
Bani Suheila, 7,561 ....A 5
Beit Hanun, 4,756 ....A 5
Deir el Balah, 10,854 ....A 5
El Ghor, 87,793 ....A 5
Gaza, *118,272 ....A 5
Jabalia, 10,508 ....A 5
Khan Yunis, 29,522 ....A 5
Rafah, 10,812 ....A 5

*City and suburbs.

66 Iran and Iraq

IRAN

INTERNAL DIVISIONS

Bakhtiari (governorate),
298,448 .... F 4
Boyer Ahmedi and Kahkiluye
(governorate) .... G 5
Central (province), 4,979,081 .. G 3
East Azerbaijan (province),
2,596,439 .... E 1
Fars (province), 1,429,804 ...... H 6
Gilan (province), 1,752,504 ..... F 2
Hamadan (governorate),
889,888 .... F 3
Ilam (governorate) .... E 4
Isfahan (province),
1,703,701 .... H 4
Kerman (province), 761,851 ..... K 6
Kermanshah (prov.), 924,717 ... E 3
Khurasan (province), 2,497,381 .. K 3
Khuzistan (prov.), 1,578,079 ... F 5
Kurdistan (prov.), 619,573 ...... E 3
Luristan (governorate),
686,307 .... F 4
Mazanderan (province),
1,841,637 .... H 2
Ports and Islands
(province), 346,410 .... H 7
Samnan (governorate),
207,786 .... J 3
Seistan and Baluchistan (prov.),
454,996 .... M 6
Southern Coast (province),
251,921 .... G 6
West Azerbaijan (province),
1,087,182 .... D 1
Yezd (governorate) .... J 5
Zenjan (governorate) .... F 2

CITIES and TOWNS

Abadan, 272,962 .... F 5
Abadeh, 16,000 .... H 5
Abarquh, 8,000 .... H 5
Abhar, 11,000 .... F 2
Aghajari, 24,000 .... E 1
Ahwaz, 206,375 .... F 5
Amul, 40,076 .... H 2
Anarak, 2,038 .... H 4
Andimeshk, 16,000 .... F 4
Aradan, 18,978 .... J 3
Arak, 71,925 .... F 3
Ardebil, 83,596 .... F 1
Ardistan, 6,645 .... H 4
Asadabad, 7,000 .... F 3
Asterabad (Gurgan),
51,181 .... J 2
Azarshahr, 6,000 .... D 2
Azna, 5,000 .... F 4
Babol, 49,973 .... H 2
Babulsar, 12,000 .... H 2
Bafq, 6,000 .... J 5
Baft, 6,000 .... K 6
Bahramabad, 21,000 .... K 5
Bam, 22,000 .... L 6
Bandar 'Abbas, 34,627 .... J 7
Bandar Ma'shur,
17,000 .... F 5
Bandar Shah, 13,000 .... H 2
Bandar Shahpur, 14,000 .... F 5
Behbehan, 39,874 .... G 5
Behshahr, 26,032 .... H 2
Bijar, 14,000 .... E 2
Birjand, 25,854 .... L 4
Borazjun, 20,000 .... G 6
Bujnurd, 31,248 .... K 2
Bukan, 9,000 .... E 2
Burujird, 71,476 .... F 3

Bushire, 26,032 .... G 6
Chalus, 15,000 .... G 2
Dalijan, 6,000 .... G 3
Damghan, 13,000 .... J 2
Darab, 13,000 .... H 6
Daran, 4,609 .... G 4
Darreh Gaz, 11,000 .... L 2
Daulatabad (Malayer), 28,434 ... F 3
Deh Bid, 4,115 .... H 5
Demavend, 5,391 .... H 3
Dizful, 84,499 .... F 4
Duzdab (Zahidan), 40,000 .... M 6
Enzeli (Pahlevi), 41,785 .... F 2
Estahabanat, 18,187 .... H 6
Fahrej (Iranshahr), 5,000 .... M 7
Fariman, 8,000 .... L 3
Farrashband, 3,532 .... G 6
Fasa, 19,000 .... H 6
Firdaus, 11,000 .... K 3
Firuzabad, 8,718 .... H 6
Firuzkuh, 4,684 .... H 3
Fumen, 9,000 .... F 2
Gach Saran .... G 5
Ganaveh, 9,000 .... G 6
Garmsar, 4,723 .... H 3
Golshan (Tabas), 10,000 .... K 4
Gulpaigan, 20,515 .... G 4
Gumishan, 6,000 .... J 2
Gunabad, 8,000 .... L 3
Gunbad-i-Qabus, 40,667 .... K 3
Gurgan, 51,181 .... J 2
Haft Kel, 10,000 .... F 5
Hamadan, 124,167 .... F 3
Hashtpar, 5,000 .... F 2
Homayunshahr, 46,836 .... G 4
Ilam, 15,000 .... E 4
Iranshahr, 5,000 .... M 7
Isfahan, 424,045 .... G 4
Jahrum, 38,236 .... H 6

Kangavar, 9,414 .... F 3
Karaj, 44,243 .... G 3
Kashan, 58,468 .... H 4
Kashmar, 17,000 .... L 3
Kazerun, 39,758 .... G 6
Kazvin, 88,106 .... F 2
Kerman, 85,404 .... K 5
Kermanshah, 187,930 .... E 3
Khaf, 5,000 .... M 3
Khoi, 47,648 .... D 1
Khorramshahr, 88,536 .... F 5
Khunsar, 10,947 .... G 4
Khur, 2,912 .... J 4
Khurramabad, 59,578 .... F 4
Lahijan, 25,725 .... F 2
Lar, 22,000 .... J 7
Mahabad, 12,000 .... D 2
Mahallat, 12,000 .... G 4
Mahan, 8,000 .... K 5
Maibud, 15,000 .... J 4
Maku, 7,000 .... D 1
Malayer, 28,434 .... F 3
Maragheh, 54,106 .... E 2
Marand, 24,000 .... D 1
Marvdasht, 25,498 .... H 6
Masjid-i-Sulaiman, 64,488 .... F 5
Meshkinshahr, 9,000 .... F 1
Mianeh, 28,447 .... E 2
Mirjawa, 11,000 .... M 6
Miyanduab, 19,000 .... D 1
Naft-i-Shah, 3,043 .... E 4
Na'in, 5,925 .... H 4
Nasratabad (Zabul), 20,000 ...... M 5
Natanz, 4,370 .... H 4
Naushahr, 8,000 .... G 2
Nehavend, 24,000 .... F 3

Nejafabad, 43,384 .... G 4
Niriz, 16,114 .... J 5
Nishapur, 33,482 .... L 2
Pahlevi (Enzeli), 41,785 .... F 2
Qain, 10,000 .... L 4
Qasr-i-Shirin, 15,904 .... E 4
Quchan, 29,133 .... L 2
Qum, 134,292 .... G 3
Rafsenjan (Bahramabad),
21,000 .... K 5
Rai, 102,825 .... H 3
Ram Hormuz, 9,000 .... F 5
Ramsar, 12,000 .... G 2
Ravar, 7,000 .... K 5
Resht, 143,557 .... F 2
Reza'iyeh, 110,749 .... D 2
Sabzawaran, 7,000 .... K 6
Saidabad (Sirjan), 20,000 .... K 6
Samnan, 31,058 .... H 3
Sanandaj, 54,578 .... E 3
Sang-i-Sar, 9,000 .... H 3
Saqqiz, 17,000 .... E 2
Sarab, 16,000 .... E 2
Sari, 44,547 .... H 2
Savanat (Estahbanat),
18,187 .... H 6
Saveh, 17,565 .... G 3
Shahabad, 12,000 .... E 3
Shahdegan, 6,000 .... F 5
Shani, 38,898 .... F 4
Shahpur, 22,000 .... D 1
Shahr-i-Kurd, 24,000 .... G 4
Shahriza, 34,220 .... H 4
Shahrud, 30,767 .... J 3
Shahsawar, 12,000 .... G 2
Shiraz, 269,865 .... H 6
Shirvan, 11,000 .... K 2

Shushtar, 24,000 .... F 5
Sinneh (Sanandaj), 54,578 .... E 3
Sirjan, 20,000 .... K 6
Sultanabad (Kashmar),
17,000 .... L 3
Sunqur, 10,433 .... E 3
Susangird, 21,000 .... F 5
Tabas, 10,000 .... K 4
Tabriz, 403,413 .... D 2
Taft, 7,000 .... J 5
Tajrish, 157,486 .... H 3
Takistan, 13,485 .... F 2
Tehran (capital), 2,719,730 ..... H 3
Tuiserkan, 12,000 .... F 3
Tun (Firdaus), 11,000 .... K 3
Turbat-i-Haidari, 35,000 .... L 3
Turbat-i-Shaikh Jam, 13,000 ..... M 3
Urmia (Reza'iyeh), 110,749 ...... D 2
Ushnuiyeh, 5,000 .... D 2
Veramin, 11,183 .... H 3
Yezd, 93,241 .... J 5
Zabul, 20,000 .... M 5
Zahidan, 39,732 .... M 6
Zarand, 5,000 .... K 5
Zarghan, 7,000 .... H 6
Zenjan, 58,714 .... F 2

OTHER FEATURES

Ab-i-Diz (river) .... F 4
Aji Chai (river) .... E 1
Arabi (isl.) .... G 7
Aras (Araks) (river) .... D 1
Atrek (river) .... J 2
Bakhtegan (lake) .... H 6
Baluchistan (region) .... M 7
Bampur (river) .... M 7
Behistun (ruins) .... F 3
Caspian (sea) .... F 1

Darya-yi-Namak (salt lake) ...... H 3
Dasht-i-Kavir (salt desert) ..... H 3
Dasht-i-Lut (desert) .... K 5
Demavend (mt.) .... H 3
Dez (Ab-i-Diz) (river) .... F 4
Elburz (range) .... H 2
Farsi (isl.) .... F 6
Hamun-i-Helmand (marsh) .... M 5
Hamun-i-Jaz-Murian
(marsh) .... L 7
Hamun-i-Sabari (lake) .... M 5
Hanjam (isl.) .... J 7
Hari Rud (river) .... M 3
Hashtadan (reg.) .... M 3
Hormuz (strait) .... J 7
Kalar, Kuh-i- (mt.) .... F 4
Karkheh (river) .... F 4
Karun (river) .... F 5
Kashaf Rud (river) .... L 2
Kharg (isl.), 647 .... F 6
Kuh, Ras el (cape) .... K 7
Kuh-i-Aladagh (mts.) .... K 2
Kuh-i-Bazraband (mts.) .... M 8
Kuh-i-Binalud (mts.) .... L 2
Kuh-i-Dinar (mts.) .... G 5
Kuh-i-Gugird (mts.) .... K 2
Kuh-i-Jagatai (mts.) .... K 2
Kuh-i-Shah Jehan (mts.) .... K 2
Kur Rud (river) .... H 6
Kurang (river) .... M 7
Maidani (cape) .... J 7
Makran (region) .... M 7
Mand Rud (river) .... G 6
Mashkel (river) .... M 7
Mehran (river) .... J 7
Mura, Qal'eh-i- (river) .... M 4
Namaksar (lake) .... M 4

IRAN and IRAQ

CONIC PROJECTION

SCALE OF MILES

0   25   50   100   150   200

SCALE OF KILOMETRES

0   25 50 100   150   200

Capitals of Countries .... ☆
Capitals of Provinces .... △
Capitals of Governorates .... ●
International Boundaries .... —·—·—
Provincial Boundaries .... —·—·—
Governorate Boundaries .... —·—·—

Copyright by C. S. HAMMOND & CO., N.Y.

Iran consists of fifteen provinces
called ostans. Attached to seven of
these provinces are eight governorates.

Namakzar (dry lake) ....L 4
Nezwar (mt.) ....H 3
Nihing (river) ....N 7
Oman (gulf) ....M 8
Pasardagae (ruins) ....H 5
Persian (gulf) ....H 6
Persepolis (ruins) ....F 6
Pusht-i-Kuh (mts.) ....E 4
Qais (isl.) ....H 7
Qarajeh Dagh (mts.) ....E 1
Qara Su (river) ....J 2
Qara Su (river) ....E 3
Qarangu (river) ....E 2
Qishm (isl.) ....J 7
Qizil Uzun (river) ....F 2
Sefid Rud (river) ....F 2
Shaikh Shu'aib (island) ....H 7
Shelagh (river) ....M 5
Shirvan (river) ....E 3
Shur (river) ....J 7
Siah Kuh (mts.) ....L 3
Silop (river) ....M 8
Susa (ruins) ....F 4
Talab (river) ....N 6
Tashk (lake) ....J 6
Urmia (lake) ....D 2
Yezd (region) ....J 5
Zagros (mts.) ....E 4
Zaindeh Rud (river) ....H 4
Zarineh (river) ....E 2
Zilbir Chai (river) ....D 1
Zuhreh Rud (river) ....F 5

IRAQ
PROVINCES

Anbar, 319,289 ....C 4
Babil, 448,023 ....D 4

CITIES and TOWNS

Ad Diwaniya, 60,553 ....D 5
'Afaq, 5,390 ....D 4
Al 'Azair, 2,255 ....E 5
Al 'Aziziya, 7,450 ....D 4
Al Falluja, 38,072 ....C 4
Al Kufa, 30,862 ....D 4
Al Kumait, 2,225 ....E 4
Al Musayib, 15,955 ....D 4
Al Qa'im, 3,372 ....B 3
Al Qaiyara, 3,060 ....C 2
Al Qosh, 3,863 ....C 2
Al Qurna, 5,638 ....E 5
'Ali Gharbi, 5,735 ....E 4
'Ali Sharqi, 1,980 ....E 4
'Amadiya, 2,578 ....C 2
'Amara, 64,847 ....E 5
An Najaf, 128,096 ....D 4
An Nasiriya, 60,405 ....D 5
'Ana, 6,884 ....B 3
'Aqra, 8,659 ....D 2
Arbela (Erbil), 90,320 ....D 2

Baghdad, 2,124,323 ....C 3
Basra, 673,623 ....E 5
Dhi Qar, 346,663 ....E 5
Diyala, 400,049 ....D 4
Dohuk ....
Erbil, 360,285 ....D 2
Karbala', 339,692 ....C 4
Kirkuk, 462,027 ....D 3
Maysan ....
Muthanna ....
Ninawa ....
Qadisiya, 500,033 ....C 5
Sulaimaniya, 408,220 ....D 4
Wasit, 335,495 ....D 4

As Busaiya, 295 ....E 5
As Salman, 1,789 ....C 5
Ash Shabicha, 249 ....C 5
Az Zubair, 41,408 ....E 5
Badra, 3,564 ....D 4
Baghdad (capital), 502,503 ..D 4
Baghdad, *1,745,328 ....D 4
Baiji, 6,785 ....C 3
Ba'quba, 34,575 ....D 4
Basra, 313,327 ....E 5
Dohuk, 16,998 ....D 2
Erbil, 90,320 ....D 2
Fao, 15,399 ....F 6
Habbaniya, 14,405 ....C 4
Hadhar, 1,019 ....C 3
Haditha, 6,870 ....C 4
Hai, 16,988 ....E 4
Halabja, 11,206 ....D 3
Hilla, 84,717 ....D 4
Hindiya, 16,436 ....D 4
Hit, 9,131 ....C 4
Karbala', 83,301 ....C 4
Khanaqin, 23,522 ....D 3
Kifri, 8,500 ....D 3
Kirkuk, 167,413 ....D 3
Kut, 42,116 ....D 4
Lailan, 1,526 ....D 3
Maidan, 354 ....D 3
Makhmur, 2,556 ....C 3
Mandali, 11,262 ....D 4
Mosul, 315,157 ....C 2
Muqdadiyah, 12,181 ....D 4
Na'maniya, 11,943 ....D 4
Qal'a Shergat, 2,434 ....C 3
Qal'at Diza, 6,250 ....D 2
Ramadi, 28,723 ....C 4
Rania, 4,090 ....D 2
Refa'i, 7,681 ....E 5
Rumaitha, 10,222 ....D 5
Rutba, 5,091 ....B 4
Ruwandiz, 5,807 ....D 2
Sa'diya, 5,285 ....D 3
Samarra, 24,746 ....C 3
Samawa, 33,473 ....D 5
Shaikh Sa'ad, 2,958 ....E 4
Shatra, 18,822 ....E 5
Shithatha, 2,326 ....C 4
Sinjar, 7,942 ....B 2
Sulaimaniya, 86,822 ....D 3
Tal Kaif, 7,482 ....C 2
Tauq, 845 ....D 3
Taza Khurmatu, 2,681 ....D 3
Tikrit, 9,921 ....C 3
Tuz Khurmatu, 13,860 ....D 3
Zakho, 14,790 ....C 2
Zorbatiya, 1,602 ....D 4

OTHER FEATURES

Adhaim (river) ....D 3
Al Hajara (plain) ....C 4
'Aneiza, Jebel (mt.) ....A 4
'Arab, Shatt-al- (river) ....F 5
'Ar'ar, Wadi (dry river) ....B 5
Babylon (ruins) ....D 4
Bahr al Milh (lake) ....C 4
Batin, Wadi al (dry river) ....E 6
Ctesiphon (ruins) ....D 4
Darbandikhan (dam) ....D 3
Euphrates (river) ....D 4
Great Zab (river) ....C 2
Hajara, Al (plain) ....D 5
Haji Ibrahim (mt.) ....D 2
Hammar, Hor al
  (lake) ....E 5
Hauran, Wadi (dry river) .....B 4
Ibrahim, Haji (mt.) ....D 2
Little Zab (river) ....D 3
Mesopotamia (region) ....B 3
Nineveh (ruins) ....C 2
Sa'diya, Hor (lake) ....E 4
Saniya, Hor (lake) ....E 5
Sha'ib Hisb, Wadi
  (dry river) ....C 5
Shatt-al-'Arab (river) ....F 5
Sinjar, Jebel (mts.) ....B 2
Siyah Kuh (mt.) ....D 2
Syrian (desert) ....B 4
Tigris (river) ....C 3
Ubaiyidh, Wadi (dry river) ...B 5
Ur (ruins) ....D 5

*City and suburbs.
†Population of sub-district.

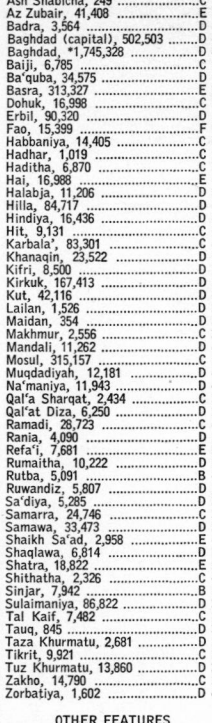

IRAN

IRAQ

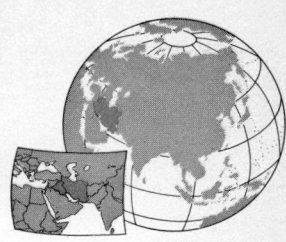

IRAN
AREA 636,293 sq. mi.
POPULATION 28,448,000
CAPITAL Tehran
LARGEST CITY Tehran
HIGHEST POINT Demavend 18,376 ft.
MONETARY UNIT rial
MAJOR LANGUAGES Persian, Azerbaijani, Kurdish
MAJOR RELIGIONS Islam, Zoroastrianism

IRAQ
AREA 167,924 sq. mi.
POPULATION 9,431,000
CAPITAL Baghdad
LARGEST CITY Baghdad
HIGHEST POINT Haji Ibrahim 11,811 ft.
MONETARY UNIT Iraqi dinar
MAJOR LANGUAGES Arabic, Kurdish
MAJOR RELIGION Islam

Topography

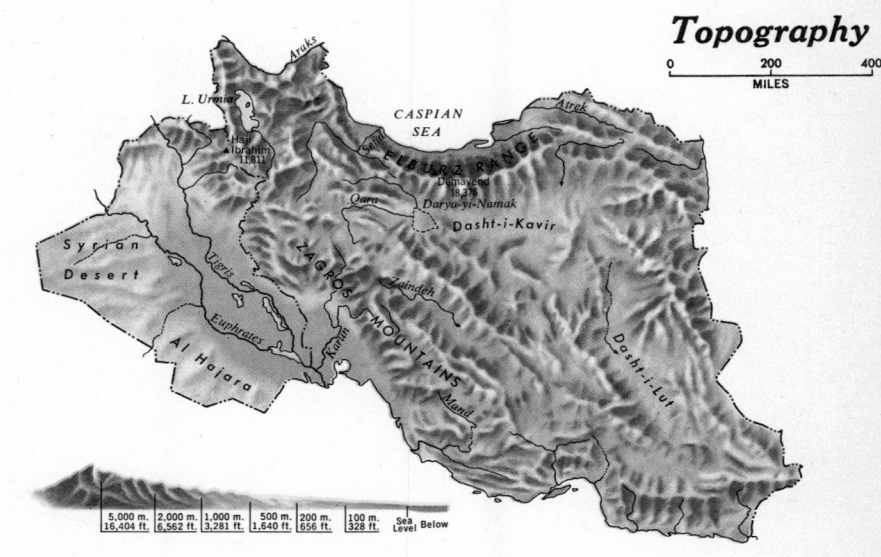

Agriculture, Industry and Resources

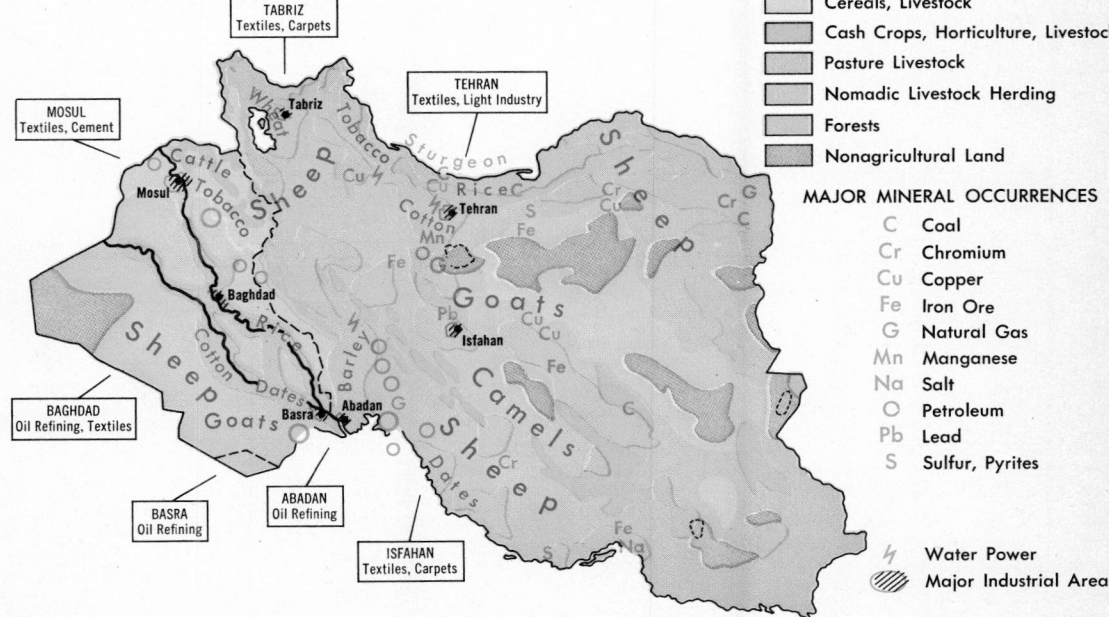

DOMINANT LAND USE

- Cereals, Livestock
- Cash Crops, Horticulture, Livestock
- Pasture Livestock
- Nomadic Livestock Herding
- Forests
- Nonagricultural Land

MAJOR MINERAL OCCURRENCES

C Coal
Cr Chromium
Cu Copper
Fe Iron Ore
G Natural Gas
Mn Manganese
Na Salt
O Petroleum
Pb Lead
S Sulfur, Pyrites

⚡ Water Power
▨ Major Industrial Areas

TABRIZ
Textiles, Carpets

TEHRAN
Textiles, Light Industry

MOSUL
Textiles, Cement

BAGHDAD
Oil Refining, Textiles

BASRA
Oil Refining

ABADAN
Oil Refining

ISFAHAN
Textiles, Carpets

INDIAN SUBCONTINENT and AFGHANISTAN

CONIC PROJECTION

SCALE OF MILES

0 50 100 200 300

SCALE OF KILOMETRES

0 50 100 200 300

Capitals of Countries .... ★
Provincial and State Capitals .... ◉
International Boundaries .... — · — · —
Provincial and State Boundaries — · —
Canals ....

Copyright by C. S. HAMMOND & CO., N. Y.

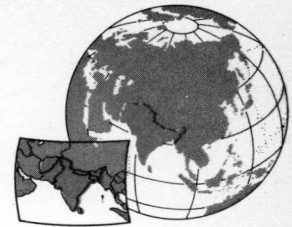

INDIA
AREA 1,261,483 sq. mi.
POPULATION 546,955,945
CAPITAL New Delhi
LARGEST CITY Calcutta (greater)
HIGHEST POINT K2 (Godwin Austen) 28,250 ft.
MONETARY UNIT Indian rupee
MAJOR LANGUAGES Hindi, English, Bihari, Telugu, Marathi, Bengali, Tamil, Gujarati, Rajasthani, Kanarese, Malayalam, Oriya, Punjabi, Assamese, Kashmiri
MAJOR RELIGIONS Hinduism, Islam, Christianity, Sikhism, Buddhism, Jainism, Zoroastrianism, Animism

PAKISTAN
AREA 310,403 sq. mi.
POPULATION 60,000,000
CAPITAL Islamabad
LARGEST CITY Karachi
HIGHEST POINT Tirich Mir 25,230 ft.
MONETARY UNIT Pakistani rupee
MAJOR LANGUAGES Urdu, English, Punjabi, Pushtu, Sindhi, Baluchi
MAJOR RELIGIONS Islam, Hinduism, Sikhism, Christianity

SRI LANKA (CEYLON)
AREA 25,332 sq. mi.
POPULATION 12,300,000
CAPITAL Colombo
LARGEST CITY Colombo
HIGHEST POINT Pidurutalagala 8,281 ft.
MONETARY UNIT Ceylonese rupee
MAJOR LANGUAGES Singhalese, Tamil, English
MAJOR RELIGIONS Buddhism, Hinduism, Christianity

AFGHANISTAN
AREA 250,000 sq. mi.
POPULATION 17,078,263
CAPITAL Kabul
LARGEST CITY Kabul
HIGHEST POINT Hindu Kush 24,556 ft.
MONETARY UNIT afghani
MAJOR LANGUAGES Pushtu, Dari, Uzbek
MAJOR RELIGION Islam

NEPAL
AREA 54,362 sq. mi.
POPULATION 10,845,000
CAPITAL Kathmandu
LARGEST CITY Kathmandu
HIGHEST POINT Mt. Everest 29,028 ft.
MONETARY UNIT Nepalese rupee
MAJOR LANGUAGES Nepali, Maithili, Tamang, Newari, Tharu
MAJOR RELIGIONS Hinduism, Buddhism

MALDIVES
AREA 115 sq. mi.
POPULATION 110,770
CAPITAL Male
LARGEST CITY Male
HIGHEST POINT 20 ft.
MONETARY UNIT Indian & Ceylonese rupee
MAJOR LANGUAGE Divehi
MAJOR RELIGION Islam

BHUTAN
AREA 18,000 sq. mi.
POPULATION 1,034,774
CAPITAL Thimphu
LARGEST CITY Thimphu
HIGHEST POINT Chomo Lhari 23,997 ft.
MONETARY UNIT Indian rupee
MAJOR LANGUAGES Tibetan dialects, Nepali
MAJOR RELIGIONS Buddhism, Hinduism

BANGLADESH
AREA 55,126 sq. mi.
POPULATION 70,000,000
CAPITAL Dacca
LARGEST CITY Dacca
HIGHEST POINT Mowdok Mual 3,292 ft.
MONETARY UNIT taka
MAJOR LANGUAGES Bengali, English
MAJOR RELIGIONS Islam, Hinduism, Christianity

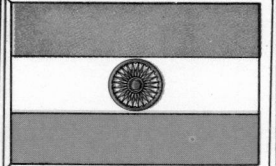
INDIA

PAKISTAN

SRI LANKA (CEYLON)

BHUTAN

AFGHANISTAN

MALDIVES

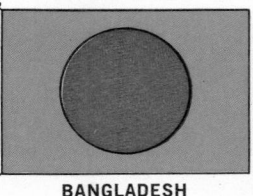
BANGLADESH

NEPAL

AFGHANISTAN
CITIES and TOWNS

Andkhui, 30,000 ....B 1
Baghlan, 92,000 ....A 1
Bala Murghab, 10,000 ....A 1
Balkh, 15,000 ....B 1
Bamian, 25,000 ....B 2
Chahar Burjak, 500 ....A 2
Charikar, 83,700 ....B 1
Daulatabad, 15,000 ....A 2
Daulat Yar, 2,000 ....B 2
Faizabad, 57,000 ....C 1
Farah, 26,400 ....A 2
Gardez, 33,000 ....B 2
Ghazni, 39,900 ....B 2
Ghurian, 10,000 ....A 2
Girishk, 10,000 ....A 2
Haibak, 35,200 ....B 1
Herat, 71,563 ....A 2
Jalalabad, 48,919 ....B 2
Jurm, 10,000 ....C 1
Juwain, 2,000 ....A 2
Kabul (cap.), 472,313 ....B 2
Kabul, *600,000 ....B 2
Kala Bist, 26,100 ....A 2
Kalat-i-Ghilzai, 40,500 ....B 2
Kandahar, 127,036 ....B 2
Kandahar, *142,000 ....B 2
Khanabad, 30,000 ....B 1
Kushk, 10,000 ....A 1
Landi Muhammad Amin Khan,
 1,000 ....A 2
Maimana, 48,750 ....A 1
Matun, 15,000 ....B 2
Mazar-i-Sharif, 43,197 ....B 1
Mukur, 10,000 ....B 2
Obeh, 5,000 ....A 2
Panjao, 3,000 ....B 2
Qala Panja, 1,000 ....C 1
Qaleh-i-Kang, 15,600 ....A 2
Rudbar, 1,000 ....A 2
Rustak, 10,000 ....C 1
Sabzawar, 5,000 ....A 2
Sar-i-Pul, 5,000 ....B 1
Shahjui, 5,000 ....B 2
Shibarghan, 50,440 ....A 1
Shindand (Sabzawar), 5,000...A 2
Taiwara, 5,000 ....A 2
Tashkurghan, 30,000 ....B 1
Zebak, 2,000 ....C 1

OTHER FEATURES

Baroghil (pass) ....C 1
Chagai (hills) ....A 3
Farah Rud (river) ....A 2
Hari Rud (river) ....A 2
Helmand (river) ....B 2
Hindu Kush (mts.) ....B 1
Jam (mt.) ....A 2
Kabul (river) ....C 2
Kunar (river) ....C 1
Kunduz (river) ....B 1
Lora (river) ....B 2
Margo, Dasht-i- (des.) ....A 2
Namaksar (salt lake) ....A 2
Paropamisus (range) ....A 2
Registan (desert) ....B 2
Tarnak (river) ....B 2
Zirreh, Gaud-i- (marsh) ....A 3

BANGLADESH
CITIES and TOWNS

Barisal, 69,936 ....G 4
Bogra, 33,784 ....F 4
Chittagong, 364,205 ....G 4
Chittagong, *437,000 ....G 4
Comilla, 54,504 ....G 4
Dacca (cap.), 556,712 ....G 4
Dacca, *829,000 ....G 4
Dinajpur, 37,711 ....F 3
Faridpur, 28,333 ....F 4
Jessore, 46,366 ....F 4
Khulna, 127,970 ....F 4
Khulna, *320,000 ....F 4
Mymensingh, 53,256 ....G 4
Narayanganj, 162,054 ....G 4
Narayanganj, *327,000 ....G 4
Noakhali, 19,874 ....G 4
Pabna, 40,792 ....F 4
Rajshahi, 56,885 ....F 4
Rangamati, 6,416 ....G 4
Rangpur, 40,634 ....F 3
Sylhet, 37,740 ....G 4

OTHER FEATURES

Bengal (bay) ....F 5
Brahamputra (riv.) ....G 3
Ganges (river) ....F 3
Sundarbans (swamp) ....F 4

BHUTAN
CITIES and TOWNS

Bumthang, 10,000 ....G 3
Paro Dzong, 35,000 ....F 3
Punakha, 12,000 ....G 3
Taga Dzong, 18,000 ....G 3
Thimphu (cap.), 50,000 ....G 3
Tongsa Dzong ....G 3

OTHER FEATURES

Chomo Lhari (mt.) ....F 3
Kula Kangri (mt.) ....G 3

INDIA
INTERNAL DIVISIONS

Andaman and Nicobar Islands
 (terr.), 115,092 ....G 6
Andhra Pradesh (state),
 43,394,951 ....D 5
Arunachal Pradesh (terr.),
 381,000 ....G 3
Assam (state), 14,630,422 .....G 3
Bihar (state), 56,387,296 ....F 4
Chandigarh (terr.), 150,000 ...D 2
Dadra and Nagar Haveli (terr.),
 69,000 ....C 4
Delhi (terr.), 4,044,281 ....D 2
Goa, Daman and Diu (terr.),
 675,000 ....C 4
Gujarat (state), 25,189,000 ....C 4
Haryana (state), 9,914,145 ....D 3
Himachal Pradesh (state),
 3,432,000 ....D 2
Jammu and Kashmir (state),
 4,615,025 ....D 2

(continued on following page)

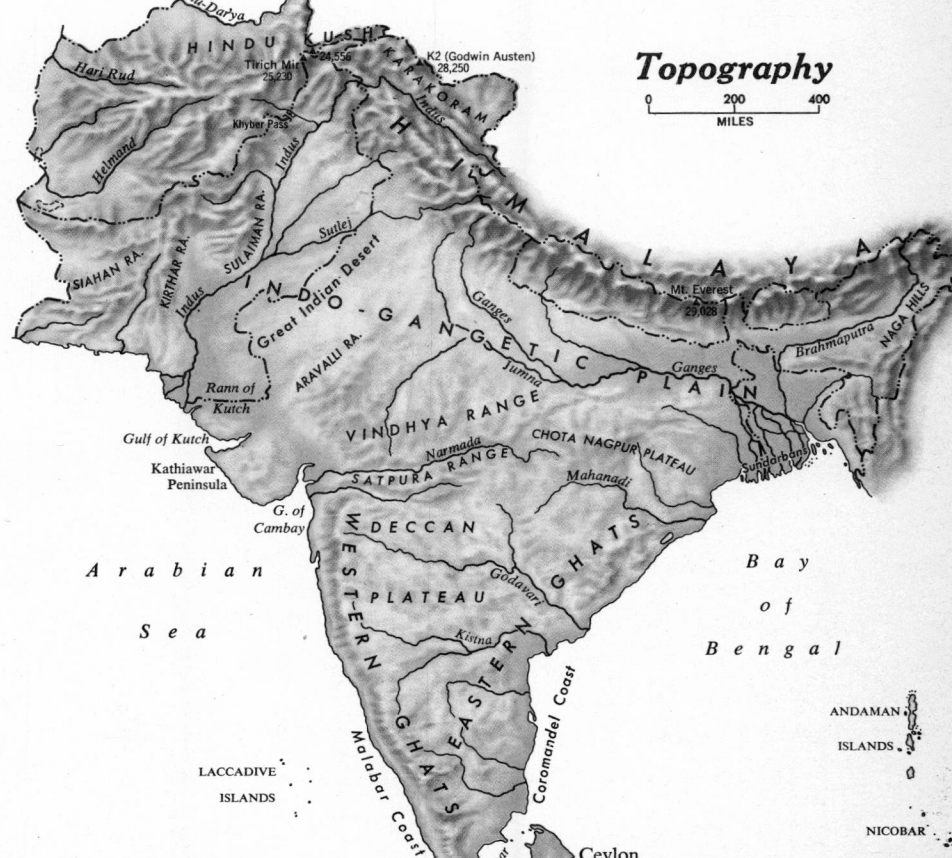

Topography

0   200   400
MILES

5,000 m. / 16,404 ft. | 2,000 m. / 6,562 ft. | 1,000 m. / 3,281 ft. | 500 m. / 1,640 ft. | 200 m. / 656 ft. | 100 m. / 328 ft. | Sea Level | Below

INDIA (continued)

Kerala (state), 20,296,000 .... D 6
Laccadive, Minicoy and Amindivi Islands (terr.), 27,000 .... C 6
Madhya Pradesh (state), 41,449,729 .... D 4
Maharashtra (state), 50,295,081 .. C 5
Manipur (state), 1,035,000 .... G 4
Meghalaya (state), 983,336 ...... G 3
Mizoram (terr.), 321,686 .... G 4
Mysore (state), 27,985,000 .... D 6
Nagaland (state), 515,551 .... G 3
Orissa (state), 20,674,000 .... E 5
Pondicherry (terr.), 430,000 ...... E 6
Punjab (state), 13,935,000 .... D 2
Rajasthan (state), 25,724,595 .... C 3
Sikkim (state), 191,000 .... F 3
Tamil Nadu (state), 33,686,953 .... D 6
Tripura (state), 1,424,000 .... G 4
Uttar Pradesh (state), 88,299,453 .... D 3
West Bengal (state), 44,440,095 .... F 4

CITIES and TOWNS

Abu Road, 17,728 .... C 4
Achalpur, 36,538 .... D 4
Achalpur, *54,028 .... D 4
Adilabad, 20,970 .... D 5
Adoni, 69,951 .... D 5
Agartala, 54,878 .... G 4
Agra, 610,328 .... D 3
Agra, *658,781 .... D 3
Ahmadabad, 1,507,921 .... C 4
Ahmadabad, *1,746,111 .... C 4
Ahmadnagar, 131,973 .... C 5
Aijal, 31,436 .... G 4
Ajanta .... D 4
Ajmer, 265,156 .... C 3
Akola, 143,919 .... D 4
Aligarh, 232,278 .... D 3
Allahabad, 521,568 .... E 3
Allahabad, *537,047 .... E 3
Alleppey, 161,279 .... D 7
Almora, 16,004 .... D 3
Almora, *16,602 .... D 3
Alwar, 72,707 .... D 3
Amalner, 46,963 .... C 4
Ambala, 87,750 .... D 2
Ambala, *200,576 .... D 2
Amravati, 177,066 .... D 4
Amreli, 34,699 .... C 4
Amritsar, 424,961 .... C 2
Amritsar, *459,179 .... C 2
Anakapalle, 46,402 .... E 5
Anantapur, 52,280 .... D 6
Anantnag, 21,087 .... D 2
Andheri, 122,401 .... B 7
Arcot, 25,029 .... D 6
Arrah, 76,766 .... E 3
Aruppukkottai, 50,200 .... D 7
Aruppukkottai, *55,977 .... D 7
Arvi, 21,478 .... D 4
Asansol, 134,058 .... F 4
Asansol, *278,350 .... F 4
Aurangabad, Bihar, 14,154 .... E 4
Aurangabad, Maharashtra, 87,579 .... D 5
Aurangabad, *97,701 .... D 5
Azamgarh, 32,391 .... E 3
Badagara, 43,908 .... D 6
Bagalkot, 39,934 .... D 5
Bahraich, 56,033 .... E 3
Baidyabati, 44,312 .... F 1
Balasore, 33,931 .... F 4
Ballia, 38,216 .... E 3
Bally, 247,844 .... F 1
Balrampur, 31,776 .... E 3
Banda, 37,744 .... D 3
Bandra, 38,099 .... B 7
Bangalore, 1,027,327 .... D 6
Bangalore, *1,648,232 .... D 6
Bankura, 62,833 .... F 4
Bansberia, 45,463 .... F 1
Baramati, 21,118 .... C 5
Barasat, 29,281 .... F 1
Barasat, *61,621 .... F 1
Bareilly, 325,560 .... D 3
Bareilly, *343,559 .... D 3
Baripada, 20,301 .... F 4
Barmer, 27,600 .... C 3
Barnagore, 143,621 .... F 1
Baroda, 400,725 .... C 4
Barpeta, 22,207 .... G 3
Barrackpore, 63,778 .... F 1
Barrackpore, *158,244 .... F 1
Barsi, 50,389 .... D 5
Basirhat, 53,943 .... F 4
Bassein, 22,598 .... C 5
Bassein, *28,238 .... C 5
Batala, 51,300 .... D 2
Beawar, 53,931 .... C 3
Belgaum, 156,105 .... C 5
Belgaum, *176,857 .... C 5
Bellary, 85,673 .... D 5
Belur, 29,737 .... F 1
Benares (Varanasi), 619,822 .... E 3
Berhampore, 62,317 .... F 4
Berhampur, 76,931 .... F 5
Bettiah, 39,990 .... E 3
Bhadrak, 25,285 .... F 4
Bhadravati, 24,495 .... D 6
Bhadravati, *65,776 .... D 6
Bhadreswar, 35,489 .... F 1
Bhagalpur, 174,538 .... F 4
Bhandara, 27,710 .... E 4
Bhandup, 33,020 .... B 7
Bharatpur, 49,776 .... D 3
Bhatinda, 52,253 .... C 2
Bhatpara, 159,219 .... F 1
Bhavnagar, 217,533 .... C 4
Bhilai, 86,116 .... E 4
Bhilwara, 43,499 .... C 3
Bhimavaram, 43,281 .... E 5
Bhir (Bir), 33,066 .... D 5
Bhiwandi, 47,630 .... C 5
Bhiwani, 58,194 .... D 3
Bhopal, 310,733 .... D 4
Bhopal, *441,939 .... D 4
Bhubaneswar, 38,211 .... F 4
Bhuj, 38,953 .... B 4
Bhuj, *40,180 .... B 4
Bhusawal, 73,994 .... D 4
Bhusawal, *79,121 .... D 4
Bidar, 32,420 .... D 5
Bihar, 78,581 .... F 3
Bijapur, 78,854 .... D 5
Bijnor, 33,821 .... D 3
Bikaner, 186,560 .... C 3
Bilaspur, 86,706 .... E 4
Bina, 27,476 .... D 4
Bir, 33,066 .... D 5
Birmitrapur, 20,301 .... E 4
Bobbili, 25,592 .... E 5
Bodhan, 30,929 .... D 5
Bodinayakkanur, 44,914 .... D 6
Bombay, *5,931,989 .... B 7
Broach, 73,639 .... C 4
Budaun, 58,770 .... D 3
Budge-Budge, 39,824 .... F 2
Bulsar, 35,028 .... C 4
Bulsar, *37,586 .... C 4
Bundi, 26,478 .... D 3
Burdwan, 147,528 .... F 4
Burhanpur, 82,090 .... D 4
Calcutta, 7,040,345 .... F 2
Calicut (Kozhikode), 315,786 .... D 6
Cambay, 51,291 .... C 4
Cannanore, 46,101 .... C 6
Cannanore, *48,960 .... B 6
Cawnpore (Kanpur), 1,163,524 .... E 3
Chaibasa, 22,019 .... F 4
Champdani, 42,129 .... F 1
Chanda, 51,484 .... D 5
Chandernagore, 67,105 .... F 1
Chandigarh, 89,321 .... D 2
Chandigarh, *110,614 .... D 2
Chapra, 75,580 .... F 3
Chembur, 85,582 .... B 7
Chhatarpur, 22,146 .... D 4
Chhindwara, 37,244 .... D 4
Chidambaram, 40,694 .... E 6
Chik Ballapur, 23,025 .... D 6
Chikmagalur, 30,253 .... D 6
Chingleput, 25,977 .... E 6
Chiplun, 17,355 .... C 5
Chiplun, *22,760 .... C 5
Chirala, 45,410 .... E 5
Chitradurga, 33,336 .... D 6
Chittoor, 47,876 .... D 6
Churu, 41,727 .... D 3
Cocanada (Kakinada), 146,332 .... E 5
Cochin, 35,076 .... D 6
Coimbatore, 393,145 .... D 6
Cooch Behar, 41,922 .... F 3
Cuddalore, 79,168 .... E 6
Cuddapah, 49,027 .... D 6
Cuttack, 198,405 .... F 4
Dabhoi, 30,841 .... C 4
Daltonganj, 25,270 .... E 4
Damoh, 46,656 .... D 4
Darbhanga, 121,438 .... F 3
Darjeeling, 40,651 .... F 3
Datia, 29,430 .... D 3
Davangere, 78,124 .... D 6
Dehra Dun, 136,469 .... D 2
Dehra Dun, *167,297 .... D 2
Delhi, *3,629,842 .... D 3
Deoghar, 35,105 .... F 4
Deolali, 37,264 .... C 5
Deoria, 28,407 .... E 3
Dewas, 34,577 .... D 4
Dhamtari, 31,552 .... E 4
Dhanbad, 57,400 .... F 4
Dhar, 28,325 .... C 4
Dharwar, 77,163 .... C 5
Dholpur, 27,412 .... D 3
Dhond, 12,912 .... C 5
Dhond, *27,168 .... C 5
Dhoraji, 48,951 .... C 4
Dhubri, 28,355 .... G 3
Dhulia, 98,893 .... C 4
Dibrugarh, 58,480 .... G 3
Dindigul, 92,947 .... D 6
Dohad, 35,483 .... C 4
Dohad, *50,434 .... C 4
Domjor, 8,670 .... F 1
Domjor, *30,843 .... F 1
Dum Dum, 20,041 .... F 1
Dum Dum, *174,177 .... F 1
Durg, 64,132 .... E 4
Durg, *204,784 .... E 4
Durgapur, *41,696 .... F 4
Dwarka, 11,912 .... B 4
Dwarka, *14,314 .... B 4
Eluru, 130,166 .... E 5
Ernakulam, 203,493 .... D 6
Ernakulam, *474,187 .... D 6
Erode, 73,762 .... D 6
Erode, *96,528 .... D 6
Etawah, 69,681 .... D 3
Faizabad, 83,717 .... E 3
Faizabad, *88,296 .... E 3
Fatehgarh, 87,793 .... D 3
Fatehgarh, *94,591 .... D 3
Fatehpur, 27,039 .... C 3
Fatehpur, 28,323 .... E 3
Ferozepore, 47,060 .... C 2
Ferozepore, *97,932 .... C 2
Firozabad, 98,611 .... D 3
Gadag, 76,614 .... D 5
Gandhinagar, 24,049 .... C 4
Ganganagar, 63,854 .... C 3
Gangtok, 6,848 .... F 3
Garden Reach, 152,347 .... F 2
Garulia, 29,041 .... F 1
Gauhati, 210,561 .... G 3
Gaya, 167,500 .... F 4
Ghat Kopar, 34,256 .... B 7
Ghaziabad, 63,190 .... D 3
Ghaziabad, *70,438 .... D 3
Ghazipur, 37,147 .... E 3
Goalpara, 13,692 .... G 3
Godhra, 52,167 .... C 4
Gonda, 43,496 .... E 3
Gondal, 45,069 .... C 4
Gopalpur, 3,536 .... F 5
Gorakhpur, 234,497 .... E 3
Gudur, 25,618 .... D 6
Gulbarga, 97,069 .... D 5
Guna, 31,031 .... D 4
Guntakal, 48,083 .... D 5
Guntur, 264,138 .... D 5
Gwalior, 361,780 .... D 3
Haflong, 3,265 .... G 3
Harda, 22,279 .... D 4
Hardoi, 36,725 .... E 3
Hardwar, 58,513 .... D 2
Hardwar, *59,960 .... D 2
Hassan, 32,172 .... D 6
Hathras, 64,045 .... D 3
Hazaribagh, 40,958 .... F 4
Hindupur, 32,445 .... D 6
Hinganghat, 36,890 .... D 4
Hingoli, 23,407 .... D 5
Hissar, 60,222 .... D 3
Honavar, 10,453 .... C 6
Hooghly-Chinsura, 83,104 .... F 1
Hoshangabad, 19,284 .... D 4
Hospet, 53,242 .... D 5
Howrah, 590,385 .... F 2
Hubli, 217,284 .... C 5
Hubli, *303,696 .... C 5
Hunza (Baltit) .... C 1
Hyderabad, 1,294,800 .... D 5
Hyderabad, *1,798,910 .... D 5
Ichchapuram, 12,961 .... F 5
Ichhapur, 12,382 .... F 1
Imphal, 67,717 .... G 4
Indore, 483,969 .... D 4
Itarsi, 33,611 .... D 4
Jabalpur, 406,214 .... D 4
Jabalpur, *497,946 .... D 4
Jagdalpur, 20,412 .... E 5
Jagtial, 20,941 .... D 5
Jaipur, 533,151 .... D 3
Jaisalmer, 8,362 .... C 3
Jajpur, 13,802 .... F 4
Jalgaon, 80,351 .... D 4
Jalna, 67,158 .... D 4
Jalor, 12,882 .... C 3
Jalpaiguri, 48,738 .... F 3
Jamalpur, 57,039 .... F 3
Jammu, 102,738 .... D 2
Jammu, *108,257 .... D 2
Jamnagar, 200,918 .... B 4
Jamshedpur, 402,462 .... F 4
Jamshedpur, *465,740 .... F 4
Jaora, 31,140 .... D 4
Jaunpur, 61,851 .... E 3
Jeypore, 25,291 .... E 5
Jhalawar, 14,643 .... D 4
Jhansi, 177,456 .... D 3
Jhansi, *216,736 .... D 3
Jhunjhunu, 24,962 .... D 3
Jind, 24,216 .... D 3
Jodhpur, 270,404 .... C 3
Jorhat, 24,953 .... G 3
Jubbulpore (Jabalpur), 406,214 .... D 4
Juhu, 9,990 .... B 7
Jullundur, 281,623 .... D 2
Jullundur, *333,938 .... D 2
Junagadh, 74,298 .... B 4
Kadayanallur, 41,249 .... D 7
Kadiri, 24,307 .... D 6
Kakinada, 146,332 .... E 5
Kalyan, 73,482 .... C 5
Kalyan, *194,334 .... C 5
Kamarhati, 190,695 .... F 1
Kamptee, 40,859 .... D 4
Kamptee, *46,643 .... D 4
Kanchipuram, 92,714 .... E 6
Kandla, 9,617 .... C 4
Kandukur, 12,436 .... E 5
Kangra, 5,775 .... D 2
Kanker, 6,487 .... E 4
Kannauj, 24,646 .... D 3
Kanpur, 1,163,524 .... E 3
Kanpur, *1,273,042 .... E 3
Karad, 33,772 .... C 5
Karaikudi, 43,698 .... D 7
Karanja, 26,440 .... D 4
Karauli, 23,696 .... D 3
Kargil .... D 2
Karikal, 22,252 .... E 6
Karkal, 15,535 .... C 6
Karnal, 72,109 .... D 3
Karur, 50,564 .... D 6
Karwar, 23,906 .... C 6
Kasaragod, 27,635 .... C 6
Kasganj, 37,559 .... D 3
Katarnian Ghat .... E 3
Katihar, 46,837 .... F 3
Katihar, *59,344 .... F 3
Katni (Murwara), 46,169 .... E 4
Kavali, 20,544 .... E 6
Kavaratti, 2,828 .... C 6
Kawardha, 10,117 .... E 4
Kendrapara, 15,830 .... F 4
Keonjhar, 12,624 .... F 4
Khamgaon, 44,432 .... D 4
Khamman, 35,888 .... D 5
Khandwa, 63,505 .... D 4
Kharagpur, 163,929 .... F 4
Khardah, 28,362 .... F 1
Khurda, 12,497 .... F 4
Kirkee, 58,496 .... C 5
Kishangarh, 25,244 .... D 3
Kishtwar, 4,140 .... D 2
Kohima, 7,246 .... G 3
Kolar, 32,587 .... D 6
Kolar Gold Fields, 167,610 .... D 6
Kolhapur, 245,206 .... C 5
Kolhapur, *259,482 .... C 5
Konnagar, 29,443 .... F 1
Koppal, 19,530 .... D 5
Koraput, 7,461 .... E 5
Kota, 205,429 .... D 3
Kotrung, 31,031 .... F 1
Kottayam, 52,685 .... D 7
Kotturu, 11,493 .... D 6
Kovur, 14,580 .... E 6
Kozhikode, 315,786 .... D 6
Kozhikode, *381,096 .... D 6
Krishnanagar, 70,440 .... F 4
Kulu, 4,886 .... D 2
Kumbakonam, 92,581 .... D 6
Kumbakonam, *96,746 .... D 6
Kumta, 16,223 .... C 6
Kurla, 98,018 .... B 7
Kurnool, 157,448 .... D 5
Lansdowne, 6,381 .... D 3
Latur, 40,913 .... D 5
Ledo .... H 3
Leh, 3,720 .... D 2
Lohardaga, 13,203 .... E 4
Lucknow, 763,604 .... E 3
Lucknow, *830,298 .... E 3
Ludhiana, 363,403 .... D 2
Lumding, 23,186 .... G 3
Machilipatnam, 126,855 .... E 5
Madh, 3,307 .... B 7
Madhubani, 28,229 .... F 3
Madras, 2,047,735 .... E 6
Madras, *2,470,288 .... E 6
Madugula, 7,688 .... E 5
Madurai, 486,480 .... D 7
Mahabaleshwar, 6,029 .... C 5
Mahbubnagar, 35,588 .... D 5
Mahe, 7,951 .... D 6
Mahoba, 24,878 .... D 3
Mahuva, 31,668 .... C 4
Mahuva, *32,732 .... C 4
Malad, 88,287 .... B 6
Malakanagiri, 2,510 .... E 5
Malegaon, 243,474 .... C 4
Maler-Kotla, 39,543 .... D 2
Malkapur, 29,687 .... D 4
Malvan, 17,828 .... C 5
Mandi, 13,034 .... D 2
Mandla, 19,416 .... E 4
Mandsaur, 41,876 .... C 4
Mandvi, 26,609 .... B 4
Mangalore, 168,646 .... C 6
Mangalore, *234,680 .... C 6
Mangrol, 21,089 .... B 4
Manmad, 23,570 .... C 4
Manmad, *31,551 .... C 4
Mannargudi, 33,558 .... E 6
Manori, 2,492 .... B 6
Marmagao, 14,140 .... C 5
Mathura, 135,166 .... D 3
Mathura, *144,485 .... D 3
Mattancheri, 83,896 .... D 7
Mau, 48,785 .... E 3
Mayuram, 51,393 .... D 6
Meerut, 244,824 .... D 3
Meerut, *335,565 .... D 3
Mehsana, 32,577 .... C 4
Mercara, 14,453 .... D 6
Mhow, 48,032 .... D 4
Midnapore, 59,532 .... F 4
Miraj, 53,345 .... D 5
Mirzapur, 113,177 .... E 4
Modasa, 16,084 .... C 4
Mominabad, 17,443 .... D 5
Monghyr, 89,768 .... F 3
Moradabad, 205,509 .... D 3
Moradabad, *221,433 .... D 3
Morvi, 50,192 .... C 4
Mulund, 56,430 .... B 6
Murud, 10,055 .... C 5
Murwara, 46,169 .... E 4
Murwara, *60,472 .... E 4
Muzaffarabad .... B 2
Muzaffarnagar, 87,622 .... D 3
Muzaffarpur, 152,831 .... E 3
Mysore, 262,136 .... D 6
Nadiad, 78,952 .... C 4
Nagapattinam, 59,063 .... E 6
Nagapattinam, *61,305 .... E 6
Nagaur, 24,296 .... C 3
Nagercoil, 136,264 .... D 7
Nagina, 30,247 .... D 3
Nagpur, 876,020 .... D 4
Nagpur, *933,344 .... D 4
Nahan, 12,439 .... D 2
Naihati, 58,457 .... F 1
Naini Tal, 14,995 .... D 3
Naini Tal, *16,080 .... D 3
Nainpur, 13,728 .... E 4
Nalgonda, 24,383 .... D 5
Nander, 81,087 .... D 5
Nandurbar, 41,055 .... C 4
Nandyal, 42,927 .... D 5
Narayanpet, 20,504 .... D 5
Narnaul, 23,959 .... D 3
Narsinghgarh, 11,558 .... D 4
Narsinghpur, 17,940 .... D 4
Nasik, 169,451 .... C 4
Nasik, *282,782 .... C 4
Nasirabad, 24,148 .... C 3
Navsari, 51,300 .... C 4
Navsari, *53,600 .... C 4
Nellore, 134,404 .... E 6
New Delhi (cap.), 324,283 .... D 3
Nimach, 36,287 .... D 4
Nirmal, 19,896 .... D 5
Nizamabad, 79,093 .... D 5
North Lakhimpur, 6,576 .... G 3
Nova Goa (Panjim), †79,437 .... C 5
Nowgong, 8,604 .... G 3
Nowgong, *38,600 .... G 3
Okha Port, 8,909 .... B 4
Okha Port, *9,630 .... B 4
Ongole, 35,804 .... E 5
Ootacamund, 50,140 .... D 6
Orai, 29,587 .... D 3
Osmanabad, 18,868 .... D 5
Pachmarhi, 653 .... D 4
Pachmarhi, *6,142 .... D 4
Palanpur, 29,139 .... C 4
Palayankottai, 51,002 .... D 7
Palghat, 77,620 .... D 6
Pali, 33,303 .... C 3
Palni, 39,832 .... D 6
Palni, *56,909 .... D 6
Panchur, 25,131 .... F 2
Pandharpur, 45,421 .... D 5
Panihati, 93,749 .... F 1
Panipat, 67,026 .... D 3
Panjim, †79,437 .... C 5
Panna, 16,737 .... E 4
Panruti, 18,754 .... D 6
Parbhani, 36,795 .... D 5
Parlakhemundi, 22,708 .... E 5
Partapgarh, 14,573 .... C 4
Parvatipuram, 25,281 .... E 5
Patan, 50,264 .... C 4
Patiala, 154,414 .... D 2
Patna, 449,471 .... F 3
Patna, *451,520 .... F 3
Phalodi, 15,722 .... C 3
Pilibhit, 57,527 .... D 3
Point Calimere .... E 6
Pondicherry, 40,421 .... E 6
Ponnani, 22,977 .... D 6
Poona, 718,220 .... C 5
Poona, *1,123,399 .... C 5
Porbandar, 74,476 .... B 4
Porbandar, *75,081 .... B 4
Port Blair, 14,075 .... G 6
Porto Novo, 15,139 .... E 6
Proddatur, 50,616 .... D 6
Pudukkottai, 50,488 .... D 6
Punch, 10,196 .... C 2
Puri, 60,815 .... F 5
Purnea, 40,602 .... F 3
Purulia, 48,134 .... F 4
Puttur, 12,498 .... D 6
Quilon, 91,018 .... D 7
Radhanpur, 15,058 .... C 4
Raichur, 63,329 .... D 5
Raigarh, 36,933 .... E 4
Raipur, 204,632 .... E 4
Rairakhol, 2,441 .... E 4
Rajahmundry, 155,450 .... E 5
Rajapalaiyam, 71,203 .... D 7
Rajapur, 8,270 .... C 5
Rajgarh, 9,095 .... D 4
Rajkot, 270,186 .... C 4
Rajnandgaon, 44,678 .... E 4
Rajpipla, 21,426 .... C 4
Rajpur, 24,812 .... F 2
Rajpura, 11,211 .... D 2
Rajpura, *27,925 .... D 2
Rameswaram, 6,801 .... D 7
Rampur, 136,349 .... D 3
Rampur, 2,079 .... D 2
Ranchi, 137,280 .... F 4
Ranchi, *176,789 .... F 4
Ratangarh, 26,631 .... C 3
Ratlam, 87,472 .... C 4
Ratnagiri, 31,091 .... C 5
Raurkela, 90,287 .... F 4
Raxaul, 9,699 .... E 3
Rayagada, 14,537 .... E 5
Renigunta, 5,942 .... E 6
Rewa, 43,065 .... E 4
Rewari, 36,994 .... D 3
Rishra, 38,535 .... F 1
Robertsganj, 6,584 .... E 4
Sadiya .... H 3
Sagar, 97,556 .... D 4
Sagar, *120,262 .... D 4
Saharanpur, 223,459 .... D 3
Salem, 297,168 .... D 6
Samalkot, 31,924 .... E 5
Sambalpur, 38,915 .... E 4
Sambhal, 68,940 .... D 3
Sangamner, 21,729 .... C 5
Sangli, 88,753 .... C 5
Sangli, *150,407 .... C 5
Santa Cruz, 101,232 .... B 7
Santipur, 51,190 .... F 4
Sardarshahr, 32,072 .... C 3
Sarnath .... E 3
Sasaram, 37,782 .... E 4
Satara, 44,353 .... C 5
Satara, *48,709 .... C 5
Satna, 38,046 .... E 4
Savantvadi, 15,120 .... C 5
Savanur, 16,930 .... D 6
Secunderabad, 187,471 .... D 5
Sehore, 28,489 .... D 4
Seoni, 30,274 .... D 4
Serampore, 91,521 .... F 1
Seringapatam, 11,423 .... D 6
Shahdol, 22,196 .... E 4
Shahjahanpur, 121,107 .... E 3
Shahjahanpur, *129,737 .... E 3
Shajapur, 17,317 .... D 4
Sheo, †56,033 .... C 3
Sheopur, 14,591 .... D 3
Shillong, Assam, 14,089 .... G 3
Shillong, Meghalaya, 73,529 .... G 3
Shillong, *130,195 .... G 3
Shimoga, 63,764 .... D 6
Shivpuri, 28,681 .... D 3
Sholapur, 398,996 .... D 5
Shorapur, 17,689 .... D 5
Sibsagar, 15,106 .... H 3
Sidhi, 5,021 .... E 4
Sidhpur, 33,850 .... C 4
Sikar, 50,636 .... D 3
Silchar, 41,062 .... G 4
Siliguri, 65,471 .... F 3
Silvassa .... B 4
Simla, 42,597 .... D 2
Singur, 7,915 .... F 1

BRITISH INDIA
U.S.S.R.
GILGIT AGENCY
AFGHANISTAN
KASHMIR & JAMMU
N.W. FRONTIER PROV.
PUNJAB
BALUCHISTAN
Indus
IRAN
BAHAWALPUR (PUNJ. ST.)
PUNJAB STATES
DELHI
RAMPUR
TIBET
CHINA
NEPAL
UNITED PROVINCES
SIKKIM
BHUTAN
ASSAM
Brahmaputra
E. ST.
KHASI HILLS
MANIPUR
TRIPURA (E. ST.)
BURMA
PUNJ. ST.
RAJPUTANA
SIND
AJMER-MERWARA
Gwadar (Oman)
GWALIOR
CENTRAL INDIA
Ganges
BENARES
BIHAR
BENGAL
Chandernagore (Fr.)
EASTERN STATES
WESTERN INDIA
GUJARAT ST.
Arabian Sea
CENTRAL PROVINCES
BERAR
E. ST.
ORISSA
Diu (Port.)
Damão (Port.)
BOMBAY
EASTERN STATES
HYDERABAD
DECCAN STATES
Bay of Bengal
Yanaon (Fr.)
Gôa (Port.)
MADRAS
MYSORE
Bangalore (Br.)
COORG
Mahé (Fr.)
Pondichéry (Fr.)
Karikal (Fr.)
M. ST.
Laccadive Islands (Madras)
Cochin (Br.)
MADRAS STATES
CEYLON
Andaman Islands (Br.)
Nicobar Islands (Br.)
British India. The provinces of British India were directly administered by Britain. A few areas were leased from the Indian princes.
Indian States. The Indian States, sometimes referred to as the "Native" or "Princely States," were under the nominal control of maharajas or other hereditary princes.
Possessions of Other Countries in India
State or Provincial Boundaries
Other Internal Boundaries

Sirohi, 14,451 C 4
Sironj, 17,288 D 4
Sirsa, 33,363 D 3
Sirsi, 21,240 D 6
Sitapur, 53,884 E 3
Skardu D 1
Sonepur, 7,108 E 4
South Suburban, 307,471 F 2
South Suburban, *513,337 F 2
Srikakulam, 35,071 E 5
Srinagar, 285,257 D 2
Sundargarh, 11,329 E 4
Surada, 8,703 E 5
Surat, 368,917 C 4
Suratgarh, 8,330 C 3
Surendranagar, 48,602 C 4
Tanda, 32,687 E 3
Tehri, 4,508 D 2
Tellicherry, 44,763 C 6
Tenali, 78,525 E 5
Tezpur, 24,159 G 3
Thana, 154,770 B 6
Thana, *164,896 B 6
Thanjavur, 120,681 D 6
Tinsukia, 28,468 H 3
Tiruchendur, 15,182 D 7
Tiruchendur, *22,752 D 7
Tiruchchirappalli, 279,283 D 6
Tirunelveli, 87,988 D 7
Tirupati, 35,845 D 6
Tiruppattur, 30,799 D 6
Tiruvannamalai, 46,441 D 6
Titagarh, 76,429 F 1
Titlagarh, 7,433 E 4
Tollygunge F 2
Tonk, 43,413 D 3
Tranquebar, 14,754 E 6
Trichur, 73,038 D 6
Trivandrum, 336,757 D 7
Trivandrum, *435,566 D 7
Trombay, 17,258 B 7
Tuensang G 3
Tumkur, 47,277 D 6
Tuni, 22,452 E 5
Tura, 8,888 G 3
Tuticorin, 150,784 D 7
Tuticorin, *157,943 D 7
Udaipur, 133,368 C 4
Udhampur, 10,263 D 2
Udipi, 24,610 C 6
Ujjain, 157,435 D 4
Ulhasnagar, 137,636 C 5
Umrer, 22,682 D 4
Unnao, 29,780 E 3
Uran, 10,229 B 7
Uttarpara, 21,132 F 1
Vaniyambadi, 42,048 D 6
Vaniyambadi, *47,918 D 6
Varanasi, 619,822 E 3
Varanasi, *643,720 E 3
Vellore, 120,643 D 6
Vellore, *138,914 D 6
Vengurla, 12,061 C 5
Venkatagiri, 17,114 D 6
Veraval, 46,637 C 4
Veraval, *60,857 C 4
Vesava, 14,580 B 7
Vidisha, 27,718 D 4
Vijayawada, 312,822 D 5
Villupuram, 43,496 D 6
Vinukonda, 11,374 D 5
Virajpet, 8,138 D 6
Viramgam, 38,955 C 4
Visakhapatnam, 285,837 E 5
Visnagar, 25,982 C 4
Vizagapatam (Visakhapatnam), 285,837 E 5
Vizianagaram, 76,808 E 5
Waltair E 5
Warangal, 178,559 D 5
Wardha, 49,113 D 4
Wun, 18,176 D 5
Yanam, 7,032 E 5
Yellamanchili, 13,556 E 5
Yellandlapad E 5
Yeola, 21,039 C 4
Yeotmal, 45,587 D 4
Ziro G 3

OTHER FEATURES

Abor (hills) G 3
Adam's Bridge (shoals) D 7
Agatti (isl.), 2,411 C 6
Amindivi (isls.), 7,854 C 6
Amini (isl.), 3,530 C 6
Anai Mudi (mt.) D 6
Andaman (isls.) G 6
Andaman (sea) G 6
Androth (isl.), 4,183 C 6
Arabian (sea) B 5
Back (bay) B 7
Baltistan (region) D 1
Banas (river) D 3
Bengal (bay) F 5
Berar (region), 4,580,302 D 4
Betwa (river) D 4
Bhima (river) D 5
Bidyadhari (river) F 2
Bombay (harb.) B 7
Brahmaputra (river) G 3
Cambay (gulf) C 4
Camorta (isl.) G 7
Car Nicobar (isl.) G 7
Chambal (river) D 3
Chenab (river) D 2
Cherial (river) F 2
Chetlat (isl.), 953 C 6
Chilka (lake) F 5
Coco (channel) G 6
Colaba (pt.) B 7
Colair (lake) E 5
Comorin (cape) D 7
Coromandel Coast (reg.) E 6
Daman (dist.), 22,390 C 4
Damodar (river) F 4
Deccan (plateau) D 6
Diu (dist.), 14,280 C 4
Duncan (passage) G 6
Eastern Ghats (mts.) D 6
Elephanta (isl.) B 7
False (pt.) F 4
False Divi (pt.) E 5
Ganges (mouths) F 4
Ganges (Ganga) (river) F 3
Ghaghara (river) E 3
Ghea (river) F 1
Goa (dist.), 589,997 C 5
Godavari (river) D 5
Godwin Austen (K2) (mt.) D 1
Golconda (ruins) D 5
Great (channel) G 7
Great Indian (des.) C 3
Great Nicobar (isl.) G 7
Hagari (river) D 6
Himalaya (mts.) D 2
Hooghly (river) F 2
Indravati (river) E 5
Indus (river) D 2
Interview (isl.) G 6
Jhelum (river) C 2
Jumna (river) E 3
K2 (mt.) D 1
Kadmat (isl.), 1,851 C 6
Kalpeni (isl.), 2,613 C 7
Kamet (mt.) D 2
Kanchenjunga (mt.) F 3
Karakoram (mts.) D 1
Kaveri (riv.) D 6
Khasi (hills) G 3
Kiltan (isl.), 1,520 C 6
Kistna (Krishna) (river) D 5
Kunlun (range) D 1
Kutch (gulf) B 4
Kutch, Rann of (salt marsh) B 4
Laccadive (isls.), 12,115 C 6
Ladakh (region), 88,651 D 2
Landfall (isl.) G 6
Little Andaman (isl.) G 6
Little Nicobar (isl.) G 7
Luni (river) C 3
Lushai (hills) G 4
Mahanadi (river) E 4
Mahim (bay) B 7
Malabar (hill) B 7
Malabar (pt.) B 7
Malabar Coast (reg.) C 6
Malad (creek) B 7
Mannar (gulf) D 7
Manori (creek) B 7
Middle Andaman (isl.) G 6
Minicoy (isl.), 4,139 C 7
Miri (hills) G 3
Mishmi (hills) H 3
Nancowry (isl.) G 7
Nanda Devi (mt.) D 2
Nanga Parbat (mt.) D 1
Narcondam (isl.) G 6
Narmada (river) D 4
Nicobar (isls.) G 7
Nine Degree (chan.) C 7
North Andaman (isl.) G 6
North Sentinel (isl.) G 6
Palk (strait) D 7
Palmyras (pt.) F 4
Pangong Tso (lake) D 2
Penganga (river) D 5
Penner (river) D 6
Periyar (lake) D 7
Pitti (isl.), 80 C 6
Pulicat (lake) E 6
Rakaposhi (mt.) C 1
Ritchies (arch.) G 6
Rutland (isl.) G 6
Salsette (isl.), 1,566,572 B 7
Sambhar (lake) C 3
Saraswati (river) F 1
Sarsati (river) F 1
Satpura (range) D 4
Shipki (pass) D 2
Soda (plains) D 1
Sombrero (channel) G 7
Son (river) E 3
South Andaman (isl.) G 6
Suheli Par (isl.) C 6
Sundarbans (swamp) F 4
Sutlej (river) C 3
Tapti (river) D 4
Tel (river) E 4
Ten Degree (chan.) G 7
Thana (creek) B 7
Tillanchong (isl.) G 7
Tolly's Nullah (river) F 2
Towers of Silence B 7
Travancore (region) D 7
Tulsi (lake) B 6
Tungabhadra (river) D 5
Vehar (lake) B 7
Vindhya (range) D 4
Wardha (river) D 4
Western Ghats (mts.) C 5
Yamuna (Jumna) (river) E 3
Zaskar (mts.) D 2

MALDIVES

Maldives, 110,770 C 7

NEPAL

CITIES and TOWNS

Bhaktapur, 33,877 F 3
Bhojpur F 3
Biratnagar, 35,355 F 3
Birganj, 10,769 F 3
Dailekh E 3
Dhangarhi E 3
Dhankuta F 3
Doti E 3
Ilam F 3
Jaleswar F 3
Janakpur, 8,928 F 3
Kathmandu (capital), 121,019 E 3
Lalitpur, 47,713 E 3
Mukhtinath E 3
Mustang E 3
Nepalganj, 15,817 E 3
Palpa E 3
Pokhara, 5,413 E 3
Pyuthan E 3
Ramechhap F 3
Sallyana E 3
Simikot E 3

OTHER FEATURES

Annapurna (mt.) E 3
Bheri (river) E 3
Dhaulagiri (mt.) E 3
Everest (mt.) F 3
Himalaya (mts.) F 3
Kanchenjunga (mt.) F 3

PAKISTAN

PROVINCES

Baluchistan, 1,400,000 B 3
Capital Territory, 50,000 C 2
North-West Frontier, 9,500,000 C 2
Punjab, 36,290,000 C 2
Sind, 11,900,000 B 3

CITIES and TOWNS

Abbottabad, 31,036 C 2
Ahmadpur East, 20,423 C 3
Attock C 2
Bahawalnagar, 36,290 C 2
Bahawalpur, 84,377 C 3
Bahawalpur, *147,000 C 3
Bannu, 31,623 C 2
Bela, 3,139 B 3
Campbellpore, 19,041 C 2
Chagai, ‡41,263 A 3
Chitral C 1
Dadu, 19,142 B 3
Dera Bugti B 3
Dera Ghazi Khan, 47,105 C 3
Dera Ismail Khan, 46,140 C 2
Dir C 1
Fort Sandeman 8,058 B 2
Gujranwala, 196,154 C 2
Gujranwala, *289,000 C 2
Gujrat, 59,608 C 2
Gwadar A 4
Hyderabad, 434,537 B 3
Hyderabad, *698,000 B 3
Islamabad (capital), 50,000 C 2
Jacobabad, 35,278 B 3
Jhang-Maghiana, 94,971 C 2
Jhang-Maghiana, *118,000 C 2
Jhelum, 52,585 C 2
Kalat, 5,321 B 3
Karachi, 1,912,598 B 4
Karachi, *3,060,000 B 4
Khairpur, 34,144 B 3
Kharan Kalat, 2,692 A 3
Kohat, 49,854 C 2
Ladgasht A 3
Lahore, 1,296,477 C 2
Lahore, *1,823,000 C 2
Larkana, 48,008 B 3
Loralai, 5,519 B 2
Lyallpur, 425,248 C 2
Lyallpur, *854,000 C 2
Malakand C 2
Mardan, 77,932 C 2
Mardan, *113,000 C 2
Mastung B 3
Mianwali, 31,398 C 2
Miram Shah C 2
Mirpur Khas, 60,861 B 3
Montgomery, 15,180 C 2
Multan, 358,201 C 2
Multan, *597,000 C 2
Murree C 2
Nawabshah, 45,651 B 3
Nowshera C 2
Nushki, 3,153 B 3
Parachinar, 22,953 B 2
Peshawar, 218,691 C 2
Peshawar, *296,000 C 2
Quetta, 106,633 B 2
Quetta, *130,000 B 2
Rahimyar Khan, 43,548 C 3
Rahimyar Khan, *130,000 C 3
Rawalpindi, 340,175 C 2
Rawalpindi, *445,000 C 2
Rohri B 3
Saidu, 15,920 C 2
Sargodha, 129,291 C 2
Sargodha, *194,000 C 2
Sehwan B 3
Shahbandar B 4
Shikarpur B 3
Sialkot, 164,346 C 2
Sialkot, *167,000 C 2
Sibi, 13,327 B 3
Sukkur, 103,216 B 3
Sukkur, *131,000 B 3
Tando Adam B 3
Tatta, 12,786 B 4
Tump A 3
Turbat, 4,578 A 3
Uch B 3
Umarkot B 3
Wana C 2

OTHER FEATURES

Arabian (sea) B 5
Baroghil (pass) C 1
Beji (river) B 3
Bolan (pass) B 3
Chagai (hills) A 3
Chenab (river) C 2
Dasht (river) A 3
Hab (river) B 3
Hindu Kush (mts.) C 1
Indus (mouths) B 4
Indus (river) B 3
Jaddi, Ras (cape) A 4
Jhelum (river) C 2
Kabul (river) C 2
Khyber (pass) C 2
Kunar (river) C 1
Kutch, Rann of (salt marsh) B 4
Lora, Hamuni-i- (swamp) A 3
Mashkel, Hamun-i (swamp) A 3
Mohenjo Daro (ruins) B 3
Muari, Ras (cape) B 4
Nal (river) B 3
Ravi (river) C 2
Siahan (range) A 3
Sulaiman (range) C 3
Sutlej (river) C 3
Talab (river) A 3
Taxila (ruins) C 2
Tirich Mir (mt.) C 1
Zhob (river) B 2

SRI LANKA (CEYLON)

CITIES and TOWNS

Anuradhapura, 29,397 E 7
Badulla, 27,088 E 7
Batticaloa, 22,957 E 7
Colombo (cap.), 551,200 D 7
Galle, 64,942 D 7
Hambantota, 5,387 E 7
Jaffna, 94,248 E 7
Kalmunai, 16,488 E 7
Kalutara, 25,286 D 7
Kandy, 67,768 E 7
Kurunegala, 21,293 E 7
Mannar, 8,988 E 7
Matara, 32,284 E 7
Moratuwa, 77,632 D 7
Mullaittivu, 4,025 E 7
Negombo, 47,026 D 7
Nuwara Eliya, 19,988 E 7
Polgahawela, 5,293 D 7
Polonnaruwa, 5,921 E 7
Puttalam, 13,250 E 7
Ratnapura, 21,582 D 7
Tangalla, 7,920 E 7
Trincomalee, 34,872 E 7
Vavuniya, 7,176 E 7

OTHER FEATURES

Adam's (peak) E 7
Adam's Bridge (shoals) D 7
Dondra (head) E 7
Kirigalpota (mt.) E 7
Mannar (gulf) D 7
Palk (strait) D 7
Pidurutalagala (mt.) E 7

*City and suburbs.
†Population of sub-division.
‡Population of district.

Agriculture, Industry and Resources
DOMINANT LAND USE
Cereals (chiefly wheat, barley, corn)
Cereals (chiefly millet, sorghum)
Cereals (chiefly rice)
Cotton, Cereals
Pasture Livestock
Nomadic Livestock Herding
Forests
Nonagricultural Land
MAJOR MINERAL OCCURRENCES
Ab Asbestos
Al Bauxite
Au Gold
Be Beryl
C Coal
Cr Chromium
Cu Copper
Fe Iron Ore
G Natural Gas
Gp Gypsum
Gr Graphite
Lg Lignite
Mg Magnesium
Mi Mica
Mn Manganese
Na Salt
O Petroleum
Ti Titanium
U Uranium
Water Power
Major Industrial Areas
LAHORE–SIALKOT Textiles, Light Industry
ASANSOL–DAMODAR VALLEY Iron & Steel, Locomotives, Chemicals
KARACHI Textiles, Oil Refining, Iron & Steel, Light Industry
AHMADABAD Cotton Textiles, Chemicals
BOMBAY-POONA Cotton Textiles, Machinery, Chemicals, Automobiles, Electrical Equipment, Oil Refining
JAMSHEDPUR Iron & Steel, Metal Products, Agricultural Equipment, Nonferrous Metals
CALCUTTA Jute & Cotton Textiles, Machinery, Chemicals, Aluminum
DACCA Textiles, Chemicals
Karachi
Lahore
Ahmadabad
Bombay
Poona
Jamshedpur
Asansol
Calcutta
Dacca
Shrimp
Herring
Mackerel
Pearls
Oysters
Coconuts
Sheep
Camels
Goats
Cattle
Wheat
Rice
Cotton
Millet
Peanuts
Tobacco
Barley
Sugar Cane
Water Buffalo
Corn
Coffee
Tea
Jute
Sorghum

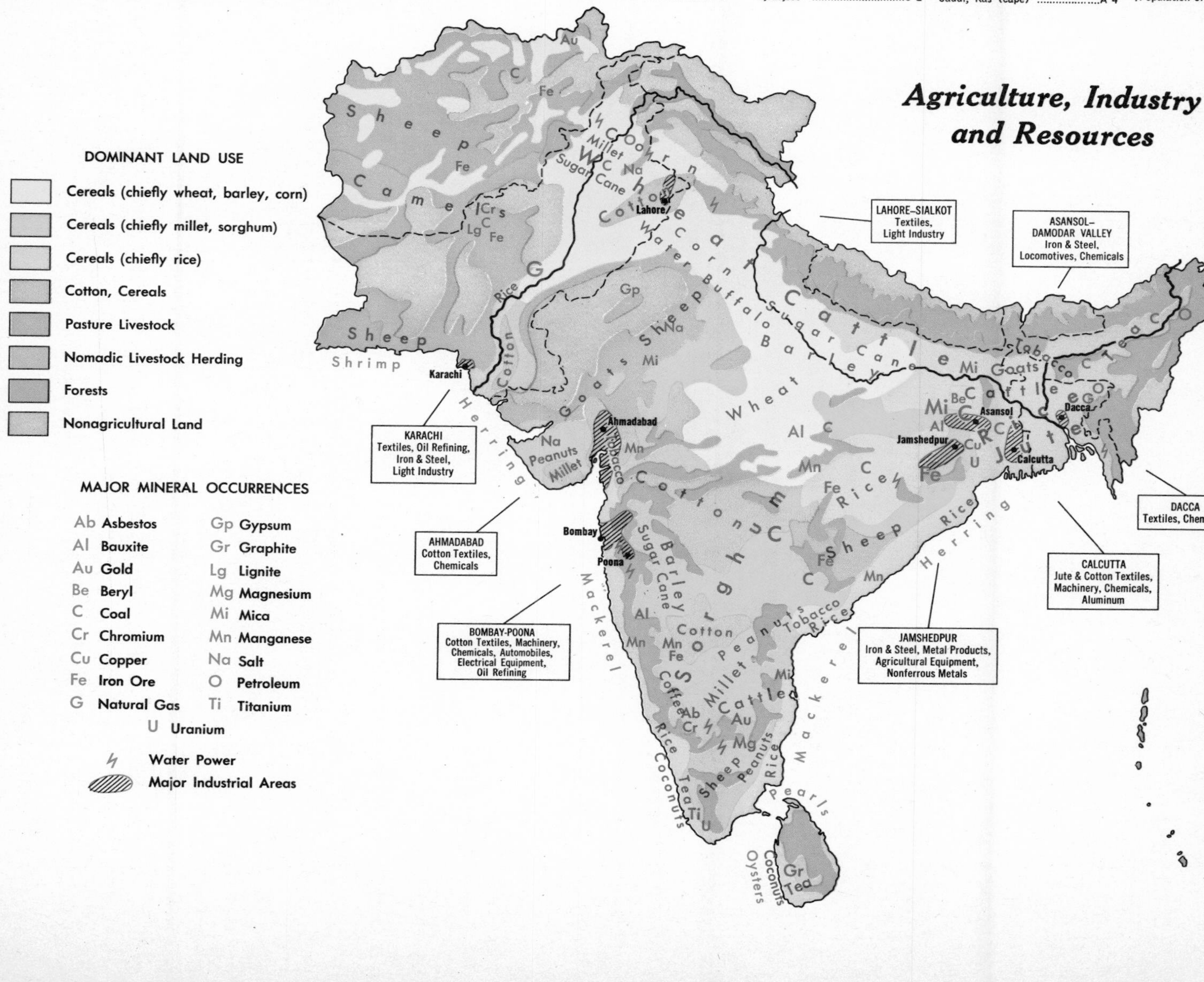

BURMA, THAILAND,
INDOCHINA
and MALAYA

CONIC PROJECTION

SCALE OF MILES

SCALE OF KILOMETRES

International Boundaries
Division and State Boundaries
Capitals of Countries
Division and State Capitals

Copyright by C.S. HAMMOND & Co., N.Y

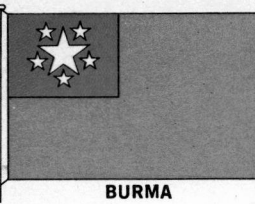

BURMA

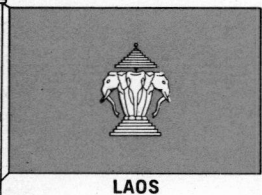

THAILAND

LAOS

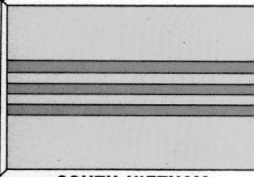

CAMBODIA

NORTH VIETNAM

SOUTH VIETNAM

MALAYSIA

SINGAPORE

BURMA
AREA 261,789 sq. mi.
POPULATION 27,000,000
CAPITAL Rangoon
LARGEST CITY Rangoon
HIGHEST POINT Hkakabo Razi 19,296 ft.
MONETARY UNIT kyat
MAJOR LANGUAGES Burmese, Karen, Shan
MAJOR RELIGIONS Buddhism, Tribal religions

THAILAND
AREA 198,456 sq. mi.
POPULATION 35,448,000
CAPITAL Bangkok
LARGEST CITY Bangkok
HIGHEST POINT Doi Inthanon 8,452 ft.
MONETARY UNIT baht
MAJOR LANGUAGES Thai, Lao, Chinese
MAJOR RELIGIONS Buddhism, Tribal religions

LAOS
AREA 91,459 sq. mi.
POPULATION 2,900,000
CAPITAL Vientiane
LARGEST CITY Vientiane
HIGHEST POINT Phu Bia 9,252 ft.
MONETARY UNIT kip
MAJOR LANGUAGES Lao, French
MAJOR RELIGION Buddhism

CAMBODIA
AREA 69,898 sq. mi.
POPULATION 6,701,000
CAPITAL Phnom Penh
LARGEST CITY Phnom Penh
HIGHEST POINT 5,948 ft.
MONETARY UNIT riel
MAJOR LANGUAGES Khmer (Cambodian),
French
MAJOR RELIGION Buddhism

NORTH VIETNAM
AREA 61,293 sq. mi.
POPULATION 21,340,000
CAPITAL Hanoi
LARGEST CITY Hanoi
HIGHEST POINT Fan Si Pan 10,308 ft.
MONETARY UNIT dong
MAJOR LANGUAGES Vietnamese, Thai, Muong,
Meo, Yao
MAJOR RELIGIONS Buddhism, Taoism,
Confucianism

SOUTH VIETNAM
AREA 66,263 sq. mi.
POPULATION 16,543,434
CAPITAL Saigon
LARGEST CITY Saigon
HIGHEST POINT Ngoc Linh 8,524 ft.
MONETARY UNIT piaster
MAJOR LANGUAGES Vietnamese, Chinese,
Khmer, Jarai, French
MAJOR RELIGIONS Buddhism, Taoism,
Confucianism, Roman Catholicism,
Cao-Dai

MALAYSIA
AREA 128,308 sq. mi.
POPULATION 10,583,000
CAPITAL Kuala Lumpur
LARGEST CITY Kuala Lumpur
HIGHEST POINT Mt. Kinabalu 13,455 ft.
MONETARY UNIT Malayan dollar
MAJOR LANGUAGES Malay, Chinese,
English, Tamil, Dayak, Kadazan
MAJOR RELIGIONS Islam, Confucianism,
Buddhism, Tribal religions, Hinduism,
Taoism

SINGAPORE
AREA 226 sq. mi.
POPULATION 2,034,000
CAPITAL Singapore
LARGEST CITY Singapore
HIGHEST POINT Bukit Timah 581 ft.
MONETARY UNIT Malayan dollar
MAJOR LANGUAGES Chinese, Malay,
Tamil, English
MAJOR RELIGIONS Confucianism, Buddhism,
Taoism, Hinduism, Islam, Christianity

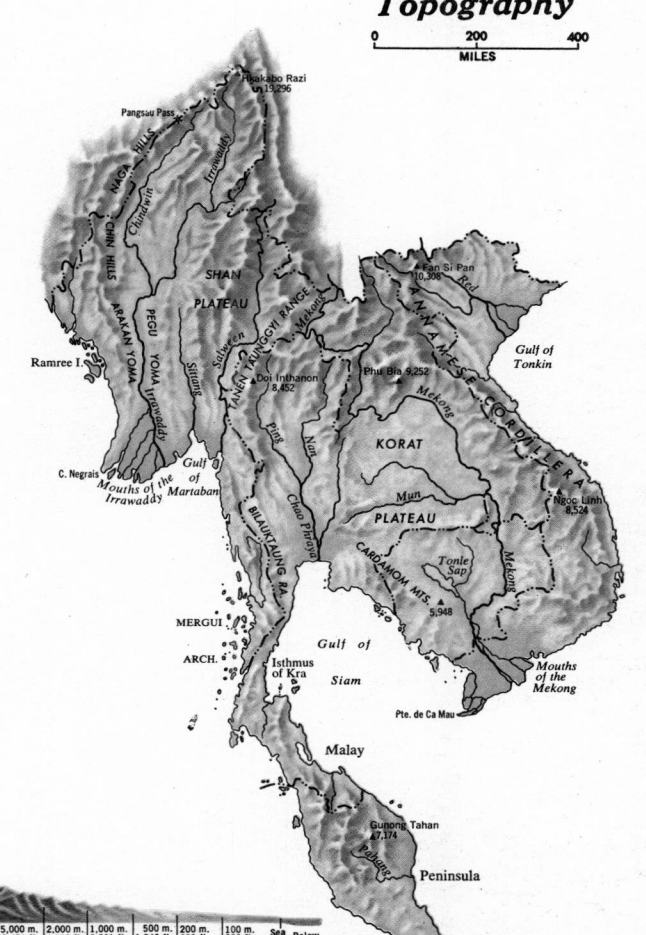

Topography

0   200   400
MILES

5,000 m. | 2,000 m. | 1,000 m. | 500 m. | 200 m. | 100 m. | Sea Level | Below
16,404 ft. | 6,562 ft. | 3,281 ft. | 1,640 ft. | 656 ft. | 328 ft.

BURMA

INTERNAL DIVISIONS

Arakan (div.) ....B 3
Chin Hills (special div.) ....B 2
Irrawaddy (div.) ....B 3
Kachin (state) ....C 1
Kawthoolei (state) ....C 3
Kayah (state) ....C 3
Magwe (div.) ....B 2
Mandalay (div.) ....B 2
Pegu (div.) ....B 3
Sagaing (div.) ....B 1
Shan (state) ....C 2
Tenasserim (div.) ....C 4

CITIES and TOWNS

Allanmyo, 15,580 ....B 3
Amarapura, 11,268 ....B 2
Amherst, 6,000 ....C 3
Athok, 4,819 ....B 3
Bassein, ‡105,000 ....B 3
Bhamo, 9,821 ....C 1
Bilin, 5,248 ....C 3
Chauk, 24,464 ....B 2
Danubyu, 9,833 ....B 3
Falam ....B 2
Fort Hertz (Putao) ....C 1
Gangaw, 3,800 ....B 2
Gyobingauk, 9,922 ....B 3
Henzada, ‡100,000 ....B 3
Insein, 27,030 ....B 3
Kalemyo, 3,158 ....B 2
Kalewa, 2,230 ....B 2
Kama, 3,523 ....B 3
Kamayut, 23,032 ....B 3
Kanbalu, 3,281 ....B 2
Kani, 2,600 ....B 2
Katha, 7,648 ....C 1
Kawlin, 3,735 ....C 2
Kyaikto, 13,154 ....C 3
Kyangin, 6,073 ....B 3
Kyaukpadaung, 5,480 ....C 2
Kyaukpyu, 7,335 ....B 3
Kyaukse, 8,659 ....C 2
Kywebwe, 3,150 ....C 3
Labutta, 12,982 ....B 3
Lashio ....C 2
Letpadan, 15,896 ....B 3
Loi-kaw ....C 3
Madauk, 4,618 ....C 3
Magwe, 13,270 ....B 2
Mahlaing, 6,543 ....B 2
Mandalay, ‡300,000 ....C 2
Martaban, 5,661 ....C 3
Ma-ubin, 23,362 ....B 3
Maungdaw, 3,772 ....B 2
Mawlaik, 2,993 ....B 2
Maymyo, 22,287 ....C 2
Meiktila, 19,474 ....C 2
Mergui, 33,697 ....C 4
Minbu, 9,096 ....B 2
Minbya, 5,783 ....B 3
Minhla, 6,470 ....B 3
Mogaung, 2,920 ....C 1
Mogok, 8,334 ....C 2
Monywa, 26,297 ....B 2
Moulmein, ‡175,000 ....C 3
Mudon, 20,136 ....C 3
Myanaung, 11,155 ....B 3
Myaungmya, 24,532 ....B 3
Myebon, 3,499 ....B 3
Myingyan, 36,439 ....C 2
Myitkyina, 12,382 ....C 1
Myitnge, 3,888 ....C 2
Myohaung, 6,534 ....B 3
Nyaunglebin, 12,155 ....C 3
Pa-an, 4,139 ....C 3
Pagan, 2,824 ....B 2
Pakokku, 30,943 ....B 2
Palaw, 5,596 ....C 4
Papun ....C 3
Paungde, 17,286 ....B 3
Pegu, 47,378 ....C 3

Putao ....C 1
Pyapon, 19,174 ....B 3
Pye, 36,997 ....B 3
Pyinmana, 22,025 ....C 3
Pyu, 10,443 ....C 3
Rangoon (capital), *1,700,000 ....C 3
Rathedaung, 2,969 ....B 2
Sagaing, 15,382 ....B 2
Sandoway, 5,172 ....B 3
Shwebo, 17,827 ....B 2
Shwegyin, 5,439 ....C 3
Shwenyaung ....C 2
Singkaling Hkamti ....B 1
Singu, 4,027 ....C 2
Sittwe, 42,329 ....A 3
Syriam, 15,296 ....C 3
Taungdwingyi, 16,233 ....C 2
Taunggyi ....C 2
Taungup, 4,065 ....B 3
Tavoy, 40,312 ....C 4
Tenasserim, 1,086 ....C 5
Tharrawaddy, 8,977 ....C 3
Thaton, 38,047 ....C 3
Thayetmyo, 11,649 ....B 3
Thazi, 7,531 ....C 2
Thongwa, 10,829 ....B 3
Thonze, 14,443 ....B 3
Toungoo, 31,569 ....C 3
Victoria Point, 1,520 ....C 5
Wakema, 20,716 ....B 3
Yamethin, 11,167 ....C 2
Yandoon, 15,245 ....B 3
Ye, 12,852 ....C 4
Yenangyaung, 24,416 ....B 2
Yesagyo, 7,880 ....C 2
Ye-u, 5,307 ....B 2

OTHER FEATURES

Amya (pass) ....C 4
Andaman (sea) ....B 4
Arakan Yoma (mts.) ....B 3
Bengal (bay) ....B 3
Bilauktaung (range) ....C 4
Chaukan (pass) ....C 1
Cheduba (isl.), 2,621 ....B 3
Chin (hills) ....B 2
Chindwin (river) ....B 2
Coco (chan.) ....B 4
Combermere (bay) ....B 3
Dawna (range) ....C 3
Great Coco (isl.) ....B 4
Great Tenasserim (river) ....C 4
Hkakabo Razi (mt.) ....C 1
Indawgyi (lake) ....C 1
Inle (lake) ....C 2
Irrawaddy (river) ....B 2
Irrawaddy, Mouths of the
(delta) ....B 4
Kaladan (river) ....B 2
Khao Luang (mt.) ....C 5
Loi Leng (mt.) ....C 2
Manipur (river) ....B 2
Martaban (gulf) ....C 4
Mekong (river) ....D 2
Mergui (arch.) ....C 5
Mon (river) ....B 2
Mu (river) ....B 2
Nam Hka (river) ....C 2
Nam Pawn (river) ....C 2
Nam Teng (river) ....C 2
Negrais (cape) ....B 3
Pakchan (river) ....C 4
Pangsau (pass) ....B 1
Pegu Yoma (mts.) ....B 3
Preparis (isl.) ....B 4
Ramree (isl.), 11,133 ....B 3
Salween (river) ....C 2
Shan (plateau) ....C 2
Sittang (river) ....C 2
Taungthonton (mt.) ....B 1
Tavoy (point) ....C 4
Tenasserim (isl.) ....C 4
Three Pagodas (pass) ....C 4
Victoria (mt.) ....B 2

(continued on following page)

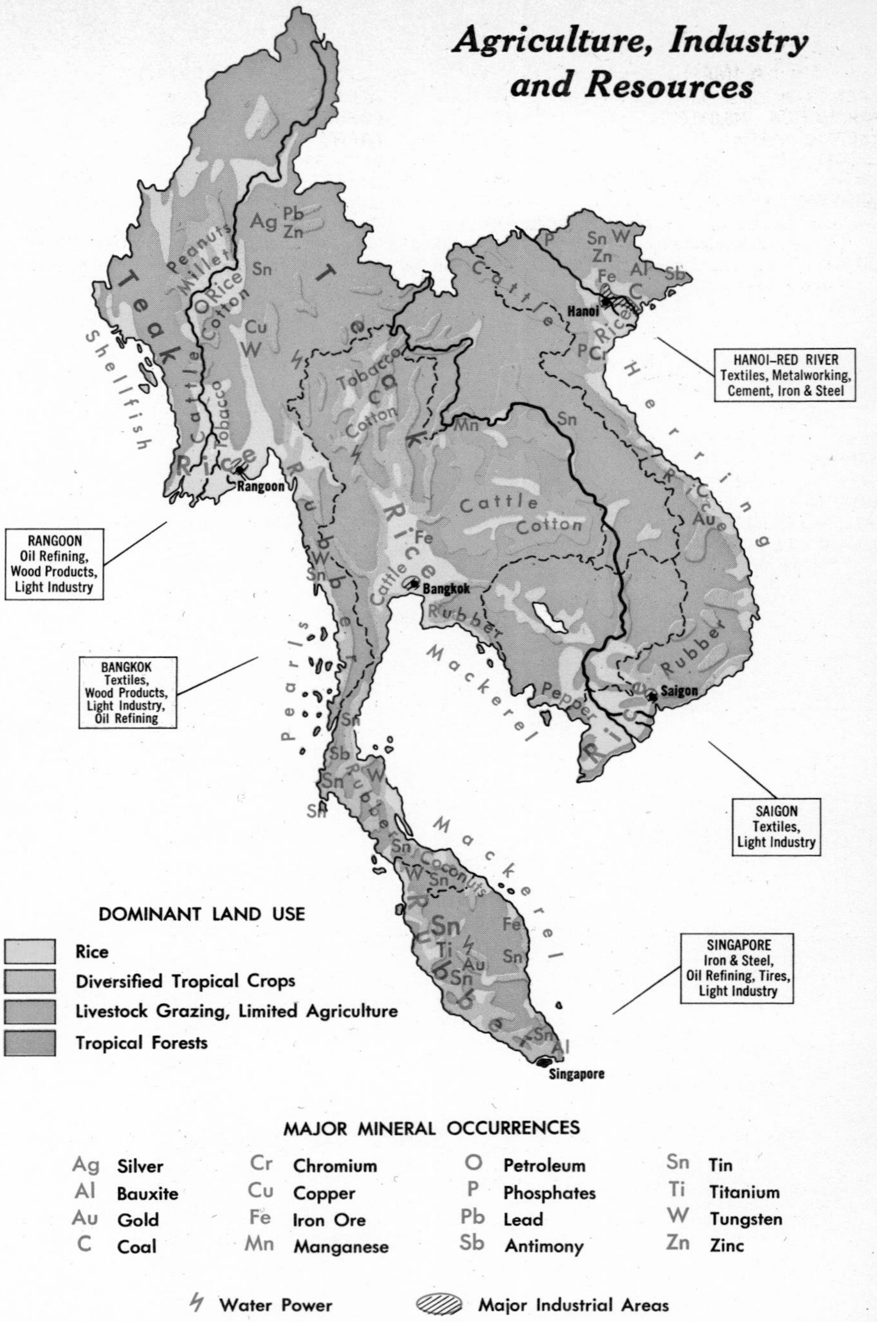

Agriculture, Industry and Resources
HANOI–RED RIVER
Textiles, Metalworking, Cement, Iron & Steel
Hanoi
RANGOON
Oil Refining, Wood Products, Light Industry
Rangoon
BANGKOK
Textiles, Wood Products, Light Industry, Oil Refining
Bangkok
SAIGON
Textiles, Light Industry
Saigon
SINGAPORE
Iron & Steel, Oil Refining, Tires, Light Industry
Singapore
Teak
Shellfish
Peanuts
Millet
Rice
Cotton
Cattle
Tobacco
Rubber
Pearls
Mackerel
Herring
Pepper
Coconuts
DOMINANT LAND USE
Rice
Diversified Tropical Crops
Livestock Grazing, Limited Agriculture
Tropical Forests
MAJOR MINERAL OCCURRENCES
Ag Silver
Al Bauxite
Au Gold
C Coal
Cr Chromium
Cu Copper
Fe Iron Ore
Mn Manganese
O Petroleum
P Phosphates
Pb Lead
Sb Antimony
Sn Tin
Ti Titanium
W Tungsten
Zn Zinc
Water Power
Major Industrial Areas

CAMBODIA

CITIES and TOWNS

Banam, †87,048 E 5
Battambang, 38,846 D 4
Cheom Ksan E 4
Chhlong, †46,108 E 4
Chong Kal, †16,918 D 4
Kampot, 12,558 E 5
Kep, 7,565 E 5
Khemarak Phouinville D 5
Kohnieh E 4
Kompong Cham, 28,534 E 4
Kompong Chhnang, 12,847 D 4
Kompong Kleang E 4
Kompong Som, 6,578 D 5
Kompong Speu, 7,453 E 5
Kompong Thom, 9,682 E 4
Kompong Trabek, †108,227 E 5
Koulen E 4
Kratie, 11,908 E 4
Krauchmar, †63,262 E 4
Moung, †88,321 D 4
Pailin, †15,536 D 4
Phnom Penh (capital), *500,000 E 5
Phsar Babau D 4
Phsar Oudong, †50,456 E 5
Phum Rovieng, †21,151 E 4
Phum Troun E 4
Poipet D 4
Prek Po E 5
Prey Veng, 8,792 E 5
Pursat, 14,329 D 4
Ream D 5
Sambor, †11,213 E 4
Siem Pang, †8,959 E 4
Siem Reap, 10,230 D 4
Sisophon, †29,581 D 4
Sre Khtum E 4
Stung Treng, 3,369 E 4
Suong E 5
Svay Rieng, 11,184 E 5
Takeo, 11,312 E 5
Virachei, †16,912 E 4

OTHER FEATURES

Angkor Wat (ruins) E 4
Dang Raek, Phanom (mts.) D 4
Joncs (plain) E 5
Kas Kong (isl.) D 5
Kas Tang (isl.) D 5
Kong, Kas (isl.) D 5
Mekong (river) E 5
Phanom Dang Raek (mts.) D 4
Preapatang (rapids) E 4
Rong, Koh (isl.) D 5
Samit (point) D 5
Se Khong (river) E 4
Se San (river) E 4
Siam (gulf) D 5
Srepok (river) E 4
Stung Sen (river) E 4
Tang, Kas (isl.) D 5
Tonle Sap (lake) D 4

LAOS

CITIES and TOWNS

Attopeu, 2,750 E 4
Ban Bung Sai E 4
Borikhane D 3
Botene D 3
Boun Neua, 2,500 D 2
Boun Tai, †1,681 D 2
Champassak, 3,500 E 4
Houei Sai, 1,500 D 2
Hua Muong D 2
Keng Kok, 2,000 E 3
Kham Keut, †31,206 E 3
Khone E 4
Khong, 1,750 E 4
Khong Sédone, 2,000 E 4
Luang Prabang, 7,596 D 3
Mahaxay, 2,000 E 3
Muong Beng, †2,305 D 2
Muong Bo D 3
Muong Hai, †476 D 2
Muong Hôm D 3
Muong Lan, †836 D 3
Muong May E 4
Muong Phalane E 3
Muong Phine E 3
Muong Phong D 3
Muong Sai, 2,000 D 2
Muong Sing, 1,091 D 2
Muong Son D 2
Muong Song Khone, 2,000 E 3
Muong Wapi E 4
Muong Yo D 2
Nam Tha, 1,459 D 2
Napé E 3
Nong Het D 3
Ou Neua, †4,300 D 2
Pak Beng, †2,964 D 3
Pak Hin Boun, 1,750 E 3
Pak Sane, 2,500 D 3
Paklay, 2,000 D 3
Pakse, 8,000 E 4
Phiafay, †17,216 E 4
Phon Tiou E 3
Phong Saly, 2,500 D 2
Sam Neua, 3,000 E 2
Saravane, 2,350 E 4
Savannakhet, 8,500 E 3
Sayaboury, 2,500 D 3
Tchepone, 1,250 E 3
Tha-deua D 3
Thakhek, 5,500 E 3
Tourakom D 3
Vang Vieng, 1,250 D 3
Vien Phou Kha D 2
Vientiane (capital), 132,253 D 3
Vientiane, *162,297 D 3
Xieng Khouang, 3,500 D 3

OTHER FEATURES

Bolovens (plateau) E 4
Hou, Nam (river) D 2
Jars (plain) D 3
Mekong (river) D 3
Nam Hou (river) D 2
Nam Tha (river) D 2
Phu Bia (mt.) D 3
Phu Co Pi (mt.) D 3
Phu Loi (mt.) D 2
Rao Co (mt.) E 3
Se Khong (river) E 4
Tha, Nam (river) D 2
Tran Ninh (plateau) D 3

MALAYSIA★

STATES

Johor, 1,236,412 D 7
Kedah, 885,775 D 6
Kelantan, 645,200 D 6
Melaka, 391,003 D 7
Negeri Sembilan, 488,318 D 7
Pahang, 405,156 D 7
Perak, 1,568,024 D 6
Perlis, 113,350 D 6
Pinang, 724,169 D 6
Selangor, 1,339,142 D 7
Terengganu, 360,388 D 6

CITIES and TOWNS

Alor Gajah, 2,135 D 7
Alor Setar, 52,915 D 6
Baling, 4,121 D 6
Bandar Maharani, 39,046 D 7
Bandar Penggaram, 39,294 D 7
Batu Gajah, 10,143 D 6
Bentong, 18,845 D 7
Butterworth, 42,504 D 6
Cameron Highlands D 6
Chukai, 10,803 D 6
Gemas, 4,873 D 7
George Town (Pinang), 234,903 C 6
Ipoh, 125,770 D 6
Johor Baharu, 74,909 F 5
Kajang, 9,630 D 7
Kampar, 24,602 D 6
Kangar, 6,064 D 6
Kelang, 75,649 D 7
Keluang, 31,181 D 7
Kota Baharu, 38,103 D 6
Kota Tinggi, 7,475 F 5
Kuala Dungun, 12,515 D 6
Kuala Lipis, 8,753 D 6
Kuala Lumpur (cap.), 325,000 D 7
Kuala Pilah, 12,024 D 7
Kuala Selangor, 2,285 D 7
Kuala Terengganu, 29,446 D 6
Kuantan, 23,034 D 7
Kulai, 7,759 F 5
Lumut, 2,947 D 6
Melaka (Malacca), 69,848 D 7
Mersing, 7,228 E 7
Pekan, 2,070 D 7
Pekan Nanas, 7,129 E 5
Pinang, 234,903 C 6
Pontian Kechil, 8,459 E 5
Port Dickson, 4,416 D 7
Port Swettenham, 16,925 D 7
Port Weld, 2,260 D 6
Raub, 15,363 D 7
Segamat, 18,445 D 7
Sematan D 6
Seremban, 52,091 D 7
Sungei Petani, 22,916 C 6
Taiping, 48,206 D 6
Tanah Merah, 775 D 6
Telok Anson, 37,042 D 6
Tumpat, 8,946 D 6

OTHER FEATURES

Aur, Pulau (isl.), 415 E 7
Belumut, Gunong (mt.) D 7
Gelang, Tanjong (point) D 6
Johor (river) F 5
Johore (str.) E 6
Kelantan (river) D 6
Langkawi, Palau (isl.), 16,535 C 6
Ledang, Gunong (mt.) D 7
Lima, Pulau (isl.) F 6
Malacca (str.) D 7
Malaya (region), 9,000,000 E 6
Pahang (river) D 7
Pangkor, Pulau (isl.), 2,580 D 6
Perak, Gunong (mt.) D 6
Perhentian (isls.), 447 D 6
Pulai (river) E 5
Pinang, Pulau (isl.), 338,898 C 6
Ramunia, Tanjong (point) F 6
Redang, Pulau (isl.), 470 D 6
Sedili Kechil, Tanjong (point) F 5
Tahan, Gunong (mt.) D 6
Temiang, Bukit (mt.) D 6
Tenggol, Pulau (isl.), 2,386 D 6
Tinggi, Pulau (isl.), 440 E 7

SINGAPORE

CITIES and TOWNS

Jurong E 6
Nee Soon, 6,043 F 6
Paya Lebar, 45,440 F 6
Serangoon, 3,798 F 6
Singapore (cap.), *1,987,900 F 6
Woodlands, 737 F 6

OTHER FEATURES

Johore (str.) E 6
Keppel (harb.) F 6
Main (str.) F 6
Singapore (str.) F 6
Tekong Besar, Pulau (isl.), 4,074 F 6

THAILAND (SIAM)

CITIES and TOWNS

Amnat, 11,335 E 4
Ang Thong, 6,458 C 4
Ayutthaya, 24,597 D 4
Ban Aranyaprathet, 11,112 D 4
Ban Kantang, 5,076 C 6
Ban Khlong Yai, 3,815 D 5
Ban Pak Phanang, 11,963 D 5
Ban Pua, 12,317 D 3
Ban Sattahip, 22,942 D 4
Ban Tha Uthen, 7,297 D 3
Bang Lamung, 9,087 D 4
Bang Saphan, 6,959 C 5
Bangkok (capital), 1,299,528 D 4
Bangkok, *2,000,000 D 4
Banphot Phisai, 6,036 C 3
Buriram, 12,579 D 4
Chachoengsao, 19,809 G 4
Chai Badan, 6,158 D 4
Chai Buri, †31,135 D 3
Chainat, 4,652 D 4
Chaiya, 3,607 C 5
Chaiyaphum, 9,633 D 4
Chang Khoeng, 6,037 C 3
Chanthaburi, 10,780 D 4
Chiang Dao, 8,017 C 3
Chiang Khan, 5,810 D 3
Chiang Rai, 11,663 C 3
Chiang Saen, 5,443 C 2
Chiengmai, 65,600 C 3
Chon Buri, 32,496 D 4
Chumphon, 9,342 C 5
Dan Sai, 6,710 D 3
Den Chai, 12,732 C 3
Hat Yai, 35,504 C 6
Hua Hin, 17,078 D 4
Kabin Buri, 3,703 D 4
Kalasin, 11,043 D 3
Kamphaeng Phet, 7,171 C 3
Kanchanaburi, 12,957 C 4
Khemmarat, 5,426 E 4
Khon Kaen, 19,591 D 3
Khorat (Nakhon Ratchasima), 41,037 D 4
Khu Khan, †122,206 E 4
Kra Buri, 3,717 C 5
Krung Thep (Bangkok) (cap.), 1,299,528 D 4
Kumphawapi, 20,759 D 3
Lae, 5,743 D 3
Lampang, 36,488 C 3
Lamphun, 10,602 C 3
Lang Suan, 4,108 C 5
Loei, 7,301 D 3
Lom Sak, 8,386 D 3
Lop Buri, 21,244 D 4
Maha Sarakham, 15,680 D 3
Mukdahan, 17,738 E 3
Nakhon Nayok, 8,048 D 4
Nakhon Pathom, 28,426 C 4
Nakhon Phanom, 14,799 D 3
Nakhon Ratchasima, 41,037 D 4
Nakhon Sawan, 34,947 D 4
Nakhon Si Thammarat, 25,919 D 5
Nan, 13,843 D 3
Nang Rong, 15,623 D 4
Narathiwat, 17,508 D 6
Ngao, †32,643 D 3
Nong Khai, 21,120 D 3
Pattani, 16,804 D 6
Phanat Nikhom, 9,307 D 4
Phangnga, 4,782 C 5
Phatthalung, 10,420 D 6
Phayao, 17,959 C 3
Phet Buri, 24,654 C 4
Phetchabun, 5,947 D 3
Phichai, 5,258 D 3
Phichit, 9,258 D 3
Phitsanulok, 30,364 D 3
Phon Phisai, 6,745 D 3
Phrae, 16,005 D 3
Phuket, 28,163 C 6
Phutthaisong, 9,315 D 4
Prachin Buri, 13,420 D 4
Prachuap Khiri Khan, 6,303 D 5
Pran Buri, 7,795 D 4
Rahaeng (Tak), 13,274 C 3
Ranong, 5,993 C 5
Rat Buri, 20,383 C 4
Rayong, 9,680 D 4
Roi Et, 12,930 D 4
Rong Kwang, †39,375 D 3
Sakon Nakhon, 16,457 E 3
Samut Prakan, 21,769 D 4
Samut Sakhon, 27,802 D 4
Samut Songkhram, 12,801 C 4
Sara Buri, 17,572 D 4
Satun, 4,369 C 6
Sawankhalok, 7,880 C 3
Selaphum, 10,395 E 3
Sing Buri, 8,384 D 4
Singora (Songkhla), 31,014 D 6
Sisaket, 9,519 E 4
Songkhla, 31,014 D 6
Sukhothai, 8,627 D 3
Suphan Buri, 13,859 C 4
Surat Thani, 19,738 C 5
Surin, 13,860 D 4
Suwannaphum, 15,731 D 4
Tak, 13,274 C 3
Takua Pa, 6,308 C 5
Thoen, 17,283 C 3
Thonburi, 403,818 D 4
Thonburi, *460,000 D 4
Trang, 17,158 C 6
Trat, 3,813 D 4
Ubon, 27,092 E 4
Udon Thani, 29,965 D 3
Uthai Thani, 10,729 C 4
Uttaradit, 9,120 D 3
Warin Chamrap, 7,067 E 4
Yala, 18,083 D 6
Yasothon, 9,717 D 4

OTHER FEATURES

Amya (pass) C 4
Bilauktaung (range) C 4
Chao Phraya, Mae Nam (river) D 4
Chi, Mae Nam (river) D 3
Chong Pak Phra (cape) C 5
Dang Raek, Phanom (mts.) D 4
Doi Inthanon (mt.) C 3
Doi Pha Hom Pok (mt.) C 2
Doi Pia Fai (mt.) D 4
Kao Prawa (mt.) C 3
Khao Luang (mt.) C 5
Khwae Noi, Mae Nam (river) C 4
Ko Chang (isl.) D 4
Ko Kut (isl.) D 5
Ko Lanta (isl.), 9,486 C 6
Ko Phangan (isl.) D 5
Ko Phuket (isl.), 75,652 C 5
Ko Samui (isl.), 30,818 D 5
Ko Tao (isl.) C 5
Ko Terutao (isl.) C 6
Ko Thalu (isls.) C 5
Kra (isthmus) C 5
Laem Pho (cape) D 6
Laem Talumphuk (cape) D 5
Luang (mt.) C 5
Mae Klong, Mae Nam (river) C 4
Mekong (river) E 3
Mulayit Taung (mt.) C 3
Mun, Mae Nam (river) D 4
Nan, Mae Nam (river) D 3
Nong Lahan (lake) D 3
Pa Sak, Mae Nam (river) D 4
Pakchan (river) C 5
Phanom Dang Raek (mts.) D 4
Ping, Mae Nam (river) C 3
Samui (str.) D 5
Siam (gulf) D 5
Tapi, Mae Nam (river) C 5
Tha Chin, Mae Nam (river) C 4
Thale Luang (lagoon) D 6
Three Pagodas (pass) C 4
Wang, Mae Nam (river) C 3

VIETNAM (NORTH)

CITIES and TOWNS

Ba Don E 3
Bac Can E 2
Bac Ninh, 22,560 E 2
Bai Thuong E 3
Bao Ha D 2
Bao Lac E 2
Cao Bang E 2
Co Lieu E 3
Con Cuong E 3
Cua Rao E 3
Dien Bien Phu D 2
Dong Hoi E 3
Ha Giang E 2
Ha Tinh E 3
Haiphong, 182,496 E 2
Haiphong, ‡*600,000 E 2
Hanoi (capital), 414,620 E 2
Hanoi, ‡*1,400,000 E 2
Hoa Binh E 2
Hoi Xuan E 2
Hon Gay, ‡100,000 E 2
Huong Khe E 3
Ke Bao E 2
Lai Chau D 2
Lang Mo E 3
Lang Son, 15,071 E 2
Lao Cai E 2
Loc Chou E 3
Luc An Chau E 2
Mon Cay E 2
Muong Khuong E 2
Nam Dinh, ‡125,000 E 2
Nghia Lo D 2
Ninh Binh E 2
Phuc Loi E 3
Phu Dien E 3
Phu Lang Thuong E 2
Phuly E 2
Phu Qui E 3
Phu Tho, 10,888 E 2
Quang Khe E 3
Quang Yen E 2
Ron E 3
Son La D 2
Son Tay, 19,213 E 2
Thai Binh, 14,739 E 2
Thai Nguyen, ‡110,000 E 2
Thanh Hoa, 31,211 E 3
That Khe E 2
Tien Yen E 2
Trung Khanh Phu E 2
Tuyen Quang E 2
Van Hoa E 2
Van Yen E 2
Vinh, 43,954 E 3
Vinh Yen E 2
Vu Liet E 3
Yen Bai E 2
Yen Minh E 2

OTHER FEATURES

Bach Long Vi, Dao (isl.) F 2
Black (river) D 2
Cat Ba, Dao (isl.) E 2
Dao Bach Long Vi (isl.) F 2
Demilitarized Zone E 3
Fan Si Pan (mt.) D 2
Lay (cape) E 3
Mui Duong (cape) E 3
Nightingale (Bach Long Vi) (isl.) F 2
Rao Co (mt.) E 3
Red (river) E 2
Sip Song Chau Thai (mts.) D 2
Song Bo (Black) (river) D 2
Song Ca (river) E 3
Song Coi (Red) (river) E 2
Tigre (isl.) E 3
Tonkin (gulf) E 3

VIETNAM (SOUTH)

CITIES and TOWNS

An Khe F 4
An Loc, 15,276 E 5
Bac Lieu (Vinh Loi), 53,841 E 5
Ban Me Thuot, 68,771 F 4
Bien Hoa, 87,135 E 5
Binh Dinh F 4
Binh Son F 4
Bong Son F 4
Bu Dop E 4
Cam Ranh, 84,281 F 5
Can Tho, 92,132 E 5
Cao Lanh, 16,482 E 5
Cap Saint-Jacques (Vung Tau), 79,270 E 5
Chau Phu, 37,175 E 5
Cheo Reo E 4
Chu Lai F 4
Da Lat, 83,992 F 5
Da Nang, 363,343 E 3
Dak Bla E 4
Dam Doi E 5
Di Linh F 5
Duong Dong D 5
Go Cong, 33,191 E 5
Go Quao E 5
Ha Tien E 5
Ham Tan, 19,323 E 5
Hoa Da F 5
Hoi An, 45,059 F 4
Hon Chong E 5
Hue, 170,884 E 3
Khanh Hoa F 4
Khanh Hung, 59,015 E 5
Kontum, 33,554 E 4
Loc Ninh E 5
Long Xuyen, 72,658 E 5
Mo Duc F 4
Moc Hoa, 3,191 E 5
My Tho, 109,967 E 5
Nha Trang, 103,184 F 4
Phan Rang, 33,377 F 5
Phan Ri F 5
Phan Thiet, 80,122 F 5
Phoc Tuy, 16,419 E 5
Phu Cuong, 28,267 E 5
Phu Loc E 5
Phu My F 4
Phu Rieng E 5
Phu Vinh (Tra Vinh), 48,485 E 5
Pleiku, 23,720 E 4
Pleime E 4
Quan Long, 59,331 E 5
Quang Nam E 4
Quang Ngai, 14,119 F 4
Quang Tri, 15,874 E 3
Qui Nhon, 116,821 F 4
Rach Gia, 66,745 E 5
Sa Dec, 51,867 E 5
Saigon (capital), 1,706,869 E 5
Song Cau F 4
Son Ha F 4
Tam Ky, 38,532 F 4
Tam Quan F 4
Tan An, 38,082 E 5
Tay Ninh, 22,957 E 5
Tra Vinh, 48,485 E 5
Truc Giang, 68,629 E 5
Tuy Hoa, 63,552 F 4
Van Gia F 4
Vinh Loi, 53,841 E 5
Vinh Long, 30,667 E 5
Vo Dat E 5
Vung Tau, 79,270 E 5

OTHER FEATURES

Batangan (cape) F 4
Bên Gôi (bay) F 4
Ca Mau (Mui Bai Bung) (pt.) E 5
Cam Ranh (bay) F 5
Chon May (bay) F 3
Chu Yang Sin (mt.) F 4
Con Son (isls.), 3,147 E 5
Cù Lao Hon (isls.) F 5
Dama, Poulo (isls.) D 5
Dao Phu Quoc (isl.) D 5
Darlac (plateau) F 4
Demilitarized Zone E 3
Dent du Tigre (mt.) E 3
Deux Frères, Les (isls.) E 5
Hon Khoai (isl.) E 5
Hon Panjang (isl.) D 5
Ia Drang (riv.) E 4
Joncs (plain) E 5
Ke Ga (point) F 5
Kontum (plateau) E 4
Lang Bian (mts.) E 4
Mekong, Mouths of the (delta) E 5
Mui Bai Bung (pt.) E 5
Mui Dinh (cape) F 5
Nam Tram (cape) F 4
Nui Ba Den (mt.) E 5
Phu Quoc, Dao (isl.) D 5
Poulo Dama (isls.) D 5
Poulo Way (isls.) D 5
Se San (river) E 4
Siam (gulf) D 5
Song Ba (river) F 4
Song Cai (river) E 4
South China (sea) F 4
Varella (cape) F 4
Way, Poulo (isls.) D 5

★See page 84 for other Malaysian entries.
*City and suburbs.
†Population of sub-division.

‡City populations courtesy of Kingsley Davis, Office of Int'l Pop. & Urban Research, Inst. of Int'l Studies, Univ. of California.

CHINA (MAINLAND)
AREA 3,691,506 sq. mi.
POPULATION 740,000,000
CAPITAL Peking
LARGEST CITY Shanghai
HIGHEST POINT Mt. Everest 29,028 ft.
MONETARY UNIT yüan
MAJOR LANGUAGES Chinese, Chuang, Uigur, Yi, Tibetan, Miao, Mongol
MAJOR RELIGIONS Confucianism, Buddhism, Taoism, Islam

CHINA (TAIWAN)
AREA 13,948 sq. mi.
POPULATION 14,577,000
CAPITAL Taipei
LARGEST CITY Taipei
HIGHEST POINT Hsinkao Shan 12,959 ft.
MONETARY UNIT new Taiwan dollar
MAJOR LANGUAGES Chinese, Formosan
MAJOR RELIGIONS Confucianism, Buddhism, Taoism, Christianity, Tribal religions

MONGOLIA
AREA 604,247 sq. mi.
POPULATION 1,300,000
CAPITAL Ulan Bator
LARGEST CITY Ulan Bator
HIGHEST POINT Tabun Bogdo 15,266 ft.
MONETARY UNIT tugrik
MAJOR LANGUAGES Mongolian, Kazakh
MAJOR RELIGION Buddhism

HONG KONG
AREA 398 sq. mi.
POPULATION 4,089,000
CAPITAL Victoria
MONETARY UNIT Hong Kong dollar
MAJOR LANGUAGES Chinese, English
MAJOR RELIGIONS Confucianism, Buddhism, Christianity

MACAO
AREA 6.2 sq. mi.
POPULATION 292,000
CAPITAL Macao
MONETARY UNIT pataca
MAJOR LANGUAGES Chinese, Portuguese
MAJOR RELIGIONS Confucianism, Buddhism, Taoism, Christianity

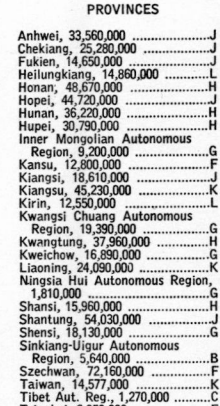

CHINA (MAINLAND)   CHINA (TAIWAN)   MONGOLIA

CHINA

PROVINCES

Anhwei, 33,560,000	J 5
Chekiang, 25,280,000	J 6
Fukien, 14,650,000	J 6
Heilungkiang, 14,860,000	L 2
Honan, 48,670,000	H 5
Hopei, 44,720,000	J 4
Hunan, 36,220,000	H 6
Hupei, 30,790,000	H 5
Inner Mongolian Autonomous Region, 9,200,000	G 3
Kansu, 12,800,000	F 4
Kiangsi, 18,610,000	J 6
Kiangsu, 45,230,000	K 5
Kirin, 12,550,000	L 3
Kwangsi Chuang Autonomous Region, 19,390,000	G 7
Kwangtung, 37,960,000	H 7
Kweichow, 16,890,000	G 6
Liaoning, 24,090,000	K 3
Ningsia Hui Autonomous Region, 1,810,000	G 4
Shansi, 15,960,000	H 4
Shantung, 54,030,000	J 4
Shensi, 18,130,000	G 5
Sinkiang-Uigur Autonomous Region, 5,640,000	B 3
Szechwan, 72,160,000	F 5
Taiwan, 14,577,000	K 7
Tibet Aut. Reg., 1,270,000	C 5
Tsinghai, 2,050,000	E 4
Yünnan, 19,100,000	F 7

CITIES and TOWNS†

Ahpa	F 5
Aicheng	G 8
Aigun	L 1
Aihui (Aigun)	L 1
Aliho	K 1
Altai	C 2
Amoy, 400,000	J 7

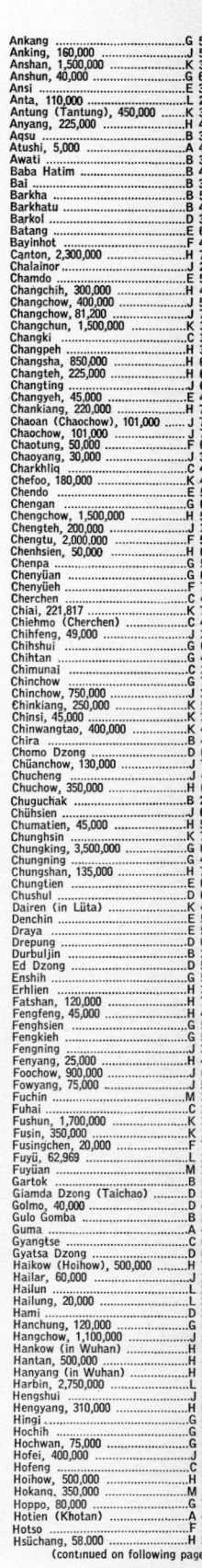

Ankang	G 5
Anking, 160,000	J 5
Anshan, 1,500,000	K 3
Anshun, 40,000	G 6
Ansi	E 3
Anta, 110,000	L 2
Antung (Tantung), 450,000	K 3
Anyang, 225,000	H 4
Aqsu	B 3
Atushi, 5,000	A 4
Awati	B 3
Baba Hatim	B 3
Bai	B 3
Barkha	B 5
Barkhatu	B 4
Barkol	J 2
Batang	D 5
Bayinhot	F 4
Canton, 2,300,000	H 7
Chalainor	J 2
Chamdo	E 5
Changchih, 300,000	H 4
Changchow, 400,000	J 6
Changchow, 81,200	J 7
Changchun, 1,500,000	L 3
Changki	C 3
Changpeh	H 3
Changsha, 850,000	H 6
Changteh, 225,000	H 6
Changting	J 6
Changyeh, 45,000	E 4
Chankiang, 220,000	H 7
Chaoan (Chaochow), 101,000	J 7
Chaochow, 101,000	J 7
Chaotung, 50,000	F 6
Chaoyang, 30,000	K 3
Charkhliq	C 4
Chefoo, 180,000	K 4
Chendo	G 6
Chengan	G 5
Chengchow, 1,500,000	H 5
Chengteh, 200,000	J 3
Chengtu, 2,000,000	F 5
Chenhsien, 50,000	H 6
Chenpa	G 5
Chenyüan	G 6
Chenyüeh	F 7
Chiai, 221,817	K 7
Chiehmo (Cherchen)	C 4
Chihfeng, 49,000	J 3
Chihshui	G 6
Chihtan	G 4
Chimunai	C 2
Chinchow	C 7
Chinchow, 750,000	J 3
Chinkiang, 250,000	K 5
Chinsi, 45,000	K 3
Chinwangtao, 400,000	K 4
Chira	B 4
Chomo Dzong	C 5
Chüanchow, 130,000	J 7
Chucheng	J 4
Chuchow, 350,000	H 6
Chuguchak	B 2
Chühsien	H 5
Chungkin	K 7
Chungking, 3,500,000	G 6
Chungning	G 4
Chungshan, 135,000	H 7
Chungtien	D 6
Chushul	C 5
Dairen (in Lüta)	K 4
Denchin	E 5
Draya	E 5
Drepung	B 2
Durbuljin	B 2
Ed Dzong	D 5
Enshih	G 5
Erhlien	H 3
Fatshan, 120,000	H 7
Fengfeng, 45,000	H 4
Fenghsien	G 5
Fengkieh	G 5
Fengning	H 3
Fenyang, 25,000	H 4
Foochow, 900,000	J 6
Fowyang, 75,000	J 5
Fuchin	M 2
Fuhai	C 2
Fushun, 1,700,000	K 3
Fusin, 350,000	K 3
Fusingchen, 20,000	F 7
Fuyü, 62,969	L 2
Fuyüan	M 2
Gartok	C 4
Giamda Dzong (Taichao)	D 5
Golmo, 40,000	E 4
Gulo Gomba	B 5
Guma	A 4
Gyangtse	C 6
Gyatsa Dzong	D 6
Haikow (Hoihow), 500,000	H 7
Hailar, 60,000	J 2
Hailun	L 2
Hailung, 20,000	L 3
Hami	C 3
Hanchung, 120,000	G 5
Hangchow, 1,100,000	J 6
Hankow (in Wuhan)	H 5
Hantan, 500,000	H 4
Hanyang (in Wuhan)	H 5
Harbin, 2,750,000	L 2
Hengshui	H 4
Hengyang, 310,000	H 6
Hingi	G 7
Hochih	G 7
Hochwan, 75,000	G 6
Hofei, 400,000	J 5
Hofeng	C 2
Hoihow, 500,000	H 7
Hoihow, 500,000	H 7
Hoko	M 2
Hoppo, 80,000	H 7
Hotien (Khotan)	A 4
Hotso	B 3
Hsüchang, 58,000	H 5

(continued on following page)

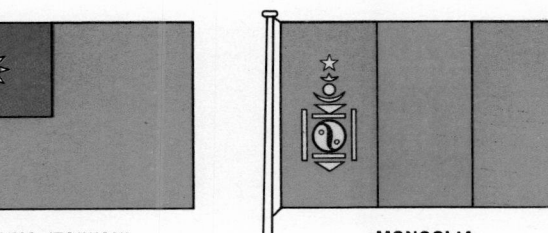

CHINA AND MONGOLIA TRANSPORTATION

Railroads	
Under Construction	
Connecting Roads	
Under Construction	
Navigable Rivers	
Canals	
Major Seaports	‡

SCALE OF MILES
0   500   1000

Map labels: U.S.S.R., MONGOLIA, CHINA, INDIA, NEPAL, BURMA, THAILAND, LAOS, N. VIETNAM, JAPAN, S. KOREA, N. KOREA, Alma-Ata, Osh, Karamai, Kodbo, Khadkhal, Ulan-Ude, Chita, Sukhe Bator, Manchouli, Aigun, Blagoveshchensk, Khabarovsk, Nenkiang, Kiamusze, Hulin, Tsitsihar, Harbin, Mutankiang, Vladivostok, Kashgar, Yarkand, Kucha, Urumchi, Turfan, Hami, Tsetserlig, Ulan Bator, Undur Khan, Choibalsan, Ierhsien, Paicheng, Changchun, Kirin, Tumen, Charkhliq, Lenghu, Yümen, Changyeh, Paiyünopo, Tsining, Chinchow, Anshan, Tantung, P'yongyang, Seoul, Pusan, Golmo, Sining, Lanchow, Tatsaitan, Paotow, Tatung, Shihkiachwang, PEKING, Tientsin, Chefoo, Tsingtao, Lienyünkang, Taiyüan, Tehchow, Tsinan, Paoki, Sian, Tungkwan, Chengchow, Süchow, Nanking, SHANGHAI, Chengtu, Siangfan, Wuhan, Hangchow, Ningpo, Chungking, Changteh, Yingtan, Kinhwa, Wenchow, Sichang, Ipin, Kweiyang, Tuyün, Chuchow, Nanping, Foochow, Kunming, Chanyi, Liuchow, Shiukwan, Amoy, Keelung, Taipei, Taiwan, Taitung, Kaohsiung, Canton, Kowloon, HONG KONG, Chankiang, Hanoi, Hainan, Gartok, Saka, Lhasa, Gyangtse, Darjeeling, Kanpur, Myitkyina, Lashio, Paoshan, Rangoon, Heiho, Batang, Gulf of Tonkin, South China Sea, East China Sea, Yellow Sea, Sea of Japan, PACIFIC OCEAN, Amur, Sungari, Hwang Ho, Yangtze Kiang, Si Kiang, Mekong, Salween, Grand Canal

CHINA (continued)

Hsünkow	L 2
Huhehot, 700,000	H 3
Huma	L 1
Hunchun, 13,246	M 3
Hunkiang	L 5
Huainan, 350,000	J 5
Huaiteh, 60,000	K 3
Huocheng	B 3
Hwangchung	J 4
Hwangling	F 4
Hwangshih, 200,000	J 5
Hwangyüan	F 4
Hweili	F 6
Hwohsien	H 4
Ichang, 150,000	H 5
Ichun, 200,000	L 2
Ierhsieh	J 2
Iliang	F 7
Ining (Kuldja), 160,000	B 3
Ipin, 275,000	F 6
Ishan	G 7
Jechiang (Charkhliq)	C 4
Jyekundo	E 5
Kaifeng, 330,000	J 5
Kailu	J 3
Kalgan, 1,000,000	J 3
Kanchow, 135,000	H 6
Kangting	F 5
Kantse	E 5
Kaohsiung, 719,899	K 7
Karamai, 43,000	B 2
Kashgar, 175,000	A 4
Kashing, 132,000	K 5
Keelung, 304,740	K 6
Kelpin (Koping)	A 3
Kenho	K 1
Keriya	B 4
Khabakhe	C 2
Khana Abasa	H 3
Khetinsiring	D 5
Khobuk-Saur (Hofeng)	C 2
Khotan	A 4
Kiamusze, 275,000	M 2
Kian, 100,000	J 6
Kiangling	H 5
Kiaoho	L 3
Kiaohsien	K 4
Kiayükwan	E 4
Kienko	G 5
Kienow	J 6
Kienshui	F 7
Kienyang, 50,000	H 6
Kinghung	E 7
Kingku	F 7
Kingpeng	J 3
Kingtehchen, 300,000	J 6
Kingyang	G 4
Kinhwa, 46,200	J 6
Kinta	E 3
Kirin, 1,200,000	L 3
Kishow	G 6
Kisi, 350,000	M 2

Kitai	C 3
Kiuchüan, 50,000	E 4
Kiukiang, 120,000	J 6
Kiungshan	H 8
Kokiu, 250,000	F 7
Kongmoon, 150,000	H 7
Koping	A 3
Kucha	B 3
Kueitun	B 3
Kulang	F 4
Kuldja, 160,000	B 3
Kungliu	B 3
Kunming, 1,700,000	F 6
Kurla	F 3
Kütsing	F 6
Kuyang	G 3
Kuyüan	G 4
Kwanghwa	H 5
Kwangnan	F 6
Kwanglin, 225,000	G 6
Kweiping	H 7
Kweisui (Huhehot), 700,000	H 3
Kweichow, 1,500,000	G 6
Kweiyang, 1,500,000	G 6
Laiyang	K 4
Lanchow, 1,500,000	F 4
Lantsang	H 6
Leiyang	H 6
Lhakang Dzong	J 6
Lhasa, 175,000	D 6
Lhatse Dzong	C 6
Lhuntse Dzong	D 6
Liangtang	G 5
Liaoyang, 250,000	K 3
Liaoyüan, 300,000	L 3
Lienyünkang, 300,000	J 5
Lihsien	H 5
Likiang	F 6
Linchwan, 45,000	J 6
Linfen	K 6
Lingling	H 6
Linhai	K 6
Linho	H 3
Linhsien	H 4
Linkow	M 2
Linping	H 7
Linsi	J 3
Linsia, 75,000	F 4
Lintsang, 45,000	E 7
Liping	G 6
Lishui	K 6
Litang	F 6
Liuchow, 250,000	G 7
Loho, 55,000	H 5
Loshan, 250,000	F 6
Loyang, 750,000	H 5
Luchow, 225,000	F 6
Luhsi	C 7
Lukchun	D 3
Lungchen, 14,000	L 2
Lungyen	G 6
Lupeh	H 5
Lüshun (Port Arthur) (in Lüta)	K 4

Lüta, $4,000,000	K 4
Maerhkang	F 5
Mahai	D 4
Manass	C 3
Manchouli, 30,000	J 2
Mangyai	D 4
Mani	C 5
Manning (Wanning)	H 8
Maralbashi	A 4
Markham Dzong	E 6
Mato	E 4
Meihsien	J 7
Mendong Gomba	C 5
Menyüan	F 4
Merket	A 4
Mienning	G 7
Mienyang	G 5
Minhsien	F 5
Mintsin	H 4
Mishan	M 2
Moho	L 1
Mowming, 15,000	H 7
Moyü (Qara Qash)	B 4
Mukden, 3,750,000	K 3
Muli	F 6
Mutankiang, 400,000	M 3
Nachü	D 5
Nanchang, 900,000	H 6
Nancheng, 50,000	J 6
Nanchung, 275,000	G 5
Nangtsien	H 6
Nanhsiung	H 6
Nanking, 2,000,000	J 5
Nanning, 375,000	G 7
Narlping, 53,445	J 5
Nanyang, 75,000	H 5
Neikiang, 240,000	F 6
Nenkiang	L 2
Ningan	M 3
Ningpo, 350,000	K 6
Ningsia (Yinchwan), 175,000	F 4
Ningsiang	H 6
Ningteh	J 6
Ningtu	J 6
Ningwu	H 4
Noh	B 5
Noho	K 2
Omin (Durbuljin)	B 2
Owpu	L 1
Pachen	C 3
Pachu (Maralbashi)	A 4
Pachung	A 3
Paicheng (Bai)	B 3
Paicheng, 75,000	L 2
Pailingmiao	H 3
Paiyin, 50,000	F 4
Paiyü	E 5
Pakhoi, 175,000	G 7
Pangkiang	H 3
Paochang	J 3
Paoki, 275,000	G 5
Paoshan	E 6
Paoting, 350,000	J 4
Paotow, 800,000	G 3

Pehan, 130,000	L 2
Peihai (Pakhoi), 175,000	G 7
Peiping (Peking) (cap.), ‡8,000,000	J 3
Peking (cap.), ‡8,000,000	J 3
Penglai	K 4
Pengpu, 400,000	J 5
Penki, 750,000	K 3
Phongdo Dzong	D 5
Pichieh	G 6
Pikiang	E 6
Pingchüan	J 3
Pingliang, 60,000	G 4
Pinglo	H 7
Pingsiang, 7,000	J 6
Pingsiang, 200,000	H 6
Pingtung, 153,953	K 7
Pingwu	G 5
Pingyang	K 6
Pingyao	H 4
Pinyang	G 7
Pishan (Guma)	A 4
Pohsien, 75,000	J 5
Pokotu	L 2
Poli	M 2
Port Arthur (in Lüta)	K 4
Poseh	F 7
Pucheng	H 6
Puerh	F 7
Putien	K 6
Qara Qash	B 4
Qara Shahr	C 3
Qaraqum	A 3
Qarghaliq	A 4
Rima	E 6
Rudok	B 5
Rungmar Thok	C 6
Saka	C 6
Sanga Cho Dzong	K 1
Sanho-	K 1
Sanming	J 6
Santai	F 5
Shahyar	B 3
Shangchih	L 3
Shanghai, ‡8,500,000	K 5
Shangnan	H 5
Shanghsien	H 5
Shangjao, 100,000	J 6
Shangkiu, 250,000	J 5
Shangnan	H 5
Shangshui, 100,000	J 5
Shanhaikwan	K 3
Shanshan	D 3
Shantan	F 4
Shaohing, 225,000	K 6
Shaoyang, 275,000	H 6
Sharasume (Altai)	C 2
Shasi, 125,000	H 5
Shentsa Dzong	D 5
Shenyang (Mukden), 3,750,000	K 3
Shigatse, 26,000	C 6
Shihchü	E 5
Shihchüan	G 5
Shihhotzu, 70,000	C 3
Shihkiachwang, 1,500,000	J 4

Shihtsuishan, 60,000	G 4
Shiukwan, 125,000	H 7
Shobando	E 5
Shwangcheng	L 2
Shwangliao	K 3
Shwangydshan, 150,000	M 2
Siaho	F 6
Siakwan, 26,200	F 6
Sian, 1,900,000	G 5
Siangfan, 150,000	H 5
Siangtan, 300,000	H 6
Siangyin	H 6
Sichang	F 6
Sienyang, 120,000	G 5
Silin	G 7
Silinhot, 20,000	J 3
Sinchu, 188,062	K 7
Sining, 250,000	F 4
Sinsiangsia	D 3
Singtai, 75,000	H 4
Sinhailien (Lienyünkang), 300,000	J 5
Sinhsien	H 4
Sinhwa	H 6
Sinyang, 125,000	H 5

Siushui	J 6
Soche (Yarkand)	A 4
Solun	K 2
Soochow, 1,300,000	K 5
Süchow, 1,500,000	J 5
Suhsien	J 5
Suihsien	H 5
Suihwa, 36,000	L 2
Suiting, 75,000	G 5
Suiteh	G 4
Sungpan	F 5
Sutsien	J 5
Süyung	F 6
Swatow, 400,000	J 7
Sienyang, 120,000	G 5
Szeping, 180,000	K 3
Tahcheng (Chuguchak)	B 2
Tahsien	G 5
Taian, 20,000	J 4
Taichao	J 3
Taichung, 407,054	J 7
Tainan, 441,556	J 7
Taipei (cap.), 1,604,543	K 7
Taitung, 69,984	K 7
Taiyüan, 2,725,000	H 4
Taklakhar	B 5
Talai, 20,000	K 2
Tali	E 6

Tangshan, 1,200,000	J 4
Tanhsien	G 8
Tantung, 450,000	K 3
Taoam, 75,000	K 2
Taocheng	E 6
Taofu	F 5
Tapanshang	H 3
Tardin	D 4
Tash Qurghan	A 4
Tashigong	C 5
Tatsaitan	D 4
Tayü	J 6
Tehchow, 45,000	J 4
Tehko	F 5
Telingha	F 4
Tehtsin	E 6
Tengchung	E 6
Tengkow	G 3
Tepao	F 7
Thok Daurakpa	C 5
Thok Jalung	B 5
Tiehling, 52,945	K 3
Tienshui, 100,000	G 5
Tientsin, ‡4,500,000	J 4
Tinghai	K 5
Tingri Dzong	C 6

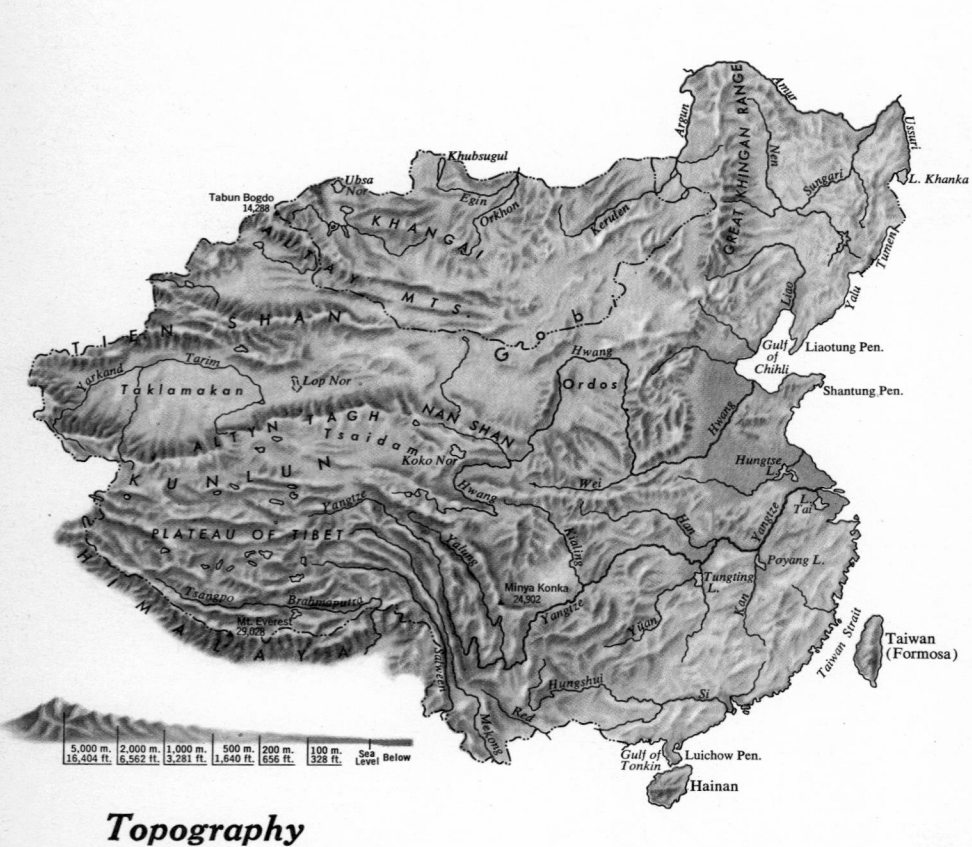

Topography

Tingsi ... G 5
Tingsin ... E 3
Tokoto ... H 3
Töling ... B 5
Tolun ... J 3
Toqsun ... C 3
Tradom ... B 6
Tsagan Usu ... E 4
Tsoachwang ... J 4
Tsangchow, 75,000 ... J 4
Tsaochwang ... J 4
Tselo (Chira) ... B 4
Tsiaotso, 300,000 ... H 4
Tsinan, 1,500,000 ... J 4
Tsingkiang, 110,000 ... J 5
Tsingkiang ... J 6
Tsingshih, 100,000 ... H 6
Tsingtao, 1,900,000 ... K 4
Tsining, 160,000 ... H 3
Tsining, 86,200 ... J 4
Tsitsihar, 1,500,000 ... K 2
Tsunyi, 275,000 ... G 6
Tsuyung ... F 6
Tuhshan ... G 6
Tulan ... E 4
Tumen ... M 3
Tungchwan ... F 6
Tungchwan, 45,000 ... G 4
Tungfang ... G 8
Tungho ... L 2
Tunghwa, 275,000 ... L 3
Tungjen ... F 4
Tungjen ... G 6
Tungkiang, 96,652 ... M 2
Tungkwan ... H 5
Tungliao, 40,000 ... K 3
Tungü ... K 2
Tunhwa, 80,000 ... L 3
Tunhwang ... D 3
Tunki, 75,000 ... J 6
Tushantze ... B 3
Turfan ... C 3
Tuyün, 60,000 ... G 6
Tzekung, 350,000 ... G 6
Tzekwei ... H 5
Tzepo, 1,750,000 ... J 4
Uch Turfan ... A 3
Ulanhot, 100,000 ... K 2
Ulughchat ... A 4
Uniket ... J 2
Urumchi, 500,000 ... C 3
Wanhsien, 175,000 ... G 5
Wanning ... H 8
Weifang, 260,000 ... J 4
Weihai, 50,000 ... K 4
Weining ... F 6
Weisi ... E 6
Wenchow, 250,000 ... J 6
Wenhsien ... F 5
Wenshan ... F 7
Wompo ... C 5
Wuchang (in Wuhan) ... H 5
Wuchang ... L 3
Wuchow, 150,000 ... H 7
Wuchung, 45,000 ... G 4
Wuchwan ... H 3
Wuhan, ‡4,250,000 ... H 5
Wuhing, 160,000 ... J 5
Wuhu, 300,000 ... J 5
Wusih, 900,000 ... K 5
Wusu ... B 3
Wuta ... G 3
Wutu ... F 5
Wuwei ... F 4
Wuyüan ... G 3
Yaan, 100,000 ... F 6
Yangchow, 210,000 ... K 5
Yangchüan, 350,000 ... H 4
Yangi Hissar ... A 4
Yarkand, 80,000 ... A 4
Yatung ... C 6
Yehsien ... K 4
Yenan ... G 4
Yenki (Qara Shahr) ... C 3
Yenki, 130,000 ... L 3
Yenyüan ... F 6
Yinchwan, 175,000 ... F 4
Yingkow, 215,000 ... K 3
Yingtak ... H 7
Yiyang, 75,000 ... H 6
Yüanling ... H 6
Yüchi ... F 7
Yüehsi ... F 6
Yühsien ... H 4
Yülin ... G 4
Yülin ... G 8
Yülin ... H 7
Yümen ... E 3
Yümen, 325,000 ... E 4
Yungan ... J 6
Yungkia (Wenchow), 250,0000 ... J 6
Yungteng ... F 4
Yünhsien ... H 5
Yüshashan ... D 4
Yüshu (Jyekundo) ... E 5
Yütien (Keriya) ... B 4
Yütze, 100,000 ... H 4

OTHER FEATURES

Achchik Kol (lake) ... C 4
Alashan (desert) ... F 4
Altay (mts.) ... C 2
Altyn Tagh (range) ... C 4
Amne Machin (mts.) ... F 5
Amur (river) ... L 2
Argun (river) ... J 1
Bagrach Kol (lake) ... C 3
Bam Tso (lake) ... D 5
Bashi (channel) ... K 7
Bayan Kara Shan (range) ... E 5
Black (river) ... F 7
Bogdo Ula (mts.) ... C 3
Bor Nor (lake) ... J 2
Chang Tang (plat.) ... B 5
Cherchen (river) ... C 4
Chihli (gulf) ... K 4
Chushan (arch.) ... K 5
Dre Chu (river) ... E 5
Dza Chu (river) ... E 5
Dzungaria (region) ... C 3
East China (sea) ... L 6
Ebi Nor (lake) ... B 2
Erh Hai (lake) ... F 6
Everest (mt.) ... C 6
Fen Ho (river) ... H 4
Formosa (Taiwan) (isl.), 12,888,478 ... K 7
Formosa (Taiwan) (str.) ... J 7
Gashun Nor (lake) ... E 3
Genghis Khan Wall (ruins) ... H 2
Gobi (desert) ... G 3
Grand (canal) ... J 4
Great Khingan (range) ... K 2
Great Wall (ruins) ... G 4
Gurla Mandhata (mt.) ... B 5
Hainan (isl.) ... G 8
Han Kiang (river) ... H 5
Hangchow (bay) ... K 5
Himalaya (mts.) ... B-D 6
Hulun Nor (lake) ... J 2
Hungtow (isl.), 2,465 ... K 7
Hwang Ho (river) ... H 5
Indus (river) ... A 5
Inner Mongolia (reg.) ... H 3
Jiggitai Tso (lake) ... C 4
Kailas (mt.) ... B 5
Kaopao (lake) ... J 5
Kara Nor (lake) ... E 4
Karakhoto (ruins) ... F 3
Karakoram (mts.) ... A 4
Kashum Tso (lake) ... C 5
Kerulen (river) ... H 2
Khanka (lake) ... M 3
Khotan (river) ... B 4
Kialing Kiang (river) ... G 5
Kiungchow (str.) ... G 7
Koko Nor (lake) ... E 4
Kumara (river) ... K 1
Kunlun (mts.) ... C 4
Kyaring Tso (lake) ... C 5
Kyaring Tso (lake) ... E 4
Liao Ho (river) ... J 3
Liaotung (pen.) ... K 4
Lighten Tso (lake) ... B 5
Lop Nor (dry lake) ... D 3
Luichow (pen.) ... G 7
Manasarowar (lake) ... B 5
Manass (river) ... C 3
Manchuria (reg.), 51,500,000 ... K 2
Matsu (isl.) ... K 6
Mekong (river) ... F 7
Min Kiang (river) ... F 5
Min Kiang (river) ... J 6
Min Shan (range) ... F 5
Minya Konka (mt.) ... F 6
Montcalm (lake) ... C 5
Muztagh (mt.) ... B 4
Muztagh Ata (mt.) ... A 4

(continued on following page)

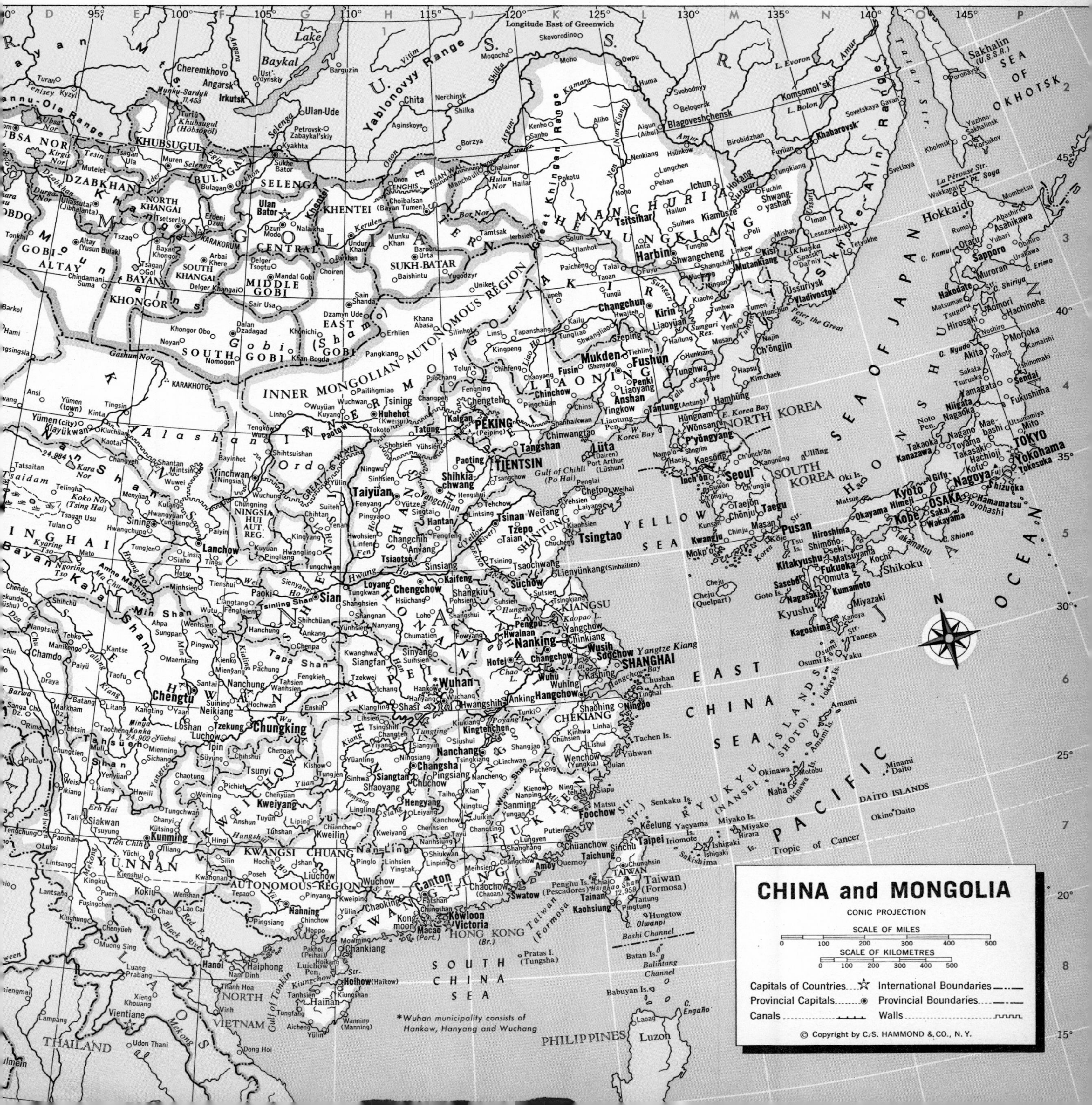

CHINA and MONGOLIA
CONIC PROJECTION
SCALE OF MILES
0 100 200 300 400 500
SCALE OF KILOMETRES
0 100 200 300 400 500
Capitals of Countries
Provincial Capitals
Canals
International Boundaries
Provincial Boundaries
Walls
© Copyright by C. S. HAMMOND & CO., N. Y.
*Wuhan municipality consists of Hankow, Hanyang and Wuchang
Longitude East of Greenwich
D 95° E 100° F 105° G 110° H 115° J 120° K 125° L 130° M 135° N 140° O 145° P

CHINA (continued)

Nam Tso (lake) ....D 5
Namcha Barwa (mt.) ....E 6
Nan Shan (range) ....E 4
Nen (river) ....K 2
Nganglaring Tso (lake) ......B 5
Ngangtse Tso (lake) ....C 5
Ngoring Tso (lake) ....E 5
Nyenchen Tanglha (range) ....C 6
Olwanpi (cape) ....K 7
Ordos (desert) ....G 4
Pangong Tso (lake) ....A 5
Penghu (isls.), 113,503 .....J 7
Pescadores (Penghu)
  (isls.), 113,503 ....J 7
Pobeda (peak) ....B 3
Po Hai (Chihli) (gulf) ......K 4
Poyang (lake) ....J 6
Pratas (isl.) ....J 7
Quemoy (isl.), 60,000 ....J 7
Red (river) ....F 7
Salween (river) ....E 5
Shamo (Gobi) (des.) ....G 3
Si Kiang (river) ....H 7
Siang Kiang (river) ....H 6
Sinkao Shan (mt.) ....H 7
South China (sea) ....H 7
Sungari (river) ....M 2
Sutlej (river) ....A 5
Tachen (isls.) ....K 6
Tahsieh Shan (range) ....C 4
Tai (lake) ....J 5
Taiwan (isl.), 12,888,478 ...J 7
Taiwan (str.) ....J 7
Taklamakan (desert) ....B 4
Tanglha (range) ....C 5
Tangra Tso (lake) ....C 5
Tapa Shan (range) ....G 5
Tarbagatay (range) ....B 2
Tarim (river) ....C 3
Tarok Tso (lake) ....B 5
Tien Chih (lake) ....E 6
Tien Shan (range) ....B 3
Tonkin (gulf) ....G 8
Trans-Himalayas (range) .....C 5
Tsaidam (swamp) ....E 4
Tsangpo (river) ....C 6
Tsing Hai (Koko Nor) (lake)..E 4
Tsinling Shan (range) ....G 5

Tungsha (Pratas) (isl.) .....J 7
Tungting (lake) ....H 6
Turfan (depr.) ....C 3
Ulan Muren (river) ....D 5
Ulugh Muztagh (mt.) ....C 4
Urungu (river) ....C 2
Ussuri (river) ....M 2
Wei Ho (river) ....G 5
West Korea (bay) ....K 4
Wu Kiang (river) ....G 6
Wuyi Shan (range) ....J 6
Yalu (river) ....L 3
Yalung Kiang (river) ....F 6
Yamdrok Tso (lake) ....D 6
Yangtze Kiang (river) ....K 5
Yarkand (river) ....B 4
Yellow (Hwang Ho) (river) ...J 4
Yellow (sea) ....K 4
Yü Kiang (river) ....G 7
Yüan Kiang (river) ....G 6
Zilling Tso (lake) ....C 5

HONG KONG

CITIES and TOWNS

Kowloon, 692,800 ....H 7
Victoria (cap.), 694,500 ....H 7
Victoria, *1,034,000 ....H 7

MACAO

CITIES and TOWNS

Macao (cap.), 262,000 ....H 7

MONGOLIA

PROVINCES

Bayan Khongor, 43,600 ....E 2

Bayan Ulegei, 45,100 ....C 2
Bulagan, 31,200 ....F 2
Central, 50,400 ....E 2
Dzabkhan, 56,800 ....E 2
Eastern, 34,300 ....H 2
East Gobi, 26,300 ....G 2
Gobi-Altay, 40,500 ....D 2
Khentei, 35,400 ....E 1
Kobdo, 44,800 ....D 2
Middle Gobi, 27,500 ....F 2
North Khangai, 60,300 ....F 2
Selenga, 43,300 ....G 2
South Gobi, 21,900 ....F 2
South Khangai, 53,800 ....F 2
Ubsa Nor, 49,000 ....D 2

CITIES and TOWNS

Arbai Khere, 6,000 ....F 2
Altay, 7,000 ....E 2
Baishintu ....
Baruun Urta, 8,000 ....H 2
Bayan Khongor, 4,400 ....F 2
Bayan Tumen (Choibalsan),
  14,000 ....H 2
Bayan Ulegei, 8,000 ....D 2
Bulagan, 8,000 ....F 2
Chindamani Suma ....
Choibalsan, 14,000 ....H 2
Dalan Dzadagad, 4,000 ....G 3
Darkhan, 30,000 ....G 2
Delger Khangai ....F 2
Delger Tsogtu ....G 2
Dzamyn Ude ....G 3
Dzun Modo, 6,000 ....G 2
Erdeni Dzuu ....F 2
Jibhalanta (Uliassutai), 7,000..E 2
Jirgalanta (Kobdo), 11,000 ..D 2
Khan Bogda ....G 3
Khongor Obo ....G 2
Khonichi ....G 3
Kobdo, 11,000 ....D 2
Mandal Gobi, 5,000 ....G 2
Munku Khan ....H 2
Muren, 9,000 ....F 2
Nalaikha, 14,000 ....G 2
Nomogon ....F 3

Noyan ....F 3
Onon ....H 2
Sain Shanda, 7,000 ....H 3
Sair Usa ....G 3
Sukhe Bator, 9,000 ....G 2
Suok ....C 2
Tamtsak ....J 2
Tsagan Ula ....F 2
Tsetserlig, 14,000 ....F 2
Tszaq ....H 2
Ulan Bator (cap.), 268,800 ..G 2
Ulangom, 10,000 ....D 2
Uliassutai, 7,000 ....E 2
Undur Khan, 7,000 ....H 2
Yugodzyr ....H 2
Yusun Bulak (Altay), 7,000 ..E 2

OTHER FEATURES

Altay (mts.) ....C 2
Bor Nor (lake) ....D 2
Durga Nor (lake) ....D 2
Dzabkhan (river) ....D 2
Egin (river) ....E 2
Genghis Khan Wall (ruins) ...H 2
Gobi (desert) ....F 2
Höbsögöl (Khubsugul) (lake)..F 1
Ider (river) ....E 2
Karakorum (ruins) ....F 2
Kerulen (river) ....G 2
Khangai (mts.) ....E 2
Khara Usu (lake) ....D 2
Khentei (mts.) ....G 2
Khubsugul (lake) ....F 1
Kirgis Nor (lake) ....D 2
Kobdo (river) ....D 2
Munku-Sardyk (mt.) ....F 1
Onon (river) ....G 2
Orkhon (river) ....F 2
Selenga (river) ....F 2
Shamo (Gobi) (des.) ....G 3
Tabun Bogdo (mt.) ....C 2
Tannu-Ola (range) ....D 1
Tesin (river) ....D 1
Ubsa Nor (lake) ....D 1

*City and suburbs.
‡Popuation of municipality.

†Populations of mainland cities over 100,000 courtesy of Kingsley Davis, Office of Int'l Pop. & Urban Research, Inst. of Int'l Studies, Univ. of California.

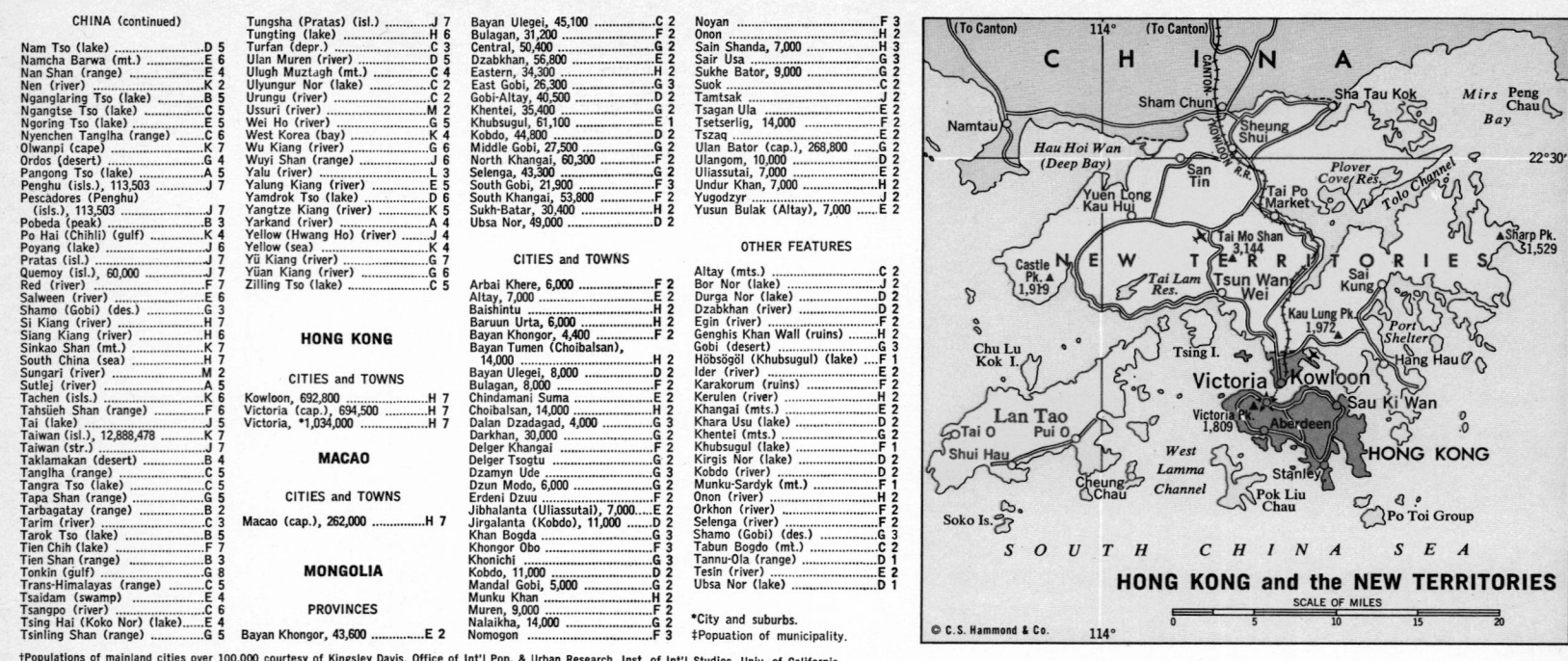

HONG KONG and the NEW TERRITORIES

SCALE OF MILES
0   5   10   15   20

© C.S. Hammond & Co.

Agriculture, Industry and Resources

DOMINANT LAND USE

Cereals (chiefly wheat, millet)
Cereals (chiefly wheat, rice, barley)
Cereals (chiefly rice, barley)
Livestock Herding, Limited Agriculture
Forests
Nonagricultural Land

MAJOR MINERAL OCCURRENCES

Ab Asbestos
Ag Silver
Al Bauxite
Au Gold
C   Coal
Cu Copper
F   Fluorspar
Fe Iron Ore
G   Natural Gas
Gp Gypsum
Hg Mercury
J   Jade
Mg Magnesium
Mn Manganese
Mo Molybdenum
Na Salt
O   Petroleum
Pb Lead
Sb Antimony
Sn Tin
Tc Talc
U   Uranium
W   Tungsten
Zn Zinc

⚡ Water Power
⚡ Major Industrial Areas

URUMCHI
Cement,
Agricultural Machinery

LANCHOW
Oil Refining,
Cement, Chemicals

PAOTOW
Iron & Steel

TAIYÜAN
Iron & Steel, Machinery,
Chemicals, Cement

HARBIN
Food Processing,
Electric Motors,
Bearings, Machinery

CHANGCHUN
Automobiles, Trucks,
Locomotives, Chemicals,
Tools, Cement

MUKDEN–ANSHAN
Iron & Steel, Machinery,
Tools, Ballbearings,
Electrical Equipment,
Chemicals

LÜTA
Steel, Railroad Equipment,
Shipbuilding, Cement,
Chemicals

PEKING–TIENTSIN
Iron & Steel, Machinery, Cement,
Textiles, Chemicals

TSINGTAO
Textiles, Tires,
Locomotives

SHANGHAI–NANKING
Iron & Steel, Machinery, Tools,
Shipbuilding, Textiles, Food
Processing, Chemicals, Paper,
Cement

WUHAN
Iron & Steel, Machinery,
Chemicals, Cement

FOOCHOW
Chemicals

SIAN
Textiles, Cement,
Electrical Equipment

CHUNGKING–RED BASIN
Iron & Steel, Machinery, Chemicals,
Sugar Refining, Fertilizer

CHANGSHA
Nonferrous Metals,
Electrical Equipment,
Iron & Steel, Tools, Cement

CANTON
Textiles, Sugar Refining,
Cement, Shipbuilding, Paper

HONG KONG
Textiles, Clothing,
Light Industry,
Shipbuilding

NANCHANG
Aircraft

TAIPEI
Machinery, Chemicals,
Textiles, Shipbuilding

TAINAN–KAOHSIUNG
Machinery, Oil Refining,
Nonferrous Metals,
Sugar Refining

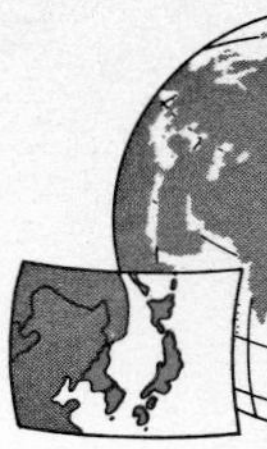

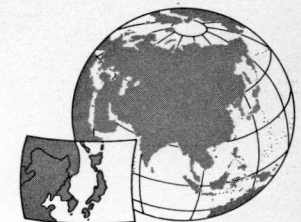

JAPAN	NORTH KOREA	SOUTH KOREA
AREA 143,622 sq. mi.	**AREA** 46,540 sq. mi.	**AREA** 38,452 sq. mi.
POPULATION 104,665,171	**POPULATION** 13,300,000	**POPULATION** 31,683,000
CAPITAL Tokyo	**CAPITAL** P'yŏngyang	**CAPITAL** Seoul
LARGEST CITY Tokyo	**LARGEST CITY** P'yŏngyang	**LARGEST CITY** Seoul
HIGHEST POINT Fuji 12,389 ft.	**HIGHEST POINT** Paektu 9,003 ft.	**HIGHEST POINT** Halla 6,398 ft.
MONETARY UNIT yen	**MONETARY UNIT** won	**MONETARY UNIT** won
MAJOR LANGUAGE Japanese	**MAJOR LANGUAGE** Korean	**MAJOR LANGUAGE** Korean
MAJOR RELIGIONS Buddhism, Shintoism	**MAJOR RELIGIONS** Confucianism, Buddhism, Christianity	**MAJOR RELIGIONS** Confucianism, Buddhism, Chondogyo, Christianity

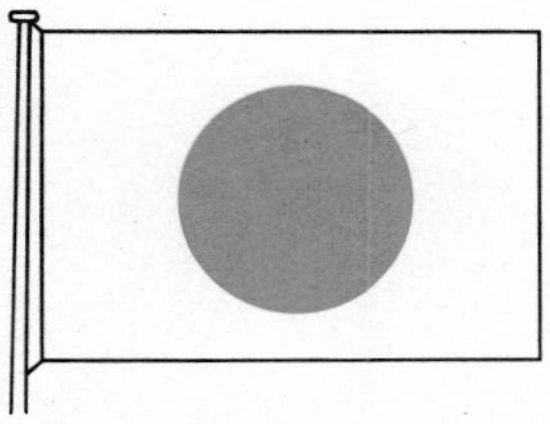

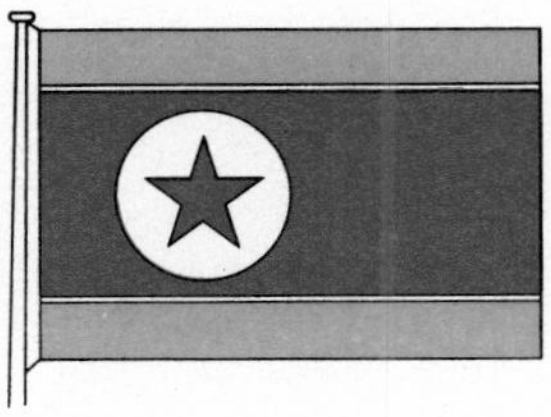

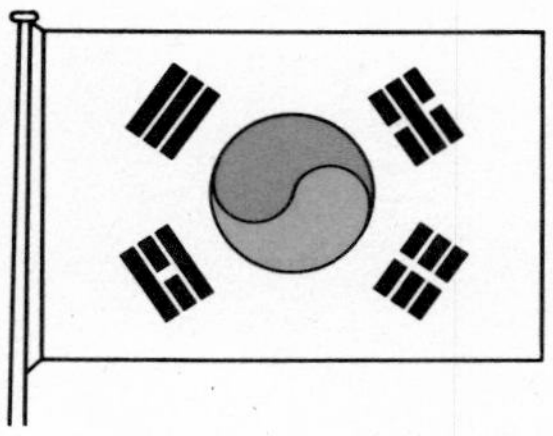

JAPAN

PREFECTURES

Aichi, 4,798,653 ....H 6
Akita, 1,279,835 ....J 4
Aomori, 1,416,591 ....K 3
Chiba, 2,701,770 ....P 2
Ehime, 1,446,384 ....F 7
Fukui, 750,557 ....G 5
Fukuoka, 3,964,611 ....D 7
Fukushima, 1,983,754 ....K 5
Gifu, 1,700,365 ....H 6
Gumma, 1,605,584 ....J 5
Hiroshima, 2,281,146 ....E 6
Hokkaido, 5,171,800 ....K 2
Hyogo, 4,309,944 ....H 7
Ibaraki, 2,056,154 ....K 5
Ishikawa, 980,499 ....H 5
Iwate, 1,411,118 ....K 4
Kagawa, 900,845 ....G 6
Kagoshima, 1,853,541 ....E 8
Kanagawa, 4,430,743 ....O 2
Kochi, 812,714 ....F 7
Kumamoto, 1,770,736 ....E 7
Kyoto, 2,102,808 ....J 7
Mie, 1,514,467 ....H 6
Miyagi, 1,753,126 ....F 4
Miyazaki, 1,080,692 ....E 8
Nagano, 1,958,007 ....J 5
Nagasaki, 1,641,245 ....D 7
Nara, 825,965 ....J 8
Niigata, 2,398,931 ....J 5
Oita, 1,187,480 ....E 7
Okayama, 1,645,135 ....F 6
Okinawa, 1,108,271 ....N 6
Osaka, 6,657,189 ....J 8
Saga, 871,885 ....E 7
Saitama, 3,014,983 ....O 2
Shiga, 853,385 ....J 7
Shimane, 821,620 ....F 6
Shizuoka, 2,912,521 ....H 6
Tochigi, 1,521,656 ....K 5
Tokushima, 815,115 ....G 7
Tokyo, 10,869,244 ....O 2
Tottori, 579,853 ....G 6
Toyama, 1,025,465 ....H 5
Wakayama, 1,026,975 ....G 6
Yamagata, 1,263,103 ....K 4
Yamaguchi, 1,543,573 ....E 6
Yamanashi, 763,194 ....J 6

CITIES and TOWNS

Abashiri, 44,195 ....M 1
Ageo, 54,776 ....O 2
Aizuwakamatsu, 104,000 ....J 5
Ajigasawa, 20,504 ....J 3
Akabira, 46,646 ....K 2
Akashi, 187,000 ....H 8
Aki, 26,605 ....F 7
Akita, 233,000 ....J 4
Akkeshi, 19,039 ....M 2
Akune, 36,026 ....E 7
Amagasaki, 532,000 ....H 8
Amagi, 44,060 ....E 7
Amaha, 18,062 ....O 3
Anan, 59,105 ....G 7
Aomori, 252,000 ....K 3
Asahi, 31,063 ....K 6
Asahikawa, 293,000 ....L 2
Ashibetsu, 52,123 ....L 2
Ashikaga, 153,000 ....J 5
Ashiya, 63,195 ....H 8
Atami, 54,540 ....J 6
Atsugi, 61,383 ....O 2
Awaji, 9,972 ....H 8
Ayabe, 48,339 ....G 6
Beppu, 144,000 ....E 7
Bibai, 63,051 ....L 2
Biratori, 12,930 ....L 2
Chiba, 407,000 ....P 2
Chichibu, 60,330 ....J 6
Chigasaki, 119,000 ....O 3
Chitose, 51,243 ....K 2
Chofu, 145,000 ....O 2
Choshi, 91,492 ....K 6
Daito, 57,107 ....J 8
Ebetsu, 44,510 ....K 2
Esashi, Hokkaido, 15,380 ....J 3
Esashi, Hokkaido, 11,401 ....L 1
Esashi, Iwate, 42,666 ....K 4
Fuchu, Hiroshima, 45,341 ....F 6
Fuchu, Tokyo, 148,000 ....O 2
Fuji, 173,000 ....J 6
Fujieda, 70,789 ....J 6
Fujisawa, 211,000 ....O 3
Fukuchiyama, 58,223 ....G 6
Fukue, 36,876 ....D 7
Fukui, 193,000 ....G 5
Fukuoka, 812,000 ....D 7
Fukushima, 225,000 ....K 5
Fukuyama, 233,000 ....F 6
Funabashi, 281,000 ....P 2
Furukawa, 52,853 ....K 4
Futtsu, 16,445 ....O 3
Gifu, 398,000 ....H 6
Gobo, 30,040 ....G 7
Gose, 35,788 ....J 8
Gosen, 38,113 ....J 5
Goshogawara, 47,433 ....K 3
Gotsu, 30,209 ....F 6
Habikino, 50,333 ....J 8
Haboro, 30,266 ....K 1
Hachinohe, 209,000 ....K 3
Hachioji, 229,000 ....O 2
Hagi, 53,905 ....E 6
Hakodate, 249,000 ....K 3
Hakui, 29,090 ....H 5
Hamada, 44,439 ....E 6
Hamamatsu, 420,000 ....H 6
Hanamaki, 62,710 ....K 4
Hanawa, 20,507 ....K 3
Hanno, 47,825 ....O 2
Haramachi, 40,643 ....K 5
Hayama, 17,617 ....O 3
Higashiosaka, 454,000 ....J 8
Hikone, 62,740 ....H 6
Himeji, 403,000 ....G 6
Himi, 62,452 ....H 5
Hirakata, 164,000 ....J 7
Hirara, 32,591 ....L 7
Hirata, 33,128 ....F 6
Hiratsuka, 151,000 ....O 3
Hiroo, 13,598 ....L 2
Hirosaki, 162,000 ....K 3
Hiroshima, 542,000 ....E 6
Hitachi, 184,000 ....K 5
Hitachiota, 36,974 ....K 5
Hitoyoshi, 44,831 ....E 7
Hofu, 94,342 ....E 6
Hondo, 39,790 ....E 7
Honjo, 38,361 ....J 4
Hyuga, 43,678 ....E 7
Ibaraki, 143,000 ....J 7
Ibusuki, 32,386 ....E 8
Ichihara, 134,000 ....P 2
Ichikawa, 236,000 ....P 2
Ichinohe, 25,165 ....K 3
Ichinomiya, 210,000 ....H 6
Ichinoseki, 57,238 ....K 4
Ide, 8,199 ....J 7
Iida, 79,145 ....H 6
Iizuka, 82,033 ....E 7
Ikeda, Hokkaido, 15,529 ....L 2
Ikeda, Osaka, 82,478 ....H 7
Ikuno, 9,466 ....G 6
Imabari, 109,000 ....F 6
Imari, 67,316 ....D 7
Imazu, 11,245 ....G 6
Ina, 51,944 ....H 6
Isahaya, 63,886 ....D 7
Ise, 104,000 ....H 6
Ishigaki, 41,315 ....L 7
Ishige, 18,481 ....P 2
Ishinomaki, 106,000 ....K 4
Ishioka, 36,789 ....K 5
Itami, 141,000 ....H 7
Ito, 59,404 ....J 6
Itoigawa, 39,332 ....H 5
Itoman, 34,065 ....N 6
Iwaizumi, 24,846 ....K 4
Iwaki, 337,000 ....K 5
Iwakuni, 106,000 ....E 6
Iwami, 18,004 ....G 6
Iwamisawa, 65,508 ....L 2
Iwanai, 25,405 ....K 2
Iwasaki, 5,432 ....J 3
Iwata, 58,940 ....H 6
Iwatsuki, 41,946 ....O 2
Iyo, 28,611 ....F 7
Izuhara, 21,989 ....D 6
Izumi, 84,771 ....J 8
Izumiotsu, 53,312 ....J 8
Izumisano, 66,521 ....G 6
Izumo, 68,765 ....F 6
Joyo, 20,038 ....J 7
Kadoma, 121,000 ....J 7
Kaga, 54,860 ....H 5
Kagoshima, 406,000 ....E 8
Kaizuka, 69,365 ....H 8
Kakogawa, 115,000 ....G 6
Kamaishi, 82,104 ....L 4
Kamakura, 136,000 ....O 3
Kameoka, 43,335 ....J 7
Kaminoyama, 38,679 ....J 4
Kamiyaku, 12,458 ....E 8
Kamo, 9,034 ....J 7
Kanazawa, 344,000 ....H 5
Kanonji, 44,200 ....F 6
Kanoya, 70,519 ....E 8
Kanuma, 77,240 ....J 5
Karatsu, 73,999 ....D 7
Kaseda, 28,565 ....D 8
Kashihara, 57,065 ....J 8
Kashiwa, 133,000 ....P 2
Kashiwazaki, 71,465 ....J 5
Kasugai, 141,000 ....H 6
Kasukabe, 42,460 ....O 2
Katsuta, 52,625 ....K 5
Katsuura, 29,133 ....K 6
Kawachi, 91,853 ....J 8
Kawachinagano, 40,109 ....J 8
Kawagoe, 148,000 ....O 2
Kawaguchi, 284,000 ....O 2
Kawanishi, 61,282 ....H 7
Kawasaki, 910,000 ....J 6
Kazusa, 12,787 ....P 3
Kembuchi, 8,013 ....L 1
Kesennuma, 59,884 ....K 4
Kikonai, 11,353 ....K 3
Kiryu, 132,000 ....J 5
Kisarazu, 54,928 ....P 3
Kishiwada, 156,000 ....J 8
Kitaibaraki, 55,334 ....K 5
Kitakata, 40,424 ....J 5
Kitakyushu, 1,042,319 ....E 6
Kitami, 74,841 ....L 2
Kizu, 10,814 ....J 7
Kobayashi, 41,922 ....E 8
Kobe, 1,288,754 ....H 7
Kochi, 242,000 ....F 7
Kodaira, 125,000 ....O 2
Kofu, 185,000 ....J 6
Kokubu, 31,249 ....E 8
Komagane, 28,327 ....H 6
Komatsu, 91,163 ....H 5
Koriyama, 240,000 ....K 5
Koshigaya, 112,000 ....P 2
Koza, 55,923 ....N 6
Kuji, 38,374 ....K 3
Kuki, 26,773 ....O 2
Kumagaya, 119,000 ....J 5
Kumamoto, 432,000 ....E 7
Kumano, 30,041 ....H 7
Kumiyama, 7,231 ....J 7
Kurashiki, 332,000 ....F 6
Kurayoshi, 50,114 ....F 6
Kure, 237,000 ....F 6
Kurume, 188,000 ....E 7
Kushikino, 31,781 ....E 8
Kushima, 36,425 ....E 8
Kushimoto, 20,252 ....G 7
Kushiro, 195,000 ....M 2
Kutchan, 19,738 ....K 2
Kyonan, 13,980 ....O 3
Kyoto, 1,418,933 ....J 7
Machida, 154,000 ....O 2
Maebashi, 225,000 ....J 5
Maibara, 13,415 ....G 6
Maizuru, 96,641 ....G 6
Mashike, 13,063 ....K 2
Masuda, 52,729 ....E 6
Matsubara, 71,406 ....H 8
Matsudo, 206,000 ....P 2
Matsue, 115,000 ....F 6
Matsumae, 19,111 ....J 3
Matsumoto, 159,000 ....H 5
Matsunaga, 34,610 ....F 6
Matsusaka, 104,000 ....H 6
Matsuto, 29,649 ....H 5
Matsuyama, 310,000 ....F 7
Mihara, 82,175 ....F 6
Miki, 38,542 ....H 7
Mikuni, 22,135 ....G 5
Minamata, 45,577 ....E 7
Minobu, 12,250 ....J 6
Minoo, 43,851 ....J 7
Misawa, 36,326 ....K 3
Mishima, 43,479 ....J 7
Mitaka, 146,000 ....O 2
Mito, 167,000 ....K 5
Mitsukaido, 36,584 ....P 2
Miura, 42,601 ....O 3
Miyako, 56,575 ....L 4
Miyakonojo, 121,000 ....E 8
Miyazaki, 212,000 ....E 8
Miyazu, 33,285 ....G 6
Miyoshi, 37,871 ....F 6
Mizusawa, 45,985 ....K 4
Mobara, 42,486 ....K 6
Mombetsu, 40,389 ....L 1
Mooka, 38,117 ....K 5
Mori, 18,330 ....K 2
Moriguchi, 164,000 ....J 7
Morioka, 191,000 ....K 4
Motobu, 15,068 ....N 6
Muko, 20,730 ....J 7
Murakami, 32,651 ....J 4
Muroran, 181,000 ....K 2
Muroto, 28,746 ....G 7
Musashino, 135,000 ....O 2
Mutsu, 39,282 ....K 3
Nachikatsuura, 24,889 ....H 7
Nagahama, Ehime, 16,193 ....F 7
Nagahama, Shiga, 49,871 ....H 6
Nagano, 280,000 ....J 5
Nagaoka, 27,522 ....J 7
Nagaoka, 159,000 ....J 5
Nagasaki, 422,000 ....D 7
Nagato, 29,246 ....E 6
Nago, 19,601 ....N 6
Nagoya, 2,036,022 ....H 6
Naha, 284,000 ....N 6
Nakaminato, 33,620 ....K 5
Nakamura, 35,717 ....F 7
Nakasato, 15,898 ....K 3
Nakatsu, 58,371 ....E 7
Nakoso, 46,731 ....K 5
Nanao, 48,715 ....H 5
Nankoku, 41,237 ....F 7
Naoetsu, 45,650 ....H 5
Nara, 191,000 ....J 8
Narashino, 64,897 ....P 2
Nayoro, 36,106 ....L 1
Naze, 44,111 ....O 5
Nemuro, 45,149 ....M 2
Neyagawa, 174,000 ....J 7
Nichinan, 57,612 ....E 8
Niigata, 379,000 ....J 5
Niihama, 130,000 ....F 6
Niimi, 34,063 ....F 6
Niitsu, 56,594 ....J 5
Nikko, 32,031 ....J 5
Nishinomiya, 357,000 ....H 8
Nishinoomote, 30,490 ....E 8
Nobeoka, 134,000 ....E 7
Noboribetsu, 39,101 ....K 2
Noda, 59,799 ....P 2
Nogata, 57,839 ....E 7
Nose, 9,906 ....J 7
Noshiro, 61,921 ....J 3
Noto, 17,719 ....H 5
Numata, 44,347 ....J 5
Numazu, 186,000 ....J 6
Obama, 35,160 ....G 6
Obihiro, 129,000 ....L 2
Oda, 42,322 ....F 6
Odate, 59,662 ....K 3
Odawara, 151,000 ....J 6
Ofunato, 38,347 ....K 4
Oga, 43,333 ....J 4
Ogaki, 134,000 ....H 6

(continued on following page)

Agriculture, Industry and Resources

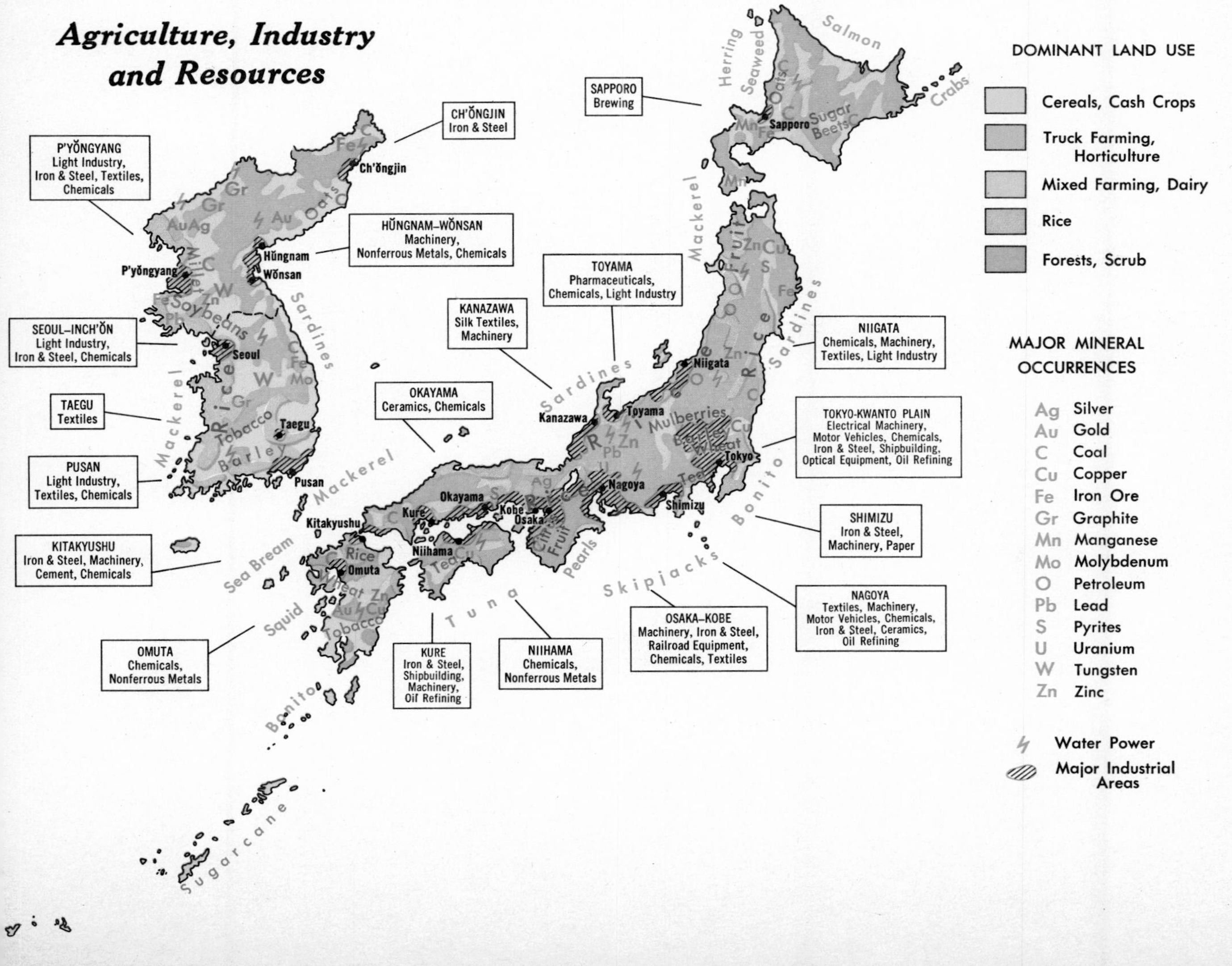

SAPPORO Brewing
CH'ŎNGJIN Iron & Steel
P'YŎNGYANG Light Industry, Iron & Steel, Textiles, Chemicals
HŬNGNAM–WŎNSAN Machinery, Nonferrous Metals, Chemicals
TOYAMA Pharmaceuticals, Chemicals, Light Industry
KANAZAWA Silk Textiles, Machinery
SEOUL–INCH'ŎN Light Industry, Iron & Steel, Chemicals
NIIGATA Chemicals, Machinery, Textiles, Light Industry
OKAYAMA Ceramics, Chemicals
TAEGU Textiles
TOKYO-KWANTO PLAIN Electrical Machinery, Motor Vehicles, Chemicals, Iron & Steel, Shipbuilding, Optical Equipment, Oil Refining
PUSAN Light Industry, Textiles, Chemicals
SHIMIZU Iron & Steel, Machinery, Paper
KITAKYUSHU Iron & Steel, Machinery, Cement, Chemicals
NAGOYA Textiles, Machinery, Motor Vehicles, Chemicals, Iron & Steel, Ceramics, Oil Refining
OSAKA–KOBE Machinery, Iron & Steel, Railroad Equipment, Chemicals, Textiles
OMUTA Chemicals, Nonferrous Metals
KURE Iron & Steel, Shipbuilding, Machinery, Oil Refining
NIIHAMA Chemicals, Nonferrous Metals
Herring
Seaweed
Salmon
Crabs
Sugar Beets
Mackerel
Sardines
Sea Bream
Squid
Tuna
Skipjacks
Bonito
Pearls
Sugarcane
Soybeans
Tobacco
Barley
Rice
Millet
Oats
Fruit
Mulberries
Wheat
Tea
Sapporo
Ch'ŏngjin
Hŭngnam
Wŏnsan
P'yŏngyang
Seoul
Taegu
Pusan
Niigata
Kanazawa
Toyama
Tokyo
Nagoya
Shimizu
Okayama
Kure
Kobe
Osaka
Niihama
Kitakyushu
Omuta
DOMINANT LAND USE
Cereals, Cash Crops
Truck Farming, Horticulture
Mixed Farming, Dairy
Rice
Forests, Scrub
MAJOR MINERAL OCCURRENCES
Ag Silver
Au Gold
C Coal
Cu Copper
Fe Iron Ore
Gr Graphite
Mn Manganese
Mo Molybdenum
O Petroleum
Pb Lead
S Pyrites
U Uranium
W Tungsten
Zn Zinc
Water Power
Major Industrial Areas

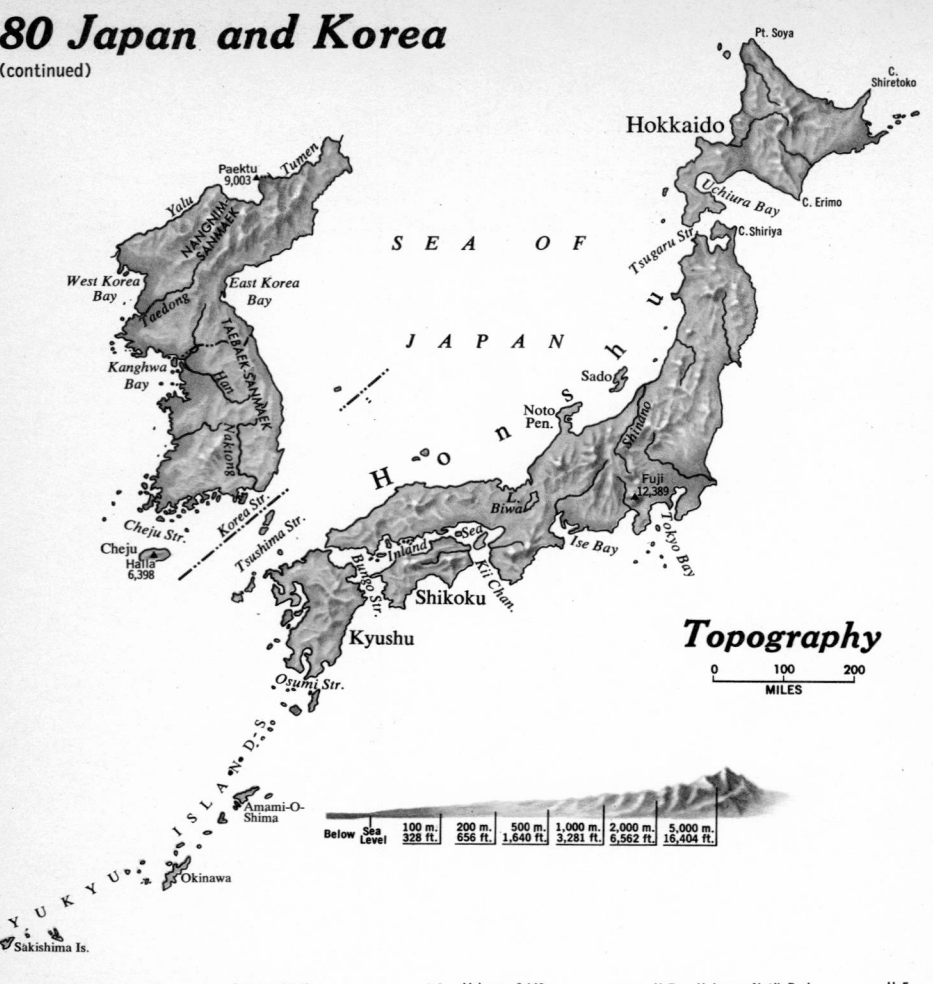

Topography

Otakine (mt.)	K 5	Shiretoko (cape)	M 1
Rebun (isl.), 8,374	K 1	Shiriya (cape)	K 3
Rikuchu-Kaigan Nat'l Park	L 4	Soya (point)	L 1
Rishiri (isl.), 17,663	K 1	Suo (sea)	E 7
Ryukyu (isls.), 1,108,271	L 7	Suruga (bay)	J 6
Sado (isl.), 102,925	J 4	Suwanose (isl.)	O 4
Sagami (bay)	O 3	Suzu (point)	H 5
Sagami (river)	O 2	Takeshima (isls.)	F 5
Saikai Nat'l Park	D 7	Tama (river)	O 2
Sakishima (isls.), 121,837	K 7	Tanega (isl.), 60,130	E 8
San'in Kaigan Nat'l Park	G 6	Tarama (isl.), 2,603	L 7
Sata (cape)	E 8	Tazawa (lake)	K 4
Setonaikai Nat'l Park	F 7	Teshio (mt.)	L 1
Shikoku (isl.), 3,975,058	F 7	Teshio (river)	L 1
Shikotan (isl.)	O 1	Tobi (isl.)	J 4
Shikotsu (lake)	L 2	Tokachi (mt.)	L 2
Shikotsu-Toya Nat'l Park	K 2	Tokachi (river)	L 2
Shimane (pen.)	F 6	Tokara (arch.), 2,722	L 5
Shimokita (pen.)	K 3	Tokuno (isl.), 18,920	L 6
Shinano (river)	H 7	Tokyo (bay)	O 2
Shiono (cape)	H 7	Tone (river)	J 5
Shiragami (cape)	K 3	Tosa (bay)	F 7
Shirane (mt.)	J 5	Towada (lake)	K 3
Shirane (mt.)	H 6	Towada-Hachimantai Nat'l Park	K 3
		Toya (lake)	K 2
		Toyama (bay)	H 5
		Tsu (isls.), 65,304	D 6
		Tsugaru (strait)	K 3
		Tsurugi (mt.)	G 7
		Tsushima (isls.), 65,304	D 6
		Tsushima (strait)	D 6
		Unzen (mt.)	D 7
		Unzen-Amakusa Nat'l Park	D 7
		Volcano (isls.)	M 4
		Wakasa (bay)	G 6
		Yaeyama (isls.), 52,012	K 7
		Yaku (isl.), 22,242	E 8
		Yonaguni (isl.), 3,671	K 7
		Yoron (isl.), 7,181	M 6
		Yoshino (river)	G 7
		Yoshino-Kumano Nat'l Park	H 7
		Zao (mt.)	K 5

KOREA (NORTH)

CITIES and TOWNS

Anju .... B 4

JAPAN (continued)

Ogi, 5,500	J 5	Suttsu, 8,043	J 2	Yokawa, 8,146	H 7	Hukusan Nat'l Park	H 5
Ohata, 13,015	K 3	Suwa, 46,276	H 6	Yokkaichi, 230,000	H 6	Harima (sea)	G 6
Oita, 243,000	E 7	Suzu, 32,122	H 5	Yokohama, 2,237,513	O 3	Hida (river)	H 6
Ojiya, 47,376	J 5	Suzuka, 115,000	H 6	Yokosuka, 340,000	O 3	Hodaka (mt.)	H 5
Okawa, 51,197	E 7	Tachikawa, 115,000	O 2	Yokote, 44,331	K 4	Hokkaido (isl.), 5,171,800	L 2
Okaya, 56,986	H 5	Tajimi, 60,175	H 6	Yonago, 108,000	F 6	Honshu (isl.), 76,757,913	J 5
Okayama, 322,000	F 6	Takada, 73,668	J 5	Yonezawa, 94,435	K 5	Ie (isl.), 7,059	N 6
Okazaki, 200,000	H 6	Takaishi, 45,679	J 8	Yono, 51,746	O 2	Iheya (isl.), 3,083	D 7
Omagari, 39,900	K 4	Takamatsu, 271,000	G 6	Yotsukura, 20,226	K 5	Iki (isl.), 45,654	D 7
Omiya, 248,000	O 2	Takaoka, 158,000	H 5	Yubari, 85,141	L 2	Ina (river)	K 5
Omu, 9,494	L 1	Takarazuka, 109,000	J 7	Yubetsu, 9,720	L 1	Inawashiro (lake)	K 5
Omura, Bonin Islands, 203	M 3	Takasaki, 184,000	J 5	Yukuhashi, 47,495	E 7	Inubo (cape)	K 6
Omura, Nagasaki, 56,425	E 7	Takatsuki, 178,000	J 7	Yuzawa, 39,879	K 4	Iriomote (isl.), 7,026	J 6
Omuta, 206,000	E 7	Takawa, 74,063	E 7	Zushi, 43,211	O 3	Iro (cape)	J 6
Onagawa, 18,080	K 4	Takayama, 53,399	H 5			Ise (bay)	H 6
Ono, 43,747	H 5	Takefu, 62,588	G 6	**OTHER FEATURES**		Ise-Shima Nat'l Park	H 6
Onoda, 43,584	E 6	Tanabe, Kyoto, 17,333	J 7			Ishigaki (isl.), 41,315	L 7
Onomichi, 90,740	F 6	Tanabe, Wakayama, 62,276	H 7	Abashiri (river)	M 1	Ishikari (bay)	L 2
Osaka, 2,980,409	J 8	Tateyama, 55,866	K 6	Abukuma (river)	K 4	Ishikari (river)	L 2
Ota, 87,898	J 5	Tendo, 43,903	K 4	Agano (river)	J 4	Ishizuchi (mt.)	F 7
Otawara, 41,026	J 7	Tenri, 54,169	J 8	Akan Nat'l Park	M 2	Iwaki (mt.)	K 3
Otsu, 164,000	J 7	Teshio, 9,493	K 1	Amakusa (isls.), 233,465	D 7	Iwate (mt.)	K 4
Owase, 34,019	H 6	Toba, 33,903	H 6	Amami (isls.), 186,193	N 5	Iwo (isl.)	M 4
Oyabe, 35,646	H 5	Tobetsu, 19,406	K 2	Amami-O-Shima (isl.), 94,348	N 5	Iyo (sea)	E 7
Oyama, 90,632	J 5	Togane, 31,922	K 6	Ara (river)	O 2	Izu (isls.), 35,592	J 6
Ozu, 40,185	F 7	Tojo, 16,886	F 6	Asahi (mt.)	J 4	Izu (pen.)	J 6
Rausu, 8,931	M 1	Tokushima, 225,000	J 7	Asama (mt.)	J 5	Japan (sea)	G 4
Rikuzentakata, 31,040	K 4	Tokuyama, 100,000	F 6	Ashizuri (cape)	F 7	Joshinetsu-Kogen Nat'l Park	J 5
Rumoi, 26,494	K 2	Tokyo (capital), 8,832,647	O 2	Aso (mt.)	E 7	Kagoshima (bay)	E 8
Ryotsu, 26,494	J 4	Tokyo, *11,350,000	O 2	Aso Nat'l Park	E 7	Kamui (cape)	K 2
Ryugasaki, 34,917	H 2	Tomakomai, 81,812	K 2	Atsumi (bay)	H 6	Kariba (mt.)	K 2
Sabae, 50,114	G 6	Tomiyama, 7,863	O 3	Awa (isl.)	J 4	Kasumiga (lagoon)	K 5
Saga, 153,000	E 7	Tondabayashi, 47,985	J 8	Awaji (isl.), 185,473	H 8	Kazan-Retto (Volcano) (isls.)	M 4
Sagamihara, 224,000	O 2	Tosa, 30,772	F 7	Bandai (mt.)	K 5	Kerama (isls.), 2,467	M 6
Saigo, 16,569	F 5	Tosashimizu, 26,725	F 7	Bandai-Asahi Nat'l Park	J 4	Kii (channel)	G 7
Saiki, 51,145	E 7	Tosu, 44,419	E 7	Biwa (lake)	H 6	Kikai (isl.), 14,231	O 5
Saito, 42,543	E 7	Tottori, 117,000	G 6	Bonin (isls.), 203	M 3	Kino (river)	G 6
Sakado, 24,854	O 2	Towada, 46,713	K 3	Boso (pen.)	K 6	Kirishima-Yaku Nat'l Park	E 8
Sakai, Ibaraki, 21,689	P 1	Toyama, 264,000	H 5	Bungo (strait)	F 7	Kita Iwo (isl.)	M 4
Sakai, Osaka, 544,000	J 8	Toyohashi, 253,000	H 6	Chichi (isl.), 203	M 3	Kita Iwo Nat'l Park	M 4
Sakaide, 61,284	G 6	Toyonaka, 334,000	J 7	Chichibu-Tama Nat'l Park	J 6	Kitakami (river)	K 4
Sakaiminato, 32,846	F 6	Toyooka, 43,259	G 6	Chokai (mt.)	J 4	Koma (river)	J 4
Sakata, 95,582	J 4	Toyota, 161,000	H 6	Chubu Sangaku Nat'l Park	H 5	Koshiki (isls.), 16,301	D 8
Saku, 55,149	J 5	Tsu, 123,000	H 6	Uchinoura, 10,036	E 8	Kuchino (isl.)	O 4
Sakurai, 49,939	J 8	Tsubame, 40,134	J 5	Ueda, 73,940	J 5	Kuju (mt.)	E 7
Sanda, 32,265	H 7	Tsuchiura, 78,971	K 5	Ugo, 25,661	K 4	Kume (isl.), 5,922	M 6
Sanjo, 74,080	J 5	Tsuruga, 54,508	J 6	Uji, 68,934	J 7	Kutcharo (lake)	M 2
Sapporo, 1,010,122	K 2	Tsuruoka, 95,615	J 4	Uozu, 46,854	H 5	Kyushu (isl.), 12,370,190	E 7
Sarufutsu, 7,450	L 1	Tsuyama, 76,007	F 6	Urakawa, 21,552	L 2	Meakan (mt.)	L 2
Sasebo, 268,000	D 7	Ube, 149,000	E 6	Urawa, 250,000	O 2	Miura (pen.)	O 3
Satte, 25,169	O 1	Ueda, 73,940	J 5	Ushibuka, 30,995	D 7	Miyako (isl.), 47,150	L 7
Sawara, 47,561	K 6	Uchinoura, 10,036	E 8	Usuki, 42,731	E 7	Miyako (isls.), 69,825	L 7
Sayama, 40,183	O 2	Ueda, 73,940	J 5	Utsunomiya, 283,000	K 5	Mogami (river)	K 4
Sendai, Kagoshima, 67,142	E 8	Uji, 68,934	J 7	Uwajima, 66,484	F 7	Motsuta (cape)	K 2
Sendai, Miyagi, 515,000	K 4	Uozu, 46,854	H 5	Wajima, 35,798	H 5	Muko (river)	H 7
Seta, 20,327	J 7	Urakawa, 21,552	L 2	Wakasa, 8,455	G 8	Muroto (point)	G 7
Shari, 18,015	M 2	Urawa, 250,000	O 2	Wakayama, 353,000	G 6	Mutsu (bay)	K 3
Shibata, 73,992	J 4	Ushibuka, 30,995	D 7	Wakkanai, 51,539	K 1	Naka (river)	K 5
Shibetsu, 36,502	M 2	Usuki, 42,731	E 7	Warabi, 69,715	O 2	Nampo-Shoto (isls.), 203	M 3
Shimabara, 44,175	E 7	Utsunomiya, 283,000	K 5	Yaizu, 77,008	J 6	Nii (isl.), 3,913	J 6
Shimizu, 230,000	J 6	Uwajima, 66,484	F 7	Yakumo, 22,487	J 2	Nikko Nat'l Park	K 5
Shimoda, 28,645	J 6	Wajima, 35,798	H 5	Yamagata, 201,000	K 4	Nojima (cape)	K 6
Shimonoseki, 276,000	H 7	Wakasa, 8,455	G 8	Yamaguchi, 103,000	E 6	Noshappu (point)	N 2
Shingu, 40,051	H 7	Wakayama, 353,000	G 6	Yamato, 64,991	J 7	Noto (pen.)	H 5
Shinjo, 43,037	K 4	Wakkanai, 51,539	K 1	Yamatokoriyama, 45,765	J 8	Nyudo (cape)	K 3
Shiogama, 58,363	K 4	Warabi, 69,715	O 2	Yamatotakada, 47,371	J 8	Oani (river)	K 3
Shiroishi, 41,928	K 4	Yaizu, 77,008	J 6	Yao, 197,000	J 8	Obitsu (river)	O 2
Shizunai, 26,533	L 2	Yakumo, 22,487	J 2	Yatabe, 20,093	P 2	Ogasawara-Gunto (Bonin) (isls.), 203	M 3
Shizuoka, 392,000	J 6	Yamagata, 201,000	K 4	Yatsushiro, 105,000	J 8	Ogasawara (isls.)	
Shobara, 29,516	F 6	Yamaguchi, 103,000	E 6	Yawata, 19,204	J 7	Ohotsk (sea)	M 1
Shuri, 28,282	N 6	Yamato, 64,991	J 7	Yawatahama, 50,005	F 7	Oki (isls.), 36,185	F 5
Soka, 102,000	O 2	Yamatokoriyama, 45,765	J 8	Yoichi, 26,154	K 2	Okinawa (isl.), 782,267	N 6
Soma, 38,430	K 5	Yamatotakada, 47,371	J 8			Okinawa (isls.), 812,339	N 6
Sonobe, 15,241	J 7	Yao, 197,000	J 8			Okushiri (isl.), 7,142	J 2
Suita, 205,000	J 7	Yatabe, 20,093	P 2			Oma (river)	K 3
Sukagawa, 46,999	K 5	Yatsushiro, 105,000	J 8			Omono (river)	K 4
Sukumo, 26,992	F 7	Yawata, 19,204	J 7			Ono (river)	E 7
Sumoto, 46,313	G 6	Yawatahama, 50,005	F 7			Ontake (mt.)	H 6
Sunagawa, 30,205	L 2	Yoichi, 26,154	K 2			Osaka (bay)	H 8
Susaki, 32,020	F 7					Oshima (isl.), 11,840	J 6
						Osumi (isls.), 82,372	E 8
						Osumi (pen.)	E 8
						Osumi (str.)	E 8

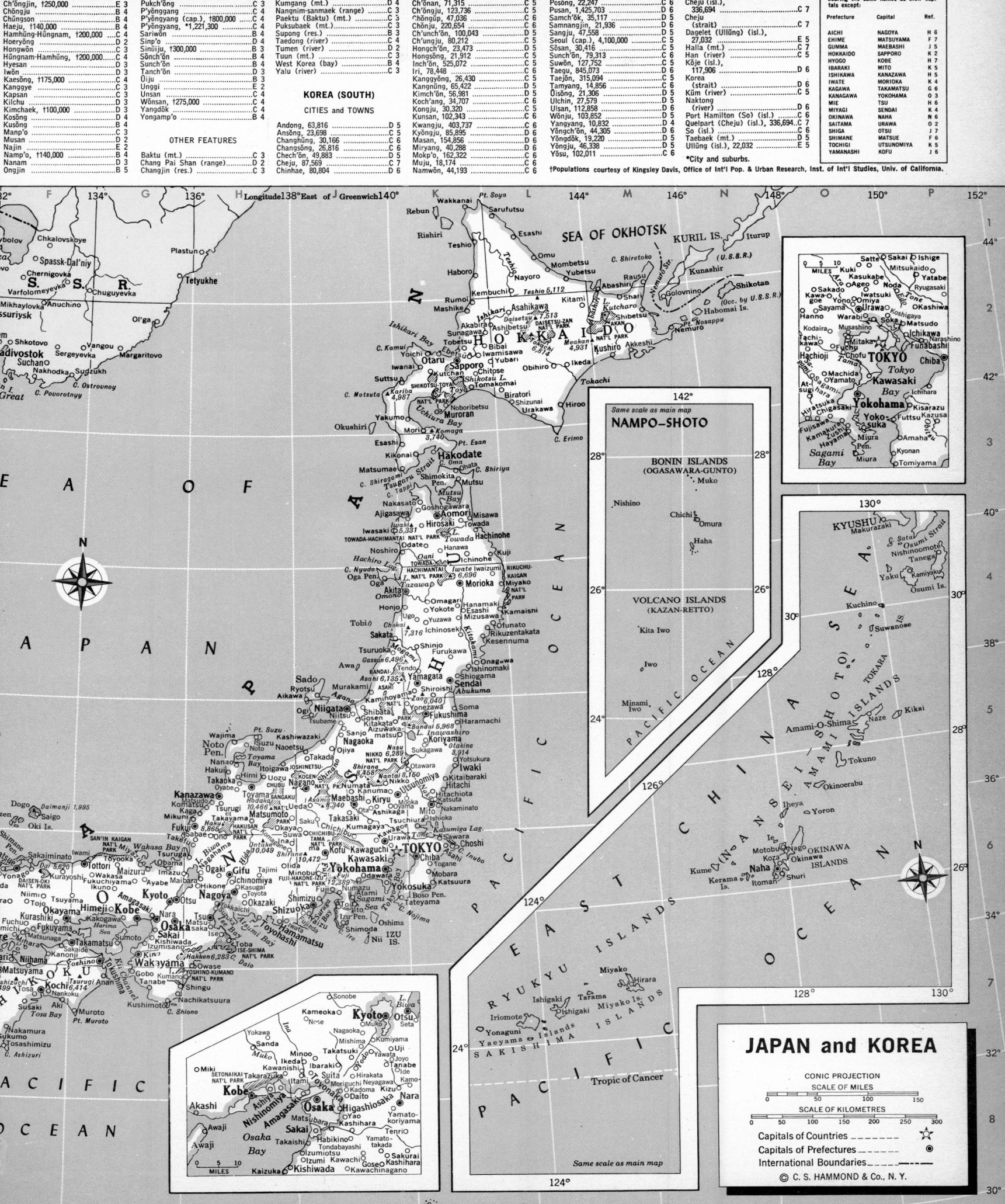

JAPAN and KOREA
CONIC PROJECTION
SCALE OF MILES
SCALE OF KILOMETRES
Capitals of Countries
Capitals of Prefectures
International Boundaries
© C. S. HAMMOND & CO., N.Y.

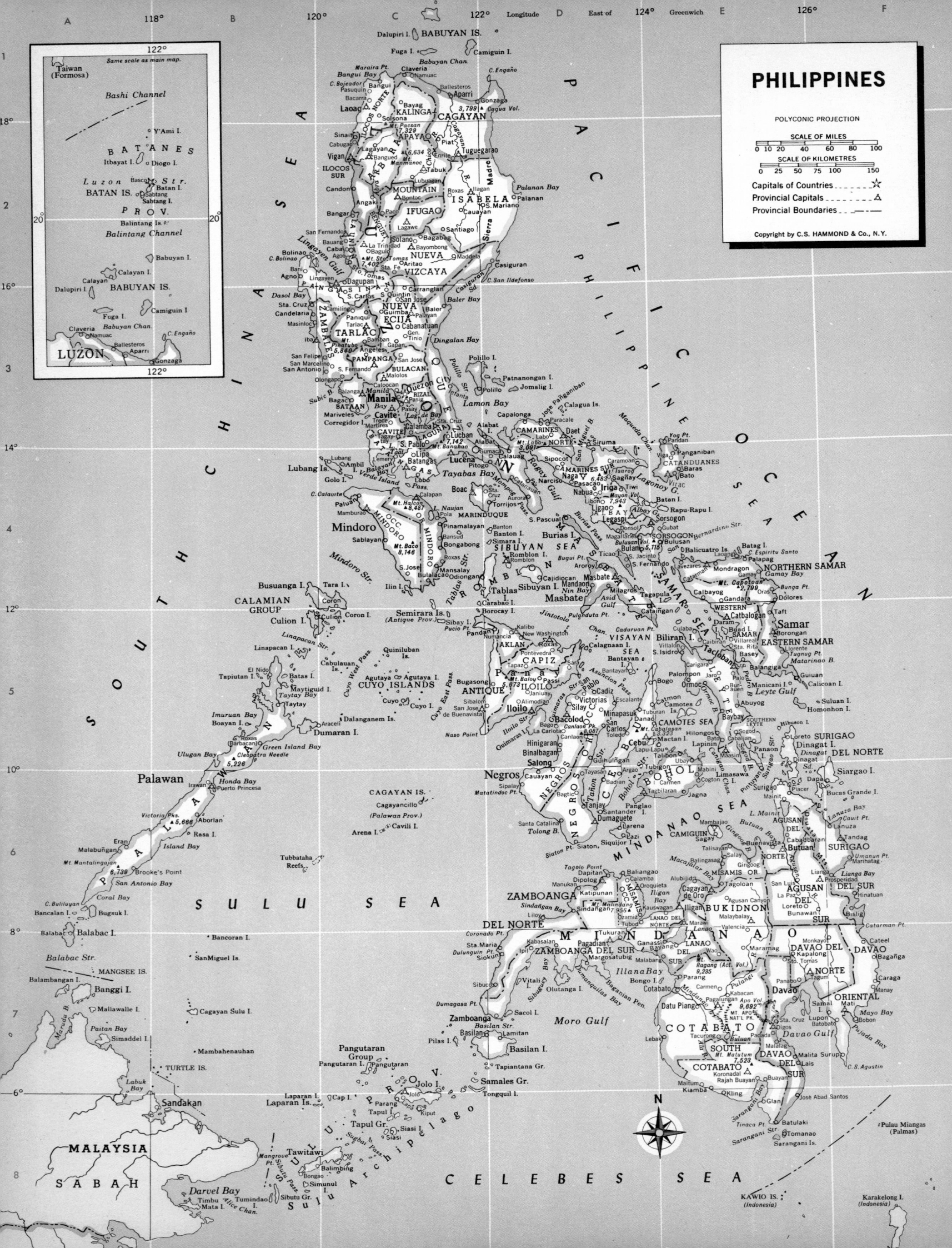

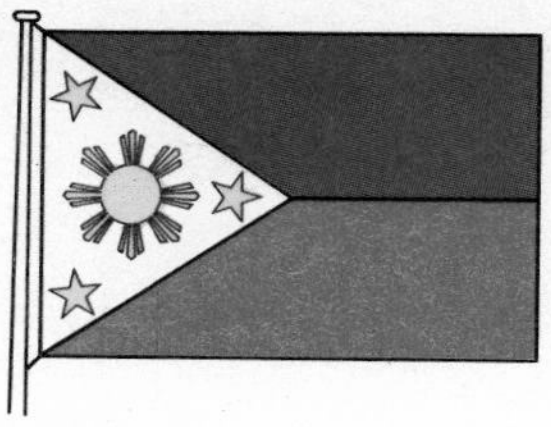

AREA 115,707 sq. mi.
POPULATION 39,079,000
CAPITAL Quezon City
LARGEST CITY Manila
HIGHEST POINT Apo 9,692 ft.
MONETARY UNIT Philippine peso
MAJOR LANGUAGES Pilipino (Tagalog), English, Spanish, Bisayan, Ilocano, Bikol
MAJOR RELIGIONS Roman Catholicism, Islam, Tribal religions

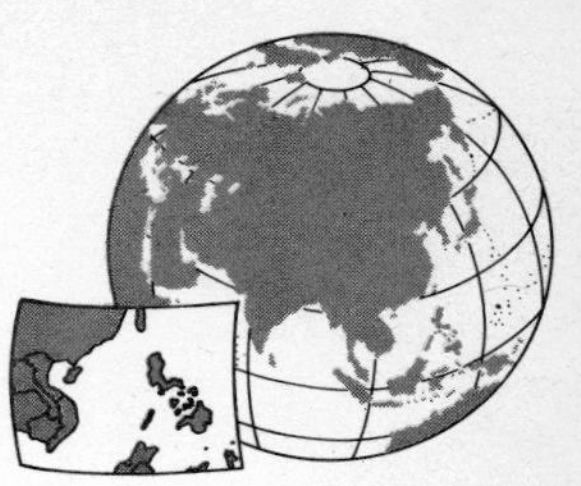

PROVINCES

Abra, 115,193	C 2
Agusan del Norte, 174,758	E 6
Agusan del Sur, 96,252	E 6
Aklan, 226,232	D 5
Albay, 514,980	D 4
Antique, 238,405	D 5
Bataan, 145,323	C 3
Batanes, 10,309	A 2
Batangas, 681,414	C 4
Benguet, 183,657	C 2
Bohol, 592,194	E 6
Bukidnon, 194,368	E 6
Bulacan, 555,819	C 3
Cagayan, 445,289	C 1
Camarines Norte, 188,091	D 3
Camarines Sur, 819,565	D 4
Camiguin, 44,717	E 6
Capiz, 315,079	D 5
Catanduanes, 156,329	E 4
Cavite, 378,138	C 3
Cebu, 1,332,847	D 5
Cotabato, 766,583	E 7
Davao del Norte, 226,728	E 7
Davao del Sur, 533,702	E 7
Davao Oriental, 132,593	F 7
Eastern Samar, 237,747	E 4
Ifugao, 76,788	C 2
Ilocos Norte, 287,333	C 1
Ilocos Sur, 338,058	C 2
Iloilo, 966,266	D 5
Isabela, 442,062	C 2
Kalinga-Apayao, 80,393	C 2
Laguna, 472,064	C 3
Lanao del Norte, 270,603	E 6
Lanao del Sur, 378,327	E 7
La Union, 293,330	C 2
Leyte, 963,364	E 5
Manila (city), 1,499,000	C 3
Marinduque, 114,586	C 4
Masbate, 335,971	D 4
Misamis Occidental, 248,371	D 6
Misamis Oriental, 343,898	E 6
Mountain, 95,001	C 2
Negros Occidental, 1,332,323	D 6
Negros Oriental, 597,761	D 6
Northern Samar, 261,424	E 4
Nueva Ecija, 608,362	C 3
Nueva Vizcaya, 138,090	C 2
Occidental Mindoro, 84,316	C 4
Oriental Mindoro, 228,998	C 4
Palawan, 162,669	B 6
Pampanga, 617,259	C 3
Pangasinan, 1,124,144	C 3
Quezon, 653,426	C 3
Rizal, 1,456,362	C 3
Romblon, 131,658	D 4
Sorsogon, 347,771	E 4
South Cotabato, 262,536	E 7
Southern Leyte, 209,608	E 5
Sulu, 326,898	B 8
Surigao del Norte, 194,981	F 5
Surigao del Sur, 165,016	F 6
Tarlac, 426,647	C 3
Western Samar, 368,823	E 4
Zambales, 213,442	C 3
Zamboanga del Norte, 281,429	D 6
Zamboanga del Sur, 742,204	D 7

CITIES and TOWNS

Abuyog, 7,018	E 5
Agoo, 6,511	C 2
Alimodian, 6,732	D 5
Alubijid, 5,105	E 6
Angeles, †102,400	C 3
Aparri, 13,167	C 1
Bacarra, 7,268	C 1
Bacolod, †156,900	D 5
Bago, †58,834	D 5
Bagtic, 6,932	D 6
Baguio, †58,000	C 2
Balangiga, 5,343	E 5
Balingasag, 5,502	E 6
Bangued, 7,602	C 2
Bantayan, 7,920	D 5
Basey, 6,240	E 5
Basilan, †209,100	C 7
Batangas, †102,100	C 4
Baybay, 10,021	E 5
Bayombong, 8,312	C 2
Binalbagan, 13,545	D 5
Bogo, 6,786	E 5
Bontoc, 5,472	C 2
Buenavista, 5,770	E 6
Bulan, 16,042	D 4
Bulusan, 5,394	E 4
Burauen, 8,677	E 5
Butuan, †110,100	E 6
Cabadbaran, 5,954	E 6
Cabanatuan, †80,000	C 3
Cadiz, †118,200	D 5
Cagayan de Oro, †78,000	E 6
Caibiran, 7,213	E 5
Calamba, 12,142	C 3
Calbayog, †103,100	E 4
Caloocan, †194,600	C 3
Camiling, 9,799	C 3
Canlaon, †26,000	D 5
Carigara, 8,299	E 5
Catarman, 8,248	E 4
Catbalogan, 14,274	E 5
Cavite, †63,000	C 3
Cebu, †332,100	D 5
Cotabato, †43,000	D 7
Daet, 19,726	D 3
Dagupan, †73,000	C 2
Danao, †37,000	D 5
Dapitan, †31,000	D 6
Datu Piang, 21,951	E 7
Davao, †337,000	E 7
Digos, 8,725	E 7
Dipolog, 15,102	D 6
Donsol, 5,509	D 4
Dumaguete, †40,000	D 6
Enrile, 5,570	C 2
Escalante, 5,304	D 5
Gapan, 6,741	C 3
General Tinio, 9,772	C 3
Gingoog, †60,000	E 6
Gubat, 8,392	E 4
Guihulñgan, 6,401	D 5
Guimba, 8,280	C 3
Guiuan, 5,865	E 5
Gumaca, 9,175	D 4
Hinigaran, 10,231	D 5
Ilagan, 6,375	C 2
Iligan, †67,000	E 6
Iloilo, †201,000	D 5
Iriga, †101,000	D 4
Janiuay, 5,840	D 5
Jaro, 7,243	E 5
Jose Pañganiban, 5,291	D 3
Kalibo, 6,025	D 5
Koronadal, 3,677	E 7
La Carlota, †56,722	D 5
Lagawe, 3,019	C 2
Lais, 7,752	E 7
Laoag, †50,198	C 1
Laoang, 8,557	E 4
Lapu-Lapu, †56,000	D 5
La Trinidad, 3,334	C 2
Lebak, 5,626	D 7
Legaspi, †69,000	D 4
Lemery, 8,617	C 4
Lianga, 5,772	E 6
Ligao, 10,547	D 4
Lingayen, 8,221	C 2
Lipa, †79,000	C 4
Lucban, 14,292	C 3
Lucena, †56,000	C 4
Maasin, 7,968	E 5
Magallanes, 6,002	D 4
Malabang, 7,884	D 7
Malalag, 5,242	E 7
Malaybalay, 7,624	E 6
Malita, 5,947	E 7
Malolos, 2,240	C 3
Mambajao, 3,880	E 6
Mandaon, 11,419	D 4
Manila, †1,499,000	C 3
Manila, *2,369,000	C 3
Marawi, †31,000	E 6
Masbate, 11,647	D 4
Mati, 7,870	F 7
Minapasuk, 10,497	D 5
Nabua, 14,146	D 4
Naga, †63,000	D 4
Olongapo, †45,330	C 3
Ormoc, †72,000	E 5
Oroquieta, 5,331	D 6
Ozamiz, †50,000	D 6
Paco, 5,475	C 2
Pagadian, 17,865	D 7
Pagalungan, 770	E 7
Palanan, 5,599	D 2
Palayan, †20,854	C 3
Palo, 8,916	E 5
Palompon, 6,399	E 5
Panabo, 5,539	E 7
Paniqui, 6,492	C 3
Parang, 5,894	E 7
Pasay, †174,100	C 3
Pinamalayan, 6,236	C 4
Prosperidad, 3,478	E 6
Puerto Princesa, 7,551	B 6
Quezon City (cap.), †545,500	C 3
Rajah Buayan, †114,000	E 7
Roxas, Capiz, †57,000	D 5
Roxas, Isabela, 5,612	C 2
Salong, 28,743	D 5
San Antonio, 8,717	B 3
San Carlos, Negros Occ., †165,200	D 5
San Carlos, Pangasinan, †73,900	C 3
San Felipe, 5,900	B 3
San Jacinto, 5,120	D 4
San Jose, Bulacan, 5,326	C 3
San Jose, Nueva Ecija, 13,444	C 3
San Jose de Buenavista, 6,364	C 5
San Marcelino, 6,841	B 3
San Pablo, Laguna, †81,000	C 3
San Pablo, Negros Occ., 13,725	D 5
Santa Cruz, Davao, 6,456	E 7
Santa Cruz, Laguna, 5,248	C 3
Santo Tomas, 9,450	E 7
Silay, †69,000	D 5
Sindañgan, 5,867	D 6
Sipocot, 5,914	D 4
Tabuk, 3,378	C 2
Tacloban, †61,000	E 5
Tacurong, 6,413	E 7
Tagaytay, †8,000	C 3
Tagbilaran, †20,250	E 6
Tagum, 5,263	E 7
Tanjay, 12,355	D 6
Tarlac, †121,400	C 3
Toledo, †73,000	D 5
Trece Martires, †5,000	C 3
Tuguegarao, 10,497	C 2
Victorias, 12,446	D 5
Vigan, 10,498	C 2
Villalon, 7,003	E 5
Virac, 9,143	E 4
Wao, 6,131	E 7
Zamboanga, †176,800	C 7

OTHER FEATURES

Abra (riv.)	C 2
Agusan (riv.)	E 6
Agutàya (isl.), 2,541	C 5
Alabat (isl.), 21,365	D 3
Albay (gulf)	D 4
Alice (chan.)	B 8
Ambil (isl.), 296	C 4
Apo (vol.)	E 7
Asid (gulf)	D 4
Asuncion (passage)	D 5
Babuyan (chan.)	C 1
Babuyan (isls.), 5,388	A 2
Baganian (pen.)	D 7
Balabac (isl.), 2,870	A 7
Balayan (bay)	C 4
Balicuatro (isls.), 8,044	E 4
Balintang (chan.)	A 2
Bancalan (isl.), 231	A 6
Bantayan (isl.), 46,593	D 5
Banton (isl.), 6,155	D 4
Bashi (chan.)	A 1
Basilan (isl.), 134,435	D 7
Batag (isl.), 4,561	E 4
Batan (isl.), Albay, 10,000	E 4
Batan (isl.), Batanes, 6,178	B 2
Batan (isls.), 10,309	A 2
Batas (isl.), 147	B 5
Bay (lag.)	C 3
Biliran (isl.), 78,707	E 5
Bohol (isl.), 531,707	E 6
Bohol (str.)	D 6
Bojeador (cape)	C 1
Bolinao (cape)	B 2
Bongo (isl.), 2,446	D 7
Borocay (isl.), 2,378	D 5
Buad (isl.), 11,549	E 5
Bucas Grande (isl.), 4,883	F 6
Bugsuk (isl.), 482	A 6
Buluan (lake)	E 7
Bulusan (vol.)	D 4
Burias (isl.), 15,494	D 4
Busuanga (isl.), 13,190	B 4
Butuan (bay)	E 6
Cabalasan (mt.)	E 5
Cabulauan (isls.), 469	C 5
Cagayan (isls.), 3,880	C 6
Cagayan (riv.)	C 2
Cagayan Sulu (isl.), 10,789	B 7
Cagua (vol.)	D 1
Calagnaan (isl.), 2,197	D 5
Calagua (isls.), 1,509	D 3
Calamian Group (isls.), 21,975	B 4
Calayan (isl.), 3,409	A 2
Calicoan (isl.), 2,557	E 5
Camiguin (isl.), 1,177	B 3
Camotes (isls.), 50,826	E 5
Camotes (sea)	E 5
Capotoan (mt.)	E 4
Carabao (isl.), 2,697	D 4
Casiguran (sound)	C 2
Catanduanes (isl.), 154,698	E 4
Cebu (isl.), 1,163,756	D 6
Cleopatra Needle (mt.)	B 5
Coral (bay)	A 6
Coron (isl.), 409	C 5
Corregidor (isl.), 65	C 3
Culion (isl.), 4,785	B 5
Cuyo (isl.), 15,541	C 5
Cuyo (isls.), 24,728	C 5
Cuyo East (passage)	C 5
Cuyo West (passage)	C 5
Dalanganem (isls.), 499	C 5
Daram (isl.), 23,310	E 5
Davao (gulf)	E 7
Dinagat (isl.), 19,543	E 5
Dingalan (bay)	C 3
Diuata (mts.)	E 6
Dumaran (isl.), 4,453	C 5
Engaño (cape)	D 1
Espiritu Santo (cape)	E 4
Fuga (isl.), 802	C 1
Golo (isl.), 1,191	C 4
Green Island (bay)	B 5
Guimaras (isl.), 56,137	D 5
Hibuson (isl.), 880	E 5
Homonhon (isl.), 2,315	E 5
Ilin (isl.), 5,379	C 4
Illana (bay)	D 7
Iloilo (str.)	D 5
Island (bay)	B 6
Itbayat (isl.), 2,365	A 2
Jintotolo (chan.)	D 5
Jolo (isl.), 165,607	C 7
Jomalig (isl.), 1,284	D 3
Lagonoy (gulf)	E 4
Lamon (bay)	C 3
Lanao (lake)	E 7
Lapinin (isl.), 9,618	E 5
Leyte (gulf)	E 5
Leyte (isl.), 1,053,782	E 5
Limasawa (isl.), 1,874	E 6
Linapacan (isl.), 922	B 5
Lingayen (gulf)	C 2
Lubang (isls.), 16,748	B 4
Luzon (isl.), 12,702,731	C 3
Luzon (str.)	A 2
Macajalar (bay)	E 6
Mactan (isl.), 50,014	E 5
Mainit (lake)	E 6
Mangsee (isls.), 143	A 7
Manicani (isl.), 1,341	E 5
Manila (bay)	C 3
Mantalingajan (mt.)	A 6
Maqueda (chan.)	D 3
Marinduque (isl.), 112,048	C 4
Masbate (isl.), 264,273	D 4
Mayon (vol.)	D 4
Maytiguid (isl.), 456	B 5
Mindanao (isl.), 4,699,475	D 7
Mindanao (riv.)	E 7
Mindanao (sea)	D 6
Mindoro (isl.), 290,394	C 4
Mindoro (str.)	C 4
Mompog (passage)	D 4
Moro (gulf)	D 7
Mount Apo Nat'l Park	E 7
Naujan (lake)	C 4
Negros (isl.), 1,862,115	D 6
Olutanga (isl.), 16,616	D 7
Palawan (isl.), 100,664	B 6
Panaon (isl.), 28,933	E 5
Panay (isl.), 1,659,832	D 5
Panglao (isl.), 24,631	D 6
Pangutaran (isl.), 8,153	C 7
Pangutaran Group (isls.), 10,235	C 7
Patnanongan (isl.), 2,760	D 3
Philippine (sea)	D 3
Pilas (isl.), 7,882	C 7
Polillo (isl.), 18,766	C 3
Quiniluban (isls.), 673	C 5
Ragang (vol.)	E 7
Ragay (gulf)	D 4
Rapu-Rapu (isl.), 6,799	E 4
Romblon (isl.), 15,178	D 4
Sabtang (isl.), 1,766	B 2
Sacol (isl.), 4,385	D 7
Samal (isl.), 33,103	E 7
Samales Group (isls.), 5,816	D 7
Samar (isl.), 733,809	E 4
Samar (sea)	E 4
San Agustin (cape)	F 7
San Bernardino (str.)	E 4
Sarangani (isls.), 4,701	E 8
Semirara (isls.), 5,993	C 5
Siargao (isl.), 38,388	F 6
Siasi (isl.), 18,353	C 8
Sibay (isl.), 1,167	C 5
Sibutu (passage)	B 8
Sibutu Group (isls.), 10,624	B 8
Sibuyan (isl.), 25,161	D 4
Sibuyan (sea)	D 4
Sierra Madre (range)	D 2
Simara (isl.), 6,510	D 4
Simunul (isl.), 6,040	B 8
Siquijor (isl.), 59,555	D 6
Subic (bay)	C 3
Sulu (arch.), 315,573	B 8
Sulu (sea)	B 6
Suluan (isl.), 834	F 5
Taal (lake)	C 4
Tablas (isl.), 71,429	D 4
Tagapula (isl.), 4,592	E 4
Tapiantana Group (isls.), 6,081	D 7
Tapul (isl.), 7,927	C 8
Tapul Group (isls.), 57,856	C 8
Tara (isl.), 385	C 4
Tawitawi (isl.), 8,257	B 8
Ticao (isl.), 47,403	D 4
Tinaca (pt.)	E 8
Tongquil (isl.), 1,662	D 8
Tubbataha (reefs)	B 6
Tumindao (isl.), 1,847	B 8
Turtle (isls.), 536	B 7
Ulugan (bay)	B 5
Umanun (pt.)	F 6
Verde Island (passage)	C 4
Victoria (peaks)	B 6
Visayan (sea)	D 5
Vitali (isl.), 3,297	D 7
Yog (pt.)	E 3

*City and suburbs.
†Population of municipality.

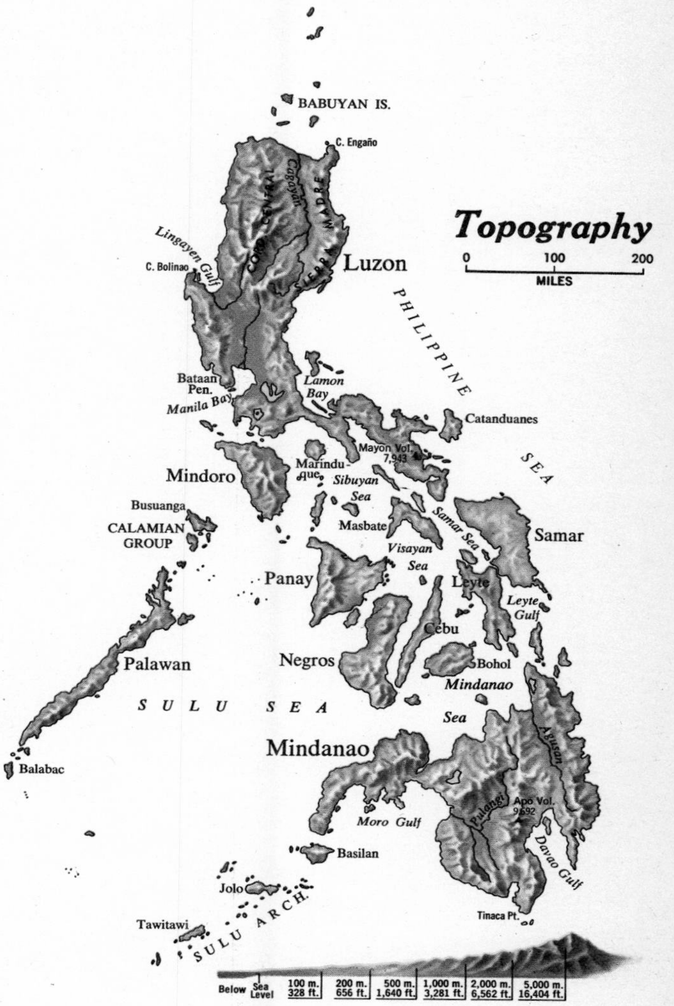

Topography
0
100
200
MILES
BABUYAN IS.
C. Engaño
Lingayen Gulf
C. Bolinao
Luzon
PHILIPPINE SEA
Bataan Pen.
Manila Bay
Lamon Bay
Catanduanes
Mayon Vol. 7,943
Mindoro
Marinduque
Sibuyan Sea
Busuanga
CALAMIAN GROUP
Masbate
Samar Sea
Samar
Visayan Sea
Panay
Leyte
Leyte Gulf
Cebu
Negros
Bohol
Palawan
S U L U   S E A
Mindanao Sea
Mindanao
Balabac
Moro Gulf
Apo Vol. 9,692
Davao Gulf
Basilan
Jolo
Tawitawi
SULU ARCH.
Tinaca Pt.
Below
Sea Level
100 m. 328 ft.
200 m. 656 ft.
500 m. 1,640 ft.
1,000 m. 3,281 ft.
2,000 m. 6,562 ft.
5,000 m. 16,404 ft.

Agriculture, Industry and Resources

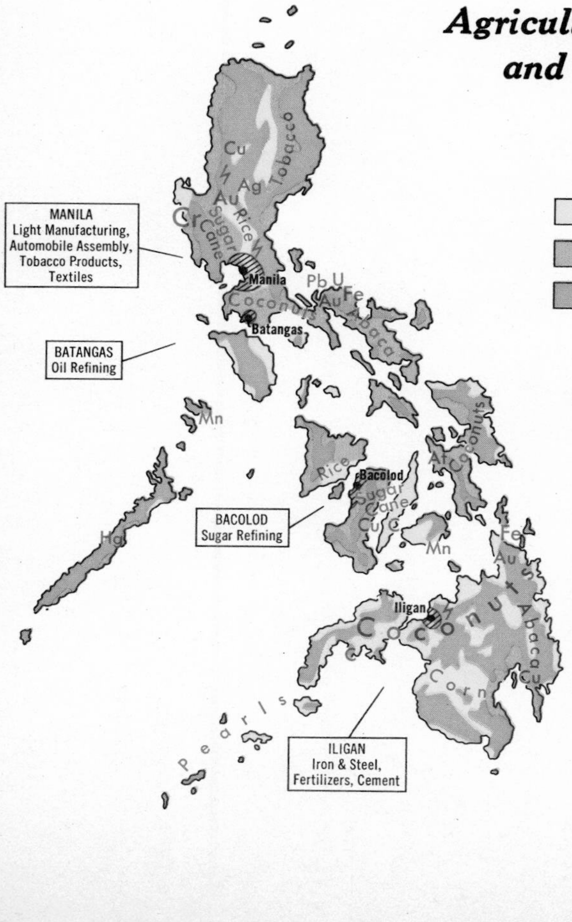

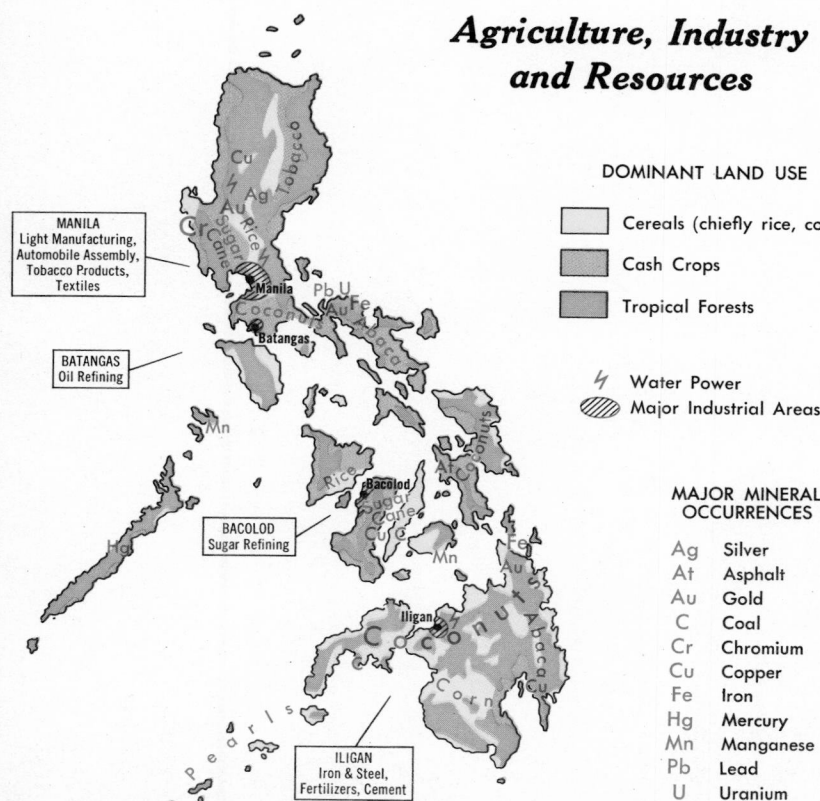

MANILA
Light Manufacturing, Automobile Assembly, Tobacco Products, Textiles
BATANGAS
Oil Refining
BACOLOD
Sugar Refining
ILIGAN
Iron & Steel, Fertilizers, Cement
Manila
Batangas
Bacolod
Iligan
Tobacco
Rice
Sugar Cane
Coconuts
Abaca
Corn
Pearls
Cu
Ag
Au
C
Pb
U
Fe
Mn
Hg

DOMINANT LAND USE

Cereals (chiefly rice, corn)
Cash Crops
Tropical Forests

Water Power
Major Industrial Areas

MAJOR MINERAL OCCURRENCES

Ag	Silver
At	Asphalt
Au	Gold
C	Coal
Cr	Chromium
Cu	Copper
Fe	Iron
Hg	Mercury
Mn	Manganese
Pb	Lead
U	Uranium

BRUNEI

CITIES and TOWNS

Bandar Seri Begawan (cap.),
37,000 ....E 4

INDONESIA

CITIES and TOWNS

Agats, 300 ....K 7
Amahai, 18,017 ....H 6
Amboina, 70,000 ....H 6
Ambon (Amboina), 70,000 .....H 6
Balikpapan, 113,000 ....F 6
Banda Atjeh, 49,000 ....A 4
Bandanaira, 13,686 ....H 6
Bandjarmasin, 264,000 ....E 6
Bandung, 1,006,000 ....H 2
Bangil, 34,112 ....J 2
Bangkalan, 129,536 ....K 2
Banjuwangi, 53,576 ....L 2
Bantul, 30,572 ....J 2
Barabai, 9,366 ....F 6
Barus, †35,716 ....B 5
Batang, 57,561 ....J 2
Batavia (Djakarta) (cap.),
3,429,000 ....H 1
Baturadja, 126,706 ....C 6
Batusangkar, 10,437 ....C 6
Bekasi, 32,012 ....H 1
Bengkajang, 117,029 ....E 5
Bengkalis, 136,433 ....C 5
Bengkulu, 31,000 ....C 6
Benteng, 7,035 ....F 6
Bindjai, 56,000 ....B 5
Bitung, 15,249 ....H 5
Blitar, 78,000 ....K 2
Blora, 49,296 ....J 2
Bodjonegoro, 161,749 ....J 2
Bogor, 172,000 ....H 2
Bondowoso, 144,215 ....L 2
Bonthain, 140,289 ....F 7
Brebes, 150,000 ....J 2
Bukittinggi, 62,000 ....B 6
Bula, 3,116 ....J 6
Bulukumba, 14,137 ....G 7
Bumiaju, 152,790 ....H 2
Buntok, 3,884 ....F 6
Demak, 142,915 ....J 2
Denpasar, 152,000 ....E 7
Djailolo, 110,170 ....H 5
Djajapura, 14,462 ....K 6
Djakarta (cap.), 3,429,000 ......H 1
Djakarta, *5,692,000 ....H 1
Djambi (Telanaipura) 139,000 ..C 6
Djemoronto, 10,350 ....J 2
Djepara, 154,025 ....J 2
Djokjakarta, 385,000 ....J 2
Djombang, 157,370 ....K 2
Dompu, 8,886 ....F 7
Fakfak, 2,430 ....J 6
Galela, 17,384 ....H 5
Garut, 167,542 ....H 2
Gorontalo, 88,000 ....G 5
Gresik, 36,790 ....K 2
Hollandia (Djajapura), 14,462 ..K 6
Indramaju, 156,117 ....H 2

Isimu, 4,304 ....G 5
Kaimana, 1,128 ....J 6
Kajuagung, 15,000 ....D 6
Kalianda, 131,073 ....D 7
Kampung Baru (Tolitoli), 8,333 ..G 5
Karangasem, 16,022 ....F 7
Kau, 17,497 ....H 5
Kebumen, 164,874 ....J 2
Kediri, 196,000 ....J 2
Kendal, 23,129 ....J 2
Kendari, 191,065 ....G 6
Kendawangan, 6,845 ....D 6
Klaten, 33,400 ....J 2
Kolaka, 118,671 ....G 6
Kotaagung, 125,314 ....C 7
Kragan, 23,786 ....J 2
Krawang, 49,867 ....H 2
Kudus, 62,130 ....J 2
Kualakurun, 4,350 ....E 6
Kuala, 8,835 ....E 6
Kuningan, 177,181 ....J 2
Kupang, 17,711 ....G 8
Kutaradja (Banda Atjeh),
49,000 ....A 4
Kutoardjo, 44,962 ....J 2
Labuan, †22,259 ....G 2
Lahat, †25,781 ....C 6
Lamongan, †34,825 ....K 2
Langsa, †47,044 ....B 5
Lawang, 140,239 ....K 2
Longiram, 7,776 ....F 6
Longnawan, †16,234 ....E 5
Lubuklinggau, 14,890 ....C 6
Lubuksikaping, 11,778 ....B 5
Lumadjang, 55,700 ....K 2
Madiun, 152,000 ....J 2
Madjalengka, 147,055 ....H 2
Madjene, 137,727 ....F 6
Magelang, 119,000 ....J 2
Magetan, 154,159 ....K 2
Makassar (Udjung Pandang),
473,000 ....F 7
Malang, 419,000 ....K 2
Malili, 5,735 ....G 6
Malinau, 9,677 ....F 5
Mamudju, †47,309 ....F 6
Manado, 160,000 ....G 5
Manokwari, 10,461 ....J 6
Sangkulirang, 8,893 ....F 6
Martapura, 153,216 ....F 6
Masamba, 115,152 ....G 6
Medan, 590,000 ....B 5
Menggala, 20,343 ....D 6
Meulaboh, 6,544 ....A 5
Merak, †36,293 ....G 1
Merauke, 5,989 ....L 7
Mindiptana, 1,577 ....L 7
Modjokerto, 64,000 ....K 2
Muarabungo, 10,706 ....C 6
Muarateweh, 6,135 ....F 6
Muntok, †25,883 ....D 6
Namlea, 16,018 ....H 6
Nangapinoh, †24,836 ....E 6
Nangatajap, 18,285 ....E 6
Negara, 10,161 ....F 6
Ngabang, †24,516 ....D 5
Ngawi, 29,220 ....J 2
Padang, 178,000 ....B 6
Padangpandjang, 32,000 ....B 6
Padangsidimpuan, †71,704 .....B 5
Painan, 12,060 ....C 6

Pajakumbuh, †74,393 ....C 6
Pakanbaru, 87,000 ....C 5
Palangkaraja, 9,000 ....E 6
Paleleh, 5,466 ....G 5
Palembang, 585,000 ....D 6
Pamangkat, 151,871 ....D 5
Pamekasan, 142,650 ....L 2
Pameungpeuk, 124,662 ....H 2
Pandeglang, 124,823 ....G 1
Pangkalanberandan, 123,806 ..B 5
Pangkalpinang, 74,000 ....D 6
Pare, 185,528 ....K 2
Parepare, 84,000 ....F 6
Pariaman, 145,812 ....B 6
Pasuruan, 78,000 ....K 2
Pati, 156,749 ....J 2
Patjitan, 44,383 ....J 2
Pekalongan, 125,000 ....J 2
Pemalang, 193,608 ....J 2
Pematangsiantar, 142,000 ....B 5
Perahumbulih, 41,951 ....C 6
Pinrang, 23,818 ....F 6
Piru, 123,633 ....H 6
Ponorogo, 49,993 ....J 2
Pontianak, 185,000 ....D 6
Poso, †141,292 ....G 6
Praja, 26,729 ....F 7
Prapat, 5,552 ....B 5
Probolinggo, 85,000 ....K 2
Purwakarta, 188,680 ....H 2
Purwodadi, †54,648 ....J 2
Purwokerto, 22,623 ....H 2
Purworedjo, 23,209 ....J 2
Putussibau, 18,781 ....F 6
Rangkasbitung, †51,176 ....G 2
Rantauprapat, 25,707 ....C 5
Rembang, 39,939 ....K 2
Rengat, †22,982 ....C 6
Ruteng, 15,814 ....F 7
Sabang, 6,747 ....B 4
Salatiga, 72,000 ....J 2
Samarinda, 87,000 ....F 6
Sambas, †53,290 ....D 5
Sampang, 47,596 ....K 2
Sanana, 23,388 ....H 6
Sanggau, †28,039 ....E 5
Sangkulirang, 8,893 ....F 6
Saparua, 53,390 ....H 6
Saumlaki, †22,732 ....J 7
Sawahlunto, 15,000 ....C 6
Semarang, 619,000 ....J 2
Semitau, 19,255 ....E 5
Sengkang, †17,948 ....G 6
Serang, †43,661 ....G 1
Serui, 2,743 ....K 6
Sibolga, 48,000 ....B 5
Sidoardjo, †40,591 ....K 2
Sigli, 4,050 ....A 4
Sindjai, 18,390 ....G 7
Singaradja, 47,000 ....E 7
Singkawang, 161,107 ....D 5
Sintang, †25,067 ....E 6
Situbondo, 30,000 ....L 2
Sorong, 9,151 ....J 6
Sragen, 32,310 ....J 2
Subang, †22,825 ....H 2
Sukabumi, 90,000 ....H 2
Sukadana, 6,899 ....E 6
Sumbawa Besar, †22,308 ......F 7

Sumedang, †74,062 ....H 2
Sumenep, 33,628 ....L 2
Surabaja, 1,556,000 ....K 2
Surakarta, 453,000 ....J 2
Tandjungbalai, 36,000 ....C 5
Tandjungkarang-Telukbetung,
164,000 ....C 7
Tandjungpandan, †39,253 ......D 6
Tandjungpriok, †140,573 ....H 1
Tandjungpura, 120,726 ....B 5
Tangerang, 181,042 ....H 2
Tapaktuan, 9,650 ....A 5
Tarakan, 24,807 ....F 5
Tarutung, 141,041 ....B 5
Tasikmalaja, †101,466 ....H 2
Tebingtinggi, 32,000 ....B 5
Tegal, 110,000 ....J 2
Telanaipura, 139,000 ....C 6
Temanggung, 8,107 ....J 2
Tenggarong, †15,516 ....F 6
Ternate, 35,000 ....H 5
Tjiamis, †80,018 ....H 2
Tjiandjur, †77,927 ....H 2
Tjidulang, †32,475 ....H 2
Tjilatjap, 78,619 ....J 2
Tjimahi, 190,718 ....H 2
Tjirebon, 176,000 ....H 2
Tjurup, 14,480 ....C 6
Tobelo, 114,430 ....H 5
Tolitoli, 8,333 ....G 5
Tondano, 129,584 ....H 5
Trenggalek, 137,762 ....K 2
Tuban, 48,123 ....K 2
Tulungagung, 43,115 ....K 2
Turen, 157,711 ....K 2
Udjung Pandang, 473,000 ......F 7
Wahai, 18,781 ....H 6
Wonogiri, 145,704 ....J 2
Wonosobo, 33,917 ....J 2

OTHER FEATURES

Alas (str.) ....A 5
Anambas (isls.), 15,700 ....D 5
Arafura (sea) ....J 8
Aru (isls.), 27,006 ....J 7
Asahan (river) ....B 5
Babar (isls.), 14,133 ....H 7
Bali (isl.), 2,196,000 ....F 7
Bali (sea) ....F 6
Banda (sea) ....H 7
Banggai (arch.), 144,747 ....G 6
Bangka (isl.), 384,000 ....D 6
Banjak (isls.), 1,696 ....B 5
Barisan (mts.) ....B 6
Barito (river) ....F 6
Batjan (isl.), 21,861 ....H 6
Batu (isls.), 60,806 ....B 6
Bawean (isl.), 47,589 ....K 2
Belitung (Billiton) (isl.),
126,000 ....D 6
Bengalen (passage) ....A 4
Berau (bay) ....J 6
Biak (isl.), 31,139 ....K 6
Billiton (isl.), 126,000 ....D 6
Binongko (isl.), 10,580 ....G 7
Bintan (isl.), 65,301 ....C 5
Bone (gulf) ....G 7
Borneo (isl.) ....E 6
Borneo (Kalimantan) (reg.),
4,243,000 ....E 5

Bosch, van den (cape) ....J 6
Bunguran (Natuna) (isls.),
15,261 ....D 5
Buru (isl.), 16,018 ....H 6
Butung (isl.), 311,000 ....G 6
Celebes (isl.), 7,665,000 ....G 6
Celebes (sea) ....G 5
Ceram (isl.), 73,453 ....H 6
Damar (isls.) ....H 7
Dampier (str.) ....J 6
Diamond (point) ....B 4
Digul (river) ....K 7
Djaja (mt.) ....K 6
Djajawidjaja (range) ....K 6
Djemadja (isl.), 3,874 ....D 5
Doberai (pen.) ....J 6
Dolak (isl.) ....K 7
Enggano (isl.), 686 ....C 7
Ewab (isls.), 76,606 ....J 7
Flores (isl.), 1,108,000 ....G 7
Flores (sea) ....F 7
Frederik Hendrik (Dolak) (isl.) ..K 7
Gebe (isl.), 5,410 ....H 6
Geelvink (Sarera) (bay) ....K 6
Good Hope (isl.) ....J 5
Gorong (isls.), 33,241 ....J 6
Halmahera (isl.), 97,133 ....H 5
Idenburg (river) ....K 6
Japen (isl.), 23,701 ....K 6
Java (head) ....J 2
Java (isl.), 69,323,000 ....J 2
Java (sea) ....E 6
Kabaena (isl.), 14,380 ....G 7
Kabia (Salajar) (isl.), 107,000 ..G 7
Kai (Ewab) (isls.), 76,606 ....J 7
Kalao (isl.), 670 ....G 7
Kalaotoa (isl.), 2,031 ....G 7
Kalimantan (reg.), 4,243,000 ..E 6
Kangean (isls.), 52,893 ....F 7
Kapuas (river) ....F 6
Karakelong (isl.), 15,276 ....H 5
Karimata (arch.), 1,623 ....D 6
Karimundjawa (isls.), 1,611 ....J 1
Kerintji (mt.) ....B 6
Kisar (isl.), 16,569 ....H 7
Komodo (isl.) ....F 7
Krakatau (Rakata) (isl.) ....C 7
Laut (isl.), 42,099 ....F 6
Leuser (mt.) ....A 5
Lingga (arch.), 39,307 ....D 5
Lingga (isl.), 14,309 ....D 5
Lombok (isl.), 1,602,000 ....F 7
Madura (isl.), 2,650,000 ....K 2
Mahakam (river) ....F 6
Makassar (str.) ....F 6
Malacca (str.) ....B 5
Mamberamo (river) ....K 6
Maoke (mts.) ....K 6
Mapia (isls.) ....J 5
Mentawai (isls.), 23,649 ....B 6
Misool (isl.), 3,022 ....J 6
Molucca (sea) ....H 6
Moluccas (isls.), 973,000 ....H 6
Morotai (isl.), 19,523 ....H 5
Muli (str.) ....K 7
Müller (mts.) ....F 6
Muna (isl.), 139,000 ....G 7
Musi (river) ....C 6
Natuna (isls.), 15,261 ....D 5
Ngundju (cape) ....F 8
Nias (isl.), 388,000 ....B 5

Obi (isls.), 6,358 ....H 6
Ombai (str.) ....H 7
Perkam (cape) ....K 6
Puting (cape), Borneo ....E 6
Puting (cape), Sumatra ....C 5
Radja Ampat Group (isls.),
17,158 ....J 6
Raja (isl.) ....E 6
Rakata (isl.) ....C 7
Rantekombola (mt.) ....F 6
Riau (arch.), 342,000 ....C 5
Rokan (river) ....C 5
Roti (isl.), 68,330 ....G 8
Rouffaer (river) ....K 6
Salajar (isl.), 107,000 ....G 7
Salawati (isl.), 5,125 ....J 6
Sandalwood (Sumba) (isl.),
311,000 ....F 7
Sangihe (isls.), 83,585 ....H 5
Sangihe (isls.), 126,931 ....H 5
Sarera (bay) ....K 6
Sawu (isls.), 78,785 ....G 8
Sawu (sea) ....G 7
Schouten (isls.), 41,647 ....K 6
Schwaner (mts.) ....E 6
Seaflower (channel) ....B 6
Sebuko (bay) ....F 6
Selatan (cape) ....E 6
Semeru (mt.) ....K 2
Siau (isl.), 29,762 ....H 5
Siberut (str.) ....B 6
Simeulue (isl.), 25,951 ....A 5
Singkep (isl.), 17,712 ....D 5
Sipora (isl.), 5,671 ....B 6
Slamet (mt.) ....J 2
Sorik Merapi (mt.) ....B 5
South Natuna (isls.), 3,318 .....D 5
Sudirman (range) ....K 6

Sula (isls.), 30,779 ....H 6
Sulawesi (Celebes) (isl.),
7,665,000 ....G 6
Sumatra (isl.), 17,345,000 ......B 5
Sumba (isl.), 311,000 ....F 7
Sumba (str.) ....F 7
Sumbawa (isl.), 625,000 ....F 7
Sunda (str.) ....C 7
Tahulandang (isl.), 13,584 ......H 5
Talaud (isls.), 28,738 ....H 5
Taliabu (isl.), 7,391 ....G 6
Tambelan (isls.), 3,551 ....D 5
Timbar (isls.), 41,233 ....J 7
Tidore (isl.), 24,064 ....H 5
Timor (sea) ....H 8
Timor, Indonesian (reg.), 866,000 ..H 8
Toba (lake) ....B 5
Tolo (gulf) ....G 6
Tomini (gulf) ....G 6
Tukangbesi (isls.), 59,775 ....G 7
Vals (cape) ....K 7
Vogelkop (Deberai) (pen.) ......J 6
Waigeo (isl.), 9,011 ....J 6
Wangiwangi (isl.), 19,719 ....G 7
West Irian (reg.), 933,000 ....K 6
Wetar (isl.), 11,383 ....H 7

MALAYSIA ★

STATES

Sabah, 633,000 ....F 4
Sarawak, 950,000 ....E 5

CITIES and TOWNS

Beaufort, †25,408 ....F 4

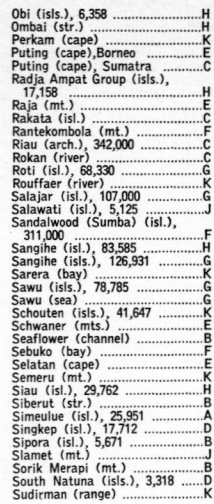
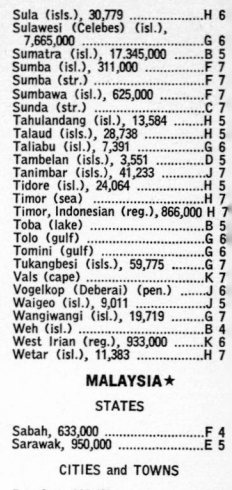
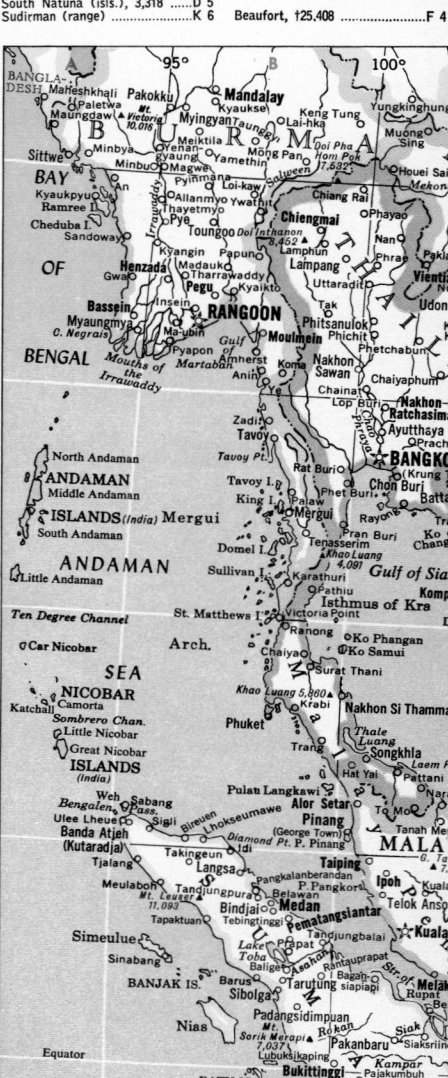

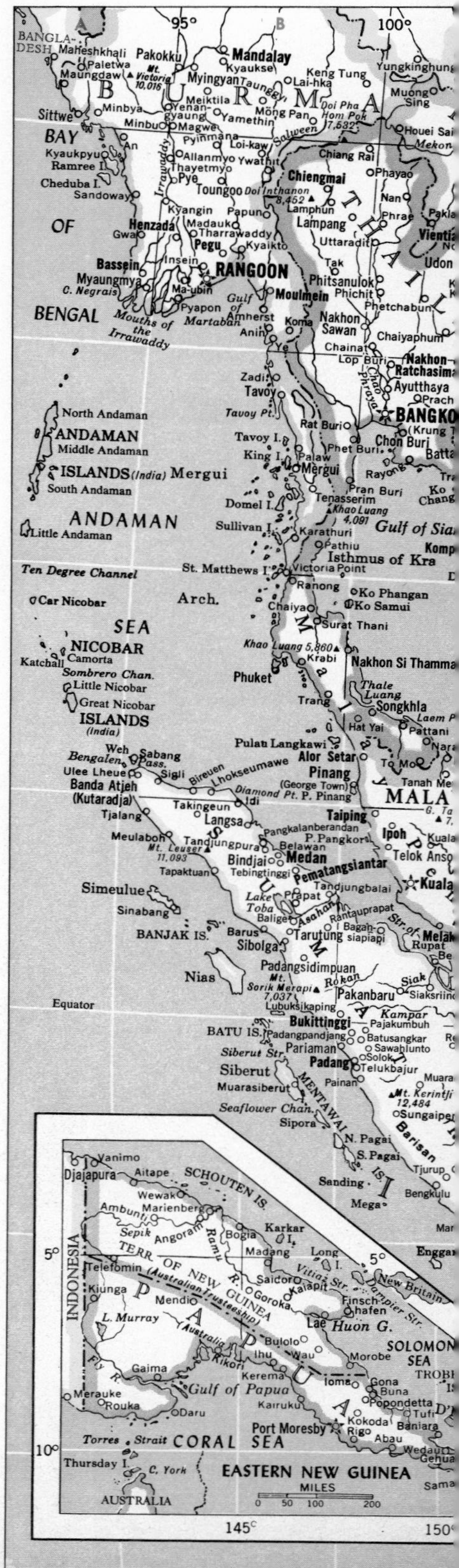

Topography

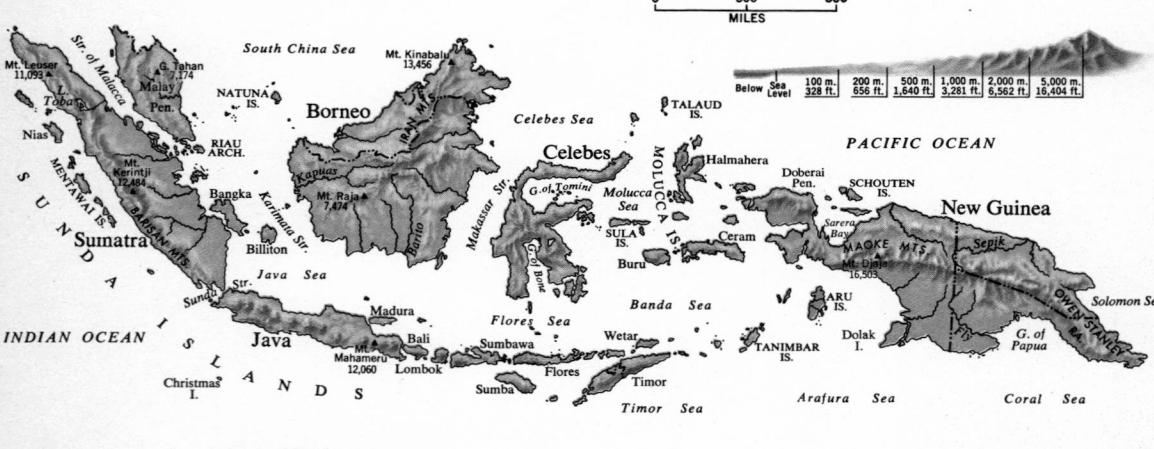

Agriculture, Industry and Resources

SINGAPORE
Iron & Steel, Oil Refining,
Tires, Light Industry

DJAKARTA
Textiles, Light Industry

DOMINANT LAND USE

- Cereals (chiefly rice, corn)
- Diversified Tropical Crops
- Forests

MAJOR MINERAL OCCURRENCES

Al Bauxite	C Coal	Mn Manganese
Au Gold	Fe Iron Ore	Ni Nickel
		O Petroleum
		Sn Tin

Major Industrial Areas

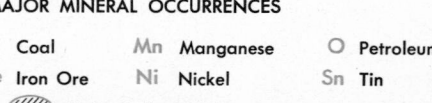

Bintulu, 5,307	E 5
Keningau, 114,645	F 4
Kota Kinabalu, 21,704	F 4
Kuching, 56,000	E 5
Kudat, 3,660	F 4
Lahad Datu, 119,534	F 5
Marudi, 2,653	E 5
Miri, 20,000	E 5
Papar, 128,210	F 4
Ranau, 117,033	F 4
Sandakan, 28,805	F 4
Sematan	D 5
Semporna, ‡16,895	F 5
Sibu, 29,630	E 5
Simanggang, 5,648	E 5
Tawau, 10,276	F 5
Victoria, 3,213	E 4

OTHER FEATURES

Balambangan (isl.)	F 4
Banggi (isl.)	F 4
Iran (mts.)	E 5
Kinabalu (mt.)	F 4
Labuan (isl.), 14,904	F 4
Labuk (bay)	F 4
Rajang (river)	E 5
Sirik (cape)	E 5

TERRITORY OF NEW GUINEA
CITIES and TOWNS

Aitape, 540	B 6
Ambunti, ‡697	B 6
Angoram, 1,822	B 6

Boqia, 639	B 6
Bulolo, 2,724	C 7
Finschhafen, 436	C 7
Goroka, 4,826	B 7
Lae, 12,392	B 7
Madang, 6,601	B 7
Morobe, 12,132	C 7
Saidor	B 7
Telefomin, ‡395	B 7
Vanimo, 512	B 6
Wau, 1,072	B 7
Wewak, 5,090	B 6

OTHER FEATURES

Dampier (str.)	B 6
Huon (gulf)	C 7
Karkar (isl.), 14,966	B 6
Long (isl.), 7,044	B 7
New Britain (isl.), 138,689	C 7
Ramu (river)	B 6
Schouten (isls.), 6,633	B 6
Sepik (river)	B 6
Solomon (sea)	C 7
Torres (str.)	A 7

PAPUA
CITIES and TOWNS

Abau, ‡3,024	C 7
Baniara, ‡1,110	C 7
Buna, 307	C 7
Daru, 3,663	B 7
Ioma, ‡3,552	B 7
Kairuku, ‡4,582	C 7
Kerema, 820	B 7
Kiunga, ‡918	B 7

Kokoda, ‡1,615	C 7
Mendi, 1,687	B 7
Popondetta, 2,139	C 7
Port Moresby (cap.), 56,206	B 7
Rigo, 1,184	C 7
Samarai, 2,201	C 8
Tufi, ‡462	C 7

OTHER FEATURES

D'Entrecasteaux (isls.), 32,288	C 7
Fly (river)	A 7
Kiriwina (isl.), 8,990	C 7
Louisiade (arch.), 11,451	D 8
Milne (bay)	C 8
Misima (isl.), 5,247	C 8
Papua (gulf)	B 7
Rossel (isl.), 1,933	D 8
Tagula (isl.), 1,654	C 8
Trobriand (isls.), 10,199	C 7
Woodlark (isl.), 1,848	C 7

PORTUGUESE TIMOR
CITIES and TOWNS

Dili (cap.), 9,753	H 7
Vila Salazar, 1,598	H 7
Viqueque, 240	H 7

OTHER FEATURES

Oe-Cusse (reg.), 21,398	G 7

★See page 74 for other Malaysian entries.
*City and suburbs.
†Population of sub-division.
‡Population of district.

INDONESIA
AREA 735,264 sq. mi.
POPULATION 119,572,000
CAPITAL Djakarta
LARGEST CITY Djakarta
HIGHEST POINT Mt. Djaja 16,503 ft.
MONETARY UNIT rupiah
MAJOR LANGUAGES Bahasa Indonesian, local Indonesian languages, Papuan languages
MAJOR RELIGIONS Islam, Tribal religions, Christianity, Hinduism

PORTUGUESE TIMOR
AREA 5,762 sq. mi.
POPULATION 590,000
CAPITAL Dili

BRUNEI
AREA 2,226 sq. mi.
POPULATION 130,000
CAPITAL Bandar Seri Begawan

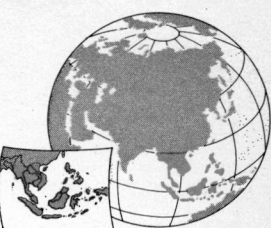

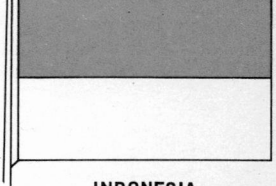

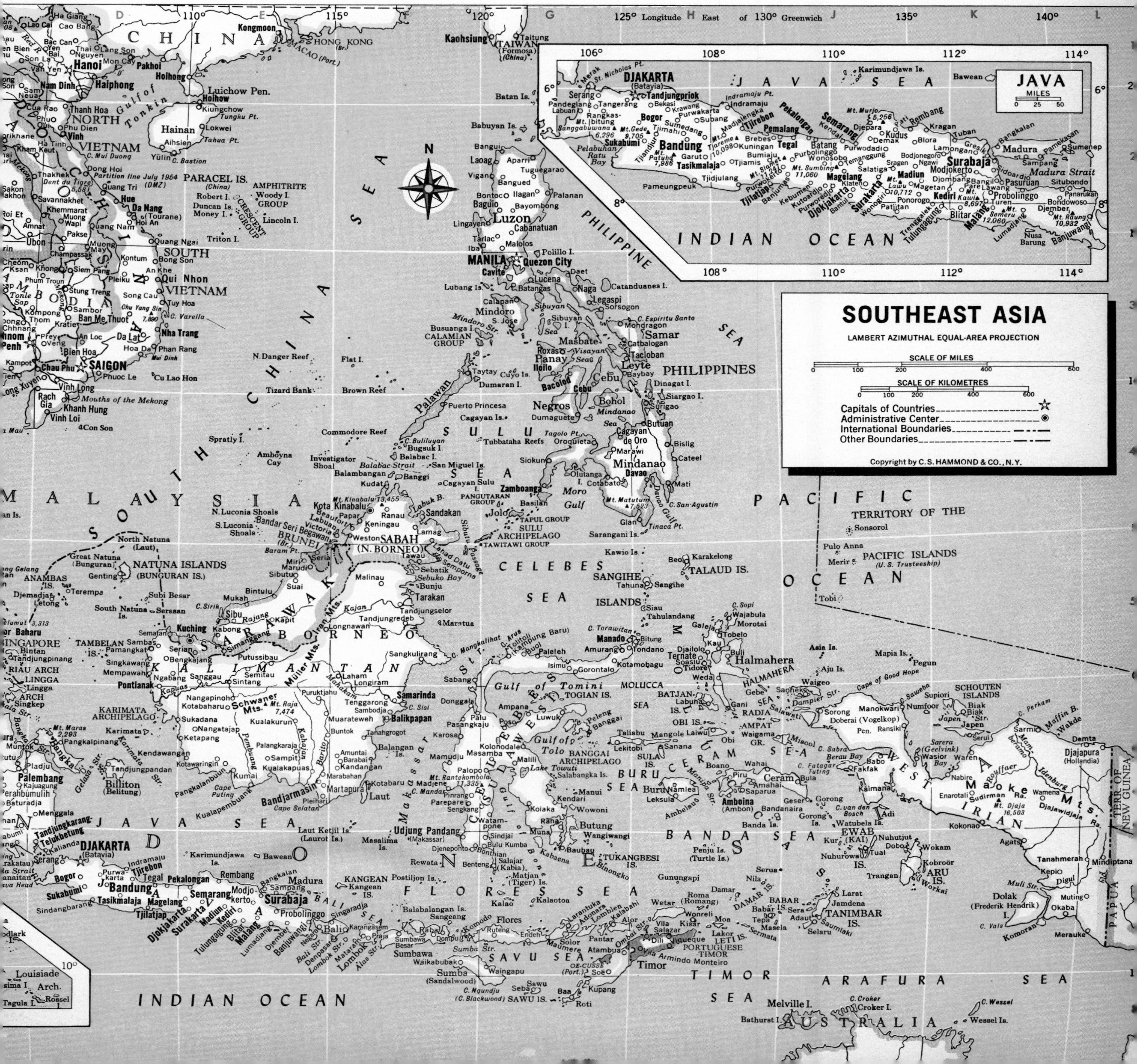

INDONESIA

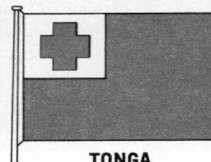

WESTERN SAMOA   **NAURU**   **TONGA**   **FIJI**

WESTERN SAMOA

AREA 1,097 sq. mi.
POPULATION 139,810
CAPITAL Apia
LARGEST CITY Apia
HIGHEST POINT Mt. Silisili 6,094 ft.
MONETARY UNIT West Samoan pound
MAJOR LANGUAGES Samoan, English
MAJOR RELIGIONS Protestantism,
    Roman Catholicism

NAURU

AREA 8.2 sq. mi.
POPULATION 7,000
MONETARY UNIT Australian dollar

TONGA

AREA 270 sq. mi.
POPULATION 83,000
CAPITAL Nuku'alofa
LARGEST CITY Nuku'alofa
HIGHEST POINT 3,389 ft.
MONETARY UNIT Tongan pound
MAJOR LANGUAGES Tongan, English
MAJOR RELIGION Protestantism

FIJI

AREA 7,015 sq. mi.
POPULATION 519,000
CAPITAL Suva
LARGEST CITY Suva
HIGHEST POINT Tomaniivi (Mt. Victoria) 4,341 ft.
MONETARY UNIT Fijian pound
MAJOR LANGUAGES Fijian, Hindi, English
MAJOR RELIGIONS Protestantism, Hinduism

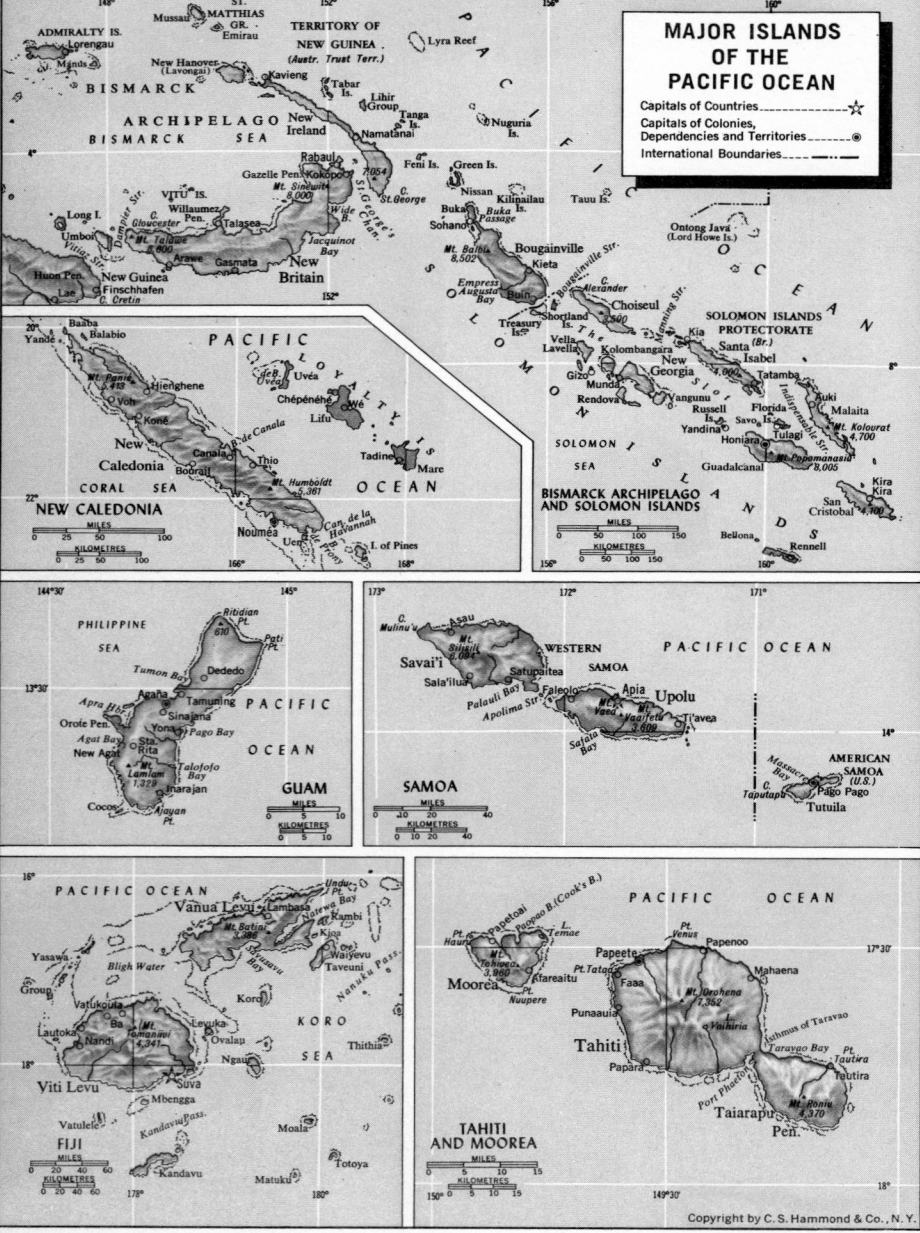

MAJOR ISLANDS OF THE PACIFIC OCEAN
Capitals of Countries ☆
Capitals of Colonies, Dependencies and Territories ◉
International Boundaries

Copyright by C. S. Hammond & Co., N.Y.

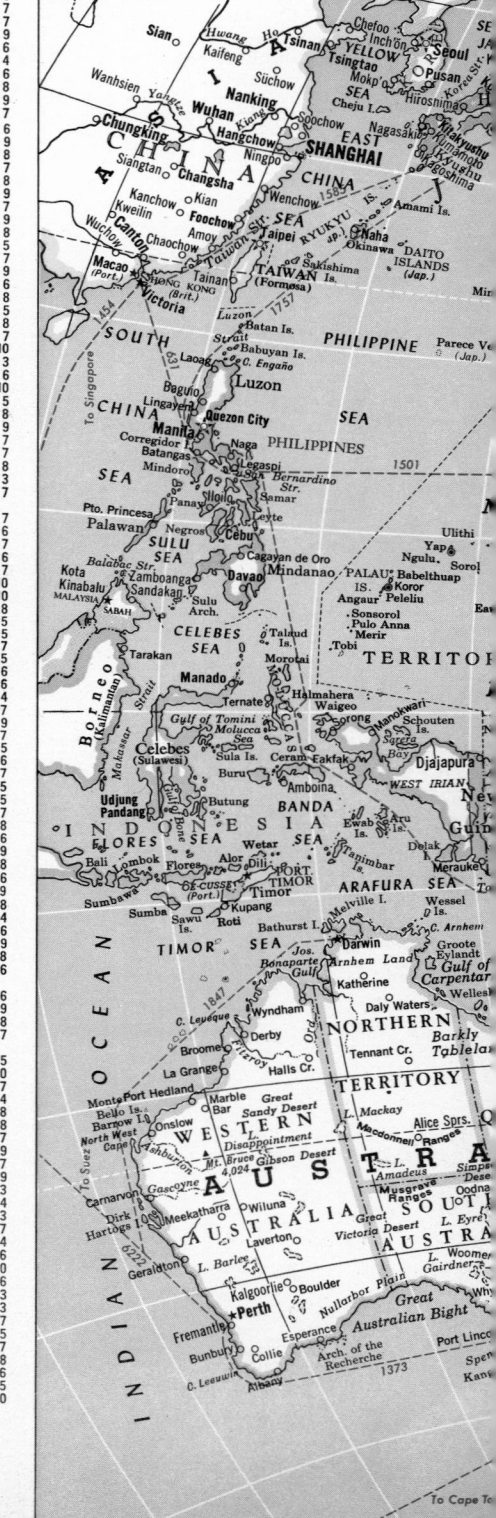

Abaing (atoll), 3,271 ....H 5
Abemama (atoll), 2,126 ....H 5
Adamstown, N 8
Adelaide, 1727,916 ....D 9
Agaña, 2,131 ....E 4
Agrihan (isl.), 64 ....E 4
Ahau, 414 ....H 7
Ailinglapalap (atoll), 1,281 ....G 5
Ailuk (atoll), 371 ....H 5
Aitutaki (atoll), 2,579 ....L 7
Alamagan (isl.), 48 ....E 4
Albany, 11,419 ....B 9
Albury, 25,112 ....H 9
Alice Springs, 6,037 ....D 7
Alofi, 1,117 ....K 7
Amanu (atoll), 117 ....N 7
Ambrym (atoll), 360 ....H 7
American Samoa, 27,159 ....J 7
Anaa (atoll), 360 ....M 7
Anatahan (isl.), 23 ....E 4
Aneityum (isl.), 300 ....H 9
Angaur (isl.), 533 ....D 5
Apataki (atoll), 108 ....M 7
Apia, 27,000 ....J 7
Armidale, 14,984 ....F 9
Arnhem Land (reg.) ....D 7
Arno (atoll), 1,198 ....H 5
Arorae (atoll), 1,830 ....H 6
Atafu (atoll), 615 ....J 6
Atiu (isl.), 1,327 ....L 8
Atuona, 663 ....M 7
Auckland, 152,200 ....H 9
Auki, 600 ....G 6
Austral (isls.), 5,053 ....L 8
Australia, 12,630,600 ....C 8
Australian Cap. Terr., 136,300 ....F 9
Avarua, 4,100 ....K 7
Babelthuap (isl.), 5,222 ....D 5
Bairiki, 1,300 ....H 5
Baker (isl.) ....J 6
Ballarat, *56,290 ....E 9
Banks (isls.), 3,250 ....G 7
Belep (isls.), 551 ....G 7
Bendigo, *42,208 ....E 9
Beru (atoll), 2,412 ....H 6
Bikini (atoll) ....G 4
Bismarck (arch.), 209,051 ....E 6
Blackall, 2,004 ....E 8
Blue Mountains, 30,731 ....E 9
Bora-Bora, 2,071 ....L 7
Bougainville (isl.), 72,661 ....F 6
Boulder, 5,234 ....C 9
Bourail, 672 ....G 8
Bowen, 5,144 ....E 7
Brisbane, 1718,822 ....F 8
Broken Hill, 30,014 ....E 9
Broome, 1,570 ....C 7
Bunbury, 15,459 ....B 9
Bundaberg, 25,402 ....E 8
Butaritari (atoll), 2,714 ....H 5
Cairns, 29,326 ....E 7
Canberra, *136,300 ....F 9
Canton (isl.), 421 ....J 6
Carnarvon, 2,956 ....B 8
Caroline (isls.), 54,563 ....E 5
Charleville, 4,871 ....E 8
Charters Towers, 7,602 ....E 7
Chatham (isls.), 520 ....J10
Chichi (isl.), 203 ....E 3
Choiseul (isl.), 6,600 ....F 6
Christchurch, 165,000 ....H10
Christmas (isl.), 367 ....L 5
Cloncurry, 2,149 ....E 7
Collie, 7,628 ....B 9
Cook (isls.), 20,000 ....K 7
Coral (sea) ....F 7
Cunnamulla, 1,980 ....E 8
Daito (isls.), 3,896 ....D 3
Daly Waters, ‡265 ....D 7
Danger (Pukapuka) (atoll), 684 ....K 7
Daru, 3,663 ....E 6
Darwin, 18,042 ....D 7
D'Entrecasteaux (isls.), 32,288 ....F 6
Derby, 1,424 ....C 7
Devonport, 14,874 ....E10
Dunedin, 77,800 ....H10
Easter (isls.), 1,598 ....Q 9
Ebon (atoll), 731 ....H 5
Efate (isl.), 10,000 ....G 7
Elato (atoll), 35 ....E 5
Ellice (isls.), 5,780 ....H 6
Eniwetok (atoll) ....G 4
Enderbury (isl.) ....J 6
Erromanga, 600 ....H 7
Esperance, 2,677 ....C 9
Espiritu Santo (isl.), 10,000 ....G 7
Fais (isl.), 230 ....E 5
Fakaofo (isl.), 740 ....J 6
Fakarava (atoll), 230 ....M 7
Fanning (isl.), 378 ....L 5
Faraulep (atoll), 176 ....E 5
Fatuhiva (isl.), 459 ....N 7
Fiji, 519,000 ....H 8
Fly (riv.) ....E 6
Fremantle, 25,284 ....B 9
French Polynesia, 109,000 ....L 8
Funafuti (atoll), 826 ....H 6
Furneaux Group (isls.), 1,234 ....E 10
Gambier (isls.), 516 ....N 8
Garapan, 4,100 ....E 4
Gardner (isl.), 230 ....J 6
Geelong, *105,059 ....E 9
Geraldton, 12,125 ....B 8
Gilbert (isls.), 44,205 ....H 6
Gilbert & Ellice Islands, 55,185 ....J 6
Gisborne, 25,600 ....H 9
Grafton, 15,951 ....F 8
Great Barrier (reef) ....E 7
Greenwich (Kapingamarangi) (atoll), 411 ....F 5
Greymouth, 8,590 ....H10
Guadalcanal (isl.), 23,922 ....G 6
Guam (isl.), 84,996 ....E 4
Gympie, 11,279 ....F 8
Ha'apai Group (isls.), 10,591 ....J 8
Halls Creek, ‡577 ....C 7
Hamilton, 67,700 ....H 9
Hao (atoll), 448 ....M 7
Hastings, 28,100 ....H 9
Hawaii (isl.), 63,468 ....L 3
Hawaii (state), 769,913 ....K 4
Hawaiian (isls.), 772,133 ....J 3
Hikueru (atoll), 115 ....M 7
Hilo, 26,353 ....L 3
Hivaoa (isl.), 1,027 ....N 6
Hobart, 53,257 ....E10
Honiara, 11,389 ....F 6
Honolulu, 324,871 ....L 3
Honolulu, *630,528 ....L 3
Hoorn (isls.), 3,000 ....J 7
Howland (isl.) ....J 6
Huahine (isl.), 2,814 ....L 7
Hughenden, 2,033 ....E 7
Hull (isl.), 583 ....J 6
Ifalik (atoll), 321 ....E 5
Invercargill, 45,300 ....H10

Ipswich, 54,531 ....F 8
Iwo (isl.) ....E 3
Jaluit (atoll), 932 ....K 5
Jarvis (isl.) ....K 6
Johnston (atoll), 1,007 ....L 4
Kalgoorlie, *19,908 ....C 9
Kandavu (isl.), 6,600 ....H 8
Kangaroo (isl.), 3,375 ....D 9
Kapingamarangi (atoll), 411 ....F 5
Katherine, 1,302 ....D 7
Kauai (isl.), 29,524 ....K 3
Kavieng, 2,142 ....E 6
Kermadec (isls.), 9 ....J 9
Kieta, 755 ....G 6
Kili (atoll), 320 ....G 5
King (isl.), 2,462 ....D 9
Kingman Reef ....K 5
Koror, 5,541 ....D 5
Kusaie, 3,648 ....G 5
Kwajalein (atoll), 3,841 ....G 5
Lae, 12,392 ....E 6
Lamotrek (atoll), 209 ....E 5
Lanai (isl.), 2,204 ....L 3
Lau Group (isls.), 15,988 ....J 7
Launceston, 37,217 ....E10
Laverton, ‡206 ....C 9
Lavongai (isl.), 7,829 ....E 6
Levuka, 1,685 ....H 7
Lifu (isl.), 6,837 ....G 8
Line (isls.), 1,180 ....K 5
Lismore, 19,784 ....F 8
Lithgow, 13,165 ....F 9
Little Makin (isl.), 1,387 ....H 5
Longreach, 3,871 ....E 8
Lord Howe (isl.), 267 ....G 9
Lord Howe (Ontong Java) (isl.), 900 ....G 6
Louisiade (archipelago), 11,451 ....F 7

Loyalty (isls.), 12,248 ....G 8
Luganville, 3,500 ....G 7
Madang, 6,601 ....E 6
Maitland, 28,428 ....F 9
Majuro (atoll), 5,957 ....H 5
Makatea (isl.), 55 ....L 7
Makin (Butaritari) (atoll), 2,714 ....H 5
Malaita (isl.), 54,000 ....G 6
Malekula (isl.), 11,200 ....G 7
Maloelap (atoll), 494 ....H 5
Mangaia (isl.), 2,002 ....L 8
Mangareva (isl.), 516 ....N 8
Manihiki (atoll), 584 ....K 7
Manra (Sydney), (isl.) ....J 6
Manua (isls.), 2,112 ....K 7
Manus (isl.), 11,088 ....E 6
Marble Bar, ‡567 ....C 8
Marcus (isl.) ....F 3
Maré (isl.), 3,410 ....G 8
Mariana (isls.), 11,827 ....E 4
Mariana Trench ....E 4
Marquesas (isls.), 5,174 ....N 6
Marshall (isls.), 19,328 ....G 4
Marutea (atoll) ....N 8
Maryborough, 20,393 ....F 8
Mataatu ....J 7
Maui (isl.), 38,691 ....L 3
Mauke (isl.), 671 ....L 8
Meekatharra, ‡1,011 ....B 8
Mehetia (isl.) ....M 7
Melanesia (reg.) ....E 5
Melbourne, 12,110,168 ....E 9
Micronesia (reg.) ....E 4
Midway (isls.), 2,220 ....J 3
Mili (atoll), 360 ....H 5

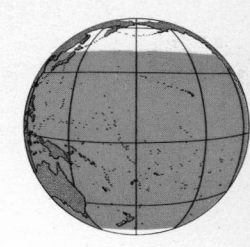

Mitiaro (isl.), 293 .... L 7
Moen (isl.), 4,966 .... F 5
Moerai, 684 .... L 8
Mokil (atoll), 393 .... G 5
Molokai (isl.), 5,089 .... L 7
Moorea (isl.), 4,370 .... L 7
Morobe, 12,132 .... E 6
Mount Gambier, 17,251 .... D 9
Mururoa (isl.) .... M 8
Namatanai, ‡2,221 .... F 6
Namonuito (atoll) .... F 5
Namorik, 490 .... G 5
Nandi, 2,542 .... H 7
Nanumea (atoll), 1,076 .... H 6
Napier, 36,700 .... H 9
Nassau (isl.), 167 .... K 7
Nauru, 7,000 .... G 6
Ndeni (isl.) .... G 6
Neiafu, 3,593 .... J 7
Nelson, 27,900 .... H10
New Britain (isl.), 138,689 .... F 6
New Caledonia (isl.), 86,802 .... G 8
Newcastle, *233,936 .... F 9
New Georgia .... F 6
New Guinea (isl.) .... E 6
New Guinea, Terr. of, 1,722,572 .... F 6
New Hebrides (isls.), 80,000 .... G 7
New Ireland (isl.), 48,774 .... F 6
New South Wales (state), 4,595,400 .... E 9
New Zealand, 2,815,000 .... H 9
Ngatik (atoll), 442 .... F 5
Ngulu (atoll), 43 .... D 5
Niihau (isl.), 237 .... K 3
Nikumaroro (Gardner) (isl.), 230 .... J 6
Ninigo Group (isls.), 1,051 .... E 6

Niuafo'ou (isl.), 599 .... J 7
Niuatoputapu (isl.), 1,294 .... J 7
Niue (isl.), 5,323 .... J 7
Niutao (atoll), 796 .... H 6
Niutao (atoll), 796 .... H 6
Norfolk Isl., 1,147 .... G 8
North (isl.), 1,956,411 .... H 9
North East New Guinea (reg.), 1,420,568 .... E 6
Northern Territory (terr.), 73,000 .... C 8
Nouméa, 41,853 .... G 8
Nouméa, *47,966 .... G 8
Nui (atoll), 569 .... H 6
Nuku'alofa, 15,685 .... J 8
Nukuhiva (isl.), 1,351 .... M 6
Nukulaelae (atoll), 354 .... H 6
Nukumanu (atoll), 678 .... F 6
Nukunono (atoll), 528 .... J 6
Nukuoro (atoll), 406 .... F 5
Oahu (isl.), 629,145 .... L 7
Ocean (isl.), 2,192 .... G 6
Oeno (isl.) .... O 8
Onotoa (atoll), 1,960 .... H 6
Ontong Java (isl.), 900 .... G 6
Orange, 22,196 .... E 9
Orona (Hull) (isl.), 583 .... J 6
Pacific Islands, Terr. of, 98,009 .... F 5
Pagan (isl.), 62 .... E 4
Pago Pago, 2,451 .... J 7
Palau (isls.), 12,291 .... D 5
Palmerston (atoll), 86 .... K 7
Palmerston North, 49,200 .... H10
Palmyra (isl.) .... K 5
Pangai, 1,670 .... J 7
Papeete, 22,278 .... M 7
Papeete, *37,485 .... M 7
Papua, 648,000 .... E 6

Peleliu (isl.), 810 .... D 5
Penrhyn (Tongareva) (atoll), 545 .... L 6
Perth, 1499,969 .... B 9
Phoenix (isls.), 1,018 .... J 6
Pines, Isle of (isl.), 978 .... G 8
Pingelap (atoll), 815 .... G 5
Pitcairn (isl.), 74 .... O 8
Polynesia (reg.) .... L 6
Ponape (isl.), 13,976 .... F 5
Port Augusta, 10,103 .... D 9
Port Hedland, 1,778 .... B 8
Port Lincoln, 8,888 .... D 9
Port Moresby, 56,206 .... E 6
Port Pirie, 15,566 .... D 9
Puka-Puka (atoll), 98 .... N 7
Pukapuka (atoll), 684 .... K 7
Pulap (atoll), 302 .... E 5
Pulo Anna (isl.), 13 .... D 5
Pulusuk (atoll), 305 .... E 5
Puluwat (atoll), 412 .... E 5
Queensland (state), 1,810,000 .... E 8
Rabaul, 8,727 .... F 6
Raiatea (isl.), 6,187 .... L 7
Raivavae (isl.), 999 .... M 8
Rakahanga (atoll), 323 .... K 7
Ralik Chain (isls.), 9,268 .... G 5
Rangiroa (atoll), 868 .... M 7
Rapa (isl.), 363 .... N 8
Rapa Nui (Easter) (isl.), 1,598 .... Q 8
Raroia (atoll), 52 .... M 7
Rarotonga (isl.), 9,971 .... K 8
Ratak Chain (isls.), 10,060 .... G 5
Reao (atoll), 255 .... N 7
Rennell (isl.), 900 .... F 7
Rimatara (isl.), 747 .... L 8
Rockhampton, 46,083 .... F 8
Roma, 5,996 .... E 8

Rongelap (atoll), 107 .... G 4
Rota (isl.), 1,344 .... E 4
Rotuma (isl.), 3,365 .... H 7
Rurutu (isl.), 1,546 .... L 8
Saipan (isl.), 9,590 .... E 4
Sala y Gómez (isl.) .... P 8
Samarai 2,201 .... E 7
Samoa (isls.), 170,159 .... J 7
San Cristobal (isl.), 8,500 .... G 7
Santa Cruz (isls.), 2,800 .... G 6
Santa Isabel (isl.), 8,548 .... F 6
Savai'i (isl.) .... J 7
Satawal (isl.) .... E 5
Senyavin (isls.) .... F 5
Society (isls.), 81,487 .... L 7
Sohano, 877 .... F 6
Solomon (isls.), 234,186 .... F 6
Solomon (sea) .... F 6
Solomon Islands Prot., 161,525 .... F 6
Sonsorol (isl.), 92 .... D 5
Sorol (atoll), 15 .... D 5
South (isl.), 798,681 .... G10
South Australia (state), 1,169,600 .... D 8
Starbuck (isl.) .... K 7
Stewart (isl.), 332 .... G10
Suva, 54,157 .... H 7
Suwarrow (Suvarov) (atoll) .... K 7
Swains (isl.), 74 .... K 7
Sydney, 12,446,345 .... F 9
Sydney (isl.) .... J 6
Tabiteuea (atoll), 4,419 .... H 6
Tahaa (isl.), 3,567 .... L 7
Takaroa (atoll), 161 .... M 7
Tamworth, 21,680 .... F 9
Tanna (isl.), 10,500 .... H 7

Taongi (atoll) .... G 4
Tarawa (atoll), 12,642 .... H 5
Tasman (sea) .... F 9
Tasmania (state), 393,700 .... E10
Taveuni (isl.), 6,351 .... H 7
Tennant Creek, 1,001 .... D 7
Tikopia (isl.), 1,400 .... G 7
Timaru, 27,800 .... H10
Tinian (isl.), 696 .... E 4
Tobi (isl.), 80 .... D 5
Tokelau (isls.), 2,000 .... J 6
Tonga, 83,000 .... J 7
Tongareva (atoll), 545 .... L 6
Tongatapu (isl.), 47,606 .... J 8
Toowoomba, 55,799 .... F 8
Torres (isls.) .... G 7
Townsville, 58,847 .... F 8
Trobriand (isls.), 10,199 .... F 6
Truk (isl.), 18,792 .... F 5
Tuamotu (archipelago), 6,148 .... M 7
Tubuai (isl.), 1,398 .... M 8
Tubuai (Austral) (isls.), 5,053 .... L 8
Tureia (atoll), 40 .... N 8
Tutuila (isl.), 24,973 .... J 7
Uahuka (isl.), 359 .... N 6
Uapou (isl.), 1,414 .... M 6
Ujelang (atoll), 281 .... F 5
Ulithi (atoll), 523 .... D 5
Upolu (isl.), 94,691 .... J 7
Uturoa, 2,394 .... L 7
Uvéa (isl.), 2,001 .... J 7
Vahitahi (atoll), 109 .... N 7
Vaitupu (atoll), 876 .... H 6
Vanua Levu (isl.), 71,933 .... H 7
Vava'u Group (isls.), 13,533 .... J 7
Victoria (state), 3,461,400 .... D 9
Vila, 7,000 .... G 7
Viti Levu (isl.), 341,784 .... H 7

Wagga Wagga, 25,819 .... E 9
Wake (isl.), 1,647 .... G 4
Wallis (isls.), 6,000 .... J 7
Wallis and Futuna, 8,546 .... J 7
Wanganui, 36,400 .... H 9
Warrnambool, 17,499 .... D 9
Washington (isl.), 437 .... L 5
Wau, 1,072 .... E 6
Wellington, 134,400 .... H 9
Western Australia (state), 991,300 .... C 8
Western Samoa, 139,810 .... J 7
Wewak, 5,090 .... E 6
Whangarei, 29,600 .... H 9

Whyalla, 22,121 .... D 9
Willis (islets), 3 .... F 7
Wiluna, ‡219 .... C 8
Woleai (atoll), 586 .... E 5
Wollongong, †162,153 .... F 9
Wonthaggi, 4,026 .... E 9
Woomera, 4,745 .... D 9
Wotje (atoll), 376 .... H 5
Wyndham, 1,156 .... C 7
Yap (isl.), 4,380 .... D 5

*City and suburbs.
†Population of metropolitan area.
‡Population of sub-district.

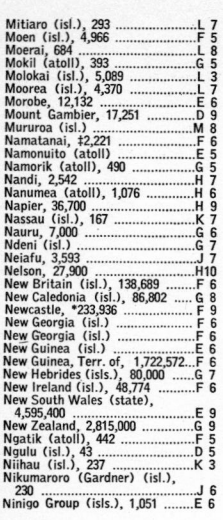

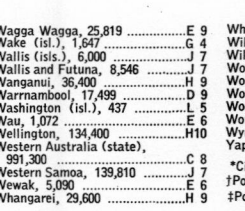

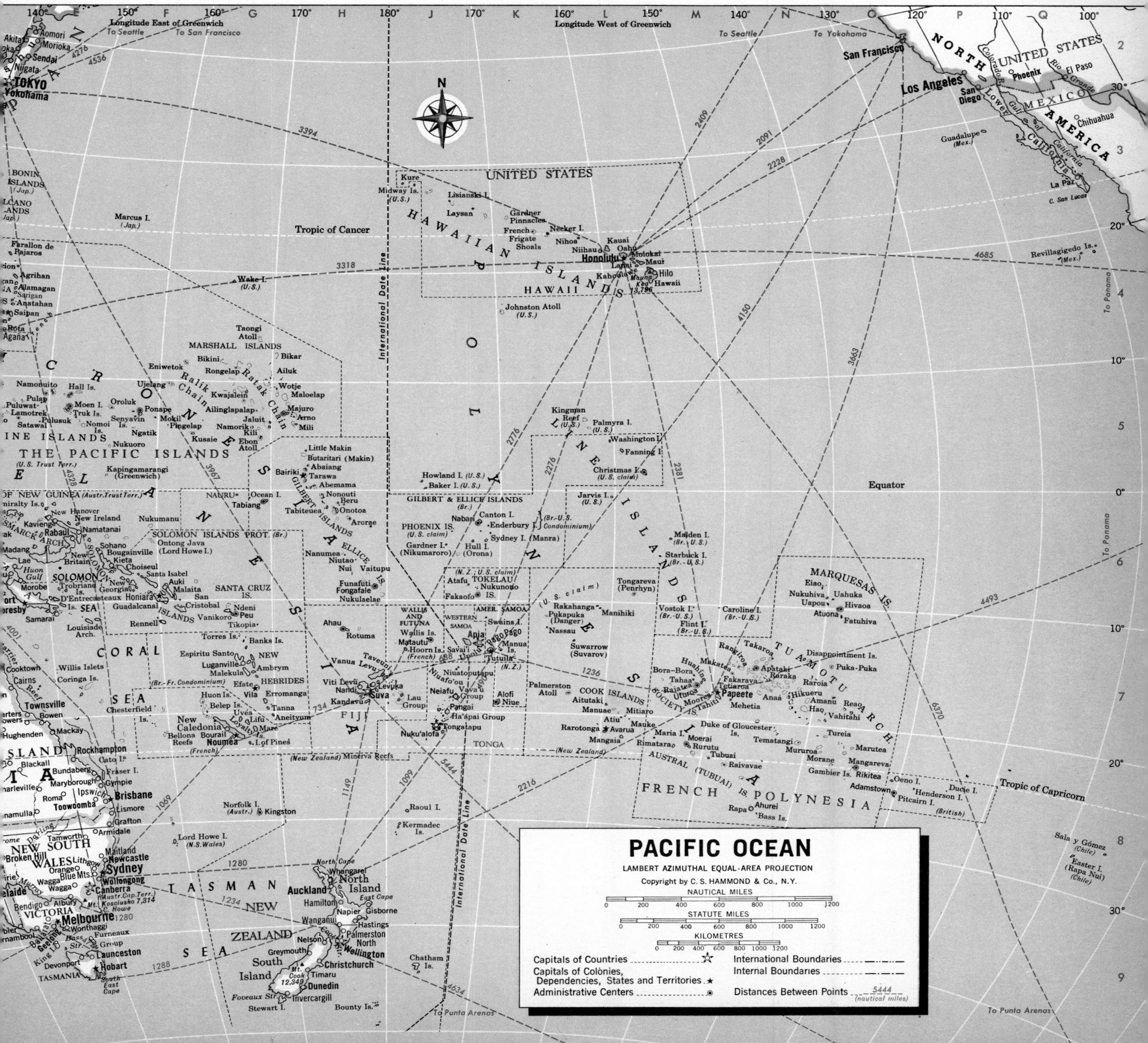

PACIFIC OCEAN
LAMBERT AZIMUTHAL EQUAL-AREA PROJECTION
Copyright by C. S. HAMMOND & Co., N.Y.

NAUTICAL MILES
STATUTE MILES
KILOMETRES

Capitals of Countries .... ★
Capitals of Colonies, Dependencies, States and Territories .★
Administrative Centers ....
International Boundaries ....
Internal Boundaries ....
Distances Between Points 5444 (nautical miles)

AUSTRALIA

BONNE PROJECTION

SCALE OF MILES

SCALE OF KILOMETRES

Capital of Country ___ ☆ State and Territorial Capitals ___ ▲

AUSTRALIAN CAPITAL TERRITORY

CITIES and TOWNS

Canberra (capital), 92,308 .....H 7
Canberra, *136,300 ....H 7

CORAL SEA ISLANDS TERRITORY

Total Population, 3

Bougainville (reef) ....H 3
Cato (isl.) ....K 4
Coral (sea) ....H 3
Coringa (islets) ....H 3
Great Barrier (reef) ....H 3
Holmes (reef) ....H 3
Lihou (reef and cays) ....H 3
Magdelaine (cays) ....H 3
Saumarez (reef) ....H 3
Willis (islets), 3 ....H 3

NEW SOUTH WALES

CITIES and TOWNS

Albury, 25,112 ....H 7
Armidale, 14,984 ....J 6
Auburn, 48,691 ....L 3
Bankstown, 159,981 ....L 3
Bathurst, 17,222 ....H 6
Blacktown, 111,488 ....K 3
Blue Mountains, 30,731 ....H 6
Botany, 31,871 ....L 4
Campbelltown, 25,695 ....L 3
Cessnock, 15,331 ....J 6
Cessnock, *34,515 ....J 6
Dubbo, 15,561 ....H 6

Goulburn, 20,871 ....J 7
Grafton, 15,951 ....J 5
Hurstville, 64,851 ....L 3
Kogarah, 47,654 ....L 3
Lismore, 19,734 ....J 5
Lithgow, 13,165 ....J 6
Liverpool, 68,959 ....L 3
Maitland, 28,428 ....J 6
Manly, 38,141 ....L 3
Newcastle, *233,936 ....J 6
Orange, 22,196 ....H 6
Parramatta, 106,996 ....K 3
Penrith, 46,357 ....L 3
Randwick, 113,634 ....L 3
Rockdale, 81,463 ....L 3
Ryde, 81,291 ....L 3
Strathfield, 26,704 ....L 3
Sutherland, 131,739 ....L 4
Sydney (capital), †2,446,345 ....L 3
Tamworth, 21,680 ....J 6
Taree, 10,560 ....J 6
Wagga Wagga, 25,819 ....H 7
Waverley, 63,607 ....L 3
Willoughby, 54,576 ....L 3
Wollongong, *149,506 ....K 4

OTHER FEATURES

Australian Alps (mts.) ....H 7
Botany (bay) ....L 3
Byron (cape) ....J 5
Darling (river) ....G 6
Great Dividing (range) ....H 7
Kosciusko (mt.) ....H 7
Lord Howe (isl.), 267 ....N 6
Murray (river) ....G 6
Murrumbidgee (river) ....H 6

NORFOLK ISLANDS

Total Population, 1,147

CITIES and TOWNS

Cascade ....L 5
Kingston ....L 5

OTHER FEATURES

Anson (bay) ....M 5
Ball (bay) ....M 5
Cable Station ....L 5
Pitt (mt.) ....L 5

QUEENSLAND

CITIES and TOWNS

Ayr, 8,674 ....H 3
Brisbane (capital), 656,222 .....K 2
Brisbane, †718,822 ....K 2
Bundaberg, 25,402 ....J 4
Cairns, 29,326 ....H 3
Charters Towers, 7,602 ....H 4
Corinda, 12,643 ....H 3
Dalby, 8,860 ....J 6
Gladstone, 12,426 ....J 4
Gold Coast, 49,481 ....J 5
Gympie, 11,229 ....J 5
Ingham, 5,354 ....H 3
Innisfail, 7,432 ....H 3
Ipswich, 54,531 ....J 5
Kingaroy, 5,080 ....J 5
Mackay, 24,578 ....H 4
Maryborough, 20,393 ....J 4
Mooroka, 16,801 ....K 2
Mount Isa, 16,877 ....F 4
Redcliffe, 27,327 ....K 1
Rockhampton, 46,083 ....J 4
Sandgate, 22,621 ....K 2
Thursday Island, 674 ....G 1
Toowoomba, 55,799 ....J 5
Townsville, 58,847 ....H 3
Warwick, 10,065 ....J 5
Wynnum, 23,191 ....K 2

OTHER FEATURES

Arafura (sea) ....E 1
Arnhem Land (region) ....E 2
Ayers Rock (mt.) ....E 5
Barkly Tableland ....F 3
Bathurst (isl.) ....D 2
Carpentaria (gulf) ....F 2

Cobourg (pen.) ....E 2
Daly (river) ....E 2
Groote Eylandt (isl.) ....F 2
Macdonnell (ranges) ....E 4
Melville (isl.) ....E 2
Simpson (desert) ....F 5
Timor (sea) ....C 2

QUEENSLAND

CITIES and TOWNS

Ayr, 8,674 ....H 3
Brisbane (capital), 656,222 .....K 2
Brisbane, †718,822 ....K 2
Bundaberg, 25,402 ....J 4
Cairns, 29,326 ....H 3
Charters Towers, 7,602 ....H 4
Corinda, 12,643 ....H 3
Dalby, 8,860 ....J 6
Gladstone, 12,426 ....J 4
Gold Coast, 49,481 ....J 5
Gympie, 11,229 ....J 5
Ingham, 5,354 ....H 3
Innisfail, 7,432 ....H 3
Ipswich, 54,531 ....J 5
Kingaroy, 5,080 ....J 5
Mackay, 24,578 ....H 4
Maryborough, 20,393 ....J 4
Mooroka, 16,801 ....K 2
Mount Isa, 16,877 ....F 4
Redcliffe, 27,327 ....K 1
Rockhampton, 46,083 ....J 4
Sandgate, 22,621 ....K 2
Thursday Island, 674 ....G 1
Toowoomba, 55,799 ....J 5
Townsville, 58,847 ....H 3
Warwick, 10,065 ....J 5
Wynnum, 23,191 ....K 2

SOUTH AUSTRALIA

CITIES and TOWNS

Adelaide (capital), †727,916 ....D 7
Elizabeth, 32,949 ....D 7
Hindmarsh, 11,352 ....D 7
Kensington and Norwood, 11,928 ..D 7
Maralinga and Woomera, 4,745 ....E 6
Marion, 50,604 ....D 8
Mitcham, 49,470 ....D 8
Mount Gambier, 17,251 ....F 7
Port Adelaide, 39,823 ....D 7
Port Augusta, 10,103 ....F 6

OTHER FEATURES

Barwon (river) ....H 5
Bulloo (river) ....G 5
Burdekin (river) ....H 3
Cape York (pen.) ....G 2
Carpentaria (gulf) ....F 2
Diamantina (river) ....G 5
Fitzroy (river) ....J 4
Flattery (cape) ....H 2
Flinders (river) ....G 3
Georgina (river) ....F 5
Great Barrier (reef) ....H 3
Great Dividing (range) ....G 3
Great Sandy (Fraser) (isl.) .....J 5
Moreton (isl.) ....L 1
Norman (river) ....G 3
Sturt (desert) ....G 5
Thomson (river) ....G 4
Torres (strait) ....G 2
York (cape) ....G 2

Port Pirie, 15,566 ....F 6
Reynella-Port Noarlunga, 11,818 ..D 7
Salisbury, 35,762 ....D 7
Unley, 38,727 ....D 7
West Torrens, 46,222 ....D 7
Whyalla, 22,121 ....F 6
Woodville, 73,878 ....D 7
Woomera and Maralinga, 4,745 ....E 6

OTHER FEATURES

Eyre (lake) ....F 5
Eyre (peninsula) ....F 6
Flinders (range) ....F 6
Frome (lake) ....F 6
Great Australian (bight) ....D 6
Investigator (strait) ....D 7
Kangaroo (isl.), 3,375 ....F 7
Murray (river) ....E 5
Musgrave (range) ....D 6
Nullarbor (plain) ....C 6
Saint Vincent (gulf) ....D 7
Simpson (desert) ....F 5
Spencer (gulf) ....F 6
Torres (lake) ....E 6
Yorke (peninsula) ....F 7

TASMANIA

CITIES and TOWNS

Burnie, 15,806 ....H 8
Deloraine, 1,793 ....H 8
Devonport, 14,874 ....H 8
Hobart (capital), 53,257 ....H 8
Hobart, †119,469 ....H 8
Launceston, 37,217 ....H 8

New Norfolk, 5,770 ....H 8
Queenstown, 4,295 ....G 8
Saint Mary's ....H 8
Ulverstone, 6,842 ....H 8
Waratah, 698 ....G 8
Wynyard, 3,355 ....G 8
Zeehan, 1,017 ....G 8

OTHER FEATURES

Bass (strait) ....H 7
Furneaux Group (isls.), 1,234 ...H 7
King (isl.), 2,462 ....G 7
Ossa (mt.) ....H 8
Tasman (pen.) ....H 8

VICTORIA

CITIES and TOWNS

Ararat, 8,233 ....G 7
Ballarat, 41,639 ....G 7
Ballarat, *56,290 ....G 7
Bendigo, 30,806 ....G 7
Bendigo, *42,208 ....G 7
Brighton, 40,617 ....M 7
Camberwell, 99,908 ....M 7
Caulfield, 76,119 ....M 7
Chelsea, 24,789 ....M 7
Coburg, 68,568 ....L 6
Dandenong, 31,698 ....M 7
Footscray, 58,823 ....L 7
Frankston, 38,718 ....M 7
Geelong, 18,129 ....G 7
Geelong, *105,059 ....L 7
Hamilton, 10,054 ....F 7
Heidelberg, 63,929 ....M 6
Horsham, 10,562 ....G 7

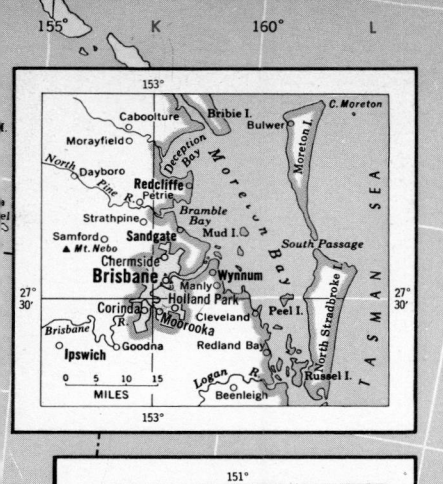

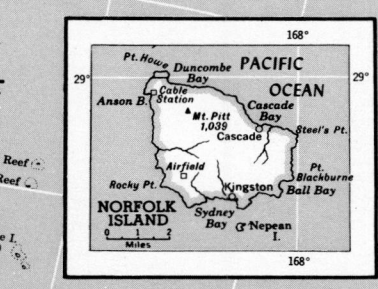

Copyright by C. S. HAMMOND & Co., N. Y.

AREA 2,967,741 sq. mi.
POPULATION 12,630,000
CAPITAL Canberra
LARGEST CITY Sydney (greater)
HIGHEST POINT Mt. Kosciusko 7,316 ft.
LOWEST POINT Lake Eyre -39 ft.
MONETARY UNIT Australian dollar
MAJOR LANGUAGE English
MAJOR RELIGIONS Protestantism, Roman Catholicism

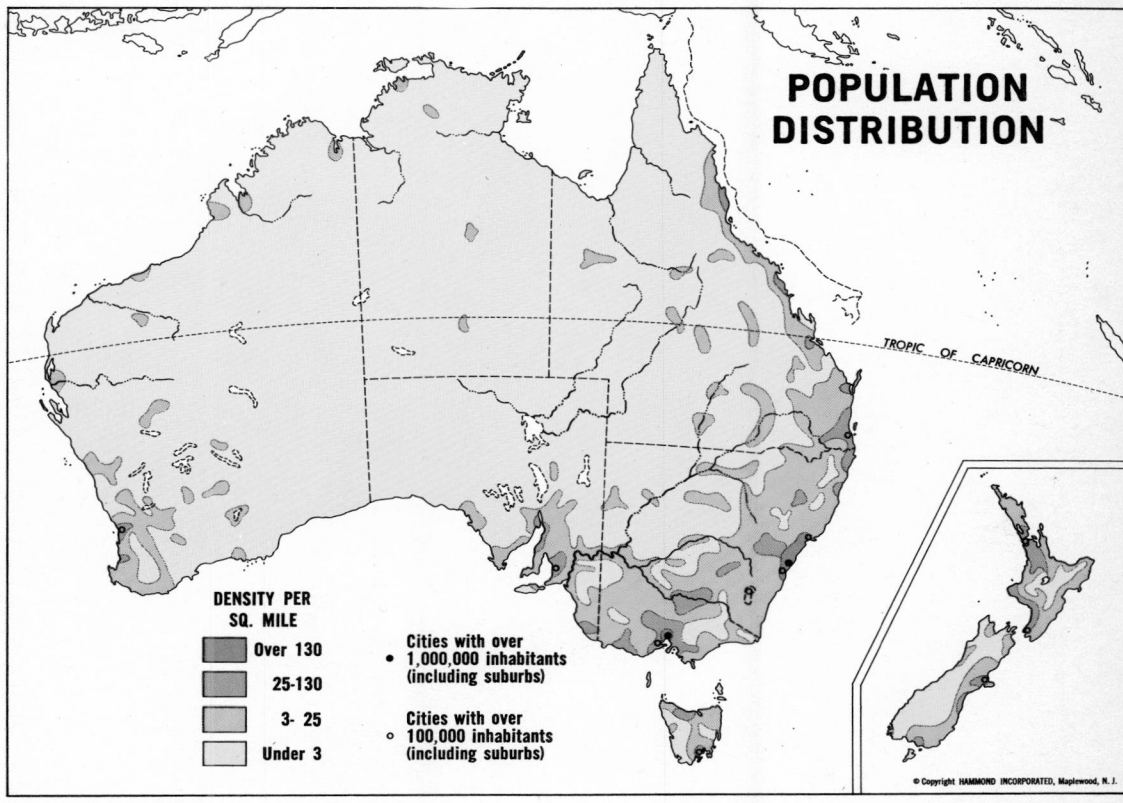

POPULATION DISTRIBUTION

DENSITY PER SQ. MILE

- Over 130
- 25-130
- 3- 25
- Under 3

● Cities with over 1,000,000 inhabitants (including suburbs)

○ Cities with over 100,000 inhabitants (including suburbs)

© Copyright HAMMOND INCORPORATED, Maplewood, N. J.

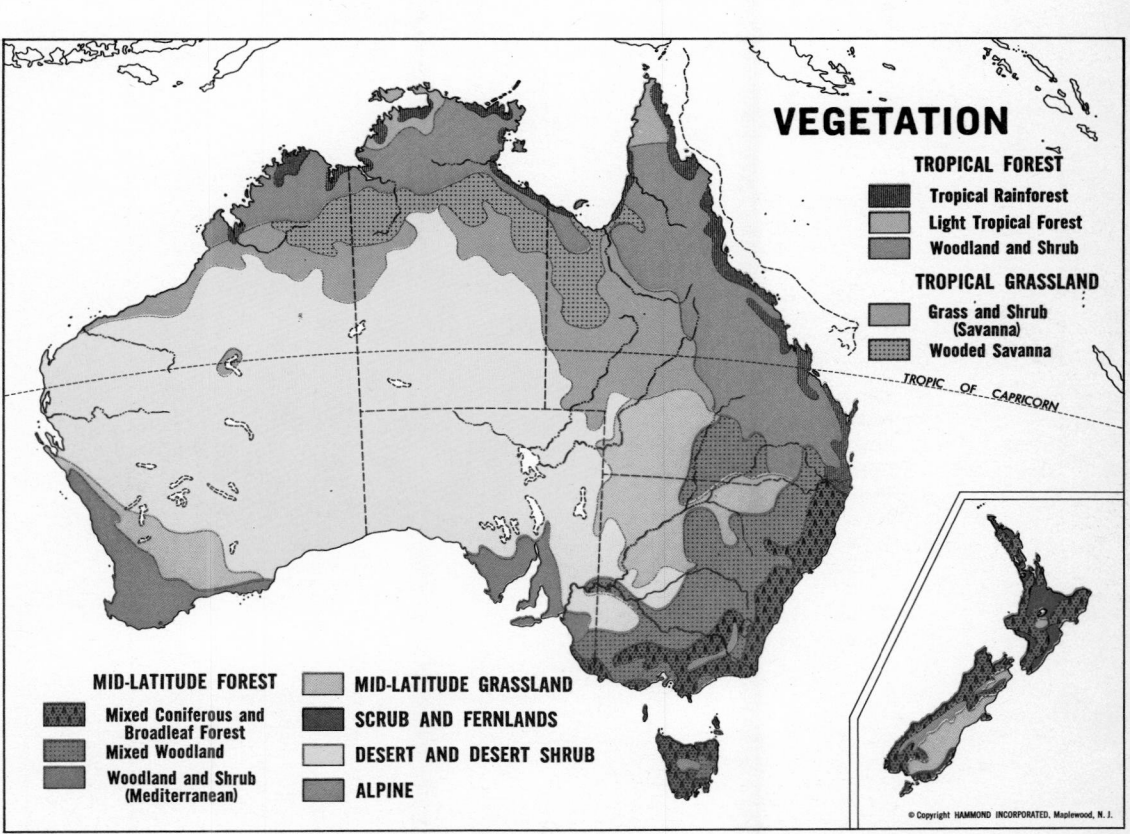

VEGETATION

TROPICAL FOREST
- Tropical Rainforest
- Light Tropical Forest
- Woodland and Shrub

TROPICAL GRASSLAND
- Grass and Shrub (Savanna)
- Wooded Savanna

MID-LATITUDE FOREST
- Mixed Coniferous and Broadleaf Forest
- Mixed Woodland
- Woodland and Shrub (Mediterranean)

MID-LATITUDE GRASSLAND

SCRUB AND FERNLANDS

DESERT AND DESERT SHRUB

ALPINE

© Copyright HAMMOND INCORPORATED, Maplewood, N. J.

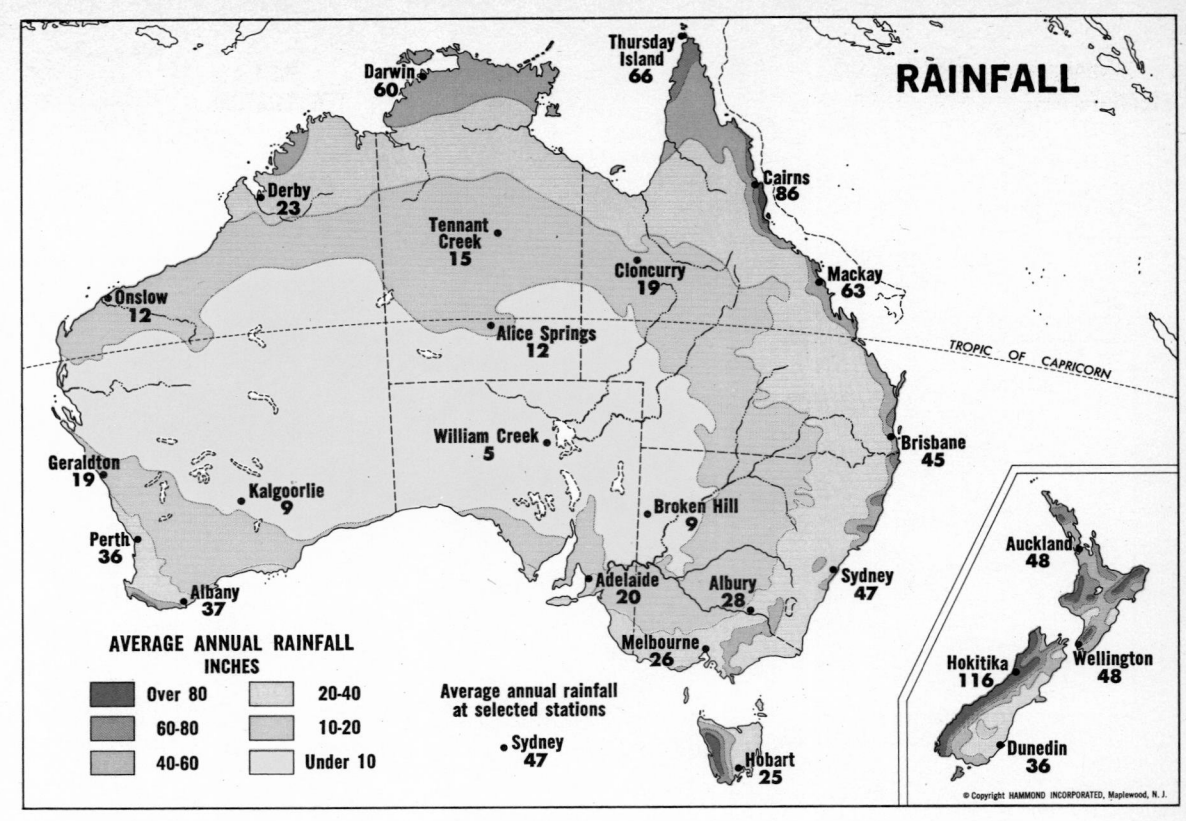

RAINFALL
Darwin 60
Thursday Island 66
Derby 23
Cairns 86
Tennant Creek 15
Cloncurry 19
Onslow 12
Mackay 63
Alice Springs 12
TROPIC OF CAPRICORN
William Creek 5
Brisbane 45
Geraldton 19
Kalgoorlie 9
Broken Hill 9
Perth 36
Auckland 48
Adelaide 20
Albury 28
Sydney 47
Albany 37
Melbourne 26
Hokitika 116
Wellington 48
Dunedin 36
Hobart 25
AVERAGE ANNUAL RAINFALL INCHES
Over 80
60-80
40-60
20-40
10-20
Under 10
Average annual rainfall at selected stations
Sydney 47
© Copyright HAMMOND INCORPORATED, Maplewood, N. J.

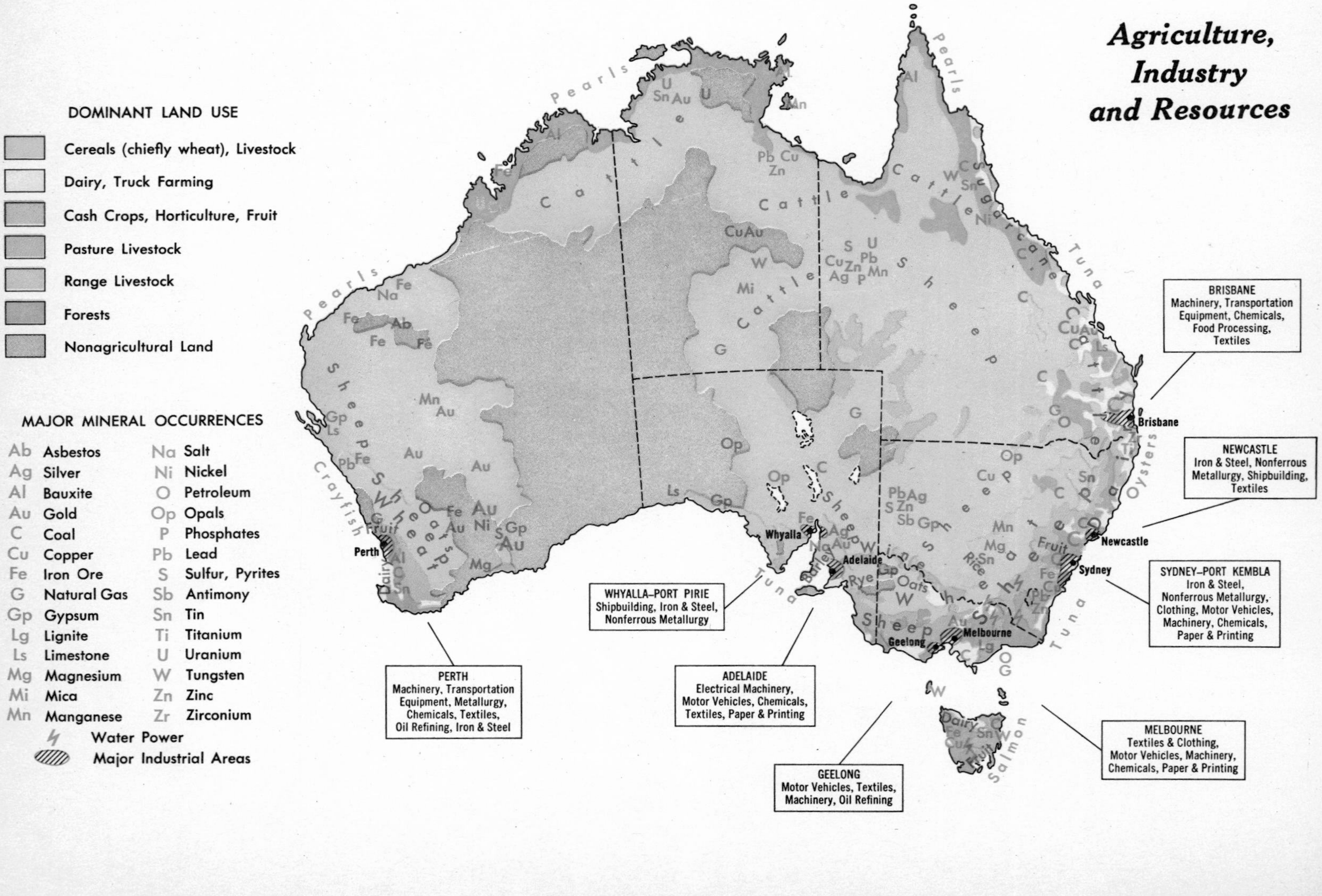

Agriculture, Industry and Resources
DOMINANT LAND USE
Cereals (chiefly wheat), Livestock
Dairy, Truck Farming
Cash Crops, Horticulture, Fruit
Pasture Livestock
Range Livestock
Forests
Nonagricultural Land
MAJOR MINERAL OCCURRENCES
Ab Asbestos
Ag Silver
Al Bauxite
Au Gold
C Coal
Cu Copper
Fe Iron Ore
G Natural Gas
Gp Gypsum
Lg Lignite
Ls Limestone
Mg Magnesium
Mi Mica
Mn Manganese
Na Salt
Ni Nickel
O Petroleum
Op Opals
P Phosphates
Pb Lead
S Sulfur, Pyrites
Sb Antimony
Sn Tin
Ti Titanium
U Uranium
W Tungsten
Zn Zinc
Zr Zirconium
Water Power
Major Industrial Areas
Pearls
Cattle
Sheep
Wheat
Oats
Crayfish
Sugarcane
Tuna
Oysters
Salmon
Fruit
Dairy
Rice
BRISBANE
Machinery, Transportation Equipment, Chemicals, Food Processing, Textiles
NEWCASTLE
Iron & Steel, Nonferrous Metallurgy, Shipbuilding, Textiles
SYDNEY–PORT KEMBLA
Iron & Steel, Nonferrous Metallurgy, Clothing, Motor Vehicles, Machinery, Chemicals, Paper & Printing
MELBOURNE
Textiles & Clothing, Motor Vehicles, Machinery, Chemicals, Paper & Printing
GEELONG
Motor Vehicles, Textiles, Machinery, Oil Refining
ADELAIDE
Electrical Machinery, Motor Vehicles, Chemicals, Textiles, Paper & Printing
WHYALLA–PORT PIRIE
Shipbuilding, Iron & Steel, Nonferrous Metallurgy
PERTH
Machinery, Transportation Equipment, Metallurgy, Chemicals, Textiles, Oil Refining, Iron & Steel
Brisbane
Newcastle
Sydney
Melbourne
Geelong
Adelaide
Whyalla
Perth

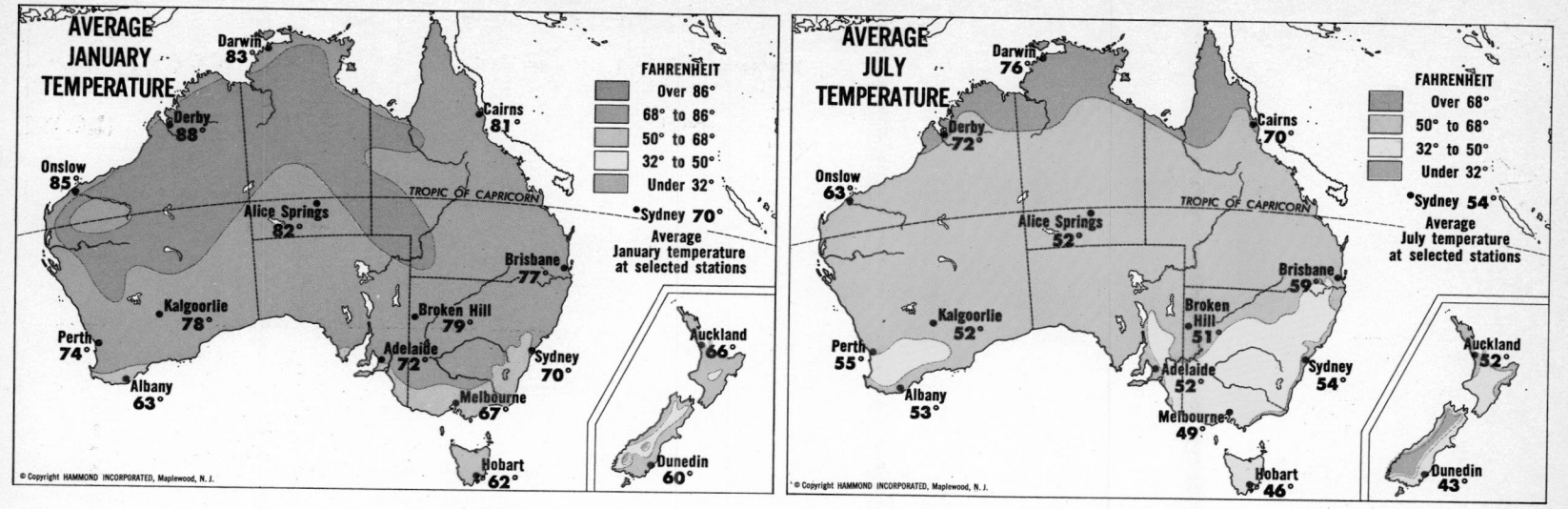

AVERAGE JANUARY TEMPERATURE

FAHRENHEIT
- Over 86°
- 68° to 86°
- 50° to 68°
- 32° to 50°
- Under 32°

•Sydney 70°
Average January temperature at selected stations

Darwin 83°
Derby 88°
Onslow 85°
Cairns 81°
TROPIC OF CAPRICORN
Alice Springs 82°
Brisbane 77°
Kalgoorlie 78°
Broken Hill 79°
Perth 74°
Adelaide 72°
Sydney 70°
Albany 63°
Melbourne 67°
Hobart 62°

Auckland 66°
Dunedin 60°

© Copyright HAMMOND INCORPORATED, Maplewood, N.J.

AVERAGE JULY TEMPERATURE

FAHRENHEIT
- Over 68°
- 50° to 68°
- 32° to 50°
- Under 32°

•Sydney 54°
Average July temperature at selected stations

Darwin 76°
Derby 72°
Onslow 63°
Cairns 70°
TROPIC OF CAPRICORN
Alice Springs 52°
Brisbane 59°
Kalgoorlie 52°
Broken Hill 51°
Perth 55°
Adelaide 52°
Sydney 54°
Albany 53°
Melbourne 49°
Hobart 46°

Auckland 52°
Dunedin 43°

© Copyright HAMMOND INCORPORATED, Maplewood, N.J.

Topography

0   150   300
MILES

INDIAN OCEAN

Timor Sea

Melville
Cobourg Pen.
C. Wessel
Torres Str.
C. York

Arnhem Land
Gulf of Carpentaria

Cape York Pen.

CORAL SEA

Daly
Victoria
Groote Eylandt

KIMBERLEY PLATEAU
Fitzroy
BARKLY TABLELAND
Mt. Bartle Frere 5,287
GREAT DIVIDING RANGE
Great Barrier Reef

Tanami Desert
Flinders
Mitchell

Great Sandy Desert
L. Mackay
Capricorn Channel

HAMERSLEY RA.
Mt. Bruce 4,024
Gibson Desert
L. Disappointment
Mt. Ziel 4,955
MACDONNELL RANGES
Georgina

North West C.

Murchison
L. Carnegie
MUSGRAVE RANGES
Mt. Woodroffe 4,970
Simpson Desert
Diamantina
Barcoo

Great Victoria Desert
L. Barlee
Lake Eyre
Sturt Desert
Barcoo
Darling

NULLARBOR PLAIN
L. Torrens
L. Frome
FLINDERS RA.
St. Mary Pk. 3,900
Lachlan
BLUE MTS.

DARLING RA.
GAWLER RA.
Eyre Pen.
Murray
GREAT DIVIDING RANGE

C. Leeuwin
Great Australian Bight
Spencer Gulf
Kangaroo I.
Mt. Kosciusko 7,316
AUSTRALIAN ALPS
C. Howe

INDIAN OCEAN

TASMAN SEA

King I.
Bass Strait
FURNEAUX GROUP

Mt. Ossa 5,305
Tasmania
South C.

Below Sea Level | 100 m. 328 ft. | 200 m. 656 ft. | 500 m. 1,640 ft. | 1,000 m. 3,281 ft. | 2,000 m. 6,562 ft. | 5,000 m. 16,404 ft.

AREA 975,920 sq. mi.
POPULATION 991,300
CAPITAL Perth
LARGEST CITY Perth
HIGHEST POINT Mt. Bruce 4,024 ft.

Topography

0 200 400
MILES

KIMBERLEY PLATEAU

Great Sandy Desert

L. Mackay

L. Disappointment

Gibson Desert

L. McLeod

L. Carnegie

L. Wells

Great Victoria Desert

L. Moore

NULLARBOR PLAIN

C. Leeuwin

Below Sea Level | 100 m. 328 ft. | 200 m. 656 ft. | 500 m. 1,640 ft. | 1,000 m. 3,281 ft. | 2,000 m. 6,562 ft. | 5,000 m. 16,404 ft.

CITIES and TOWNS

Albany, 11,419 ....B 6
Armadale, 3,463 ....A 1
Augusta, ⊙3,238 ....A 6
Beverley, ⊙1,773 ....B 1
Boddington, ⊙761 ....B 2
Boulder, 5,234 ....C 5
Bridgetown, 1,569 ....B 6
Brookton, ⊙1,341 ....B 2
Broome, 1,570 ....C 2
Bruce Rock, ⊙2,142 ....B 5
Bunbury, 15,459 ....A 2
Busselton, 4,278 ....A 6
Capel, ⊙2,132 ....A 2
Carnamah, ⊙996 ....A 5
Carnarvon, 2,956 ....A 4
Collie, 7,628 ....A 2
Coolgardie, ⊙762 ....C 5
Coorow, ⊙808 ....B 5

Corrigin, ⊙2,099 ....B 6
Cranbrook, ⊙1,419 ....B 6
Cuballing, ⊙732 ....B 2
Cue, ⊙430 ....B 4
Cunderdin, ⊙2,114 ....B 5
Dalwallinu, ⊙2,425 ....B 5
Dampier, 1,080 ....B 3
Dandaragan ⊙619 ....A 5
Denmark, ⊙1,775 ....B 6
Derby, 1,424 ....C 2
Donnybrook, 981 ....A 2
Esperance, 2,677 ....C 6
Exmouth Gulf, ⊙2,248 ....A 3
Fremantle, 25,284 ....A 1
Geraldton, 12,125 ....A 5
Gingin, ⊙1,021 ....A 1
Gnowangerup, 981 ....B 6
Goomalling, ⊙1,567 ....B 1
Gosnells, 7,135 ....A 1
Halls Creek, ⊙577 ....D 2
Harvey, 2,066 ....A 2
Jarrahdale, ⊙1,728 ....B 2

Kalamunda-Gooseberry Hill, 3,068 ....B 1
Kalgoorlie, 9,174 ....C 5
Kalgoorlie, ▫19,908 ....C 5
Katanning, 3,506 ....B 6
Kellerberrin, 1,343 ....B 5
Kojonup, ⊙2,711 ....B 6
Kwinana, 1,272 ....A 1
Lake Grace, ⊙1,986 ....B 6
Learmonth ....A 3
Leonora, ⊙623 ....C 5
Mandurah, 2,730 ....A 2
Manjimup, 3,186 ....B 6
Marble Bar, ⊙567 ....C 3
Meekatharra, ⊙1,011 ....B 4
Menzies, ⊙404 ....C 5
Merredin, 3,599 ....B 5
Midland, 9,335 ....A 1
Mingenew, ⊙978 ....A 5
Moora, 1,185 ....B 5
Morawa, ⊙1,718 ....A 5
Mount Barker, 1,594 ....B 6

Mount Magnet, ⊙1,016 ....B 5
Mukinbudin, ⊙869 ....B 5
Mullewa, ⊙1,825 ....A 5
Nannup, ⊙1,272 ....B 6
Narrogin, 4,861 ....B 2
Nedlands, 23,320 ....A 1
Norseman, 1,863 ....C 6
Northam, 7,400 ....B 1
Northampton, ⊙2,021 ....A 5
Nullagine, ⊙211 ....C 3
Nungarin, ⊙539 ....B 5
Onslow, ...A 3
Pardoo, ...B 3
Pemberton, 930 ....A 6
Perenjori, ⊙1,311 ....B 5
Perth (cap.), ‡499,969 ....A 1
Pingelly, ⊙1,453 ....B 2
Port Hedland, 1,778 ....B 3
Quairading, ⊙1,687 ....B 1
Ravensthorpe, ⊙782 ....B 6
Rockingham, 3,767 ....A 1
Roebourne, ⊙702 ....B 3
South Perth, 32,042 ....A 1
Subiaco, 16,621 ....A 1
Tableland, ⊙1,815 ....D 2
Three Springs, ⊙1,038 ....A 5
Toodyay, ⊙1,388 ....B 1
Wagin, 1,750 ....B 2
Wandering, ⊙611 ....B 2
Wanneroo, 612 ....A 1
Waroona, 1,013 ....A 2
Wickepin, ⊙1,380 ....B 2
Williams, ⊙1,193 ....B 2
Wiluna, ⊙219 ....C 4
Wundowie, 1,040 ....B 1
Wyalkatchem, ⊙1,252 ....B 5
Wyndham, 1,156 ....E 1
Yalgoo, ⊙392 ....A 5
Yampi Sound, ...C 2
York, 1,421 ....B 1

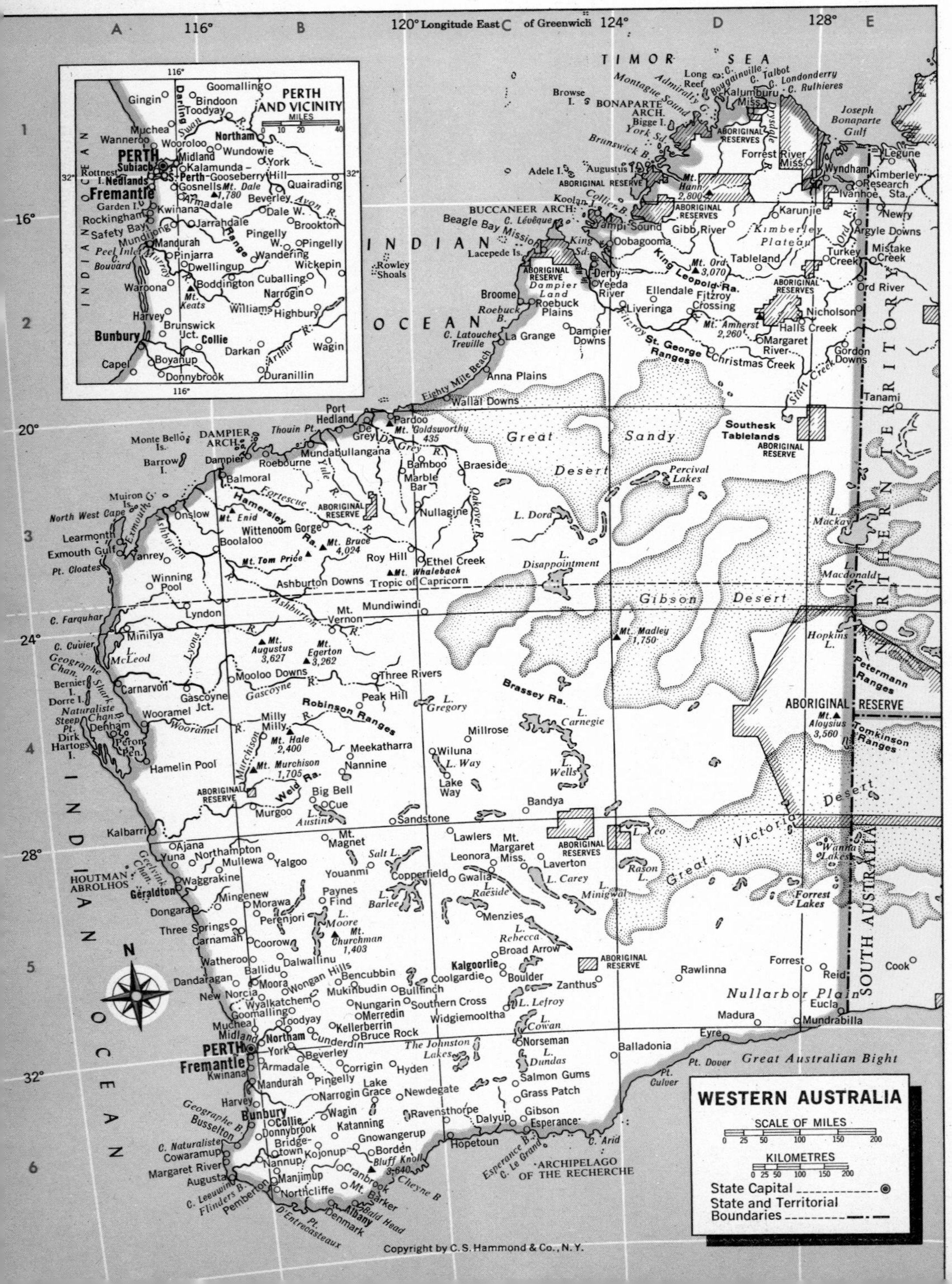

OTHER FEATURES

Adele (isl.) ....C 1
Admiralty (gulf) ....D 1
Aloysius (mt.) ....E 4
Amherst (mt.) ....D 2
Arid (cape) ....C 6
Arthur (riv.) ....A 3
Ashburton (riv.) ....B 3
Augustus (isl.) ....D 1
Augustus (mt.) ....B 4
Austin (lake) ....B 4
Avon (riv.) ....A 1
Bald (head) ....B 6
Barlee (lake) ....B 5
Barrow (isl.) ....A 3
Bernier (isl.) ....A 4
Bigge (isl.) ....D 1
Bluff Knoll (mt.) ....B 6
Bonaparte (arch.) ....D 1
Bougainville (cape) ....D 1
Bouvard (cape) ....A 2
Brassey (range) ....C 4
Browse (isl.) ....C 1
Bruce (mt.) ....B 3
Brunswick (bay) ....C 2
Buccaneer (arch.) ....C 2
Carey (lake) ....C 5
Carnegie (lake) ....C 4
Cheyne (bay) ....B 6
Churchman (mt.) ....B 5
Cloates (pt.) ....A 3
Collier (bay) ....C 1
Cowan (lake) ....C 5
Culver (pt.) ....D 6
Cuvier (cape) ....A 4
Dale (mt.) ....B 1
Dampier (arch.) ....B 3
Dampier Land (reg.) ....C 2
Darling (range) ....A 1
De Grey (riv.) ....B 3
D'Entrecasteaux (pt.) ....B 6
Dirk Hartogs (isl.) ....A 4
Disappointment (lake) ....C 3
Dora (lake) ....C 3
Dorre (isl.) ....A 4
Dover (pt.) ....D 6
Drysdale (riv.) ....D 1
Dundas (lake) ....C 6
Egerton (mt.) ....B 4
Eighty Mile (beach) ....C 2
Enid (mt.) ....B 3
Esperance (bay) ....C 6
Exmouth (gulf) ....A 3
Farquhar (cape) ....A 4
Fitzroy (riv.) ....D 2
Flinders (bay) ....A 6
Fortescue (riv.) ....B 3
Garden (isl.) ....A 1
Gascoyne (riv.) ....B 4
Geelvink (chan.) ....A 5
Geographe (bay) ....A 6
Geographe (chan.) ....A 4
Gibson (des.) ....D 3
Goldsworthy (mt.) ....C 3
Great Australian (bight) ....E 6
Great Sandy (des.) ....C 3
Great Victoria (des.) ....D 5
Gregory (lake) ....C 4
Hale (mt.) ....B 4
Hamersley (range) ....B 3
Hann (mt.) ....D 1
Hopkins (lake) ....E 4
Houtman Abrolhos (isls.) ....A 5

Indian Ocean ....A 5
Johnston, The (lakes) ....C 6
Joseph Bonaparte (gulf) ....E 1
Keats (mt.) ....A 2
Kimberley (plat.) ....D 1
King (sound) ....C 2
King Leopold (range) ....D 2
Koolan (isl.) ....C 1
Lacepede (isls.) ....C 2
Latouche Treville (cape) ....C 2
Leeuwin (cape) ....A 6
Lefroy (lake) ....C 5
Le Grand (cape) ....C 6
Lévêque (cape) ....C 2
Londonderry (cape) ....D 1
Long (reef) ....D 1
Lyons (riv.) ....A 4
Macdonald (lake) ....E 3
Mackay (lake) ....E 3
Madley (mt.) ....D 4
McLeod (lake) ....A 4
Minigwal (lake) ....C 5
Montague (sound) ....D 1
Monte Bello (isls.) ....A 3
Moore (lake) ....B 5
Muiron (isls.) ....A 3
Murchison (mt.) ....B 4
Murchison (riv.) ....B 4
Murray (riv.) ....A 2
Naturaliste (cape) ....A 6
Naturaliste (chan.) ....A 4
North West (cape) ....A 3
Nullarbor (plain) ....D 5
Oakover (riv.) ....C 3
Ord (mt.) ....D 2
Ord (riv.) ....E 2
Peel (inlet) ....A 2
Percival (lakes) ....D 3
Peron (pen.) ....A 4
Petermann (ranges) ....E 4
Raeside (lake) ....C 5
Rason (lake) ....D 5
Rebecca (lake) ....C 5
Recherche (arch.) ....C 6
Robinson (ranges) ....B 4
Roebuck (bay) ....C 2
Rottnest (isl.) ....A 1
Rowley (shoals) ....B 2
Rulhieres (cape) ....D 1
Saint George (ranges) ....D 2
Salt (lake) ....B 5
Shark (bay) ....A 4
Southesk Tablelands ....D 3
Steep (pt.) ....A 4
Sturt (creek) ....D 2
Swan (riv.) ....A 1
Talbot (cape) ....D 1
Thouin (pt.) ....B 3
Timor (sea) ....D 1
Tomkinson (ranges) ....E 4
Tom Price (mt.) ....B 3
Wanna (lakes) ....E 5
Way (lake) ....C 4
Weld (range) ....B 4
Wells (lake) ....C 4
Whaleback (mt.) ....B 3
Wooramel (riv.) ....A 4
Yeo (lake) ....D 5
York (sound) ....C 1
Yule (riv.) ....B 3

⊙ Population of district.
‡ Population of met. area.
▫ Population of urban area.

WESTERN AUSTRALIA

SCALE OF MILES

KILOMETRES

State Capital ⊚
State and Territorial Boundaries

PERTH AND VICINITY

MILES

PERTH

Fremantle

AREA 520,280 sq. mi.
POPULATION 73,000
CAPITAL Darwin
LARGEST CITY Darwin
HIGHEST POINT Mt. Ziel 4,955 ft.

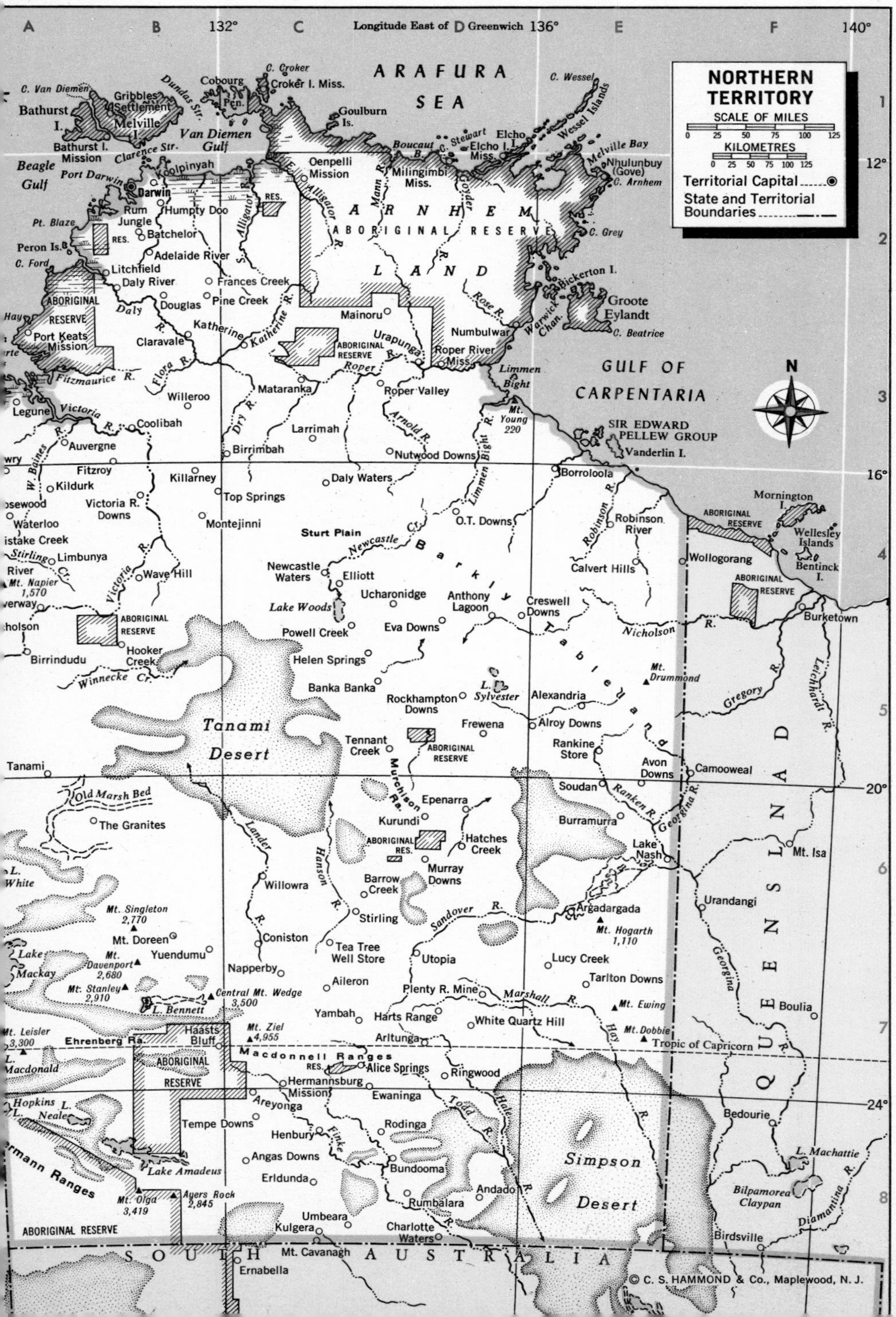

CITIES and TOWNS

Adelaide River, ⊙300	B 2
Aileron,	C 7
Alexandria,	E 5
Alice Springs, 6,037	D 7
Alroy Downs,	E 5
Andado,	D 8
Angas Downs,	C 8
Anthony Lagoon, ⊙162	D 4
Areyonga,	C 7
Argadargada,	E 6
Aritunga,	D 7
Auvergne,	B 3
Avon Downs, ⊙231	E 5
Banka Banka,	C 5
Barrow Creek,	D 6
Batchelor, ⊙551	B 2
Bathurst Island Mission,	B 1
Birdum,	C 3
Birrimbah,	C 3
Birrindudu,	A 5
Bundooma,	D 8
Burramurra,	E 6
Calvert Hills,	E 4
Charlotte Waters,	D 8
Claravale,	B 3
Coniston,	C 7
Coolibah,	B 3
Creswell Downs,	E 4
Daly River, ⊙237	B 2
Daly Waters, ⊙265	C 3
Darwin (cap.), 18,042	B 2
Douglas,	B 2
Elliott, ⊙234	C 4
Epenarra,	D 6
Erldunda,	C 8
Eva Downs,	D 5
Ewaninga,	D 8
Fitzroy,	B 4
Frewena,	D 5
Harts Range, ⊙95	D 7
Hatches Creek, ⊙74	D 6
Helen Springs,	C 5
Henbury,	C 8
Humpty Doo,	B 2
Inverway,	A 4
Katherine, 1,302	B 3
Kildurk,	A 4
Killarney,	B 4
Koolpinyah,	B 2
Kulgera, ⊙229	C 8
Kurundi,	D 6
Lake Nash, ⊙113	E 6
Larrimah, ⊙88	C 3
Legune,	A 3
Limbunya,	B 4
Litchfield,	B 2
Lucy Creek,	E 7
Mainoru,	C 3
Mataranka, ⊙114	C 3
Mistake Creek,	A 4
Montejinni,	C 4
Mount Cavanagh,	C 8
Mount Doreen,	B 7
Murray Downs,	D 6
Napperby,	C 7
Newcastle Waters,	C 4
Newry,	A 3
Nutwood Downs,	D 3
O.T. Downs,	D 4
Pine Creek, ⊙577	C 2
Plenty River Mine,	D 7
Powell Creek,	C 5
Rankine Store,	E 5
Ringwood,	D 7
Robinson River,	E 4
Rockhampton Downs,	D 5
Rodinga,	D 8
Roper River Mission, ⊙357	D 3
Roper Valley,	D 3
Rosewood,	A 4
Rum Jungle,	B 2
Soudan,	E 6
Stirling,	C 6
Tanami,	A 5
Tarlton Downs,	E 7
Tea Tree Well Store,	C 7
Tempe Downs,	C 8
Tennant Creek, 1,001	C 5
The Granites,	C 6
Top Springs,	C 4
Ucharonidge,	D 4
Umbeara,	C 8
Urapunga,	D 3
Utopia,	D 7
Victoria River Downs,	B 4
Waterloo,	A 4
Wave Hill, ⊙289	B 4
White Quartz Hill,	D 7
Willeroo,	B 3
Willowra,	C 6
Wollogorang, ⊙87	F 4
Yambah,	C 7

OTHER FEATURES

Amadeus (lake)	B 8
Arafura (sea)	D 1
Arnhem (cape)	E 2
Arnhem Land (reg.)	D 2
Arnold (riv.)	D 3
Barkly Tableland	D 4
Bathurst (isl.)	A 1
Beagle (gulf)	A 2
Beatrice (cape)	E 3
Bennett (lake)	B 7
Bickerton (isl.)	E 2
Blaze (pt.)	A 1
Boucaut (bay)	D 1
Carpentaria (gulf)	E 3
Central Wedge (mt.)	C 7
Clarence (str.)	B 1
Cobourg (pen.)	C 1
Conner (mt.)	B 8
Croker (cape)	C 1
Daly (riv.)	B 2
Davenport (mt.)	B 7
Dobbie (mt.)	E 7
Drummond (mt.)	D 5
Dry (riv.)	C 3
Dundas (str.)	B 1
East Alligator (riv.)	C 2
Ehrenberg (range)	B 7
Elcho (isl.)	D 1
Ewing (mt.)	E 7
Finke (riv.)	C 8
Fitzmaurice (riv.)	B 3
Flora (riv.)	B 3
Ford (cape)	A 2
Georgina (riv.)	E 6
Goulburn (isls.)	C 1
Goyder (riv.)	D 2
Grey (cape)	E 2
Groote Eylandt (isl.)	E 2
Hale (riv.)	D 8
Hanson (riv.)	C 6
Hay (cape)	A 2
Hay (dry riv.)	E 7
Hogarth (mt.)	E 6
Hopkins (lake)	A 8
Joseph Bonaparte (gulf)	A 3
Katherine (riv.)	C 3
Lander (riv.)	C 6
Leisler (mt.)	A 7
Limmen (bight)	D 3
Limmen Bight (riv.)	D 4
Macdonald (lake)	B 7
Macdonnell (ranges)	C 7
MacKay (lake)	A 7
Mann (riv.)	D 2
Marshall (riv.)	D 7
Melville (bay)	E 2
Melville (isl.)	B 1
Murchison (range)	D 6
Napier (mt.)	A 4
Neale (lake)	A 8
Newcastle (creek)	C 4
Nicholson (riv.)	E 5
Old Marsh Bed	B 6
Olga (mt.)	B 8
Peron (isls.)	A 2
Petermann (ranges)	A 8
Port Darwin (inlet)	B 2
Ranken (riv.)	E 6
Robinson (riv.)	E 4
Roper (riv.)	C 3
Rose (riv.)	D 2
Sandover (riv.)	D 6
Simpson (des.)	E 8
Singleton (mt.)	B 6
Sir Edward Pellew Group (isls.)	E 3
South Alligator (riv.)	C 2
Stanley (mt.)	B 7
Stewart (cape)	D 1
Stirling (creek)	A 4
Sturt (plain)	C 4
Sylvester (lake)	D 5
Tanami (des.)	A 5
Timor (sea)	A 2
Todd (riv.)	D 8
Vanderlin (isl.)	E 3
Van Diemen (cape)	A 1
Van Diemen (gulf)	B 1
Victoria (riv.)	B 3
Warwick (chan.)	E 3
Wessel (cape)	E 1
Wessel (isls.)	E 1
West Baines (riv.)	A 4
White (lake)	A 6
Winnecke (creek)	B 5
Woods (lake)	C 4
Young (mt.)	D 3
Ziel (mt.)	C 7

⊙ Population of district.

NORTHERN TERRITORY

SCALE OF MILES

0 25 50 75 100 125

KILOMETRES

0 25 50 75 100 125

Territorial Capital .... ⊙
State and Territorial Boundaries ....

Longitude East of Greenwich

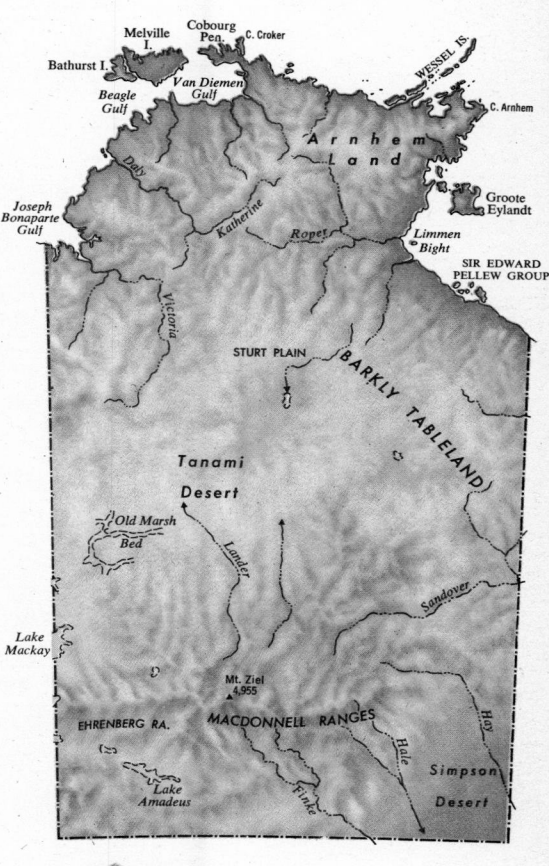

Topography

0 100 200
MILES

| 5,000 m. 16,404 ft. | 2,000 m. 6,562 ft. | 1,000 m. 3,281 ft. | 500 m. 1,640 ft. | 200 m. 656 ft. | 100 m. 328 ft. | Sea Level Below |

AREA 380,070 sq. mi.
POPULATION 1,169,600
CAPITAL Adelaide
LARGEST CITY Adelaide
HIGHEST POINT Mt. Woodroffe 4,970 ft.

CITIES and TOWNS

Adelaide (cap.), ‡727,916 ..B 6
Angaston, 1,887 ....F 6
Balaklava, 1,199 ....F 6
Barmera, 1,484 ....G 7
Beachport, ⊙1,903 ....G 6
Berri, 2,232 ....G 7
Bordertown, 1,758 ....F 6
Brighton, 22,620 ....A 8
Burnside, 38,758 ....B 8
Burra, 1,342 ....F 6
Campbelltown, 32,083 ....B 7
Ceduna, 1,406 ....D 5
Clare, 1,579 ....F 5
Cleve, ⊙2,817 ....E 5
Colonel Light Gardens,
  3,404 ....A 8
Coober Pedy, ...D 3
Crystal Brook, 1,235 ....E 5
Elizabeth, 32,949 ....B 7
Elliston, ⊙1,424 ....D 5
Enfield, 80,261 ....B 7
Gawler, 6,645 ....B 6
Gladstone, 1,035 ....F 5
Glenelg, 14,762 ....A 8
Gumeracha, ⊙2,654 ....C 7
Hindmarsh, 11,352 ....A 7
Hope Valley-Tea Tree
  Gully, ⊙21,314 ....B 7
Jamestown, 1,282 ....F 5
Kadina, 3,022 ....E 6
Kapunda, 1,119 ....F 6
Keith, 1,097 ....G 7
Kensington and Norwood,
  11,928 ....B 8
Kimba, ⊙1,703 ....E 5
Kingscote, 1,071 ....E 6
Kingston, 1,065 ....G 7
Lameroo, ⊙1,947 ....G 6
Leigh Creek, 1,014 ....F 4
Lobethal, 1,098 ....C 7
Loxton, 2,418 ....G 6
Maitland, 1,017 ....E 6
Mannum, 2,034 ....F 6
Maralinga and Woomera,
  4,745 ....B 3
Marion, 66,950 ....A 8
Meadows, ⊙2,824 ....B 8
Meningie, ⊙4,104 ....F 7
Millicent, 4,533 ....F 7
Minlaton, ⊙2,504 ....E 6
Mitcham, 49,470 ....B 8
Moonta, 1,122 ....E 5
Mount Barker, 1,934 ....C 8
Mount Gambier, 17,251 ......G 7
Murray Bridge, 5,957 ....F 6
Nangwarry, 977 ....G 7
Naracoorte, 4,378 ....G 7
Nuriootpa, 2,041 ....F 6
Orroroo, ⊙1,228 ....F 5
Payneham, 16,844 ....B 7
Penola, 1,383 ....G 7
Peterborough, 3,117 ....F 5
Pinnaroo, ⊙1,717 ....G 6
Port Adelaide, 39,823 ......A 7

Port Augusta, 10,103 ....E 5
Port Lincoln, 8,888 ....E 6
Port Pirie, 15,566 ....E 5
Prospect, 21,411 ....B 7
Radium Hill, ...G 5
Renmark, 6,275 ....G 5
Reynella-Port Noarlunga,
  11,818 ....A 8
Robe, ⊙941 ....F 7
Salisbury, 35,762 ....B 7
Snowtown, ⊙1,694 ....E 5
Stirling-Bridgewater,
  4,487 ....B 8
Strathalbyn, 1,449 ....F 6
Streaky Bay, ⊙2,134 ....D 5
Tailem Bend, 1,947 ....F 6
Tanunda, 1,986 ....C 6
Thebarton, 12,296 ....A 7
Tumby Bay, ⊙2,793 ....E 6
Unley, 39,727 ....B 8
Victor Harbor, 3,128 ....F 6
Waikerie, ⊙3,818 ....G 6
Wallaroo, 2,094 ....E 5
West Torrens, 46,222 ....A 8
Whyalla, 22,121 ....E 5
Willunga, ⊙2,190 ....F 6
Wilmington, ⊙828 ....F 5
Woodville, 73,878 ....A 7
Woomera and Maralinga,
  4,745 ....E 4
Yorketown, ⊙2,734 ....E 6

OTHER FEATURES

Acraman (lake) ....D 5
Alberga, The (riv.) ....F 6
Alexandrina (lake) ....F 6
Anxious (bay) ....D 5
Arckaringa (creek) ....D 2
Barcoo (creek) ....F 3
Barossa (res.) ....C 6
Birksgate (range) ....A 2
Blanche (lake) ....F 3
Brady (mt.) ....D 3
Cadibarrawirracanna
  (lake) ....D 3
Callabonna (lake) ....F 3
Catastrophe (cape) ....D 6
Coffin (bay) ....D 6
Coffin Bay (pen.) ....D 6
Coopers (Barcoo) (creek) ..F 3
Coorong, The (lag.) ....F 6
Dey Dey (lake) ....B 3
Encounter (bay) ....F 6
Everard (lake) ....D 4
Everard (ranges) ....D 3
Eyre (pen.) ....D 5
Eyre North (lake) ....E 3
Eyre South (lake) ....E 3
Finke (riv.) ....C 1
Flinders (range) ....F 4
Frome (lake) ....G 4
Gairdner (lake) ....D 4
Gawler (ranges) ....E 5
Gawler (riv.) ....B 6
Gilles (lake) ....E 5
Goyders (lag.) ....F 2
Great Australian (bight) ..A 5
Great Victoria (des.) .....B 3
Gregory (lake) ....F 3

Hack (mt.) ....F 4
Hamilton, The (riv.) ......D 2
Harris (lake) ....D 4
Head of Bight (bay) ....B 4
Indian Ocean ....E 6
Investigator (str.) ....E 6
Investigator Group (isls.) .D 5
Island (lag.) ....E 4
Jaffa (cape) ....G 7
Kangaroo (isl.), 3,375 ....E 7
Lacepede (bay) ....F 7
Little Para (riv.) ....B 7
Lofty (mt.) ....B 8
Macfarlane (lake) ....E 5
Macumba, The (riv.) ....E 2
Maurice (lake) ....B 3
Meramangye (lake) ....C 3
Morris (mt.) ....B 2
Mount Bold (res.) ....B 8
Murray (riv.) ....F 6
Musgrave (ranges) ....B 2
Neales, The (riv.) ....E 3
Neptune (isls.) ....D 6
Northumberland (cape) .....G 7
Nukey Bluff (mt.) ....D 5
Nullarbor (plain) ....A 4
Nurrari (lakes) ....B 3
Nuyts (arch.) ....C 5
Nuyts (cape) ....C 5
Onkaparinga (riv.) ....B 8
Peera Peera Poolanna
  (lake) ....F 2
Saint Mary (peak) ....F 4
Saint Vincent (gulf) ......F 6
Serpentine (lakes) ....A 3
Simpson (des.) ....E 1
Sir Joseph Banks Group
  (isls.) ....E 6
South Para (riv.) ....C 7
Spencer (cape) ....E 6
Spencer (gulf) ....E 6
Stevenson, The (riv.) .....D 2
Streaky (bay) ....D 5
Strzelecki (creek) ....G 3
Stuart (range) ....D 3
Sturt (des.) ....F 2
Sturt (riv.) ....B 8
The Alberga (riv.) ....D 2
The Coorong (lag.) ....F 6
The Hamilton (riv.) ....D 2
The Macumba (riv.) ....E 2
The Neales (riv.) ....E 3
The Stevenson (riv.) ......D 2
The Warburton (riv.) ......F 2
Thistle (isl.) ....E 6
Torrens (lake) ....E 4
Torrens (riv.) ....C 7
Warburton, The (riv.) .....F 2
Warren (res.) ....C 7
Whidbey (isls.) ....C 3
Wilkinson (lakes) ....C 3
Wilson Bluff (prom.) ......A 4
Woodroffe (mt.) ....B 2
Wright (lake) ....B 2
Yarle (lakes) ....B 3
Yorke (pen.) ....E 6

⊙ Population of district.
‡ Population of met. area.

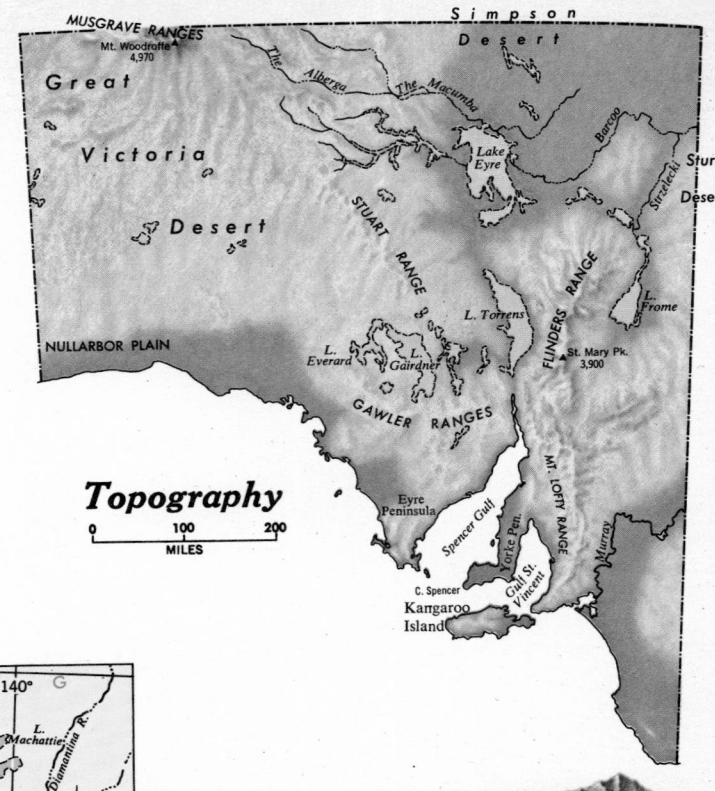

Topography

Musgrave Ranges, Mt. Woodroffe 4,970
Simpson Desert
Great Victoria Desert
Nullarbor Plain
Stuart Range
Flinders Range
L. Torrens
L. Eyre
L. Gairdner
L. Everard
Gawler Ranges
Eyre Peninsula
Spencer Gulf
Yorke Pen.
Gulf St. Vincent
Mt. Lofty Range
Murray
St. Mary Pk. 3,900
Sturt Desert
L. Frome
C. Spencer
Kangaroo Island

0   100   200
MILES

Below Sea Level | 100 m. 328 ft. | 200 m. 656 ft. | 500 m. 1,640 ft. | 1,000 m. 3,281 ft. | 2,000 m. 6,562 ft. | 5,000 m. 16,404 ft.

ADELAIDE AND VICINITY

Roseworthy
Tanunda
Gawler
Lyndoch
Virginia
Williamstown
Elizabeth
Barossa Res.
Outer Harbor
Salisbury
Birdwood
Port Adelaide
Enfield
Woodville
Prospect
Campbelltown
Gumeracha
West Torrens
Hindmarsh
Payneham
Lobethal
Thebarton
Kensington and Norwood
Lenswood
Glenelg
Unley
Uraidla
Woodside
Marion
Burnside
Mitcham
Hahndorf
Brighton
Colonel Light Gardens
Stirling-Bridgewater
Nairne
Reynella-Port Noarlunga
Mt. Bold Res.
Noarlunga
Kangarilla
Mt. Barker
Meadows

SOUTH AUSTRALIA

SCALE OF MILES
0   25   50   75   150

KILOMETRES
0   25   50   75   150

State Capital .... ⊛
State and Territorial
Boundaries ....

Copyright by C.S. Hammond & Co., N.Y.

CORAL SEA ISLANDS TERR.
Total Population
3

PHYSICAL FEATURES

...ougainville (reef)	C 2
...inders (reefs)	D 3
...reat Barrier (reef)	C 3
...eralds (cays)	D 3
...olmes (reef)	D 2
...arion (reef)	E 3
...sprey (reef)	C 2
...aumarez (reef)	E 4

QUEENSLAND

CITIES and TOWNS

...scot, 16,450	E 2
...yr, 8,674	C 3
...almoral, 15,758	E 2
...loela, 3,537	D 5
...owen, 5,144	D 3
...risbane (cap.), 656,222	D 2
...risbane, ‡718,822	D 2
...undaberg, 25,402	D 5
...airns, 29,326	C 3
...aloundra, 3,657	E 5
...amp Hill, 12,392	E 2
...ardwell, 5,640	C 3
...harleville, 4,871	C 5
...harters Towers, 7,602	C 4
...hermside, 26,189	D 2
...amp Hill, 12,392	E 3
...oopers Plains, 16,817	E 3
...orinda, 12,643	D 3
...alby, 8,860	D 5
...ast Brisbane, 10,780	E 3
...kibin, 13,224	D 3
...sk, ⊙6,120	E 5
...eebung, 17,850	E 2
...ladstone, 12,426	D 4
...reenslopes, 13,351	E 3
...old Coast, 49,481	E 6
...oondiwindi, 3,529	D 6
...ympie, 11,279	E 5
...olland Park, 22,645	E 3
...ome Hill, 3,507	C 3
...ala, 18,705	D 3
...dooroopilly, 15,321	D 3
...ngham, 5,354	C 3
...nisfail, 7,432	C 3
...swich, 54,531	D 5
...ngreach, 3,871	B 4

Mackay, 24,578	D 4
Mareeba, 4,799	C 3
Maryborough, 20,393	E 5
Mary Kathleen	A 4
Mirani, ⊙5,379	D 4
Mitchelton, 13,998	D 2
Moorooka, 16,801	D 3
Mount Isa, 16,877	A 4
Mount Morgan, 4,055	D 4
Nambour, 6,219	E 5
Newmarket, 12,212	D 2
Nundah, 15,609	E 2
Redcliffe, 27,327	E 5
Rockhampton, 46,083	D 4
Roma, 5,996	D 5
Sandgate, 22,621	D 2
Stafford, 17,692	D 2
Stanthorpe, 3,641	D 6
Taroom, ⊙3,367	D 5
Toowoomba, 52,139	D 5
Townsville, 58,847	C 3
Warwick, 10,065	D 6
Weipa,	B 2
Windsor, 14,023	E 5
Wynnum, 23,191	E 5
Yeppoon, 3,418	D 4
Yeronga, 11,769	D 3

OTHER FEATURES

Albatross (bay)	B 2
Alice (riv.)	C 4
Archer (riv.)	B 2
Balonne (riv.)	D 6
Banks (isl.)	B 1
Barcoo (creek)	A 4
Barkly Tableland	A 4
Bartle Frere (mt.)	C 3
Beal (range)	B 5
Belyando (riv.)	C 4
Bentinck (isl.)	A 3
Bigge (range)	D 5
Bowling Green (cape)	C 3
Bramble (bay)	E 2
Brisbane (riv.)	E 2
Brisbane Airport	E 2
Broad (sound)	D 4
Bulimba (creek)	E 3
Bulloo (lake)	B 6
Bulloo (riv.)	B 6
Bunker Group (isls.)	E 4
Burdekin (riv.)	C 3
Cabbage Tree (creek)	D 2
Cape York (pen.)	B 2
Capricorn (chan.)	D 4
Capricorn Group (isls.)	E 4
Carnarvon (range)	D 5
Carpentaria (gulf)	A 2

Caryapundy (swamp)	B 6
Clarke (range)	C 4
Cloncurry (riv.)	B 4
Coleman (riv.)	B 2
Comet (riv.)	D 5
Condamine (riv.)	D 5
Coopers (Barcoo) (creek)	B 5
Coral (sea)	C 1
Culgoa (riv.)	C 6
Cumberland (isls.)	D 4
Curtis (isl.)	D 4
Darling Downs	D 5
Dawson (riv.)	D 5

Diamantina (riv.)	B 4
Direction (cape)	B 2
Downfall (creek)	D 2
Drummond (range)	C 5
Duifken (pt.)	B 2
Endeavour (str.)	B 1
Enoggera (creek)	D 2
Fitzroy (riv.)	D 4
Flattery (cape)	C 2
Flinders (riv.)	B 3
Fraser (isl.)	E 5
Galilee (lake)	C 4
Georgina (riv.)	A 4

AREA 667,000 sq. mi.
POPULATION 1,810,000
CAPITAL Brisbane
LARGEST CITY Brisbane
HIGHEST POINT Mt. Bartle Frere 5,287 ft.

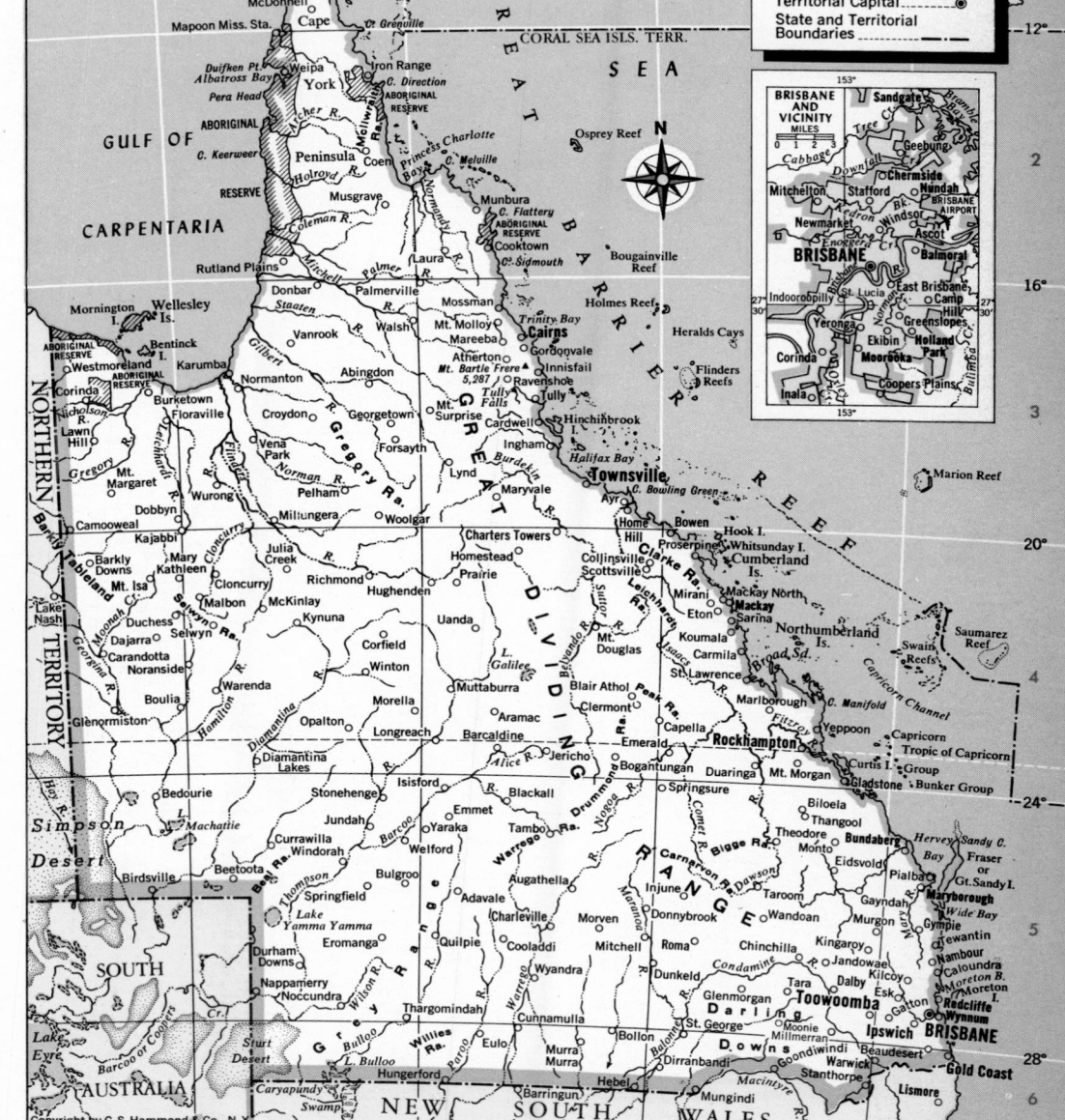

QUEENSLAND

SCALE OF MILES
0 50 100 150 200
KILOMETRES
0 50 100 150 200

Territorial Capital ....⊚
State and Territorial
Boundaries ....

Copyright by C.S. Hammond & Co., N.Y.

Topography

0 100 200
MILES

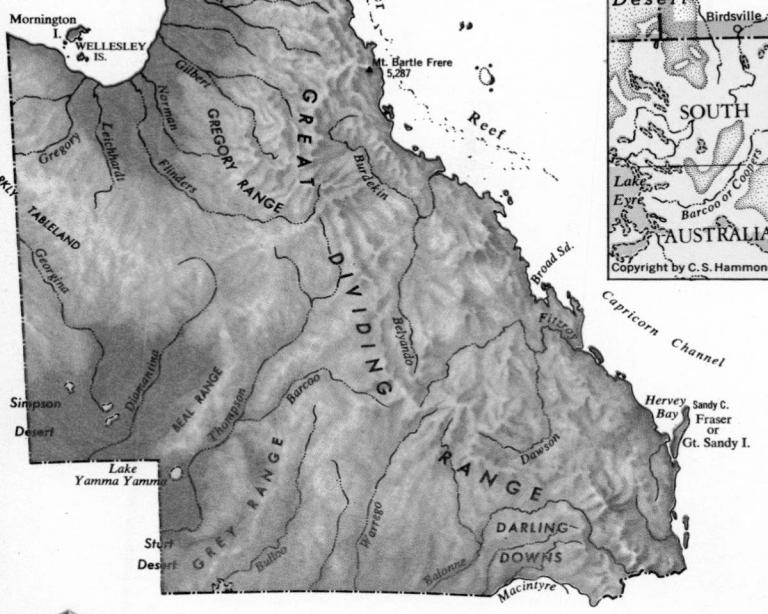

5,000 m. 2,000 m. 1,000 m. 500 m. 200 m. 100 m. Sea Below
16,404 ft. 6,562 ft. 3,281 ft. 1,640 ft. 656 ft. 328 ft. Level

Gilbert (riv.)	B 3
Great Dividing (range)	C 4
Great Sandy (Fraser) (isl.)	E 5
Gregory (range)	B 3
Gregory (riv.)	A 3
Grenville (cape)	B 1
Grey (range)	B 5
Halifax (bay)	C 3
Hamilton (riv.)	B 4
Hervey (bay)	E 5
Hinchinbrook (isl.)	C 3
Holroyd (riv.)	B 2
Hook (isl.)	D 4
Isaacs (riv.)	D 4
Kedron (brook)	D 2
Keerweer (cape)	B 2
Leichhardt (range)	C 4
Leichhardt (riv.)	A 3
Machattie (lake)	B 5
Macintyre (riv.)	D 6
Manifold (cape)	D 4
Maranoa (riv.)	C 5

Mary (riv.)	E 5
McIlwraith (range)	B 2
Melville (cape)	C 2
Mitchell (riv.)	B 3
Moonah (creek)	A 4
Moreton (bay)	E 5
Moreton (isl.)	E 5
Mornington (isl.)	A 3
Nicholson (riv.)	A 3
Nogoa (riv.)	D 4
Norman (creek)	D 3
Norman (riv.)	B 3
Normanby (riv.)	C 2
Northumberland (isls.)	D 4
Oxley (creek)	C 6
Palmer (riv.)	C 6
Paroo (riv.)	C 6
Peak (range)	D 4
Pera (head)	B 2
Prince of Wales (isl.)	B 1
Princess Charlotte (bay)	C 2
Sandy (cape)	E 5

Selwyn (range)	B 4
Sidmouth (cape)	B 2
Simpson (des.)	A 5
Staaten (riv.)	B 3
Sturt (des.)	B 5
Suttor (riv.)	C 4
Swain (reefs)	E 4
Thompson (riv.)	B 5
Torres (str.)	B 1
Trinity (bay)	C 3
Tully (falls)	C 3
Warrego (range)	C 5
Warrego (riv.)	C 5
Wellesley (isls.)	A 3
Whitsunday (isl.)	D 4
Wide (bay)	E 5
Willies (range)	C 6
Wilson (riv.)	B 5
Yamma Yamma (lake)	B 5
York (cape)	B 1

⊙ Population of district.
‡ Population of met. area.

AUSTRALIAN CAPITAL
TERRITORY
Total Population
136,300

CITIES and TOWNS

Canberra (cap.),
  Australia, 92,308.....E 4
Canberra, ‡136,300.....E 4
Jervis Bay.............F 4

OTHER FEATURES

Saint George (head)....F 4

NEW SOUTH WALES

CITIES and TOWNS

Aberdeen, 1,127........F 3
Abermain, ...F 3
Adaminaby, ...E 5
Adelong, ...D 4
Albert, ...D 3
Albury, 25,112........D 5
Alstonville, ...G 1
Ardlethan, ...D 4
Ariah Park, ...D 4
Armidale, 14,984......F 2
Ashfield, 41,933......J 3

Ashford, ⊙2,930.......F 1
Ashley, ...E 1
Attunga, ...F 2
Auburn, 48,691........J 3
Baan Baa, ...E 2
Ballina, 4,931........G 1
Balpunga, ...A 3
Balranald, 1,490......B 4
Bangalow, ...G 1
Bankstown, 159,981....J 3
Baradine, ...E 2
Barellan, ...D 4
Bargo, ...E 4
Barham, 1,139.........C 4
Barmedman, ...D 4

Barooga, 1,425........C 4
Barraba, ...F 2
Barringun, ...C 1
Baryulgil, ...G 1
Batemans Bay-
  Batehaven, 1,445....F 4
Bathurst, 17,222......E 3
Batlow, 1,448.........E 4
Berry, ...F 4
Bibbenluke, ⊙2,220....E 5
Bigga, ...E 4
Binda, ...E 4
Bingara, 1,504........F 1
Binnalong, ...E 4
Binnaway, ...E 2
Birriwa, ...E 3
Belmont, ...F 3

Belmore, ...J 3
Bemboka, ...E 5
Benanee, ...B 4
Bendemeer, ...F 2
Bermagui, ...F 5
Berrigan, ⊙6,641......C 4
Bermagui, ...F 5
Baulkham Hills, 24,873.H 3
Bega, 3,925...........E 5
Bellata, ...F 1
Bellbird-Cessnock,
  15,331.............F 3
Bellingen, 1,390......G 2
Belmont, ...F 3

Blayney, 1,909........E 3
Blue Mountains, 30,731.F 3
Bobadah, ...D 3
Bodalla, ...F 5
Bogan Gate, ...D 3
Boggabilla, ...F 1
Boggabri, 1,199.......F 2
Bomaderry-Nowra, 9,633.F 4
Bombala, 1,495........E 5
Bonalbo, ...G 1
Bondi, ...K 3
Bonnyrigg, ...H 3
Booligal, ...C 3
Boomi, ⊙2,654.........E 1
Booroorban, ...C 4

Boorowa, 1,181........E 4
Boree Creek, ...D 4
Botany, 31,871........J
Bourke, 3,262.........D
Bowral, 5,210.........E 4
Bowraville, 883.......G 2
Braidwood, ...E 4
Branxton-Greta, 2,539..F
Bredbo, ...E
Brewarrina, 1,255.....D
Bribbaree, ...E
Broken Hill, 30,036...A
Browning, ...E
Brunswick Heads, 1,068.G
Bugaldie, ...E

NEW SOUTH WALES
AREA 309,433 sq. mi.
POPULATION 4,595,400
CAPITAL Sydney
LARGEST CITY Sydney
HIGHEST POINT Mt. Kosciusko 7,316 ft.

VICTORIA
AREA 87,884 sq. mi.
POPULATION 3,461,400
CAPITAL Melbourne
LARGEST CITY Melbourne
HIGHEST POINT Mt. Bogong 6,508 ft.

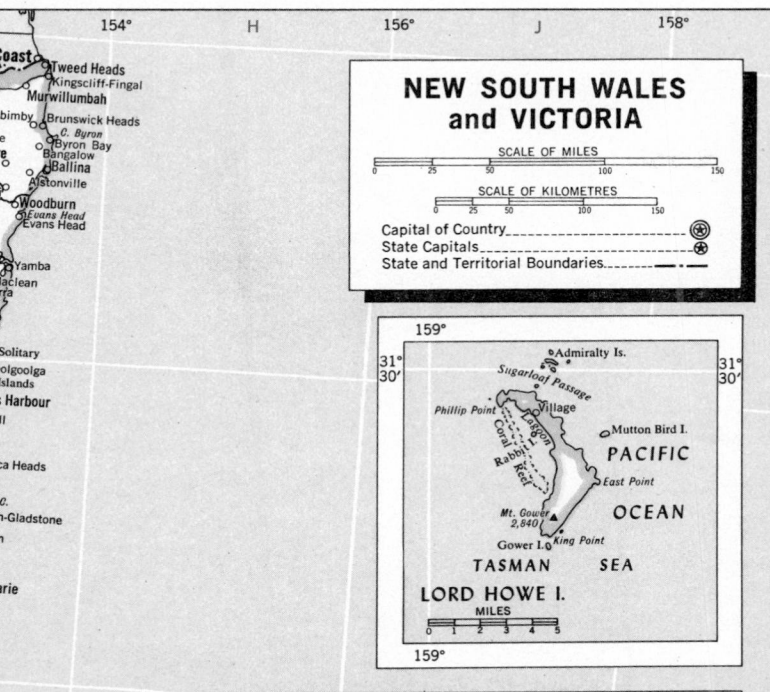

NEW SOUTH WALES and VICTORIA

SCALE OF MILES

SCALE OF KILOMETRES

Capital of Country ⊛
State Capitals ★
State and Territorial Boundaries ▬▬▬

Topography

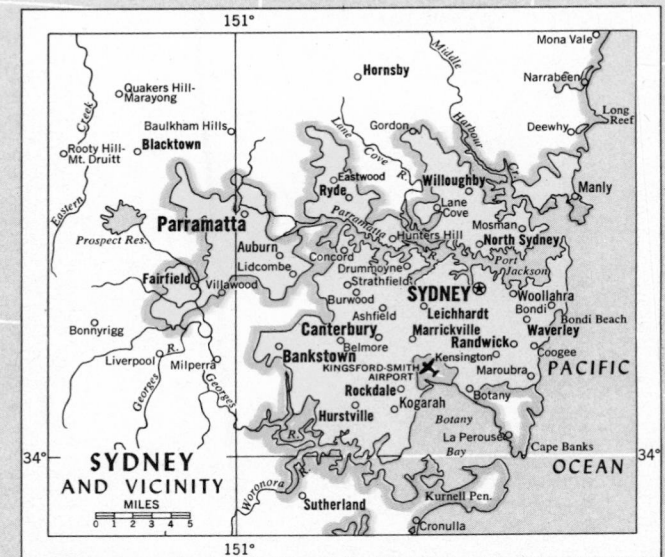

SYDNEY AND VICINITY

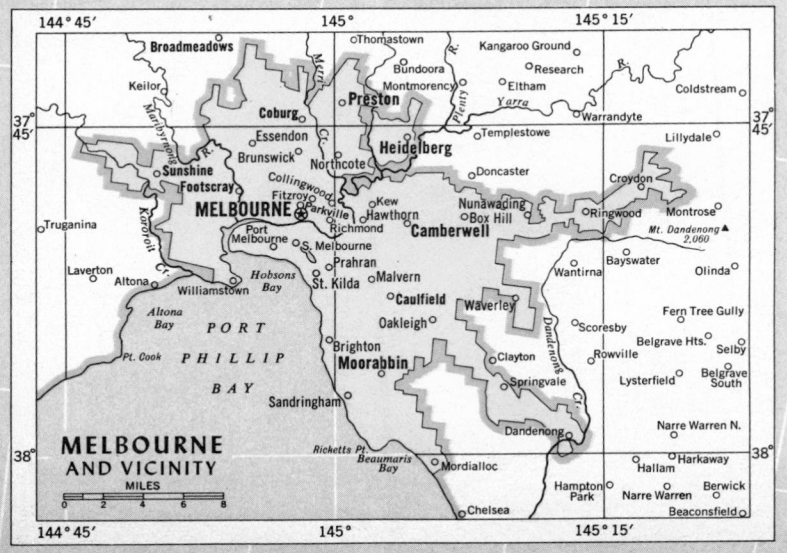

MELBOURNE AND VICINITY

(continued on following page)

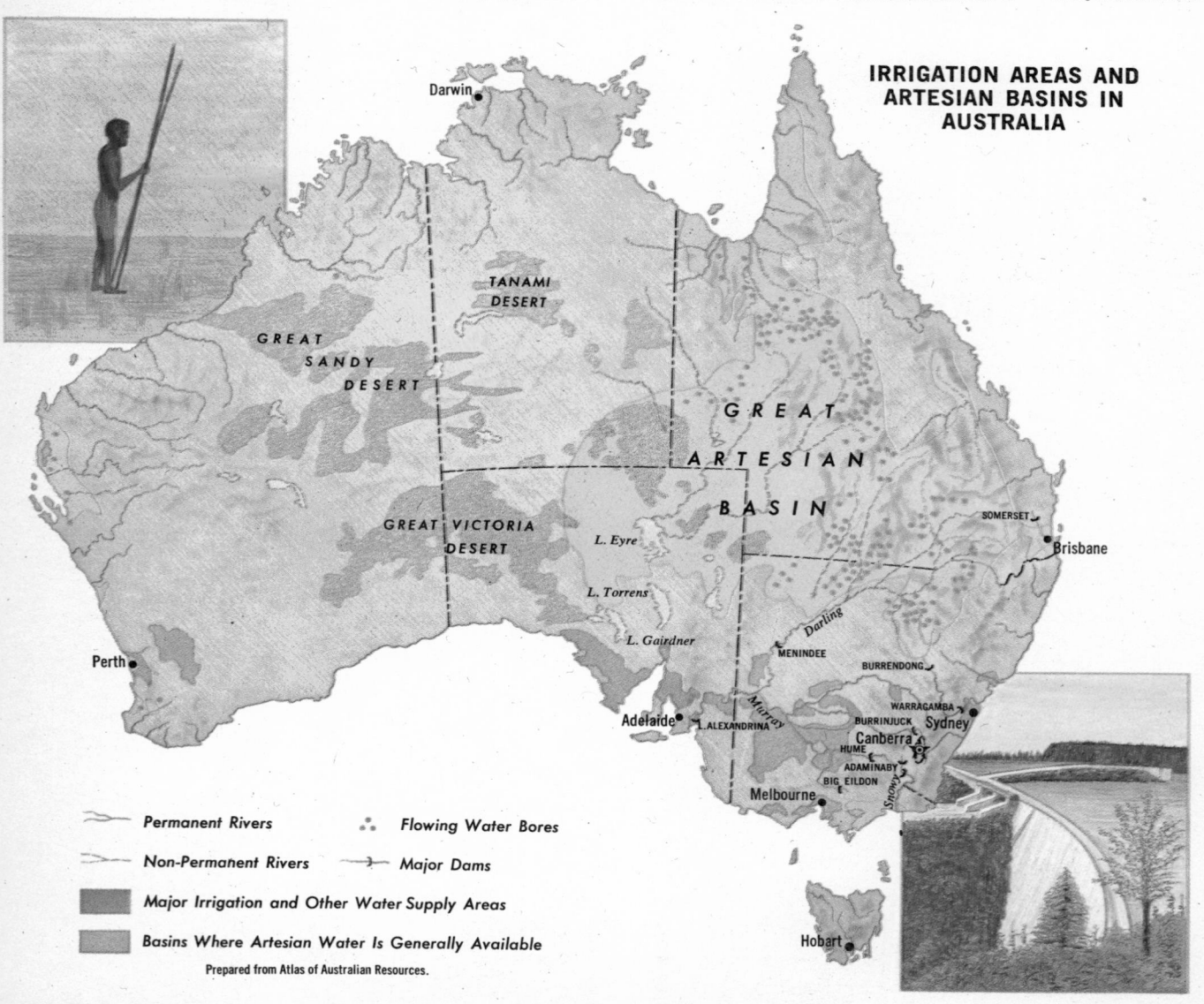

IRRIGATION AREAS AND ARTESIAN BASINS IN AUSTRALIA

Darwin

GREAT SANDY DESERT

TANAMI DESERT

GREAT VICTORIA DESERT

GREAT ARTESIAN BASIN

L. Eyre

L. Torrens

L. Gairdner

Perth

SOMERSET

Brisbane

MENINDEE

BURRENDONG

Darling

WARRAGAMBA

Adelaide

L. ALEXANDRINA

Murray

BURRINJUCK

Sydney

HUME

Canberra

ADAMINABY

BIG EILDON

Snowy

Melbourne

Hobart

Permanent Rivers · · · Flowing Water Bores

Non-Permanent Rivers → Major Dams

Major Irrigation and Other Water Supply Areas

Basins Where Artesian Water Is Generally Available

Prepared from Atlas of Australian Resources.

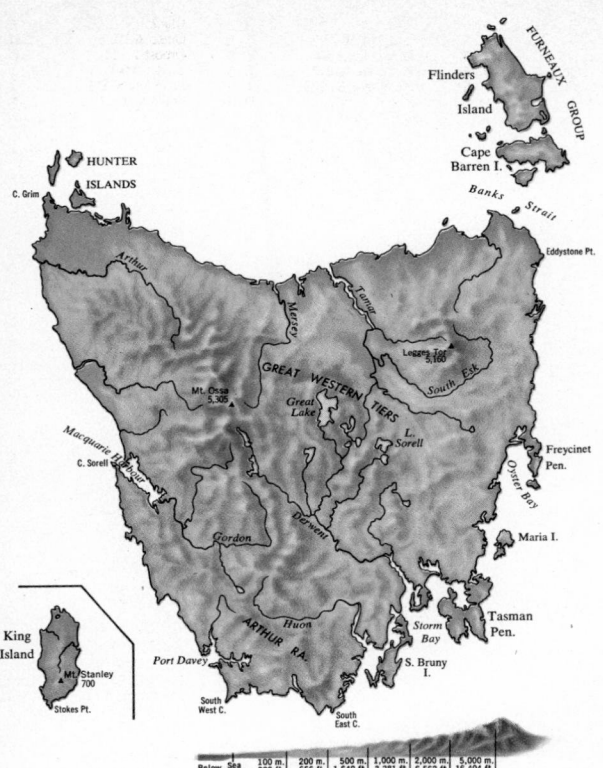

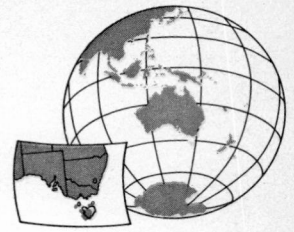

AREA 26,215 sq. mi.
POPULATION 393,700
CAPITAL Hobart
LARGEST CITY Hobart
HIGHEST POINT Mt. Ossa, 5,305 ft.

⊙ Population of district.
‡ Population of met. area.

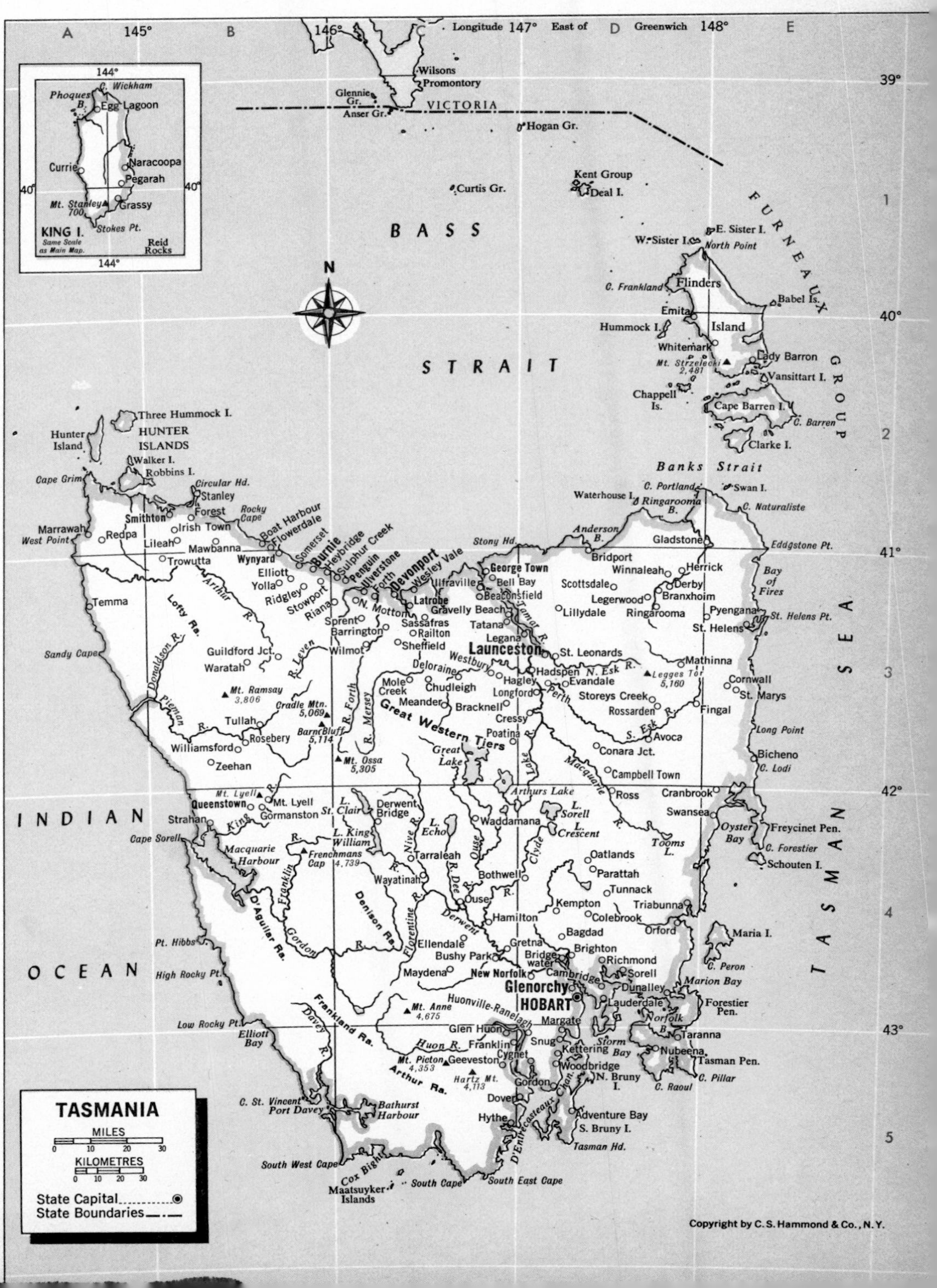

Topography

0   30   60
MILES

TASMANIA

MILES
0   10   20   30
KILOMETRES
0   10   20   30

State Capital .... ◉
State Boundaries ----

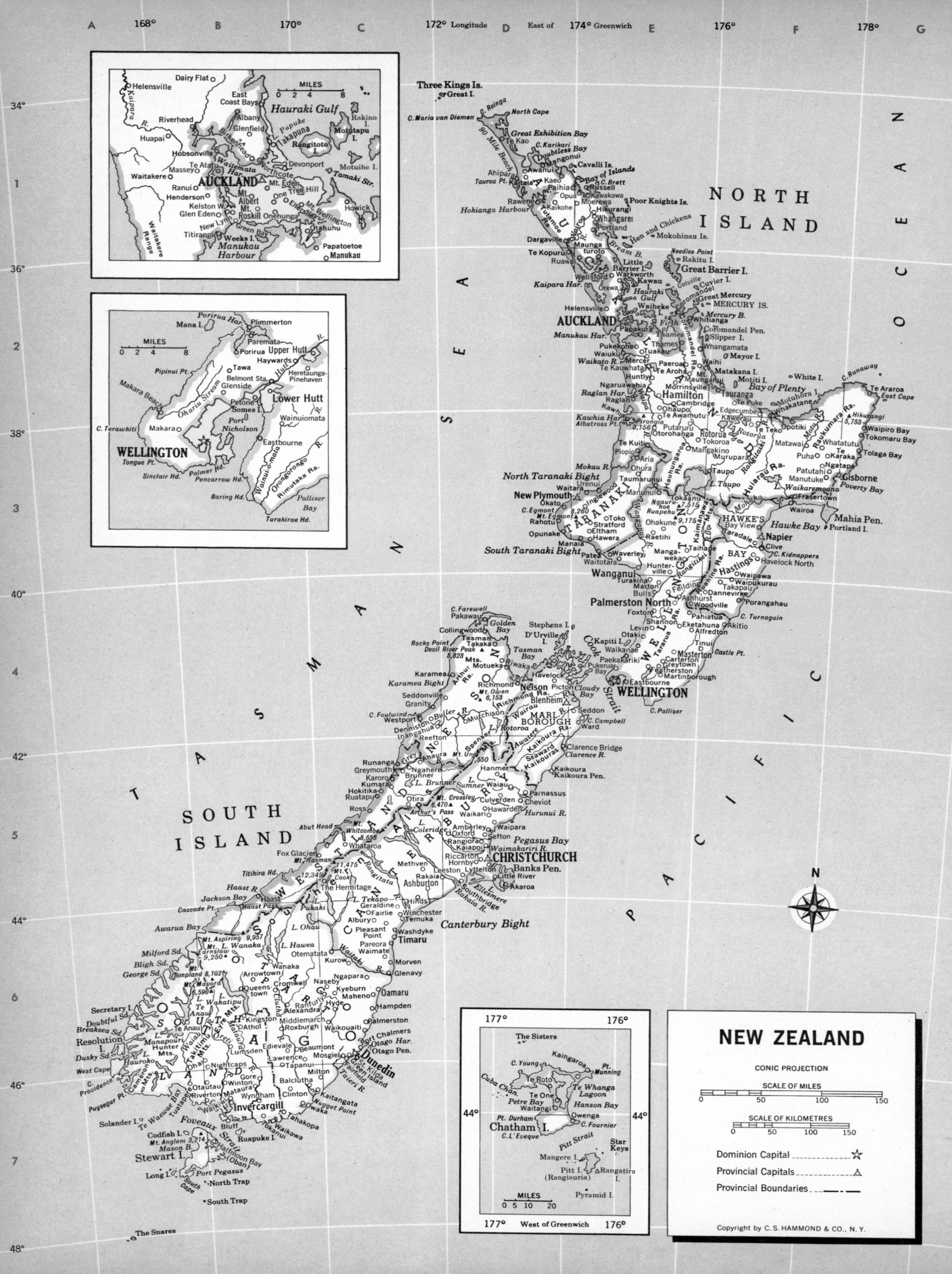

NEW ZEALAND

CONIC PROJECTION

SCALE OF MILES

SCALE OF KILOMETRES

Dominion Capital .... ☆
Provincial Capitals .... △
Provincial Boundaries .... ─ ─ ─

Copyright by C. S. HAMMOND & CO., N.Y.

Topography

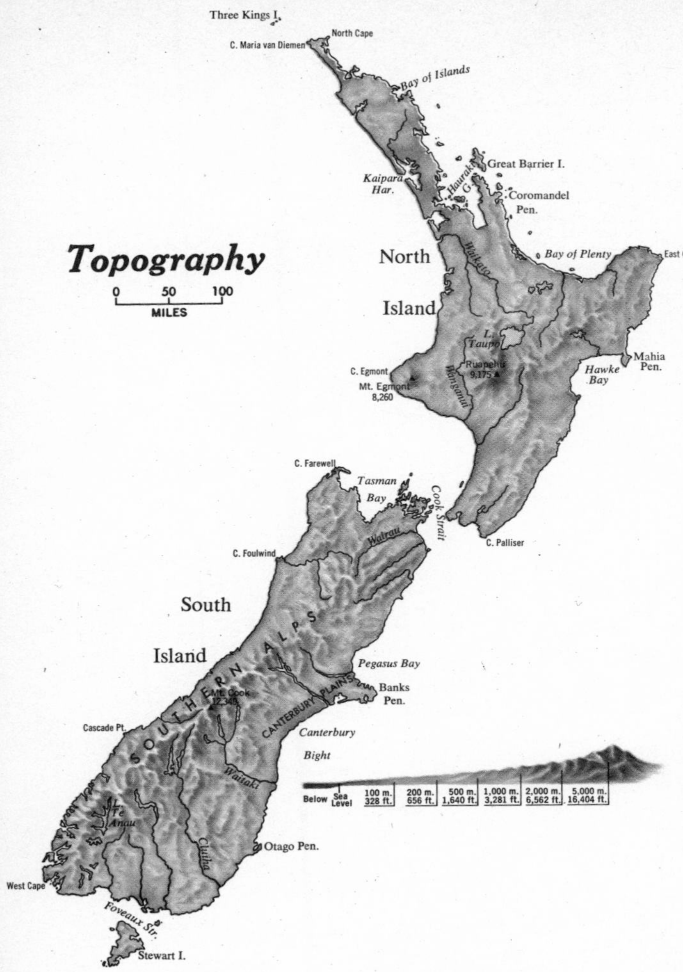
0 50 100
MILES
Three Kings I.
North Cape
C. Maria van Diemen
Bay of Islands
Great Barrier I.
Kaipara Har.
Hauraki G.
Coromandel Pen.
North
Island
Waikato
Bay of Plenty
East Cape
L. Taupo
Ruapehu 9,175
Wanganui
C. Egmont
Mt. Egmont 8,260
Mahia Pen.
Hawke Bay
C. Farewell
Tasman Bay
Cook Strait
C. Palliser
C. Foulwind
Wairau
South
Island
SOUTHERN ALPS
Mt. Cook 12,349
CANTERBURY PLAINS
Pegasus Bay
Banks Pen.
Canterbury Bight
Cascade Pt.
Waitaki
Clutha
Otago Pen.
West Cape
Foveaux Str.
Stewart I.
Below Sea Level
100 m. 328 ft.
200 m. 656 ft.
500 m. 1,640 ft.
1,000 m. 3,281 ft.
2,000 m. 6,562 ft.
5,000 m. 16,404 ft.

AREA 103,736 sq. mi.
POPULATION 2,815,000
CAPITAL Wellington
LARGEST CITY Auckland
HIGHEST POINT Mt. Cook 12,349 ft.
MONETARY UNIT New Zealand dollar
MAJOR LANGUAGES English, Maori
MAJOR RELIGION Protestantism

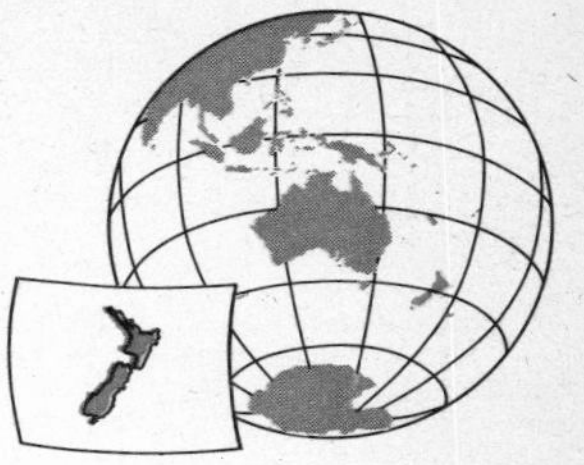

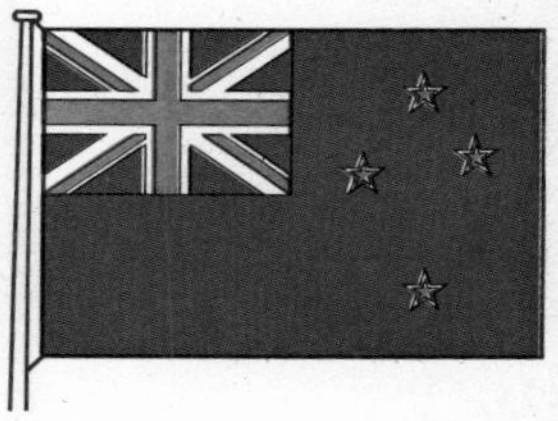

DISTRICTS

Auckland (prov. dist.), 1,189,811 ....E 2
Canterbury (prov. dist.), 385,981 ....C 5
Hawke's Bay (prov. dist.), 128,300 ....F 3
Marlborough (prov. dist.), 30,200 ....D 4
Nelson (prov. dist.), 68,300 ....D 4
Otago (prov. dist.), 290,100 ....A 6
Otago (land dist.), 183,200 ....B 6
Southland (land dist.), 106,900....A 6
Taranaki (prov. dist.), 101,200 ..E 3
Wellington (prov. dist.), 537,100 ....E 4
Westland (prov. dist.), 24,100.....C 5

CITIES and TOWNS

Alexandra, 3,160 ....B 6
Ashburton, 12,950 ....C 5
Ashhurst, 922 ....E 4
Auckland, 152,200 ....B 1
Auckland, †588,400 ....B 1
Balclutha, 4,570 ....B 7
Bay View, 945 ....F 3
Belmont Hill, 1,119 ....B 2
Birkenhead, 12,800 ....B 1
Blenheim, 13,950 ....D 4
Bluff, 3,300 ....B 7
Bulls, 1,803 ....E 4
Cambridge, 6,060 ....E 2
Carterton, 3,640 ....E 4
Christchurch, 165,000 ....D 5
Christchurch, †256,300 ....D 5
Clive, 1,017 ....F 3
Cromwell, 1,062 ....B 6
Dannevirke, 5,780 ....F 4
Dargaville, 3,910 ....D 1
Devonport, 11,100 ....C 1
Dunedin, 77,800 ....C 6
Dunedin, †109,800 ....C 6
Eastbourne, 4,610 ....B 3
East Coast Bays, 13,150 ....B 1
Edgecumbe, 1,277 ....F 2
Ellerslie, 4,260 ....B 1
Eltham, 2,319 ....E 3
Fairfield, 1,106 ....C 6
Featherston, 1,857 ....E 4
Feilding, 9,360 ....E 4
Foxton, 2,830 ....E 4
Geraldine, 1,876 ....C 6
Gisborne, 25,600 ....G 3
Gisborne, †28,500 ....G 3
Glen Eden, 6,230 ....B 1
Glenfield, 16,450 ....B 1
Gore, 8,380 ....B 7
Green Bay, 2,022 ....B 1
Green Island, 5,990 ....C 7
Greymouth, 8,590 ....C 5
Greytown, 1,715 ....E 4
Hamilton, 67,700 ....E 2
Hamilton, †68,000 ....E 2
Hastings, 28,100 ....F 3
Hastings, †39,200 ....F 3
Havelock North, 5,950 ....F 3
Hawera, 8,210 ....E 3
Helensville, 1,305 ....B 1
Henderson, 5,780 ....B 1
Heretaunga-Pinehaven, 4,990.......C 2
Hikurangi, 1,091 ....E 1
Hobsonville. 1,612 ....B 1
Hokitika, 3,310 ....C 5
Hornby, 6,780 ....D 5
Howick, 9,890 ....C 1
Huntly, 5,420 ....E 2
Hutt, †118,400 ....B, C 2
Inglewood, 2,003 ....E 3
Invercargill, 45.300 ....B 7
Invercargill, †47,800 ....B 7
Kaiapoi, 3,610 ....D 5
Kaikohe, 3,120 ....D 1
Kaikoura, 1,571 ....D 5
Kaitaia, 3,110 ....D 1
Kaitangata, 1,208 ....C 7
Kawakawa, 1,032 ....E 1
Kawerau, 6,010 ....F 3
Kelston West, 5,490 ....B 1
Levin, 11,950 ....E 4
Lower Hutt, 58,700 ....C 2
Lyttelton, 3,510 ....D 5
Mangakino, 1,466 ....E 3
Manukau, 84,700 ....C 1
Martinborough, 1,462 ....E 4
Marton, 4,780 ....E 4
Massey ....B 1
Masterton, 17,950 ....E 4
Mataura, 2,720 ....B 7
Milton, 1,861 ....C 7
Moerewa, 1,090 ....E 1
Morrinsville, 4,530 ....E 2
Mosgiel, 8,100 ....C 6
Motueka, 3,840 ....D 4
Mount Albert, 25,700 ....B 1
Mount Eden, 18,400 ....B 1
Mount Maunganui, 7,210 ....F 2
Mount Roskill, 34,400 ....B 1
Mount Wellington, 19,650 ....C 1
Murupara, 2,670 ....F 3
Napier, 36,700 ....F 3
Napier, †39,900 ....F 3
Nelson, 27,900 ....D 4
Nelson, †28,400 ....D 4
New Lynn, 10,150 ....B 1
New Plymouth, 32,300 ....D 3
New Plymouth, †35,800 ....D 3
Ngaruawahia, 3,790 ....E 2
Northcote, 8,640 ....B 1
Oamaru, 13,350 ....C 6
Ohai, 939 ....A 6
Ohakune, 1,458 ....E 3
One Tree Hill, 12,900 ....B 1
Onehunga, 16,050 ....B 1
Opotiki, 2,560 ....F 3
Opua, 151 ....D 1
Orewa, 1,357 ....E 2
Otahuhu, 10,000 ....C 1
Otaki, 3,660 ....E 4
Otematata, 3,890 ....B 6
Otorohanga, 1,951 ....E 3
Paekakariki, 1,934 ....E 4
Pahiatua, 2,590 ....E 4
Palmerston North, 49,200 ....E 4
Palmerston North, †50,900 ....E 4
Papakura, 12,950 ....E 2
Papatoetoe, 21,400 ....C 1
Patea, 2,013 ....E 3
Petone, 10,200 ....B 2
Picton, 2,610 ....D 4
Pinehaven (Heretaunga-Pinehaven), 4,990 ....C 2
Plimmerton-Paremata, 3,910 ....B 2
Porirua, 24,900 ....B 2
Port Chalmers, 3,040 ....C 6
Pukekohe, 6,800 ....E 2
Pukerua Bay, 1,220 ....E 4
Putaruru, 4,500 ....E 3
Queenstown, 1,634 ....B 6
Raetihi, 1,376 ....E 3
Raglan, 1,019 ....E 2
Ranfurly, 946 ....B 6
Rangiora, 4,270 ....D 5
Ranui, 1,897 ....B 1
Reefton, 1,730 ....C 5
Riccarton, 7,220 ....D 5
Richmond, 4,870 ....D 4
Riverton, 1,258 ....A 7
Riwaka, 993 ....D 4
Rotorua, 27,600 ....F 3
Rotorua, †35,300 ....F 3
Runanga, 1,683 ....C 5
Saint Kilda, 6,720 ....C 7
Shannon, 1,544 ....E 4
Stratford, 5,470 ....E 3
Taihape, 2,880 ....E 3
Takapuna, 23,800 ....B 1
Taradale ....F 3
Taumarunui, 6,080 ....E 3
Taupo, 8,530 ....F 3
Tauranga, 25,500 ....F 2
Tauranga, †33,500 ....F 2
Tawa, 10,200 ....B 2
Te Anau, 951 ....A 6
Te Aroha, 3,220 ....E 2
Te Atatu ....B 1
Te Awamutu, 6,780 ....E 3
Te Karaka, 637 ....F 3
Te Kuiti, 4,830 ....E 3
Temuka, 3,190 ....C 6
Te Puke, 3,090 ....F 2
Thames, 5,680 ....E 2
The Hermitage, 306 ....C 5
Timaru, 27,800 ....C 6
Timaru, †28,400 ....C 6
Titirangi, 5,740 ....B 1
Tokoroa, 12,450 ....F 3
Tuakau, 1,677 ....E 2
Tuatapere, 954 ....A 7
Upper Hutt, 19,750 ....B 2
Waihi, 3,170 ....F 2
Waikanae, 1,570 ....E 4
Waimate, 3,300 ....C 6
Wainuiomata, 15,000 ....B 3
Waipawa, 1,848 ....F 3
Waipukurau, 3,670 ....F 4
Wairoa, 5,190 ....F 3
Waitangi, 179 ....D 7
Waitara, 4,870 ....E 3
Waiuku, 1,759 ....E 2
Wanganui, 36,400 ....E 3
Wanganui, †38,500 ....E 3
Warkworth, 1,200 ....E 2
Waverley, 1,062 ....E 3
Wellington (capital), 134,400 ....A 3
Wellington, †175,500 ....A 3
Wellsford, 1,431 ....E 2
Westport, 5,230 ....C 4
Whakatane, 9,080 ....F 2
Whangarei, 29,600 ....E 1
Whangarei, †31,600 ....E 1
Winton, 1,740 ....B 7
Woodville, 1,529 ....F 4

OTHER FEATURES

Abut (head) ....B 5
Arthur (range) ....D 4
Arthur's (pass) ....C 5
Aspiring (mt.) ....B 6
Awarua (bay) ....A 6
Banks (pen.) ....D 5
Bligh (sound) ....A 6
Breaksea (sound) ....A 6
Bream (bay) ....E 1
Brett (cape) ....E 1
Brunner (lake) ....C 5
Buller (river) ....D 4
Cameron (mts.) ....A 7
Campbell (cape) ....E 4
Canterbury (bight) ....D 6
Cascade (point) ....A 6
Castle (point) ....F 4
Chatham (isl.), 467 ....D 7
Chatham (isls.), 520 ....D 7
Christina (mt.) ....B 6
Clarence (river) ....E 5
Cloudy (bay) ....E 4
Clutha (river) ....B 6
Codfish (isl.) ....A 7
Coleridge (lake) ....C 5
Colville (cape) ....E 2
Cook (mt.) ....C 5
Cook (strait) ....E 4
Coromandel (pen.) ....E 2
Coromandel (range) ....E 2
Crossley (mt.) ....C 5
Cuvier (isl.), 12 ....E 2
D'Urville (isl.), 91 ....D 4
Devil River (peak) ....D 4
Durham (pt.) ....D 7
Dusky (sound) ....A 6
Earnslaw (mt.) ....B 6
East (cape) ....G 2
Egmont (mt.) ....D 3
Ellesmere (lake) ....D 6
Eyre (mts.) ....B 6
Farewell (cape) ....D 4
Foulwind (cape) ....C 4
Foveaux (strait) ....A 7
George (sound) ....A 6
Golden (bay) ....D 4
Great Barrier (isl.), 272 ....F 2
Great Mercury (isl.), 7 ....E 2
Grey (river) ....C 5
Hauhangaroa (range) ....E 3
Hauraki (gulf) ....E 2
Hawea (lake) ....B 6
Hawke's (bay) ....F 3
Hen and Chickens (isls.) ....E 1
Hikurangi (mt.) ....G 2
Hokianga (harb.) ....D 1
Hunter (mts.) ....A 6
Hurunui (river) ....D 5
Hutt (river) ....C 2
Islands, Bay of (bay) ....E 1
Jackson (bay) ....B 5
Kaikoura (pen.) ....D 5
Kaikoura (range) ....D 4
Kaimanawa (mts.) ....E 3
Kaipara (harb.) ....D 2
Kapiti (isl.), 2 ....E 4
Karamea (bight) ....C 4
Karikari (cape) ....D 1
Kawau (isl.), 103 ....E 2
Kawhia (harb.) ....E 3
Kidnappers (cape) ....F 3
Little Barrier (isl.), 4 ....E 2
Mahia (pen.) ....G 3
Mana (isl.), 5 ....B 2
Manapouri (lake) ....A 6
Manukau (harb.) ....D 2
Maria van Diemen (cape) ....D 1
Mason (bay) ....A 7
Matakana (isl.), 396 ....F 2
Mataura (river) ....B 6
Mayor (isl.), 47 ....F 2
Mercury (bay) ....F 2
Mercury (isls.), 7 ....F 2
Milford (sound) ....A 6
Mokau (river) ....E 3
Mokohinau (isls.), 7 ....E 1
Motiti (isl.), 7 ....F 2
Motuhora (isl.) ....F 2
Motuihe (isl.), 6 ....C 1
Motutapu (isl.), 27 ....C 1
Munning (point) ....E 7
Needles (point) ....E 2
Ninety-Mile (beach) ....D 1
North (isl.), 1,956,411 ....F 1
North Taranaki (bight) ....D 3
Nugget (point) ....C 7
Ohariu (stream) ....B 2
Otago (pen.), ...C 6
Owen (mt.) ....D 4
Palliser (bay) ....C 3
Palliser (cape) ....E 4
Pegasus (bay) ....D 5
Pitt (isl.), 53 ....E 7
Plenty (bay) ....F 2
Poor Knights (isls.) ....E 1
Port Nicholson (inlet) ....B 3
Port Pegasus (inlet) ....B 7
Portland (isl.), 14 ....G 3
Poverty (bay) ....G 3
Pukaki (lake) ....B 6
Pupuke (lake) ....B 1
Puysegur (point) ....A 7
Pyramid (isl.) ....E 7
Rakino (isl.), 5 ....C 1
Rakitu (isl.), 2 ....E 2
Rangatira (isl.) ....E 7
Rangiauria (Pitt) (isl.), 53........E 7
Rangitoto (isl.), 48 ....C 1
Raukumara (range) ....F 3
Reinga (cape) ....D 1
Resolution (isl.) ....A 6
Richmond (range) ....D 4
Rimutaka (range) ....B 3
Rocks (point) ....C 4
Rotorua (lake) ....E 3
Ruahine (range) ....E 4
Ruapehu (mt.) ....E 3
Ruapuke (isl.) ....B 7
Runaway (cape) ....G 2
Secretary (isl.) ....A 6
Slipper (isl.), 4 ....E 2
Somes (isl.), 2 ....B 2
South (isl.), 798,681 ....B 5
South Taranaki (bight) ....D 3
Southern Alps (range) ....C 5
Spenser (mts.) ....D 5
Stephens (isl.), 9 ....D 4
Stewart (isl.), 332 ....A 7
Sumner (lake) ....D 5
Taieri (river) ....C 7
Tasman (bay) ....D 4
Tasman (mt.) ....C 5
Tasman (sea) ....B 3
Taupo (lake) ....E 3
Tauroa (point) ....D 1
Te Anau (lake) ....A 6
Tekapo (lake) ....C 5
Three Kings (isls.) ....C 1
Titihiri (head) ....B 5
Tongue (point) ....A 3
Turnagain (cape) ....F 4
Tutumoe (range) ....D 1
Una (mt.) ....D 5
Waiau (river) ....A 6
Waiheke (isl.), 2,013 ....E 2
Waikato (river) ....E 2
Waimakariri (river) ....D 5
Wairau (river) ....D 4
Wairoa (river) ....E 1
Waitaki (river) ....C 6
Wakatipu (lake) ....B 6
Wanaka (lake) ....B 6
Wanganui (river) ....E 3
West (cape) ....A 6
Whitcombe (mt.) ....C 5
White (isl.) ....F 2

†Population of urban area.

Agriculture, Industry and Resources

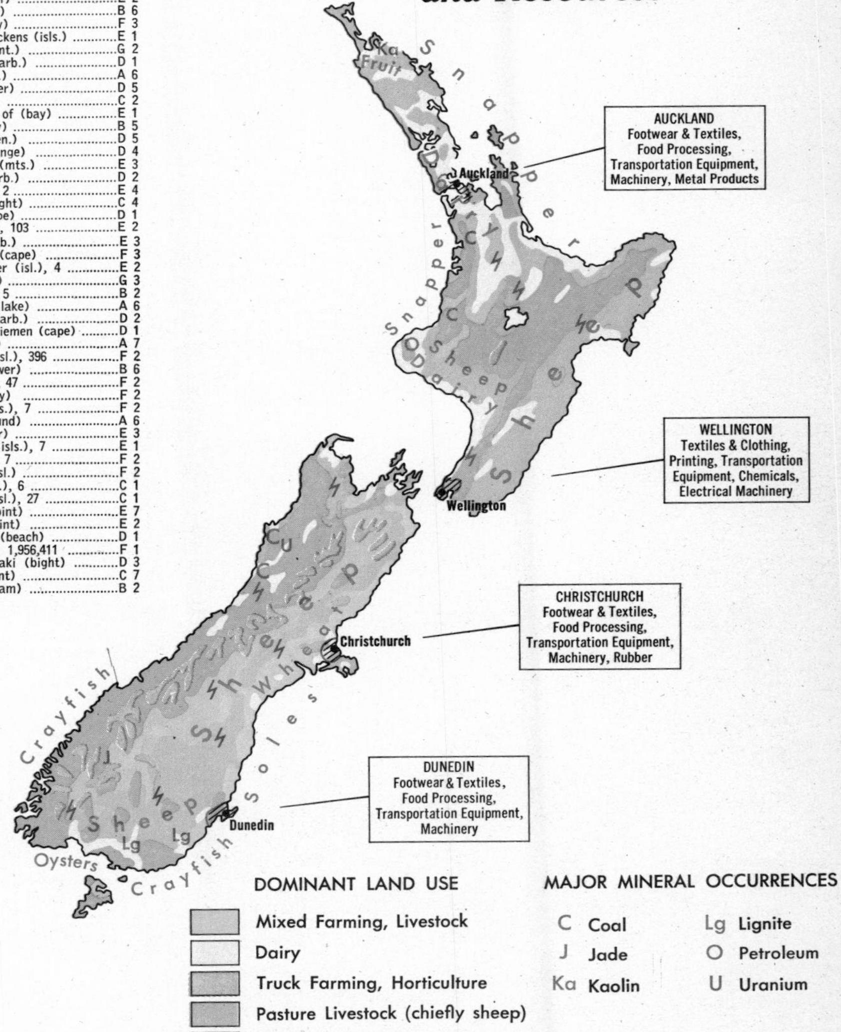
Ka
Fruit
Snapper
Auckland
AUCKLAND
Footwear & Textiles,
Food Processing,
Transportation Equipment,
Machinery, Metal Products
Sheep
Dairy
Wellington
WELLINGTON
Textiles & Clothing,
Printing, Transportation
Equipment, Chemicals,
Electrical Machinery
Christchurch
CHRISTCHURCH
Footwear & Textiles,
Food Processing,
Transportation Equipment,
Machinery, Rubber
Wheat
Soles
Crayfish
Dunedin
DUNEDIN
Footwear & Textiles,
Food Processing,
Transportation Equipment,
Machinery
Lg
Oysters

DOMINANT LAND USE

- Mixed Farming, Livestock
- Dairy
- Truck Farming, Horticulture
- Pasture Livestock (chiefly sheep)
- Livestock Herding
- Forests
- Nonagricultural Land

MAJOR MINERAL OCCURRENCES

- C Coal
- J Jade
- Ka Kaolin
- Lg Lignite
- O Petroleum
- U Uranium
- Water Power
- Major Industrial Areas

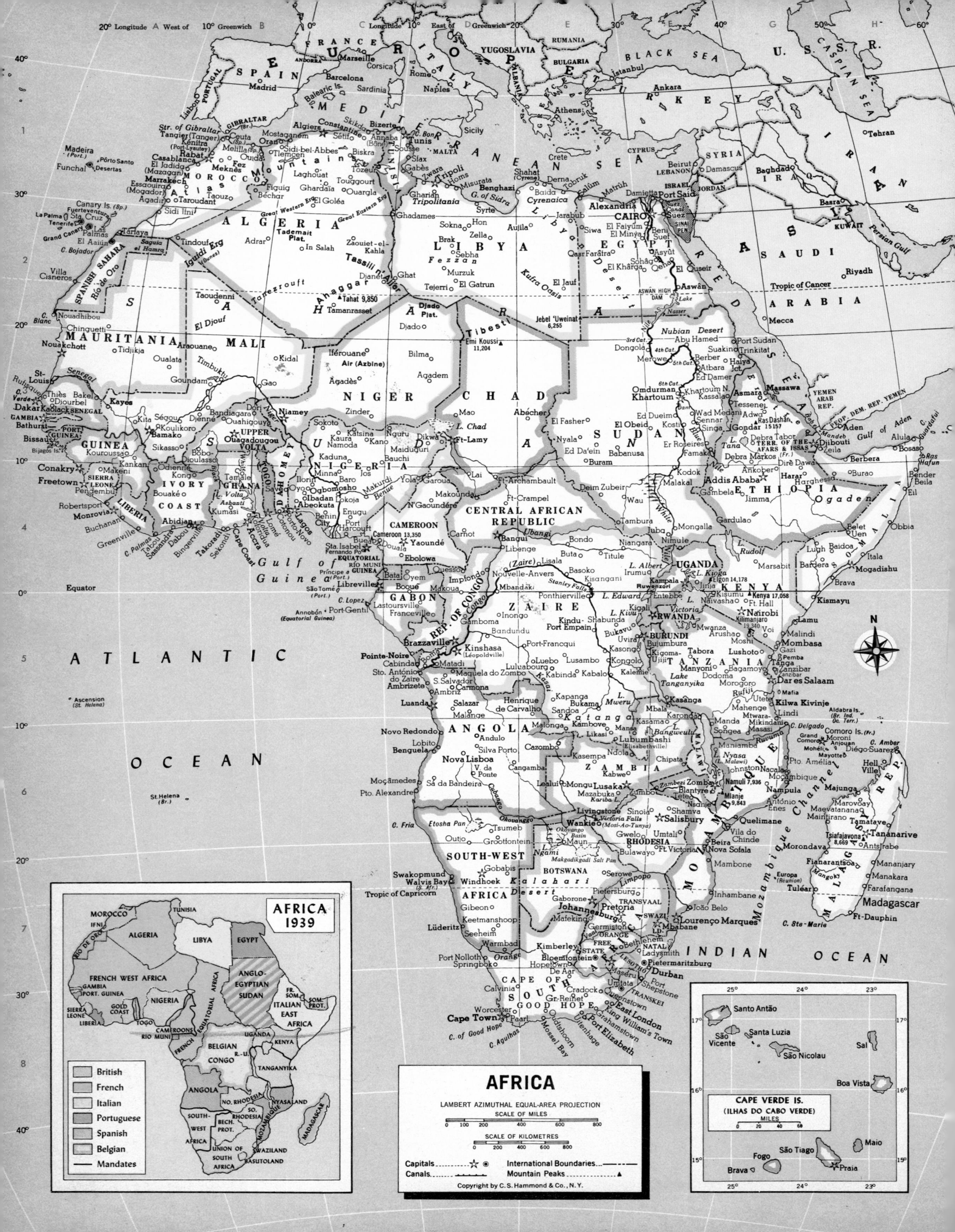

AFRICA

LAMBERT AZIMUTHAL EQUAL-AREA PROJECTION

SCALE OF MILES

0 100 200   400   600   800

SCALE OF KILOMETRES

0   200   400   600   800

Capitals .... ★ ◉   International Boundaries ....
Canals ....   Mountain Peaks .... ▲

Copyright by C. S. Hammond & Co., N.Y.

AFRICA 1939

- British
- French
- Italian
- Portuguese
- Spanish
- Belgian
- — Mandates

CAPE VERDE IS.
(ILHAS DO CABO VERDE)

MILES

0   20   40   60

Africa 103

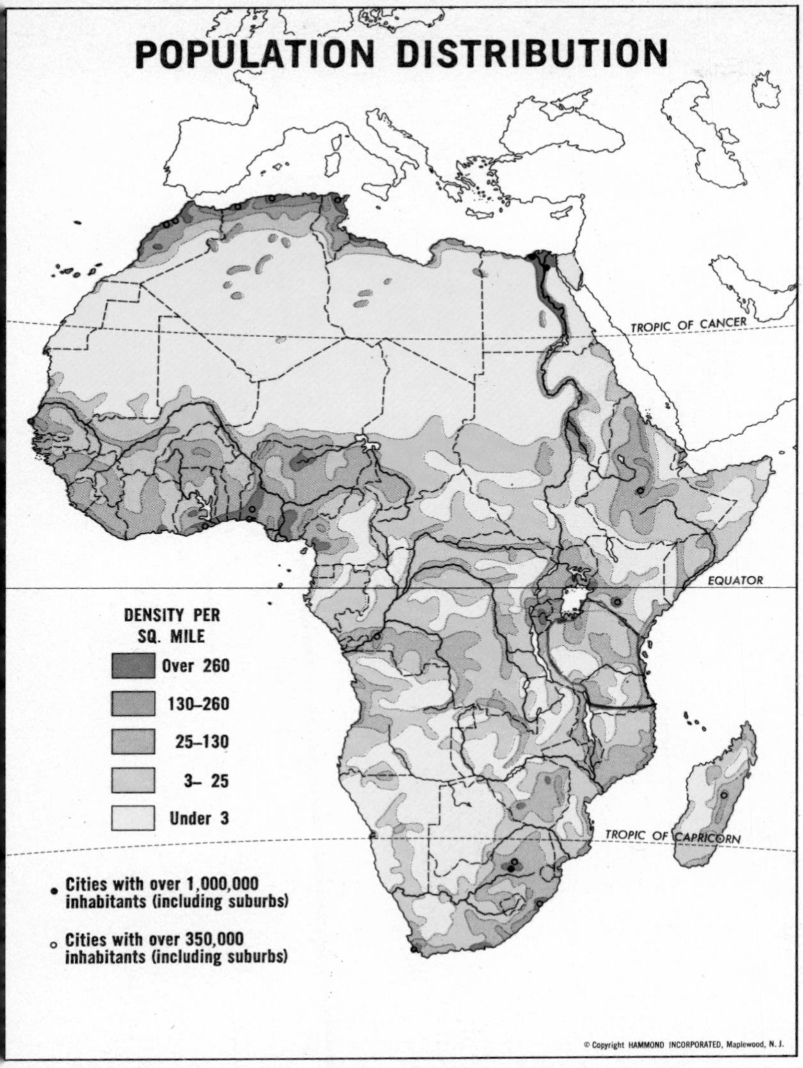
POPULATION DISTRIBUTION
TROPIC OF CANCER
EQUATOR
TROPIC OF CAPRICORN
DENSITY PER SQ. MILE
Over 260
130–260
25–130
3– 25
Under 3
• Cities with over 1,000,000 inhabitants (including suburbs)
○ Cities with over 350,000 inhabitants (including suburbs)
© Copyright HAMMOND INCORPORATED, Maplewood, N. J.

AREA 11,682,000 sq. mi.
POPULATION 345,000,000
LARGEST CITY Cairo
HIGHEST POINT Kilimanjaro 19,340 ft.
LOWEST POINT Qattara Depression -436 ft.

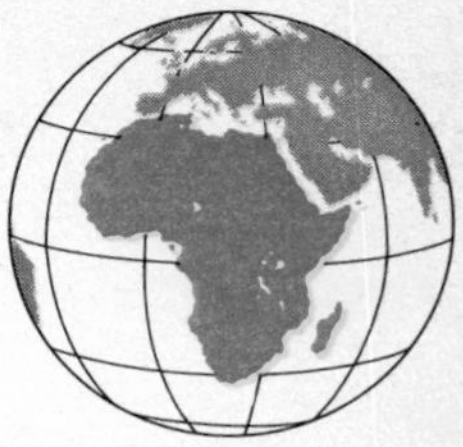

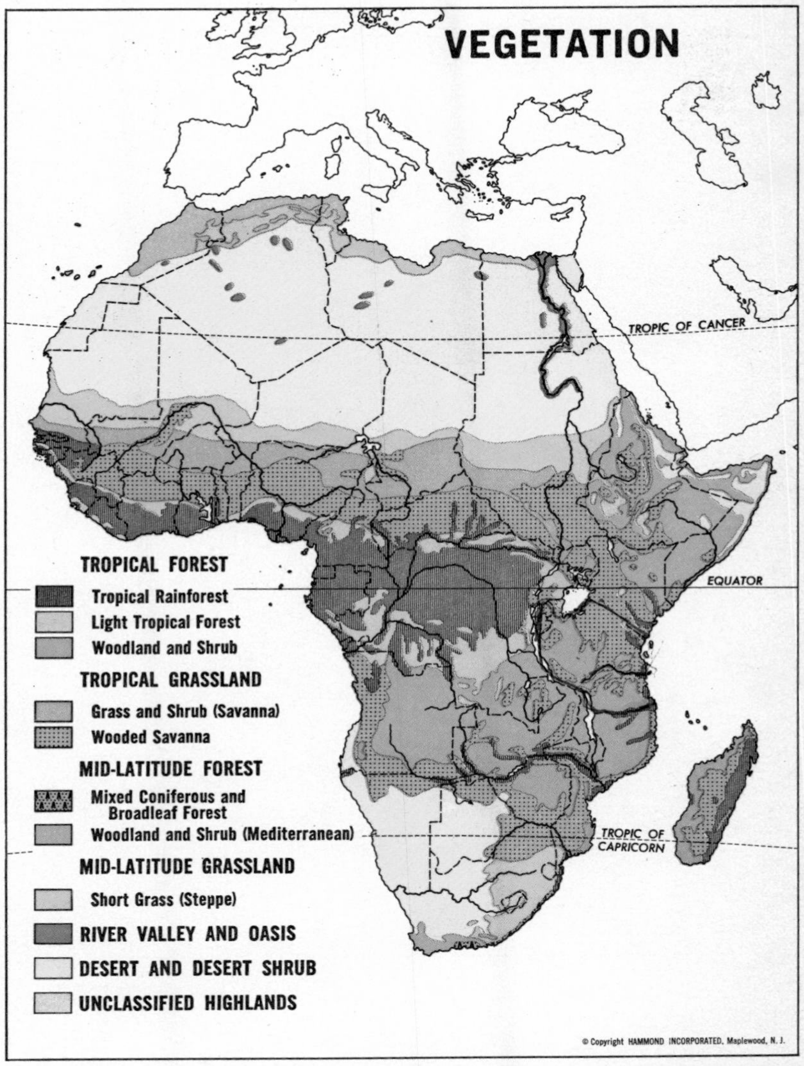
VEGETATION
TROPIC OF CANCER
EQUATOR
TROPIC OF CAPRICORN
TROPICAL FOREST
Tropical Rainforest
Light Tropical Forest
Woodland and Shrub
TROPICAL GRASSLAND
Grass and Shrub (Savanna)
Wooded Savanna
MID-LATITUDE FOREST
Mixed Coniferous and Broadleaf Forest
Woodland and Shrub (Mediterranean)
MID-LATITUDE GRASSLAND
Short Grass (Steppe)
RIVER VALLEY AND OASIS
DESERT AND DESERT SHRUB
UNCLASSIFIED HIGHLANDS
© Copyright HAMMOND INCORPORATED, Maplewood, N. J.

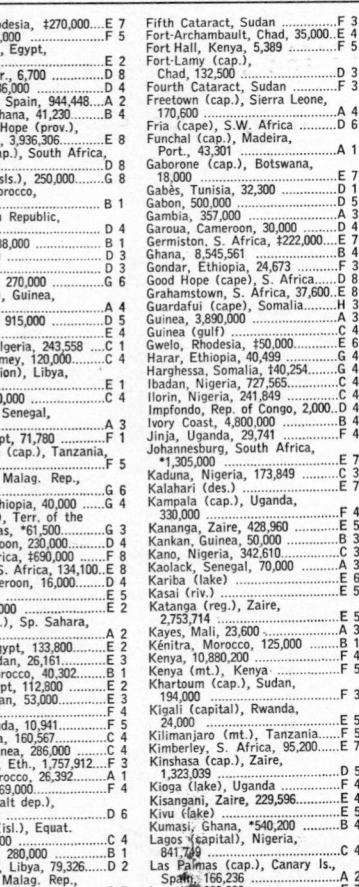

Abécher, Chad, 19,650 ....E 3
Abéokuta, Nigeria, 217,201 ....C 4
Abidjan (cap.), Ivory Coast, *425,000 ....B 4
Accra (capital), Ghana, *848,825 ....B 4
Addis Ababa (cap.), Ethiopia, 644,120 ....F 4
Aden (gulf) ....G 3
Adwa, Ethiopia ....F 3
Afars and Issas, Terr. of the 125,050 ....G 3
Agulhas (cape), S. Africa ....D 8
Ahaggar (mts.), Algeria ....C 2
Albert (lake) ....F 4
Alexandria, Egypt, 1,803,900....E 1
Algeria, 13,547,000 ....C 1
Algiers (cap.), Algeria, *1,800,000 ....C 1
Angola, 5,430,000 ....D 6
Annaba, Algeria, *223,000 ....C 1
Annobón (isl.), Equat. Guinea, 1,408 ....C 5
Antsirabe, Malag. Rep., 29,914....G 6
Ascension (isl.), St. Helena, 1,486 ....A 5
Asmara, Ethiopia, 190,500 ....F 3
Aswân, Egypt, 127,700 ....F 2
Asyût, Egypt, 154,100 ....F 2
Atbara, Sudan, 36,000 ....F 3
Atlas (mts.) ....B 1
Bamako (capital), Mali, *182,000 ....B 3
Bangui (cap.), Central African Rep., *240,000 ....D 4
Bata, Equat. Guinea, 27,024....D 4
Bathurst (cap.), Gambia, *48,333 ....A 3
Beira, Mozambique, †58,235 ....F 6
Benghazi, Libya, 137,295....D 1
Benguela, Angola, 23,256....D 6
Beni Suef, Egypt, 78,829 ....F 2
Benin City, Nigeria, 116,774....C 4
Biskra, Algeria, 59,275....C 1
Bissau (cap.), Port. Guinea, 20,000 ....A 3
Bizerte, Tunisia, 51,700....C 1
Blanc (cape) ....A 2
Blantyre, Malawi, 109,461 ....F 6
Bloemfontein (cap.), O.F.S., S. Africa, ‡147,000 ....E 7
Blue Nile (riv.) ....F 3
Bobo-Dioulasso, Upper Volta, 56,100 ....B 3
Boma, Zaire, 33,143 ....D 5
Bon (cape), Tunisia ....D 1
Bône (Annaba), Algeria, *223,000 ....C 1
Botswana, 629,000 ....E 7
Bouaké, Ivory Coast, 100,000....B 4
Brazzaville (cap.), Rep. of Congo, *200,000 ....D 5
British Indian Ocean Territory, 2,000 ....G 5
Broken Hill, Zambia, ‡67,200....E 6
Bujumbura (cap.), Burundi, 90 000 ....F 5
Bukavu, Zaire, 134,861 ....E 5
Bulawayo, Rhodesia, ‡270,000....E 7
Burundi, 3,475,000 ....F 5
Cairo (capital), Egypt, 4,219,853 ....E 2
Calvinia, S. Afr., 6,700 ....D 8
Cameroon, 5,836,000 ....D 4
Canary (isls.), Spain, 944,448....A 2
Cape Coast, Ghana, 41,230....B 4
Cape of Good Hope (prov.), South Africa, 3,936,306....E 8
Cape Town (cap.), South Africa, ‡817,000 ....D 8
Cape Verde (isls.), 250,000....G 8
Casablanca, Morocco, 1,320,000 ....B 1
Central African Republic, 1,518,000 ....D 4
Ceuta, Spain, 88,000 ....B 1
Chad, 3,510,000 ....D 3
Chad (lake) ....D 3
Comoro (isls.), 270,000 ....G 6
Conakry (cap.), Guinea, *197,267 ....A 4
Congo, Rep. of, 915,000 ....D 5
Congo (riv.) ....E 4
Constantine, Algeria, 243,558 ....C 1
Cotonou, Dahomey, 120,000....C 4
Cyrenaica (region), Libya, 450,954 ....E 1
Dahomey, 2,640,000 ....C 4
Dakar (cap.), Senegal, *661,000 ....A 3
Damietta, Egypt, 71,780 ....F 1
Dar es Salaam (cap.), Tanzania, 272,821 ....F 5
Diégo-Suarez, Malag. Rep., 40,237 ....G 6
Dire Dawa, Ethiopia, 40,000 ....G 4
Djibouti (cap.), Terr. of the Afars & Issas, *61,500....G 3
Douala, Cameroon, 230,000....D 4
Durban, S. Africa, ‡690,000 ....F 8
East London, S. Africa, 134,100..E 8
Ebolowa, Cameroon, 16,000....D 4
Edward (lake) ....E 5
Egypt, 33,329,000 ....E 2
El Aaiún (cap.), Sp. Sahara, 10,000 ....A 2
El Faiyûm, Egypt, 133,800....E 2
El Fasher, Sudan, 26,161....E 3
El Jadida, Morocco, 40,302....B 1
El Minya, Egypt, 112,800 ....E 2
El Obeid, Sudan, 53,000....E 3
Elgon (mt.) ....F 4
Entebbe, Uganda, 10,941....F 5
Enugu, Nigeria, 160,567....C 4
Equatorial Guinea, 286,000 ....C 4
Eritrea (reg.), Eth., 1,757,912....F 3
Essaouira, Morocco, 26,392....A 1
Ethiopia, 24,769,000....F 4
Etosha Pan (salt dep.), S. W. Africa ....D 6
Fernando Po (isl.), Equat. Guinea, 78,000 ....C 4
Fez, Morocco, 280,000 ....B 1
Fezzan (reg.), Libya, 79,326....D 2
Fianarantsoa, Malag. Rep., 45,790 ....G 7
Fifth Cataract, Sudan ....F 3
Fort-Archambault, Chad, 35,000..E 4
Fort Hall, Kenya, 5,389 ....F 5
Fort-Lamy (cap.), Chad, 132,500 ....D 3
Fourth Cataract, Sudan ....F 3
Freetown (cap.), Sierra Leone, 170,600 ....A 4
Fria (cape), S.W. Africa ....D 6
Funchal (cap.), Madeira, Port., 43,301 ....A 1
Gaborone (cap.), Botswana, 18,000 ....E 7
Gabès, Tunisia, 32,300 ....D 1
Gabon, 500,000 ....D 5
Gambia, 357,000 ....A 3
Garoua, Cameroon, 30,000 ....D 4
Germiston, S. Africa, ‡222,000....E 7
Ghana, 8,545,561 ....B 4
Gondar, Ethiopia, 24,673 ....F 3
Good Hope (cape), S. Africa....D 8
Grahamstown, S. Africa, 37,600..E 8
Guardafui (cape), Somalia....H 3
Guinea, 3,890,000 ....A 3
Guinea (gulf) ....C 4
Gwelo, Rhodesia, ‡50,000....E 6
Harar, Ethiopia, 40,499 ....G 4
Harghessa, Somalia, †40,254....G 4
Ibadan, Nigeria, 727,565....C 4
Ilorin, Nigeria, 241,849 ....C 4
Impfondo, Rep. of Congo, 2,000..D 4
Ivory Coast, 4,800,000 ....B 4
Jinja, Uganda, 29,741 ....F 4
Johannesburg, South Africa, *1,305,000 ....E 7
Kaduna, Nigeria, 173,849 ....C 3
Kalahari (des.) ....E 7
Kampala (cap.), Uganda, 330,000 ....F 4
Kananga, Zaire, 428,960 ....E 5
Kankan, Guinea, 50,000 ....B 3
Kano, Nigeria, 342,610....C 3
Kaolack, Senegal, 70,000 ....A 3
Kariba (lake) ....E 6
Kasai (riv.) ....E 5
Katanga (reg.), Zaire, 2,753,714 ....E 5
Kayes, Mali, 23,600 ....A 3
Kénitra, Morocco, 125,000 ....B 1
Kenya, 10,880,200 ....F 4
Kenya (mt.), Kenya ....F 5
Khartoum (cap.), Sudan, 194,000 ....F 3
Kigali (capital), Rwanda, 24,000 ....E 5
Kilimanjaro (mt.), Tanzania....F 5
Kimberley, S. Africa, 95,200....E 7
Kinshasa (cap.), Zaire, 1,323,039 ....D 5
Kioga (lake), Uganda ....F 4
Kisangani, Zaire, 229,596....E 4
Kivu (lake) ....E 5
Kumasi, Ghana, *540,200 ....B 4
Lagos (capital), Nigeria, 841,749 ....C 4
Las Palmas (cap.), Canary Is., Spain, 166,236 ....A 2
Lesotho, 930,000 ....E 7
Liberia, 1,200,000 ....B 4
Libreville (cap.), Gabon, *57,000 ....C 4
Libya, 1,900,000 ....D 2
Libyan (des.) ....E 2
Likasi, Zaire, 146,394 ....E 6
Limpopo (riv.) ....E 7
Livingstone, Zambia, ‡33,440 ....E 6
Lobito, Angola, 50,164 ....D 6
Lokoja, Nigeria, 13,103 ....C 4
Lomé (cap.), Togo, *149,879....C 4
Lourenço Marques (cap.), Mozambique, *177,929 ....F 7
Luanda (cap.), Angola, 400,000..D 5
Lubumbashi, Zaire, 318,000 ....E 6
Lusaka (cap.), Zambia, ‡238,200 ....E 6
Madagascar (isl.) ....G 7
Madeira (isls.), Port., 268,700....A 1
Maiduguri, Nigerja, 162,316....D 3
Majunga, Malag. Rep., 47,654....G 6
Malagasy Republic, 7,011,563 ....G 6
Malawi, 4,530,000 ....F 6
Mali, 4,929,000 ....B 3
Marrakech, Morocco, 295,000....A 1
Maseru (cap.), Lesotho, 18,797..E 8
Matadi, Zaire, 110,436 ....D 5
Maun, Botswana, 4,591 ....E 6
Mauritania, 1,140,000 ....A 3
Mbabane (cap.), Swaziland, 13,803 ....F 7
Mbandaka, Zaire, 107,910 ....E 4
Meknès, Morocco, 235,000 ....B 1
Melilla, Spain, 77,000 ....B 1
Merowe, Sudan, 1,620 ....F 3
Mogadishu (Mogadiscio) (cap.), Somalia, 172,677 ....G 4
Mombasa, Kenya, 234,400 ....G 5
Monrovia (cap.), Liberia, *100,000 ....A 4
Morocco, 15,577,000 ....B 1
Moroni (cap.), Comoro Is., 11,515 ....G 6
Mostaganem, Algeria, 75,332 ....B 1
Mozambique, 7,376,000 ....F 6
Mozambique (channel) ....G 6
Nairobi (cap.), Kenya, 477,600..F 5
Nasser (lake) ....F 2
Natal (prov.), S. Afr., 2,979,920..F 7
Ndola, Zambia, ‡150,800 ....E 6
N'Gaoundéré, Cam., 15,000 ....D 4
Niamey (cap.), Niger, *122,672..C 3
Niger, 4,016,000 ....C, D 3
Niger (river) ....C 3
Nigeria, 66,174,000 ....C 4
Nile (river) ....F 2
Nouakchott (cap.), Mauritania, 14,500 ....A 3
Nova Lisboa, Angola, 109,000 ....D 6
Nubian (des.), Sudan ....F 2
Nyasa (lake) ....F 6
Omdurman, Sudan, 206,000....F 3
Oran, Algeria, *393,000 ....B 1
Orange (river) ....D 7
Orange Free State (prov.), South Africa, 1,386,547....E 7
Ouagadougou (cap.), Upper Volta, *100,000 ....B 3
Oujda, Morocco, 150,000....B 1
Oyo, Nigeria, 130,290 ....C 4
Palmas (cape) ....B 4
Pemba (isl.), Tanzania, 164,321 ....G 5
Pietermaritzburg (cap.), Natal, S. Africa, ‡128,598 ....F 7
Pointe-Noire, Rep. of Congo, 100,000 ....D 5
Port Elizabeth, S. Africa, ‡448,000 ....E 8
Port Harcourt, Nigeria, 208,237..C 4
Port Said, Egypt, 283,400 ....F 1
Port Sudan, Sudan, 110,000....F 3
Porto-Novo (cap.), Dahomey, 80,000 ....C 4
Portuguese Guinea, 530,000....A 3
Praia (cap.), Cape Verde Is., 3,628 ....G 8
Pretoria (cap.), S. Africa, 479,700 ....E 7
Qena, Egypt, 57,417 ....F 2
Quelimane, Moz., †62,717 ....F 6
Rabat (cap.), Morocco, *435,000 ....B 1
Red (sea) ....F 2
Rhodesia, 5,310,000 ....E 6
Río de Oro (reg.), Sp. Sahara...A 2
Río Muni (terr.), Equat. Guinea, 203,000 ....C 4
Rudolf (lake), Kenya ....F 4
Rufisque, Senegal, 50,000 ....A 3
Rwanda, 3,500,000 ....F 5
Ruwenzori (range) ....E 4
Sahara (desert) ....C 2
Saint Helena (isl.), 4,707 ....B 6
Saint-Louis, Senegal, 50,000....A 3
Salisbury (cap.), Rhodesia, ‡423,000 ....F 6
Santa Cruz (cap.), Canary Is., Spain, 82,620 ....A 2
Santa Isabel (cap.), Equat. Guinea, 37,237 ....C 4
Sekondi-Takoradi, Ghana, *209,400 ....B 4
Senegal, 3,780,000 ....A 3
Serowe, Botswana, 35,000 ....E 7
Sétif, Algeria, 98,337 ....C 1
Sfax, Tunisia, 65,000 ....D 1
Sidi-bel-Abbès, Algeria, 91,527....C 1
Sierra Leone, 2,512,000 ....A 4
Sinai (pen.), Egypt, 49,769 ....F 2
Sixth Cataract, Sudan ....F 3
Skikda, Algeria, 72,742 ....C 1
Sohâg, Egypt, 61,944 ....F 2
Somalia, 2,730,000 ....G 4
Sousse, Tunisia, 48,200 ....D 1
South Africa, 21,282,000 ....E 7
South-West Africa, 615,000 ....D 7
Spanish Sahara (prov.), Spain, 63,000 ....A 2
Stanley (falls), Zaire ....E 4
Sudan, 15,312,000 ....E 3
Suez, Egypt, 264,500 ....F 2
Suez (canal), Egypt ....F 1
Swaziland, 411,879 ....F 7
Tamale, Ghana, 40,443....B 4
Tamatave, Malag. Rep., 53,173...G 6
Tana (lake), Ethiopia....F 3
Tananarive (cap.), Malag. Rep., *447,016 ....G 6
Tanga, Tanzania, 61,058 ....F 5
Tanganyika (lake) ....F 5
Tangier, Morocco, 160,000....B 1
Tanzania, 12,896,000 ....F 5
Taouz, Morocco, 641 ....B 1
Thiès, Senegal, 70,000 ....A 3
Third Cataract, Sudan ....E 3
Tibesti (mts.) ....D 2
Timbuktu, Mali, 14,900 ....B 3
Tlemcen, Algeria, 87,210....B 1
Togo, 2,004,711 ....C 4
Transkei (prov.), S. Africa, 1,439,195 ....E 8
Transvaal (prov.), S. Africa, 6,273,477 ....E 7
Tripoli (cap.), Libya, 247,365....D 1
Tripolitania (reg.), Libya, 1,034,089 ....D 1
Tuléar, Malag. Rep., 33,842....G 7
Tunis (cap.), Tunisia, *800,000....D 1
Tunisia, 5,027,000 ....C 1
Ubangi (river) ....E 3
Uganda, 9,764,000 ....F 4
Uitenhage, S. Africa, 63,400....E 8
Umtali, Rhodesia, ‡50,000 ....F 6
Umtata (cap.), Transkei, South Africa, 17,200....E 8
Upper Volta, 5,330,000 ....B 3
Vaal (riv.), S. Africa ....E 7
Verde (cape), Senegal ....A 3
Victoria (falls) ....E 6
Victoria (lake) ....F 5
Volta (lake), Ghana ....B 4
Volta (river) ....C 4
Wad Medani, Sudan, 48,000 ....F 3
Walvis Bay, S. Africa, 12,234....D 7
White Nile (river)....F 4
Windhoek (cap.), S.W. Africa, 36,050 ....D 7
Yaoundé (cap.), Cameroon, 130,000 ....D 4
Zaire, 21,637,876 ....E 5
Zaire (Congo) (riv.) ....E 4
Zambezi (river) ....E 6
Zambia, 4,056,995 ....E 6
Zanzibar, Tanzania, *95,047 ....G 5
Zanzibar (isl.), Tanzania, 190,494 ....G 5
Zomba (cap.), Malawi, 19,666....F 6

*City and suburbs.
†Population of sub-district.
‡Population of urban or met. area.

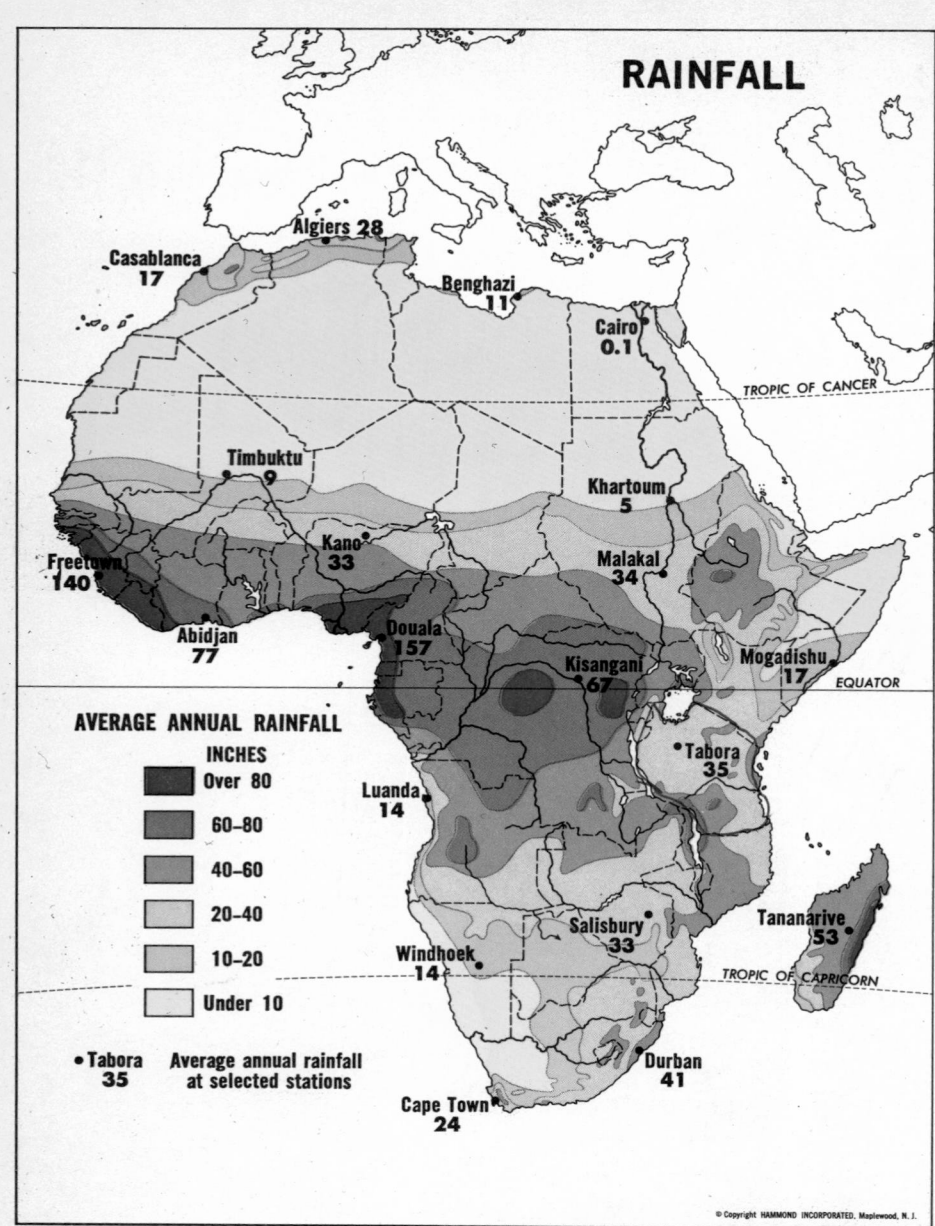

RAINFALL

Algiers **28**

Casablanca **17**

Benghazi **11**

Cairo **0.1**

TROPIC OF CANCER

Timbuktu **9**

Khartoum **5**

Kano **33**

Malakal **34**

Freetown **140**

Abidjan **77**

Douala **157**

Kisangani **67**

Mogadishu **17**

EQUATOR

Tabora **35**

AVERAGE ANNUAL RAINFALL
INCHES

- Over 80
- 60–80
- 40–60
- 20–40
- 10–20
- Under 10

Luanda **14**

•Tabora
35 Average annual rainfall at selected stations

Salisbury **33**

Windhoek **14**

Tananarive **53**

TROPIC OF CAPRICORN

Durban **41**

Cape Town **24**

© Copyright HAMMOND INCORPORATED, Maplewood, N.J.

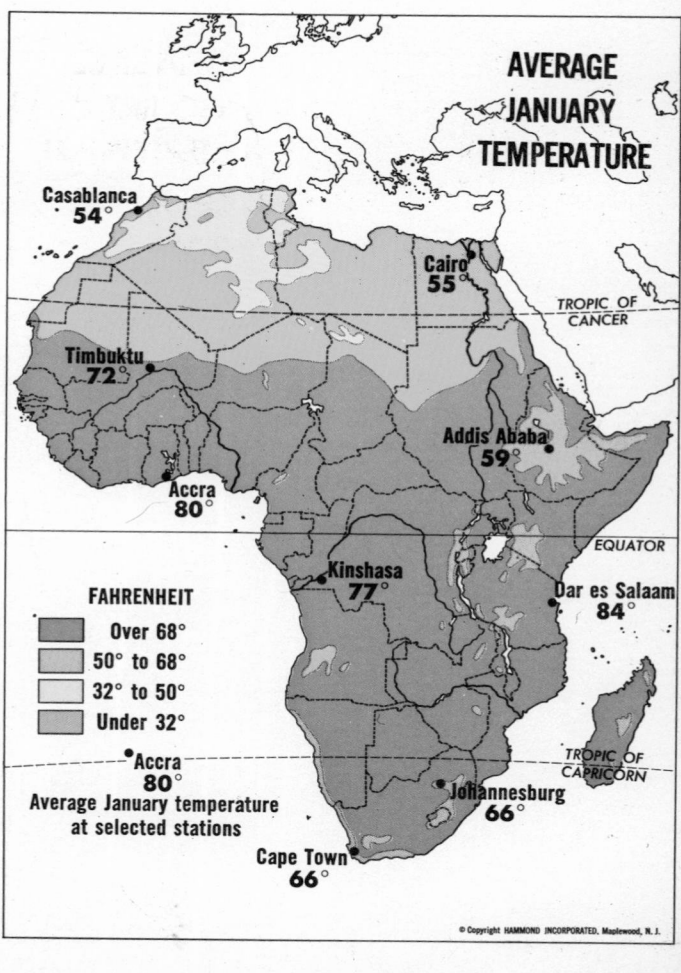

AVERAGE JANUARY TEMPERATURE

Casablanca **54**

Cairo **55**

TROPIC OF CANCER

Timbuktu **72°**

Addis Ababa **59**

Accra **80°**

EQUATOR

Kinshasa **77°**

Dar es Salaam **84°**

FAHRENHEIT

- Over 68°
- 50° to 68°
- 32° to 50°
- Under 32°

•Accra
80°
Average January temperature at selected stations

Johannesburg **66°**

TROPIC OF CAPRICORN

Cape Town **66°**

© Copyright HAMMOND INCORPORATED, Maplewood, N.J.

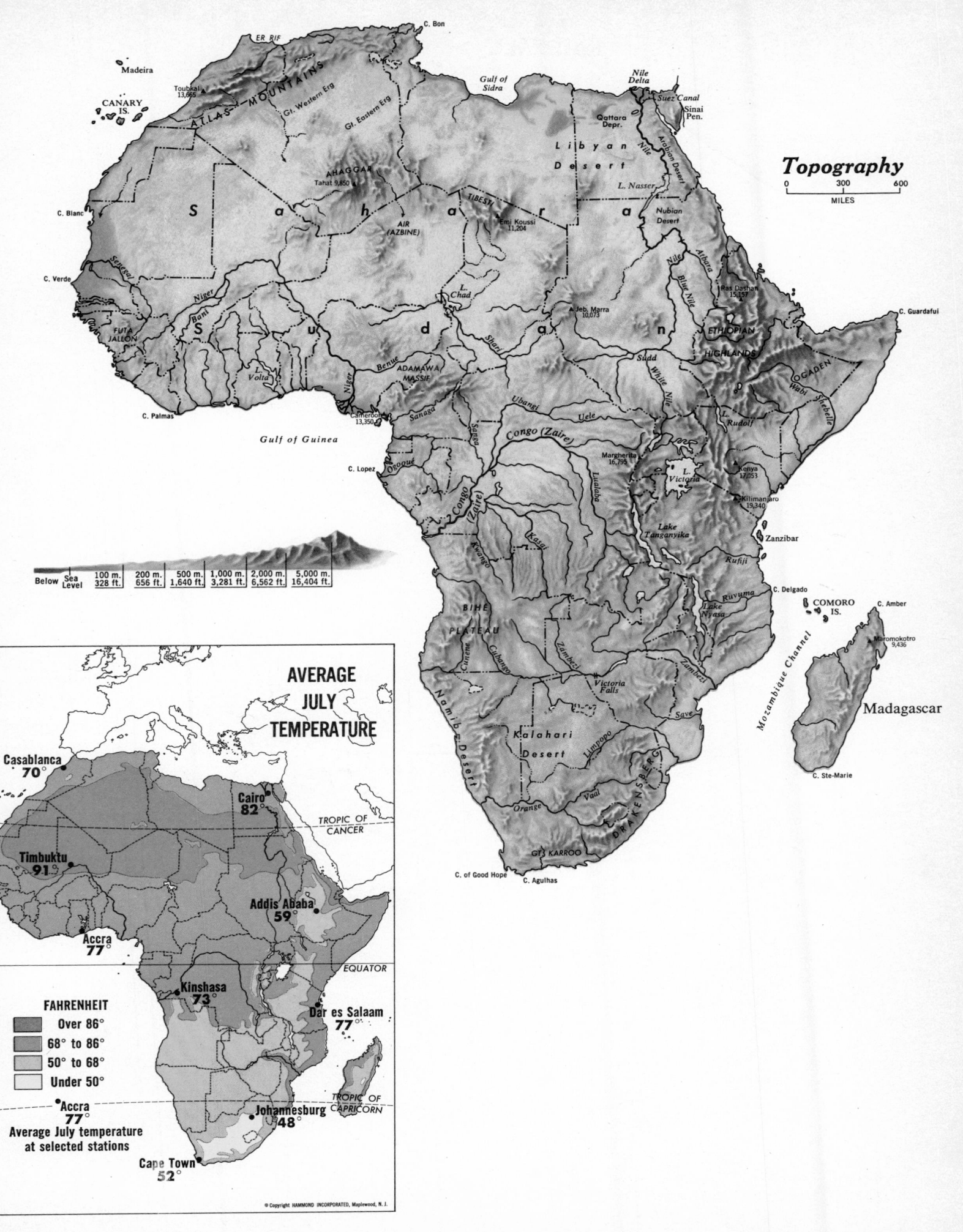

Topography

```
0        300      600
        MILES
```

Madeira

CANARY IS.

ER RIF

C. Bon

ATLAS MOUNTAINS

Toubkal 13,665

Gt. Western Erg

Gt. Eastern Erg

Gulf of Sidra

Nile Delta

Suez Canal

Sinai Pen.

Qattara Depr.

Libyan Desert

L. Nasser

Nubian Desert

Arabian Desert

S a h a r a

AHAGGAR Tahat 9,850

AIR (AZBINE)

TIBESTI

Emi Koussi 11,204

C. Blanc

C. Verde

Senegal

Niger

Boni

FUTA JALLON

S   u   d   a   n

L. Chad

Shari

A Jeb. Marra 10,073

Blue Nile

Atbara

Nile

Ras Dashan 15,157

ETHIOPIAN HIGHLANDS

C. Guardafui

OGADEN

L. Volta

Benue

Sanaga

ADAMAWA MASSIF

C. Palmas

Cameroon 13,350

Gulf of Guinea

C. Lopez

Ogooue

Sangha

Ubangi

Uele

White Nile

Sudd

Congo (Zaire)

Wabi Shebelle

L. Rudolf

Congo (Zaire)

Lualaba

Kasai

Margherita 16,795

L. Victoria

Kenya 17,053

Kilimanjaro 19,340

Lake Tanganyika

Zanzibar

Kwango

Kwilu

Rufiji

Lake Nyasa

Ruvuma

C. Delgado

COMORO IS.

C. Amber

Maromokotro 9,436

BIHE PLATEAU

Cunene

Cubango

Zambezi

Victoria Falls

Zambezi

Save

Mozambique Channel

Madagascar

Namib Desert

Kalahari Desert

Limpopo

Vaal

Orange

DRAKENSBERG

GT. KARROO

C. of Good Hope

C. Agulhas

C. Ste-Marie

```
Below Sea    100 m.    200 m.    500 m.    1,000 m.   2,000 m.   5,000 m.
Level        328 ft.   656 ft.   1,640 ft. 3,281 ft.  6,562 ft.  16,404 ft.
```

AVERAGE JULY TEMPERATURE

Casablanca 70°

Cairo 82°

TROPIC OF CANCER

Timbuktu 91°

Addis Ababa 59°

Accra 77°

EQUATOR

Kinshasa 73°

Dar es Salaam 77°

TROPIC OF CAPRICORN

FAHRENHEIT

	Over 86°
	68° to 86°
	50° to 68°
	Under 50°

Accra 77°
Average July temperature at selected stations

Johannesburg 48°

Cape Town 52°

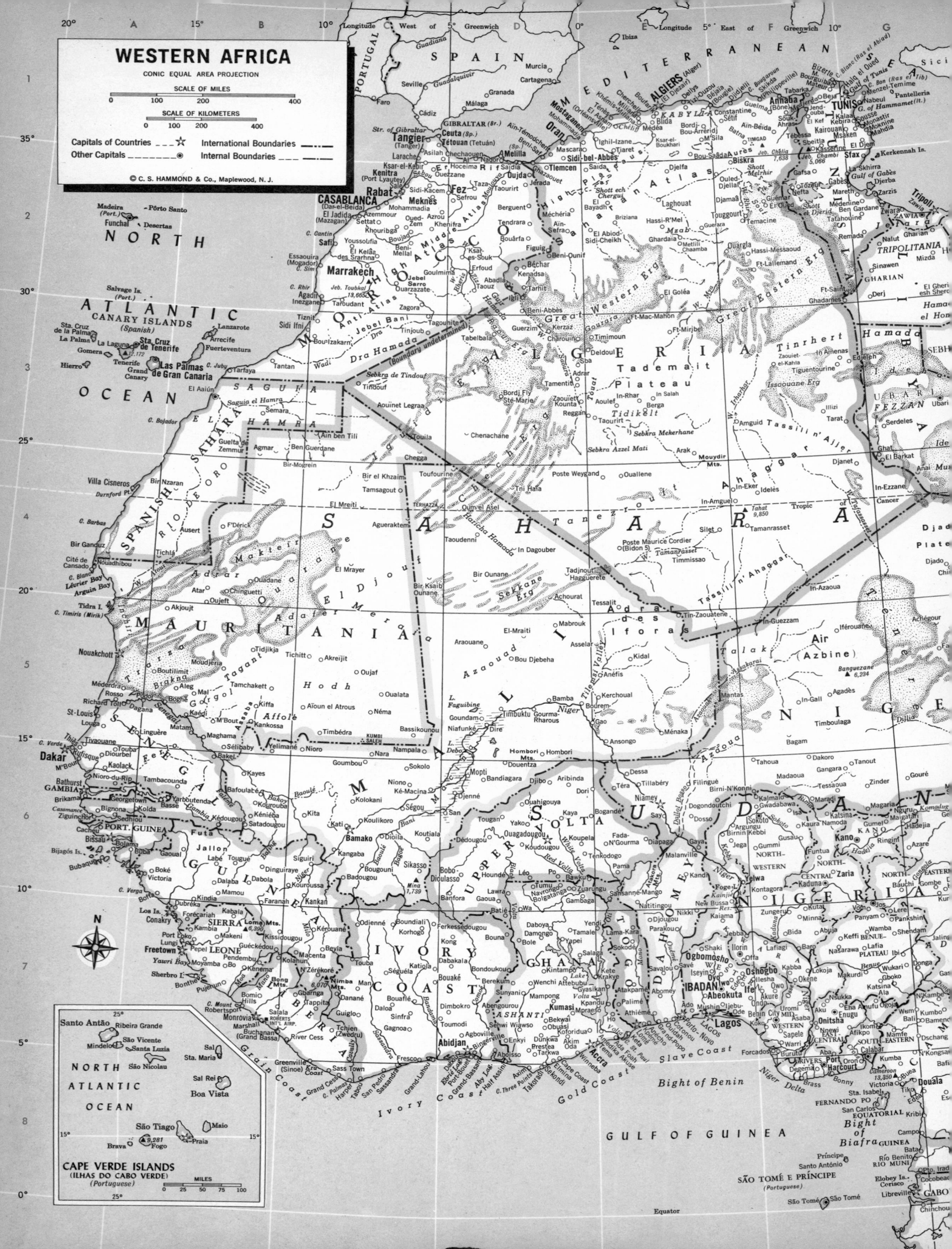

WESTERN AFRICA

CONIC EQUAL AREA PROJECTION

SCALE OF MILES
0   100   200   400

SCALE OF KILOMETERS
0   100   200   400

Capitals of Countries ____★____   International Boundaries _____
Other Capitals _____◉   Internal Boundaries ___ ___ ___

© C. S. HAMMOND & Co., Maplewood, N. J.

CAPE VERDE ISLANDS
(ILHAS DO CABO VERDE)
(Portuguese)

Santo Antão
Ribeira Grande
São Vicente
Mindelo · Santa Luzia
São Nicolau
Sal
Sta. Maria
Sal Rei
Boa Vista

NORTH
ATLANTIC
OCEAN

São Tiago
Maio
Brava ▲9,281 Praia
Fogo

MILES
0   25   50   75   100

ALGERIA
AREA 919,595 sq. mi.
POPULATION 13,547,000
CAPITAL Algiers
LARGEST CITY Algiers
HIGHEST POINT Tahat 9,850 ft.
MONETARY UNIT Algerian franc
MAJOR LANGUAGES Arabic, Berber, French
MAJOR RELIGION Islam

DAHOMEY
AREA 44,290 sq. mi.
POPULATION 2,640,000
CAPITAL Porto-Novo
LARGEST CITY Cotonou
HIGHEST POINT Atakora Mts. 2,083 ft.
MONETARY UNIT CFA franc
MAJOR LANGUAGES Fon, Somba, Yoruba, Bariba, French
MAJOR RELIGIONS Tribal religions, Islam, Roman Catholicism

GAMBIA
AREA 4,003 sq. mi.
POPULATION 357,000
CAPITAL Bathurst
LARGEST CITY Bathurst
HIGHEST POINT 100 ft.
MONETARY UNIT West African pound
MAJOR LANGUAGES Mandingo, Fulani, Wolof, English
MAJOR RELIGIONS Islam, Tribal religions, Christianity

GHANA
AREA 91,843 sq. mi.
POPULATION 8,545,561
CAPITAL Accra
LARGEST CITY Accra
HIGHEST POINT Togo Hills 2,900 ft.
MONETARY UNIT cedi
MAJOR LANGUAGES Twi, Fante, Dagomba, Ewe, Ga, English
MAJOR RELIGIONS Tribal religions, Christianity

GUINEA
AREA 94,925 sq. mi.
POPULATION 3,890,000
CAPITAL Conakry
LARGEST CITY Conakry
HIGHEST POINT Nimba Mts. 6,070 ft.
MONETARY UNIT Guinean franc
MAJOR LANGUAGES Fulani, Mandingo, Susu, French
MAJOR RELIGIONS Islam, Tribal religions

IVORY COAST
AREA 124,503 sq. mi.
POPULATION 4,800,000
CAPITAL Abidjan
LARGEST CITY Abidjan
HIGHEST POINT Nimba Mts. 5,745 ft.
MONETARY UNIT CFA franc
MAJOR LANGUAGES Bale, Bete, Senufu, French
MAJOR RELIGIONS Tribal religions, Islam

LIBERIA
AREA 43,000 sq. mi.
POPULATION 1,200,000
CAPITAL Monrovia
LARGEST CITY Monrovia
HIGHEST POINT Wutivi 5,584 ft.
MONETARY UNIT Liberian dollar
MAJOR LANGUAGES Kru, Kpelle, Bassa, Vai, English
MAJOR RELIGIONS Christianity, Tribal religions

MALI
AREA 463,948 sq. mi.
POPULATION 4,929,000
CAPITAL Bamako
LARGEST CITY Bamako
HIGHEST POINT Hombori Mts. 3,789 ft.
MONETARY UNIT Malian franc
MAJOR LANGUAGES Bambara, Senufu, Fulani, Soninke, French
MAJOR RELIGIONS Islam, Tribal religions

MAURITANIA
AREA 397,954 sq. mi.
POPULATION 1,140,000
CAPITAL Nouakchott
LARGEST CITY Nouakchott
HIGHEST POINT 2,972 ft.
MONETARY UNIT CFA franc
MAJOR LANGUAGES Arabic, French, Wolof
MAJOR RELIGION Islam

MOROCCO
AREA 172,413 sq. mi.
POPULATION 15,577,000
CAPITAL Rabat
LARGEST CITY Casablanca
HIGHEST POINT Jeb. Toubkal 13,665 ft.
MONETARY UNIT dirham
MAJOR LANGUAGES Arabic, Berber, French
MAJOR RELIGIONS Islam, Judaism

NIGER
AREA 489,189 sq. mi
POPULATION 4,016,000
CAPITAL Niamey
LARGEST CITY Niamey
HIGHEST POINT Banguezane 6,234 ft.
MONETARY UNIT CFA franc
MAJOR LANGUAGES Hausa, Songhai, Fulani, French
MAJOR RELIGIONS Islam, Tribal religions

NIGERIA
AREA 356,669 sq. mi.
POPULATION 66,174,000
CAPITAL Lagos
LARGEST CITY Lagos
HIGHEST POINT Vogel 6,700 ft.
MONETARY UNIT naira
MAJOR LANGUAGES Hausa, Yoruba, Ibo, Fulani, Tiv, Kanuri, Ibibio, English
MAJOR RELIGIONS Islam, Christianity

PORTUGUESE GUINEA
AREA 13,948 sq. mi.
POPULATION 530,000
CAPITAL Bissau
LARGEST CITY Bissau
HIGHEST POINT 689 ft.
MONETARY UNIT Portuguese escudo
MAJOR LANGUAGES Balante, Fulani, Mandjako, Mandingo, Portuguese
MAJOR RELIGIONS Islam, Tribal religions, Roman Catholicism

SENEGAL
AREA 75,750 sq. mi.
POPULATION 3,780,000
CAPITAL Dakar
LARGEST CITY Dakar
HIGHEST POINT Futa Jallon 1,640 ft.
MONETARY UNIT CFA franc
MAJOR LANGUAGES Wolof, Fulani, Serer, French
MAJOR RELIGIONS Islam, Tribal religions, Roman Catholicism

SIERRA LEONE
AREA 27,925 sq. mi.
POPULATION 2,512,000
CAPITAL Freetown
LARGEST CITY Freetown
HIGHEST POINT Loma Mts. 6,390 ft.
MONETARY UNIT leone
MAJOR LANGUAGES Mende, Temne, Vai, English
MAJOR RELIGIONS Tribal religions, Islam, Christianity

SPANISH SAHARA
AREA 102,702 sq. mi.
POPULATION 63,000
CAPITAL El Aaiún
LARGEST CITY El Aaiún
HIGHEST POINT 2,700 ft.
MONETARY UNIT Spanish peseta
MAJOR LANGUAGES Arabic, Spanish
MAJOR RELIGION Islam

TOGO
AREA 21,853 sq. mi.
POPULATION 2,004,711
CAPITAL Lomé
LARGEST CITY Lomé
HIGHEST POINT Agou 3,445 ft.
MONETARY UNIT CFA franc
MAJOR LANGUAGES Ewe, Kabre, Gurma, French
MAJOR RELIGIONS Tribal religions, Roman Catholicism, Islam

TUNISIA
AREA 63,378 sq. mi.
POPULATION 5,027,000
CAPITAL Tunis
LARGEST CITY Tunis
HIGHEST POINT Jeb. Chambi 5,066 ft.
MONETARY UNIT Tunisian dinar
MAJOR LANGUAGES Arabic, French
MAJOR RELIGION Islam

UPPER VOLTA
AREA 105,841 sq. mi.
POPULATION 5,330,000
CAPITAL Ouagadougou
LARGEST CITY Ouagadougou
HIGHEST POINT 2,352 ft.
MONETARY UNIT CFA franc
MAJOR LANGUAGES Mossi, Lobi, Fulani, Bobo, French
MAJOR RELIGIONS Islam, Tribal religions, Roman Catholicism

CAPE VERDE ISLANDS
AREA 1,557 sq. mi.
POPULATION 250,000
CAPITAL Praia

SÃO TOMÉ E PRÍNCIPE
AREA 372 sq. mi.
POPULATION 66,000
CAPITAL São Tomé

Topography

0   200   400   600
MILES

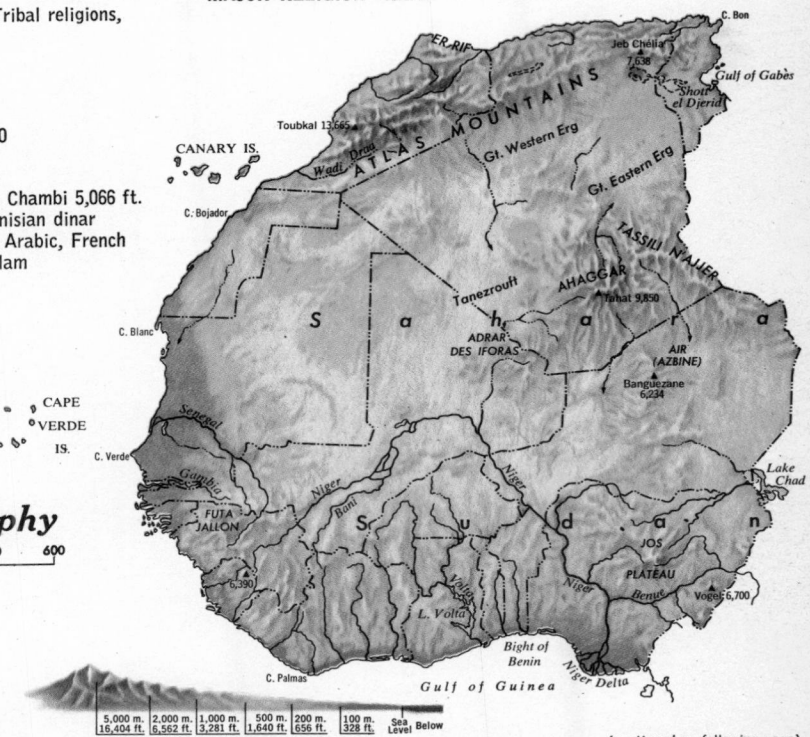

(continued on following page)

(continued)

ALGERIA

CITIES and TOWNS

Abadla, 7,288 .... D 2
Adrar, 13,332 .... D 3
Aïn-Béïda, 30,757 .... F 1
Aïn-Sefra, 16,818 .... D 2
Aïn-Témouchent, 33,481 .... D 1
Algiers (cap.), 943,142 .... E 1
Algiers, *1,800,000 .... E 1
Amguid .... F 3
Annaba, 152,006 .... F 1
Annaba, *223,000 .... F 1
Aoulef, 11,285 .... E 3
Arak .... E 3
Batna, 69,090 .... F 1
Béchar, 46,505 .... D 2
Béjaïa, 64,876 .... F 1
Beni-Abbès, 3,943 .... D 2
Beni-Ounif, 5,271 .... D 2
Beni-Saf, 23,368 .... D 1
Berga .... E 3
Bidon 5 (Poste Maurice Cordier) .... E 4
Biskra, 59,275 .... F 2
Blida, 99,238 .... E 1
Bordj-Bou-Arréridj, 43,494 .... E 1
Bordj Fly Sainte-Marie .... D 3
Boufarik, 33,881 .... E 1
Bougie (Béjaïa), 64,876 .... F 1
Bou-Saâda, 26,262 .... E 1
Briziana, 7,498 .... E 2
Charouïn .... D 3
Cherchell, 27,464 .... E 1
Constantine, 243,558 .... F 1
Deldoul .... F 3
Dellys, 23,718 .... E 1
Djamaâ, 25,925 .... F 2
Djanet .... F 4
Djelfa, 30,304 .... E 2
Djidjelli, 35,371 .... F 1
Edjeleh .... F 3
El Abiod-Sidi-Cheikh, 10,512 .... E 2
El Asnam, 69,745 .... E 1
El Bayadh, 24,770 .... E 2
El Djezair (Algiers) (cap.), 943,142 .... E 1
El Goléa, 16,679 .... E 2
El Oued, 43,547 .... F 2
Fort-Lallemand .... F 2
Fort-Mac-Mahon .... E 3
Fort-Miribel .... E 3
Ghardaïa, 46,609 .... E 2
Ghazaouet, 20,785 .... D 2
Guelma, 39,817 .... F 1
Guémar, 20,394 .... F 2
Guerara, 14,173 .... E 2
Guerzim .... D 3
Hassi-Messaoud .... F 2
Hassi-R'Mel .... E 2
Idelès .... F 4
Ighil-Izane, 43,547 .... E 1
Igli, 2,912 .... D 2
Illizi, 4,000 .... F 3
In-Amenas .... F 3
In-Amguel .... E 4
In-Eker .... F 4
In-Rhar .... E 3
In Salah, 12,645 .... E 3
Kenadsa, 7,258 .... D 2
Kerzaz, 2,492 .... D 3
Khémis-Miliana, 36,530 .... E 1
Ksar-el-Boukhari, 30,338 .... E 1
Laghouat, 38,166 .... E 2
Mascara, 43,108 .... D 1
Méchéria, 12,151 .... D 2
Médéa, 53,567 .... E 1
Metlili Chaamba, 17,999 .... E 2
Miliana, 28,410 .... E 1
Mohammadia, 38,441 .... D 1
Mostaganem, 75,332 .... D 1
M'Sila, 36,930 .... E 1
Oran, 327,493 .... D 1
Oran, *393,000 .... D 1
Ouallene .... E 4
Ouargla, 48,323 .... F 2
Ouled-Djellal, 14,597 .... F 2
Philippeville (Skikda), 72,742 .... F 1
Poste Maurice Cordier .... E 4
Poste Weygand .... D 4
Reggan, 11,075 .... D 3
Saïda, 38,348 .... E 2
Sba .... D 3
Sétif, 98,337 .... F 1
Sidi-bel-Abbès, 91,527 .... D 1
Silet .... E 4
Skikda, 72,742 .... F 1
Souk-Ahras, 42,680 .... F 1
Tabelbala, 1,972 .... D 3
Tamanrasset, 16,298 .... F 4
Tamentit .... D 3
Taourirt .... E 3
Tarat .... F 3
Tarhit .... D 2
Tébessa, 46,148 .... F 1
Temacine .... F 2
Ténès, 22,881 .... E 1
Tiaret, 40,934 .... E 1
Tiguentourine .... F 3
Timimoun, 15,349 .... E 3
Tindouf, 3,414 .... C 3
Tizi-Ouzou, 53,546 .... E 1
Tlemcen, 87,210 .... D 2
Touggourt, 50,159 .... F 2
Zaouiet-el-Kahla, 1,080 .... F 3
Zaouïet-Kounta, 11,455 .... D 3

OTHER FEATURES

Adrar des Iforas (plat.) .... E 4
Ahaggar (range) .... F 4
Aouïnet Legraa (well) .... C 3
Atlas (mts.) .... E 2
Aurés (mts.) .... F 1
Azzel Mati, Sebkra (lake) .... E 3
Bougaroun (cape) .... F 1
Chech Erg (des.) .... D 3
Chélia (mt.) .... F 1
Chéliff (riv.) .... E 1
Chenachane (well) .... D 3
Chergui, Shott Ech (salt lake) .... E 2
Gourara (oasis), 28,893 .... E 3
Great Eastern Erg (des.) .... F 2
Great Western Erg (des.) .... E 2
High Plateaus (ranges) .... D 2
Iguidi Erg (des.) .... C 3
In-Ezzane (well) .... G 4
In-Guezzam (well) .... F 5
Irharhar, Wadi (dry riv.) .... F 3
Issaouane Erg (des.) .... F 3
Kabylia (reg.) .... E 1
Medjerda (riv.) .... F 1
Mekerhane, Sebkra (salt lake) .... E 3
Melrhir, Shott (salt lake) .... F 2
Mouydir (mts.) .... E 3
Mya, Wadi (dry riv.) .... E 2
Mzab (oasis), 52,500 .... E 2
Raoui Erg (des.) .... D 3
Rhir, Wadi (dry riv.) .... F 2
Sahara (des.) .... E 4
Saharan Atlas (mts.) .... E 2
Saoura, Wadi (dry riv.) .... D 3
Souf (oasis), 92,014 .... F 2
Tademait (plat.) .... E 3
Tahat (mt.) .... F 4
Tamanrasset, Wadi (dry river) .... E 4
Tanezrouft (des.) .... E 4
Tassili n'Ahaggar (plat.) .... E 4
Tassili n'Ajjer (plat.) .... F 3
Tidikelt (oasis), 17,280 .... E 3
Timgad (ruins) .... F 1
Timmissao (well) .... E 4
Tindouf, Sebkra de (salt lake) .... C 3
Tinrhert Hamada (des.) .... F 3
Tni Haïa (well) .... D 4
Touat (oasis), 35,537 .... E 3
Touila (well) .... C 3

CAPE VERDE ISLANDS

CITIES and TOWNS

Mindelo, 7,312 .... A 7
Praia (cap.), 3,628 .... B 8
Ribeira Grande, †17,573 .... B 7
Sal Rei, †3,309 .... B 8
Santa Maria, †2,626 .... B 8

OTHER FEATURES

Boa Vista (isl.), 3,309 .... B 8
Brava (isl.), 8,646 .... B 8
Fogo (isl.), 25,457 .... B 8
Maio (isl.), 2,718 .... B 8
Sal (isl.), 2,626 .... B 7
Santa Luzia (isl.) .... B 8
Santo Antão (island), 36,703 .... A 7
São Nicolau (island), 13,894 .... B 8
São Tiago (island), 86,835 .... B 8
São Vicente (island), 21,361 .... B 7

DAHOMEY

CITIES and TOWNS

Abomey, 19,000 .... E 7
Athiémé, 1,782 .... E 7
Cotonou, 120,000 .... E 7
Djougou, 7,000 .... E 7
Grand-Popo, 2,545 .... E 7
Kandi, 5,100 .... E 6
Malanville, 1,900 .... E 6
Natitingou, 2,260 .... E 6
Nikki .... E 7
Ouidah, 18,915 .... E 7
Parakou, 10,600 .... E 7
Porto-Novo (cap.), 80,000 .... E 7
Savalou, 5,000 .... E 7
Savé, 6,262 .... E 7

OTHER FEATURES

Atakora (mts.) .... E 6
Benin (bight) .... E 8
Guinea (gulf) .... E 8
Ouémé (riv.) .... E 7
Slave Coast (reg.) .... E 7

GAMBIA

CITIES and TOWNS

Basse, 1,639 .... B 6
Bathurst (cap.), 31,800 .... A 6
Bathurst, *48,333 .... A 6
Brikama, 4,195 .... A 6
Georgetown, 1,592 .... A 6

GHANA

CITIES and TOWNS

Accra (cap.), 337,828 .... D 7
Accra, *848,825 .... D 7
Ada Foah, 3,332 .... E 7
Akim Oda, 19,666 .... D 7
Amedika Akuse, 3,638 .... E 7
Attebubu, 4,216 .... D 7
Axim, 5,619 .... D 8
Bawku, 12,719 .... D 6
Bekwai, 9,093 .... D 7
Berekum, 11,148 .... D 7
Bole, 3,118 .... D 7
Bolgatanga, 5,515 .... D 6
Cape Coast, 41,230 .... D 7
Daboya, 1,579 .... D 7
Damongo, 6,575 .... D 7
Dunkwa, 12,689 .... D 7
Elmina, 8,534 .... D 8
Enkyi, 4,007 .... D 7
Gambaga, 2,936 .... D 6
Gyasikan, 4,989 .... D 7
Half Assini, 4,575 .... D 8
Ho, 14,519 .... E 7
Keta, 16,719 .... E 7
Kete Krakye, 3,928 .... E 7
Kintampo, 4,678 .... D 7
Koforidua, 34,856 .... D 7
Kpandu, 8,070 .... D 7
Kumasi, 281,600 .... D 7
Kumasi, *340,200 .... D 7
Lawra, 3,237 .... D 6
Mampong, 7,943 .... D 7
Mpraeso, 5,193 .... D 7
Navrongo, 5,274 .... D 6
Obuasi, 22,818 .... D 7
Prestea, 13,246 .... D 7
Salaga, 4,199 .... D 7
Sehwi Wiawso, 4,430 .... D 7
Sekondi, 34,513 .... D 8
Sekondi-Takoradi, 128,200 .... D 8
Sekondi-Takoradi, *209,400 .... D 8
Sunyani, 12,160 .... D 7
Takoradi, 40,937 .... D 8
Tamale, 40,443 .... D 7
Tarkwa, 13,545 .... D 7
Tema, 14,937 .... E 7
Tumu, 2,773 .... D 6
Wa, 14,342 .... D 6
Wenchi, 10,672 .... D 7
Winneba, 25,376 .... D 7
Yapei, 515 .... D 7

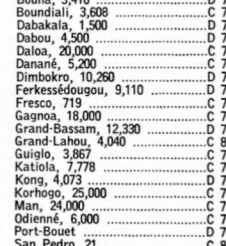

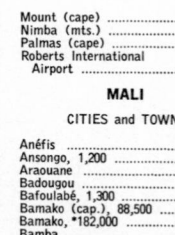

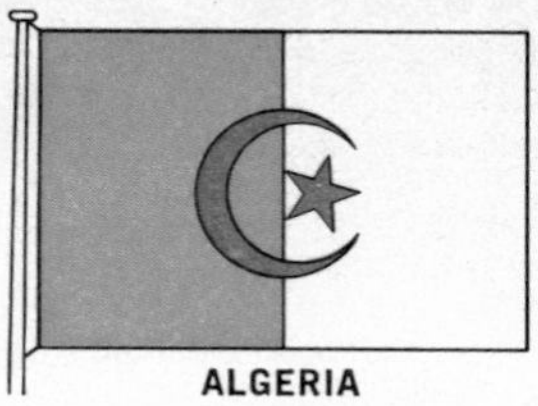
ALGERIA

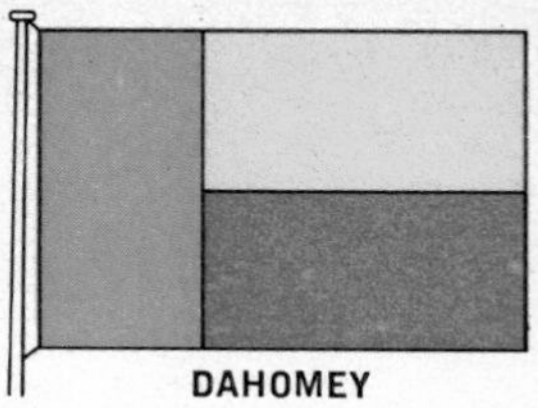
DAHOMEY

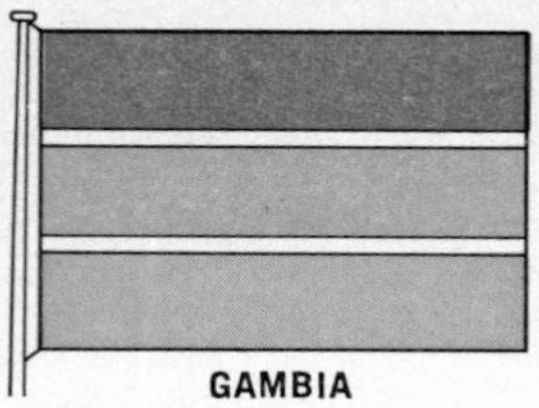
GAMBIA

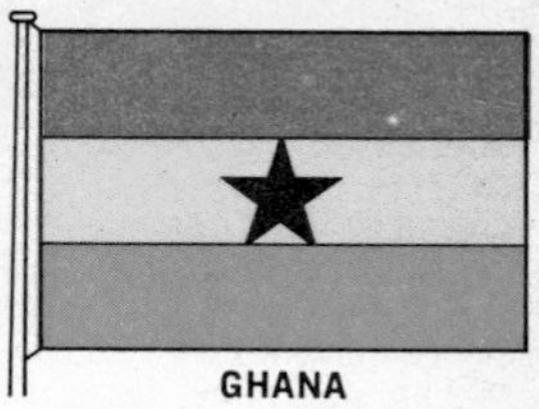
GHANA

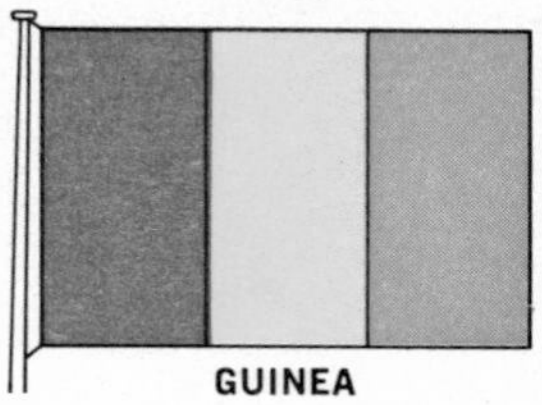
GUINEA

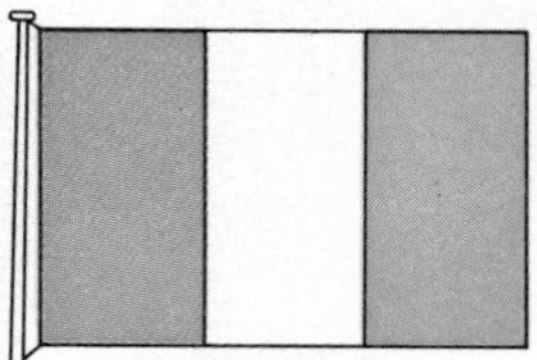
IVORY COAST

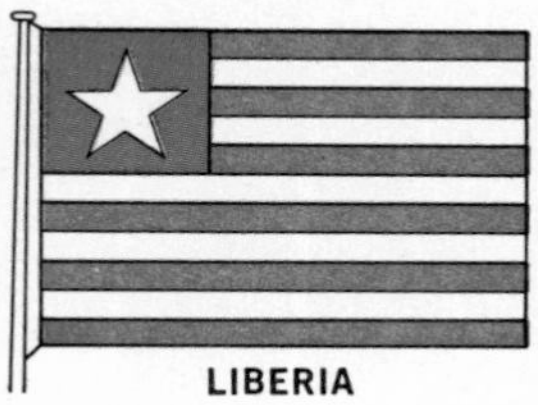
LIBERIA

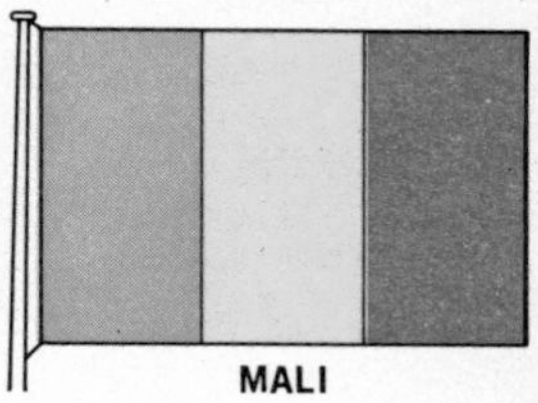
MALI

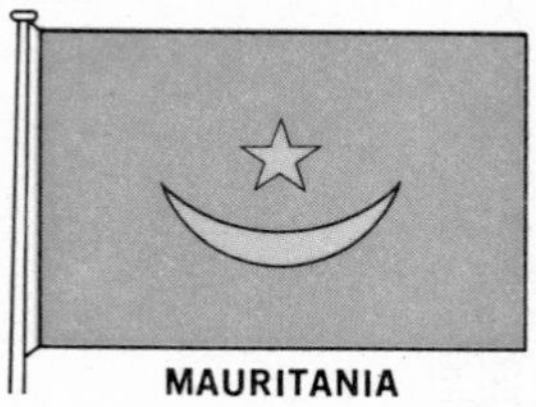
MAURITANIA

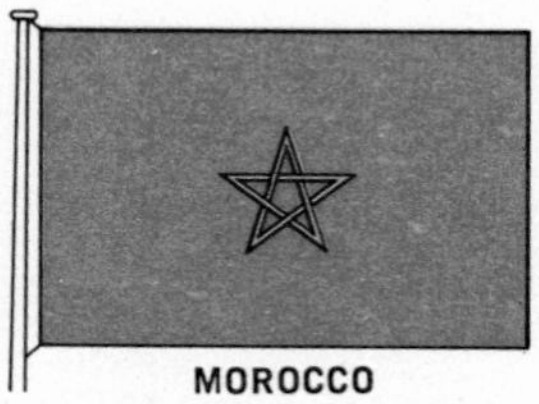
MOROCCO

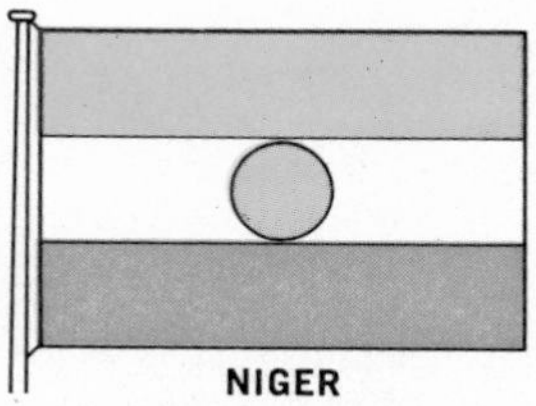
NIGER

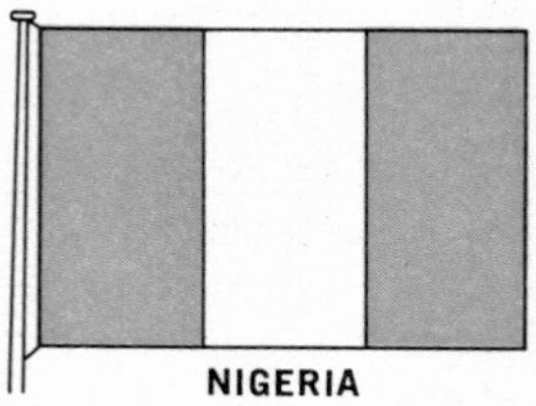
NIGERIA

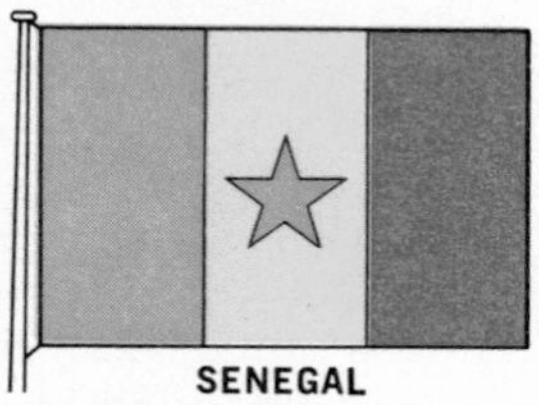
SENEGAL

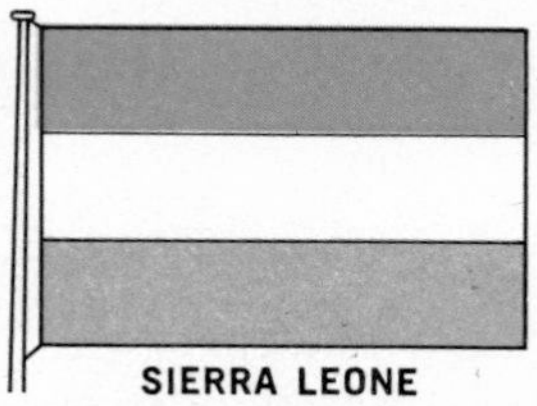
SIERRA LEONE

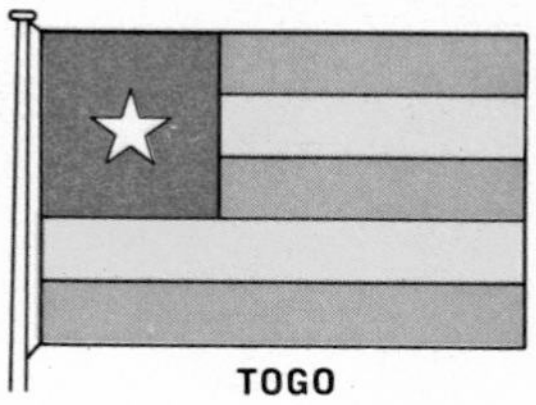
TOGO

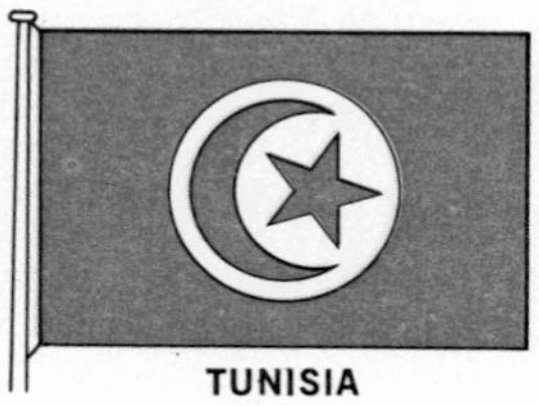
TUNISIA

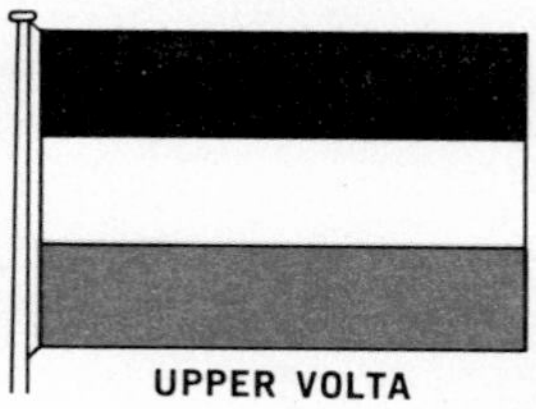
UPPER VOLTA

Yendi, 16,096 .... D 7
Zuarungu, 1,278 .... D 6

OTHER FEATURES

Ashanti (region), 1,109,133 .... D 7
Black Volta (riv.) .... D 6
Gold Coast (reg.) .... D 8
Guinea (gulf) .... E 8
Oti (riv.) .... E 7
Saint Paul (cape) .... E 7
Three Points (cape) .... D 8
Volta (lake) .... D 7
Volta (riv.) .... E 7
White Volta (riv.) .... D 6

GUINEA

CITIES and TOWNS

Beyla, 6,035 .... C 7
Boffa, 1,014 .... B 6
Boké, 6,000 .... B 6
Conakry (capital), 43,000 .... B 7
Conakry, *197,267 .... B 7
Dabola, 5,600 .... B 6
Dalaba, 5,450 .... B 6
Dinguiraye, 2,600 .... B 6
Dubréka, 740 .... B 7
Faranah, 4,000 .... B 6
Forécariah, 5,250 .... B 7
Gaoual, 3,208 .... B 6
Guéckédou, 1,421 .... B 7
Kankan, 50,000 .... C 6
Kérouané .... C 7
Kindia, 25,000 .... B 6
Kissidougou, 12,000 .... B 7
Kouroussa, 6,100 .... C 6
Labé, 11,609 .... B 6
Macenta, 22,500 .... C 7
Mamou, 9,000 .... B 6
N'Zérékoré, 11,000 .... C 7
Siguiri, 12,000 .... C 6
Tougué, 9,810 .... B 6
Victoria, 1,913 .... B 6

OTHER FEATURES

Bafing (riv.) .... B 6
Futa Jallon (mts.) .... B 6
Los (isls.) .... B 7
Milo (riv.) .... C 7
Niger (riv.) .... C 6
Nimba (mts.) .... C 7
Verga (cape) .... B 6

IVORY COAST

CITIES and TOWNS

Abengourou, 18,000 .... D 7
Abidjan (capital), 180,000 .... D 7
Abidjan, *425,000 .... D 7
Aboisso, 3,310 .... D 7
Agboville, 15,475 .... D 7
Bingerville, 2,500 .... D 7
Bondoukou, 5,216 .... D 7
Bouaflé, 5,000 .... C 7
Bouaké, 100,000 .... D 7
Bouna, 3,410 .... D 7
Boundiali, 3,608 .... C 7
Dabakala, 1,500 .... D 7
Dabou, 4,500 .... D 7
Daloa, 20,000 .... C 7
Danané, 5,200 .... C 7
Dimbokro, 10,260 .... D 7
Ferkessédougou, 9,110 .... D 7
Fresco, 719 .... C 7
Gagnoa, 18,000 .... C 7
Grand-Bassam, 12,330 .... D 7
Grand-Lahou, 4,040 .... C 8
Guiglo, 3,867 .... C 7
Katiola, 7,778 .... C 7
Kong, 4,073 .... D 7
Korhogo, 25,000 .... C 7
Man, 24,000 .... C 7
Odienné, 6,000 .... C 7
Port-Bouet .... D 7
San Pedro, 21 .... C 8
Sassandra, 5,300 .... D 7
Séguéla, 7,598 .... C 7
Sinfra, 5,965 .... C 7
Tabou, 3,030 .... C 8
Touba, 1,217 .... C 7
Toumodi, 3,000 .... D 7

OTHER FEATURES

Aby (lag.) .... D 8
Bandama (riv.) .... C 7
Cavally (riv.) .... C 7
Comoé (riv.) .... D 7
Ebrié (lag.) .... D 8
Ivory Coast (reg.) .... C 8
Sassandra (riv.) .... C 7

LIBERIA

CITIES and TOWNS

Bomi Hills, 2,441 .... B 7
Buchanan, 11,909 .... B 7
Gbarnga, 2,810 .... C 7
Grand Bassa (Buchanan), 11,909 .... B 7
Grand Cess .... C 8
Greenville, 3,962 .... C 8
Harper, 6,095 .... C 8
Kolahun .... C 7
Marshall .... B 7
Monrovia (capital), 85,000 .... B 7
Monrovia, *100,000 .... B 7
River Cess .... C 7
Robertsport, 2,417 .... B 7
Salala .... B 7
Sass Town .... C 8
Sinoe (Greenville), 3,962 .... C 8
Tappita .... C 7
Tchien, 945 .... C 7
Zwedru (Tchien), 945 .... C 7

OTHER FEATURES

Bong (mts.) .... B 7
Cavally (riv.) .... C 7
Grain Coast (reg.) .... B 8
Kru Coast (reg.), 21,280 .... C 8
Mano (riv.) .... B 7
Mount (cape) .... B 7
Nimba (mts.) .... C 7
Palmas (cape) .... C 8
Roberts International Airport .... B 7

MALI

CITIES and TOWNS

Anéfis .... E 5
Ansongo, 1,200 .... E 5
Araouane .... D 5
Badougou .... C 6
Bafoulabé, 1,300 .... B 6
Bamako (cap.), 88,500 .... C 6
Bamako, *182,000 .... C 6
Bamba .... D 5
Bandiagara, 6,700 .... D 6
Bou Djebeha .... D 5
Bougouni, 5,500 .... C 6
Bourem, 2,700 .... E 5
Dioila, 1,900 .... C 6
Dire, 3,300 .... D 5
Djenné, 8,200 .... D 6
Douentza, 7,100 .... D 6
Gao, 15,400 .... E 5
Goumbou, 5,000 .... C 6
Goundam, 10,000 .... D 5
Gourma-Rharous, 2,700 .... D 5
Hombori, 3,600 .... D 5
Kangaba, 6,200 .... C 6
Kati, 5,900 .... C 6
Kayes, 23,600 .... B 6
Ké-Macina, 3,100 .... C 6
Kéniéba, 800 .... B 6
Kerchoual .... E 5
Kidal, 1,200 .... E 5
Kita, 8,600 .... C 6
Kolokani, 7,300 .... C 6
Koulikoro, 10,000 .... C 6
Kourouba, 807 .... B 6
Koutiala, 11,300 .... C 6
Mabrouk .... D 5
Ménaka, 1,400 .... E 5
Mopti, 32,000 .... D 6
Nampala .... C 5
Nara, 2,500 .... C 5
Niafunké, 5,100 .... D 5
Niono, 4,000 .... C 6
Nioro, 11,000 .... C 5
San, 14,900 .... D 6
Satadougou, 180 .... B 6
Ségou, 27,200 .... C 6
Sikasso, 21,800 .... C 6
Sokolo, 3,457 .... C 6
Taoudenni .... D 4
Tessalit .... E 4
Timbuktu, 14,900 .... D 5
Tin-Zaouatene .... E 5
Yelimané, 1,700 .... B 5

OTHER FEATURES

Achourat (well) .... D 4
Adrar des Iforas (plat.) .... E 4
Asselar (well) .... D 5
Azaouad (reg.) .... D 5
Azaouak (dry riv.) .... E 5
Bafing (riv.) .... B 6
Bagoé (riv.) .... C 6
Bakoy (riv.) .... B 6
Bani (riv.) .... C 6
Baoulé (riv.) .... C 6
Bir Ounane (well) .... D 4
Chech Erg (des.) .... D 3
Debo (lake) .... D 5
El-Mraiti (well) .... D 5
Faguibine (lake) .... D 5
Falémé (riv.) .... B 6
Haricha Hamada (des.) .... D 4
Hombori (mts.) .... D 5
In Dagouber (well) .... D 4
Macina (depr.) .... D 6
Mina (mt.) .... C 6
Niger (riv.) .... D 5
Oum el Asel (well) .... D 4
Sahara (des.) .... D 4
Sekkane (des.) .... D 4
Tadjnout Hagguerete (well) .... D 4
Terhazza (ruins) .... C 4
Tilemsi (valley) .... E 5
Toufourine (well) .... C 4

MAURITANIA

CITIES and TOWNS

Aïoun el Atrous, 3,054 .... C 5
Akjoujt, 2,500 .... B 5
Akreïjit .... C 5
Aleg, 1,000 .... B 5
Atar, 7,120 .... B 4
Bassikounou .... C 5
Bir Mogrein, 1,052 .... B 4
Boghé, 2,316 .... B 5
Boutilimit, 3,000 .... B 5
Chinguetti, 600 .... B 4
Cité de Cansado .... A 4
F'Dérick, †900 .... B 4
Kaédi, 11,000 .... B 5
Kankossa, †13,000 .... B 5
Kiffa, 2,600 .... B 5
Maghama, 3,157 .... B 5
Mal .... B 5
M'Bout, 1,400 .... B 5
Méderdra, 1,473 .... A 5
Moudjéria, 753 .... B 5
Néma, 2,946 .... C 5
Nouadhibou, 11,250 .... A 4
Nouakchott (capital), 14,500 .... A 5
Ouadane .... B 4
Oualata, 1,285 .... C 5
Oujaf .... C 5
Oujeft .... B 4
Rosso, 3,923 .... A 5
Sélibaby, 2,600 .... B 5
Tamchakett, 641 .... B 5
Tamsagout .... C 4
Tazadit .... A 4
Tichitt, 1,000 .... C 5
Tidjikja, 5,900 .... B 5
Timbédra, 1,200 .... C 5

OTHER FEATURES

Adafer (reg.) .... B 5
Adrar (reg.), 50,920 .... B 4
Affolé (reg.) .... B 5
Agmar (well) .... B 3
Agueraktem (well) .... C 4
Aïn ben Tili (well) .... C 3
Arguin (bay) .... A 4
Assaba (reg.), 100,000 .... B 5
Atoui, Wadi (dry riv.) .... B 4
Ben Guerdane (well) .... B 3
Bir el Khzaim (well) .... C 4
Blanc (cape) .... A 4
Brakna (reg.), 82,020 .... B 5
Chegga (well) .... C 3
Djouf, El (des.) .... C 4
El Mrayer (well) .... C 4
El Mreïti (well) .... C 4
Gorgol (reg.), 54,037 .... B 5
Hodh (reg.), 183,945 .... C 5
Iguidi Erg (des.) .... C 3
Inchiri (reg.), 15,443 .... A 5
Kumbi Saleh (ruins) .... C 5
Lévrier (bay) .... A 4
Makteïr (des.) .... B 4
Meraia (reg.) .... C 5
Mirik (Timiris) (cape) .... A 5
Ouarane (reg.) .... B 4
Sahara (des.) .... C 4
Senegal (riv.) .... B 5
Tagant (reg.), 52,703 .... B 5
Tidra (isl.) .... A 5
Timiris (cape) .... A 5
Touila (well) .... C 3
Trarza (reg.), 105,737 .... A 5

MOROCCO

CITIES and TOWNS

Agadir, 16,695 .... C 2
Al Hoceima, 11,262 .... D 1
Asilah, 10,839 .... C 1
Azemmour, 12,449 .... C 2
Azrou, 14,143 .... C 2
Beni-Mellal, 28,933 .... C 2
Berguent, 2,607 .... D 2
Bouârfa, 8,775 .... D 2
Bou-Izakarn, 661 .... C 3
Boujad, 14,728 .... C 2
Casablanca, 1,320,000 .... C 2
Chechaouen, 13,712 .... D 1
Dar-el-Beida (Casablanca), 1,320,000 .... C 2
El Jadida, 40,302 .... C 2
El Kelâa des Srarhna, 10,187 .... C 2
Erfoud, 4,491 .... D 2
Essaouira, 26,392 .... B 2
Fédala (Mohammedia), 35,010 .... C 2
Fez, 280,000 .... D 2
Figuig, 12,108 .... D 2
Goulmima, 1,804 .... C 2
Inezgane, 6,917 .... C 2
Jerada, 18,872 .... D 2
Kénitra, 125,000 .... C 2
Khenifra, 18,503 .... C 2
Khouribga, 40,838 .... C 2
Ksar-el-Kebir, 34,035 .... C 2
Ksar-es-Souk, 6,554 .... D 2
Larache, 30,763 .... C 1

Western Africa 109

Marrakech, 295,000 ....C 2
Mazagan (El Jadida), 40,302 ....C 2
Meknès, 235,000 ....C 2
Mogador (Essaouira), 26,392 ....B 2
Mohammedia, 35,010 ....C 2
Nador, 17,583 ....D 1
Ouarzazate, 4,200 ....C 2
Oued-Zem, 18,640 ....C 2
Ouezzane, 26,203 ....C 2
Oujda, 150,000 ....D 2
Petitjean (Sidi-Kacem), 19,478 ....C 2
Port-Lyautey (Kénitra), 125,000 ....C 2
Rabat (capital), 227,445 ....C 2
Rabat, *435,000 ....C 2
Safi, 125,000 ....C 2
Saïdia, 1,102 ....D 2
Salé, 75,799 ....C 2
Sefrou, 21,478 ....D 2
Settat, 29,617 ....C 2
Sidi Ifni, 12,751 ....B 3
Sidi-Kacem, 19,478 ....C 2
Tagounite, 354 ....C 3
Tangier (Tanger), 160,000 ....C 1
Tantan, 2,153 ....B 3
Taourirt, 7,343 ....D 2
Taouz, 641 ....D 2
Tarfaya, 1,521 ....B 3
Taroudant, 17,141 ....C 2
Taza, 31,667 ....D 2
Tendrara, 1,563 ....D 2
Tétouan (Tetuán), 120,000 ....C 1
Tinjoub ....C 3
Tiznit, 7,694 ....B 3
Youssoufia, 8,302 ....C 2
Zagora, 2,200 ....C 2

OTHER FEATURES

Anti-Atlas (ranges) ....C 3
Atlas (mts.) ....C 2
Bani, Jebel (mts.) ....C 3
Cantin (cape) ....C 2
Dra Hamada (des.) ....C 3
Dra, Wadi (dry riv.) ....C 3
Er Rif (range) ....D 2
Gibraltar (str.) ....C 1
High Atlas (ranges) ....C 2
Juby (cape) ....B 3
Middle Atlas (ranges) ....C 2
Moulouya (riv.) ....D 2
Rhéris, Wadi (dry riv.) ....D 2
Rhir (cape) ....B 2
Rif, Er (range) ....D 2
Sarro, Jebel (mts.) ....C 2
Sebou (riv.) ....C 2
Sim (cape) ....B 2
Toubkal, Jebel (mt.) ....C 2
Ziz, Wadi (dry riv.) ....D 2

NIGER

CITIES and TOWNS

Agadès, 7,100 ....F 5
Bilma, 1,500 ....G 5
Birni-N'Konni, 7,900 ....E 6
Bosso, 509 ....G 6
Chirfa ....G 4
Dakoro, 2,400 ....F 6
Dessa ....E 6
Diffa, 477 ....G 6
Djado ....G 4
Dogondoutchi, 7,700 ....E 6
Dosso, 3,500 ....E 6
Fachi, 1,060 ....G 5
Filingué, 6,000 ....E 6
Gangara ....F 6
Gaya, 4,200 ....E 6
Gouré, 2,100 ....G 6
Iférouane ....F 5
In-Gall, 1,555 ....F 5
Madama ....G 4
Madaoua, 2,800 ....F 6
Magaria, 4,000 ....F 6
Mainé-Soroa, 1,500 ....G 6
Maradi, 22,400 ....F 6
N'Guigmi, 4,000 ....G 6
Niamey (cap.), 42,000 ....E 6
Niamey, *122,672 ....E 6
Say, 2,700 ....E 6
Tahoua, 18,100 ....F 6
Tanout, 1,600 ....F 6
Téra, 6,600 ....E 6
Tessaoua, 6,700 ....F 6
Tillabéry, 1,600 ....E 6
Zinder, 24,000 ....F 6

OTHER FEATURES

Achégour (well) ....G 5
Agadem (well) ....G 5
Aïr (mts.) ....F 5
Anaye (well) ....G 5
Assakarai (dry riv.) ....E 5
Azaoua (reg.) ....E 5
Azbine (Aïr) (mts.) ....F 5
Bagam (well) ....F 5
Banguezane (mt.) ....F 5
Bedouaram (well) ....G 5
Chad (lake) ....G 6
Dallol Bosso (dry riv.) ....E 6
Dillia (dry riv.) ....G 5
Djado (plat.) ....G 4
El War (well) ....G 4
In-Azaoua (well) ....F 4
Mantas (well) ....F 5
Niger (riv.) ....E 6
Sudan (reg.) ....E 6
Talak (reg.) ....E 5
Ténéré (des.) ....G 5
Timboulaga (well) ....F 5
Tummo (El War) (well) ....G 4
Zoo Baba (well) ....G 5

NIGERIA

STATES

Benue-Plateau, 4,009,408 ....F 7
East-Central, 6,223,831 ....F 7
Kano, 5,774,842 ....F 6
Kwara, 2,406,265 ....E 7
Lagos, 1,443,567 ....E 7
Mid-Western, 2,535,839 ....F 7
North-Central, 4,098,305 ....F 6
North-Eastern, 7,815,443 ....F 6
North-Western, 5,733,296 ....F 6
Rivers, 1,544,314 ....F 8
South-Eastern, 4,626,317 ....F 7
Western, 9,487,576 ....E 7

CITIES and TOWNS

Aba, 151,923 ....F 7
Abeokuta, 217,201 ....E 7
Abuja ....F 7
Ado, 182,673 ....E 7
Afikpo ....F 7
Aku, 20,809 ....F 7
Akure, 38,853 ....F 7
Argungu ....E 6
Asaba, 17,387 ....F 7
Azare ....G 6
Baga ....G 6
Bama ....G 6
Baro ....F 7
Bauchi ....F 6
Benin City, 116,774 ....F 7
Bida ....F 7
Birnin Kebbi ....E 6
Biu ....G 6
Bonny ....F 8
Brass ....F 8
Burutu, 6,784 ....F 7
Calabar, 46,705 ....F 7
Deba Habe ....G 6
Degema ....F 8
Dikwa ....G 6
Donga ....G 7
Ede, 156,036 ....E 7
Eha Amufu, 29,434 ....F 7
Enugu, 160,567 ....F 7
Forcados ....F 7
Funtua ....F 6
Gashaka ....G 7
Gbogo ....F 7
Geidam ....G 6
Gombe ....G 6
Gumel ....F 6
Gummi ....F 6
Gusau, 40,202 ....F 6
Gwadabawa ....F 6
Hadejia ....G 6
Ibadan, 727,565 ....E 7
Ibi ....F 7
Ife, 150,818 ....E 7
Ijebu-Ode, 27,558 ....E 7
Ikom ....F 7
Ilesha, 192,302 ....E 7
Ilorin, 241,849 ....E 7
Isa ....F 6
Iseyin, 49,680 ....E 7
Iwo, 183,907 ....E 7
Jalingo ....G 7
Jebba ....E 6
Jega ....E 6
Jos, 38,527 ....F 7
Kabba, 7,305 ....F 7
Kaduna, 173,849 ....F 6
Kaiama ....E 7
Kalmalo ....F 6
Kano, 342,610 ....F 6
Katsina, 52,672 ....F 6
Katsina Ala ....F 7
Kaura Namoda ....F 6
Keffi ....F 7
Koko ....F 7
Kontagora ....F 6
Kukawa ....G 6
Kumo ....G 7
Kuta ....F 7
Lafia ....F 7
Lafiagi ....F 7
Lagos (cap.), 841,749 ....E 7
Lere ....F 7
Lokoja, 13,103 ....F 7
Maiduguri, 162,316 ....G 6
Maigatari ....F 6
Makurdi ....F 7
Minna ....F 7
Mubi ....G 6
Mushin, 169,287 ....E 7
Nasarawa ....F 7
New Bussa, 10,000 ....E 6
Nguru, 23,084 ....G 6
Nnewi, 28,777 ....F 7
Nsukka ....F 7
Numan ....G 7
Offa, 20,668 ....E 7
Ogbomosho, 370,963 ....E 7
Ogoja ....F 7
Okene, 32,602 ....F 7
Ondo, 36,233 ....F 7
Onitsha, 189,067 ....F 7
Oron ....F 8
Oshogbo, 242,336 ....F 7
Owo, 30,662 ....F 7
Oyo, 130,290 ....E 7
Pankshin ....F 7
Panyam ....F 7
Port Harcourt, 208,237 ....F 8
Ringim ....F 6
Sapele, 33,638 ....F 7
Shaki, 22,983 ....E 7
Shendam ....F 7
Sokoto, 47,643 ....F 6
Toungo ....G 7
Uromi, 22,339 ....F 7
Vom ....F 7
Wamba ....F 7
Warri, 19,526 ....F 7
Wukari ....F 7
Yan ....G 7
Yelwa ....F 6
Yola ....G 7
Zaria, 192,706 ....F 6
Zungeru ....F 7

OTHER FEATURES

Adamawa (reg.) ....G 7
Benin (bight) ....E 8
Benue (riv.) ....F 7
Biafra (bight) ....F 8
Bornu (reg.) ....G 6
Chad (lake) ....G 6
Cross (riv.) ....F 7
Donga (riv.) ....G 7
Foge (isl.) ....F 6
Gongola (riv.) ....G 6
Guinea (gulf) ....E 8
Hadejia (riv.) ....F 6
Kaduna (riv.) ....F 6
Kainji (res.) ....E 6
Kebbi (riv.) ....E 6
Komadugu Yobe (riv.) ....G 6
Niger (delta) ....F 8
Niger (riv.) ....F 7
Osse (riv.) ....F 7
Slave Coast (reg.) ....E 7
Sokoto (riv.) ....F 6
Sudan (reg.) ....F 6
Vogel (peak) ....G 7

PORTUGAL—Madeira

CITIES and TOWNS

Funchal, 43,301 ....A 2

OTHER FEATURES

Desertas (isls.) ....A 2
Madeira (island), 265,432 ....A 2
Madeira (islands), 268,700 ....A 2
Pôrto Santo (island), 3,505 ....A 2
Salvage (isls.) ....A 2

PORTUGUESE GUINEA

CITIES and TOWNS

Bissau (capital), 20,000 ....A 6
Bolama, †4,642 ....A 6
Buba ....B 6
Bubaque ....A 6
Cacheu, †70,233 ....A 6

OTHER FEATURES

Bijagós (isls.), 9,332 ....A 6

SÃO TOMÉ E PRÍNCIPE

CITIES and TOWNS

Santo António, †4,605 ....F 8
São Tomé (capital), 7,364 ....F 8

OTHER FEATURES

Príncipe (isl.), 4,605 ....F 8
São Tomé (isl.), 58,880 ....F 8

SENEGAL

CITIES and TOWNS

Bakel, 2,500 ....B 6
Bignona, 5,432 ....A 6
Dagana, 4,000 ....A 5
Dakar (cap.), 550,000 ....A 6
Dakar, *661,000 ....A 6
Diourbel, 30,000 ....A 6
Kaolack, 70,000 ....A 6
Kédougou, 1,938 ....B 6
Louga, 15,000 ....A 5
Matam, 5,000 ....B 5
M'Bour, 15,000 ....A 6
Nioro-du-Rip, 2,788 ....A 6
Podor, 5,000 ....A 5
Richard Toll, 894 ....A 5
Rufisque, 50,000 ....A 6
Saint-Louis, 50,000 ....A 5
Sedhiou, 2,419 ....A 6
Tambacounda, 10,027 ....B 6
Thiès, 70,000 ....A 5
Tivaouane, 8,000 ....A 5
Touba, 2,575 ....A 6
Yarboutenda ....B 6
Ziguinchor, 30,000 ....A 6

OTHER FEATURES

Casamance (riv.) ....A 6
Falémé (riv.) ....B 6
Ferlo (reg.) ....B 6
Gambia (riv.) ....B 6
Senegal (riv.) ....B 5
Verde (cape) ....A 6

SIERRA LEONE

CITIES and TOWNS

Bo, 26,613 ....B 7
Bonthe, 6,230 ....B 7
Freetown (capital), 170,600 ....B 7
Kabala, 4,610 ....B 7
Kambia, 3,700 ....B 7
Kenema, 13,246 ....B 7
Lungi, 2,170 ....B 7
Makeni, 12,304 ....B 7
Moyamba, 4,564 ....B 7
Pendembu, 2,696 ....B 7
Pepel ....B 7
Port Loko, 5,809 ....B 7
Pujehun, 2,034 ....B 7

OTHER FEATURES

Loma (mts.) ....B 7
Moa (riv.) ....B 7
Sherbro (isl.), 6,894 ....B 7
Yawri (bay) ....B 7

SPAIN—Canary Islands, Ceuta and Melilla

CITIES and TOWNS

Arrecife, 12,748 ....B 3
Ceuta, 88,000 ....C 1
La Laguna, 15,899 ....A 3
Las Palmas de Gran Canaria, 166,236 ....B 3
Melilla, 77,000 ....D 1
Santa Cruz de la Palma, 9,928 ....A 3
Santa Cruz de Tenerife, 82,620 ....A 3

OTHER FEATURES

Canary (isls.), 944,448 ....A 3
Fuerteventura (island), 18,138 ....B 3
Gomera (isl.), 27,790 ....A 3
Grand Canary (island), 400,837 ....A 3
Hierro (isl.), 7,957 ....A 3
Lanzarote (isl.), 34,805 ....B 3
La Palma (isl.), 67,141 ....A 3
Tenerife (isl.), 387,767 ....A 3

SPANISH SAHARA

CITIES and TOWNS

El Aaiún (cap.), 10,000 ....B 3
Semara, 1,000 ....B 3
Villa Cisneros, 4,000 ....A 4

OTHER FEATURES

Atoui, Wadi (dry riv.) ....B 4
Ausert (well) ....B 4
Barbas (cape) ....A 4
Bir Ganduz (well) ....A 4
Bir Nzaran (well) ....B 4
Blanc (cape) ....A 4
Bojador (cape) ....B 3
Durnford (pt.) ....A 4
Guelta de Zemmur (well) ....B 3
Río de Oro (reg.) ....B 4
Saguia el Hamra (dry riv.) ....B 3
Saguia el Hamra (region) ....B 3
Tichlá (well) ....B 4

TOGO

CITIES and TOWNS

Anécho, ‡11,040 ....E 7
Atakpamé, ‡18,008 ....E 7
Kpémé, 2,229 ....E 7
Lama-Kara ....E 7
Lomé (cap.), 90,600 ....E 7
Lomé, *149,879 ....E 7
Palimé, ‡20,331 ....E 7
Sansanné-Mango ....E 6
Sokodé, ‡30,271 ....E 7

OTHER FEATURES

Guinea (gulf) ....E 8
Mono (riv.) ....E 7
Oti (riv.) ....E 7
Slave Coast (reg.) ....E 7

TUNISIA

CITIES and TOWNS

Beja, 28,100 ....F 1
Ben Gardane, 2,138 ....G 2
Bizerte, 51,700 ....F 1
El Djem, 6,800 ....G 1
El Kef, 23,200 ....F 1
Fort-Saint ....F 2
Gabès, 32,300 ....F 2
Gafsa, 32,400 ....F 2
Halq el Oued, 27,500 ....G 1
Jendouba, 14,800 ....F 1
Kairouan, 46,200 ....F 1
Kalaa-Kebira, 16,800 ....F 1
Kasserine, 9,800 ....F 1
La Skhirra, 1,500 ....G 2
Mahdia, 10,900 ....G 1
Mareth, 153 ....F 2
Mateur, 15,600 ....F 1
Médenine, 8,000 ....F 2
Menzel Bourguiba, 36,700 ....F 1
Menzel-Temime, 12,500 ....G 1
Moknine, 18,500 ....G 1
Monastir, 16,500 ....G 1
Msaken, 27,500 ....G 1
Nabeul, 34,100 ....G 1
Nefta, 15,000 ....F 2
Remada, 1,866 ....F 2
Sbeitla, 4,000 ....F 1
Sfax, 65,000 ....G 2
Sousse, 48,200 ....G 1
Tabarka, 356 ....F 1
Tatahouine, 3,100 ....G 2
Tozeur, 11,820 ....F 2
Tunis (cap.), 662,000 ....G 1
Tunis, *800,000 ....G 1
Zarzis, 30,080 ....G 2

OTHER FEATURES

Abiad, Ras el (Blanc) (cape) ....G 1
Blanc (cape) ....G 1
Bon (cape) ....G 1
Chambi, Jebel (mt.) ....F 2
Djerba (isl.), 62,445 ....G 2
Djerid, Shott el (salt lake) ....F 2
Gabès (gulf) ....G 2
Hammamet (gulf) ....G 1
Jefara (reg.) ....G 2
Kerkennah (isls.), 13,704 ....G 2
Merjerda (riv.) ....F 1
Tib, Ras el (Bon) (cape) ....G 1
Tunis (gulf) ....G 1

UPPER VOLTA

CITIES and TOWNS

Aribinda, 3,150 ....D 6
Banfora, 4,511 ....D 6
Batié, 1,335 ....D 6
Bobo-Dioulasso, 56,100 ....D 6
Bogandé, 3,125 ....E 6
Dédougou, 3,680 ....D 6
Diapaga, 3,050 ....E 6
Djibo ....D 6
Dori, 3,500 ....D 6
Fada-N'Gourma, 4,867 ....E 6
Gaoua, 5,907 ....D 6
Houndé, 1,153 ....D 6
Kaya, 10,304 ....D 6
Koudougou, 7,940 ....D 6
Koupela, 3,800 ....D 6
Léo, 2,139 ....D 6
Ouagadougou (capital), 77,500 ....D 6
Ouagadougou, *100,000 ....D 6
Ouahigouya, 12,960 ....D 6
Pama, 1,411 ....E 6
Po, 4,000 ....D 6
Tenkodogo, 6,561 ....E 6
Tougan, 5,000 ....D 6
Yako, 5,110 ....D 6

OTHER FEATURES

Black Volta (riv.) ....D 6
Red Volta (riv.) ....D 6
Sudan (reg.) ....E 6
White Volta (riv.) ....D 6

*City and suburbs.
†Population of sub-district or division.
‡Population of commune

Agriculture, Industry and Resources

DOMINANT LAND USE

- Cereals, Horticulture, Livestock
- Market Gardening, Diversified Tropical Crops
- Plantation Agriculture
- Oases
- Pasture Livestock
- Nomadic Livestock Herding
- Forests
- Nonagricultural Land

MAJOR MINERAL OCCURRENCES

Al	Bauxite	Gp	Gypsum
Au	Gold	Mn	Manganese
C	Coal	Na	Salt
Co	Cobalt	O	Petroleum
Cr	Chromium	P	Phosphates
Cu	Copper	Pb	Lead
D	Diamonds	Sb	Antimony
Fe	Iron Ore	Sn	Tin
G	Natural Gas	Ti	Titanium
Gn	Granite	Zn	Zinc

Water Power
Major Industrial Areas

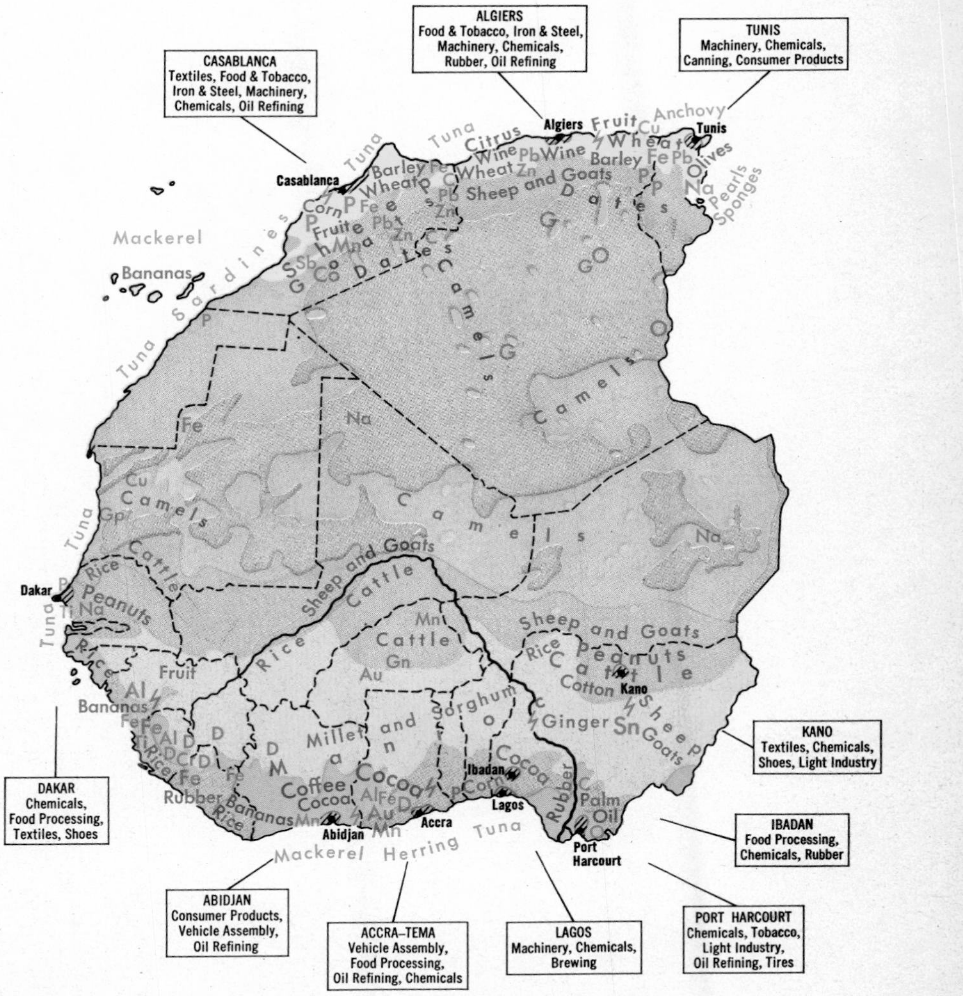

ALGIERS
Food & Tobacco, Iron & Steel, Machinery, Chemicals, Rubber, Oil Refining
TUNIS
Machinery, Chemicals, Canning, Consumer Products
CASABLANCA
Textiles, Food & Tobacco, Iron & Steel, Machinery, Chemicals, Oil Refining
Casablanca
Algiers
Tunis
Mackerel
Bananas
Sardines
Tuna
Citrus
Wine
Barley
Wheat
Fruit
Anchovy
Sheep and Goats
Dates
Camels
Sponges
Pearls
Cattle
Rice
Peanuts
Dakar
Millet and Sorghum
Ginger
Cocoa
Coffee
Rubber
Palm Oil
Cotton
Kano
Ibadan
Lagos
Accra
Abidjan
Port Harcourt
Mackerel Herring Tuna
KANO
Textiles, Chemicals, Shoes, Light Industry
DAKAR
Chemicals, Food Processing, Textiles, Shoes
IBADAN
Food Processing, Chemicals, Rubber
ABIDJAN
Consumer Products, Vehicle Assembly, Oil Refining
ACCRA–TEMA
Vehicle Assembly, Food Processing, Oil Refining, Chemicals
LAGOS
Machinery, Chemicals, Brewing
PORT HARCOURT
Chemicals, Tobacco, Light Industry, Oil Refining, Tires

LIBYA

EGYPT

CHAD

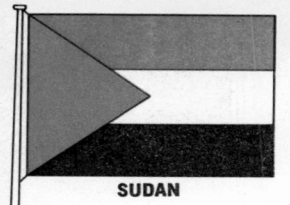

SUDAN

ETHIOPIA

LIBYA
AREA 679,359 sq. mi.
POPULATION 1,900,000
CAPITAL Tripoli
LARGEST CITY Tripoli
HIGHEST POINT Bette Pk. 7,500 ft.
MONETARY UNIT Libyan dinar
MAJOR LANGUAGES Arabic, Berber
MAJOR RELIGION Islam

TERRITORY OF THE AFARS AND ISSAS
AREA 8,498 sq. mi.
POPULATION 125,050
CAPITAL Djibouti

EGYPT
AREA 386,100 sq. mi.
POPULATION 33,329,000
CAPITAL Cairo
LARGEST CITY Cairo
HIGHEST POINT Jeb. Katherina 8,651 ft.
MONETARY UNIT Egyptian pound
MAJOR LANGUAGE Arabic
MAJOR RELIGIONS Islam, Christianity

CHAD
AREA 495,753 sq. mi.
POPULATION 3,510,000
CAPITAL Fort-Lamy
LARGEST CITY Fort-Lamy
HIGHEST POINT Emi Koussi 11,204 ft.
MONETARY UNIT CFA franc
MAJOR LANGUAGES Arabic, Bagirmi, French
MAJOR RELIGIONS Islam, Tribal religions

SUDAN
AREA 967,495 sq. mi.
POPULATION 15,312,000
CAPITAL Khartoum
LARGEST CITY Omdurman
HIGHEST POINT Jeb. Marra 10,073 ft.
MONETARY UNIT Sudanese pound
MAJOR LANGUAGES Arabic, Dinka, Nubian, Beja, Nuer
MAJOR RELIGIONS Islam, Tribal religions

ETHIOPIA
AREA 471,776 sq. mi.
POPULATION 24,764,000
CAPITAL Addis Ababa
LARGEST CITY Addis Ababa
HIGHEST POINT Ras Dashan 15,157 ft.
MONETARY UNIT Ethiopian dollar
MAJOR LANGUAGES Amharic, Galla, Tigrinya, Somali, Sidamo
MAJOR RELIGIONS Coptic Christianity, Islam

NORTHEASTERN AFRICA
CONIC EQUAL-AREA PROJECTION

SCALE OF MILES
0 50 100   200   300

SCALE OF KILOMETERS
0 50 100   200   300

Capitals of Countries .... ☆
Other Capitals .... ⊛
International Boundaries ....
Internal Boundaries ....

© C. S. HAMMOND & Co., Maplewood, N.J.

AFARS & ISSAS, TERR.

CITIES and TOWNS

Ali Sabieh, 2,000 ......H 5
Dikhil, 1,000 ......H 5
Djibouti (capital), 41,200 ......H 5
Djibouti, *61,500 ......H 5
Obock, 582 ......H 5
Tadjoura, 2,000 ......H 5

OTHER FEATURES

Abbe (lake) ......H 5
Aden (gulf) ......J 5
Bab el Mandeb (str.) ......H 5

CHAD

CITIES and TOWNS

Abécher, 19,650 ......D 5
Abou Deïa, 1,100 ......C 6
Adré ......D 5
Ain-Galakka ......C 4
Am-Dam, 1,002 ......D 5
Am-Timan, 1,500 ......D 5
Aozi ......C 3
Aozou ......C 3
Arada ......D 4
Ati, 6,000 ......C 5
Baïbokoum, 3,138 ......C 6
Bardaï, 800 ......C 3
Biltine, 4,000 ......D 5

Bokoro, 4,700 ......C 5
Bol, 1,500 ......B 5
Bongor, 11,000 ......C 5
Bousso, 1,800 ......C 5
Doba, 7,375 ......C 6
Fada, 1,500 ......D 4
Faya (Largeau), 5,200 ......C 4
Fianga, 923 ......C 6
Fort-Archambault, 35,000 ......C 6
Fort-Lamy (capital), 132,500 ......C 5
Fort-Lamy, *91,688 ......C 5
Goré ......C 6
Gouro ......C 4
Ham ......C 5
Kélo, 6,067 ......C 6
Koro Toro ......C 4
Koumra, 6,351 ......C 6
Kouno ......C 5
Kyabé, 3,000 ......C 6
Lai, 8,000 ......C 6
Largeau, 5,200 ......C 4
Léré, 3,500 ......B 6
Madadi ......D 4
Mangueigne, 1,700 ......D 5
Mao ......C 5
Massakori, 2,000 ......C 5
Masséna, 1,700 ......C 5
Melfi, 3,000 ......C 5
Mogororo ......D 5
Moïssala, 3,000 ......C 6
Mongo, 7,000 ......C 5
Moundou, 34,100 ......C 6
Moussoro ......C 5
Oum Chalouba ......D 4

Oum Hadjer, 4,500 ......D 5
Ouanianga-Kébir ......D 4
Pala, 4,200 ......B 6
Rig Rig, 286 ......B 5
Wour ......C 3
Yarda ......C 4
Ziguei ......C 5
Zouar ......C 3

OTHER FEATURES

Baguirmi (region), 81,666 ......C 5
Bahr el 'Ghazal (dry riv.) ......C 5
Batha (riv.) ......C 5
Bodélé (depr.) ......C 4
Borku (region), 21,962 ......C 4
Chad (lake) ......C 5
Domar (dry riv.) ......C 4
Emi Koussi (mt.) ......C 4
Ennedi (plat.) ......D 4
Fittri (lake) ......C 5
Haouach, Wadi (dry riv.) ......C 5
Jef Jef (plat.) ......D 3
Kanem (region), 261,108 ......C 4
Logone (riv.) ......C 5
Maro (dry riv.) ......C 6
Mbéré (riv.) ......C 6
Mourdi (depr.) ......D 4
Pendé (riv.) ......C 6
Sahara (des.) ......C 3
Salamat (riv.) ......C 6
Sara (riv.) ......C 6
Shari (riv.) ......C 5

Sudan (reg.) ......C 5
Tibesti (mts.) ......C 3
Wadaï (region), 314,775 ......D 5

EGYPT

CITIES and TOWNS

Abnûb, 27,751 ......J 4
Abu Qurqâs, 19,318 ......J 4
Akhmîn, 41,580 ......F 2
Alexandria, 1,803,900 ......J 2
Aswân, 127,700 ......F 3
Asyût, 154,100 ......J 4
Bâris, 1,347 ......F 3
Baris ......F 3
Beni Mazar, 30,583 ......J 4
Beni Suef, 78,829 ......J 3
Biba, 20,773 ......J 4
Bûlaq, 928 ......F 2
Bur Sa'îd (Port Said), 283,400 ......K 3
Cairo (cap.), 4,219,853 ......J 3
Dairût, 24,364 ......J 4
Damanhur, 146,300 ......J 3
Damietta, 71,780 ......J 3
Disûq, 39,473 ......J 3
Dumyât (Damietta), 71,780 ......J 3
Dûsh, 794 ......F 3
El 'Alamein, 593 ......F 1
El 'Arish, 29,973 ......F 1
El Bawiti, 2,478 ......E 2
El Faiyûm, 133,800 ......J 3
El Fashn, 25,961 ......J 4

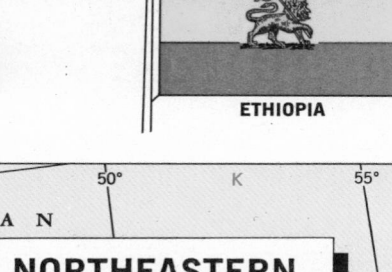

ALEXANDRIA
(El Iskandariya)

MEDITERRANEAN SEA

Abu Qir Bay
Rosetta (Rashid)
Port Said (Bur Sa'id)
Port Fuad
Damietta (Dumyât)
Damanhur
Disûq
El Mansura
El Qantara (Occ. by Israel)
El Mahalla el Kubra
Tanta
Zifta
Ismailia
Suez Canal
Shibin el Kom
Zagazig
Minûf
Qalyûb
Benha
Heliopolis
Imbâba
Giza
CAIRO (El Qâhira)
Bitter Lakes
Port Taufiq
PYRAMIDS
MEMPHIS
Suez
Gulf of Suez
Helwân
Birket Qârûn
Sinnûris
El Faiyûm
El Wasta
Beni Suef
Biba
El Fashn
Maghâgha
Beni Mazar
Samalût
El Minya
Abu Qurqâs
Mallawi
Dairût
Manfalût
Abnûb
Asyût

Gulf of Suez
Arabian Desert
Ghard Abu Muharik

Topography

0 200 400 600
MILES

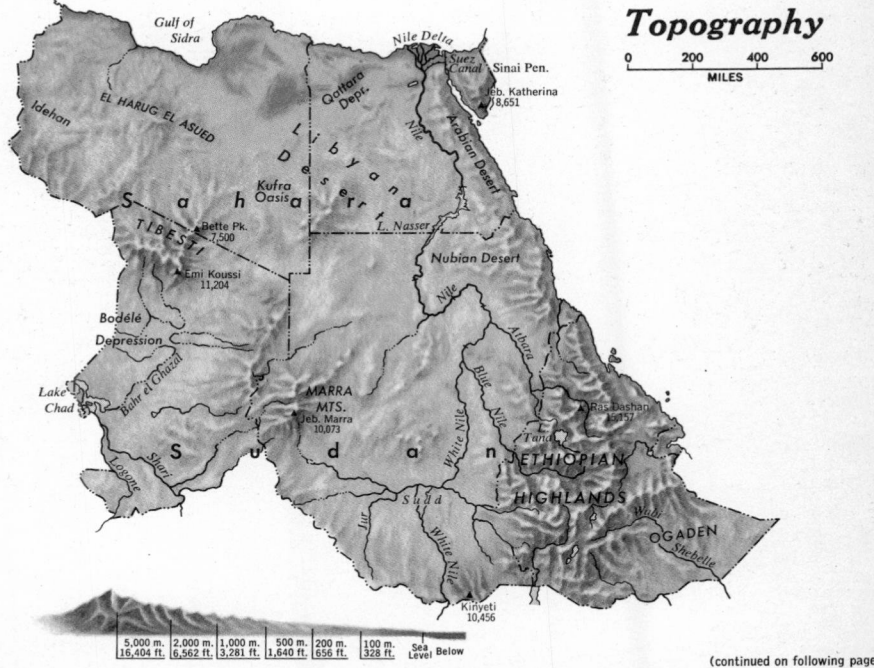

Gulf of Sidra
Nile Delta
Sinai Pen.
Suez Canal
Jeb. Katherina 8,651
Qattara Depr.
El Harug el Asued
Idehan
Libyan Desert
Kufra Oasis
L. Nasser
Nubian Desert
Arabian Desert
Nile
TIBESTI
Bette Pk. 7,500
Emi Koussi 11,204
Bodélé Depression
Lake Chad
Bahr el Ghazal
Shari
Logone
Sobat
White Nile
Blue Nile
Atbara
MARRA MTS.
Jeb. Marra 10,073
Sudan
Sahara
Ras Dashan 15,157
Tana
ETHIOPIAN HIGHLANDS
OGADEN
Shebele
Kiriyeti 10,456

5,000 m. / 16,404 ft. | 2,000 m. / 6,562 ft. | 1,000 m. / 3,281 ft. | 500 m. / 1,640 ft. | 200 m. / 656 ft. | 100 m. / 328 ft. | Sea Level | Below

IRAN
IRAQ
Tigris
Euphrates
NEUTRAL ZONE
45° 50° K 55°
H J
A
SAUDI ARABIA
Cancer
Nile
Bahr Yusef
ARABIAN DESERT
Farasan Is.
Abha
'ASIR
San'a
Kamaran I. (P.D.R. Yemen)
Hodeida
YEMEN ARAB REPUBLIC
Ta'izz
Mocha
Thio
Edd
Hanish Is.
Assab
Perim
Bab el Mandeb
Danakil
Obock
Tadjoura
Djibouti
Dikhil
L. Abbe
Ali Sabieh
Zeila
PEOPLES DEM. REP. OF YEMEN
Mukalla
Aden
Gulf of Aden
Cape Guardafui
Alula
Candala
Bereda
Bosaso (Bender Kassim)
Bargal
Ras Hafun
Hafun (Dante)
Bulhar
Berbera
Las Dureh
Karin
Ankhor
Surud Ad 7,900
Erigavo
Hordio
Skushuban
Bender Beila
NORTH- EAST SOMALIA
Upper Sheikh
Burao
Gardo
Garoe
MIJIRTEIN
Callis
Negro Bay
Harghessa
Dire Dawa
Adadle
Borama
Odweina
Ainabo
Halin
Las Anod
Taleh
Harar
Jijiga
HARAR
Awareh
Fefan
Bohotleh
Domo
El Hamure
Dagabur
El Bur
Wardere
Galadi
Garad
MUDUGH
INDIAN OCEAN
Gerlogubi
Gorrahei
Dusa Mareb
Obbia
Ginir
Imi
Wabi Shebele
Callafo
MENDEBO
El Carre
El Der
Mustahil
Ferfer
Belet Uen
HIRAN
El Bur
Harardera
Ganale Dorya
Filtu
Dolo
Lugh
Hodur
Tijeglo
El Dere
Marek
UPPER JUBA
Mandera
Dawa

(continued on following page)

(continued)

EGYPT (continued)

El Hammam, 3,664 E 1
El Iskandariya (Alexandria), 1,803,900 J 2
El Karnak, 14,121 F 2
El Khârga, 9,277 F 2
El Mahalla el Kubra, 225,700 J 3
El Mansûra, 191,700 K 3
El Minya, 112,800 J 4
El Qâhira (Cairo) (cap.), 4,219,853 J 3
El Qantara, 11,201 K 3
El Qasr, 1,789 E 2
El Quseir, 4,336 F 2
El Tûr, 418 F 2
El Wasta, 11,283 J 3
Gaza, 87,793 F 1
Gaza, *118,272 F 1
Gemsa, 225 F 2
Girga, 42,017 F 2
Giza, 571,249 J 3
Heliopolis, 124,774 J 3
Helwân, 94,385 J 3
Hurghada, 2,012 F 2
Idfu, 25,105 F 3
Imbâba, 226,300 J 3
Ismailia, 156,500 K 3
Isna, 25,342 F 2
Kôm Ombo, 21,783 F 3
Luxor, 35,074 F 2
Maghâgha, 28,650 J 4
Mallawi, 52,614 J 4
Manfalût, 28,540 J 4
Matrûh, 9,254 E 1
Minûf, 41,914 J 3
Mût, 3,496 E 2
Port Fuad, 12,881 K 3
Port Safâga, 1,448 F 2
Port Said, 283,400 K 3
Port Taufiq, 26,075 K 3
Qalyub, 43,202 J 3
Qasr Farâfra, 747 E 2
Qena, 57,417 F 2
Ras Ghârib, 5,857 F 2
Rashid (Rosetta), 32,368 J 2
Rosetta, 32,368 J 2
Rudeis F 2
Salûm, 1,348 E 1
Samalût, 17,368 J 4
Shibin el Kom, 54,910 J 3
Sidi Barrani, 1,583 E 1
Sinnûris, 31,831 J 3
Siwa, 3,839 E 2
Sohâg, 61,944 F 2
Suez, 264,500 K 3
Tahta, 36,165 F 2
Tanta, 230,400 J 3
Zagazig, 151,300 J 3
Zifta, 31,421 J 3

OTHER FEATURES

Abu Qir (bay) J 2
Abydos (ruins) F 2
'Allaqi, Wadi (dry riv.) F 3
'Aqaba (gulf) G 2
Arabian (des.) F 2
Aswân (dam) F 3
Aswân High (dam) F 3
Baharîya (oasis), 6,779 E 2
Bahr Yusef (stream) J 4
Bânâs, Ras (cape) G 3
Berenice (ruins) F 3
Birket Qârûn (lake) J 3
Bir Taba (well) F 2
Bitter (lakes) K 3
Dakhla (oasis), 21,586 E 2
Eastern (Arabian) (des.) F 2
Farâfra (oasis), 747 E 2
Foul (bay) G 3
Ghard Abu Muharik (des.) J 4
Gilf Kebir (plat.) E 3
Great Sand Sea (des.) E 2
Katherina, Jebel (mt.) F 2
Khârga (oasis), 12,346 F 2
Libyan (des.) E 2
Libyan (plat.) E 1
Mediterranean (sea) E 1
Memphis (ruins) J 3
Muhammad, Ras (cape) F 2
Nasser (lake) F 3
Nile (riv.) F 2
Pyramids (ruins) J 3
Qattâra (depr.) E 2
Red (sea) G 3
Sahara (des.) E 3
Salûm (gulf) E 1
Sinai (mt.) F 2
Sinai (pen.), 49,769 F 2
Siwa (oasis), 3,839 E 2
Suez (canal) K 3
Suez (gulf) F 2
Tiran (str.) F 2
'Uweinat, Jebel (mt.) E 3

ETHIOPIA

GOVERNORATES

Arusi, 1,092,565 G 6
Begemdir and Simen, 2,125,069 G 5
Eritrea, 1,757,912 G 4
Gamu-Gofa, 563,749 G 6
Gojjam, 1,414,944 G 5
Harar, 1,540,211 H 6
Ilubabor, 1,061,208 F 6
Kaffa, 876,836 G 6
Mendebo, 353,736 H 6
Shoa, 2,614,689 G 6
Sidamo, 2,242,515 G 7
Tigre, 3,104,451 H 5
Wallaga, 2,386,218 G 6
Wallo, 2,946,924 H 5

CITIES and TOWNS

Addis Ababa (capital), 644,120 G 6
Addis Alam, 7,789 G 6
Adigrat G 5
Adi Ugri G 5
Adola G 6
Adwa G 5
Agordat G 4
Aksum, 11,596 G 5
Ankober, 12,871 H 6
Arba Minch G 6
Asmara, 190,500 G 4
Asosa F 5
Assab H 5
Asselle, 9,523 G 6
Awareh H 6
Awash H 6
Bako G 6
Bedessa H 6
Beica F 6
Burei G 6
Burye, 18,139 G 5
Callafo H 6
Chilga G 5
Dagabur H 6
Dallol G 5
Dangila, 2,351 G 5
Debra Birhan G 6
Debra Markos, 20,096 G 5
Debra Tabor G 5
Dembidollo F 6
Dessye, 40,000 G 5
Dilla G 6
Dire Dawa, 40,000 H 6
Dolo H 7
Domo J 6
Edd H 5
El Carre H 6
El Der H 6
Filtu H 6
Gabredarre H 6
Galadi J 6
Gambela, 9,955 F 6
Gardula G 6
Gedo G 6
Gerlogubi H 6
Ginir H 6
Goba, 6,389 H 6
Gondar, 24,673 G 5
Gore G 6
Gorrahei H 6
Hadama, 7,293 G 6
Harar, 40,499 H 6
Harkiko G 4
Hosseina, 5,803 G 6
Imi H 6
Jijiga H 6
Jimma, 39,559 G 6
Jiran G 6
Karkabat G 4
Keren G 4
Koma G 6
Lalibela G 5
Magdala G 5
Maji G 6
Makale, 16,873 G 5
Massawa, 25,000 G 4
Masslo G 6
Mega G 7
Mendi G 6
Mersa Fatma H 5
Metamma G 5
Miesso, 32,960 H 6
Murle G 6
Mustahil H 6
Nakamti, 5,889 G 6
Nakfa G 4
Negelli G 6
Nejo G 6
Saio (Dembidollo) F 6
Soddu, 5,595 G 6
Sokota G 5
Tessenei G 4
Thio H 5
Tori F 6
Umm Hajar G 5
Waka G 6
Waldia G 5
Wardere J 6
Wota G 6
Yaballo G 6
Yirga Alam G 6
Zula G 4

OTHER FEATURES

Abaya (lake) G 6
Abbai (riv.) G 5
Abbe (lake) H 5
Akobo (riv.) F 6
Amhara (reg.) G 5
Assale (lake) H 5
Awash (riv.) H 5
Bale (mt.) G 6
Baraka (dry riv.) G 4
Baro (riv.) G 6
Billate (riv.) G 6
Blue Nile (Abbai) (riv.) G 5
Buri (pen.) H 4
Chamo (lake) G 6
Dahlak (arch.) H 4
Dahlak (isl.) H 4
Danakil (reg.) H 5
Dawa (riv.) H 7
Fafan (riv.) H 6
Ganale Dorya (riv.) H 6
Gughe (mt.) G 6
Haud (reg.) J 6
Kasar, Ras (cape) G 4
Ogaden (reg.) H 6
Omo (riv.) G 6
Ras Dashan (mt.) G 5
Red (sea) G 3
Rudolf (lake) G 7
Simen (mts.) G 5
Stefanie (lake) G 7
Takkaze (riv.) G 5
Tana (lake) G 5
Wabi (riv.) H 6
Wabi Shebelle (riv.) H 6
Zwai (lake) G 6

LIBYA

PROVINCES

Baida, 88,016 D 1
Benghazi, 278,826 D 2
Derna, 84,112 D 1
Gharian, 180,883 B 1
Homs, 136,679 B 1
Misurata, 145,894 C 1
Sebha, 47,436 B 2
Tripoli, 379,925 B 1
Ubari, 31,890 B 2
Zawia, 190,708 B 1

CITIES and TOWNS

Ajedabia, †15,430 D 1
Aujila, †2,993 D 2
Baida, 12,799 D 1
Barce (El Marj), 10,645 D 1
Benghazi, 137,295 D 1
Beni Ulid, †4,293 C 1
Berken, †3,114 B 2
Bir Hakeim D 1
Brak, †7,042 B 2
Bu Ngem C 1
Buzeima D 3
Cyrene (Shahat), †6,266 D 1
Derj, †2,272 B 1
Derna, 21,432 D 1
Edri, †4,271 B 2
El Abiar, †14,260 D 1
El Agheila, †852 C 1
El Azizia, †18,753 B 1
El Bardi, †3,755 D 1
El Barkat, †11,476 B 3
El Ergh D 2
El Fogaha, †607 C 2
El Gatrun, †11,660 B 3
El Gezira D 2
El Gheria esh Sherqia B 1
El Jauf, †4,330 D 3
El Marj, 10,645 D 1
Ez Zuetina, †2,430 D 1
Ghadames, †2,636 A 2
Gharian, †10,807 B 1
Ghat, †1,639 B 3
Homs, †13,864 B 1
Hon, †3,435 C 2
Jaghbub (Jarabub), †1,101 D 2
Jarabub, †1,101 D 2
Marada, †2,172 C 2
Marsa el Awegia C 1
Marsa el Brega, †2,797 D 1
Marsa el Hariga D 1
Marsa Susa, †2,062 D 1
Mekili, †703 D 1
Misurata, †36,850 C 1
Mizda, †2,508 B 1
Murzuk, †3,863 B 2
Nalut, †9,010 B 1
Ras Lanuf C 1
Sebha, †9,804 B 2
Serdeles B 2
Shahat, †6,266 D 1
Sinawen, †715 B 1
Sokna, †1,873 C 2
Soluk, †12,395 D 1
Suk el Juma, †81,123 B 1
Syrte, 7,093 C 1
Tagrifet C 2
Tarhuna, †25,502 B 1
Tejerri B 3
Tesawa B 2
Tmessa, 4,806 C 2
Tobruk, 15,867 D 1
Tokra, †5,900 D 1
Traghen, †2,952 B 2
Tripoli (capital), 247,365 B 1
Ubari, †1,711 B 2
Umm el Abid C 2
Waddan, †3,519 C 2
Wau el Kebir C 2
Zawia, †28,349 B 1
Zella, †2,560 C 2
Zliten, †17,950 C 1
Zuila, †1,839 C 2
Zwara, †14,578 B 1

OTHER FEATURES

Ain Dawa (well) D 3
Akhdar, Jebel (mts.) D 1
'Amir, Ras (cape) D 1
Anai (well), †1,795 B 3
Ben Ghnema, Jebel (mts.) C 2
Bette (peak) C 3
Bey el Kebir, Wadi (dry riv.) B 1
Bishiara (well) D 3
Bomba (gulf) D 1
Calansho, Serir (des.) D 2
Calansho Sand Sea (desert) D 2
Cyrenaica (region), 450,954 D 1
Fezzan (region), 79,326 B 2
Great Sand Sea (des.) D 2
Harug el Asued, El (mts.) C 2
Homra, Hamada el (desert) B 2
Hosenofu (well) D 3
Idehan (des.) B 2
Idehan Murzuk (des.) B 2
Jalo (oasis), 3,910 D 2
Jefara (reg.) B 1
Jofra (oasis), 8,827 C 2
Kufra (oasis), 5,509 D 3
Leptis Magna (ruins) B 1
Libyan (des.) D 2
Libyan (plat.) D 1
Mediterranean (sea) C 1
Nefusa, Jebel (mts.) B 1
Rebiana (oasis), †666 D 3
Rebiana Sand Sea (des.) D 3
Sabratha (ruins) B 1
Sahara (des.) D 3
Sarra (well) D 3
Shati, Wadi esh (dry riv.) B 2
Sidra (gulf) C 1
Soda, Jebel es (mts.) C 2
Tazerbo (oasis), †1,307 D 2
Tibesti, Serir (des.) C 3
Tinrhert Hamada (des.) B 2
Tripolitania (region), 1,034,089 B 1
'Uweinat, Jebel (mt.) E 3
Wau en Namus (well) C 3
Zelten, Jebel (mts.) D 2

SUDAN

PROVINCES

Bahr el Ghazal, 1,238,779 E 6
Blue Nile, 2,724,968 F 5
Darfur, 1,467,688 D 5
Equatoria, 1,129,388 E 6
Kassala, 1,413,069 G 4
Khartoum, 749,932 F 4
Kordofan, 2,022,201 E 5
Northern, 982,046 E 3
Upper Nile, 1,110,769 F 6

CITIES and TOWNS

Abu Hamed F 4
Abu Matariq E 5
Abu Zabad E 5
Abwong F 6
Abyei E 6
Adarama G 4
Adok F 6
Akobo F 6
Amadi F 6
'Aqiq G 4
Argo, 2,329 F 4
Aroma, 3,451 G 4
Atbara, 36,000 F 4
Aweil, 2,438 E 6
Ayod F 6
Babanusa E 5
Bara, 4,885 F 5
Bentiu E 6
Berber, 10,977 F 4
Bor F 6
Bo River Post E 6
Buram E 5
Deim Zubeir E 6
Delgo F 3
Derudeb G 4
Dilling, 5,596 E 5
Dongola, 3,350 F 4
Dungunab G 3
Ed Da'ein E 5
Ed Damer, 5,458 F 4
Ed Debba F 4
Ed Dueim, 12,319 F 5
El Abbasiya, 2,846 F 5
El Fasher, 26,161 E 5
El Fifi D 5
El Geteina F 5
El Hilla E 5
El Khandaq F 4
El Obeid, 53,000 E 5
El Odaiya E 5
En Nahud, 16,499 E 5
Er Rahad, 6,706 F 5
Er Roseires, 3,927 F 5
Famaka F 5
Fangak F 6
Fashoda (Kodok), 9,100 F 6
Gabras E 5
Gallabat G 5
Gebeit Mine G 3
Gedaref, 17,537 G 5
Geneina, 11,817 D 5
Gogrial E 6
Goz Regeb G 4
Haiya Junction G 4
Halaib G 3
Heiban F 5
Juba, 10,660 F 7
Kadugli, 4,716 E 5
Kafia Kingi D 6
Kajok E 6
Kaka F 5
Kapoeta F 7
Karima, 5,989 F 4
Karora G 4
Kassala, 40,000 G 4
Kerma F 4
Khartoum (capital), 194,000 F 4
Khartoum North, 40,000 F 4
Khashm el Girba G 5
Kodok, 9,100 F 6
Kongor F 6
Korti F 4
Kosti, 22,688 F 5
Kubbum D 5
Kurmuk, 1,647 F 5
Kutum D 5
Lado F 6
Loka F 7
Malakal, 9,680 F 6
Maridi, 839 E 7
Marsa Oseif G 3
Melut, 334 F 5
Merowe, 1,620 F 4
Meshra' er Req E 6
Mongalla F 6
Muglad, 3,735 E 5
Muhammad Qol G 3
Musmar G 4
Nagishot F 7
Nasir F 6
Nimule F 7
Nyala, 12,278 E 5
Nyamlell E 6
Nyerol F 6
Omdurman, 206,000 F 4
Opari F 7
Pibor Post F 6
Port Sudan, 110,000 G 4
Raga E 6
Rashad, 1,683 F 5
Rejaf F 7
Renk F 5
Rufa'a, 9,137 F 5
Rumbek, 2,944 E 6
Sennar, 8,093 F 5
Shambe F 6
Shendi, 11,031 F 4
Shereik F 4
Showak, 2,171 G 5
Singa, 9,436 F 5
Sinkat, 5,175 G 4
Sodiri, 1,804 E 5
Suakin, 4,228 G 4
Suki, 7,388 F 5
Tali Post F 6
Talodi, 2,736 F 5
Tambura E 6
Tendelti, 7,555 F 5
Tokar, 16,802 G 4
Tombe F 6
Tonga F 6
Tonj, 2,071 E 6
Torit, 2,353 F 7
Towot F 6
Trinkitat G 4
Umm Keddada, 2,410 E 5
Umm Ruwaba, 7,805 F 5
Wad Medani, 48,000 F 5
Wankai E 6
Wau, 8,009 E 6
Yambio, 3,890 E 7
Yei, 739 F 7
Yirol, 1,895 F 6
Zalingei, 3,314 D 5

OTHER FEATURES

Abu Dara, Ras (cape) G 3
Abu Habl, Wadi (dry riv.) F 5
Abu Shagara, Ras (cape) G 3
Abu Tabari (well) E 4
Adda (riv.) D 6
Akobo (riv.) F 6
'Amur, Wadi (dry riv.) G 4
Asoteriba, Jebel (mt.) G 3
Atbara (riv.) G 4
Bahr Azoum (riv.) D 5
Bahr el 'Arab (riv.) E 6
Bahr ez Zeraf (riv.) F 6
Baraka (dry riv.) G 4
Blue Nile (riv.) F 5
Dar Hamid (region) F 5
Dar Masalit (reg.), 323,616 D 5
Dinder (riv.) G 5
El 'Atrun (oasis) E 4
Fifth Cataract F 4
Fourth Cataract F 4
Gabgaba, Wadi (dry riv.) F 3
Gezira, El (reg.) F 5
Ghalla, Wadi el (dry riv.) E 5
Hadarba, Ras (cape) G 3
Howar, Wadi (dry riv.) E 4
Ibra, Wadi (dry riv.) D 5
Jebel Abyad (plat.) E 4
Jebel Aulia (dam) F 4
Jur (riv.) E 6
Kasar, Ras (cape) G 4
Kinyeti (mt.) F 7
Laqiya 'Umran (well) E 3
Libyan (desert) E 3
Lol (dry riv.) E 6
Lotagipi (swamp) F 6
Marra, Jebel (mt.) D 5
Meroe (ruins) F 4
Milk, Wadi el (dry riv.) E 4
Muqaddam, Wadi (dry riv.) F 4
Napata (ruins) F 4
Naqa (ruins) F 4
Nasser (lake) F 3
Nile (riv.) F 4
Nuba (mts.) E 5
Nubian (des.) F 3
Nukheila (oasis) E 4
Nuri (ruins) F 4
Oda, Jebel (mt.) G 3
Pibor (riv.) F 6
Red (sea) G 3
Sahara (des.) E 3
Second Cataract F 3
Selima (oasis) E 3
Sennar (dam) F 5
Setit (riv.) G 5
Sixth Cataract F 4
Sobat (riv.) F 6
Suakin (arch.) G 4
Sudan (reg.) E 5
Sudd (swamp) F 6
Sue (riv.) E 6
Third Cataract E 3
'Uweinat, Jebel (mt.) E 3
White Nile (riv.) F 5

Agriculture, Industry and Resources

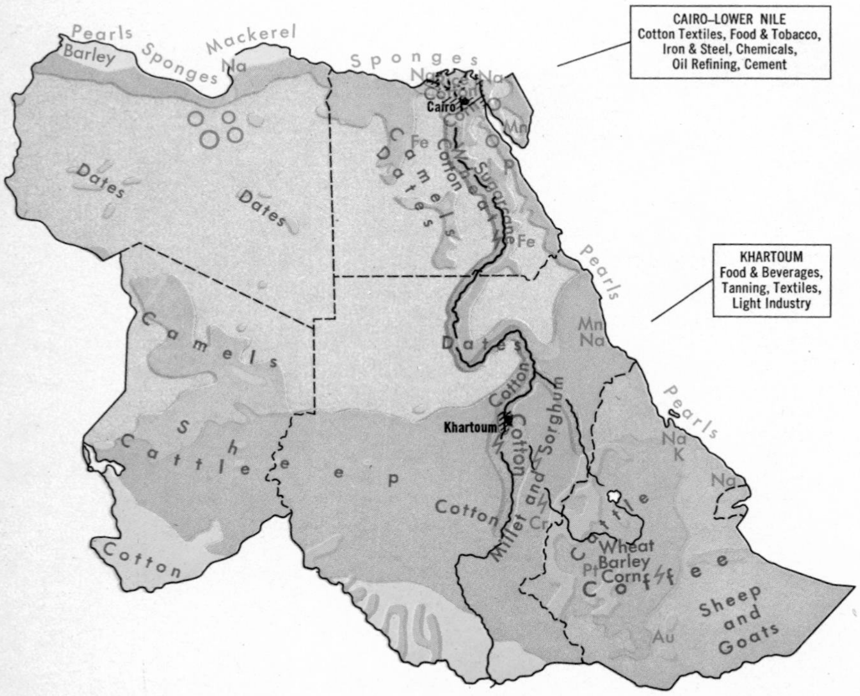

CAIRO–LOWER NILE
Cotton Textiles, Food & Tobacco, Iron & Steel, Chemicals, Oil Refining, Cement
KHARTOUM
Food & Beverages, Tanning, Textiles, Light Industry
Pearls
Barley
Sponges
Mackerel
Na
Cairo
Camels
Dates
Cotton
Sugar
Fe
Pearls
Mn
Khartoum
Sorghum
Millet
Cattle
Sheep
Wheat
Barley
Corn
Coffee
Sheep and Goats
Au
K
Cr
Pt

DOMINANT LAND USE

Cereals, Horticulture, Livestock
Cash Crops, Mixed Cereals
Cotton, Cereals
Market Gardening, Diversified Tropical Crops
Plantation Agriculture
Oases
Pasture Livestock
Nomadic Livestock Herding
Forests
Nonagricultural Land

MAJOR MINERAL OCCURRENCES

Au Gold
Cr Chromium
Fe Iron Ore
K Potash
Mn Manganese
Na Salt
O Petroleum
P Phosphates
Pt Platinum

Water Power
Major Industrial Areas

*City and suburbs.
†Population of sub-district or division.

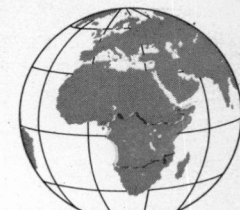

ANGOLA
AREA 481,351 sq. mi.
POPULATION 5,475,000
CAPITAL Luanda
LARGEST CITY Luanda
HIGHEST POINT Mt. Moco 8,593 ft.
MONETARY UNIT Portuguese escudo
MAJOR LANGUAGES Mbundu, Kongo, Lunda, Portuguese
MAJOR RELIGIONS Tribal religions, Roman Catholicism

BURUNDI
AREA 10,747 sq. mi.
POPULATION 3,475,000
CAPITAL Bujumbura
LARGEST CITY Bujumbura
HIGHEST POINT 8,858 ft.
MONETARY UNIT Rwanda-Burundi franc
MAJOR LANGUAGES Kirundi, French
MAJOR RELIGIONS Tribal religions, Roman Catholicism

CAMEROON
AREA 183,568 sq.mi.
POPULATION 5,836,000
CAPITAL Yaoundé
LARGEST CITY Douala
HIGHEST POINT Cameroon 13,350 ft.
MONETARY UNIT CFA franc
MAJOR LANGUAGES Fang, Bamileke, Fulani, Duala, French, English
MAJOR RELIGIONS Tribal religions, Christianity, Islam

CENTRAL AFRICAN REPUBLIC
AREA 240,534 sq. mi.
POPULATION 1,518,000
CAPITAL Bangui
LARGEST CITY Bangui
HIGHEST POINT Gao 4,659 ft.
MONETARY UNIT CFA franc
MAJOR LANGUAGES Banda, Gbaya, Sango, French
MAJOR RELIGIONS Tribal religions, Christianity, Islam

REPUBLIC OF CONGO
AREA 175,676 sq. mi.
POPULATION 915,000
CAPITAL Brazzaville
LARGEST CITY Brazzaville
HIGHEST POINT Leketi Mts. 3,412 ft.
MONETARY UNIT CFA franc
MAJOR LANGUAGES Kongo, Bateke, Lingala, French
MAJOR RELIGIONS Christianity, Tribal religions

EQUATORIAL GUINEA
AREA 10,832 sq. mi.
POPULATION 286,000
CAPITAL Santa Isabel
LARGEST CITY Santa Isabel
HIGHEST POINT 9,868 ft.
MONETARY UNIT peseta
MAJOR LANGUAGES Fang, Bubi, Spanish
MAJOR RELIGIONS Tribal religions, Christianity

GABON
AREA 103,346 sq. mi.
POPULATION 500,000
CAPITAL Libreville
LARGEST CITY Libreville
HIGHEST POINT Ibounzi 5,165 ft.
MONETARY UNIT CFA franc
MAJOR LANGUAGES Fang and other Bantu languages, French
MAJOR RELIGIONS Tribal religions, Christianity

KENYA
AREA 224,960 sq. mi.
POPULATION 10,880,200
CAPITAL Nairobi
LARGEST CITY Nairobi
HIGHEST POINT Kenya 17,058 ft.
MONETARY UNIT East African shilling
MAJOR LANGUAGES Kikuyu, Luo, Kavirondo, Kamba, Swahili, English
MAJOR RELIGIONS Tribal religions, Christianity

MALAWI
AREA 45,483 sq. mi.
POPULATION 4,530,000
CAPITAL Zomba
LARGEST CITY Blantyre
HIGHEST POINT Mlanje 9,843 ft.
MONETARY UNIT Malawi pound
MAJOR LANGUAGES Chichewa, Yao, English
MAJOR RELIGIONS Tribal religions, Islam

RWANDA
AREA 10,169 sq. mi.
POPULATION 3,500,000
CAPITAL Kigali
LARGEST CITY Kigali
HIGHEST POINT Karisimbi 14,780 ft.
MONETARY UNIT Rwanda-Burundi franc
MAJOR LANGUAGES Kinyarwanda, French
MAJOR RELIGIONS Tribal religions, Roman Catholicism

SOMALIA
AREA 246,200 sq. mi.
POPULATION 2,730,000
CAPITAL Mogadishu
LARGEST CITY Mogadishu
HIGHEST POINT Surud Ad 7,900 ft.
MONETARY UNIT somalo
MAJOR LANGUAGES Somali, Arabic, Italian, English
MAJOR RELIGIONS Islam, Roman Catholicism

TANZANIA
AREA 362,819 sq. mi.
POPULATION 12,896,000
CAPITAL Dar es Salaam
LARGEST CITY Dar es Salaam
HIGHEST POINT Kilimanjaro 19,340 ft.
MONETARY UNIT East African shilling
MAJOR LANGUAGES Nyamwezi-Sukuma, Swahili, English
MAJOR RELIGIONS Tribal religions, Christianity, Islam

UGANDA
AREA 92,674 sq. mi.
POPULATION 9,764,000
CAPITAL Kampala
LARGEST CITY Kampala
HIGHEST POINT Margherita 16,795 ft.
MONETARY UNIT East African shilling
MAJOR LANGUAGES Ganda, Acholi, Teso, Nyoro, Soga, Nkole, English
MAJOR RELIGIONS Tribal religions, Christianity

ZAIRE
AREA 905,563 sq. mi.
POPULATION 21,637,876
CAPITAL Kinshasa
LARGEST CITY Kinshasa
HIGHEST POINT Margherita 16,795 ft.
MONETARY UNIT zaire
MAJOR LANGUAGES Luba, Mongo, Kongo, Kinyarwanda, Zande, Lingala, Swahili, French
MAJOR RELIGIONS Tribal religions, Christianity

ZAMBIA
AREA 290,586 sq. mi.
POPULATION 4,056,995
CAPITAL Lusaka
LARGEST CITY Lusaka
HIGHEST POINT Sunzu 6,782 ft.
MONETARY UNIT kwacha
MAJOR LANGUAGES Bemba, Tonga, Lozi, Luvale, Nyanje, English
MAJOR RELIGIONS Tribal religions

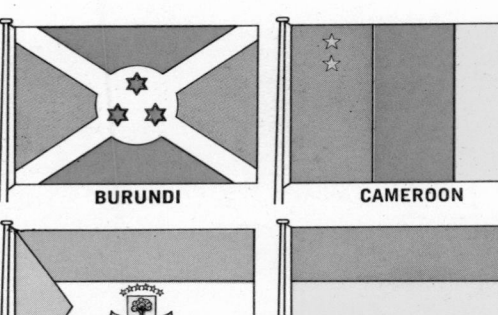

BURUNDI   CAMEROON   CENTRAL AFRICAN REP.   REPUBLIC OF CONGO

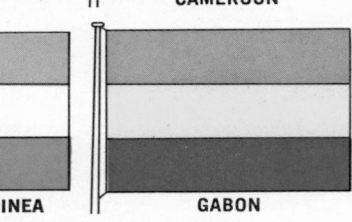

EQUATORIAL GUINEA   GABON   KENYA   MALAWI   RWANDA

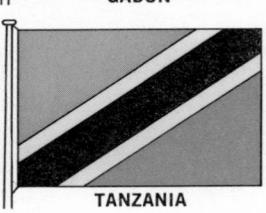   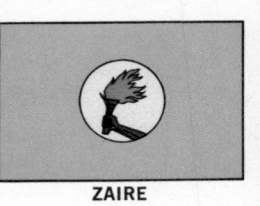 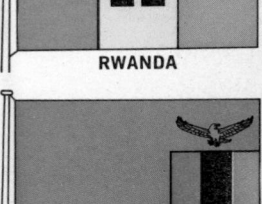

SOMALIA   TANZANIA   UGANDA   ZAIRE   ZAMBIA

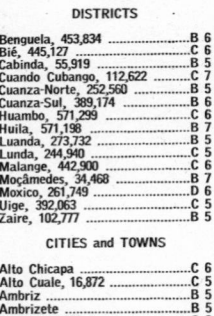
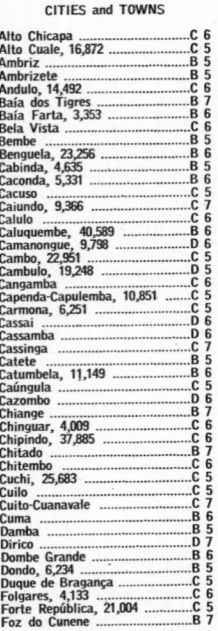

CAMEROON (continued)					OTHER FEATURES		CENTRAL AFRICAN REPUBLIC		
Kontcha	B 2	N'Gaoundéré, 15,000	B 2				CITIES and TOWNS		
Kousséri, 2,000	B 1	N'Kambe, 4,000	B 2		Adamawa (reg.)	B 2			
Kribi, 7,000	A 3	N'Konqsamba, 39,800	B 2		Benue (riv.)	A 2	Baboua, 2,000	C 2	
Kumba, 10,000	A 3	Poli, 700	B 2		Biafra (bight)	A 3	Bakala, 1,000	D 2	
Kumbo	B 2	Rei-Bouba, 3,500	B 2		Cameroon (mt.)	A 2	Bambari, 32,000	D 2	
Lomié, 10,127	A 2	Sangmélima, 4,800	B 3		Cross (riv.)	A 2	Bangassou, 28,000	D 2	
Mamfé, 10,000	A 2	Tibati, 4,000	B 2		Dja (riv.)	A 3	Bangui (capital), 111,266	C 3	
Maroua, 24,979	B 1	Tiko, 15,000	A 3		Donga (riv.)	B 3	Bangui, *240,000	C 3	
M'Balmayo, 5,500	B 3	Victoria, 15,000	A 3		Logone (riv.)	B 2	Bania	C 3	
Meiganga, 2,000	B 2	Yabassi	B 3		Lom (riv.)	B 2	Batangafo, 7,500	C 2	
Mokolo, 5,145	B 1	Yaoundé (cap.), 130,000	B 3		Mbéré (riv.)	B 2	Berbérati, 40,000	C 3	
Moloundou, 8,575	C 3	Yokadouma	B 3		Sanaga (riv.)	B 3			
		Yoko	B 2						

Birao	D 2	Fort-de-Possel, 500	C 2	M'Bres, 7,000	D 2
Bocaranga, 4,000	C 2	Fort-Sibut, 526	C 2	Mobaye	D 2
Boda	C 3	Gaza	C 2	Mouka	C 2
Bossangoa, 36,000	C 2	Goubéré	E 2	Ndélé, 4,013	D 2
Bossembele, 1,700	C 3	Grimari, 1,400	C 2	Ngourou	C 2
Bouali	C 3	Hyrra Banda	D 2	Nola, 500	C 3
Bouar, 29,000	C 2	Ippy, 6,000	D 2	Obo, 3,000	E 2
Bouca, 3,000	C 2	Kaka	E 2	Ouadda	D 2
Bozoum, 4,700	C 2	Kembé	D 2	Ouanda-Djalé	D 2
Bria, 25,000	D 2	Kouango	D 2	Ouango, 2,000	D 2
Bangui, *240,000	C 3	Kouki	C 2	Paoua, 3,500	C 2
Carnot, 4,000	C 3	Koundé	B 2	Rafaï, 8,891	D 2
Damara, 800	C 2	Koundé	C 2	Yalinga, 1,500	D 2
Djéma	E 2	Makounda	C 2	Zako	C 2
Fort-Crampel, 5,000	C 2	M'Baiki, 18,000	C 3		

Zémio, 1,500	D 2	Shinko (riv.)	D 2
Zemongo	E 2	Ubangi (riv.)	C 3

OTHER FEATURES

Bamingui (riv.)	C 2
Dar Rounga (region), 25,000	C 2
Kadeï (mt.)	C 3
Kadeï (riv.)	C 3
Kotto (riv.)	D 2
Lobaye (riv.)	C 3
Pendé (riv.)	C 3
Sara (riv.)	C 2
Shari (riv.)	C 2

CONGO, REPUBLIC OF

CITIES and TOWNS

Boko, 800	B 4
Brazzaville (capital), 94,000	B 4
Brazzaville, *200,000	C 4
Djambala, 2,000	B 4
Dolisie, 20,000	B 4
Dongou, 2,190	C 3
Epéna, 8,446	C 3
Ewo, 700	B 4
Fort-Rousset, 5,082	C 4
Gamboma, 1,700	C 4
Ikelemba, 400	C 4
Impfondo, 2,000	C 3
Kayes, 1,500	B 4
Kellé, 1,282	B 4
Kibangou, 1,000	B 4
Kinkala, 1,000	B 4
Komono, 750	B 4
Loudima, 400	B 4
Madingo, 2,500	B 4
Makoua, 2,000	C 3
Mindouli, 1,600	B 4
Mossaka, 2,128	C 4
Mossendjo, 3,000	B 4
M'Pouya	C 4
M'Vouti	B 4
Okoyo, 2,464	C 3
Ouesso, 4,464	C 3
Pangala	B 4
Pointe-Noire, 100,000	B 4
Sembé	B 3
Sibiti, 1,000	B 4
Souanké, 280	B 3
Zanaga, 800	B 4

OTHER FEATURES

Alima (riv.)	B 4
Congo (riv.)	C 4
Crystal (mts.)	B 4
Kouilou (riv.)	B 4
Niari (riv.)	B 4
Sanga (riv.)	C 3
Ubangi (riv.)	C 3

EQUATORIAL GUINEA

TERRITORIES

Fernando Po, 78,000	A 3
Río Muni, 203,000	A 3

CITIES and TOWNS

Bata, 27,024	B 3
Puerto Iradier	A 3
Río Benito, 14,503	A 3
San Carlos, 19,933	A 3
Santa Isabel (capital), 37,237	A 3

OTHER FEATURES

Corisco (isl.)	A 3
Elobey (isls.)	A 3
Fernando Po (island), 78,000	A 3

GABON

CITIES and TOWNS

Bitam, 2,080	B 3
Booué, 114	B 4
Cocobeach, 100	B 3
Franceville, 2,000	B 4
Kango, 300	B 4
Koula-Moutou, 3,170	B 4
Lalara, 1,333	B 3
Lambaréné, 7,000	B 4
Lastoursville, 2,000	B 4
Lekoni, 3,020	B 4
Libreville (capital), *57,000	A 3
Makokou, 1,150	B 3
Mayumba, 1,000	A 4
M'Bigou, 1,500	B 4
Mekambo, 800	B 3
Mimongo, 350	B 4
Minvoul, 200	B 3
Mitzic, 1,180	B 3
Moanda, 2,700	B 4
Mouila, 1,800	B 4
N'Dendé, 1,560	B 4
N'Djolé, 500	B 4
Okondja, 1,600	B 4
Oyem, 3,050	B 3
Port-Gentil, 30,000	A 4
Setté-Cama, 1,609	A 4
Tchibanga, 2,080	B 4

OTHER FEATURES

Crystal (mts.)	B 4
Ibounzi (mt.)	B 3
Ivindo (riv.)	B 3
Lopez (cape)	A 4
N'Dogo (lag.)	A 4
N'Gounié (riv.)	B 4
N'Komi (lag.)	A 4
Ogooué (riv.)	A 4
Onangué (lake)	A 4
Pongara (pt.)	A 4

KENYA

PROVINCES

Central, 1,664,000	G 4
Coast, 924,800	G 4
Eastern, 1,899,200	G 4
Nairobi (city district), 477,600	G 4
North Eastern, 244,200	G 3
Nyanza, 2,115,900	F 4
Rift Valley, 2,219,400	G 3
Western, 1,335,100	G 3

CITIES and TOWNS

Baragoi	G 3
Eldoret, 16,900	G 3
El Wak	H 3
Embu, 5,213	G 4
Fort Hall, 5,389	G 4
Garissa	G 4
Garsen	G 4
Gazi, 6,452	G 4
Gilgil	G 4
Hadu	G 4
Isiolo, 5,445	G 3
Kajiado	G 4
Kakamega	F 3
Karungu	F 4
Kericho, 10,900	G 4
Kiambu	G 4
Kibwezi	G 4
Kipini	H 4
Kisii	F 4
Kisumu, 30,700	G 4
Kitale, 11,500	G 3
Kitui	G 4
Konza	G 4
Kwale	G 4
Laisamis	G 3
Lamu, 5,828	H 4
Lodwar	G 3
Lokitaung	G 3
Lolgorien	G 4
Machakos	G 4
Magadi	G 4
Malindi, 5,818	H 4
Marsabit	G 3
Meru	G 4
Mombasa, 234,400	G 4
Moyale	G 3
Nairobi (capital), 477,600	G 4
Naivasha	G 4
Nakuru, 47,800	G 4
Namanga	G 4
Nanyuki, 11,200	G 3
Ngong	G 4
North Horr	G 3
Nyeri, 9,900	G 4
Port Victoria	F 3
Rumuruti	G 3
South Horr	G 3
Thika, 18,100	G 4
Thomson's Falls, 5,316	G 3
Todenyang	G 3
Tsavo	G 4
Vanga	G 4
Voi	G 4
Wajir	H 3
Witu	H 4

OTHER FEATURES

Dawa (riv.)	H 3
Elgon (mt.)	F 3
Formosa (bay)	H 4
Galana (riv.)	G 4
Gedi (ruins)	H 4
Kavirondo (gulf)	F 4
Kenya (mt.)	G 4
Lorian (swamp)	G 3
Lotagipi (swamp)	F 2
Nyira (mt.)	H 4
Patta (isl.)	H 4
Royal Tsavo Nat'l Park	G 4
Rudolf (lake)	G 3
Tana (riv.)	G 4
Victoria (lake)	F 4

MALAWI

CITIES and TOWNS

Bandawe	F 6
Blantyre, 109,461	F 7
Chilumbe	F 7
Chipoka	F 7
Chiromo	F 7
Chitipa, 1,429	F 5
Cholo, 1,394	F 7
Dedza, 2,318	F 6
Dowa, 750	F 6
Fort Johnston, 1,467	G 6
Karonga, 1,128	F 5
Kasungu, 1,628	F 6
Lilongwe, 19,425	F 6
Livingstonia	F 5
Mchinji, 831	F 6
Mzimba, 4,156	F 5
Ncheu, 1,118	F 6
Nkhata Bay, 1,188	F 6
Nkhota Kota, 1,117	F 6
Nsanje, 1,373	G 7
Salima, 2,307	F 6
Zomba (cap.), 19,666	G 7

OTHER FEATURES

Chilwa (lake)	G 7
Malawi (Nyasa) (lake)	F 6
Mlanje (mt.)	G 7
Nyasa (lake)	F 6
Shire (riv.)	G 7

RWANDA

CITIES and TOWNS

Butare, 3,714	E 4
Cyangugu, 3,956	E 4
Gisenyi, 3,956	E 4
Kigali (cap.), 24,000	E 4
Nyabisindu, 1,010	F 4

OTHER FEATURES

Kagera Nat'l Park	E 4
Karisimbi (mt.)	E 4
Kivu (lake)	E 4
Ruzizi (riv.)	E 4

SOMALIA

PROVINCES

Benadir, 392,189	H 3
Hiran, 176,603	J 3
Lower Juba, 113,774	H 3
Mijirtein, 82,710	J 1
Mudugh, 141,197	J 2
North-East	J 1
North-West	H 2
Upper Juba, 362,397	H 3

CITIES and TOWNS

Adadle	H 2
Afgoi, ⊙16,575	H 3
Afmadu, ⊙2,580	H 3
Alula, ⊙6,063	K 1
Ankhor	J 2
Audegle, ⊙8,865	H 3
Baduen	J 2
Baidoa, ⊙14,962	H 3
Balad, ⊙1,936	H 3
Barawa (Brava), ⊙6,168	H 3
Bardera, ⊙7,874	H 3
Bargal, ⊙2,222	K 1
Belet Uen, ⊙11,426	J 3
Bender Beila, ⊙6,084	K 2
Bender Kasim (Bosaso), ⊙7,560	J 1
Berbera, ⊙12,219	H 2
Bereda, ⊙5,323	K 1
Birikao (Bur Gavo)	H 4
Bohotleh	J 2
Borama, ⊙3,244	H 2
Bosaso, ⊙7,560	J 1
Brava, ⊙6,168	H 3
Bulo Burti, ⊙5,247	J 3
Bur Acaba, ⊙10,924	H 3
Burao, ⊙12,617	J 2
Bur Gavo	H 4
Candala, ⊙3,213	K 1
Coriolei, ⊙4,341	H 3
Dante (Hafun)	K 1
Dif	H 3
Dinsor, ⊙4,301	H 3
Dusa Mareb, ⊙3,125	J 2
Eil, ⊙2,234	J 2
El Athale (Itala), ⊙900	J 3
El Bur, ⊙3,224	J 3
El Dere, ⊙10,924	J 3
El Hamurre	J 2
Erigavo, ⊙4,279	J 1
Ferfer	J 2
Galkayu, ⊙9,477	J 2
Garad	J 2
Gardo, ⊙4,076	J 2
Garoe, ⊙5,672	J 2
Gowben	K 1
Hafun	K 1
Harardera, ⊙824	J 3
Harghessa, ⊙40,254	H 2
Hodur, ⊙3,137	H 3
Hordio	K 1
Iddan	J 2

(continued on following page)

CENTRAL AFRICA

CYLINDRICAL EQUAL-AREA PROJECTION

SCALE OF MILES
0 50 100   300

SCALE OF KILOMETERS
0 50 100   200   300

Capitals of Countries ⋯⋯⋯ ☆
Other Capitals ⋯⋯⋯ ⊙
International Boundaries — — —
Internal Boundaries ⋯⋯⋯

© C. S. HAMMOND & Co., Maplewood, N.J.

Topography

0   200   400   600
MILES

Below Sea Level	100 m. 328 ft.	200 m. 656 ft.	500 m. 1,640 ft.	1,000 m. 3,281 ft.	2,000 m. 6,562 ft.	5,000 m. 16,404 ft.

116 Central Africa

(continued)

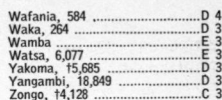

SOMALIA (continued)

Iet, ◉1,370 H 3
Itala, ◉900 J 3
Jamama, ◉22,030 H 3
Jelib, ◉3,232 H 3
Johar, ◉13,156 H 3
Kismayu, ◉17,872 H 4
Las Anod, ◉2,441 J 2
Las Dureh J 1
Las Khoreh, ◉2,245 J 1
Lugh, ◉3,768 H 3
Marek J 3
Margherita (Jamama), ◉22,030 H 3
Merka, ◉56,385 H 3
Mogadishu, 172,677 J 3
Obbia, ◉2,106 J 2
Odweina, ◉1,422 J 2
Skushuban, ◉1,384 J 1
Taleh J 2
Tijeglo, ◉5,459 H 3
Uanle Uen, ◉9,650 H 3
Upper Sheikh J 2
Villabruzzi (Johar), ◉13,156 J 3
Vittorio d'Africa H 3
Zeila, ◉1,226 H 1

OTHER FEATURES

Aden (gulf) J 1
Chiamboni, Ras (cape) H 4
Guardafui (cape) K 1
Guban (reg.) H 1
Hafun, Ras (cape) K 1
Haud (plat.) J 2
Juba (riv.) H 3
Negro (bay) J 2
Nogal (reg.) J 2
Surud Ad (mt.) J 1
Wabi Shebelle (riv.) H 3

TANZANIA

PROVINCES

Arusha, 610,474 G 4
Coast, 511,506 G 5
Dar es Salaam (city), 272,821 G 5
Dodoma, 709,380 G 5
Iringa, 689,905 G 5
Kigoma, 473,443 F 4
Kilimanjaro, 652,722 G 4
Mara, 544,125 F 4
Mbeya, 969,053 F 5
Morogoro, 685,104 G 5
Mtwara, 1,041,146 G 5
Mwanza, 1,055,883 F 4
Pemba, 164,321 H 5
Ruvuma, 393,043 G 6
Shinyanga, 899,468 F 4
Singida, 457,938 F 5
Tabora, 562,871 F 5
Tanga, 771,060 G 5
West Lake, 658,712 F 4
Zanzibar (city), 95,047 F 4
Zanzibar (rural), 95,447 G 5

CITIES and TOWNS

Arusha, 32,452 G 4
Bagamoyo, 5,112 G 5
Biharamulo, 1,011 F 4
Bukene, 2,288 F 4
Bukoba, 8,141 F 4
Chake Chake, 4,862 G 5
Chunya, 2,398 F 5
Dar es Salaam (capital), 272,821 G 5
Dodoma, 23,559 G 5
Geita, 3,066 F 4
Handeni G 5
Ifakara, †21,101 G 5
Iringa, 21,746 G 5
Itigi, †6,633 F 5
Kahama, 3,211 F 4
Kaliua, †13,071 F 5
Karema, †3,171 F 5
Kasanga, †10,462 F 5
Kasulu F 4
Kibara, †18,827 F 4
Kibaya, †4,422 G 5
Kibondo F 4
Kigoma-Ujiji, 21,369 E 4
Kilosa, 4,458 G 5
Kilwa Kivinje, 2,790 G 5
Kilwa Masoko G 5
Kinyangiri, †14,111 G 4
Kipili, †2,964 F 5
Kisiju, †26,298 G 5
Kitunda, †2,491 F 5
Kizimkazi, 992 G 5
Koani, 1,102 G 5
Kondoa, 4,514 G 4
Kongwa, †27,411 G 5
Korogwe, 6,675 G 5
Lindi, 13,352 G 5
Liwale, †22,205 G 5
Longido, †1,998 G 4
Lushoto, 1,803 G 4
Mahenge, †32,047 G 5
Makumbako G 5
Manyoni, †4,362 G 5
Masasi G 6
Mbamba Bay, †10,936 G 6
Mbeya, 12,479 F 5
Mbulu, †7,004 G 4
Mchinga, †5,778 H 5
Mohoro-Kikobo, †6,112 G 5
Mombo, †29,782 G 4
Morogoro, 25,262 G 5
Moshi, 26,864 G 4
Mpanda, †4,220 F 5
Mpwapwa, 2,429 G 5
Mtwara-Mikindani, 20,413 H 6
Murongo, †20,118 F 4
Musoma, 15,412 F 4
Muwale F 5
Mwadui, 7,383 F 4
Mwanza, 34,861 F 4
Mwaya, †15,940 F 5
Mwesi, †803 F 5
Nachingwea, 3,751 G 6
Newala, †7,458 G 6
Ngara F 4
Njombe F 5
Nzega, 2,386 F 4
Pangani, 2,955 G 5
Rungwa, †903 F 5
Sadani, †760 G 5
Same, †8,105 G 4
Sekenke F 4
Shinyanga, 5,135 F 4
Singida, 9,478 F 4
Songea, 5,430 G 6
Sumbawanga, †34,106 F 5
Tabora, 21,012 F 5
Tanga, 61,058 G 4
Tukuyu, 4,089 F 5
Tunduru G 6
Urambo, †16,625 F 4
Utete, †5,642 G 5
Uvinza, †12,812 F 5
Wete, 8,469 G 4
Zanzibar, 68,490 G 5
Zanzibar, *95,047 G 5

OTHER FEATURES

Eyasi (lake) F 4
Gombe (riv.) F 4
Great Ruaha (riv.) G 5
Juani (isl.), 696 G 5
Kalambo (falls) F 5
Kanzi (cape) G 5
Kilimanjaro (mt.) G 4
Kilombero (riv.) G 5
Kungwe (mt.) F 5
Mafia (isl.), 15,459 H 5
Manyara (lake) G 4
Masai (steppe) G 4
Mbarangandu (riv.) G 5
Mbemkuru (riv.) G 5
Meru (mt.) G 4
Natron (lake) G 4
Ngorongoro (crater) F 4
Njombe (riv.) F 5
Nyasa (lake) F 6
Olduvai Gorge (canyon) G 4
Pangani (riv.) G 4
Pemba (isl.), 164,321 H 5
Rufiji (riv.) G 5
Rukwa (lake) F 5
Rungwa (riv.) F 5
Rungwe (mt.) F 5
Ruvuma (riv.) G 4
Serengeti Nat'l Park F 4
Tanganyika (lake) E 5
Victoria (lake) F 4
Wami (riv.) G 5
Wembere (riv.) F 4
Zanzibar (isl.), 190,494 G 5

UGANDA

CITIES and TOWNS

Arua, 4,645 F 3
Atura, 119 F 3
Butiaba, 1,216 F 3
Entebbe, 10,941 F 4
Fort Portal, 8,317 F 3
Gulu, 4,770 F 3
Hoima, 1,056 F 3
Jinja, 29,741 F 3
Kaabong F 3
Kabale, 10,919 E 4
Kampala (capital), 330,000 F 3
Kasese, 1,564 F 3
Katwe, 2,057 F 4
Kilembe F 3
Kitgum, 3,454 F 3
Lira, 2,929 F 3
Masaka, 4,785 F 4
Masindi, 1,571 F 3
Mbale, 23,539 F 3
Mbarara, 3,844 F 4
Moroto, 2,082 F 3
Moyo, 2,009 F 3
Mubende, 1,878 F 3
Namasagali F 3
Pakwach, 1,467 F 3
Rhino Camp, 3,478 F 3
Soroti, 6,645 F 3
Tororo, 6,365 F 3
Yumbe, 949 F 3

OTHER FEATURES

Albert (lake) F 3
Edward (lake) E 4
Elgon (mt.) F 3
George (lake) F 4
Kioga (lake) F 3
Margherita (mt.) E 3
Murchison (falls) F 3
Owen Falls (dam) F 3
Queen Elizabeth Nat'l Park F 4
Ruwenzori (range) E 3
Sese (isls.) F 4
Victoria (lake) F 4

ZAIRE

PROVINCES

Bandundu, 2,600,556 C 4
Bas-Zaïre, 1,504,361 B 4
Equateur, 2,431,812 D 3
Haut-Zaïre, 3,356,419 E 3
Kasai-Occidental, 2,433,861 D 4
Kasai-Oriental, 1,872,231 D 5
Katanga, 2,753,714 E 5
Kinshasa (city), 1,323,039 C 4
Kivu, 3,361,883 E 4

CITIES and TOWNS

Aba F 3
Abumombazi, †5,773 D 3
Aketi, 15,339 D 3
Ango E 3
Avakubi E 3
Bagata C 4
Balangala D 3
Bambesa E 3
Bambili E 3
Banana B 5
Bandundu, 74,467 C 4
Banzyville, 6,608 D 3
Baraka E 4
Basankusu, 5,613 C 3
Basoko D 3
Basongo D 4
Batama E 3
Baudouinville E 5
Befale, 3,407 D 3
Bena-Dibele D 4
Beni E 3
Bikoro, 6,491 C 4
Boende, 391 D 4
Bokungu, 4,952 D 4
Bolobo C 4
Bolomba, 5,636 C 3
Boma, 33,143 B 5
Bomboma, 1,319 C 3
Bomongo, 4,827 C 3
Bondo, 453 D 3
Bongandanga, 4,476 D 3
Bosobolo, 2,809 D 3
Budjala, 415 C 3
Bukama E 5
Bukavu, 134,861 E 4
Bumba, 5,182 D 3
Bunia, 12,410 E 3
Bunkeya E 6
Busanga, †2,792 D 6
Businga, 2,827 D 3
Busu-Djanoa, †5,520 D 3
Buta, 10,845 D 3
Butembo, 9,980 E 3
Dekese D 4
Demba D 5
Dibaya D 5
Dibaya-Lubue C 4
Dilolo D 6
Dimbelenge D 5
Djolu, 2,516 D 3
Djugu F 3
Djuma C 4
Dongo, 559 C 3
Doruma E 3
Dungu E 3
Elila E 4
Equateur C 3
Etoile E 6
Faradje E 3
Feshi C 5
Fizi E 4
Gandajika D 5
Gemena, 8,135 D 3
Goma, 14,115 E 4
Gombari E 3
Gumba-Mobeka, †7,023 C 3
Idiofa C 4
Ikela, 3,166 D 4
Imese, 115 C 3
Ingende, 6,730 C 4
Inongo C 4
Irumu E 3
Isangi D 3
Isangila B 5
Isiro, 17,430 E 3
Kabalo E 5
Kabare E 4
Kabinda D 5
Kabongo E 5
Kabunda E 6
Kahemba C 5
Kalehe E 4
Kalemie, 29,934 E 5
Kalima E 4
Kaloko E 5
Kama E 4
Kambove (with Shinkolobwe), 14,517 E 6
Kamina, 20,915 D 5
Kanda Kanda D 5
Kaniama D 5
Kapanga D 5
Kasaji D 6
Kasangulu C 4
Kasenyi E 3
Kasese E 4
Kasongo E 4
Kasongo-Lunda C 5
Katako-Kombe D 4
Katana E 4
Katenga E 5
Kazumba D 5
Kenge C 4
Kibombo E 4
Kikwit, 111,960 C 5
Kilo E 3
Kilwa E 5
Kindu-Port Empain, 19,385 E 4
Kiniama E 6
Kinshasa (capital), 1,323,039 C 4
Kipushi, 22,602 E 6
Kirundu E 4
Kisangani, 229,596 E 3
Kolwezi, 45,192 E 6
Komba D 3
Kongolo, 10,434 E 5
Kungu, 7,912 C 3
Kutu, †2,072 C 4
Kwamouth C 4
Libenge, 2,632 C 3
Lienartville E 3
Likasi, 146,394 E 6
Likati D 3
Lisala, 574 D 3
Lodja, 7,227 D 4
Lokolama D 4
Lomela, †7,757 D 4
Loto D 4
Lotumbe C 4
Luashi D 6
Lubefu D 4
Lubudi, 5,915 E 5
Lubumbashi, 318,000 E 6
Lubutu E 4
Luebo D 5
Luena E 5
Luishia E 6
Lukula B 4
Luluabourg, 428,960 D 5
Lunyama E 5
Luofu E 4
Luozi B 5
Luputa D 5
Lusambo, 9,395 D 4
Lusangi E 4
Madimba C 5
Malonga D 6
Mambasa E 3
Manono, 12,234 E 5
Masi-Manimba C 4
Masisi E 4
Matadi, 110,436 B 5
Mbandaka, 107,910 C 3
Mbuji-Mayi, 256,154 D 5
Moanda B 5
Moba E 5
Moliro E 5
Monga D 3
Monkoto, 5,209 D 4
Monveda D 3
Mungbere E 3
Mushie, 12,118 C 4
Mutshatsha D 6
Muyumba E 5
Mwadingusha E 6
Mwanza E 5
Mwene Ditu D 5
Mwenga E 4
Niangara E 3
Niemba E 5
Nouvelle-Anvers, †4,330 C 3
Nyunzu E 5
Oshwe C 4
Panda E 6
Pangi E 4
Penge D 5
Piana-Mwanga E 5
Poie D 4
Poko E 3
Ponthierville D 4
Port-Francqui D 4
Punia E 4
Pweto E 5
Rutshuru E 4
Sakania E 6
Sampwe E 5
Sandoa D 5
Shabunda E 4
Shinkolobwe (with Kambove), 14,517 E 6
Songololo B 5
Thysville, 16,369 C 5
Titule E 3
Tolo C 4
Tondo C 4
Tshela B 4
Tshikapa D 5
Tshofa D 5
Uvira E 4
Vanga C 4
Wafania, 584 D 4
Waka, 264 D 3
Wamba E 3
Watsa, 6,077 E 3
Yakoma, †5,685 D 3
Yangambi, 18,849 D 3
Zongo, †4,128 C 3

OTHER FEATURES

Albert (lake) F 3
Albert Nat'l Park E 4
Aruwimi (riv.) E 3
Bomu (riv.) D 3
Congo (riv.) C 4
Edward (lake) E 4
Elila (riv.) E 4
Fimi (riv.) C 4
Garamba Nat'l Park E 3
Giri (riv.) C 3
Itimbiri (riv.) D 3
Ituri (for.) E 3
Karisimbi (mt.) E 4
Kasai (riv.) C 4
Kivu (lake) E 4
Kwa (riv.) C 4
Kwango (riv.) C 5
Kwilu (riv.) C 5
Léopold II (lake) C 4
Lindi (riv.) E 3
Livingstone (falls) B 5
Loange (riv.) C 5
Lokoro (riv.) C 4
Lomami (riv.) D 4
Lomela (riv.) D 4
Lowa (riv.) E 4
Lua (riv.) C 3
Lualaba (riv.) E 4
Luapula (riv.) E 6
Lubilash (riv.) D 5
Lufira (riv.) E 5
Luilaka (riv.) D 4
Lukenie (riv.) D 4
Lukuga (riv.) E 5
Lulua (riv.) D 5
Luvua (riv.) E 5
Margherita (mt.) E 3
Mweru (lake) E 5
Marungu (mts.) E 5
Ruwenzori (range) E 3
Ruzizi (riv.) E 4
Sankuru (riv.) D 4
Stanley (falls) E 3
Stanley Pool (lake) C 4
Tanganyika (lake) E 5
Tshuapa (riv.) D 4
Tumba (lake) C 4
Ubangi (riv.) C 3
Uele (riv.) E 3
Ulindi (riv.) E 4
Upemba (lake) E 5
Upemba Nat'l Park E 5
Virunga (range) E 4
Zaire (Congo) (riv.) C 4

ZAMBIA

CITIES and TOWNS

Abercorn (Mbala), ‡5,200 F 5
Balovale, 2,260 D 6
Bancroft (Chililabombwe), ‡39,900 E 6
Broken Hill (Kabwe), ‡67,200 E 6
Chilanga, 2,510 E 7
Chililabombwe, ‡39,900 E 6
Chingola, ‡92,800 E 6
Chinsali, 1,110 F 6
Chipata, ‡13,300 F 6
Chisamba, 790 E 6
Choma, ‡11,300 E 7
Feira, 310 E 7
Fort Rosebery (Mansa), ‡5,700 E 6
Isoka, 1,370 F 6
Kabompo, 990 D 6
Kabwe, ‡67,200 E 6
Kafue, 2,490 E 7
Kalabo, 2,420 D 6
Kalomo, 2,560 E 7
Kapiri Mposhi, 440 E 6
Kasama, ‡8,900 F 6
Kasempa, 670 E 6
Kawambwa, 1,430 E 5
Kitwe, ‡179,300 E 6
Lealui D 6
Livingstone, ‡43,000 E 7
Luanshya, ‡90,400 E 6
Lukulu D 6
Lundazi, 1,750 F 6
Lusaka (capital), ‡238,200 E 7
Luwingu, 850 E 6
Mankoya, 1,600 D 6
Mansa, ‡5,700 E 6
Mazabuka, ‡9,400 E 7
Mbala, ‡5,200 F 5
Mongu, ‡10,700 D 7
Monze, ‡4,300 E 7
Mpika, 660 F 6
Mporokoso, 790 F 5
Mpulungu, 1,830 F 5
Mufulira, ‡101,200 E 6
Mumbwa, 1,400 E 6
Mwinilunga, 700 D 6
Nakonde F 5
Namwala, 880 E 7
Nchanga, 35,030 E 6
Ndola, ‡150,800 E 6
Nkana, 54,500 E 6
Petauke, 1,640 F 6
Roan Antelope, 36,300 E 6
Senanga, 1,500 D 7
Serenje, 1,650 F 6
Sesheke, 910 D 7
Solwezi, 1,930 E 6

OTHER FEATURES

Bangweulu (lake) F 6
Barotseland (reg.), 417,000 D 7
Chambeshi (riv.) F 6
Dongwe (riv.) D 6
Kabampo (riv.) D 6
Kafue (riv.) E 7
Kariba (dam) E 7
Kariba (lake) E 7
Kwando (riv.) D 7
Luangwa (riv.) F 6
Mosi-Ao-Tunya (Victoria) (falls) E 7
Mulungushi (dam) E 6
Mweru (lake) E 5
Sunzu (mt.) F 5
Tanganyika (lake) E 5
Victoria (falls) E 7
Zambezi (riv.) D 7

*City and suburbs.
†Population of sub-district or division.
‡Population of urban area.
◉Population of municipality.

Agriculture, Industry and Resources

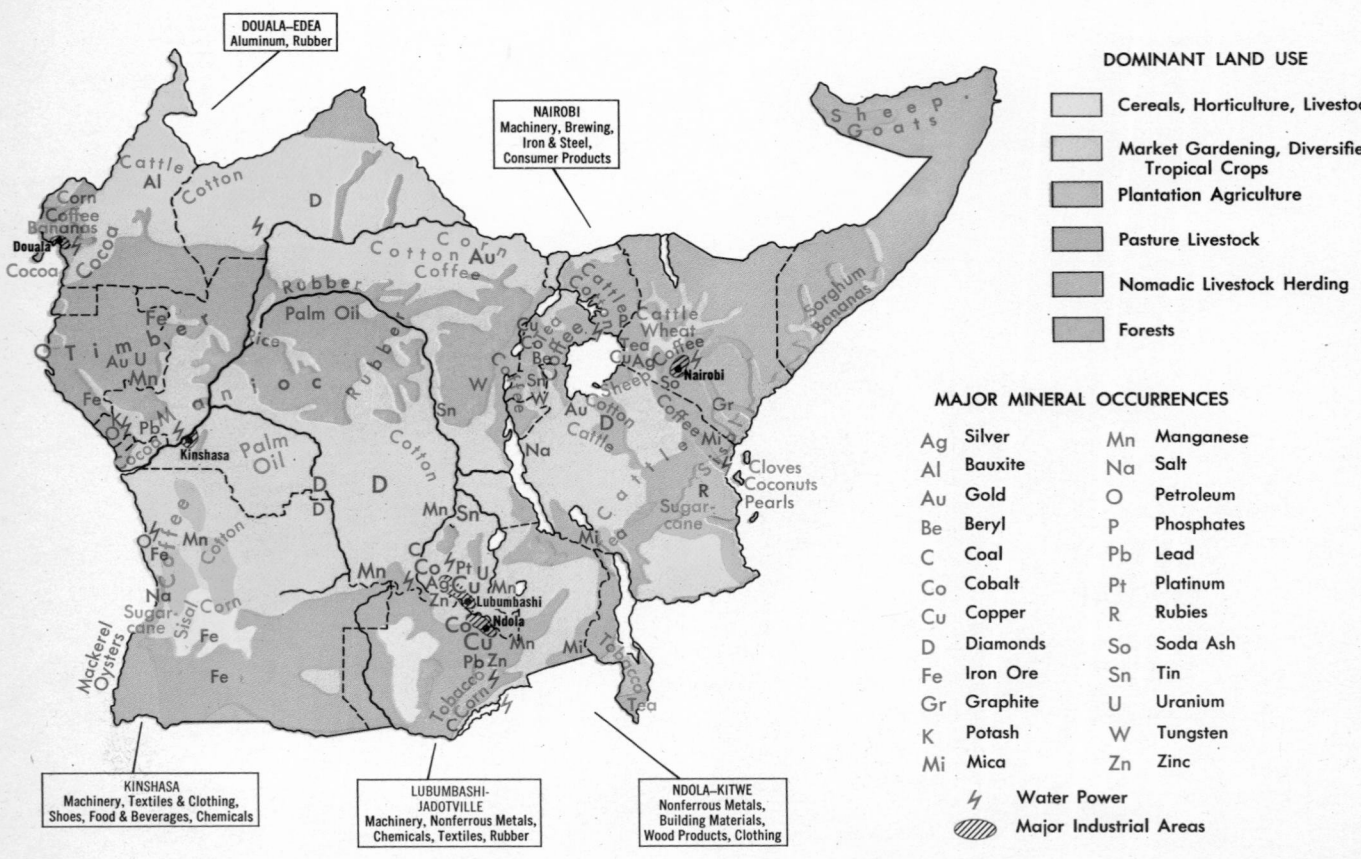

DOUALA–EDEA
Aluminum, Rubber
NAIROBI
Machinery, Brewing, Iron & Steel, Consumer Products
KINSHASA
Machinery, Textiles & Clothing, Shoes, Food & Beverages, Chemicals
LUBUMBASHI-JADOTVILLE
Machinery, Nonferrous Metals, Chemicals, Textiles, Rubber
NDOLA–KITWE
Nonferrous Metals, Building Materials, Wood Products, Clothing
Douala
Kinshasa
Nairobi
Lubumbashi
Ndola
Sheep
Goats
Cattle
Cotton
Corn
Coffee
Bananas
Cocoa
Rubber
Palm Oil
Timber
Manioc
Wheat
Sisal
Sugar-cane
Cloves
Coconuts
Pearls
Tobacco
Tea
Mackerel
Oysters
Sorghum
DOMINANT LAND USE
Cereals, Horticulture, Livestock
Market Gardening, Diversified Tropical Crops
Plantation Agriculture
Pasture Livestock
Nomadic Livestock Herding
Forests
MAJOR MINERAL OCCURRENCES
Ag Silver
Al Bauxite
Au Gold
Be Beryl
C Coal
Co Cobalt
Cu Copper
D Diamonds
Fe Iron Ore
Gr Graphite
K Potash
Mi Mica
Mn Manganese
Na Salt
O Petroleum
P Phosphates
Pb Lead
Pt Platinum
R Rubies
So Soda Ash
Sn Tin
U Uranium
W Tungsten
Zn Zinc
Water Power
Major Industrial Areas

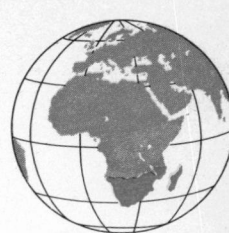

SOUTH-WEST AFRICA
AREA 317,838 sq. mi.
POPULATION 615,000
CAPITAL Windhoek
LARGEST CITY Windhoek
HIGHEST POINT Brandberg 8,550 ft.
MONETARY UNIT rand
MAJOR LANGUAGES Ovambo, Hottentot, Herero, Afrikaans, English
MAJOR RELIGIONS Tribal religions, Protestantism

BOTSWANA
AREA 219,815 sq. mi.
POPULATION 629,000
CAPITAL Gaborone
LARGEST CITIES Serowe and Kanye
HIGHEST POINT Tsodilo Hill 5,922 ft.
MONETARY UNIT pound sterling
MAJOR LANGUAGES Setswana, Shona, Bushman, English
MAJOR RELIGIONS Tribal religions, Protestantism

RHODESIA
AREA 150,332 sq. mi.
POPULATION 5,310,000
CAPITAL Salisbury
LARGEST CITY Salisbury
HIGHEST POINT Mt. Inyangani 8,517 ft.
MONETARY UNIT Rhodesian pound
MAJOR LANGUAGES English, Shona, Ndabele
MAJOR RELIGIONS Tribal religions, Protestantism

SOUTH AFRICA
AREA 471,663 sq. mi.
POPULATION 21,282,000
CAPITALS Cape Town, Pretoria
LARGEST CITY Johannesburg
HIGHEST POINT Injasuti 11,182 ft.
MONETARY UNIT rand
MAJOR LANGUAGES Afrikaans, English, Xhosa, Zulu, Sesotho, Pedi
MAJOR RELIGIONS Protestantism, Roman Catholicism, Islam, Hinduism

MOZAMBIQUE
AREA 302,328 sq. mi.
POPULATION 7,376,000
CAPITAL Lourenço Marques
LARGEST CITY Lourenço Marques
HIGHEST POINT Mt. Binga 7,992 ft.
MONETARY UNIT Portuguese escudo
MAJOR LANGUAGES Makua, Thonga, Shona, Portuguese
MAJOR RELIGIONS Tribal religions, Roman Catholicism

MALAGASY REPUBLIC
AREA 226,657 sq. mi.
POPULATION 7,011,563
CAPITAL Tananarive
LARGEST CITY Tananarive
HIGHEST POINT Maromokotro 9,436 ft.
MONETARY UNIT CFA franc
MAJOR LANGUAGES Malagasy, French
MAJOR RELIGIONS Tribal religions, Roman Catholicism, Protestantism

MAURITIUS
AREA 709 sq. mi.
POPULATION 823,000
CAPITAL Port Louis
LARGEST CITY Port Louis
HIGHEST POINT 2,711 ft.
MONETARY UNIT Mauritius rupee
MAJOR LANGUAGES English, French, French Creole, Hindi
MAJOR RELIGIONS Hinduism, Christianity

LESOTHO
AREA 11,716 sq. mi.
POPULATION 930,000
CAPITAL Maseru
LARGEST CITY Maseru
HIGHEST POINT 11,425 ft.
MONETARY UNIT rand
MAJOR LANGUAGES Sesotho, English
MAJOR RELIGIONS Tribal religions, Christianity

SWAZILAND
AREA 6,704 sq. mi.
POPULATION 411,879
CAPITAL Mbabane
LARGEST CITY Mbabane
HIGHEST POINT Emlembe 6,109 ft.
MONETARY UNIT rand
MAJOR LANGUAGES Swazi, English
MAJOR RELIGIONS Tribal religions, Christianity

RÉUNION
AREA 969 sq. mi.
POPULATION 436,000
CAPITAL St-Denis

SEYCHELLES
AREA 109 sq. mi.
POPULATION 51,396
CAPITAL Victoria

COMORO ISLANDS
AREA 838 sq. mi.
POPULATION 270,000
CAPITAL Moroni

RHODESIA

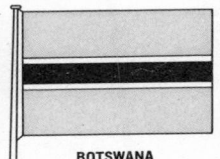
BOTSWANA

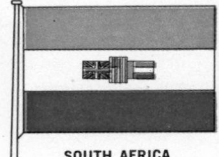
SOUTH AFRICA

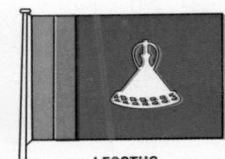
LESOTHO

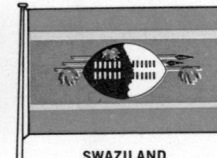
SWAZILAND

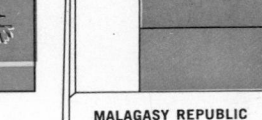
MALAGASY REPUBLIC

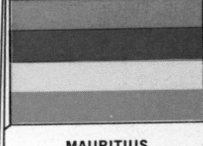
MAURITIUS

Agriculture, Industry and Resources

DOMINANT LAND USE

- Cereals, Horticulture, Livestock
- Market Gardening, Diversified Tropical Crops
- Plantation Agriculture
- Pasture Livestock
- Nomadic Livestock Herding
- Forests
- Nonagricultural Land

MAJOR MINERAL OCCURRENCES

Ab	Asbestos	Mn	Manganese
Ag	Silver	Na	Salt
Au	Gold	Ni	Nickel
Be	Beryl	P	Phosphates
C	Coal	Pb	Lead
Cr	Chromium	Pt	Platinum
Cu	Copper	Sb	Antimony
D	Diamonds	Sn	Tin
Fe	Iron Ore	U	Uranium
Gr	Graphite	V	Vanadium
Lt	Lithium	W	Tungsten
Mg	Magnesium	Zn	Zinc
Mi	Mica		

⚡ Water Power
🔲 Major Industrial Areas

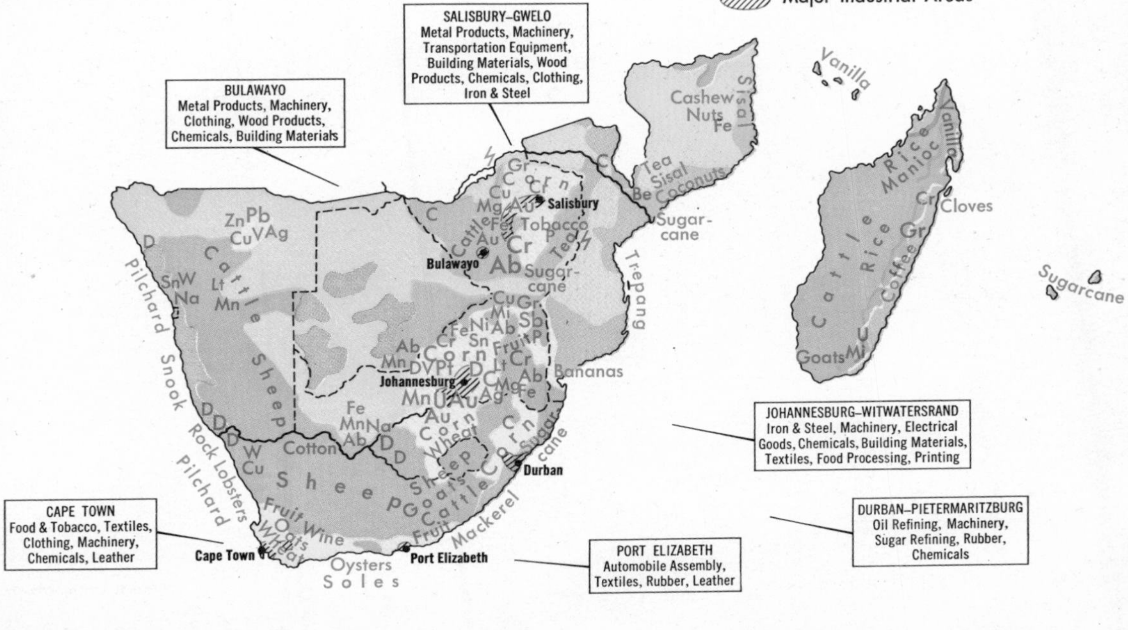

SALISBURY–GWELO
Metal Products, Machinery, Transportation Equipment, Building Materials, Wood Products, Chemicals, Clothing, Iron & Steel

BULAWAYO
Metal Products, Machinery, Clothing, Wood Products, Chemicals, Building Materials

JOHANNESBURG–WITWATERSRAND
Iron & Steel, Machinery, Electrical Goods, Chemicals, Building Materials, Textiles, Food Processing, Printing

CAPE TOWN
Food & Tobacco, Textiles, Clothing, Machinery, Chemicals, Leather

PORT ELIZABETH
Automobile Assembly, Textiles, Rubber, Leather

DURBAN–PIETERMARITZBURG
Oil Refining, Machinery, Sugar Refining, Rubber, Chemicals

BOTSWANA

CITIES and TOWNS

Bobonong, 7,490	D 4
Dinokwe, 1,422	D 4
Francistown, 3,225	D 4
Gaborone (cap.), 18,000	D 4
Ghanzi, 889	C 4
Kalkfontein, 1,470	C 4
Kanye, 35,000	C 5
Kasane, 391	D 3
Khuis, 615	C 5
Lehututu, 1,350	C 4
Lephepe, 2,770	D 4
Lobatse, 3,949	D 5
Machaneng, 1,709	D 4
Mahalapye, 13,199	D 4
Maun, 4,591	C 3
Mochudi, 17,712	D 4
Molepolole, 29,625	C 4
Palapye, 5,137	D 4
Ramotswa, 10,549	C 4
Serowe, 35,000	D 4
Serule, 1,507	D 4
Shakawe, 4,359	C 3
Shoshong, 7,022	D 4
Tonota, 9,892	C 4
Tshabong, 978	C 5
Tshane, 630	C 4
Tsau, 2,963	C 4

OTHER FEATURES

Chobe (riv.)	C 3
Kalahari (des.)	C 4
Limpopo (riv.)	D 4
Mababe (depr.)	C 3
Makgadikgadi (salt pan)	D 3
Molopo (riv.)	C 5
Ngami (lake)	C 4
Ngamiland (reg.), 42,395	C 3
Okavango (basin)	C 3
Shashi (riv.)	D 4
Tati (riv.)	D 4
Tsodilo Hill (mt.)	C 3
Xau (lake)	D 4

BRITISH INDIAN OCEAN TERR.

PHYSICAL FEATURES

Aldabra (isls.), 100	H 1

COMORO ISLANDS

CITIES and TOWNS

Dzaoudzi, 196	H 2
Fomboni, 3,229	G 2
Mitsamiouli, 3,196	G 2
Moroni (cap.), 11,515	G 2
Mutsamudu, 7,652	G 2

OTHER FEATURES

Anjouan (isl.), 83,486	G 2
Grand Comoro (island), 118,443	G 2
Mayotte (isl.), 32,494	G 2
Mohéli (isl.), 9,525	G 2

LESOTHO

CITIES and TOWNS

Leribe, 3,799	D 5
Mafeteng, 5,050	D 5
Maseru (cap.), 18,797	D 5
Mohaleshoek, 3,753	D 6

MALAGASY REPUBLIC

PROVINCES

Diégo Suarez, 575,424	H 2
Fianarantsoa, 1,720,922	H 3
Majunga, 839,654	H 3
Tamatave, 1,096,235	H 3
Tananarive, 1,692,607	H 3
Tuléar, 1,086,721	G 4

CITIES and TOWNS

Ambalavao, 6,045	H 4
Ambanja, 5,198	H 2
Ambato Boina, 3,108	H 3
Ambatofinandrahana, 2,039	H 4
Ambatolampy, 10,504	H 3
Ambatondrazaka, 14,297	H 3
Ambilobe, 7,877	H 2
Amboasary, 2,260	H 4
Ambodifototra, 1,080	J 3
Ambohimahasoa, 5,114	H 4
Ambositra, 15,131	H 4
Ambovombe, 3,161	H 5
Ampanihy, 2,078	G 4
Analalava, 3,061	H 2
Andapa, 8,296	H 2
Andilamena, 2,767	H 3
Ankazoabo, 1,528	G 4
Anororoa, 2,445	H 3
Antalaha, 18,083	J 2
Antsalova, 1,867	G 3
Antsirabe, 29,914	H 3
Antsohihy, 7,618	H 2
Arivonimamo, 7,011	H 3
Bealanana, 2,820	H 2
Befandriana, 2,714	H 3
Bekily, 1,556	G 4
Belo-sur-Tsiribihina, 4,391	G 3
Beroroha, 1,549	G 4
Besalampy, 2,519	G 3
Betioky, 2,256	G 4
Betroka, 4,071	H 4
Brickaville, 1,750	H 3
Diégo-Suarez, 40,237	H 2
Fandriana, 3,406	H 3
Farafangana, 10,753	H 4
Fénérive, 7,080	H 3
Fianarantsoa, 45,790	H 4
Fort-Dauphin, 12,677	H 5
Hell-Ville, 9,481	H 2
Ifanadiana, 1,090	H 4
Ihosy, 6,578	H 4
Ivohibe, 1,150	H 4
Maevatanana, 5,147	H 3
Mahabo, 2,821	G 4
Mahanoro, 4,930	H 3
Maintirano, 4,594	G 3
Majunga, 47,654	H 3
Manakara, 17,567	H 4
Mananara, 3,163	J 3
Mananjary, 13,019	H 4
Mandritsara, 6,025	H 3
Manja, 4,671	G 4
Maroantsetra, 7,184	H 3
Marolambo, 953	H 3
Marovoay, 18,074	H 3
Miandrivazo, 2,485	G 3
Midongy Sud, 959	H 4
Mitsinjo, 1,204	H 3
Morafenobe, 725	G 3
Moramanga, 10,706	H 3
Morombe, 6,684	G 4
Morondava, 15,032	G 4
Nosy-Varika, 938	H 4
Port-Bergé, 3,345	H 3
Sambava, 6,198	J 2
Soalala, 774	G 3
Soanierana-Ivongo, 2,592	H 3
Tamatave, 53,173	H 3

(continued on following page)

Map labels: Vanilla, Cashew Nuts, Sisal, Tea, Sisal, Be, Coconut, Rice, Manioc, Cr, Cloves, Vanilla, Rice, Cattle, Coffee, Sugarcane, Goats, Mi, ZnPb, CuVAg, Gr, Cu, Cr, Mn, Mg, Cu, Salisbury, Cattle, Au, Cr, Ab, Tobacco, Corn, Bulawayo, Sugarcane, Cu, Cr, Fe, Ni, Ab, Sb, Fruit, Pt, Corn, Cr, Mg, Bananas, Johannesburg, Au, Ag, Mn, Na, Fe, Mn, Na, Ab, D, V, Pt, Cr, Corn, Wheat, Cotton, Ab, D, D, D, D, W, Cu, Sheep, Goats, Cattle, Corn, Cane, Durban, SnW, Na, Mn, Cattle, Sheep, Pilchard, Snoek, Rock Lobsters, Pilchard, Fruit, Wine, Fruit, Cape Town, Oysters, Soles, Port Elizabeth, Mackerel, Trepang

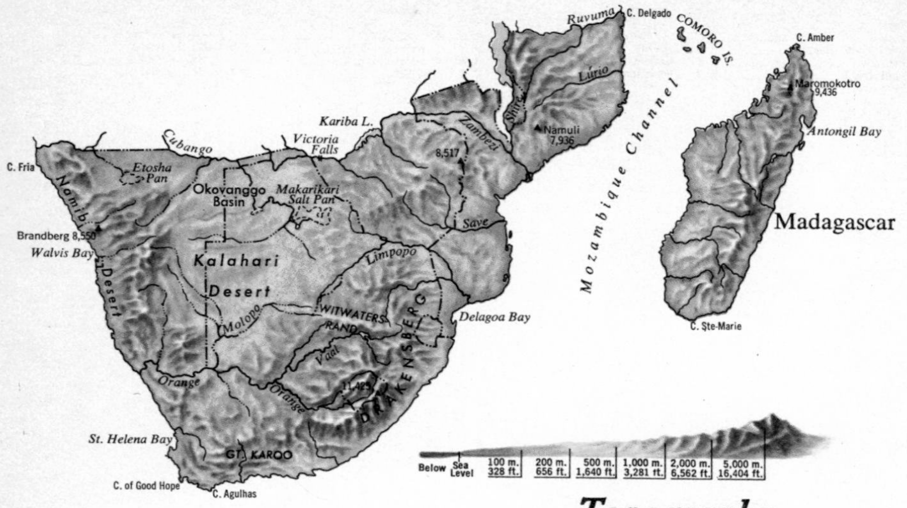
Ruvuma
C. Delgado
COMORO IS.
C. Amber
Maromokotro
9,436
Lúrio
Shire
Namuli
7,936
Zambezi
Mozambique Channel
Antongil Bay
Madagascar
Kariba L.
Victoria Falls
Cubango
C. Fria
Etosha Pan
Namib
Okovanggo Basin
Makarikari Salt Pan
8,517
Save
Brandberg 8,550
Walvis Bay
Kalahari
Desert
Limpopo
Molopo
WITWATERSRAND
DRAKENSBERG
Delagoa Bay
Vaal
Orange
St. Helena Bay
GT. KAROO
C. of Good Hope
C. Agulhas
C. Ste-Marie
Below Sea Level
100 m. 328 ft.
200 m. 656 ft.
500 m. 1,640 ft.
1,000 m. 3,281 ft.
2,000 m. 6,562 ft.
5,000 m. 16,404 ft.

Topography

0 200 400 600
MILES

MALAGASY REPUBLIC (continued)

Tananarive (capital), 332,885 .... H 3
Tananarive, *447,016 .... H 3
Tsiroanomandidy, 9,956 .... H 3
Tuléar, 33,842 .... G 4
Vangaindrano, 2,665 .... H 4
Vatomandry, 3,739 .... H 3
Vohémar, 3,622 .... J 2
Vohipeno .... H 4

OTHER FEATURES

Alaotra (lake) .... H 3
Amber (cape) .... H 2
Antongil (bay) .... J 3
Barren (isls.) .... G 3
Betsiboka (riv.) .... H 3
Boby, Pic (mt.) .... H 4
Chesterfield (isl.) .... G 3
Ikopa (riv.) .... H 3
Itasy (lake) .... H 3
Madagascar (isl.) .... G 4
Mahajamba (bay) .... H 2
Mananara (riv.) .... H 4
Mananbao (riv.) .... G 3
Mangoky (riv.) .... G 4
Mangoro (riv.) .... H 3
Maromokotro (mt.) .... H 2
Masoala (pen.) .... J 3
Menarandra (riv.) .... H 4
Mozambique (chan.) .... G 3
Nossi-Bé (isl.), 26,462 .... H 2
Onilahy (riv.) .... G 4
Radama (isls.) .... H 2
Saint-André (cape) .... G 3
Sainte-Marie (cape) .... G 5
Sainte-Marie (isl.), 9,090 .... J 3
Saint-Sébastien (cape) .... H 2
Sofia (riv.) .... H 3
Tsiafajavona (mt.) .... H 3
Tsiribihina (riv.) .... G 3

MAURITIUS

CITIES and TOWNS

Curepipe, 49,000 .... G 5
Mahébourg, 13,005 .... G 5
Port Louis (capital), 131,000 .... G 5
Poudre d'Or, 1,208 .... G 5
Quatre Bornes, 28,389 .... G 5
Souillac, 2,606 .... G 5

MOZAMBIQUE

DISTRICTS

Cabo Delgado, 542,165 .... F 2
Gaza, 675,150 .... E 4
Inhambane, 583,772 .... E 4
Lourenço Marques, 436,897 .... E 5
Manica e Sofala, 781,070 .... E 3
Moçambique, 1,444,555 .... F 2
Niassa, 276,810 .... F 2
Tete, 470,100 .... E 3
Zambézia, 1,363,619 .... F 3

CITIES and TOWNS

Alto Molócuè, †50,093 .... F 3
António Enes, †33,245 .... G 3
Bartolomeu Dias .... F 4
Beira, †58,235 .... F 3
Bela Vista, 206 .... E 5
Caniçado, †30,647 .... E 4
Chemba, †28,317 .... E 3
Chibuto, †122,989 .... E 4
Chicoa, †11,852 .... E 3
Cóbuè, †6,305 .... F 2
Dona Ana, †10,894 .... F 3
Entre-Rios, †28,475 .... F 2
Errego, †80,886 .... F 3
Espungabera, †37,353 .... E 4
Fíngoè, †14,926 .... E 2
Furancungo, †18,185 .... E 2
Homoíne, †57,959 .... E 4
Ibo, †4,394 .... G 2
Inhambane, †22,016 .... F 4
Inhaminga, †21,280 .... F 3
Inharrime, †40,721 .... F 4
João Belo, †48,959 .... E 5
Lourenço Marques (cap.), 65,716 .... E 5
Lourenço Marques, *177,929 .... E 5
Lumbo, †14,357 .... G 3
Lúrio, †9,932 .... G 2
Macia, †83,412 .... E 4
Macomia, †12,913 .... F 2
Magude, †44,183 .... E 5
Máguè, †10,695 .... E 3
Malvérnia, †11,373 .... E 4
Mandimba .... F 2
Manhiça, †6,267 .... E 5
Maniamba, †11,708 .... F 2
Manjacaze, †63,626 .... E 5
Marromeu, †33,096 .... F 3
Marrupa, †15,540 .... F 2
Massinga, †80,526 .... F 4
Maúa, †29,346 .... F 2
Meconta, †28,187 .... F 3
Mecúfi, †26,290 .... G 2
Mecula, †5,203 .... F 2
Memba, †51,703 .... G 2
Milange, †76,466 .... F 3
Moamba, 993 .... E 5
Moatize, †30,885 .... E 3
Mocambique, †12,166 .... G 3
Mocímboa da Praia, †28,335 .... G 2
Mocuba, †43,484 .... F 3
Mogincual, †21,786 .... G 3
Moma, †64,685 .... F 3
Montepuez, †46,667 .... F 2
Mopeia, †28,683 .... F 3
Morrumbala, †56,457 .... F 3
Morrumbene, †68,094 .... F 4
Mossuril, †25,494 .... G 2
Muecate, †35,068 .... F 2
Mueda, †51,229 .... F 2
Nacala, †43,439 .... G 2
Namacurra, †38,037 .... F 3
Namarrói, †55,925 .... F 3
Nampula, †104,648 .... F 3
Nova Mambone, †12,498 .... F 4
Nova Freixo, †146,186 .... F 2
Nova Luzitânia, †68,678 .... E 3
Nova Sofala, †16,468 .... F 4
Pafúri, †1,883 .... E 4
Palma, †15,451 .... G 2
Panda, †35,462 .... E 4
Pebane, †18,826 .... F 3
Porto Amélia, †21,005 .... G 2
Quelimane, †62,717 .... F 3
Quionga, †2,486 .... G 2
Quissanga, †11,463 .... G 2
Quissico, †69,940 .... F 4
Ribáuè, †29,689 .... F 3
Tete, †38,196 .... E 3
Vila Cabral, †28,701 .... F 2
Vila Coutinho, †41,193 .... E 2
Vila de Maganja, †52,722 .... F 3
Vila de Manica, †14,151 .... E 3
Vila de Sena, †46,616 .... E 3
Vila do Chinde, †25,617 .... F 3
Vila do Dondo, †39,683 .... F 3
Vila Fontes, †29,434 .... E 3
Vila Gouveia, †18,449 .... E 3
Vila Luísa, 294 .... E 5
Vilanculos, †67,041 .... E 4
Vila Paiva de Andrada †44,692 .... E 3
Vila Pery, †36,406 .... E 3
Zumbo, †9,978 .... E 3

OTHER FEATURES

Angoche (isl.) .... G 3
Bazaruto (isl.) .... F 4
Binga (mt.) .... E 3
Caça Nat'l Park .... E 3
Changane (riv.) .... E 4
Chilwa (lake) .... F 3
Delagoa (bay) .... E 5
Delgado (cape) .... G 2
Ligonha (riv.) .... F 3
Lugenda (riv.) .... F 2
Lúrio (riv.) .... F 2
Mazoe (riv.) .... E 3
Mozambique (chan.) .... G 3
Namuli (mt.) .... F 3
Nyasa (lake) .... E 2
Ruvuma (riv.) .... F 2
São Sebastião (cape) .... F 4
Save (riv.) .... E 4
Shire (riv.) .... E 3
Zambezi (riv.) .... E 3

RÉUNION

CITIES and TOWNS

Le Port, 13,281 .... F 5
Saint-André, 1,501 .... G 5
Saint-Benoît, 4,095 .... G 5
Saint-Denis (capital), 37,047 .... F 5
Saint-Denis, *65,614 .... F 5
Saint-Joseph, 5,969 .... G 6
Saint-Louis, 7,753 .... F 5
Saint-Pierre, 8,752 .... F 6

OTHER FEATURES

Bassas da India (isl.) .... F 4
Europa (isl.) .... G 4
Glorioso (isls.) .... H 2
Juan de Nova (isl.) .... G 3
Piton des Neiges (mt.) .... G 5

RHODESIA

CITIES and TOWNS

Beitbridge, 760 .... E 4
Bindura, 5,530 .... E 3
Bulawayo, 245,590 .... D 3
Bulawayo, ‡270,000 .... D 3
Chipinga, 1,730 .... E 4
Dett, 2,180 .... D 3
Eiffel Flats, 4,230 .... E 3
Enkeldoorn, 1,600 .... E 3
Fort Victoria, 11,350 .... E 4
Fort Victoria, ‡12,000 .... E 4
Gatooma, 20,960 .... D 3
Gatooma, ‡23,000 .... D 3
Gwaai, †2,160 .... D 3
Gwanda, 5,880 .... D 4
Gwelo, 46,230 .... D 3
Gwelo, ‡50,000 .... D 3
Hartley, 7,170 .... E 3
Inyanga, 310 .... E 3
Kariba, 5,950 .... D 3
Marandellas, 10,980 .... E 3
Marandellas, ‡11,000 .... E 3
Matetsi, 220 .... D 3
Matopos, †9,390 .... D 4
Mazoe, 410 .... E 3
Melsetter, 680 .... E 3
Mount Darwin, 1,250 .... E 3
Plumtree, 1,690 .... D 4
Que Que, 32,860 .... D 3
Que Que, ‡37,000 .... D 3
Rusape, 3,960 .... E 3
Salisbury (capital), 385,530 .... E 3
Salisbury, ‡423,000 .... E 3
Selukwe, 3,030 .... E 3
Shabani, 15,810 .... E 4
Shabani, ‡17,000 .... E 4
Shamva, 750 .... E 3
Sinoia, 13,250 .... D 3
Sinoia, ‡14,000 .... D 3
Tuli, †1,580 .... D 4
Umtali, 45,510 .... E 3
Umtali, ‡50,000 .... E 3
Umvuma, 1,750 .... D 3
Wankie, 20,190 .... D 3
Wankie, ‡21,000 .... D 3
West Nicholson, 2,640 .... D 4

OTHER FEATURES

Inyanga National Park, 580 .... E 3
Kariba (lake) .... D 3
Lundi (riv.) .... E 4
Mashonaland (reg.), 1,445,070 .... E 3
Matabeleland (reg.), 894,100 .... D 3
Mazoe (riv.) .... E 3
Mosi-Ao-Tunya (Victoria falls) .... C 3
Mushandike National Park .... D 4
Sabi (riv.) .... E 3
Sanyati (riv.) .... D 3
Shangani (riv.) .... D 3
Shashi (riv.) .... D 4
Umvukwe (range) .... E 3
Victoria (falls) .... C 3
Zambezi (riv.) .... E 3
Zimbabwe Nat'l Park .... E 4

SEYCHELLES

CITIES and TOWNS

Anse Boileau, ◉2,399 .... H 5
Anse Royale, ◉2,373 .... H 5
Cascade, ◉1,583 .... H 5
Victoria (cap.), 14,000 .... H 5

OTHER FEATURES

Assumption (isl.), 31 .... H 1
Astove (isl.), 50 .... H 2
Cerf (isl.), 34 .... H 5
Cosmoledo (isls.), 57 .... H 1
Curieuse (isl.) .... H 5
Felicité (isl.) .... J 5
Frigate (isl.), 94 .... J 5
La Digue (isl.), 1,842 .... J 5
Mahé (isl.), 33,478 .... H 5
Morne Seychellois (mt.) .... H 5
North (isl.), 53 .... H 5
Praslin (isl.), 3,886 .... H 5
Sainte Anne (isl.), 32 .... H 5
Silhouette (isl.), 780 .... H 5

SOUTH AFRICA

PROVINCES

Cape of Good Hope, 3,936,306 .... C 6
Natal, 2,979,920 .... E 5
Orange Free State, 1,386,547 .... D 4
Transkei, 1,439,195 .... D 6
Transvaal, 6,273,477 .... D 4

CITIES and TOWNS

Aberdeen, 5,100 .... C 6
Adelaide, 7,000 .... D 6
Alberton, 44,800 .... H 6
Alexander Bay, 2,073 .... B 5
Aliwal North, 10,700 .... D 6
Barberton, 13,200 .... E 5
Barkly East, 3,650 .... D 6
Beaufort West, 16,300 .... C 6
Bellville, 42,500 .... F 6
Benoni, 126,700 .... J 6
Bethal, 16,600 .... D 5
Bethlehem, 31,400 .... D 5
Bloemfontein, 146,200 .... C 5
Bloemfontein, ‡147,000 .... C 5
Bloubergstrand, 230 .... E 6
Boksburg, 83,300 .... J 6
Botrivier, 937 .... F 7
Brakpan, 84,400 .... J 6
Brandvlei, 1,419 .... B 6
Brits, 11,800 .... D 5
Britstown, 2,834 .... C 6
Burgersdorp, 10,000 .... D 6
Butterworth, 2,367 .... D 6
Caledon, 4,300 .... G 7
Calvinia, 6,700 .... B 6
Cape Town (capital), 625,000 .... E 6
Cape Town, ‡817,000 .... E 6
Carnarvon, 4,800 .... C 6
Ceres, 6,200 .... B 6
Christiana, 6,800 .... D 5
Clanwilliam, 2,216 .... B 6
Colesberg, 6,800 .... D 6
Cradock, 21,300 .... D 6
Daleside, 1,103 .... H 7
De Aar, 16,600 .... C 6
Dibeng, 911 .... C 5
Douglas, 5,200 .... C 5
Dundee, 16,600 .... E 5
Durban, 662,900 .... E 5
Durban, ‡690,000 .... E 5
Durbanville, 3,057 .... F 6
East London, 134,100 .... D 6
Edenburg, 3,118 .... D 5
Edenvale, 30,200 .... H 6
Eersterivier, 1,826 .... F 6
Elliot, 3,517 .... D 6
Eloff, 970 .... J 6
Empangeni, 9,900 .... E 5
Ermelo, 22,800 .... E 5
Eshowe, 4,800 .... E 5
Estcourt, 12,900 .... D 5
Ficksburg, 10,300 .... D 5
Fort Beaufort, 9,900 .... D 6
Franschhoek, 1,534 .... F 6
Garies, 1,103 .... B 6
George, 19,600 .... C 6
Germiston, 189,600 .... H 6
Germiston, ‡222,000 .... H 6
Glencoe, 10,000 .... E 5
Goodwood, 82,600 .... F 6
Gordon's Bay, 900 .... F 7
Graaff-Reinet, 17,700 .... C 6
Grabouw, 5,200 .... F 7
Grahamstown, 37,600 .... D 6
Grasmere, 3,338 .... H 7
Greytown, 9,800 .... E 5
Griquatown, 2,526 .... C 5
Harrismith, 16,200 .... D 5
Hawston, 1,211 .... G 7
Heidelberg, 12,200 .... J 7
Heilbron, 7,900 .... D 5
Henley on Klip, 717 .... H 7
Hermanus, 5,200 .... G 7
Hopetown, 2,631 .... C 5
Howick, 4,900 .... E 5
Humansdorp, 3,128 .... C 6
Ingwavuma, 655 .... E 5
Irene, 1,284 .... H 6
Jagersfontein, 3,893 .... D 6
Jameson Park, 447 .... J 7
Johannesburg, 595,083 .... H 6
Johannesburg, *1,305,000 .... H 6
Keimoes, 2,997 .... C 5
Kempton Park, 56,200 .... J 6
Kenhardt, 2,833 .... C 5
Kimberley, 95,200 .... C 5
King William's Town, 15,000 .... D 6
Kirkwood, 7,400 .... D 6
Kleinmond, 639 .... F 7
Klerksdorp, 60,400 .... D 5
Knysna, 13,900 .... C 6
Koffiefontein, 2,987 .... D 5
Kokstad, 10,000 .... D 6
Kommetjie, 280 .... E 7
Kraaifontein, 4,800 .... F 6
Kroonstad, 50,700 .... D 5
Krugersdorp, 100,500 .... H 6
Kuilsrivier, 7,200 .... F 6
Kuruman, 7,000 .... C 5
Ladybrand, 8,000 .... D 5
Ladysmith, 27,900 .... D 5
Lambert's Bay, 3,211 .... B 6
Louis Trichardt, 14,800 .... E 4
Lydenburg, 8,000 .... E 4
Maclear, 3,550 .... D 6
Mafeking, 6,200 .... C 5
Malmesbury, 8,800 .... B 6
Margate, 2,915 .... E 6
Matatiele, 3,251 .... D 6
Messina, 12,500 .... D 4
Meyerton, 17,100 .... H 7
Middelburg, C. of Good Hope, 11,700 .... D 6
Middelburg, Transvaal, 25,100 .... D 5
Molteno, 4,600 .... D 6
Montagu, 5,800 .... C 6
Moorreesburg, 4,000 .... B 6
Moroka, 2,673 .... H 6
Mossel Bay, 15,600 .... C 6
Nelspruit, 31,700 .... E 5
Newcastle, 16,900 .... E 5
Nigel, 38,400 .... J 7
Noupoort, 7,200 .... C 6
Nylstroom, 6,700 .... D 4
Odendaalsrus, 17,500 .... D 5
Okiep, 2,973 .... B 5
Onrusrivier, 398 .... G 7
Oudtshoorn, 25,800 .... C 6
Paarl, 48,800 .... F 6
Parow, 48,100 .... F 6
Parys, 15,400 .... D 5
Pietermaritzburg, 111,000 .... E 5
Pietermaritzburg, ‡128,598 .... E 5
Pietersburg, 35,700 .... D 4
Piet Retief, 8,100 .... D 5
Piketberg, 4,500 .... B 6
Pinelands, 14,100 .... F 6
Pinetown, 21,100 .... E 5
Pniel, 1,309 .... F 6
Port Alfred, 6,600 .... D 6
Port Elizabeth, 374,100 .... D 6
Port Elizabeth, ‡448,000 .... D 6
Port Nolloth, 2,624 .... B 5
Port Saint Johns, 1,172 .... D 6
Port Shepstone, 4,200 .... E 6
Postmasburg, 10,000 .... C 5
Potchefstroom, 51,800 .... D 5
Potgietersrus, 12,700 .... D 4
Pretoria (capital), 479,700 .... D 5
Prieska, 7,600 .... C 5
Prince Albert, 4,500 .... C 6
Queenstown, 42,200 .... D 6
Randfontein, 45,400 .... G 6
Reitz, 7,000 .... D 5
Richmond, 2,692 .... C 6
Riversdale, 1,386 .... H 7
Riversdale, 5,100 .... C 6
Robertson, 8,200 .... C 6
Roodeport-Maraisburg, 115,600 .... H 6
Rustenburg, 32,500 .... D 5
Saldanha, 2,243 .... B 6
Senekal, 7,400 .... D 5
Simonstown, 8,900 .... E 7
Somerset East, 9,800 .... D 6
Somerset West, 9,500 .... F 6
Springbok, 4,100 .... B 5
Springfontein, 2,860 .... C 6
Springs, 142,300 .... J 6
Standerton, 22,500 .... D 5
Stanger, 11,200 .... E 5
Stellenbosch, 29,900 .... F 6
Strand, 21,200 .... F 7
Stutterheim, 10,600 .... D 6
Swellendam, 4,900 .... C 6
Taung, 860 .... C 5
Thabazimbi, 8,800 .... D 4

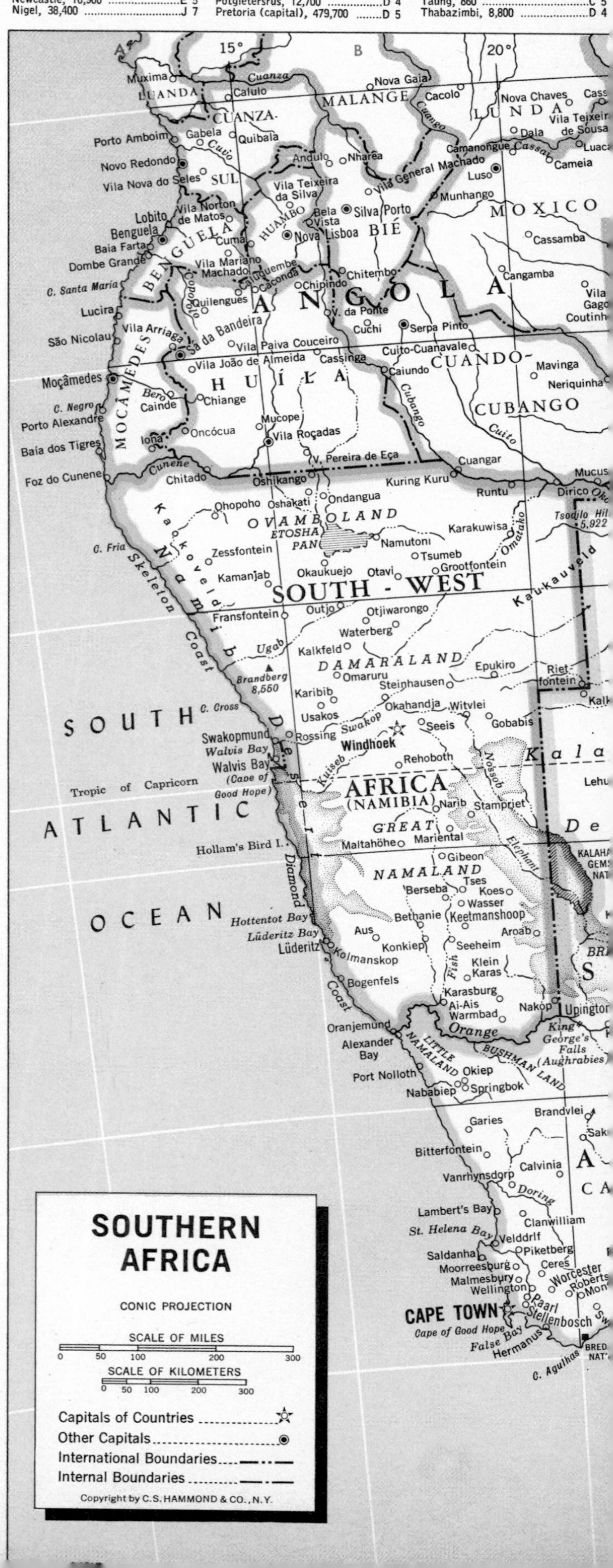
15°
B
20°
Muxima
LUANDA
Calulo
Cuanza
Nova Gaia
MALANGE
Cacolo
Nova Chaves
LUNDA
Vila Teixeira de Sousa
CUANZA-SUL
Porto Amboim
Gabela
Quibala
Novo Redondo
Vila Nova do Seles
Andulo
Nharea
Vila General Machado
Camanongue
Luso
Cameia
Vila Teixeira da Silva
Munhango
MOXICO
Lobito
Vila Norton de Matos
Benguela
BENGUELA
HUAMBO
Bela Vista
Silva Porto
Nova Lisboa
BIÉ
Baia Farta
Dombe Grande
Cuma
Vila Mariano Machado
Cassamba
Chitembo
Cangamba
C. Santa Maria
Quilengues
Chipindo
ANGOLA
Lucira
V. da Ponte
Cuchi
Serpa Pinto
São Nicolau
Vila Arriaga
Sá da Bandeira
Vila Paiva Couceiro
Cuito-Cuanavale
CUANDO-CUBANGO
Mavinga
Vila João de Almeida
Cassinga
Caiundo
Neriquinha
Moçâmedes
HUÍLA
MOÇÂMEDES
Bero
Caínde
Chiange
C. Negro
Porto Alexandre
Mucope
Vila Roçadas
Oncócua
Baía dos Tigres
Iona
V. Pereira de Eça
Cuangar
Foz do Cunene
Cunene
Chitado
Oshikango
Kuring Kuru
Runtu
Dirico
Ondangua
Ohopoho
Oshakati
OVAMBOLAND
ETOSHA PAN
Karakuwisa
C. Fria
Zessfontein
Namutoni
Tsumeb
Grootfontein
Kamanjab
Okaukuejo
Otavi
SOUTH-WEST
Kaukauveld
Skeleton Coast
Kaokoveld
Fransfontein
Outjo
Otjiwarongo
Waterberg
Kalkfeld
Ugab
DAMARALAND
Epukiro
Omaruru
Brandberg 8,550
Karibib
Steinhausen
Okahandja
Witvlei
Gobabis
C. Cross
Usakos
Seeis
Swakopmund
Rossing
Swakop
Windhoek
Walvis Bay
Rehoboth
SOUTH ATLANTIC OCEAN
Tropic of Capricorn
(Cape of Good Hope)
AFRICA (NAMIBIA)
Narib
Stampriet
Kuiseb
Hollam's Bird I.
GREAT NAMALAND
Maltahöhe
Mariental
Gibeon
Tses
Berseba
Koes
Wasser
Bethanie
Keetmanshoop
Hottentot Bay
Lüderitz Bay
Lüderitz
Aus
Konkiep
Aroab
Seeheim
Kolmanskop
Klein Karas
Bogenfels
Karasburg
Ai-Ais
Warmbad
Nakop
Upington
Oranjemund
Alexander Bay
LITTLE NAMALAND
Orange
King George's Falls (Aughrabies)
BUSHMAN LAND
Port Nolloth
Okiep
Nababiep
Springbok
Garies
Brandvlei
Bitterfontein
Calvinia
Vanrhynsdorp
Doring
Lambert's Bay
Clanwilliam
St. Helena Bay
Velddrif
Piketberg
Saldanha
Ceres
Moorreesburg
Worcester
Malmesbury
Wellington
Paarl
Robertson
CAPE TOWN
Stellenbosch
Cape of Good Hope
False Bay
Hermanus
C. Agulhas
SOUTHERN AFRICA
CONIC PROJECTION
SCALE OF MILES
0 50 100 200 300
SCALE OF KILOMETERS
0 50 100 200 300
Capitals of Countries
Other Capitals
International Boundaries
Internal Boundaries
Copyright by C.S. HAMMOND & CO., N.Y.

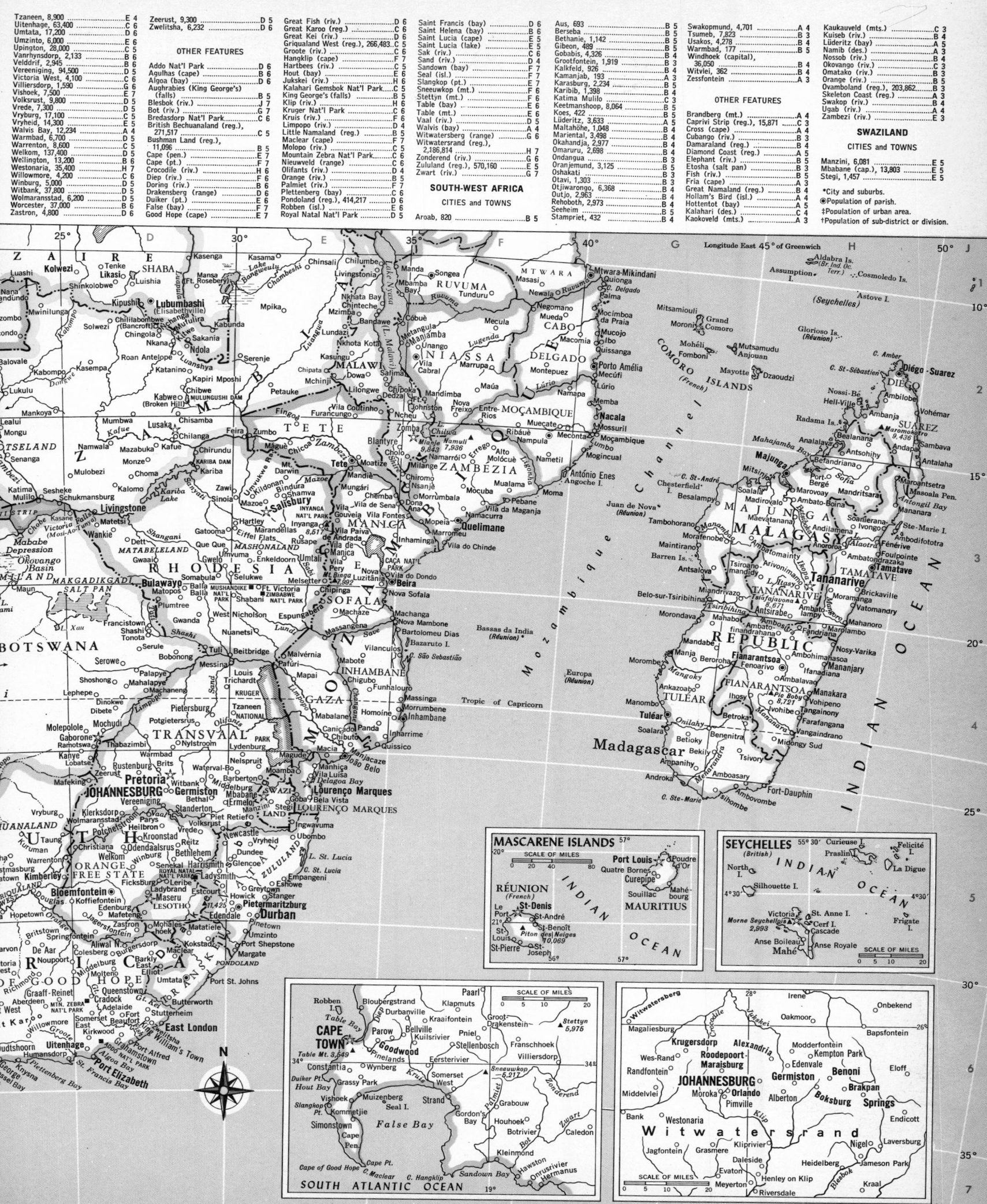

SOUTH AMERICA

LAMBERT AZIMUTHAL EQUAL-AREA PROJECTION

SCALE OF MILES

0 100 200 400 600

SCALE OF KILOMETRES

0 100 200 400 600

Capitals of Countries .... ☆

International Boundaries ___ _ _ ___

Canals _ _ _ _ _ _ _ _ _ _

© C.S. HAMMOND & Co., N.Y.

GALAPAGOS ISLANDS
(ARCHIPIELAGO DE COLON)
(ECUADOR)

SCALE OF MILES

0 50 100 150

PACIFIC   OCEAN

I. Pinta
I. Marchena
I. Santiago
I. Chaves
I. Fernandina   I. San Cristóbal
Isla Isabela
I. Floreana   I. Española

Equator

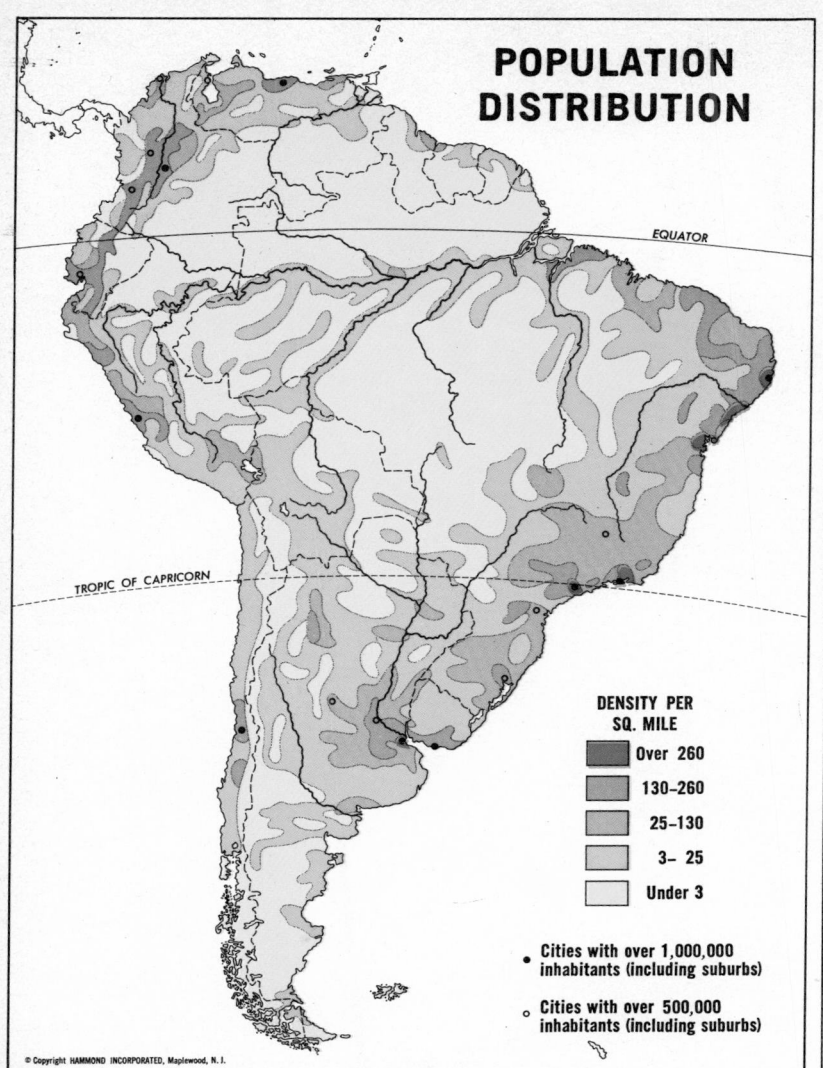

POPULATION DISTRIBUTION

AREA 6,875,000 sq. mi.
POPULATION 186,000,000
LARGEST CITY Buenos Aires (greater)
HIGHEST POINT Cerro Aconcagua 22,831 ft.
LOWEST POINT Salina Grande -131 ft.

DENSITY PER SQ. MILE

- Over 260
- 130–260
- 25–130
- 3– 25
- Under 3

• Cities with over 1,000,000 inhabitants (including suburbs)
○ Cities with over 500,000 inhabitants (including suburbs)

© Copyright HAMMOND INCORPORATED, Maplewood, N.J.

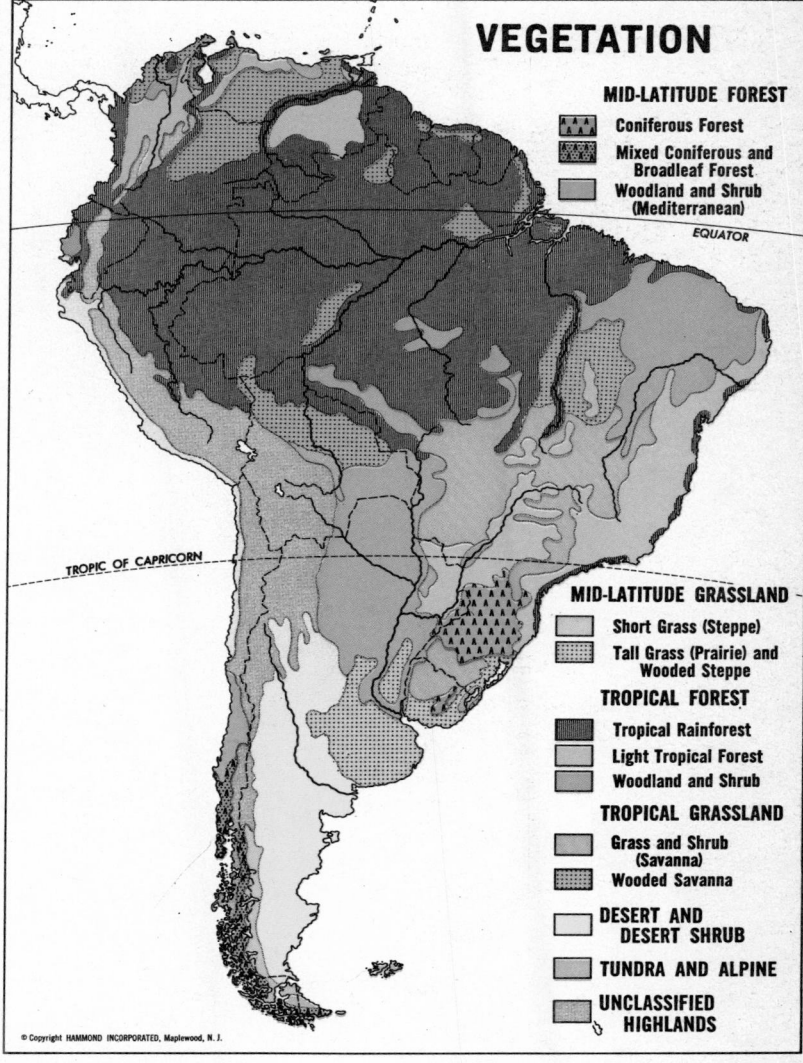

VEGETATION

MID-LATITUDE FOREST
- Coniferous Forest
- Mixed Coniferous and Broadleaf Forest
- Woodland and Shrub (Mediterranean)

MID-LATITUDE GRASSLAND
- Short Grass (Steppe)
- Tall Grass (Prairie) and Wooded Steppe

TROPICAL FOREST
- Tropical Rainforest
- Light Tropical Forest
- Woodland and Shrub

TROPICAL GRASSLAND
- Grass and Shrub (Savanna)
- Wooded Savanna

DESERT AND DESERT SHRUB

TUNDRA AND ALPINE

UNCLASSIFIED HIGHLANDS

© Copyright HAMMOND INCORPORATED, Maplewood, N.J.

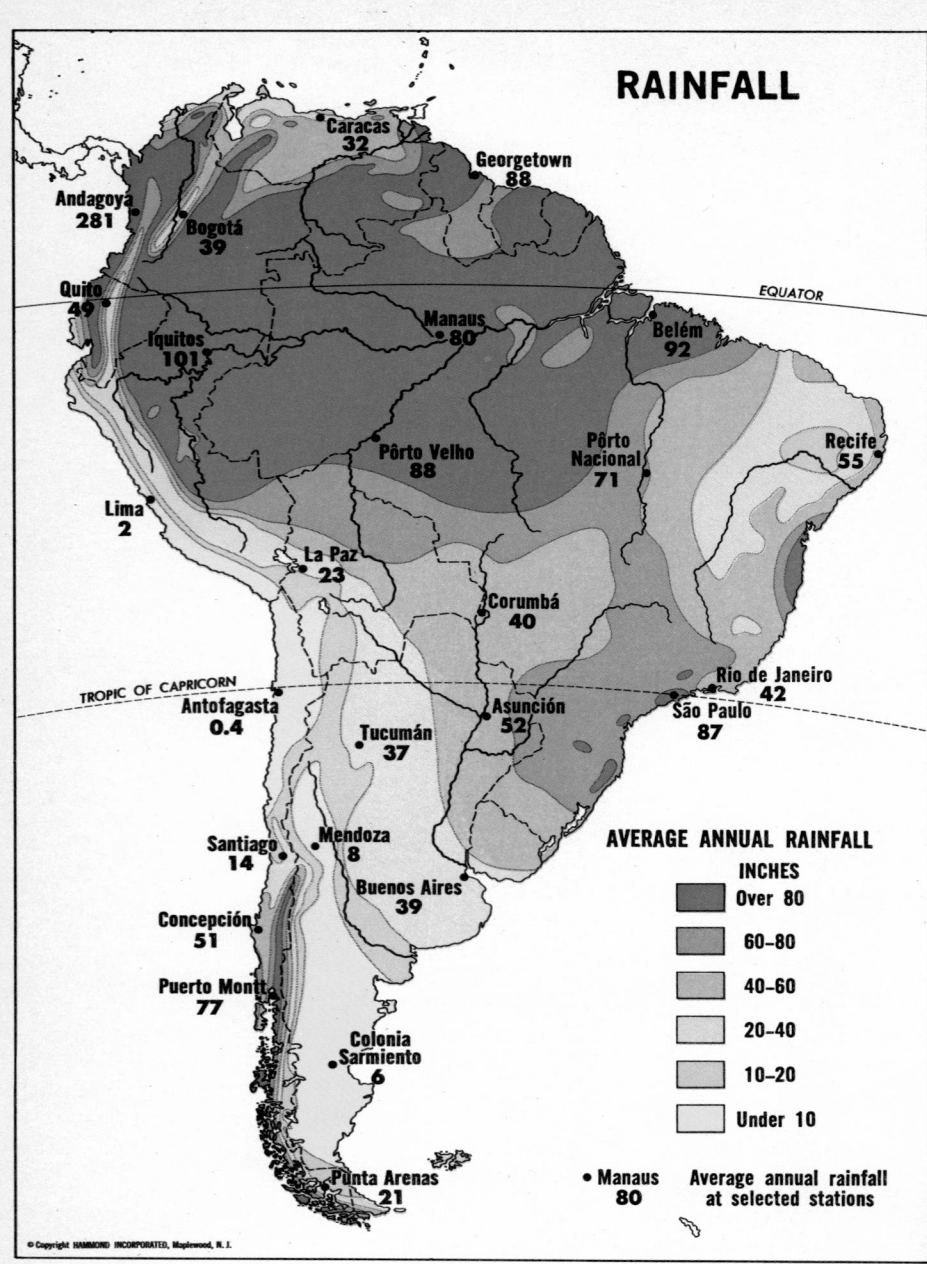

RAINFALL

Caracas 32
Georgetown 88
Andagoya 281
Bogotá 39
Quito 49
Iquitos 101
Manaus 80
Belém 92
Pôrto Velho 88
Pôrto Nacional 71
Recife 55
Lima 2
La Paz 23
Corumbá 40
EQUATOR
TROPIC OF CAPRICORN
Antofagasta 0.4
Tucumán 37
Asunción 52
Rio de Janeiro 42
São Paulo 87
Santiago 14
Mendoza 8
Buenos Aires 39
Concepción 51
Puerto Montt 77
Colonia Sarmiento 6
Punta Arenas 21

© Copyright HAMMOND INCORPORATED, Maplewood, N.J.

AVERAGE ANNUAL RAINFALL

INCHES

- Over 80
- 60–80
- 40–60
- 20–40
- 10–20
- Under 10

• Manaus 80 Average annual rainfall at selected stations

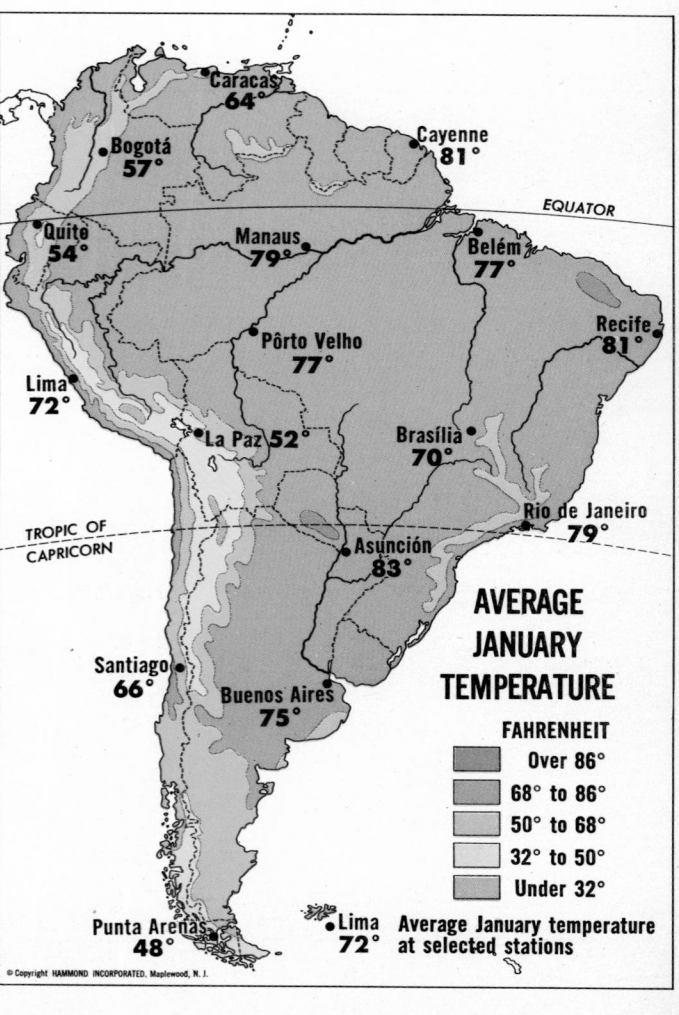

Caracas 64°
Bogotá 57°
Cayenne 81°
Quito 54°
Manaus 79°
Belém 77°
Lima 72°
Pôrto Velho 77°
Recife 81°
La Paz 52°
Brasília 70°
EQUATOR
TROPIC OF CAPRICORN
Asunción 83°
Rio de Janeiro 79°
Santiago 66°
Buenos Aires 75°
Punta Arenas 48°

AVERAGE JANUARY TEMPERATURE

FAHRENHEIT

- Over 86°
- 68° to 86°
- 50° to 68°
- 32° to 50°
- Under 32°

• Lima 72° Average January temperature at selected stations

© Copyright HAMMOND INCORPORATED, Maplewood, N.J.

Topography

0   300   600
MILES

Pta. Gallinas
Pico Cristóbal Colón 19,029
Delta del Orinoco
Lake Maracaibo
Goajira
ANDES MOUNTAINS
Magdalena
Meta
Orinoco
Angel Fall
Guaviare
Orinoco
LLANOS
GUIANA HIGHLANDS
Negro
I. de Marajó
Esequibo
Amazon
Gulf of Guayaquil
Putumayo
Japurá
Amazon
Marañón
Juruá
Purus
Madeira
Tapajós
Xingu
Tocantins
Amazon
Tocantins
C. de São Roque
Parnaíba
Pta. Aguja
Huascarán 22,205
Ucayali
SELVAS
Guaporé
São Francisco
Caatingas
Beni
Mamoré
PLANALTO DE MATO GROSSO
Araguaia
Tocantins
BRAZILIAN
L. Titicaca
L. Poopó
Desaguadero
Pilcomayo
GRAN CHACO
Paraná
Campos
Rio Grande
HIGHLANDS
Vol. Llullaillaco 22,057
Bermejo
Paraguay
Iguassú Falls
Ojos del Salado 22,572
Salado
Uruguay
Paraná
L. dos Patos
ANDES
PAMPAS
Salado
MOUNTAINS
Aconcagua 22,831
Rio de la Plata
C. San Antonio
Colorado
Colorado
Negro
G. San Matías
Pen. Valdés
PATAGONIA
Chubut
I. de Chiloé
G. San Jorge
Pen. Taitao
FALKLAND ISLANDS
ARCH. REINA ADELAIDA
Str. of Magellan
Tierra del Fuego
Cape Horn

5,000 m. 16,404 ft. | 2,000 m. 6,562 ft. | 1,000 m. 3,281 ft. | 500 m. 1,640 ft. | 200 m. 656 ft. | 100 m. 328 ft. | Sea Level | Below

AVERAGE JULY TEMPERATURE

Caracas 70°
Cayenne 81°
Bogotá 56°
EQUATOR
Quito 54°
Manaus 81°
Belém 79°
Lima 59°
Pôrto Velho 75°
Recife 75°
La Paz 45°
Brasília 66°
TROPIC OF CAPRICORN
Rio de Janeiro 70°
Asunción 64°
Santiago 46°
Buenos Aires 48°
Punta Arenas 35°

FAHRENHEIT

Over 86°
68° to 86°
50° to 68°
32° to 50°
Under 32°

Lima 59°   Average July temperature at selected stations

124 Venezuela

INTERNAL DIVISIONS

Amazonas (terr.), 12,831 .... E 5
Anzoátegui (state),
501,394 .... F 3
Apure (state), 158,487 .... D 4
Aragua (state), 429,344 .... E 3
Barinas (state), 193,914 .... D 4
Bolívar (state), 383,315 .... F 4
Carabobo (state), 512,173 .... D 2
Cojedes (state), 95,177 .... D 3
Delta Amacuro (terr.), 34,278 .... H 3
Dependencias Federales (terr.),
1,000 .... E 2
Distrito Federal, 2,009,561 .... E 2
Falcón (state), 408,051 .... D 2
Guárico (state), 330,147 .... E 3
Lara (state), 611,192 .... C 2
Mérida (state), 335,428 .... C 3
Miranda (state), 702,603 .... E 2
Monagas (state), 316,732 .... G 3
Nueva Esparta (state),
112,611 .... G 2
Portuguesa (state),
284,523 .... D 3
Sucre (state), 493,840 .... G 2
Táchira (state), 525,840 .... B 3
Trujillo (state), 382,441 .... C 3
Yaracuy (state), 222,041 .... D 2
Zulia (state), 1,342,994 .... B 2

CITIES and TOWNS

Acarigua, 30,683 .... D 3
Achaguas, 1,934 .... D 4
Adícora, 563 .... D 2
Aguada Grande, 1,601 .... D 2
Agua Fría, 539 .... D 2
Agua Linda, 25 .... C 3
Aguasay, 1,458 .... G 3
Altagracia, 7,362 .... C 2
Altagracia de Orituco, 13,013 .... E 3
Amuay, 998 .... D 2
Anaco, 23,105 .... F 3
Aparurén .... G 5
Apurito, 739 .... D 4
Arabopó .... H 5
Aragua de Barcelona,
8,241 .... F 3
Aragua de Maturín,
2,643 .... G 3
Araure, 12,316 .... D 3
Aricagua, 730 .... C 3
Arichuna, 983 .... D 3
Arismendi, 1,243 .... F 4
Aroa, 6,356 .... D 2
Atapirire, 203 .... F 3
Bachaquero, 14,490 .... C 2
Baragua, 831 .... C 2
Barbacoas, 1,579 .... E 3
Barcelona, 42,379 .... F 2
Barinas, 25,748 .... C 3
Barinitas, 7,208 .... C 3
Barquisimeto, 280,086 .... D 2
Barrancas, Barinas, 3,154 .... C 3
Barrancas, Monagas,
4,189 .... G 3
Betijoque, 3,915 .... C 3
Biruaca, 631 .... E 4
Biscucuy, 3,900 .... D 3
Bobare, 970 .... D 2
Bobures, 2,159 .... C 3
Boca de Aroa, 1,674 .... D 2
Boca del Mangle, 1,075 .... E 4
Boca del Pao, 283 .... F 3
Bocono, 10,430 .... C 3
Borbón, 373 .... F 3
Borojó, 367 .... D 2
Bruzual, 556 .... D 4
Buena Vista, Anzoátegui, 2,335 .... F 3
Buena Vista, Apure, 786 .... D 4
Buena Vista, Falcón, 786 .... C 2
Cabimas, 141,314 .... C 2
Cabruta, 813 .... E 4
Cabudare, 4,480 .... D 2
Cabure, 1,440 .... D 2
Cachipo, 1,091 .... G 3
Cacuri, 45 .... F 5
Cagua, 16,233 .... E 2
Caicara, 4,776 .... G 3
Caicara de Orinoco, 3,281 .... E 4
Calabozo, 15,739 .... E 3
Calderas, 857 .... C 3
Camaguán, 1,917 .... E 3
Camatagua, 1,419 .... E 3
Campo Claro, 1,620 .... C 3
Candelaria, 188 .... E 2
Cantaura, 14,068 .... F 3
Capatárida, 1,278 .... C 2
Capure, 459 .... H 3
Carabobo, Bolívar .... H 4

Carabobo, Carabobo,
2,319 .... D 3
Caracas (cap.) 786,710 .... E 2
Caracas, *2,064,033 .... E 2
Carache, 2,635 .... C 3
Carapa, 115 .... G 3
Cariaco, 4,281 .... G 2
Caribén, 25 .... E 4
Caripe, 3,583 .... G 2
Caripito, 21,598 .... G 2
Carirubana, 3,421 .... D 2
Carmelo, 1,944 .... C 2
Carora, 23,227 .... C 2
Carrasquero, 1,353 .... B 2
Carúpano, 38,197 .... G 2
Casanay, 3,561 .... G 2
Casigua, Falcón, 406 .... C 2
Casigua, Zulia, 5,320 .... B 3
Caucagua, 4,705 .... E 2
Cazorla, 657 .... E 3
Chaguaramas, 1,363 .... E 3
Chichiriviche, 2,512 .... D 2
Chivacoa, 12,871 .... D 2
Choroní, 352 .... E 2
Churuguara, 4,458 .... C 2
Ciudad Bolívar, 63,266 .... G 3
Ciudad Bolivia, 2,080 .... C 3
Ciudad de Nutrias, 541 .... D 3
Ciudad Guayana, 127,681 .... G 3
Ciudad Ojeda, 53,745 .... C 2
Ciudad Piar, 4,598 .... F 3
Clarines, 2,018 .... F 3
Cojoro, 156 .... C 2
Colón, 169 .... E 6

Comunidad, 44 .... E 6
Coporito, 659 .... H 3
Coro, 45,506 .... D 2
Corozo Pando, 286 .... E 3
Cúa, 5,567 .... E 2
Cubiro, 1,742 .... D 2
Cuchivero, 122 .... F 4
Cumaná, 69,937 .... F 2
Cumanacoa, 7,354 .... F 2
Cunaviche, 596 .... E 4
Curiapo, 375 .... H 3
Dabajuro, 3,927 .... C 2
Delicias, 1,398 .... B 3
Democracia, 12 .... E 6
Dolores, 1,122 .... D 3
Duaca, 5,771 .... D 2
Ejido, 5,457 .... C 3
El Almacén, 31 .... G 4
El Amparo de Apure, 1,087 .... C 4
El Baúl, 1,550 .... D 3
El Callao, 5,039 .... G 4
El Calvario, 567 .... E 3
El Carmen .... E 7
El Chaparro, 1,703 .... F 3
El Cristo, 328 .... G 4
El Dorado, 2,094 .... H 4
El Empedrado, 1,739 .... C 3
El Guapo, 842 .... F 2
El Manteco, 999 .... G 4
El Miamo, 269 .... H 4
Elorza, 2,121 .... D 4
El Palmar, 1,986 .... G 4
El Pao, Anzoátegui, 586 .... F 3
El Pao, Bolívar, 2,115 .... G 3

El Pao, Cojedes, 1,081 .... D 3
El Perú, 1,487 .... H 4
El Pilar, 3,326 .... G 2
El Rastro, 748 .... E 3
El Roque, 348 .... E 2
El Samán de Apure, 1,099 .... D 4
El Socorro, 3,153 .... E 3
El Sombrero, 5,712 .... E 3
El Tigre, 41,961 .... F 3
El Tocuyo, 14,560 .... C 3
El Toro, 199 .... D 1
El Vigía, 8,874 .... C 3
El Vínculo, 1,224 .... D 2
El Yagual, 435 .... D 4
Encontrados, 2,991 .... B 3
Esperanza, 15 .... C 3
Espino, 470 .... E 3
Garcitas, 1,224 .... C 3
Guacara, 11,353 .... D 2
Guachara, 462 .... D 4
Guadaramas, 461 .... E 3
Guaina .... G 5
Guana, 87 .... G 5
Guanare, 18,452 .... D 3
Guanarito, 1,048 .... D 3
Guanoco, 437 .... G 2
Guanta, 8,048 .... F 2
Guardatinajas, 704 .... E 3
Guarenas, 646 .... E 2
Guárico, 3,653 .... D 3
Guariquén, 633 .... G 2
Guasdualito, 4,586 .... C 4
Guasimal, 303 .... C 3
Guasipati, 3,446 .... H 4

Guayabal, 40 .... E 6
Guayabal, 841 .... E 3
Güiria, 11,061 .... H 2
Guri, 158 .... G 4
Guzmán Blanco, 151 .... E 6
Higuerote, 3,852 .... E 2
Icabarú, 475 .... H 5
Irapa, 4,532 .... H 2
Juangriego, 4,505 .... G 2
Judibana, 4,375 .... D 2
Jusepín, 2,471 .... G 3
Kavanayén, 401 .... H 4
La Aduana, 106 .... H 3
La Asunción, 5,517 .... G 2
La Canoa, 256 .... G 3
La Ceiba, 13 .... G 4
La Ceiba, Trujillo, 199 .... C 3
La Concepción, 18,015 .... B 2
La Concepción, 9,488 .... C 2
La Esmeralda, 30 .... F 6
La Esperanza .... G 5
La Fría, 4,771 .... B 3
La Grita, 7,866 .... C 3
La Guaira, 20,497 .... E 2
Lagunetas, 522 .... G 4
La Horqueta, 330 .... G 3
La Inglesa, 100 .... C 3
La Leona, 327 .... G 3
La Luz, 414 .... D 3
La Margarita .... H 3
La Paragua, 833 .... G 4
Las Bonitas, 306 .... F 4
Las Lajitas .... F 4

© C.S. HAMMOND & Co., N.Y.

Map

VENEZUELA
MERCATOR PROJECTION

SCALE OF MILES
0 25 50 75 100 125

SCALE OF KILOMETRES
0 25 50 75 100 125

Capitals of Countries .... ☆
State Capitals .... ◉
International Boundaries .... — · — · —
State Boundaries .... — — —
Canals .... ————

Venezuela 125

Las Mercedes, 5,410 ....E 3
Las Piedras, Falcón, 2,068 ....C 2
Las Piedras, Zulia, 2,069 ....B 2
Las Trincheras, 157 ....F 4
Las Vegas, 1,190 ....D 3
La Tigra, 234 ....H 4
La Trinidad, 141 ....D 4
La Trinidad de Arauca, 68 ....D 3
La Trinidad de Orichuna, 820 ....D 4
La Unión, 1,068 ....E 3
La Urbana, 444 ....E 4
La Vela de Coro, 4,963 ....D 2
La Victoria, Apure, 109 ....D 4
La Victoria, Aragua, 22,293 ....E 2
Libertad, Barinas, 1,218 ....D 3
Libertad, Cojedes, 1,000 ....D 3
Los Castillos, 92 ....G 3
Los Taques, 2,097 ....C 2
Los Teques, 36,073 ....E 2
Macareo Santo Niño, 376 ....H 3
Machiques, 11,115 ....B 3
Macuro, 899 ....H 2
Macuto, 7,041 ....E 2
Maiquetía, 75,687 ....E 2
Mantecal, Apure, 987 ....D 4
Mantecal, Bolívar, 21 ....F 4
Maparari, 1,330 ....D 2
Mapire, 658 ....F 4
Maporal, 224 ....C 4
Maracaibo, 625,101 ....C 2
Maracaibo, *655,000 ....C 2
Maracay, 185,655 ....E 2
Marigüitar, 3,075 ....G 2
Maripa, 802 ....F 4
Maroa, 417 ....E 6
Matu, 87 ....F 4
Maturín, 54,362 ....G 3
Mene de Mauroa, 3,597 ....C 2
Mene Grande, 11,673 ....C 3
Mérida, 46,339 ....C 3
Mesa Bolívar, 1,227 ....C 3
Mirimire, 1,473 ....D 2
Moitaco, 364 ....F 4
Morganito, 103 ....E 5
Morón, 7,079 ....D 2
Mucuchachí, 391 ....C 3
Mucuchíes, 1,034 ....C 3
Naricual, 656 ....F 2
Nirgua, 7,371 ....D 2
Nuevo Mamo, 284 ....G 3
Obispos, 651 ....D 3
Ocumare de la Costa, 1,332 ....E 2
Ocumare del Tuy, 15,006 ....E 2
Onoto, 1,090 ....F 3
Ortiz, 1,309 ....E 3
Ospino, 1,590 ....D 3
Palmarejo, 943 ....C 2
Palmarito, Apure, 1,176 ....D 4
Palmarito, Guárico, 74 ....F 3
Palmarito, Mérida, 903 ....C 3
Papelón, 414 ....D 3
Paraguaipoa, 1,443 ....C 2
Paraíso de Chabasquén, 2,324 ....D 3
Pariaguán, 6,236 ....F 3
Parmana, 322 ....F 4
Pedernales, 788 ....G 3
Pedregal, 1,483 ....C 2
Peraitepuí, 81 ....H 5
Piacoa, 377 ....H 3
Pimichín, 19 ....E 6
Píritu, Anzoátegui, 1,438 ....F 2
Píritu, Falcón, 1,859 ....D 2
Píritu, Portuguesa, 4,879 ....D 3
Platanal, 8 ....F 6
Porlamar, 21,787 ....G 2
Pozuelos, 6,488 ....F 2
Pregonero, 2,894 ....C 3
Pueblo Nuevo, 2,680 ....D 1
Puerto Ayacucho, 5,465 ....E 5
Puerto Cabello, 52,493 ....E 2
Puerto Cumarebo, 8,029 ....D 2
Puerto de Nutrias, 565 ....D 3
Puerto Hierro, 1,096 ....H 2
Puerto La Cruz, 59,033 ....F 2
Puerto Miranda, 374 ....E 4
Puerto Páez, 767 ....E 4
Puerto Píritu, 2,407 ....F 2
Punta Cardón, 7,461 ....C 2
Punta de Mata, 6,525 ....G 3
Punta de Piedras, 2,342 ....F 2
Punto Fijo, 34,457 ....D 2
Puruey, 343 ....F 4
Puruname, 8 ....E 6
Quibor, 7,046 ....D 3
Quiriquire, 7,393 ....G 3
Quisiro, 816 ....C 2
Río Caribe, 7,774 ....G 2
Río Chico, 2,612 ....F 2
Río Claro, 1,374 ....D 3
Río Tocuyo, 1,650 ....C 2
Rosario, 10,442 ....B 2
Rubio, 11,774 ....B 4
Sabaneta, Barinas, 1,997 ....D 3
Sabaneta, Falcón, 414 ....D 2
Samariapo, 19 ....E 5
San Antonio, Monagas, 3,337 ....G 2
San Antonio, Zulia, 510 ....C 3
San Antonio de Caparo, 1,412 ....C 4
San Antonio del Táchira, 14,247 ....B 4
San Antonio de Orinoco, 48 ....E 6
San Antonio de Tabasca, 434 ....G 3
Sanare, 3,599 ....D 3
San Carlos, Cojedes, 11,934 ....D 3
San Carlos, Zulia, 686 ....C 2
San Carlos del Zulia, 14,480 ....C 3
San Carlos de Río Negro, 474 ....E 7
San Casimiro, 3,485 ....E 3
San Cristóbal, 149,063 ....B 4
San Diego de Cabrutica, 455 ....F 3
San Felipe, Yaracuy, 28,744 ....D 2
San Felipe, Zulia, 570 ....B 3
San Félix, 424 ....C 2
San Fernando, 24,470 ....E 4
San Fernando de Atabapo, 898 ....E 5
San Francisco, 967 ....C 2
San Ignacio, 697 ....B 2
San José, Amazonas ....E 5
San José, Zulia, 2,991 ....B 3
San José de Amacuro, 22 ....H 3
San José de Areocuar, 1,000 ....G 2
San José de Guanipa, 20,746 ....G 3
San José de la Costa, 505 ....D 2
San José de Río Chico, 3,368 ....F 2
San José de Tiznados, 504 ....E 3
San Juan de Colón, 8,944 ....B 3
San Juan de las Galdonas, 1,104 ....G 2
San Juan de los Cayos, 1,191 ....D 2
San Juan de los Morros, 28,556 ....E 3
San Juan de Manapiare, 46 ....E 5
San Juan de Payara, 945 ....E 4
San Lorenzo, Falcón, 527 ....D 2
San Lorenzo, Zulia, 1,552 ....C 3
San Luis, 1,266 ....D 2
San Mateo, 1,849 ....F 3
San Mauricio, 43 ....E 3
San Pedro de las Bocas, 288 ....G 4
San Rafael, 6,390 ....C 2
San Rafael de Atamaica, 597 ....E 4
San Rafael de Orituco, 991 ....E 3
San Sebastián, 4,090 ....E 2
Santa Ana, Anzoátegui, 3,609 ....F 3
Santa Ana, Táchira, 3,677 ....B 4
Santa Bárbara, Amazonas ....E 6
Santa Bárbara, Barinas, 2,029 ....C 4
Santa Bárbara, Monagas, 1,720 ....G 3
Santa Bárbara, Zulia, 105 ....C 3
Santa Catalina, Barinas, 425 ....D 4
Santa Catalina, Delta Amacuro, 440 ....H 3
Santa Cruz, 3,224 ....C 3
Santa Cruz de Bucaral, 1,829 ....D 2
Santa Cruz del Zulia, 2,041 ....B 3
Santa Cruz de Mara, 1,919 ....C 2
Santa Cruz de Orinoco, 419 ....F 3
Santa Elena, 752 ....H 5
Santa Inés, Anzoátegui, 917 ....F 3
Santa Inés, Barinas, 257 ....C 3
Santa Isabel ....F 7
Santa Lucía, 563 ....D 3
Santa María, Bolívar, 468 ....G 3
Santa Mariá de Erebató, 468 ....F 5
Santa María de Ipire, 3,167 ....F 3
Santa María del Orinoco, 57 ....E 4
Santa Rita, Guárico, 306 ....E 3
Santa Rita, Zulia, 5,342 ....C 2
Santa Rosa, Anzoátegui, 1,036 ....F 3
Santa Rosa, Apure, 27 ....D 4
Santa Rosa, Barinas, 957 ....D 3
Santa Rosa de Amanadona, 163 ....E 7
Santa Rosalía, 239 ....F 4
Santa Teresa del Tuy, 6,958 ....E 2
San Timoteo, 2,823 ....C 3
San Tomé, 5,625 ....F 3
San Vicente, Amazonas, 14 ....E 5
San Vicente, Apure, 252 ....D 4
Sarare, 2,664 ....D 3
Seboruco, 2,440 ....B 3
Simaraña ....G 5
Sinamaica, 1,345 ....B 2
Siquisique, 2,579 ....D 2
Solano ....E 6
Soledad, 5,653 ....G 3
Sucre, 65 ....D 3
Suripa, 128 ....D 4
Tamatama, 35 ....F 6
Táriba, 9,835 ....B 4
Temblador, 2,041 ....G 3
Tia Juana, 5,846 ....C 2
Timotes, 2,548 ....C 3
Tinaco, 4,485 ....D 3
Tinaquillo, 8,142 ....D 3
Tocópero, 721 ....D 2
Tocuyo de la Costa, 3,351 ....D 2
Torunos, 676 ....C 3
Tovar, 9,614 ....C 3
Trujillo, 18,957 ....C 3
Tucacas, 3,853 ....D 2
Tucupido, 7,016 ....F 3
Tucupita, 9,922 ....H 3
Tumeremo, 3,926 ....H 4
Tupí, 91 ....D 2
Turén, 341 ....D 3
Turiamo, 31 ....E 2
Turmero, 7,639 ....E 2
Upata, 12,717 ....G 3
Urachiche, 3,630 ....D 2
Uracoa, 858 ....G 3
Urica, 1,577 ....F 3
Urimán, 237 ....G 5
Urumaco, 941 ....C 2
Uruyén ....G 5
Uverito, 336 ....F 3
Valencia, 177,199 ....E 2
Valencia, *224,552 ....E 2
Valera, 46,643 ....C 3
Valle de Guanape, 3,254 ....F 3
Valle de la Pascua, 24,308 ....F 3
Villa Bruzual, 10,278 ....D 3
Villa de Cura, 19,945 ....E 2
Villa Frontado, 1,597 ....G 2
Yaguaraparo, 2,673 ....G 2
Yaritagua, 14,740 ....D 2
Yavita, 49 ....E 6
Yerichaña ....F 5
Yoco, 2,181 ....G 2
Zanja de Lira, 58 ....E 3
Zaraza, 10,084 ....F 3
Zuata, 783 ....F 3

OTHER FEATURES

Amacuro (river) ....H 4
Angel (Salto Angel) (fall) ....G 5
Apongua (river) ....H 5
Apure (river) ....E 4
Arauca (river) ....E 4
Arichuna (river) ....D 4
Aro (river) ....F 4
Atabapo (river) ....E 6
Auyantepui (mt.) ....G 5
Baria (river) ....E 7
Blanquilla, La (isl.), 46 ....F 2
Bolívar (mt.) ....C 3
Bolívar (mt.) ....G 4
Canagua (river) ....C 3
Caño Capure (river) ....H 3
Caño Macareo (river) ....H 3
Caño Mánamo (river) ....G 3
Capanaparo (river) ....E 4
Caparo (river) ....C 4
Caroní (river) ....G 4
Carrao (river) ....G 5
Caruai (river) ....H 5
Casiquiare, Brazo (river) ....E 6
Catatumbo (river) ....B 3
Caura (river) ....F 5
Cerbatana, La (mts.) ....E 4
Chicanán (river) ....H 4
Chimantá–tepuí (mt.) ....G 5
Chivapure (river) ....E 4
Cinaruco (river) ....D 4
Coche (isl.) ....F 2
Codera (cape) ....F 2
Cojedes (river) ....D 3
Cuao (river) ....E 5
Cubagua (isl.) ....F 2
Cuchivero (river) ....F 4
Cuquenán (river) ....H 5
Curutú (river) ....G 5
Cuyuni (river) ....H 4
Delgado Chalbaud (mt.) ....G 6
Dragons Mouth (strait) ....H 2
Duida (mt.) ....F 6
Erebato (river) ....F 5
Gran Sabana, La (plain) ....G 5
Guainía (river) ....E 6
Guampí (mts.) ....F 4
Guanare (river) ....D 3
Guanare Viejo (river) ....D 3
Guanipa (river) ....G 3
Guárico (res.) ....E 3
Guárico (river) ....E 3
Guayapo (mts.) ....E 5
Güere (river) ....F 3
Guri (dam) ....G 4
Guri (res.) ....G 4
Hermanos, Los (isls.) ....F 2
Icabaru (river) ....G 5
Imataca (mts.) ....H 4
Imeri (mts.) ....F 7
La Blanquilla (isl.), 46 ....F 2
La Grand Sabana (plain) ....G 5
La Orchila (isl.), 35 ....F 2
Las Aves (isl.), 6 ....E 2
La Tortuga (isl.), 25 ....F 2
Los Hermanos (isls.) ....F 2
Los Monjes (isls.) ....C 1
Los Roques (isls.), 537 ....E 2
Los Testigos (isls.), 59 ....G 2
Macanao (pen.) ....F 2
Maigualida (mts.) ....F 4
Manapire (river) ....E 3
Maracaibo (lake) ....C 3
Margarita (isl.), 85,296 ....F 2
Mavaca (river) ....F 6
Médanos (isthmus) ....D 2
Merevari (river) ....E 4
Mérida (mts.) ....C 3
Meta (river) ....E 4
Monjes, Los (isls.) ....C 1
Morichal Largo (river) ....G 3
Neblina (Phelps) (pk.) ....E 7
Negro (river) ....E 7
Nuria (mts.) ....H 4
Ocamo (river) ....F 6
Orchila, La (isl.), 35 ....F 2
Orinoco (delta) ....H 3
Orinoco (river) ....G 3
Orituco (river) ....E 3
Pacaraima (mts.) ....G 5
Pao (river) ....D 3
Pao (river) ....F 3
Paragua (river) ....G 4
Paraguaná (peninsula), 104,535 ....C 1
Paria (gulf) ....H 2
Paria (pen.) ....G 2
Parida, La (Bolívar) (mt.) ....G 4
Parima (mts.) ....F 6
Perijá (mts.) ....B 2
Phelps (pk.) ....E 7
Portuguesa (river) ....D 3
Roques, Los (isls.), 537 ....E 2
Roraima (mt.) ....H 5
Salto Angel (fall) ....G 5
Sarare (river) ....C 4
Serpents Mouth (strait) ....H 3
Siapa (river) ....E 7
Sipapo (river) ....E 5
Suapure (river) ....E 4
Suripá (river) ....C 4
Tapirapecó (mts.) ....F 7
Testigos, Los (isls.), 59 ....G 2
Tigre (river) ....G 3
Tocuco (river) ....B 3
Tocuyo (river) ....D 2
Tortuga, La (isl.), 25 ....F 2
Tramán–tepuí (mt.) ....G 5
Triste (gulf) ....D 2
Turagua (mts.) ....F 4
Tuy (river) ....E 2
Unare (river) ....F 3
Valencia (lake) ....E 2
Venamo (mt.) ....H 4
Venamo (river) ....H 4
Venezuela (gulf) ....C 2
Ventuari (river) ....E 5
Votamo (river) ....F 6
Yatua (river) ....E 7
Yuruari (river) ....H 4
Zuata (river) ....F 3
Zulia (river) ....B 3

*City and suburbs.

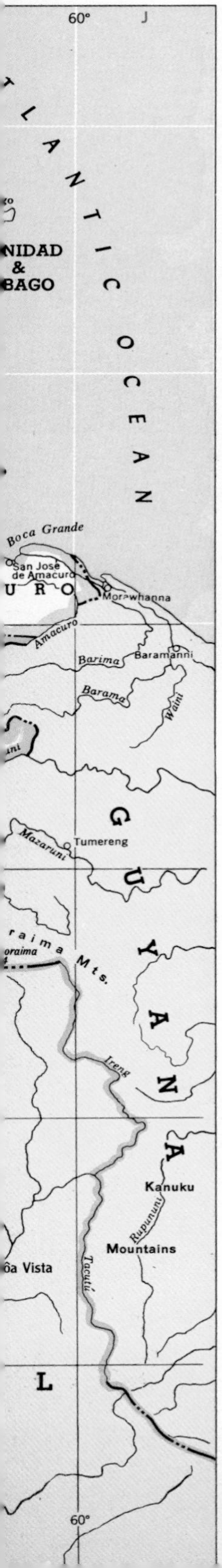

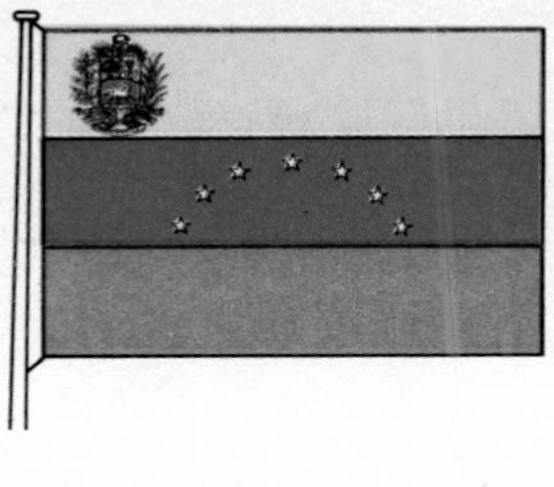

AREA 352,143 sq. mi.
POPULATION 10,398,907
CAPITAL Caracas
LARGEST CITY Caracas
HIGHEST POINT Pico Bolívar 16,427 ft.
MONETARY UNIT bolívar
MAJOR LANGUAGE Spanish
MAJOR RELIGION Roman Catholicism

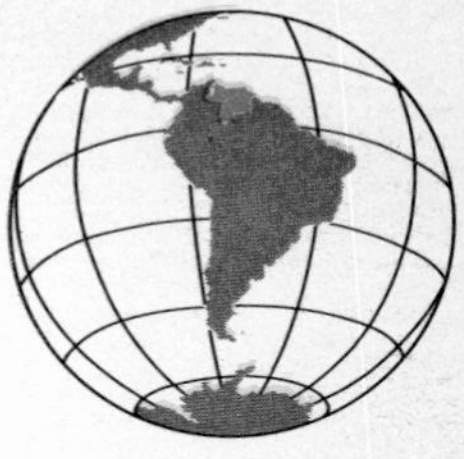

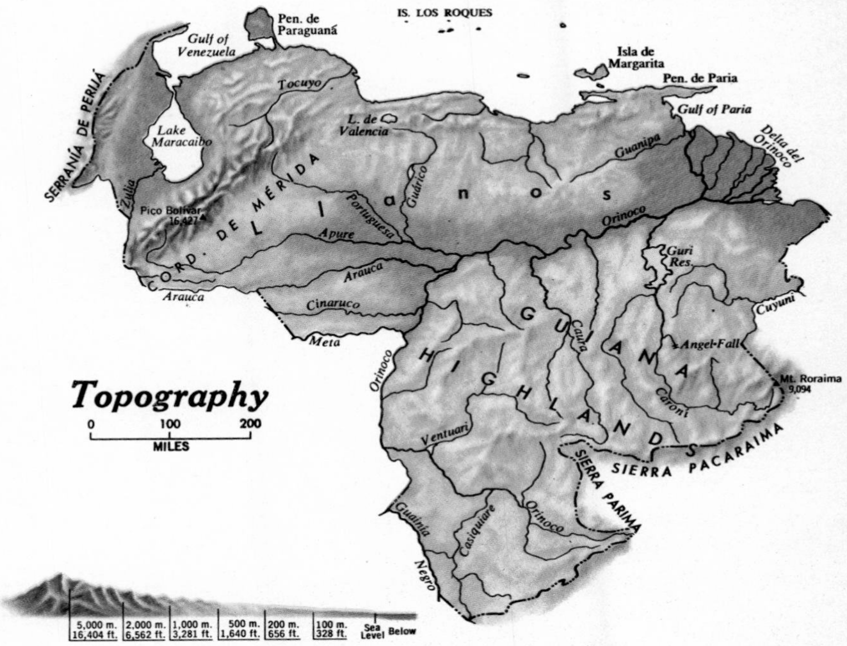
Pen. de Paraguaná
IS. LOS ROQUES
Isla de Margarita
Pen. de Paria
Gulf of Paria
Gulf of Venezuela
Tocuyo
L. de Valencia
Lake Maracaibo
SERRANÍA DE PERIJÁ
Guanipa
Delta del Orinoco
Pico Bolívar 16,427
CORD. DE MÉRIDA
L l a n o s
Apure
Portuguesa
Guárico
Orinoco
Guri Res.
Cuyuni
Arauca
Cinaruco
Meta
Caura
G U I A N A
Angel Fall
Mt. Roraima 9,094
H I G H L A N D S
Caroni
Ventuari
SIERRA PACARAIMA
SIERRA PARIMA
Casiquiare
Guainía
Negro
0 100 200
MILES
5,000 m. 16,404 ft.
2,000 m. 6,562 ft.
1,000 m. 3,281 ft.
500 m. 1,640 ft.
200 m. 656 ft.
100 m. 328 ft.
Sea Level
Below

Topography

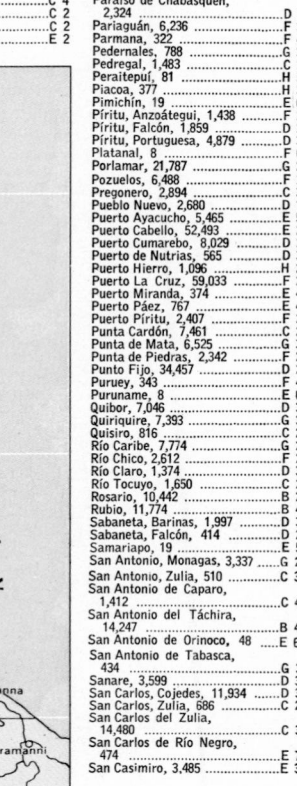

Agriculture, Industry and Resources

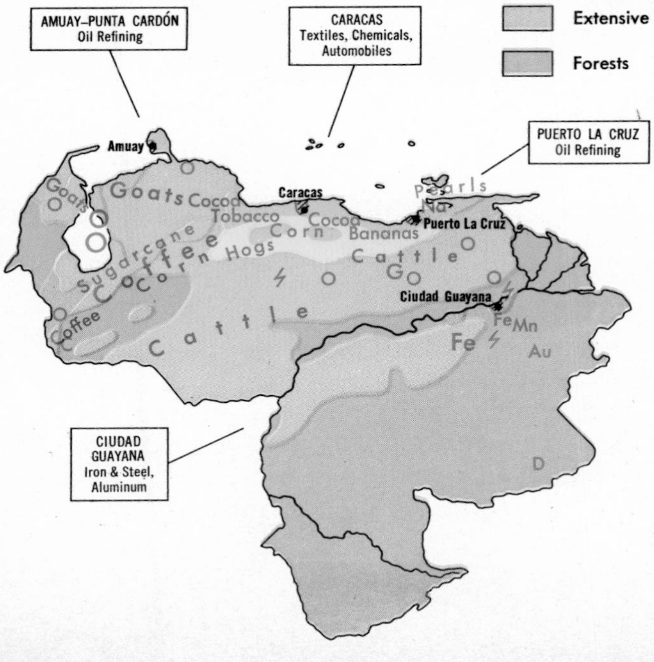
AMUAY–PUNTA CARDÓN
Oil Refining
CARACAS
Textiles, Chemicals, Automobiles
PUERTO LA CRUZ
Oil Refining
CIUDAD GUAYANA
Iron & Steel, Aluminum
Amuay
Caracas
Puerto La Cruz
Ciudad Guayana
Goats
Cocoa
Tobacco
Coffee
Sugarcane
Corn
Hogs
Bananas
Cattle
Pearls
Fe
Mn
Au
D

DOMINANT LAND USE

- Diversified Tropical Crops (chiefly plantation agriculture)
- Upland Cultivated Areas
- Upland Livestock Grazing, Limited Agriculture
- Extensive Livestock Ranching
- Forests

MAJOR MINERAL OCCURRENCES

- Au Gold
- C Coal
- D Diamonds
- Fe Iron Ore
- G Natural Gas
- Mn Manganese
- Na Salt
- O Petroleum
- Water Power
- Major Industrial Areas

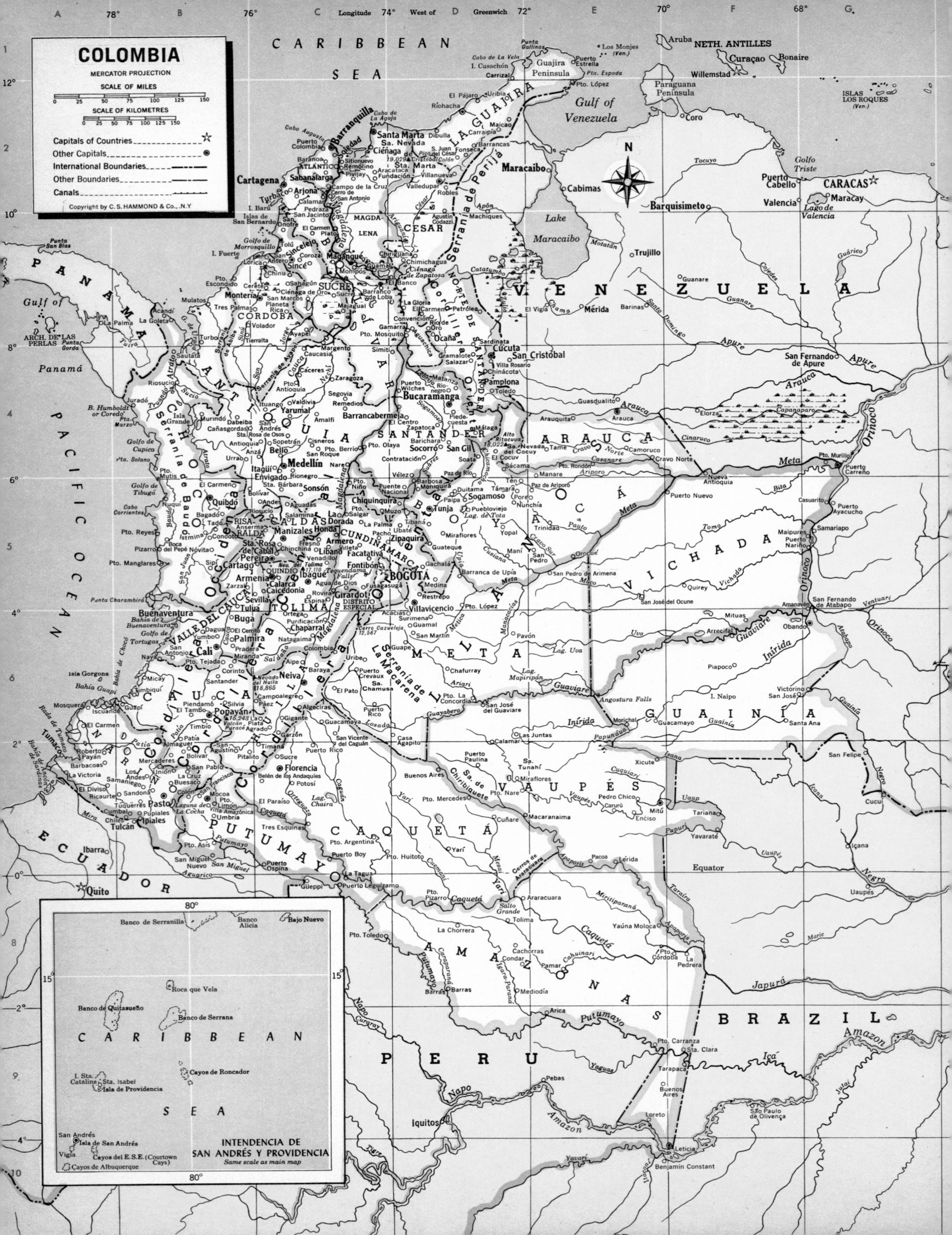

COLOMBIA

MERCATOR PROJECTION

SCALE OF MILES

0 25 50 75 100 125 150

SCALE OF KILOMETRES

0 25 50 75 100 125 150

Capitals of Countries _____ ☆
Other Capitals _____ ◉
International Boundaries _____
Other Boundaries _____
Canals _____

Copyright by C. S. HAMMOND & Co., N.Y.

INTENDENCIA DE
SAN ANDRÉS Y PROVIDENCIA
Same scale as main map

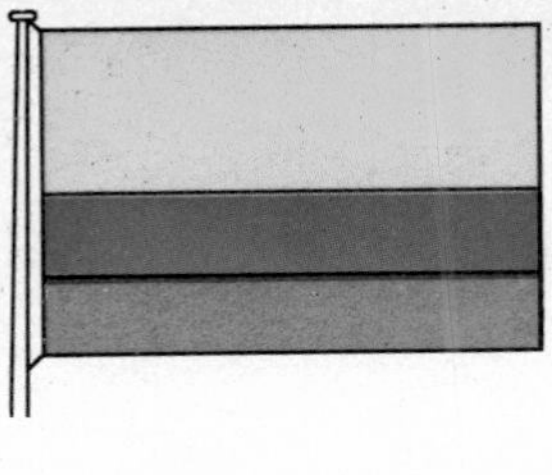

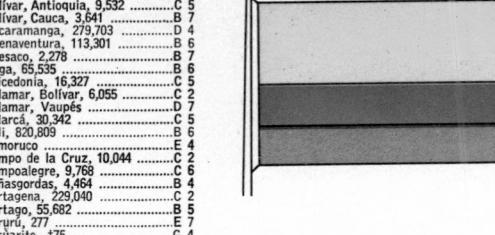

AREA 439,513 sq. mi.
POPULATION 21,117,000
CAPITAL Bogotá
LARGEST CITY Bogotá
HIGHEST POINT Pico Cristóbal Colón 19,029 ft.
MONETARY UNIT Colombian peso
MAJOR LANGUAGE Spanish
MAJOR RELIGION Roman Catholicism

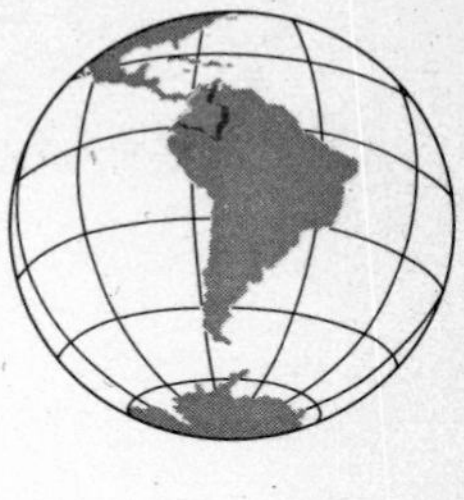

INTERNAL DIVISIONS

Amazonas (intendency), 16,000...D 8
Antioquia (dept.), 3,031,000........C 4
Arauca (commissary), 32,000......E 4
Atlántico (dept.), 903,000 ....C 2
Bolívar (dept.), 849,000 ....C 3
Boyacá (dept.), 1,194,000 ....D 5
Caldas (dept.), 810,000 ....C 5
Caquetá (intendency), 157,000....C 7
Cauca (dept.), 696,000 ....B 6
Cesar (dept.), 357,000 ....D 3
Chocó (dept.), 210,000 ....B 4
Córdoba (dept.), 760,000 ....C 3
Cundinamarca (dept.),
1,187,000 ....C 5
Distrito Especial, 2,416,000 ....C 5
Guainía (comm.), 5,000 ....F 6
Guajira, La (dept.), 173,000 .....D 2
Huila (dept.), 485,000 ....C 6
La Guajira (dept.), 173,000 ....D 2
Magdalena (dept.), 683,000 ......D 3
Meta (dept.), 248,000 ....D 6
Nariño (dept.), 787,000 ....B 7
Norte de Santander (dept.),
615,000 ....D 4
Putumayo (comm.), 77,000 ....C 7
Quindío (dept.), 346,000 ....C 5
Risaralda (dept.), 512,000...........C 5
San Andrés y Providencia
(intendency), 27,000 ....B10
Santander (dept.), 1,137,000 ....D 4
Sucre (dept.), 361,000 ....C 3
Tolima (dept.), 902,000 ....C 5
Valle del Cauca (dept.),
2,114,000 ....B 6
Vaupés (commissary), 18,000 ....E 7
Vichada (commissary), 9,000 ....F 5

CITIES and TOWNS

Acacías, 6,508 ....D 6
Acandí, 1,686 ....B 3
Agrado, 2,751 ....C 6
Agua de Dios, 7,401 ....C 5
Aguachica, 8,556 ....D 3
Aguadas, 10,822 ....C 5
Agustín Codazzi, 11,673 ....D 3
Aipe, 3,404 ....C 6
Algeciras, 3,778 ....C 6
Almaguer, 1,251 ....B 7
Amalfi, 4,667 ....C 4
Amanavén, †1,164 ....G 6
Andes, 11,135 ....C 5
Anserma, 14,129 ....B 5
Antioquia, 6,002 ....B 4
Anza, 680 ....C 4
Aracataca, 5,304 ....D 2
Araracuara ....E 8
Arauca, 4,280 ....E 4
Arauquita, 413 ....E 4
Arjona, 16,510 ....C 2
Armenia, 162.837 ....B 5
Armero, 17,495 ....C 5
Ayapel, 5,610 ....C 3
Bagado, 865 ....B 5
Baranoa, 14,064 ....C 2
Baraya, 2,696 ....C 6
Barbacoas, 4,011 ....A 7
Barbosa, 6,018 ....D 5
Barichara, 2,798 ....D 4
Barrancabermeja, 59,625 ....C 4
Barrancas, 2,010 ....D 2
Barranco de Loba, 1,648 ....C 3
Barranquilla, 816,706 ....C 2
Belén de los Andaquíes, 1,420....C 7
Bello, 127,377 ....C 4
Boca del Pepé, 566 ....B 5
Bogotá (cap.), 2,037,904 ....D 5
Bogotá, *2,416,000 ....D 5
Bolívar, Antioquia, 9,532 ....C 5
Bolívar, Cauca, 3,641 ....B 7
Bucaramanga, 279,703 ....D 4
Buenaventura, 113,301 ....B 6
Buesaco, 2,278 ....B 7
Buga, 65,535 ....B 6
Caicedonia, 16,327 ....C 5
Calamar, Bolívar, 6,055 ....C 2
Calamar, Vaupés ....D 7
Calarcá, 30,342 ....C 5
Cali, 820,809 ....B 6
Camoruco ....E 4
Campo de la Cruz, 10,044 ....C 2
Campoalegre, 9,768 ....C 6
Cañasgordas, 4,464 ....B 4
Cartagena, 229,040 ....C 2
Cartago, 55,682 ....B 5
Carurú, 277 ....E 7
Casuarito, †75 ....G 4
Caucasia, 5,616 ....C 4
Cereté, 11,849 ....C 3
Cerro de San Antonio, 3,397 ......C 2
Chaparral, 13,261 ....C 6
Chimichagua, 5,093 ....D 3
Chinácota, 4,081 ....D 4
Chinchiná, 15,944 ....C 5
Chinú, 7,552 ....C 3
Chiquinquirá, 16,926 ....C 5
Chiriguaná, 6,516 ....D 3
Ciénaga, 142,893 ....C 2
Ciénaga de Oro, 8,047 ....C 3
Cisneros, 7,554 ....C 4
Colombia, 1,599 ....C 6
Colón, 1,133 ....B 7
Condoto, 4,094 ....B 5
Contratación, 3,117 ....D 4
Convención, 7,371 ....D 3
Corinto, 5,008 ....B 6
Corozal, 14,000 ....C 3
Cravo Norte, 566 ....F 4
Cúcuta, 207.091 ....D 4
Cumbal, 2,549 ....B 7
Cuñare ....D 7
Dabeiba, 4,218 ....B 4
Dagua, 4,635 ....B 6
Dibulla ....D 2
Duitama, 31,865 ....D 5
El Banco, 14,889 ....D 3
El Carmen, Chocó, 1,689 ....B 5
El Carmen, Norte de Santander,
2,737 ....D 3
El Carmen de Bolívar, 19,196....C 3
El Cerrito, 12.200 ....B 6
El Cocuy, 2,869 ....D 4
El Tambo, 4,003 ....B 6
Envigado, 40,686 ....C 4
Espinal, 22,791 ....C 5
Facatativá, 20,742 ....C 5
Florencia, 17,709 ....C 7
Fonseca, 5,190 ....D 2
Fontibón ....C 5
Fresno, 7,058 ....C 5
Fundación, 14,128 ....D 2
Fusagasugá, 18,755 ....C 5
Gachalá, 1,253 ....D 5
Gamarra, 4,664 ....D 3
Garzón, 11,999 ....C 6
Gigante, 4,594 ....C 6
Girardot, 66,584 ....C 5
Gramalote, 3,098 ....D 4
Guacamaya ....C 6
Guamal, Magdalena, 4,695 ....C 3
Guamal, Meta, 2,113 ....D 6
Guape ....D 6
Guapí, 3,066 ....B 6
Guateque, 4,646 ....D 5
Honda, 19,945 ....C 5
Ibagué, 178,821 ....C 5
Ipiales, 23,320 ....B 7
Iscuandé, 1,777 ....A 6
Istmina, 3,996 ....B 5
Itagüí, 101,066 ....C 4
Ituango, 3,466 ....C 4
Juradó, 708 ....B 4
La Cruz, 4,014 ....B 7
La Dorada, 26,168 ....C 5
La Gloria, 2,915 ....D 3
La Palma, 4,594 ....C 5
La Plata, 5,863 ....C 6
La Unión, 3,875 ....B 7
Leticia, 4,013 ....F10
Líbano, 18,640 ....C 5
Lorica, 12,880 ....C 3
Los Andes, 1,392 ....B 7
Macaranaima ....E 7
Magangué, 27,354 ....C 3
Maicao, 9,347 ....D 2
Maipures ....F 5
Majagual, 2,197 ....C 3
Málaga, 9,674 ....D 4
Manare ....E 4
Maní, 586 ....D 5
Manizales, 267,543 ....C 5
Matanza, 1,264 ....D 4
Medellín, 967,825 ....C 4
Medina, 893 ....D 5
Mercaderes, 2,376 ....B 7
Micay ....B 6
Miraflores, Boyacá, 3,257 ....D 5
Miraflores, Vaupés, 245 ....E 7
Miranda, 5,527 ....B 6
Mitú, 1,623 ....E 7
Mituas ....F 6
Mocoa, 2,571 ....B 7
Mompós, 10,965 ....C 3
Moniquirá, 4,882 ....D 5
Montería, 167,446 ....B 3
Morichal, †2,512 ....E 6
Mosquera, 766 ....A 6
Murindó, 319 ....B 4
Muzo, 792 ....D 5
Natagaima, 8,372 ....C 6
Naya ....B 6
Neiva, 111,727 ....C 6
Nóvita, 883 ....B 5
Nueva Antioquia, †236 ....F 5
Nunchía, 461 ....D 5
Nuquí, 1,500 ....B 5
Obando ....G 6
Ocaña, 28,028 ....D 3
Orocué, 1,600 ....E 5
Ortega, 4,450 ....C 6
Pacho, 7,192 ....C 5
Pacoa, †960 ....G 6
Páez, 1,570 ....C 6
Paipa, 3,105 ....D 5
Palmira, 164,394 ....B 6
Pamplona, 25,502 ....D 4
Pasto, 123,153 ....B 7
Patía, 3,045 ....B 6
Paz de Ariporo, 1,216 ....E 5
Paz de Río, 2,748 ....D 4
Pedraza, 1,757 ....C 2
Pereira, 224,421 ....C 5
Piedecuesta, 12,278 ....D 4
Pitalito, 10,818 ....B 7
Pivijay, 8,200 ....C 2
Planeta Rica, 5,959 ....C 3
Plato, 13,364 ....C 3
Popayán, 58,500 ....B 6
Pore, 193 ....D 5
Potosí, 1,149 ....C 7
Pradera, 11,223 ....B 6
Puente Nacional, 2,913 ....D 5
Puerto Asís, 2,902 ....B 7
Puerto Berrío, 15,812 ....C 4
Puerto Carreño, 1,115 ....G 4
Puerto Colombia, 7,143 ....C 2
Puerto Escondido, 1,543 ....B 3
Puerto Leguízamo, 3,014 ....C 8
Puerto López, La Guajira ....E 2
Puerto López, Meta, 3,586 ....D 5
Puerto Murillo, †1,014 ....G 4
Puerto Nariño, †926 ....F 5
Puerto Rico, Caquetá, †10,328 ....C 7
Puerto Rico, Meta ....C 6
Puerto Rondón, 951 ....E 4
Puerto Salgar, 6,398 ....C 5
Puerto Tejada, 14,863 ....B 6
Puerto Wilches, 4,635 ....D 4
Pupiales, 2,432 ....B 7
Purificación, 7,044 ....C 6
Quibdó, 19,989 ....B 5
Remedios, 2,090 ....C 4
Remolino, 3,373 ....C 2
Restrepo, 2,603 ....D 5
Ricaurte, 866 ....A 7
Río de Oro, 2,482 ....D 3
Riohacha, 11,708 ....D 2
Rionegro, Antioquia, 2,708 ....D 4
Rionegro, Santander, 12,541 ......C 4
Riosucio, Caldas, 11,274 ....C 5
Riosucio, Chocó, 1,817 ....B 4
Roberto Payán, 402 ....A 7
Robles, 4,278 ....D 2
Rovira, 4,582 ....C 5
Sabanalarga, 20,254 ....C 2
Sácama, 54 ....D 4
Sahagún, 11,560 ....C 3
Salamina, 14,263 ....C 5
Salazar, 3,020 ....D 4
Samaniego, 3,181 ....B 7
San Agustín, 3,250 ....B 7
San Andrés, Antioquia, 1,773 .....C 4
San Andrés, San Andrés y
Providencia, 9,040 ....A10
San Antero, 6,596 ....C 3
San Felipe, 187 ....G 7
San Francisco, 1,248 ....B 7
San Gil, 18,518 ....D 4
San Jacinto, 10,210 ....C 3
San José del Guaviare, 215 ....D 6
San José del Ocuné, 105 ....E 5
San Juan del César, 9,347 ....D 2
San Marcos, 7,083 ....C 3
San Martín, 6,739 ....D 6
San Onofre, 10,737 ....C 3
San Pablo, 4,103 ....B 7
San Roque, 3,272 ....C 4
San Vicente del Caguán, 1,764....C 6
Sandoná, 6,776 ....B 7
Santa Bárbara, 7,779 ....C 5
Santa Isabel, 468 ....B 9
Santa Marta, 137,474 ....D 2
Santa Rosa de Cabal, 31,646 .....C 5
Santa Rosa de Osos, 6,860 ....C 4
Santander, 11,426 ....B 6
Santiago, 929 ....B 7
Sardinata, 2,964 ....D 3
Segovia, 9,234 ....C 4
Sevilla, 26,757 ....C 5
Sibundoy-Las Casas, 1,999 ....B 7
Silvia, 3,180 ....B 6
Simití, 2,825 ....C 4
Sincé, 10,631 ....C 3
Sincelejo, 44,001 ....C 3
Sipí, 155 ....B 5
Sitionuevo, 5,969 ....C 2
Soatá, 4,361 ....D 4
Socorro, 13,716 ....D 4
Sogamoso, 32,274 ....D 5
Soledad, 37,617 ....C 2
Sonsón, 16,955 ....C 5
Sopetrán, 3,646 ....C 4
Sucre, Bolívar, 3,035 ....C 3
Sucre, Caquetá ....C 7
Tadó, 1,947 ....B 5
Támara, 1,034 ....D 5
Tame, 3,063 ....E 4
Tibaná, 924 ....D 5
Tierralta, 4,415 ....C 3
Timaná, 2,999 ....C 7
Timbío, 4,145 ....B 6
Timbiquí, 1,406 ....B 6
Toledo, 2,314 ....D 4
Tolú, 7,954 ....C 3
Trinidad, 572 ....E 5
Tuluá, 56,539 ....B 5
Tumaco, 25,145 ....A 7
Tunja, 40,451 ....D 5
Túquerres, 10,698 ....B 7
Turbaco, 14,255 ....C 2
Turbo, 7,375 ....B 3
Ubaté, 6,261 ....D 5
Uribia, 1,763 ....D 2
Urrao, 7,712 ....B 4
Valdivia, 2,264 ....C 4
Valledupar, 120,009 ....D 2
Vélez, 7,033 ....D 4
Venadillo, 6,931 ....C 5
Villanueva, 8,288 ....D 2
Villa Amazónica, 1,344 ....B 7
Villa Rosario, 5,184 ....D 4
Villavicencio, 45,277 ....D 5
Villeta, 5,280 ....C 5
Yarumal, 16,823 ....C 4
Yavaraté, †1,963 ....F 7
Yopal, 2,878 ....D 5
Yumbo, 15,270 ....B 6
Zapatoca, 7,305 ....D 4
Zaragoza, 2,134 ....C 4
Zarzal, 17,768 ....B 5
Zipaquirá, 22,648 ....D 5

OTHER FEATURES

Abibe (mts.) ....B 4
Aguja (cape) ....C 2
Albuquerque (cays) A10
Alicia (bank) ....B 8
Alto Ritacuva (mt.) ....D 4
Amazon (Amazonas) (river) ....E 9
Ancón de Sardinas (bay) ....A 7
Angostura (falls) ....E 6
Apaporis (river) ....F 8
Araracuara (mts.) ....E 7
Arauca (river) ....E 4
Ariari (river) ....D 6
Ariguaní (river) ....D 3
Ariporo (river) ....E 4
Atabapo (river) ....G 6
Atrato (river) ....B 4
Augusta (cape) ....C 2
Ayapel (mts.) ....C 4
Bajo Nuevo (shoal) ....C 8
Baudó (mts.) ....B 5
Baudó (river) ....B 5
Bita (river) ....F 5
Caguán (river) ....C 7
Cahuinari (river) ....E 8
Caquetá (river) ....E 8
Caraparaná (river) ....D 8
Casanare (river) ....E 4
Cauca (river) ....C 4
Cazueleja (mt.) ....C 6
Central (mts.) ....C 5
César (river) ....D 2
Chaira (lagoon) ....C 7
Chamusa (mts.) ....C 6
Charambirá (point) ....B 5
Chiribiquete (mts.) ....D 7
Chocó (bay) ....B 6
Cocha (lake) ....D 7
Cocuy (mts.) ....D 4
Coredó (Humboldt) (bay) ....B 4
Corrientes (cape) ....B 5
Courtown (Este Sudeste)
(cays) A10
Cravo Norte (river) ....E 4
Cravo Sur (river) ....E 5
Cristóbal Colón (mt.) ....D 2
Cuemaní (river) ....D 7
Cupica (gulf) ....B 4
Cuquiari (river) ....E 7
Cusiana (river) ....D 5
Este Sudeste (cays) A10
Gallinas (point) ....E 1
Grande (isl.) ....B 4
Guainía (river) ....F 6
Guajira (pen.) ....E 1
Guapí (bay) ....A 6
Guaviare (river) ....F 6
Guayabero (river) ....D 6
Huila (mt.) ....C 6
Humboldt (Coredó) (bay) ....B 4
Igara-Paraná (river) ....D 8
Inírida (river) ....F 6
Isana (river) ....F 7
Lebrija (river) ....D 4
Llanos (plains) ....D 5
Losada (river) ....C 6
Macarena (mts.) ....D 6
Magdalena (river) ....C 3
Manacacías (river) ....D 6
Mapiripán (lake) ....E 6
Marzo (cape) ....B 4
Mesai (river) ....D 7
Meta (river) ....E 5
Metica (river) ....D 6
Miritiparaná (river) ....E 8
Morrosquillo (gulf) ....C 3
Muco (river) ....E 5
Naipo (isl.) ....F 6
Nechi (river) ....C 4
Occidental, Cordillera (mts.) ....B 5
Oriental, Cordillera (mts.) ....D 5
Orinoco (river) ....G 5
Orteguaza (river) ....C 7
Papunáua (river) ....E 6
Patía (river) ....B 6
Pauto (river) ....E 5
Perijá (mts.) ....D 2
Providencia (isl.), 2,318 ....B 9
Pupurí (river) ....F 7
Puracé (volcano) ....B 6
Putumayo (river) ....E 9
Quitasueño (bank) ....A 8
Riosucio (river) ....C 5
Roncador (cays) ....B 9
Saldaña (river) ....C 6
Salto Grande (falls) ....D 8
San Andrés (isl.), 14,413 ....A10
San Jorge (river) ....C 3
San Juan (river) ....B 5
Santa Marta, Nev. de (range)...D 2
Serrana (bank) ....B 9
Serranilla (bank) ....B 8
Sinú (river) ....B 3
Sogamoso (river) ....D 4
Solano (point) ....B 4
Suárez (river) ....D 4
Taraíra (river) ....F 8
Tequendama (falls) ....C 5
Tibugá (gulf) ....B 5
Tolima (mt.) ....C 5
Tomo (river) ....F 5
Tortugas (gulf) ....B 6
Truandó (river) ....B 4
Tumaco (inlet) ....A 6
Tunahí (mts.) ....E 7
Upía (river) ....D 5
Urabá (gulf) ....B 3
Uva (lake) ....E 6
Uva (river) ....E 6
Vaupés (river) ....E 7
Vela (cape) ....D 1
Vela, Roca que (cay) ....B 8
Vichada (river) ....F 5
Yarí (river) ....D 8
Zapatosa (swamp) ....D 3

*City and suburbs.

Agriculture, Industry and Resources

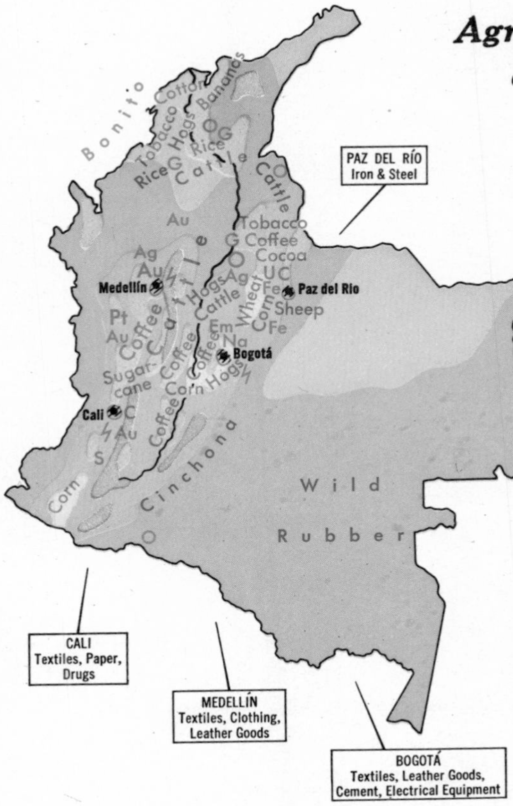

DOMINANT LAND USE

- Diversified Tropical Crops (chiefly plantation agriculture)
- Upland Cultivated Areas
- Upland Livestock Grazing, Limited Agriculture
- Extensive Livestock Ranching
- Forests
- Nonagricultural Land

MAJOR MINERAL OCCURRENCES

Ag	Silver	G	Natural Gas
Au	Gold	Na	Salt
C	Coal	O	Petroleum
Em	Emeralds	Pt	Platinum
Fe	Iron Ore	S	Sulfur
		U	Uranium

Water Power

Major Industrial Areas

Topography

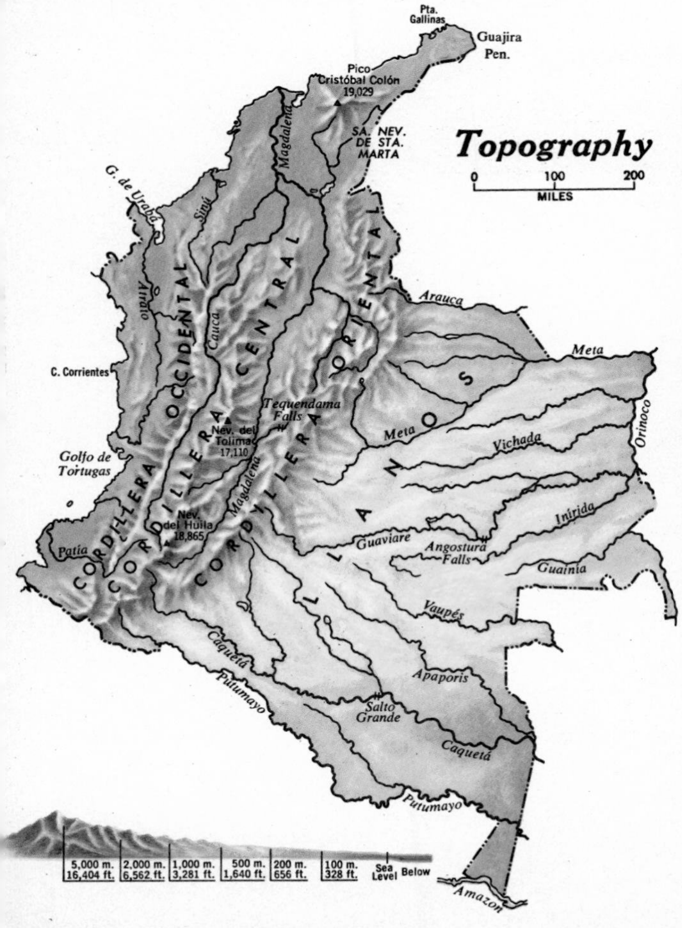

PERU and ECUADOR

BIPOLAR OBLIQUE CONIC CONFORMAL PROJECTION

SCALE OF MILES

0 50 100 150 200

SCALE OF KILOMETRES

0 50 100 150 200

Capitals of Countries .... ☆

Other Capitals .... ⊙

International Boundaries ....

Other Boundaries ....

Copyright by C. S. Hammond & Co., N.Y.

PROVINCES OF ECUADOR
INDICATED BY NUMBERS

1 Imbabura	C-2	5 Bolívar	C-3
2 Cotopaxi	C-3	6 Chimborazo	C-3
3 Tungurahua	C-3	7 Cañar	C-4
4 Los Ríos	C-3	8 El Oro	C-4

GALÁPAGOS ISLANDS
(ARCHIPIÉLAGO DE COLÓN)
(Ecuador)
Same scale as main map

PACIFIC OCEAN

I. Culpepper (Darwin)
I. Wenman (Wolf)
I. Pinta
I. Marchena
Pta. Albemarle
I. Genovesa
Equator
B. de Banks
I. San Salvador (Santiago)
Fernandina
I. Isabel
I. Baltra
Pinzón
I. Sta. Cruz (Chaves)
Isla
Isabela
Sta. Cruz
Villamil
I. Sta. Fe
C. Rosa
Pto. Baquerizo Moreno
I.S. Cristóbal
El Progreso
Floreana
I. Sta. María (Floreana)
I. Española

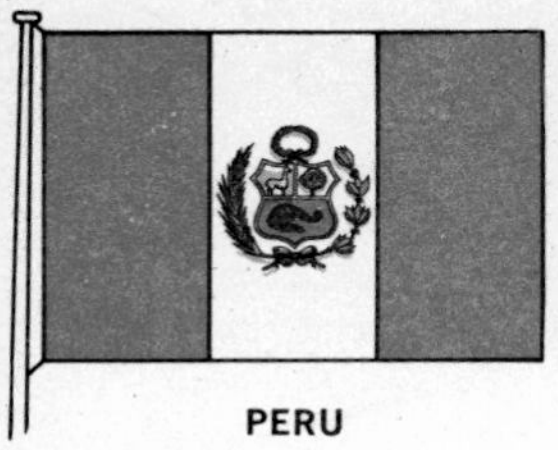

PERU

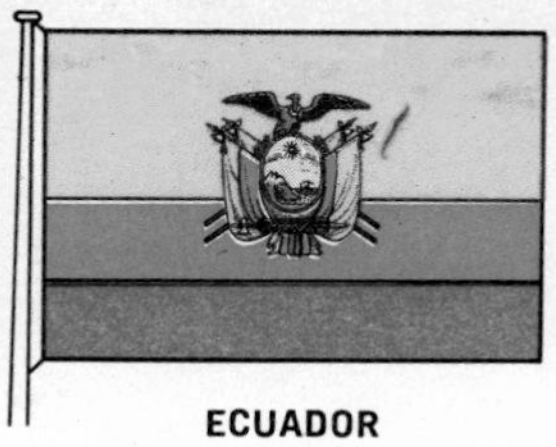

ECUADOR

PERU

AREA 496,222 sq. mi.
POPULATION 13,586,300
CAPITAL Lima
LARGEST CITY Lima
HIGHEST POINT Huascarán 22,205 ft.
MONETARY UNIT sol
MAJOR LANGUAGES Spanish, Quechua, Aymara
MAJOR RELIGION Roman Catholicism

ECUADOR

AREA 109,483 sq. mi.
POPULATION 6,144,000
CAPITAL Quito
LARGEST CITY Guayaquil
HIGHEST POINT Chimborazo 20,561 ft.
MONETARY UNIT sucre
MAJOR LANGUAGES Spanish, Quechua
MAJOR RELIGION Roman Catholicism

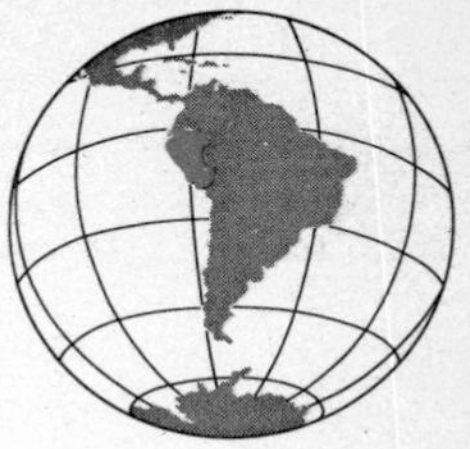

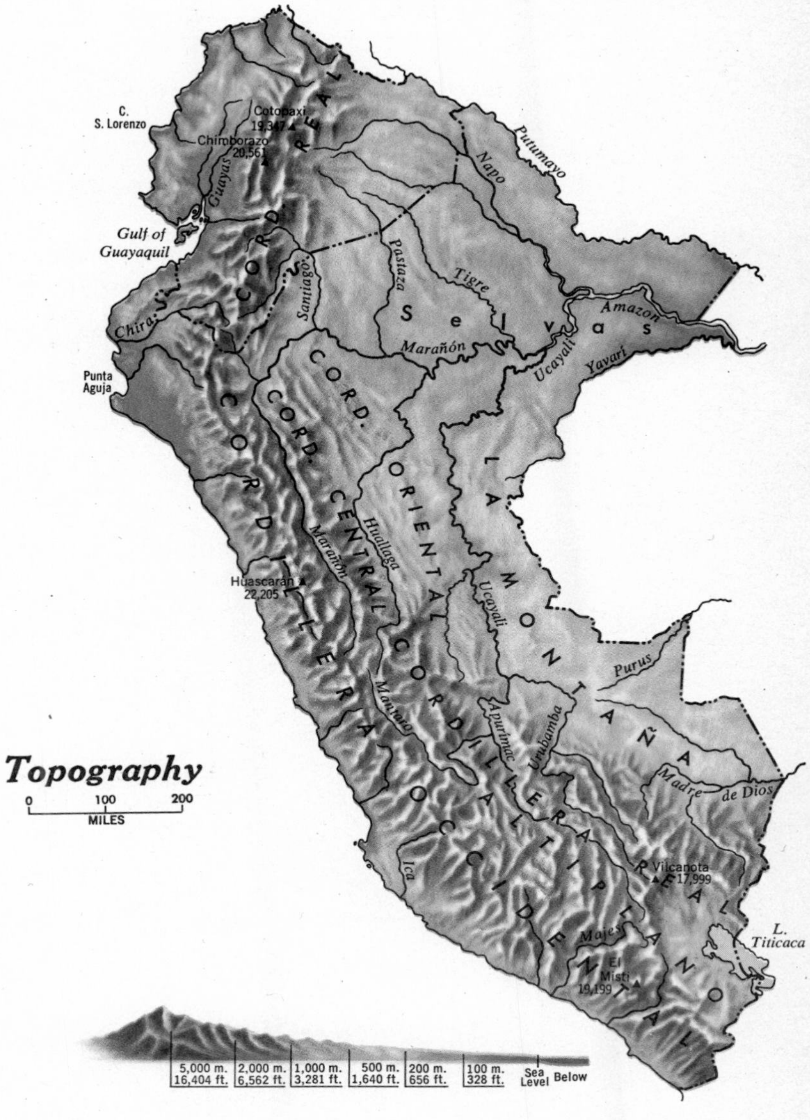

PERU

DEPARTMENTS

Amazonas, 171,100 .... C 5
Ancash, 744,700 .... D 7
Apurímac, 330,400 .... F10
Arequipa, 518,300 .... F10
Ayacucho, 474,100 .... E 9
Cajamarca, 1,007,600 .... C 6
Callao (province), 335,400 .... D 9
Cuzco, 756,100 .... F 9
Huancavelica, 367,100 .... E 9
Huánuco, 430,100 .... D 7
Ica, 362.700 .... E10
Junín, 699,100 .... E 8
La Libertad, 784,900 .... C 6
Lambayeque, 485,500 .... B 6
Lima, 3,155,800 .... D 8
Loreto, 504,600 .... E 5
Madre de Dios, 24,200 .... G 8
Moquegua, 68,800 .... G11
Pasco, 188,000 .... E 8
Piura, 922,300 .... B 5
Puno, 848,200 .... G10
San Martín, 229,400 .... D 6
Tacna, 93,900 .... G11
Tumbes, 84,000 .... B 4

CITIES and TOWNS

Abancay, 9,053 .... F 9
Acarí, 1,428 .... E10
Acobamba, 2,167 .... E 9
Acolla, 4,415 .... E 8
Acomayo, Cuzco, 1,874 .... G 9
Acomayo, Huánuco, 1,198 .... E 7
Acora, 941 .... H11
Acuracay, 96 .... F 5
Aija, 1,710 .... D 7
Alca, 539 .... F10
Ambo, 1,606 .... D 8
Ancón, 3,760 .... D 8
Andahuaylas, 4,674 .... F 9
Andamarca, 339 .... E 8
Anta, 2,574 .... F 9
Antabamba, 2,294 .... F10
Aplao, 1,316 .... F11
Aquia, 897 .... D 8
Arequipa, 194,700 .... G11
Ascope, 3,845 .... C 6
Astillero .... H 9
Atalaya, 816 .... E 8
Atico, 297 .... F11
Ayabaca, 3,415 .... C 5
Ayacucho, 28,500 .... F 9
Ayavirí, 7,553 .... G10
Azángaro, 4,771 .... H10
Bagua, 2,343 .... C 5
Balsapuerto, 203 .... D 5
Bambamarca, 4,281 .... C 6
Barranca, Lima, 11,320 .... C 8
Barranca, Loreto, 184 .... D 5
Bartra Antiguo .... E 4
Bartra Nuevo .... E 4
Bayóvar .... B 5
Bellavista, 2,129 .... C 5
Bolívar, 1,057 .... D 6
Bolognesi .... F 6
Bolognesi, 516 .... F 8
Borja, 300 .... D 5
Bretaña, 766 .... E 5
Buldibuyo, 616 .... D 7
Caballococha, 1,197 .... G 4
Cabana, 1,910 .... C 7
Cabo Blanco .... B 5
Cahuapanas, 125 .... D 5
Cailloma, 607 .... G10
Cajabamba, 5,253 .... C 6
Cajacay, 809 .... D 8
Cajamarca, 28,200 .... C 6
Cajatambo, 2,257 .... D 8
Calca, 3,489 .... G 9
Callalli, 133 .... G10
Callao, 335,400 .... D 9
Camaná, 5,120 .... F11
Candarave, 859 .... G11
Cangallo, 1,578 .... E 9
Canta, 2,491 .... D 8
Capachica, 193 .... H10
Carás, 4,033 .... D 7
Caravelí, 1,954 .... F10
Carhuás, 2,175 .... D 7
Carumás, 727 .... G11
Cascas, 2,403 .... C 6
Casma, 4,975 .... C 7
Castilla, 29,541 .... B 5
Castrovirreyna, 784 .... E 9
Catacaos, 12,135 .... B 5
Celendín, 5,646 .... D 6
Cerro Azul, 1,571 .... D 9
Cerro de Pasco, 23,400 .... D 8
Chachapoyas, 6,860 .... D 6
Chala, 1,054 .... E10
Chalhuanca, 2,840 .... F10
Chancay, 6,145 .... D 8
Chao .... C 7
Chepén, 16,119 .... C 6
Chicama, 1,362 .... C 6
Chiclayo, 140,800 .... C 6
Chilca (Pucusana), 1,331 .... D 9
Chilete, 1,105 .... C 6
Chimbote, 102,800 .... C 7
Chincha Alta, 26,500 .... D 9
Chiquián, 3,354 .... D 8
Chirinos, 490 .... C 5
Chivay, 2,320 .... G10
Chorrillós, 31,703 .... D 9
Chosica .... D 8
Chota, 4,961 .... C 6
Chulucanas, 19,714 .... B 5
Chupaca, 2,180 .... E 9
Chuquibamba, 2,983 .... F10
Chuquibambilla, 1,423 .... F 9
Churín, 610 .... D 8
Cocachacra, 2,869 .... G11
Cocama .... G 8
Cojata, 763 .... H10
Colasay, 466 .... C 5
Colcamar, 1,370 .... D 6
Conaica, 1,408 .... E 9
Concepción, 4,184 .... E 8
Concordia, 66 .... E 5
Contamana, 4,708 .... E 6
Contumazá, 2,532 .... C 6
Coracora, 4,116 .... F10
Córdova, 620 .... E10
Corongo, 2,241 .... D 7
Cotahuasi, 1,618 .... F10
Culebras .... C 7
Cumaría .... F 7
Cutervo, 4,702 .... C 6
Cuyocuyo, 708 .... H10
Cuzco, 108,900 .... F 9
Desaguadero, 948 .... H11
Deustua, 416 .... G10
Dos de Mayo, 970 .... E 6
Echarate, 374 .... F 9
El Portugués .... C 7
Esperanza, 261 .... G 7
Ferreñafe, 12,112 .... C 6
Fitzcarrald .... G 8
Francisco de Orellana, 306 .... F 4
Guadalupe, 2,896 .... E 9
Güeppi .... E 3
Huacho, 29,400 .... D 8
Huacrachuco, 757 .... D 7
Hualgayoc, 1,223 .... C 6
Hualla, 2,586 .... F 9
Huallanca, Ancash, 491 .... D 7
Huallanca, Huánuco, 1,202 .... D 7
Huamachuco, 5,730 .... D 6
Huancabamba, 3,215 .... C 5
Huancané, 4,053 .... H10
Huancapi, 2,415 .... E 9
Huancavelica, 11,039 .... E 9
Huancayo, 95,000 .... E 9
Huanchaco, 1,006 .... C 7
Huanta, 5,728 .... E 9
Huánuco, 34,500 .... E 7
Huaral, 11,481 .... D 8
Huaráz, 20,345 .... D 7
Huari, 2,467 .... D 7
Huariaca, 1,534 .... E 8
Huarmey, 5,232 .... C 8
Huarochirí, 2,125 .... D 9
Huarocondo, 2,921 .... F 9
Huaura, 1,442 .... D 8
Huaylas, 1,258 .... C 7
Iberia, 526 .... F 5
Ica, 72,300 .... E10
Ichuña, 183 .... G11
Ilave, 4,278 .... H11
Ilo, 9,986 .... G11
Imperial, 6,345 .... D 9
Inambari, 9 .... H 9
Iñapari, 159 .... H 8
Intutu, 344 .... E 4
Iparia, 171 .... E 7
Iquitos, 76,100 .... F 4
Jaén, 4,420 .... C 5
Jauja, 12,751 .... E 8
Jayanca, 4,240 .... B 6
Jeberos, 1,842 .... D 5
Juanjuí, 5,105 .... D 6
Juli, 3,874 .... H11
Juliaca, 35,000 .... G10
Jumbilla, 876 .... C 5
Junín, 5,004 .... E 8
Lagunas, 3,637 .... E 5
La Huaca, 1,863 .... B 5
La Jalca, 1,401 .... D 6
La Joya, 1,305 .... G11
Lamas, 7,139 .... D 6
Lambayeque, 10,629 .... B 6
Lampa, 3,123 .... G10
Lamud, 2,609 .... C 6
Lanlacuni Bajo, 229 .... G 9
La Oroya, 32,600 .... D 8
Las Piedras, 13 .... H 9
Las Yaras, 367 .... G11
La Tina .... B 5
La Unión, 2,013 .... D 7
Leimebamba, 1,026 .... D 6
Lima (capital), *2,541,300 .... D 8
Limbani, 903 .... H10
Lircay, 2,077 .... E 9
Llata, 2,255 .... D 7
Lobitos, 3,071 .... B 5
Locumba, 349 .... G11
Lomas, 111 .... E10
Lucerna .... H 9
Lurín, 2,741 .... D 9
Machupicchu, 1,026 .... F 9
Macusani, 1,601 .... G10
Madre de Dios, †802 .... G 9
Máncora, 7,943 .... B 5
Manú, †686 .... G 9
Marcapata, 334 .... G 9
Marcona, 6,744 .... E10
Margos, 1,195 .... D 8
Masisea, 1,520 .... E 7
Matarani F11
Matucana, 2,883 .... D 8
Mavila .... H 8
Mazán, 411 .... F 4
Mazocruz, 156 .... H11
Mendoza, 1,002 .... D 6
Miraflores, 52,142 .... G11
Mishagua .... F 8
Moho, 1,377 .... H10
Mollendo, 12,483 .... F11
Monsefú, 11,141 .... C 6
Moquegua, 7,795 .... G11
Morales, 2,430 .... D 6
Morococha, 6,519 .... D 8
Morropón, 4,730 .... C 5
Motupe, 1,286 .... C 6
Moyobamba, 8,373 .... D 6
Nauta, 1,905 .... F 5
Nazca, 13,587 .... E10
Negritos, 14,810 .... B 5
Nueva Alejandría, †264 .... F 5
Nuñoa, 2,137 .... G10
Ocoña, 1,207 .... F11
Ocros, 1,204 .... D 8
Ollachea, 903 .... G 9
Ollantaytambo, 1,632 .... F 9
Olmos, 3,628 .... C 5
Omaguas .... F 4
Omas, 217 .... D 9
Omate, 856 .... G11
Orcotuna, 2,716 .... E 8
Orellana, 1,596 .... E 6
Otuzco, 4,311 .... C 6
Oxapampa, 2,535 .... E 8
Oyón, 2,171 .... D 8
Pacasmayo, 11,956 .... C 6
Pachiza, 1,307 .... D 6
Paijan, 5,815 .... C 6
Paita, 9,615 .... B 5
Palpa, 2,615 .... E10
Pampachiri, 448 .... F10
Pampacolca, 1,876 .... F10
Pampas, 2,495 .... E 9
Panao, 1,262 .... E 7
Pantoja, 528 .... E 3
Parinari, 126 .... E 5
Paruro, 1,905 .... F 9
Pataz, 324 .... D 6
Pativilca, 15,325 .... D 8
Paucarbamba, 715 .... E 9
Paucartambo, Cuzco, 1,928 .... E 8
Paucartambo, Pasco, 1,717 .... G 9
Pevas, 696 .... G 4
Picota, 2,014 .... D 6
Pimentel, 6,252 .... B 6
Pinquén .... G 9
Pisac, 1,230 .... G 9
Pisco, 27,300 .... D 9
Piura, 111,400 .... B 5
Pizacoma, 86 .... H11
Pomabamba, 2,522 .... D 7
Porvenir .... E 5
Poto, 161 .... H10
Pozuzo, 121 .... E 8
Puca Barranca .... F 4
Pucallpa, 45,600 .... E 7
Pucará, 1,119 .... G10
Pucaurco, 12 .... G 4
Pucusana, 1,331 .... D 9
Puerto Alianza .... D 5
Puerto América, 150 .... D 5
Puerto Arturo .... F 3
Puerto Bermúdez, 230 .... E 8
Puerto Caballas E10
Puerto Chicama, 3,002 .... C 6
Puerto Eten, 2,192 .... B 6
Puerto José Pardo .... D 4
Puerto Leguía, Loreto .... D 4
Puerto Leguía, Puno .... G 9
Puerto Maldonado, 3,518 .... H 9
Puerto Morín .... C 7
Puerto Ocopa, 1,304 .... E 8
Puerto Pardo .... F 7
Puerto Pizarro .... B 4
Puerto Portillo, 49 .... F 7
Puerto Prado, 419 .... E 8
Puerto Samanco, 1,733 .... C 7
Puerto Tahuantinsuyo .... G 9
Puerto Victoria .... E 7
Puno, 32,100 .... G10
Punta de Bombón, 3,943 .... F11
Punta Moreno .... C 6
Puquina, 1,030 .... G11
Puquio, 8,144 .... F10
Putina, 3,512 .... H10
Querecotillo, 6,205 .... B 5
Quicacha, 299 .... F10
Quilca, 171 .... F11
Quillabamba, 8,644 .... F 9
Quince Mil .... G 9
Ramón Castilla, †8,106 .... G 5
Recuay, 1,755 .... D 7
Requena, 3,931 .... F 5
Reventazón .... B 6
Rioja, 4,361 .... D 6
Salaverry, 4,605 .... C 7
San José, 2,612 .... B 6
San José de Sisa, 4,190 .... D 6
San Juan, 717 .... E10
San Lorenzo, 84 .... H 8
San Martín .... E 3
San Miguel, Ayacucho, 1,271 .... F 9
San Miguel, Cajamarca, 1,871 .... C 6
San Pedro de Lloc, 7,497 .... C 6
San Ramón, 3,016 .... E 8
San Vicente de Cañete, 7,184 .... D 9
Saña, 18,421 .... C 6
Sandia, 3,026 .... H10
Santa, 2,966 .... C 7
Santa Clotilde, 824 .... E 4
Santa Cruz, Cajamarca, 1,729 .... C 6
Santa Cruz, Loreto, 739 .... E 5
Santa Elena, 271 .... F 5
Santa Isabel de Sihuas, 118 .... F11
Santa María de Nanay, 123 .... F 4
Santiago, 1,613 .... E10
Santiago de Cao, 1,033 .... C 6
Santiago de-Chocorvos, 344 .... E 9
Santiago de Chuco, 4,649 .... C 7
Santo Tomás, Amazonas, 1,097 .... C 6
Santo Tomás, Cuzco, 1,659 .... G10
Santo Tomás de Andoas, 65 .... D 4
Saposoa, 4,456 .... D 6
Saquena, 688 .... F 5
Satipo, 2,499 .... E 8
Sauce, 1,761 .... D 6
Sayán, 1,764 .... D 8
Sechura, 5,157 .... B 5
Sicuani, 10,664 .... G10
Sihuas, 1,404 .... D 7
Sullana, 43,500 .... B 5
Sumbay G10
Sumbilca, 1,365 .... D 8
Supe, 2,499 .... D 8
Tacna, 41,200 .... G11
Tahuamanu, †4,011 .... H 8
Talara, 39,600 .... B 5
Tambo de Mora, 1,128 .... D 9
Tambo Grande, 4,404 .... B 5
Tamshiyacu, 1,623 .... F 5
Tarapoto, 13,907 .... D 6
Tarata, 2,673 .... H11
Tarma, 15,452 .... E 8
Tarqui .... E 3
Tayabamba, 1,519 .... D 7
Ticaco, 1,206 .... H11
Tingo María, 5,208 .... D 7
Tiruntán, 847 .... E 6
Tocache, 1,607 .... D 7
Tonegrama .... D 4
Topara, 1,437 .... D 9
Toquepala G11
Torata, 669 .... G11
Tournavista .... E 7
Trujillo, 156,200 .... C 7
Tumbes, 30,000 .... B 4
Ubinas, 348 .... G11
Uchiza, 1,006 .... D 7
Unini .... F 8
Urcos, 2,733 .... G 9
Urubamba, 3,325 .... F 9
Vinchos, 473 .... E 9
Virú, 2,647 .... C 7
Vitor, 117 .... G11
Yambrasbamba, 306 .... D 5
Yanahuanca, 962 .... D 8
Yanaoca, 1,146 .... G10
Yauca, 2,364 .... E10
Yauli, 1,696 .... D 8
Yauri, 2,834 .... G10
Yauyos, 1,456 .... E 9
Yunguyo, 2,506 .... H11
Yurimaguas, 11,655 .... E 5
Zarumilla, 3,499 .... B 4
Zorritos, 2,862 .... B 4

OTHER FEATURES

Acarí (river) E10
Aguaytía (river) .... E 7
Aguja (point) .... B 5
Amazon (river) .... F 4
Andes, Cordillera de los (mts.) F10
Apurímac (river) .... F 9
Azángaro (river) G10
Azul, Cordillera (mts.) .... E 7
Blanca, Cordillera (mts.) .... D 7
Blanco (cape) .... B 5
Blanco (river) .... F 6
Boquerón, El (pass) .... E 7
Cañete (river) .... D 9
Casma (river) .... C 7
Chimbote (bay) .... C 7
Chincha (isls.) .... D 9
Chira (river) .... B 5
Coles (point) G11
Cóndor, Cordillera del (mts.) .... C 5
Coropuna, Nudo (mt.) F10
Corrientes (river) .... E 4
El Boquerón (pass) .... E 7
El Misti (mt.) G11
Ene (river) .... E 8
Ferrol (pen.) .... C 7
Grande (river) E10
Guañape (isls.) .... C 7
Heath (river) .... H 9
Huallaga (river) .... D 5
Huasaga (river) .... D 4
Huascarán (mt.) .... D 7
Huayabamba (river) .... D 6
Ica (river) E10
Inambari (river) .... H 9
Independencia (bay) D10
Junín (lake) .... E 8
La Montaña (reg.) .... F 8
Lachay (Salinas) (point) .... D 8
Las Piedras (river) .... G 8
Las Viejas (isl.) D10
Lobos de Afuera (isls.) .... B 6
Lobos de Tierra (isl.) .... B 6
Locumba (river) G11
Madre de Dios (river) .... G 9
Majes (river) F11
Mantaro (river) .... E 8
Manú (river) .... G 8
Marañón (river) .... E 5
Mayo (river) .... D 6
Misti, El (mt.) G11
Montaña, La (reg.) .... F 8
Morona (river) .... D 5
Nanay (river) .... E 4
Napo (river) .... F 4
Negra, Cordillera (mts.) .... D 7
Negra (point) .... B 6
Ñermete (point) .... B 5
Nudo Coropuna (mt.) F10
Occidental, Cordillera (mts.) F10
Ocoña (river) F11
Oriental, Cordillera (mts.) H10
Pachitea (river) .... E 7
Paita (bay) .... B 5
Pampas (river) .... E 9
Paracas (pen.), †727 .... D 9
Parinacochas (lake) F10
Pariñas (point) .... B 5
Pastaza (river) .... D 5
Pativilca (river) .... D 8
Perené (river) .... E 8
Pichis (river) .... E 8
Piedras, Las (river) .... G 8
Pisco (bay) .... D 9
Pisco (river) .... D 9
Pirua (river) .... B 5
Puinagua, Canal de (river) .... E 5
Purus (river) .... G 8
Putumayo (river) .... G 4
Rímac (river) .... D 9
Salinas (Lachay) (point) .... D 8
Sama (river) G11

(continued on following page)

PERU (continued)	
San Gallán (isl.)	D 9
San Lorenzo (isl.)	D 9
San Nicolás (bay)	E10
Santa (river)	C 7
Santiago (river)	H 8
Sechura (bay)	B 5
Tahuamanu (river)	H 8
Tambo (river)	G11
Tambopata (river)	H 9
Tapiche (river)	E 6
Tigre (river)	E 4
Titicaca (lake)	H10
Tumbes (river)	B 4
Ucayali (river)	F 5
Urituyacu (river)	D 5
Urubamba (river)	F 8
Viejas, Las (isl.)	D10
Vilcabamba, Cordillera (mts.)	F 9
Vilcanota (mt.)	G10
Vitor (river)	F11
Yaguas (river)	G 4
Yavarí (river)	G 5
Yavero (river)	F 9

ECUADOR

PROVINCES

Azuay, 274,642	C 4
Bolívar, 131,651	C 3
Cañar, 112,733	C 4
Carchi, 94,649	C 2
Chimborazo, 276,668	C 3
Colón, Archipiélago de (terr.), 2,391	C 8
Cotopaxi, 154,971	C 3
El Oro, 160,650	C 4
Esmeraldas, 124,881	C 2
Guayas, 979,223	B 4
Imbabura, 174,039	C 3
Loja, 285,448	C 4
Los Ríos, 250,062	C 3
Manabí, 612,542	B 3
Morona-Santiago, 25,503	C 4
Napo, 24,253	D 3
Pastaza, 13,693	D 3
Pichincha, 587,835	C 3

CITIES and TOWNS

Alausí, 6,676	C 4
Ambato, 53,372	C 3
Andoas Nuevo	D 3
Arapicos	D 3
Archidona	D 3
Arenillas, 3,925	B 4
Atuntaqui, 8,759	C 2
Azogues, 8,075	C 4
Baba, 693	C 3
Babahoyo, 16,444	C 3
Balao, 213	C 4
Balao	B 4
Balzar, 6,588	C 3
Bolívar, 410	C 2
Cajabamba, 2,094	C 3
Calceta, 4,946	C 3
Cañar, 4,935	C 4

Tungurahua, 178,709	C 3
Zamora-Chinchipe, 11,464	C 5

CITIES and TOWNS

Atacames, 4,097	C 4
Catarama, 2,424	C 3
Cayambe, 8,101	C 3
Celica, 3,467	B 4
Chone, 12,832	B 3
Chunchi, 2,388	C 3
Coca	D 3
Cojimíes, 1,538	B 3
Cononaco	E 3
Cuenca, 60,402	C 4
Cuyabeno	E 3
Daule, 7,428	C 3
Edén	D 3
El Ángel, 4,009	C 2
El Corazón, 1,118	C 3
El Progreso	C 3
El Pun, 612	D 2
Esmeraldas, 33,403	C 2
Farfán	C 3
Floreana	B10

Canelos	D 3
Cariamanga, 5,381	C 5
Carondelet, 318	C 2
Catacocha, 3,796	C 4
Catamayo, 4,097	C 4
Chone, 12,832	B 3
Coca	D 3
Girón, 1,914	C 4
Gualaceo, 3,065	C 4
Gualaquiza, 635	C 4
Guale	B 3
Guamote, 2,640	C 4
Guano, 4,455	C 3
Guaranda, 9,900	C 3
Guayaquil, 738,591	B 4
Ibarra, 25,835	C 3
Jama, 1,743	B 3
Jipijapa, 13,367	B 4
La Libertad, 13,565	B 4
La Tola, 650	C 2
Latacunga, 14,856	C 3
Loja, 26,785	C 4
Loreto	D 3
Macará, 5,027	C 5
Machachi, 3,951	C 3
Machala, 29,036	B 4
Machalilla, 615	B 3
Manglaralto, 799	B 3
Manta, 33,622	B 3
Méndez, 527	C 4

Mera	C 3
Miazal	D 4
Milagro, 28,148	C 4
Montecristi, 4,540	B 3
Morona	D 4
Mulaló, 427	C 3
Napo	D 3
Nuevo Rocafuerte, 435	E 3
Otavalo, 8,630	C 3
Paján, 1,818	B 3
Palanda	C 5
Papallacta	C 3
Pasaje, 13,215	C 4
Paute, 1,511	C 4
Pedernales, 610	B 2
Peñipe, 2,545	C 3
Pillaro, 2,714	C 3
Piñas, 3,344	C 4
Playas, 5,067	B 4
Portoviejo, 32,228	B 3
Posorja, 2,086	B 4
Puerto Baquerizo Moreno	C 9
Puerto de Cayo, 713	B 3
Pujilí, 2,534	C 3
Putumayo	D 2
Puyo, 2,290	D 3
Quevedo, 20,602	C 3
Quito (capital), 496,410	C 3
Río Tigre	D 4
Riobamba, 41,625	C 3
Rocafuerte, 4,349	B 3
Rosa Zárate, 1,662	C 3
Salinas, 5,460	B 4
San Gabriel, 6,803	D 2
San Lorenzo, 575	C 2
San Miguel, 2,410	C 3
San Miguel de Salcedo, 3,442	C 3
Sangolquí, 5,501	C 3
Santa Ana, 3,940	B 3
Santa Cruz	B 9
Santa Elena, 4,241	B 4
Santa Isabel, 1,602	C 4
Santa Rosa, 8,935	C 4
Santa Rosa de Sucumbíos, 132	D 2
Santo Domingo de los Colorados, 6,951	C 3
Saraguro, 1,562	C 4
Sarayacu	D 3
Sigsig, 1,228	C 4
Sigüe	D 2
Sucre, 2,578	B 3
Sucúa, 1,153	C 4
Tabacundo, 2,009	C 3
Tachina	C 2
Tena, 1,029	D 3
Tulcán, 16,448	C 2
Valdez, 3,358	C 2
Viche, 230	C 2
Villamil	B 9
Vinces, 5,901	C 3
Yacuambí, 405	C 4
Yaguachi, 2,996	C 4
Yaupi	D 4
Zamora, 1,030	C 5
Zapotillo, 460	B 5
Zaruma, 9,000	C 4
Zumba, 450	C 5

OTHER FEATURES

Aguarico (river)	D 3
Albemarle (point)	B 9
Ancón de Sardinas (bay)	C 2
Antisana (mt.)	D 3
Baltra (isl.)	B 9
Banks (bay)	B 9
Bobonaza (river)	D 3
Cayambe (mt.)	D 3
Chaves (Santa Cruz) (isl.), 626	C 9
Chimborazo (mt.)	C 3
Cotopaxi (mt.)	C 3
Cristóbal (point)	B 9
Culpepper (isl.)	B 8
Curaray (river)	D 3
Darwin (Culpepper) (isl.)	B 8
Esmeraldas (river)	C 2
Española (isl.)	C10
Fernandina (isl.)	B 9
Floreana (Santa María) (isl.), 46	B10
Galápagos (isls.), 2,391	C 8
Galera (point)	B 2
Genovesa (isl.)	C 9
Guayaquil (gulf)	B 4
Guayas (river)	C 4
Isabel (bay)	B 9
Isabela (isl.), 336	B 9
La Puntilla (cape)	B 4
Manta (bay)	B 3
Marchena (isl.)	B 9
Mira (river)	C 2
Napo (river)	D 3
Naranjal (river)	C 4
Pasado (cape)	B 3
Pastaza (river)	D 4
Pindo (river)	D 3
Pinta (isl.)	B 9
Pinzón (isl.)	B 9
Puná (isl.), 5,459	B 4
Puntilla, La (cape)	B 4
Putumayo (river)	E 2
Rosa (cape)	B10
San Cristóbal (isl.), 1,404	C 9
San Francisco (cape)	B 2
Sangay (mt.)	C 4
San Lorenzo (cape)	B 3
San Miguel (river)	D 2
San Salvador (isl.)	B 9
Santa Cruz (isl.), 626	C 9
Santa Elena (bay)	B 3
Santa Fé (isl.)	C 9
Santa María (isl.), 46	B10
Santiago (San Salvador) (isl.)	C 9
Tumbes (river)	B 4
Wenman (isl.)	B 8
Wolf (Wenman) (isl.)	B 8
Zamora (river)	B 4

FRENCH GUIANA

DISTRICTS

Cayenne, 36,187	E 3
St-Laurent-du-Maroni, 8,205	E 3

CITIES and TOWNS

Camopi, 1276	E 3
Cayenne (cap.), 19,668	E 3
Cayenne, *24,581	E 3
Counamama	E 3
Edmond	E 3
Grand-Santi, 60	E 3
Guisambourg	E 3
Inini	E 4
Iracoubo, 504	E 3
Kaw, 258	E 3
Kourou, 868	E 3
Macouria (Tonate), 301	E 3
Mana, 568	E 3
Maripa	E 4
Maripasoula, 166	D 4
Montsinéry, 107	E 3
Organobo	E 3
Oscar	E 3
Ouanary, 79	F 3
Ouaqui	E 3
P. I. (Paul Isnard), 147	E 3
Paul Isnard, 147	E 3
Régina	E 3
Rémire, 650	E 3
Roura, 84	E 3
Saint-Élie, 78	E 3
Saint-Georges-de-l'Oyapoc, 502	F 4
Saint-Jean	E 3
Saint-Laurent-du-Maroni, 3,486	E 3
Saül, 81	E 4
Saut-Tigre	E 3
Sinnamary, 1,355	E 3
Tonate, 301	E 3

OTHER FEATURES

Approuague (river)	E 4
Béhague (point)	F 3
Camopi (river)	E 4
Chaîne Granitique (range)	E 4
Comté (river)	E 3
Connétable (isls.)	F 3
Devil's (isl.)	E 3
Granitique, Chaîne (range)	E 4
Inini (river)	E 4
Itany (river)	D 4
Mana (river)	E 3
Maroni (river)	D 4
Marouini (river)	E 4
Oyapock (river)	E 4
Rémire (river)	E 3
Salut (isls.)	E 3
Sinnamary (river)	E 3
Tampoc (river)	E 4

GUYANA

DISTRICTS

East Berbice, 115,511	C 3
East Demerara, 256,908	B 2
Essequibo, 29,729	B 2
Essequibo Islands, 15,728	B 2
Mazaruni-Potaro, 12,029	A 2
North West, 12,809	A 2
Rupununi, 10,031	A 2
West Berbice, 26,524	C 2
West Demerara, 81,061	B 2

CITIES and TOWNS

Adventure, 507	B 2
Anna Regina, 848	B 2
Apoteri	B 3
Arakaka	B 2
Atkinson Field	B 2
Aurora	B 2
Baramanni	B 2
Baramita	B 1
Bartica, 2,352	B 2
Charity, 838	B 2
Christianburg-Wismar-Mackenzie, 5,843	B 2
Dadanawa	B 3
Danielstown, 478	C 2
Enmore	C 2
Enterprise	C 2
Epira	A 3
Five Stars	A 3
Fort Wellington	C 2
Georgetown (cap.), 97,190	C 2
Georgetown, *102,688	B 2
Imbaimadai	A 3
Ituni	A 3
Kamakusa	A 3
Kamarang, 510	A 3
Kurupukari	B 3
Lethem	B 3
Lumid Pau	B 3
Mabaruma, 343	B 1
Mahaica, 8,646	C 2
Mahaicony, 8,272	C 2
Morawhanna, 305	B 1
Mount Everard	B 2
New Amsterdam, 14,300	C 2
Orealla	C 3
Paradise	C 2
Parika, 577	B 2
Pickersgill, 334	B 2
Port Kaituma	B 1
Queenstown, 1,067	B 2
Rockstone	B 2
Rosignol, 1,204	C 2
Skeldon, 4,367	C 2
Springlands, 181	C 2
Suddie, 512	B 2
Takama	C 2
Tumatumari	B 3
Tumereng	A 3
Vreed-en-Hoop, 3,156	B 2
Yupukari	B 3

OTHER FEATURES

Akarai (mts.)	B 5
Amakara (river)	A 2
Amuku (mts.)	B 3
Barama (river)	A 2
Barima (river)	B 1
Berbice (river)	C 3
Canje (river)	C 2
Courantyne (river)	C 3
Cuyuni (river)	A 2
Demerara (river)	B 2
Enwarak (mt.)	B 3
Essequibo (river)	B 2
Great (fall)	B 3
Ireng (river)	B 3
Kaieteur (fall)	B 3
Kamaria (falls)	B 2
Kanuku (mts.)	B 3
Kurungiku (mts.)	B 3

Agriculture, Industry and Resources

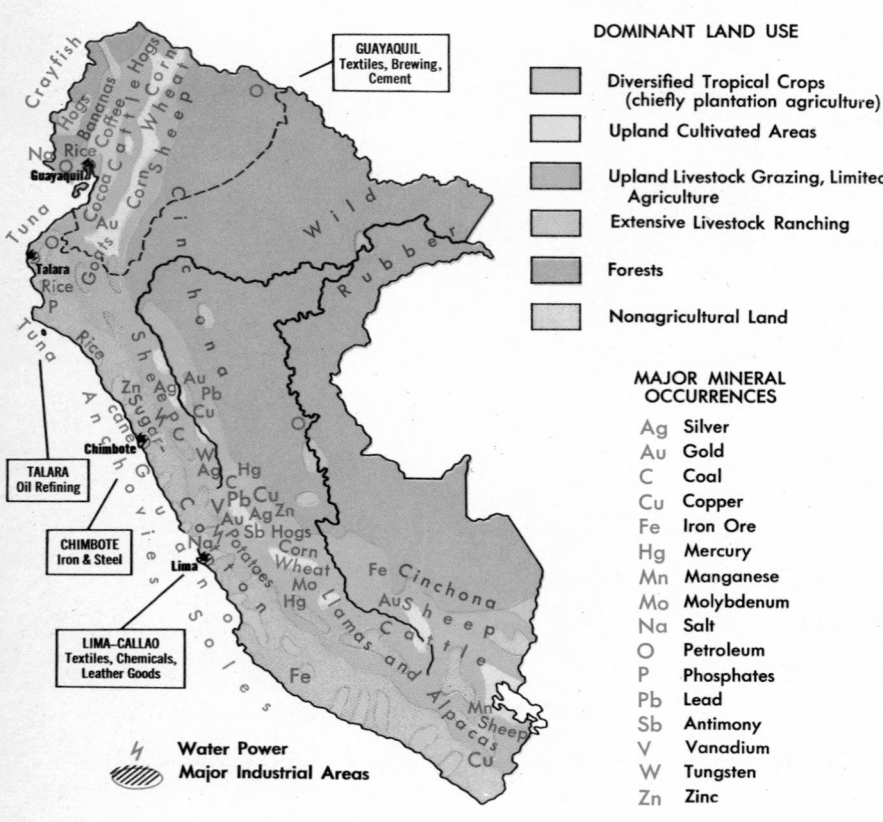

DOMINANT LAND USE

- Diversified Tropical Crops (chiefly plantation agriculture)
- Upland Cultivated Areas
- Upland Livestock Grazing, Limited Agriculture
- Extensive Livestock Ranching
- Forests
- Nonagricultural Land

MAJOR MINERAL OCCURRENCES

Ag	Silver
Au	Gold
C	Coal
Cu	Copper
Fe	Iron Ore
Hg	Mercury
Mn	Manganese
Mo	Molybdenum
Na	Salt
O	Petroleum
P	Phosphates
Pb	Lead
Sb	Antimony
V	Vanadium
W	Tungsten
Zn	Zinc

⚡ Water Power
Major Industrial Areas

GUAYAQUIL
Textiles, Brewing, Cement

TALARA
Oil Refining

CHIMBOTE
Iron & Steel

LIMA-CALLAO
Textiles, Chemicals, Leather Goods

Agriculture, Industry and Resources

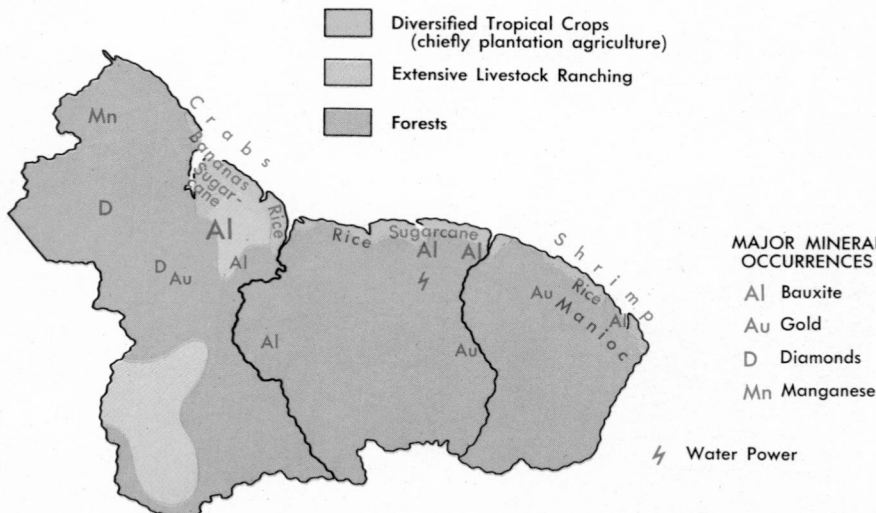

DOMINANT LAND USE

- Diversified Tropical Crops (chiefly plantation agriculture)
- Extensive Livestock Ranching
- Forests

MAJOR MINERAL OCCURRENCES

Al	Bauxite
Au	Gold
D	Diamonds
Mn	Manganese

⚡ Water Power

*City and suburbs.
†Population of district.

GUYANA
AREA 83,000 sq. mi.
POPULATION 763,000
CAPITAL Georgetown
LARGEST CITY Georgetown
HIGHEST POINT Mt. Roraima 9,094 ft.
MONETARY UNIT Guyana dollar
MAJOR LANGUAGES English, Hindi
MAJOR RELIGIONS Christianity, Hinduism, Islam

SURINAM
AREA 55,144 sq. mi.
POPULATION 389,000
CAPITAL Paramaribo
LARGEST CITY Paramaribo
HIGHEST POINT Julianatop 4,200 ft.
MONETARY UNIT Surinam guilder
MAJOR LANGUAGES Dutch, Hindi, Indonesian
MAJOR RELIGIONS Christianity, Islam, Hinduism

FRENCH GUIANA
AREA 35,135 sq. mi.
POPULATION 48,000
CAPITAL Cayenne
LARGEST CITY Cayenne
HIGHEST POINT 2,723 ft.
MONETARY UNIT French franc
MAJOR LANGUAGE French
MAJOR RELIGIONS Roman Catholicism, Protestantism

Kuyuwini (river)	B 4
Kwitaro (river)	B 4
Leguan (isl.), 6,567	B 2
Marudi (mts.)	B 5
Mazaruni (river)	B 2
Moruka (river)	B 2
New (river)	C 4
Pakaraima (mts.)	A 3
Playa (point)	B 1
Pomeroon (river)	B 2
Potaro (river)	B 3
Pururi (river)	B 2
Roraima (mt.)	A 3
Rupununi (river)	B 4
Sororieng (mt.)	B 2
Surwakwima (fall)	B 2
Takutu (river)	B 4
Venamo (mt.)	A 3
Waini (river)	B 2
Wenamu (river)	A 2

Cottica	D 4
Domburg, 1,200	D 3
Groningen, 800	D 3
Huwelijkszorg	D 3
Kwakoegron	D 3
Kwatta	D 2
Lelydorp, 300	D 4
Magalie	D 3
Marienburg, 3,500	D 2
Moengo, 2,100	D 2
Nieuw-Amsterdam, 1,400	D 2
Nieuw-Nickerie, 7,400	C 2
Paramaribo (cap.), 110,867	D 2
Paramaribo, *182,100	D 2
Paranam	D 3
Saramaccapolder	D 2
Totness, 1,300	C 3
Wageningen, 800	C 3
Zanderij	D 3

OTHER FEATURES

Bakhuys (mts.)	C 3
Coeroeni (river)	C 4
Commewijne (river)	D 3
Coppename (river)	D 3
Corantijn (river)	C 4
Cottica (river)	D 3
Eilerts-de-Haan (mts.)	C 4
Frederik Willem IV (falls)	C 4
Julianatop (mt.)	D 3
Kayser (mts.)	D 3
Lely (mts.)	D 3
Litani (river)	D 4
Marowijne (river)	D 3
Nickerie (river)	C 3
Orange (mts.)	D 4
Saramacca (river)	D 3
Sipaliwini (river)	D 4
Suriname (river)	D 3
Tapanahoni (river)	D 3
Toekomstig (res.)	D 4
Van Blommestein (lake)	D 3
Wilhelmina (mts.)	C 4

*City and suburbs.

SURINAM

DISTRICTS

Brokopondo, 1,376	D 4
Commewijne, 18,796	D 3
Coronie, 4,069	C 3
Marowijne, 10,074	D 4
Nickerie, 24,730	C 3
Para	D 3
Paramaribo, 122,634	D 2
Saramacca, 10,979	C 3
Suriname, 80,870	D 3

CITIES and TOWNS

Ajoewa	C 4
Alalapadu	D 4
Albina, 1,000	D 3
Asidonhoppo	D 4
Berg-en-Dal	D 3
Bitagron	D 3
Brokopondo	D 3
Burnside	C 2
Calcutta, 1,100	D 3

†Population of municipality.

Topography

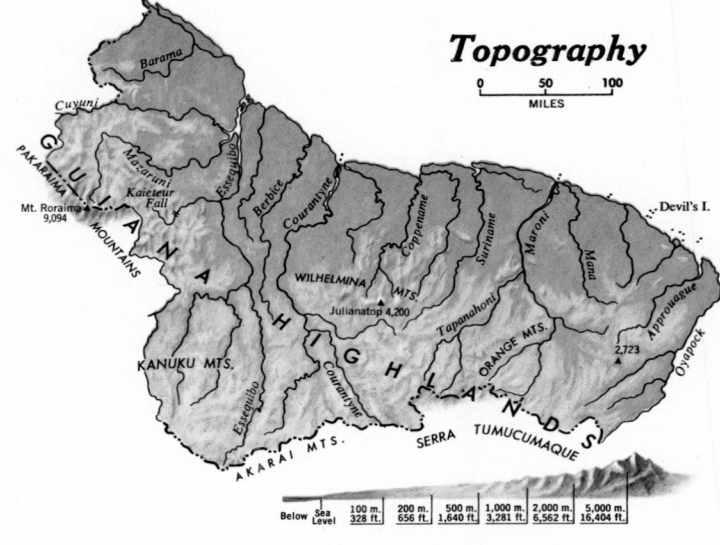

Below Sea Level | 100 m. 328 ft. | 200 m. 656 ft. | 500 m. 1,640 ft. | 1,000 m. 3,281 ft. | 2,000 m. 6,562 ft. | 5,000 m. 16,404 ft.

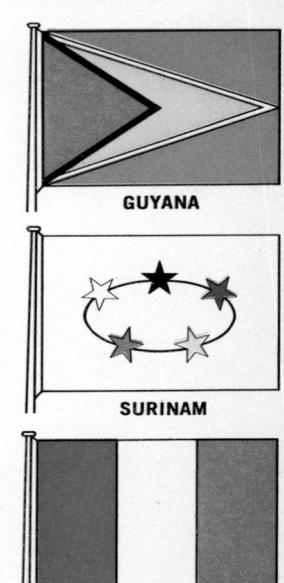

GUYANA

SURINAM

FRENCH GUIANA

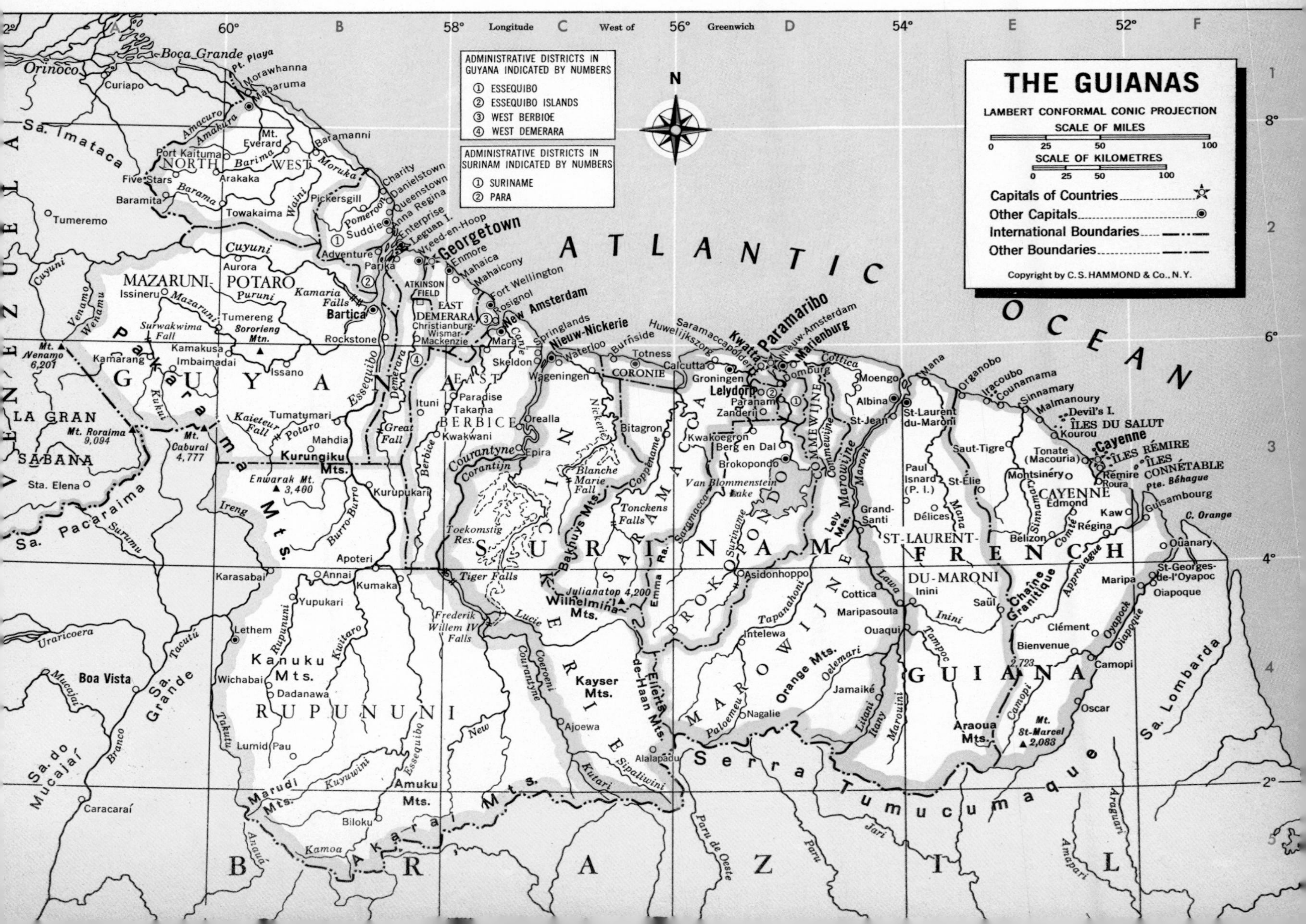

THE GUIANAS

LAMBERT CONFORMAL CONIC PROJECTION

SCALE OF MILES
0 — 25 — 50 — 100

SCALE OF KILOMETRES
0 — 25 — 50 — 100

Capitals of Countries .... ☆
Other Capitals .... ◉
International Boundaries .... — — —
Other Boundaries .... — · —

Copyright by C.S. HAMMOND & Co., N.Y.

ADMINISTRATIVE DISTRICTS IN GUYANA INDICATED BY NUMBERS
① ESSEQUIBO
② ESSEQUIBO ISLANDS
③ WEST BERBICE
④ WEST DEMERARA

ADMINISTRATIVE DISTRICTS IN SURINAM INDICATED BY NUMBERS
① SURINAME
② PARA

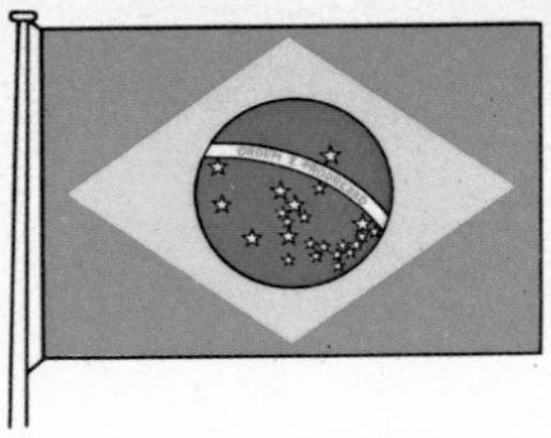

AREA 3,284,426 sq. mi.
POPULATION 90,840,000
CAPITAL Brasília
LARGEST CITY São Paulo (greater)
HIGHEST POINT Pico da Neblina 9,889 ft.
MONETARY UNIT cruzeiro
MAJOR LANGUAGE Portuguese
MAJOR RELIGION Roman Catholicism

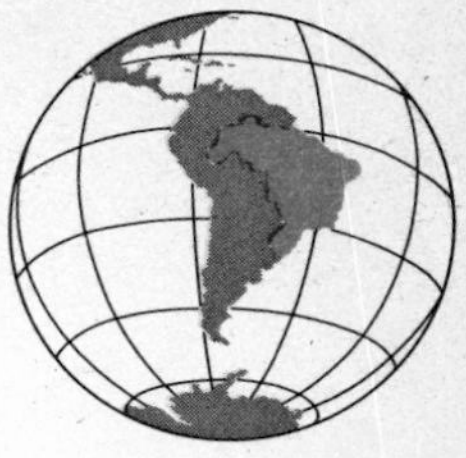

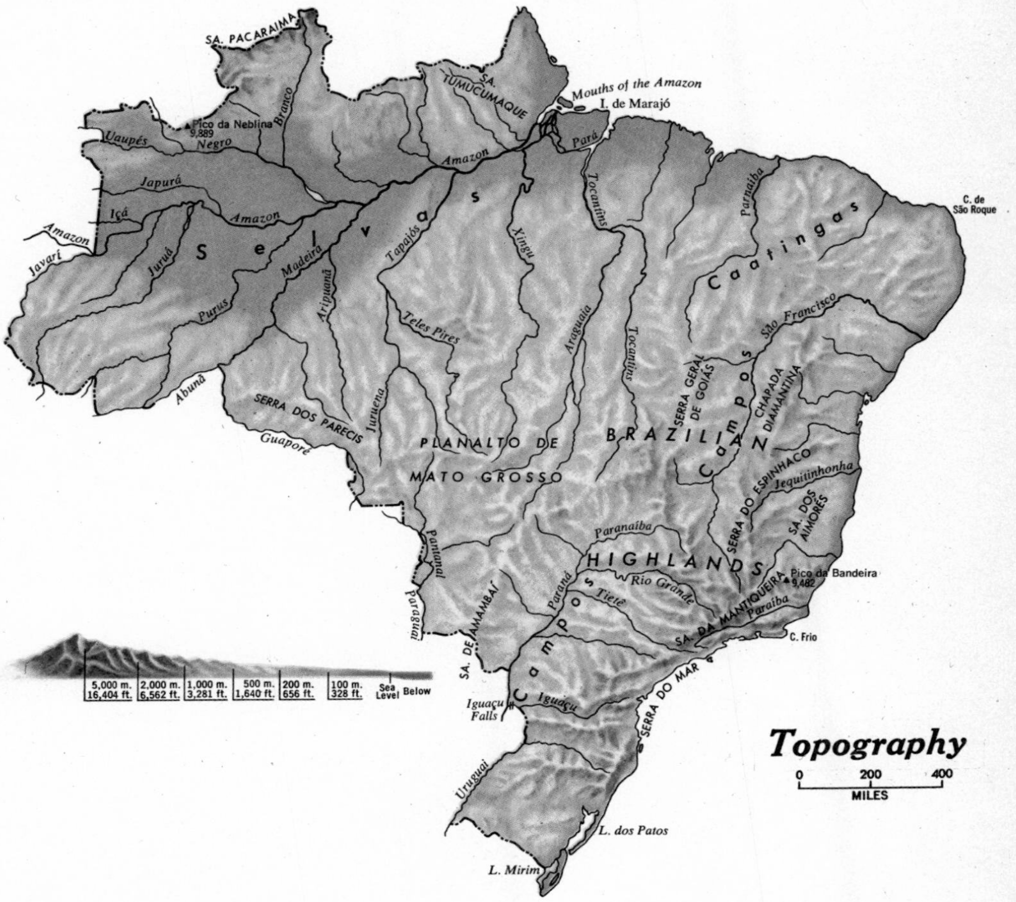

Topography

0 200 400 MILES

STATES and TERRITORIES

Acre, 196,000 ... G10
Alagoas, 1,381,000 ... G 5
Amapá (terr.), 100,000 ... D 2
Amazonas, 875,000 ... G 9
Bahia, 6,778,000 ... F 6
Ceará, 3,764,000 ... G 4
Espírito Santo, 1,446,000 ... F 7
Federal District, 348,000 ... E 6
Goiás, 2,950,000 ... D 6
Guanabara, 4,007,000 ... F 8, †E 3
Guaporé (Rondônia) (terr.), 97,000 ... H10
Maranhão, 3,314,000 ... E 4
Mato Grosso, 1,293,000 ... B 6
Minas Gerais, 11,230,000 ... E 7, †D 2
Pará, 1,872,000 ... C 4
Paraíba, 2,219,000 ... G 4
Paraná, 6,743,000 ... D 9, †B 4
Pernambuco, 4,645,000 ... G 5
Piauí, 1,391,000 ... F 4
Rio de Janeiro, 4,340,000 ... F 8, †E 3
Rio Grande do Norte, 1,271,000 ... G 4
Rio Grande do Sul, 6,397,000 ... C10
Rondônia (terr.), 107,000 ... H10
Roraima (terr.), 40,000 ... H 8
Santa Catarina, 2,624,000 ... D 9
São Paulo, 16,081,000 ... D 8, †B 2
Sergipe, 838,000 ... G 5

CITIES and TOWNS

Abaeté, 7,988 ... E 7
Abaetetuba, 11,196 ... D 3
Acaraú, 3,042 ... F 3
Acopiara, 3,953 ... G 4
Acorizal, 892 ... C 6
Açu, 8,158 ... G 4
Afuá, 600 ... D 3
Agudos, 6,564 ... †B 3
Alagoa Grande, 12,115 ... H 4
Alagoinhas, 38,246 ... G 6
Alcobaça, 1,812 ... G 7
Alegre, 7,487 ... †F 2
Alegrete, 33,735 ... B10
Além Paraíba, 18,399 ... †E 2
Alenquer, 7,027 ... C 3
Alfenas, 16,051 ... †C 2
Alfredo Chaves, 1,209 ... F 8
Altamira, 2,939 ... C 3
Alto Araguaia, 2,077 ... C 7
Alto Longa, 784 ... F 4
Alto Parnaiba, 1,300 ... E 5
Altos, 5,056 ... F 4
Amambaí, 2,601 ... C 8
Amarante, 3,199 ... F 4
Amargosa, 6,059 ... F 6
Americana, 32,000 ... †C 3
Amparo, 14,348 ... †C 3
Anápolis, 48,847 ... D 7
Andaraí, 2,510 ... F 6
Angra dos Reis, 10,634 ... †D 3
Anicuns, 3,642 ... D 7
Andrelândia, 4,617 ... †D 2
Antonina, 8,520 ... †B 4
Aparecida, 15,290 ... †D 3
Apiaí, 2,728 ... †B 4
Aquidauana, 11,997 ... C 8
Aracaju, *156,243 ... G 5
Aracati, 11,016 ... G 4
Araçatuba, 53,563 ... †A 2
Araçuaí, 6,763 ... F 7
Araguacema, 1,745 ... D 5
Araguaiana, 568 ... C 6
Araguari, 35,520 ... D 7
Araioses, 1,487 ... F 3
Araranguá, 7,775 ... D10
Araraquara, 58,076 ... †B 2
Araras, 23,898 ... †C 3
Arari, 4,004 ... E 3
Araxá, 24,041 ... E 7
Arcoverde, 18,008 ... G 5
Areia Branca, 8.904 ... G 4
Aripuanã, 178 ... B 5
Arraias, 1,446 ... E 6
Assis, 30,207 ... †A 3
Aurora, 3,622 ... G 4
Avaré, 20,334 ... †B 3
Bacabal, *19,753 ... E 4
Bagé, 47,930 ... C10
Bahia (Salvador), *892,392 ... G 6
Baião, 2,265 ... D 3
Baixo Guandu, 6,975 ... F 7
Balsas, 1,946 ... E 4
Bambuí, 8,148 ... †C 2
Barão dé Cocais, 7,223 ... †E 1
Barbacena, 41,931 ... †E 2
Barcelos, 1,904 ... H 9
Bariri, 8,403 ... †B 3
Barra, 7,237 ... F 5
Barra-do-Bugres, 658 ... B 6
Barra-do-Corda, 3,723 ... E 4
Barra do Piraí, 29,398 ... †E 3
Barra Mansa, 47,398 ... †D 3
Barras, 3,388 ... F 4
Barreiras, 7,175 ... E 6
Barreirinha, 701 ... B 3
Barreirinhas, 2,184 ... F 3
Barreiros, 10,402 ... H 5
Barretos, 39,950 ... †B 2
Batalha, 15,559 ... F 3
Batatais, 15,266 ... †C 2
Baturité, 7,198 ... G 4
Bauru, *110,961 ... †B 3
Bebedouro, 18,249 ... †B 2
Bela Vista, 8,878 ... C 8
Bela Vista de Goiás, 2,687 ... D 7
Belém, *563,996 ... E 3
Belmonte, 7,897 ... G 6
Belo Horizonte, *1,167,026 ... †D 1
Belo Horizonte, ‡1,300,000 ... †D 1
Beneditinos, 828 ... F 4
Benjamin Constant, 3,224 ... G 9
Bento Gonçalves, 13,662 ... C10
Bertolínia, 714 ... F 4
Betim, 8,963 ... †D 2
Bicas, 7,469 ... †E 2
Birigui, 18,721 ... †A 2
Blumenau, 46,591 ... D 9
Boa Esperança, 9,263 ... †D 2
Boa Vista, 10,180 ... H 8
Bôca do Acre, 2,994 ... G10
Bocaiúva, 5,952 ... E 7
Boiaçu, 180 ... H 8
Bom Conselho, 6,840 ... G 5
Bom Despacho, 13,568 ... †D 1
Bom Jesus, 1,431 ... E 5
Bom Jesus da Lapa, 6,107 ... F 6
Bom Retiro, 1,601 ... D10
Bom Sucesso, 6,173 ... †D 2
Borba, 1,304 ... H 9
Botucatu, 33,878 ... †B 3
Bragança, 12,848 ... E 3
Bragança Paulista, 27,328 ... †C 3
Brasiléia, 1,902 ... G10
Brasília (capital), 130,968 ... D 6
Brasília, ‡379,699 ... D 6
Brasília, 3,182 ... F 7
Brumado, 7,054 ... F 6
Brusque, 16,127 ... D 9
Buri, 2,666 ... †B 3
Buriti, 1,951 ... F 3
Buriti Alegre, 5,042 ... D 7
Buriti dos Lopes, 1,812 ... F 3
Cabedelo, 10,738 ... H 4
Cabo Frio, 13,117 ... †F 3
Caçador, 10,480 ... D 9
Caçapava, 7,987 ... †D 3
Caçapava do Sul, 6,712 ... C10
Cáceres, 8,246 ... B 7
Cachoeira, 11,415 ... G 6
Cachoeira do Arari, 2,532 ... D 3
Cachoeira do Sul, 38,661 ... C10
Cachoeiro de Itapemirim, *110,301 ... G 8
Caeté, 10,840 ... †E 1
Caetite, 4,823 ... F 6
Cafelândia, 6,573 ... †B 2
Caiapônia, 2,476 ... C 7
Caicó, 15,826 ... G 4
Cajàzeiras, 15,884 ... G 4
Cajuru, 4,971 ... †C 2
Camaquã, 9,732 ... C10
Cambará, 6,028 ... †A 3
Cametá, 5,695 ... D 3
Camocim, 10,788 ... F 3
Campanha, 6,178 ... †D 2
Campina Grande, *157,149 ... G 4
Campinas, *252,145 ... †C 3
Campina Verde, 4,464 ... D 7
Campo Belo, 15,742 ... †D 2
Campo Florido, 1,307 ... †B 1
Campo Formoso, 3,925 ... F 5
Campo Grande, *111,205 ... C 8
Campo Largo, 7,915 ... †B 4
Campo Maior, 13,939 ... F 4
Campos, *389,045 ... †F 2
Campos Altos, 5,243 ... †C 1
Cananéia, 1,948 ... †C 4
Canavieiras, 10,264 ... G 6
Cândido Mendes, 819 ... E 3
Canguaretama, 4,261 ... H 4
Canindé, 5,854 ... G 4
Canoas, *122,040 ... D10
Canoinhas, 9,252 ... D 9
Cantagalo, 3,479 ... †E 3
Canto do Buriti, 1,636 ... F 5
Canutama, 977 ... G 9
Capanema, 9,678 ... E 3
Capão Bonito, 6,829 ... †B 4
Capela, 5,172 ... G 5
Caraguatatuba, 4,655 ... †D 3
Carandaí, 2,792 ... †E 2
Carangola, 11,896 ... †E 2
Caratinga, *123,344 ... †E 1
Caraúbas, 3,066 ... G 4
Caravelas, 3,096 ... G 7
Carinhanha, 2,163 ... E 6
Carolina, 8,137 ... E 4
Caruaru, *115,414 ... G 5
Carutapera, 2,477 ... E 3
Casa Branca, 8,980 ... †C 2
Casa Nova, 1,525 ... F 5
Cascatinha, 19,497 ... †E 3
Cascavel, 3,336 ... G 4
Cássia, 7,034 ... †C 2
Castanhal, 9,528 ... E 3
Castelo, 5,729 ... F 8
Castelo do Piauí, 1,185 ... F 4
Castro, 9,249 ... †B 4
Castro Alves, 7,388 ... G 6
Cataguases, 21,476 ... †E 2
Catalão, 11,471 ... D 7
Catanduva, 37,307 ... †B 2
Catolé do Rocha, 5,217 ... G 4
Cavalcante, 660 ... D 6
Caxambu, 10,491 ... †D 2
Caxias, *124,403 ... F 4
Caxias do Sul, *110,241 ... D10
Ceará (Fortaleza), *846,069 ... G 3
Ceará-Mirim, 8,290 ... H 4
Ceres, 6,895 ... D 7
Cêrro Azul, 1,460 ... †B 4
Chaves, 428 ... D 3
Cicero Dantas, 2,972 ... G 5
Coari, 5,908 ... H 9
Codajás, 1,505 ... H 9
Codó, *100,933 ... E 4
Colatina, *140,729 ... F 7
Colinas, 2,972 ... F 4
Conceição da Barra, 2,229 ... G 7
Conceição do Araguaia, 2,332 ... D 5
Concórdia, 5,864 ... D 9
Conde, 4,190 ... G 5
Conselheiro Lafaiete, 29,208 ... †E 2
Corinto, 12,247 ... E 7
Cornélio Procópio, 17,524 ... D 8
Coroatá, 7,720 ... F 3
Coromandel, 5,148 ... E 7
Corrente, 2,214 ... E 5
Correntina, 2,636 ... E 6
Corumbá, 36,744 ... B 7
Coxim, 1,371 ... C 7
Crateús, 14,572 ... F 4
Crato, 27,649 ... G 4
Criciúma, 25,331 ... D10
Cristalina, 3,810 ... E 7
Cruz Alta, 33,190 ... C10
Cruzeiro, 27,005 ... †D 3
Cruzeiro do Sul, 2,826 ... G10
Cubatão, 18,885 ... †C 3
Cuiabá, 43,112 ... C 6
Curaça, 1,264 ... G 5
Curitiba, *616,548 ... †B 4
Currais Novos, 7,782 ... G 4
Curuçá, 3,871 ... E 3
Cururupu, 4,822 ... E 3
Curvelo, 21,772 ... E 7
Diamantina, 14,252 ... F 7
Diamantino, 645 ... B 6
Dianópolis, 2,145 ... E 5
Divinópolis, 41,544 ... †D 2
Dois Córregos, 7,272 ... †B 3
Dom Pedrito, 15,429 ... C10
Dores do Indaiá, 10,354 ... E 7
Dourados, 10,757 ... C 8
Duque de Caxias, *324,261 ... †E 3
Eirunepé, 3,023 ... G10
Eldorado, 1,524 ... †B 4
Erechim, 24,941 ... C 9
Erval, 1,404 ... C11
Escada, 13,761 ... H 5
Esperança, 9,105 ... G 4
Esplanada, 3,792 ... G 5
Estância, 16,106 ... G 5
Exu, 2,549 ... G 4
Faro, 1,434 ... B 3
Feira de Santana, *136,000 ... G 5
Fernandópolis, 14,375 ... †A 2
Ferreira Gomes, 439 ... D 2
Ferros, 2,456 ... F 7
Flores, 2,102 ... G 4
Floriano, 16,063 ... F 4
Florianópolis, *130,012 ... E 9
Formiga, 18,763 ... †D 2
Formosa, 9,449 ... E 6
Fortaleza, *846,069 ... G 3
Foz do Iguaçu, 7,407 ... C 9
Franca, 47,244 ... †C 2
Fronteiras, 1,320 ... F 4
Frutal, 8,252 ... †B 2
Garanhuns, 34,050 ... G 5
Garça, 18,155 ... †B 3
Gilbués, 588 ... E 5
Goiana, 19,026 ... H 4
Goiandira, 3,169 ... E 7
Goiânia, *345,085 ... D 7
Goiás, 7,121 ... D 6
Governador Valadares, *124,606 ... F 7
Grajaú, 2,539 ... E 4
Granja, 5,074 ... F 3
Guacuí, 7,724 ... †F 2
Guajará-Mirim, 7,115 ... H10
Guamá, 2,470 ... E 3
Guarabira, 15,848 ... H 4
Guarapuava, *126,080 ... C 9
Guaratinguetá, 38,293 ... †D 3
Guarujá, 6,506 ... †C 4
Guarulhos, *119,572 ... †C 3
Guarus, 21,492 ... †F 2
Guaxupé, 14,168 ... †C 2
Guimarães, 1,512 ... E 3
Guiratinga, 4,203 ... C 7
Gurupá, 912 ... D 3
Gurupi, 4,148 ... D 5
Humaitá, 1,192 ... H10
Ibaiti, 3,628 ... †A 3
Ibiá, 6,999 ... E 7
Ibipetuba, 2,298 ... F 5
Ibitinga, 8,881 ... †B 2
Icó, 5,586 ... G 4
Icoraci, 11,512 ... D 3
Igarapava, 9,083 ... †C 2
Igarapé-Miri, 2,591 ... D 3
Iguape, 5,465 ... †C 4
Iguatu, 16,540 ... G 4
Ijuí, 19,671 ... C10
Ilhéus, *100,687 ... G 6
Imbituba, 6,638 ... D10
Imbituva, 3,290 ... †A 4
Imperatriz, 9,004 ... E 4
Inhumas, 8,298 ... D 7
Ipameri, 8,987 ... E 7
Ipiaú, 13,164 ... G 6
Ipu, 7,724 ... F 4
Irati, 12,764 ... †A 4
Itabaiana, Paraíba, 11,847 ... H 4
Itabaiana, Sergipe, 11,050 ... G 5
Itaberaba, 8,555 ... F 6
Itabira, 15,539 ... F 7
Itabirito, 10,511 ... †E 2
Itabuna, 54,268 ... G 6
Itacoatiara, 8,818 ... B 3
Itaguatins, 1,596 ... D 4
Itaí, 1,601 ... †B 3
Itajaí, 38,889 ... D 9
Itajubá, 31,262 ... †D 3
Itamarandiba, 2,404 ... F 7
Itanhaém, 5,376 ... †C 4
Itapecerica, 7,696 ... †D 2
Itapecuru-Mirim, 3,385 ... F 3
Itapemirim, 4,095 ... F 8
Itaperuna, 18,095 ... †F 2
Itapetininga, 29,468 ... †B 3
Itapeva, 13,510 ... †B 3
Itapicuru, 900 ... G 5
Itapipoca, 7,186 ... G 3
Itapira, 16,859 ... †C 3
Itapiranga, 477 ... B 3
Itápolis, 7,430 ... †B 2
Itaporanga, 5,328 ... G 4
Itaqui, 13,223 ... B10
Itararé, 12,812 ... †B 4
Itariri, 1,318 ... †C 4
Itatiba, 12,336 ... †C 3
Itaúna, 22,319 ... †D 2
Itu, 23,435 ... †C 3
Ituaçu, 1,431 ... F 6
Ituberá, 4,097 ... G 6
Ituiutaba, 29,724 ... D 7
Itumbiara, 12,575 ... D 7
Iturama, 1,518 ... †A 1
Ituverava, 11,890 ... †C 2
Jaboticabal, 20,231 ... †B 2
Jacareí, 28,131 ... †D 3
Jacarèzinho, 14,813 ... †A 3
Jacobina, 12,373 ... F 5
Jacupiranga, 2,144 ... †B 4
Jaguaquara, 5,363 ... F 6
Jaguarão, 12,336 ... C11
Jaguariaíva, 6,465 ... †B 4
Jaicós, 1,308 ... F 4
Januária, 9,741 ... E 6
Jaraguá, 3,813 ... D 6
Jardim, 3,104 ... G 4
Jataí, 14,022 ... D 7
Jaú, 31,229 ... †B 3
Jequié, 40,158 ... F 6
Jequitinhonha, 5,410 ... F 7
Jeremoabo, 3,177 ... G 5
Joaçaba, 7,921 ... D 9
João Pessoa, *189,096 ... H 4
João Pinheiro, 3,433 ... E 7
Joaquim Tavora, 3,574 ... †B 3
Joinville, 44,255 ... D 9
Juàzeiro, 21,196 ... G 5
Juàzeiro do Norte, 53,421 ... F 4
Juiz de Fora, *194,135 ... †E 2
Jundiaí, *124,368 ... †C 3
Lábrea, 2,080 ... G10
Laguna, 17,451 ... D10
Lajes, 35,112 ... D 9
Lambari, 6,825 ... †D 2
Lapa, 7,167 ... D 9
Laranjeiras, 4,296 ... G 5
Laranjeiras do Sul, 3,802 ... C 9
Lavras, 23,793 ... †D 2
Leme, 11,785 ... †C 3
Lençóis, 2,483 ... F 6
Leopoldina, 17,726 ... †E 2
Lima Duarte, 3,554 ... †E 2
Limeira, 45,256 ... †C 3
Limoeiro, 21,252 ... H 4
Limoeiro do Norte, 5,705 ... G 4
Linhares, 5,751 ... F 7
Lins, 32,204 ... †B 2
Londrina, *226,332 ... D 8
Lorena, 26,068 ... †D 3
Luís Correia, 1,523 ... F 3
Luz, 5,633 ... †D 1
Luziânia, 4,849 ... E 7
Luzilândia, 3,434 ... F 3
Macaé, 19,830 ... †F 3
Macapá, 27,585 ... D 2
Macau, 11,876 ... G 4
Macaúbas, 2,504 ... F 6
Maceió, *221,250 ... H 5
Machado, 8,373 ... †C 2
Mafra, 12,981 ... D 9
Magé, 10,712 ... †E 3
Mallet, 1,816 ... D 9
Manacapuru, 2,584 ... H 9
Manaus, *249,797 ... H 9
Manga, 2,000 ... E 6
Manhuaçu, 10,546 ... †E 2
Manhumirim, 9,477 ... †E 2
Manicoré, 2,268 ... H 9
Marabá, 8,533 ... D 4
Maragogipe, 12,575 ... G 6
Maranguape, 8,715 ... G 3
Marapanim, 3,542 ... E 3
Marechal-Deodoro, 5,269 ... H 5
Mariana, 6,378 ... †E 2
Marília, *107,305 ... †A 3
Marques de Valença, 18,935 ... †D 3
Massapê, 4,760 ... G 3
Mata de São João, 8,117 ... G 6
Mato Grosso, 520 ... B 6
Maués, 4,161 ... B 3
Mazagão, 919 ... B 3
Miguel Alves, 4,537 ... F 4
Mimoso do Sul, 5,278 ... †F 2
Minas Novas, 1,708 ... F 7
Mineiros, 5,105 ... C 7
Miracema, 9,810 ... †E 2
Mirador, 818 ... B 4
Miranda, 2,075 ... C 8
Mirassol, 13,674 ... †B 2
Mocajuba, 1,352 ... D 3
Mococa, 14,306 ... †C 2
Mogi das Cruzes, *111,554 ... †C 3
Mogi-Mirim, 18,345 ... †C 3
Monte Alegre, 3,911 ... C 3
Monte Alegre de Minas, 4,464 ... D 7
Monte Aprazível, 7,235 ... †A 2
Monte Azul, 4,860 ... F 6
Monteiro, 6,028 ... G 4
Montenegro, 14,491 ... D10
Monte Santo, 1,607 ... G 5
Montes Claros, *121,428 ... E 7
Morrinhos, 9,879 ... D 7
Morro do Chapéu, 2,039 ... F 5
Mossoró, 38,833 ... G 4
Mucugê, 723 ... F 6
Mucuri, 603 ... G 7
Mundo Novo, 3,237 ... F 5
Muqui, 4,262 ... F 8
Muriaé, 22,571 ... †E 2
Muzambinho, 18,073 ... †C 2
Natal, *239,590 ... H 4

(continued on following page)

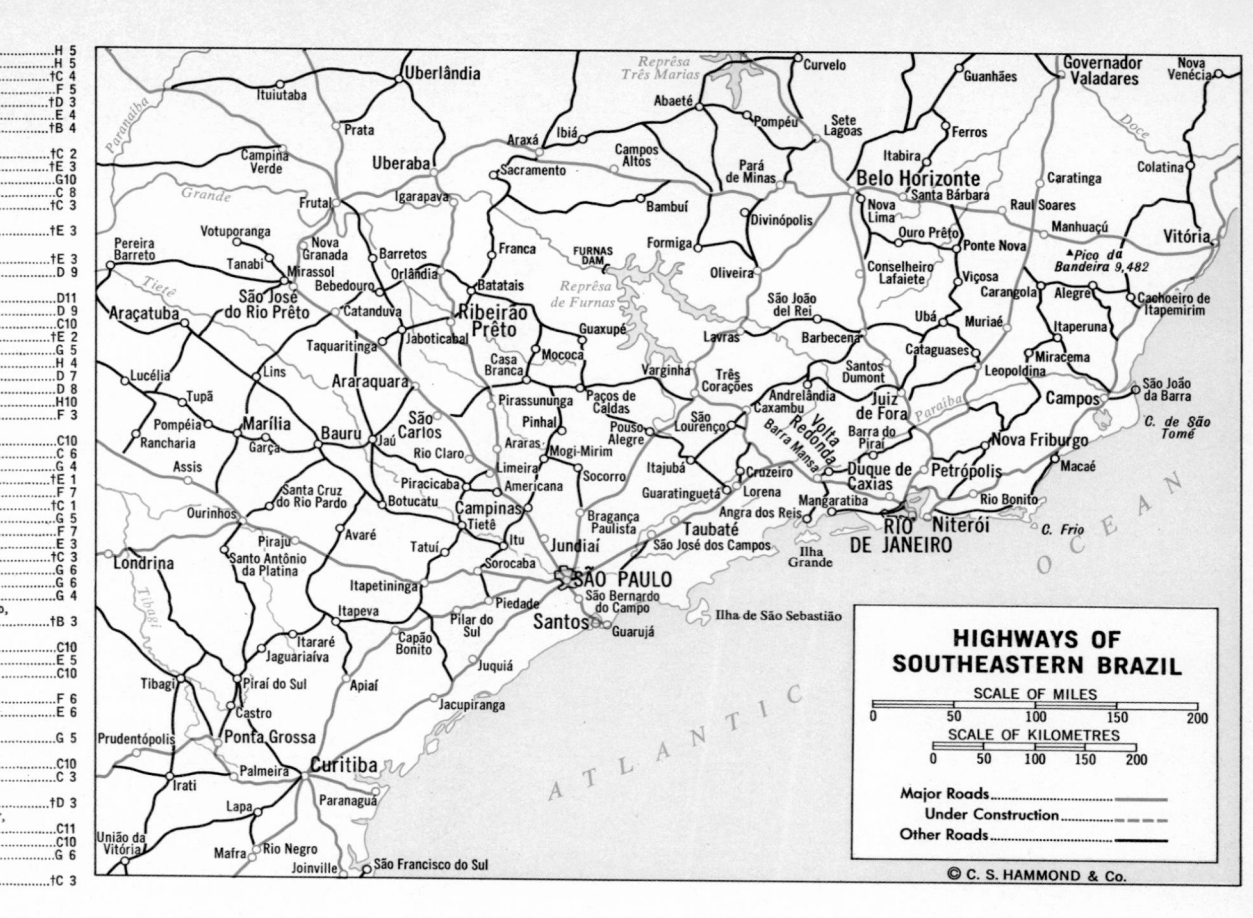

HIGHWAYS OF SOUTHEASTERN BRAZIL

SCALE OF MILES
0   50   100   150   200

SCALE OF KILOMETRES
0   50   100   150   200

Major Roads
Under Construction
Other Roads

© C. S. HAMMOND & Co.

Agriculture, Industry and Resources

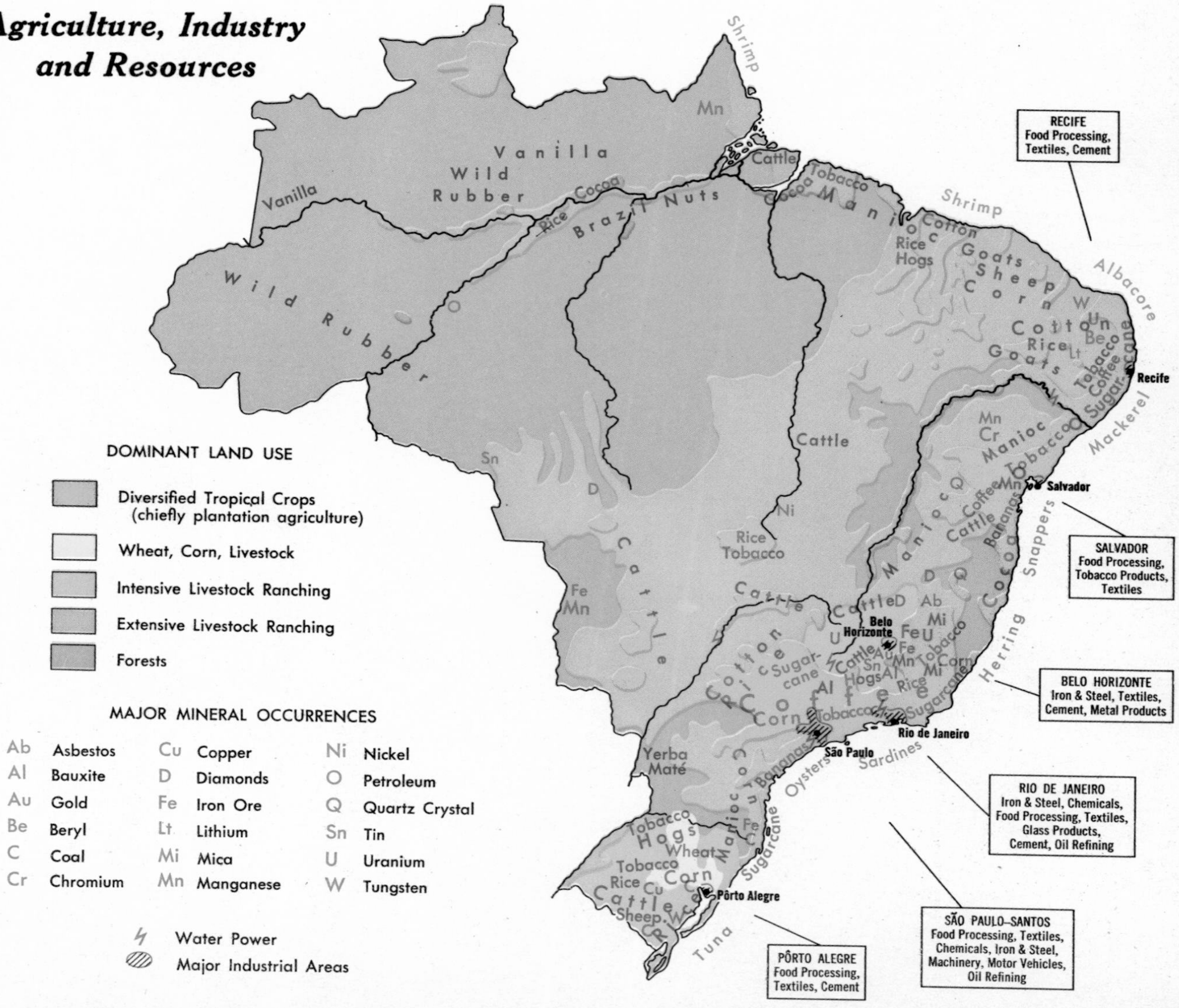

DOMINANT LAND USE

- Diversified Tropical Crops (chiefly plantation agriculture)
- Wheat, Corn, Livestock
- Intensive Livestock Ranching
- Extensive Livestock Ranching
- Forests

MAJOR MINERAL OCCURRENCES

Ab	Asbestos	Cu	Copper	Ni	Nickel
Al	Bauxite	D	Diamonds	O	Petroleum
Au	Gold	Fe	Iron Ore	Q	Quartz Crystal
Be	Beryl	Lt	Lithium	Sn	Tin
C	Coal	Mi	Mica	U	Uranium
Cr	Chromium	Mn	Manganese	W	Tungsten

⚡ Water Power

Major Industrial Areas

RECIFE
Food Processing, Textiles, Cement

SALVADOR
Food Processing, Tobacco Products, Textiles

BELO HORIZONTE
Iron & Steel, Textiles, Cement, Metal Products

RIO DE JANEIRO
Iron & Steel, Chemicals, Food Processing, Textiles, Glass Products, Cement, Oil Refining

SÃO PAULO–SANTOS
Food Processing, Textiles, Chemicals, Iron & Steel, Machinery, Motor Vehicles, Oil Refining

PÔRTO ALEGRE
Food Processing, Textiles, Cement

Brazil 135

Santo Ângelo, 25,415 .... C10
Santo Antônio da Platina, 9,378 .... †A 3
Santo Antonio do Leverger, 2,028 .... C 6
Santos, *313,771 .... †C 3
Santos Dumont, 20,414 .... †E 2
São Bento, 7,094 .... E 3
São Bernardo do Campo, 61,645 .... †C 3
São Borja, 20,339 .... C10
São Caetano do Sul, *135,095 .... †C 3
São Carlos, 50,010 .... †C 3
São Cristóvão, 7,624 .... G 5
São Domingos, 907 .... E 6
São Félix, 5,993 .... G 6
São Fidélis, 6,145 .... †F 2
São Francisco, 4,074 .... E 6
São Francisco do Sul, 11,593 .... E 9
São Gabriel, 22,967 .... C10
São João da Boa Vista, 25,226 .... †C 2
São João del Rei, 34,654 .... †D 2
São João do Piauí, 2,688 .... F 5
São João dos Patos, 2,590 .... F 4
São João Nepomuceno, 9,436 .... †E 2
São Joaquim da Barra, 13,853 .... †C 2
São José, 3,295 .... D 9
São José da Laje, 5,822 .... H 5
São José de Mipibu, 5,179 .... H 4
São José do Rio Pardo, 14,186 .... †C 2
São José do Rio Prêto, 66,476 .... †B 2
São José dos Campos, 55,349 .... †D 3
São José dos Pinhais, 7,574 .... D 9
São Leopoldo, 41,023 .... D10
São Lourenço, 14,680 .... †D 3
São Lourenço do Sul, 6,877 .... C10
São Luís, *218,783 .... F 3
São Luís Gonzaga, 12,926 .... C10
São Manuel, 10,009 .... †B 3
São Mateus, 6,075 .... G 7
São Miguel Arcanjo, 3,633 .... †C 3
São Miguel dos Campos, 6,511 .... G 5
São Miguel Paulista, 39,644 .... †C 3
São Paulo, *5,684,706 .... †C 3
São Paulo, ‡6,300,000 .... †C 3
São Pedro, 4,474 .... †C 3
São Pedro do Piauí, 2,139 .... F 4
São Raimundo Nonato, 3,751 .... F 5
São Roque, 12,409 .... †C 3
São Sebastião, 3,490 .... †D 3
São Sebastião do Paraíso, 14,451 .... †C 2
São Simão, 5,742 .... †C 2
São Vicente, 73,578 .... †C 4
Senador Pompeu, 8,210 .... G 4
Sena Madureira, 1,962 .... G10
Senhor do Bonfim, 13,958 .... F 5
Serra do Navio, 9 .... C 2
Serra Talhada, 12,164 .... G 4
Serrinha, 10,284 .... G 5
Sertânia, 7,556 .... G 5
Sertanópolis, 6,469 .... D 8
Sete Lagoas, 36,302 .... E 7
Sitio da Abadia, 482 .... E 6
Silvânia, 2,920 .... D 7
Sobral, 32,281 .... G 3
Socorro, 6,402 .... †C 3
Sorocaba, *142,835 .... †C 3
Soure, 6,666 .... D 3
Taquaritinga, 11,624 .... †B 2
Tarauacá, 2,292 .... G10
Tatuí, 22,550 .... †C 3
Taubaté, 64,863 .... E 8
Tefé, 2,781 .... G 9
Teófilo-Otoni, *134,476 .... F 7
Teresina, *184,836 .... F 4
Teresópolis, 29,540 .... †E 3
Tibagi, 1,746 .... †A 4
Tietê, 8,729 .... †C 3
Tijucas, 4,420 .... D 9
Tocantínia, 1,414 .... D 5
Tocantinópolis, 4,927 .... D 4
Três Corações, 17,498 .... †D 2
Três Lagoas, 14,520 .... C 8
Três Pontas, 11,534 .... †D 2
Três Rios, 22,246 .... †E 3
Tubarão, 20,615 .... D10
Tucano, 4,007 .... G 5
Tupã, 28,723 .... †A 2
Tupanciretã, 8,659 .... C10
Tutóia, 3,337 .... F 3
Uaupés, 571 .... G 9
Ubá, 21,767 .... †E 2
Ubaíra, 2,352 .... G 6
Ubaitaba, 3,581 .... G 6
Ubatuba, 3,748 .... †D 3
Uberaba, *100,634 .... †C 1
Uberlândia, *101,149 .... E 7
Unaí, 4,214 .... E 7
União, 4,296 .... F 4
União da Vitória, 15,822 .... D 9
União dos Palmares, 10,406 .... H 5
Uruaçu, 4,392 .... D 5
Uruçuí, 2,233 .... E 4
Urucurituba, 520 .... B 3
Uruguaiana, 48,358 .... B10
Valença, 17,137 .... G 6
Valença do Piauí, 3,046 .... F 4
Valparaíso, 7,974 .... D 8
Varginha, 24,944 .... †D 2
Vera Cruz, 5,535 .... †B 3
Viana, 5,385 .... E 3
Viçosa, Alagoas, 7,285 .... G 5
Viçosa, Minas Gerais, 9,342 .... †E 2
Vigia, 7,246 .... E 3
Visconde do Rio Branco, 12,363 .... †E 2
Viseu, 1,606 .... E 3
Vitória, *121,843 .... G 8
Vitória da Conquista, 46,778 .... F 6
Vitória de Santo Antão, 27,053 .... G 4
Volta Redonda, *118,114 .... †D 3
Votuporanga, 18,722 .... †B 2
Xapecó, 8,465 .... C 9
Xapuri, 2,000 .... G10
Xique-Xique, 5,467 .... F 5

OTHER FEATURES

Abacaxis (river) .... B 4
Abunã (river) G10
Acaraí (range) .... B 2
Acre (river) G10
Amambaí (range) .... C 7
Amaparí (river) .... C 2
Amazon (river) .... C 3
Anauá (river) .... B 2
Aporé (river) .... D 7
Araguaia (river) .... D 6
Araguarí (river) .... D 2
Araruama (lagoon) .... †E 3
Arinos (river) .... B 5
Aripuanã (river) .... A 4
Balsas (river) .... E 5
Bananal (isl.) .... D 5
Bandeira, Pico da (mt.) .... F 8
Branco (river) .... H 8
Buzios (cape) .... †F 3
Canumã (river) .... B 4
Capim (river) .... D 3
Carajás (range) .... D 4
Cardoso (isl.) .... †C 4
Cassiporé (cape) .... D 2
Caviana (isl.) .... D 2
Chavantes (range) .... D 5
Claro (river) .... D 7
Coluene (river) .... C 6
Comprida (isl.) .... †C 4
Cuiabá (river) .... B 7
Doce (river) .... F 7
Dois Irmãos (range) .... F 5
Erepecuru (river) .... B 3
Espigão Mestre (Geral) (range) .... E 6
Espinhaço (range) .... F 7
Estrondo (range) .... D 4
Feia (lake) .... †F 3
Feio (river) .... †B 2
Formosa (range) .... C 5
Frio (cape) .... †F 3
Furnas (dam) .... †C 2
Furnas (res.) .... †C 2
Geral (range) .... D 9
Geral de Goiás (range) .... E 6
Gi-Paraná (river) H10
Gradaús (range) .... D 4
Grajaú (river) .... E 4
Grande (isl.) .... †D 3
Grande (river) .... †B 1, D 8
Guanabara (bay) .... †E 3
Guaporé (river) H10
Guariba (river) .... B 5
Gurguéia (river) .... E 5
Gurupi (range) .... E 4
Gurupi (river) .... E 3
Ibicuí (river) C10
Içá (river) .... G 9
Iguaçu (river) .... C 9
Iguazú (falls) .... C 9
Ilha Grande (bay) .... †D 3
Iriri (river) .... C 4
Itapecuru (river) .... F 4
Itararé (river) .... †B 3
Ivaí (river) .... C 8
Jacuipe (river) .... F 5
Jaguaribe (river) .... G 4
Japurá (river) .... G 9
Jari (river) .... C 3
Javarí (river) .... F 9
Jequitinhonha (river) .... F 7
Juruá (river) G10
Juruena (river) .... B 5
Madeira (river) .... A 4
Manso (river) .... C 6
Mantiqueira (range) .... †D 3
Mar (range) .... †C 4, E 9
Maracá (isl.) .... D 2
Marajó (isl.) .... D 3
Mato Grosso (plateau) .... B 6
Mirim (lagoon) C11
Moji Guaçu (river) .... †C 2
Mortes (Manso) (river) .... D 6
Neblina, Pico da (mt.) .... G 8
Negro (river) .... H 9
Nhamundá (river) .... B 3
Norte (range) .... B 5
Orange (cape) .... D 1
Orgãos (range) .... †E 3
Oyapock (river) .... C 2
Pacajá Grande (river) .... D 4
Pacaraima (range) .... H 8
Papagaio (river) .... B 6
Pará (river) .... D 3
Paracatu (river) .... E 7
Paraguaçu (river) .... F 6
Paraguai (river) .... B 8
Paraíba (river) .... †E 2
Paranã (river) .... E 6
Paraná (river) .... C 8
Paranapanema (river) .... †B 3, C 8
Paranapiacaba (range) .... †B 4
Paranatinga (river) .... C 6
Pardo (river) .... †B 2, D 8
Pardo (river) .... F 6
Parecis (range) .... B 6
Parnaíba (river) .... E 5
Paru (river) .... C 3
Patos (lagoon) D10
Peixoto (dam) .... †C 2
Penitente (range) .... E 5
Piauí (range) .... F 5
Piauí (river) .... F 3
Piracambu (range) .... E 3
Purus (river) .... H 9
Ribeira (river) .... †B 4
Roncador (range) .... D 5
Roosevelt (river) .... A 5
Santa Catarina (isl.), 98,520 .... E 9
São Francisco (river) .... F 5
São Lourenço (river) .... C 7
São Marcos (bay) .... F 3
São Roque (cape) .... H 4
São Sebastião (isl.), 1,823 .... †D 3
São Tomé (cape) .... G 8
Sapucaí (river) .... †D 2
Sepetiba (bay) .... †D 3
Sete Quedas (falls) .... C 9
Tacutú (river) .... B 2
Tapajós (river) .... B 4
Taquarí (river) .... C 7
Teles Pires (river) .... B 5
Tibagi (river) .... †A 4
Tietê (river) .... †B 2, D 8
Tocantins (river) .... D 4
Tombador (range) .... B 6
Trombetas (river) .... B 3
Tumucumaque (range) .... C 2
Turvo (river) .... †B 2
Uaupés (river) .... G 9
Uraricuera (river) .... H 8
Urucún, Morro do (mt.) .... B 7
Uruguai (river) .... C 9
Verde (river) .... C 7
Xingu (river) .... C 3

‡Population of metropolitan area.
*Population of municipality.
†Keys refer to map on page 135.

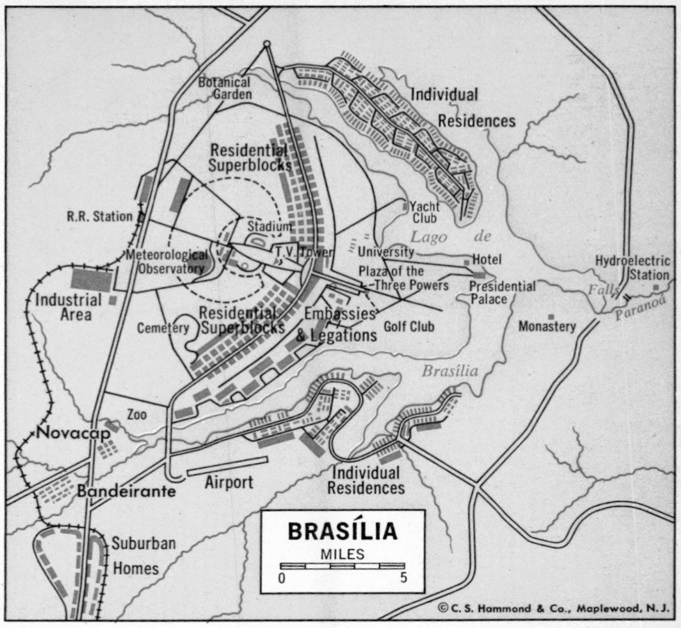
Botanical Garden
Individual Residences
Residential Superblocks
R.R. Station
Stadium
Yacht Club
Lago de
Meteorological Observatory
T.V. Tower
University
Hotel
Hydroelectric Station
Plaza of the Three Powers
Presidential Palace
Falls
Paranoá
Industrial Area
Cemetery
Residential Superblocks
Embassies & Legations
Golf Club
Monastery
Brasília
Zoo
Novacap
Bandeirante
Airport
Individual Residences
Suburban Homes
BRASÍLIA
MILES
0
5
© C. S. Hammond & Co., Maplewood, N. J.

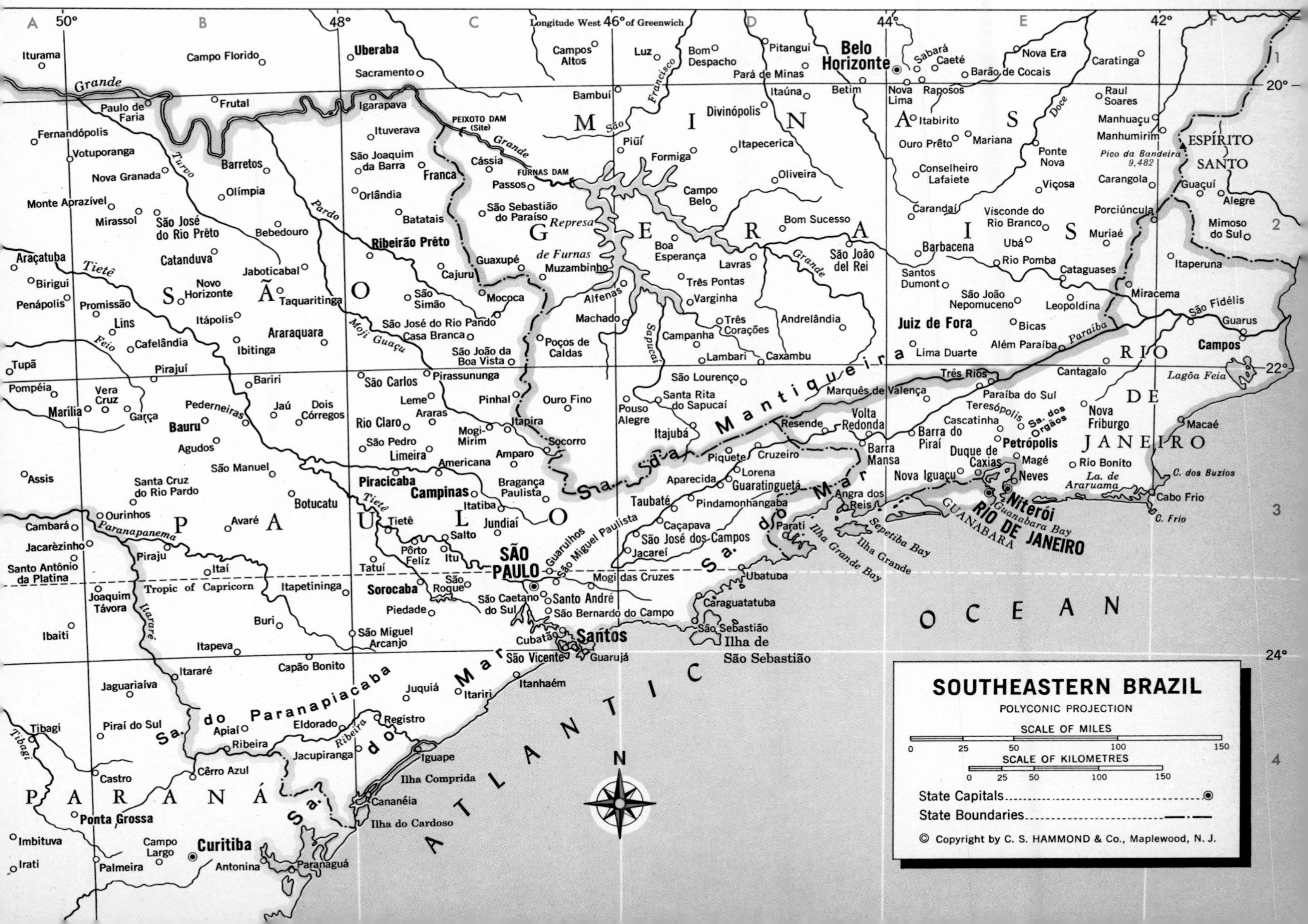
Longitude West 46° of Greenwich
50°
48°
44°
42°
20°
22°
24°
M I N A S
G E R A I S
S Ã O
P A U L O
P A R A N Á
ESPÍRITO SANTO
R I O
D E
J A N E I R O
O C E A N
A T L A N T I C
Grande
Tietê
Paranapanema
Tropic of Capricorn
Sa. da Mantiqueira
Sa. do Mar
Sa. do Paranapiacaba
Represa de Furnas
PEIXOTO DAM (Site)
FURNAS DAM
Belo Horizonte
SÃO PAULO
RIO DE JANEIRO
Niterói
Curitiba
Santos
Campinas
Sorocaba
Juiz de Fora
Uberaba
Ribeirão Prêto
Guanabara Bay
Sepetiba Bay
Ilha Grande
Ilha Grande Bay
Ilha de São Sebastião
Ilha Comprida
Ilha do Cardoso
Pico da Bandeira 9,482
C. dos Buzios
C. Frio
Lagôa Feia
SOUTHEASTERN BRAZIL
POLYCONIC PROJECTION
SCALE OF MILES
0 25 50 100 150
SCALE OF KILOMETRES
0 25 50 100 150
State Capitals
State Boundaries
© Copyright by C. S. HAMMOND & Co., Maplewood, N. J.

DEPARTMENTS

Beni, 181,000 ....C 3
Chuquisaca, 427,400 ....C 6
Cochabamba, 741,100 ....C 5
La Paz, 1,433,000 ....A 6
Oruro, 317,700 ....B 5
Pando, 29,900 ....A 2
Potosí, 807,400 ....B 7
Santa Cruz, 432,300 ....E 5
Tarija, 191,600 ....D 7

CITIES and TOWNS

Abapó, 466 ....D 6
Acchilla, 208 ....C 7
Achacachi, 3,621 ....A 5

Aiquile, 3,465 ....C 6
Alcalá, 236 ....C 6
Alejandría ....A 3
Alto Seco ....D 6
Amarete, 992 ....A 4
Amboró ....D 5
Ananea, 302 ....A 4
Ancoraimes, 769 ....A 5
Andamarca ....B 6
Añimbo, 443 ....C 7
Anzaldo, 1,056 ....C 5
Apolo, 1,043 ....B 4
Aquío ....D 6
Araca ....A 5
Arampampa, 829 ....B 5
Araní, 2,200 ....C 5
Arcopongo ....B 5

Aroma ....B 6
Arque, 1,254 ....B 5
Arroyo Grande ....A 2
Ascención, 2,097 ....D 2
Asunción ....A 2
Asunta, 45 ....B 5
Atén, 199 ....A 4
Ayacucho, 729 ....D 5
Ayata, 479 ....A 4
Azurduy, 1,234 ....C 6
Barrera ....B 3
Baures, 592 ....D 3
Bella Flor ....A 2
Bella Vista ....E 3
Berenguela ....A 5
Bermejo ....C 8

Betanzos, 1,097 ....C 6
Bolívar ....B 3
Bolpebra ....A 2
Boyuibe, 537 ....D 7
Buena Hora ....E 4
Buena Vista ....B 2
Buena Vista, 435 ....D 5
Cabezas, 298 ....D 6
Cachuela Esperanza, 1,073 ...C 2
Caiza, 838 ....C 7
Cajuata, 447 ....B 5
Calacoto, 415 ....A 5
Calamarca, 802 ....A 5
Calcha ....C 7
Calcha ....B 7
Callapa, 636 ....A 5
Camacho ....C 7

Camargo, 1,609 ....C 7
Camatindi ....D 7
Camiri, 4,969 ....D 7
Cañas ....C 7
Candelaria ....F 5
Canquella, 148 ....A 5
Capinota, 1,734 ....B 5
Capirenda ....D 7
Caquiaviri, 760 ....A 5
Carabuco, 626 ....A 4
Caracollo, 909 ....B 5
Caranavi ....B 4
Carandaití, 1,403 ....D 7
Carangas ....A 6
Caraparí, 351 ....D 7
Carmen ....B 2
Carrizal ....C 7

Cataricahua, 3,240 ....B 6
Cavari, 249 ....B 5
Cavinas ....B 3
Chachacomani, 159 ....C 7
Chaguaya, 643 ....B 6
Challacollo, 284 ....B 6
Challacota ....A 6
Challana ....B 4
Challapata, 2,529 ....B 6
Chaqui, 291 ....C 6
Charagua, 1,185 ....D 6
Charaña, 794 ....A 5
Chayanta, 1,272 ....B 6
Chiguana, 154 ....A 7
Chiñijo, 27 ....A 4
Chivé ....A 3

Chocaya, 444 ....B 7
Choquecota ....A 6
Chorrillos ....A 2
Chulumani, 2,362 ....B 5
Chuma, 931 ....A 4
Chuquichambi ....B 6
Chuquichuqui ....C 6
Cliza, 3,121 ....C 5
Cobija, 2,537 ....A 2
Cocapata ....C 5
Cochabamba, 157,000 ....C 5
Cohoni, 890 ....A 5
Coipasa ....A 6
Collpa, 481 ....C 5
Colquechaca, 1,070 ....B 6
Colquiri, 806 ....B 5

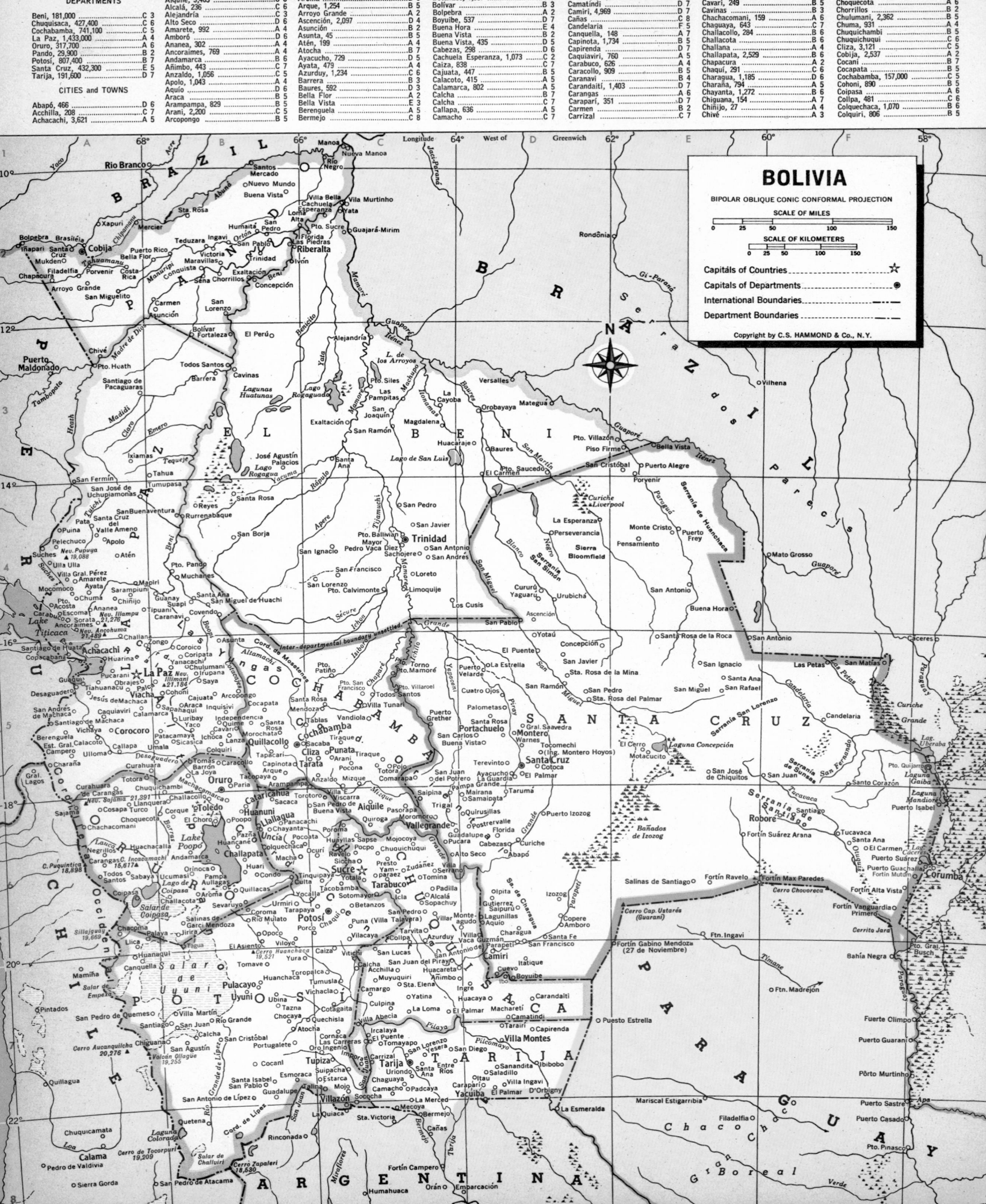

BOLIVIA

BIPOLAR OBLIQUE CONIC CONFORMAL PROJECTION

SCALE OF MILES
0   25   50   100   150

SCALE OF KILOMETERS
0   25 50   100   150

Capitals of Countries ....☆
Capitals of Departments ....◉
International Boundaries ....
Department Boundaries ....

Copyright by C.S. Hammond & Co., N.Y.

AREA 424,163 sq. mi.
POPULATION 4,804,000
CAPITALS La Paz, Sucre
LARGEST CITY La Paz
HIGHEST POINT Nevada Ancohuma 21,489 ft.
MONETARY UNIT Bolivian peso
MAJOR LANGUAGES Spanish, Quechua, Aymara
MAJOR RELIGION Roman Catholicism

Topography

0   100   200
MILES

Below Sea Level	100 m. 328 ft.	200 m. 656 ft.	500 m. 1,640 ft.	1,000 m. 3,281 ft.	2,000 m. 6,562 ft.	5,000 m. 16,404 ft.

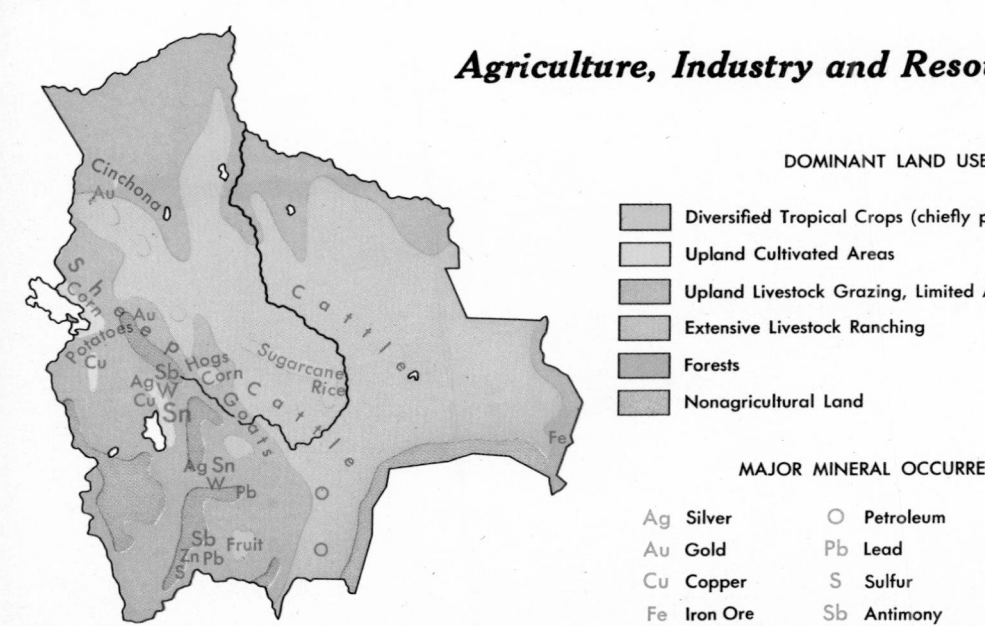

Agriculture, Industry and Resources

DOMINANT LAND USE

- Diversified Tropical Crops (chiefly plantation agriculture)
- Upland Cultivated Areas
- Upland Livestock Grazing, Limited Agriculture
- Extensive Livestock Ranching
- Forests
- Nonagricultural Land

MAJOR MINERAL OCCURRENCES

Ag	Silver	O	Petroleum	Sn	Tin
Au	Gold	Pb	Lead	W	Tungsten
Cu	Copper	S	Sulfur	Zn	Zinc
Fe	Iron Ore	Sb	Antimony		

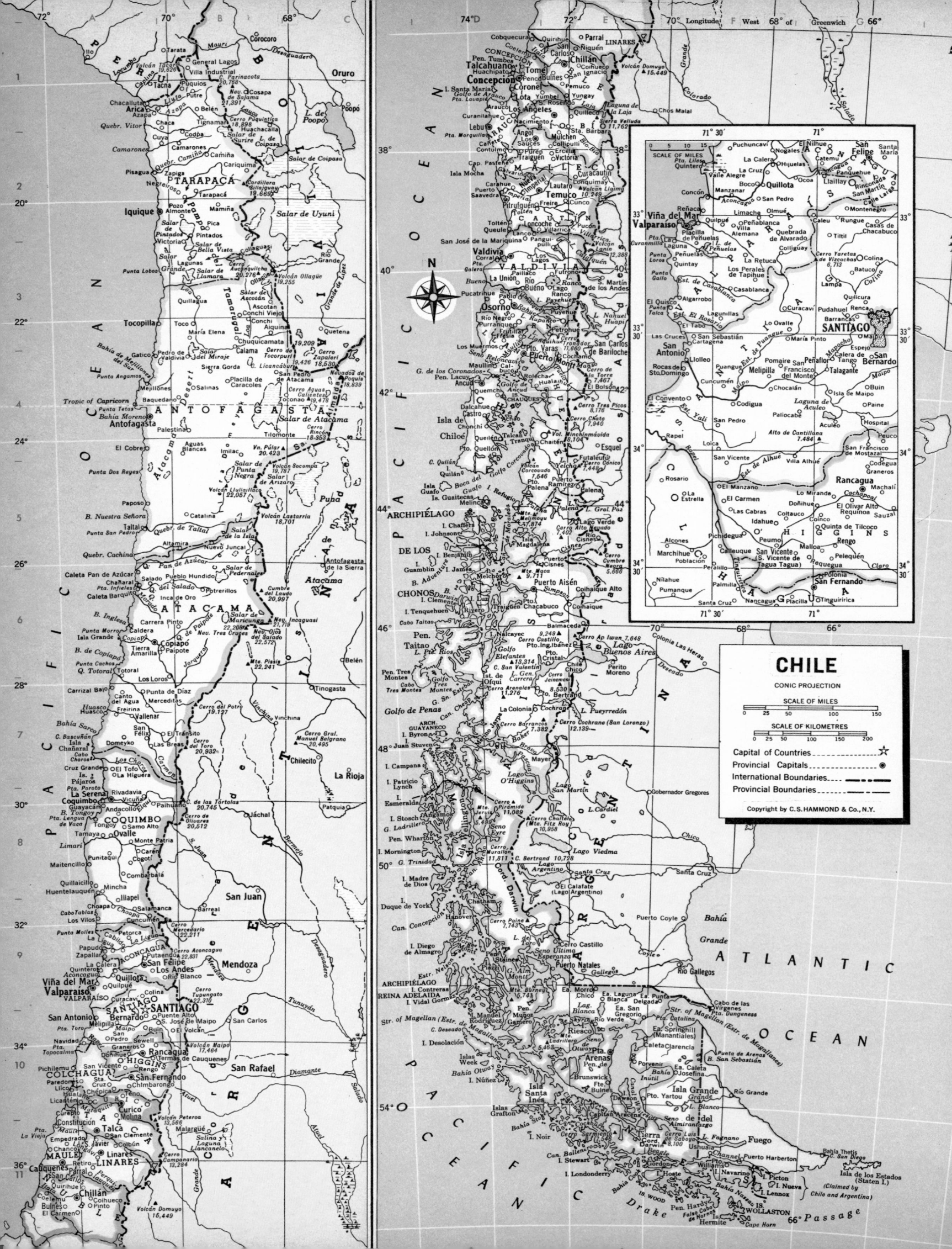

CHILE

CONIC PROJECTION

SCALE OF MILES

0 25 50 100 150

SCALE OF KILOMETRES

0 25 50 100 150 200

Capital of Countries .... ☆

Provincial Capitals .... ⊙

International Boundaries .... ▬ ▬ ▬

Provincial Boundaries .... ▬ ▬ ▬

Copyright by C.S. HAMMOND & Co., N.Y.

Topography

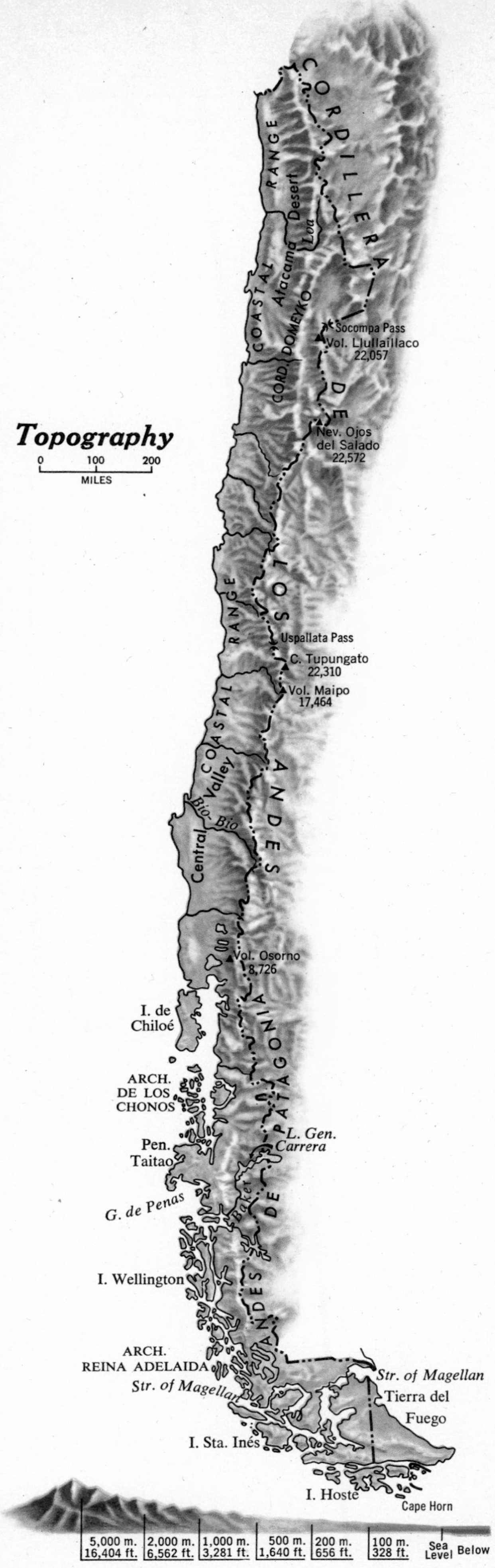
0 100 200
MILES
CORDILLERA DE LOS ANDES
COASTAL RANGE
Atacama Desert
Loa
CORD. DOMEYKO
Socompa Pass
Vol. Llullaillaco
22,057
Nev. Ojos
del Salado
22,572
Uspallata Pass
C. Tupungato
22,310
Vol. Maipo
17,464
Central Valley
Bío Bío
ANDES
Vol. Osorno
8,726
I. de
Chiloé
ARCH.
DE LOS
CHONOS
Pen.
Taitao
L. Gen.
Carrera
G. de Penas
Baker
ANDES DE PATAGONIA
I. Wellington
ARCH.
REINA ADELAIDA
Str. of Magellan
Str. of Magellan
Tierra del
Fuego
I. Sta. Inés
I. Hoste
Cape Horn
5,000 m. 16,404 ft.
2,000 m. 6,562 ft.
1,000 m. 3,281 ft.
500 m. 1,640 ft.
200 m. 656 ft.
100 m. 328 ft.
Sea Level
Below

AREA 292,257 sq. mi.
POPULATION 8,834,820
CAPITAL Santiago
LARGEST CITY Santiago
HIGHEST POINT Ojos del Salado 22,572 ft.
MONETARY UNIT Chilean escudo
MAJOR LANGUAGE Spanish
MAJOR RELIGION Roman Catholicism

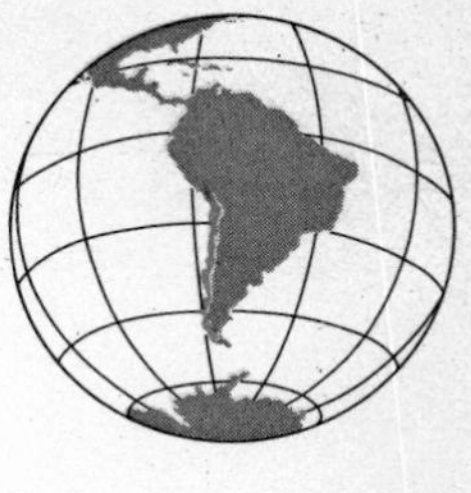

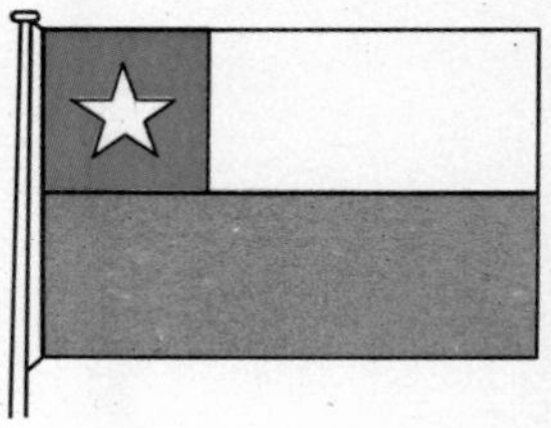

PROVINCES

Aconcagua, 160,821 ....A 9
Aisén, 51,022 ....D 6
Antofagasta, 250,665 ....B 4
Arauco, 98,810 ....D 1
Atacama, 152,326 ....B 6
Bío-Bío, 193,002 ....D 1
Cautín, 420,682 ....E 2
Chiloé, 110,728 ....D 4
Colchagua, 167,899 ....A10
Concepción, 638,118 ....D 1
Coquimbo, 336,821 ....A 8
Curicó, 113,710 ....A10
Linares, 189,010 ....A11
Llanquihue, 197,986 ....D 3
Magallanes, 88,706 ....E10
Malleco, 176,060 ....E 2
Maule, 82,339 ....A11
Ñuble, 314,738 ....E 1
O'Higgins, 306,739 ....A10
Osorno, 158,673 ....D 3
Santiago, 3,217,870 ....A 9
Talca, 231,088 ....A11
Tarapacá, 174,730 ....B 2
Valdivia, 275,404 ....D 3
Valparaíso, 726,953 ....A 9

CITIES and TOWNS

Achao, †11,501 ....D 4
Aculeo, 20 ....G 4
Aguas Blancas, †203 ....B 4
Aiquina, 105 ....B 3
Alcones, 682 ....F 5
Algarrobo, †3,941 ....F 3
Altamira, 93 ....B 5
Ancud, †22,127 ....D 4
Andacollo, †9,987 ....A 8
Angol, †35,995 ....D 1
Antofagasta, †126,252 ....A 4
Arauco, †20,018 ....D 1
Arica, †92,394 ....A 1
Ascotán, 23 ....B 3
Azapa, 225 ....A 1
Balmaceda, 735 ....E 6
Baquedano, 1,412 ....A 4
Barrancas, †184,241 ....G 3
Batuco, 1,125 ....G 3
Belén, †925 ....B 1
Boco, 1,655 ....F 2
Buin, †31,233 ....G 4
Bulnes, †16,107 ....E 1
Cabildo, †13,018 ....A 9
Calama, †71,983 ....B 3
Calbuco, †21,673 ....D 4
Caldera, †3,268 ....A 6
Calera de Tango, †6,198 ....G 4
Caleta Barquito, 932 ....A 6
Caleta Clarencia, 60 ....E10
Caleta Pan de Azúcar, 8 ....A 6
Caleu, 187 ....G 2
Calle Larga, †7,172 ....G 2
Calleuque ....F 5
Camarones, 259 ....B 2
Camiña, 234 ....B 2
Cañete, †15,179 ....D 2
Canto del Agua, 269 ....A 7
Capitán Pastene, 1,669 ....D 2
Carahue, †12,733 ....D 2
Carén, 225 ....A 8
Cariquima, 20 ....B 2
Carrera Pinto, 68 ....B 6
Carrizal Bajo, 207 ....A 7
Cartagena, †7,124 ....F 3
Casablanca, †12,292 ....F 3
Castro, †22,682 ....D 4
Catalina, †1,637 ....B 5
Catemu, †8,728 ....G 2
Cauquenes, †38,476 ....A11
Cerro Castillo, †537 ....E 9
Chaca, 37 ....B 1
Chacalluta, 75 ....A 1
Chaitén, †4,067 ....E 4
Chañaral, †36,949 ....A 6
Chanco, †12,433 ....A11
Chépica, †11,199 ....A10
Chile Chico, 1,926 ....E 6
Chillán, †102,361 ....A11
Chimbarongo, †17,592 ....A10
Choapa, 258 ....A 9
Chocalán, 187 ....F 4
Chonchi, †8,911 ....D 4
Chuquicamata, 24,798 ....B 3
Cobquecura, †6,298 ....D 1
Cochamó, †5,042 ....E 3
Codegua, †6,757 ....G 4
Codigua, 530 ....F 4
Codpa, †950 ....B 1
Coelemu, †11,967 ....D 1
Cogotí, 212 ....A 8
Coihaique, †24,032 ....E 6
Coihaique Alto, 24 ....E 6
Coihueco, †17,276 ....A11
Coinco, †4,942 ....G 5
Colbún, †12,924 ....A11
Colina, †18,058 ....G 3
Collaguasi, 8 ....B 3
Colliguay, 102 ....F 3
Collipulli, †15,058 ....E 2
Coltauco, †11,857 ....F 5
Combarbalá, †17,332 ....A 8
Concepción, †189,929 ....D 1
Conchi, 9 ....B 3
Conchi Viejo, 17 ....B 3
Concón, 5,381 ....F 2
Constitución, †23,543 ....A11
Contulmo, †13,987 ....D 2
Copiapó, †51,809 ....B 6
Coquimbo, †55,360 ....A 8
Coronel, †73,568 ....D 1
Corral, †5,533 ....D 3
Cruz Grande, 478 ....A 7
Cunco, †18,836 ....E 2
Cuncumén, Coquimbo, 1,052 ....A 9
Cuncumén, Santiago ....F 4
Curacautín, †15,862 ....E 2
Curacaví, †11,481 ....G 3
Curanilahue, †21,207 ....D 1
Curepto, †13,020 ....A10
Curicó, †59,621 ....A10
Cuya, 86 ....B 2
Dalcahue, †7,084 ....D 4
Domeyko, 1,814 ....A 7
Doñihue, †8,837 ....G 5
El Carmen, Ñuble, †13,226 ....A11
El Carmen, O'Higgins, 625 ....F 5
El Cobre, 7 ....A 4
El Convento, 733 ....F 4
El Manzano, 1,073 ....F 5
El Ñilhue, 341 ....G 1
El Olivar Alto, †5,414 ....G 5
El Quisco, †2,152 ....E 3
El Tabo, †2,180 ....F 3
El Tofo, 1,175 ....A 7
El Tránsito, 235 ....B 7
El Volcán, 250 ....B10
Empedrado, †7,887 ....A11
Ercilla, †8,061 ....E 2
Espejo, 3,481 ....G 3
Estancia Caleta Josefina, †1,042 ....F10
Estancia Laguna Blanca, 119 ....E 9
Estancia Morro Chico, †785 ....E 9
Estancia Punta Delgada, 233 ....E 9
Estancia San Gregorio, †1,156 ....E 9
Estancia Springhill (Manantiales), 291 ....F10
Freire, †23,313 ....E 2
Freirina, †5,523 ....A 7
Fresia, †15,359 ....D 3
Frutillar, †12,721 ....D 3
Fuerte Bulnes, 18 ....E10
Futaleufú, †2,366 ....E 4
Futrono, †7,109 ....E 3
Galvarino, †9,495 ....D 2
Gatico, 16 ....A 4
General Lagos, †810 ....B 1
Graneros, †13,523 ....G 5
Guayacán, 1,514 ....A 8
Hijuelas, †7,128 ....F 2
Hospital, 460 ....G 4
Huachipato, †16,336 ....D 1
Hualaihué, 391 ....E 4
Hualañé, †6,912 ....A10
Huara, †1,934 ....B 2
Huasco, †4,971 ....A 7
Huentelauquén, 355 ....A 8
Idahue, 1,832 ....F 5
Illapel, †20,660 ....A 8
Imalac, 27 ....B 4
Inca de Oro, 1,406 ....B 6
Iquique, †64,900 ....A 2
Isla de Maipo, †12,903 ....G 4
La Calera, †28,728 ....F 2
La Colonia, 41 ....D 7
La Cruz, †8,907 ....F 2
La Estrella, †3,707 ....F 5
La Higuera, †6,991 ....A 7
La Laguna, 316 ....F 2
La Ligua, †15,719 ....A 9
La Retuca, 173 ....F 3
La Serena, †71,898 ....A 8
La Unión, †32,010 ....D 3
Lago Ranco, †12,767 ....D 3
Lago Verde, 193 ....E 5
Lagunas, †5,653 ....B 3
Lagunillas, 468 ....F 3
Lampa, †10,220 ....G 3
Lanco, †14,479 ....D 2
Las Breas, 14 ....B 7
Las Cabras †12,119 ....F 5
Las Cruces, 612 ....F 3
Lautaro, †26,011 ....E 2
Lebu, †16,946 ....D 1
Licantén, †6,354 ....A10
Limache, †22,472 ....F 2
Linares, †61,011 ....A11
Llaillay, †14,074 ....G 2
Llico, 330 ....A10
Llolleo, 9,846 ....F 4
Lo Miranda, 2,270 ....G 5
Lo Ovalle, 129 ....F 3
Loica, 446 ....F 4
Loncoche, †17,539 ....D 2
Longaví, †15,909 ....A11
Lonquimay, †9,524 ....E 2
Los Andes, †30,408 ....B 9
Los Ángeles, †89,810 ....D 1
Los Lagos, †14,934 ....D 3
Los Loros, 269 ....A 6
Los Muermos, †9,296 ....D 3
Los Perales de Tapihue, 176 ....F 3
Los Sauces, †7,613 ....D 2
Los Vilos, †10,453 ....A 9
Lota, †51,548 ....D 1
Machalí, †28,415 ....G 5
Maipú, †117,872 ....G 3
Maitencillo, 31 ....A 8
Malloa, †9,742 ....G 5
Mamiña, 341 ....B 2
Manantiales, 291 ....F10
Manzanar, 248 ....F 2
Marchihue, †4,451 ....F 5
María Elena, 9,572 ....B 3
María Pinto, †5,980 ....G 3
Maullín, †14,544 ....D 4
Mayer, 29 ....E 7
Mejillones, †3,333 ....A 4
Melinca, 166 ....D 5
Melipilla, †49,306 ....F 4
Merceditas, 33 ....B 7
Mincha, †11,329 ....A 8
Molina, †30,398 ....A10
Montenegro, 327 ....G 2
Monte Patria, †18,927 ....A 8
Mulchén, †23,379 ....E 1
Nacimiento, †17,651 ....D 1
Nancagua, †11,076 ....F 6
Navidad, †6,618 ....A10
Negreiros, †1,144 ....B 2
Nilahue, 428 ....E 6
Ñiquén, †13,640 ....E 1
Nogales, †18,529 ....F 2
Nueva Imperial, †30,286 ....D 2
Nuevo Juncal, 2 ....B 5
Ocoa, 871 ....G 2
Ollagüe, 333 ....B 3
Olmué, †8,804 ....F 2
Osorno, †105,793 ....D 3
Ovalle, †53,433 ....A 8
Paihuano, †6,048 ....B 8
Paillaco, †13,612 ....D 3
Paine, †21,876 ....G 4
Paipote, 2,278 ....B 6
Palena, †2,508 ....E 5
Palestina, 7 ....B 4
Paliocabe, 77 ....F 4
Palmilla, †12,429 ....F 6
Panguipulli, †32,834 ....E 2
Panquehue, †4,230 ....G 2
Paposo, 87 ....A 5
Papudo, †2,594 ....A 9
Paredones, †7,404 ....A10
Parral, †30,427 ....A11
Pedro de Valdivia, 11,028 ....B 4
Pelequen, 1,068 ....G 5
Pemuco, †7,577 ....E 1
Peñablanca, 5,586 ....F 2
Peñaflor, †37,788 ....G 4
Penco, †33,962 ....D 1
Peñuelas, 359 ....F 3
Peralillo, †7,965 ....F 5
Petorca, †8,343 ....A 9
Petrohué, 40 ....E 3
Peuco, 211 ....G 4
Peumo, †11,308 ....F 5
Pica, †1,487 ....B 2
Pichidegua, †13,550 ....F 5
Pichilemu, †8,042 ....A10
Pintados, 144 ....B 2
Pinto, †8,687 ....A11
Pisagua, †1,880 ....A 2
Pitrufquén, †16,797 ....D 2
Placilla, †6,411 ....F 6
Placilla de Caracoles, 2 ....B 4
Placilla de Peñuelas, 1,495 ....F 2
Población, 1,026 ....F 5
Polonia ....G 6
Pomaire, 1,366 ....F 4
Porvenir, †3,600 ....E10
Potrerillos, 6,168 ....B 6
Pozo Almonte, †1,798 ....B 2
Puangue ....F 4
Pucatrihue, 60 ....D 3
Puchuncaví, †7,542 ....F 2
Pucón, †16,872 ....E 2
Pudahuel, 172 ....G 3
Pueblo Hundido, 2,123 ....B 6
Puente Alto, †81,031 ....B10
Puerto Aisén, †15,000 ....E 6
Puerto Bertrand, 52 ....E 7
Puerto Chacabuco, 130 ....D 6
Puerto Cisnes, †2,800 ....E 5
Puerto Cristal, 698 ....E 6
Puerto Ingeniero Ibáñez, †1,900 ....E 6
Puerto Montt, †86,750 ....E 4
Puerto Natales, †13,577 ....E 9
Puerto Palena, 105 ....D 5
Puerto Quellón, †7,734 ....D 4
Puerto Ramírez, 82 ....E 5
Puerto Saavedra, 805 ....D 2
Puerto Varas, †21,003 ....E 3
Puerto Williams, †949 ....F11
Puerto Yartou, 14 ....E10
Pumanque, †3,137 ....F 6
Punitaqui, †16,167 ....A 8
Punta Arenas, †64,958 ....E10
Punta de Díaz, 11 ....B 7
Puquios, 105 ....B 1
Purén, †11,604 ....D 2
Purranque, †18,201 ....D 3
Putaendo, †12,806 ....A 9
Putre, †855 ....B 1
Puyehue, 39 ....E 3
Quebrada de Alvarado, 429 ....F 2
Queilén, †6,055 ....D 4
Quemchi, †6,707 ....D 4
Queule, 235 ....D 2
Quilicura, †22,644 ....G 3
Quillagua, 288 ....B 3
Quillaicillo, 195 ....A 8
Quilleco, †16,043 ....E 1
Quillota, †49,202 ....F 2
Quilpué, †56,399 ....F 2
Quinta de Tilcoco, †6,513 ....G 5
Quintay, 166 ....F 3
Quintero, †11,847 ....F 2
Quirihue, †11,178 ....E 1
Rancagua, †95,030 ....G 5
Rapel, 699 ....F 4
Reñaca, 1,267 ....F 2
Renca, †67,168 ....G 3
Rengo, †28,230 ....G 5
Requegua, 1,699 ....G 5
Requíhoa, †10,730 ....G 5
Retiro, †15,146 ....A11
Rinconada San Martín, †4,118 ....G 2
Río Blanco, 456 ....B 9
Río Bueno, †28,469 ....D 3
Río Cisnes, 244 ....E 5
Río Negro, †15,582 ....D 3
Río Verde, †554 ....E10
Rivadavia, 443 ....A 7
Rocas de Santo Domingo, †4,114 ....F 4
Rolecha, 573 ....D 4
Rosario, †3,383 ....F 5
Rungue, 312 ....G 2
Salado, 1,375 ....A 6
Salamanca, †18,741 ....A 9
Salinas, 7 ....B 4
Samo Alto, †5,689 ....A 8
San Antonio, †53,100 ....F 3
San Bernardo, †117,766 ....G 4
San Carlos, †30,651 ....E 1
San Clemente, †23,273 ....A11
San Felipe, †34,292 ....G 2
San Félix, 495 ....A 7
Sán Fernando, †44,160 ....G 6
San Francisco de Mostazal, †11,439 ....G 4
San Francisco del Monte, †14,897 ....G 4
San Ignacio, †13,523 ....E 1
San Javier, †27,592 ....A11
San José de la Mariquina, 2,878 ....D 2
San José de Maipo, †9,601 ....B10
San Pablo, †7,978 ....D 3
San Pedro, Santiago, †8,255 ....F 4
San Pedro, Valparaíso, 1,420 ....F 2
San Pedro de Atacama, 515 ....C 4
San Rosendo, †14,337 ....E 1
San Sebastián, 494 ....F 3
San Vicente, 230 ....F 4
San Vicente (San Vicente de Tagua Tagua), †28,333 ....F 5
Santa Bárbara, †14,345 ....E 1
Santa Cruz, †19,338 ....F 6
Santa María, †8,162 ....G 2
Santiago (capital), 2,596,929 ....G 3
Sewell, 10,866 ....A10
Sierra Gorda, †8,805 ....B 4
Talagante, †23,619 ....G 4
Talca, †102,522 ....A11
Talcahuano, †150,011 ....D 1
Taltal, †7,417 ....A 5
Tamaya, 248 ....A 8
Tarapacá, 130 ....B 2
Temuco, †146,039 ....E 2
Teno, †17,675 ....A10
Termas de Cauquenes, 210 ....B10
Tierra Amarilla, †6,842 ....A 6
Tignamar, 226 ....B 1
Tilomonte, 3 ....B 4
Tiltil, †9,198 ....G 2
Tinguiririca, 1,012 ....G 6
Toco, †8,734 ....B 3
Toconao, 452 ....C 4
Tocopilla, †22,301 ....A 3
Toltén, †16,265 ....D 2
Tomé, †44,480 ....D 1
Tongoy, 935 ....A 8
Totoral, 109 ....A 6
Traiguén, †21,084 ....D 2
Valdivia, †90,942 ....D 3
Valle Alegre, 241 ....F 2
Vallenar, †41,907 ....A 7
Valparaíso, †251,459 ....E 2
Victoria, Malleco, †28,382 ....E 2
Victoria, Tarapacá, 4,943 ....B 3
Vicuña, †13,806 ....A 8
Villa Alemana, †37,547 ....F 2
Villa Alhué, †5,078 ....G 4
Villa Industrial, 28 ....B 1
Villarrica, †23,924 ....E 2
Viña del Mar, †184,332 ....F 2
Yumbel, †21,858 ....E 1
Yungay, †10,725 ....E 1
Zapallar, †2,894 ....A 9

OTHER FEATURES

Aconcagua (river) ....F 2
Aculeo (lagoon) ....G 4
Adventure (bay) ....D 5
Aguas Calientes (mt.) ....C 4
Alhué (river) ....F 4
Almirantazgo (bay) F11
Almeida (mts.) ....C 4
Almirante Montt (gulf) ....D 9
Alto Nevado (mt.) ....E 5
Ancho (channel) ....D 8
Ancud (gulf) ....D 4
Angamos (isl.) ....D 8
Angamos (point) ....A 4
Ap Iwan (mt.) ....E 6
Arauco (gulf) ....D 1
Arenales (mt.) ....D 7
Ascotán (salt deposit) ....B 3
Atacama (desert) ....B 4
Atacama (salt deposit) ....C 4
Aucanquilcha (mt.) ....B 3
Azapa (river) ....B 1
Baker (river) ....D 7
Ballenero (channel) E11
Barrancos (mt.) ....D 7
Bascuñán (cape) ....A 7
Beagle (channel) E11
Bella Vista (salt deposit) ....B 3
Benjamín (isl.), 16 ....D 5
Bertrand (mt.) ....D 8
Bío-Bío (river) ....E 2
Blanca (lagoon) E10
Blanco (lake) F10
Bravo (river) ....D 7
Brunswick (pen.) E10

(continued on following page)

DOMINANT LAND USE

- Cereals, Livestock
- Mediterranean Agriculture (cereals, fruit, livestock)
- Pasture Livestock
- Extensive Livestock Ranching
- Limited Seasonal Grazing
- Forests
- Nonagricultural Land

MAJOR MINERAL OCCURRENCES

Ag	Silver	Hg	Mercury
Au	Gold	Id	Iodine
C	Coal	Mn	Manganese
Cu	Copper	Mo	Molybdenum
Fe	Iron Ore	N	Nitrates
G	Natural Gas	Na	Salt
Gp	Gypsum	O	Petroleum
		S	Sulfur

⚡ Water Power   ▨ Major Industrial Areas

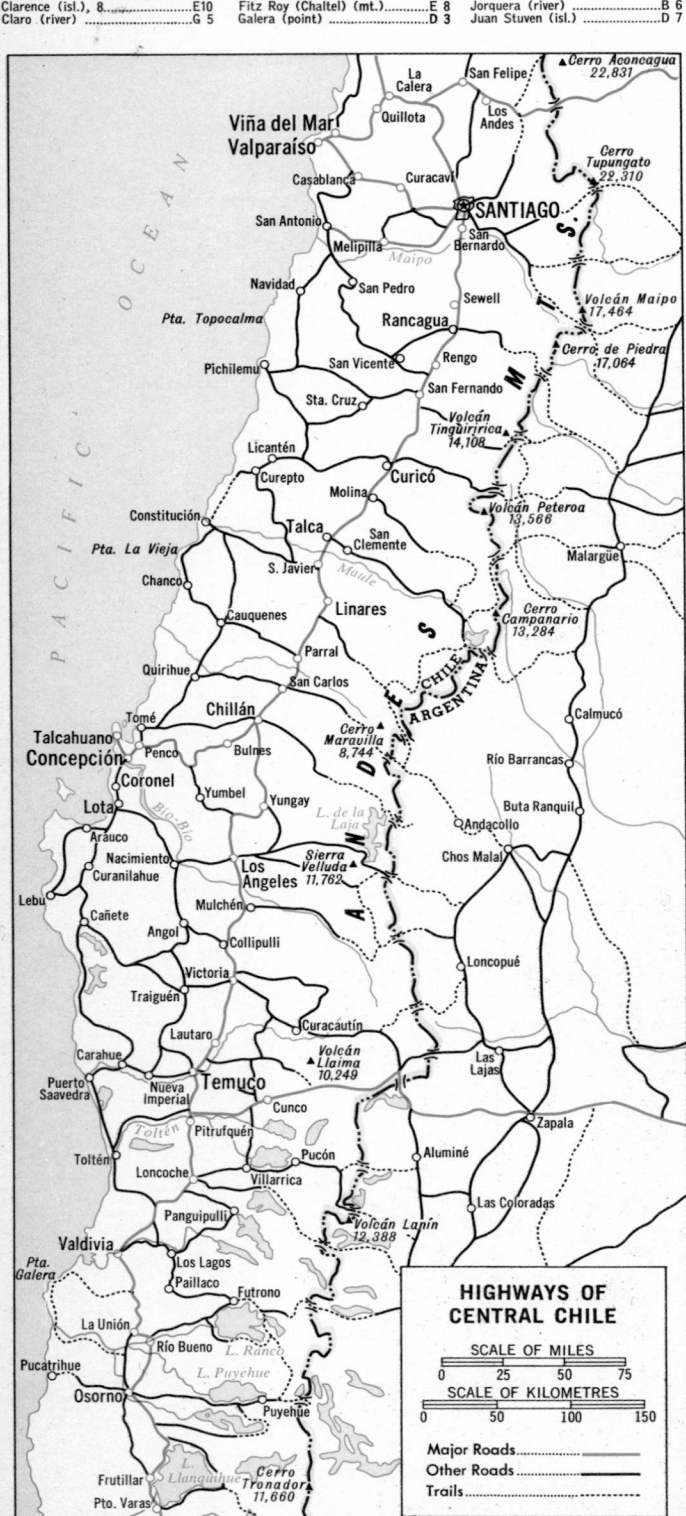

Viña del Mar
Valparaíso
SANTIAGO
(map labels include: La Calera, San Felipe, Cerro Aconcagua 22,831, Quillota, Los Andes, Casablanca, Curacaví, Cerro Tupungato 22,310, San Antonio, Melipilla, Maipo, San Bernardo, Navidad, San Pedro, Sewell, Pta. Topocalma, Rancagua, Volcán Maipo 17,464, Pichilemu, San Vicente, Rengo, Cerro de Piedra 17,064, Sta. Cruz, San Fernando, Licantén, Curicó, Volcán Tinguiririca 14,108, Constitución, Molina, Talca, Volcán Peteroa 13,566, Pta. La Vieja, San Clemente, Malargüe, Chanco, S. Javier, Maule, Linares, Cerro Campanario 13,284, Cauquenes, Parral, Río Barrancas, Quirihue, San Carlos, Tomé, Chillán, Calmucó, Talcahuano, Penco, Bulnes, Cerro Maravilla 8,744, Concepción, Coronel, Yumbel, Yungay, Buta Ranquil, Lota, L. de la Laja, Andacollo, Arauco, Nacimiento, Los Angeles, Sierra Velluda 11,762, Chos Malal, Curanilahue, Mulchén, Lebu, Cañete, Angol, Collipulli, Loncopué, Victoria, Traiguén, Las Lajas, Carahue, Lautaro, Curacautín, Volcán Llaima 10,249, Puerto Saavedra, Nueva Imperial, Temuco, Cunco, Zapala, Pitrufquén, Pucón, Aluminé, Toltén, Loncoche, Villarrica, Las Coloradas, Panguipulli, Volcán Lanín 12,388, Valdivia, Los Lagos, Pta. Galera, Paillaco, Futrono, La Unión, Río Bueno, L. Ranco, L. Puyehue, Pucatrihue, Osorno, Puyehue, Frutillar, Llanquihue, Cerro Tronador 11,660, Pto. Varas, Puerto Montt, ANDES, CHILE-ARGENTINA)

HIGHWAYS OF CENTRAL CHILE

SCALE OF MILES
0   25   50   75

SCALE OF KILOMETRES
0   50   100   150

- Major Roads
- Other Roads
- Trails

© C. S. HAMMOND & CO.

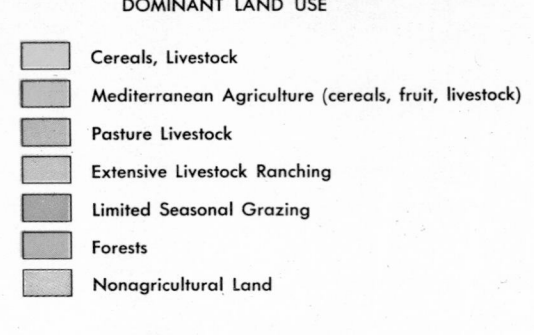

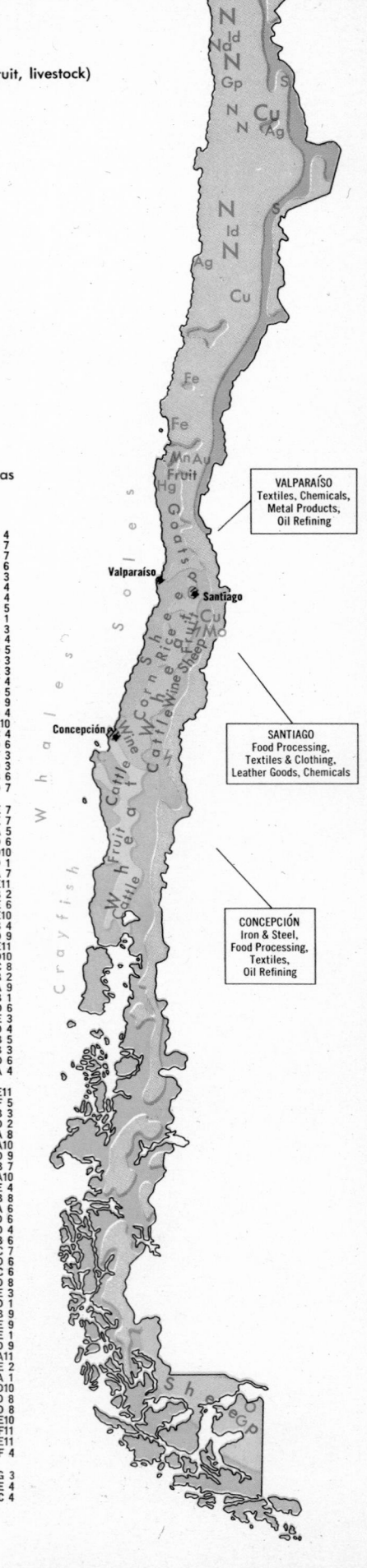

VALPARAÍSO
Textiles, Chemicals, Metal Products, Oil Refining

SANTIAGO
Food Processing, Textiles & Clothing, Leather Goods, Chemicals

CONCEPCIÓN
Iron & Steel, Food Processing, Textiles, Oil Refining

PROVINCES

Buenos Aires, 6,734,548	D 4
Catamarca, 172,407	C 2
Chaco, 535,443	D 2
Chubut, 142,195	C 6
Córdoba, 1,759,997	D 3
Corrientes, 543,226	E 2
Distrito Federal (fed. dist.), 2,966,816	H 7
Entre Ríos, 803,505	E 3
Formosa, 178,458	D 1
Jujuy, 239,783	C 1
La Pampa, 158,489	C 4
La Rioja, 128,270	C 2
Mendoza, 825,535	C 4
Misiones, 391,094	F 2
Neuquén, 111,008	C 4
Río Negro, 192,595	C 5
Salta, 412,652	D 1
San Juan, 352,461	C 3
San Luis, 174,251	C 3
Santa Cruz, 52,853	C 6
Santa Fe, 1,865,537	D 3
Santiago del Estero, 477,156	D 2
Tierra del Fuego, Antártida e Islas del Atlántico Sur (terr.), 13,452	C 7
Tucumán, 780,348	C 2

CITIES and TOWNS

Abra Pampa, 1,391	C 1
Acebal, 2,026	F 6
Acevedo, 1,057	F 6
Acuña, 805	G 5
Adolfo Alsina, 5,836	D 4
Aguilares, 9,816	C 2
Aimogasta, 2,721	C 2
Alberti, 4,447	G 7
Alcaraz, 376	F 6
Alcorta, 3,781	F 6
Alejandra, 881	F 5
Allen, 11,389	C 4
Alpachiri, 733	D 4
Alta Gracia, 11,570	D 3
Aluminé, 744	B 4
Alvear, 4,252	E 2
Ameghino, 2,770	D 3
Aminga, 480	C 2
Añatuya, 11,753	D 2
Anchorena, 862	C 4
Andacollo, 587	B 4
Andalgalá, 3,260	C 2
Angélica, 434	E 5
Anguil, 734	D 4
Antofagasta de la Sierra, 462	C 2
Apóstoles, 6,507	E 2
Arrecifes, 7,635	F 6
Arribeños, 1,739	F 7
Arroyo Seco, 5,193	F 6
Ascensión, 1,775	F 7
Astra, 1,019	C 6
Avellaneda, †329,626	G 7
Ayacucho, 9,220	E 4
Azul, 28,609	D 4
Bahía Blanca, †150,354	D 4
Bahía Thetis, †438	C 7
Baibiene, 380	G 4
Baigorrita, 1,206	F 7
Balcarce, 15,210	E 4
Balnearia, 4,306	D 3
Bañado de Ovanta, 198	C 2
Bandera, 2,035	D 2
Baradero, 10,194	G 6
Barrancas, 1,953	F 6
Barranqueras, 19,779	E 2
Barreal, 1,790	C 3
Basavilbaso, 6,614	G 6
Batavia, 457	C 3
Beazley, 1,070	C 3
Belén, 5,469	C 2
Bella Vista, Corrientes, 8,334	E 2
Bella Vista, Tucumán, 6,816	C 2
Bell Ville, 15,796	D 3
Bernardo de Irigoyen, 1,400	F 2
Bolívar, 14,010	D 4
Bovril, 1,955	G 5
Bragado, 16,104	F 7
Buenos Aires (capital), 3,549,000	H 7
Buenos Aires, *9,070,000	H 7
Bustinza, 918	F 6
Cachi, 491	C 2
Cafayate, 2,407	C 2
Calchaqui, 2,782	F 5
Caleta Olivia, 3,639	C 6
Caleufú, 1,197	D 4
Camarones, 501	D 5
Campana, 14,452	G 6
Campo Gallo, 2,336	D 2
Cañada de Gómez, 12,354	F 6
Cañada Honda, 345	C 3
Canals, 5,359	D 3
Cañuelas, 5,614	G 7
Carabelas, 3,476	F 6
Carcarana, 4,516	F 6
Carlos Casares, 7,558	F 7
Carlos Tejedor, 2,897	D 4
Carmen de Areco, 4,411	F 7
Carmen de Patagones, 5,423	D 5
Caseros, 4,975	D 4
Casilda, 11,023	F 6
Castelli, Buenos Aires, 3,263	H 7
Castelli, Chaco, 4,131	D 2
Catamarca, 45,929	C 2
Catriló, 1,794	D 4
Cayasta, 592	F 5
Cayastacito, 483	F 5
Cereales, 367	D 4
Ceres, 6,525	D 2
Chabas, 2,937	F 6
Chacabuco, 12,530	F 7
Chajarí, 9,075	G 5
Chamical, 3,756	C 3
Charadai, 1,872	D 2
Charata, 8,953	D 2
Chascomús, 9,105	H 7
Chepes, 2,941	C 3
Chicoana, 1,093	C 2
Chilecito, 9,809	C 2
Chivilcoy, 23,386	F 7
Choele-Choel, 3,079	C 4
Chos Malal, 2,874	C 4
Chumbicha, 2,188	C 2
Cinco Saltos, 10,196	C 4
Cipolletti, 19,862	C 4
Clarke, 506	F 6
Clodomira, 4,685	D 2
Clorinda, 10,043	E 2
Colón, Buenos Aires, 5,628	F 6

AREA 1,072,070
POPULATION 23,983,000
CAPITAL Buenos Aires
LARGEST CITY Buenos Aires
HIGHEST POINT Cerro Aconcagua 22,831 ft.
MONETARY UNIT Argentine peso
MAJOR LANGUAGE Spanish
MAJOR RELIGION Roman Catholicism

Agriculture, Industry and Resources

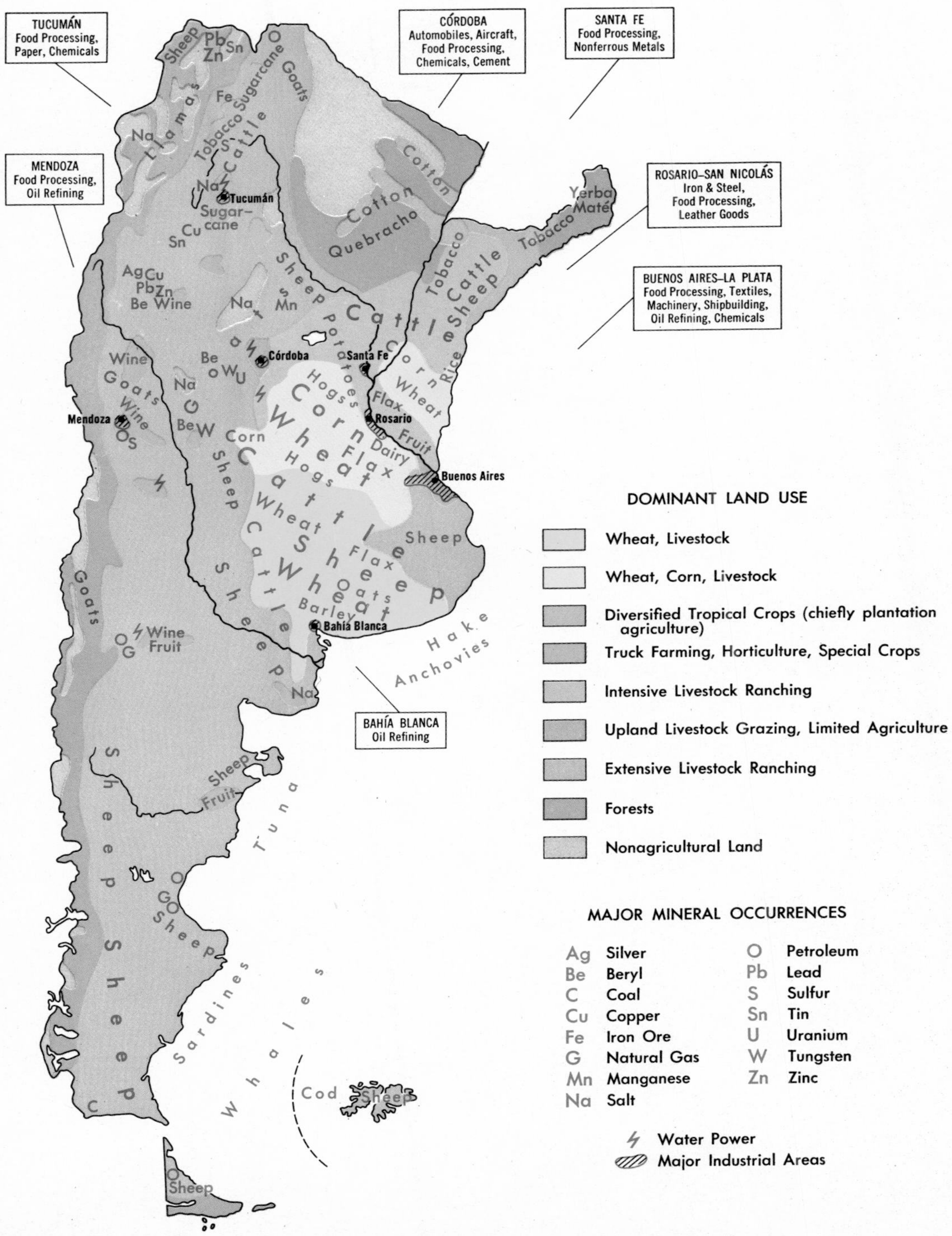

TUCUMÁN
Food Processing, Paper, Chemicals

MENDOZA
Food Processing, Oil Refining

CÓRDOBA
Automobiles, Aircraft, Food Processing, Chemicals, Cement

SANTA FE
Food Processing, Nonferrous Metals

ROSARIO–SAN NICOLÁS
Iron & Steel, Food Processing, Leather Goods

BUENOS AIRES–LA PLATA
Food Processing, Textiles, Machinery, Shipbuilding, Oil Refining, Chemicals

BAHÍA BLANCA
Oil Refining

DOMINANT LAND USE

- Wheat, Livestock
- Wheat, Corn, Livestock
- Diversified Tropical Crops (chiefly plantation agriculture)
- Truck Farming, Horticulture, Special Crops
- Intensive Livestock Ranching
- Upland Livestock Grazing, Limited Agriculture
- Extensive Livestock Ranching
- Forests
- Nonagricultural Land

MAJOR MINERAL OCCURRENCES

Ag	Silver	O	Petroleum
Be	Beryl	Pb	Lead
C	Coal	S	Sulfur
Cu	Copper	Sn	Tin
Fe	Iron Ore	U	Uranium
G	Natural Gas	W	Tungsten
Mn	Manganese	Zn	Zinc
Na	Salt		

⚡ Water Power
▨ Major Industrial Areas

Colón, Entre Ríos, 6,813	G 6
Colonia Elisa, 1,338	E 2
Colonia Las Heras, 1,880	C 6
Comandante Fontana, 1,686	D 2
Comandante Luis Piedrabuena, 1,441	C 6
Comodoro Rivadavia, 35,966	C 6
Concepción, Corrientes, 2,593	E 2
Concepción, Tucumán, 15,832	C 2
Concepción del Uruguay, 36,486	G 6
Concordia, 56,654	G 5
Copacabana, 957	C 2
Córdoba, †589,153	D 3
Coronda, 4,656	F 6
Coronel Bogado, 1,264	F 6
Coronel Brandsen, 3,803	H 7
Coronel Dorrego, 7,245	D 4
Coronel Moldes, 1,695	C 2
Coronel Pringles, 12,844	D 4
Coronel Suárez, 11,133	D 4
Corral de Bustos, 3,900	D 3
Corrientes, 97,507	E 2
Cosquín, 7,746	D 3
Crespo, 5,706	F 6
Cruz del Eje, 15,563	C 3
Cuadro Nacional, 1,879	C 3
Curuzú Cuatiá, 16,567	G 5
Cutral-Có, 11,292	C 4
Deán Funes, 13,840	D 3
Del Carril, 475	G 7
Diamante, 10,948	F 6
Díaz, 1,288	F 6
Doblas, 902	D 4
Dolavón, 1,277	C 5
Dolores, 14,438	E 4
Dudignac, 1,503	F 7
Eduardo Castex, 4,020	D 4
El Bolsón, 2,607	B 5
El Calafate, 377	B 7
El Chorro, 377	D 1
Eldorado, 2,778	F 2
El Huecu, 298	B 4
Elisa, 579	F 5
El Maitén, 2,382	B 5
Elortondo, 3,514	F 6
El Pintado, 388	D 1
El Quebrachal, 1,212	D 2
Embárcación, 6,371	D 1
Emilio Ayarza, 1,357	F 7
Empedrado, 3,735	E 2
Enrique Carbó, 956	G 6
Ensenada, †35,030	H 7
Escobar, 3,693	G 7
Esperanza, 10,035	F 5
Esquel, 9,900	B 5
Esquina, 7,619	G 5
Famatina, 1,330	C 2
Federación, 4,247	G 5
Fernández, 3,115	D 2
Fiambalá, 1,450	C 2
Firmat, 4,051	F 6
Fives Lille, 667	G 7
Formosa, 36,499	E 2
French, 4,007	F 7
Frías, 11,862	C 2
Gaimán, 1,286	C 5
Gálvez, 2,475	F 6
Gálvez, 7,891	F 6
Gan Gan, 381	C 5
General Acha, 4,709	C 4
General Alvarado, 3,537	E 4
General Alvear, Buenos Aires, 2,548	F 7
General Alvear, Mendoza, 12,325	C 3
General Arenales, 2,182	F 7
General Belgrano, 3,789	G 7
General Campos, 1,400	G 5
General Conesa, 716	C 5
General Galarza, 2,435	G 6
General Juan Madariaga, 7,073	E 4
General José de San Martín, 5,390	E 2
General La Madrid, 3,572	D 4
General Las Heras, 3,820	G 7
General Lavalle, 1,663	E 4
Gral. M. M. de Güemes, 8,748	D 1
General O'Brien, 2,988	F 7
General Paz, 1,689	C 2
General Pico, 11,121	D 4
General Roca, 21,969	C 4
General San Martín, 2,501	D 4
General Villegas, 4,738	D 4
Gobernador Crespo, 6,000	F 5
Gobernador Gregores, 772	C 6
Gobernador Mansilla, 947	G 6
Godoy Cruz, 80,024	C 3
Goya, 30,011	G 4
Gualeguay, 16,542	G 6
Gualeguaychú, 29,863	G 6
Guandacol, 1,255	C 2
Guardia Mitre, 746	D 5
Guatrache, 1,259	D 4
Guaymallén, 85,718	C 3
Hasenkamp, 1,789	F 5
Helvecia, 3,390	F 5
Hernández, 283	F 6
Hernando, 4,869	D 3
He-radura, 1,679	E 2
Herrera, 1,685	D 2
Huinca Renancó, 4,391	D 3
Humahuaca, 2,530	C 1
Humberto, 3,434	F 5
Ibarreta, 4,366	D 2
Ibicuy, 3,356	G 6
Icaño, Catamarca, 1,114	C 2
Icaño, Santiago del Estero, 1,926	D 2
Iglesia, 575	C 3
Ingeniero Huergo, 3,083	C 4
Ingeniero Jacobacci, 2,656	C 5
Ingeniero Luiggi, 1,665	D 4
Intendente Alvear, 2,760	D 4
Irigoyen, 3,500	F 6
Itacaruaré, 422	F 2
Jáchal, 6,886	C 3
Jaramillo, 437	C 6
Jesús María, 6,284	D 3
Joaquín V. González, 3,274	D 2
Jobson, 7,667	F 5
José de San Martín, 1,143	B 5
José M. Micheo, 1,165	G 7
Juan B. Arruabarrena, 1,997	G 5
Juan B. Molino, 1,483	F 6
Juan Ortíz, 6,240	F 6
Juan Pujol, 625	G 5
Juárez, 7,602	D 4
Jujuy, 44,188	C 1
Juncal, 943	F 7
Junín, 36,149	F 7
Junín de los Andes, 1,183	B 4
La Banda, 23,772	D 2
Labougle, 503	G 5
Laboulaye, 9,032	D 3
La Clarita, 389	G 5
La Cumbre, 3,961	C 3
La Esmeralda, 348	D 2
La Falda, 2,847	D 3
La Gallareta, 3,736	F 5
Lago Argentino (El Calafate), 567	B 7
Laguna Paiva, 7,196	F 5
Lanús, 381,561	G 7
La Paz, Entre Ríos, 11,028	G 5
La Paz, Mendoza, 2,502	C 3
La Plata, †330,310	H 7
La Quiaca, 6,290	C 1
La Rioja, 35,431	C 2
Las Flores, 9,287	E 4
Las Lajas, 1,805	B 4
Las Lomitas, 1,650	D 1
Las Palmas, 3,590	E 2
Las Parejas, 1,973	F 6
Las Plumas, 182	C 5
Las Rosas, 6,153	F 6
Las Varillas, 5,950	D 3
La Toma, 2,352	G 4
Lavalle, 1,571	G 4
Leleque, 401	B 5
Lezama, 1,962	H 7
Libertador General San Martín, Jujuy, 5,051	D 1
Libertador General San Martín, Misiones, 2,267	E 2
Lincoln, 12,695	F 4
Lobería, 7,916	E 4
Lobos, 8,372	G 7
Lomas de Zamora, †275,219	G 7
Loncopué, 856	B 4
Los Antiguos, 709	B 6
Los Menucos, 1,749	C 5
Los-Toldos, 5,342	F 7
Lucas González, 1,145	G 6
Luján, 19,176	G 7
Lules, 4,828	C 2
Macachín, 1,793	D 4
Maciel, 1,832	F 6
Magdalena, 4,114	H 7
Maipú, 5,469	E 4
Makallé, 1,462	E 2
Malabrigo, 1,532	F 4
Malargüe, 4,523	C 4
Manucho, 2,800	F 5
Maquinchao, 1,851	C 5
Mar del Plata, 141,886	E 4
Marcos Juárez, 9,556	D 3
Marcos Paz, 4,115	G 7
Margarita, 1,461	F 5
María Grande, 2,819	F 5
Mburucuyá, 2,555	E 2
Médanos, Buenos Aires, 2,229	D 4
Médanos, Entre Ríos, 647	G 6
Mencué, 208	C 5
Mendoza, 109,122	C 3
Mercedes, Buenos Aires, 16,932	G 7

(continued on following page)

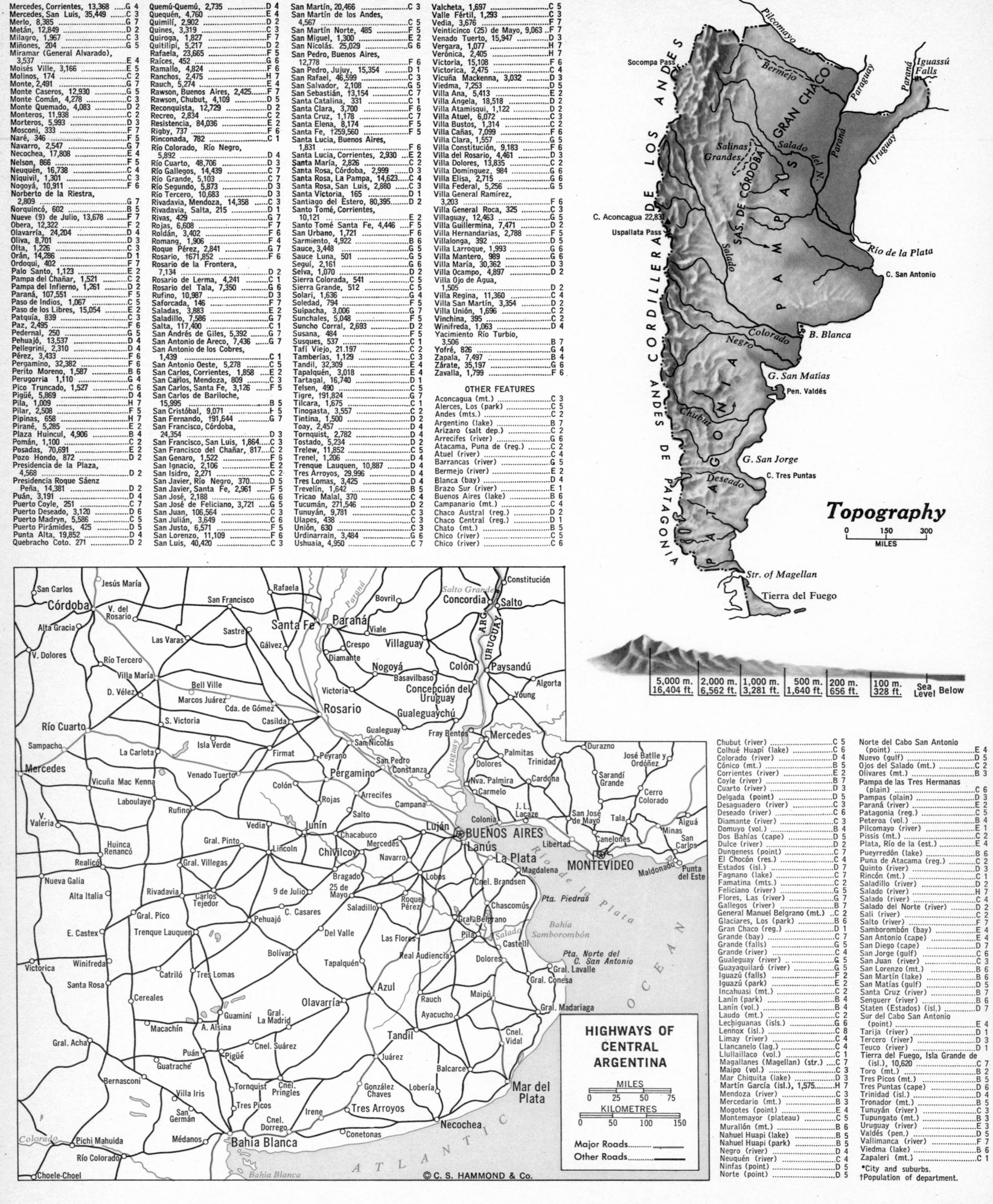

Mercedes, Corrientes, 13,368 ...G 4
Mercedes, San Luis, 35,449 ...C 3
Merlo, 8,385 ...D 2
Metán, 12,849 ...D 2
Milagro, 1,967 ...G 5
Miñones, 204 ...G 5
Miramar (General Alvarado), 3,537 ...E 5
Moisés Ville, 3,166 ...E 5
Molinos, 174 ...G 2
Monte, 2,491 ...G 2
Monte Caseros, 12,930 ...G 5
Monte Comán, 4,278 ...C 4
Monte Quemado, 4,083 ...D 2
Monteros, 11,938 ...D 3
Morteros, 5,993 ...D 3
Mosconi, 333 ...F 5
Naré, 346 ...G 7
Navarro, 2,547 ...G 7
Necochea, 17,808 ...F 5
Nelson, 866 ...F 5
Neuquén, 16,738 ...C 4
Niquivil, 1,301 ...G 5
Nogoyá, 10,911 ...F 6
Norberto de la Riestra, 2,809 ...G 7
Norquincó, 602 ...B 5
Nueve (9) de Julio, 13,678 ...D 3
Obera, 12,322 ...G 4
Olavarría, 24,204 ...D 4
Oliva, 8,701 ...D 3
Olta, 1,173 ...C 4
Orán, 14,286 ...D 1
Ordoqui, 402 ...F 7
Palo Santo, 1,123 ...E 2
Pampa del Chañar, 1,521 ...E 2
Pampa del Infierno, 1,261 ...D 2
Paraná, 107,551 ...F 6
Paso de Indios, 1,067 ...B 5
Paso de los Libres, 15,054 ...E 2
Patquía, 839 ...C 3
Paz, 2,495 ...F 6
Pedernal, 250 ...D 4
Pehuajó, 13,537 ...D 4
Pellegrini, 2,310 ...D 4
Pérez, 3,433 ...F 6
Pergamino, 32,382 ...F 6
Perito Moreno, 1,587 ...B 6
Perugorria, 1,110 ...G 4
Pico Truncado, 1,527 ...C 6
Pigüé, 5,869 ...D 4
Pila, 1,009 ...H 7
Pilar, 2,508 ...G 7
Pipinas, 658 ...H 7
Piraré, 5,285 ...G 4
Plaza Huincul, 4,906 ...B 4
Pomán, 1,100 ...C 2
Posadas, 70,691 ...G 4
Pozo Hondo, 872 ...D 2
Presidencia de la Plaza, 4,568 ...E 2
Presidencia Roque Sáenz Peña, 14,381 ...D 2
Puán, 3,191 ...D 4
Puerto Coyle, 251 ...C 7
Puerto Deseado, 3,120 ...D 6
Puerto Madryn, 5,586 ...C 5
Puerto Pirámides, 425 ...D 5
Punta Alta, 19,852 ...D 4
Quebracho Coto. 271 ...D 2

Quemú-Quemú, 2,735 ...D 4
Quequén, 4,760 ...E 4
Quimilí, 2,902 ...D 2
Quines, 3,319 ...C 3
Quiroga, 1,827 ...F 7
Quitilipi, 5,217 ...E 2
Rafaela, 23,665 ...F 5
Raíces, 452 ...G 6
Ramallo, 2,475 ...H 7
Ranchos, 2,475 ...E 4
Rauch, 5,274 ...E 4
Rawson, Buenos Aires, 2,425 ...F 7
Rawson, Chubut, 4,109 ...D 5
Reconquista, 12,729 ...F 2
Recreo, 2,834 ...D 2
Resistencia, 84,036 ...E 2
Rigby, 737 ...F 6
Rinconada, 782 ...C 1
Río Colorado, Río Negro, 5,892 ...D 4
Río Cuarto, 48,760 ...D 3
Río Gallegos, 14,439 ...C 7
Río Grande, 5,103 ...C 7
Río Segundo, 5,873 ...D 3
Río Tercero, 10,683 ...D 3
Rivadavia, Mendoza, 14,358 ...C 3
Rivadavia, Salta, 215 ...D 1
Rojas, 6,608 ...F 7
Roldán, 3,402 ...F 6
Romang, 1,906 ...F 5
Roque Pérez, 2,841 ...G 7
Rosario, 1671,852 ...F 6
Rosario de la Frontera, 7,134 ...D 2
Rosario de Lerma, 4,241 ...C 1
Rosario del Tala, 7,350 ...G 6
Rufino, 10,987 ...D 3
Saforcada, 146 ...F 7
Saladas, 3,883 ...G 4
Saladillo, 7,586 ...G 7
Salta, 117,400 ...C 1
San Andrés de Giles, 5,392 ...G 7
San Antonio de Areco, 7,436 ...G 7
San Antonio de los Cobres, 1,439 ...C 1
San Antonio Oeste, 5,278 ...C 5
San Carlos, Corrientes, 1,858 ...E 2
San Carlos, Mendoza, 809 ...C 3
San Carlos, Santa Fe, 3,126 ...F 5
San Carlos de Bariloche, 15,995 ...B 5
San Cristóbal, 9,071 ...F 5
San Fernando, 191,644 ...G 7
San Francisco, Córdoba, 24,354 ...D 3
San Francisco de San Luis, 1,864 ...C 3
San Francisco del Chañar, 817 ...D 2
San Genaro, 1,522 ...F 6
San Ignacio, 2,106 ...G 4
San Isidro, 2,271 ...G 7
San Javier, Río Negro, 370 ...D 5
San Javier, Santa Fe, 2,961 ...F 5
San José, 2,188 ...G 6
San José de Feliciano, 3,721 ...G 6
San Juan, 106,564 ...C 3
San Julián, 3,649 ...C 7
San Justo, 6,571 ...F 5
San Lorenzo, 11,109 ...F 6
San Luis, 40,420 ...C 3

San Martín, 20,466 ...C 3
San Martín de los Andes, 4,567 ...C 3
San Martín Norte, 485 ...F 5
San Miguel, 1,300 ...E 2
San Nicolás, 25,029 ...F 6
San Pedro, Buenos Aires, 12,778 ...F 6
San Pedro, Jujuy, 15,354 ...D 1
San Rafael, 46,599 ...C 3
San Salvador, 2,108 ...G 6
San Sebastián, 13,154 ...C 7
Santa Catalina, 331 ...C 1
Santa Clara, 3,700 ...F 6
Santa Cruz, 1,178 ...C 7
Santa Elena, 8,174 ...F 5
Santa Fe, 1,259,560 ...F 5
Santa Lucía, Buenos Aires, 1,831 ...F 6
Santa Lucía, Corrientes, 2,930 ...C 2
Santa María, 2,826 ...C 2
Santa Rosa, Córdoba, 2,999 ...D 3
Santa Rosa, La Pampa, 14,623 ...C 4
Santa Rosa, San Luis, 2,880 ...C 3
Santa Victoria, 165 ...D 1
Santiago del Estero, 80,395 ...D 2
Santo Tomé, Corrientes, 10,121 ...E 2
Santo Tomé Santa Fe, 4,446 ...F 5
San Urbano, 1,721 ...F 6
Sarmiento, 4,922 ...B 6
Sauce, 3,448 ...G 5
Sauce Luna, 501 ...G 5
Seguí, 2,161 ...G 6
Selva, 1,070 ...D 2
Sierra Colorada, 541 ...C 5
Sierra Grande, 512 ...C 5
Solari, 1,636 ...G 4
Soledad, 794 ...F 5
Suipacha, 3,006 ...G 7
Sunchales, 5,048 ...F 5
Suncho Corral, 2,693 ...D 2
Susana, 484 ...F 5
Susques, 537 ...C 1
Tafí Viejo, 21,197 ...C 2
Tamberías, 1,129 ...C 3
Tandil, 32,309 ...E 4
Tapalqué, 3,018 ...D 4
Tartagal, 16,740 ...D 1
Telsen, 490 ...C 5
Tigre, 191,824 ...G 7
Tilcara, 1,675 ...C 1
Tinogasta, 3,557 ...C 2
Tintina, 1,500 ...D 2
Toay, 2,457 ...C 4
Tornquist, 2,782 ...D 4
Tostado, 5,234 ...E 2
Trelew, 11,852 ...C 5
Trenel, 1,206 ...C 4
Trenque Lauquen, 10,887 ...D 4
Tres Arroyos, 29,996 ...E 4
Tres Lomas, 3,425 ...D 4
Trevelín, 1,642 ...B 5
Tricao Malal, 370 ...C 4
Tucumán, 271,546 ...C 2
Tunuyán, 9,781 ...C 3
Ulapes, 438 ...C 3
Unión, 630 ...D 3
Urdinarrain, 3,484 ...G 6
Ushuaia, 4,950 ...C 7

Valcheta, 1,697 ...C 5
Valle Fértil, 1,293 ...C 3
Vedia, 3,676 ...F 7
Veinticinco (25) de Mayo, 9,063 ...F 7
Venado Tuerto, 15,947 ...E 3
Vergara, 1,077 ...H 7
Verónica, 2,405 ...H 7
Victoria, 15,108 ...F 6
Victorica, 2,475 ...C 4
Vicuña Mackenna, 3,032 ...D 3
Viedma, 7,253 ...D 5
Villa Ana, 5,413 ...E 2
Villa Ángela, 18,518 ...D 2
Villa Atamisqui, 1,122 ...D 2
Villa Atuel, 6,072 ...C 4
Villa Bustos, 1,314 ...D 2
Villa Cañas, 7,099 ...F 6
Villa Clara, 1,557 ...G 5
Villa Constitución, 9,183 ...F 6
Villa del Rosario, 4,461 ...D 3
Villa Dolores, 13,835 ...C 2
Villa Domínguez, 984 ...G 6
Villa Elisa, 2,715 ...G 6
Villa Federal, 5,256 ...G 5
Villa General Ramírez, 3,203 ...F 6
Villa General Roca, 325 ...C 3
Villaguay, 12,463 ...F 6
Villa Guillermina, 7,471 ...F 5
Villa Hernandarias, 2,788 ...F 5
Villalonga, 392 ...C 5
Villa Larroque, 1,993 ...G 6
Villa Mantero, 989 ...G 6
Villa María, 30,362 ...D 3
Villa Ocampo, 4,897 ...D 2
Villa Ojo de Agua, 1,505 ...D 2
Villa Regina, 11,360 ...C 4
Villa San Martín, 3,354 ...D 2
Villa Unión, 1,696 ...C 2
Vinchina, 395 ...C 2
Winifreda, 1,063 ...D 4
Yacimiento Río Turbio, 3,506 ...B 7
Yofré, 826 ...B 4
Zapala, 7,497 ...B 4
Zárate, 35,197 ...G 6
Zavalla, 1,799 ...F 6

OTHER FEATURES

Aconcagua (mt.) ...C 3
Alerces, Los (park) ...C 5
Andes (mts.) ...C 2
Argentino (lake) ...B 7
Arizaro (salt dep.) ...C 1
Arrecifes (river) ...G 6
Atacama, Puna de (reg.) ...C 4
Atuel (river) ...C 4
Barrancas (river) ...C 4
Bermejo (river) ...E 2
Blanca (bay) ...D 5
Brazo Sur (river) ...E 1
Buenos Aires (lake) ...B 6
Campanario (mt.) ...C 4
Chaco Austral (reg.) ...D 2
Chaco Central (reg.) ...D 1
Chato (mt.) ...B 5
Chico (river) ...C 5
Chico (river) ...C 6

Chubut (river) ...C 5
Colhué Huapí (lake) ...C 6
Colorado (river) ...D 4
Cónico (mt.) ...B 5
Corrientes (river) ...E 2
Coyle (river) ...B 7
Cuarto (river) ...D 3
Delgada (point) ...D 5
Desaguadero (river) ...C 3
Deseado (river) ...C 6
Diamante (river) ...C 4
Domuyo (vol.) ...B 4
Dos Bahías (cape) ...D 5
Dulce (river) ...D 2
Dungeness (point) ...C 7
El Chocón (res.) ...C 4
Estados (isl.) ...D 7
Fagnano (lake) ...C 7
Famatina (mts.) ...C 2
Feliciano (river) ...G 5
Flores, Las (river) ...G 7
Gallegos (river) ...B 7
General Manuel Belgrano (mt.) ...C 2
Glaciares, Los (park) ...B 7
Gran Chaco (reg.) ...D 1
Grande (bay) ...C 7
Grande (falls) ...C 4
Grande (river) ...C 4
Gualeguay (river) ...G 6
Guayaquirái (river) ...G 4
Iguazú (falls) ...F 2
Iguazú (park) ...E 2
Incahuasi (mt.) ...C 2
Lanín (park) ...B 4
Lanín (mt.) ...B 4
Laudo (mt.) ...C 2
Lechiguanas (isls.) ...G 6
Lennox (isl.) ...C 7
Limay (river) ...C 4
Llancanelo (lag.) ...C 4
Llullaillaco (vol.) ...C 1
Magallanes (Magellan) (str.) ...C 7
Maipo (vol.) ...B 3
Mar Chiquita (lake) ...D 3
Martín García (isl.), 1,575 ...H 7
Mendoza (river) ...C 3
Mercedario (mt.) ...B 3
Mogotes (point) ...E 4
Montemayor (plateau) ...C 5
Muralión (mt.) ...B 6
Nahuel Huapí (lake) ...B 5
Nahuel Huapí (park) ...B 5
Negro (river) ...D 4
Neuquén (river) ...C 4
Ninfas (point) ...D 5
Norte (point) ...D 5

Norte del Cabo San Antonio (point) ...E 4
Nuevo (gulf) ...D 5
Ojos del Salado (mt.) ...C 2
Olivares (mt.) ...B 3
Pampa de las Tres Hermanas (plain) ...C 6
Pampas (plain) ...D 3
Paraná (river) ...F 2
Patagonia (reg.) ...B 5
Peteroa (vol.) ...B 4
Pilcomayo (river) ...E 1
Pissis (mt.) ...C 2
Plata, Río de la (est.) ...E 4
Pueyrredón (lake) ...B 6
Puna de Atacama (reg.) ...C 1
Quinto (river) ...D 3
Rincón (mt.) ...C 3
Saladillo (river) ...D 4
Salado (river) ...H 7
Salado (river) ...D 2
Salado del Norte (river) ...D 2
Sali (river) ...C 2
Salto (river) ...D 1
Samborombón (bay) ...E 4
San Antonio (cape) ...E 4
San Diego (cape) ...C 7
San Jorge (gulf) ...C 6
San Juan (river) ...C 3
San Lorenzo (mt.) ...B 6
San Martín (lake) ...B 6
San Matías (gulf) ...D 5
Santa Cruz (river) ...B 7
Senguerr (river) ...C 6
Staten (Estados) (isl.) ...D 7
Sur del Cabo San Antonio (point) ...E 4
Tarija (river) ...D 1
Tercero (river) ...D 3
Teuco (river) ...D 1
Tierra del Fuego, Isla Grande de (isl.), 10,620 ...C 7
Toro (mt.) ...B 3
Tres Picos (mt.) ...D 4
Tres Puntas (cape) ...D 6
Trinidad (isl.) ...D 5
Tronador (mt.) ...B 5
Tunuyán (river) ...C 3
Tupungato (mt.) ...B 3
Uruguay (river) ...F 7
Valdés (pen.) ...D 5
Vallimanca (river) ...F 7
Viedma (lake) ...B 6
Zapaleri (mt.) ...C 1

*City and suburbs.
†Population of department.

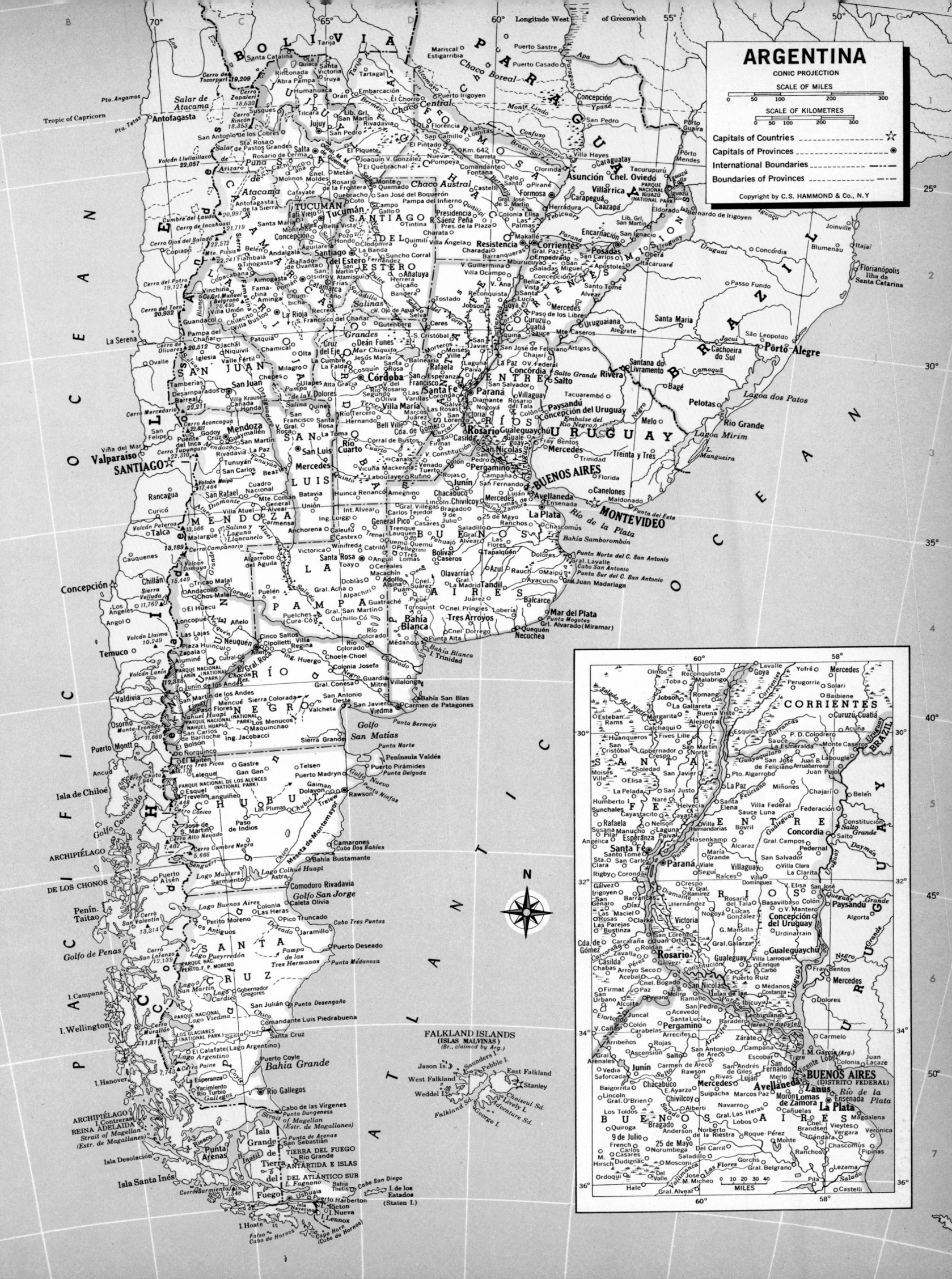

ARGENTINA

CONIC PROJECTION

SCALE OF MILES

0 50 100   200   300

SCALE OF KILOMETRES

0 50 100   200   300

Capitals of Countries _____ ☆
Capitals of Provinces _____ ◉
International Boundaries _____
Boundaries of Provinces _____

Copyright by C.S. HAMMOND & Co., N.Y

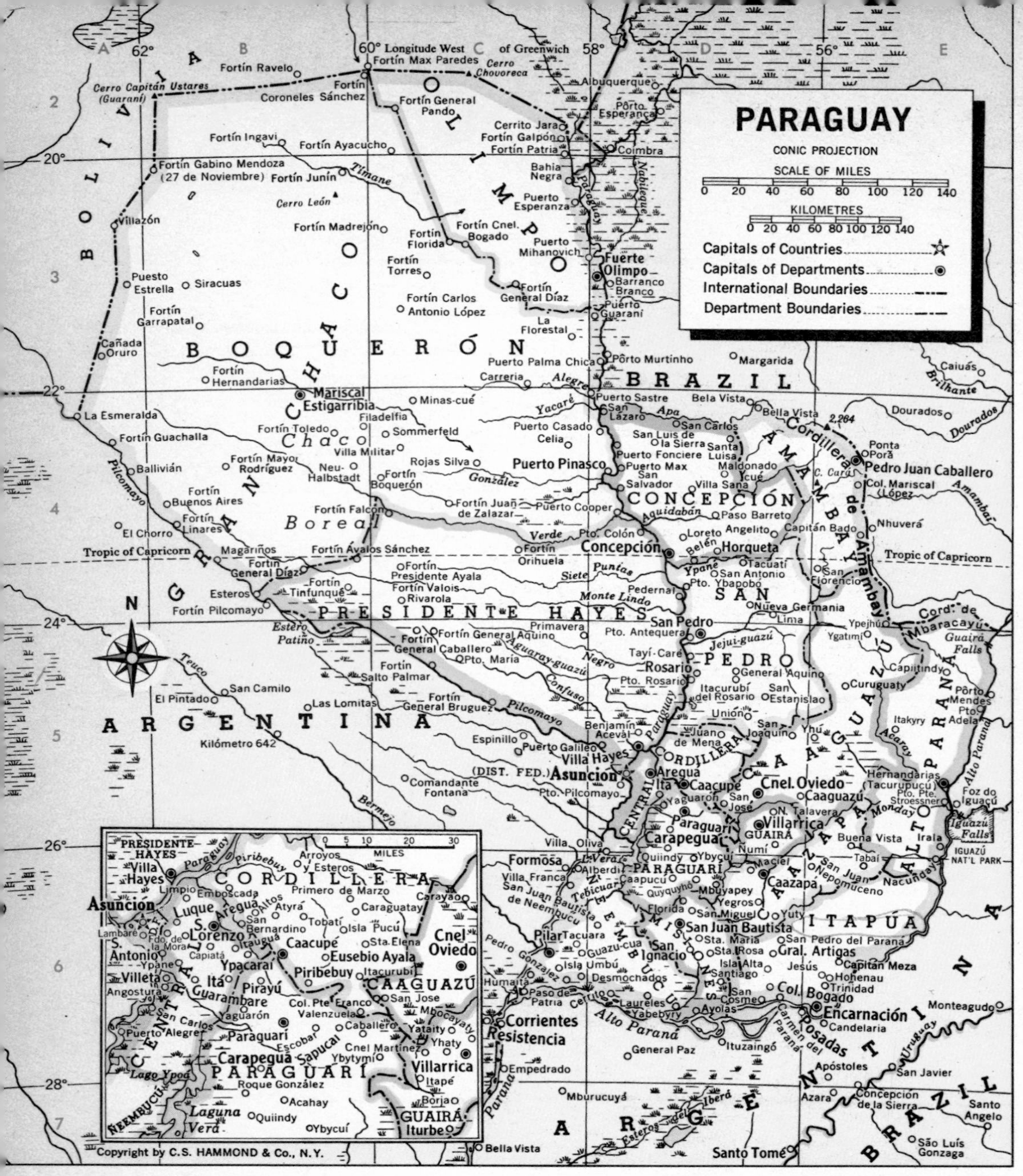

PARAGUAY

CONIC PROJECTION

SCALE OF MILES

0 20 40 60 80 100 120 140

KILOMETRES

0 20 40 60 80 100 120 140

⭐ Capitals of Countries

◉ Capitals of Departments

International Boundaries

Department Boundaries

PARAGUAY

DEPARTMENTS

Alto Paraná, 24,067	E 5
Amambay, 34,505	E 4
Boquerón, 40,405	B 3
Caaguazú, 125,138	D 6
Caazapá, 92,401	D 6
Central, 229,073	A 6
Concepción, 85,690	D 4
Cordillera, 188,313	D 5
Distrito Federal, 288,882	A 6
Guairá, 114,949	D 6
Itapúa, 149,821	E 6
Misiones, 59,441	D 6
Ñeembucú, 57,878	D 5
Olimpo, 3,854	C 3
Paraguarí, 203,012	D 6
Presidente Hayes, 29,870	C 5
San Pedro, 91,804	D 5

CITIES and TOWNS

Acahay, 2,622	B 7
Alberdi, 1,787	B 7
Altos, 1,348	B 6
Areguá, 3,699	B 6
Arroyos y Esteros, 1,447	B 6
Asunción (cap.), 350,000	A 6
Atyrá, 1,246	D 6
Ayolas, 321	D 6
Bahía Negra 415	C 3
Belén, 2,523	D 4
Bella Vista, 2,331	D 4
Benjamín Aceval, 3,463	D 5
Borja, 625	C 7
Buena Vista, 1,954	C 6
Caacupé, 6,329	B 6
Caaguazú, 2,291	E 5
Caapucú, 1,513	C 6
Caazapá, 3,079	D 6
Caballero, 1,553	C 6
Cañada Oruro, †442	A 3
Capiatá, 2,062	B 6
Capitán Bado, 257	E 4
Capitán Meza, 306	E 6
Caraguatay, 1,935	D 6
Carapeguá, 2,628	B 6
Carayaó, 1,376	C 6
Carmen del Paraná, 1,813	D 6
Cerrito, 801	C 5
Concepción, 33,500	D 4
Corone Bogado, 3,885	D 6
Coronel Martínez, 1,270	C 6
Coronel Oviedo, 9,468	C 6
Curuguaty, 497	E 5
Desmochados, 681	C 6
Emboscada, 1,040	B 6
Encarnación, 35,000	E 6
Escobar, 567	C 6
Eusebio Ayala, 2,532	C 6
Fernando de la Mora, 10,194	A 6
Filadelfia, 12,639	C 4
Fortín General Díaz, Boquerón, †508	B 4
Fuerte Olimpo, 2,588	D 3
General Aquino, 1,162	D 5
General Artigas, 3,450	E 6
Guarambaré, 3,167	A 6
Guazú-cuá, 153	D 6
Hernandarias, 1,646	E 5
Hohenau, 1,877	E 6
Horqueta, 5,095	D 4
Humaitá, 781	C 6
Irala, 295	E 5
Isla Pucú, 1,938	B 6
Isla Umbú, 202	C 6
Itá, 6,265	B 6
Itacurubí de la Cordillera, 2,137	C 6
Itacurubí del Rosario, 1,776	D 5
Itakyry, 788	E 5
Itapé, 1,235	C 6
Itauguá, 3,064	B 6
Iturbe, 3,274	C 7
Jesús, 1,814	D 6
Juan de Mena, 1,450	D 6
Lambaré, 8,300	B 6
Laureles, 380	D 6
Lima, 751	D 5
Limpio, 1,438	B 6
Loreto, 1,866	D 4
Luque, 11,008	B 6
Maciel, 400	D 6
Mariscal Estigarribia, 1,824	B 4
Mbocayaty, 701	C 6
Mbuyapey, 1,310	C 6
Ñacunday, †119	E 6
Natalicio Talavera, 1,020	D 5

Nueva Germania, 511	D 4
Ñumí, 346	D 5
Paraguarí, 4,880	C 6
Paso de Patria, 608	C 6
Pedro González, 377	E 4
Pedro Juan Caballero, 10,355	E 4
Pilar, 10,500	C 6
Pirayú, 2,753	B 6
Piribebuy, 4,038	B 6
Primero de Marzo, 672	C 6
Puerto Adela, 46	E 5
Puerto Antequera, 1,123	D 5
Puerto Casado, 1,891	C 4
Puerto Guaraní, 1,055	C 3
Puerto Mihanovich, 132	C 3
Puerto Pinasco, 3,872	C 4
Puerto Presidente Stroessner, †764	E 5
Puerto Sastre, 1,408	C 4
Quiindí, 2,851	B 7
Quyuyhó,, 1,168	C 6
Roque González, 1,436	B 7
Rosario, 3,313	D 5
San Antonio, Central, 4,247	B 6
San Bernardino, 570	B 6
San Carlos, Concepción, 870	D 4
San Cosme, 554	D 6
San Estanislao, 3,569	D 5
San Ignacio, 5,141	D 6
San Joaquín, 421	C 6
San José, 2,802	B 6
San Juan Bautista, 5,972	D 6
San Juan Bautista de Ñeembucú, 454	C 6
San Juan Nepomuceno, 3,118	D 6
San Lázaro, 807	D 4
San Lorenzo, 8,593	A 6
San Miguel, 1,034	D 6
San Pedro, 3,306	D 5
San Pedro del Paraná, 2,263	D 6
San Salvador, 1,569	C 6
Santa Elena, 1,364	C 6
Santa María, 754	D 6
Santa Rosa, 2,641	D 6
Santiago, 1,689	D 6
Sapucaí, 1,708	B 6
Tabaí, 528	E
Tacuara, 54	D 6
Tacuatí, 615	D 5
Tacurupucú (Hernandarias), 2,311	E 5
Tobatí, 2,520	B 6
Trinidad, 518	E 6
Unión, 806	D 5
Valenzuela, 994	D 6
Villa Florida, 1,141	D 6
Villa Franca, 374	C 6
Villa Hayes, 4,712	A 6
Villa Oliva, 813	A 6
Villarrica, 30,500	C 6
Villeta, 3,020	A 6
Yabebyry, 486	C 6
Yaguarón, 2,763	B 6
Yataity, 1,050	C 6
Ybycuí, 3,056	B 7
Ybytimí, 1,410	B 6
Yegros, 1,158	C 6
Ygatimí, 370	E 5
Yhú, 1,240	D 6
Ypacaraí, 5,281	B 6
Ypané, 1,469	A 6
Ypejhú, 64	E 4
Yuty, 2,573	C 7

OTHER FEATURES

Acaray (river)	E 5
Aguaray-guazú (river)	C 5
Alegre (river)	C 3
Alto Paraná (river)	E 5
Amambay, Cord. de (mts.)	E 4
Apa (river)	D 4
Aquidabán (river)	D 4
Capitán Ustarés (hill)	B 4
Cará (mt.)	E 4
Chaco Boreal (reg.)	B 4
Chovoreca (hill)	C 2
Confuso (river)	C 5
González (river)	C 4
Gran Chaco (reg.)	B 5
Guairá (falls)	E 5
Guaraní (Cap. Ustarés) (hill)	B 4
León (mt.)	D 4
Mbaracayú (mts.)	E 4
Monday (river)	E 5
Monte Lindo (river)	C 4
Negro (river)	D 5
Paraguay (river)	C 5
Pilcomayo (river)	C 5
Siete Puntas (river)	C 4
Tebicuary (river)	D 6

Copyright by C.S. HAMMOND & Co., N.Y.

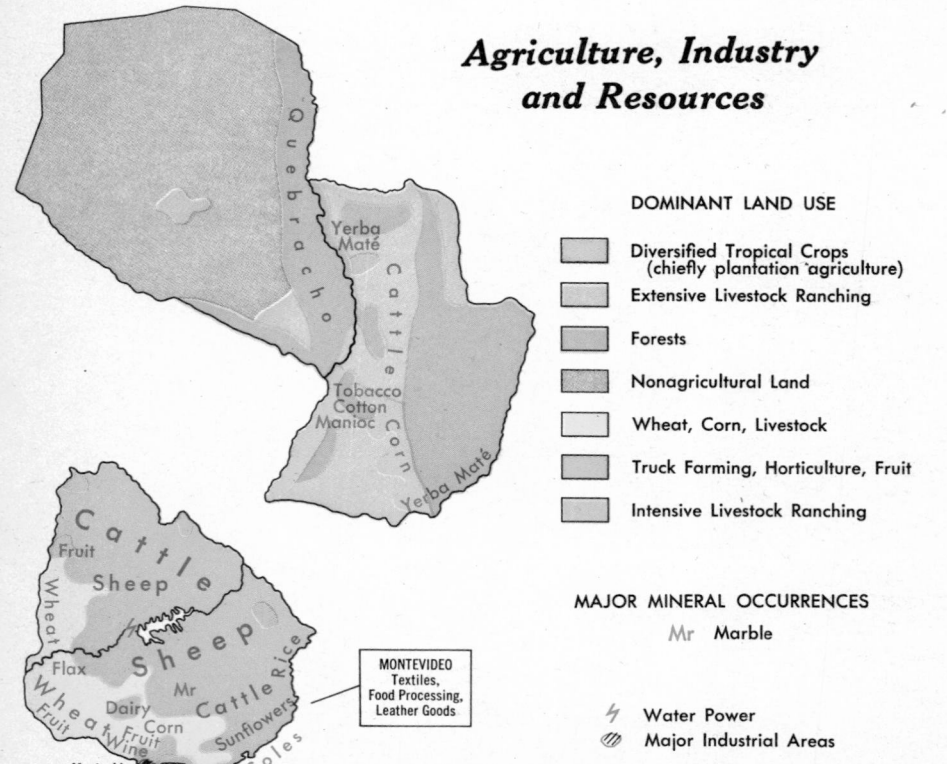

Agriculture, Industry and Resources

DOMINANT LAND USE

Diversified Tropical Crops (chiefly plantation agriculture)

Extensive Livestock Ranching

Forests

Nonagricultural Land

Wheat, Corn, Livestock

Truck Farming, Horticulture, Fruit

Intensive Livestock Ranching

MAJOR MINERAL OCCURRENCES

Mr Marble

MONTEVIDEO Textiles, Food Processing, Leather Goods

⚡ Water Power

Major Industrial Areas

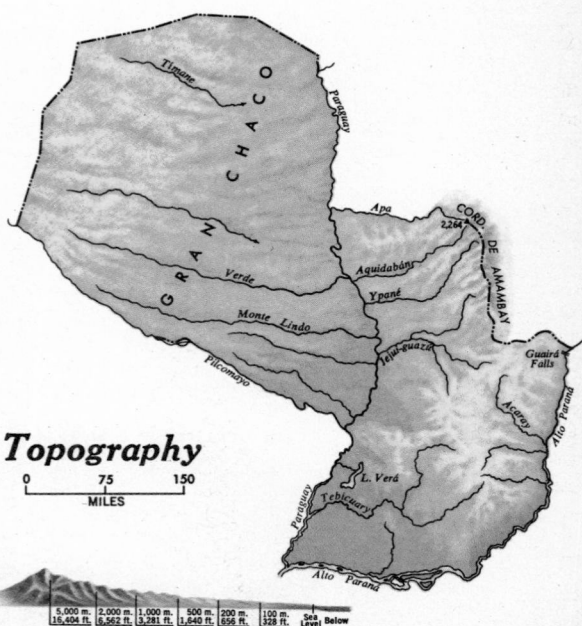

Topography

0 75 150

MILES

5,000 m. 2,000 m. 1,000 m. 500 m. 200 m. 100 m. Sea Below
16,404 ft. 6,562 ft. 3,281 ft. 1,640 ft. 656 ft. 328 ft. Level

PARAGUAY

AREA 157,047 sq. mi.
POPULATION 2,314,000
CAPITAL Asunción
LARGEST CITY Asunción
HIGHEST POINT Amambay Range 2,264 ft.
MONETARY UNIT guaraní
MAJOR LANGUAGES Spanish, Guaraní
MAJOR RELIGION Roman Catholicism

URUGUAY

AREA 72,172 sq. mi.
POPULATION 2,900,000
CAPITAL Montevideo
LARGEST CITY Montevideo
HIGHEST POINT Mirador Nacional 1,644 ft.
MONETARY UNIT Uruguayan peso
MAJOR LANGUAGE Spanish
MAJOR RELIGION Roman Catholicism

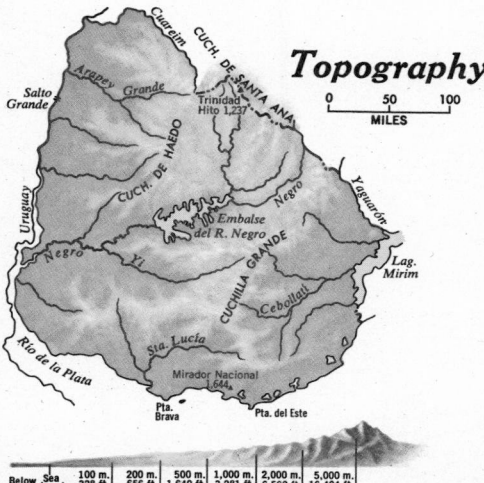

Topography

0   50   100
MILES

Below Sea Level | 100 m. 328 ft. | 200 m. 656 ft. | 500 m. 1,640 ft. | 1,000 m. 3,281 ft. | 2,000 m. 6,562 ft. | 5,000 m. 16,404 ft.

URUGUAY

CONIC PROJECTION

SCALE OF MILES
0   20   40   60

SCALE OF KILOMETRES
0   20   40   60

Capitals of Countries ....☆
Department Capitals ....●
International Boundaries ....
Department Boundaries ....

NORTH AMERICA

LAMBERT AZIMUTHAL EQUAL-AREA PROJECTION

SCALE OF MILES
0 100 200   400   600   800

SCALE OF KILOMETRES
0   200   400   600   800

Capitals of Countries .... ★
International Boundaries .... — · — · —
Other Boundaries .... — — — —
Canals

© C.S. HAMMOND & Co., N.Y.

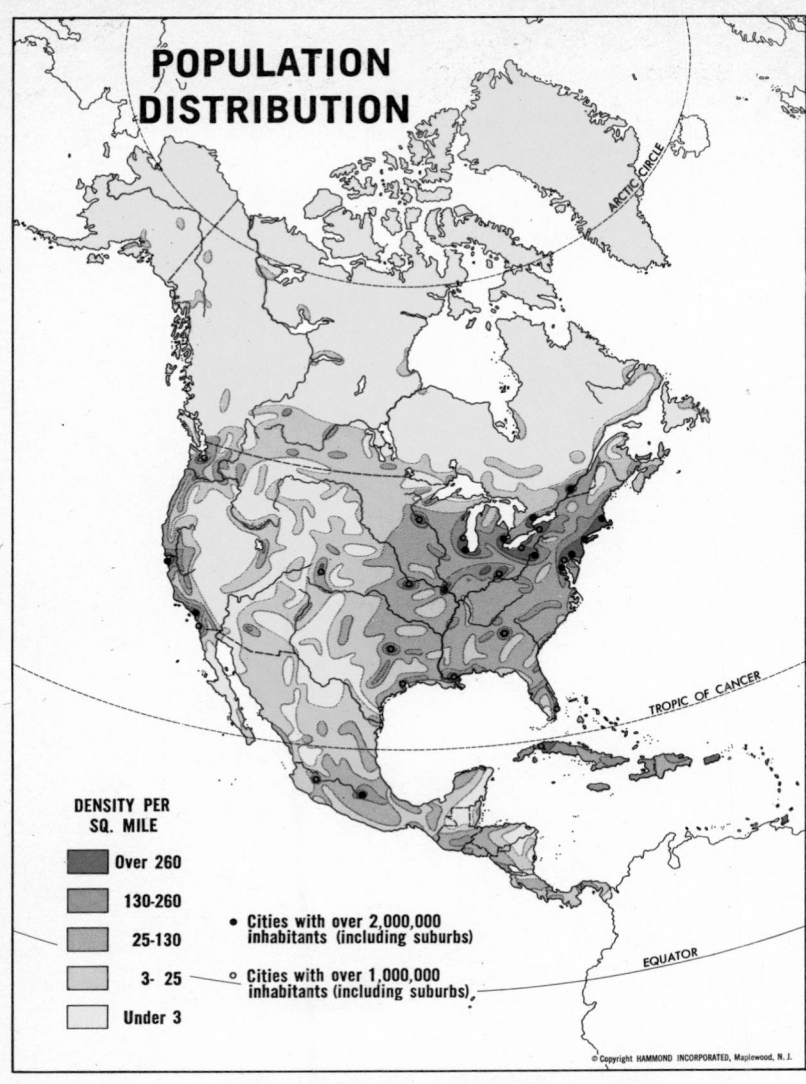

POPULATION DISTRIBUTION

DENSITY PER SQ. MILE
- Over 260
- 130-260
- 25-130
- 3-25
- Under 3

● Cities with over 2,000,000 inhabitants (including suburbs)

○ Cities with over 1,000,000 inhabitants (including suburbs)

ARCTIC CIRCLE

TROPIC OF CANCER

EQUATOR

© Copyright HAMMOND INCORPORATED, Maplewood, N.J.

AREA 9,363,000 sq. mi.
POPULATION 314,000,000
LARGEST CITY New York
HIGHEST POINT Mt. McKinley 20,320 ft
LOWEST POINT Death Valley -282 ft.

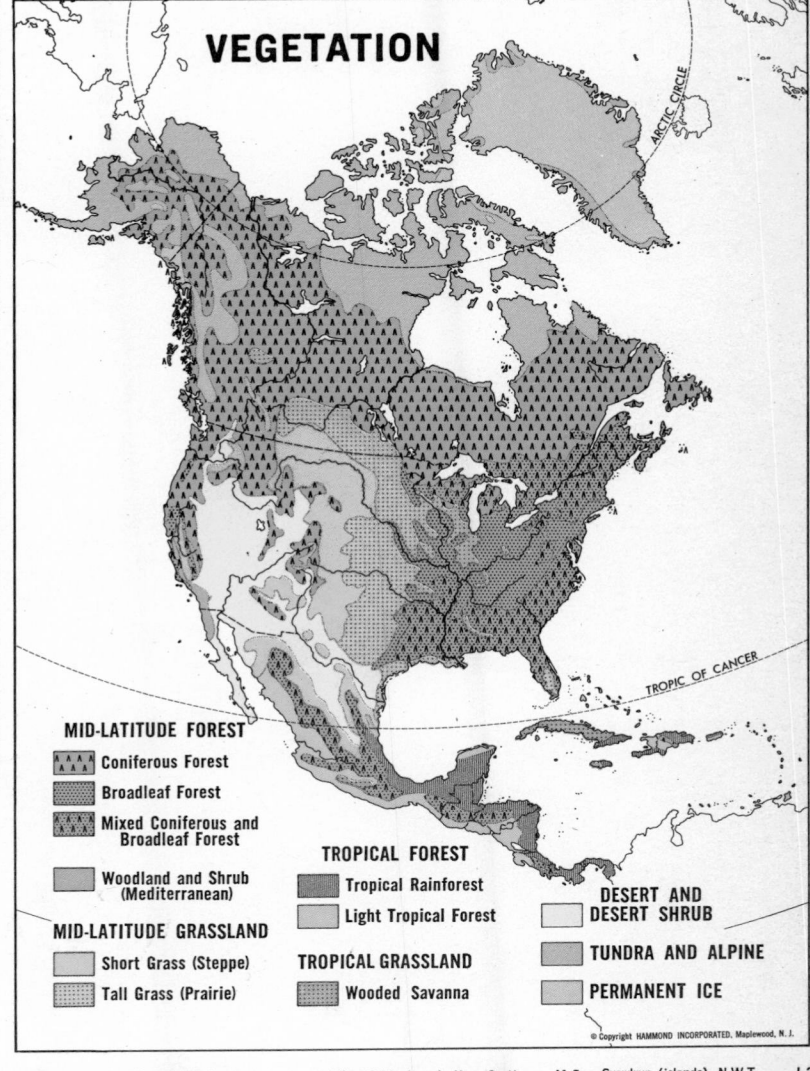

VEGETATION

MID-LATITUDE FOREST
- Coniferous Forest
- Broadleaf Forest
- Mixed Coniferous and Broadleaf Forest
- Woodland and Shrub (Mediterranean)

MID-LATITUDE GRASSLAND
- Short Grass (Steppe)
- Tall Grass (Prairie)

TROPICAL FOREST
- Tropical Rainforest
- Light Tropical Forest

TROPICAL GRASSLAND
- Wooded Savanna

DESERT AND DESERT SHRUB

TUNDRA AND ALPINE

PERMANENT ICE

© Copyright HAMMOND INCORPORATED, Maplewood, N.J.

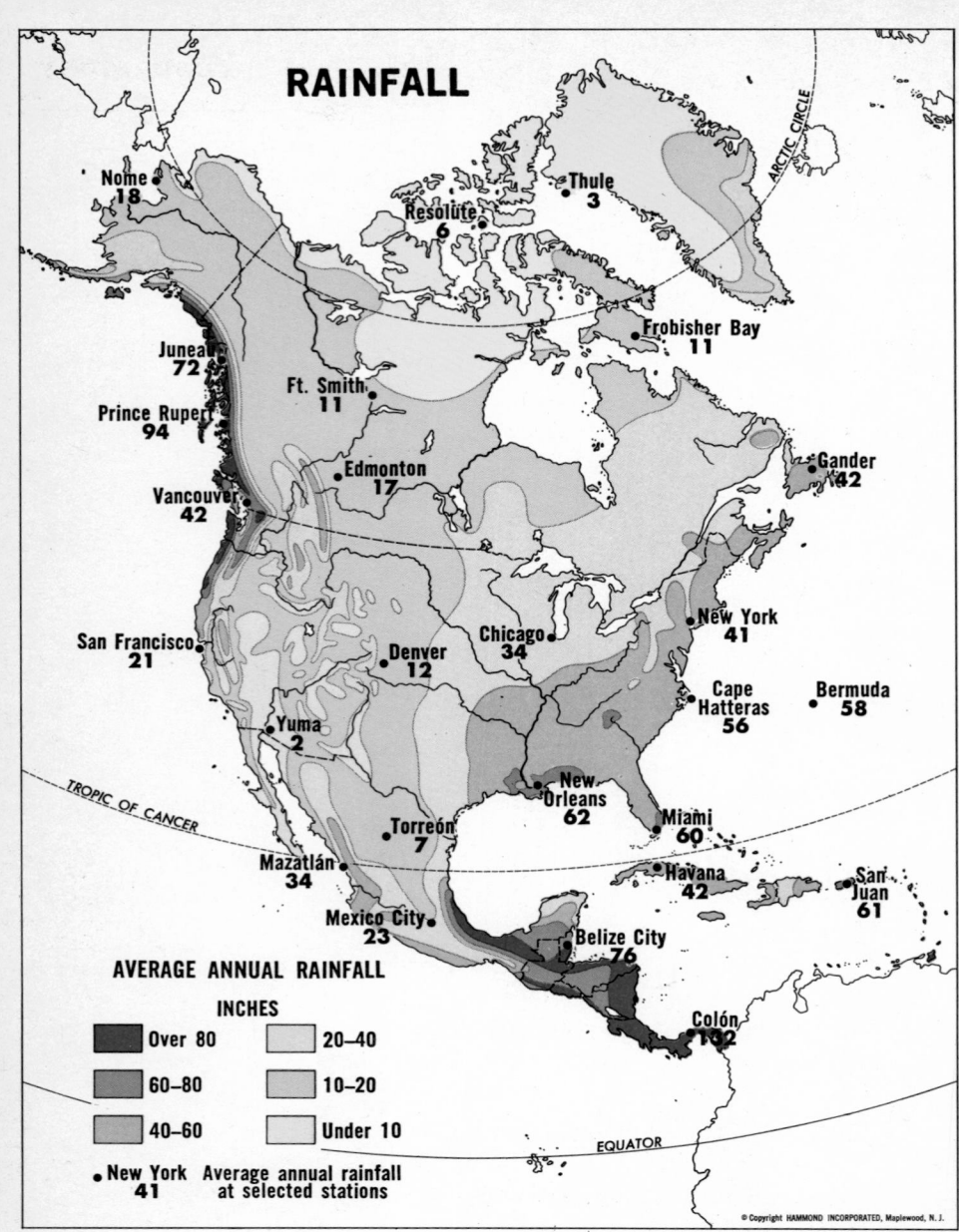

RAINFALL

Nome
18

Thule
3

Resolute
6

Frobisher Bay
11

Juneau
72

Ft. Smith
11

Prince Rupert
94

Gander
42

Vancouver
42

Edmonton
17

San Francisco
21

Denver
12

Chicago
34

New York
41

Cape Hatteras
56

Bermuda
58

Yuma
2

New Orleans
62

Miami
60

Torreón
7

Havana
42

San Juan
61

Mazatlán
34

Mexico City
23

Belize City
76

Colón
152

AVERAGE ANNUAL RAINFALL

INCHES

- Over 80
- 60–80
- 40–60
- 20–40
- 10–20
- Under 10

• New York   Average annual rainfall
  41   at selected stations

TROPIC OF CANCER

EQUATOR

© Copyright HAMMOND INCORPORATED, Maplewood, N.J.

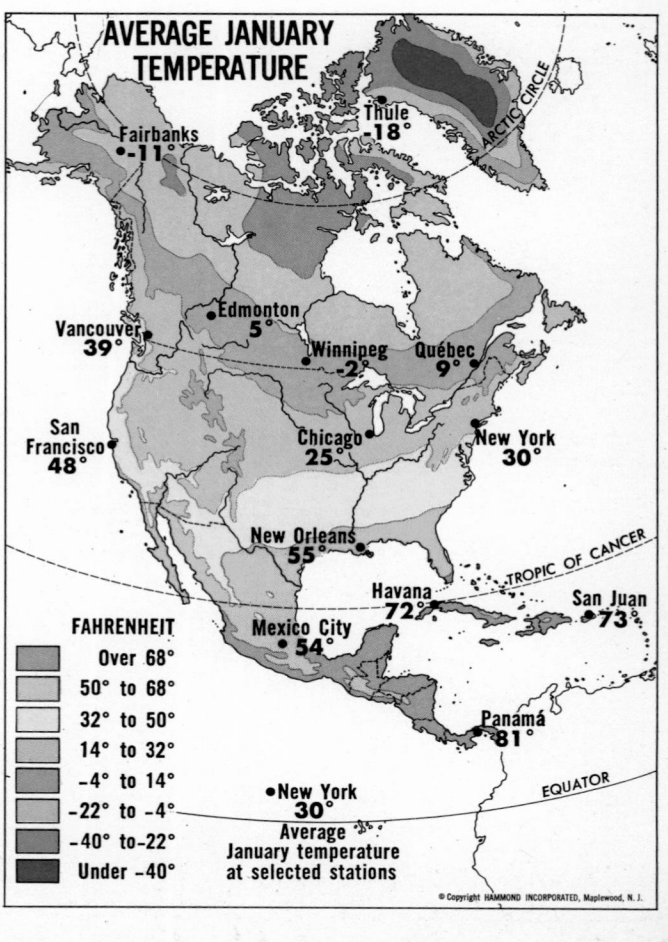

AVERAGE JANUARY TEMPERATURE

Fairbanks
-11°

Thule
-18°

Vancouver
39°

Edmonton
5°

Winnipeg
-2°

Québec
9°

San Francisco
48°

Chicago
25°

New York
30°

New Orleans
55°

Havana
72°

San Juan
73°

Mexico City
54°

Panamá
81°

FAHRENHEIT

- Over 68°
- 50° to 68°
- 32° to 50°
- 14° to 32°
- -4° to 14°
- -22° to -4°
- -40° to -22°
- Under -40°

• New York
  30°
  Average
  January temperature
  at selected stations

TROPIC OF CANCER

EQUATOR

© Copyright HAMMOND INCORPORATED, Maplewood, N.J.

Topography

ARCTIC OCEAN

QUEEN
ELIZABETH
SVERDRUP
ISLANDS IS.

Greenland

C. Morris
Jesup

Ellesmere

Baffin
Bay

Disko I.

Beaufort
Sea

Banks
I.

Parry
Channel

Victoria
I.

Baffin

Baffin
Island

Davis Strait

C. Farewell

St. Lawrence
I.

Bering Strait

Pt. Barrow

Seward
Pen.

BROOKS RANGE

Yukon

Great Bear
L.

Foxe
Basin

Southampton
I.

Hudson Str.

C. Chidley

Labrador
Sea

Bering
Sea

Mt.
McKinley
20,320

Kenai
Pen.

Mackenzie

Great
Slave L.

Ungava
Peninsula

Churchill

ALEUTIAN ISLANDS

Alaska
Pen.

Kodiak
I.

Gulf
of
Alaska

Logan
19,850

Peace

Athabasca

L.
Athabasca

Hudson
Bay

Newfoundland

C. Race

ALEXANDER
ARCH.

Saskatchewan

Nelson

L.
Winnipeg

Albany

Eastmain

Cape Breton
I.

QUEEN
CHARLOTTE
IS.

Vancouver
I.

Fraser

Columbia

Rainier
14,410

Snake

COAST RANGES

ROCKY MOUNTAINS

Missouri

Red

L.
Superior

L.
Michigan

L.
Huron

Ontario

Erie

Nova
Scotia

C. Cod

Long I.

PACIFIC
OCEAN

C. Mendocino

COLUMBIA
PLATEAU

Great
Basin

Mt.
Whitney
14,495

COLORADO
PLATEAU

Platte

Arkansas

Missouri

OZARK
PLATEAU

Ohio

Tennessee

APPALACHIAN MTS.

C. Hatteras

ATLANTIC
OCEAN

Bermuda

Lower California

Gulf of
California

Colorado

Rio Grande

SIERRA MADRE OCCIDENTAL

MEXICAN PLATEAU

SIERRA MADRE ORIENTAL

Red

GREAT PLAINS

GULF COASTAL PLAIN

ATLANTIC COASTAL PLAIN

Florida
Pen.

C. Kennedy

BAHAMA IS.

Puerto
Rico

C. San Lucas

Gulf of Mexico

Bay of
Campeche

Citlaltépetl
18,855

Yucatán
Pen.

GREATER
ANTILLES

Cuba

Jamaica

Hispaniola

LESSER ANTILLES

Caribbean   Sea

Trinidad

Isthmus
of
Tehuantepec

L.
Nicaragua

Chirripó Grande
12,530

Isthmus of
Panama

0   400   800
MILES

5,000 m.   2,000 m.   1,000 m.   500 m.   200 m.   100 m.   Sea
16,404 ft.   6,562 ft.   3,281 ft.   1,640 ft.   656 ft.   328 ft.   Level   Below

AVERAGE JULY TEMPERATURE

ARCTIC CIRCLE

Thule
41°

Fairbanks
57°

Vancouver
59°

Edmonton
61°

Winnipeg
66°

Québec
66°

San
Francisco
61°

Chicago
75°

New York
73°

New Orleans
83°

TROPIC OF CANCER

Havana
81°

San Juan
81°

Mexico City
61°

Panamá
81°

EQUATOR

FAHRENHEIT

Over 86°
68° to 86°
50° to 68°
32° to 50°
14° to 32°
Under 14°

• New York
73°
Average
July temperature
at selected stations

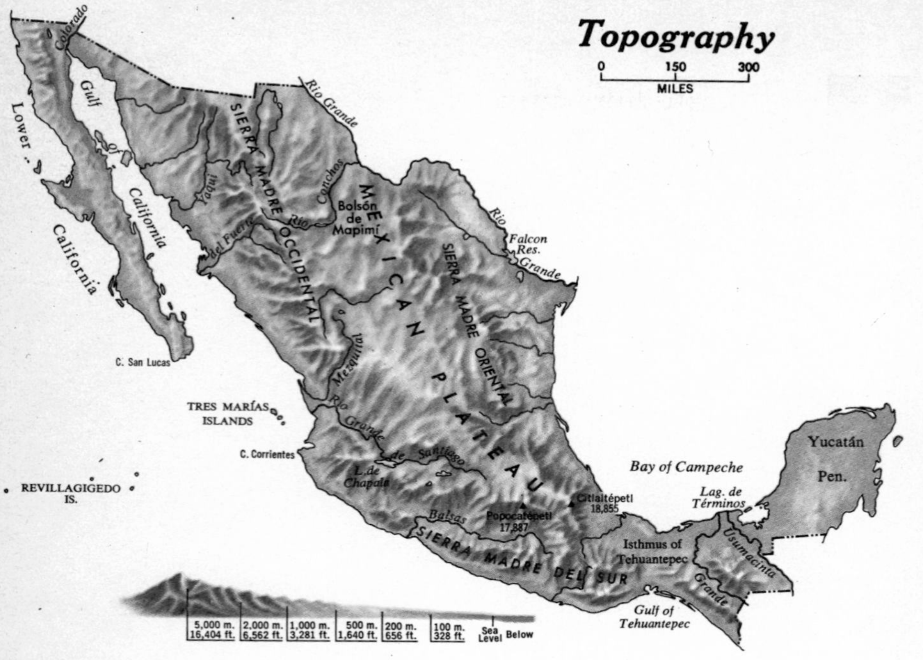

STATES and TERRITORIES

Aguascalientes, 334,936 .... H 6
Baja California, 856,773 .... B 1
Baja California (terr.), 123,786 .... C 3
Campeche, 250,391 .... O 7
Chiapas, 1,578,180 .... N 8
Chihuahua, 1,730,012 .... F 2
Coahuila, 1,140,989 .... H 3
Colima, 240,235 .... G 7
Distrito Federal, 7,005,855 .... L 1
Durango, 919,381 .... G 4
Guanajuato, 2,285,249 .... J 6
Guerrero, 1,573,098 .... J 8
Hidalgo, 1,156,177 .... K 6
Jalisco, 3,322,750 .... H 6
México, 3,797,861 .... K 7
Michoacán, 2,341,556 .... H 7
Morelos, 620,392 .... K 7
Nayarit, 547,992 .... G 6
Nuevo León, 1,653,808 .... K 4
Oaxaca, 2,011,946 .... L 8
Puebla, 2,483,770 .... L 7
Querétaro, 464,226 .... J 6
Quintana Roo (terr.), 91,044 .... P 7
San Luis Potosí, 1,257,028 .... J 5
Sinaloa, 1,273,228 .... F 4
Sonora, 1,092,458 .... D 2
Tabasco, 766,346 .... N 7
Tamaulipas, 1,438,350 .... K 4
Tlaxcala, 418,334 .... N 1
Veracruz, 3,813,613 .... L 7
Yucatán, 774,011 .... P 6
Zacatecas, 949,663 .... H 5

CITIES and TOWNS

Acámbaro, 80,259 .... J 7
Acaponeta, 29,829 .... G 5
Acapulco de Juárez, 234,866 .... J 8
Acatlán, 22,507 .... K 7
Acatzingo, 14,809 .... N 2
Acayucan, 36,352 .... M 8
Aconchi, 2,313 .... D 2
Actopan, 26,608 .... Q 1
Agualeguas, 5,536 .... J 3
Agua Prieta, 21,627 .... E 1
Aguascalientes, 222,105 .... H 6
Aguililla, 20,752 .... H 7
Ahuacatlán, 14,180 .... G 6
Ajalpan, 20,413 .... L 7
Alamos, 24,123 .... E 3
Aldama, Chihuahua, 14,117 .... G 2
Aldama, Tamaulipas, 15,336 .... L 5
Aljojuca, 5,520 .... O 1
Allende, Chihuahua, 11,039 .... G 3
Allende, Coahuila, 12,736 .... J 2
Allende, Nuevo León, 14,263 .... J 4
Almoloya del Río, 3,692 .... K 1
Altamira, 28,667 .... K 5
Altar, 3,811 .... D 1
Altotonga, 31,231 .... P 1
Alvarado, 33,152 .... M 7
Amatlán de los Reyes, 21,011 .... P 2
Amealco, 26,222 .... K 6
Ameca, 42,016 .... H 6
Amecameca de Juárez, 21,753 .... L 1
Amozoc de Mota, 13,381 .... N 2
Angostura, 29,709 .... E 4
Apan, 21,550 .... M 1
Apatzingán de la Constitución, 67,384 .... J 7
Apizaco, 20,998 .... N 1
Aquiles Serdán, 5,159 .... G 2
Aramberri, 16,051 .... J 5
Arandas, 41,958 .... H 6
Arcelia, 25,631 .... J 7
Arizpe, 4,415 .... D 1
Armería, 16,334 .... G 7
Arriaga, 23,582 .... N 8
Arteaga, 17,455 .... H 7
Ascensión, 8,810 .... E 1
Atlixco, 72,256 .... M 2
Atotonilco, 35,297 .... H 6
Autlán de Navarro, 30,853 .... G 7
Ayutla de los Libres, 23,668 .... K 8
Azcapotzalco, 545,513 .... L 1
Azoyú, 23,554 .... K 8
Bacadéhuachi, 1,470 .... D 2
Bacerac, 2,306 .... E 1
Bácum, 17,598 .... D 3
Badiraguato, 28,995 .... F 4
Balancán, 27,241 .... O 8
Balleza, 15,122 .... F 3
Batopilas, 8,780 .... F 3
Baviácora, 4,202 .... E 2
Bavispe, 2,048 .... E 1
Benjamín Hill, 5,807 .... D 1
Boca del Río, 27,884 .... Q 1
Buenaventura, 14,629 .... F 2
Burgos, 5,529 .... K 4
Cadereyta, 28,093 .... K 6
Cadereyta Jiménez, 30,429 .... K 4
Calera, 13,030 .... H 5
Calkiní, 24,503 .... O 6
Calpulalpan, 14,633 .... M 1
Calvillo, 24,039 .... H 6
Campeche, 81,147 .... O 7
Cananea, 21,824 .... D 1
Canatlán, 63,871 .... G 4
Cancún .... Q 6
Candela, 2,202 .... J 3
Carbo, 3,242 .... D 2
Cárdenas, S. Luis Potosí, 18,091 .... K 6
Cárdenas, Tabasco, 78,477 .... N 8
Carmen, 71,240 .... N 7
Casas Grandes, 11,207 .... F 1
Catemaco, 23,671 .... M 7
Cedral, 12,426 .... J 5
Celaya, 143,703 .... J 6
Celestún, 1,535 .... O 6
Cerralvo, 6,831 .... J 3
Cerritos, 18,868 .... K 5
Chalchihuites, 11,347 .... G 5
Chalco, 41,145 .... M 1
Champotón, 27,581 .... O 7
Chapulco, 2,807 .... O 2
Charcas, 22,388 .... J 5
Chetumal, 34,237 .... Q 7
Chiapa de Corzo, 22,640 .... N 8
Chiautempan, 33,820 .... N 1
Chicoloapan de Juárez, 8,995 .... M 1
Chietla, 26,921 .... M 2
Chignahuapan, 29,556 .... N 1
Chignautla, 8,348 .... N 1
Chihuahua, 363,850 .... G 2
Chilapa, 53,263 .... K 8
Chilpancingo, 56,904 .... K 8
China, 9,018 .... K 4
Chocamán, 7,270 .... P 2
Choix, 27,515 .... E 3
Cholula, 20,913 .... M 1
Cihuatlán, 16,314 .... G 7
Cintalapa, 31,252 .... M 8
Ciudad Acuña, 32,760 .... J 2
Ciudad Camargo, Chihuahua, 29,185 .... G 3
Ciudad Camargo, Tamaulipas, 16,097 .... K 3
Ciudad Delicias, 64,385 .... G 2
Ciudad del Maíz, 35,502 .... K 5
Ciudad de Valles, 71,098 .... K 5
Ciudad Guerrero, 35,631 .... F 2
Ciudad Guzmán, 48,142 .... H 7
Ciudad Juárez, 436,054 .... F 1
Ciudad Lerdo, 53,551 .... H 4
Ciudad Madero, 89,994 .... L 5
Ciudad Mante, 79,130 .... K 5
Ciudad Miguel Alemán, 18,134 .... K 3
Ciudad Obregón, 181,972 .... E 3
Ciudad Río Bravo, 70,814 .... K 4
Ciudad Serdán, 25,288 .... O 2
Ciudad Victoria, 94,304 .... K 5
Coalcomán de Matamoros, 13,480 .... H 7
Coatepec, 34,161 .... P 1
Coatzacoalcos, 108,818 .... M 7
Cocula, 20,273 .... G 6
Colima, 72,074 .... H 7
Colón, 20,392 .... K 6
Colotlán, 14,316 .... H 5
Comala, 13,715 .... G 7
Comalcalco, 71,651 .... N 7
Comitán, 38,137 .... O 8
Comondú, 30,872 .... D 3
Compostela, 59,422 .... G 6
Concepción del Oro, 15,711 .... J 4
Concordia, 21,023 .... G 5
Córdoba, 92,870 .... P 2
Cosalá, 16,202 .... F 4
Cosamaloapan de Carpio, 75,412 .... M 7
Cosautlán de Carvajal, 8,015 .... P 1
Coscomatepec de Bravo, 19,890 .... P 2
Cosío, 7,031 .... H 5
Cosoleacaque, 20,251 .... M 7
Cotija, 17,296 .... H 7
Coyame, 3,798 .... G 2
Coyoacán, 338,850 .... L 1
Coyotepec, 8,658 .... L 1
Coyuca, 25,128 .... J 7
Coyuca de Benítez, 36,032 .... J 8
Coyutla, 12,008 .... L 6
Cozumel, 12,634 .... Q 6
Cuatrociénegas de Carranza, 9,512 .... H 3
Cuauhtémoc, 65,160 .... F 2
Cuautitlán, 40,622 .... L 1
Cuautla Morelos, 67,869 .... L 2
Cuencamé, 31,170 .... H 4
Cuernavaca, 159,909 .... L 2
Cuicatlán, 45,013 .... L 8
Cuitlahuac, 13,078 .... P 2
Culiacán, 358,812 .... F 4
Cumpas, 6,186 .... D 2
Cuna de la Independencia Nacional, 71,212 .... J 6
Cunduacán, 42,872 .... N 7
Doctor Arroyo, 45,889 .... K 5
Durango, 192,934 .... G 4
Ejutla de Crespo, 34,890 .... L 8
El Ebano, 20,571 .... K 5
El Fuerte, 62,001 .... E 3
El Oro, Durango, 18,668 .... G 4
El Oro, México, 17,086 .... K 7
El Salto, 19,604 .... G 5
Empalme, 32,541 .... D 2
Encarnación de Díaz, 29,533 .... H 6
Ensenada, 113,320 .... A 1
Escuinapa de Hidalgo, 30,763 .... G 5
Esculntla, 13,754 .... N 9
Etchojoa, 53,767 .... E 3
Fortín de las Flores, 21,370 .... P 2
Fresnillo, 101,316 .... H 5
Frontera, 43,007 .... N 7
Galeana, Chihuahua, 3,176 .... F 1
Galeana, Nuevo León, 39,143 .... J 4
García de la Cadena, 4,755 .... H 6
General Bravo, 6,063 .... K 4
General Cepeda, 13,332 .... J 4
Gómez Palacio, 135,743 .... G 4
González, 23,748 .... K 5
Guadalajara, 1,196,218 .... H 6
Guadalupe, Nvo. León, 153,454 .... J 4
Guadalupe, Zacatecas, 31,976 .... H 5
Guadalupe-Bravos, 9,649 .... F 1
Guadalupe Victoria, 27,450 .... G 4
Guadalupe y Calvo, 31,131 .... F 2
Guanacevi, 12,036 .... G 4
Guanajuato, 65,258 .... J 6
Guasave, 148,475 .... E 4
Guaymas, 84,730 .... D 3
Gutiérrez Zamora, 20,534 .... L 6
Halachó, 8,547 .... O 6
Hecelchakán, 10,974 .... O 6
Hermosillo, 206,663 .... D 2
Heroica Caborca, 29,486 .... C 1
Heroica Huamantla, 26,191 .... N 1
Heroica Nogales, 52,865 .... D 1
Hidalgo, 21,434 .... K 4
Hopelchén, 23,509 .... P 7
Huajuapan de León, 83,939 .... L 8
Huaquechula, 16,702 .... M 2
Huatabampo, 43,963 .... D 3
Huatusco de Chicuellar, 20,621 .... P 2
Huauchinango, 37,211 .... L 6
Huehuetlán, 6,962 .... M 2
Huejotzingo, 21,728 .... M 1
Huejutla de Reyes, 45,771 .... K 6
Huetamo de Núñez, 35,414 .... J 7
Hueyotlipan, 6,786 .... M 1
Huimanguillo, 70,525 .... N 8
Huitzuco, 28,159 .... K 7
Huixtla, 25,884 .... N 9
Hunucmá, 10,600 .... O 6
Ignacio de la Llave, 16,345 .... Q 2
Iguala, 60,980 .... K 7
Imuris, 5,853 .... D 1
Indé, 11,969 .... G 4
Irapuato, 175,966 .... J 6
Isla de Aguada .... O 7
Isla Mujeres, 10,469 .... Q 6
Ixmiquilpan, 35,851 .... K 6
Ixtacalco, 474,700 .... L 1
Ixtapalapa, 533,569 .... L 1
Ixtlán del Río, 16,228 .... G 6
Izamal, 16,188 .... P 6
Izúcar de Matamoros, 44,074 .... M 2
Jala, 11,174 .... G 6
Jalacingo, 15,436 .... P 1
Jalapa Enríquez, 127,081 .... P 1
Jalpa, Tabasco, 29,904 .... N 7
Jalpa, Zacatecas, 26,050 .... H 6
Jalpan, 15,319 .... K 6
Jáltipan, 19,676 .... M 8
Jaumave, 13,504 .... K 5
Jerez de Garcia Salinas, 49,202 .... H 5
Jico, 14,153 .... P 1
Jilotepec, 34,866 .... K 7
Jiménez, Chihuahua, 27,044 .... G 3
Jiménez, Coahuila, 8,019 .... J 2
Jojutla de Juárez, 31,196 .... L 2
Jonacatepec, 7,478 .... M 2
Jonuta, 14,227 .... N 7
Juan Aldama, 13,661 .... H 4
Juárez, 1,664 .... J 3
Juchipila, 14,517 .... H 6
Juchique de Ferrer, 14,094 .... Q 1
Juchitán de Zaragoza, 178,388 .... M 8
La Barca, 40,331 .... H 6
La Concordia, 15,296 .... N 9
La Cruz, Chihuahua, 3,899 .... G 3
La Cruz, Sinaloa, 19,055 .... F 5
Lagos, 66,273 .... J 6
La Paz, 49,637 .... D 5
La Piedad, 51,484 .... H 6
La Trinitaria, 28,028 .... N 9
La Yesca, 9,010 .... G 6
León, 453,976 .... J 6
Libres, 12,973 .... O 1
Linares, 49,397 .... K 4
Llera de Canales, 21,117 .... K 5
Loreto, 21,544 .... J 5
Los Mochis, 165,612 .... E 4
Los Reyes, 33,879 .... H 7
Macuspana, 75,013 .... N 8
Madera, 32,367 .... F 2
Magdalena, 13,485 .... D 1
Manuel Benavides, 5,135 .... H 2
Manzanillo, 46,170 .... G 7
Mapastepec, 16,911 .... N 9
Mapimí, 19,053 .... G 4
Martínez de la Torre, 62,707 .... L 6
Mascota, 15,260 .... G 6
Matamoros, Coahuila, 44,103 .... H 4
Matamoros, Tamaulipas, 182,887 .... L 4
Matehuala, 48,368 .... J 5
Maxcanú, 10,620 .... O 6
Mazapil, 28,656 .... J 4
Mazatán, 1,561 .... E 2
Mazatlán, 171,835 .... F 5
Melchor Múzquiz, 45,945 .... J 3
Melchor Ocampo, 4,180 .... H 4
Melchor Ocampo del Balsas, 23,248 .... H 8
Meoquí, 27,000 .... G 2
Mérida, 253,856 .... P 6
Mexicali, 390,411 .... B 1
Mexico City (México) (capital), 3,025,564 .... L 1
Mexico City, *7,157,000 .... L 1
Mezquital, 4,663 .... G 5
Miacatlán, 12,579 .... L 2
Mier, 5,916 .... K 3
Miguel Azua, 15,330 .... H 4
Minatitlán, 89,412 .... M 8
Mineral del Monte, 10,943 .... K 6
Miquihuana, 3,099 .... K 5
Misantla, 44,268 .... P 1
Mocorito, 49,957 .... F 4
Moctezuma, S. L. Potosí, 13,628 .... J 5
Moctezuma, Sonora, 3,476 .... E 2
Monclova, 80,252 .... J 3
Montemorelos, 34,067 .... K 4
Monterrey, 830,336 .... J 4
Morelia, 209,507 .... J 7
Morelos, 4,721 .... J 2
Morelos Cañada, 11,463 .... O 2
Moroleón, 33,765 .... J 6
Motozintla de Mendoza, 31,518 .... N 9
Motul, 21,087 .... P 6
Mulegé, 19,282 .... C 3
Muna, 6,147 .... P 6
Naco, 3,639 .... D 1
Nacozari de García, 3,483 .... E 1
Nadadores, 3,869 .... J 3
Nanacamilpa, 8,658 .... M 1
Naolinco de Victoria, 11,077 .... P 1
Naranjos, 21,371 .... L 6
Naucalpan, 373,605 .... L 1
Nautla, 9,425 .... L 6
Nava, 5,669 .... J 2
Navojoa, 69,792 .... E 3
Nazas, 13,189 .... G 4
Nieves, 19,938 .... H 5
Nochistlán, Oaxaca, 58,609 .... L 8
Nochistlán, Zacatecas, 28,463 .... H 6
Nogales, 19,158 .... P 2
Nombre de Dios, 17,742 .... G 5
Nonoava, 4,054 .... F 3
Nopalucan, 8,401 .... O 1
Nueva Casas Grandes, 25,333 .... F 1
Nueva Ciudad Guerrero, 4,065 .... K 3
Nuevo Laredo, 150,922 .... J 3
Nuevo Morelos, 2,245 .... K 5
Oaxaca de Juárez, 156,587 .... L 8
Ocampo, Chihuahua, 4,947 .... E 2
Ocampo, Coahuila, 10,072 .... H 3
Ocampo, Tamaulipas, 15,998 .... K 5
Ocotlán, 43,394 .... H 6
Ocotlán de Morelos, 45,752 .... L 8
Ojinaga, 23,854 .... G 2
Ojocaliente, 20,283 .... H 5
Ometepec, 23,604 .... K 8
Opódepe, 3,312 .... D 2
Oriental, 7,375 .... O 1
Orizaba, 92,728 .... P 2
Otumba de Gómez Farías, 11,960 .... M 1
Oxkutzcab, 10,295 .... P 7
Ozuluama, 22,382 .... L 6
Ozumba, 11,013 .... M 1
Pachuca, 84,543 .... K 6
Padilla, 13,643 .... K 5
Palenque, 22,684 .... O 8
Palizada, 7,445 .... O 7
Palmar de Bravo, 15,898 .... O 2
Palmillas, 2,420 .... K 5
Pánuco, 49,077 .... K 6
Papantla de Olarte, 94,623 .... L 6
Paraíso, 30,439 .... N 7
Parral, 61,729 .... G 3
Parras, 32,664 .... H 4
Pátzcuaro, 44,591 .... J 7
Pedro Montoya, 10,760 .... K 6
Pénjamo, 89,548 .... J 6
Peñón Blanco, 10,541 .... H 4
Perote, 23,556 .... P 1
Petatlán, 31,088 .... J 8
Peto, 11,986 .... P 6
Piedras Negras, 65,883 .... J 2
Pijijiapan, 20,350 .... N 9
Pitiquito, 6,100 .... D 1
Pochutla, 84,033 .... L 9
Poza Rica de Hidalgo, 121,341 .... L 6
Progreso, 22,100 .... P 6

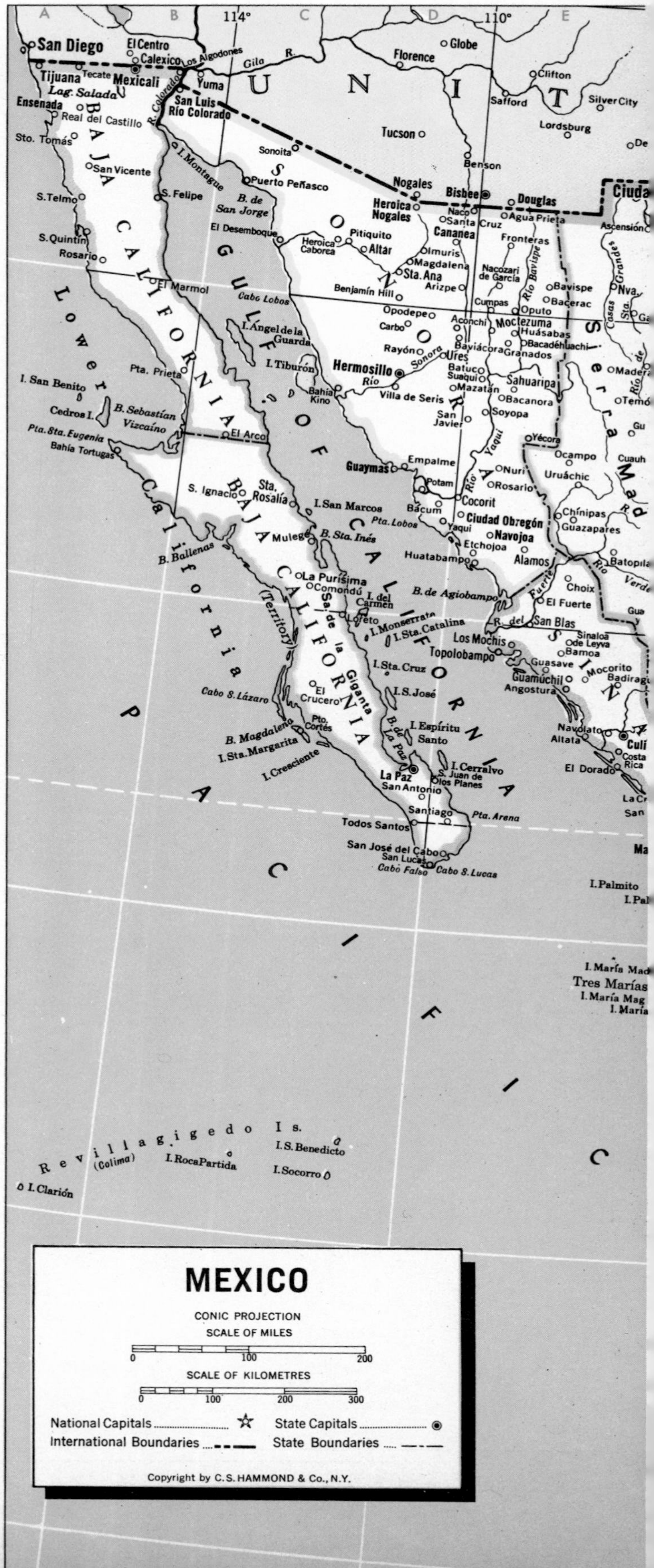

Copyright by C. S. HAMMOND & Co., N.Y.

AREA   761,601 sq. mi.
POPULATION   48,313,438
CAPITAL   Mexico City
LARGEST CITY   Mexico City
HIGHEST POINT   Citlaltépetl 18,855 ft.
MONETARY UNIT   Mexican peso
MAJOR LANGUAGE   Spanish
MAJOR RELIGION   Roman Catholicism

States Indicated by Numbers

1	Tlaxcala	6	Querétaro
2	Morelos	7	Guanajuato
3	Distrito Federal	8	Aguascalientes
4	México	9	Nayarit
5	Hidalgo	10	Colima

HIGHWAYS OF MIDDLE AMERICA

0   200   400   600 MI.
0   200   400   600 KM.

Limited Access Highways
Major Highways
Other Important Roads
U.S. Interstate Numbers
U.S. Route Numbers
Other Route Numbers

© C. S. HAMMOND & Co., Maplewood, N.J.

Agriculture, Industry and Resources

CHIHUAHUA
Nonferrous Metals

PIEDRAS NEGRAS
Iron & Steel

MONCLOVA
Iron & Steel,
Chemicals

MONTERREY—SALTILLO
Iron & Steel, Nonferrous Metals,
Metalworking, Chemicals,
Food Processing

TORREÓN
Nonferrous Metals,
Chemicals, Textiles

SAN LUIS POTOSÍ
Nonferrous Metals,
Textiles

TAMPICO
Oil Refining, Chemicals,
Food Processing

SALAMANCA
Chemicals, Textiles,
Food Processing

VERACRUZ LLAVE
Iron & Steel, Textiles,
Metalworking

GUADALAJARA
Metalworking, Textiles,
Food Processing,
Leather Products

ORIZABA
Textiles,
Cement

MEXICO CITY—PUEBLA
Metalworking, Textiles, Leather
Products, Food Processing,
Chemicals, Automobile Assembly

DOMINANT LAND USE

Wheat, Livestock
Cereals (chiefly corn), Livestock
Diversified Tropical Cash Crops
Cotton, Mixed Cereals
Livestock, Limited Agriculture
Range Livestock
Forests
Nonagricultural Land

Water Power
Major Industrial Areas

MAJOR MINERAL OCCURRENCES

Ag	Silver	G	Natural Gas	O	Petroleum
Au	Gold	Gr	Graphite	Pb	Lead
C	Coal	Hg	Mercury	S	Sulfur
Cu	Copper	Mn	Manganese	Sb	Antimony
F	Fluorspar	Mo	Molybdenum	Sn	Tin
Fe	Iron Ore	Na	Salt	W	Tungsten
				Zn	Zinc

GUATEMALA
AREA 42,042 sq. mi.
POPULATION 5,200,000
CAPITAL Guatemala
LARGEST CITY Guatemala
HIGHEST POINT Tajumulco 13,845 ft.
MONETARY UNIT quetzal
MAJOR LANGUAGES Spanish, Quiché
MAJOR RELIGION Roman Catholicism

BRITISH HONDURAS
AREA 8,867 sq. mi.
POPULATION 122,000
CAPITAL Belmopan
LARGEST CITY Belize City
HIGHEST POINT Victoria Peak, 3,681 ft.
MONETARY UNIT British Honduran dollar
MAJOR LANGUAGES English, Spanish, Mayan
MAJOR RELIGIONS Protestantism, Roman Catholicism

EL SALVADOR
AREA 8,260 sq. mi.
POPULATION 3,418,455
CAPITAL San Salvador
LARGEST CITY San Salvador
HIGHEST POINT Santa Ana 7,825 ft.
MONETARY UNIT colón
MAJOR LANGUAGE Spanish
MAJOR RELIGION Roman Catholicism

HONDURAS
AREA 43,277 sq. mi.
POPULATION 2,495,000
CAPITAL Tegucigalpa
LARGEST CITY Tegucigalpa
HIGHEST POINT Las Minas 9,347 ft.
MONETARY UNIT lempira
MAJOR LANGUAGE Spanish
MAJOR RELIGION Roman Catholicism

NICARAGUA
AREA 45,698 sq. mi.
POPULATION 1,984,000
CAPITAL Managua
LARGEST CITY Managua
HIGHEST POINT Cerro Mocotón 6,913 ft.
MONETARY UNIT córdoba
MAJOR LANGUAGE Spanish
MAJOR RELIGION Roman Catholicism

COSTA RICA
AREA 19,575 sq. mi.
POPULATION 1,800,000
CAPITAL San José
LARGEST CITY San José
HIGHEST POINT Chirripó Grande 12,530 ft.
MONETARY UNIT colón
MAJOR LANGUAGE Spanish
MAJOR RELIGION Roman Catholicism

PANAMA
AREA 29,209 sq. mi.
POPULATION 1,425,343
CAPITAL Panamá
LARGEST CITY Panamá
HIGHEST POINT Vol. Chiriquí 11,401 ft.
MONETARY UNIT balboa
MAJOR LANGUAGE Spanish
MAJOR RELIGION Roman Catholicism

CANAL ZONE
AREA 647 sq. mi.
POPULATION 44,650
CAPITAL Balboa Heights

Agriculture, Industry and Resources

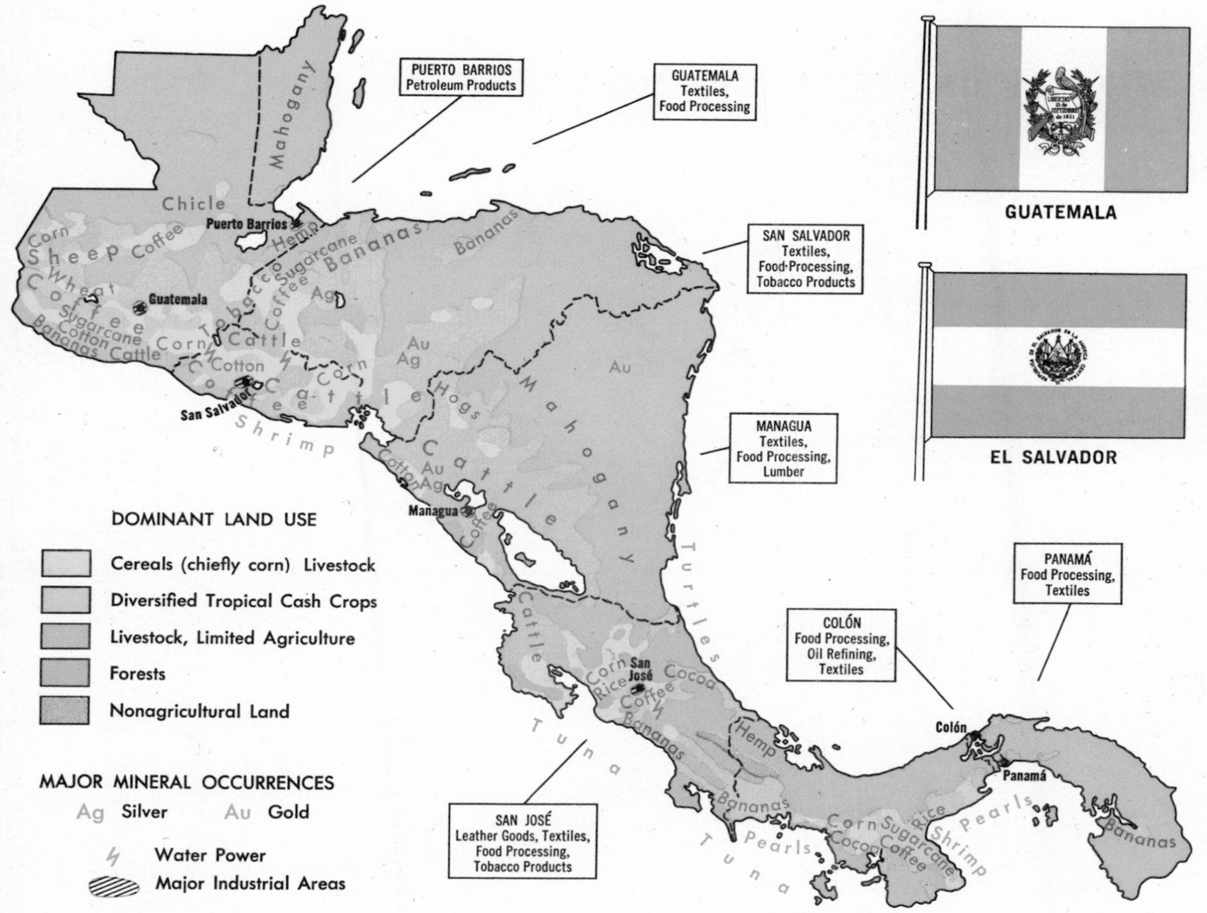

PUERTO BARRIOS Petroleum Products

GUATEMALA Textiles, Food Processing

SAN SALVADOR Textiles, Food-Processing, Tobacco Products

MANAGUA Textiles, Food Processing, Lumber

PANAMÁ Food Processing, Textiles

COLÓN Food Processing, Oil Refining, Textiles

SAN JOSÉ Leather Goods, Textiles, Food Processing, Tobacco Products

DOMINANT LAND USE

- Cereals (chiefly corn) Livestock
- Diversified Tropical Cash Crops
- Livestock, Limited Agriculture
- Forests
- Nonagricultural Land

MAJOR MINERAL OCCURRENCES

Ag Silver   Au Gold

⚡ Water Power

▨ Major Industrial Areas

GUATEMALA

EL SALVADOR

HONDURAS

NICARAGUA

COSTA RICA

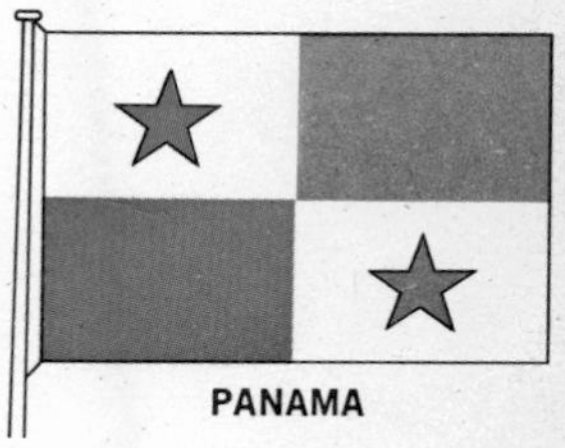

PANAMA

BRITISH HONDURAS

CITIES and TOWNS

Belize City, 37,000 ....C 2
Belize City, *48,421 ....C 2
Belmopan (capital) ....C 2
Benque Viejo, 1,607 ....C 2
Cayo, 1,890 ....C 2
Corozal Town, 3,171 ....C 1
Hill Bank, 78 ....C 2
Monkey River Town, 417 ....C 2
Orange Walk Town, 2,157 ....C 1
Punta Gorda, 1,789 ....C 2
San José, 365 ....C 2

San Pedro, 170 ....D 2
Stann Creek Town, 5,287 ....C 2

OTHER FEATURES

Ambergris (cay), †572 ....D 1
Belize (river) ....C 2
Bokel (cay) ....D 2
Cockscomb (mts.) ....C 2
Corker (cay), †360 ....D 2
Glovers (reef) ....D 2
Half Moon (cay) ....D 2
Hondo (river) ....C 1

Honduras (gulf) ....D 2
Mauger (cay) ....D 2
New (river) ....C 2
Saint Georges (cay), †34 ....D 2
Sarstún (river) ....C 3
Turneffe (isls.), 99 ....D 2

CANAL ZONE

CITIES and TOWNS

Balboa, 2,568 ....H 6
Cristóbal, 817 ....G 6

COSTA RICA

CITIES and TOWNS

Alajuela, 25,195 ....E 6
Atenas, 963 ....E 6
Atlanta ....E 5
Bagaces, 1,175 ....E 5
Beverly ....E 5
Boruca, †1,049 ....F 6
Buenos Aires, ‡4,624 ....F 6
Cañas, 2,991 ....E 5
Carmen ....E 5
Cartago, 19,038 ....F 6
Chomes, ‡1,991 ....E 5

Ciudad Quesada, 3,696 ....E 5
El Salvador ....F 5
Esparta, 2,860 ....E 5
Filadelfia, 1,574 ....E 5
Golfito, 6,859 ....F 6
Grecia, 4,862 ....E 6
Guácimo, 5,731 ....F 5
Guápiles, 983 ....F 5
Heredia, 20,523 ....E 6
Las Juntas, 827 ....E 5
Liberia, 11,171 ....E 5
Limón, 30,676 ....F 6
Miramar, 1,122 ....E 5
Nicoya, 3,196 ....E 5
Orotina, 1,749 ....E 6

Palmares, 1,529 ....F 6
Paquera ....F 6
Paraíso, 4,427 ....F 6
Pejivalle ....F 6
Platanilla ....F 6
Playa Bonita ....F 5
Puerto Cortés, 1,757 ....F 6
Puntarenas, 27,527 ....E 6
Quepos, 1,858 ....F 6
San Ignacio, 315 ....F 6
San José (cap.), 182,961 ....F 5
San José, *408,000 ....F 5
San Marcos, 411 ....F 5
San Ramón, 6,444 ....E 5
Santa Cruz, 3,849 ....E 5

Santa Rosa, ‡1,750 ....E 5
Santo Domingo, 3,333 ....F 6
Sibube ....F 6
Siquirres, 2,157 ....F 5
Turrialba, 8,629 ....F 5
Vesta ....F 6

OTHER FEATURES

Blanca (point) ....F 5
Blanco (cape) ....F 6
Blanco (mt.) ....F 6
Burica (point) ....F 6
Cahuita (point) ....F 6
Caño (isl.) ....F 6

(continued on following page)

COSTA RICA (continued)

Carreta (point)		F 6
Chirripó Grande (mt.)		F 6
Coronada (bay)		F 6
Cuilapa Miravalles (volcano)		E 5
Dulce (gulf)		F 6
Góngora (mt.)		F 6
Guionos (point)		E 5
Irazú (mt.)		F 6
Judas (point)		F 6
Llerena (point)		E 5
Matapalo (cape)		F 6
Nicoya (gulf)		E 6
Nicoya (pen.)		E 6
Papagayo (gulf)		E 5
Salinas (bay)		E 5
San Juan (river)		E, F 5
Santa Elena (cape)		D 5
Talamanca (range)		F 6
Velas (cape)		D 5

EL SALVADOR

CITIES and TOWNS

Acajutla, 5,310		B 4
Ahuachapán, 16,180		B 4

Atiquizaya, 7,878		C 3
Chalatenango, 7,209		C 3
Cojutepeque, 16,084		C 4
Estanzuelas, 2,785		C 4
Ilobasco, 6,432		C 4
Intipucá, 3,683		D 4
Jucuarán, 1,600		C 4
La Libertad, 7,015		C 4
La Palma, 1,992		C 4
La Unión, 16,459		D 4
Metapán, 4,896		C 3
Nueva San Salvador (Santa Tecla), 36,944		C 4
Puerto de la Concordia		C 4
San Francisco Gotera, 4,638		C 4
San Miguel, 50,668		D 4
San Salvador (cap.), 349,725		C 4
Santa Ana, 102,301		B 4
Santa Rosa de Lima, 6,297		D 4
Santa Tecla, 36,944		C 4
San Vicente, 19,887		C 4
Sensuntepeque, 6,791		C 4
Sonsonate, 32,675		C 4
Suchitoto, 5,758		C 4
Texistepeque, 1,723		C 4
Usulután, 17,796		C 4
Zacatecoluca, 16,189		C 4

OTHER FEATURES

Fonseca (gulf)		D 4
Güija (lake)		C 3
Lempa (river)		C 4
Remedios (point)		B 4
Santa Ana (mt.)		C 4

GUATEMALA

CITIES and TOWNS

Amatitlán, 12,225		B 3
Antigua, 13,576		B 3
Asunción Mita, 6,341		C 3
Cahabón, 939		C 3
Chahal, 323		C 2
Chajul, 4,187		B 3
Champerico, 3,823		A 3
Chichicastenango, 2,099		B 3
Chimaltenango, 9,077		B 3
Chinaja		B 2
Chiquimula, 14,760		C 3
Chisec, 812		B 2
Coatepeque, 13,657		A 3
Cobán, 9,073		B 2
Comalapa, 9,202		B 3

Cubulco, 1,676		B 3
Cuilapa, 3,657		B 3
Cuilco, 728		B 2
Dolores, 630		C 2
El Cambio		C 2
El Porvenir		B 3
El Progreso, 3,458		B 3
Escuintla, 24,832		B 3
Flores, 1,503		C 2
Guatán, 4,425		C 2
Guatemala (cap.), 700,000		B 3
Huehuetenango, 10,185		B 2
Ipala, 3,190		C 3
Izabal		C 3
Iztapa, 751		B 3
Jacaltenango, 3,873		A 3
Jalapa, 10,035		B 3
Jutiapa, 7,747		C 3
La Gomera, 1,397		B 3
La Libertad, 770		B 2
Livingston, 3,026		C 2
Los Amates, 1,131		C 3
Masagua, 1,100		B 3
Matías de Gálvez		C 3
Mazatenango, 19,506		A 3
Momostenango, 3,148		B 3
Morales, 1,710		C 3
Nejapa		B 3

Ocós, 576		A 3
Panzós, 1,803		C 2
Puerto Barrios, 22,242		C 3
Quezaltenango, 45,195		A 3
Quezaltepeque, 2,578		C 3
Rabinal, 4,155		B 3
Retalhuleu, 14,366		A 3
Río Hondo, 1,300		C 3
Sacapulas, 1,407		B 3
Salamá, 4,442		B 3
San Andrés, 939		B 2
San Felipe, 2,916		A 3
San José, 5,771		B 4
San Juan de Dios		B 3
San Luis, 763		C 2
San Luis Jilotepeque, 5,795		C 3
San Marcos, 5,569		A 3
San Martín Jilotepeque, 2,806		B 3
San Mateo Ixtatán, 2,892		B 2
San Miguel		B 3
San Pedro Carchá, 3,966		B 2
Santa Ana, 239		C 2
Santa Ana Mixtán		B 3
Santa Cruz del Quiché, 6,472		B 3
Santa Rosa de Lima, 734		B 3
Sipacate		B 3
Solola, 3,957		B 3
Tacaná, 900		A 3

Tejutla, 973		B 3
Totonicapán, 7,292		B 3
Yaloch		C 2
Zacapa, 11,173		C 3

OTHER FEATURES

Atitlán (lake)		B 3
Atitlán (volcano)		B 3
Azul (river)		C 2
Chixoy (river)		B 2
Dulce (Izabal) (lake)		C 3
Güija (lake)		C 3
Honduras (gulf)		C 2
Izabal (lake)		C 3
Minas (mts.)		C 3
Motagua (river)		C 3
Pasión (river)		B 2
Petén-Itzá (lake)		B 2
Sarstun (river)		C 2
Tacaná (volcano)		A 3
Tajumulco (volcano)		A 3
Tres Puntas (cape)		C 3
Usumacinta (river)		B 2

HONDURAS

CITIES and TOWNS

Ahuás, 3,491		E 3
Amapala, 3,491		D 4
Balana		E 3
Balfate, 602		D 3
Belén, 201		C 3
Brus Laguna, 1,247		E 3
Caratasca		F 3
Catacamas, 4,751		D 3
Cedros, 1,177		D 3
Chichicaste		C 3
Choloma, 6,678		C 3
Choluteca, 17,350		D 4
Colorado		D 3
Comayagua, 11,247		D 3
Comayagüela		D 3
Concepción de María, 653		D 4
Concordia, 644		D 3
Copán, 2,190		C 3
Corquín, 2,817		C 3
Cruta		F 3
Danlí, 8,242		D 3
Donel		E 3
El Dulce Nombre, 145		E 3

Topography

El Paraíso, Copán, 1,787	C 3
El Paraíso, El Paraíso, 5,758	D 4
El Porvenir, 529	D 3
El Progreso, 8,718	D 3
El Triunfo, 2,136	D 4
Goascorán, 1,184	D 4
Gracias, 2,484	C 3
Guaimaca, 2,620	D 3
Gualpatanta	E 3
Guanaja, 1,253	E 2
Guarita, 599	C 3
Guayape, 610	D 3
Iriona, 119	E 2
Jacaleapa, 992	D 3
Jesús de Otoro, 2,775	C 3
Jutiapa, 1,711	D 2
Juticalpa, 7,912	D 3
La Ceiba, 33,934	D 2
La Concepción	E 3
La Esperanza, 2,000	C 3
La Guata, 281	D 3
La Paz, 5,542	C 3
La Protección	C 3
Lauterique, 272	D 4
Limón, 1,934	E 3
Manto, 943	D 3
Marcala, 1,968	C 3
Melcher	D 3

Morazán, 3,924	D 3
Morocelí, 1,472	D 3
Nacaome, 4,376	D 4
Namasigüe, 1,024	D 4
Naranjito, 3,291	D 4
Nueva Armenia, 866	D 3
Nueva Ocotepeque, 4,608	C 3
Olanchito, 5,008	D 3
Omoa, 1,384	E 3
Paso Real	E 3
Patuca	C 3
Pespire, 1,758	D 4
Puerto Castilla	D 2
Puerto Cortés, 21,600	D 2
Roatán, 1,883	D 2
Sabanagrande, 1,657	D 4
Salado	D 3
San Esteban, 763	D 3
San Francisco, 1,122	D 3
San Francisco de la Paz, 1,971	D 3
San Juan de Flores, 1,174	D 3
San Luís, 2,631	C 3
San Marcos, 1,576	C 3
San Pedro Sula, 90,538	C 3
San Pedro Zacapa, 765	C 3
Santa Bárbara, 6,129	C 3
Santa Cruz de Yojoa, 1,833	D 3

Topography

0   75   150
MILES

| 5,000 m. 16,404 ft. | 2,000 m. 6,562 ft. | 1,000 m. 3,281 ft. | 500 m. 1,640 ft. | 200 m. 656 ft. | 100 m. 328 ft. | Sea Level | Below |

Santa Rita, 3,976	D 3
Santa Rosa de Aguán, 1,701	E 2
Santa Rosa de Copán, 9,109	C 3
Siguatepeque, 9,462	D 3
Sinuapa, 882	C 3
Sonaguera, 1,344	D 3
Sulaco, 1,071	D 3
Tegucigalpa (cap.), 253,283	D 3
Tela, 14,103	D 2
Teupasenti, 829	D 3
Tocoa, 1,605	E 3
Trinidad, 2,817	C 3
Trujillo, 4,656	F 3
Uji	D 2
Utila, 967	D 2
Villa de San Antonio, 2,287	D 3
Yocón, 269	D 3
Yorito, 869	D 3
Yoro, 4,129	D 3
Yuscarán, 1,854	D 4

OTHER FEATURES

Aguán (river)	D 3
Bahía (isls.), 9,702	D 2
Bonacca (Guanaja) (isl.), 2,039	E 2
Brus (lagoon)	E 2
Camarón (cape)	E 2
Caratasca (cays)	F 2
Caratasca (lagoon)	F 2
Cholutaca (river)	D 4
Cisne (isls.), 28	F 2
Coco (river)	E 3
Colón (mts.)	E 3
Esperanza (mts.)	E 3
Falso (cape)	F 3
Fonseca (gulf)	C 4
Gorda (cay)	F 2
Guanaja (isl.), 2,039	E 2
Half Moon (reefs)	F 3
Honduras (cape)	E 2
Honduras (gulf)	D 2
Patuca (point)	E 3
Patuca (river)	E 3
Paulaya (river)	E 3
Pigeon (cays)	F 3
Pija (mts.)	D 3
Roatán (isl.), 6,552	E 3
San Pablo, Sierra de (mts.)	E 3
Segovia (Coco) (river)	F 3
Sico (river)	E 3
Sulaco (river)	D 3
Swan (Cisne) (isls.), 28	F 2
Ulúa (river)	D 3
Utila (isl.), 1,111	D 2
Vivario (cays)	F 3
Wanks (Coco) (river)	F 3
Yojoa (lake)	D 3

NICARAGUA

CITIES and TOWNS

Acoyapa, 1,755	E 5
Alamikamba	F 4
Barra de Río Grande	F 4
Bilwaskarma	F 3
Bluefields, 9,292	F 4
Boaco, 4,656	E 4
Bocay	E 3
Bonanza, 2,175	F 3
Bragman's Bluff (Puerto Cabezas), 5,983	F 3
Cabo Gracias a Dios, 511	F 3
Camoapa, 2,617	E 4

Chichigalpa, 6,657	D 4
Chinandega, 22,409	D 4
Ciudad Darío, 3,851	D 4
Comalapa, 441	E 4
Condega, 2,229	D 4
Corinto, 9,177	D 4
Cuicuina	F 3
Cuyu Tigni	F 3
Diriamba, 10,499	D 5
El Gallo	F 4
El Jicaral, 239	D 4
El Jícaro, 1,114	D 4
El Sauce, 2,944	D 4
El Viejo, 7,190	D 4
Esquipulas, 1,636	E 4
Estelí, 12,742	E 4
Granada, 28,507	E 5
Greytown (San Juan del Norte), 199	F 5
Jalapa, 1,868	E 4
Jinotega, 7,693	E 4
Jinotepe, 9,113	D 5
Juigalpa, 6,146	E 4
La Conquista, 364	D 5
La Cruz, 155	E 4
Laguna de Perlas	F 4
La Libertad, 1,355	E 4
La Paz Central, 4,431	D 4
La Paz de Oriente, 828	E 5
La Trinidad, 2,340	D 4
León, 44,053	D 4
Managua (capital), 262,047	D 4
Masatepe, 4,831	D 5
Masaya, 23,402	D 5
Matagalpa, 15,030	E 4
Mateare, 1,254	D 4
Morrito, 324	E 5
Moyogalpa, 1,252	E 5
Muleculus	E 4
Muy Muy, 691	E 4
Muy Muy Viejo	E 4
Nagarote, 5,241	D 4
Nandaime, 5,051	D 5
Ocotal, 4,339	D 4
Ocotal	E 4
Palsagua	E 4
Playa Grande	D 4
Poneloya, 995	D 4
Poteca	E 3
Prinzapolka, 230	F 4
Puerto Cabezas, 5,983	F 3
Quilalí, 710	E 4
Rama (El Rama), 600	E 4
Rivas, 7,721	D 5
San Carlos, 1,547	E 5
Sandy Bay	F 3
San Francisco	E 5
San Jorge, 1,657	D 5
San Juan del Norte, 199	F 5
San Juan del Sur, 2,103	D 5
San Miguelito, 885	E 5
San Pedro	E 4
San Rafael del Norte, 1,298	E 4
San Rafael del Sur, 2,411	D 5
San Ramón, 436	E 4
Santa Cruz	E 4
Santo Domingo, 1,779	E 4
Santo Tomás, 1,530	E 4
Siuna, 3,743	F 3
Somotillo, 1,435	D 4
Somoto, 3,743	D 4
Telpaneca, 1,019	D 4
Terrabona, 690	E 4
Teustepe, 764	E 4
Tipitapa, 3,600	D 4
Tunki	E 4
Waspán, 973	E 3
Yablis	F 4

OTHER FEATURES

Alargate (reef)	F 3
Coco (river)	E 3
Cosegüina (point)	D 4
Dariense (range)	E 4
Dipilto (range)	D 4
Escondido (river)	F 4
Fonseca (gulf)	D 4
Gorda (point)	F 5
Gracias a Dios (cape)	F 3
Grande (river)	F 4
Great Corn (isl.), 1,896	F 4
Huapí (mts.)	E 4
Isabelia (range)	E 4
King (cays)	F 4
Kukalaya (river)	F 4
Little Corn (isl.)	F 4
Managua (lake)	D 4
Miskito (cays)	F 3
Monkey (point)	F 4
Mosquito Coast (reg.)	E 4
Nicaragua (lake)	E 5
Ometepe (isl.), 12,556	E 5
Pearl (cays)	F 4
Perlas (lagoon)	F 4
Prinzapolca (river)	F 4
Salinas (bay)	E 5
San Juan (river)	E, F 5
San Juan del Norte (bay)	F 5
Solentiname (isls.)	E 5
Tuma (river)	E 4
Tyra (cays)	F 4
Waspuk (river)	E 3
Wawa (river)	F 4
Zapatera (isl.)	E 5

PANAMA

CITIES and TOWNS

Aguadulce, 8,192	G 6
Alanje, †1,544	F 6
Almirante, 4,134	F 6
Antón, 3,022	G 6
Bajo Boquete, 2,625	F 6
Belén	G 6
Bocas del Toro, 2,462	F 6
Calobre, †1,933	G 6
Cañazas, †5,516	G 6
Capira, †2,168	G 6
Carreto	H 6
Chepo, †598	H 6
Chimán, †972	H 6
Chiriquí Grande, †1,517	F 6
Chitré, 12,575	G 7
Chorrera, 26,026	H 6
Coclé del Norte, †1,329	G 6
Colón, 67,641	H 6
David, 35,538	F 6
Dolega, †3,710	F 6
El Real	H 6
Garachiné, †1,471	H 6
Guabito, †3,531	F 6
Gualaca, †3,125	F 6
Horconcitos	F 6
La Concepción, 9,179	F 6
La Palma, 1,845	H 6
Las Palmas, †3,115	G 6
Las Tablas, 3,571	G 7
Loma Escobar (La Pintada)	G 6
Los Santos, 3,940	G 7
Mandinga	H 6
Miguel de la Borda	G 6
Miramar, †132	G 6
Montijo, †3,600	G 6
Natá, 8,446	G 6
Nuevo Chagres	G 6
Ocú, 15,267	G 7

Olá, †987	G 6
Panamá (cap.), 418,013	H 6
Parita, †2,320	G 6
Pedasí, †1,302	G 7
Penonomé, 5,067	G 6
Playón Chico	H 6
Playón Grande	H 6
Portobelo, 1626	H 6
Potrerillos	F 6
Puerto Armuelles, 12,022	F 6
Puerto Obaldía	J 6
San Carlos, †1,421	H 6
San Cristóbal	G 6
San Félix, †1,314	F 6
San Francisco, †1,576	G 6
Santa Fé, †1,768	G 6
Santiago, 14,391	G 6
Soná, 4,066	G 6
Tocumen, 15,905	H 6
Tolé, †4,734	F 6
Tonosí, †1,301	G 7

OTHER FEATURES

Azuero (pen.)	G 7
Bastimentos (isl.), 574	F 6
Brewster (mt.)	H 6
Burica (point)	F 6
Cébaco (isl.)	G 7
Chepo (river)	H 6
Chiriquí (gulf)	F 7
Chiriquí (lagoon)	F 6
Chiriquí (volcano)	F 6
Chucunaque (river)	J 6
Coiba (isl.)	F 7
Colón (isl.)	F 6
Contreras (isls.)	F 7
Darién (mts.)	J 6
Escudo de Veraguas (isl.)	G 6
Gatun (lake)	G 6
Gorda (point)	H 6
Jicarón (isl.)	F 7
Ladrones (isls.)	F 7
Manzanillo (point)	H 6
Montijo (gulf)	G 7
Mosquito (gulf)	G 6
Mulatas (arch.)	J 6
Panamá (gulf)	H 7
Pando (mt.)	F 6
Parida (isl.)	F 6
Parita (gulf)	G 6
Perlas (arch.)	H 6
Puercos (prom.)	H 7
Rey (isl.)	H 6
Rincón (point)	H 6
San Blas (gulf)	H 6
San Blas (range)	H 6
San José (isl.)	H 6
San Miguel (bay)	H 6
Santiago (mt.)	F 6
Secas (isls.)	F 7
Tabasará (mts.)	F 6
Taboga (isl.), 1,747	H 6
Tiburón (cape)	J 6
Urabá (gulf)	J 6
Valiente (pen.)	G 6

City and suburbs.
†Population of sub-district.
‡Population of district.

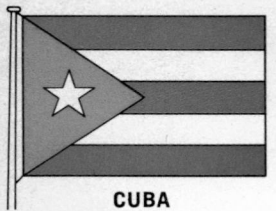
CUBA

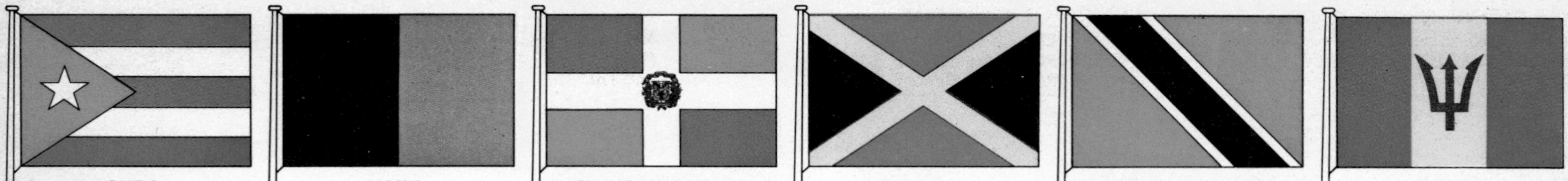

HAITI

DOMINICAN REPUBLIC

JAMAICA

TRINIDAD AND TOBAGO

BARBADOS

CUBA
AREA 44,206 sq. mi.
POPULATION 8,553,395
CAPITAL Havana
LARGEST CITY Havana
HIGHEST POINT Pico Turquino 6,561 ft.
MONETARY UNIT Cuban peso
MAJOR LANGUAGE Spanish
MAJOR RELIGION Roman Catholicism

HAITI
AREA 10,694 sq. mi.
POPULATION 4,867,190
CAPITAL Port-au-Prince
LARGEST CITY Port-au-Prince
HIGHEST POINT Pic La Selle 8,793 ft.
MONETARY UNIT gourde
MAJOR LANGUAGES Creole French, French
MAJOR RELIGION Roman Catholicism

DOMINICAN REPUBLIC
AREA 18,704 sq. mi.
POPULATION 4,011,589
CAPITAL Santo Domingo
LARGEST CITY Santo Domingo
HIGHEST POINT Pico Duarte 10,417 ft.
MONETARY UNIT Dominican peso
MAJOR LANGUAGE Spanish
MAJOR RELIGION Roman Catholicism

JAMAICA
AREA 4,411 sq. mi.
POPULATION 1,972,000
CAPITAL Kingston
LARGEST CITY Kingston
HIGHEST POINT Blue Mountain Peak, 7,402 ft.
MONETARY UNIT Jamaican pound
MAJOR LANGUAGE English
MAJOR RELIGIONS Protestantism, Roman Catholicism

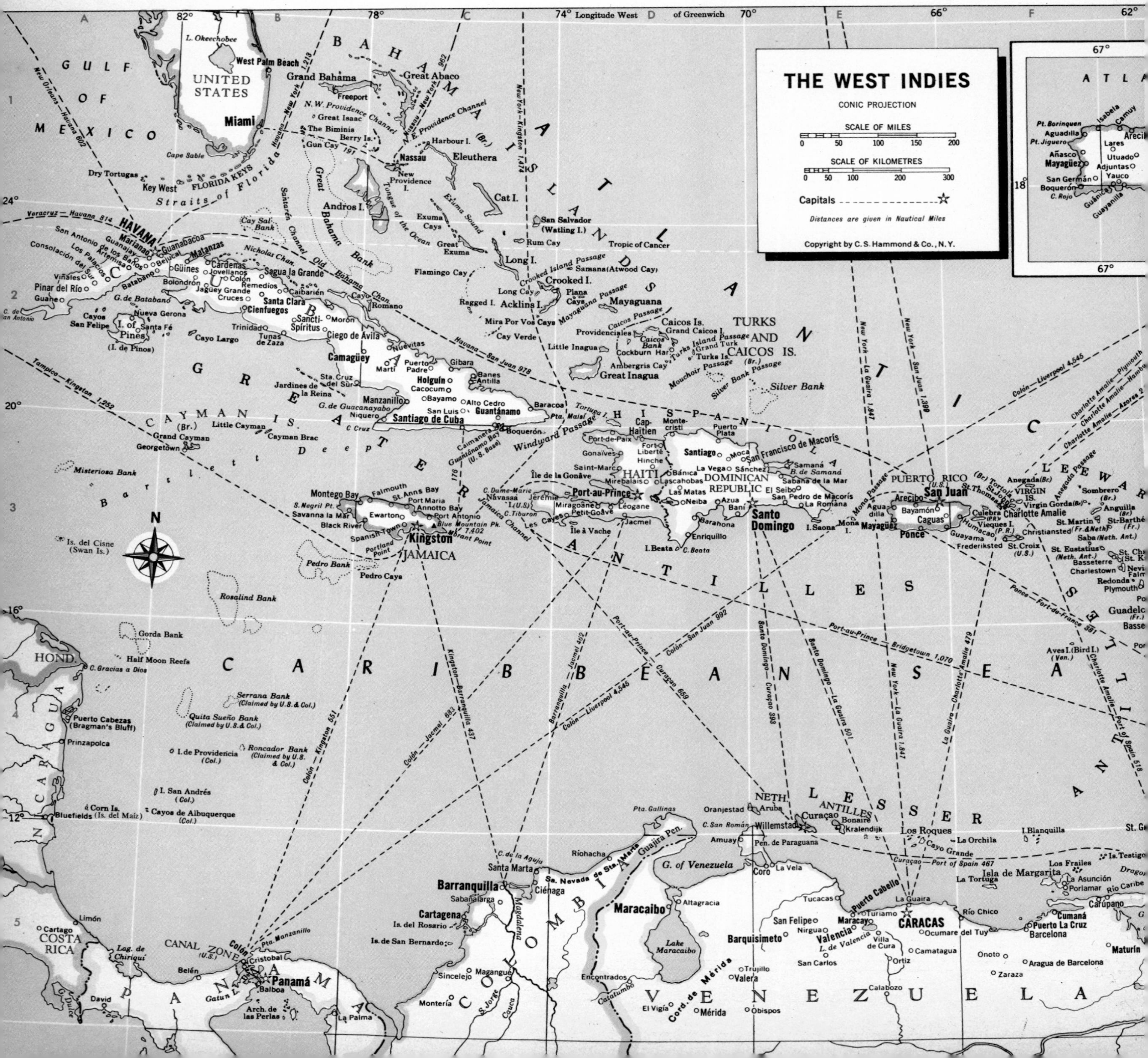

THE WEST INDIES

CONIC PROJECTION

SCALE OF MILES
0   50   100   150   200

SCALE OF KILOMETRES
0   50   100   200   300

Capitals - - - - - - - ☆

Distances are given in Nautical Miles

Copyright by C. S. Hammond & Co., N.Y.

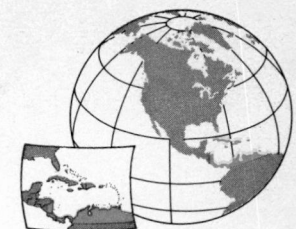

TRINIDAD AND TOBAGO
AREA 1,980 sq. mi.
POPULATION 1,040,000
CAPITAL Port of Spain
LARGEST CITY Port of Spain
HIGHEST POINT Mt. Aripo 3,084 ft.
MONETARY UNIT Trinidad and Tobago dollar
MAJOR LANGUAGES English, Hindi
MAJOR RELIGIONS Roman Catholicism, Protestantism, Hinduism, Islam

BARBADOS
AREA 166 sq. mi.
POPULATION 253,620
CAPITAL Bridgetown
LARGEST CITY Bridgetown
HIGHEST POINT Mt. Hillaby 1,104 ft.
MONETARY UNIT East Caribbean dollar
MAJOR LANGUAGE English
MAJOR RELIGION Protestantism

BAHAMA ISLANDS
AREA 4,404 sq. mi.
POPULATION 168,838
CAPITAL Nassau
MONETARY UNIT Bahaman dollar
MAJOR LANGUAGE English
MAJOR RELIGIONS Roman Catholicism, Protestantism

VIRGIN ISLANDS (U.S.)
AREA 133 sq. mi.
POPULATION 62,468
CAPITAL Charlotte Amalie
MONETARY UNIT U.S. dollar
MAJOR LANGUAGES English, Creole
MAJOR RELIGIONS Roman Catholicism, Protestantism

VIRGIN ISLANDS (BR.)
AREA 59 sq. mi.
POPULATION 10,484
CAPITAL Road Town
MONETARY UNIT British West Indian dollar
MAJOR LANGUAGES English, Creole
MAJOR RELIGION Protestantism

NETHERLANDS ANTILLES
AREA 390 sq. mi.
POPULATION 220,000
CAPITAL Willemstad
MONETARY UNIT Antilles guilder
MAJOR LANGUAGES Dutch, Papiamento, English
MAJOR RELIGIONS Roman Catholicism, Protestantism

PUERTO RICO
AREA 3,435 sq. mi.
POPULATION 2,712,033
CAPITAL San Juan
MONETARY UNIT U.S. dollar
MAJOR LANGUAGES Spanish, English
MAJOR RELIGION Roman Catholicism

BERMUDA
AREA 21 sq. mi.
POPULATION 52,000
CAPITAL Hamilton
MONETARY UNIT Bermuda dollar
MAJOR LANGUAGE English
MAJOR RELIGION Protestantism

ANTIGUA
Barbuda (isl.), 1,145 ....G 3
Redonda (isl.) ....F 3
Saint John's (cap.), 24,367 ......G 3

BAHAMA ISLANDS
Acklins (isl.), 1,160 ....C 2
Andros (isl.), 7,460 ....B 2
Atwood (Samana) (cay), 32 .....D 2
Berry (isls.), 266 ....B 1
Biminis, The (isls.), 1,576 ....B 1
Cat (isl.), 3,131 ....C 1
Crooked (isl.), 764 ....D 2
Eleuthera (isl.), 7,247 ....C 1
Exuma (cays), 220 ....C 1
Exuma (Great Exuma) (isl.), 2,854 ....C 2
Grand Bahama (isl.), 7,847 .....B 1
Great Abaco (isl.), 4,746 ....C 1
Great Exuma (isl.), 2,854 ....C 2
Great Inagua (isl.), 1,240 ....D 2
Great Issac (isl.), 5 ....B 1
Gun (cay), 3 ....B 1
Harbour (isl.), 997 ....C 2
Long (cay), 22 ....C 2
Long (isl.), 4,176 ....C 2
Mayaguana (isl.), 707 ....D 2
Nassau (cap.), *100,000 ....C 1
New Providence (isl.), 100,000 ...C 1
Plana (cays), 3 ....D 2
Ragged (isl.), 371 ....C 2
Rum (cay), 77 ....C 2
Samana (cay), 32 ....C 1
San Salvador (isl.), 968 ....C 1
Tongue of the Ocean (chan.) ...C 1
Watling (San Salvador) (isl.), 968 ....C 1

BARBADOS
Bridgetown (cap.), 12,430 ....G 4

BERMUDA
Bermuda (isl.) ....H 3
Castle (harb.) ....H 2
Great (sound) ....H 3
Hamilton (cap.), 3,000 ....H 3
Hamilton, *14,156 ....H 3
Harrington (sound) ....G 3
Ireland (isl.) ....H 2
Saint David's (isl.) ....H 2
Saint George, 1,335 ....H 2
Saint George's (isl.) ....H 2
Somerset (isl.) ....G 3

CAYMAN ISLANDS
Total Population, 10,652

Cayman Brac (isl.), 1,240 ......B 3
Georgetown (cap.), 4,106 ......B 3
Grand Cayman (isl.), 9,309 ....B 3
Little Cayman (isl.), 23 ....B 3

CUBA
Bayamo, 45,400 ....C 2
Camagüey, 178,600 ....B 2
Cárdenas, 67,400 ....B 2
Ciego de Ávila, 54,700 ....B 2
Cienfuegos, 91,800 ....B 2
Florida (isl.) ....B 1
Guanabacoa, 41,000 ....B 2
Guantánamo, 135,100 ....C 2
Güines, 45,000 ....B 2
Havana (cap.), *1,577,200 ......B 2
Holguín, 100,500 ....C 2
Manzanillo, 91,200 ....C 2
Marianao, 454,700 ....B 2
Matanzas, 84,100 ....B 2
Pinar del Río, 67,600 ....A 2
Pines (Pinos) (isl.), 20,630 .....A 2
Sagua la Grande, 35,200 ....B 2
Sancti-Spíritus, 62,500 ....B 2
San Felipe (cay), 391 ....A 2

Santa Clara, 137,700 ....B 2
Santiago de Cuba, 259,000 ....B 2
Viñales, 1,602 ....A 2
Windward (passage) ....C 3

DOMINICA
Roseau (cap.), *16,677 ....G 4

DOMINICAN REPUBLIC
Barahona, 37,889 ....D 3
La Romana, 36,722 ....E 3
La Vega, 31,085 ....D 3
Puerto Plata, 32,181 ....D 3
San Francisco de Macorís, 43,941 ....E 3
San Pedro de Macorís, 42,473 ...E 3
Santiago, 155,151 ....D 3
Santo Domingo (cap.), 671,402 ...E 3

GRENADA
Carriacou (isl.), 6,958 ....G 4
Gouyave, 2,356 ....F 4
Grenadines (isls.), 5,612 ....G 4
Saint George's (cap.), *26,843 ...F 5

GUADELOUPE
Basse-Terre (cap.), 16,000 .....F 4
Saint-Barthélemy (isl.), 2,351 ...F 3
Saint-Martin (isl.), 5,062 ....F 3

HAITI
Cap-Haïtien, 30,000 ....D 3
Gonâve (isl.), 45,411 ....D 3
Jérémie, 1199,598 ....D 3
Léogâne, 1140,607 ....D 3
Les Cayes, *95,446 ....D 3
Port-au-Prince (cap.), *352,681 ...D 3
Tortuga (Tortue) (isl.), 13,723 ...D 2

JAMAICA
Blue Mountain (peak) ....C 3
Jamaica (channel) ....C 3
Kingston (cap.), *376,520 ......C 3
Montego Bay, 23,610 ....B 3
Pedro (cays) ....C 3
Port Antonio, 7,830 ....C 3
Savanna la Mar, 9,789 ....B 3
Spanish Town, 14,706 ....C 3

MARTINIQUE
Forte-de-France (cap.), 100,000 ...G 4
Pelée (vol.) ....G 4

MONTSERRAT
Total Population, 12,300

Plymouth (cap.), 3,000 ....F 3

NETHERLANDS ANTILLES
Aruba (isl.), 58,868 ....E 4
Bonaire (isl.), 5,755 ....E 4
Curaçao (isl.), 196,170 ....E 4
Saba (isl.), 1,094 ....F 3
Saint Eustatius (isl.), 1,020 .....F 3
Sint Maarten (Saint Martin) (isl.), 4,970 ....F 3
Willemstad (cap.), *94,133 .....E 4

PUERTO RICO
Aguadilla, 21,031 ....F 1
Arecibo, 35,484 ....F 1
Bayamón, 147,552 ....G 1
Caguas, *95,661 ....G 1
Cataño, 26,459 ....G 1
Cayey, 21,562 ....G 1
Culebra (isl.), 732 ....G 1
Guayama, 20,318 ....G 1
Humacao, 12,411 ....G 1
Mayagüez, *85,857 ....F 1
Mona (isl.), 6 ....E 3
Ponce, *158,981 ....F 1
San Juan (cap.), *851,247 .....G 1
Vieques (isl.), 7,767 ....G 1

SAINT CHRISTOPHER-NEVIS-ANGUILLA
Anguilla (isl.), 5,605 ....F 3
Basseterre (cap.), 15,726 ....F 3
Sombrero (isl.), 5 ....F 3

SAINT LUCIA
Castries (cap.), *15,291 ....G 4

SAINT VINCENT
Bequia (isl.) ....G 4
Canouan (isl.) ....G 4
Grenadines (isls.), 6,428 ....G 4
Kingstown (cap.), *23,482 ......G 4
Union (isl.) ....G 4

TRINIDAD AND TOBAGO
Port of Spain (cap.), *250,000 ...G 5
Scarborough, 1,931 ....G 5
Tobago (isl.), 36,850 ....G 5
Trinidad (isl.), 973,250 ....G 5

TURKS AND CAICOS IS.
Total Population, 6,000

Caicos (isls.), 2,200 ....D 2
Cockburn Harbour, 866 ....D 2
Grand Turk (isl.), 2,339 ....D 2
Providenciales (isl.), 510 ....D 2
Turks (isl.), 3,800 ....D 2

VIRGIN ISLANDS (BRITISH)
Anegada (isl.), 290 ....H 1
Road Town (cap.), 2,183 ....H 1

VIRGIN ISLANDS (U.S.)
Charlotte Amalie (cap.), 12,220 ...H 1
Saint Croix (isl.), 31,779 ....H 1
Saint John (isl.), 1,729 ....H 1
Saint Thomas (isl.), 28,960 ....G 1

WEST INDIES
Antilles Gtr. (isls.), 22,094,100 ...D 3
Antilles, Lesser, 2,749,000 .....F 4
Hispaniola (isl.), 8,878,800 ....D 2
Leeward (isls.), 599,300 ....F 3
Navassa (isl.) ....C 3
Windward (isls.), 2,149,750 ....G 4

*City and suburbs.
†Population of commune.
‡Population of met. area.

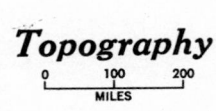

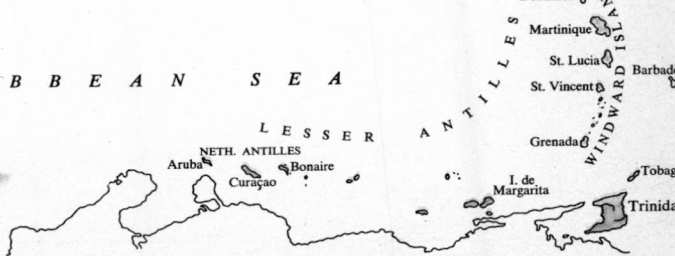

Topography

MILES
0   100   200

| Below Sea Level | 100 m. 328 ft. | 200 m. 656 ft. | 500 m. 1,640 ft. | 1,000 m. 3,281 ft. | 2,000 m. 6,562 ft. | 5,000 m. 16,404 ft. |

158 West Indies

(continued)

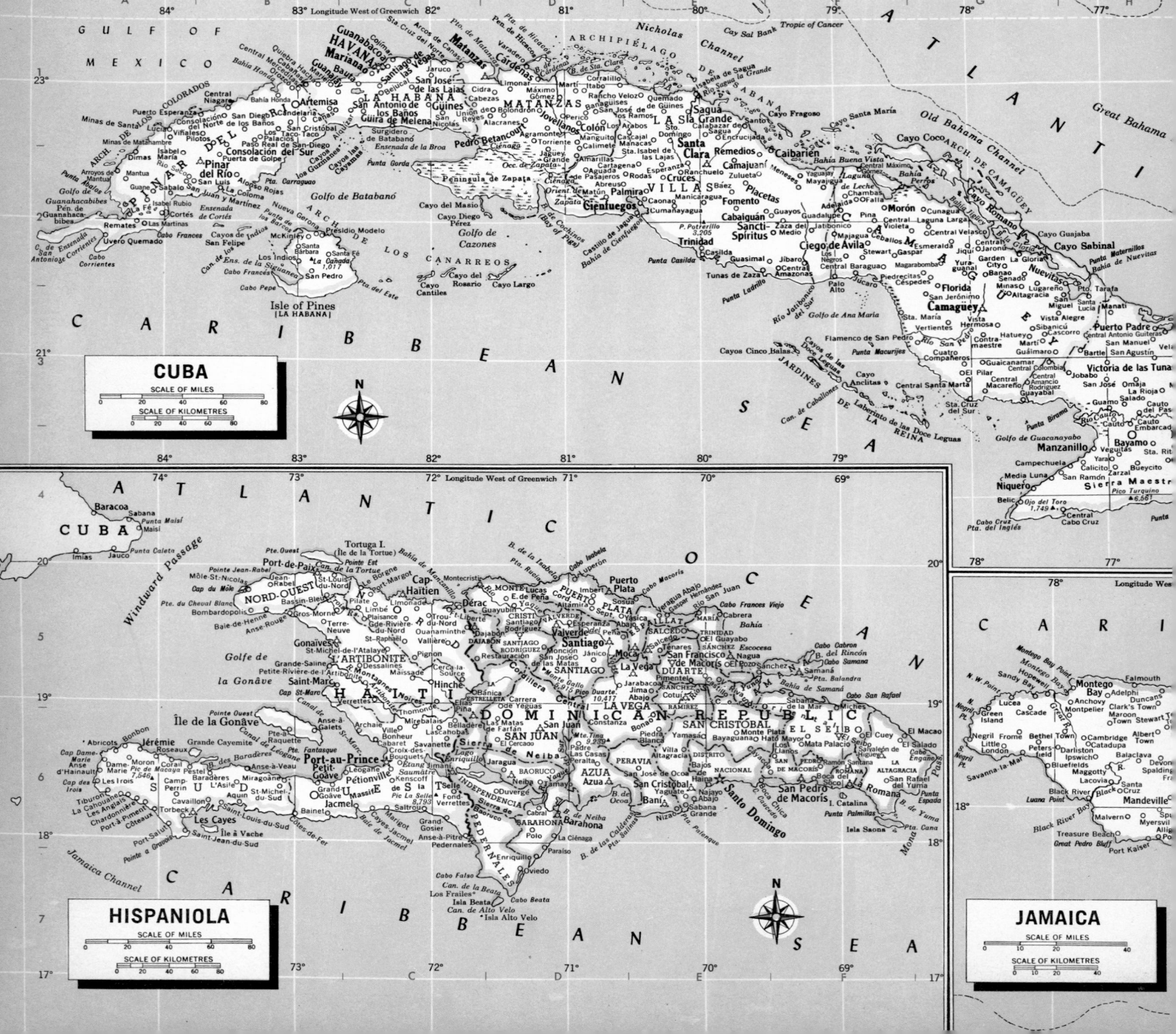

- Camagüey (arch.) G 2
- Cantiles (cay) C 3
- Cárdenas (bay) D 1
- Carraguao (point) B 2
- Casilda (point) E 2
- Cauto (river) H 3
- Cayamas (cays) C 2
- Cazones (gulf) C 2
- Cienfuegos (bay) D 2
- Cinco Balas (cays) E 3
- Cochinos (bay) D 2
- Coco (cay) G 1
- Corrientes (cape) A 2
- Corrientes (inlet) A 2
- Cortés (inlet) B 2
- Cristal, Sierra del (mts.) J 4
- Cruz (cape) G 4
- Diego Pérez (cay) C 2
- Doce Leguas (cays) F 3
- Este (point) C 3
- Fragoso (cay) F 1
- Francés (cape) A 2
- Gorda (point) C 2
- Gran Piedra (mt.) J 4
- Guacanayabo (gulf) G 4
- Guajaba (cay) H 2
- Guanahacabibes (gulf) A 2
- Guanahacabibes (pen.) A 2
- Guantánamo (bay) J 4
- Guantánamo Bay U.S. Naval Reserve J 4
- Guarico (point) K 3
- Guzmanes (cays) B 2
- Hicacos (pen.) D 1
- Hicacos (point) D 1
- Honda (bay) B 1
- Indios (chan.) B 2
- Inglés (point) G 4
- Jardines de la Reina (arch.) F 3
- Jatibonico del Sur (river) F 3
- Jigüey (bay) G 2
- Laberinto de las Doce Leguas (cays) F 3
- La Cañada (mt.) B 2
- La Gloria (bay) G 2
- Ladrillo (point) E 2
- Largo (cay) D 2
- Leche (lagoon) F 2
- Los Barcos (point) B 2
- Los Canarreos (arch.) C 2
- Los Colorados (arch.) A 1
- Lucrecia (cape) J 3
- Macurijes (point) F 3
- Maestra, Sierra (mts.) H 4
- Maisí (point) K 4
- Mangle (point) J 3
- Masio (cay) C 2
- Matanzas (bay) D 1
- Matanzas (point) H 2
- Mayarí (river) J 4
- Nicholas (chan.) E 1
- Nipe (bay) J 3
- Nuevitas (bay) H 2
- Ojo del Toro (mt.) G 4
- Old Bahama (chan.) G 1
- Pepe (cape) B 1
- Perros (bay) G 2
- Pigs (Cochinos) (bay) D 2
- Pines (isl.), 20,630 G 3
- Potrerillo (peak) E 2
- Quemado (point) A 4
- Romano (cay) G 2
- Rosario (cay) C 2
- Sabana (arch.) E 1
- Sabinal (cay) H 2
- Sagua la Grande (river) E 1
- San Antonio (cape) A 2
- San Felipe (cays) B 2
- San Pedro (river) G 3
- Santa Clara (bay) D 1
- Santa María (cay) F 1
- Siguanea (bay) B 2
- Tabacal (point) H 4
- Toa, Cuchillas de (mts.) K 4
- Tortuguilla (point) K 4
- Turquino (peak) H 4
- Zapata (pen.) C 2
- Zapata Occidental (swamp) D 2
- Zapata Oriental (swamp) D 2

DOMINICAN REPUBLIC

PROVINCES

- Azua, 91,511 D 6
- Baoruco, 66,572 D 6
- Barahona, 112,914 D 6
- Dajabón, 50,780 D 5
- Distrito Nacional, 817,467 E 6
- Duarte, 200,813 E 5
- El Seibo, 132,795 F 6
- Espaillat, 139,579 E 5
- Independencia, 32,580 D 6
- La Altagracia, 87,180 F 6
- La Estrelleta, 53,228 C 5
- La Romana, 56,955 F 6
- La Vega, 293,694 D 6
- María Trinidad Sánchez, 97,043 E 5
- Montecristi, 69,276 D 5
- Pedernales, 12,547 D 7
- Peravia, 127,587 E 6
- Puerto Plata, 185,800 D 5
- Salcedo, 89,773 E 5
- Samaná, 53,893 E 5
- San Cristóbal, 324,395 E 6
- San Juan, 191,065 D 6
- San Pedro de Macorís, 105,490 F 6
- Sánchez Ramírez, 106,177 E 5
- Santiago, 386,269 D 5
- Santiago Rodríguez, 49,598 D 5
- Valverde, 76,608 D 5

CITIES and TOWNS

- Altamira, 1,573 D 5
- Azua, 18,584 D 6
- Bajos de Haina, 10,396 E 6
- Baní, 23,716 E 6
- Bánica, 1,303 D 5
- Barahona, 37,889 D 6
- Bayaguana, 2,947 E 6
- Bonao E 6
- Cabral, 5,575 D 6
- Cabrera, 1,899 E 5
- Castillo, 3,191 E 5
- Cayacoa E 6
- Ciudad Trujillo (Santo Domingo) (cap.), 671,402 E 6
- Constanza, 4,316 D 6
- Cotuí, 7,574 E 5
- Dajabón, 6,027 D 5
- Duvergé, 7,979 D 6
- El Cercado, 3,369 D 6
- El Cuey F 6
- El Guayabo E 5
- El Pozo E 5
- El Salado F 6
- El Seibo, 8,958 F 6
- Elías Piña, 5,099 C 6
- Enriquillo, 4,103 D 7
- Esperanza, 10,684 D 5
- Gaspar Hernández, 2,222 E 5
- Guayubín, 1,369 D 5
- Hato Mayor, 9,985 F 6
- Imbert, 4,321 D 5
- Jánico, 1,117 D 5
- Jarabacoa, 6,329 E 5
- Jaragua, 4,853 D 6
- Jimaní, 2,248 C 6
- La Romana, 36,722 F 6
- La Vega, 31,085 D 5
- Las Matas de Farfán, 7,138 D 6
- Los Llanos, 1,849 F 6
- Lucas E. de Peña D 5
- Luperón, 1,991 D 5
- Mata Palacio F 6
- Miches, 4,410 F 6
- Moca, 18,965 D 5
- Moncíon, 2,007 D 5
- Montecristi, 8,252 C 5
- Monte Plata, 3,636 E 6
- Nagua, 13,937 E 5
- Najayo Abajo E 6
- Neiba, 10,194 D 6
- Nizao, 3,178 E 6
- Oviedo, 2,117 D 7
- Padre Las Casas, 2,953 D 6
- Paraíso, 3,496 D 7
- Pedernales, 5,919 C 7
- Peña D 5
- Peralta D 6
- Pimentel, 5,954 E 5
- Polo D 6
- Puerto Plata, 32,181 D 5
- Ramón Santana, 4,139 F 6
- Restauración, 1,784 D 5
- Río San Juan, 2,764 E 5
- Sabana de la Mar, 6,841 F 5
- Sabana Grande de Palenque, 1,950 E 6
- Salcedo, 11,459 E 5
- Salvaleón de Higüey, 21,741 F 6
- Samaná, 4,435 F 5
- Sánchez, 6,583 E 5
- San Cristóbal, 25,829 E 6
- San Francisco de Macorís, 43,941 E 5
- San José de las Matas, 3,228 D 5
- San José de Ocoa, 9,382 E 6
- San Juan, 32,248 D 6
- San Pedro de Macorís, 42,473 E 6
- San Rafael del Yuma, 1,944 F 6
- Santiago, 155,151 D 5
- Santiago Rodríguez, 9,637 D 5
- Santo Domingo (cap.), 671,402 E 6
- Sosúa, 4,204 E 5
- Tamayo, 4,177 D 6
- Tenares, 2,663 E 5
- Valverde, 27,111 D 5
- Villa Altagracia, 10,300 E 6
- Villa Riva 2,165 E 5
- Yaguate, 1,854 E 6
- Yamasá, 2,642 E 6
- Yásica Abajo E 5

OTHER FEATURES

- Alto Velo (chan.) C 7
- Alto Velo (isl.) D 7
- Balandra (point) F 5
- Baoruco, Sierra de (mts.) D 6
- Beata (cape) D 7
- Beata (chan.) C 7
- Beata (isl.) C 7
- Cabrón (cape) F 5
- Calderas (bay) D 6
- Cana (point) F 6
- Catalina (isl.) F 6
- Caucedo (cape) E 6
- Central, Cordillera (range) D 5
- Duarte (peak) D 5
- Engaño (cape) F 5
- Enriquillo (lake) C 6
- Escocesa (bay) E 5
- Espada (point) F 6
- Falso (cape) C 7
- Francés Viejo (cape) E 5
- Gallo (mt.) D 5
- Isabela (bay) D 5
- Isabela (cape) D 5
- Los Frailes (isl.) C 7
- Macorís (cape) E 5
- Manzanillo (bay) C 5
- Mona (passage) F 6
- Neiba (bay) D 6
- Neiba (mt.) D 6
- Ocoa (bay) D 6
- Oriental, Cordillera (range) F 6
- Palenque (point) E 6
- Palmillas (point) F 6
- Rincón (bay) F 5
- Rucia (point) D 5
- Salinas (point) E 6
- Samaná (bay) F 5
- Samaná (cape) F 5
- San Rafael (cape) F 5
- Saona (isl.) F 6
- Septentrional, Cord. (range) D 5
- Tina (mt.) D 6
- Yaque del Norte (river) D 5
- Yaque del Sur (river) D 6
- Yuma (bay) F 6
- Yuna (river) E 5

HAITI

DEPARTMENTS

- Artibonite, 748,357 C 5
- Nord, 747,360 C 5
- Nord-Ouest, 247,326 B 5
- Ouest, 1,983,826 C 6
- Sud, 1,041,232 A 6

CITIES and TOWNS

- Abricots, †26,612 B 6
- Anse-à-Pitre, †16,195 C 6
- Anse-à-Veau, †41,690 B 6
- Anse-d'Hainault, †18,416 A 6
- Anse-Rouge, †14,657 B 5
- Aquin, †95,283 B 6
- Archaie, †52,221 C 6
- Baie-de-Henne, †6,927 B 5
- Baradères, †33,575 B 6
- Bassin-Bleu, †23,623 B 5
- Belladère, †35,706 C 6
- Bombardopolis, †13,556 B 5
- Bonbon, †8,711 A 6
- Camp-Perrin, †25,398 A 6
- Cap-Haïtien, 30,000 C 5
- Cavaillon, †50,479 A 6
- Cayes-Jacmel, †39,726 C 6
- Cerca-la-Source, †20,671 C 5
- Chardonnière, †15,270 A 6
- Corail, †47,936 A 6
- Côteaux, †28,327 A 6
- Côtes-de-Fer, †122,568 B 6
- Croix-des-Bouquets, †83,250 C 6
- Dame-Marie, †27,430 A 2
- Dessalines, †86,348 C 5
- Fort-Liberté, †26,942 C 5
- Gonaïves, †99,140 B 5
- Grand-Goâve, †60,589 B 6
- Grand-Gosier, †29,102 C 6
- Grande-Rivière-du-Nord, †29,904 C 5
- Grande-Saline, †30,628 B 5
- Gros-Morne, †90,116 B 4
- Hinche, †63,796 C 5
- Jacmel, †199,598 C 6
- Jean-Rabel, †55,834 B 5
- Jérémie, †92,500 A 6
- Kenscoff, †24,219 C 6
- La Cahouane A 6
- Lascahobas, †29,760 C 6
- Le Borgne, †51,325 C 5
- Léogane, †140,607 C 6
- Les Anglais, †15,321 A 6
- Les Cayes, †95,446 B 6
- Limbé, †52,315 C 5
- Limonade, †21,395 C 5
- Maissade, †26,568 C 5
- Marigot, †65,402 C 6
- Miragoâne, †50,059 B 6
- Mirebalais, †78,060 C 6
- Môle-Saint-Nicolas, †14,352 B 5
- Moron, †17,020 A 6
- Ouanaminthe, †55,717 C 5
- Pestel, †33,007 A 6
- Pétionville, †52,221 C 6
- Petit-Goâve, †123,157 B 6
- Petite-Rivière-de-l'Artibonite, †65,772 B 5
- Pignon, †15,512 C 5
- Pilate, †40,293 C 5
- Plaisance, †47,896 C 5
- Pointe-à-Raquette B 6
- Port-à-Piment, †14,072 A 6
- Port-au-Prince (cap.), 265,000 C 6
- Port-au-Prince, *352,681 C 6
- Port-de-Paix, †54,016 B 5
- Port-Margot, †33,043 C 5
- Port-Salut, †41,055 A 6
- Roseaux, †25,984 A 6
- Saint-Jean-du-Sud, †18,923 B 6
- Saint-Louis-du-Nord, †44,898 B 5
- Saint-Louis-du-Sud, †42,807 B 6
- Saint-Marc, †61,359 B 5
- Saint-Michel-de-l'Atalaye, †68,813 C 5
- Saint-Raphaël, †25,708 C 5
- Saltrou, †57,067 C 6
- Savanette, †55,505 C 6
- Terre-Neuve, †15,953 B 5
- Thomonde, †15,660 C 6
- Tiburon, †9,860 A 6
- Torbeck, †66,480 A 6
- Trou-du-Nord, †29,324 C 5
- Vallière, †16,089 C 5
- Verrettes, †39,327 C 5

OTHER FEATURES

- Artibonite (river) C 5
- Baradères (bay) B 6
- Cheval Blanc (point) B 5
- Dame-Marie (cape) A 6
- Est (point) C 4
- Fantasque (point) B 6
- Gonâve (gulf) B 5
- Gonâve (isl.), 45,411 B 6
- Grande Cayemite (isl.) B 6
- Gravois (point) A 6
- Irois (cape) A 6
- Jean-Rabel (point) B 5
- La Selle (mts.) C 6
- La Selle (peak) C 6
- Macaya (peak) A 6
- Manzanillo (bay) C 5
- Môle (cape) B 5
- Noires (mts.) C 5
- Ouest (point) B 4
- Ouest (point) B 6
- Saint-Marc (cape) B 5
- Saint-Marc (chan.) B 6
- Saumâtre (lake) C 6
- Tortue (chan.) C 5
- Tortue (isl.), 13,723 C 4
- Tortuga (Tortue) (isl.), 13,723 C 4
- Trois-Rivières (river) B 5
- Vache (isl.) B 6
- Windward (passage) A 5

JAMAICA

CITIES and TOWNS

- Adelphi H 5
- Albany, 1,590 J 6
- Albert Town, 1,650 H 6
- Alley J 7
- Alligator Pond H 6
- Anchovy H 5
- Annotto Bay, 3,559 K 6
- Balaclava, 1,153 H 6
- Bath, 1,979 K 6
- Bethel Town G 6
- Black River, 3,077 H 6
- Bluefields H 6
- Bog Walk, 2,808 J 6
- Brown's Town, 3,899 H 6
- Buff Bay, 2,821 K 6
- Cambridge H 6
- Castleton J 6
- Catadupa H 6
- Chapelton, 4,417 J 6
- Christiana, 4,404 H 6
- Claremont, 1,417 J 6
- Clark's Town, 1,543 H 6
- Darliston H 6
- Devon H 6
- Discovery Bay J 5
- Ewarton J 6
- Falmouth, 3,727 H 5
- Four Paths J 6
- Frankfield, 2,123 H 6
- Golden Grove K 6
- Green Island G 6
- Hayes J 6
- Highgate, 3,313 J 6
- Hope Bay K 6
- Hopewell G 5
- Kingston (cap.), 123,403 K 6
- Kingston, *376,520 K 6
- Lacovia H 6
- Linstead, 3,781 J 6
- Lionel Town, 2,664 J 7
- Little London G 6
- Lluidas Vale J 6
- Lucea, 2,803 G 5
- Maggotty H 6
- Malvern H 6
- Manchioneal K 6
- Mandeville, 8,416 H 6
- Maroon Town H 6
- May Pen, 14,085 J 6
- Moneague J 6
- Montego Bay, 23,610 H 5
- Moore Town K 6
- Morant Bay, 5,054 K 7
- Myersville H 6
- Negril G 6
- Ocho Rios, 4,570 J 6
- Old England H 6
- Old Harbour, 4,192 J 6
- Oracabessa, 1,313 J 5
- Petersfield G 6
- Port Antonio, 7,830 K 6
- Port Kaiser H 7
- Port Maria, 3,998 J 6
- Port Morant, 2,284 K 6
- Port Rhoades J 6
- Port Royal, 37,673 J 6
- Porus, 2,723 H 6
- Richmond J 6
- Runaway Bay J 5
- Saint Ann's Bay, 5,087 J 5
- Saint Margaret's Bay K 6
- Sandy Bay G 5
- Santa Cruz, 1,426 H 6
- Savanna la Mar, 9,789 G 6
- Spaldings, 2,003 H 6
- Spanish Town, 14,706 J 6
- Stewart Town H 6
- Tobolski J 6
- Treasure Beach H 6
- Trinityville K 6
- Trout Hall J 6
- Ulster Spring H 6
- Williamsfield H 6
- Yallahs K 6

OTHER FEATURES

- Black (river) H 6
- Black River (bay) G 6
- Blue (mts.) K 6
- Blue Mountain (peak) K 6
- Galina (point) J 6
- Grande (river) K 6
- Great (river) H 6
- Great Pedro Bluff (prom.) H 6
- Long (bay) H 7
- Luana (point) G 6
- Minho (river) J 6
- Montego (bay) G 5
- Montego Bay (point) G 5
- North East (point) K 6
- North Negril (point) G 6
- North West (point) G 5
- Old Harbour (bay) J 6
- Portland (point) J 7
- Sir John's (peak) K 6
- South East (point) K 6
- South Negril (point) G 6

*City and suburbs.
†Population of commune.
‡Population of met. area.

LEGEND
Capitals of Countries
Provincial Capitals
International Boundaries
Provincial Boundaries
Copyright by C. S. HAMMOND & Co., N.Y.
BAHAMA IS.
OCEAN
CARIBBEAN SEA
Santiago de Cuba
Guantánamo
Baracoa
Kingston
Spanish Town
Port Antonio
Montego Bay
May Pen

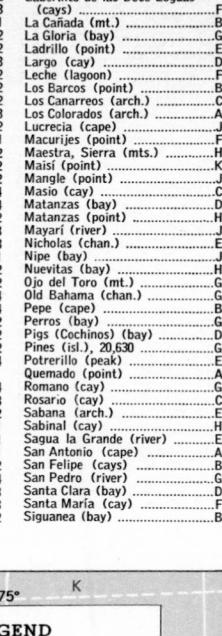

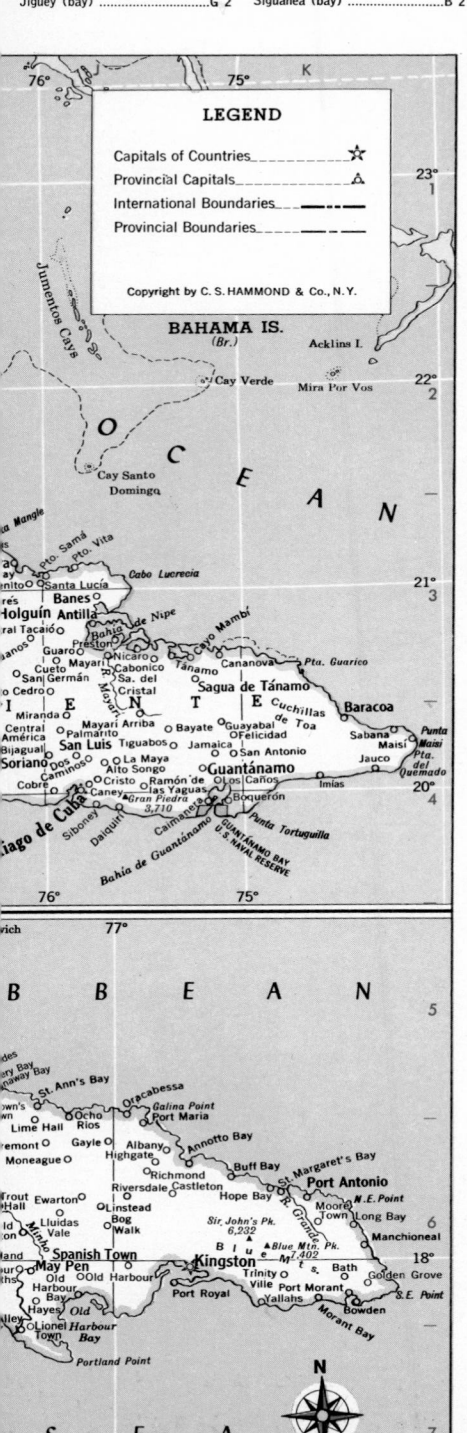

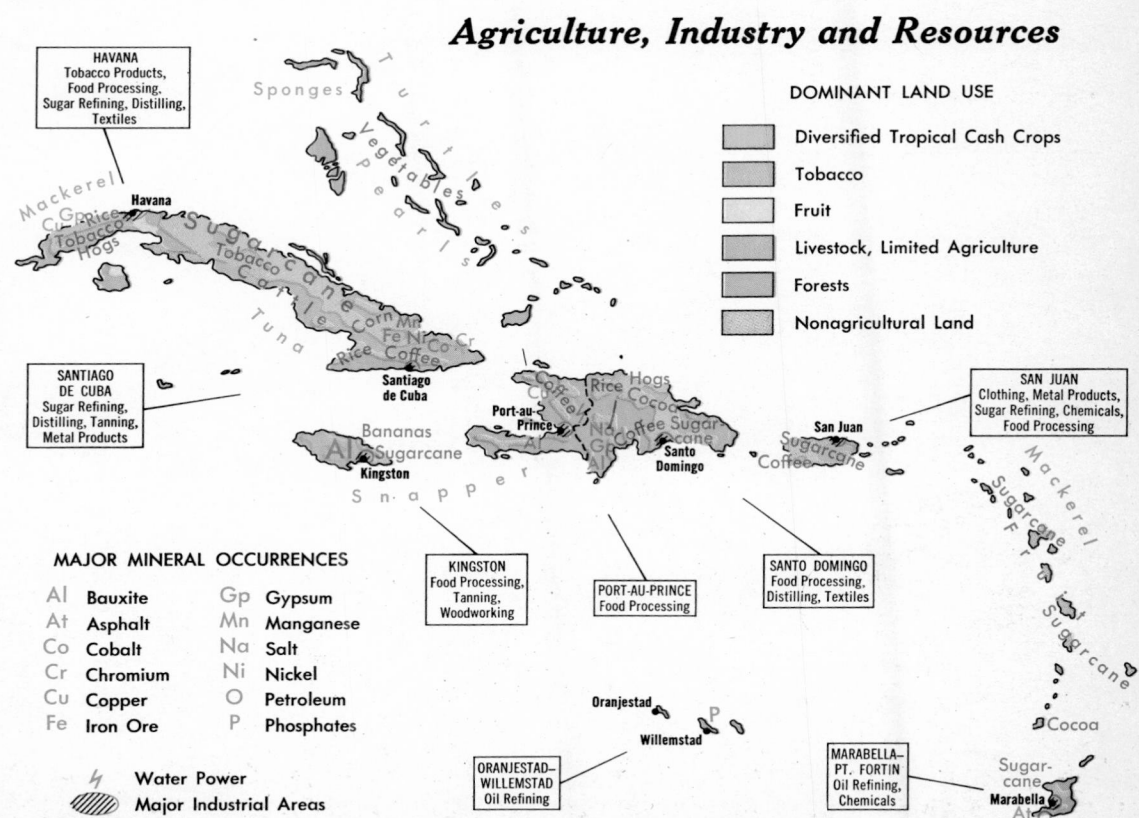

Agriculture, Industry and Resources

DOMINANT LAND USE
Diversified Tropical Cash Crops
Tobacco
Fruit
Livestock, Limited Agriculture
Forests
Nonagricultural Land
MAJOR MINERAL OCCURRENCES
Al Bauxite
At Asphalt
Co Cobalt
Cr Chromium
Cu Copper
Fe Iron Ore
Gp Gypsum
Mn Manganese
Na Salt
Ni Nickel
O Petroleum
P Phosphates
Water Power
Major Industrial Areas
HAVANA
Tobacco Products, Food Processing. Sugar Refining, Distilling, Textiles
SANTIAGO DE CUBA
Sugar Refining, Distilling, Tanning, Metal Products
KINGSTON
Food Processing, Tanning, Woodworking
PORT-AU-PRINCE
Food Processing
SANTO DOMINGO
Food Processing, Distilling, Textiles
SAN JUAN
Clothing, Metal Products, Sugar Refining, Chemicals, Food Processing
ORANJESTAD–WILLEMSTAD
Oil Refining
MARABELLA–PT. FORTIN
Oil Refining, Chemicals

PUERTO RICO

DISTRICTS

Aguadilla, 284,983 .... A 1
Arecibo, 270,492 .... C 1
Bayamón, 359,499 .... D 1
Guayama, 335,305 .... D 2
Humacao, 283,481 .... F 2
Mayagüez, 267,731 .... B 2
Ponce, 308,988 .... C 2
San Juan, 601,554 .... E 1

CITIES and TOWNS

Adjuntas, 5,319 .... B 2
Aguada, 4,590 .... A 1
Aguadilla, 21,031 .... A 1
Aguas Buenas, 3,426 .... E 2
Aibonito, 7,582 .... D 2
Añasco, 4,416 .... A 1
Ángeles, †2,817 .... B 2
Arecibo, 35,484 .... B 1
Arroyo, 5,429 .... E 3
Arus .... C 3
Bahomamey, †146 .... A 1
Bajadero .... C 1
Barceloneta, 4,515 .... C 1
Barranquitas, 4,508 .... D 2
Bayamón, 147,552 .... D 1
Boquerón, †2,790 .... A 3
Cabo Rojo, 7,181 .... A 2
Caguas, 63,215 .... E 2
Caguas, ‡95,661 .... E 2
Camuy, 3,892 .... B 1
Carolina, 94,271 .... E 1
Cataño, 26,459 .... D 1
Cayey, 21,562 .... D 2
Ceiba, 2,147 .... F 2
Central Aguirre, 1,237 .... D 3
Ciales, 4,046 .... C 1
Cidra, 6,306 .... D 2
Coamo, 12,077 .... D 2
Comerío, 6,297 .... D 2
Coquí, 2,643 .... D 3
Corozal, 5,211 .... D 1
Corral Viejo .... C 2
Coto Laurel, 1,761 .... C 2
Culebra, 611 .... G 1
Dewey (Culebra), 611 .... G 1
Dorado, 4,388 .... D 1
Ensenada, 1,268 .... B 3
Esperanza, †1,312 .... G 2
Fajardo, 18,249 .... F 1
Florida, 1,716 .... C 1
Guánica, 8,979 .... B 3
Guayama, 20,318 .... E 3
Guayanilla, 5,189 .... B 3
Guaynabo, 55,310 .... D 1
Gurabo, 6,290 .... E 2
Hatillo, 2,760 .... B 1
Hato Rey, †60,539 .... E 1
Hormigüeros, 6,531 .... A 2
Humacao, 12,411 .... E 2
Isabela, 9,515 .... A 1
Isabel Segunda, 2,378 .... G 2
Jayuya, 3,826 .... C 2
Jobos, 2,720 .... D 3
Juana Díaz, 8,765 .... C 2
Juncos, 7,985 .... E 2
Lajas, 3,391 .... A 3
Lares, 4,545 .... B 2
Las Marias, 474 .... B 2
Las Piedras, 4,636 .... E 2
Levittown, 17,079 .... D 1
Loíza, 2,707 .... E 1
Loíza Aldea, 3,350 .... E 1
Luquillo, 2,459 .... F 1
Manatí, 13,483 .... C 1
Maricao, 1,492 .... B 2
Maunabo, 1,829 .... E 3
Mayagüez, 68,872 .... A 2
Mayagüez, ‡85,857 .... A 2
Moca, 2,378 .... A 1
Morovis, 2,892 .... D 1
Naguabo, 4,169 .... F 2
Naranjito, 3,283 .... D 1
Orocovis, 3,684 .... C 2
Palmer, 1,456 .... F 1
Palo Seco, †489 .... D 1
Parquera, 1,028 .... A 3
Patillas, 2,543 .... E 3
Peñuelas, 3,169 .... B 2
Playa de Fajardo .... F 1
Playa de Humacao, 1,912 .... F 2
Playa de Ponce, †15,574, ... C 3
Ponce, 128,233 .... C 3
Ponce, ‡158,981 .... C 3
Puerto Nuevo, †37,644 .... D 1
Puerto Real, 1,502 .... A 2
Puerto Real (Playa de Fajardo) .... F 1
Punta Santiago (Playa de Humacao), 1,912 .... F 2
Quebradillas, 2,840 .... B 1
Rincón, 1,538 .... A 1
Río Blanco, †2,659 .... F 2
Río Grande, 4,164 .... E 1
Río Piedras, †3,761 .... E 1
Rosario, 640 .... A 2
Sabana Grande, 5,561 .... B 2
Sabana Seca, 5,023 .... D 1
Salinas, 4,461 .... D 3
San Antonio, 2,484 .... A 1
San Germán, 11,613 .... A 2
San Juan (capital), 452,749 .... E 1
San Juan, ‡851,247 .... E 1
San Lorenzo, 7,702 .... E 2
San Sebastián, 7,169 .... B 1
Santa Isabel, 4,495 .... C 3
Santurce, †128,232 .... E 1
Tallaboa, 1,155 .... B 3
Toa Alta, 3,199 .... D 1
Toa Baja, 2,026 .... D 1
Trujilo Alto, 18,477 .... E 1
Utuado, 11,573 .... B 2
Vega Alta, 8,688 .... D 1
Vega Baja, 17,089 .... C 1
Vieques (Isabel Segunda), 2,378 .... G 2
Villalba, 4,134 .... C 2
Yabucoa, 5,119 .... E 2
Yauco, 12,922 .... B 2

OTHER FEATURES

Aguadillo (bay) .... A 1
Algarrobo (pt.) .... A 2
Añasco (bay) .... A 1
Arenas (pt.) .... F 2
Bauta (river) .... C 2
Bayamón (river) .... D 1
Boquerón (bay) .... A 3
Borinquen (pt.) .... A 1
Cabullón (pt.) .... C 3
Caja de Muertos (isl.) .... C 3
Camuy (river) .... B 1
Candelero (pt.) .... F 2
Canovanas (river) .... E 1
Caonillas (lake) .... C 2
Carite (lake) .... E 2
Carraízo (lake) .... E 1
Cayey, Sierra de (mts.) .... D 2
Central, Cordillera (range) .... C 2
Cerro Gordo (pt.) .... D 1
Coamo (res.) .... D 3
Coamo (river) .... D 3
Culebra (isl.), 732 .... G 1
Culebrinas (river) .... A 1
Culebrita (isl.) .... G 2
El Toro (mt.) .... F 2
El Yunque (mt.) .... F 1
Este (pt.) .... G 2
Fajardo (river) .... F 1
Figuras (pt.) .... E 3
Fosforescente (bay) .... A 3
Grande de Añasco (river) .... B 2
Grande de Arecibo (river) .... C 1
Grande de Loíza (river) .... E 1
Grande de Manatí (river) .... C 1
Guajataca (lake) .... B 1
Guanajibo (pt.) .... A 2
Guanajibo (river) .... A 2
Guánica (lake) .... B 3
Guaniquilla (pt.) .... A 2
Guayabal (lake) .... C 2
Guayanés (pt.) .... F 2
Guayanés (river) .... E 2
Guayanilla (bay) .... B 3
Guayo (lake) .... B 2
Guilarte (mt.) .... B 2
Honda (bay) .... F 2
Humacao (river) .... E 2
Jacaguas (river) .... C 2
Jaicoa (mts.) .... B 1
Jiguero (pt.) .... A 1
Jobos (bay) .... D 3
La Bandera (pt.) .... F 1
Lima (pt.) .... F 2
Lobo (cay) .... G 1
Luquillo, Sierra de (mts.) .... E 2
Manglillo (pt.) .... B 3
Mayagüez (bay) .... A 2
Miquillo (pt.) .... F 1
Molinos (pt.) .... G 1
Mona (passage) .... A 2
Negra (pt.) .... G 2
Nigua (river) .... D 2
Ola Grande (pt.) .... D 3
Palmas Altas (pt.) .... C 1
Patillas (lake) .... E 2
Peñón (pt.) .... B 1
Petrona (pt.) .... D 3
Pirata (mt.) .... F 2
Plata (river) .... D 2
Puerca (pt.) .... F 2
Puerto Medio Mundo (bay) .... F 2
Puerto Nuevo (pt.) .... C 1
Punta, Cerro de (mt.) .... C 2
Ramey A.F.B., 7,507 .... A 1
Rincón (bay) .... D 3
Rojo (cape) .... A 3
Salinas (pt.) .... D 1
San José (lake) .... E 1
San Juan, Cabezas de (prom.) .... F 1
San Juan National Hist. Site .... D 1
Sardina (pt.) .... A 1
Soldado (pt.) .... G 2
Sucia (bay) .... A 3
Tanamá (river) .... B 1
Torrecilla (lagoon) .... E 1
Tortuguero (lake) .... D 1
Tuna (pt.) .... E 3
Vacía Talega (pt.) .... E 1
Viento (pt.) .... E 3
Vieques (isl.), 7,767 .... G 2
Vieques (passage) .... F 2
Vieques (sound) .... G 2
Yagüez (river) .... A 2
Yauco (lake) .... B 2
Yeguas (pt.) .... F 3

ANTIGUA
Total Population, 63,000

CITIES and TOWNS

All Saints, 2,077 .... D11
Cedar Grove, 899 .... E11
Falmouth, 239 .... E11
Freetown, 1,026 .... E11
Jennings, 850 .... D11
Johnsons Point, 339 .... D11
Liberta, 1,988 .... E11
Old Road, 1,178 .... D11
Parham, 1,123 .... E11
Saint John's (capital) 24,367 .... E11
Willikies, 1,330 .... E11

OTHER FEATURES

Antigua (isl.), 54,304 .... E11
Boggy (peak) D11
Boon (pt.) E11
Green (isl.) E11
Guiana (isl.) E11
Long (isl.) E11
Saint John's (harb.) D11
Standfast (pt.) E11
Willoughby (bay) E11

BARBADOS

CITIES and TOWNS

Bathsheba .... B 8
Belleplaine .... B 8
Bridgetown (capital), 12,430 .... B 9
Carlton .... B 8
Cave Hill .... B 9
Checker Hall .... B 8
Codrington .... B 8
Crab Hill .... B 8
Crane .... C 9
Drax Hall .... B 8
Ellerton .... B 9
Greenland .... B 8
Holetown .... B 8
Kendal .... B 8
Lodge Hill .... B 8
Marchfield .... B 9
Maxwell .... B 9
Maxwell Hill .... B 9
Mount Standfast .... B 8
Portland .... B 8
Rose Hill .... B 8
Rouen .... B 9
Saint Lawrence .... B 9
Saint Martins .... B 9
Scarboro .... B 9
Seawell .... B 9
Six Mens .... B 8
Speightstown, 2,415 .... B 8
Spring Hall .... B 8
Welchman Hall .... B 8

OTHER FEATURES

Carlisle (bay) .... B 9
Hillaby (mt.) .... B 8
Long (bay) .... B 9
North (pt.) .... B 8
Oistins (bay) .... B 9
Pelican (isl.) .... B 9
Ragged (pt.) .... C 8
Sam Lord's Castle .... C 9
South (pt.) .... B 9

DOMINICA
Total Population, 70,302

CITIES and TOWNS

Barroui .... E 6
Castle Bruce, 1,474 .... F 6
Coulihaut, 972 .... E 6
Delice, 377 .... F 7
Grand Bay, 2,385 .... F 7
Hampstead, 559 .... E 5
La Plaine, 746 .... F 6
Laudat, 364 .... E 6
Mahaut, 1,688 .... E 6
Marigot, 3,200 .... E 6
Petit Soufrière, 799 .... F 6
Portsmouth, 4,146 .... E 5
Rosalie, 781 .... F 6
Roseau (capital), 10,157 .... E 7
Roseau, *16,677 .... E 7
Saint Joseph, 2,646 .... E 6
Salybia, 297 .... F 6
Soufrière, 934 .... E 7
Vieille Case, 1,372 .... E 5
Wesley, 2,063 .... F 5

OTHER FEATURES

Capuchin (cape) .... E 5
Carib Reserve, 1,974 .... F 6
Clyde (river) .... F 6
Crampton (pt.) .... F 5
Diablotin, Morne (mt.) .... E 6
Dominica (passage) .... E 5
Douglas (bay) .... E 5
Grand (bay) .... F 7
Jaquet (pt.) .... E 5
Layou (river) .... E 6
Martinique (passage) .... E 7
Micotrin (mt.) .... F 6
Pagoua (bay) .... F 6
Prince Rupert (bay) .... E 5
Roseau (river) .... E 7
Scotts (head) .... E 7
Soufrière (bay) .... E 7
Trois Pitons, Morne (mt.) .... E 6

GRENADA
Total Population, 105,000

CITIES and TOWNS

Crochu .... D 8
Gouyave, 2,356 .... C 8
Grand Anse .... C 9
Grand Roy .... C 8
Grenville, 1,747 .... D 8
Hermitage .... D 8
La Taste .... D 8
Marquis .... D 8
Mount Tivoli .... D 8
Providence .... D 9
Saint George's, (capital), 9,000 .... C 9
Saint George's, *26,843 .... C 9
Sauteurs, 925 .... D 8
Union .... D 8
Victoria, 1,692 .... D 8
Woburn .... C 9
Woodford .... C 8

OTHER FEATURES

Bedford (pt.) .... D 8
David (pt.) .... D 8
Great Bacolet (pt.) .... D 8
Green (isl.) .... D 8
Grenville (bay) .... D 8
Gros (pt.) .... C 8
Halifax (harb.) .... C 8
Irvins (bay) .... D 8
Les Tantes (isls.) .... D 7
Molinière (pt.) .... C 8
Prickly (pt.) .... C 9
Ronde (isl.) .... D 7
Saint Catherine (mt.) .... D 8
Saline (pt.) .... C 9
Sinai (mt.) .... D 8
Telescope (pt.) .... D 8

GUADELOUPE
Total Population, 324,000

CITIES and TOWNS

Anse-Bertrand, 2,597 .... B 5
Baie-Mahault, 2,518 .... A 6
Baillif, 3,056 .... A 7
Baninier .... A 7
Basse-Terre (capital), 16,000 .... A 7
Bouillante, 1,993 .... A 6
Bourg-des-Saintes, 1,174 .... A 7
Capesterre, 7,000 .... A 7
Capesterre, 861 .... B 7
Deshaies, 754 .... A 6
Ferry .... A 6
Gosier, 5,000 .... B 6
Gourbeyre, 3,024 .... A 7
Goyave, 1,191 .... A 6
Grand-Bourg, 3,299 .... B 7
Grippon .... B 6
Lamentin, 1,457 .... A 6
Le Moule, 8,000 .... B 6
Les Abymes, 6,600 .... B 6
Morne-à-l'Eau, 10,000 .... A 6
Petit-Bourg, 3,896 .... A 6
Petit-Canal, 1,725 .... A 6
Pigeon .... A 6
Pointe-à-Pitre, 50,000 .... B 6
Pointe-Noire, 2,473 .... A 6
Port-Louis, 5,000 .... B 5
Saint-Claude, 4,800 .... A 7
Saint-François, 3,200 .... B 6
Saint-Louis, 1,500 .... B 7
Sainte-Anne, 3,573 .... B 6
Sainte-Marguerite .... B 6
Sainte-Marie .... A 6
Sainte-Rose, 3,043 .... A 6
Trois-Rivières, 1,743 .... A 7
Vieux-Fort, 1,213 .... B 7
Vieux-Habitants, 1,621 .... A 7

OTHER FEATURES

Allègre (pt.) .... A 6
Antigues (pt.) .... A 5
Basse-Terre (isl.), 134,601 .... A 6
Châteaux (pt.) .... B 6
Constant, Morne (hill) .... B 7
Désirade (isl.), 1,559 .... B 6
Fajou (isl.) .... A 6
Grand Cul-de-Sac Marin (bay) .... A 6
Grand Îlet (isl.) .... A 7
Grande-Terre (isl.), 150,576 .... B 5
Grande Vigie (pt.) .... B 5
Guadeloupe (isl.), 285,177 .... B 6
Guadeloupe (passage) .... A 5
Kahouanne (isl.) .... A 6
Marie-Galante (isl.), 15,870 .... B 7
Nord (pt.) .... B 7
Nord-Est (bay) .... B 6
Petit Cul-de-Sac Marin (bay) .... A 6
Petite-Terre (isls.) .... B 6
Saintes (isls.), 3,272 .... A 7
Saintes, Canal des (chan.) .... A 7
Salée (river) .... A 6
Sans Toucher (mt.) .... A 6
Soufrière (mt.) .... A 7
Terre-de-Bas (isl.), 1,795 .... A 7
Terre-de-Haut (isl.), 1,477 .... A 7
Vieux-Fort (pt.) .... A 7

MARTINIQUE
Total Population, 332,000

CITIES and TOWNS

Ajoupa-Bouillon, 1,397 .... C 5
Anses-d'Arlet, 1,102 .... C 7
Basse-Pointe, 2,324 .... C 5
Belle-Fontaine, 1,082 .... C 6
Carbet, 2,593 .... C 6
Case-Pilote, 1,625 .... C 6
Diamant, 629 .... D 7
Ducos, 1,976 .... D 6
Fond-Lahaye .... C 6
Fonds-Saint-Denis, 780 .... C 6
Fort-de-France (capital), 100,000 .... C 6
Fort-Desaix .... D 6
François, 3,195 .... D 6
Grande-Rivière, 1,493 .... C 5
Gros-Morne, 979 .... D 6
Lamentin, 6,721 .... D 6
Lorrain, 1,848 .... D 5
Macouba, 1,329 .... C 5
Marigot, 1,449 .... D 5
Marin, 1,789 .... D 7
Morne-Rouge, 2,655 .... C 5
Morne-Vert, 493 .... C 6
Prêcheur, 2,312 .... C 5
Rivière-Pilote, 2,039 .... D 7
Rivière-Salée, 1,725 .... D 7
Robert, 2,077 .... D 6
Saint-Esprit, 3,214 .... D 6
Saint-Joseph, 1,995 .... C 6
Saint-Pierre, 5,556 .... C 6
Sainte-Anne, 960 .... D 7
Sainte-Luce, 1,243 .... D 7
Sainte-Marie, 2,933 .... D 5
Schoelcher, 10,817 .... C 6
Trinité, 3,566 .... D 6
Trois-Îlets, 1,400 .... D 6
Vauclin, 2,908 .... D 6
Vert-Pré .... D 6

OTHER FEATURES

Cabet, Pitons du (mt.) .... C 6
Cabri (isl.) .... D 7
Caravelle (pen.) .... D 6
Cul-de-Sac du Marin (bay) .... D 7
Diable (pt.) .... D 5
Ferré (cape) .... E 7
Fort-de-France (bay) .... C 6
Galion (bay) .... D 6
Lézarde (river) .... D 6
Long, Îlet (isl.) .... D 6
Lorrain (river) .... D 5
Martinique (passage) .... C 5
Pelée (vol.) .... C 5
Pilote (river) .... D 7
Ramièrs, Îlet-à- (isl.) .... C 6
Ramville, Îlet (isl.) .... D 6
Robert (harb.) .... D 6
Rocher du Diamant (isl.) .... C 7
Rose (pt.) .... D 6
Saint-Martin (cape) .... C 5
Saint-Pierre (bay) .... C 6
Salines (pt.) .... D 7
Salomon (pt.) .... C 7
Vauclin (mt.) .... D 6

NETHERLANDS ANTILLES

CITIES and TOWNS

Aresji .... D 9
Ascension .... F 8
Bacuna .... E 8
Balashi E10
Boven Bolivia .... E 8
Bubali D10
Bushiribana E10
Dokterstuin .... D 8
Druif D10
Emmastad .... G 9
Entrejo .... E 8
Fontein .... E 8
Fuik .... G 9
Groot Sint Joris .... G 9
Hato .... G 8
Kralendijk (capital), Bonaire, 839 .... E 8
Lago E10
Lagoen .... F 8
Montanja di Reij .... G 9
New Port .... G 9
Noord di Salinja .... E 8
Onima .... E 8
Oranjestad (capital), Aruba, 15,398 .... D10
Otrabanda .... F 9
Patrick .... F 8
Rincon .... E 8
Rooi .... E 8
Sabana Westpunt .... F 8
Santa Barbara .... G 9
Santa Catharina .... G 9
Savaneta E10
Savonet .... F 8
Sint Anna D10
Sint Jan .... D 8
Sint Kruis .... F 8
Sint Martha .... F 8
Sint Michiel .... F 9
Sint Nicolaas E10
Sint Willebrordus .... F 8
Terra Corra .... E 8
Westpunt D10
Willemstad (capital), 43,547 .... F 9
Willemstad, *94,133 .... F 9

OTHER FEATURES

Aruba (isl.), 58,868 .... E 9
Basora (pt.) E10
Bonaire (isl.), 5,755 .... E 9
Bullen (bay) .... F 8
Caracas (bay) .... G 9
Curaçao (isl.), 196,170 .... G 7
Goto (lake) .... D 8
Jamanota (mt.) E10
Kanon (pt.) .... G 9
Klein Bonaire (isl.) .... E 8
Kudarebe (pt.) .... D 9
Lac (bay) .... D 9
Lacre (pt.) .... E 9
Malmok (mt.) .... E 8
Noord (pt.) .... D 8
Noord (pt.) .... F 8
Paarden (bay) D10
Palm (beach) D10
Pekelmeer (lake) .... E 9
Piscadera (bay) .... F 9
Schottegat (bay) .... G 9
Sint Anna (bay) .... F 9
Sint Christoffel Berg (mt.) .... F 8
Sint Joris (bay) .... G 9
Slag (bay) .... D 8
Vierkant (pt.) .... E 8

SAINT CHRISTOPHER-NEVIS-ANGUILLA
Total Population, 56,000

CITIES and TOWNS

Basseterre (capital), 15,726 .... C10
Cayon, 1,524 .... C10
Charlestown, 2,852 .... C11
Cotton Ground, 747 .... C11
Dieppe Bay, 949 .... C10
Gingerland D11
Golden Rock C10
Newcastle, 361 .... D11
Old Road, 1,206 .... C10
Sadlers Village, 1,091 .... C10
Sandy Point, 3,608 .... C10
Tabernacle, 1,250 .... C10
Zion Hill D11

OTHER FEATURES

Brimstone (hill) C10
Dogwood (pt.) D11
Fort (pt.) C11
Great Salt (pond) D10
Heldens (pt.) C10
Horse Shoe (pt.) C11
Misery (mt.) C10
Monkey (hill) C10
Muddy (pt.) C10
Narrows, The (str.) D11
Nevis (isl.), 12,762 .... D11
Nevis (peak) D11
North Friars (bay) D10
Palmetto (pt.) C10
Saint Christopher (isl.), 38,291 .... D10
Saint Kitts (Saint Christopher) (isl.), 38,291 .... D10
South Friars (bay) C10

SAINT LUCIA
Total Population, 110,000

CITIES and TOWNS

Anse la Raye, 2,053 .... F 6
Canaries, 1,676 .... G 6
Castries (capital), 4,353 .... G 6
Castries, *15,291 .... G 6
Choc .... G 5
Choiseul, 513 .... F 7
Dauphin .... G 5
Dennery, 2,252 .... G 6
Gros Islet, 1,016 .... G 5
Laborie, 1,591 .... G 7
Marigot .... G 6
Marquis .... G 6
Micoud, 2,040 .... G 6
Praslin .... G 6
Soufrière, 2,692 .... F 6
Vieux Fort, 3,228 .... G 7

OTHER FEATURES

Beaumont (pt.) .... F 6
Canaries, Piton (mt.) .... G 6
Cannelles (pt.) .... G 7
Cannelles (river) .... G 6
Cap (pt.) .... G 5
Choc (bay) .... G 5
Fond d'Or (bay) .... G 6
Gimie (mt.) .... G 6
Grand Caille (pt.) .... F 6
Grand Cul de Sac (river) .... G 6
Gros Islet (bay) .... G 5
Gros Piton (mt.) .... G 6
Maria (isl.) .... G 7
Ministre (pt.) .... G 7
Moule à Chique (cape) .... G 7
Petit Piton (mt.) .... G 6
Pigeon (isl.) .... G 5
Port Castries (harb.) .... G 6
Port Praslin (bay) .... G 6
Roseau (river) .... G 6
Saint Lucia (chan.) .... G 5
Saint Vincent (passage) .... G 7
Savannes (bay) .... G 7
Sorcière, La (mt.) .... G 6
Soufrière (bay) .... F 6
Vierge (pt.) .... G 6
Vieux Fort (river) .... G 6

SAINT VINCENT
Total Population, 89,129

CITIES and TOWNS

Barrouallie, †2,459 .... A 9
Calliaqua, †3,589 .... A 9
Camden Park .... A 9
Chateaubelair, †2,173 .... A 8
Colonarie, †1,550 .... A 9
Georgetown, †2,645 .... A 8
Kingstown (capital), 17,258 .... A 9
Kingstown, *23,482 .... A 9
Layou, †3,060 .... A 9
Turema .... A 8
Wallibu .... A 8

OTHER FEATURES

Colonarie (pt.) .... A 9
Cumberland (bay) .... A 8
Dark (head) .... A 8
De Volet (pt.) .... A 8
Espagnol (pt.) .... A 8
Greathead (bay) .... A 9
Kingstown (bay) .... A 9
Owia (bay) .... A 8
Porter (pt.) .... A 8
Richmond (peak) .... A 8
Saint Andrew (mt.) .... A 9
Saint Vincent (passage) .... A 8
Soufrière (mt.) .... A 8
Yambu (head) .... A 9

TRINIDAD and TOBAGO

CITIES and TOWNS

Arima, 10,982 .... B10
Arouca, 4,781 .... B10
Basse Terre B11
Biche, 1,986 .... B10
Blanchisseuse, 205 .... B10
California A11
Carapichaima B10
Caroni, 678 .... B10
Cedros, 1,388 .... A11
Chaguanas, 3,509 .... A10
Chaguaramas A10
Couva, 3,567 .... B10
Cunapo B10
Débé, 2,189 .... B11
Ecclesville B11
Flanagin Town B10
Fullarton A11
Fyzabad, 1,869 .... A11
Gran Couva B11
Grande Rivière, 301 .... B10
Guaico B10
Guayaguayare, 287 .... B11
La Brea, 4,828 .... A11
La Lune, 252 .... B11
Marabella, 8,937 .... A11
Matelot, 289 .... B10
Matura B10
Mayaro, 1,828 .... B11
Moruga, 656 .... B11
Mucurapo, 2,851 .... A10
Nestor B10
Palo Seco A11
Peñal, 3,594 .... B11
Piarco B10
Point Fortin, 8,753 .... A11
Port-of-Spain (capital), 86,150 .... A10
Port-of-Spain, *250,000 .... A10
Princes Town, 6,681 .... B11
Redhead, 302 .... B10
Rio Claro, 2,174 .... B11
Sadhoowa B11
Saint Joseph, 4,079 .... B10
Saint Joseph B11
San Fernando, 39,830 .... A11
San Francique A11
San Juan, 19,064 .... A10
Sangre Grande, 5,087 .... B10
Sans Souci, 295 .... B10
Siparia, 4,174 .... B11
Tabaquite B11
Tableland B11
Tacarigua, 6,704 .... B10
Talparo B10
Toco, 979 .... B10
Tunapuna, 11,287 .... B10
Upper Manzanilla B10
Valencia, 370 .... B10
Waterloo A10

OTHER FEATURES

Aripo, El Cerro del (mt.) B10
Boca Grande (passage) A10
Casa Cruz (cape) B11
Chacachacare (isl.) A10
Chupara (pt.) B10
Cocos (bay) B10
Dragons Mouth (passage) A10
Erin (bay) A11
Erin (pt.) A11
Galeota (pt.) B11
Galera (pt.) C10
Guapo (bay) A11
Guatuaro (pt.) B11
Icacos (pt.) A11
Matura (bay) B10
Mayaro (bay) B11
Monos (isl.) A10
Nariva (swamp) B10
Oropuche (river) B10
Ortoire (river) B11
Paria (gulf) A10
Pitch (lake) A11
Serpents Mouth (passage) A11
Tamana (mt.) B10
Trinidad (isl.), 973,250 .... A 9
Tucuche, El (mt.) B10
U.S. Naval Base A10

VIRGIN ISLANDS (BRITISH)

CITIES and TOWNS

Road Town (capital), 2,183 .... D 3
West End, 105 .... C 4

OTHER FEATURES

Flanagan (passage) .... D 4
Frenchman (cay) .... C 4
Great Thatch (isl.) .... C 4
Great Tobago (isl.) .... B 3
Jost Van Dyke (isl.), 124 .... C 3
Little Tobago (isl.) .... B 3
Narrow, The (str.) .... C 4
Norman (isl.) .... D 4
Peter (isl.) .... D 4
Road (bay) .... D 3
Sage (mt.) .... D 4
Sir Francis Drake (chan.) .... D 4
Tortola (isl.), 8,939 .... D 3

VIRGIN ISLANDS (U. S.)

CITIES and TOWNS

Bethlehem .... E 4
Canebay .... E 3
Charlotte Amalie (capital), 12,220 .... B 4
Christiansted, 3,020 .... F 4
Cruz Bay, †1,497 .... C 4
Diamond .... F 4
East End, †26 .... D 4
Emmaus .... C 4
Fredensdal .... F 4
Frederiksted, 1,531 .... E 4
Grove Place .... E 4
Kingshill .... F 4
Longford .... F 4
Negro Bay .... E 4

OTHER FEATURES

Altona (lagoon) .... F 4
Annaly (bay) .... E 3
Baron Bluff (prom.) .... E 3
Bordeaux (mt.) .... C 4
Brass (isls.) .... A 4
Buck (isl.) .... G 3
Buck Island (chan.) .... F 3
Buck Island Reef National Mon. .... G 3
Butler (bay) .... E 4
Caneel (bay) .... B 4
Capella (isls.) .... B 5
Christiansted National Hist. Site .... F 4
Coral (bay) .... C 4
Crown (mt.) .... A 4
Dutchcap (cay) .... A 4
Eagle (mt.) .... E 4
East (pt.) .... G 4
Flanagan (passage) .... D 4
Flat (cays) .... A 4
Grass (pt.) .... G 4
Great (pond) .... F 4
Great Pond (bay) .... F 4
Green (cay) .... F 4
Hams Bluff (prom.) .... E 3
Hans Lollik (isls.) .... B 4
Hassel (isl.) .... B 4
Jersey (bay) .... B 4
Krause (lagoon) .... F 4
Leeward (passage) .... B 4
Long (pt.) .... B 4
Long (pt.) .... E 4
Lovango (cay) .... C 4
Magens (bay) .... B 4
Maho (bay) .... C 4
Narrows, The (str.) .... C 4
Nulliberg (mt.) .... B 4
Perseverance (bay) .... A 4
Picara (pt.) .... B 4
Pillsbury (sound) .... B 4
Privateer (pt.) .... D 4
Pull (pt.) .... F 3
Ram (head) .... C 4
Red (pt.) .... D 4
Reef (bay) .... C 4
Saba (isl.) .... A 4
Saint Croix (isl.), 31,779 .... G 4
Saint James (isls.) .... B 4
Saint John (isl.), 1,729 .... C 4
Saint Thomas (harb.) .... B 4
Saint Thomas (isl.), 28,960 .... A 4
Salt (cay) .... A 4
Salt (river) .... F 4
Salt River (bay) .... F 3
Sandy (pt.) .... D 4
Savana (isl.) .... A 4
Southwest (cape) .... E 4
Tague (bay) .... G 4
Thatch (cay) .... B 4
Turner Hole (bay) .... G 4
U.S. Naval Air Sta. .... A 4
Vagthus (pt.) .... F 4
Virgin (passage) .... A 4
Virgin Islands National Park .... C 4
Water (isl.) .... A 4
Westend Saltpond (lagoon) .... E 4

*City and suburbs.
†Population of municipality or sub-division.

PUERTO RICO
AND THE LESSER ANTILLES

Copyright by C.S. HAMMOND & CO., N.Y.

National, Territorial and Colonial Capitals .... ☆	International Boundaries ....
	Senatorial District Boundaries ....
Lesser Administrative Centers ...... ⊛	Railroads ....

ISLANDS	POLITICAL UNITS
Puerto Rico	Commonwealth of the United States
St. Thomas & St. John St. Croix	} Virgin Islands — U.S. Territory
Curaçao, Aruba Bonaire	} Neth. Antilles-Integral Part of Neth. Realm
Guadeloupe	French Overseas Department
Martinique	French Overseas Department
Dominica, St. Lucia, St. Vincent, Grenada	} Associated Members of the British Commonwealth
St. Christopher & Nevis, Antigua	}
Trinidad	Trinidad & Tobago
Barbados	} Independent Members of the British Commonwealth

CANADA

SCALE

0 50 100 200 300 400 500MI.

0 50 100 200 300 400 500 KM.

Capitals of Countries .... ☆
Provincial & Territorial Capitals △
International Boundaries
Provincial Boundaries
Canals

© C.S. HAMMOND & Co., N.Y.

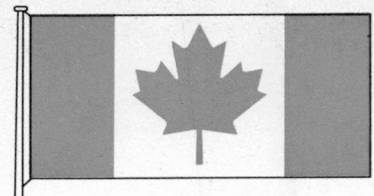

AREA 3,851,809 sq. mi.
POPULATION 21,489,000
CAPITAL Ottawa
LARGEST CITY Montréal
HIGHEST POINT Mt. Logan 19,850 ft.
MONETARY UNIT Canadian dollar
MAJOR LANGUAGES English, French
MAJOR RELIGIONS Protestantism, Roman Catholicism

QUEEN ELIZABETH ISLANDS

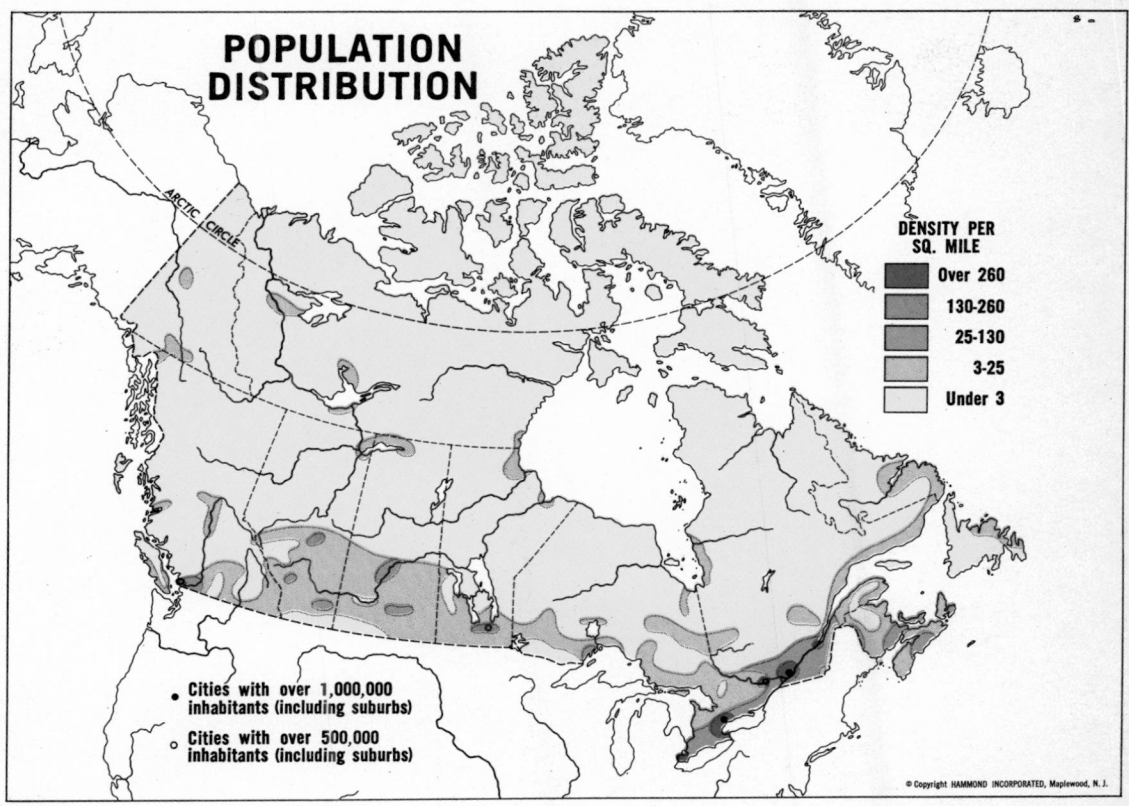

POPULATION DISTRIBUTION

DENSITY PER SQ. MILE

- Over 260
- 130-260
- 25-130
- 3-25
- Under 3

● Cities with over 1,000,000 inhabitants (including suburbs)

○ Cities with over 500,000 inhabitants (including suburbs)

© Copyright HAMMOND INCORPORATED, Maplewood, N.J.

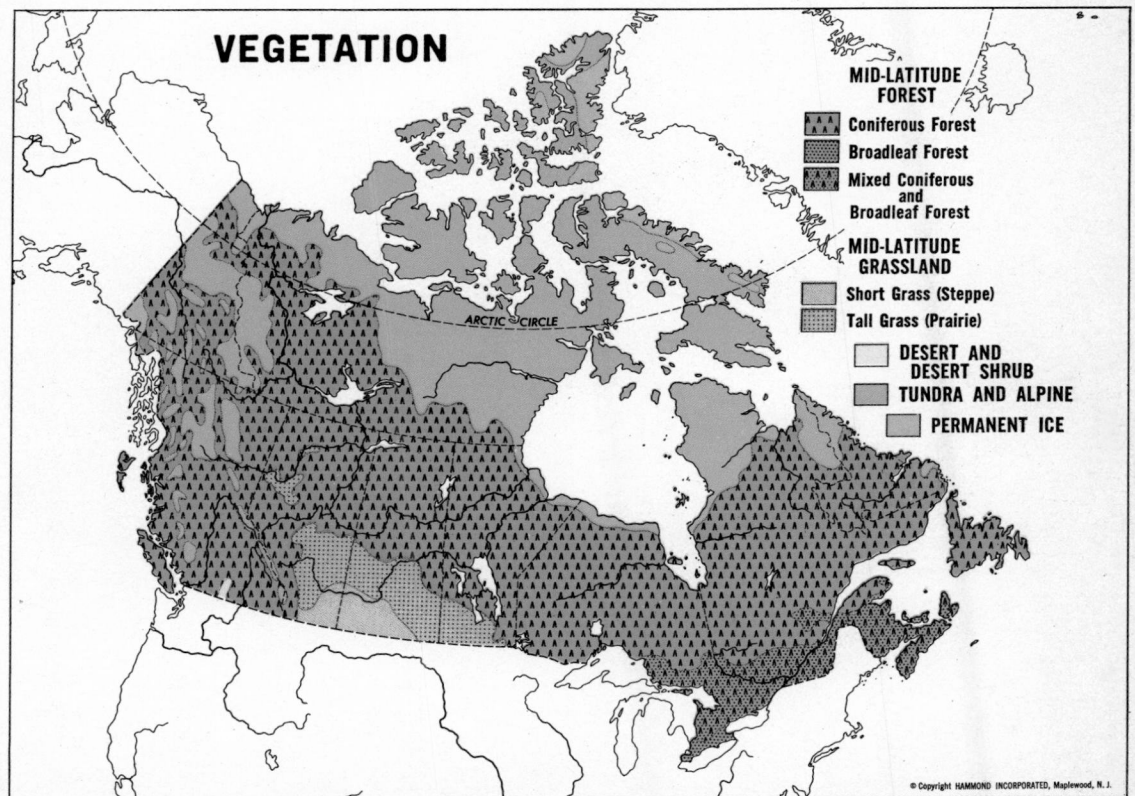

VEGETATION

MID-LATITUDE FOREST
- Coniferous Forest
- Broadleaf Forest
- Mixed Coniferous and Broadleaf Forest

MID-LATITUDE GRASSLAND
- Short Grass (Steppe)
- Tall Grass (Prairie)

- DESERT AND DESERT SHRUB
- TUNDRA AND ALPINE
- PERMANENT ICE

© Copyright HAMMOND INCORPORATED, Maplewood, N.J.

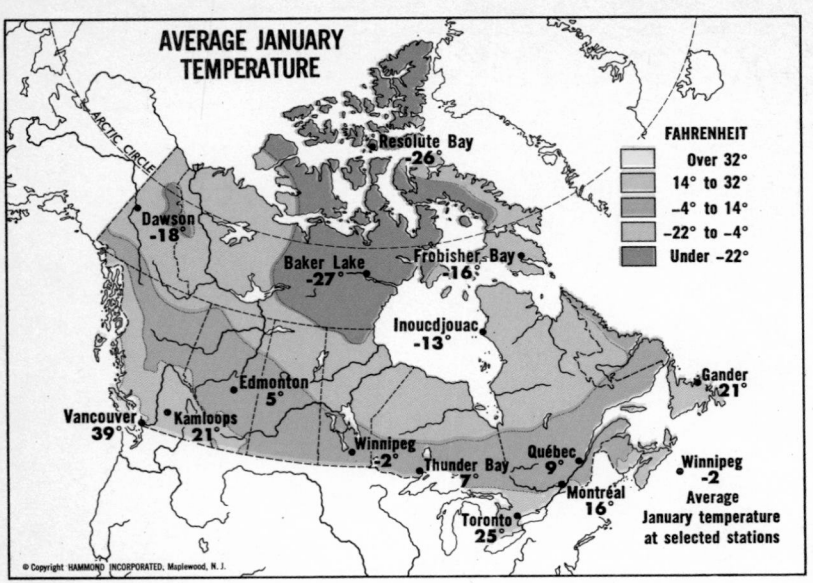

AVERAGE JANUARY TEMPERATURE
ARCTIC CIRCLE
FAHRENHEIT
Over 32°
14° to 32°
-4° to 14°
-22° to -4°
Under -22°
Resolute Bay -26°
Dawson -18°
Baker Lake -27°
Frobisher Bay -16°
Inoucdjouac -13°
Edmonton 5°
Gander 21°
Vancouver 39°
Kamloops 21°
Winnipeg -2°
Thunder Bay 7°
Québec 9°
Montréal 16°
Toronto 25°
Winnipeg -2
Average January temperature at selected stations
© Copyright HAMMOND INCORPORATED, Maplewood, N. J.

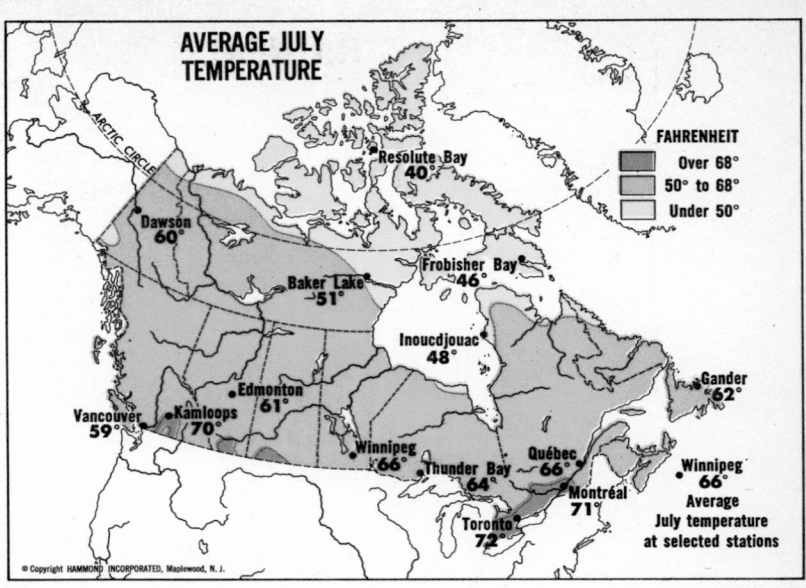

AVERAGE JULY TEMPERATURE
ARCTIC CIRCLE
FAHRENHEIT
Over 68°
50° to 68°
Under 50°
Resolute Bay 40°
Dawson 60°
Frobisher Bay 46°
Baker Lake 51°
Inoucdjouac 48°
Edmonton 61°
Gander 62°
Vancouver 59°
Kamloops 70°
Winnipeg 66°
Thunder Bay 64°
Québec 66°
Montréal 71°
Toronto 72°
Winnipeg 66°
Average July temperature at selected stations
© Copyright HAMMOND INCORPORATED, Maplewood, N. J.

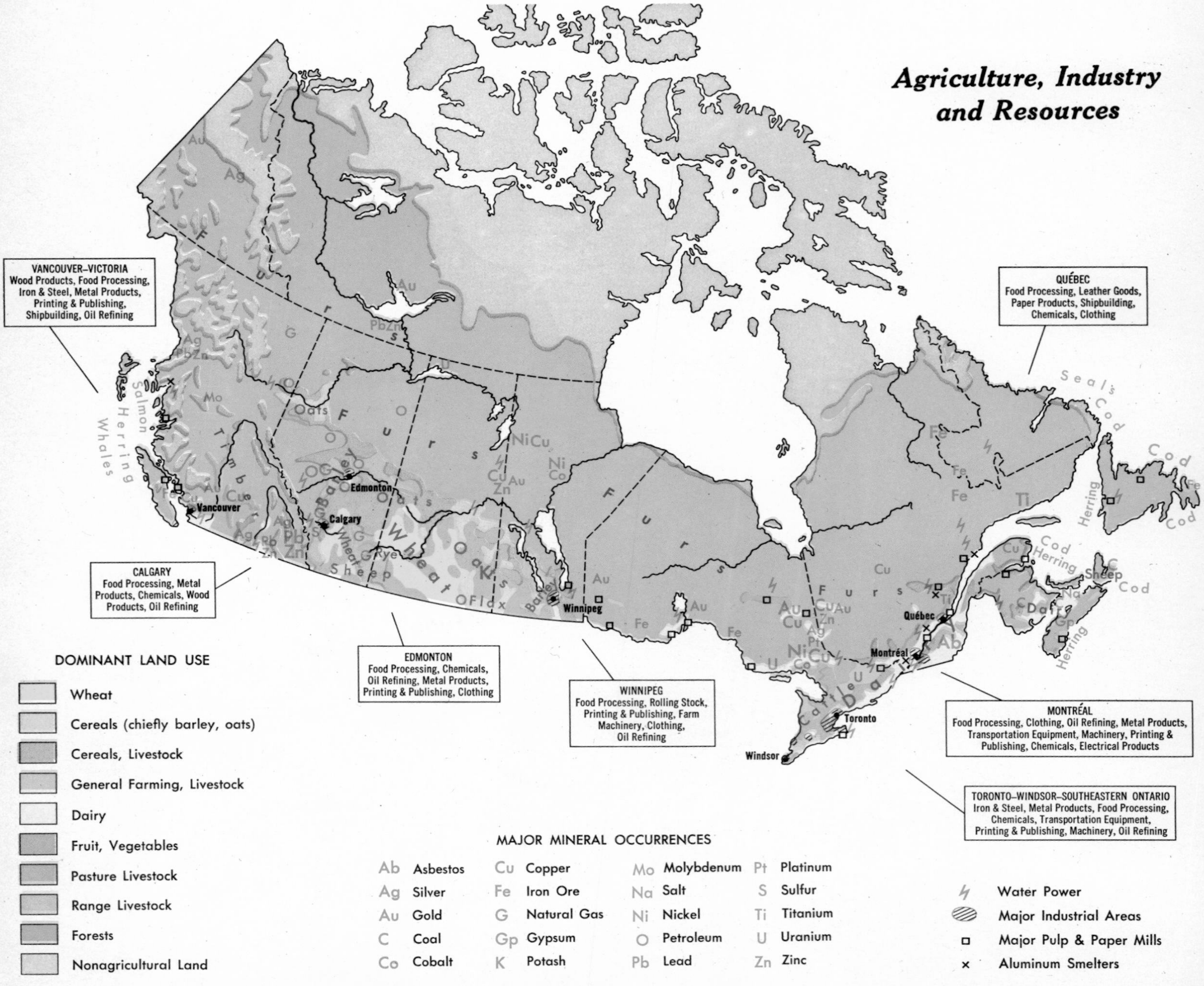

Agriculture, Industry and Resources
VANCOUVER–VICTORIA
Wood Products, Food Processing, Iron & Steel, Metal Products, Printing & Publishing, Shipbuilding, Oil Refining
QUÉBEC
Food Processing, Leather Goods, Paper Products, Shipbuilding, Chemicals, Clothing
CALGARY
Food Processing, Metal Products, Chemicals, Wood Products, Oil Refining
EDMONTON
Food Processing, Chemicals, Oil Refining, Metal Products, Printing & Publishing, Clothing
WINNIPEG
Food Processing, Rolling Stock, Printing & Publishing, Farm Machinery, Clothing, Oil Refining
MONTRÉAL
Food Processing, Clothing, Oil Refining, Metal Products, Transportation Equipment, Machinery, Printing & Publishing, Chemicals, Electrical Products
TORONTO–WINDSOR–SOUTHEASTERN ONTARIO
Iron & Steel, Metal Products, Food Processing, Chemicals, Transportation Equipment, Printing & Publishing, Machinery, Oil Refining
Vancouver
Calgary
Edmonton
Winnipeg
Québec
Montréal
Toronto
Windsor
Salmon
Herring
Whales
Seals
Cod
DOMINANT LAND USE
Wheat
Cereals (chiefly barley, oats)
Cereals, Livestock
General Farming, Livestock
Dairy
Fruit, Vegetables
Pasture Livestock
Range Livestock
Forests
Nonagricultural Land
MAJOR MINERAL OCCURRENCES
Ab Asbestos
Ag Silver
Au Gold
C Coal
Co Cobalt
Cu Copper
Fe Iron Ore
G Natural Gas
Gp Gypsum
K Potash
Mo Molybdenum
Na Salt
Ni Nickel
O Petroleum
Pb Lead
Pt Platinum
S Sulfur
Ti Titanium
U Uranium
Zn Zinc
Water Power
Major Industrial Areas
Major Pulp & Paper Mills
Aluminum Smelters

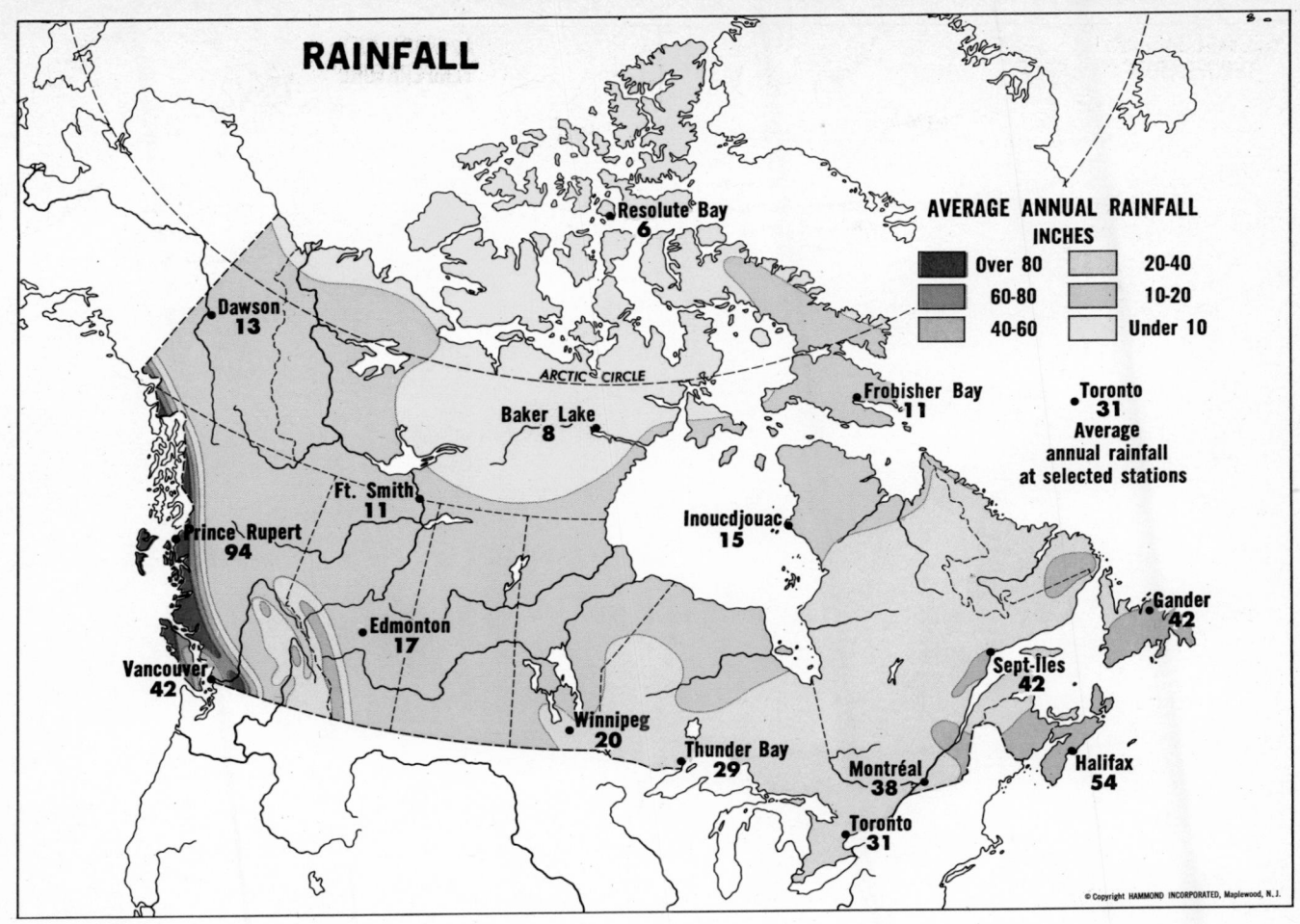

RAINFALL

AVERAGE ANNUAL RAINFALL
INCHES

- Over 80
- 60-80
- 40-60
- 20-40
- 10-20
- Under 10

Resolute Bay 6

Dawson 13

ARCTIC CIRCLE

Frobisher Bay 11

Toronto 31
Average
annual rainfall
at selected stations

Baker Lake 8

Ft. Smith 11

Prince Rupert 94

Inoucdjouac 15

Gander 42

Edmonton 17

Vancouver 42

Sept-Îles 42

Winnipeg 20

Thunder Bay 29

Montréal 38

Halifax 54

Toronto 31

© Copyright HAMMOND INCORPORATED, Maplewood, N. J.

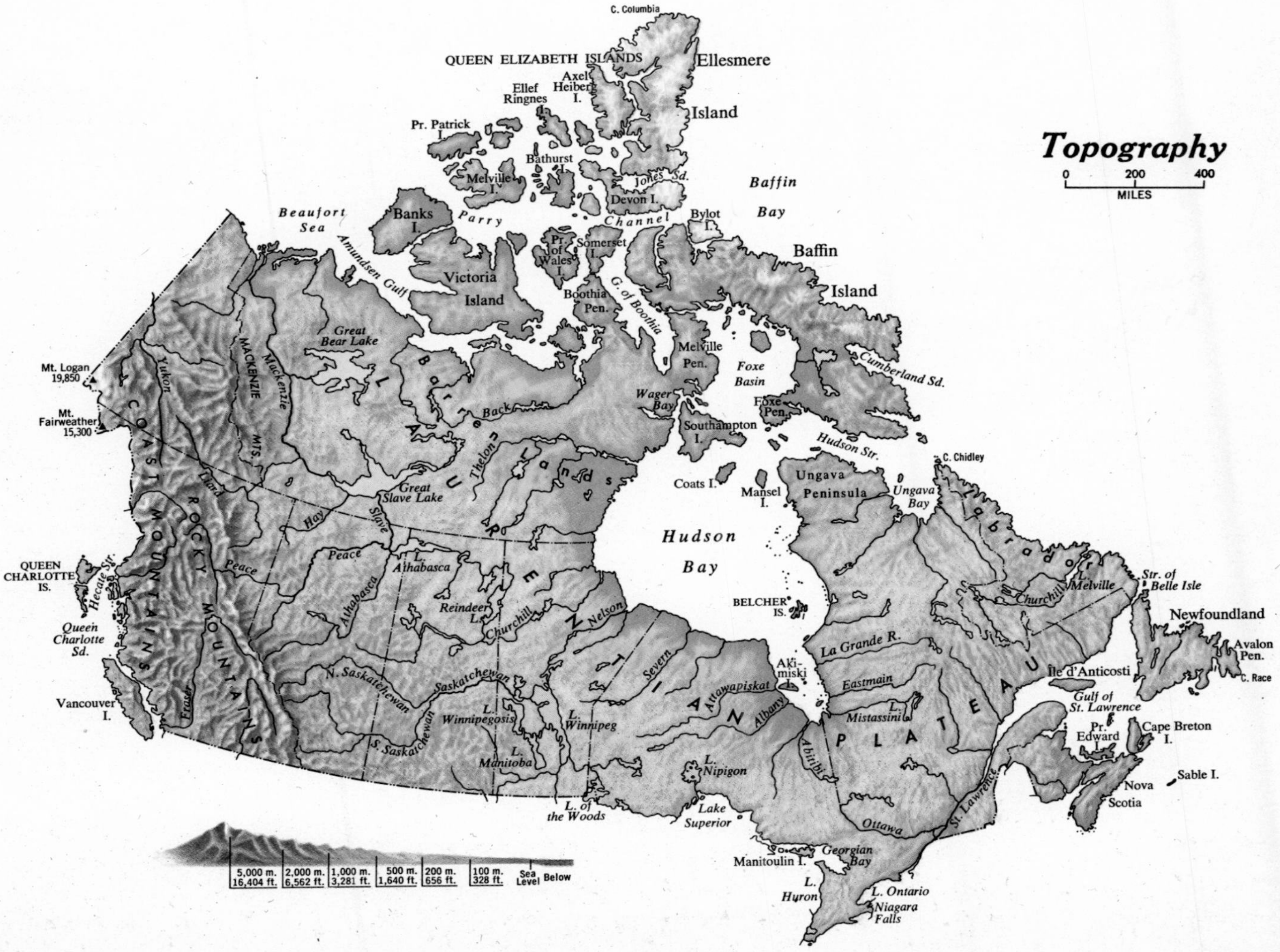

Topography

0   200   400
MILES

C. Columbia

QUEEN ELIZABETH ISLANDS   Ellesmere

Ellef Ringnes I.   Axel Heiberg I.   Island

Pr. Patrick I.

Bathurst I.

Melville I.   Jones Sd.   Baffin Bay

Beaufort Sea   Banks I.   Parry Channel   Devon I.

Bylot I.

Amundsen Gulf   Victoria Island   Pr. of Wales   Somerset   G. of Boothia   Baffin Island

Boothia Pen.

Great Bear Lake   Melville Pen.   Cumberland Sd.

Mt. Logan 19,850   MACKENZIE MTS.   Foxe Basin

Mt. Fairweather 15,300   Yukon   Mackenzie   Back   Wager Bay   Foxe Pen.

Great Slave Lake   Southampton I.   Hudson Str.   C. Chidley

Thelon   Coats I.   Ungava Peninsula   Ungava Bay

COAST MOUNTAINS   Liard   Mansel I.

ROCKY MOUNTAINS   Slave   Hudson Bay   La Grande R.

QUEEN CHARLOTTE IS.   Peace   Peace   Athabasca   Reindeer   Churchill   BELCHER IS.   Aki-miski   Eastmain   L. Melville   Str. of Belle Isle

Hecate Str.   Fraser   Athabasca   Nelson   Churchill   Newfoundland

Queen Charlotte Sd.   N. Saskatchewan   Saskatchewan   Severn   Attawapiskat   Mistassini   Gulf of St. Lawrence   Avalon Pen.   C. Race

Vancouver I.   S. Saskatchewan   Winnipegosis   L. Winnipeg   Albany   L A U R E N T I A N   PLATEAU   Pr. Edward I.   Cape Breton I.   Ile d'Anticosti

Manitoba   Abitibi   Sable I.   Nova Scotia

L. Nipigon   St. Lawrence

L. of the Woods   Lake Superior   Ottawa

Manitoulin I.   Georgian Bay

L. Huron   L. Ontario   Niagara Falls

5,000 m. 16,404 ft. | 2,000 m. 6,562 ft. | 1,000 m. 3,281 ft. | 500 m. 1,640 ft. | 200 m. 656 ft. | 100 m. 328 ft. | Sea Level | Below

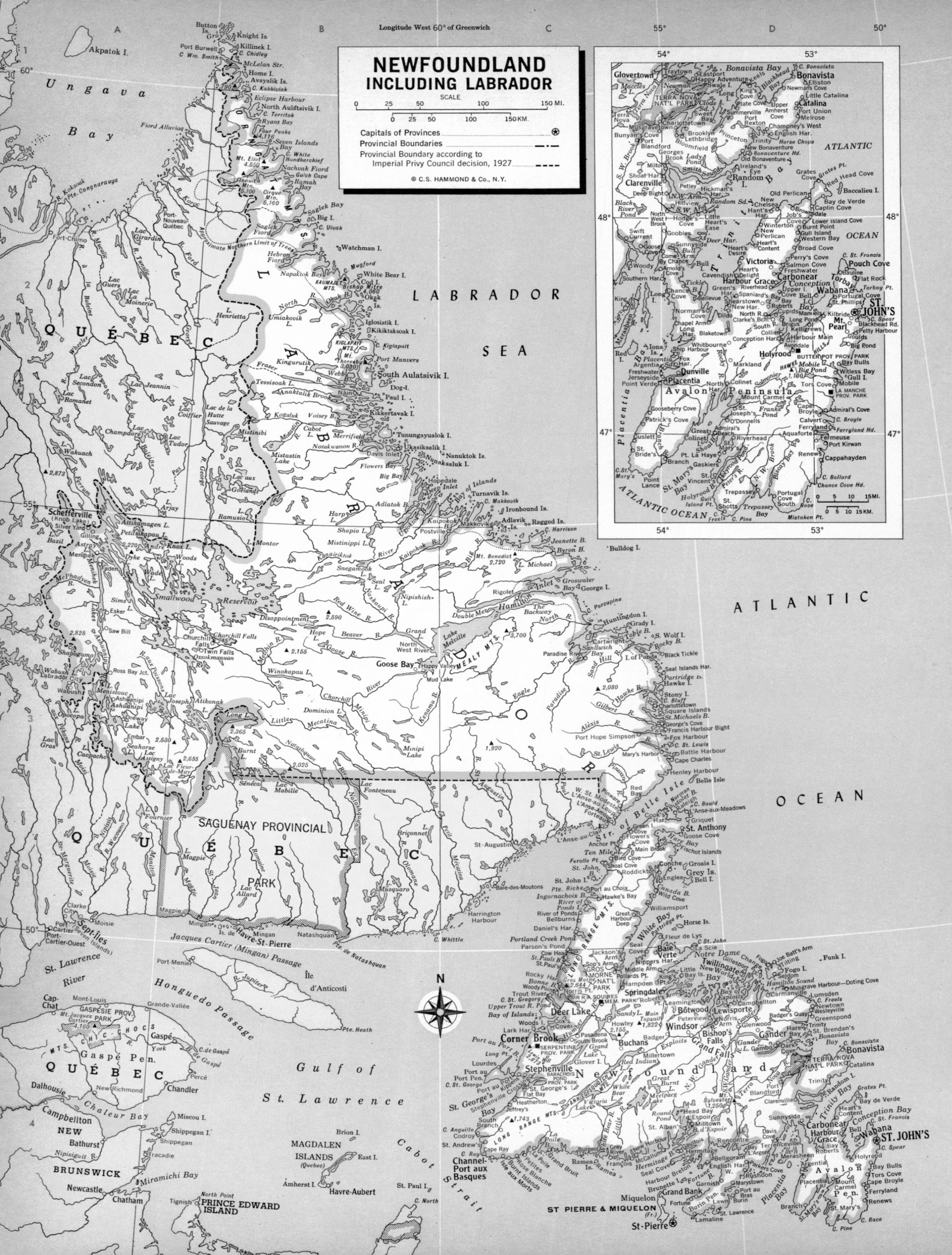

CITIES and TOWNS

Admiral's Beach, 402	D	2
Admiral's Cove, 121	D	2
Anchor Point, 275	C	3
Aquaforte, 186	D	2
Argentia, 13	C	2
Arnold's Cove, 919	C	2
Avondale, 944	D	2
Badger, 1,187	C	4
Badger's Quay, 904	D	4
Baie Verte, 2,397	C	4
Battle Harbour, 75	C	3
Bauline, 297	D	2
Bay Bulls, 1,011	D	2
Bay de Verde, 826	D	2
Bay L'Argent, 453	D	4
Bay Roberts, 3,702	D	2
Bellburns, 165	C	3
Belleoram, 530	C	4
Bellevue, 293	D	2
Bird Cove, 339	C	3
Bishop's Falls, 4,133	C	4
Blackhead Road, 1,672	D	2
Black Tickle, 164	C	3
Blaketown, 399	D	2
Bloomfield, 597	D	2
Bonavista, 4,215	D	2
Botwood, 4,115	C	4
Branch, 516	D	2
Brigus, 746	D	2
Broad Cove, 198	D	2
Brooklyn, 167	D	2
Brownsdale, 189	D	2
Buchans, 1,907	C	4
Bunyan's Cove, 494	C	2
Burgeo, 2,226	C	4
Burin, 2,586	C	4
Burnt Islands, 799	C	4
Burnt Point, 257	D	2
Calvert, 470	D	2
Campbellton, 730	D	4
Cape Broyle, 677	D	2
Cape Ray, 302	C	4
Caplin Cove, 164	D	2
Carbonear, 4,732	D	2
Carmanville, 839	D	4
Cartwright, 752	C	3
Catalina, 1,131	D	2
Cavendish, 286	D	2
Champney's West, 195	D	2
Chance Cove, 446	D	2
Change Islands, 609	D	4
Channel-Port aux Basques, 5,942	C	4
Chapel Arm, 659	D	2
Charlottetown, 309	D	2
Churchill Falls, 2,357	B	3
Clarenville, 2,193	C	2
Clarke's Beach, 877	D	2
Codroy, 321	C	4
Colinet, 264	D	2
Colliers, 650	D	2
Come By Chance, 364	C	2
Conception Harbour, 783	D	2
Conche, 505	C	3
Cook's Harbour, 325	C	3
Corner Brook, 26,309	C	4
Cow Head, 501	C	4
Cox's Cove, 797	C	4
Cupids, 691	D	2
Cuslett, 124	C	2
Daniel's Harbour, 415	C	3
Dark Cove, 1,198	D	4
Davis Inlet, 193	B	2
Deep Bight, 169	C	2
Deer Lake, 4,421	C	4
Dildo, 878	D	2
Dunville, 1,742	D	2
Eastport, 438	D	1
Elliston, 551	D	2
Englee, 1,050	C	3
English Harbour West, 393	C	4
Fermeuse, 404	D	2
Ferryland, 716	D	2
Flat Bay, 357	C	4
Flat Rock, 680	D	2
Fleur de Lys, 672	C	3
Flowers Cove, 372	C	3
Fogo, 1,155	D	4
Forteau, 312	C	3
Fortune, 2,164	C	4
Fox Harbour, 214	C	3
Fox Harbour, 685	D	2
François, 220	C	4
Freshwater, 1,562	C	2
Freshwater, 222	D	2
Gambo, 491	D	4
Gander, 7,748	D	4
Garnish, 618	C	4
Gaskiers, 300	D	2
Gaultois, 509	C	4
Georges Brook, 209	D	2
Gillesport, 314	D	4
Glenwood, 979	D	4
Glovertown, 1,915	C	1
Goobies, 137	D	2
Goose Bay, 496	B	3
Gooseberry Cove, 145	C	2
Goose Cove, 239	C	2
Goose Cove, 349	C	3
Goulds, 4,695	D	2
Grand Bank, 3,476	C	4
Grand Falls, 7,677	C	4
Grates Cove, 328	D	2
Great Harbour Deep, 329	C	3
Green Island Cove, 224	C	3
Green's Harbour, 710	D	2
Greenspond, 449	D	4
Grey River, 204	C	4
Griquet, 825	C	3
Gull Island, 361	D	2
Hampden, 739	C	4
Hant's Harbour, 522	D	2
Happy Adventure, 364	D	2
Happy Valley, 4,937	B	3
Harbour Breton, 2,196	C	4
Harbour Grace, 2,771	D	2
Harbour Main, 652	D	2
Hare Bay, 1,485	D	4
Hawke's Bay, 462	C	3
Head of Bay d'Espoir, 514	C	4
Heart's Content, 599	D	2
Heart's Delight, 543	D	2
Heart's Desire, 347	D	2
Heatherton, 329	C	4
Hermitage, 520	C	4
Hickman's Harbour, 414	D	2
Hillview, 281	D	2
Hodge's Cove, 391	D	2
Holyrood, 1,282	D	2
Hopedale, 375	B	2
Howley, 409	C	4
Isle aux Morts, 1,158	C	4
Jackson's Arm, 491	C	4
Jeffrey's, 280	C	4
Jerseyside, 1,061	B	3
Job's Cove, 182	D	2
Joe Batt's Arm, 886	D	4
Keels, 146	D	1
Kelligrews, 2,046	D	2
Kilbride, 2,148	D	2
King's Cove, 271	D	1
King's Point, 651	C	4
Kippens, 1,383	C	4
Labrador City, 7,622	A	3
Lamaline, 553	C	4
L'Anse-au-Clair, 233	C	3
L'Anse-au-Loup, 448	C	3
La Poile, 173	C	4
Lark Harbour, 590	C	4
La Scie, 1,255	C	4
Lawn, 1,000	C	4
Lethbridge, 657	D	2
Lewisporte, 3,175	C	4
Little Bay Islands, 394	C	4
Little Catalina, 722	D	2
Little Heart's Ease, 395	D	2
Long Harbour, 376	D	2
Long Pond, 1,758	D	2
Lourdes, 903	C	4
Lower Island Cove, 406	D	2
Lumsden, 630	D	4
Main Brook, 590	C	3
Makkovik, 292	C	2
Manuels, 1,006	D	2
Markland, 311	D	2
Mary's Harbour, 134	C	3
Marystown, 4,960	D	4
McCallum, 216	C	4
Melrose, 378	D	2
Middle Arm, 474	C	4
Millertown, 316	C	4
Milltown, 712	C	4
Milton, 290	C	2
Mount Carmel, 435	D	2
Mount Pearl, 7,211	D	2
Musgrave Harbour-Doting Cove, 1,238	D	4
Musgravetown, 586	C	2
Nain, 708	B	2
New Chelsea, 215	D	2
New Harbour, 704	D	2
Newmans Cove, 235	D	2
New Perlican, 308	D	2
Newtown, 513	D	4
Nippers Harbour, 275	C	4
Norman's Cove, 997	D	2
Norris Arm, 1,191	C	4
Norris Point, 986	C	4
North Harbour, 146	D	2
North River, 256	D	2
North West Brook, 302	C	2
North West River, 931	B	3
O'Donnells, 268	D	2
Old Perlican, 597	D	2
Paradise River, 146	C	3
Parkers Cove, 405	D	4
Parson's Pond, 491	C	3
Pasadena, 964	C	4
Patrick's Cove, 170	C	2
Perry's Cove, 165	D	2
Peterview, 953	C	4
Petley, 177	D	2
Petty Harbour, 940	D	2
Pinware, 186	C	3
Placentia, 2,211	C	2
Plate Cove, 517	D	2
Point La Haye, 320	D	2
Point Lance, 133	C	2
Point Leamington, 940	C	4
Point Verde, 309	C	2
Pollards Point, 439	C	4
Port au Bras, 393	D	4
Port au Choix, 861	C	3
Port au Port, 605	C	4
Port Blandford, 779	C	2
Port Hope Simpson, 232	C	3
Port Kirwan, 159	D	2
Port Rexton, 384	D	2
Portugal Cove, 1,411	D	2
Portugal Cove South, 371	D	2
Port Union, 578	D	2
Pouch Cove, 1,483	D	2
Princeton, 180	D	2
Raleigh, 292	C	3
Ramea, 1,208	C	4
Red Bay, 296	C	3
Red Head Cove, 234	D	2
Rencontre East, 235	C	4
Renews, 497	D	2
Rigolet, 182	C	3
Riverhead, 329	D	2
River of Ponds, 258	C	3
Robert's Arm, 1,044	C	4
Rocky Harbour, 982	C	4
Roddickton, 1,239	C	3
Rose Blanche, 703	C	4
Rushoon, 506	D	4
Saint Alban's, 1,941	C	4
Saint Andrew's, 257	C	4
Saint Anthony, 2,593	C	3
Saint Brendan's, 276	D	4
Saint Bride's, 598	C	2
Saint George's, 2,082	C	4
Saint John's (cap.), 88,102	D	2
Saint John's, ‡131,814	D	2
Saint Joseph's, 305	D	2
Saint Lawrence, 2,173	C	4
Saint Mary's, 375	D	2
Saint Paul's, 347	C	4
Saint Phillips, 573	D	2
Saint Shotts, 226	D	2
Saint Vincent's, 593	D	2
Salmon Cove, 653	D	2
Seal Cove, 698	C	3
Seal Cove, 457	C	4
Seldom, 442	D	4
Ship Harbour, 255	D	2
Shoal Cove, 236	C	3
Shoal Harbour, 715	C	2
Sop's Arm, 382	C	4
South Branch, 339	C	4
South Brook, 802	C	4
Southern Harbour, 679	C	2
South River, 554	D	2
Spaniard's Bay, 1,764	D	2
Springdale, 3,224	C	4
Stephenville, 7,770	C	4
Stephenville Crossing, 2,129	C	4
Summerville, 374	D	2
Sunnyside, 716	D	2
Sweet Bay, 192	D	2
Swift Current, 426	C	2
Terrenceville, 700	D	4
Tilting, 406	D	4
Torbay, 2,090	D	2
Tors Cove, 325	D	2
Traytown, 344	D	1
Trepassey, 1,443	D	2
Trinity, 577	D	2
Trinity, 288	D	4
Trout River, 689	C	4
Twillingate, 1,437	C	4
Upper Island Cove, 1,819	D	2
Victoria, 1,601	D	2
Wabana, 5,421	D	2
Wabush, 3,387	A	3
Wesleyville, 1,142	D	4
Western Bay, 430	D	2
West Saint Modeste, 294	C	3
Whitbourne, 1,235	D	2
Wild Cove, 172	C	3
Windsor, 6,644	C	4
Winterton, 794	D	2
Witless Bay, 754	D	2
Woody Point, 300	C	4

AREA 156,185 sq. mi.
POPULATION 620,000
CAPITAL St. John's
LARGEST CITY St. John's
HIGHEST POINT Cirque Mtn. 5,160 ft.
SETTLED IN 1610
ADMITTED TO CONFEDERATION 1949
PROVINCIAL FLOWER Pitcher Plant

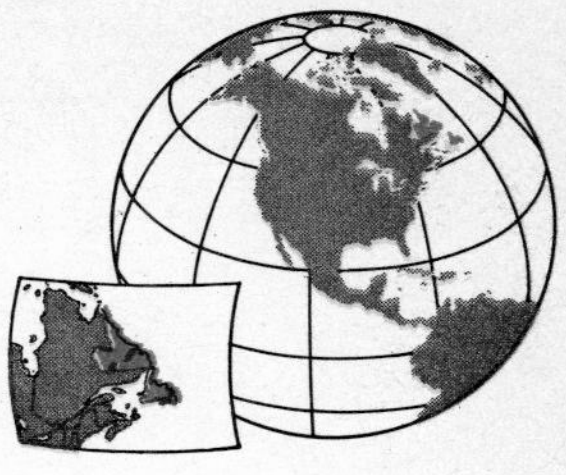

Agriculture, Industry and Resources

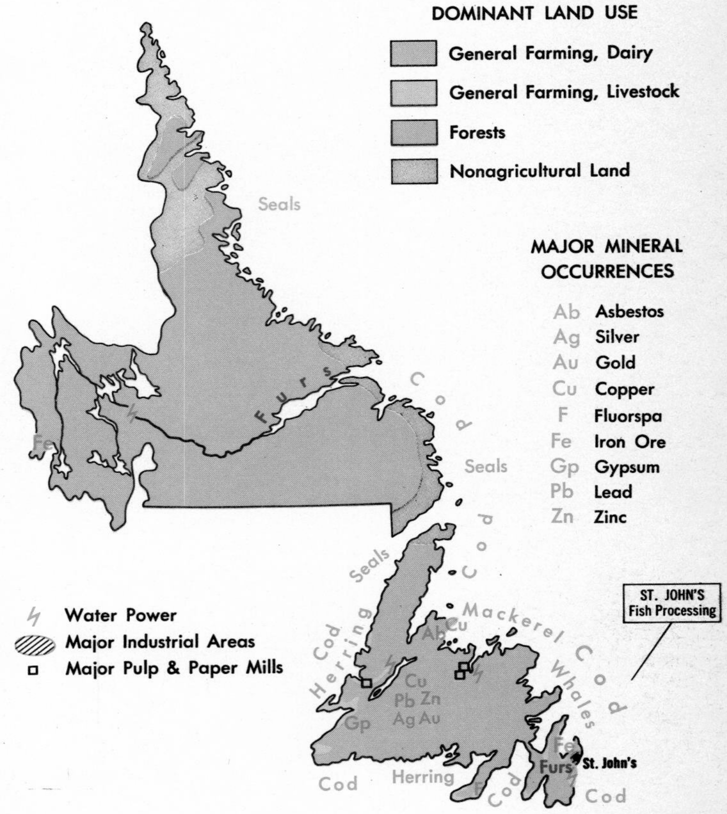
DOMINANT LAND USE
General Farming, Dairy
General Farming, Livestock
Forests
Nonagricultural Land
MAJOR MINERAL OCCURRENCES
Ab Asbestos
Ag Silver
Au Gold
Cu Copper
F Fluorspa
Fe Iron Ore
Gp Gypsum
Pb Lead
Zn Zinc
Water Power
Major Industrial Areas
Major Pulp & Paper Mills
Seals
Furs
Cod
Fe
Seals
Seals
Cod
Herring
Mackerel
Cod
Whales
Ab
Cu
Cu
Pb Zn
Ag Au
Gp
Fe
Furs
St. John's
ST. JOHN'S
Fish Processing
Cod
Herring
Cod
Cod

OTHER FEATURES

Alexis (riv.)	C	3
Anguille (cape)	C	4
Annieopscotch (mts.)	C	4
Ashuanipi (lake)	A	3
Ashuanipi (riv.)	A	3
Atikonak (lake)	B	3
Attikamagen (lake)	A	3
Avalon (pen.)	D	2
Barachois Pond Prov. Park	C	4
Bauld (cape)	C	3
Bell (isl.)	C	3
Bell (isl.), 6,079	D	2
Belle Isle (isl.), 25	C	3
Belle Isle (str.)	C	3
Blackhead (bay)	D	2
Bonavista (bay)	D	1
Bonavista (cape)	D	1
Bonne (bay)	C	4
Broyle (cape)	D	2
Bull Arm (inlet)	D	2
Burin (pen.)	C	4
Butter Pot Prov. Park	D	2
Cabot (str.)	B	4
Canada (bay)	C	3
Chidley (cape)	B	1
Churchill (falls)	B	3
Churchill (riv.)	B	3
Cirque (mt.)	B	2
Clode (sound)	D	2
Conception (bay)	D	2
Deep (inlet)	B	2
Double Mer (lake)	C	3
Dyke (lake)	A	3
Eagle (riv.)	C	3
Espoir (bay)	C	4
Exploits (bay)	C	4
Exploits (riv.)	C	4
Fogo (isl.), 4,094	D	4
Fortune (bay)	C	4
Freels (cape)	D	3
Gander (lake)	D	4
Gander (riv.)	D	4
Glover (isl.)	C	4
Goose (riv.)	B	3
Grand (lake)	B	3
Grand (lake)	C	4
Grates (pt.)	D	2
Great Colinet (isl.)	D	2
Grey (isls.)	C	3
Groais (isl.)	C	3
Gros Morne (mt.)	C	4
Gros Morne Nat'l Park	C	4
Groswater (bay)	C	3
Hamilton (inlet)	C	3
Hamilton (sound)	D	4
Hare (bay)	C	3
Hawke (hills)	D	2
Hebron (fjord)	B	2
Hermitage (bay)	C	4
Holyrood (bay)	D	2
Horse (isls.)	C	3
Horse Chops (head)	D	2
Humber (riv.)	C	4
Ingornachoix (bay)	C	3
Innuit (mt.)	B	2
Ireland's Eye (isl.)	D	2
Islands (bay)	C	4
Kaipokok (bay)	B	2
Kanairiktok (riv.)	B	3
Kaumajet (mts.)	B	2
Kingurutuk (lake)	B	2
Labrador (reg.), 28,166	B	2
Labrador (sea)	C	2
La Manche Prov. Park	D	2
La Poile (bay)	C	4
Little Mecatina (riv.)	B	3
Long (isl.)	C	2
Long (lake)	A	3
Long (pt.)	C	4
Long Range (mts.)	C	4
Main Topsail (mt.)	C	4
Makkovik (cape)	C	2
McLelan (str.)	B	1
Mealy (mts.)	C	3
Meelpaeg (lake)	C	4
Melville (lake)	C	3
Menihek (lakes)	A	3
Merasheen (isl.)	C	2
Mistaken (pt.)	D	2
Mistastin (lake)	B	2
Nachvak (fjord)	B	2
Naskaupi (riv.)	B	3
Newfoundland (isl.), 493,938	C	4
Newman (sound)	D	2
New World (isl.), 4,563	C	4
Norman (cape)	C	3
North Aulatsivik (isl.)	B	2
Notre Dame (bay)	C	4
Okak (bay)	B	2
Ossokmanuan (res.)	B	3
Petitsikapau (lake)	A	3
Pine (cape)	D	2
Pinware (riv.)	C	3
Pistolet (bay)	C	3
Placentia (bay)	C	2
Ponds (isl.), 164	C	3
Port au Port (bay)	C	4
Port au Port (pen.)	C	4
Port Manvers (harb.)	B	2
Race (cape)	D	2
Ramah (bay)	B	2
Ramea (isls.), 1,208	C	4
Random (isl.), 1,353	D	2
Random (sound)	D	2
Ray (cape)	C	4
Red (isl.)	C	2
Red Indian (lake)	C	4
Red Wine (riv.)	B	3
Rocky (riv.)	D	2
Round (pond)	C	4
Saglek (bay)	B	2
Saint Francis (cape)	D	2
Saint George (cape)	C	4
Saint George's (bay)	C	4
Saint John (bay)	C	3
Saint John (cape)	C	3
Saint Lawrence (gulf)	B	4
Saint Lewis (cape)	C	3
Saint Mary's (bay)	C	2
Saint Mary's (cape)	C	2
Saint Michaels (bay)	C	3
Salmonier (riv.)	D	2
Sandwich (bay)	C	3
Serpentine Prov. Park	C	4
Shabogamo (lake)	A	3
Shoal (bay)	D	2
Sir R.A. Squires Mem. Park	C	4
Smallwood (res.)	B	3
Smith (sound)	D	2
South Aulatsivik (isl.)	B	2
Spear (cape)	D	2
Swale (isl.)	D	1
Sylvester (mt.)	C	4
Terra Nova (riv.)	C	2
Terra Nova Nat'l Park	D	2
Territok (cape)	B	2
Thoresby (mt.)	B	2
Tickle (bay)	D	2
Torbay (pt.)	D	2
Torngat (mts.)	B	2
Trespassey (bay)	D	2
Trinity (bay)	D	2
Tunungayualok (isl.)	B	2
Ukasiksalik (isl.), 193	B	2
Victoria (lake)	C	4
Wabush (lake)	A	3
White (bay)	C	3
White Bear (lake)	C	4
White Handkerchief (cape)	B	2

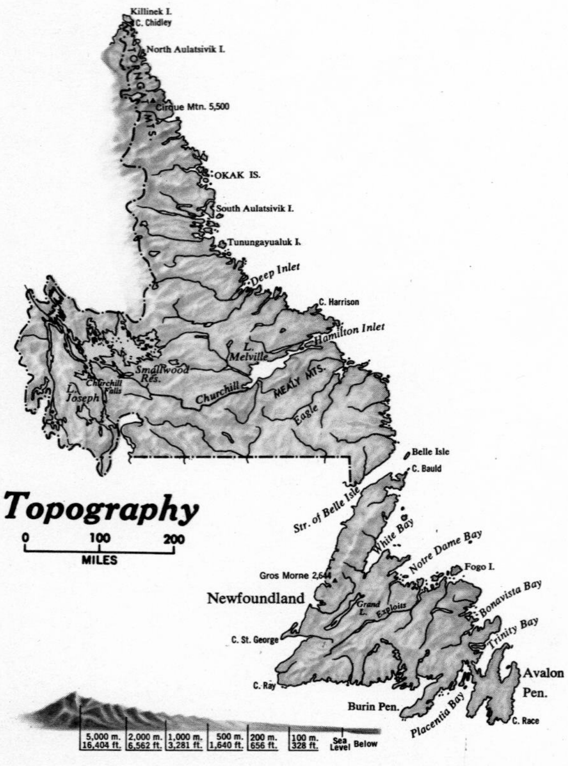
Killinek I.
C. Chidley
North Aulatsivik I.
Cirque Mtn. 5,500
OKAK IS.
South Aulatsivik I.
Tunungayualuk I.
Deep Inlet
C. Harrison
Hamilton Inlet
Melville
Smallwood Res.
Churchill Falls
Churchill
MEALY MTS.
Eagle
Joseph
Belle Isle
C. Bauld
Str. of Belle Isle
White Bay
Notre Dame Bay
Fogo I.
Gros Morne 2,644
Newfoundland
Grand L.
Exploits
Bonavista Bay
Trinity Bay
C. St. George
C. Ray
Burin Pen.
Placentia Bay
Avalon Pen.
C. Race
Topography
0 100 200
MILES
5,000 m. 16,404 ft.
2,000 m. 6,562 ft.
1,000 m. 3,281 ft.
500 m. 1,640 ft.
200 m. 656 ft.
100 m. 328 ft.
Sea Level
Below

SAINT PIERRE & MIQUELON

CITIES and TOWNS

Saint-Pierre (cap.), 4,565	C	

OTHER FEATURES

Miquelon (isl.), 621	C	4
Saint Pierre (isl.), 4,565	C	4

‡ Population of metropolitan area.

NOVA SCOTIA

COUNTIES

Annapolis, 21,841 ....C 4
Antigonish, 16,814 ....F 3
Cape Breton, 129,075 ....H 3
Colchester, 37,735 ....E 3
Cumberland, 35,160 ....D 3
Digby, 20,345 ....C 4
Guysborough, 12,864 ....G 3
Halifax, 261,461 ....E 4
Hants, 28,935 ....D 4
Inverness, 20,375 ....G 2
Kings, 44,975 ....D 3
Lunenburg, 38,422 ....D 4
Pictou, 46,104 ....F 3
Queens, 12,950 ....C 4
Richmond, 12,734 ....H 3
Shelburne, 16,661 ....C 5
Victoria, 7,823 ....H 2

CITIES and TOWNS

Yarmouth, 24,682 ....C 5

Abercrombie, 532 ....F 3
Alder Point, 844 ....H 2
Aldershot, 1,729 ....D 3
Amherst◉, 9,966 ....D 3
Annapolis Royal◉, 758 ....C 4
Antigonish◉, 5,489 ....F 3
Arcadia, 425 ....B 5
Arichat◉, 829 ....H 3
Auburn, 519 ....C 4
Aylesford, 956 ....D 4
Baddeck◉, 831 ....H 2
Barrington Passage, 551 .....C 5
Bear River, 733 ....C 4
Beaverbank, 958 ....E 4
Belliveau Cove, 486 ....B 4
Belmont, 663 ....E 3
Berwick, 1,412 ....D 4

Bible Hill, 3,505 ....E 3
Block House, 418 ....D 4
Blue Rock, 394 ....D 4
Bras d'Or, 655 ....H 2
Bridgetown, 1,039 ....C 4
Bridgewater, 5,231 ....D 4
Brookfield, 658 ....E 3
Brooklyn, 1,253 ....D 4
Caledonia, 459 ....C 4
Cambridge Station, 699 ......D 3
Canning, 809 ....D 3
Canso, 1,209 ....H 3
Cape North, 118 ....H 2
Centreville, 552 ....D 3
Chester, 1,031 ....D 4
Chester Basin, 588 ....D 4
Chéticamp, 1,016 ....G 2
Church Point, 258 ....B 4
Clark's Harbour, 1,082 ......C 5
Clementsport, 479 ....C 4
Comeauville, 365 ....B 4
Concession, 404 ....B 4
Conquerall Bank, 480 ....D 4

Conway, 363 ....C 4
Dartmouth, 64,770 ....E 4
Debert, 703 ....E 3
Deep Brook, 494 ....C 4
Digby◉, 2,363 ....C 4
Dominion, 2,879 ....J 2
Donkin, 910 ....J 2
East Chester, 485 ....D 4
East Chezzetcook, 617 ....E 4
Ellershouse, 424 ....D 4
Elmsdale, 758 ....E 4
Enfield, 1,056 ....E 4
Fall River, 969 ....E 4
Falmouth, 759 ....D 3
Florence, 1,958 ....H 2
Freeport, 475 ....B 4
Glace Bay, 22,440 ....J 2
Gold River, 448 ....D 4
Granville Ferry, 445 ....C 4
Great Village, 494 ....E 3
Grosses Coques, 360 ....B 4
Guysborough◉, 494 ....G 3
Halifax, ‡222,637 ....E 4
Halifax (cap.)◉, 122,035 .....E 4

Halifax, ‡222,637 ....E 4
Hantsport, 1,447 ....D 3
Havre Boucher, 385 ....G 3
Head of Jeddore, 445 ....E 4
Head of Saint Margarets
  Bay, 644 ....E 4
Heatherton, 368 ....G 3
Hebron, 463 ....B 5
Herring Cove, 1,487 ....E 4
Hilden, 803 ....F 3
Hopewell, 439 ....F 3
Hubbards, 427 ....D 4
Ingonish, 338 ....H 2
Ingonish Beach, 640 ....H 2
Inverness, 1,846 ....G 2
Joggins, 777 ....D 3
Judique, 409 ....G 3
Kentville◉, 5,198 ....D 3
Kingston, 1,429 ....D 4
Lakeside, 1,687 ....E 4
Lantz, 661 ....E 4
L'Ardoise West, 432 ....H 3
Lawrencetown, 512 ....C 4

Lequille, 526 ....C 4
Little Dover, 585 ....G 3
Liverpool◉, 3,654 ....C 4
Lockeport, 1,208 ....C 5
Louisbourg, 1,582 ....J 3
Louisdale, 1,036 ....G 3
Lower Wedgeport, 561 ....C 5
Lower West Pubnico, 743 .....C 5
Lower Woods Harbour,
  589 ....C 5
Lunenburg◉, 3,215 ....D 4
Lyons Brook, 441 ....F 3
Mabou, 421 ....G 2
Maccan, 492 ....D 3
Mahone Bay, 1,333 ....D 4
Main-à-Dieu, 394 ....J 2
Meaghers Grant, 388 ....E 4
Melvern Square, 427 ....C 4
Meteghan, 909 ....B 4
Meteghan Centre, 368 ....B 4
Meteghan River, 414 ....B 4
Middle Musquodoboit,
  638 ....E 3

Middleton, 1,870 ....C 4
Middlewood, 395 ....D 4
Milford Station, 650 ....E 3
Milton, 1,854 ....C 4
Mira Road, 1,503 ....H 2
Monastery, 418 ....G 3
Mount Uniacke, 813 ....E 4
Mulgrave, 1,196 ....G 3
Musquodoboit Harbour,
  768 ....E 4
New Germany, 584 ....D 4
New Glasgow, 10,849 ....F 3
New Minas, 1,503 ....D 3
Newport, 471 ....D 3
New Road, 1,333 ....C 4
New Victoria, 1,377 ....J 2
New Waterford, 9,579 ......J 2
Nictaux, 578 ....C 4
North Sydney, 8,604 ....H 2
Oxford, 1,473 ....D 3
Parkers Cove, 395 ....C 4
Parrsboro, 1,807 ....D 3
Petit-de-Grat, 1,032 ....H 3

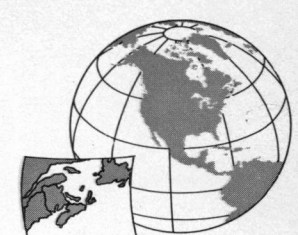

Petit-Étang, 438 ....G 2
Pictou⊙, 4,250 ....F 3
Pictou Landing, 435 ....F 3
Pomquet, 387 ....G 3
Porters Lake, 840 ....E 4
Port Hastings, 565 ....G 3
Port Hawkesbury, 3,372 ...G 3
Port Hood⊙, 523 ....G 2
Port Maitland, 419 ....B 5
Port Morien, 470 ....H 3
Port Williams, 638 ....D 3
Pugwash, 644 ....E 3
Reserve Mines, 2,529 ....H 2
River Bourgeois, 445 ....H 3
River Hébert, 862 ....D 3
River John, 468 ....E 3
Riverport, 371 ....D 4
Sackville, 5,701 ....E 4
Saint Croix, 375 ....D 3
Saint Peters, 663 ....H 3
Sambro, 556 ....E 4
Saulnierville, 481 ....B 4
Sheet Harbour, 1,062 .....F 4

Shelburne⊙, 2,689 ....C 5
Shubenacadie, 633 ....E 3
Somerset, 371 ....D 3
Springhill, 5,262 ....E 3
Stellarton, 5,357 ....F 3
Stewiacke, 1,040 ....E 3
Sydney⊙, 33,230 ....H 2
Sydney Mines, 8,991 ....H 2
Sydney River, 2,009 ....H 2
Tatamagouche, 568 ....E 3
Terence Bay, 1,134 ....E 4
Thorburn, 1,019 ....F 3
Three Mile Plains, 1,163 ...D 4
Timberlea, 1,770 ....E 4
Trenton, 3,331 ....F 3
Troy, 441 ....G 3
Truro⊙, 13,047 ....E 3
Tusket, 423 ....C 5
Upper Musquodoboit, 362 ..F 3
Waterville, 552 ....D 3
Waverley, 1,419 ....E 4
Wedgeport, 840 ....C 5
Wellington, 411 ....E 4

West Arichat, 549 ....G 3
West Dover, 362 ....E 4
Western Shore, 774 ....D 4
Westmount, 1,790 ....H 2
Westport, 380 ....B 4
Westville, 3,898 ....F 3
Weymouth, 604 ....C 4
Whites Lake, 432 ....E 4
Wilmot Station, 597 ....D 3
Windsor⊙, 3,775 ....D 3
Wolfville, 2,861 ....D 3
Yarmouth⊙, 8,516 ....B 5

OTHER FEATURES

Ainslie (lake) ....G 2
Annapolis (basin) ....C 4
Annapolis (riv.) ....C 4
Aspy (bay) ....H 2
Avon (riv.) ....D 4
Barachois (pt.) ....G 4
Bedford (basin) ....E 4
Boularderie (isl.), 1,902 ...H 2
Bras d'Or (lake) ....H 3
Breton (cape) ....J 3
Brier (isl.), 380 ....B 4
Canso (cape) ....H 3
Canso (str.) ....G 3
Cape Breton (isl.),
  162,989 ....J 2
Cape Breton Highlands
  Nat'l Park ....H 2
Cape Sable (isl.), 3,151 ....C 5
Caribou (isl.), 35 ....F 3
Carleton (riv.) ....C 4
Chebogue (harb.) ....B 5
Chedabucto (bay) ....G 3
Chéticamp (isl.), 63 ....G 2
Chignecto (bay) ....D 3
Chignecto (isth.) ....D 3
Cobequid (bay) ....E 3
Country (harb.) ....G 3
Craignish (hills) ....G 3
Cumberland (basin) ....D 3
Digby Gut (chan.) ....C 4
Digby Neck (pen.) ....B 4
Egmont (cape) ....H 2
Fourchu (cape) ....H 3
Fundy (bay) ....C 3
Gabarus (bay) ....H 3
Gaspereau (lake) ....D 4
George (cape) ....G 3
Georges (bay) ....G 3
Gold (riv.) ....D 4
Great Bras d'Or (chan.) .....H 2
Greville (bay) ....D 3
Guysborough (riv.) ....G 3
Halifax (harb.) ....E 4
Hébert (riv.) ....D 3
Ingonish North (bay) ....H 2
Janvrin (isl.), 162 ....G 3
Jeddore (harb.) ....F 4
John (cape) ....E 3
Joli (pt.) ....D 5
Jordan (riv.) ....C 5
Kejimkujik Nat'l Park ....C 4
Kennetcook (riv.) ....E 3
La Have (isl.), 7 ....D 4
La Have (riv.) ....D 4
Liscomb (isl.), 12 ....G 4
Lomond, Loch (lake) ....H 3
Long (isl.), 846 ....B 4
Louisbourg Nat'l Hist.
  Park ....J 3
Mabou Highlands (hills) ....G 2
Madame (isl.), 3,767 ....H 3
Mahone (bay) ....D 4
Malagash (pt.) ....E 3
McNutt (isl.), 20 ....C 5
Medway (riv.) ....C 4
Merigomish (harb.) ....F 3
Mersey (riv.) ....C 4
Minas (basin) ....D 3
Minas (chan.) ....D 3
Mira (bay) ....H 2
Musquodoboit (riv.) ....E 3
Necum Teuch (harb.) ....F 4
Negro (cape) ....C 5
North (cape) ....H 1
North (mt.) ....D 3
North Bay Ingonish (bay) ..H 2
North East Margaree (riv.) ..H 2
Northumberland (str.) ......E 2
Nuttby (mt.) ....E 3
Ohio (riv.) ....D 4
Panuke (lake) ....D 3
Pennant (pt.) ....E 4
Percé (cape) ....J 2
Petit-de-Grat (isl.), 1,032 ...H 3
Petpeswick (head) ....F 4
Pictou (harb.) ....F 3
Pictou (isl.), 69 ....F 3
Ponhook (lake) ....D 4
Port Hood (isl.), 39 ....G 2
Port Joli (harb.) ....D 5
Prim (pt.) ....C 4

Roseway (riv.) ....C 4
Rossignol (lake) ....C 4
Sable (cape) ....C 5
Sable (isl.), 12 ....J 5
Saint Andrews (chan.) ......H 2
Saint Ann's (bay) ....H 2
Saint Lawrence (bay) ....H 1
Saint Lawrence (cape) ......H 1
Saint Margarets (bay) ....E 4
Saint Mary's (bay) ....B 4
Saint Mary's (riv.) ....F 3
Saint Paul (isl.), 10 ....H 1
Saint Peters (bay) ....H 3
Salmon (riv.) ....E 3
Scatarie (isl.), 8 ....J 2
Scots (bay) ....D 3
Seal (isl.), 10 ....B 5
Sheet (harb.) ....F 4
Sherbrooke (harb.) ....F 4
Shubenacadie (lake) ....E 3
Shubenacadie (riv.) ....E 3
Sissiboo (riv.) ....C 4
Sober (isl.), 113 ....F 4
Split (cape) ....D 3
Stewiacke (riv.) ....E 3

Sydney (harb.) ....H 2
Tor (bay) ....G 3
Tusket (riv.) ....C 4
Verte (bay) ....D 2
West (riv.) ....F 3
West Liscomb (riv.) ....F 4
Whitehaven (bay) ....G 3
Yarmouth (sound) ....B 5

PRINCE EDWARD ISLAND

COUNTIES

Kings, 18,424 ....F 2
Prince, 42,082 ....D 2
Queens, 51,135 ....E 2

CITIES and TOWNS

Alberton, 973 ....E 2

Borden, 624 ....E 2
Bunbury, 527 ....F 2
Charlottetown (cap.)⊙,
  19,133 ....E 2
Cornwall, 557 ....E 2
Elmsdale, 403 ....D 2
Georgetown⊙, 767 ....F 2
Hunter River, 362 ....E 2
Kensington, 1,086 ....E 2
Miminegash, 417 ....D 2
Miscouche, 750 ....D 2
Montague, 1,608 ....F 2
Morell, 387 ....F 2
Mount Stewart, 413 ....F 2
Murray Harbour, 367 ......F 2
Murray River, 478 ....F 2
North Rustico, 767 ....E 2
O'Leary, 795 ....D 2
Parkdale, 2,313 ....E 2
Saint Edward, 537 ....D 2
Saint Eleanors, 1,621 ......E 2
Saint Peters, 370 ....F 2
Sherwood, 3,807 ....E 2
Souris, 1,393 ....F 2
Stanhope, 203 ....E 2

Summerside⊙, 9,439 ....E 2
Tignish, 1,060 ....D 2
Victoria, 171 ....E 2
Wilmot, 737 ....E 2

OTHER FEATURES

Bedeque (bay) ....E 2
Cardigan (bay) ....F 2
Cascumpeque (bay) ....E 2
East (pt.) ....G 2
Egmont (bay) ....D 2
Hillsborough (bay) ....E 2
Malpeque (bay) ....E 2
North (pt.) ....E 1
Panmure (isl.), 45 ....F 2
Prince Edward Island
  Nat'l Park ....E 2
Saint Lawrence (gulf) ....F 2
Tracadie (bay) ....F 2
⊙ County seat.

‡ Population of metropolitan
  area.

PRINCE EDWARD ISLAND

AREA 2,184 sq. mi.
POPULATION 110,000
CAPITAL Charlottetown
LARGEST CITY Charlottetown
HIGHEST POINT 465 ft.
SETTLED IN 1720
ADMITTED TO CONFEDERATION 1873
PROVINCIAL FLOWER Lady's Slipper

NOVA SCOTIA

AREA 21,425 sq. mi.
POPULATION 767,000
CAPITAL Halifax
LARGEST CITY Halifax
HIGHEST POINT Cape Breton Highlands 1,747 ft.
SETTLED IN 1605
ADMITTED TO CONFEDERATION 1867
PROVINCIAL FLOWER Trailing Arbutus or
  Mayflower

Topography

0   30   60
MILES

Agriculture, Industry and Resources

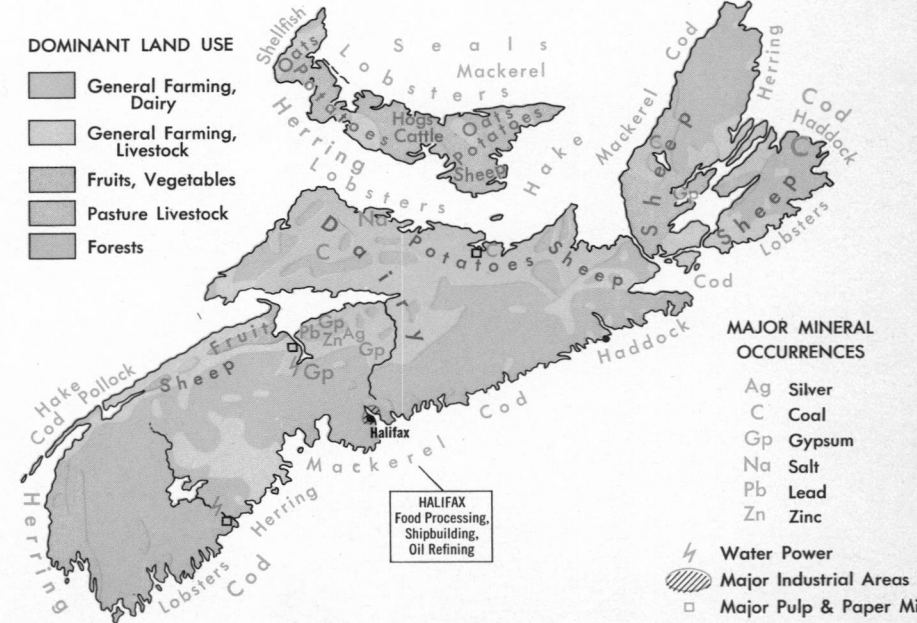

DOMINANT LAND USE

General Farming, Dairy
General Farming, Livestock
Fruits, Vegetables
Pasture Livestock
Forests

MAJOR MINERAL OCCURRENCES

Ag   Silver
C   Coal
Gp   Gypsum
Na   Salt
Pb   Lead
Zn   Zinc

⚡ Water Power
▨ Major Industrial Areas
◻ Major Pulp & Paper Mills

HALIFAX
Food Processing,
Shipbuilding,
Oil Refining

COUNTIES

Albert, 16,307 .... F 3
Carleton, 24,428 .... C 2
Charlotte, 24,551 ...... C 3
Gloucester, 74,752 ..... E 1
Kent, 24,901 .... E 2
King's, 33,285 .... E 3
Madawaska, 34,976 ...... B 1
Northumberland, 51,561 . D 2
Queen's, 12,486 .... D 3
Restigouche, 41,289 .... C 1
Saint John, 92,162 ..... D 3
Sunbury, 21,268 .... D 3
Victoria, 19,796 .... C 1
Westmorland, 98,669 .... F 2
York, 64,126 .... C 3

CITIES and TOWNS

Acadie Siding, 112 .... E 2
Acadieville, 144 .... E 2
Adamsville, 119 .... E 2
Albert Mines, 130 .... F 3
Alcida, 222 .... E 1
Aldouane, 83 .... E 2
Allardville, 712 .... E 1
Alma, 425 .... F 3
Anagance, 109 .... E 3
Apohaqui, 352 .... E 3
Argyle, 63 .... C 2
Armstrong Brook, 321 .... E 1
Aroostook, 550 .... C 2
Arthurette, 299 .... C 2
Astle, 194 .... D 2
Atholville, 2,108 .... D 1
Aulac, 128 .... F 3
Back Bay, 567 .... D 3
Baie-Sainte-Anne, 735 .... F 1
Baie-Verte, 177 .... F 2
Bailey, 143 .... C 3
Bairdsville, 171 .... C 2
Baker Brook, 561 .... B 1
Balmoral, 896 .... D 1
Barker's Point, 1,882 .... D 3
Barnaby River, 87 .... E 2
Barnettville, 182 .... D 2
Bartibog Bridge, 163 .... E 1
Bas-Caraquet, 1,685 .... F 1
Bass River, 129 .... E 2
Bath, 920 .... C 2
Bathurst⊙, 16,674 .... E 1
Bathurst Mines, 45 .... D 1
Bayfield, 178 .... G 2
Bayside, 207 .... C 3
Beaver Brook Station, 276 .... E 1
Beaver Harbour, 355 .... D 3

Beechwood, 349 .... C 2
Beersville, 85 .... E 2
Belledune, 784 .... E 1
Bellefleur, 145 .... C 1
Bellefond, 294 .... E 1
Belleisle Creek, 179 .... E 3
Benjamin, 65 .... E 1
Benton, 149 .... C 3
Beresford, 2,325 .... E 1
Berry Mills, 349 .... E 2
Bertrand, 1,094 .... F 1
Berwick, 130 .... E 3
Black Point, 150 .... D 1
Black River, 91 .... E 3
Black River Bridge, 335 ..... E 2
Blackville, 915 .... D 2
Blissfield, 130 .... D 2
Bloomfield Ridge, 218 .... D 2
Blue Cove, 519 .... E 1
Bocabec, 59 .... C 3
Boiestown, 332 .... D 2
Bonny River, 134 .... D 3
Bosse, 134 .... B 1
Bourgeois, 306 .... F 2
Brantville, 1,072 .... F 1
Breau-Village, 249 .... F 2
Brest, 117 .... C 2
Bridgedale, 416 .... F 3
Briggs Corner, 138 .... E 2

Bristol, 771 .... C 2
Brockway, 68 .... C 3
Browns Flats, 262 .... D 3
Buctouche, 1,964 .... F 2
Burnsville, 179 .... E 1
Burton⊙, 357 .... D 3
Burtts Corner, 487 .... D 2
Caissie-Village, 34 .... F 2
Cambridge-Narrows, 416 ...... E 3
Campbellton, 10,335 .... D 1
Canaan Road, 130 .... E 2
Canaan Station, 102 .... E 2
Canterbury, 528 .... C 3
Cap-Bateau, 466 .... F 1
Cape Tormentine, 261 .... G 2
Cap Lumière, 305 .... F 2
Cap-Pelé, 2,081 .... F 2
Caraquet, 3,441 .... E 1
Caron Brook, 191 .... B 1
Carrolls Crossing, 188 ...... D 2
Castalia, 199 .... D 4
Central Blissville (Bailey),
  143 .... D 3
Centre-Acadie, 151 .... E 2
Centre-Saint-Simon, 517 ..... E 1
Centreville, 566 .... C 2
Chance Harbour, 181 .... D 3
Charlo, 1,621 .... D 1
Chartersville, 320 .... F 2
Chatham, 7,833 .... E 2

Chatham Head, 1,440 .... E 2
Chipman, 1,977 .... E 2
Clair, 704 .... B 1
Clarendon, 105 .... D 3
Cliffordvale, 110 .... C 2
Clifton, 231 .... E 1
Cloverdale, 133 .... C 2
Coal Branch, 89 .... E 2
Coal Creek, 71 .... E 2
Cocagne, 234 .... F 2
Cocagne Cape, 258 .... F 2
Codys, 67 .... E 3
Coldstream, 160 .... C 2
Coles Island, 121 .... E 3
College Bridge, 545 .... F 2
Collette, 178 .... E 2
Connell, 107 .... C 2
Connors, 231 .... B 1
Cork Station, 70 .... D 3
Cornhill, 83 .... E 3
Cross Creek, 241 .... D 2
Cumberland Bay, 246 .... E 2
Dalhousie⊙, 6,255 .... D 1
Dalhousie Junction, 275 ..... D 1
Darlington, 585 .... D 1
Daulnay, 539 .... E 1
Dawsonville, 208 .... C 1
Debec, 222 .... C 2
Dieppe, 4,277 .... F 2
Dipper Harbour, 109 .... D 3

Doaktown, 938 .... D 2
Dorchester⊙, 1,199 .... F 2
Dorchester Crossing, 574 .... F 2
Douglas Harbour, 46 .... D 3
Douglastown, 637 .... E 1
Drummond, 637 .... C 1
Duguayville, 372 .... E 1
Dumbarton, 59 .... C 3
Dumfries, 257 .... C 3
Dupuis Corner, 218 .... F 2
Durham Bridge, 182 .... D 2
East Shediac, 585 .... F 2
Edmundston⊙, 12,365 .... B 1
Eel River Bridge, 487 .... D 1
Eel River Crossing, 1,075 ... D 1
Elgin, 283 .... F 3
Elmwood, 78 .... C 2
Enniskillen, 77 .... D 3
Evandale, 33 .... E 3
Evangeline, 298 .... F 1
Fairhaven, 118 .... C 4
Fairvale, 444 .... E 3
Fairvale, 2,050 .... E 3
Ferry Road, 520 .... E 1
Fielding, 31 .... C 2
Five Fingers, 148 .... C 1
Flatlands, 280 .... D 1
Florenceville, 584 .... C 2
Fontaine, 318 .... F 2
Forest City, 55 .... C 3

Fosterville, 71 .... C 3
Four Falls Corner, 97 .... C 2
Fox Creek, 488 .... F 2
Fredericton (cap.)⊙,
  24,254 .... D 3
Fredericton Junction, 615 ... D 3
Gagetown⊙, 609 .... D 3
Gardner Creek, 47 .... E 3
Geary, 1,023 .... D 3
Germantown, 71 .... F 3
Gillespie, 88 .... C 2
Glassville, 174 .... C 2
Glencoe, 143 .... D 1
Glenlivet, 231 .... D 1
Gloucester Junction, 167 .... E 1
Gondola Point, 850 .... D 3
Grafton, 359 .... C 2
Grand Bay, 1,066 .... D 3
Grande-Anse, 545 .... E 1
Grand Falls, 4,516 .... C 1
Grand Falls Hill, 559 .... C 1
Grand Harbour, 556 .... D 4
Gray Rapids, 307 .... E 2
Gunningsville, 1,669 .... F 2
Hammondvale, 127 .... E 3
Hampstead, 118 .... D 3
Hampton⊙, 1,748 .... E 3
Harcourt, 163 .... E 2
Hardwicke, 93 .... E 1
Hardwood Ridge, 222 .... E 2

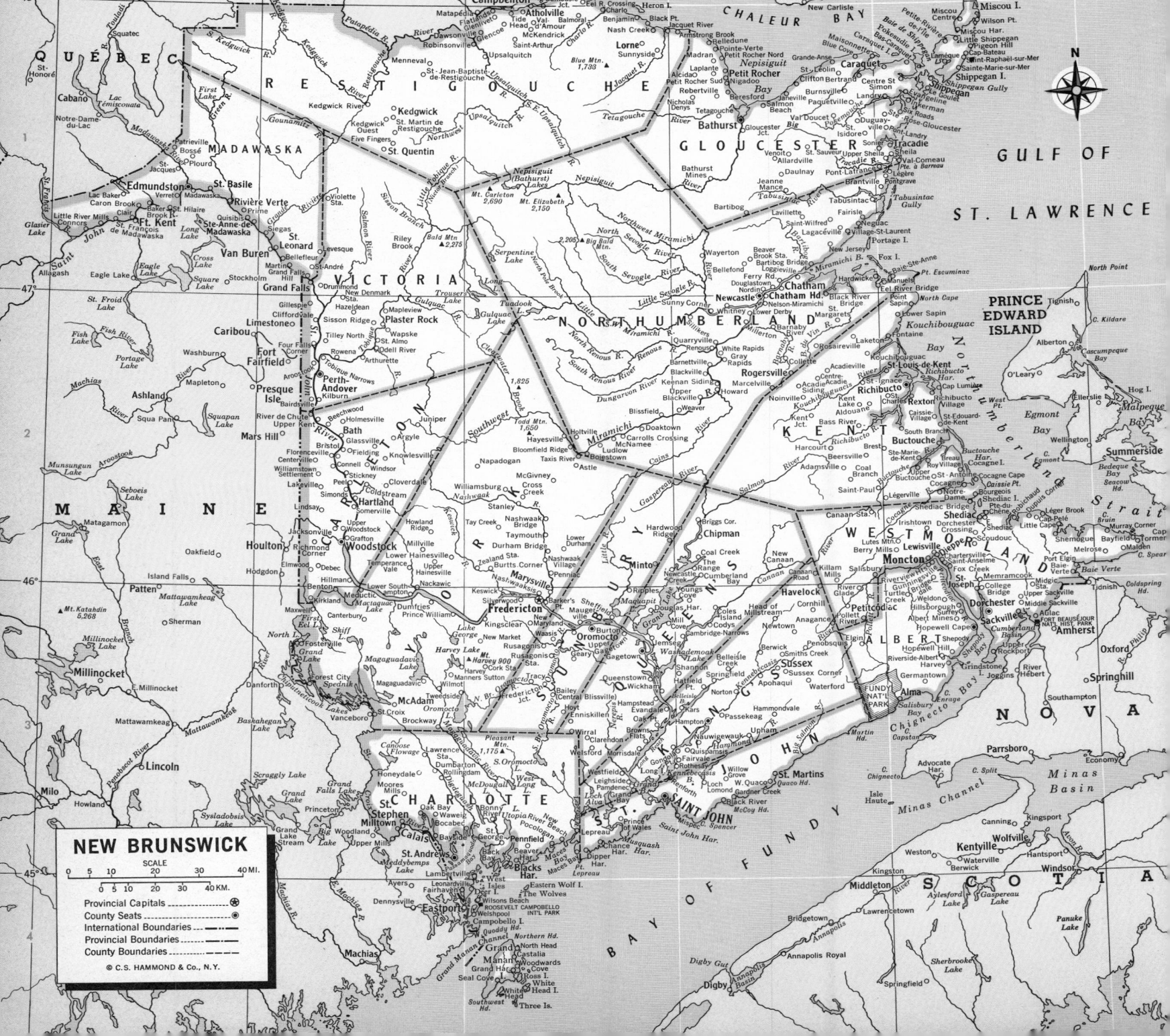

Hartland, 1,009 C 2
Harvey, 54 F 3
Harvey, 383 D 3
Hatfield Point, 181 E 3
Havelock, 513 E 3
Hayesville, 120 D 2
Hazeldean, 213 C 2
Head of Millstream, 86 E 3
Hillman, 159 C 2
Hillsborough, 781 F 3
Holmésville, 251 C 2
Holtville, 300 D 2
Honeydale, 90 C 3
Hopewell Cape⊙, 162 F 3
Hopewell Hill, 164 F 3
Howard, 176 E 2
Howland Ridge, 56 C 2
Hoyt, 97 D 3
Inkerman, 500 F 1
Irishtown, 194 F 2
Jacksonville, 372 C 2
Jacquet River, 866 E 1
Janeville, 164 E 1
Jeanne Mance, 97 E 1
Jemseg, 185 D 3
Juniper, 585 C 2
Kars, 76 E 3
Kedgwick, 1,065 C 1
Kedgwick Ouest, 101 C 1
Kedgwick River, 25 C 1
Keenan Siding, 74 E 2
Kent Junction, 105 E 2
Kent Lake, 50 E 2
Keswick, 308 D 3
Kilburn, 167 C 2
Killam Mills, 60 E 2
Kingsclear, 132 D 3
Kirkland, 91 C 3
Knowlesville, 58 C 2
Kouchibouguac, 151 F 2
Lac Baker, 360 B 1
Lagacéville, 261 E 1
Laketon, 127 E 2
Lakeville, 325 C 2
Lambertville, 181 C 3
Lamèque, 933 F 1
Landry, 268 E 1
Laplante, 240 E 1
Lavillette, 500 E 1
Lawrence Station, 221 C 3
Léger Brook, 339 F 2
Légère, 514 F 1
Légerville, 199 F 2
Le Goulet, 1,155 F 1
Leighside, 597 D 3
Leonardville, 179 C 4
Lepreau, 162 D 3
Levesque, 225 C 1

Lewisville, 3,710 F 2
Lindsay, 108 C 2
Little Cape, 454 F 2
Little River Mills, 110 B 1
Little Shippegan, 100 F 1
Loch Lomond, 137 E 3
Loggieville, 877 E 1
Lorne, 999 D 1
Lower Derby, 260 E 2
Lower Durham, 115 D 2
Lower Hainesville, 119 C 2
Lower Millstream, 199 E 3
Lower Sapin, 186 F 2
Lower Southampton, 118 C 2
Ludlow, 193 D 2
Lutes Mountain, 234 E 2
Maces Bay, 133 D 3
Madran, 245 E 1
Magaguadavic, 121 C 3
Maisonnette, 620 E 1
Malden, 112 G 2
Manners Sutton, 199 D 3
Manuels, 546 F 1
Mapleview, 110 C 2
Marcelville, 78 E 2
Martin, 115 C 1
Marysville, 3,872 D 2
Maugerville, 346 D 3
Maxwell, 61 C 3
McAdam, 2,224 C 3
McGivney, 232 D 2
McKendrick, 594 D 1
McNamee, 189 D 2
Meductic, 172 C 3
Melrose, 144 F 2
Memramcook, 366 F 2
Menneval, 169 C 1
Middle Sackville, 311 F 3
Midgic Station, 211 F 3
Mill Cove, 227 D 3
Millerton, 199 E 2
Milltown, 1,893 C 3
Millville, 352 C 2
Minto, 3,880 D 2
Miscou Centre, 473 F 1
Miscou Harbour, 86 F 1
Mispec, 132 E 3
Moncton, 47,891 F 2
Moores Mills, 138 C 3
Morrisdale, 162 D 3
Murray Corner, 178 G 2
Nackawic, 1,324 C 2
Napadogan, 123 D 2
Nash Creek, 268 D 1
Nashwaak Bridge, 237 D 2
Nashwaaksis, 7,353 D 3
Nashwaak Village, 141 D 2
Nauwigewauk, 313 E 3

Neguac, 1,498 E 1
Nelson-Miramichi, 1,580 E 2
New Canaan, 44 E 2
Newcastle⊙, 6,460 E 2
Newcastle Creek, 205 D 2
New Denmark Station, 315 C 1
New Jersey, 117 E 1
New Market, 95 D 3
New Maryland, 643 D 3
New River Beach, 78 D 3
Newtown, 89 E 3
Nicholas Denys, 241 D 1
Nigadoo, 597 E 1
Noinville, 39 E 2
Nordin, 303 E 1
North Head, 649 D 4
Norton, 1,149 E 3
Notre-Dame, 362 F 2
Oak Bay, 232 C 3
Oak Point, 100 D 3
Odell River, 166 C 2
Oromocto, 11,427 D 3
Pamdenec, 422 D 3
Paquetville, 479 E 1
Passekeag, 169 E 3
Patrieville, 140 B 1
Peel, 82 C 2
Pennfield, 267 D 3
Penniac, 407 D 2
Penobsquis, 79 E 3
Perth-Andover⊙, 2,108 C 2
Petitcodiac, 1,569 E 3
Petite-Rivière-de-l'Île, 477 F 1
Petit Rocher, 1,624 E 1
Petit Rocher Nord, 414 E 1
Petit Rocher Sud, 538 E 1
Pigeon Hill, 445 F 1
Plaster Rock, 1,331 C 2
Plourd, 336 B 1
Pocologan, 108 D 3
Pointe-du-Chêne, 484 F 2
Pointe-Verte, 524 E 1
Point Sapin, 349 F 2
Pollett River, 64 E 3
Pontgrave, 202 F 1
Pont-Lafrance, 856 E 1
Pont-Landry, 562 F 1
Port Elgin, 553 F 2
Prime, 73 B 1
Prince of Wales, 131 D 3
Prince William, 236 C 3
Quarryville, 312 E 2
Queenstown, 105 D 3
Quisibis, 138 B 1
Quispamsis, 2,215 E 3
Renforth, 1,606 E 3
Renous, 211 E 2

Rexton, 755 F 2
Richardsville, 892 D 1
Richibucto⊙, 1,850 E 2
Richibucto Village, 357 F 2
Richmond Corner, 54 C 2
Riley Brook, 166 C 1
Ripples, 230 D 3
River de Chute, 57 C 2
River Glade, 242 E 3
Riverside-Albert, 509 F 3
Riverview Heights, 6,525 F 2
Rivière Verte, 1,657 B 1
Robertville, 954 E 1
Robichaud, 350 F 2
Robinsonville, 202 C 1
Rogersville, 1,077 E 2
Rollingdam, 124 C 3
Rosaireville, 87 E 2
Rothesay, 1,038 E 3
Rowena, 104 C 2
Roy, 115 F 2
Rusagonis, 182 D 3
Rusagonis Station, 76 D 3
Sackville, 3,180 F 3
Saint Almo, 53 C 2
Saint-André, 315 C 1
Saint Andrews⊙, 1,812 C 3
Saint-Anselme, 1,150 F 2
Saint-Antoine, 756 F 2
Saint-Arthur, 521 D 1
Saint Basile, 3,085 B 1
Saint-Charles, 381 F 2
Saint Croix, 50 C 3
Sainte-Anne-de-Madawaska, 1,253 B 1
Saint-Édouard-de-Kent, 207 F 2
Sainte-Marie-de-Kent, 269 F 2
Sainte-Marie-sur-Mer, 430 F 1
Sainte-Rose-Gloucester, 479 F 1
Saint François de Madawaska, 511 B 1
Saint George, 977 D 3
Saint Hilaire, 199 B 1
Saint-Ignace, 382 F 2
Saint-Isidore, 477 E 1
Saint-Jacques, 1,072 B 1
Saint-Jean-Baptiste-de-Restigouche, 293 C 1
Saint John⊙, 89,039 E 3
Saint John, ‡106,744 E 3
Saint-Joseph, 687 F 3
Saint-Léolin, 694 E 1
Saint Leonard, 1,478 C 1
Saint-Louis-de-Kent, 992 F 2
Saint Margarets, 213 E 2
Saint Martin de Restigouche, 145 C 1
Saint Martins, 484 E 3
Saint-Paul, 314 E 2
Saint Quentin, 2,093 C 1
Saint-Raphaël-sur-Mer, 588 F 1
Saint Sauveur, 626 E 1
Saint Stephen, 3,409 C 3
Saint-Wilfred, 307 E 1
Salisbury, 1,070 E 2
Salmon Beach, 382 E 1
Scoudouc, 250 F 2
Séal Cove, 613 D 4
Shannon, 72 E 3
Shediac, 2,203 F 2
Shediac Bridge, 347 F 2
Sheffield, 112 D 3
Sheila, 854 F 1
Shemogue, 189 F 2
Shepody, 88 F 3
Shippegan, 2,043 F 1
Siegas, 393 C 1
Sillikers, 275 E 2
Silverwood, 935 D 3
Simonds, 236 C 2
Sisson Ridge, 166 C 2
Six Roads, 441 F 1
Smiths Creek, 195 E 3
Somerville, 362 C 2
Sonier, 443 E 1
South Branch, 143 F 2
Springfield, 139 E 3
Stanley, 388 D 2
Stickney, 266 C 2
Sunny Corner, 572 E 2
Sunnyside, 79 D 1
Surrey, 286 F 3
Sussex, 3,942 E 3

AREA 28,354 sq. mi.
POPULATION 624,000
CAPITAL Fredericton
LARGEST CITY Saint John
HIGHEST POINT Mt. Carleton 2,690 ft.
SETTLED IN 1611
ADMITTED TO CONFEDERATION 1867
PROVINCIAL FLOWER Purple Violet

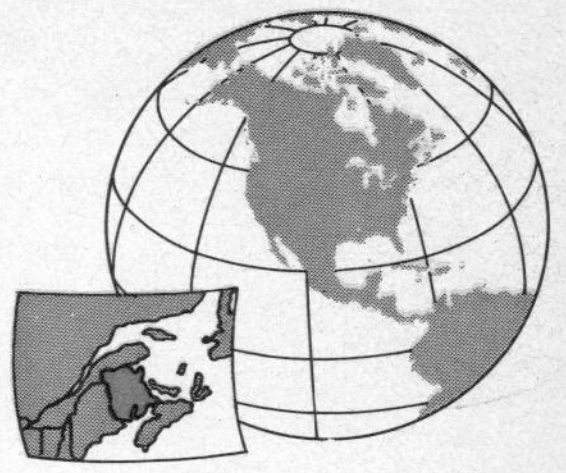

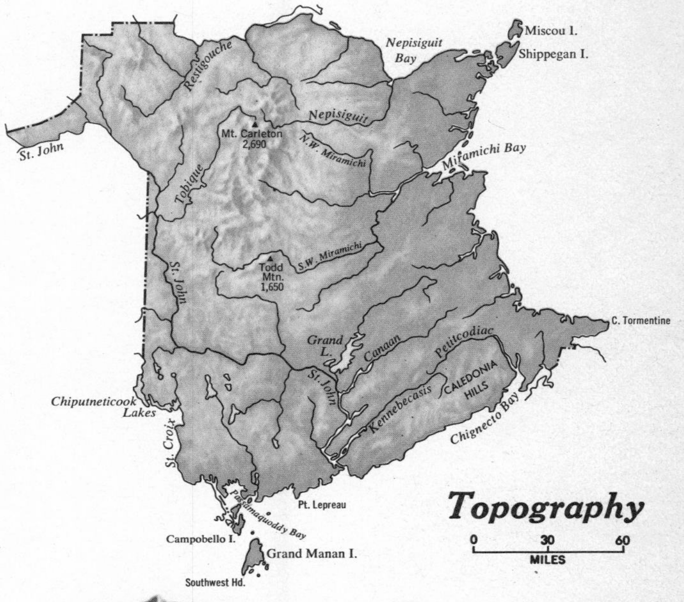

Miscou I.
Shippegan I.
Nepisiguit Bay
Restigouche
Nepisiguit
St. John
Mt. Carleton 2,690
N.W. Miramichi
Miramichi Bay
Tobique
St. John
Todd Mtn. 1,650
S.W. Miramichi
C. Tormentine
Grand L.
Canaan
Petitcodiac
Chiputneticook Lakes
St. John
Kennebecasis
CALEDONIA HILLS
Chignecto Bay
St. Croix
Passamaquoddy Bay
Pt. Lepreau
Campobello I.
Grand Manan I.
Southwest Hd.
Topography
0 30 60
MILES

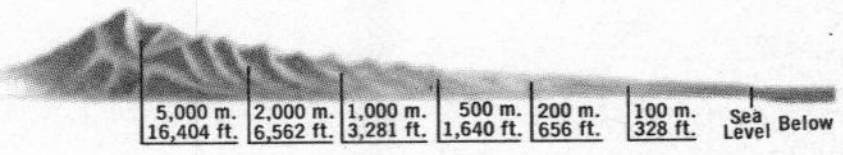

5,000 m. 16,404 ft.
2,000 m. 6,562 ft.
1,000 m. 3,281 ft.
500 m. 1,640 ft.
200 m. 656 ft.
100 m. 328 ft.
Sea Level
Below

Agriculture, Industry and Resources

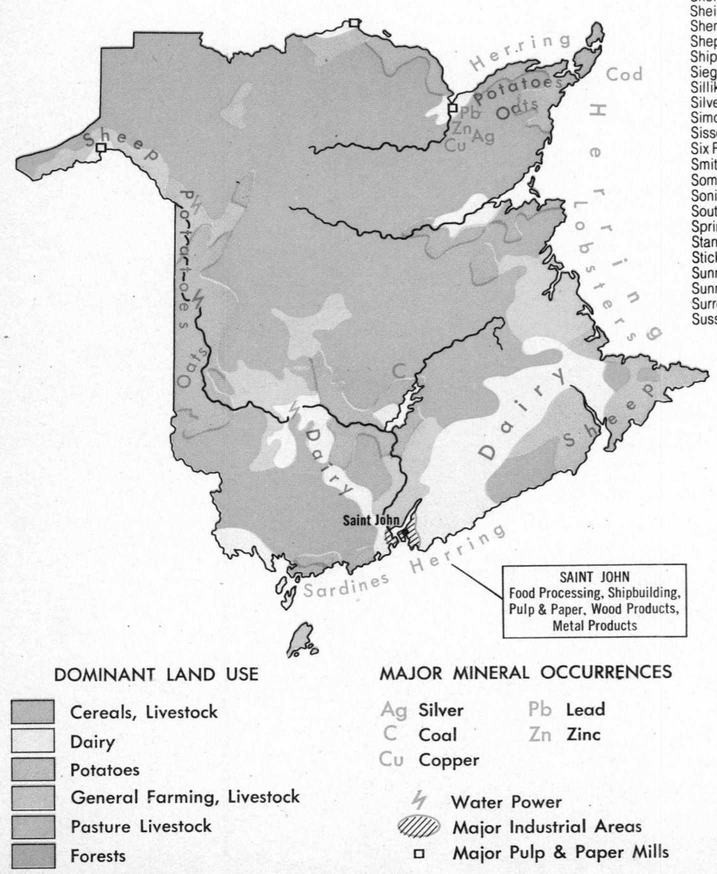

Herring
Cod
Potatoes
Pb
Oats
Zn
Ag
Cu
Sheep
Herring
Lobsters
Dairy
Sheep
Dairy
Saint John
Herring
Sardines
SAINT JOHN
Food Processing, Shipbuilding, Pulp & Paper, Wood Products, Metal Products
DOMINANT LAND USE
Cereals, Livestock
Dairy
Potatoes
General Farming, Livestock
Pasture Livestock
Forests
MAJOR MINERAL OCCURRENCES
Ag Silver
C Coal
Cu Copper
Pb Lead
Zn Zinc
Water Power
Major Industrial Areas
Major Pulp & Paper Mills

Sussex Corner, 700 E 3
Tabusintac, 253 E 1
Taxis River, 172 D 2
Tay Creek, 177 D 2
Taymouth, 280 D 2
Temperance Vale, 323 C 2
Tetagouche, 359 E 1
The Range, 88 E 2
Thibault, 231 C 1
Tide Head, 797 D 1
Tilley North, 226 C 2
Tobique Narrows, 169 C 2
Tracadie, 2,222 F 1
Tracy, 610 D 3
Turtle Creek, 200 F 3
Tweedside, 125 C 3
Upham, 132 E 3
Upper Blackville, 224 E 2
Upper Buctouche, 155 F 2
Upper Gagetown, 299 D 3
Upper Hainesville, 217 C 2
Upper Kent, 301 C 2
Upper Mills, 143 C 3
Upper Rockport, 17 F 3
Upper Sackville, 234 F 3
Upper Sheila, 748 E 1
Upper Woodstock, 336 C 2
Upsalquitch, 135 D 1
Val-Comeau, 495 F 1
Val d'Amour, 580 D 1
Val Doucet, 486 E 1
Veniot, 560 E 1
Verret, 900 B 1
Village-Saint-Laurent, 164 E 1
Violette Station, 128 C 1
Waasis, 176 D 3
Wapske, 210 C 2
Waterford, 132 E 3
Waweig, 124 C 3
Wayerton, 161 E 1
Weaver, 112 E 2
Weldon, 199 F 3
Welsford, 293 D 3
Welshpool, 172 D 4
Westfield, 461 D 3
West Quaco, 102 E 3
White Head, 178 D 4
White Rapids, 304 E 2
Whitney, 282 E 2
Wickham, 86 D 3
Williamsburg, 333 D 2
Williamstown Settlement, 197 C 2
Willow Grove, 336 E 3
Wilmot, 127 C 3
Wilson Point, 70 F 1
Wilsons Beach, 911 D 4
Windsor, 56 C 2

Wirral, 115 D 3
Woodstock⊙, 4,846 C 2
Woodwards Cove, 180 D 4
Youngs Cove, 118 E 3
Zealand Station, 442 D 2

OTHER FEATURES

Bald (mt.) C 1
Bartibog (riv.) E 1
Bay du Vin (riv.) E 2
Big Tracadie (riv.) E 1
Buctouche (harb.) F 2
Buctouche (riv.) F 2
Campobello (isl.), 1,274 D 4
Canaan (riv.) E 2
Carleton (mt.) D 1
Chaleur (bay) E 1
Chignecto (bay) F 3
Chiputneticook (lakes) C 3
Cocagne (isl.) F 2
Cumberland (basin) F 3
Deer (isl.), 730 D 4
Digdeguash (riv.) C 3
Escuminac (bay) D 1
Escuminac (pt.) F 1
Fort Beauséjour Nat'l Hist. Park F 3
Fundy (bay) E 3
Fundy Nat'l Park E 3
Gaspereau (riv.) D 2
Grand (bay) D 3
Grand (lake) C 3
Grand (lake) D 3
Grande (riv.) C 1
Grand Manan (chan.) C 4
Grand Manan (isl.), 2,547 D 4
Green (riv.) B 1
Hammond (riv.) E 3
Harvey (lake) C 3
Heron (isl.) D 1
Kedgwick (riv.) C 1
Kennebecasis (riv.) E 3
Keswick (riv.) C 2
Kouchibouguac (bay) F 2
Kouchibouguacis (riv.) E 2
Lepreau (riv.) D 3
Little (riv.) D 2
Long (isl.) D 3
Long Reach (inlet) D 3
Maces (bay) D 3
Mactaquac (lake) C 3
Madawaska (riv.) B 1
Magaguadavic (lake) C 3
Magaguadavic (riv.) C 3
Miramichi (bay) E 1

Miscou (isl.), 728 F 1
Miscou (pt.) F 1
Musquash (harb.) D 3
Nashwaak (riv.) D 2
Nepisiguit (bay) E 1
Nepisiguit (riv.) D 1
Nerepis (riv.) D 3
Northern (head) D 4
North Sevogle (riv.) D 1
Northumberland (str.) F 2
Northwest Miramichi (riv.) D 1
Oromocto (lake) C 3
Oromocto (riv.) D 3
Passamaquoddy (bay) C 3
Patapédia (riv.) C 1
Petitcodiac (riv.) F 3
Pokemouche (riv.) E 1
Pokesudie (isl.), 368 F 1
Pollett (riv.) E 3
Quaco (head) E 3
Renous (riv.) D 2
Restigouche (riv.) C 1
Richibucto (harb.) F 2
Richibucto (riv.) E 2
Roosevelt Campobello Int'l Park D 4
Saint Croix (riv.) C 3
Saint Francis (riv.) A 1
Saint John (harb.) E 3
Saint John (riv.) C 2
Saint Lawrence (gulf) F 1
Salisbury (bay) F 3
Salmon (riv.) C 1
Salmon (riv.) E 2
Shediac (isl.) F 2
Shepody (bay) F 3
Shippegan (bay) E 1
Shippegan (gully) F 1
Shippegan (isl.), 7,745 F 1
South Sevogle (riv.) D 1
Southwest (head) D 4
Southwest Miramichi (riv.) D 2
Spear (cape) G 2
Spednik (lake) C 3
Spencer (cape) E 3
Tabusintac (gully) F 1
Tabusintac (riv.) E 1
Tetagouche (riv.) D 1
Tobique (riv.) C 2
Upsalquitch (riv.) D 1
Utopia (lake) D 3
Verte (bay) G 2
Washademoak (lake) E 3
West (isls.), 974 D 4
White Head (isl.), 178 D 4

⊙ County seat.
‡ Population of metropolitan area.

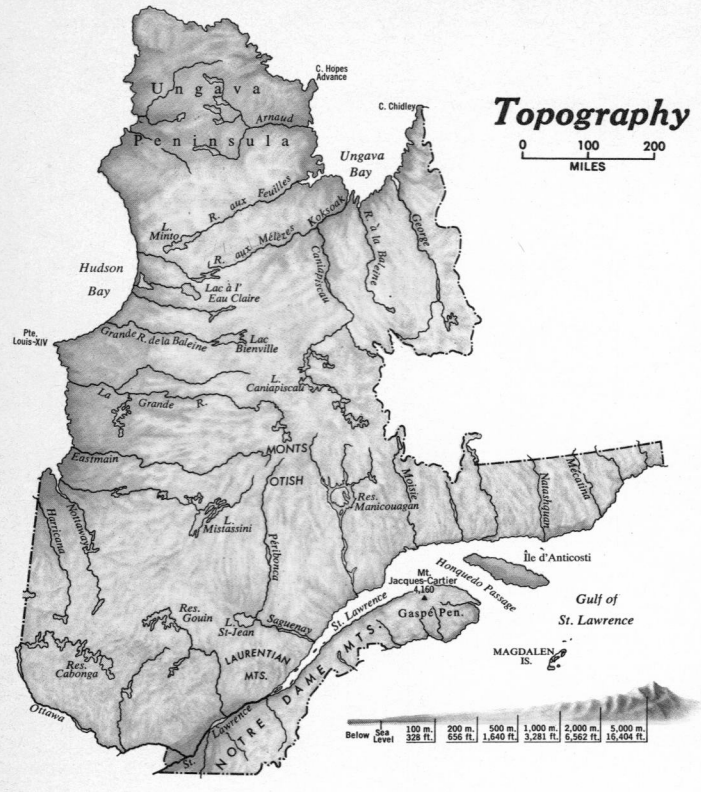

Topography

0   100   200
MILES

Below | 100 m. | 200 m. | 500 m. | 1,000 m. | 2,000 m. | 5,000 m.
Sea Level | 328 ft. | 656 ft. | 1,640 ft. | 3,281 ft. | 6,562 ft. | 16,404 ft.

QUÉBEC
COUNTIES

Argenteuil, 31,319..........C 4
Arthabaska, 51,524.........E 4
Bagot, 23,591...............E 4
Beauce, 63,960.............G 3
Beauharnois, 52,137........C 4
Bellechasse, 23,517........G 3
Berthier, 27,288............D 3
Bonaventure, 41,701........C 2
Brome, 15,311..............E 4
Chambly, 231,590...........J 4
Champlain, 113,150.........E 2
Charlevoix-Est, 16,780......G 2
Charlevoix-Ouest, 13,650....G 2
Châteauguay, 53,737........D 4
Chicoutimi, 163,348.........G 1
Compton, 21,367............F 4
Deux-Montagnes, 52,369.....C 4
Dorchester, 32,473..........G 3

Drummond, 64,144..........E 4
Frontenac, 27,293..........G 4
Gaspé-Est, 41,727..........D 1
Gaspé-Ouest, 18,754........C 1
Gatineau, 55,729...........B 3
Hull, 109,946..............B 4
Huntingdon, 15,358.........C 4
Iberville, 20,400...........C 4
Île-de-Montréal, 1,959,143...H 4
Île-Jésus, 228,010..........H 4
Joliette, 52,088............C 3
Kamouraska, 26,264.........H 2
Labelle, 30,582............B 3
Lac-Saint-Jean-Est,
  45,220.................F 1
Lac-Saint-Jean-Ouest,
  57,074.................E 1
Laprairie, 61,691...........H 4
L'Assomption, 62,198.......D 4
Lévis, 62,776..............F 3
L'Islet, 23,187............G 2
Lotbinière, 27,373.........F 3

Maskinongé, 21,257.........D 3
Matane, 30,261.............B 1
Matapédia, 26,856..........B 2
Mégantic, 58,020...........F 3
Missisquoi, 33,953.........D 4
Montcalm, 21,546...........C 3
Montmagny, 26,307.........G 3
Montmorency No. 1,
  20,401.................F 2
Montmorency No. 2, 5,435...G 3
Napierville, 12,067.........D 4
Nicolet, 30,004.............E 3
Papineau, 31,793...........B 4
Pontiac, 19,570............A 3
Portneuf, 51,540...........E 3
Québec, 423,162...........F 3
Richelieu, 47,093..........D 4
Richmond, 41,044..........E 4
Rimouski, 64,263...........C 1
Rivière-du-Loup, 39,488.....H 2
Rouville, 31,759...........D 4
Saguenay, 111,272..........H 1

CITIES and TOWNS

Saint-Hyacinthe, 50,494.....D 4
Saint-Jean, 45,892.........D 4
Saint-Maurice, 108,366.....D 3
Shefford, 62,361...........E 4
Sherbrooke, 101,470........E 4
Soulanges, 11,449..........C 4
Stanstead, 36,266..........F 4
Témiscouata, 23,189........J 2
Terrebonne, 139,945........H 4
Vaudreuil, 36,593..........C 4
Verchères, 35,273..........J 4
Wolfe, 16,197.............F 4
Yamaska, 15,206...........E 3

Acton Vale, 4,564..........E 4
Albanel, 788...............E 1
Alma◉, 22,622.............F 1
Amqui◉, 3,797............B 2
Ancienne-Lorette, 8,304.....H 3
Angers, 881...............B 4
Anjou, 33,886.............H 4
Armagh, 987...............G 3
Arthabaska◉, 4,479........F 3
Arvida, 18,448.............F 1
Asbestos, 9,749...........F 4
Ayer's Cliff◉, 873.........E 4
Aylmer, 7,198.............B 4
Bagotville, 6,041..........G 1
Baie-Comeau, 12,109.......A 1
Baie-de-Shawinigan, 847....E 3
Baie-des-Sables, 638.......A 1
Baie-d'Urfé, 3,881.........H 4
Baie-Saint-Paul◉, 4,163....G 2
Baie-Trinité, 734..........B 1
Beaconsfield, 19,389.......H 4
Beauceville, 2,098.........G 3
Beauceville-Est◉, 2,192....G 3
Beauharnois◉, 8,121.......D 4
Beaulieu, 659.............E 4
Beaumont, 630............F 3
Beauport, 14,681..........G 3
Beaupré, 2,862............G 2
Bécancour◉, 8,182.........E 3
Bedford◉, 2,786..........E 4
Beebe Plain, 1,236........E 4
Bélair, 4,505.............H 3
Beloeil, 12,274...........D 4
Bernierville, 2,415........F 3
Berthierville◉, 4,080.......D 3
Bic, 1,157................J 1
Black Lake, 4,123.........F 3
Blainville, 9,630..........H 4
Bois-des-Filion, 4,061......H 4
Bolduc, 1,496............G 4
Bonaventure, 1,179........C 2
Boucherville, 19,997.......J 4
Breakeyville, 800.........J 3
Bromont, 1,089...........F 4
Bromptonville, 2,771.......F 4
Brossard, 23,452..........H 4
Brownsburg, 3,481.........C 4
Buckingham, 7,304........B 4
Cabano, 3,063............J 2
Calumet, 764.............C 4
Candiac, 5,185............J 4
Cap-à-l'Aigle, 679.........G 2
Cap-Chat, 3,868..........B 1
Cap-de-la-Madeleine,
  31,463.................E 3
Caplan, 693..............C 2
Cap-Rouge, 1,750.........H 3
Cap-Saint-Ignace, 1,338....G 2
Cap-Santé◉, 610.........F 3

Carignan, 3,340...........J 4
Carleton, 899.............C 2
Caughnawaga, 3,982......H 4
Causapscal, 2,965........B 2
Chambly, 11,469..........J 4
Chambord, 1,106.........E 1
Champlain, 632...........E 3
Chandler, 3,843..........D 2
Charlemagne, 4,111.......H 4
Charlesbourg, 33,443.....H 3
Charny, 5,175............J 3
Châteauguay, 15,797......H 4
Châteauguay-Centre,
  17,942.................H 4
Château-Richer◉, 3,111...F 3
Chénéville, 718...........B 4
Chicoutimi◉, 33,893......G 1
Chicoutimi-Jonquière,
  ‡133,703...............G 1
Chicoutimi-Nord, 14,086...G 1
Chute-aux-Outardes,
  1,930..................A 1
Clermont, 3,386..........G 2
Coaticook, 6,569.........F 4
Coleraine, 1,474..........F 3
Contrecoeur, 2,694.......D 4
Cookshire◉, 1,484........F 4
Coteau-du-Lac, 838.......C 4
Coteau-Landing, 846......C 4
Côte-Saint-Luc, 24,375....H 4
Courcelles, 679...........G 4
Courville, 6,222..........J 3
Cowansville, 11,920.......E 4
Crabtree, 1,706..........D 4
Danville, 2,566...........E 4
Daveluyville, 998.........E 3
Deauville, 761............E 4
Dégelis, 3,046...........J 2
Delson, 2,941...........H 4
Desbiens, 1,813..........E 1
Deschaillons-sur-Saint-
  Laurent, 1,176..........E 3
Deschambault, 995........E 3
Deschênes, 1,806.........B 4
Deux-Montagnes, 8,631....H 4
Didyme, 720.............E 1
Disraëli, 3,384...........F 4
Dolbeau, 7,633...........E 1
Dollard-des-Ormeaux,
  25,217.................H 4
Donnacona, 5,940........F 3
Dorion, 6,209............C 4
Dorval, 20,469...........H 4
Douville, 3,267...........D 4
Drummondville◉, 31,813...E 4
Drummondville-Sud,
  8,989..................E 4
East Angus, 4,715........F 4
East Broughton, 1,380.....F 3
East Broughton Station,
  1,127..................F 3
Escoumins, 1,968.........H 1
Farnham, 6,496..........E 4
Ferme-Neuve, 1,990......B 3
Forestville, 1,606.........H 1
Frampton, 711...........G 3
Francoeur, 1,186.........F 3
Gaspé, 17,211...........D 1
Gatineau, 22,321.........B 4
Giffard, 13,135..........J 3
Girardville, 933...........E 1
Glenwood Domaine, 3,997..B 1
Godbout, 653............A 1
Gracefield, 1,049.........A 3
Granby, 34,385...........E 4
Grande-Rivière, 1,330.....D 2
Grandes-Bergeronnes,
  802...................H 1
Grande-Vallée, 779.......D 1
Grand'Mère, 17,137......E 3
Greenfield Park, 15,348....J 4
Grenville, 1,495..........C 4
Hampstead, 7,033........H 4
Ham-Sud◉, 64...........F 4
Hauterive, 13,181........A 1
Hébertville-Station, 1,163..F 1
Hemmingford, 810........D 4
Henryville, 666...........D 4
Hudson, 4,345...........C 4
Hull◉, 63,580...........B 4
Huntingdon, 3,087.......C 4
Iberville, 9,331..........D 4
Île-Bizard, 2,950.........H 4
Île-Perrot, 4,021.........G 4
Inverness◉, 362.........F 3
Joliette◉, 20,127........D 3
Jonquière, 28,430........F 1
Kénogami, 10,970........F 1
Kirkland, 2,917..........H 4
Labelle, 1,492...........C 3
Lac-au-Saumon, 1,314.....B 2
Lac-aux-Sables, 844.......E 3
Lac-Beauport, 42.........F 3
Lac-Bouchette, 954.......E 1
Lac-Brome◉, 4,063.......E 4
Lac-Carré, 660...........C 3
Lac-Etchemin, 2,789......G 3
Lachine, 44,423..........H 4
Lachute◉, 11,813........C 4
Lac-Mégantic◉, 6,770....G 4
Lacolle, 1,254...........D 4
Lac-Saint-Charles, 1,693...H 3
Lafontaine, 2,980........C 4
La Guadeloupe, 1,934....F 4
La Malbaie◉, 4,036......G 2
Lambton, 747............F 4
L'Ange-Gardien, 1,605....F 3
L'Annonciation, 2,162.....C 3
Lanoraie, 1,151..........D 4
La Pérade, 1,123.........E 3
La Pocatière, 4,256.......H 2
La Prairie◉, 8,309........J 4
La Providence, 4,709......J 4
La Salle, 72,912.........H 4
L'Ascension, 1,034.......F 1
L'Assomption◉, 4,915....D 4
La Station-du-Coteau, 885..C 4

La Tuque, 13,099.........E 2
Laurentides, 1,746........D 4
Laurier-Station, 946.......F 3
Laurierville, 922..........F 3
Lauzon, 12,809..........J 3
Laval, 228,010...........H 4
Lavaltrie, 1,261..........D 4
Le Moyne, 8,194.........J 4
Lennoxville, 3,859........F 4
L'Épiphanie, 2,752........D 4
Léry, 2,247..............J 4
Les Méchins, 792.........B 1
Lévis, 16,597............J 3
Linière, 1,220............G 3
L'Islet, 1,195............G 2
L'Islet-sur-Mer, 772.......G 2
L'Isle-Verte, 1,360........G 1
Longueuil◉, 97,590......J 4
Loretteville◉,
  11,644.................H 3
Lorraine, 3,145..........H 4
Louiseville◉, 4,042.......E 3
Luceville, 1,411..........J 1
Lyster, 879.............F 3
Magog, 13,281...........E 4
Maniwaki◉, 6,689........B 3
Manouane, 751..........C 2
Manseau, 756...........E 3
Maple Grove, 1,708.......H 4
Maria, 1,157............C 2
Marieville◉, 4,563.......D 4
Mascouche, 8,812........H 4
Maskinongé, 996........E 3
Masson, 2,336...........B 4

Massueville, 632.........E 4
Matane◉, 11,841........B 1
Melocheville, 1,601.......H 4
Mercier, 4,011..........H 4
Mistassini, 3,601.........E 1
Mont-Carmel, 800........H 2
Montebello, 1,285........B 4
Mont-Joli, 6,698.........J 1
Montmagny◉, 12,432.....G 3
Montmorency, 4,949......J 3
Montréal◉, 1,214,352....H 4
Montréal-Est, 5,076......H 4
Montréal-Nord, 89,139....H 4
Mont-Rolland, 1,503......C 4
Mont-Royal, 21,561......H 4
Mont-Saint-Hilaire, 5,758..D 4
Morin Heights, 710.......C 4
Murdochville, 2,891......C 1
Napierville, 1,987........D 4
Neuville, 798............F 3
New Carlisle, 1,384......D 2
New Richmond, 3,957.....C 2
Nicolet, 4,714...........E 3
Nitro, 1,827.............D 4
Nominingue, 699.........B 3
Normandin, 1,823........E 1
North Hatley, 728........F 4
Notre-Dame-de-la-Doré,
  1,127..................E 1
Notre-Dame-des-Anges,
  790...................E 3

Agriculture, Industry and Resources

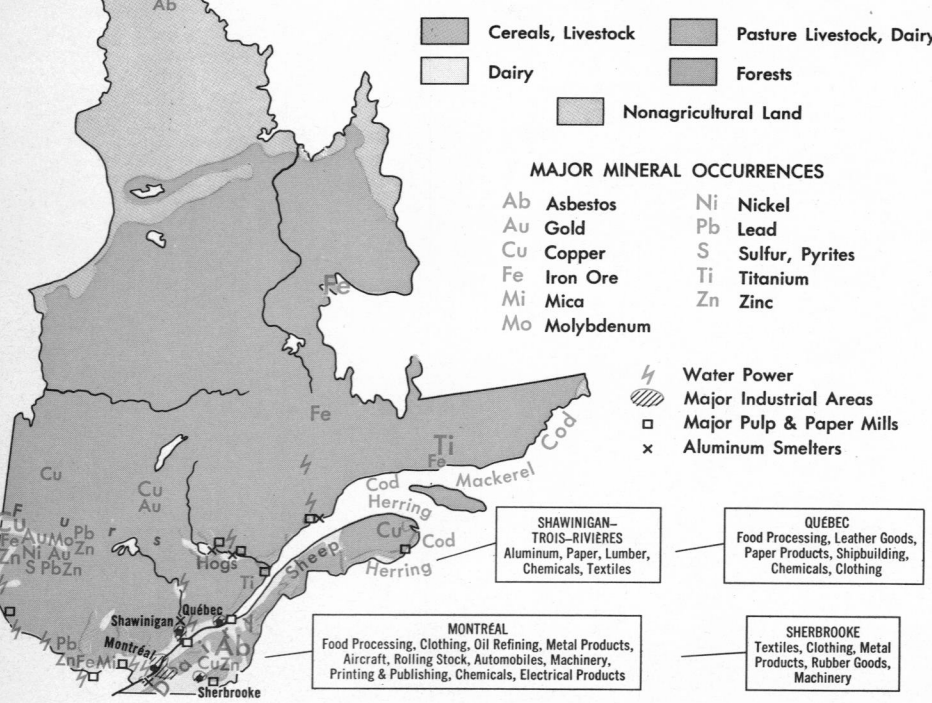

DOMINANT LAND USE

Cereals, Livestock

Pasture Livestock, Dairy

Dairy

Forests

Nonagricultural Land

MAJOR MINERAL OCCURRENCES

Ab Asbestos
Au Gold
Cu Copper
Fe Iron Ore
Mi Mica
Mo Molybdenum

Ni Nickel
Pb Lead
S   Sulfur, Pyrites
Ti Titanium
Zn Zinc

⚡ Water Power
▨ Major Industrial Areas
□ Major Pulp & Paper Mills
× Aluminum Smelters

SHAWINIGAN–TROIS-RIVIÈRES
Aluminum, Paper, Lumber, Chemicals, Textiles

QUÉBEC
Food Processing, Leather Goods, Paper Products, Shipbuilding, Chemicals, Clothing

MONTRÉAL
Food Processing, Clothing, Oil Refining, Metal Products, Aircraft, Rolling Stock, Automobiles, Machinery, Printing & Publishing, Chemicals, Electrical Products

SHERBROOKE
Textiles, Clothing, Metal Products, Rubber Goods, Machinery

QUÉBEC
SOUTHERN PART

SCALE
0 5 10   20   30   40 MI.
0 5 10   20   30   40 KM.

National Capital — ⊛   Provincial & State
Provincial Capital — ⊛   Boundaries ____
County Seats — ◉   County Boundaries ----
International Boundaries

Notre-Dame-des-
 Laurentides, 5,080......H 3
Notre-Dame-des-Prairies,
 3,541..........................D 3
Notre-Dame-
 d'Hébertville, 1,506....F 1
Notre-Dame-du-Bon-
 Conseil, 1,048............E 4
Notre-Dame-du-Lac◉,
 2,107..........................J 2
Nouvelle, 722................C 2
Omerville, 1,102............E 4
Ormstown, 1,517............D 4
Orsainville, 12,520.........H 3
Otterburn Park, 3,512.....J 4
Ouiatchouan, 1,217.........E 1
Outremont, 28,552.........H 4
Pabos-Mills, 668.............D 2
Papineauville◉, 1,384.....C 4
Paspébiac, 1,317............D 2
Percé◉, 5,617.................D 2
Petite-Matane, 668..........B 1
Petit-Saguenay (Saint-
 François-d'Assise),
 691..............................G 1
Pierrefonds, 33,010.........H 4
Pierreville, 1,455............E 3
Pincourt, 5,899..............H 4
Pintendre, 796................J 3
Plaisance, 651................F 4
Plessisville, 7,204...........E 3
Pointe-à-la-Croix, 753.....C 2
Pointe-au-Pic, 1,231........F 2
Pointe-aux-Outardes, 836..A 1

Pointe-aux-Trembles,
 35,567........................J 4
Pointe-Calumet, 2,214.....G 4
Pointe-Claire, 27,303......H 4
Pointe-au-Lac, 1,314.......E 3
Pointe-Gatineau, 15,640..B 4
Pointe-Lebel, 756...........A 1
Pont-Rouge, 3,272..........G 1
Port-Alfred, 9,228..........G 1
Portneuf, 1,347..............F 1
Price, 2,740...................A 1
Princeville, 3,829...........E 3
Québec (cap.), 186,088...H 3
Québec, ‡480,502..........H 3
Quyon, 879....................A 4
Rawdon, 2,740...............D 4
Repentigny, 19,520.........J 4
Restigouche, 1,155.........C 2
Richelieu, 1,777..............D 4
Richmond, 4,317............E 3
Rigaud, 2,138................C 4
Rimouski◉, 26,887..........J 1
Rimouski-Est, 2,069.......J 1
Rivière-à-Pierre, 691.......F 1
Rivière-du-Loup◉, 12,760..H 2
Rivière-du-Moulin, 4,393..G 1
Rivière-Portneuf, 987.......H 1
Robertsonville, 1,294.......F 3
Roberval◉, 8,330............E 1
Rock Forest, 793.............F 4
Rock Island, 1,341..........F 4
Rosemère, 6,710.............H 4
Rougemont, 853.............D 4
Roxboro, 7,633..............H 4

Roxton Falls, 1,139.........E 4
Sacré-Coeur-de-Jésus,
 1,252..........................H 1
Saint-Adelphe, 708.........E 3
Saint-Agapitville, 1,493...F 3
Saint-Alban, 770.............E 3
Saint-Alexandre-de-
 Kamouraska, 927.........H 2
Saint-Alexis-des-Monts,
 1,905..........................D 3
Saint-Amable, 1,051.......J 4
Saint-Ambroise, 1,629....F 1
Saint-Anaclet, 955..........J 1
Saint-André-Avellin, 1,088..B 4
Saint-André-Est, 1,201....C 4
Saint-Anselme, 1,400.......J 3
Saint-Antoine, 5,831.......H 4
Saint-Antonin, 748..........H 2
Saint-Aubert, 952...........G 2
Saint-Augustin-de-
 Québec, 688...............H 3
Saint-Basile-le-Grand,
 4,402..........................J 4
Saint-Basile-Sud, 1,731...F 3
Saint-Bernard-sur-Mer,
 667..............................G 2
Saint-Boniface-de-
 Shawinigan, 2,581........D 3
Saint-Bruno, 1,276..........F 1
Saint-Bruno-de-
 Montarville, 15,780......J 4
Saint-Camille-de-
 Bellechasse, 774..........G 3
Saint-Casimir, 1,239.......E 3

Saint-Césaire, 2,279........D 4
Saint-Charles, 969..........G 3
Saint-Charles-de-
 Drummond, 2,266.........E 4
Saint-Charles-de-
 Mandeville, 900...........D 3
Saint-Chrysostome, 1,077..D 4
Saint-Coeur-de-Marie,
 1,218..........................F 1
Saint-Côme, 914.............D 3
Saint-Constant, 4,139......H 4
Saint-Cyprien
 743..............................J 2
Saint-Cyrille, 1,125.........E 4
Saint-Damien-de-
 Buckland, 1,799...........G 3
Saint-David-de-
 Falardeau, 770.............F 1
Saint-Denis, 899.............D 4
Saint-Domaine, 1,722......E 4
Saint-Donat-de-
 Montcalm, 1,536..........C 3
Sainte-Adelaide-de-
 Pabos, 853...................D 2
Sainte-Adèle, 2,581........C 4
Sainte-Agathe, 646.........F 3
Sainte-Agathe-des-
 Monts, 5,532................C 3
Sainte-Angèle-de-Mérici,
 688..............................J 1
Sainte-Anne-de-Beaupré,
 1,797..........................F 2

Sainte-Anne-de-Bellevue,
 4,976..........................H 4
Sainte-Anne-des-Monts◉,
 5,546..........................C 1
Sainte-Anne-des-Plaines,
 2,093..........................H 4
Sainte-Blandine, 941.......J 1
Sainte-Catherine, 913.....F 3
Sainte-Claire-de-Joliette,
 1,490..........................G 3
Sainte-Croix◉, 1,545......F 3
Sainte-Famille-
 d'Orléans◉, 295...........G 3
Sainte-Félicité, 816.........B 1
Sainte-Foy, 68,385.........H 3
Sainte-Geneviève, 2,847..H 4
Sainte-Geneviève-de-
 Batiscan◉, 556.............E 3

Sainte-Hedwidge-de-
 Roberval, 641..............E 1
Sainte-Hélène-de-
 Kamouraska, 656..........H 2
Sainte-Hénédine, 533......F 3
Sainte-Jeanne-d'Arc, 936..E 1
Sainte-Julie-de-
 Verchères, 1,214...........J 4
Sainte-Julienne◉, 839.....D 4
Saint-Justine, 980...........G 3
Saint-Éleuthère, 1,083.....H 2
Sainte-Marie,
 4,307..........................G 3
Sainte-Martine◉, 1,931...D 4
Saint-Émile, 2,645..........H 3
Sainte-Monique, 697.......F 1
Sainte-Perpétue-de-
 L'Islet, 1,048................H 2

Saint-Éphrem-de-Tring, 954..G 3
Sainte-Pudentienne, 799..E 4
Sainte-Scholastique◉,
 14,787........................C 4
Saint-Esprit, 937............D 4
Sainte-Thècle, 1,725.......E 3
Sainte-Thérèse, 17,175...H 4
Sainte-Thérèse-Ouest,
 7,278..........................H 4
Saint-Étienne-des-Grès,
 870..............................E 3
Saint-Eugène, 656..........G 2
Saint-Eustache, 9,479.....H 4
Saint-Eustache-Est, 4,993..H 4
Saint-Fabien, 1,537.........J 1
Saint-Félicien, 4,952.......E 1
Saint-Félix-de-Valois,
 1,455..........................D 3

AREA 594,860 sq. mi.
POPULATION 6,023,000
CAPITAL Québec
LARGEST CITY Montréal
HIGHEST POINT Mt. Jacques Cartier 4,160 ft.
SETTLED IN 1608
ADMITTED TO CONFEDERATION 1867
PROVINCIAL FLOWER White Garden Lily

COUNTIES
indicated by numbers:
1 Iberville.............D4
2 Napierville.........D4
3 Rouville.............E4
4 St-Hyacinthe......D4
5 Île-de-Montréal...C4
6 Deux-Montagnes...C4
7 Hull...................B4
8 Beauharnois........D4
9 Laprairie.............D4
10 Île-Jésus...........H4
11 Richelieu...........D4
12 Vaudreuil..........C4

Internal divisions represent Municipal Counties

Saint-Féréol-les-Neiges, 692	G 2	Saint-Joseph, 4,945	E 4
Saint-Flavien, 645	F 3	Saint-Joseph-de-Beauce, 2,893	G 3
Saint-François-d'Assise, 691	G 1	Saint-Joseph-de-la-Rivière-Bleue, 1,429	J 2
Saint-François-du-Lac⊙, 1,001	E 3	Saint-Joseph-de-Sorel, 3,290	D 4
Saint-Fulgence, 999	G 1	Saint-Jovite, 3,132	C 3
Saint-Gabriel, 3,383	D 3	Saint-Lambert, 18,616	J 4
Saint-Gédéon, Frontenac, 1,174	G 4	Saint-Laurent, 62,955	H 4
Saint-Gédéon, Lac-St-Jean-E., 885	F 1	Saint-Léonard, 52,040	H 4
Saint-Georges, Beauce, 7,554	G 3	Saint-Léonard-d'Aston, 995	E 3
Saint-Georges, Champlain, 2,061	E 3	Saint-Léon-de-Standon, 830	G 3
Saint-Georges-de-Cacouna, 1,001	H 2	Saint-Léon-le-Grand, 695	B 2
Saint-Georges-Ouest, 6,000	G 3	Saint-Liboire⊙, 667	E 4
Saint-Germain-de-Grantham, 1,104	E 3	Saint-Louis-de-Terrebonne, 1,113	H 1
Saint-Gilles, 694	F 3	Saint-Louis-du-Ha! Ha!,733	H 2
Saint-Grégoire, 655	D 4	Saint-Luc, 4,850	D 4
Saint-Grégoire-de-Greenlay, 694	E 4	Saint-Marc-des-Carrières, 2,650	E 3
Saint-Henri, 1,160	J 3	Saint-Méthode-de-Frontenac, 793	F 3
Saint-Honoré, Beauce, 1,045	G 4	Saint-Michel-de-Bellechasse, 967	G 3
Saint-Honoré, Chicoutimi, 1,055	F 1	Saint-Michel-des-Saints, 1,647	D 3
Saint-Hubert, 36,854	J 4	Saint-Nazaire-de-Chicoutimi, 884	F 1
Saint-Hubert-de-Témiscouata, 832	J 2	Saint-Nicolas, 1,975	J 3
Saint-Hyacinthe‡, 24,562	D 4	Saint-Noël, 910	B 1
Saint-Isidore, 736	J 4	Saint-Odilon, 704	G 3
Saint-Isidore-de-Laprairie, 749	D 4	Saint-Ours, 838	D 4
Saint-Jacques, 1,975	D 4	Saint-Pacôme, 1,809	H 2
Saint-Jean⊙, 32,863	D 4	Saint-Pamphile, 3,542	H 3
Saint-Jean-Chrysostome, 1,905	J 3	Saint-Pascal, 2,513	H 2
Saint-Jean-de-Boischatel, 1,685	J 3	Saint-Paul-de-Montminy, 746	H 3
Saint-Jean-de-Dieu, 1,148	J 1	Saint-Paulin, 809	D 3
Saint-Jean-de-Matha, 943	D 3	Saint-Paul-l'Ermite, 3,165	J 4
Saint-Jean-Port-Joli⊙, 1,795	G 2	Saint-Philippe-de-Néri, 701	H 2
Saint-Jérôme, Lac-St-Jean-E., 1,910	F 1	Saint-Pie, 1,709	E 4
Saint-Jérôme, Terrebonne⊙, 26,524	H 4	Saint-Pierre, 6,801	H 4
Saint-Joachim, 920	G 2	Saint-Prime, 2,350	E 1
Saint-Joachim-de-Tourelle, 1,021	C 1	Saint-Prosper-de-Dorchester, 1,696	G 3
		Saint-Raphaël, 1,216	G 3
		Saint-Raymond, 4,036	F 3
		Saint-Rédempteur, 1,652	J 3
		Saint-Régis, 727	J 4
		Saint-Rémi, 2,282	D 4
		Saint-Roch-de-l'Achigan, 962	D 4

Saint-Roch-de-Richelieu, 721	D 4	Verchères⊙, 1,840	J 4
Saint-Romuald-d'Etchemin⊙, 8,394	J 3	Verdun, 74,718	H 4
Saint-Sauveur-des-Monts, 1,846	C 4	Victoriaville, 22,047	F 3
Saint-Siméon, 1,186	G 2	Villeneuve, 4,062	J 3
Saint-Thomas-de-Joliette, 728	D 4	Warwick, 2,847	F 4
Saint-Timothée, 1,613	D 4	Waterloo⊙, 4,936	E 4
Saint-Tite, 3,130	E 3	Waterville, 1,476	F 4
Saint-Ubald, 809	E 3	Weedon-Centre, 1,429	F 4
Saint-Ulric, 936	B 1	Westmount, 23,606	H 4
Saint-Urbain-de-Charlevoix, 1,172	G 2	Windsor, 6,023	F 4
Saint-Victor, 1,017	G 3	Wottonville, 683	F 4
Saint-Zacharie, 1,390	G 3	Yamachiche⊙, 1,147	E 3
Saint-Zotique, 1,243	C 4		
Sault-au-Mouton, 951	H 1	**OTHER FEATURES**	
Sawyerville, 864	F 4		
Sayabec, 1,789	B 1	Alma (isl.)	F 1
Scotstown, 917	F 4	Aylmer (lake)	F 4
Senneville, 1,412	G 4	Baskatong (res.)	B 3
Shawbridge, 969	C 4	Batiscan (riv.)	E 2
Shawinigan, 27,792	E 3	Bécancour (riv.)	F 3
Shawinigan-Sud, 11,470	E 3	Bonaventure (isl.)	D 1
Sherbrooke⊙, 80,711	F 4	Bonaventure (riv.)	C 1
Sillery, 13,932	J 3	Brome (lake)	E 4
Sorel⊙, 19,347	D 4	Brompton (lake)	F 4
Squatec, 950	J 2	Cascapédia (riv.)	C 1
Stanstead Plain, 1,192	F 4	Chaleur (bay)	C 1
Sully, 776	H 2	Champlain (lake)	D 4
Sutton, 1,684	E 4	Chaudière (riv.)	G 3
Tadoussac⊙, 1,010	H 1	Chic-Chocs (mts.)	C 1
Templeton, 3,684	B 4	Chicoutimi (riv.)	F 1
Terrebonne, 9,212	H 4	Coudres (isl.), 1,522	G 2
Thetford Mines, 22,003	F 3	Deschênes (lake)	A 4
Thurso, 3,219	B 4	Deux Montagnes (lake)	H 4
Touraine, 6,978	B 4	Ditton (riv.)	F 4
Tourville, 818	H 3	Forillon Nat'l Park	J 4
Tracy, 11,842	D 4	Fort Chambly Nat'l Hist. Park	J 4
Tring-Jonction, 1,283	F 3	Gaspé (bay)	D 1
Trois-Pistoles, 4,678	H 1	Gaspé (cape)	D 1
Trois-Rivières, 55,869	E 3	Gaspé (pen.)	C 1
Trois-Rivières-Ouest, 8,057	E 3	Gaspésie Prov. Park	B 1
Upton, 818	E 4	Gatineau (riv.)	B 3
Val-Brillant, 690	B 1	Îles (pass.)	E 2
Valcourt, 2,411	E 4	Jacques-Cartier (mt.)	C 1
Val-David, 1,627	C 3	Jacques-Cartier (riv.)	F 2
Vallée-Jonction, 1,295	G 3	Kénogami (lake)	F 1
Valleyfield, 30,173	D 4	Kiamika (res.)	B 3
Val-Saint-Michel, 2,050	H 3	La Maurice Nat'l Park	E 3
Vanier, 9,717	J 3	Laurentides Prov. Park	F 2
Varennes, 2,382	J 4	La Vérendrye Prov. Park	A 2
Vaudreuil, 3.843	G 4	Lièvre (riv.)	B 3
		Lièvres (isl.)	H 2
		Maskinongé (riv.)	D 3
		Matane (riv.)	B 1
		Matane Prov. Park	B 1
		Matapédia (riv.)	C 1
		Matawin (riv.)	D 3

Mégantic (lake)	G 4	Pontiac (co.), 19,570	B 3
Memphremagog (lake)	E 4	Saguenay (co.), 111,272	D 2
Mercier (dam)	A 3	Témiscamingue (county), 54,656	B 3
Métabetchouane (riv.)	F 1		
Mille Îles (riv.)	H 4	**CITIES and TOWNS**	
Montmorency (riv.)	F 2		
Mont-Tremblant Prov. Park	C 3	Aguanish, 442	E 2
Nicolet (riv.)	E 3	Amos⊙, 6,984	B 3
Nominingue (lake)	B 3	Angliers, 404	B 3
Nord (riv.)	C 4	Baie-du-Poste, 1,598	C 2
Orléans (isl.), 5,435	F 3	Barraute, 1,288	B 3
Ottawa (riv.)	B 4	Belleterre, 614	B 3
Ouareau (riv.)	D 4	Betsiamites, 1,574	D 3
Patapédia (riv.)	B 2	Cadillac, 1,102	B 3
Péribonca (riv.)	F 1	Chapais, 2,914	B 3
Petite Nation (riv.)	B 4	Chibougamau, 9,701	C 3
Prairies (riv.)	H 4	Clarke City, 750	D 2
Rimouski (riv.)	J 1	Dolbeau, 7,633	C 2
Ristigouche (riv.)	B 2	Duparquet, 786	B 3
Saguenay (riv.)	G 1	Dupuy, 439	B 3
Sainte-Anne (riv.)	B 1	Évain, 605	B 3
Sainte-Anne (riv.)	G 2	Forestville, 1,606	D 3
Saint-François (lake)	F 4	Fort-Chimo, 693	F 2
Saint-François (riv.)	E 4	Fort-George, 1,280	B 3
Saint-Jean (lake)	E 1	Gagnon, 3,787	D 2
Saint Lawrence (gulf)	D 2	Godbout, 653	D 2
Saint Lawrence (riv.)	H 1	Hauterive, 13,181	D 3
Saint-Louis (lake)	H 4	Havre-St-Pierre, 2,999	E 2
Saint-Maurice (riv.)	E 3	Inoucdjouac, 525	E 1
Saint-Pierre (lake)	E 3	La Reine, 450	B 3
Shawinigan (riv.)	E 3	La Sarre, 5,185	B 3
Shipshaw (riv.)	F 1	La Tabatière, 475	F 2
Soeurs (isl.)	H 4	Lebel-sur-Quevillon, 2,936	B 3
Témiscouata (lake)	H 2	Lorrainville, 906	B 3
Tremblant (lake)	C 3	Macamic, 1,705	B 3
Trente et un Milles (lake)	B 3	Malartic, 5,347	B 3
Verte (isl.), 175	H 1	Manicouagan, 500	D 2
Yamaska (riv.)	D 4	Matagami, 2,411	B 3
York (riv.)	D 1	Micoua, 851	D 3
		Moisie, 570	D 2
⊙ County seat.		Noranda, 10,741	B 3
‡ Population of metropolitan area.		Normétal, 1,851	B 3
		Nouveau-Comptoir, 514	B 2
QUÉBEC, NORTHERN		Obedjiwan, 712	B 3
		Parent, 452	B 3
INTERNAL DIVISIONS		Port-Cartier, 3,730	D 2
		Port-Cartier-Ouest, 500	D 2
Abitibi (co.), 112,244	B 2	Port-Menier, 394	E 3
Abitibi (terr.), 21,308	B 3	Poste-de-la-Baleine, 987	B 1
Chicoutimi (county), 163,348	C 2	Povungnituk, 676	C 1
Lac-Saint-Jean-Ouest (county), 57,074	C 2	Rivière-au-Tonnerre, 520	D 2
Mistassini (terr.), 2,702	B 2	Rouyn, 17,821	B 3
Nouveau-Québec (terr.), 10,002	E 1	Rupert House, C.S.	D 1

Saglouc, 402	E 1		
Saint-Augustin, 916	F 1		
Schefferville, 3,271	D 2		
Senneterre, 4,303	B 3		
Sept-Îles, 24,320	D 2		
Témiscaming, 2,428	B 3		
Val-d'Or, 17,421	B 3		
Ville-Marie, 1,995	B 3		
OTHER FEATURES			
Anticosti (isl.), 419	E 3		
Baleine, Grand Rivière de la (riv.)	B 1		
Betsiamites (riv.)	C 2		
Bienville (lake)	B 3		
Cabonga (res.)	B 3		
Caniapiscau (riv.)	D 1		
Daniel-Johnson (dam)	D 2		
Dozois (res.)	B 3		
Eastmain (riv.)	B 3		
George (riv.)	F 2		
Gouin (res.)	B 3		
Grande Rivière, La (riv.)	B 2		
Guillaume-Delisle (lake)	B 1		
Harricana (riv.)	B 3		
Honguedo (passg.)	D 1		
Hudson (bay)	A 1		
Hudson (str.)	F 1		
Jacques-Cartier (passg.)	E 3		
James (bay)	B 2		
Koksoak (riv.)	D 1		
La Vérendrye Prov. Park	B 3		
Louis-XIV (pt.)	B 2		
Manicouagan (res.)	D 2		
Mistassini (lake)	C 3		
Mistassini (riv.)	C 2		
Moisie (riv.)	D 2		
Natashquan (riv.)	E 2		
Nottaway (riv.)	B 2		
Nouveau-Québec (crater)	F 1		
Otish (mts.)	D 2		
Ottawa (riv.)	B 3		
Reed (mt.)	D 2		
Romaine (riv.)	E 2		
Saguenay (riv.)	C 3		
Saguenay Prov. Park	C 2		
Saint Lawrence (gulf)	E 3		
Saint Lawrence (riv.)	D 3		
Ungava (bay)	E 1		
Ungava (pen.)	E 1		
Wolstenholme (cape)	E 1		
Wright (mt.)	D 2		

NORTHERN QUÉBEC

SCALE

0 50 100 150 200 MI.

0 50 100 150 200 KM.

Provincial Capital	⊛	Provincial Boundaries	
County Seats	⊙	County Boundaries	
International Boundaries		Territorial Boundaries	

© C.S. HAMMOND & Co., N.Y.

ONTARIO, NORTHERN

INTERNAL DIVISIONS

Algoma (terr. dist.), 121,937	D 3
Cochrane (terr. dist.), 95,836	D 2
Kenora (terr. dist.), 53,230	C 2
Manitoulin (terr. dist.), 10,931	D 3
Nipissing (terr. dist.), 78,867	E 3
Parry Sound (terr. dist.), 30,244	E 3
Rainy River (terr. dist.), 25,750	B 3
Renfrew (terr. dist.), 90,875	E 3
Sudbury (terr. dist.), 198,079	D 3
Thunder Bay (terr. dist.), 145,390	C 3
Timiskaming (terr. dist.), 46,485	D 3

CITIES and TOWNS

Atikokan, 6,007	B 3
Blind River, 3,450	D 3
Capreol, 3,470	D 3
Chalk River, 1,094	E 3
Chapleau, 3,365	D 3
Cochrane⊙, 4,965	D 3
Coniston, 2,907	D 3
Copper Cliff, 4,089	D 3
Deep River, 5,671	E 3
Dryden, 6,939	B 3
Elliot Lake, 8,727	D 3
Espanola, 6,045	D 3
Fort Albany	D 2
Fort Frances⊙, 9,947	C 3
Geraldton, 3,178	C 3
Haileybury⊙, 5,280	D 3
Hearst, 3,501	D 3
Huntsville, 9,784	E 3
Iroquois Falls, 7,271	D 3
Kapuskasing, 12,834	D 3
Kenora⊙, 10,952	B 3
Kirkland Lake, 13,599	D 3
Levack, 2,948	D 3
Manitouwadge, 3,258	C 3
Mattawa, 2,881	E 3

Moose Factory, 849	D 2
Moosonee, 1,793	D 2
New Liskeard, 5,488	E 3
North Bay⊙, 49,187	E 3
Parry Sound⊙, 5,842	D 3
Pembroke⊙, 16,544	E 3
Renfrew, 9,173	E 3
Sault Sainte Marie⊙, 80,332	D 3
South Porcupine, 4,843	D 3
Sturgeon Falls, 6,662	E 3
Sudbury, 90,535	D 3
Sudbury, ‡155,424	D 3
Thunder Bay⊙, 108,411	C 3
Thunder Bay, ‡112,093	C 3
Timmins, 28,542	D 3
Wawa, 4,375	C 3

OTHER FEATURES

Abitibi (lake)	E 3
Abitibi (riv.)	D 2
Albany (riv.)	C 2
Attawapiskat (riv.)	C 2
Big Trout (lake)	B 2
Caribou (isl.), 3	C 2
Eabamet (lake)	C 2
Ekwan (riv.)	C 2
English (riv.)	B 2
Groundhog (riv.)	D 3
Hannah (bay)	D 2
Henrietta Maria (cape)	D 1
Hudson (bay)	D 1
James (bay)	D 2
Kapuskasing (riv.)	D 3
Kenogami (riv.)	C 2
Lake of the Woods (lake)	B 3
Lake Superior Prov. Park	D 3
Mattagami (riv.)	D 3
Michipicoten (isl.), 4	C 3
Mille Lacs (lake)	B 3
Missinaibi (riv.)	D 2
Nipigon (lake)	C 3
North Caribou (lake)	B 2
Ogidaki (mt.)	D 3
Ogoki (riv.)	C 2
Ottawa (riv.)	E 3
Pipestone (riv.)	B 2
Polar Bear Prov. Park	D 2
Quetico Prov. Park	B 3
Rainy (riv.)	B 3
Red (lake)	B 2
Sachigo (riv.)	B 2
Saint Joseph (lake)	B 2

Sandy (lake)	B 2
Seine (riv.)	B 3
Seul (lake)	B 2
Severn (riv.)	B 2
Sibley Prov. Park, 2	C 3
Slate (isls.), 4	C 3
Superior (lake)	C 3
Sutton (riv.)	C 2
Thunder (bay)	C 3
Timagami (lake)	E 3
Timiskaming (lake)	E 3
Winisk (riv.)	C 2
Winnipeg (riv.)	A 2
Woods (lake)	B 3

ONTARIO

INTERNAL DIVISIONS

Algoma (terr. dist.), 121,937	J 5
Brant (county), 96,767	D 4
Bruce (county), 47,385	C 3
Cochrane (terr. dist.), 95,836	J 4
Dufferin (county), 21,200	D 3
Dundas (county), 17,457	J 2
Durham (county), 47,494	F 3
Elgin (county), 66,608	C 5
Essex (county), 306,399	B 5
Frontenac (county), 101,692	H 3
Glengarry (county), 18,480	K 2
Grenville (county), 24,316	J 3
Grey (county), 66,403	D 3
Haldimand (county), 32,673	E 5
Haliburton (county), 9,081	F 2
Halton (county), 190,469	E 4
Hastings (county), 99,393	G 3
Huron (county), 52,951	C 4
Kenora (terr. dist.), 53,230	G 5
Kent (county), 101,118	B 5
Lambton (county), 114,314	B 5
Lanark (county), 42,259	H 3
Leeds (county), 50,093	H 3
Lennox and Addington (county), 28,359	G 3
Manitoulin (terr. dist.), 10,931	B 2
Middlesex (county), 282,014	C 4

Muskoka (dist. munic.), 31,938	E 3
Niagara (reg. munic.), 347,328	E 4
Nipissing (terr. dist.), 78,867	F 2
Norfolk (county), 54,099	D 5
Northumberland (county), 48,162	G 3
Ontario (county), 196,257	E 3
Ottawa-Carleton (reg. munic.), 471,931	J 2
Oxford (county), 80,349	D 4
Parry Sound (terr. dist.), 30,244	D 2
Peel (county), 259,402	E 4
Perth (county), 62,973	C 4
Peterborough (county), 87,804	F 3
Prescott (county), 27,832	K 2
Prince Edward (county), 20,640	G 3
Rainy River (terr. dist.), 25,750	H 5
Renfrew (county), 90,875	G 2
Russell (county), 16,287	J 2
Simcoe (county), 171,433	E 3
Stormont (county), 61,302	K 2
Sudbury (terr. dist.), 198,079	J 5
Thunder Bay (terr. dist.), 145,390	H 5
Timiskaming (terr. dist.), 46,485	K 5
Toronto (metro. munic.), 2,086,017	K 4
Victoria (county), 34,242	F 3
Waterloo (county), 254,037	D 4
Wellington (county), 108,581	D 4
Wentworth (county), 401,883	D 4
York (reg. munic.), 166,060	E 4

CITIES and TOWNS

Acton, 5,031	D 4
Ailsa Craig, 608	C 4
Ajax, 12,515	E 4
Alban, 420	D 1
Alcona Beach, 659	E 3
Alexandria, 3,240	K 2

Alfred, 1,230	K 2
Alliston, 3,176	E 3
Almonte, 3,696	H 2
Alton, 506	H 3
Alvinston, 702	B 5
Amherstburg, 5,169	A 5
Amherst View, 3,121	H 3
Angus, 3,174	E 3
Arkona, 469	C 4
Armstrong, 574	H 4
Arnprior, 6,016	H 2
Arthur, 1,414	D 4
Athens, 1,071	J 3
Atherley, 392	E 3
Atikokan, 6,007	G 5
Atwood, 690	D 4
Aurora, 13,614	J 3
Aylmer, 4,755	C 5
Ayr, 1,272	D 4
Ayton, 423	D 3
Baden, 959	D 4
Bala, 462	E 2
Bancroft, 2,394	G 2
Barrie⊙, 27,676	E 3
Barry's Bay, 1,432	G 2
Batawa, 667	G 3
Batchwana Bay, 586	J 5
Bath, 810	H 3
Bayfield, 503	C 4
Bay Ridges, 8,500	K 4
Bayside, 1,732	G 3
Beachburg, 549	H 2
Beachville, 995	D 4
Beardmore, 754	H 5
Beaverton, 1,485	E 3
Beeton, 1,061	E 3
Belle River, 2,877	B 5
Belleville⊙, 35,128	G 3

Belmont, 798	C 5
Bethany, 325	F 3
Bewdley, 446	F 3
Blackburn, 3,841	J 2
Blenheim, 3,490	C 5
Blind River, 3,450	J 5
Bloomfield, 730	G 4
Blyth, 814	C 4
Bobcaygeon, 1,518	F 3
Bolton, 2,984	J 4
Bonfield, 694	E 1
Bothwell, 810	C 5
Bourget, 835	J 2
Bowmanville, 8,947	F 4
Bracebridge⊙, 6,903	E 2
Bradford, 3,401	E 3
Braeside, 522	H 2
Bramalea, 23,083	J 4
Brampton⊙, 41,211	J 4
Brantford⊙, 64,421	D 4
Bridgenorth, 1,380	F 3
Bridgeport, 2,375	D 4
Brigden, 582	B 5
Brighton, 2,956	G 3
Brights Grove, 730	B 4
Britt, 500	D 2
Brockville⊙, 19,765	J 3
Brougham, 367	K 4
Bruce Mines, 505	J 5
Brussels, 908	C 4
Burford, 1,291	D 4
Burgessville, 329	D 4
Burk's Falls, 891	E 2
Burlington, 87,023	E 4
Cache Bay, 727	D 1
Caesarea, 352	F 3
Caledon East, 910	J 4
Caledonia, 3,183	E 4

Callander, 1,190	E 1
Campbellford, 3,522	G 3
Cannington, 1,083	E 3
Cape Croker, 681	D 3
Capreol, 3,470	K 5
Caramat, 520	H 5
Cardiff, 525	F 2
Cardinal, 1,865	J 3
Carleton Place, 5,020	H 2
Carlisle, 488	D 4
Carp, 678	H 2
Cartier, 740	J 5
Casselman, 1,337	J 2
Cayuga⊙, 1,084	E 5
Chalk River, 1,094	G 1
Chapleau, 3,365	J 5
Charing Cross, 436	B 5
Chatham⊙, 35,317	B 5
Chatsworth, 399	D 3
Chelmsford, 7,501	K 5
Chesley, 1,693	C 3
Chesterville, 1,252	J 2
Chute-à-Blondeau, 420	K 2
City View, 4,500	J 2
Claremont, 592	K 3
Clarence Creek, 411	J 2
Clarksburg, 389	D 3
Clifford, 555	D 4
Clinton, 3,154	C 4
Cobalt, 2,197	K 5
Cobden, 926	H 2
Coboconk, 477	F 3
Cobourg⊙, 11,282	F 4
Cochrane⊙, 4,965	K 5
Colborne, 1,588	G 3
Colborne, 759	D 5
Colchester, 752	B 6
Coldwater, 759	E 3
Collingwood, 9,775	D 3
Collins Bay, 2,089	H 3
Comber, 642	B 5
Coniston, 2,907	D 1
Consecon, 332	G 3
Cookstown, 887	E 3
Copper Cliff, 4,089	J 5
Cornwall⊙, 47,116	K 2
Corunna, 3,052	B 5
Cottam, 530	B 5
Courtice, 519	F 4
Courtland, 574	D 5
Courtright, 590	B 5
Coverdale, 670	F 4
Crediton, 409	C 4
Creemore, 978	D 3
Creighton, 1,294	B 5
Crysler, 481	J 2
Cumberland, 581	J 2
Cumberland Beach, 477	E 3
Dashwood, 434	C 4
Deep River, 5,671	G 1
Delaware, 627	C 4
Delhi, 3,894	D 5
Delta, 465	H 3
Deseronto, 1,863	G 3
Dorchester, 1,796	C 4
Drayton, 752	D 4
Dresden, 2,369	B 5
Drumbo, 460	D 4
Dryden, 6,939	G 5
Dubreuilville, 654	J 5
Dundalk, 1,022	D 3
Dundas, 17,208	D 4
Dunnville, 5,576	E 5
Durham, 2,448	D 3
Dutton, 878	C 5
East York, 104,784	J 4
Echo Bay, 493	J 5
Eganville, 1,395	G 2
Egmondville, 492	C 4
Elk Lake, 627	K 5
Elliot Lake, 8,727	B 1
Elmira, 4,730	D 4
Elmvale, 1,103	E 3
Elmwood, 345	C 3
Elora, 1,904	D 4
Embro, 703	D 4
Embrun, 1,452	J 2
Emeryville, 1,719	B 5
Emo, 768	F 5
Englehart, 1,721	K 5
Erieau, 509	C 5
Erin, 1,446	D 4
Espanola, 6,045	B 5
Essex, 4,002	B 5
Etobicoke, 282,686	E 4
Everett, 405	E 3
Exeter, 3,354	C 4
Falconbridge, 1,136	D 1
Fauquier, 643	J 4
Fenelon Falls, 1,616	F 3
Fergus, 5,433	D 4
Field, 655	E 1
Finch, 397	J 2
Flesherton, 524	D 3
Foleyet, 637	J 5
Fordwich, 325	C 4
Forest, 2,355	C 4
Formosa, 370	C 3
Fort Erie, 23,113	E 5

AREA 412,582 sq. mi.
POPULATION 7,707,000
CAPITAL Toronto
LARGEST CITY Toronto
HIGHEST POINT Ogidaki Mtn. 2,183 ft.
SETTLED IN 1749
ADMITTED TO CONFEDERATION 1867
PROVINCIAL FLOWER White Trillium

NORTHERN ONTARIO

SCALE

0 25 50 100 150 200 MI.

0 25 50 100 150 200 KM.

Provincial Capital .... ⊛ Provincial and
County Seats ....⊙ State Boundaries
International Boundaries — — — County Boundaries — — —

© C.S. HAMMOND & Co., N.Y.

(continued on following page)

Fort Frances⊙, 9,947	F 5
Foxboro, 590	G 3
Frankford, 1,862	G 3
Fraserdale, 337	J 5
Galt, 38,897	D 4
Gananoque, 5,212	H 3
Garson, 4,447	D 1
Georgetown, 17,053	E 4
Geraldton, 3,178	H 5
Glencoe, 1,387	C 5
Glen Miller, 736	G 3
Glen Robertson, 345	K 2
Glen Walter, 656	K 2
Glen Williams, *1,127	K 4
Goderich⊙, 6,813	C 4
Gogama, 578	D 4
Goodwood, 356	E 3
Gore Bay⊙, 770	B 2
Gorrie, 380	C 4
Grafton, 395	G 4
Grand Bend, 696	C 4
Grand Valley, 904	D 4
Granton, 350	C 4
Gravenhurst, 7,133	E 3
Green Valley, 363	K 2
Grimsby, 15,770	E 4
Guelph⊙, 60,087	D 4
Hagersville, 2,292	D 5
Haileybury⊙, 5,280	K 5
Haliburton, 899	F 2
Hamilton, 309,173	E 4
Hamilton, ‡498,523	E 4
Hampton, 597	F 4
Hanover, 5,063	C 3
Harriston, 1,785	C 4
Harrow, 1,971	B 5

Harrowsmith, 550	H 3
Hastings, 938	G 3
Havelock, 1,225	G 3
Hawkesbury, 9,276	K 2
Hawk Junction, 396	J 5
Hearst, 3,501	J 5
Hensall, 970	C 4
Hepworth, 372	C 3
Hespeler, 6,343	D 4
Highgate, 424	C 5
Hillsburgh, 674	D 4
Holland Landing, 896	E 3
Hornepayne, 1,826	J 5
Hudson, 543	G 4
Huntsville, 9,784	E 2
Huron Park, 1,217	C 4
Ignace, 334	G 5
Ingersoll, 7,783	C 4
Ingleside, 899	J 2
Inglewood, 367	D 4
Innerkip, 584	D 4
Iron Bridge, 874	A 1
Iroquois, 1,224	J 2
Iroquois Falls, 7,271	J 5
Jarvis, 965	D 5
Johnstown, 414	J 3
Kakabeka Falls, 325	G 5
Kanata, 4,635	J 2
Kapuskasing, 12,834	J 5
Keene, 334	F 3
Keewatin, 2,112	F 5
Kemptville, 2,413	J 2
Kenora⊙, 10,952	F 4
Keswick, 1,031	E 3
Killaloe Station, 810	G 2
Killarney, 475	C 2

Kincardine, 3,239	C 3
King City, 2,091	J 3
Kingston⊙, 59,047	H 3
Kingsville, 4,076	B 6
Kinmount, 371	F 3
Kiosk, 332	F 1
Kirkland Lake, 13,599	K 5
Kitchener⊙, 111,804	D 4
Kitchener, ‡226,846	D 4
Komoka, 698	C 5
Lakefield, 2,245	F 3
Lambeth, 3,023	C 5
Lanark, 861	J 2
Lancaster, 617	K 2
Langton, 478	D 5
Lansdowne, 520	H 3
Latchford, 535	K 5
Leamington, 10,435	B 5
Lefroy, 629	E 3
Levack, 2,948	J 5
Limoges, 355	J 2
Lincoln, 14,247	E 4
Lindsay, 12,746	F 3
Linwood, 482	D 4
Lion's Head, 467	C 2
Listowel, 4,677	C 4
Little Britain, 337	F 3
Little Current, 1,565	B 2
Lively, 3,000	C 1
London⊙, 223,222	C 5
London, ‡286,011	C 5
Longlac, 1,400	H 5
Long Sault, 965	K 2
L'Orignal⊙, 1,405	K 2
Lucan, 1,178	C 4
Lucknow, 1,047	C 4

Lyn, 556	J 3
Lynden, 454	D 4
MacTier, 794	E 2
Madawaska, 371	G 2
Madoc, 1,353	G 3
Maitland, 670	J 3
Mallorytown, 347	J 3
Manitouwadge, 3,258	H 5
Manitowaning, 437	C 2
Manotick, 476	J 2
Maple Grove, 550	F 4
Marathon, 2,409	H 5
Markdale, 1,236	D 3
Markham, 36,684	K 4
Markstay, 491	D 1
Marmora, 1,350	G 3
Martintown, 394	K 2
Massey, 1,278	C 1
Matachewan, 549	J 5
Matheson, 721	K 5
Mattawa, 2,881	F 1
Mattice, 860	J 5
Maxville, 846	K 2
Maynooth, 328	G 2
McGregor, 665	B 5
Meaford, 4,045	D 3
Merlin, 757	B 5
Merrickville, 930	J 2
Metcalfe, 473	J 2
Midhurst, 342	E 3
Midland, 10,992	D 3
Mildmay, 963	C 3
Millbrook, 908	F 3
Milton⊙, 7,018	E 4
Milverton, 1,193	C 4
Minemoya, 458	B 2

Minden⊙, 697	F 3
Mississauga, 156,070	J 4
Mitchell, 2,545	C 4
Monkton, 550	C 4
Moonbeam, 920	J 5
Moose Creek, 391	K 2
Morrisburg, 2,055	J 3
Mount Albert, 705	E 3
Mount Brydges, 1,484	C 5
Mount Forest, 3,037	D 4
Mount Hope, 565	E 4
Mount Pleasant, 574	D 4
Nairn, 461	C 1
Nakina, 673	H 4
Napanee⊙, 4,638	G 3
Naughton, 1,076	C 1
Neustadt, 579	D 3
Newburgh, 820	H 3
Newbury, 338	C 5
Newcastle, 1,942	F 4
New Hamburg, 3,008	D 4
New Liskeard, 5,488	K 5
Newmarket⊙, 18,941	E 3
Niagara Falls, 67,163	E 4
Niagara-on-the-Lake, 12,552	E 4
Nipigon, 2,141	H 5
Nobel, 484	D 2
Nobleton, 1,356	J 3
Noelville, 856	D 1
North Bay⊙, 49,187	F 1
North Gower, 363	J 2
North York, 504,150	J 4
Norton, 332	E 4
Norwich, 1,806	D 5
Norwood, 1,183	F 3

Nottawa, 401	D 3
Oakville, 61,483	E 4
Odessa, 1,020	H 3
Oil Springs, 570	B 5
Omemee, 777	F 3
Onaping, 1,317	J 5
Orangeville⊙, 8,074	D 4
Orillia, 24,040	E 3
Orleans, 2,810	J 2
Orono, 1,276	F 4
Osgoode, 823	J 2
Oshawa, 91,587	F 4
Ottawa (cap.), Canada⊙, 302,341	H 4
Ottawa-Hull, ‡602,510	J 2
Otterville, 754	D 5
Owen Sound, 18,469	D 3
Paincourt, 324	B 5
Painswick, 727	E 3
Paisley, 793	C 3
Pakenham, 371	H 2
Palmerston, 1,855	D 4
Paris, 6,483	D 4
Parkhill, 1,167	C 4
Parry Sound⊙, 5,842	E 2
Pefferlaw, 432	E 3
Pelham, 9,997	E 4
Pembroke⊙, 16,544	J 2
Penetanguishene, 5,497	D 3
Perkinsfield, 368	E 3
Perth⊙, 5,537	H 3
Petawawa, 5,784	G 2
Peterborough⊙, 58,111	F 3
Petrolia, 4,044	B 5
Pickering, 2,537	K 4
Pickering Beach, 621	G 4

Picton⊙, 4,875	G 3
Plantagenet, 909	K 2
Plattsville, 526	D 4
Point Anne, 373	G 3
Point Edward, 2,773	B 4
Porcupine, 1,303	J 5
Port Burwell, 700	D 5
Port Carling, 617	E 2
Port Colborne, 21,420	E 5
Port Credit, 9,442	J 4
Port Dover, 3,407	D 5
Port Elgin, 2,855	C 3
Port Hope, 8,872	F 4
Port Lambton, 714	B 5
Port Loring, 331	E 2
Port McNicoll, 1,450	E 3
Port Perry, 2,977	F 4
Port Rowan, 856	D 5
Port Stanley, 1,725	C 5
Pottageville, 381	J 3
Powassan, 1,163	F 1
Prescott⊙, 5,165	J 3
Preston, 16,723	D 4
Princeton, 456	D 4
Rainy River, 1,196	F 5
Red Rock, 1,407	H 5
Renfrew, 9,173	J 2
Richmond, 2,522	J 2
Richmond Hill, 32,384	J 4
Ridgetown, 2,836	C 5
Ripley, 448	C 3
Rockcliffe Park, 2,138	J 2
Rockland, 3,649	J 2
Rockwood, 996	D 4
Rodney, 1,016	C 5
Rolphton, 418	G 1

OTHER FEATURES

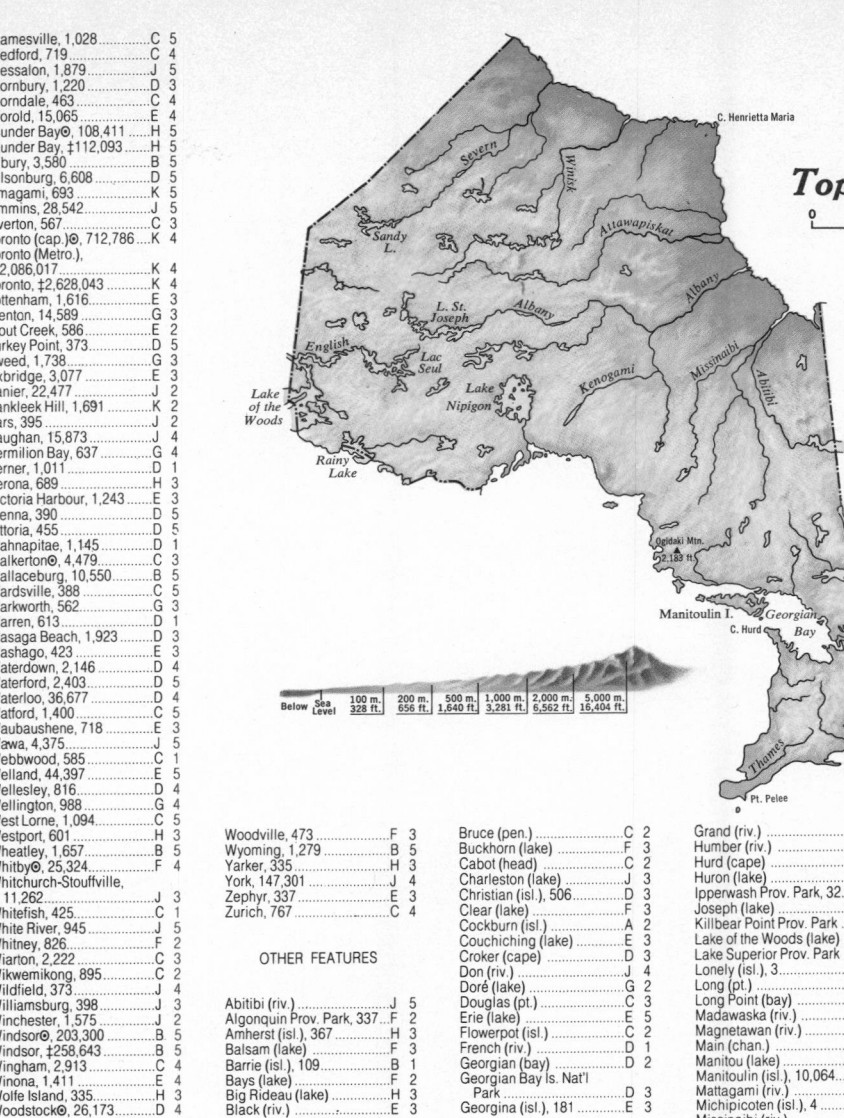

Topography

0   100   200
MILES

Below Sea Level | 100 m. 328 ft. | 200 m. 656 ft. | 500 m. 1,640 ft. | 1,000 m. 3,281 ft. | 2,000 m. 6,562 ft. | 5,000 m. 16,404 ft.

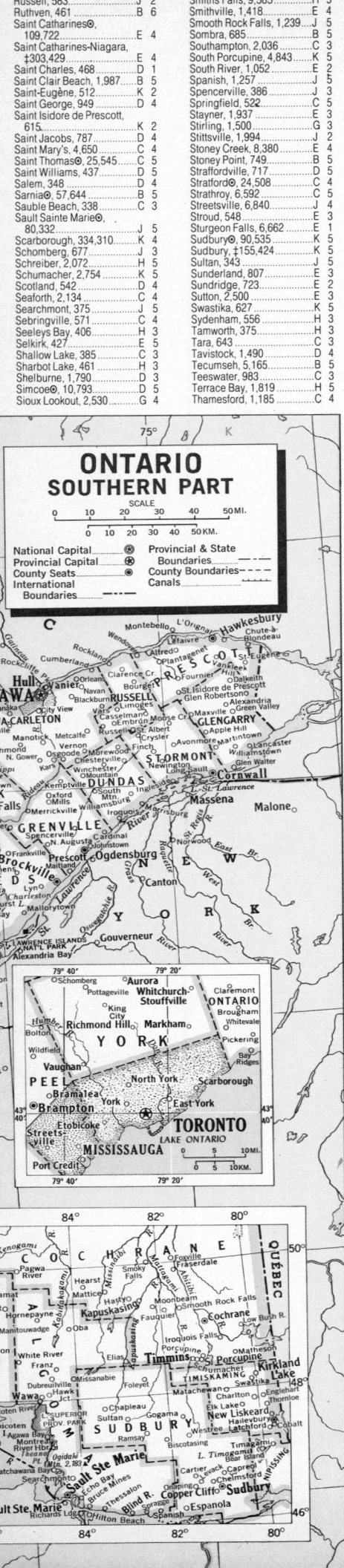

ONTARIO SOUTHERN PART

SCALE
0 10 20 30 40 50 MI.
0 10 20 30 40 50 KM.

National Capital .... ⊛
Provincial Capital .... ⊛
County Seats .... ●
International Boundaries ......
Provincial & State Boundaries ......
County Boundaries ------
Canals ......

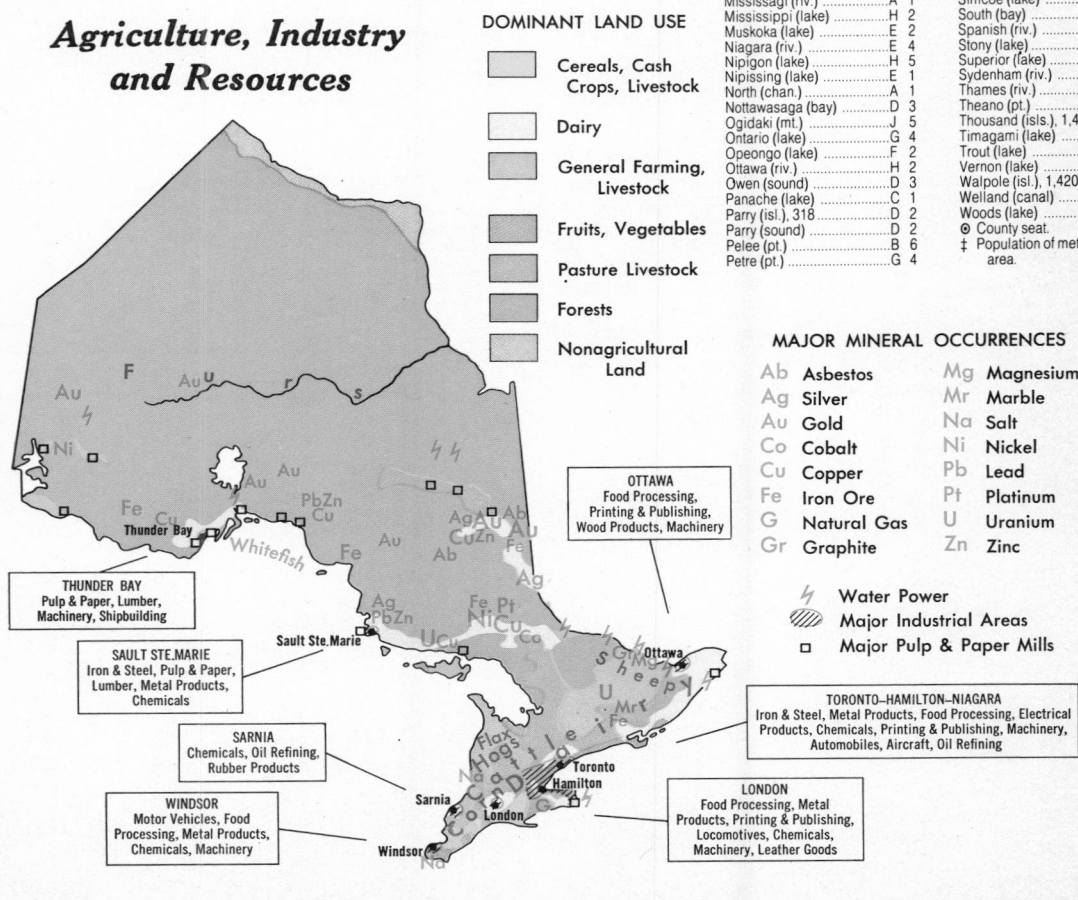

Agriculture, Industry and Resources

DOMINANT LAND USE

Cereals, Cash Crops, Livestock
Dairy
General Farming, Livestock
Fruits, Vegetables
Pasture Livestock
Forests
Nonagricultural Land

MAJOR MINERAL OCCURRENCES

Ab	Asbestos	Mg	Magnesium
Ag	Silver	Mr	Marble
Au	Gold	Na	Salt
Co	Cobalt	Ni	Nickel
Cu	Copper	Pb	Lead
Fe	Iron Ore	Pt	Platinum
G	Natural Gas	U	Uranium
Gr	Graphite	Zn	Zinc

Water Power
Major Industrial Areas
Major Pulp & Paper Mills

OTTAWA
Food Processing, Printing & Publishing, Wood Products, Machinery

THUNDER BAY
Pulp & Paper, Lumber, Machinery, Shipbuilding

SAULT STE. MARIE
Iron & Steel, Pulp & Paper, Lumber, Metal Products, Chemicals

SARNIA
Chemicals, Oil Refining, Rubber Products

WINDSOR
Motor Vehicles, Food Processing, Metal Products, Chemicals, Machinery

TORONTO–HAMILTON–NIAGARA
Iron & Steel, Metal Products, Food Processing, Electrical Products, Chemicals, Printing & Publishing, Machinery, Automobiles, Aircraft, Oil Refining

LONDON
Food Processing, Metal Products, Printing & Publishing, Locomotives, Chemicals, Machinery, Leather Goods

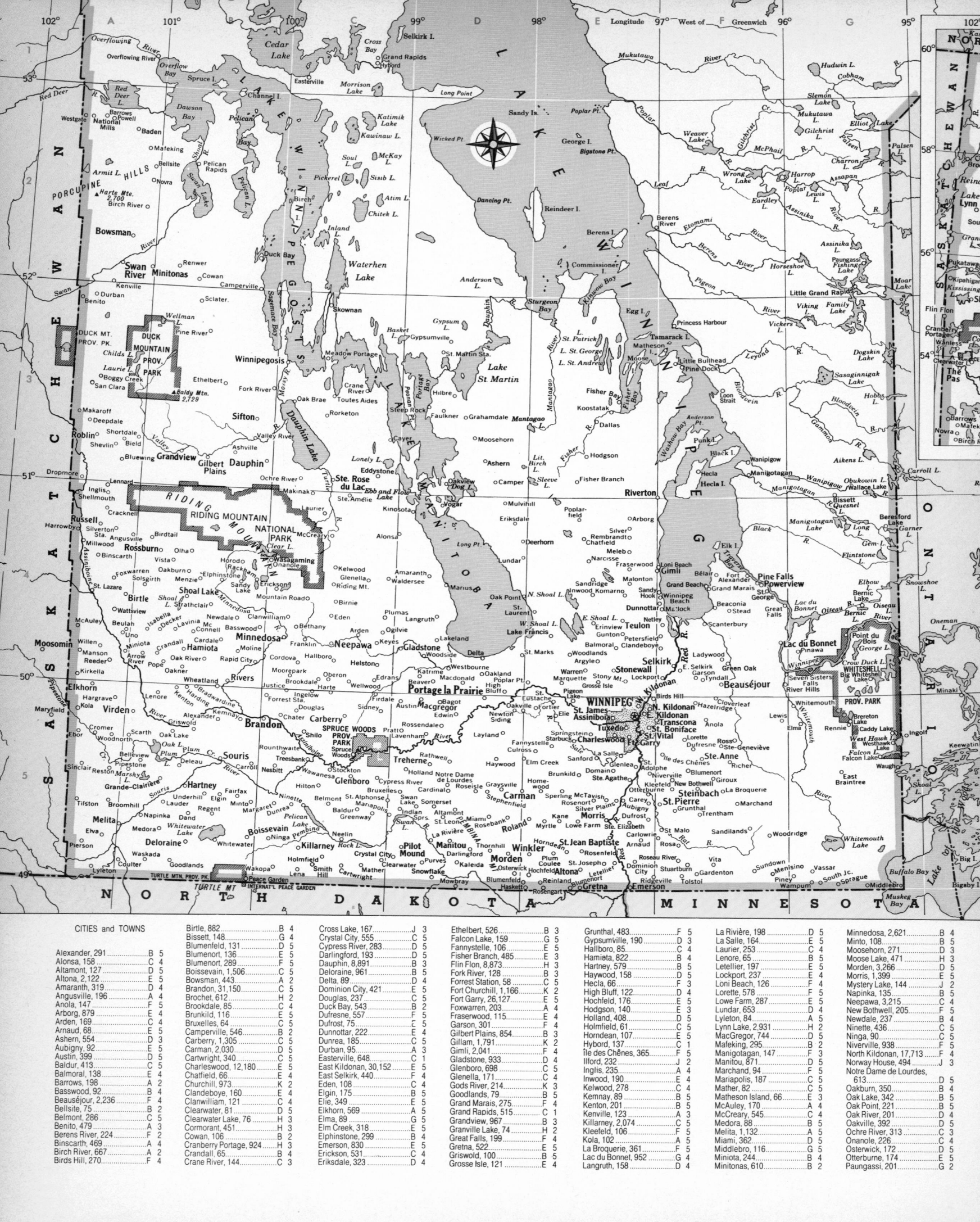

CITIES and TOWNS

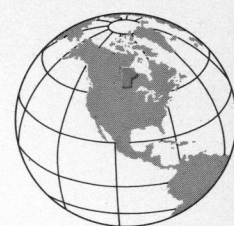

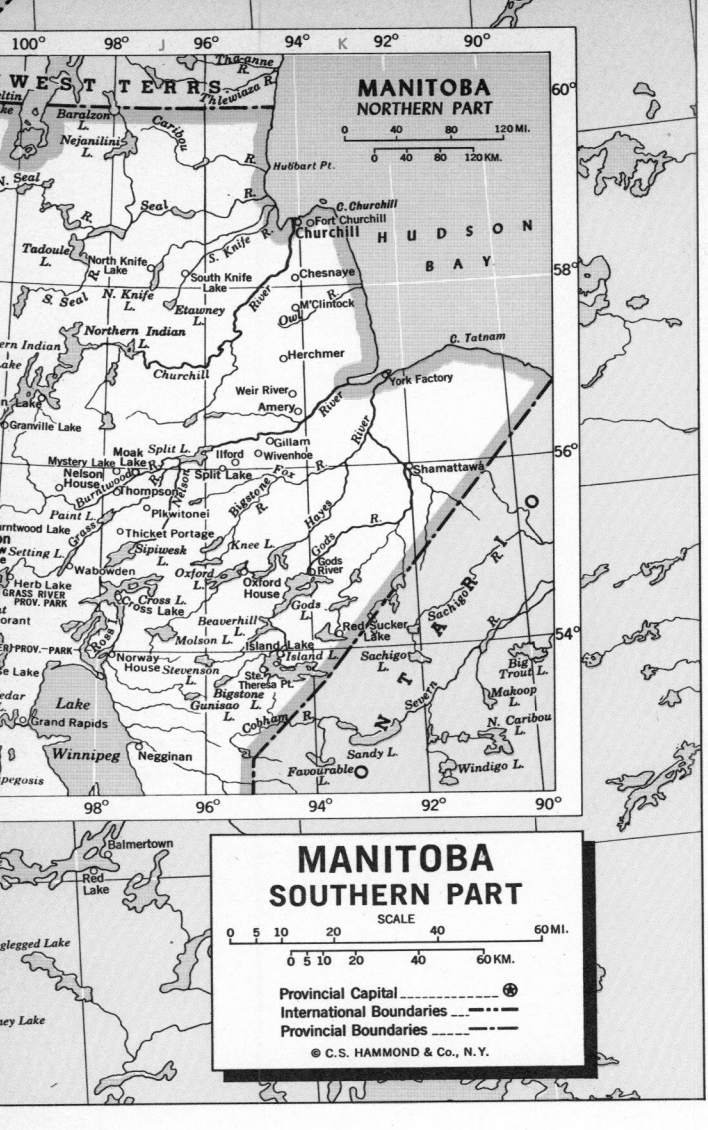

MANITOBA NORTHERN PART
SCALE
0 40 80 120 MI.
0 40 80 120 KM.

MANITOBA SOUTHERN PART
SCALE
0 5 10 20 40 60 MI.
0 5 10 20 40 60 KM.

Provincial Capital ⊕
International Boundaries
Provincial Boundaries
© C.S. HAMMOND & Co., N.Y.

AREA 251,000 sq. mi.
POPULATION 979,000
CAPITAL Winnipeg
LARGEST CITY Winnipeg
HIGHEST POINT Baldy Mtn. 2,729 ft.
SETTLED IN 1812
ADMITTED TO CONFEDERATION 1870
PROVINCIAL FLOWER Prairie Crocus

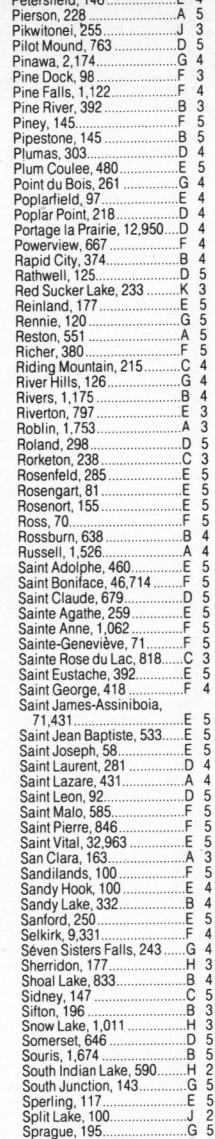

Agriculture, Industry and Resources

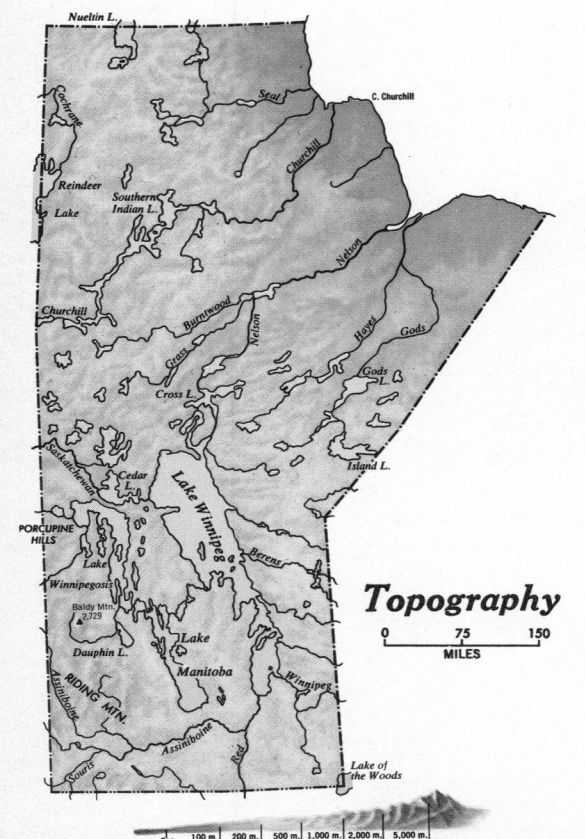

Topography
0 75 150 MILES

100 m. 200 m. 500 m. 1,000 m. 2,000 m. 5,000 m.
Below Sea Level 328 ft. 656 ft. 1,640 ft. 3,281 ft. 6,562 ft. 16,404 ft.

DOMINANT LAND USE

Cereals (chiefly barley, oats)
Cereals, Livestock
Dairy
Livestock
Forests
Nonagricultural Land

MAJOR MINERAL OCCURRENCES

Au Gold
Co Cobalt
Cu Copper
Na Salt
Ni Nickel
O Petroleum
Pb Lead
Pt Platinum
Zn Zinc

⚡ Water Power
Major Industrial Areas
▫ Major Pulp & Paper Mills

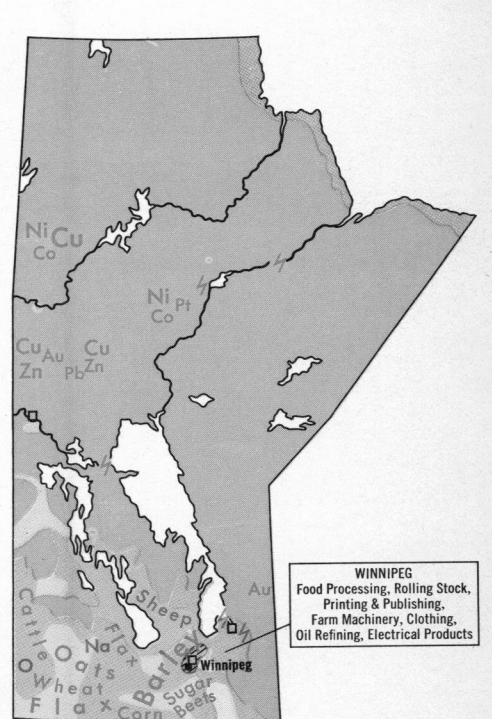

WINNIPEG
Food Processing, Rolling Stock, Printing & Publishing, Farm Machinery, Clothing, Oil Refining, Electrical Products

Topography

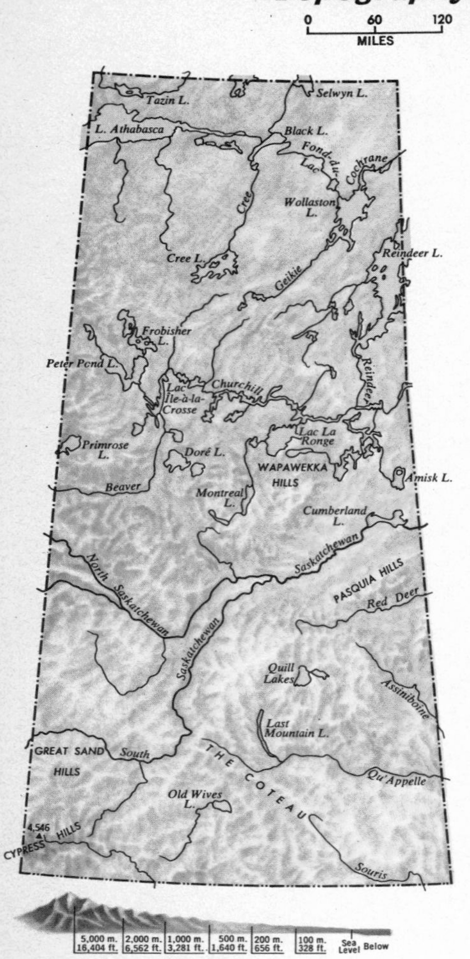

CITIES and TOWNS

Abbey, 246 C 5
Aberdeen, 288 E 3
Abernethy, 253 H 5
Air Ronge, 239 M 3
Alameda, 370 J 6
Alida, 230 K 6
Allan, 712 E 4
Alsask, 819 B 4
Alvena, 143 E 3
Aneroid, 163 D 6
Annaheim, 182 G 3
Antler, 115 K 6
Arborfield, 418 H 2
Archerwill, 302 H 3
Arcola, 539 J 6
Arran, 120 K 4
Asquith, 355 D 3
Assiniboia, 2,675 E 6
Avonlea, 391 G 5
Aylesbury, 88 F 5
Aylsham, 170 H 2
Balcarres, 678 H 5
Balgonie, 518 G 5
Batoche, 27 E 3
Battleford, 1,803 C 3
Beatty, 97 G 3
Beauval, 436 L 3
Beechy, 342 D 5
Bellevue, 122 F 3
Bengough, 650 F 6
Bethune, 291 F 5
Bienfait, 823 J 6
Biggar, 2,607 C 3
Big River, 836 D 2
Birch Hills, 696 F 3
Birsay, 123 D 4
Bjorkdale, 223 H 3
Black Lake, 471 M 2
Bladworth, 125 E 4
Blaine Lake, 671 D 3
Borden, 187 D 3
Bradwell, 100 E 4
Bredenbury, 472 K 5
Briercrest, 130 F 5
Broadview, 959 J 5
Brock, 205 C 4
Broderick, 115 E 4
Brownlee, 121 F 5
Bruno, 728 F 3
Buchanan, 442 J 4
Buffalo Narrows, 794 L 3
Bulyea, 109 G 5
Burstall, 507 B 5
Cabri, 737 C 5
Cadillac, 217 D 6
Calder, 186 K 4
Camsell Portage, 87 L 2
Cando, 193 C 3
Canoe Lake, 138 L 3
Canora, 2,603 J 4
Canwood, 325 E 2
Carievale, 229 K 6
Carlyle, 1,101 J 6
Carmel, 90 F 3
Carnduff, 1,075 K 6
Caron, 96 F 5
Carragana, 137 J 3
Carrot River, 953 H 2
Central Butte, 522 E 5
Ceylon, 279 G 6
Chamberlain, 161 F 5
Chaplin, 368 E 5
Chelan, 101 H 3
Chitek Lake, 131 D 2
Choiceland, 456 G 2
Christopher Lake, 143 F 2
Churchbridge, 973 J 5
Clair, 86 G 3
Climax, 341 C 6
Cochin, 163 C 2
Coderre, 161 E 5
Codette, 175 H 2
Coleville, 482 B 4
Colonsay, 526 F 4
Conquest, 261 D 4
Consul, 205 B 6
Coronach, 379 F 6
Craik, 503 F 4
Crane Valley, 84 F 6
Craven, 126 G 5
Creelman, 197 H 6
Creighton, 1,857 N 4
Crooked River, 106 H 3
Cudworth, 799 F 3
Cupar, 573 G 5
Cutbank, 217 E 4
Cut Knife, 560 B 3
Dalmeny, 417 E 3
Davidson, 1,043 E 4
Debden, 340 E 2
Delisle, 653 D 4
Delmas, 161 C 3
Denare Beach, 235 M 4
Denzil, 287 B 3
Deschambault Lake, 127 M 3
Dilke, 130 F 5
Dinsmore, 421 D 4
Dodsland, 404 C 4
Dollard, 92 C 6
Domremy, 208 F 3
Dorintosh, 87 L 4
Drake, 238 G 4
Drinkwater, 118 F 5
Dubuc, 153 J 5
Duck Lake, 584 E 3
Duff, 90 H 5
Dundurn, 354 E 4
Duval, 133 G 4
Dysart, 243 H 5
Earl Grey, 243 G 5
Eastend, 784 C 6
Eatonia, 610 B 4
Ebenezer, 140 J 4
Edam, 334 C 2
Edenwold, 129 G 5
Elbow, 361 E 4
Eldorado, 289 L 2
Elfros, 253 H 4
Elrose, 573 D 4
Elstow, 150 E 4
Endeavour, 193 J 3
Englefeld, 218 G 3
Ernfold, 100 D 5
Erwood, 94 J 3
Esterhazy, 2,896 K 5
Estevan, 9,150 J 6
Eston, 1,418 C 4
Eyebrow, 181 E 5
Fairlight, 127 K 6
Fenwood, 112 H 4
Ferland, 109 D 6
Fillmore, 396 H 6
Findlater, 96 F 5
Fiske, 85 C 4
Flaxcombe, 99 B 4
Fleming, 183 K 5
Flin Flon, 471 N 4
Foam Lake, 1,331 H 4
Fond du Lac, 328 L 2
Forget, 118 J 6
Fort Qu'Appelle, 1,606 H 5
Fosston, 119 H 3
Fox Valley, 489 B 5
Francis, 159 H 5
Frenchman Butte, 86 B 2
Frobisher, 245 J 6
Frontier, 249 C 6
Gainsborough, 375 K 6
Garrick, 120 G 2
Gerald, 174 K 5
Girvin, 86 F 4
Gladmar, 131 G 6
Glaslyn, 357 C 2
Glenavon, 340 J 5
Glen Ewen, 223 K 6
Glenside, 94 E 4
Glentworth, 126 E 6
Golden Prairie, 144 B 5
Goodeve, 169 H 4
Goodsoil, 219 L 4
Gorlitz, 94 J 4
Govan, 354 G 4
Grand Coulee, 131 G 5
Gravelbourg, 1,428 E 6
Grayson, 260 J 5
Green Lake, 450 L 4
Grenfell, 1,350 J 5
Griffin, 90 H 6
Gronlid, 138 G 2
Guernsey, 142 F 4
Gull Lake, 1,156 C 5
Hafford, 580 D 3
Hague, 431 E 3
Halbrite, 166 H 6
Hanley, 390 E 4
Harris, 254 D 4
Hawarden, 190 E 4
Hazel Dell, 105 H 4
Hazenmore, 127 D 6
Hazlet, 198 C 5
Hepburn, 305 E 3
Herbert, 1,024 D 5
Herschel, 89 C 4
Hitchcock, 91 J 6
Hodgeville, 399 E 5
Hoey, 95 F 3
Holdfast, 399 F 5
Hubbard, 119 H 4
Hudson Bay, 1,971 J 3
Humboldt, 3,881 F 3
Hyas, 215 J 4
Île-à-la-Crosse, 908 L 3
Imperial, 486 F 4
Indian Head, 1,810 H 5
Invermay, 412 J 4
Ituna, 960 H 4
Jansen, 241 G 4
Kamsack, 2,783 K 4
Kayville, 84 F 6
Kelliher, 460 H 4
Kelvington, 1,053 H 3
Kenaston, 402 E 4
Kendal, 90 H 5
Kennedy, 264 J 5
Kenosee Park, 103 J 6
Kerrobert, 1,180 C 4
Khedive, 91 G 6
Killaly, 139 J 5
Kincaid, 306 D 6
Kindersley, 3,451 B 4
Kinistino, 767 F 3
Kinoosao, 95 N 3
Kipling, 927 J 5
Kisbey, 260 J 6
Krydor, 136 D 3
Kuroki, 167 H 4
Kyle, 509 C 5
Lacadena, 84 C 5
Lac Vert, 111 G 3
Lafleche, 715 E 6
Laird, 218 E 3
Lake Alma, 173 G 6
Lake Lenore, 392 G 3
La Loche, 1,136 L 3
Lampman, 830 J 6
Lancer, 199 C 5
Landis, 297 C 3
Lang, 183 G 6
Langenburg, 1,236 K 5
Langham, 535 E 3
Lanigan, 1,430 F 4
La Ronge, 906 L 3
Lashburn, 494 B 2
Leader, 1,105 B 5
Leask, 439 E 2
Lebret, 278 H 5
Leipzig, 87 C 3
Lemberg, 409 H 5
Leoville, 399 D 2
Leross, 91 H 4
Leroy, 435 G 4
Leslie, 87 H 4
Lestock, 452 G 4
Liberty, 141 F 4
Limerick, 178 E 6
Lintlaw, 212 H 3
Lipton, 401 H 5
Livelong, 126 C 2
Lloydminster, 3,953 A 2
Lone Rock, 120 A 2
Loon Lake, 348 B 1
Loreburn, 252 E 4
Love, 133 G 2
Lucky Lake, 378 D 5
Lumsden, 900 G 5
Luseland, 728 B 3
Macdowall, 173 E 2
Macklin, 829 A 3
MacNutt, 184 K 4
Macoun, 172 H 6
Macrorie, 120 E 4
Maidstone, 691 B 2
Major, 164 B 4
Makwa, 126 C 2
Manitou Beach, 118 F 4
Mankota, 424 D 6
Manor, 409 K 6
Maple Creek, 2,268 B 6
Marcelin, 306 E 3
Marchwell, 129 K 5
Marengo, 133 B 4
Margo, 225 H 4
Marquis, 131 F 5
Marsden, 241 B 3
Marshall, 195 B 2
Martensville, 870 E 3
Maryfield, 408 K 6
Mayfair, 134 D 2
Maymont, 167 D 3
McKague, 91 G 3
McLean, 178 G 5
Meacham, 186 F 3
Meadow Lake, 3,435 C 1
Meath Park, 251 F 2
Medstead, 172 C 2
Melfort, 4,725 G 3
Melville, 5,375 J 5
Mendham, 163 B 5
Meota, 233 C 2
Mervin, 198 C 2
Meyronne, 142 E 6
Midale, 647 H 6
Middle Lake, 292 F 3
Mikado, 90 J 4
Milden, 239 D 4
Milestone, 483 G 5
Minton, 215 G 6
Mistatim, 165 H 3
Molanosa, 213 M 4
Montmartre, 510 H 5
Moose Jaw, 31,854 F 5
Moosomin, 2,407 K 5
Morse, 455 D 5
Mortlach, 310 E 5
Mossbank, 460 E 6
Mozart, 93 G 4
Muenster, 280 F 3
Naicam, 711 G 3
Neilburg, 298 B 3
Neuanlage, 107 E 3
Neudorf, 469 J 5
Neville, 154 D 6
Nipawin, 4,057 H 2
Nokomis, 533 F 4
Norquay, 513 J 4
North Battleford, 12,698 C 3
North Portal, 189 J 6
Odessa, 224 H 5
Ogema, 457 G 6
Ormiston, 173 F 6
Osler, 182 E 3
Outlook, 1,767 E 4
Oxbow, 1,380 J 6
Paddockwood, 230 F 2
Pambrun, 91 D 6
Pangman, 242 G 6
Paradise Hill, 344 B 2
Parkside, 112 E 2
Paynton, 204 B 2
Pelican Narrows, 265 N 3
Pelly, 426 K 4
Pennant, 215 C 5
Pense, 270 G 5
Perdue, 411 D 3
Piapot, 160 B 6
Pierceland, 271 K 4
Pilger, 109 F 3
Pilot Butte, 403 G 5
Pine House, 427 M 3
Pleasantdale, 153 G 3
Plenty, 208 C 4
Plunkett, 152 F 4
Ponteix, 786 D 6
Porcupine Plain, 830 H 3
Preeceville, 1,118 J 4
Prelate, 407 B 5
Prince Albert, 28,464 F 2
Prud'homme, 260 F 3
Punnichy, 451 G 4
Qu'Appelle, 451 H 5
Quill Lake, 566 G 3
Quinton, 195 G 4
Rabbit Lake, 206 D 2
Radisson, 416 D 3
Radville, 1,024 G 6
Rama, 188 H 4
Raymore, 523 G 4
Redvers, 846 K 6
Regina (cap.), 139,469 G 5
Regina, ‡140,734 G 5
Regina Beach, 334 F 5
Regway, 19 G 6
Reserve, 153 J 3
Rhein, 295 J 4
Rhineland, 84 D 5
Riceton, 112 G 5
Richmound, 208 B 5
Ridgedale, 169 H 2
Riverhurst, 264 E 5
Rocanville, 891 K 5
Roche Percée, 167 J 6
Rockglen, 550 F 6
Rosetown, 2,614 D 4
Rose Valley, 591 H 3
Rosthern, 1,431 E 3
Rouleau, 395 G 5
Rush Lake, 162 D 5
Saint Benedict, 193 F 3
Saint Brieux, 367 G 3
Saint Front, 94 G 3
Saint Gregor, 125 G 3
Saint Louis, 387 F 3
Saint Victor, 85 F 6
Saint Walburg, 656 B 2
Saltcoats, 509 J 4
Sandy Bay, 494 N 3
Saskatoon, 126,449 E 3
Saskatoon, ‡126,449 E 3
Sceptre, 234 B 5
Scott, 254 C 3
Sedley, 268 H 5
Semans, 331 G 4
Senlac, 94 B 3
Shamrock, 105 E 5
Shaunavon, 2,244 C 6
Sheho, 320 H 4
Shellbrook, 1,048 E 2
Shell Lake, 255 D 2
Simmie, 100 C 6
Simpson, 239 F 4
Sintaluta, 272 H 5
Smeaton, 315 G 2
Smiley, 124 B 4
Snowden, 87 G 2
Sonningdale, 106 D 3
Southey, 548 G 5
Sovereign, 91 D 4
Spalding, 329 G 3

Agriculture, Industry and Resources

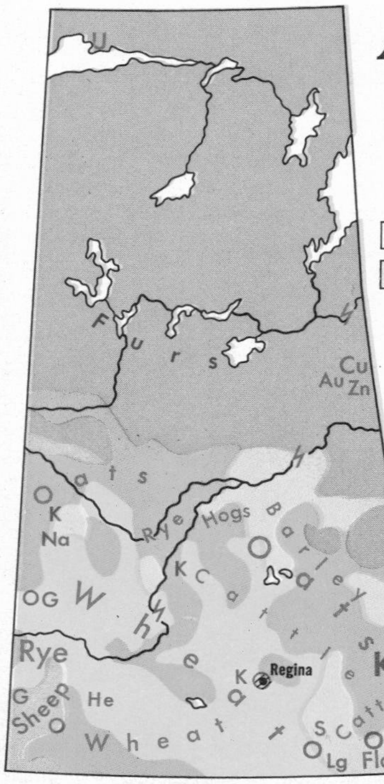

DOMINANT LAND USE

- Wheat
- Cereals (chiefly barley, oats)
- Cereals, Livestock
- Livestock
- Forests

MAJOR MINERAL OCCURRENCES

Au	Gold	Na	Salt
Cu	Copper	O	Petroleum
G	Natural Gas	S	Sulfur
He	Helium	U	Uranium
K	Potash	Zn	Zinc
Lg	Lignite		

- Water Power
- Major Industrial Areas

REGINA
Food Processing, Machinery, Oil Refining

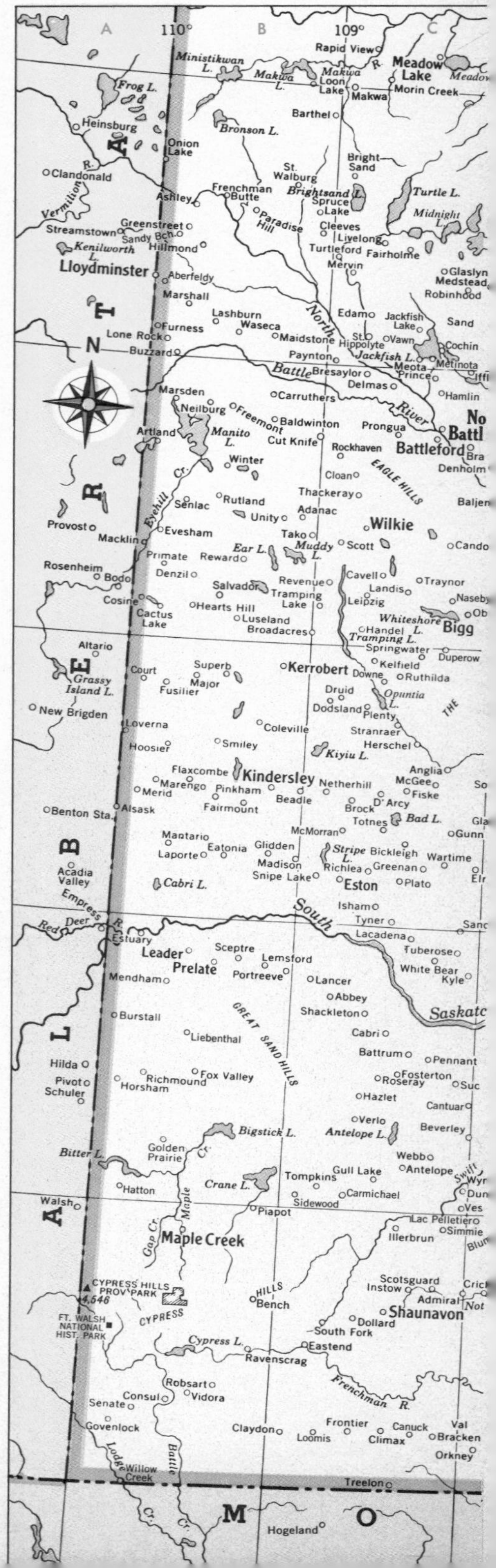

Speers, 117 .... D 3
Spiritwood, 719 .... J 3
Springside, 350 .... J 4
Springwater, 99 .... C 4
Spruce Lake, 106 .... B 2
Spy Hill, 384 .... K 5
Star City, 543 .... G 3
Stenen, 225 .... J 4
Stewart Valley, 138 .... D 5
Stockholm, 357 .... J 5
Stony Rapids, 147 .... M 2
Storthoaks, 177 .... K 6
Stoughton, 751 .... H 6
Strasbourg, 759 .... G 4
Strongfield, 110 .... E 4
Sturgis, 617 .... J 4
Success, 101 .... D 5
Swift Current, 15,415 .... D 5
Sylvania, 125 .... G 3
Tantallon, 174 .... K 5
Theodore, 434 .... J 4
Tisdale, 2,798 .... H 3
Togo, 227 .... K 4
Tompkins, 353 .... C 5
Torquay, 377 .... H 6
Tramping Lake, 241 .... B 3
Tribune, 136 .... H 6
Tugaske, 196 .... E 5
Turnor Lake, 276 .... L 3
Turtleford, 419 .... B 2
Tuxford, 153 .... F 5
Tyvan, 86 .... H 5

Unity, 2,294 .... B 3
Uranium City, 1,867 .... L 2
Val Marie, 307 .... D 6
Vanguard, 315 .... D 6
Vanscoy, 244 .... C 4
Vawn, 119 .... C 2
Veregin, 197 .... K 4
Vibank, 275 .... H 5
Viceroy, 152 .... F 6
Viscount, 395 .... F 4
Vonda, 258 .... F 3
Wadena, 1,382 .... H 4
Wakaw, 1,009 .... F 3
Waldeck, 242 .... D 5
Waldheim, 606 .... E 3
Wapella, 518 .... K 5
Warman, 781 .... E 3
Waseca, 115 .... B 2
Waskesiu Lake, 154 .... E 2
Watrous, 1,541 .... F 4
Watson, 840 .... G 3
Wawota, 536 .... J 6
Webb, 105 .... C 5
Weekes, 183 .... J 3
Weirdale, 108 .... F 2
Weldon, 254 .... F 2
Welwyn, 231 .... K 5
Weyburn, 8,815 .... H 6
White City, 129 .... H 5
White Fox, 354 .... G 2
Whitewood, 1,098 .... J 5
Wilcox, 189 .... G 5

Wilkie, 1,642 .... C 3
Willow Bunch, 482 .... F 6
Windthorst, 188 .... J 5
Wiseton, 181 .... D 4
Wishart, 269 .... H 4
Wollaston Lake, 115 .... M 2
Wolseley, 975 .... H 5
Wood Mountain, 86 .... E 6
Wroxton, 92 .... K 4
Wymark, 199 .... D 5
Wynyard, 1,932 .... G 4
Yarbo, 160 .... K 5
Yellow Creek, 163 .... F 3
Yellow Grass, 500 .... H 6
Yorkton, 13,430 .... J 4
Young, 496 .... F 4
Zealandia, 155 .... D 4
Zenon Park, 346 .... H 2

OTHER FEATURES

Allan (hills) .... E 4
Amisk (lake) .... M 4
Assiniboine (riv.) .... J 3
Athabasca (lake) .... L 2
Battle (creek) .... B 6
Battle (riv.) .... B 3
Bear (lake) .... C 4
Beaver (hills) .... H 4
Beaver (riv.) .... L 4

Beaverlodge (lake) .... L 2
Brightsand (lake) .... B 2
Candle (lake) .... F 2
Carrot (riv.) .... J 2
Churchill (riv.) .... M 3
Coteau, The (hills) .... D 4
Cowan (lake) .... D 2
Cree (lake) .... L 3
Cumberland (lake) .... J 1
Cypress (hills) .... C 6
Cypress Hills Prov. Park .... B 6
Delaronde (lake) .... E 2
Diefenbaker (lake) .... E 4
Doré (lake) .... L 3
Duck Mountain Prov. Park .... K 3
Eagle (hills) .... C 3
Eaglehill (lake) .... D 4
Fond du Lac (riv.) .... M 2
Fort Walsh Nat'l Hist. Park .... A 6
Frenchman (riv.) .... B 6
Frobisher (lake) .... L 3
Gardiner (dam) .... D 4
Good Spirit (lake) .... J 4
Goodspirit Prov. Park .... J 4
Great Sand (hills) .... B 5
Greenwater Lake Prov.
   Park, 13 .... H 3
Île-à-la-Crosse (lake) .... L 3
Jackfish (lake) .... C 2
Lac La Ronge Prov. Park .... M 3
La Ronge (lake) .... M 3
Last Mountain (lake) .... F 4

Lenore (lake) .... G 3
Makwa (riv.) .... B 1
Manito (lake) .... B 3
Meadow Lake Prov. Park .... B 1
Meeting (lake) .... D 2
Missouri Coteau (hills) .... F 6
Montreal (lake) .... E 1
Moose Jaw (riv.) .... G 5
Moose Mountain Prov.
   Park .... J 6
Nipawin Prov. Park .... G 1
North Saskatchewan (riv.) .... D 3
Old Wives (lake) .... E 5
Pasquia (hills) .... J 2
Peter Pond (lake) .... L 3

Pheasant (hills) .... J 5
Prince Albert Nat'l Park,
   182 .... E 1
Qu'Appelle (riv.) .... J 5
Quill (lakes) .... G 4
Redberry (lake) .... D 3
Red Deer (riv.) .... N 3
Reindeer (lake) .... N 3
Rivers (lake) .... F 6
Saskatchewan (riv.) .... J 1
Souris (riv.) .... J 6
South Saskatchewan (riv.) .... C 5
Sturgeon (lake) .... E 2
Swift Current (creek) .... D 5
Tazin (lake) .... L 2

Thickwood (hills) .... D 2
Tobin (lake) .... H 2
Torch (riv.) .... H 2
Touchwood (hills) .... G 4
Turtle (lake) .... C 2
Wapawekka (hills) .... M 2
Waskesiu (lake) .... E 2
Willow Bunch (lake) .... F 6
Witchekan (lake) .... D 2
Wollaston (lake) .... N 2
Wood (mt.) .... E 6
Wood (riv.) .... E 6

AREA 251,700 sq. mi.
POPULATION 933,000
CAPITAL Regina
LARGEST CITY Regina
HIGHEST POINT Cypress Hills 4,546 ft.
SETTLED IN 1774
ADMITTED TO CONFEDERATION 1905
PROVINCIAL FLOWER Prairie Lily

‡ Population of metropolitan area.

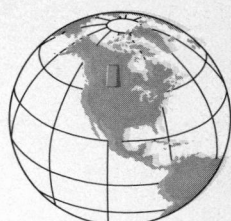

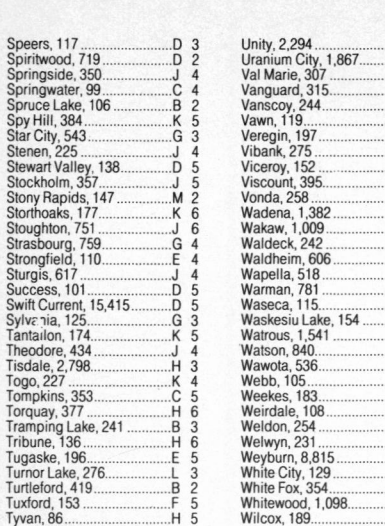

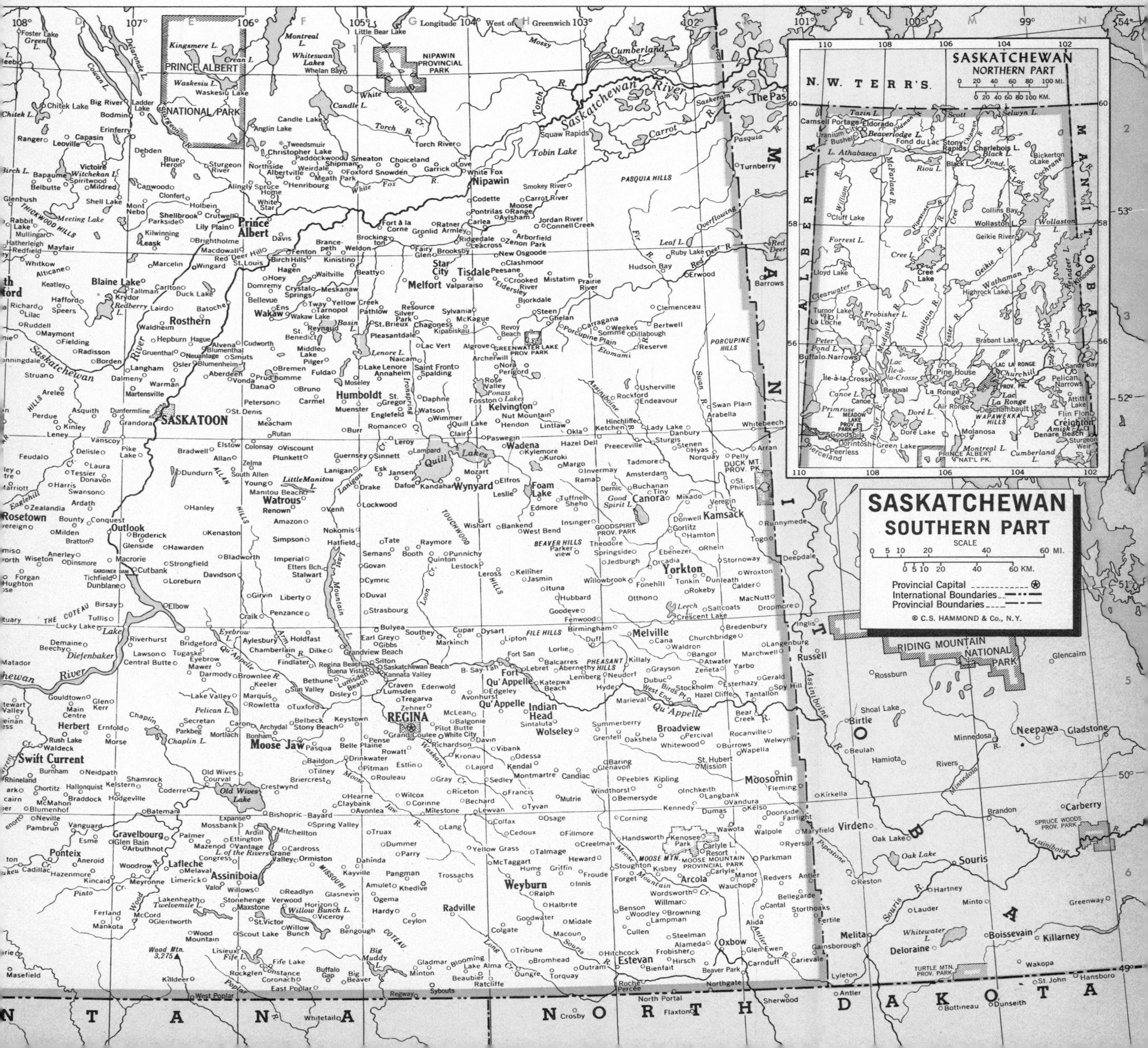

SASKATCHEWAN NORTHERN PART

SASKATCHEWAN SOUTHERN PART

SCALE

Provincial Capital .... ⊛
International Boundaries
Provincial Boundaries

© C.S. HAMMOND & Co., N.Y.

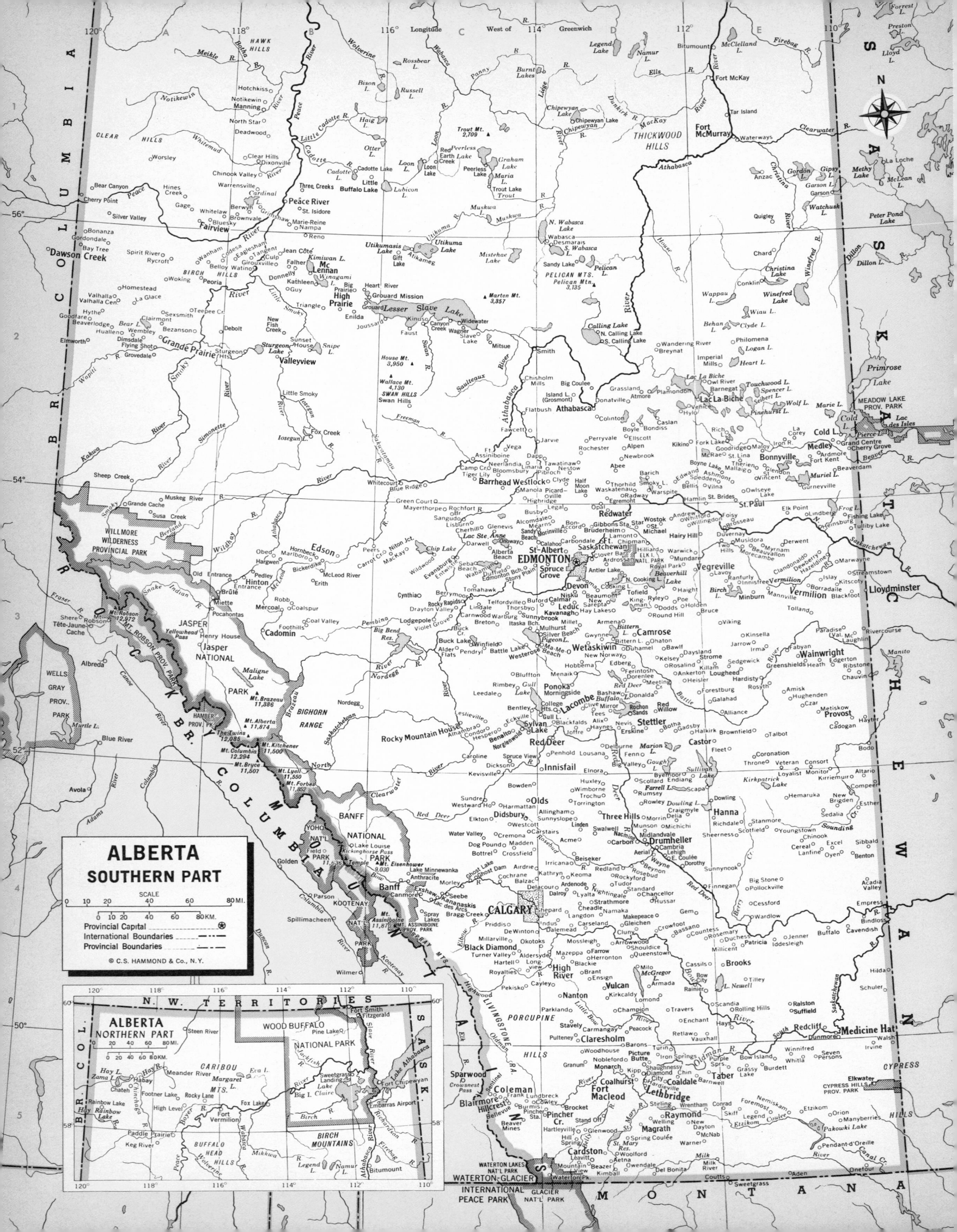

ALBERTA
SOUTHERN PART

SCALE
0 10 20 40 60 80 MI.
0 10 20 40 60 80 KM.

Provincial Capital .... ⊛
International Boundaries _._._._._
Provincial Boundaries _____

© C.S. HAMMOND & Co., N.Y.

ALBERTA
NORTHERN PART
20 40 60 80 MI.
0 20 40 60 80KM.

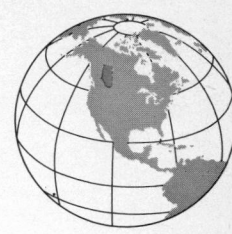

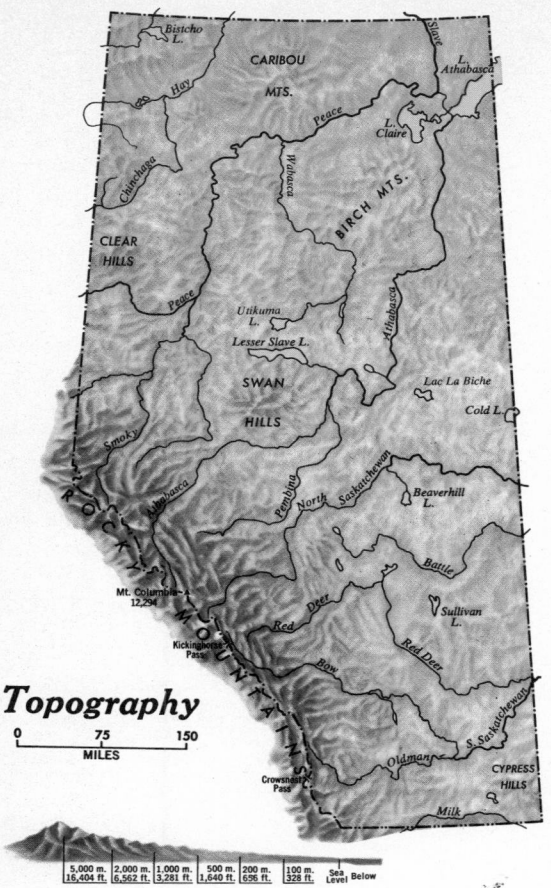

Topography

```
0      75      150
       MILES
```

5,000 m. 2,000 m. 1,000 m. 500 m. 200 m. 100 m. Sea Level Below
16,404 ft. 6,562 ft. 3,281 ft. 1,640 ft. 656 ft. 328 ft.

AREA 255,285 sq. mi.
POPULATION 1,614,000
CAPITAL Edmonton
LARGEST CITY Edmonton
HIGHEST POINT Mt. Columbia 12,294 ft.
SETTLED IN 1861
ADMITTED TO CONFEDERATION 1905
PROVINCIAL FLOWER Wild Rose

Agriculture, Industry and Resources

DOMINANT LAND USE

- Wheat
- Cereals (chiefly barley, oats)
- Cereals, Livestock
- Dairy
- Pasture Livestock
- Range Livestock
- Forests
- Nonagricultural Land

MAJOR MINERAL OCCURRENCES

- C Coal
- G Natural Gas
- Na Salt
- O Petroleum
- S Sulfur

- ⚡ Water Power
- Major Industrial Areas

EDMONTON
Food Processing, Chemicals, Oil Refining, Metal Products, Printing & Publishing, Clothing

CALGARY
Food Processing, Metal Products, Chemicals, Wood Products, Oil Refining

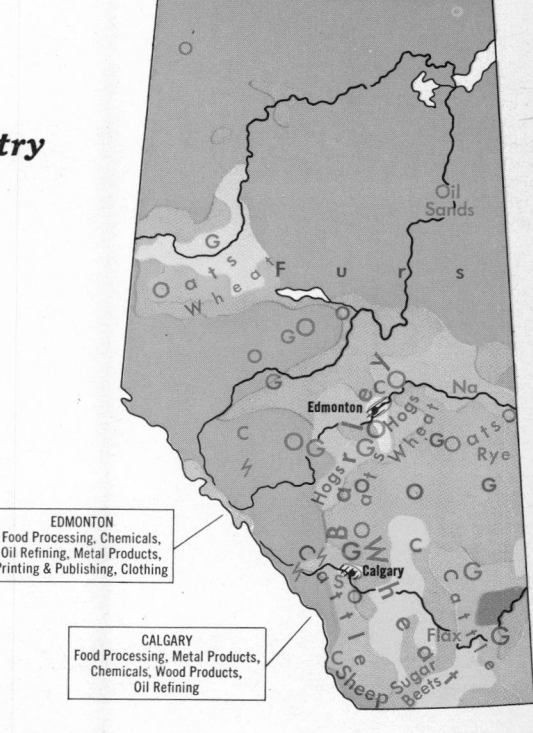

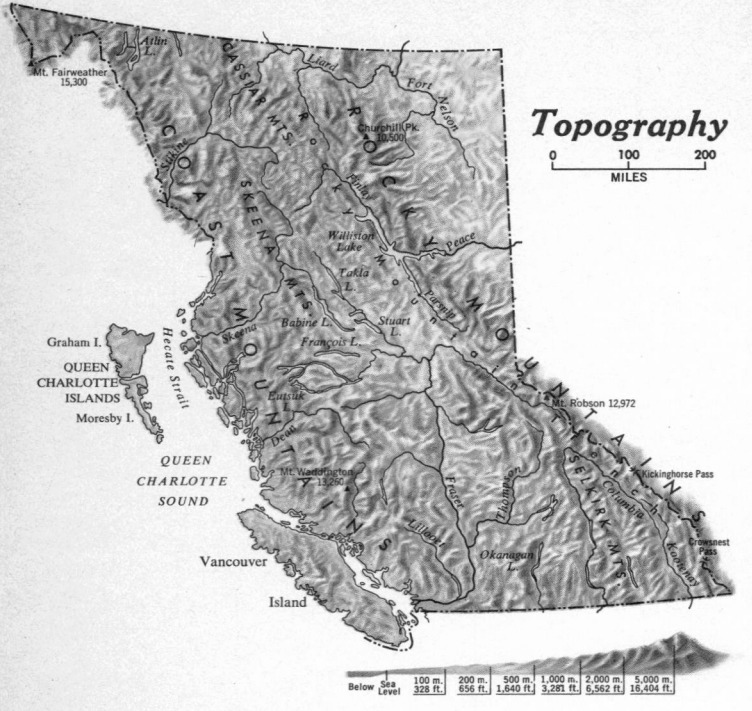

Topography

```
0    100    200
    MILES
```

Below Sea Level | 100 m. 328 ft. | 200 m. 656 ft. | 500 m. 1,640 ft. | 1,000 m. 3,281 ft. | 2,000 m. 6,562 ft. | 5,000 m. 16,404 ft.

Agriculture, Industry and Resources

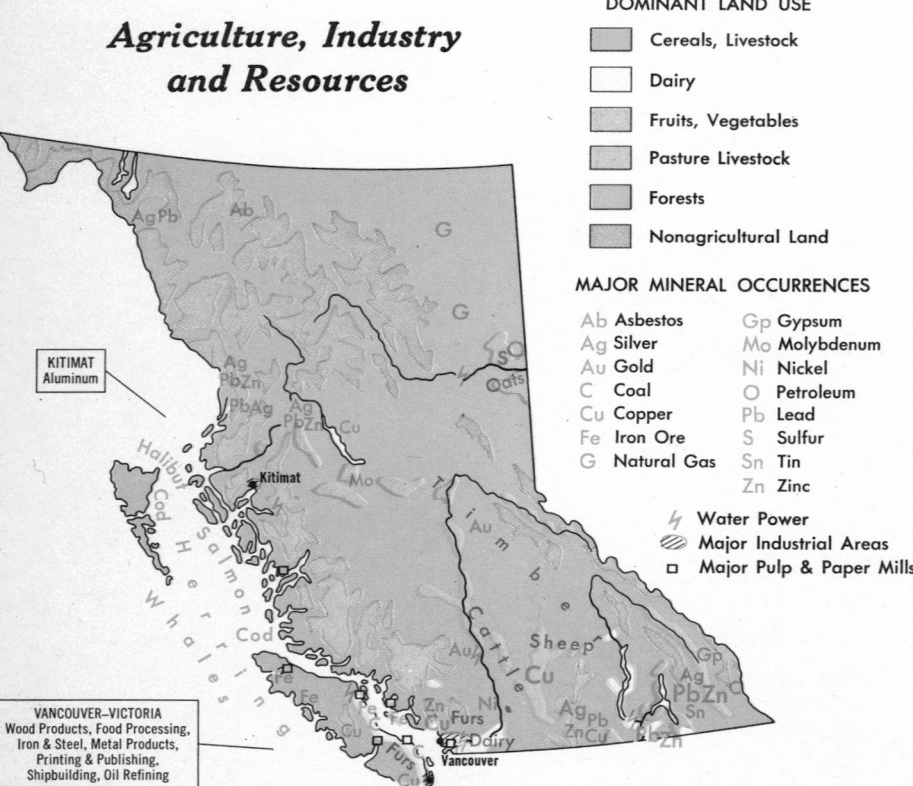

KITIMAT Aluminum

VANCOUVER–VICTORIA
Wood Products, Food Processing,
Iron & Steel, Metal Products,
Printing & Publishing,
Shipbuilding, Oil Refining

DOMINANT LAND USE

- Cereals, Livestock
- Dairy
- Fruits, Vegetables
- Pasture Livestock
- Forests
- Nonagricultural Land

MAJOR MINERAL OCCURRENCES

Ab	Asbestos	Gp	Gypsum
Ag	Silver	Mo	Molybdenum
Au	Gold	Ni	Nickel
C	Coal	O	Petroleum
Cu	Copper	Pb	Lead
Fe	Iron Ore	S	Sulfur
G	Natural Gas	Sn	Tin
		Zn	Zinc

⚡ Water Power
〰 Major Industrial Areas
□ Major Pulp & Paper Mills

CITIES and TOWNS

Abbotsford, 706............L 3
Albert Head, 330...........J 4
Alert Bay, 760.............D 5
Alexandria, 168............F 4
Armstrong, 1,648..........H 5
Ashcroft, 1,916...........G 5
Ashton Creek, 318.........H 5
Athalmer, 255.............K 5
Atlin, 258................J 1
Avola, 265................H 4
Balfour, 195..............J 5
Barrière, 829.............H 4
Bear Lake, 302............F 3
Beaverdell, 241...........H 5
Bella Coola, 273..........D 4
Big Eddy, 654.............H 4
Birch Island, 219.........H 4
Blue River, 475...........H 4
Boston Bar, 548...........G 5
Bowen Island, 351.........K 3
Bowser, 169...............H 2

Brackendale, 692..........F 5
Bralorne, 379.............F 5
Britannia Beach, 738......K 2
Brouse, 446...............J 5
Burnaby, ●125,660.........K 3
Burns Lake, 1,259.........D 3
Cache Creek, 1,013........G 4
Campbell River, ●10,000...E 5
Campbell River, 9,770.....E 5
Canal Flats, 902..........K 5
Cassiar, 1,073............K 1
Castlegar, 3,072..........J 5
Cawston, 642..............H 5
Caycuse, 297..............J 3
Cedarside, 218............H 4
Celista, 178..............H 5
Central Saanich, ●5,136...K 3
Chase, 1,212..............H 5
Charlie Lake, 214.........G 2
Chase River, 728..........J 3
Chemainus, 2,129..........J 3
Cherry Creek, 449.........G 5
Cherryville, 284..........H 5
Chetwynd, 1,260...........G 2

Chilliwack, 9,135.........M 3
Chilliwack, ●23,739.......M 3
Clearbrook, 3,653.........L 3
Clearwater, 513...........G 4
Clinton, 905..............G 4
Coal Harbour, 334.........D 5
Cobble Hill, 280..........K 3
Coldstream, ●3,602........H 5
Comox, 3,980..............H 2
Coquitlam, ●53,073........K 3
Courtenay, 7,152..........E 5
Cranbrook, 12,000.........K 5
Crawford Bay, 244.........J 5
Creston, 3,204............J 5
Crofton, 972..............J 3
Cultus Lake, 554..........M 3
Cumberland, 1,718.........E 5
Dawson Creek, 11,885......G 2
Delta, ●45,860............K 3
Departure Bay, 3,744......J 3
Donald, 235...............J 4
Duncan, 4,388.............J 3
East Kelowna, 826.........H 5
Eddontenajon, 180.........K 2

Edgewater, 346............J 5
Elko, 196.................K 5
Endako, 242...............E 3
Enderby, 1,158............H 5
Errington, 464............J 3
Esquimalt, ●12,922........K 4
Extension, 181............J 3
Falkland, 375.............H 5
Fernie, 4,422.............K 5
Field, 358................J 4
Flood, 295................M 3
Forest Grove, 238.........G 4
Fort Fraser, 385..........E 3
Fort Langley, 1,342.......L 3
Fort Nelson, 2,289........M 2
Fort Saint James, 1,483...E 3
Fort Saint John, 8,264....G 2
Franklin River, 187.......H 3
Fraser Lake, 1,292........E 3
Fraser Mills, ●157........K 3
Fruitvale, 1,379..........J 5
Gabriola Island, 655......J 3
Galiano Island, 412.......K 3
Ganges, 333...............K 3
Gibsons, 1,934............K 3
Gillies Bay, 543..........H 2
Giscome, 416..............F 3
Golden, 3,012.............J 4
Gold River, 1,896.........D 5
Grand Forks, 3,173........H 6
Granisle, 451.............D 3
Granthams Landing, 404....J 3
Greenwood, 868............H 5
Grindrod, 283.............H 5
Hagensborg, 315...........D 4
Haney, 3,221..............L 3
Harrison Hot Springs, 598..M 3
Hatzic, 547...............L 3
Hazelton, 351.............D 2
Hedley, 385...............G 5
Heffley Creek, 503........G 5
Hendrix Lake, 341.........G 4
Heriot Bay, 187...........E 5
Hixon, 385................F 3
Holberg, 333..............C 5
Honeymoon Bay, 546........J 3
Hope, 3,153...............M 3
Houston, ●2,232...........D 3
Houston, 905..............D 3
Hudson Hope, 1,116........F 2
Hudson's Hope, ●1,741.....F 2
Huntingdon, 202...........L 3
Invermere, 1,065..........J 5
Iooo, 308.................K 3
Jaffray, 193..............K 5
Kaleden, 640..............H 5
Kamloops, 26,168..........G 5
Kaslo, 755................J 5
Kelly Lake, 231...........G 4
Kelowna, 19,412...........H 5
Kemano, 346...............D 3
Kent, ●2,966..............M 3
Keremeos, 605.............H 5
Kimberley, 7,641..........K 5
Kinnaird, 2,846...........J 5
Kitimat, 11,824...........C 3
Kitsault, 343.............C 2
Kitwanga, 217.............D 2
Kokish, 222...............D 5
Lac La Hache, 417.........G 4
Ladysmith, 3,664..........J 3
Lake Cowichan, 2,364......J 3

Lang Bay, 285.............E 5
Langley, ●21,936..........L 3
Langley, 4,684............L 3
Lantzville, 565...........J 3
Lillooet, 1,514...........G 5
Lion's Bay, 396...........K 3
Lone Butte, 206...........G 4
Louis Creek, 289..........H 4
Lower Nicola, 361.........G 5
Lower Post, 206...........K 1
Lumby, 940................H 5
Lytton, 494...............G 5
Mackenzie, ●2,332.........F 2
Mackenzie, 1,976..........F 2
Madeira Park, 351.........J 2
Maple Bay, 509............K 3
Maple Ridge, ●24,476......L 3
Masset, 975...............B 2
Matsqui, ●23,554..........L 3
Mayne Island, 293.........K 3
McBride, 658..............H 4
McConnell Creek, 233......D 2
McLure, 193...............H 4
Merritt, 5,289............G 5
Merville, 227.............E 5
Mesachie Lake, 266........J 3
Metchosin, 540............K 4
Mica Creek, 772...........H 4
Midway, 502...............H 6
Mill Bay, 347.............C 2
Milnes Landing, 254.......J 4
Mission, ●10,220..........L 3
Mission City, 3,649.......L 3
Moberly, 175..............J 4
Monte Lake, 176...........G 5
Montrose, 1,137...........J 5
Nakusp, 1,163.............J 5
Nanaimo, 14,948...........J 3
Naramata, 461.............H 5
Nelson, 9,400.............J 5
New Denver, 644...........J 5
New Hazelton, 475.........D 2
New Westminster, 42,835...K 3
Nicholson, 619............J 4
Nicomen Island, 527.......L 3
Nootka, 2.................D 5
North Bend, 424...........G 5
North Cowichan, ●12,170...J 3
North Pender Island, 407..K 3
North Saanich, ●3,601.....K 3
North Vancouver, ●57,861..K 3
North Vancouver, 31,847...K 3
Nukko Lake, 182...........F 2
Oak Bay, ●18,426..........K 4
Ocean Falls, 1,085........D 4
Okanagan Centre, 266......H 5
Okanagan Falls, 621.......H 5
Okanagan Landing, 656.....H 5
Okanagan Mission, 857.....H 5
Old Barkerville, 3........G 3
Oliver, 1,615.............H 5
One Hundred Mile House,
  1,120...................G 4
Osoyoos, 1,285............H 5
Oyama, 326................H 5
Parksville, 2,169.........J 3
Parson, 306...............J 4
Peachland, ●1,446.........G 5
Penticton, 18,146.........H 5
Pine Valley, 264..........F 2
Pitt Meadows, ●2,771......L 3
Popkum, 286...............M 3
Port Alberni, 20,063......H 3
Port Alice, 1,507.........D 5
Port Clements, 406........B 3
Port Coquitlam, 19,560....L 3
Port Edward, 1,019........B 3
Port Hammond, 1,556.......L 3
Port Hardy, ●1,761........D 5
Port McNeill, 934.........D 5
Port Moody, 10,778........L 3
Port Renfrew, 362.........J 4
Pouce-Coupé, 595..........G 2
Powell River, ●13,726.....E 5
Prince George, 33,101.....F 3
Prince Rupert, 15,747.....B 3
Princeton, 2,601..........G 5
Procter, 183..............J 5
Qualicum Beach, 1,245.....J 3
Queen Charlotte, 665......A 3
Quesnel, 6,252............F 4
Radium Hot Springs, 393...J 5
Rayleigh, 652.............G 5
Revelstoke, 4,867.........J 5
Richmond, ●62,121.........K 3
Riondel, 572..............J 5
Robson, 1,046.............J 5
Rossland, 3,896...........H 6
Royston, 532..............H 2
Rutland, 3,279............H 5
Saanich, ●65,040..........K 3
Salmo, 872................J 5
Salmon Arm, ●7,793........H 5
Salmon Arm, 1,981.........H 5
Saltair, 1,008............J 3
Sandspit, 459.............B 3
Sardis, 1,194.............M 3
Saseenos, 574.............J 3
Saturna Island, 174.......K 3
Savona, 670...............G 5
Sayward, 465..............D 5
Sechelt, 590..............J 3
Seventy Mile House, 225...G 4
Shawnigan Lake, 213.......J 3
Shoreacres, 345...........J 5
Sicamous, 814.............H 5
Sidney, 4,868.............K 3
Silverton, 246............J 5
Slocan, 346...............J 5
Slocan Park, 360..........J 5
Smithers, 3,864...........D 3
Sointula, 575.............D 5
Sooke, 836................J 4
Sorrento, 269.............H 5
South Fort George, 1,282..F 3
South Hazelton, 483.......D 2
South Slocan, 278.........J 5

South Wellington, 460.....J 3
Sparwood, ●2,990..........K 5
Sparwood, 2,154...........K 5
Spences Bridge, 199.......G 5
Sproat Lake, 321..........H 3
Squamish, 6,121...........F 5
Squamish, 1,597...........F 5
Stewart, ●1,357...........C 2
Stoner, 182...............F 3
Summerland, ●5,551........H 5
Surrey, ●98,601...........K 3
Tahsis, 1,351.............D 5
Tasu, 331.................A 4
Taylor, 605...............G 2
Telkwa, 712...............D 3
Terrace, ●9,991...........C 3
Terrace, 7,820............C 3
Thrums, 365...............J 5
Tofino, 461...............E 5
Trail, 11,149.............J 6
Ucluelet, 1,018...........E 6
Union Bay, 407............H 2
Upper Fraser, 339.........F 3
Valemount, 693............H 4
Valleyview, 3,787.........G 5
Vananda, 497..............E 5
Vancouver, 426,256........K 3
Vancouver, ‡1,082,352.....K 3
Vancouver (Greater),
  ●1,028,334..............K 3
Vanderhoof, 1,653.........E 3
Vavenby, 331..............H 4
Vernon, 13,283............H 5

Victoria (cap.), 61,761...K 4
Victoria, ‡195,800........K 4
Warfield, 2,132...........J 5
Wasa, 355.................K 5
Wells, 409................G 3
Westbank, 747.............H 5
West Vancouver, ●36,440...K 3
Westwold, 434.............G 5
White Rock, 10,349........K 3
Williams Lake, 4,072......F 4
Willow River, 422.........F 3
Wilmer, 200...............J 5
Wilson Creek, 408.........J 3
Windermere, 421...........J 5
Winfield, 875.............H 5
Winlaw, 383...............J 5
Woodfibre, 408............K 2
Woss Lake, 394............D 5
Wynndel, 579..............J 5
Yahk, 192.................K 5
Yale, 224.................M 2
Yarrow, 1,039.............M 3
Ymir, 292.................J 5
Youbou, 1,109.............J 3
Zeballos, 186.............D 5

OTHER FEATURES

Adams (riv.)..............H 4
Alberni (inlet)...........H 3
Alsek (riv.)..............H 1

BRITISH COLUMBIA

```
SCALE
0  15  30    60    90    120 MI.
0  15  30    60    90    120 KM.
```

Provincial Capital .... ⊛
State Capital .... ◉
International Boundaries .. – ·· – ··
Provincial Boundaries .... – · – · –

© C.S. HAMMOND & Co., N.Y.

Aristazabal (isl.)	C 4	
Assiniboine (mt.)	K 5	
Atlin (lake)	J 1	
Babine (lake)	E 3	
Banks (isl.)	B 3	
Barkley (sound)	E 6	
Bennett, W.A.C. (dam)	F 2	
Bowron Lake Prov. Park	G 3	
Bryce (mt.)	J 4	
Burke (chan.)	D 4	
Burnaby (mt.)	B 4	
Bute (inlet)	E 5	
Caamaño (sound)	C 4	
Calvert (isl.)	C 4	
Canoe (riv.)	H 4	
Cariboo (mts.)	G 3	
Cassiar (mts.)	K 2	
Chatham (sound)	B 3	
Chilcotin (riv.)	E 4	
Chilko (riv.)	E 4	
Chilkoot (pass)	J 1	
Churchill (peak)	L 2	
Clayoquot (sound)	D 5	
Clearwater (riv.)	G 4	
Coast (mts.)	D 3	
Columbia (lake)	K 5	
Columbia (mt.)	J 4	
Columbia (riv.)	H 4	
Cowichan (lake)	J 3	
Crowsnest (pass)	K 5	
Dean (chan.)	D 4	
Dease (lake)	K 2	
Dixon Entrance (chan.)	A 3	
Douglas (chan.)	C 3	
Duncan (riv.)	J 5	
Dundas (isl.)	B 3	
Elk (riv.)	K 5	
Eutsuk (lake)	D 3	
Fairweather (mt.)	H 1	
Finlay (riv.)	E 1	
Flores (isl.)	D 5	
Fort Nelson (riv.)	M 2	
François (lake)	D 3	
Fraser (riv.)	F 4	
Galiano (isl.)	K 3	
Gardner (canal)	C 3	
Garibaldi Prov. Park	F 5	
Georgia (str.)	J 3	
Glacier Nat'l Park	J 4	
Golden Ears Prov. Park	L 2	
Graham (isl.)	A 3	
Grenville (chan.)	C 3	
Hamber Prov. Park	H 4	
Harrison (lake)	M 2	
Hazelton (mts.)	C 2	
Hecate (str.)	B 3	
Howe (sound)	K 2	
Hunter (isl.)	C 4	
Iskut (riv.)	B 2	
Jervis (inlet)	E 5	
Johnstone (str.)	D 5	
Juan de Fuca (str.)	J 4	
Kates Needle (mt.)	A 1	
Kechika (riv.)	K 2	
Kenney (dam)	E 3	
Kettle (riv.)	H 5	
Kickinghorse (pass)	J 4	
King (isl.)	D 4	
Klinaklini (riv.)	E 4	
Knight (inlet)	E 5	
Knox (cape)	A 3	
Kokanee Glacier Prov. Park	J 5	
Koocanusa (lake)	K 6	
Kootenay (lake)	K 5	
Kootenay (riv.)	K 5	
Kootenay Nat'l Park	J 4	
Kunghit (isl.)	B 4	
Kyuquot (sound)	D 5	
Langara (isl.)	A 3	
Liard (riv.)	L 2	
Lillooet (riv.)	F 5	
Lower Arrow (lake)	H 5	
Malaspina (str.)	J 3	
Manning Prov. Park, 23	G 5	
Masset (inlet)	A 3	
Milbanke (sound)	C 4	
Monashee (mts.)	H 4	
Moresby (isl.)	B 3	
Morice (riv.)	D 3	
Mount Assiniboine Prov. Park	K 5	
Mount Edziza Prov. Park and Rec. Area	B 1	
Mount Revelstoke Nat'l Park	H 4	
Mount Robson Prov. Park	H 3	
Muncho Lake Prov. Park	L 2	
Muskwa (riv.)	M 2	
Nanika (dam)	D 3	
Nass (riv.)	C 2	
Nechako (riv.)	E 3	
Nootka (isl.)	D 5	
Nootka (sound)	D 5	
North Thompson (riv.)	G 4	
Observatory (inlet)	C 2	
Okanagan (lake)	H 5	
Okanogan (riv.)	H 6	
Omineca (mts.)	D 2	
Ootsa (lake)	D 3	
Pacific Rim Nat'l Park	E 6	
Parsnip (riv.)	F 2	
Peace (riv.)	G 2	
Pine (riv.)	G 2	
Pitt (isl.)	C 3	
Pitt (lake)	L 2	
Porcher (isl.)	B 3	
Portland (canal)	B 2	
Portland (inlet)	C 2	
Princess Royal (isl.)	C 3	
Principe (chan.)	B 3	
Prophet (riv.)	M 2	
Purcell (mts.)	J 5	
Quatsino (sound)	C 5	
Queen Charlotte (isls.), 2,390	B 3	
Queen Charlotte (sound)	C 4	
Queen Charlotte (str.)	D 5	
Quesnel (lake)	G 3	
Rivers (inlet)	D 4	
Robson (mt.)	H 3	
Rocky (mts.)	F 2	
Rose (pt.)	B 3	
Saint James (cape)	B 4	
Salmon (riv.)	L 3	
Scott (cape)	C 5	
Seechelt (inlet)	J 2	
Seechelt (pen.)	J 2	
Selkirk (mts.)	J 4	
Seymour (inlet)	D 4	
Shuswap (lake)	H 4	
Sikanni Chief (riv.)	F 1	
Sir Sandford (mt.)	H 4	
Skeena (mts.)	C 2	
Skeena (riv.)	C 3	
Skidegate (inlet)	B 3	
Slocan (lake)	J 5	
Smith (sound)	C 4	
Stave (lake)	L 3	
Stikine (riv.)	B 1	
Stone Mountain Prov. Park	L 2	
Strathcona Prov. Park	E 5	
Stuart (lake)	E 3	
Tagish (lake)	J 1	
Tahtsa (lake)	D 2	
Takla (lake)	D 2	
Taku (riv.)	K 1	
Teslin (lake)	K 1	
Tetachuck (lake)	D 3	
Texada (isl.)	J 2	
Thompson (riv.)	G 5	
Tiedemann (mt.)	E 4	
Tweedsmuir Prov. Park	D 3	
Upper Arrow (lake)	H 5	
Valdes (isl.)	K 3	
Vancouver (isl.), 381,297	D 5	
Waddington (mt.)	E 4	
Wells Gray Prov. Park	H 4	
Whitesail (lake)	D 3	
Williston (lake)	F 2	
Work (chan.)	C 3	
Yellowhead (pass)	H 4	
Yoho Nat'l Park	J 4	

AREA 366,255 sq. mi.
POPULATION 2,161,000
CAPITAL Victoria
LARGEST CITY Vancouver
HIGHEST POINT Mt. Fairweather 15,300 ft.
SETTLED IN 1806
ADMITTED TO CONFEDERATION 1871
PROVINCIAL FLOWER Dogwood

‡ Population of metropolitan area.
● Population of municipality.

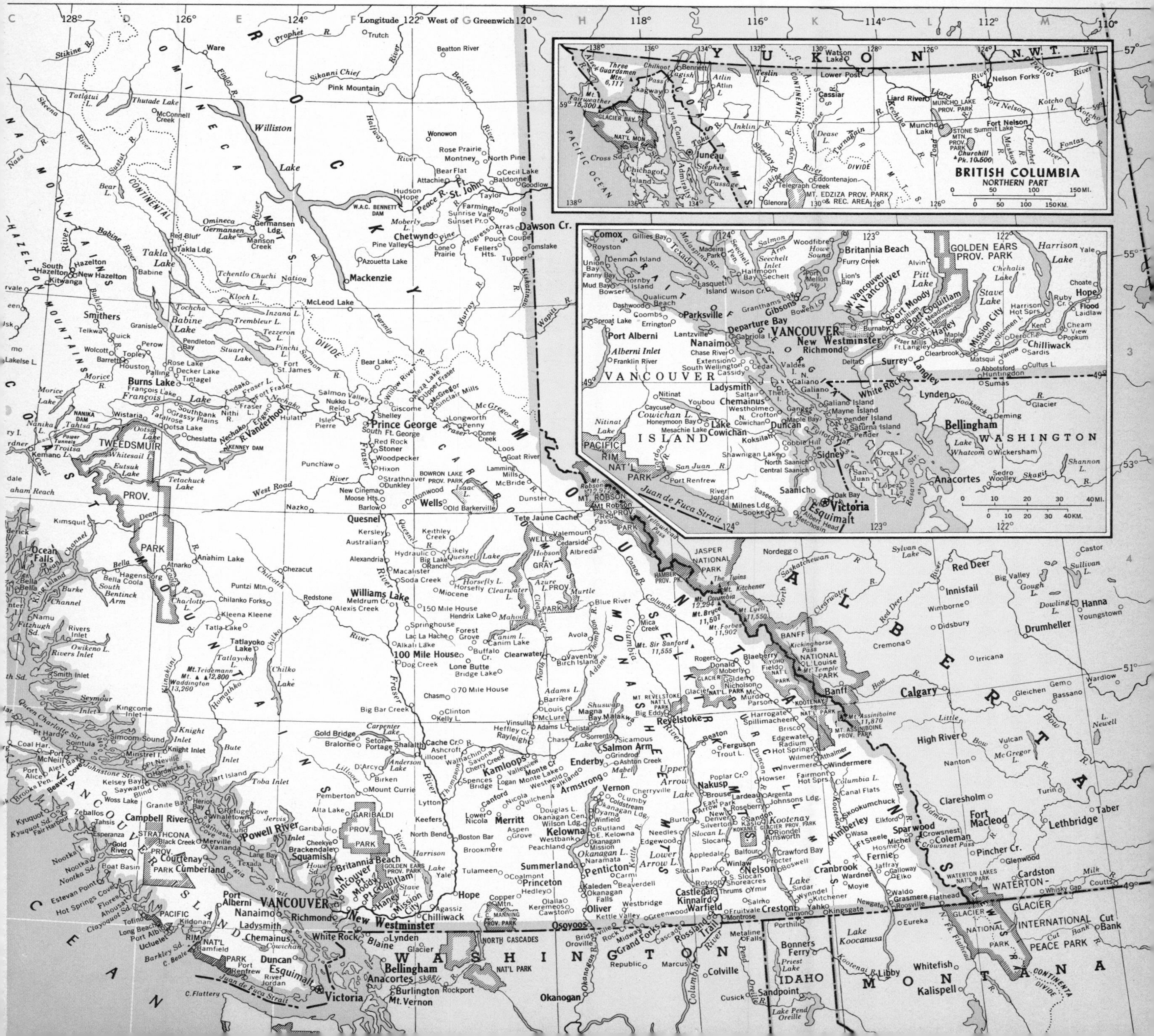

DOMINANT LAND USE

 Forests

Nonagricultural Land

MAJOR MINERAL OCCURRENCES

Ab Asbestos   Cu Copper
Ag Silver   Fe Iron Ore
Au Gold   O Petroleum
C Coal   Pb Lead
                 Zn Zinc

Topography

0   200   400
MILES

5,000 m.   2,000 m.   1,000 m.   500 m.   200 m.   100 m.   Sea
16,404 ft. 6,562 ft. 3,281 ft. 1,640 ft. 656 ft. 328 ft. Level
                                                              Below

Agriculture, Industry and Resources

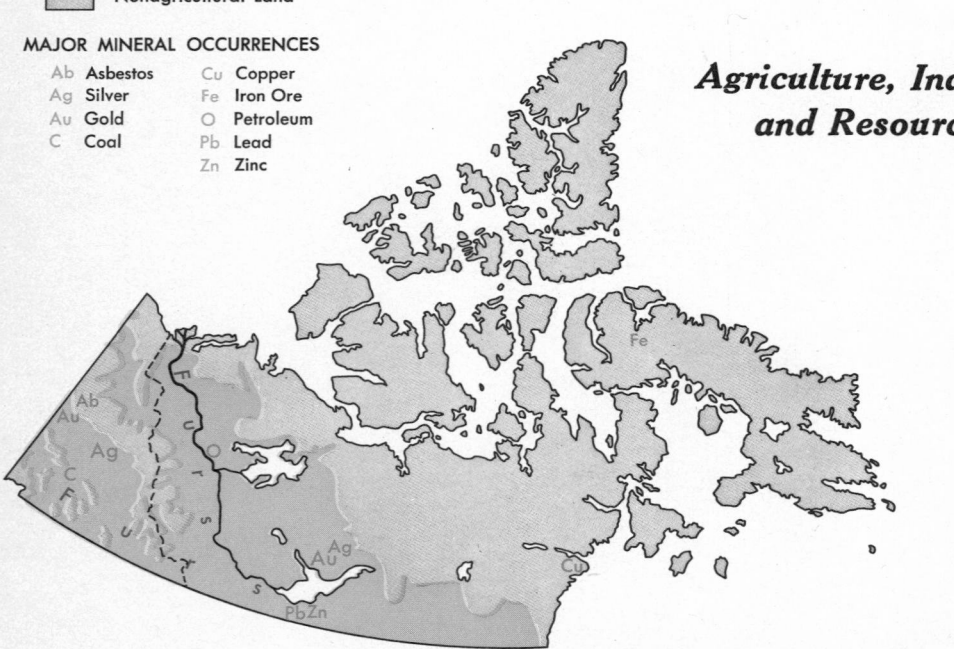

Prince Albert (pen.)	G 2
Prince Albert (sound)	G 2
Prince Charles (isl.)	L 3
Prince Gustav Adolf (sea)	H 2
Prince of Wales (isl.)	J 2
Prince of Wales (str.)	G 2
Prince Patrick (isl.)	F 2
Prince Regent (inlet)	J 2
Queen Elizabeth (isls.)	H 1
Queen Maud (gulf)	H 3
Queens (chan.)	J 2
Raanes (pen.)	K 2
Rae (isth.)	K 3
Rae (riv.)	G 3
Rae (str.)	J 3
Ramparts (riv.)	E 3
Resolution (isl.)	M 3
Richard Collinson (inlet)	G 2
Richards (isl.)	E 3
Richardson (mts.)	E 3
Robeson (chan.)	M 1
Roes Welcome (sound)	K 3
Royal Geographical Society (isls.)	J 3
Russell (isl.)	J 2
Sabine (pen.)	H 2
Salisbury (isl.)	L 3
Seahorse (pt.)	L 3
Selwyn (lake)	H 4
Sherman (inlet)	J 3
Simpson (riv.)	K 3
Sir James MacBrien (mt.)	F 3
Slave (riv.)	G 3

Smith (bay)	L 2
Smith (cape)	L 2
Smith (sound)	L 2
Snare (riv.)	G 3
Snowbird (lake)	H 3
Somerset (isl.)	J 2
South (bay)	K 3
Southampton (isl.)	K 3
South Nahanni (riv.)	E 3
Stallworthy (cape)	L 1
Steensby (inlet)	L 2
Stefansson (isl.)	H 2
Sverdrup (chan.)	J 1
Sverdrup (isls.)	J 2
Talbot (inlet)	L 2
Taltson (riv.)	G 3
Tathlina (lake)	G 3
Tha-anne (riv.)	J 3
Thelon (riv.)	H 3
Thlewiaza (riv.)	J 3
Trout (lake)	G 3
Ungava (bay)	M 4
Vansittart (isl.)	K 3
Victoria (isl.)	G 2
Victoria (str.)	H 3
Viscount Melville (sound)	G 2
Wager (bay)	K 3
Wales (isl.)	K 3
Walsingham (cape)	M 3
Wellington (chan.)	J 2
Wholdaia (lake)	H 3
Winter (harb.)	H 2
Wollaston (pen.)	G 3

YUKON TERRITORY

AREA 207,076 sq. mi.
POPULATION 17,000
CAPITAL Whitehorse
LARGEST CITY Whitehorse
HIGHEST POINT Mt. Logan 19,850 ft.
SETTLED IN 1897
ADMITTED TO CONFEDERATION 1898
PROVINCIAL FLOWER Fireweed

Wood Buffalo Nat'l Park	G 3
Wynniatt (bay)	G 2
Yathkyed (lake)	J 3
Yellowknife (riv.)	G 3

YUKON

CITIES and TOWNS

Bear Creek, 4	E 3

Beaver Creek, 120	D 3
Burwash Landing, 67	D 3
Carcross, 188	E 3
Carmacks, 348	E 3
Clinton Creek, 381	D 3
Cowley, 11	E 3
Dawson, 762	E 3
Destruction Bay, 82	E 3
Dominion, 12	E 3
Donjek, 11	D 3
Eagle River, 12	E 3
Elsa, 298	E 3
Faro, 863	E 3
Fort Selkirk, 3	E 3
Haines Junction, 179	E 3
Herschel, 5	E 3

NORTHWEST TERRITORIES

AREA 1,304,903 sq. mi.
POPULATION 34,000
CAPITAL Yellowknife
LARGEST CITY Yellowknife
HIGHEST POINT Barbeau Peak 8,540 ft.
SETTLED IN 1800
ADMITTED TO CONFEDERATION 1870
PROVINCIAL FLOWER Mountain Avens

Keno Hill, 79	E 3
Mayo, 462	E 3
McCabe Creek, 12	E 3
Old Crow, 206	E 3
Pelly Crossing, 141	E 3
Ross River, 317	E 3
Stewart Crossing, 43	E 3
Stewart River, 4	D 3
Swift River, 33	E 3
Tagish, 4	E 3
Teslin, 340	E 3
Toobally Lake, 1	F 3
Tuchitua Lake, 17	F 3
Upper Liard, 219	F 3
Watson Lake, 553	E 3
Whitehorse (cap.), 11,217	E 3

OTHER FEATURES

Alsek (riv.)	E 3
British (mts.)	D 3
Cassiar (mts.)	E 3
Frances (lake)	E 3
Herschel (isl.)	E 3
Hess (riv.)	E 3
Hyland (riv.)	F 3
Keele (peak)	E 3
Klondike (riv.)	E 3
Kluane (lake)	E 3
Kluane Nat'l Park	D 3
Logan (mt.)	D 3
Mackenzie (bay)	E 3
Mackenzie (mts.)	E 3

Macmillan (riv.)	E 3
Mayo (lake)	E 3
Ogilvie (mts.)	E 3
Peel (riv.)	E 3
Pelly (mts.)	E 3
Pelly (riv.)	E 3
Porcupine (riv.)	E 3
Richardson (mts.)	E 3
Rocky (mts.)	F 4
Saint Elias (mt.)	D 3
Saint Elias (mts.)	D 3
Selwyn (mts.)	E 3
Stewart (riv.)	E 3
Teslin (riv.)	E 3
White (riv.)	D 3
Yukon (riv.)	E 3

YUKON AND NORTHWEST TERRITORIES

SCALE
0 50 100 200 300 MI.
0 50 100 200 300 KM.

Territorial Capitals ⊛
International Boundaries
Provincial & Territorial Boundaries
District Boundaries

All islands in Hudson and James Bays lie within the District of Keewatin.

© Copyright by C. S. HAMMOND & Co.

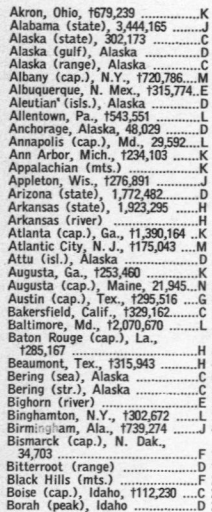

Akron, Ohio, †679,239....K 2	Boston (cap.), Mass., †2,753,700.M 2	Connecticut (state), 3,032,217...M 2	Golden Gate (chan.), Calif. ....B 3	Kennedy (cape), Fla. ....L 5	Minneapolis, Mihn., †1,813,647...H 1	Oregon (state), 2,091,385....B 2
Alabama (state), 3,444,165....J 4	Brazos (river), Tex. ....G 4	Connecticut (river)....M 2	Grand Canyon Nat'l Park, Ariz...D 3	Kentucky (state), 3,219,311....J 3	Minnesota (state), 3,805,069....H 1	Orlando, Fla., 1428,003....K 5
Alaska (state), 302,173....C 5	Bridgeport, Conn., †388,953....M 2	Corpus Christi, Tex., 1284,832...G 5	Grand Rapids, Mich., 1539,225...J 2	Kentucky (lake)....J 3	Mississippi (state), 2,216,912....J 4	Ozark (mts.)....H 3
Alaska (gulf), Alaska....D 6	Brooks (range), Alaska....C 5	Cumberland (river)....J 3	Great Salt (lake), Utah....D 2	Knoxville, Tenn., 1400,337....K 3	Mississippi (river)....J 4	Paterson, N. J., 1,358,794....M 2
Alaska (range), Alaska....C 6	Buffalo, N.Y., †1,349,211....L 2	Dallas, Tex., 11,555,950....G 4	Greensboro, N.C., 1603,895....K 3	Lancaster, Pa., 1319,693....L 2	Missouri (state), 4,677,399....H 3	Pennsylvania (state), 11,793,909..L 2
Albany (cap.), N.Y., †720,786....M 2	California (state), 19,953,134...B 3	Davenport, Iowa, 1362,638....H 2	Greenville, S.C., 1299,502....K 4	Lansing (cap.), Mich., 1378,423..K 2	Mitchell (mt.), N.C. ....K 3	Pensacola, Fla., 1243,075....J 4
Albuquerque, N. Mex., 1,315,774..E 3	Canadian (river)....F 3	Dayton, Ohio, 1850,266....K 3	Hamilton, Ohio, 1226,207....K 3	Las Vegas, Nev., 1273,288....C 3	Mobile, Ala., 1376,690....J 4	Peoria, Ill., 1341,979....J 2
Aleutian* (isls.), Alaska....D 6	Canaveral (Kennedy) (cape), Fla. ....L 5	Death Valley (depr.), Calif. ....C 3	Harrisburg (cap.), Pa., 1410,626..L 2	Lawrence, Mass., 1232,395....M 2	Montana (state), 694,409....E 1	Philadelphia, Pa., 14,817,914....M 2
Allentown, Pa., 1,543,551....L 2	Canton, Ohio, 1372,210....K 2	Delaware (state), 548,104....L 3	Hartford (cap.), Conn., 1663,891....M 2	Lexington, Ky., 1174,323....K 3	Montgomery (cap.), Ala., 1201,325....J 4	Phoenix (cap.), Ariz., 1968,487...D 4
Anchorage, Alaska, 48,029....D 6	Cape Fear (river), N.C. ....L 3	Delaware (bay)....M 3	Hatteras (cape), N.C. ....M 3	Lima, Ohio, 1171,472....K 2	Montpelier (cap.), Vt., 8,609....M 2	Pierre (cap.), S. Dak., 9,699....F 2
Annapolis (cap.), Md., 29,592....L 3	Carson City (cap.), Nev., 15,468..C 3	Denver (cap.), Colo., 11,227,529..F 3	Havasu (lake)....D 4	Lincoln (cap.), Nebr., 1167,972...G 2	Nantucket (isl.), Mass. ....N 2	Pikes (peak), Colo. ....F 3
Ann Arbor, Mich., 1234,103....K 2	Cascade (range)....B 2	Des Moines (cap.), Iowa, 1286,101....H 2	Hawaii (state), 769,913....F 6	Little Rock (cap.), Ark., 1323,296....H 3	Nashville (cap.), Tenn., 1540,982..J 3	Pittsburgh, Pa., 12,401,245....L 2
Appalachian (mts.)....K 3	Cedar Rapids, Iowa, 1163,213...H 2	Detroit, Mich., 14,199,931....K 2	Hawaii (isl.), Hawaii....F 6	Long (isl.), N.Y. ....M 2	Nebraska (state), 1,483,791....F 2	Platte (river), Nebr. ....G 2
Appleton, Wis., 1276,891....J 2	Champlain (lake)....M 2	District of Columbia, 756,510....L 3	Helena (cap.), Mont., 22,730....D 1	Los Angeles, Calif., 17,032,075..C 4	Nevada (state), 488,738....C 3	Pontchartrain (lake), La. ....J 5
Arizona (state), 1,772,482....D 4	Charleston, S.C., 1303,849....L 4	Dover (cap.), Del., 17,488....L 3	Honolulu (cap.), Hawaii, 1629,176....F 5	Louisiana (state), 3,643,180....H 4	Newark, N.J., 11,856,556....M 2	Portland, Maine, 1141,625....N 2
Arkansas (state), 1,923,295....H 3	Charleston (cap.), W. Va., †229,515....K 3	Duluth, Minn., 1265,350....H 1	Houston, Tex., 11,985,031....G 5	Louisville, Ky., 1826,553....J 3	New Hampshire(state), 737,681..M 2	Portland, Oreg., 11,009,129....B 1
Arkansas (river)....H 3	Charlotte, N.C., 1409,370....K 3	Durham, N.C., 1190,388....L 3	Huntington, W. Va., 1253,743....K 3	Lowell, Mass., 1212,860....M 2	New Haven, Conn., 1355,538....M 2	Potomac (river)....L 3
Atlanta (cap.), Ga., 11,390,164....K 4	Chattahoochee (river)....J 4	El Paso, Tex., 1359,291....E 4	Huntsville, Ala., 1228,239....J 4	Lubbock, Tex., 1179,295....F 4	New Jersey (state), 7,168,164....M 3	Providence (cap.), R.I., 1914,110..M 2
Atlantic City, N. J., 1175,043....M 3	Chattanooga, Tenn., 1304,927...J 3	Erie, Pa., 1263,654....K 2	Huron (lake), Mich. ....K 2	Macon, Ga., 1206,342....K 4	New Mexico (state), 1,016,000...E 4	Racine, Wis., 1170,838....J 2
Attu (isl.), Alaska....A 5	Chesapeake (bay)....L 3	Erie (lake)....K 2	Idaho (state), 713,008....D 2	Madison (cap.), Wis., 1290,272...H 2	New Orleans, La., 11,045,809....H 5	Rainier (mt.), Wash. ....B 1
Augusta, Ga., 1253,460....K 4	Cheyenne (cap.), Wyo., 40,914..F 2	Eugene, Oreg., 1213,358....B 2	Illinois (state), 11,113,976....J 3	Maine (state), 993,663....N 1	Newport News, Va., 1292,159....L 3	Raleigh (cap.), N.C., 1228,453...L 3
Augusta (cap.), Maine, 21,945...N 2	Chicago, Ill., †6,978,947....J 2	Evansville, Ind., 1232,775....J 3	Indiana (state), 5,193,669....J 3	Maryland (state), 3,922,399....L 3	New York (state), 18,190,740....L 2	Reading, Pa., 1296,382....L 2
Austin (cap.), Tex., 1295,516....G 4	Cimarron (river)....G 3	Everglades (swamp), Fla. ....K 5	Indianapolis (cap.), Ind., 11,109,882....J 3	Massachusetts (state), 5,689,170....M 2	New York, N.Y., 11,528,649....M 2	Red (river)....H 4
Bakersfield, Calif., 1329,162....C 3	Cincinnati, Ohio, 11,384,911....K 3	Fayetteville, N.C., 1212,042....L 3	Iowa (state), 2,825,041....H 2	Maui (isl.), Hawaii....F 5	Norfolk, Va., 1680,600....L 3	Red River of the North (river)...G 1
Baltimore, Md., †2,070,670....L 3	Cleveland, Ohio, 12,064,194....K 2	Flint, Mich., 1496,658....K 2	Jackson (cap.), Miss., 1258,906..H 4	Mauna Kea (mt.), Hawaii....F 6	North Carolina(state), 5,082,059..L 3	Rhode Island (state), 949,723....M 2
Baton Rouge (cap.), La., †285,167....H 4	Coast (range)....B 2	Florida (state), 6,789,443....K 5	Jacksonville, Fla., 1528,865....K 5	Mauna Loa (mt.), Hawaii....F 6	North Dakota (state), 617,761....F 1	Richmond (cap.), Va., 1518,319..L 3
Beaumont, Tex., 1315,943....H 4	Cod (cape), Mass. ....N 2	Florida (keys), Fla. ....K 6	Jefferson City (cap.), Mo., 32,407....H 3	May (cape), N. J. ....M 3	Oahu (isl.), Hawaii....E 5	Rio Grande (river)....E 4
Bering (sea), Alaska....B 5	Colorado (state), 2,207,259....E 3	Ft. Smith, Ark., 1160,421....H 3	Jersey City, N. J., 1609,266....M 2	McKinley (mt.), Alaska....D 5	Oakland, Calif., 361,561....B 3	Roanoke, Va., 1181,436....K 3
Bering (strait), Alaska....C 5	Colorado (river)....D 4	Ft. Wa̧yne, Ind., 1280,455....J 2	Juneau (cap.), Alaska, 13,556...E 6	Mead (lake)....D 3	Ohio (state), 10,652,017....J 2	Rochester, N.Y., 1882,667....L 2
Bighorn (river)....E 2	Colorado (river), Tex. ....G 4	Ft. Worth, Tex., 1762,086....G 4	Kalamazoo, Mich., 1201,550....J 2	Memphis, Tenn., 1770,120....J 3	Ohio (river)....J 3	Rockford, Ill., 1272,063....J 2
Binghamton, N.Y., 1302,672....L 2	Colorado Sprs., Colo., 1235,972..F 3	Frankfort (cap.), Ky., 121,356...K 3	Kansas (state), 2,249,071....G 3	Mendocino (cape), Calif. ....B 3	Oklahoma (state), 2,559,253....G 3	Rocky (mts.)....E 2
Birmingham, Ala., 1739,274....J 4	Columbia (cap.), S.C., 1322,880..K 4	Fresno, Calif., 1413,053....C 3	Kansas City, Kans.-Mo., 11,256,649....H 3	Mexico (gulf)....J 5	Oklahoma City (cap.), Okla., 1640,889....G 3	Sacramento (cap.), Calif., 1800,592....B 3
Bismarck (cap.), N. Dak., 34,703....F 1	Columbia (river)....B 1	Galveston, Tex., 1169,812....H 5	Kauai (isl.), Hawaii....E 5	Miami, Fla., 11,267,792....K 5	Olympia (cap.), Wash., 23,111...B 1	Saginaw, Mich., 1219,743....K 2
Bitterroot (range)....D 1	Columbus, Ga., 1238,584....J 4	Gary, Ind., 1633,367....J 2		Michigan (state), 8,875,083....J 1	Olympic Nat'l Park, Wash. ....A 1	Saint John (river), Maine....N 1
Black Hills (mts.)....F 2	Columbus (cap.), Ohio, 1916,228..K 3	Georgia (state), 4,589,575....K 4		Michigan (lake)....J 2	Omaha, Nebr., 1541,453....G 2	Saint Lawrence (river), N.Y. ....N 1
Boise (cap.), Idaho, 1112,230....C 2	Concord (cap.), N.H., 30,022....M 2	Gila (river)....D 4		Milwaukee, Wis., 11,403,887....J 2	Ontario (lake), N.Y. ....H 1	Saint Louis, Mo., 12,363,017....H 3
Borah (peak), Idaho....D 2		Glacier Nat'l Park, Mont. ....D 1				Saint Paul (cap.), Minn., 309,980....H 1

AREA 3,615,123 sq. mi.
POPULATION 203,235,298
CAPITAL Washington
LARGEST CITY New York
HIGHEST POINT Mt. McKinley 20,320 ft.
MONETARY VALUE U.S. dollar
MAJOR LANGUAGE English
MAJOR RELIGIONS Protestantism, Roman Catholicism, Judaism

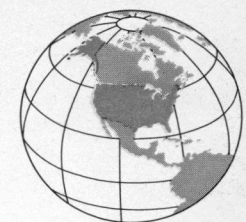

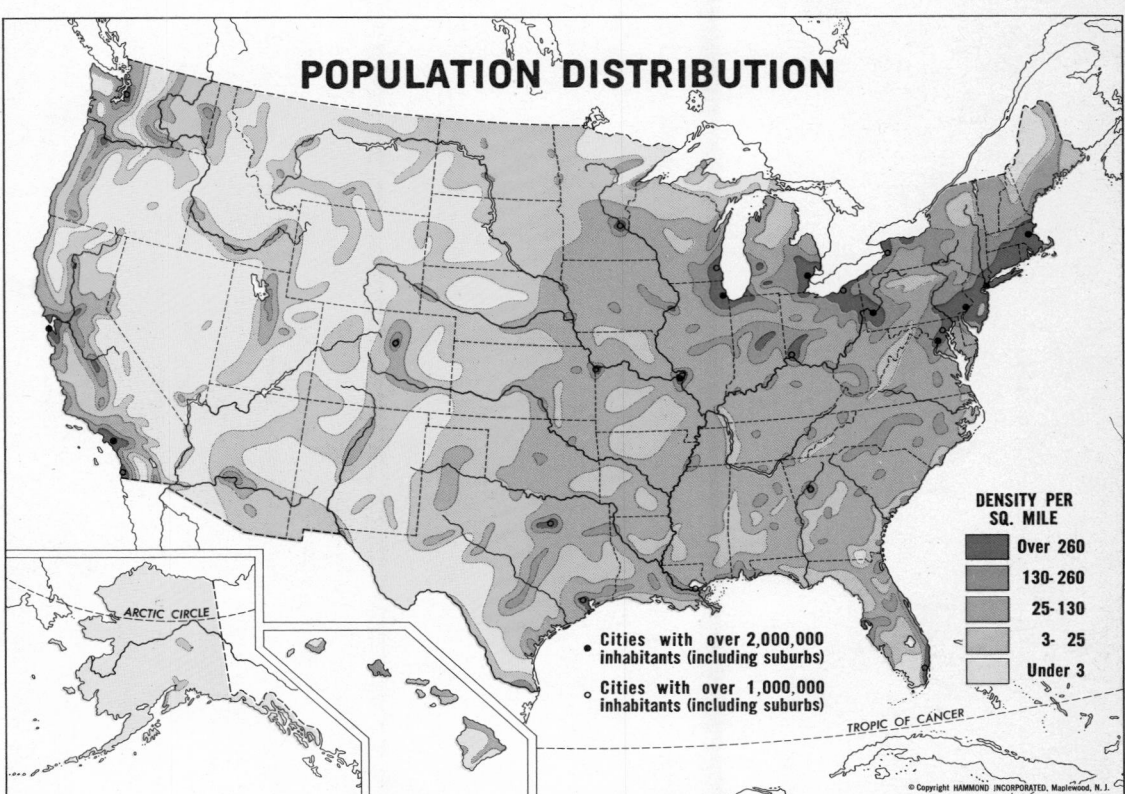

POPULATION DISTRIBUTION

ARCTIC CIRCLE

• Cities with over 2,000,000 inhabitants (including suburbs)
○ Cities with over 1,000,000 inhabitants (including suburbs)

TROPIC OF CANCER

DENSITY PER SQ. MILE
- Over 260
- 130- 260
- 25- 130
- 3- 25
- Under 3

© Copyright HAMMOND INCORPORATED, Maplewood, N. J.

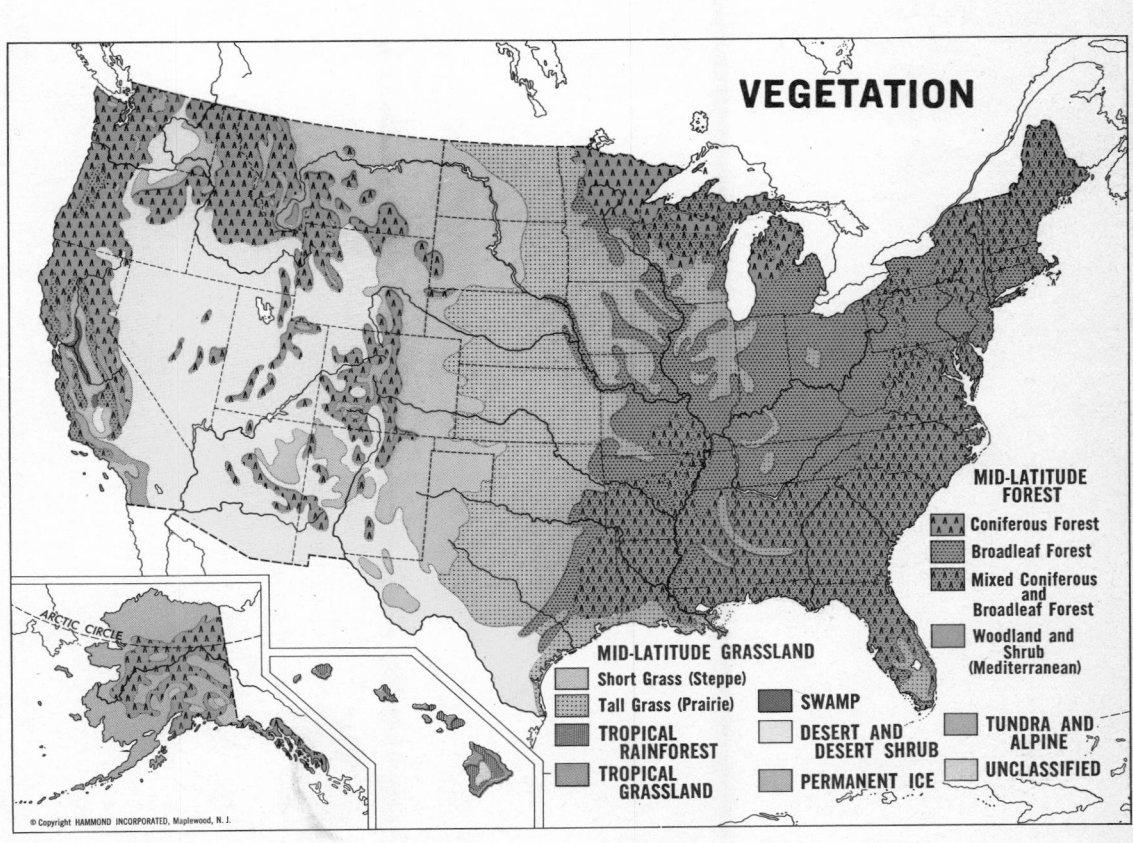

VEGETATION

ARCTIC CIRCLE

MID-LATITUDE FOREST
- Coniferous Forest
- Broadleaf Forest
- Mixed Coniferous and Broadleaf Forest
- Woodland and Shrub (Mediterranean)

MID-LATITUDE GRASSLAND
- Short Grass (Steppe)
- Tall Grass (Prairie)

TROPICAL RAINFOREST
TROPICAL GRASSLAND

- SWAMP
- DESERT AND DESERT SHRUB
- PERMANENT ICE

- TUNDRA AND ALPINE
- UNCLASSIFIED

© Copyright HAMMOND INCORPORATED, Maplewood, N. J.

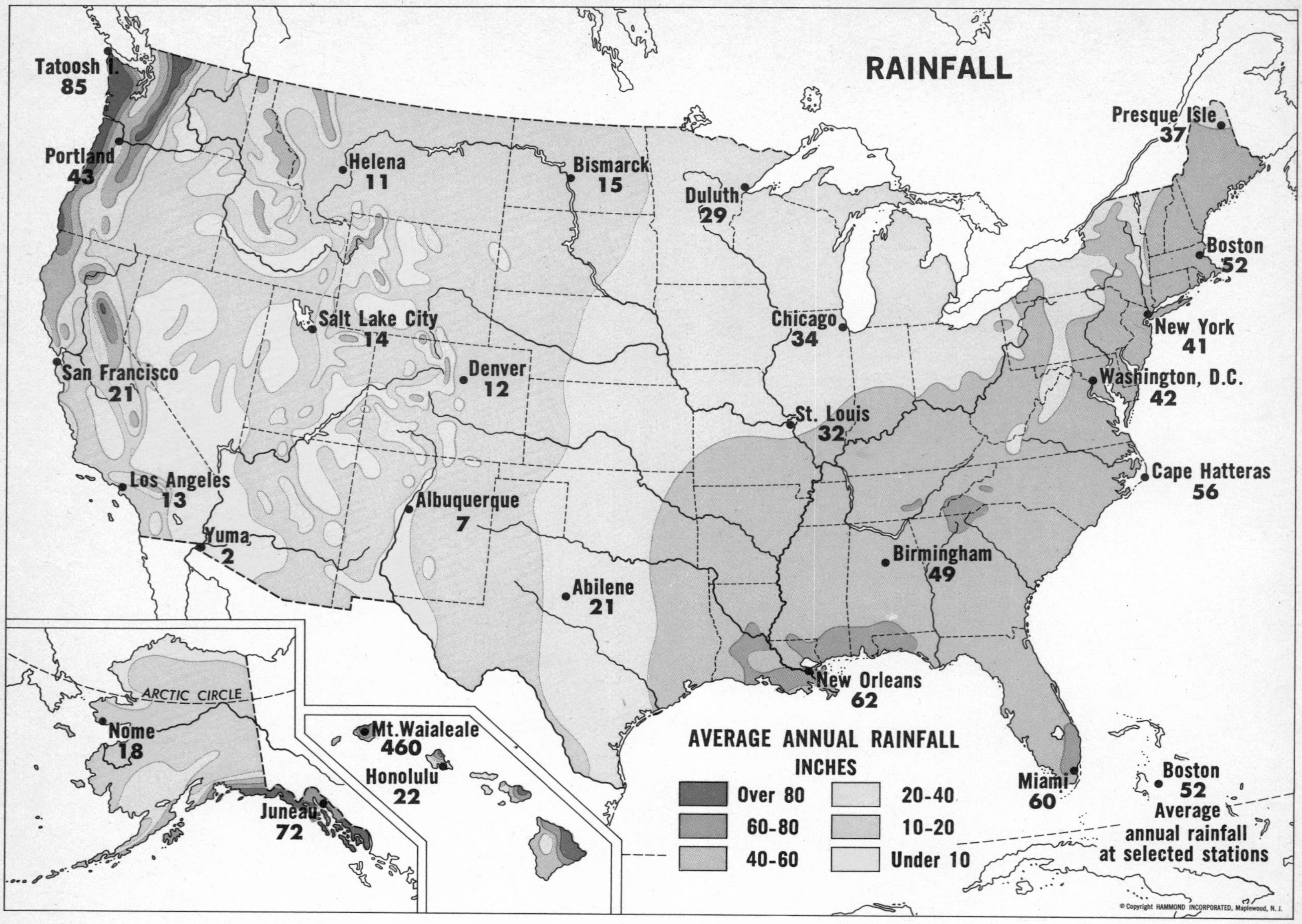

RAINFALL

Tatoosh I.
85

Portland
43

Helena
11

Bismarck
15

Duluth
29

Presque Isle
37

Boston
52

Chicago
34

Salt Lake City
14

San Francisco
21

Denver
12

St. Louis
32

New York
41

Washington, D.C.
42

Los Angeles
13

Albuquerque
7

Cape Hatteras
56

Yuma
2

Abilene
21

Birmingham
49

New Orleans
62

ARCTIC CIRCLE

Nome
18

Mt. Waialeale
460

Honolulu
22

Juneau
72

AVERAGE ANNUAL RAINFALL
INCHES

Over 80	20-40
60-80	10-20
40-60	Under 10

Miami
60

Boston
52
Average
annual rainfall
at selected stations

© Copyright HAMMOND INCORPORATED, Maplewood, N.J.

AVERAGE JANUARY TEMPERATURE

Seattle
39°

Bismarck
9°

Minneapolis
12°

San Francisco
48°

Denver
30°

St. Louis
31°

Chicago
25°

New York
30°

Washington
34°

Los Angeles
55°

Phoenix
52°

Dallas
46°

Atlanta
43°

Chicago
25°
Average January
temperature at
selected stations

New Orleans
55°

ARCTIC CIRCLE

Fairbanks
-11°

Honolulu
73°

Miami
69°

TROPIC OF CANCER

FAHRENHEIT

Over 68°	14° to 32°
50° to 68°	-4° to 14°
32° to 50°	Under -4°

© Copyright HAMMOND INCORPORATED, Maplewood, N.J.

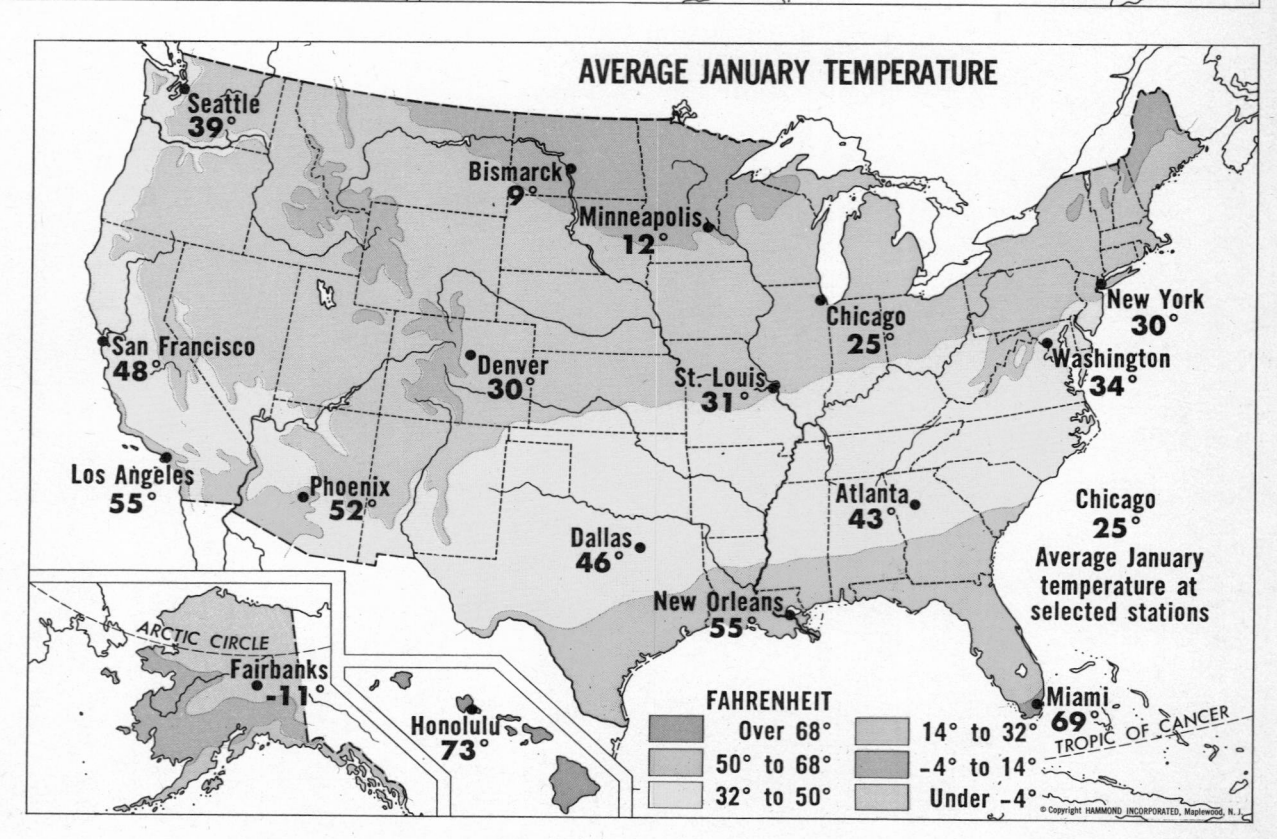

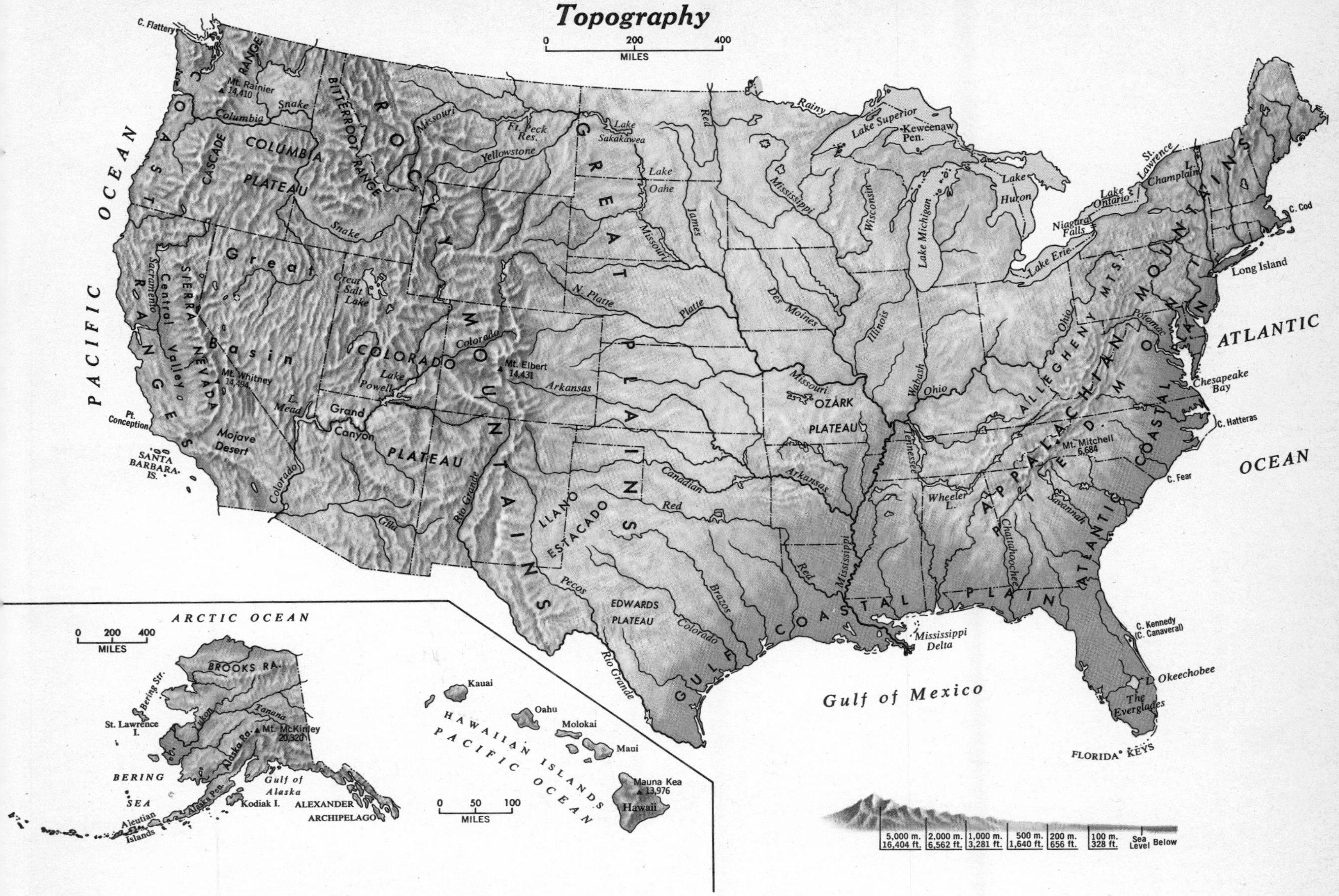

Topography

MILES
0 200 400

C. Flattery

PACIFIC OCEAN

COAST RANGE
CASCADE RANGE
Mt. Rainier 14,410
Columbia
Snake
COLUMBIA PLATEAU
BITTERROOT RANGE
ROCKY
Yellowstone
Great Salt Lake
SIERRA NEVADA
Sacramento
Central Valley
Mt. Whitney 14,494
Great Basin
Lake Powell
Lake Mead
Grand Canyon
COLORADO
Colorado
Mt. Elbert 14,431
Pt. Conception
SANTA BARBARA IS.
Mojave Desert
PLATEAU
MOUNTAINS
Colorado
Rio Grande
Gila

Missouri
Ft. Peck Res.
N. Platte
Platte
Arkansas
LLANO ESTACADO
Pecos
EDWARDS PLATEAU
Rio Grande
GREAT
Lake Sakakawea
Lake Oahe
James
Red
Missouri
Des Moines
Platte
Canadian
Red
Colorado
Brazos
PLAINS
GULF COASTAL PLAIN

Rainy
Lake Superior
Keweenaw Pen.
Wisconsin
Lake Michigan
Missouri
Mississippi
Illinois
Wabash
Ohio
OZARK PLATEAU
Arkansas
Red
Mississippi
Mississippi Delta

Lake Huron
Lake Erie
Lake Ontario
St. Lawrence
L. Champlain
Niagara Falls
Ohio
Potomac
Mt. Mitchell 6,684
Wheeler L.
Chattahoochee
Savannah
ALLEGHENY MTS.
APPALACHIAN MOUNTAINS
ATLANTIC COASTAL PLAIN

C. Cod
Long Island
ATLANTIC
Chesapeake Bay
C. Hatteras
OCEAN
C. Fear

Gulf of Mexico

C. Kennedy (C. Canaveral)
L. Okeechobee
The Everglades
FLORIDA KEYS

ARCTIC OCEAN
MILES
0 200 400
BROOKS RA.
St. Lawrence I.
Yukon
Tanana
Alaska Ra.
Mt. McKinley 20,320
BERING SEA
Gulf of Alaska
Kodiak I.
ALEXANDER ARCHIPELAGO
Aleutian Islands

HAWAIIAN ISLANDS
PACIFIC OCEAN
Kauai
Oahu
Molokai
Maui
MILES
0 50 100
Mauna Kea 13,976
Hawaii

5,000 m. 16,404 ft. | 2,000 m. 6,562 ft. | 1,000 m. 3,281 ft. | 500 m. 1,640 ft. | 200 m. 656 ft. | 100 m. 328 ft. | Sea Level | Below

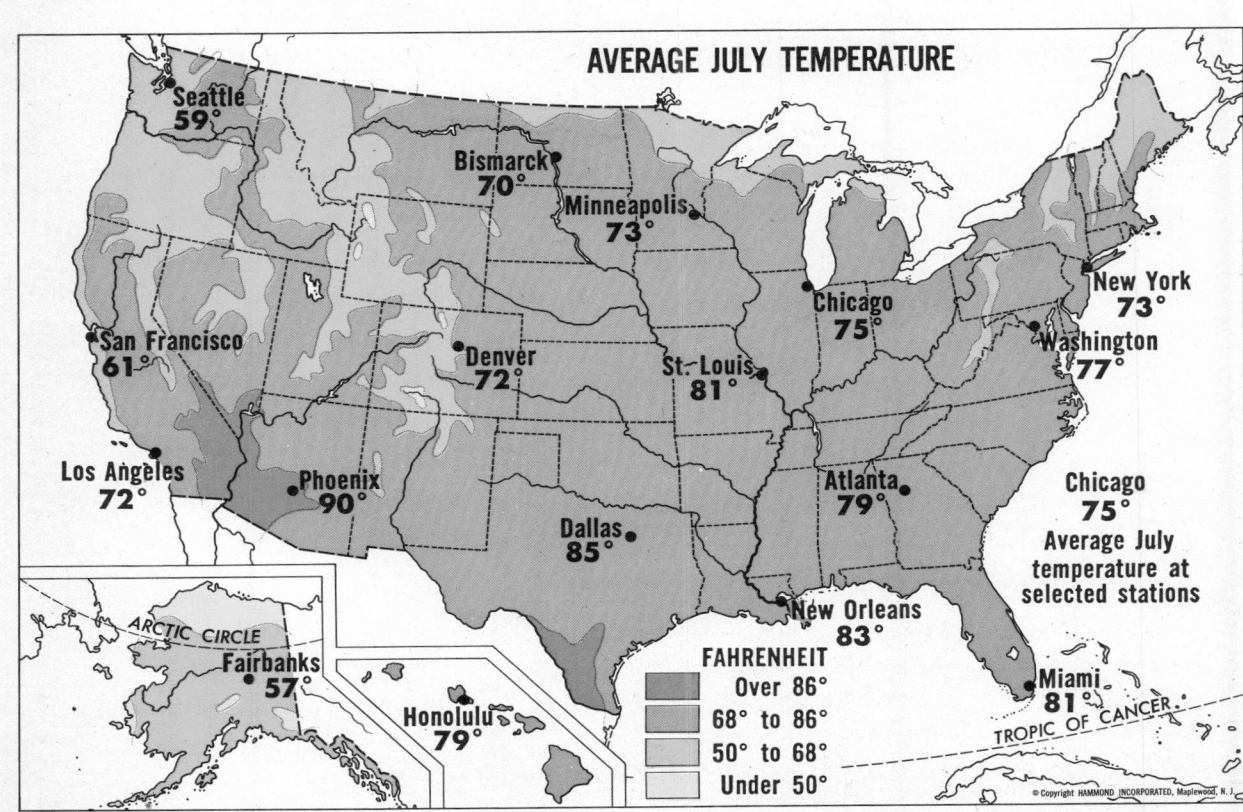

AVERAGE JULY TEMPERATURE

Seattle 59°
Bismarck 70°
Minneapolis 73°
New York 73°
Chicago 75°
Washington 77°
San Francisco 61°
Denver 72°
St. Louis 81°
Los Angeles 72°
Phoenix 90°
Atlanta 79°
Dallas 85°
New Orleans 83°
Miami 81°

Chicago
75°
Average July temperature at selected stations

ARCTIC CIRCLE
Fairbanks 57°
Honolulu 79°

TROPIC OF CANCER

FAHRENHEIT
Over 86°
68° to 86°
50° to 68°
Under 50°

(continued)

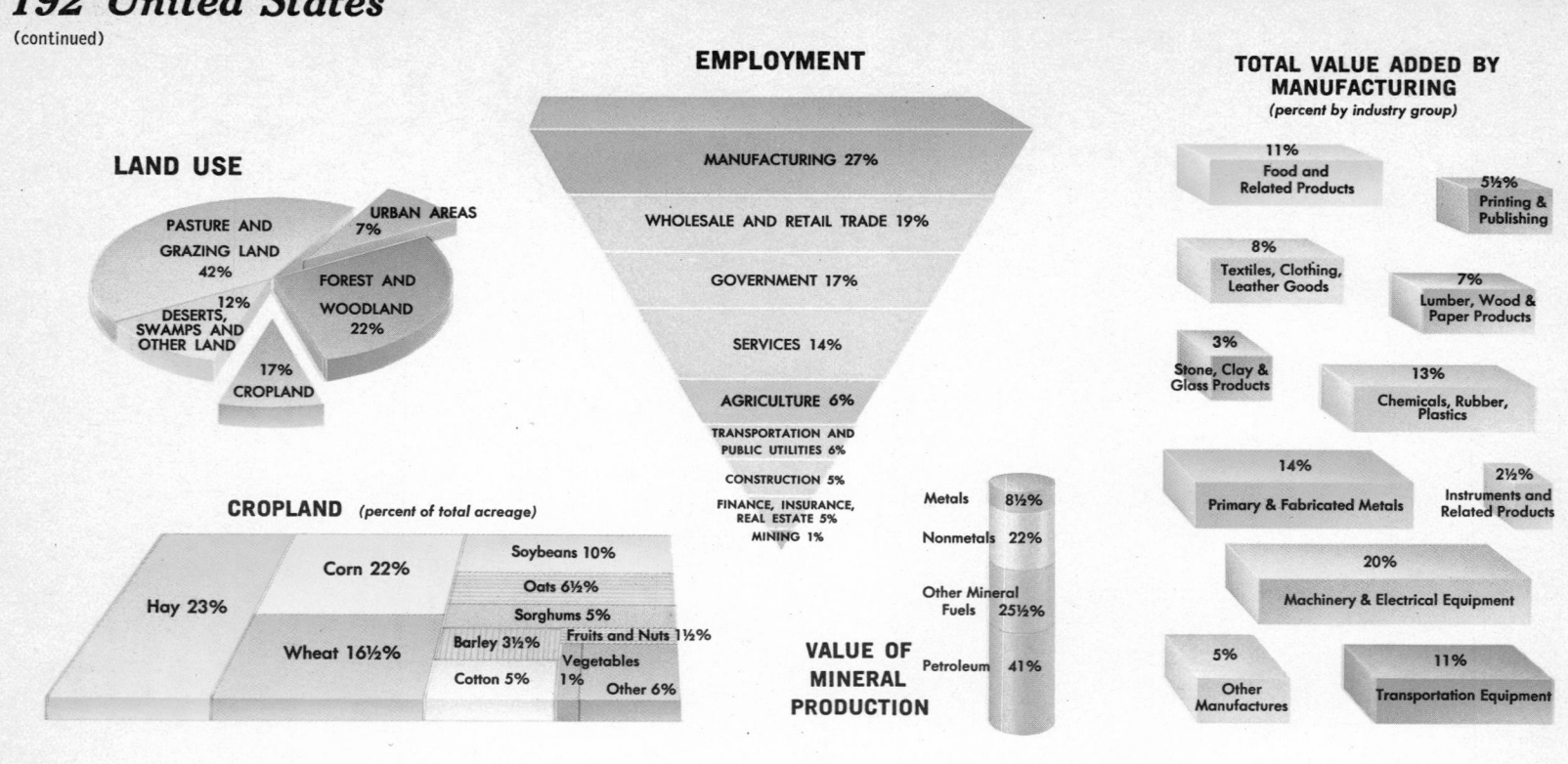

LAND USE

PASTURE AND GRAZING LAND 42%
URBAN AREAS 7%
FOREST AND WOODLAND 22%
12% DESERTS, SWAMPS AND OTHER LAND
17% CROPLAND

EMPLOYMENT

MANUFACTURING 27%
WHOLESALE AND RETAIL TRADE 19%
GOVERNMENT 17%
SERVICES 14%
AGRICULTURE 6%
TRANSPORTATION AND PUBLIC UTILITIES 6%
CONSTRUCTION 5%
FINANCE, INSURANCE, REAL ESTATE 5%
MINING 1%

TOTAL VALUE ADDED BY MANUFACTURING

(percent by industry group)

11% Food and Related Products
5½% Printing & Publishing
8% Textiles, Clothing, Leather Goods
7% Lumber, Wood & Paper Products
3% Stone, Clay & Glass Products
13% Chemicals, Rubber, Plastics
14% Primary & Fabricated Metals
2½% Instruments and Related Products
20% Machinery & Electrical Equipment
5% Other Manufactures
11% Transportation Equipment

CROPLAND *(percent of total acreage)*

Hay 23%
Corn 22%
Wheat 16½%
Soybeans 10%
Oats 6½%
Sorghums 5%
Barley 3½%
Fruits and Nuts 1½%
Vegetables 1%
Cotton 5%
Other 6%

VALUE OF MINERAL PRODUCTION

Metals 8½%
Nonmetals 22%
Other Mineral Fuels 25½%
Petroleum 41%

Agriculture, Industry and Resources

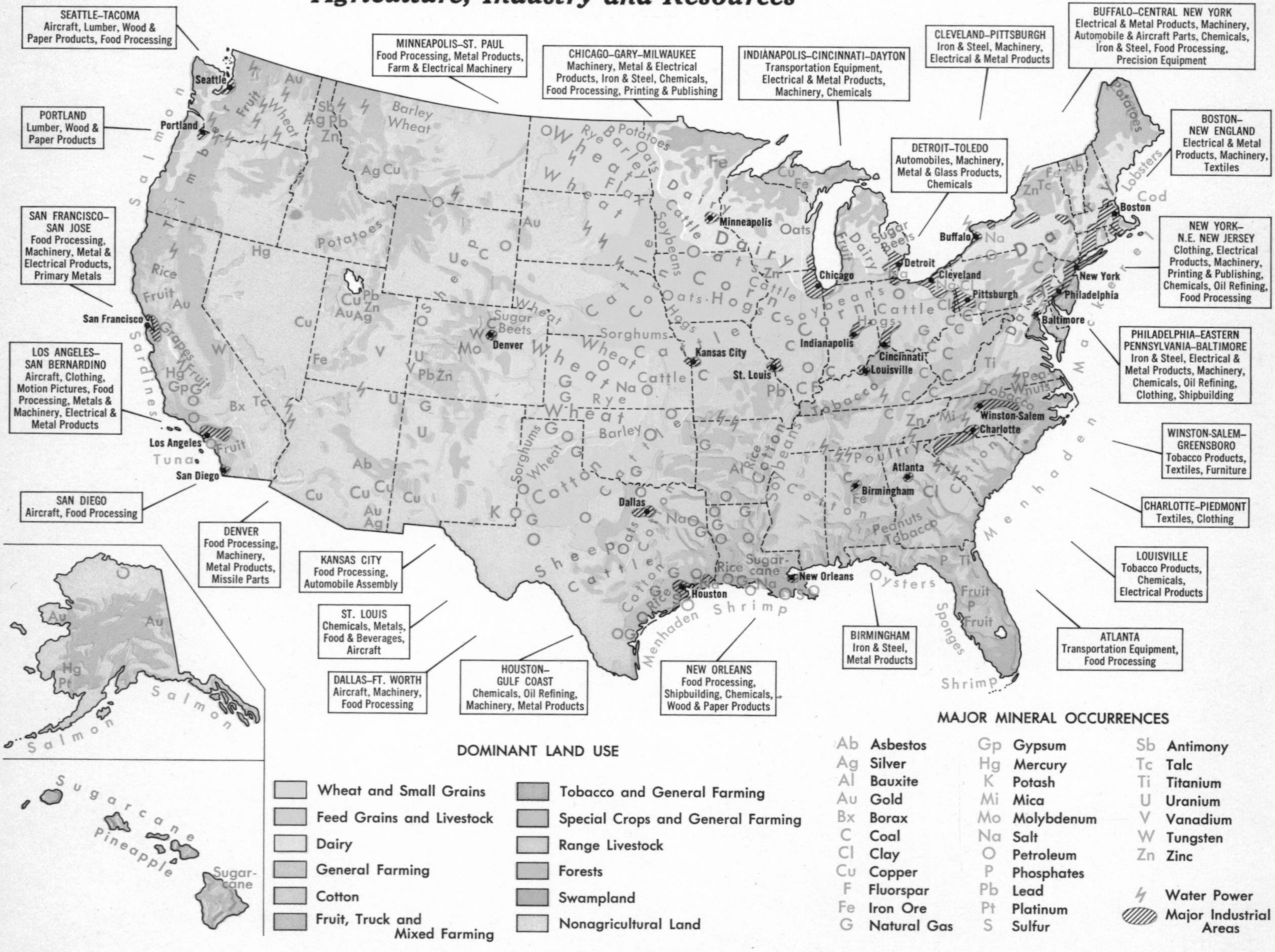

SEATTLE–TACOMA
Aircraft, Lumber, Wood & Paper Products, Food Processing
MINNEAPOLIS–ST. PAUL
Food Processing, Metal Products, Farm & Electrical Machinery
CHICAGO–GARY–MILWAUKEE
Machinery, Metal & Electrical Products, Iron & Steel, Chemicals, Food Processing, Printing & Publishing
INDIANAPOLIS–CINCINNATI–DAYTON
Transportation Equipment, Electrical & Metal Products, Machinery, Chemicals
CLEVELAND–PITTSBURGH
Iron & Steel, Machinery, Electrical & Metal Products
BUFFALO–CENTRAL NEW YORK
Electrical & Metal Products, Machinery, Automobile & Aircraft Parts, Chemicals, Iron & Steel, Food Processing, Precision Equipment
PORTLAND
Lumber, Wood & Paper Products
DETROIT–TOLEDO
Automobiles, Machinery, Metal & Glass Products, Chemicals
BOSTON–NEW ENGLAND
Electrical & Metal Products, Machinery, Textiles
SAN FRANCISCO–SAN JOSE
Food Processing, Machinery, Metal & Electrical Products, Primary Metals
NEW YORK–N.E. NEW JERSEY
Clothing, Electrical Products, Machinery, Printing & Publishing, Chemicals, Oil Refining, Food Processing
LOS ANGELES–SAN BERNARDINO
Aircraft, Clothing, Motion Pictures, Food Processing, Metals & Machinery, Electrical & Metal Products
PHILADELPHIA–EASTERN PENNSYLVANIA–BALTIMORE
Iron & Steel, Electrical & Metal Products, Machinery, Chemicals, Oil Refining, Clothing, Shipbuilding
WINSTON-SALEM–GREENSBORO
Tobacco Products, Textiles, Furniture
SAN DIEGO
Aircraft, Food Processing
CHARLOTTE–PIEDMONT
Textiles, Clothing
DENVER
Food Processing, Machinery, Metal Products, Missile Parts
KANSAS CITY
Food Processing, Automobile Assembly
LOUISVILLE
Tobacco Products, Chemicals, Electrical Products
ST. LOUIS
Chemicals, Metals, Food & Beverages, Aircraft
ATLANTA
Transportation Equipment, Food Processing
BIRMINGHAM
Iron & Steel, Metal Products
DALLAS–FT. WORTH
Aircraft, Machinery, Food Processing
HOUSTON–GULF COAST
Chemicals, Oil Refining, Machinery, Metal Products
NEW ORLEANS
Food Processing, Shipbuilding, Chemicals, Wood & Paper Products
Seattle
Portland
San Francisco
Los Angeles
San Diego
Denver
Minneapolis
Chicago
Detroit
Buffalo
Boston
Cleveland
Pittsburgh
New York
Philadelphia
Baltimore
Indianapolis
Cincinnati
Louisville
Kansas City
St. Louis
Winston-Salem
Charlotte
Atlanta
Birmingham
Dallas
Houston
New Orleans
Salmon
Sardines
Tuna
Shrimp
Oysters
Sponges
Menhaden
Mackerel
Lobsters
Cod
Sugarcane
Pineapple
DOMINANT LAND USE
Wheat and Small Grains
Feed Grains and Livestock
Dairy
General Farming
Cotton
Fruit, Truck and Mixed Farming
Tobacco and General Farming
Special Crops and General Farming
Range Livestock
Forests
Swampland
Nonagricultural Land
MAJOR MINERAL OCCURRENCES
Ab Asbestos
Ag Silver
Al Bauxite
Au Gold
Bx Borax
C Coal
Cl Clay
Cu Copper
F Fluorspar
Fe Iron Ore
G Natural Gas
Gp Gypsum
Hg Mercury
K Potash
Mi Mica
Mo Molybdenum
Na Salt
O Petroleum
P Phosphates
Pb Lead
Pt Platinum
S Sulfur
Sb Antimony
Tc Talc
Ti Titanium
U Uranium
V Vanadium
W Tungsten
Zn Zinc
Water Power
Major Industrial Areas